D1097045

An Index to Oxfordian Publications

including Oxfordian books and selected articles from non-Oxfordian periodicals

Fifth Edition
September 2023

Editor
James A. Warren

Published by
VERITAS PUBLICATIONS
Cary, North Carolina

All rights reserved.

ISBN 979-8-9861351-7-5
Published September 10, 2023

The "stamp" on the cover—the image resembling a postage stamp with the picture of Edward de Vere on it—was created by Faddon W. Heron in the early 1940s. Heron was one of the earliest advocates of the plan for what became the popular Famous American series of U.S. commemorative postage stamps issued 1940-1941. His Oxfordian publications are listed on page 121.

*The strange, difficult, contradictory man who emerges as the real Shakespeare,
Edward de Vere, the 17th Earl of Oxford,
is not just plausible but fascinating and wholly believable.*

David McCullough[1]

*I think Oxford wrote Shakespeare. If you don't agree, there are some
awful funny coincidences to explain away.*

Orson Welles[2]

*I'm falling in love with this idea that the real Shakespeare was Edward de Vere,
the Earl of Oxford. . . . It is astonishing what the Edward de Vere camp has turned up
in the way of research to explain all kinds of mysteries of the plays and the life
of the so-called Shakespeare. Very, very interesting stuff.*

Anne Rice[3]

*I no longer believe that . . . the actor from Stratford was the author of the works
that have been ascribed to him. Since reading* "Shakespeare" Identified *by J. Thomas Looney,
I am almost convinced that the assumed name conceals the personality of
Edward de Vere, Earl of Oxford. . . . The man of Stratford seems to have nothing at all
to justify his claim, whereas Oxford has almost everything.*

Sigmund Freud[4]

*The Oxfordians have presented a very strong – almost fully convincing – case
for their point of view. . . . If I had to rule on the evidence presented,
it would be for the Oxfordians.*

U.S. Supreme Court Justice Harry Blackmun[5]

---

[1] "Forward" to *The Mysterious William Shakespeare* (Ogburn 1984).
[2] Quoted in *Persona Grata* (Cecil Beaton & Kenneth Tyson 1954).
[3] Quoted in *Shakespeare Oxford Newsletter*, vol. 38/3 (Summer 2002).
[4] *An Autobiographical Study* (1935).
[5] Quoted in "Opinions of the Justices," *American University Law Review*, vol. 37/3 (1988).

SHAKESPEARE IDENTIFIED
in Edward de Vere, 17th Earl of Oxford

By J. THOMAS LOONEY

Demy 8vo. Cloth. **21s.** net. Illustrated.

This book has aroused, if not the traditional storm, at least a good strong wind of controversy. Inevitably a certain amount of scoffing was waiting ready for it. Thanks to the rather wild speculations of the Baconian cryptogramists, it has become the custom to take up an attitude of amused scepticism towards any attempt to study the matter of Shakespearean identity. Many great men and scholars, though, have considered the question a real one and worthy of their attention. In an article by E. Nesbit, in the New Witness, obviously inspired by this book, a list is given of men who are known to have been either doubters or frank unbelievers in the Stratfordian authorship. It includes Disraeli, James Russell Lowell, W. H. Mallock, W. Hepworth Dixon, Sir Lewis Morris, Bismarck, Byron, Henry Hallam, Coleridge, Emerson, Palmerston, Cardinal Newman, Dickens, Oliver Wendell Holmes, J. G. Whittier, Thomas Davidson, John Bright, Lord Penzance, Walt Whitman and Gladstone. Mr. Looney's is probably the most serious endeavour that has yet been made to solve the mystery.

" It is impossible here even to indicate the array of chronological fact and biographical details marshalled against the Stratfordian. They are startling enough. Very ingenious, too, is Mr. Looney's success in tracing a conformity between De Vere's life and the plots of Shakespearean plays."—W. L. GEORGE in *The World*.

THE POEMS OF EDWARD DE VERE
With biographical introduction and notes

By J. THOMAS LOONEY

Small Quarto. **6s.** net. Cloth.

Most of the critics of *Shakespeare Identified*, even those frankly hostile to Mr. Looney's theory, were agreed that Mr. Looney had performed a good service in bringing forward the early and acknowledged work of this little-known Elizabethan. Mr. Looney has now prepared an edition of these poems, including several which he finds reason to attribute to De Vere, or which have some connection with his work. The book contains a long biographical and critical introduction, as well as some additional matter bearing on the controversy.

SHAKESPEARE'S LAW
By SIR GEORGE GREENWOOD

Cr. 8vo. **2s. 6d.** net. Boards.

In this book, Sir George Greenwood, having dealt with Shakespeare's handwriting, turns his attention to his knowledge of law. Mr. Holbrook Jackson, in a recent speech, alluding to the announcement of this book, said : " Sir George Greenwood is so impartial in his views of Shakespeare that he is one of the few critics of the poet whom we can trust."

Advertisement from the end pages of Lt.-Col. J. E. Tenant's
In the Clouds Above Baghdad: Being the Records an an Air Commander,
published by Cecil Palmer (1920).

CONTENTS

PART I: INDEXES

PART II: SOURCES – PERIODICALS

IIc: REGULAR OXFORDIAN COLUMNS IN NON-OXFORDIAN PERIODICALS

IId: OXFORDIAN PIECES IN NON-OXFORDIAN PERIODICALS

PART III: SOURCES – BOOKS

IIIA. NON-FICTION BOOKS AND PAMPHLETS OF SPECIAL INTEREST

Listed in chronological order.

IIIB. OXFORDIAN EDITIONS OF SHAKESPEAREAN ERA PLAYS

Introduced and annotated from an Oxfordian perspective.

IIIC. FICTION BOOKS AND DRAMATIC/MUSICAL WORKS OF SPECIAL INTEREST

Inspired by the idea of Edward de Vere as Shakespeare. Listed in chronological order.

IIID: COLLECTIONS OF ARTICLES BY OXFORDIAN AUTHORS

CONTENTS

CONTENTS

PART IV: SOURCES – AUDIO-VISUAL AND OTHER

PART V: CODA

*   *   *   *   *   *   *

ABBREVIATIONS
(in alphabetical order by abbreviation)

BC	Brief Chronicles: An Interdisciplinary Journal of Authorship Studies [Stritmatter]
BTC	Building the Case for Edward de Vere as Shakespeare [Altrocchi]
CY	Contested Year [Anderson, McNeil, Waugh]
DS	Discovering Shakespeare [Wright]
DSP	Dating Shakespeare's Plays [Gilvary]
DVN	De Vere Society Newsletter
EAM	East Anglian Magazine
EDV	Edward de Vere Newsletter [Green]
ER	Elizabethan Review, The [Goldstein]
ES	Early Shakespeare [Feldman/Hope]
EVR	Ever Reader, The [Boyle]
FF	First Folio
GO	Great Oxford [Malim, de Vere Society]
LC	Literature Criticism 1400-1800, vol. 193
LS	Lame Storyteller [Moore/Goldstein]
MS	My Shakespeare [Leahy]
NM	Necessary Mischief [Cutting]
NSJ	Neues Shake-speare Journal (German) [Laugwitz]
OXV	Oxfordian Vistas [Miller]
POV	Poems of Edward de Vere [Looney]
PR	Poet's Rage, A [Boyle]
RCA	Report My Cause Aright: SOS 50th Anniversary Anthology
REF	Reflections on the True Shakespeare (Goldstein)
SA	Shakespeare and His Authors [Leahy]
SAH	Shakespeare and His Rivals [McMichael & Glenn]
SAL	Shakespeare and the Law [Stritmatter]
SAR	Shakespearean Authorship Review
SAS	Shakespeare Authorship Sourcebook [Stritmatter]
SBD?	Shakespeare Beyond Doubt? [Shahan & Waugh]
SC	Shakespeare Cross-Examination
SCV	Shakespeare Criticism
SE	Shakespeare's Education [Fox/Goldstein]
SF	Shakespeare Fellowship
SFF	Shakespeare First Folio [Stritmatter]
SFA	Shakespeare Fellowship (American)
SFC	Shakespeare Fellowship Circulars
SFE	Shakespeare Fellowship (English)
SFI	Such Fruits Out of Italy [Magri/Goldstein]
SFQ	Shakespeare Fellowship Quarterly
SI	"Shakespeare" Identified [Looney]
SM	Shakespeare Matters
SMO	Shakespeare, Marlowe and Other Elizabethans [Feldman/Hope]
SOF	Shakespeare Oxford Fellowship
SON	Shakespeare Oxford Newsletter
SOS	Shakespeare Oxford Society
SSN	Spear-shaker Newsletter [Caruana]
SSR	Spear-shaker Review [Caruana]
TLR	Tennessee Law Review
TFF	The First Folio [Stritmatter]
TMWS	The Mysterious William Shakespeare [Ogburn]
TOX	The Oxfordian
TYLS	Twelve Years in the Life of Shakespeare [Whittemore]

INTRODUCTION TO THE FIFTH EDITION

In January 1945, the editors of the *Shakespeare Fellowship Quarterly* noted that since J. Thomas Looney had published *"Shakespeare" Identified* in 1920 "some 50 books, pamphlets and widely published magazine articles have been issued, amplifying and corroborating Mr. Looney's original discoveries."[6] Several hundred reviews of those books had also been published, as had some 1,100 other articles and letters discussing the Oxfordian idea in journals, magazines and newspapers in England, the United States and Canada. An additional 400 pieces had also been published in periodicals that the Shakespeare Fellowship distributed to its members. In sum, by early 1945 nearly 2,000 books, pamphlets, articles, reviews and letters to editors had been published addressing the idea that Edward de Vere, 17th Earl of Oxford—and not William Shakspere of Stratford-upon-Avon—was the real author of the works traditionally attributed to William Shakespeare. Today, the number (including documentaries, movies and other audio-video materials) surpasses 12,000.

An Index to Oxfordian Publications is designed to serve as a guide through that wealth of information for general readers interested in learning more about the extent of research into the Oxfordian answer to the Shakespeare authorship question, and as a reference tool for scholars already aware of much of the research that has been conducted on various topics and who need to find specific books or articles.

This Fifth Edition includes 3,000 items added since the Fourth Edition was published in 2017. These include Oxfordian items published over the past six years, as well as more than 2,000 older items I uncovered during five research trips to the United Kingdom beginning in 2018. Of primary importance among them are the 400 items in the papers given to me by J. Thomas Looney's grandson. These papers had been stored in a desk drawer in 1952 and forgotten about until rediscovered in 2019. They now form the J. Thomas Looney Archives in the Senate House Library at the University of London. Also of special importance are the thousands of Oxfordian items in the archives of several early Oxfordian scholars and organizations, as described below.

Among the "new" older items I found in those archives—and in the British Library and elsewhere—were complete sets of articles for the four non-Oxfordian periodicals that ran regular Oxfordian columns edited by the Shakespeare Fellowship (UK) or the Shakespeare Oxford Society (U.S.): in the UK these include *The Hackney Spectator* (1922-1925), *The Shakespeare Pictorial* (1929-1936) and *The East Anglian Magazine* (1937-1941); and, in the United States several decades later, Louis Marder's *Shakespeare Newsletter* (1979-1991).

With these and other new listings from older and recent publications, the *Index* now includes nearly every known publication commenting on the Oxfordian idea. Among these are 700 stand alone items (books, pamphlets and audio-visual productions), 3,600 pieces in general circulation periodicals, and more than 7,400 pieces in periodicals distributed to members of Oxfordian organizations. An additional 300 pieces not reprinted from elsewhere appeared in Oxfordian collections, for a total of more than 12,000. These pieces were written by 1,440 authors. Not every author listed has been convinced that Edward de Vere wrote Shakespeare's works, but almost all have had something substantive to say about the question of his authorship.

---

[6] *Shakespeare Fellowship Quarterly*, vol VI, no. 1 (Jan. 1945): 10.

⎯⎯⎯⎯⎯⎯◗◖⎯⎯⎯⎯⎯⎯

The *Index* is organized into two main parts. The first includes an author index, a title index, and lists of reviews of books and A/V materials of special interest to Oxfordians. Parts II-IV contain the sources of the materials indexed in Part I: Part II reprints the tables of contents of every Oxfordian periodical ever published, and lists pieces addressing the Oxfordian idea in general circulation periodicals. Part III identifies books and pamphlets of special interest to Oxfordian, non-fiction and fiction, in chronological order, and presents tables of contents of collections of Oxfordian materials. Part IV is a listing of audio-visual materials of special interest, in chronological order. All publications have been cross-referenced with each other as well as incorporated into the indexes in Part I. Further details can be found in the Table of Contents.

The *Index* complements two other publications that I have already released and a third currently in preparation, which lay out the context in which the Oxfordian pieces indexed here were published. The first is *Shakespeare Revolutionized: The First Hundred Years of J. Thomas Looney's "Shakespeare Identified*, of which Heward Wilkinson wrote, "this massive, extraordinary, and extremely riveting history is not neutral; it is transformative; and it alters the identity of the movement. It is monumental history, history which creates a new sense of time and being for peoples."[7] The second is *Shakespeare Investigated: Publications of the Shakespeare Fellowship, 1922-1936*, which reprints the full text of 335 early Oxfordian pieces. And third, currently being prepared, is *Shakespeare Discussed*, which reprints the full text of more than 500 letters exchanged between early Oxfordians, 1920-1945. More than half are either from or to J. Thomas Looney.

Supplementing these books are new editions of fifteen out-of-print books from the first decades of the Oxfordian era that I have brought back into print over the past five years. These new editions have modern layouts and fonts, scholarly introductions, annotations, bibliographies and indexes. More information about them is included in the final pages of this volume.

This *Index* also serves as a complement to the Shakespeare Online Authorship Resources (SOAR) cataloue developed by Bill Boyle and available at the New England Shakespeare Oxford Library (NESOL), whose website is www.shakespeareoxford library.org. This essential database can be searched by subject, and it provides easy access to the full text of thousands of Oxfordian pieces. SOAR also includes summaries of hundreds of the most important articles and chapters of Oxfordian books. Eventually all items listed in this *Index* will be included in the SOAR database, with links to the full texts of all those for which copyright restrictions do not apply.

And, this *Index* supports the work of the Shakespeare Oxford Fellowship's Data Preservation Committee, which works to preserve Oxfordian documents that tell the story of the Oxfordian movement as well as the research and analysis of the authorship question.

⎯⎯⎯⎯⎯⎯◗◖⎯⎯⎯⎯⎯⎯

With only a few exceptions, this *Index* lists only print publications—books, pamphlets and pieces in periodicals—and audio-visual recordings. A few online publications are

---

[7] *De Vere Society Newsletter*, vol. 28/4 (October 2021): 36-43.

included, such as *The Ever Reader*, published online by the Shakespeare Oxford Society in the 1990s. The most prominent authorship or Oxfordian websites and blogs are noted, but their contents are not included. Current online discussions, though of great value, are also excluded because they are different in tone and function from printed materials. and because their contents change frequently.

In this Fifth Edition I have expanded the list of books of interest to Oxfordians to include several dozen that aren't Oxfordian publications *per se*, but which touch on the authorship question and provide information useful for understanding the context in which "Shakespeare" lived and wrote. Among them are:

Cyndia S. Clegg: *Press Censorship in Elizabethan England* (1997)

Frank Harris: *The Man Shakespeare and His Tragic Life-story* (1909)

Alfred Hart: *Shakespeare and the Homilies, and Other Pieces of Research into the Elizabethan Drama* (1934)

Leah S. Marcus: *Puzzling Shakespeare: Local Reading and Its Discontents* (1988)

Penny McCarthy: *Pseudonymous Shakespeare* (2006)

Annabel M. Patterson: *Censorship and Interpretation: The Conditions of Writing and Reading in Early Modern England* (1984)

Janet W. Starner & Barbara H. Traister: *Anonymity in Early Modern England* (2011)

E. M. W. Tillyard: *The Elizabethan World Picture* (1941).

In past editions of this *Index*, I included only those items in periodicals for which I had definite information; leads on additional pieces not yet investigated or found were removed from my working draft before publication. In this edition, however, I have left in several dozen incomplete listings, such as the following:

Weekly Dispatch
> Date?   [Not yet found. Cecil Palmer stated that the first review of *"Shakespeare" Identified* appeared in this publication. (See SFE, March 1952, p. 4) for details.)]

I have also included a small number of unpublished items. One example is this listing:

Ruth Loyd Miller
> 1974   [Five-page letter to the *American Bar Association Journal*, dated December 6, 1974, in response to "Who Wrote Shakespeare?" in the October 1974 issue; unpublished, but is item DVS129 in the De Vere Society Archives at Brunel University.]

The *Index* has grown so lengthy that even after moving from the 7.5 x 9.25 inch size of the previous four editions to the current 8 x 10 inch size, I have had to omit the following sections to stay within the printer's maximum of 828 pages:

• A Chronological Listing of All Oxfordian Publications, 1920 to the Present;

• A Chronological Listing of All Oxfordian Events, 1920 to the Present;

• Contents of Archives of Oxfordian Materials in Public Institutions in England. Information on these five sets of papers can be found on the websites of the following intitutions:

Concordia University, Library, Special Collections Room
Archives of the Shakespeare Fellowship/Shakespearean Authorship Trust
Archives of the De Vere Society

University of London, Senate House Library, Special Collections Room
Archives of Katharine E. Eggar
Archives of J. Thomas Looney

University of Liverpool, Jones Library
Archives of Gerald H. Rendall.

In future editions of the *Index*, in addition to adding newly published pieces and newly found older materials, I hope to add materials in several important areas not yet fully investigated. These include the following:

• Archives of major Oxfordian scholars not yet located, which need to be found and examined;

• Unpublished manuscripts in the archives already located, which need to be assessed for publication;

• Lists of talks/presentations given at Oxfordian conferences, which are yet to be compiled;

• A more extensive listing of articles about the Oxfordian idea in encyclopedias;

• Country Indexes of Oxfordian Events and Publications for countries such as Austria, France, Germany, Holland, Sweden and Australia, which aren't yet compiled.

For Holland, for instance, I am aware of but haven't yet located a copy of Pieter N. Helsloot's 2004 Dutch language biography of Edward de Vere, *Edward de Vere: Onvermijdelijk Shakespeare*. I am also aware of an article by Dr. Gunning that appeared in *De Amsterdammer*, the leading Dutch paper of the time, on May 12, 1923, but don't yet have a copy of it.

I also know that K. D. W. Boissevain wrote an essay on Edward de Vere that was published in *Haagsch Maandblad* in Holland, but don't have any more information than that. I recently learned that in 1941 Boissevain was translating into Dutch Charles Barrell's article on the Ashbourne Portrait published in *Scientific American* in January 1940. I also came across a reference to a Charles Boissevain who gave a lecture on Edward de Vere at the Lyceum de Suisse in Geneva that was published in *La Tribune de Geneva* on February 1, 1938. Were these two Boissevains the same person? I don't know. Much work remains to be done to tell the story of the Oxfordian movement in Holland, England, the United States and many other countries.

As in previous editions, the *Index* is intended to guide readers not just through Oxfordian research and findings published over the past century, but also to make better known the individuals active in the Oxfordian movement. Readers might be surprised to learn that more than 1,440 people have contributed to discussion of the Oxfordian answer to the Shakespeare authorship question in the periodical literature – some by only one article or letter – but others by scores of items, all the way up to Richard F. Whalen, with 184 articles, reviews and letters, not to mention several Oxfordian books.

Most Oxfordians are aware of the contributions being made by those currently researching and publishing their work, and also of such early luminaries as J. Thomas Looney, Percy Allen, Col. Bernard R. Ward and Capt. Bernard M. Ward, Eva Turner Clark, and Charles W. Barrell. They are probably also aware of the seminal contributions made in the intervening decades by Charlton and Dorothy Ogburn, Charlton Ogburn, Jr., and Ruth Loyd Miller. But they might not be much aware of the important contributions made by other Oxfordians whose articles are still worth reading. Among them are Louis P. Bénézet, Gwynneth M. Bowen, Gordon G. Cyr, Col. Montagu Douglas, Father Francis Edwards, Katherine E. Eggar, A. Bronson Feldman, Admiral H. H. Holland, Richard C. Horne, Jr., Morse Johnson, William Kent, Harold W. Patience, Canon Gerald H. Rendall, Esther Singleton, Gilbert Slater, David W. T. C. Vessey, and Ruth M. D. Wainewright.

Many of these people are well worth remembering not only for the quality of their research, but also for their efforts to keep the Oxfordian flame alive during the long decades of the past 100 years. Perhaps the most important benefit of this *Index* comes not from the articles and books indexed in it, but simply from the reminder it offers Oxfordians today that they are part of a long and arduous effort to garner rightful recognition of Edward de Vere, 17th Earl of Oxford, as the author of the greatest literary creations in human history.

⎯⎯⎯◆⎯⎯⎯

In closing, I am happy to acknowledge the guidance of Bill Boyle, whose assistance was instrumental in turning my database of current Oxfordian newsletters into the First Edition of this *Index* (2012). His making available the issues of older newsletters enabled me to prepare the Second Edition (2013), and his encouragemnt led me to begin the effort to seek out and incorporate Oxfordian articles in non-Oxfordian periodicals into the Third Edition (2015). I am grateful for his continuing encouragement, which led to the greatly expanded Fourth Edition (2017) and Fifth Edition (2023).

Jim Warren
September, 2023

"SHAKESPEARE" IDENTIFIED
By J. THOMAS LOONEY

There is no cipher, no cryptogram, no mystery in this important treatment of the Shakespearean controversy. Its straightforward attitude must appeal to all intelligent readers, whether Shakespeare scholars or not. The growing doubts regarding the claims of William Shakespeare of Stratford are here crystallized, and a logical presentment of the known facts, backed by newly discovered evidence, strongly points to Edward de Vere, Seventeenth Earl of Oxford, as the real author of the plays. *Net $5.00.*

Stokes Books advertistment
in *The Atlantic Monthley*, June 1920.

PART I: INDEXES

IA. INDEX OF AUTHORS

Adamson, T. L. (continued)
Shorter pieces
1943, Aug.	[letter: need for discussion to reach consensus on Oxfordian ideas]	SF News-l. (E), vol. 4/5: 67-68
1946, March	Oxfordians v. Baconians: A Public Debate	SF News-letter (E), p. 4
1955, Spring	Shakespeare and Oxford in the Lecture Room [repr. in BTC, vol. 4: 127-132]	SF News-letter (E), p. 7-8
1955, Spring	[review of *The Renaissance Man of England, Revised Edition,* by Dorothy and Charlton Ogburn (1955)]	SF News-letter (E), p. 12
1955, Sept.	Shakespeare, Earl of Rutland?	Literary Guide, p. 19-20
1956, Spring	[review of *Shakespeare* by Charles. J. Sisson]	SF News-letter (E), p. 10
1958, Spring	[report on Gwynneth Bowen's Jan. 16 lecture "Reign of King John"]	SF News-letter (E), p. 3
1958, Autumn	Mr. J. Shera Atkinson (d. 1958) [obituary]	SF News-letter (E), p. 8
1959, Spring	Mr. Percy Allen (1875-1959) [obituary] [repr. in BTC, vol. 5: 329-30]	Sh. Authorship Rev. no. 1: 22-23
1962, Spring	Charlton Ogburn (1882-1962) [obituary] [repr. in BTC, vol. 5: 81-82]	Sh. Authorship Rev. no. 7: 19
1966, Autumn	Mr. H. S. Shield (d. 1966) [obituary]	Sh. Authorship Rev. no. 16: 26

Addison, William
1973	*Essex Worthies: A Biographical Companion to the County.* London: Phillimore. [excerpt, "History of de Vere Family," repr. in SON, vol. 18/3 (Summer 1982): 10-12; and in BTC, vol. 6: 200-08]	

Adler, Mortimer J.
2002, Nov.	["Who Wrote *Hamlet*? The Great Shakespeare Hoax" by Max Weismann reprints Adler's Nov. 7, 1997 letter stating his conviction that Edward de Vere wrote the works of Shakespeare, and recommends reading SI]	Great Ideas Online, no. 203: 7-8

Adler, Tony
1994, Nov.	The Big Whodunnit	Stagebill (Chicago), p. 14

Agate, James
1943, July 18	Shakespeare, Bacon, or Both?" [review of *Shakespeare: New Views for Old* by R. S. Eagle]	Sunday Times, p. 2

Aitchiff
1930, Sept. 27	Week After Week	Graphic, p. 486

Aitken, T. M.
Books and pamphlets
1948	*The Inspiration of Shakespeare* [pamphlet, with Sir H. S. Lawrence]. Printed Privately.	

Shorter pieces
1938, Jan. 20	A New Shakespeare Candidate [letter]	British Weekly, p. 314
1939, April	A Criticism of "An Enquiry" Response by Percy Allen, same pub, p. 9-20. Response by Bernard M. Ward, same pub., p. 20-24.	SF News-letter (E), no. 14, Supplement, p. 5-9
1939, April	Queen Elizabeth – Oxford – Son Theory: A Reply to Allen and Ward	SF News-l. (E), no. 14, Supplement 2, p. 1-4
1947, Oct.	Woman's Hand in Shakespeare [letter] [repr. in *The Inspiration of Shakespeare* (pamphlet)]	Int'l Women's News
1953, April	[review of *Lord Oxford and the Shakespeare Group* by Col. Douglas]	SF News-letter (E), p. 9
1957, Spring	Lt. Col. Montagu W. Douglas (d. 1957) [obituary]	SF News-letter (E), p. 11

Akrigg, G. P. V.
Books
1968	*Shakespeare and the Earl of Southampton.* London: H. Hamilton; and Cambridge: Harvard University Press.	

Shorter pieces
1980	[review of *Shakespeare By Hilliard* by Leslie Hotson (1977)]	Mod. Philology, v. 77: 427-29

Alberge, Dalya
1996, April 23	McKellen Scorns Much Literary Ado About Nothing	Times (London), p. 4
2012, Aug. 19	Suzman "mad as a snake" with Rylance Over Bard "Myths"	Observer, p. 5
2012, Oct. 13	Zounds! He's Cracked the de Vere Code	Sunday Times
2013, March 31	National Shakespearean Scholars United to See Off Claims of "Bard Deniers" [review of *Shakespeare Beyond Doubt*]	Observer, p. 23
2015, Feb. 1	Has the Mystery of Shakespeare's Sonnets Finally Been Solved?	Observer, p. 13

Author Index

Alderman, Sidney S.
  1956, May   To the Editor and Readers of *The Shakespeare Newsletter*   Sh. Newsl., vol. 6/3: 18
       [letter, with 21 other signers]

Alexander, Ben
  2011   Susan Vere and the River Avon [letter]   Oxfordian, vol. 13: 4
  2012, Sum/Fall   Lady Susan de Vere [letter]   Sh. Ox. Newsl., vol. 48/3: 8

Alexander, James
  2019, Jan.   [review of *Shakespeare's Dark Lady: Amelia Bassano Lanier:*   De Vere Soc. Newsl., vol. 26/1:
       The Woman Behind Shakespeare's Plays? by John Hudson]   42-44
  2019, April   Elizabethan Treasures: Miniatures by Hilliard and Oliver (National   De Vere Soc. Newsl., vol. 26/2:
       Portrait Gallery, London (21 February – 19 May 2019)   38-43

Alexander, Mark A.
Blog: www.sourcetext.com/sourcebook
Shorter pieces
  2000, Winter   Shakespeare's "Bad Law:" Journey Through the History of the   Sh. Ox. Newsl., vol. 35/4: 1, 9-13
       Arguments [repr. in RCA, p. 44-54; and in EVR, vol. 10]
  2001   Shakespeare's Knowledge of Law: History of the Argument   Oxfordian, vol. 4: 51-120
       [repr. in *Sh. and the Law* (Stritmatter, 2022): 115-70]
  2001, Fall   [letter: importance of the Shakespeare Fellowship]   Sh. Matters, vol. 1/1: 2
  2004   [letter: Regnier's *University of Miami Law Review* article]   Oxfordian, vol. 7: 170

Alexander, Peter
  1932, Jan.   [review of *Shakespeare's Plays in the Order of Their Writing* by   Rev. Eng. St., vol. 8/29: 102
       Eva Turner Clark
  1962, July 27   Who Was Shakespeare? [reviews of *The Shakespeare Claimants* by   Times Lit. Sup., is. 3152: 542
       H. Gibson and *The Authorship of Shakespeare* by J. McManaway]

Alexander, Ted
  2002, Nov. 27   Defends Oxfordians [letter]   Globe and Mail, p. A22

Alexis, Louis E. M.
  1975   At Last the Truth about Shakespeare: Every Word Doth Almost   ISIS (Oxford), p. 20-23
       Sell His Name
  1975, Winter   British Oxfordian Develops Theory on "Dram of Eale" Problem   Sh. Ox. Newsl., vol. 11/1: 5
  1975, Summer   Plato and Clown William   Sh. Ox. Newsl., vol. 11/2: 19-22
  1978, Summer   Common Sense About "Shake-Speare"   Sh. Ox. Newsl., vol. 14/3: 6-7

Alford, Stephen
  2012   *The Watchers: A Secret History of the Reign of Elizabeth I.* Allen Lane.

Aljumily, Refat
  2015   Applying Hierarchical and Non-Hierarchical Linear and Non-Linear   Soc. Sci., vol. 4/3: 758-99
       Clustering Methods to the "Shakespeare Authorship Question"

Allen, D. F.
  1937, July   The Annual Dinner   SF News-letter (E), no. 4: 6
  1938, July   The Annual Dinner   SF News-letter (E), no. 10: 2

Allen, Ernest
Books and pamphlets
  1937   *When Shakespeare Died.* [pamphlet]
  1933   *Lord Oxford & "Shakespeare:" A Reply to John Drinkwater* [with Percy Allen]. London: Denis Archer.
Shorter pieces
  1932, July   Annual Dinner   Sh. Pictorial, no. 53: 116
  1933, May 17   The Oxfordians: A Reply to John Drinkwater [with Percy Allen]   Manchester Guardian, p. 5
  1935, Oct.   [letter: evidence in the *Sonnets* points to Lord Oxford]   Sh. Pictorial, no. 92: 158
  1936, July   Claimants to "Shakespeare" Authorship   Sh. Pictorial, no. 101: 116
       [resp. by E.S., Aug., no. 102: 128]
  1936, Sept.   [letter: reply to E.S.]   Sh. Pictorial, no. 103: 136
  1936, Nov.   Criticism from Australia   Sh. Pictorial, no. 105: 180
  1937, Sept.   [Shakespearean page]   East Anglian Mag., vol. 2/12:
       [repr. in BTC, vol. 2: 34-37 with title "Shakespeare's Sonnets."]   537-38
  1937, Dec.   [letter: Shakespeare's Sonnets]   East Ang. Mag., vol. 3/3: 142
  1938, March   [letter: Sir Christopher Hatton as Malvolio?]   SF News-letter (E), no. 8: 13

Allen, Ernest (continued)

1939, Feb.	Where are Shakespeare's Portraits?	East Ang. Mag., vol. 4/5: 183-84
1939, April	Curious "Tributes" to Shakespeare	East Ang. Mag., vol. 4/6: 311-12
1940, April	Who Was Cheveril?	SF News-letter (E), p. 5-6

Allen, Percy

Books and pamphlets [All have been reprinted in *Complete Writings on Shakespeare by Percy Allen* (7 volumes). Edited by James A. Warren. Cary, NC: Veritas Publications. 2022.]

1928	*Shakespeare as a Topical Dramatist.* [pamphlet published by the Poetry League]
1928	*Shakespeare, Jonson, and Wilkins as Borrowers.* London: Cecil Palmer. [2nd ed. 1972. New York: Russell & Russell]
1929	*Open Letter.* [pamphlet: Shakespeare Fellowship Circular] [June]
1929	*Shakespeare and Chapman as Topical Dramatists.* London: Cecil Palmer.
1930	*The Case for Edward de Vere, 17th Earl of Oxford, as "Shakespeare".* London: Cecil Palmer.
1930	*The Case for Edward de Vere, 17th Earl of Oxford, as "Shakespeare"* (booklet). London: Cecil Palmer.
1931	*The Oxford-Shakespeare Case Corroborated.* London: Cecil Palmer. [excerpt repr. in BTC, vol. 1: 358-80]
1932	*The Life Story of Edward de Vere as "William Shakespeare."* Intro. by Capt. B. M. Ward, p. xi-xv. London: Cecil Palmer.
1933	*Lord Oxford & "Shakespeare": A Reply to John Drinkwater* (with Ernest Allen). London: Denis Archer. [excerpt, "Note by Percy Allen," repr. in BTC, vol. 1: 382-404]
1933	*The Plays of Shakespeare & Chapman in Relation to French History.* With an introduction by Marjorie Bowen. London: Denis Archer. [Intro. repr. in BTC, vol. 1: 333-47]
1934	*Anne Cecil, Elizabeth & Oxford.* London: Denis Archer. [excerpt repr. in BTC, vol. 5: 402-419]
1936	*An Enquiry into the Relations Between Lord Oxford as "Shakespeare," Queen Elizabeth and the Fair Youth.* London: Percy Allen. [repr. in BTC, vol. 3: 407-27]
1943	*Who Were the Dark Lady and Fair Youth of the Sonnets?* [pamphlet printed privately]
1947	*Talks with Elizabethans: Revealing the Mystery of "William Shakespeare."* London: Rider and Company. [The Library of Congress lists Hester Dowden as the author.]

Periodicals edited

1940, April-1945, Nov.: *Shakespeare Fellowship News-letter* (English)

Shorter pieces [All have been reprinted in *Complete Writings on Shakespeare by Percy Allen* (7 volumes). Edited by James A. Warren. Cary, NC: Veritas Publications. 2022]

1923, May 19	Hamlet's Identity with an Elizabethan [by PA] [repr. in *Billboard*, Aug. 25, 1923, p. 64]	Christian Sci. Monitor, p. D7
1928, March 31	[letter: resp. to Ivor Brown's March 31 review of *Borrowers*]	Sat. Review, vol. 145: 388
1928, April 4	[letter: resp. to its March 20 review of *Borrowers*, with editor's reply]	Man. Guardian, p. 5
1928, April 14	[letter: resp. to Ivor Brown's April 7 reply, & reply by editor & Brown]	Sat. Review, vol. 145: 462-63
1928, June 15	With Hamlet in Hackney [review of *The 17th Earl of Oxford* by B. M. Ward] [by PA]	Christian Sci. Monitor, p. 11
1928, July	The Historic Originals of Ophelia	Sh. Review, vol. 1/3: 166-71
1928, July 3	Versatile Elizabethan: Willfull Young Earl [review of *The 17th Earl of Oxford* by B. M. Ward] [by PA]	Christian Sci. Monitor, p. 12
1928, Aug. 18	Musings Over the Shakespearean First Folio [by PA]	Christian Sci. Monitor, p. 7
1929, Jan. 18	The Rhyme-Linked Order of Shakespeare's Sonnets [by PA]	Christian Sci. Monitor, p. 4
1929, Feb. 7	Elizabeth and Essex [letter]	Times Lit. Sup., is. 1410: 98
1929, March 2	[letter: resp. to Ivor Brown's Feb. 23 review of *Topical Dramatists*, with reply by Brown]	Sat. Review, vol. 147: 281
1929, March 28	[letter: resp. to Byrne's March 21 review of *Topical Dramatists*]	Times Lit. Sup., is. 1417: 260
1930, April	[letter: resp. to G. B. Harrison's January review of two of his books; with reply by Harrison]	Rev. Eng. St., vol. 6/22: 196-8
1930, April 2	[letter: resp. to its March 12 review of *Case*]	Eastbourne Gazette., p. 25
1929, April 4	[letter: further resp. to Byrne's March 21 review]	Times Lit. Sup., is. 1418: 276
1929, May 24	One Theory as to the Authorship of Shakespeare's Sonnets	Christian Sci. Monitor, p. 9
1929, May 30	[letter: resp. to the May 23 review of *Topical Dramatists*]	Stage, p. 15
1929, June 5	Authorship of the Sonnets [letter: resp. to Eagle's May 18 article]	Telegraph
1929, Sept.	[letter: resp. to Harrison's Aug. review]	London Mercury, vol. xx/119
1929, Sept. 12	[letter: comments on a Chapman play]	Times Lit. Sup., is. 1441: 705
1929, Sept. 26	[letter: resp. to A. S. Ferguson's Sept. 19 letter]	Times Lit. Sup., is. 1443: 746
1929, Dec. 27	How Shakespeare Wrote *King Lear*	Christian Sci. Monitor, p. 7

Author Index

Allen, Percy (continued)

1934, Oct. 3	Shakespearean Topicalities [review of *Shakespeare, Oxford, and Elizabethan Times* by Adm. Hubert H. Holland]	Christian Sci. Mon., p. WM10
1935, June	Our Year's Activities	Sh. Pictorial, no. 88: 93
1935, July	[review of *Sunlight on Shakespeare's Sonnets* by G. W. Phillips]	Sh. Pictorial, no. 89: 112
1935, Oct. 3	Lord Oxford as Shakespeare [letter: resp. to Lawrence's Oct. 3 article]	Times Lit. Sup., is. 1757: 612
1935, Nov.	Yet Another Contender [letter: Shakespeare Monument at Stratford] [response to George Corlius' Oct. article]	Sh. Pictorial, no. 93: 172
1935, Dec. 4	*Hamlet*, Topically [rev. of *What Happens in Hamlet* by J. Do. Wilson]	Christian Sci. Mon., p. WM12
1936, Feb.	More *Hamlet* Problems [review of *The MS. of Shakespeare's Hamlet*]	Sh. Pictorial, no. 96: 36
1936, Feb. 8	Thomas Sackville [letter]	Times Lit. Sup., is. 1775: 116
1936, May	Shakespeare's Imagery [review of the book by Caroline Spurgeon]	Sh. Pictorial, no. 99: 84
1936, May 9	Stage or Study [letter: resp. to Gregg: *Hamlet* Q2 supports de Vere]	Times Lit. Sup., is. 1788: 400
1936, July 18	Names in *The Winter's Tale* [letter: resp. to Griffin's June 6 letter]	Times Lit. Sup., is. 1798: 600
1936, Aug.	Topical Events in Drama of Shakespeare's Age	Sh. Pictorial, no. 102: 132
1936, Oct.	Another Bombshell for the Orthodox [review of *The Problem of Hamlet – A Solution* by A. S. Cairncross (1936)]	Sh. Pictorial, no. 104: 164
1937, Jan.	Shakespearean Adventures in Canada and the United States	SF News-letter (E), no. 1: 2-7
1937, Jan. 2	The Date of *Hamlet* [letter: resp. to Dec. 19 review of Cairncross] [repr. in SFE, no. 2: 9-10 (March 1937)] Response by Cairncross, TLS, Jan. 9, p. 28.	Times Lit. Sup., is. 1822: 12
1937, March	Dr. Cairncross and *Hamlet* [letter to the *Times Literary Sup.* repr.]	SF News-letter (E), no. 2: 9-10
1937, April 28	Was Oxford Shakespeare? [letter: response to Cooke's April 20 letter]	West. Morning News, p. 11
1937, May	Lord Oxford as Shakespeare [repr. in BTC, vol. 2: 5-13] Response in *The Bury Free Press*, April 24.	East Angl. Mag., vol. 2/5: 340-45
1937, May	Shakespeare and Montaigne	SF News-letter (E), no. 3: 5-7
1937, Sept. 18	Montaigne and *Twelfth Night* [letter]	Times Lit. Sup., is. 1859: 675
1937, Nov. 27	The 17th Earl of Oxford	Sunday Times, p. 16
1938, Jan.	[review of *I, William Shakespeare* by Leslie Hotson]	SF News-letter. (E), no. 7: 3-5
1938, Jan.	Shakespearean Page [The Question of Locality]	East Ang. Mag., vol. 3/4: 172-73
1938, Feb.	Shakespeare Upon a Platform Stage	Drama
1938, March	[response to Gilbert Slater's "The Rival Poet of the *Sonnets*"]	SF News-letter (E), no. 8: 3-5
1938, April	Shakespearean Page [more thoughts on the question of locality]	East Ang. Mag., vol. 3/6: 309-10
1938, May	Shakespeare's *Coriolanus*	SF News-letter (E), no. 9: 6-7
1938, May	[review of *Shakespeare Rediscovered* by Clara L de Chambrun]	SF News-letter (E), no. 9: 7-9
1938, June	Shakearean Page [Chronology of the Plays]	East Ang. Mag., vol. 3/8: 371-72
1938, July	Recent Books on the *Sonnets*	SF News-letter (E), no. 10: 8-9
1938, July	Pirate Publishers [letter: *Macbeth* was abbreviated acting version]	Sh. Pictorial, no. 125: 107
1938, July 31	Shakespeare and Herbert Lawrence, 1769 [letter]	Sunday Times, p. 10
1938, Aug	Shakespearean Page [the De Vere star] [repr. In BTC, vol. 2: 56-58]	East Ang. Mag., vol. 3/10: 487-8
1938, Sept.	The First Anti-Stratfordian [review of *The Life and Adventures of Common Sense* by Herbert Lawrence (1769)]	SF News-letter (E), no. 11: 1-5
1938, Sept.	[review of *Elizabeth and Sixtus* by H. Kendra Baker (1938)]	SF News-letter (E), no. 11: 8-9
1938, Nov.	Shakespearean Page [*The Life and Adventures of Common Sense* by Herbert Lawrence (1769)]	East Ang. Mag., vol. 4/1: 13-14
1938, Nov.	Commentary on *Life and Adventures of Common Sense* by Herbert Lawrence (1769)	SF News-letter (E), no. 12: 2-16
1938, Nov.	How Lawrence Acquired His Information	SF News-letter (E), no. 12: 17-18
1939, Jan.	Opening Spencer's Grave [letter]	Sh. Pictorial, no. 143: 8
1939, Feb. 10	Who Was Shakespeare? [letter: resp. to Barrett, with reply by Barrett]	John O'London's Weekly, p. 821
1939, April	Mr. Percy Allen's Reply [in the Supplement to the issue]	SF News-letter (E), vol. 14 Supplement: 9-20
1939, Aug.	The Other View-point [response to Hipperson's July article]	East Ang. Mag., vol. 4/9: 434-35
1940, Jan.	MOAI Doth Sway My Life	East Ang. Mag., vol. 5/1: 16-17
1940, May	Shakespeare's *Cymbeline* and East Anglia	East Ang. Mag., vol. 5/4: 153-54
1941, April	The "Ashbourne" Portrait of Shakespeare [review of the pamphlet by Gerald H. Rendall]	East Ang. Mag., vol. 5/6: 229-30
1941, Oct.	Did Queen Elizabeth Bear a Child?	SF News-letter (E), p. 3
1941, Oct.	Actors and the Oxford-Shakespeare Case	SF News-letter (E), p. 3-4

1942, Oct.	Sir Edward Vere and Mr. Barrell's Discovery	SF News-letter (E), p. 2
1942, April	How Lord Oxford Paid His Way	SF News-letter (E), p. 2
1942, April	Mr. Charles Barrell and Our American Branch	SF News-letter (E), p. 3
1942, April	Melford Hall and Shakespeare	SF News-letter (E), p. 3-4
1942, April	Mr. Charles Boissevain and Mons. H. R. Leonormand; Mr. Osbert Sitwell on Shakespeare	SF News-letter (E) p. 4
1940, April	[letter to *Times Lit. Sup.*, Lyly's *Endimion* and Lord Oxford; not printed]	SF News-letter (E), p. 6
1942, Oct.	Peele's Sonnet on Oxford (1590)	SF News-letter (E), p. 3-4
1942, Oct.	[letter to BBC World Service re Bacon; not printed]	SF News-letter (E), p. 4
1943, May	Peele's Verses in Polyhymmus II	SF News-letter (E), page 4
1943, Oct.	[review of *A Comparative Study of Shakespeare's Bad Quartos* by Alfred Hart]	SF News-letter (E), p. 2
1944, May	John Thomas Looney (1870-1944)	SF News-letter (E), p. 2-4
1944, May	The Symbolism of *Pericles* and *Winter's Tale*	SF News-letter (E), p. 4-5
1944, May	The Elizabethan Mind [review of *The Elizabethan World Picture* by E. M. W. Tillyard	SF News-letter (E), page 6
1944, May	Francis Bacon's Share in the Shakespeare Folio of 1623	SF News-letter (E), p. 8
1945, May	Frederick Bligh Bond	SF News-letter (E), p. 3
1945, May	The Group Theory and Some Modern Intellectuals	SF News-letter (E), p. 4
1945, Nov.	Oxford as the Water-Bearer	SF News-letter (E), p. 4-5
1946, March	[review of *Elizabethan Plays and Players* by G. B. Harrison (1945)]	SF News-letter (E), p. 4-5
1950, April	Much Ado About Nothing—A Burlesque of the Oxford-Howard-Arundel Quarrel [repr. in Clark, *Hidden Allusions*, 3rd ed., Ruth Loyd Miller, editor, p. 549-51 (1974)]	SF News-letter (E), p. 4-5
1951, April	*King Lear* in Relation to French History (repr. in BTC, vol. 4: 112-4)	SF News-letter (E), p. 6
1951, July-Aug.	Shakespearer or Bacon—or Oxford? I. The Composite Shakespeare	Open Forum, vol. 1/1: 48-52
1953, April	[review of *This Star of England* by Dorothy and Charlton Ogburn] [repr. in BTC, vol. IV, p. 117-118]	SF News-letter (E), p. 6-7

Allen, Ron
Books
1998	*Who Were Shake-speare? The Ultimate Who-dunit.* San Diego: Silverado.	

Shorter pieces
1999, Spring	[letter: role of Edward de Vere in the writing of Shakespeare's plays]	Sh. Ox. Newsl., vol. 35/1: 22

Allsop, Kenneth
1962, June 7	"The Day Those Tudor Beatniks Dreamed Up Shaksper"	Daily Mail, p. 12.

Allvine, Glendon
1947, June 29	[letter: Oxford's literary genius]	NY Herald Tribune, p. II-7

Alter, Alexandra
2010, April 2	"The Shakespeare Whodunit: A Scholar Tackles Doubters on Who Wrote the Plays" [interview with James Shapiro]	Wall St. Journal, p. W4
2010, April 9	"The Plays the Thing – Shakespeare Still has His Doubters [review of *Contested Will* by James Shapiro]	Wall St. Journal, p. W12
2011, April 2	"Just Asking: Hollywood Weighs in [review of *Anonymous*]	Wall St. Journal, p. W4

Altrocchi, Julia C.
1959, Spring	Ships and Spears in Genoa [repr. in BTC, vol. 5: 6-15] Response by H. S. Shield, Autumn 1959, p. 24. Response to Shield by Gwynneth M. Bowen, same issue, p. 24.	Sh. Authorship Rev. #1: 8-11
1959, Autumn	Edward de Vere and the Commedia Dell' Arte [repr. in SON, 42/1: 24-25 (Winter 2006); and in BTC, vol. 5: 28-30]	Sh. Authorship Rev. #2: 3-4
1960, Autumn	The Names of Shakespeare's Characters	Sh. Authorship Rev. #4: 20
1971, March	From Mrs. Julia Cooley Altrocchi	Sh. Ox. Newsl., vol. 7/1: 3
1971, June 1	The Diamond Tablet	Sh. Ox. Newsl., vol. 7/2: 6-7
2007, Sum.	Note for Sir John Sheppard [poem written during his April 1952 lecture at the University of California]	Sh. Ox. Newsl., vol. 43/3: 3
2007, Summer	The Ghost of Edward de Vere Speaks [reprint of a poem]	Sh. Ox. Newsl., vol. 43/3: 16

Altrocchi, Paul H.

Books

2010	*Malice Aforethought: The Killing of a Unique Genius.* Xlibris.
2000	*Most Greatly Lived: A Biographical Novel of Edward de Vere, Seventeenth Earl of Oxford, Whose Pen Name was William Shakespeare.* Xlibris Corp.

Books edited

2014	*Building the Case for Edward de Vere as Shakespeare, vol. 6: Wonder of Our Stage.* iUniverse.com.
2014	*Building the Case for Edward de Vere as Shakespeare, vol. 7: Avalanche of Falsity.* iUniverse.com.
2014	*Building the Case for Edward de Vere as Shakespeare, vol. 8: To All the World Must Die.* iUniverse.com.
2014	*Building the Case for Edward de Vere as Shakespeare, vol. 9: Soul of the Age.* iUniverse.com.
2014	*Building the Case for Edward de Vere as Shakespeare, vol. 10: Moniment.* iUniverse.com.

Books co-edited with Hank Whittemore

2009	*Building the Case for Edward de Vere as Shakespeare, vol. 1: The Great Shakespeare Hoax.* iUniverse.com.
2009	*Building the Case for Edward de Vere as Shakespeare, vol. 2: Nothing Truer Than Truth.* iUniverse.com.
2009	*Building the Case for Edward de Vere as Shakespeare, vol. 3: Shine Forth.* iUniverse.com.
2009	*Building the Case for Edward de Vere as Shakespeare, vol. 4: My Name Be Buried.* iUniverse.com.
2009	*Building the Case for Edward de Vere as Shakespeare, vol. 5: So Richly Spun.* iUniverse.com.

Shorter pieces

2001, Winter	Stone Coffin Underneath	Sh. Ox. Newsl., vol. 36/4: 19, 27
2001, July	I Never Saw a Stupider Face!	De Vere Soc. Newsl., p. 25-29
2001, Fall	A Portrait Analysis of William Cecil: A Heretofore Untold Story Hidden in Plain Sight?	Sh. Matters, vol. 1/1: 8-11, 20
2002, Summer	It Was Not "Ye Plague:" Oxfordian Mythology and de Vere's Death	Sh. Matters, vol. 1/4: 1, 14-16
2002, Winter	The Queen Elizabeth Pregnancy Portrait: Who Designed it & Who Did the Cover-ups? [repr. in BTC, vol. 10: 177-212] Response by Marlene Benjamin, Spring 2002, p. 3.	Sh. Matters, vol. 1/2: 8-16
2002, Fall	And in This Corner . . . the Sanders Portrait	Sh. Matters, vol. 2/1: 1, 23-25
2002, Fall	The Probable Identity of the Sanders Portrait	Sh. Matters, vol. 2/1: 26-29
2003, Summer	Aeolian Stinking Pitch: Tempestuous Shipwreck on the Island of Vulcano	Sh. Ox. Newsl., v. 39/3: 3, 18-20
2003, Summer	Sleuthing an Enigmatic Latin Annotation	Sh. Matters, vol. 2/4: 16-19
2003, Fall	William Camden: What Did He Say, and When Did He Say It?	Sh. Matters, vol. 3/1: 1, 12-16
2004, Winter	Capturing Student Interest in the Authorship Debate: Studying Intentional Droeshout Portrait Errors	Sh. Ox. Newsl., vol. 40/1: 9-10
2004, Spring	My Turk: Why the Nickname?	Sh. Matters, vol. 3/3: 22-24
2004, Summer	Updates to My Turk: Why the Nickname?	Sh. Matters, vol. 3/4: 2
2004, Spring	Edward de Vere Studies Conference at Concordia University	Sh. Ox. New., vol. 40/2: 1, 10-11
2004, Summer	Poison Power: Natural Death or Murder Most Foul?	Sh. Matters, vol. 3/4: 26-30
2005	Searching for the Oxfordian "Smoking Gun" in Elizabethan Letters	Oxfordian, vol. 8: 110-123
2005, Spring	Edward de Vere as Translator of Ovid's *Metamorphoses*	Sh. Ox. Newsl., vol. 41/2: 6-9
2005, Summer	A Royal Shame: The Origins and History of the Prince Tudor Theory Response by John Shahan, Fall 2005, p. 2.	Sh. Matters, vol. 4/4: 1, 12-17
2006, Spring	Bermoothes: An Intriguing Enigma Response by Christopher Paul, Summer 2006, p. 30-32.	Sh. Matters, vol. 5/3: 10-15
2006, Fall redux	Ideational Change: Why Is It So Difficult? [revised version reprinted in BTC, vol. 9: 427-44] Response by Alan Tarica, Winter 2007, p. 30.	Sh. Ox. Newsl., vol. 42/4: 24-29
2007, Winter	Shakespeare, Not Arthur Brooks, Wrote *Tragicall Historye of Romeus & Juliet*	Sh. Ox. Newsl., vol. 43/1: 22-26
2007, Spring	Roscius Annotation Revisited: Epicurean Discovery or Ambiguous Tidbit? [with Alan H. Nelson]	Sh. Ox. Newsl., vol. 43/2: 2, 9-13
2008, Summer	Is a Powerful Authorship Smoking Gun Buried in Westminster Abbey?	Sh. Ox. Newsl., vol. 44/3: 1, 3-13
2009, Winter	William Shakespeare, "Our Roscius"	Sh. Quarterly, vol. 60/4: 460-69
2010, May	Searching For Shakespeare's Earliest Published Works	Sh. Ox. Newsl., vol. 46/1: 3-6, 15
2017, Winter	[letter: the first 'How I Became an Oxfordian' Series; and Morse Johnson's tribute to Gordon and Helen Cyr]	Sh. Ox. Newsl., vol. 53/1: 4

Altschuler, Eric L.

1998, Oct. 23	Searching For Shakespeare in the Stars	Physicsworld.com
2003, June	Searching for Shake-speare in the Stars [letter]	De Vere Soc. Newsl., p. 26

Anderson, Mark K./Margo (continued)

1996, Winter	A Little More than Kuhn, and Less than Kind: Examining the Headlines with *The Structure of Scientific Revolutions* in Mind [repr. in EVR, vol. 2 (Winter 1996)	Sh. Ox. Newsl., vol. 32/1: 12-14
1996, Fall	Shakespeare's Bible Brings Truth to Light [repr. in BTC, vol. 7: 378-84; in EVR, vol. 4 (Winter 1997); and in NSJ, vol. 1: 99-106 (Dec. 1997)] Response/high praise by Charlton Ogburn, Winter 1996, p. 21.	Sh. Ox. Newsl., vol. 32/4: 8-15
1997, Spring	Meet the New Bard: Concordia University Festivities	Sh. Ox. Newsl., v. 33/2: 1, 10-13
1997, Summer	Beauty and the Paradigm [repr. in EVR, vol. 6 (Winter 1998)]	Sh. Ox. Newsl., v. 33/3: 1, 10-12
1997, Fall	Paradigm Shift: Beauty and "Bottom's Dream" [repr. in EVR, vol. 6]	Sh. Ox. Newsl., vol. 33/4: 19-21
1998, Spring	[review of *The Art of Shakespeare's Sonnets* by Helen Vendler] [repr. in EVR, vol. 8 (Spr. 1999)]	Sh. Ox. Newsl., vol. 34/1: 16-17
1998, Summer	The Zen of Shake-speare	Sh. Ox. Newsl., vol. 34/2: 18, 24
1998, Oct. 29	Losing Voice; Losing Face; Gaining Vision: Charlton Ogburn, Jr. [repr. in SON, vol. 34/3: 6-7 (Fall 1998)]	Valley Advocate (Springfield)
1998, Fall	Paradigm Shift: Sex, Lies and Psalm 51 [repr. in BTC, vol. 8: 114-18]	Sh. Ox. Newsl., vol. 34/3: 21, 27
1999, Winter	Did Shakespeare Stop Writing in 1604? [repr. in BTC, vol. 8: 46-47]	Sh. Ox. Newsl., vol. 34/4: 17
1999, Winter	Paradigm Shift: Revisiting "Apis Lapis" [repr. in BTC, vol. 8: 48-51]	Sh. Ox. Newsl., vol. 34/4: 19, 24
1999, Spring	Paradigm Shift: Moment of Truth . . . *Harper's Mag.* Folio Articles	Sh. Ox. Newsl., vol. 35/1: 1, 4-5+
1999, April	Thy Countenance Shakes Spears [repr. in LC, p. 57-78]	Harpers, vol. 298: 46-49
1999, Summer	Paradigm Shift: Thomas of Woodstock – A "Prequel" to *Richard II*? [repr. from *Valley Advocate* (July 17, 1999); also in EVR, vol. 10 (2000); and in BTC, vol. 8: 114-18]]	Sh. Ox. Newsl., vol. 35/2: 4-6
1999, Nov. 7	Who Wrote Shakespeare? Was it the William We Know? [prom. placement in upper left hand corner of Focus' front page]	Boston Globe, p. Focus 1
2000, Winter	Paradigm Shift: Ophelia's Difference, Or, "To Catch the Conscience of the Counselor" [repr. in BTC, vol. 9: 183-91] Response by Dan Wright, Summer 2000, p. 21.	Sh. Ox. Newsl., vol. 35/4: 17-19+
2000, Spring	Ophelia's Difference [letter]	Sh. Ox. Newsl., vol. 36/1: 29
2000, Summer	Nero Caesar: The *First Folio*'s Straight-Man	Sh. Ox. Newsl., vol. 36/2: 5, 24
2001, Winter	The Upstart Crow's Other Plumage [repr. in BTC, vol. 9: 176-82]	Sh. Ox. Newsl., vol. 36/4: 20-21+
2001, Spring	Ingenuity of Imposition	Sh. Ox. Newsl., vol. 37/1: 19, 22
2001, Summer	Introducing "Phorionymous;" More on Batillus	Sh. Ox. Newsl., vol. 37/2: 16
2002, Summer	Paradigm Shift: Richard Roe on Shakespeare in Italy	Sh. Matters, vol. 1/4: 24-25, 28
2003, Winter	More on *Pierce Penniless*	Sh. Matters, vol. 2/2: 26-28
2003, Fall	Burghley's Bribe: de Vere's Dower? [with Tekastiaks]	Sh. Matters, vol. 3/1: 25-27
2004, Winter	An Interview with Derran Charlton	Sh. Matters, vol. 3/2: 28-29+
2005, Sept.	Interview (with John Riley)	Against the G., v.. 17/4: 48-51
2005, Sept. 26	[letter: resp. to Ron Rosenbaum's Sept. 19 article] Reply by Ron Rosenbaum, 26 Sept. 2005, p. 4.	NY Observer, p. 26
2006, Winter	Bird by Bird: Mark Anderson Interview with James Newcomb	Sh. Matters, vol. 5/2: 24-26+
2006, Spring	[letter: resp. to D. Gontar's "Ox. and Eliza;" in same issue, p. 2-3]	Sh. Matters, vol. 5/3: 3
2007	[letter: praise for *The Oxfordian*'s first ten years]	Oxfordian, vol. 10: 164-164
2008, Winter	News: Shakespeare Video Game: In Search of an Author; More Red Herrings . . . and an Oxfordian Silver Bullet	Sh. Matters, vol. 7/2: 4-5
2008, Spring	News: New England Authorship Conference	Sh. Matters, vol. 7/3: 19-20
2008, Fall	News: Mark Anderson reports from Sin City; M. Rylance Wins Tony	Sh. Matters, vol. 7/4: 4, 14
2010, Winter	News: 2010: A Blockbuster Year for Authorship Studies	Sh. Matters, vol. 9/1: 4
2011, July	[letter: second edition of *"Shakespeare" By Another Name*]	De Vere Soc. Newsl., v. 18/2: 24
2011, July 28	Wikipedia's Shakespeare Problem: Wikipedia is a little too sure we know who authored *Hamlet*	IEEE Spectrum
2011, Oct. 27	[letter: resp. to James Shapiro's Oct. 17 review of *Anonymous*]	New York Times, p. A24
2011, Fall	In Memoriam: Noemi Magri (d. 2011)	Sh. Ox. Newsl., vol. 47/3: 5
2013	Doubter Response to Question #19: Could the Plays Have Been Written By Someone Who Never Left England?	Sh. Beyond Doubt?, p. 178-79
2014	Foreword, in BTC, vol. 8: xiv-xxv	
2015	Melville's *Billy Budd* and the Disguises of Authorship [with Roger Stritmatter and Elliott Stone]	New England Review, vol. 36/1: 100-31

Appleyard, Bryan

2001, Oct. 30	Tragedy of Errors [review of *Anonymous*]	Sunday Times, p. 4
2004, April 25	Theatre: Global Domination [Interview with Mark Rylance] [repr. in DVN (April 2004), p. 28]	Times (London)

Arendt, Paul

2007, Sept. 10   Another View on *I Am Shakespeare* [letter]   Guardian, p. 25.

Arnold, Frazer

1959, July	[review of *The Six Loves of "Shakespeare"* by Louis P. Bénézet]	Am. Bar Assoc. Journ., vol. 45/7: 738-9
1962, Nov.	[review of *Shake-Speare: The Real Man Behind the Name* by Dorothy Ogburn & Charlton Ogburn, Jr (1962)]	Am. Bar Assoc. Journ., vol. 48/11: 1070

Arnold, Gary

1997, April 25   Much Ado About Shakespearean Actor [Derek Jacobi is "very beguiled by the Earl of Oxford theory."]   Washington Times, p. 12

Arthur, Charles

1998, Nov. 5   Shakespeare's Identity 'is in the stars'   Independent, p. 7

Ashe, Geoffrey

1964, Autumn   Sir John Harington and the Authorship Question   Sh. Authorship Rev. #12: 9-12

Ashelford, Jane

1979   Shakespeare and the "Dead Indian"   Bard, vol. 2/3: 95-99

Ashley, Celeste

1980, Spring   [letter: Oxford as translator of Golding's Ovid's *Metamorphoses*]   Sh. Ox. Newsl., vol. 16/2: 5

Ashley, L. R. Newsl.

1986	[rev. of *The Mysterious William Shakespeare* by Ch. Ogburn, Jr.]	Biblio. D'Hum. et Ren., vol. 48: 125-209
1995	[rev. of *Shakespeare: Who Was He?* by Richard F. Whalen (1994)]	Biblio. D'Hum. et Ren., vol. 57: 643-701
1997	[rev. of *Shakespeare, In Fact* by Irvin Matus (1994)]	Biblio. D'Hum. et Ren., vol. 59: 365-409

Asquith, Clare

2005	*Shadowplay: The Hidden Beliefs and Coded Politics of William Shakespeare*. New York: PublicAffairs.
2018	*Shakespeare and the Resistance: The Earl of Southampton, the Essex Rebellion, and the Poems that Challenged Tudor Tyranny*. New York: Public Affairs.

Assante, Katharine

1987, Fall	[letter to the Earl of Oxford (in the form of a poem)]	Sp. Sh. Rev., issue 1/1: 10
1989, Spring	[letter to the Earl of Oxford (in the form of a poem)]	Sh. Ox. Newsl., vol. 25/2: 17

Astley-Lock, John L.

1941, Oct.	[letter: excerpt reprinted]	SF News-letter (A), vol. 2/6: 71
1947, May 30	Infra-Red Peers Into Mystery of Shakespeare [Barrell's work on the Hampton court portrait]	Chicago Tribune, p. 8
1947, Autumn	Latin Anagram on the Title-p. of Peacham's *Minerva Britanna* [repr. in BTC, vol. 4: 29-32; and in OXV, p. 311-314, as "Mente, Vide Bori – Tibi Nom, De Vere"]	SF Quarterly, vol. VIII/3: 36-38
1948, Dec. 20	Check and Mate [letter]	Chicago Tribune, p. 20

Astrea

1923, June   [review of *The Mystery of "Mr. W. H."* by Col. Bernard R. Ward]   Baconiana, vol. XVII/65: 155

Athos.

1921, Oct. 27   The Real Shakespeare [review of SI]   Bulletin, vol. 42: 25

Atkins, Harold

1979, Aug.   Who was the Bard of Avon?   Telegraph

Atkins, Trudy

1992, Spring   [letter: the intransigence of Stratfordians]   Sh. Ox. Newsl., vol. 28/2: 11

Atkinson, A. D.

1949, Aug. 20   Additional Florio-Shakespeare Resemblances   Notes & Queries

Author Index

Baker, Norman
    1961   *William Shakespeare's Conspiracy: A Play*

Baker, Simon
    2007, Sept.   Where There's a Will [review of *Shakespeare* by Bill Bryson (2007)]   Spectator, p. 200

Bakewell, Joan
    1990, April 22   Much Ado About Nothing   Sunday Times, p. 4E

Baldwin, T. W.
    1940, June   Light on the Dark Lady [an exchange of letters with Pauline K.   PMLA, vol. 55/2: 598-602
                    Angell: Baldwin-Angell-Baldwin-Angell]

Ball, Mrs. George A.
    1941, Oct.   [letter: the Oxford theory]   SF News-letter (A), vol. 2/6: 72

Banks-Smith, Nancy
    1989, July 5   Shakespeare and the Loonies   Guardian, p. 46

Barber, Nicholas
    1994, Oct. 30   Television [*Bard on the Box* episode "Battle of Wills:" rival groups   Independent, p. 21
                    contest the authorship]

Barber, Ros (Dr. Rosalind Barber)
Books
    2012   *The Marlowe Papers: A Novel in Verse*. London: Sceptre. Repr. in 2013: New York: St. Martin's Press.
    2013   *Shakespeare: The Evidence – The Authorship Question Clarified*. [A web-based publication, continually
                    updated]
Shorter pieces
    2009, Summer   Shakespeare Authorship Doubt in 1593   Crital Survey, vol. 21/2: 83-110
    2010   Exploring Biographical Fictions: The Role of Imagination in Writing   Rethinking History,
                  and Reading Narrative   vol. 14/2: 165-87
    2013   Doubter response to Question #186: Does Shakespeare's dramatic   Sh. Beyond Doubt?, p. 186
                  verse seem to be different from Marlowe's
                  [see DoubtAboutWill.org/exposing]
    2013, July   [letter: establishing the authorship issue as a valid question]   De Vere Soc. Newsl., v. 20/2: 31
    2014, Winter   Shakespeare Authorship Trust Conference Report   Sh. Ox. Newsl., vol. 50/1: 1, 6
    2014, May   Shakespeare: The Evidence   De Vere Soc. New., v. 21/2: 36-7
    2016   Shakespeare and Warwickshire Dialect [repr. in *Shakespeare*   J. Early Mod. St., v. 5: 91-118
                  Authorship Sourcebook (Stritmatter 2019, 2022): 351-81]
    2018   My Shakespeare—Christopher Marlowe, in *My Shakespeare*
                  (Leahy): 85-111

Barley, Annie L.
    1923, Nov. 2   Alternative Solutions   Hackney Spectator, p. 2

Barnaby, Andrew
    2004, Winter   [review of *Monstrous Adversary* by Alan Nelson (2003)]   Renaissance Qt., vol. 57/4: 1529

Barnard, Francis P.
    1929, Sept. 10   Shakespeare and *Richard III*: Destruction of Records and   Morning Post, p. 9
                  Documents [letter]

Barnett, Lori
    2002, Feb. 24   Sins of Omission [letter: response to Niederkorn]   New York Times, A&L: E6

Barnes, Bart
    1990, Nov. 20   Geico Chairman David L. Kreeger Dies   Wall St. Journal, p. A1

Barnes, Clive
    1971, Nov. 29   Earl Who Wrote Shakespeare [review of *Masquerade*, Gertrude   New York Times, p. 57
                  Gale's play based on the Prince Tudor thesis]

Baron, Dennis
Books
    1997   *De Vere is Shakespeare: Evidence From the Biography and Wordplay*. Introduction by Christopher H.
                  Dams. Cambridge: Oleander Press.
Shorter pieces
    1997, June   [letter: resp. to Michael Llewellyn's Feb. review]   De Vere Soc. New., v. 2/9: 10-11

Barrell, Charles Wisner (continued)

1944, April	Newly Discovered Oxford-Shakespeare Pictorial Evidence [repr. in BTC, vol. 3: 37-44]	SF Quarterly, vol. V/2: 24-27
1944, July	Lord Oxford as Supervising Patron of Shakespeare's Theatrical Company [repr. in BTC, vol. 3: 61-78]	SF Quarterly, vol. V/3: 33-40
1944, Oct.	New Milestone in Shakespearean Research: Contemporary Proof that the Earl of Oxford's Literary Nickname was "Gentle Master William" [repr. in BTC, vol. 3: 116-54]	SF Quarterly, vol. V/4: 49-66
1945, Jan.	Sole Author of *Renowned Victorie*: Gabriel Harvey testifies in the Oxford-Shakespeare case [repr. in BTC, vol. 3: 176-79]	SF Quarterly, vol. VI/1: 11-12
1945, April	Earliest Authenticated "Shakespeare" Transcript Found With Oxford's Personal Poems [repr. in BTC, vol. 3: 180-90]	SF Quarterly, vol. VI/2: 22-26
1945, April	Rare Military Volume Sponsored by Lord Oxford issued by "Shakespeare's" First Publisher [repr. in BTC, vol. 3: 191-96]	SF Quarterly, vol. VI/2: 30-32
1945, May	[letter to Percy Allen, dated March 8, 1945 (excerpts)]	SF News-letter (E), p. 4
1945, July	The Wayward Water-Bearer Who Wrote "Shakespeare's" Sonnet 109 [repr. in BTC, vol. 3: 197-202; and in OXV, p. in 107-20]	SF Quarterly, vol. VI/3: 37-39
1945, Oct.	Creature of Their Own Creating: An Answer to the Present Day School of Shakespearean Biography [repr. in BTC, vol. 3: 220-24]	SF Quarterly, vol. VI/4: 59-60
1945, Oct.	Genesis of a Henry James Story [repr. in BTC, vol. 3: 225-27]	SF Quarterly, vol. VI/4: 63-64
1946, Jan.	Exploding the Ancient Play Cobbler Fallacy [repr. in BTC, vol. 3: 228-37]	SF Quarterly, vol. VII/1: 3-7
1946, Jan.	A Literary Pirate's Attempt to Publish *The Winter's Tale* in 1594 [repr. in BTC, vol. 3: 247-72]	SF Quarterly, vol. VII/1: 20-31
1946, Feb.	Verifying the Secret History of *Shake-speare's Sonnets* [repr. in BTC, vol. 4: 345-59]	Tomorrow
1946, July	The Playwright Earl Publishes "Hamlet's Book" [repr. in BTC, vol. 3: 273-88]	SF Quarterly, vol. VII/3: 35-42
1946, Oct.	Shakespeare's *Henry V* Can Be Identified As "Harry of Cornwall" in Henslowe's Diary [repr. in BTC, vol. 3: 293-02]	SF Quarterly, vol. VII/4: 49-54
1946, Oct.	Proof That Shakespeare's Thought and Imagery Dominate Oxford's Own Statement of Creative Principles [repr. in BTC, vol. 3: 316-35]	SF Quarterly, vol. VII/4: 61-69
1947, Spring	Queen Elizabeth's Master Showman Shakes a Spear in Her Defense [repr.in SON, vol. 7/2: 7-18 (Spring 1947); and BTC 3: 336-57]	SF Quarterly, vol. VIII/1: 4-11
1947, Spring	The Arundel-Arundell Mix-Up	SF Quarterly, vol. VIII/1: 13-14
1947, Autumn	Pictorial Clues and Key Initials [repr. in OXV, p. 315-17; and in BTC, vol. 4: 33-34]	SF Quarterly, vol. VIII/3: 38-39
1947, Autumn	Historical Background of *The Merchant of Venice*: The Jew in London [repr. in BTC, vol. 4: 35-42]	SF Quarterly, vol. VIII/3: 44
1947, Autumn	[letter: resp. to drama editor Brooks Atkinson's Dec. 1947 article] [repr. in BTC, vol. 4: 38-42]	SF Quarterly, vol. VIII/3: 45-47
1947, Autumn	New Proof that *Henry VIII* Was Written Before the Spring of 1606 [repr. in BTC, vol. 4: 43-45]	SF Quarterly, vol. VIII/3: 47-48
1948, Winter	Dr. John Dover Wilson's "New" *Macbeth* Is a Masterpiece Without a Master [repr. in Clark, *Hidden Allusions*, 3rd ed., Ruth Loyd Miller, editor, p. 855-64 (1974); and in BTC, vol. 4: 46-60]	SF Quarterly, vol. VIII/4: 58-64
1948, Spring	Rarest Contemporary Description of "Shakespeare" Proves Poet to have been a Nobleman [repr. in BTC, vol. 4: 63-77]	SF Quarterly, vol. IX/1/1: 1-7
1948, Summer	Oxford vs. Other "Claimants" of the Edwards Shakespearean Honors, 1593 [repr. in BTC, vol. 4: 80-86]	SF Quarterly, vol. IX/2: 9-12
1948, Autumn	In deed as in name--Vere nobilis for he was W . . . (?) . . . [repr. in BTC, vol. 4: 87-91]	SF Quarterly, vol. IX/3: 17-18+
1948, Autumn	John Lyly as Both Oxford's and Shakespeare's "Honest Steward" [repr. in BTC, vol. 4: 92-101]	SF Quarterly, vol. IX/3: 19-24
1949	"Afterword" to *"Shakespeare" Identified* by J. Thomas Looney. 2nd edition. New York: Duell, Sloan & Pearce.	
1972	The Strange Silence of William Shakespeare's Son-in-Law, Dr. John Hall of Stratford-on-Avon: "My father-in-law died Thursday' in *Oxfordian*	

Vistas, Ruth Loyd Miller, editor, p. 286-89. [Written in 1972 specifically for Ruth Loyd Miller's edition of SI]

Barrett, Jr., Robert M.

1999, Winter	Interview: Bob Barrett [conducted by William E. Boyle] [repr. in BTC, vol. 8: 37-42; and in EVR, vol. 9 (Fall 1999), and in *Sh. Authorship Sourcebook*, R. Stritmatter, editor (2022), p. 79-85]	Sh. Ox. Newsl., vol. 34/4: 11-13
2003, Spring	Concordia's Annual Edward de Vere Studies Conference	Sh. Ox. Newsl., vol. 39/2: 6-7, 24
2006, Fall	Shakespeare, Meet Robert Frost: Teaching the Authorship Question to Ninth Graders in Kitsap County, Washington [repr. in *Sh. Authorship Source* (Stritmatter, 2019, 2022): 16-23]	Sh. Matters, vol. 6/1: 1, 9-11

Barrett, W. P.

1939, Feb. 10	Who Was Shakespeare? III: The Traditional View	John O'London's W., p. 733-34
1939, Feb. 21	[letter: Shakspere was Shakespeare]	John O'London's W., p. 822

Barron, Randall

Books

1996	*The Great Shakespeare Hoax*. Bloomington: 1st Books.	
2000	*Shakespeare and the Queen*. Bloomington: 1st Books.	
2000	*Shakespeare Through the Looking Glass*. Bloomington: 1st Books.	

Shorter pieces

1993, Summer	Edmund Ironside	Sh. Ox. Newsl., vol. 29/3a: 10-11
1993, Fall	Edward De Vere's Will [repr. in BTC, vol. 7: 201-05]	Sh. Ox. Newsl., vol. 29/4: 1-3
1994, Autumn	A New Shakespeare Poem?	Sh. Ox. Newsl., vol. 30/4: 6-8
1995, Winter	Shipwreck in the Waters of Orthodoxy [de Vere listed as 'alias Shakespeare' in index of *England's Helicon*, ed. by Hyder E. Rollins, published by Harvard University Press, 1935]	Sh. Ox. Newsl., vol. 31/1a: 3-4

Barsi-Greene, Margaret (compiler and arranger)

1973	*I, Prince Tudor, Wrote Shakespeare: An Autobiography from His Two Ciphers in Poetry and Prose*. Boston: Branden Press.

Barton, Anne

2006, May 11	The One and Only [reviews of five recent books on Shakespeare biography] [see comments on this article in SM, vol. 6/3 (Spring 2007)]	New York Review, p. 27

Barton, John

2003, Winter	Prospero's Island	Sh. Ox. Newsl., v. 39/1: 2, 4, 9+
2005, Summer	The Grandsire Phrase in *Romeo and Juliet* [with Derran Charlton]	Sh. Ox. Newsl., vol. 41/3: 17-18
2010, August	Monsters of the 16-17th Century, no. 4 [with Elizabeth Imlay]	De Vere Society N., vol. 17/2: 31

Bassett, Kate

2007, Sept. 9	[review of *The Big Secret Live* by M. Rylance and M. Warchus]	Independent

Basso, Hamilton

1950, April 8	The Big Who-Done-It [review of *"Shakespeare" Identified*, 2nd ed.]	New Yorker, p. 113-4, 117-9

Batchelor, H. Crouch

Books and pamphlets

1924	*The Shakespeare Myth: A Challenge* [with Lord Sydenham of Combe]. [pamphlet: repr. from *The English Review*, p. 221-29 (Aug. 1924)]

Shorter pieces

1924, Aug.	The "Shakespeare" Myth: A Challenge [with Lord Sydenham of] Combe [reprinted as a pamphlet]	English Review, p. 221-29
1924, Oct.	Challengers Challenged [with Lord Sydenham, reply to responses]	English Review, p. 461
1924, Nov.	The "Shakespearean" Myth [letter]	English Review, p. 603-04

Bate, Jonathan

Books

2008	*The Genius of Shakespeare*. 10th Anniversary Edition. New York: Oxford University Press. [See esp. "Ch. 3: The Authorship Controversy," p. 65-100]
2019	*How the Classics Made Shakespeare*. Princeton: Princeton University Press.

Shorter pieces

1993, Feb. 12	The Bard for All Causes	Times Lit. Sup., is. 4689: 12
1995, April 9	Snobbish About Shakespeare	Telegraph, p. 11

Bate, Jonathan (continued)

1997, May 1	Bard Belief Belief [review of *Alias Shakespeare* by Joseph Sobran]
	    Response by Nancy A. Holz, May 15, p. A23.
	    Response by Patrick R. Sullivan, May 15, p. A23.
	    Reply by Joseph Sobran, May 15, p. A23.
		Wall St. Journal, p. A16

1999, April	Golden Lads and Chimney-Sweepers [repr. in LC, p. 57-78]	Harper's Mag., vol. 298: 60-62
2010, April 4	The Question of Who Wrote Shakespeare's Plays . . . Why It Was Asked in the First Place [review of *Contested Will* by J. Shapiro]	Telegraph, p. 25
2013, April 26	A Player, Not a Gentleman [review of *Shakespeare Beyond Doubt*, edited by Paul Edmonson and Stanley Wells]	New Statesman, vol. 142: 44
2017, Jan. 2	Shakespeare Study Turns Into a Comedy of Errors	Times (London), p. 22

2023, May 28	Was Shakespeare Really a Woman? And Does Taylor Swift Know
	    Him Best? [review of *Shakespeare Was a Woman and Other
	    Heresies* by Elizabeth Winkler]
	        Response by Winkler, May 28.
		Telegraph

Batiuk, Tom

1987, 98, Fall	Funky Winkerbean [comic strip mentions Edward de Vere]	Sh. Ox. Newsletter, vol. 34/3: 2

Bauer, Henry

2004	[reviews of *Shakespeare's Unorthodox Biography* by Diana Price and *Alias Shakespeare* by Joseph Sobran]	J. Sci. Expl., vol. 18: 149

Bayley, John

1962	The Shakespeare Fringe [review of *The Shakespeare Claimants* by H. M. Gibson]	L'Opinion, p. 8

Baylor, Charles C.

2018, Winter	[letter: response to Draya's Winter 2018 "Queen's Guilt" article]	Sh. Ox. Newsletter, vol. 54/2: 4-5
2021, Fall	[letter: hidden messages in the canon]	Sh. Ox. Newsletter, vol. 57/4: 3

Baxter, Frank C.

1959, July 6	Shakespeare Not Ghost Written [letter]	Los Angeles Times, p. B4

Baxter, James Phinney

1915	*The Greatest of All Literary Problems, the Authorship of the Shakespeare Works: An Exposition of All Points at issue from Their Inception to the Present Moment.* New York: AMS Press.

Baxter, Robert

2022, Oct.	Preview of *Shakespeare and religio mentis: A Study of Christian Hermetism in Four Plays* by Jane E. Nelson	De Vere Soc. NL., v. 29/4: 35-44
2022, Oct.	[letter: *My Lady Rich: Her Teares and Joy*, a CD]	De Vere Soc. NL, v. 29/4: 31-32

Bayam, Nina

1996, June	Delia Bacon, History's Odd Woman Out	New Eng. Quar., v. 34/8: 223-49

Bayley, Harold

1902	*The Tragedy of Sir Francis Bacon.* [excerpt repr. in BTC, vol. 1: 160-162]

Bayley, John

1962, July 20	The Shakespearean Fringe [review of *The Shakespeare Claimants* by H. M. Gibson]	South Notts Echo, p. 7

Bayley, M. F.

1933, April	Bacon's and Shakespeare's Manuscripts in One Portfolio Response by J. Denam Parsons in the June 193 issue.	Sh. Pictorial, no. 62: 60

Baylor, Charles

2021, Summer	[letter: Shakespeare's/Oxford's religion]	Sh. Ox. Newsletter, vol. 57/3: 4

Beam, Alex

2009, Sept. 25	The Shakespeare Truthers: Search for the "Real" Shakespeare is Collective Madness	Boston Globe

Beane, Connie J.

2010, May	Shakespeare and "The King of Hungary's 'Peace'"	Sh. Ox. Newsl., v. 46/1: 1, 14-15
2013, Fall	[letter: Dating *Macbeth*]	Sh. Ox. Newsl., vol. 49/3: 8
2016	Reconsidering the Jephthah Allusion in *Hamlet*	Oxfordian, vol. 18: 23-40
2018, Sept.	The True Story of Edward Webbe and *Troublesome Travailes*	Oxfordian, vol. 20: 105-30

Author Index

Beaton, Alisa
1988, Fall-Wint.	Shake-Speare's History Plays: A Medium for the Masses	Sh. Newsl., vol. 38/3-4: 44
1990, Fall	Cherchez La Femme	Sh. Newsl., vol. 40/3: 42

Beaton, Cecil
1954	*Persona Grata* [with Kenneth Tyson]. New York: G. P. Putnam's Sons. [Quotes Orson Welles on Oxford]	

Beauclerk, Charles
2010	*Shakespeare's Lost Kingdom: The True History of Shakespeare and Elizabeth*. New York: Grove Press. [Chapter 6 repr. as "Identity Crisis" in *A Poet's Rage*, edited by William E. Boyle]	
2020	*Take Physic, Pomp!* [with Sarah Beauclerk]	

Periodicals edited

1988 (Jan-Mar): *The De Vere Society Newsletter* (no. 1-3)

Shorter pieces
1987, Summer	[letter: to SOS President Charlton Ogburn, Jr.]	Sh. Ox. Newsl., vol. 23/3: 4-5
1987, Fall	News From The De Vere Society: Lady Diana is Direct Descendant of Edward de Vere	Spear-shaker Rev., issue 1/1: 36
1988	Foreword, in *The Mystery of William Shakespeare* by Charlton Ogburn [an abridged version published in the UK of *The Mysterious William Shakespeare* (1984)]	
1988, April	Introductory Remarks	De Vere Soc. Newsl., no. 2: 2
1988, April	Reply to Lord Dacre	De Vere Soc. Newl., no. 2: 14-15
1988, Summer	[letter: SOS President Charlton Ogburn, Jr. re the Trial]	Sh. Ox. Newsletter, vol. 24/3: 6-7
1988, Aug.	Introductory Remarks	De Vere Soc. Newsl., no. 3: 3-4
1988, Aug.	A Peculiar Parable [short story]	De Vere Soc. Newl., no. 3: 53-69
1988, Jan.	Introductory Remarks	De Vere Soc. Newsl., no. 1: 2
1988, Winter	News From The De Vere Society	Spear-shaker Rev., is. 1/2: 38-39
1991, Summer	An Open Letter to American Oxfordians: Ordered & Professional Approaches to Capturing Hearts/Minds of Public Opinion	Sh. Ox. Newsletter, vol. 27/3: 10
1991, Aug.	An Open Letter to American Oxfordians	Spear-shaker Rev., is. 5: 19-20
1991, Aug.	[letter: admiration for *The Spear-shaker*]	Spear-shaker Rev., is. 5: 25
1994, Autumn	William O. Hunt of Chicago (d. 1994): A Recollection	Sh. Ox. Newsl., vol. 30/4: 12-13
1994, Autumn	What Was the Author's Motivation in Writing This Work?	Sh. Ox. Newsl., vol. 30/4: 18
1994, Autumn	Sir Philip Sidney Satirized in *Merry Wives of Windsor* [repr. in BTC, vol. 8: 168-76]	Eliz. Review, vol. 2/2: 3-10
1995, Aug.	The Shakespeare Authorship Question: Why It Matters [repr. in EVR, vol. 1 (Fall 1995)]	De Vere Soc. Newsl., v. 2/2: 5-7
1995, Autumn	Who Really Wrote the Plays of "William Shakespeare?"	Sh. Ox. Newsl., vol. 31/4: 4-5
1995, Autumn	Edward de Vere and the Psychology of Feudalism [repr. in BTC, vol. 8: 233-54; and in LC, p. 36-45]	Eliz. Review, vol. 3/2: 35-52
1996, Winter	To Our Members: from new President Charles Vere	Sh. Ox. Newsl., vol. 32/1: 1, 11
1996, Winter	Explanation for Revoking Invitation to Joseph Sobran to Speak at SOS Conference	Sh. Ox. Newsl., vol. 32/1: 6
1996, Winter	Prince Charles' Views	Sh. Ox. Newsl., vol. 32/1: 7
1996, Spring	Board of Trustees Votes in a New Era: Fundraising Now the Key	Sh. Ox. Newsl., vol. 32/2: 6-7
1996, Summer	How Are the Mighty Fallen? [repr. in BTC, vol. 7: 359-62]	Sh. Ox. Newsl., vol. 32/3: 7, 22
1997, Winter	Branagh's Sound and Fury [review of Branagh's *Hamlet*]	Sh. Ox. Newsl., v. 33/1: 2, 14-15
1997, Winter	Writing History: The Facts are the Facts, but Interpretation is All [with William E. Boyle & Charles Boyle] [repr. in *A Poet's Rage*, p. 5-14] Response by Richard Whalen, SON, Spring 1997, p. 21.	Sh. Ox. Newsl., vol. 33/1: 1, 6-7+
1997, Spring	Parting Is Such Sweet Sorrow	Sh. Ox. Newsletter, vol. 33/2: 3
1997, Summer	At the Bath Debate: The Case for Oxford [repr. in BTC, vol. 7: 404-07]	Sh. Ox. Newsl., vol. 33/3: 5, 12
1998, Oct.	Shakespeare's Sovereign Conception [summary]	De Vere Soc. Newsl., v. 3/1: 3-5
2002, April 14	Don't Call me Lord – Traitors Have Stolen My Birthright	Daily Mail, p. 2
2003, Spring	Obituaries: John Louther: a Recollection; G. Grant Gifford	Sh. Ox. Newsl., vol. 39/2: 20
2005	[review of *The Truth Will Out* by B. James and W. D. Rubinstein]	Oxfordian, vol. 8: 140-145
2005, Spring	[letter: pursuit of the truth in the authorship question]	Sh. Matters, vol. 4/3: 2
2007	[letter: thanks to the editors of *The Oxfordian* for ten great years]	Oxfordian, vol. 10: 164-164
2008, Winter	Isabel Holden (1915-2007): In Memoriam	Sh. Matters, vol. 7/2: 1, 18-20
2009	Eulogy in Commemoration of the Life of Isabel Holden	Discovering Sh., p. 1-3

Beauclerk, Charles (continued)

2021, Spring	Introduction to the 2020 Autumn Conference Webinar	De Vere Soc. Newsl., v. 28/1: 6-7
2022, April	Interview with Charles Beauclerk, DVS Founder (1986) and Honorary President, Part 1	De Vere Soc. New., v. 29/2: 24-5
2022, April	Interview with Charles Beauclerk, Part 2	De Vere Soc. New., v. 29/3: 5-22
2023, Jan.	Presentation: The Meaning of Power in Shakespeare	De Vere Soc. Newsl., v. 30/1: 6-8

Beauclerk, Charles Sidney De Vere

1931, July 18	Shakespeare Identified At Last	Accrington Observer

Beauregard, Sue-Ellen

1994, Nov. 1	[review of *Shakespeare—Who Was He? The Oxford Challenge to the Bard of Avon* by Richard F. Whalen (1994)]	Booklist, vol. 91/5: 486-87

Beazley, Raymond

1929, Sept. 11	Shakespeare and *Richard III*: An Historical Enigma [letter]	Morning Post, p. 6

Becker, Margaret
Plays

2013	*Snatches From History: A Play in Five Acts* [Acts 1-3 printed in SM, vol. 12/3 (Summer 2013): 20-27; Acts 4-5 printed in SM, vol. 12/4 (Fall 2013): 29-33]	

Shorter pieces

2017, Spring	Look at the Lighter Side	Sh. Ox. Newsl., vol. 53/2: 31
2015, Fall	[letters: resemblances and misidentifications of portraits of Edward de Vere and others]	Sh. Ox. Newsl., vol. 51/4: 4-5
2020, Winter	Misprison and the Essex Rebellion [letter]	Sh. Ox. Newsl., vol. 56/1: 2
2023, Summer	Understanding Ben Jonson's "To the Memory of My Beloved, the Author"	Sh. Ox. Newsl., vol. 59/3: 15-16

Beesley, F.

1951, May 18	Mr. Brophy and Shakespeare [letter]	Truth, p. 533
1951, June 8	Mr. Brophy and Shakespeare [letter]	Truth, p. 620

Beggs, Mary

1995, March 16	Who What Where [many believe the Earl of Oxford was the author]	Commercial Appeal

Begley, Walter

1903	*Is It Shakespeare?* London: John Murray.	

Bell, Allan

2020, Winter	Acrostic: Greater Opportunities	Sh. Ox. Newsl., vol. 56/1: 28-29

Bell, James H.

1980, April 11	Orwell and Oxford [letter] [repr. in SON, vol. 16/1: 12, Winter, 1980]	Washington Star

Benedick

2009, Winter	Benedick and Beatrice's Excellent Adventure	Sh. Matters, v. 8/1: 1, 13-18+

Bénézet, Louis P.
Books and pamphlets

1937	*Shakspere, Shakespeare, and De Vere.* Manchester, NH: Granite State Press. [excerpts repr. in SFA, vol. 3/58: 67 (August 1942); and in BTC, vol. 4: 202-212]	
1947-48	*The Shakespeare Hoax: An Improbable Narrative* [pamphlet] [repr. from the *Dartmouth Quarterly*, Nov. 1947; described in SFQ, vol. VIII/4 : 56 (Winter 1947-48); repr. in BTC, vol. 4: 4-11]	
1958	*The Six Loves of "Shake-Speare."* New York: Pageant Press. [repr. in BTC, vol. 4: 287-324]	

Shorter pieces

1937	[response to review of Oxfordian books by Edwin Edgett]	Boston Transcript
1939, Dec.	Organization of the Shakespeare Fellowship, American Branch [repr. in BTC, vol. 2: 89-91]	SF News-letter (A), vol. 1/1: 1
1939, Dec.	President Louis Bénézet's Message [repr. in BTC, vol. 2, p. 70-71]	SF News-letter (A), vol. 1/1: 2
1939, Dec.	Youthful Minds Are Open	SF News-letter (A), vol. 1/1: 4
1940, Feb.	Rapid Growth of Research Fellowship Means Means End of Pompous Obstructionists [as editor]	SF News-letter (A), vol. 1/2: 7
1940, June/July	Shakespeare and Ben Jonson [repr. in BTC, vol. 2:107-108]	SF News-letter (A), vol. 1/4: 5
1940, Dec.	Shake-scene and Shake-Rags	SF News-letter (A), vol. 2/1: 4

Bennett, Tom
    1998, Oct. 22   Charlton Ogburn Obituary   Atlantic Monthly, p. C6

Bensley, Edward
    1931, April 18   The Oxford-Shakespeare Case Corroborated [letter: resp. to Percy Allen]   Notes & Q., vol. 160/16: 283

Benson, Jon (Doug Hollman)
Books
    2016   *The Death of Shakespeare As It Was Accomplisht in 1616 & The Causes Thereof, Part One*. Annapolis, MD: Nedward, LLC.
    2016   *The Reader's Companion to The Death of Shakespeare, Part One*. Annapolis, MD: Nedward, LLC.
    2023   *The Death of Shakespeare As It Was Accomplisht in 1616 & The Causes Thereof, Part Two*. Annapolis, MD: Nedward, LLC.

Shorter pieces
    2023, Sept.   A Conversation with Jon Benson [interview with Phoebe Nir]   Oxfordian, vol. 25: 319-23

Benson, Jr., Jon
    1991, Spring   Interview with Professor Cavaliero Academico   Sh. Ox. Newsl., vol. 27/2: 8-10

Bentley, Richard
    1961   *Shakespeare Cross-Examination* [editor]. American Bar Association. [A collection of articles from the *American Bar Association Journal*] [excerpt repr. in SON, vol. 30/2a: 15-16 (Spring 1994); and in BTC, vol. 7: 240-41]

Shorter pieces
    1959, Feb.   Elizabethan Whodunit: Who was "William Shakespeare"?   Am. Bar Assoc. Journ., vol. 45/2: 204-08
        [repr. in SC, p. 1-16]
        Response by Louis P. Bénézet and others, June, p. 106-25.
        [repr. in *Sh. and His Rivals* (McMichael & Glenn 1962): 193-203]
    1959, Nov.   Elizabethan Whodunit: Supplementary Notes   Am. Bar Assoc. Journ., vol. 15/11: 1160+
        [repr. in SC, page 58-78]

Berg, Scott A.
    1978   *Max Perkins: Editor of Genius*. New York: E. P. Dutton. Repr. in 2015: New York: New American Library.

Berkeley Lab News Center
    2011, Spring   Have Genome Scientists Uncovered Shakespeare's Literary DNA?   Sh. Ox. Newsl., vol. 47/2: 7-8

Berlyne, Alex
    1991, April 9   [commentary on Channel 2's "Who Was Shakespeare?"]   Jerusalem Post, p. 5

Berman, Lois René
Periodicals edited
    2016, April – 2019, Oct.: *The De Vere Society Newsletter* (vol. 23/3 – vol. 26/4)
Shorter pieces
    2019, Oct.   The Wanamaker Theatre's *Bartholomew Fair* and the Story of Vere   De Vere Soc. NL, v. 26/4: 35-42

Berman, Ronald
    1976, Fall   The Shakespeare Industry   Sewane Review, v. 84/4: 657-68

Berney, Charles V.
Books
    2017   *Shakespeare Confidential*. Somerville, MA: Forever Press.
Shorter pieces
    1996, Summer   What's in a Name?   Sh. Ox. Newsl., vol. 32/3: 11
    1999   Mathematical Models of Stratfordian Persistence   Oxfordian, vol. 2: 138-144
    1999, Summer   Adventures of a Contestant   Sh. Ox. Newsl., vol. 35/2: 5
    1999, Fall   The Legend of the Round-Earthers   Sh. Ox. Newsl., vol. 35/3: 5
    2000, Summer   [letter: kudos to Charles Boyle and Mark Anderson for tackling issue of incest]   Sh. Ox. Newsl., vol. 36/2: 21-22
    2000, Fall   Sir Walter Scott as Paleo-Oxfordian, Part 1   Sh. Ox. Newsl., vol. 36/3: 17
        Response by Richard Whalen, Winter 2001, p. 23.
    2001, Winter   [letter" "Supposes" and Greene's *Groatsworth of Wit*]   Sh. Ox. Newsl., vol. 36/4: 24
    2001, Spring   *Midsummer Night's Dream* on Film: From Hollywood Extravaganza to British Opera   Sh. Ox. Newsl., v. 37/1: 17, 23+
    2001, Fall   Confidential Video Bard: *Love's Labour's Lost*: BBC vs. Branagh   Sh. Matters, vol. 1/1: 18-19
    2002, Winter   From Fellowship President Dr. Charles Berney   Sh. Matters, vol. 1/2: 4
    2002, Winter   Moorer's Marathon, or Three Plays in One Day   Sh. Matters, vol. 1/2: 30-31

Bethell, Tom (continued)

1999, April	The Ghost of Shakespeare: Who, in Fact, Was the Bard: The Usual Suspect from Stratford, or Edward de Vere, 17th Earl of Oxford? [repr. in LC, p. 57-78]	Harper's Mag., v. 298: 35-62
1999, April	A Never Writer [repr. in LC, p. 57-78]	Harper's Mag., vol. 298: 36-8
1999, April 10	Studious, Not Snobbish	Washington Post, p. A19

Bethune, Brian

1999, July 5	International Man of Mystery	Maclean's, p. 52
2010, April	What's Behind the Shakespeare Wars	Maclean's, p. 60

Bettany, F. G.

1928, May 6	A Favourite of Elizabeth [review of *Seventeenth Earl* by Capt. Ward]	Sunday Times, p. 8

Betts, Hannah

2005, June 11	Who Says that Rylance is Golden?	Times (London), p. 27

Bevington, David M.

Books

1968	*Tudor Drama and Politics: A Critical Approach to Topical Meaning*. Cambridge: Harvard University Press.	
2010	*Shakespeare and Biography*. Oxford and New York: Oxford University Press.	

Shorter pieces

1989, August	[review of "The Shakespeare Mystery"] [documentary by Al Austin]	Eleven Mag., p. 14-15
1993, Autumn	[letter: congratulations on success of new venture]	Eliz. Review, vol. 1/2: 5
2010	"Shakespeare, William," in *Encyclopedia Britannica, 15th ed.: Macropaedia: Knowledge in Depth*, vol. 27: 253-72 [with John Russell Brown & John Bew Spencer; repeats many points rebutted by Oxfordian scholars many times since 1920, with no notice of the rebuttals]	

Bewley, Dorna

2006, June 2	[letter: confusion between hamlets and hamlettes] [repr. in DVN (Feb. 2007), p. 22-23]	Times Lit. Sup., is. 5383: 17
2007, June	The Ashbourne Portrait [with Jeremy Crick] Response by Christopher Paul, Oct. 2007, p. 29-30.	De Vere Soc. Newsl., p. 24-35

Bianchi, Julie Sandys

2017, Fall	Brevity and the Soul of Witlessness	Sh. Ox. Newsl., vol. 53/4: 13-16
2019, Winter	SOF Hires PR Director	Sh. Ox. Newsl., vol. 55/1: 1
2019, Spring	Marketing Ourselves to the Public [with Joan Leon, Shelly Maycock & Kathryn Sharpe]	Sh. Ox. Newsl., vol. 55/2: 20
2019, Fall	SOF Annual Conference Sets New Attendance Record [with others]	Sh. Ox. Newsl., v. 55/4: 1, 18-32

Bianculli, David

1989, April 4	[review of "The Shakespeare Mystery"] [documentary by Al Austin] [repr. in SON, vol. 25/2: 9 (Spring 1989)]	New York Post

Biederman, Patricia W.

1992, April 23	What Manner of Birthday Gift Be This? The Authorship Question Surrounding Shakespeare's Writings Never Ends	Los Angeles Times, p. 8
1992, April 23	For the Bard, Slings and Arrows [lecture by the Earl of Burford]	Los Angeles Times, p. WSJ1

Billington, Michael

2007, Sept. 3	"I Am Shakespeare" [review of *The Big Secret Live* by Mark Rylance and Matthew Warchus] Response by David Johnson, Sept. 8, p. 39. Response by Paul Arendt, Sept. 10, p. 25.	Guardian

Binyon, Michael

1987, Sept. 26	All's Well That Ends Well As Judges Back Bard	Times (London), p. 5

Bird, Charles J.

1999, July	Shakespeare und Lord Burleigh	Neues Sh. Journal, vol. 4: 117-20
1999, Aug.	Springtime in Hesperides	De Vere Soc. Newsl., v. 3/4: 3-8
1999, Aug.	[letter: efforts to get media coverage in newspapers and on TV]	De Vere Soc. Newsl., vol. 3/4: 9
2000	Shakespeare und der "Caleygreyhound"	Neues Sh. Journal, vol. 5: 109-16
2000, Oct.	Did You Know? (John de Vere)	De Vere Soc. Newsl., p. 19
2000, Oct.	Thomas Creede's 'Truth' Motto	De Vere Soc. Newsl., p. 29-31

2000, Oct.	[letter: Jolly's May 2000 "Burghley's Library" article]	De Vere Soc. Newsl., p. 22-23
2003, Winter	Wounded Truth - Some Further Thoughts	Sh. Matters, vol. 2/2: 29
2003, Feb.	King Edward III at Castle Hedingham	De Vere Soc. Newsl., p. 12-15
2004	Oxford's Early Years, in *Great Oxford* (Malim): 13-15	
2005, May	Would You Not Deem it Breathed?: Exhibition at Castle Hedingham	De Vere Soc. Newsl., p. 30-31
2008, June	'A per se A' and Apis Lapis	De Vere Soc. New., v. 15/2: 27-9
2016, April	New Evidence for de Vere From Tilbury Church	De Vere Soc. New., v. 23/2: 25-9

Bisol, Anna L.

| 1995, Oct. 4 | Was Shakespeare Really Shakespeare? – Lecturer [Grace Cali, SOS Member] Asks Who Wrote Classic Literature | Telegram & Gazette, p. 1 |

Bjerring, Jens-Christian

| 2014, Feb. | Problems in Epistemic Space [eses Edward de Vere's authorship in considering "epistemic space"] | J. Phil. Logic, p. 153-70 |

Björkman, Edwin

| 1920, Aug. | Shakespeare? [review of *"Shakespeare" Identified*] | Bookman, vol. 51/6:677-82 |

Black, James

| 2006, Feb. 1 | The Bard or Not the Bard: Answers to Correspondents | Daily Mail, p. 55 |

Black, Michael & Pauline Black

| 2016 | *Shakespeare Unravelled – Court Plays: The 1623 Deception*. Croydon, UK: CPI Books. | |

Blackadar, Bruce

| 1991, Oct. 5 | [refers to Tom Bethel and *The Atlantic*] | Toronto Star, p. F5 |

Blackmore, Malcolm

2008, June	Fedor Kusmich and the Authorship Question]	De Vere Soc. Newsl., v. 15/2: 7-9
2009, Feb.	[letter: the great Yorick skull story]	De Vere Soc. Newsl., v. 16/1: 27
2010, Feb.	[letter: dating of *Judgement at Paris*]	De Vere Soc. Newsl., v. 17/1: 26

Blackmun, Harry A.; William J. Brennan, Jr.; John Paul Stevens

| 1988, Spring | Opinions of the Justices | Am. U. Law Review, vol. 37/3: 819-26 |

Blair, James

| 2010, May 6 | [letter: response to Terry Teachout's April 17 article] | Wall St. Journal, p. A18 |

Blair, William Paul

| 1996, Fall | [letter: praise for most recent issue of the *Newsletter*] | Sh. Ox. Newsl., vol. 32/4: 21 |

Blake, Darrol

Plays

| 1977/2019 | *Nothing Truer Than Truth: The Life and Times of Edward de Vere, Sometimes Known as William Shakespeare.* | |

Shorter pieces

| 2020, Jan. | Nothing Truer than Truth [with Oliver Kinsey] | De Vere S. New., v. 27/1: 18-20 |

Blakey, Bob

| 1989, April 17 | Was Shakespeare a Fake? Some Scholars Think So | Calgary Herald, p. D2 |

Blakley, Rhys and Ben Hoyle

| 2011, Oct. 19 | Shakespeare as U.S. Likes It: Film Credits New Leading Man [review of *Anonymous*] | Times (London), p. 19 |

Blanding, Michael

| 2021 | *North by Shakespeare: A Rogue Scholar's Quest for the Truth Behind the Bard's Work*. New York: Hachette Books. | |

Blank, Daniel M.

| 2011, Oct. 27 | [letter: resp. to James Shapiro's April 11 review of *Anonymous*] | Times (London), p. A24 |

Blatty, William P.

| 1965 | *I, Billy Shakespeare*. Garden City, NY: Doubleday. | |

Blennerhassett, Leslie

| 2007, Sept. 12 | [letter: joining the doubters] | Birmingham Daily P., p. 13 |

Bloch, Howard

| 2000 | [letter: statistical analysis and dating the plays] | Oxfordian, vol. 3: 122-123 |

Bloom, Harold
Books
1994   *The Western Canon: The Books and School of the Ages*. New York: Riverhead Books. [see esp. p. 56-7, 347-49]

Shorter pieces
1999, April A Salvo for Lucy Negro   Harper's Mag., v. 298: 55-57
      [repr. in LC, p. 57-78, and in MEM, vol. 2: 195-98 (2015)]

Blume, Georg
2002, May Vorwort   Neues Sh. Journal, vol. 7: 13
2002, May Briefe, 1964-1985 [Correspondence with Gwynneth Bowen, Neues Sh. Journal, vol. 7: 14-37
      Dr. Hans Henning, Dr. Anselm Schlösser, Dr. W. Habicht,
      Sir John Gielgud and others]
2002, May Vorwort und Einleitung zu "Ein neues Shakespearebild" Neues Sh. Journal, vol. 7: 38
2002, May Bericht über ein neues Shakespeare-Bild (nach J. Thomas Looney Neues Sh. Journal, vol. 7: 39-64
      und Dorothy und Charlton Ogburn)
2002, May Briefe 1985-1994 [Correspondence with Gabriele Bock, The Shake- Neues Sh. Journal, vol. 7: 65-114
      speare Oxford Society, Charlton Ogburn, Helen Cyr, Vivian
      Elliot, Dr. Christian Thomsen]
      [p. 104: Georg Blume March 23, 1992 letter (English) to Ch. Ogburn]
      [p. 104-6: Charlton Ogburn April 4, 1992 letter (German) to Georg Blume]
      [p. 106-7: Ch. Ogburn Dec. 26, 1992 letter (German) to Georg Blume]
      [p. 108-09: Ch. Ogburn Dec. 29, 1993 letter (German) to Georg Blume]
2002, May Notwendige Schlußbemerkung   Neues Sh. Journal, vol. 7: 115

Blumenfeld, Samuel
2010, June [letter: John Gross's March review of *Contested*   Commentary, vol. 129/6: 6
      Will [reply by John Gross, same issue, p. 7-8]

Blumenthal, Walter H.
Books
1961   *Paging Mr. Shakespeare: A Critical Challenge*. New York: University Publishers.
1963   *Shakespeare: Veneration vs. Verity: Critical Comments From a Sceptic*. Lexington.
1965   *Who Knew Shakespeare? What Was His Reputation in His Lifetime?* Iowa City, IA: Prairie Press.
Shorter pieces
1966   One Cannot Flesh the Shakespeare Figure   Manuscripts, vol. 18: 20-31

Blunden, Mark
2009, April 23 Shakespeare Did Not Write His Own Plays, Claims Jacobi. Evening Standard, p. 19

Boas, F. S.
1930, June 11 Sidelight on Shakespeare [review of Allen's *Case*]   Listener, vol. 23: 1041
1933, Dec. 3 Anthologies With a Purpose [review of *Shakespeare, Oxford and* Observer, p. 3
      Elizabethan Times by Hubert Holland (1933)

Bodell, Alan
2020, Oct. [letter: Gilvary's article on J. Thomas Looney]   De Vere Soc. New., v. 27/4: 41-2

Bodell, Evelyn
1943, May [letter to Percy Allen, dated Occtober 14, 1942 (excerpts)] SF News-letter (E), p. 1

Boehm, Mike
2001, May 27 [review of *The Beard of Avon* by Amy Freed]   Los Angeles Times, p. 1

Boettger, Carol
1996, Winter That Way Madness Lies: Elegy Conference still leaves questions Sh. Ox. Newsl., vol. 32/1: 2, 24
1996, Spring Events at the World Shakespeare Congress: visions and revisions Sh. Ox. Newsl., vol. 32/2: 2, 23

Boileau, Ethel
1937, Nov. Shakespeare and Bacon [letters]   East Angl. Mag., vol. 3/2: 80-81

Boissevain, Charles
1929, Feb. 4 [review of *The Shakespeare Problem*] [a lecture given to the Journal de Geneve
      Anglo-Genevese Society]
1937, Dec. [letter: response to Rendall]   East Angl. M., vol. 3/3: 140-41
1942, Feb. [letter: authorship interest in the History Society of Geneva] SF News-letter (A), vol. 3/2: 24

Boissevain, K.D.W.

1930, Nov.	[letter: Colonel Ward re Oxford in Holland in 1585, citing entries in the Farnese Library]	Sh. Pictorial, no. 33: 16
1931, Sept.	[essay on de Vere]	Haagsch Maandblad

Bokenham, T. D.

1966, Spring	[letter: topical allusions in *King John*]	Sh. Authorship Rev. #15: 21-22
1967, Spring	"Ben Jonson, Shakespeare and the 1623 *Folio*" [summary of his Dec. 1, 1966 lecture] [repr. in BTC, vol. 5: 230-231]	Sh. Authorship Rev. #17: 17-18

Bompas, George C.

1902   *The Problem of the Shakespeare Plays*. London: S. Low, Marston & Company. [excerpt, "The Argument," Chapters 2 and 3, repr. in BTC, vol. 1: 163-83] [other editions: 1974, Folcroft, PA: Folcroft Library Editions; 1976, Norwood, PA: Norwood Editions; 1977, Philadelphia: R. West]

Bond, Jonathan

2009   *The De Vere Code: Proof of the True Author of Shake-speares Sonnets*. Canterbury: Real Press.

Bone, Captain F. D.

1941, April	Castle Hedingham	SF News-letter (A), v. 2/3: 33-34
1941, April	[letter]	SF News-letter (A), vol. 2/3: 36

Bone, James

2002, June 24	Poem Not Shakespeare's After All, Scholar Admits [repr. in DVS, p. 5-6, July 2002]	Sunday Times

Bongiorno, Dominick L.

1999, Spring	The Choice of 'fitchew' in *Othello*	Sh. Newsletter, vol. 49/1: 7
	Response by Richard Whalen in SON, vol. 36/1: 23 (2000).	

Borkin, Joseph

1959, May 31	[letter: Louis B. Wright's May 20 letter]	Washington Post., p. E4

Boule, Margie

1999, Nov. 30	Millennium Is Worth 1,000 Queries	Oregonian, p. C1

Bowen, Gwynneth M.

Books and pamphlets

1951   *Shakespeare's Farewell: The Date and Authorship of The Tempest* [pamphlet]. Inglethorpe, Buxton: printed privately. [repr. in BTC, vol. 5: 360-376]

Periodicals edited (co-editor)

1954, Sept.-1958, Autumn: *Shakespeare Fellowship News-letter (English)*
1959, Spring-1974, Summer: *Shakespearean Authorship Review* (issues 1-29)

Shorter pieces

1948, April	[letter: Sir Christopher Hatton as Shallow (not printed by TLS)]	SF News-letter (E), p. 6
1952, Sept.	[review of *Shakespeare's Identity: William Stanley, 6th Earl of Derby* by A. W. Titherley (1952)]	SF News-letter (E), p. 6-7
1953, April	[letter: wishful thinking and the authorship issue]	SF News-letter (E), p. 11-12
1954, April	Sir Edmund Chambers (1866-1954)	SF News-letter (E), p. 6
1954, April	[letter: *This Star of England* by Dorothy and Charlton Ogburn]	SF News-letter (E), p. 13
1954, Sept.	The Wounded Name [see correction in Spring 1955, p. 14] [repr. in BTC, vol. 4: 123-26]	SF News-letter (E), p. 7-8
1954, Sept.	[letter: Shakespeare Fellowship Study Circle]	SF News-letter (E), p. 12
1955, Spring	Falstaff, Tarlton and *The Famous Victories*	SF News-letter (E), p. 9-10
1955, Spring	[correction to her article "The Wounded Name"]	SF News-letter (E), p. 14
1955, Autumn	[report on Christmas Humphreys' April 22, 1955 Talk "Who Wrote Shakespeare – A Lawyer Enquires"]	SF News-letter (E), p. 2-3
1955, Autumn	Chronology in the Melting Pot	SF News-letter (E), p. 5-6
1956, Spring	The Banished Duke	SF News-letter (E), p. 5-6
1956, Spring	Coronation Sonnet	SF News-letter (E), p. 7-9
	Response by J. Shera Atkinson, Autumn 1956, p. 10-11. Reply by Bowen, Spring 1957, p. 11-12.	
1956, Autumn	[letter: Freud and Shakespeare]	SF News-letter (E), p. 3-4
1956, Autumn	Francis L. Nichols [obituary]	SF News-letter (E), p. 12
1957, Spring	[review of *The Shakespeare First Folio* by W. W. Greg (1955)]	SF News-letter (E), p. 10-11

Bowen, Gwynneth (continued)

1957, Autumn	[review of *Shakespeare's Sources* by Kenneth Muir (1957)]	SF News-letter (E), p. 9
1958, Spring	[letter: Lambin's recent letter on Oxford in Milan]	SF News-letter (E), p. 11
1957, Spring	[letter: Coronation Sonnet]	SF News-letter (E), p. 11-12
1958, Spring	[report on Katharine Eggar's Nov. 9, 1957 talk "What We Learn of de Vere from Shakespeare's Fools and Clowns"]	SF News-letter (E), p. 2
1958, Spring	Shakespeare and the Trussells of Billesley	SF News-letter (E), p. 6
1958, Autumn	[report on Ruth Wainewright's March 18, 1958 lecture "*All's Well that Ends Well* and the Authorship Question"]	SF News-letter (E), p. 2
1958, Autumn	Annual Dinner	SF News-letter (E), p. 3
1958, Autumn	Shakespeare's Early Style	SF News-letter (E), p. 3-6
1959, Spring	Ave Atque Vale	Sh. Authorship Rev. #1: 3-5
1959, Spring	Debate at the Old Vic – The Shakespeare Mystery [repr. in BTC, vol. 5: 19-23]	Sh. Authorship Rev. #1: 14-17
1959, Autumn	[review of *The Six Loves of Shake-speare* by Louis Bénézet (1958)] [repr. in BTC, vol. 5: 31-35]	Sh. Authorship Rev. #2: 9-12
1959, Autumn	[report of "Secrets of the Sonnets," a recorded dramatic reading edited by H. K. Kennedy-Skipton (18 Apr. 1959)]	Sh. Authorship Rev. #2: 15-16
1959, Autumn	John R. Mez (d. 1959) [obituary]	Sh. Authorship Rev. #2: 23
1959, Autumn	[letter: H. S. Shield's comments on Altrocchi's "Ships" article]	Sh. Authorship Rev. #2: 24
1960, Spring	Shakespeare to His Sovereign	Sh. Authorship Rev. #3: 6-8
1960, Spring	[report on Katharine Eggar's Nov. 28, 1959 talk "Ferdinando Stanley: An Undetected Pupil of Edward de Vere"]	Sh. Authorship Rev. #3: 18-19
1960, Autumn	Oxford Exonerated	Sh. Authorship Rev. #4: 2-9
1960, Autumn	[report on G. A. Morison's April 9, 1960 talk "Interest in the Authorship Question in the U.S."]	Sh. Authorship Rev. #4: 15-16
1960, Autumn	Oxford Did Go to Milan [repr. in BTC, vol. 5: 48-50]	Sh. Authorship Rev. #4: 48-50
1961, Spring	[report on John MacDonald's Jan. 14, 1961 lecture "Poems on Shakespeare By His Contemporaries," with comments by G. Bowen]	Sh. Authorship Rev. #5: 18-19
1961, Spring	Editorial Reply Regarding Spinola's Letter [repr. in BTC, vol. 5: 61-62]	Sh. Authorship Rev. #5: 23-24
1961, Autumn	Incomparable Pair and "The Works of William Shakespeare" [repr. in BTC, vol. 5: 63-69]	Sh. Authorship Rev. #6: 2-8
1961, Autumn	[report on Ruth Wainewright Lecture, "Macbeth and the Authorship Question"] [repr. in BTC, vol. 5: 77-79]	Sh. Authorship Rev. #6: 15-16
1961, Autumn	Annual Dinner [20 April 1961]	Sh. Authorship Rev. #6: 17-18
1962, Spring	Shakespeare and His Contemporaries	Sh. Authorship Rev. #7: 1-6
1962, Spring	A Shakespeare Allusion Continued?	Sh. Authorship Rev. #7: 10-12
1962, Autumn	[review of *The Shakespeare Claimants* by H. N. Gibson (1962)] [repr. in BTC, vol. 5: 112-113]	Sh. Authorship Rev. #8: 15-17
1963, Spring	J. Howard Dellinger (d. 1962) [obituary]	Sh. Authorship Rev. #9: 20
1963, Spring	T. B. Hart (1963) [obituary]	Sh. Authorship Rev. #9: 20
1963, Autumn	[review of *The Case for Shakespeare's Authorship of 'The Famous Victories'* by Seymour M. Pitcher (1961)] [repr. in BTC, vol. 5: 124-129]	Sh. Authorship Rev. #10: 10-14
1963, Autumn	[report on Gwynneth Bowen's March 14, 1963 talk "The Case for Edward de Vere as "Shakespeare"]	Sh. Authorship Rev. #10: 17-20
1963, Autumn	[report on Hilda Amphlett's April 30, 1963 talk "The Haunts of Edward de Vere"]	Sh. Authorship Rev. #10: 21
1964, Spring	Stratfordian Quatercentenary [repr. in BTC, vol. 5: 132-133]	Sh. Authorship Rev. #11: 3
1964, Spring	The Verdict of History [literary scholars vs. historians]	Sh. Authorship Rev. #11: 10-12
1964, Autumn	Reverberations [repr. in BTC, vol. 5: 146-149]	Sh. Authorship Rev. #12: 7-9
1964, Autumn	[report on Professor L. S. Penrose's March 12, 1964 lecture "Shakespeare's Knowledge of Medicine"[	Sh. Authorship Rev. #12: 15-16
1965, Spring	[review of *Shakespeare* by Peter Alexander (1964)]	Sh. Authorship Rev. #13: 12-17
1965, Autumn	Hackney, Harsnett, and the Devils in *King Lear* [repr. in OXV, p. 237-43; and in BTC, vol. 5: 160-167]	Sh. Authorship Rev. #14: 2-7
1965, Autumn	[report on Ruth Wainewright's March 17, 1965 lecture "Conflicting Dates for Various Candidates"] [repr. in BTC, vol. 5: 176-78]	Sh. Authorship Rev. #14: 13-15
1966, Spring	Sir Edward Vere and His Mother, Anne Vavasor [repr. in BTC, vol. 5: 183-187]	Sh. Authorship Rev. #15: 4-7

Bowen, Pamella M.

    1998, Summer   Unexpected Help From Neil Simon   Sh. Ox. Newsl., vol. 34/2: 17

    2007, Fall   [letter: *Macbeth*]   Sh. Matters, vol. 7/1: 2

Bowers, Fredson T.

    1937, March   Gascoigne and the Oxford Cipher [review of *A Hundreth Sundrie Flowres* by George Gascoigne, edited by Bernard M. Ward]   Mod. Lang. Notes, vol. 52/3: 183-86

Boyce, Burke

    1949   *Cloak of Folly*. New York: Harper.

Boyce, Tom

    1993, Winter   [letter: CD: *Joyne Hands: Music of Thomas Morley*]   Sh. Ox. Newsl., vol. 29/1a: 17

Boyd, Bentley

    1989, Aug. 7   Was the Earl the Bard? Defenders of an Oxford Nobleman Take Center Stage in the Long-Running Drama Over Whether Sh. Really Wrote His Plays   Chicago Tribune, Sec. 5: 1-2

    1989, Sept. 18   The Bard: Oxford Earl or "the Stratford man"?   Washington Post, p. B4

Boyd, Michael

    2005, May   [letter: redevelopment of the Royal Shakespeare theatre]   De Vere Soc. Newsl., p. 29

Boyle, Charles

Books

    1993   *To Catch the Conscience of the King: Leslie Howard and the 17th Earl of Oxford* (pamphlet). Northampton, MA: Oxenford Press. [revised and repr. in *Another Hamlet*]

    2013   *Another Hamlet: The Mystery of Leslie Howard*. Somerville, MA: Forever Press. [1ST ed. 2011]

Shorter pieces

    1988, April 28   [letter: Wilborn Hampton's April 26 "Freud" article] [both repr. in SON, vol. 24/2: 8-9]   New York Times

    1988, Summer   [letter: Oxford bearing the canopy]   Sh. Ox. Newsl., vol. 34/2: 21

    1989, Sept. 8   Baring the Bard [letter: Jeffrey Gantz's Aug. 11 article] [both repr. in SON, vol. 22/4: 12-13 (Fall 1989)]   Boston Phoenix

    1993, Summer   [letter: petitioning the Shakespearean Association of America]   Sh. Ox. Newsl., vol. 29/3a: 9

    1994, Autumn   Bitter Fruit: Troilus and Cressida in Queen Elizabeth's Court [repr. in PR, p. 143-52]   Eliz. Review, vol. 2/2: 11-18

    1996, Winter   Notes Towards an Elizabethan *Twelfth Night*   Ever Reader, vol. 2

    1996, Winter   [letter: the crown signature]   Sh. Ox. Newsl., vol. 32/1: 23

    1996, Spring   Lessons From a Seminar [repr. in PR, p. 1-4; in EVR, vol. 3 (Sum. 1996); and in German in NSJ, vol. 3: 151-54 (Jan. 1999)]   Sh. Ox. Newsl., vol. 32/2: 4

    1997, Summer   [review of *Alias Shakespeare* by Joseph Sobran (1997)]   Sh. Ox. Newsl., vol. 33/3: 16

    1998, Fall   [review of *Who Were Shakespeare?* by Ron Allen (1998)]   Sh. Ox. Newsl., vol. 34/3: 22

    1999, Winter   [letter: Roger Stritmatter's brilliant Fall 1998 First Folio article]   Sh. Ox. Newsl., vol. 34/4: 21

    2000, Winter   Why *Pericles* Was Not Included in the *First Folio* [repr. in BTC, vol. 9: 250-58] Response by Chuck Berney, Summer 2000, p. 21-22.   Sh. Ox. Newsl., vol. 35/4: 6-8

    2001, Winter   Elizabeth's Glass   Sh. Ox. Newsl., v. 36/4: 1, 15-17

    2021, Sept.   Adapting Shakespeare to the Screen   Oxfordian, vol. 23: 365-372

    1997, Winter   Writing History: The Facts are the Facts, But Interpretation is All [with William E. Boyle and Charles Burford (Beauclerk)] [repr. in *A Poet's Rage*, p. 5-14] Response by Richard Whalen, SON, Spring 1997, p. 21.   Sh. Ox. Newsl., vol. 33/1: 1, 6-7+

Boyle, James

    2006   *The Shakespeare Chronicles: A Novel*. Lulu Press.

Boyle, James D. A.

    1988, Spring   The Search for an Author: Shakespeare and the Framers   Am U. Law Rev., vol. 37/3: 625-43

    1988, Spring   Brief of Appellee William Shakespeare (or Shakspere) of Stratford-Upon-Avon   Am U. Law Rev., vol. 37/3: 725-97

    1998, Spring   Reply Brief of Appellee William Shakespeare (or Shakspere) of Stratford-Upon-Avon   Am U. Law Rev., vol. 37/3: 809-17

Boyle, William E. (Bill) (continued)

1999, Spring	*Harper's* Story Generates Commentary, Coverage	Sh. Ox. Newsl., vol. 35/1: 3
1999, Spring	The Invisible Men	Sh. Ox. Newsl., vol. 35/1: 20
1999, Summer	Media: Follow-up to *Harper's*, *Chronicle of Higher Education* Stories	Sh. Ox. Newsl., vol. 35/2: 2
1999, Summer	And Meet the Once and Future Descendant? Is Prince William Descended From Shakespeare?	Sh. Ox. Newsl., vol. 35/2: 3
1999, Summer	Shakespeare, Southampton and *The Sonnets* [repr. in BTC, vol. 8: 73-74]	Sh. Ox. Newsl., vol. 35/2: 24
1999, Fall	23rd Annual Conference Caps an Eventful Year	Sh. Ox. Newsl., vol. 35/3: 1, 3-5
1999, Fall	Shakespeare, Southampton and the *Sonnets*: Conference Explores Competing Theories	Sh. Ox. Newsl., vol. 35/3: 6-7, 22
1999, Fall	3rd Earl of Southampton and the Order of the Garter [summary of a talk by John Rollett] [repr. in BTC, vol. 8: 119-21]	Sh. Ox. Newsl., vol. 35/3: 7
1999, Fall	Shakespeare and Religion: Conference Panel Highlights Sticking Points for Scholars [with Roger Stritmatter and Daniel Wright]	Sh. Ox. Newsl., vol. 35/3: 8-9
2000, Winter	Society Opens Its Library, Establishes an Endowment [with William Peel and Jack Shuttleworth]	Sh. Ox. Newsl., vol. 35/4: 1, 4-5
2000, Spring	Whose Handwriting? The Annotations in Oxford's *Geneva Bible*	Sh. Ox. Newsl., vol. 36/1: 3
2000, Spring	4th Annual Edward de Vere Studies Conference	Sh. Ox. Newsl., vol. 36/1: 10-11+
2000, Spring	Paradigm Earthquake Strikes Amherst, Mass. [Stritmatter's successful Ph.D. defense]	Sh. Ox. Newsl., vol. 36/1: 1, 8-9
2000, Spring	From the Editor: Edward de Vere's Last Known Letter; Paradigms Shifting and Shaking	Sh. Ox. Newsl., vol. 36/1: 28
2000, Summer	*U.S. News & World Report* Features Shakespeare Mystery; Authorship Encounters with William F. Buckley, Jr.	Sh. Ox. Newsl., vol. 36/2: 3, 24
2000, Summer	News: Folger Library's Ashbourne Portrait Now on Public Display	Sh. Ox. Newsl., vol. 36/2: 4
2000, Summer	From the Editor: The Ashbourne Portrait; Folger's Authorship Policy	Sh. Ox. Newsl., vol. 36/2: 20
2000, Fall	Stratford (Ontario) Hosts 24th Annual Conference	Sh. Ox. Newsl., vol. 36/3: 1, 3-4
2000, Fall	*Hamlet*, the Comedy	Sh. Ox. Newsl., vol. 36/3: 20
2001, Winter	The Bad Boy is Back: *NY Times* Trumpets Marlowe	Sh. Ox. Newsl., vol. 36/4: 3
2001, Winter	The ABCs of the Authorship Debate	Sh. Ox. Newsl., vol. 36/4: 22
2001, Spring	James Edmund Fitzgerald (1943-2001) [obituary]	Sh. Ox. Newsl., vol. 37/1: 3
2001, Spring	From the Editor: As We Like It; Goodbye to a Friend: Goodby to a Friend: James Fitzgerald	Sh. Ox. Newsl., vol. 37/1: 20
2002, Winter	Tender Airs, Tudor Heirs [with Roger Stritmatter]	Sh. Matters, vol. 1/2: 3
2002, Spring	Smithsonian Showdown and *NY Times* Feature Article Rock the Authorship Debate	Sh. Matters, vol. 1/3: 1, 6-7
2002, Spring	From the Editors: Making News; State of the Debate [with Stritmatter]	Sh. Matters, vol. 1/3: 3
2002, Spring	New Documents Vindicate Barrell [with Roger Stritmatter]	Sh. Matters, vol. 1/3: 3
2002, Summer	Swan Song for *Funeral Elegy*: Prof. Donald Foster Concedes It's Not Shakespeare [with Roger Stritmatter]	Sh. Matters, vol. 1/4: 1, 4
2002, Summer	Why the Ashbourne Portrait Matters [with Roger Stritmatter]	Sh. Matters, vol. 1/4: 3
2002, Summer	From the Editors: Oxford is Shakespeare: Any Questions? [with Roger Stritmatter]	Sh. Matters, vol. 1/1: 1, 3, 20
2002, Fall	From the Editor: Editorial changes; Books and Book Reviews	Sh. Matters, vol. 2/1: 3
2002, Fall	Elizabethan History and the "Bag of Secrets"	Sh. Matters, vol. 2/1: 5
2002, Fall	Recent Developments: The Folger and the Ashbourne Portrait	Sh. Matters, vol. 2/1: 10
2003, Winter	Searching for Shakespeare: How the Sanders Portrait Quest Leads Straight to Authorship	Sh. Matters, vol. 2/2: 1, 10-11
2003, Winter	From the Editor: Who's Afraid of the Big, Bad Earl?	Sh. Matters, vol. 2/2: 3
2003, Winter	Shakespeare and Rule of Law Panel Discussion Attracts SRO Crowd	Sh. Matters, vol. 2/2: 7
2003, Winter	Stritmatter, Ross Debate Oxford's Bible	Sh. Matters, vol. 2/2: 8
2003, Winter	Moot Court Debate on the Authorship Question	Sh. Matters, vol. 2/2: 9
2003, Winter	Ashbourne Portrait Followup	Sh. Matters, vol. 2/2: 11
2003, Winter	Much Ado About Something Airs on PBS	Sh. Matters, vol. 2/2: 30-31
2003, Winter	Fellowship in Cambridge: Conf. Brings Together Shakespeareans [with Lynne Kositsky and Richard F. Whalen]	Sh. Matters, vol. 2/2: 1, 6
2003, Spring	From the Editor: As We Like It?; John Louther, 1924-2003	Sh. Matters, vol. 2/3: 3
2003, Summer	7th Annual De Vere Studies Conference	Sh. Matters, vol. 2/4: 1, 8-12

Author Index

Boyle, William E. (Bill) (continued)

2020, Summer	Archives Matter: Reprint of Col. Bernard R. Ward's "What Lurks Behind Shakespeare's Historical Plays, from *Shakespeare Pictorial*, Sept. 1929, p. 16.	Sh. Ox. Newsl., vol. 56/3: 34-35
2020, Fall	Reasonable Doubts, Reasonable Theories	Sh. Ox. Newsl., vol. 56/4: 23-25
2021, Winter	[letter: response to John Hamill]	Sh. Ox. Newsl., vol. 57/1: 30-31
2021, Fall	Tales from the Archives: The Drayton Collection; History of the Evered Foundation [with R. Euchner, T. Deer & K. Sharpe]	Sh. Ox. Newsl., vol. 57/4: 29-32
2022, Spring	SOF Spring Symposium Report	Sh. Ox. Newsl., v. 58/2: 1, 27-28
2023, Winter	In Memoriam: James S. Hardigg (2022-2020)	Sh. Ox. Newsl., vol. 59/1: 5
2023, Spring	Tales from the Archives: Cataloguing Shakespeare: Introducing the Authorship Question into the Library Science Literature	Sh. Ox. Newsl., vol. 59/2: 31-32
2023, Summer	In Memoriam: Helen Heightsman Gordon (1932-1922)	Sh. Ox. Newsl., vol. 59/3: 10
2023, Summer	Tales from the Archives: Mad North north-west	Sh. Ox. Newsl., vol. 59/3: 16-18
2023, Summer	Thomas Nashe: A Person or a Persona?	Sh. Ox. Newsl., vol. 59/3: 26-27

Braben, Shirley

2007, Spring	[letter: Thomas Smith and Hill Hall]	Sh. Ox. Newsl., vol. 43/2: 21

Brackmann, Bernd

2015, Summer	Biography, Genius, and Inspiration	Brief Chronicles, vol. VI: 23-32

Brackmann, Elke

2011, July	[review of *Shakespeare: The Concealed Poet* by Robert Detobel] [with Jan. H. Scheffer]	De Vere Soc. New., v. 18/2: 36-8
2016, Dec.	Teaching the Sonnets and de Vere's Biography at School – Opportunities and Risks [with Robert Detobel] [repr. in *Sh. Authorship Sourcebook* (Stritmatter 2019, 2022): 117-41]	Brief Chron., vol. VII: 83-100

Brady, Tera

2011, Oct. 28	Anonymous [review of *Anonymous*]	Irish Times (Dublin), p. 16

Brame, Michael

Books [all with Galina Popova]

2002	*Shakespeare's Fingerprints*. Vashon Island, WA: Adonis Editions.	
2004	*Secret Shakespeare's Adventures of Freeman Jones*. Vashon Island, WA: Adonis Editions.	
2004	*What Thing Is Love?* (poems of Edward de Vere). adonis-editions.com.	

Shorter pieces

1999, Jan.	Behind and Beyond Shakespeare's Wordplay	Ling. Analy., v. 29/3-4: 349+
2000, Jan.	Sweet Will's Big O	Ling. Analy., v. 30/3-4: 359+
2000, Jan.	Will I Am	Ling. Analy., v. 30/3-4: 397+
2003, Fall	Illicit Reversal [with Galina Popova]	Sh. Matters, vol. 3/1: 28-29
2004, Winter	[letter, with Galina Popova: Pushkin and Shakespeare]	Sh. Matters, vol. 3/2: 2
2004, Spring	[letter, with Galina Popova: *Monstrous Adversary* by Alan Nelson]	Sh. Matters, vol. 3/3: 2
2004, Summer	Was Shakespeare Gay? [with Galina Popova]	Sh. Matters, vol. 3/4: 34-36
2004, Fall	[letter: linguistic fingerprints]	Sh. Matters, vol. 4/1: 2-3

Brand, Alice Blarden

1976	Antony and Cleopatra and the Nature of Their Sexuality	Bard, vol. 1/3: 98-107

Brandt, Bruce E.

2010-11	[review of *Contested Will* by James Shapiro (2010)]	Choice, vol. 48

Brantley, Ben

2011, Oct. 29	Author? Who Cares? The Play's the Thing [review of *Anonymous*]	New York Times, Arts, p. 1, 6

Bravin, Jess

1992, April 24	Much Ado About Real Shakespeare	Los Angeles Times, p. 1
1992, April 28	Claiming the Bard's Mantle: Descendants Contend That the Earl of Oxford Was the Author	Los Angeles Times, p. SDF1
2009, Apr. 18-19	Justice Stevens Renders an Opinion on Who Wrote Sh.'s Plays Responses by David Elmore, Paul Dawson, Martha K. Hogan, & Royal S. Dellinger on 25 April 2009. Response by *First Things*, June/July 2009, p. 68-72.	Wall St. Journal, p. A1-2

Brazil, Robert
Books
1999   *The True Story of the Shakespeare Publications, vol. 1: Edward de Vere and the Shakespeare Printers.* Repr. in 2010: Seattle: Cortical Output.

2013   *Angel Day, The English Secretary, and the Seventeenth Earl of Oxford.* Cortical Output.

Periodicals edited
2002, Spring-2002, Fall: *Shakespeare Oxford Newsletter*, vol. 38/2-38/4

Shorter pieces

1999, Summer	Edward de Vere and the Shakespeare Quartos, Part 1 [repr. in BTC, vol. 8: 86-94]	Sh. Ox. Newsl., vol. 35/2: 1, 16+
1999, Fall	Edward de Vere and the Shakespeare Quartos, Part 2 [repr. in BTC, vol. 8: 95-102] See also Peter W. Dickson, SON, vol. 35/3: 15, 23-24 (1999).	Sh. Ox. Newsl., vol. 35/3: 1, 10+-
1999, Fall	The Thomas Creede Connection [repr. in BTC, vol. 8: 106-13]	Sh. Ox. Newsl., vol. 35/3: 12-13
1999, Fall	James Roberts and Oxford: another key publishing relationship [repr. in BTC, vol. 8: 103-05]	Sh. Ox. Newsl., vol. 35/3: 14
1999	Unpacking *The Merry Wives*	Oxfordian, vol. 2: 117-137
2002, Spring	Supreme Court Justice John Paul Stevens Argues for Oxford's Authorship of Shakespeare	Sh. Ox. Newsl., vol. 38/2: 3, 21
2002, Spring	New Evidence Confirms Oxford's Birth Date	Sh. Ox. Newsl., vol. 38/2: 6-7
2002, Summer	Stylometrics and the *Funeral Elegy* Affair [with Wayne Shore]	Sh. Ox. Newsl., vol. 38/3: 1, 8
2002, Summer	Countess Anne's Book: New Light on a 1581 Translation of Sermons on Saint Paul	Sh. Ox. Newsl., vol. 38/3: 18-21
2002, Fall	26th Annual SON Conference Held in Nation's Capitol	Sh. Ox. Newsl., v. 38/4: 1, 17-19
2002, Fall	[review of *Bedside Bathtub & Armchair Companion to Shakespeare* by Riley/McAllister (2001)]	Sh. Ox. Newsl., vol. 38/4: 21
2002, Fall	[review of *Infinite Variety: The Folger Shakespeare Library* by Esther Ferington (2002)]	Sh. Ox. Newsl., vol. 38/4: 21
2002, Fall	[review of *The Real Shakespeare* by Marilyn Savage Gray (2001)]	Sh. Ox. Newsl., vol. 38/4: 21
2002, Fall	[letter: Carl Caruso's "Maiden and Mermaid" article] Reply by Robert Brazil, Fall 2002, p. 2. Additional response by Caruso, Winter 2003, p. 2.	Sh. Matters, vol. 2/1: 2
2003, Winter	Trevor-Roper, Elizabethan Scholar, Dies (1914-2003)	Sh. Ox. Newsl., vol. 39/1: 7
2003, Winter	Oxfordian News: Shakespeare and the Stars; Tudor "Angel" Coins; Weir Talks	Sh. Ox. Newsl., vol. 39/1: 7-8
2003, Winter	Oxford and the Turk	Sh. Ox. Newsl., vol. 39/1: 16-18
2006, Spring	Oxford's Heraldry Explained [Barbara Burris's Sum. 2003 article]	Sh. Matters, vol. 5/3: 1, 15-25

Breitwieser, Ludwig
1963   *Der falsche und der wahre Shakespeare.* Offenbach.

Bremer, Nolan
2000, Spring   [letter: bequest of Tal Wilson]   Sh. Ox. Newsl., vol. 36/1: 29

Brennan, Michael G. (editor)
2022   *English Travellers to Venice 1450-1600.* London: Routledge. [with nine-page essay on Edward de Vere]

Brennan, Patricia
1997, Aug. 23   On Shakespeare and Cadfael [profile of Derek Jacobi]   New York Times, p. TV36

Brennan, Jr., William J.; Harry A. Blackmun; John Paul Stevens
1988, Spring   Opinions of the Justices   Am U. Law Rev., v. 37/3: 819-26

Brereton, Cloudesley
1937, May   "Shakespeare"—A "Stage Manager" [letter]   East Ang. M., vol. 2/8: 361-62

Brewer, Caroline
2000, April 23   Book Value Between Elegant Covers [profile of Oxfordian Leonard Hansen]   Record (Bergen C., NJ), p. L1

Brewster, Eleanor
1964   *Oxford, Courtier to the Queen: A Biography.* New York: Pageant Press.
1972   *Oxford and His Elizabethan Ladies.* Philadelphia: Dorrance.

Bridgers, Sue E.
1993   *Keeping Christina.* New York: HarperCollins Publishers.

Bridgewater, H.
Books and pamphlets
    1938   *Shakespeare and Italy* [pamphlet, repr. from *Baconiana*, October 1938]
    1942   *Bacon or Shakspere: Does It Matter?* [pamphlet]
Shorter pieces
    1935, Dec.   [letter: missing plays of the Earl of Oxford]   Sh. Pictorial, no. 94: 191
    1938, Oct.   Shakespeare and Italy [reprinted as a pamphlet]   Baconiana

Briggs, Arthur E.
    1960, April   Did Shaxper Write Shakespeare? [repr. in SC, p. 93-97]   Am. Bar Assoc. Journ., vol. 46/4: 410-12

Briggs, Nate
    2015, Winter   Shakespeare Full Circle   Sh. Ox. Newsl., vol. 51/1: 31-32

Broach, Elise
    2005   *Shakespeare's Secret*. New York: Henry Holt and Co.

Brock, H. I.
    1928, Nov. 25   Seeking a True Shakespeare Portrait   New York Times, p. SM6

Broder, C.
    1964, June 2   The Real "Shakespeare"? [excerpt in SAR, #14: 21 (Autumn 1965)]   Hackney Gazette

Broderick, James F.
Books [with Darren W. Miller]
    2008   *Web of Conspiracy: A Guide to Conspiracy Theory Sites on the Internet*. Medford, NJ: Information Today.
Shorter pieces
    2013   Doubter Response to Question 55: What other theories might be   Sh. Beyond Doubt?, p. 212-13
            compared to the Sh. authorship conspiracy theory and why?

Brody, Burton H.
    1989, June 3   Earl of Oxford Preferred [George Rickey's May 11 review of   New York Times, p. 14
            Frontline's "The Shakespeare Mystery"]

Brokaw, Leslie
    2006, June 25   She's Bringing Shakespeare Controversy to Film   Boston Globe
            [Cheryl Eagan-Donovan]

Bronte, Lydia
    1989, Spring   "The Shakespeare Mystery" [repr. in BTC, vol. 6: 393-95]   Sh. Ox. Newsl., vol. 25/2: 12-13

Brook, Peter
    2014   *The Quality of Mercy: Reflections on Shakespeare*. New York: Theatre Communications Group.
            [See esp. "Alas, Poor Yorick, or What if Shakespeare Fell off the Wall?" p. 3-17]

Brooke, Tucker
    1931, Autumn   [review of *Hidden Allusions in Shakespeare's Plays* by Eva T. Clark]   Yale Review, vol. 21: 215
    1938, April   [review of *The Man Who Was Shakespeare* by Eva T. Clark (1937)]   J. of Eng. & Germanic Phil-
                                               ology, vol. 37/2: 311-12

Brookman, Belinda
    1988, April 6   Group Persuades "Jurors" Bard Really Earl, Not Will   Palm Beach Post
            [repr. in SON, vol. 24/2: 9, Spring 1988]

Brooks, Alden
Books
    1937   *Will Shakspere: Factotum and Agent*. New York: Round Table Press. Repr. in 1974: New York: AMS
            Press. ["Introduction" repr. in BTC, vol. 4: 213-222]

Shorter pieces
    1949, Sept. 3   A Look at the Register [letter: response to Burgess]   Sat. Review, p. 26
            [repr. in *Sh. and His Rivals* (McMichael & Glenn 1962): 190-92]

Brooks, Andree
    2011, Oct. 27   [letter: James Shapiro's Oct. 17 review of *Anonymous*]   Times (London), p. A24

Brooks, Helen
    1962, Sept. 14   The Truth Is Out! [letter: regrets that the *Post* wasted space to review   Washington Post, p. A14
            Ogburn's book]

Browning, Olive H.
1955, Spring	[review of *Who Was Shakespeare?* by Hilda Amphlett (1955)]	SF News-letter (E), p. 10-11
1955, Autumn	Annual Dinner	SF News-letter (E), p. 1-2

Brownlow, Frank
1997	[review of *Alias Shakespeare* by Joe Sobran (1997)]	Chronicles, vol. 21/8: 26

Brunel University and the Shakespearean Authorship Trust
2007, Summer	2007 John Silberrad Memorial Lectures at Shakespeare's Globe	Sh. Ox. Newsl., vol. 43/3: 22-23

Brunner, Karl
1952	[review of *Der wahre Shakespeare* by Charlton Ogburn]	Sh. Jahrbuch, b. 87/88: 211-3

Bryan, Aubrey
1994, Nov.	[review of *Shakespeare—Who Was He?* by Richard Whalen (1994)]	Library Journal, vol. 119/18: 78

Bryant, J. A., Jr.
1997	[review of *Shakespeare, In Fact* by Irvin Matus (1994)]	Sewanee Review, vol. 105: 96

Buckley, Eric R.
1937, May	Was Shakespeare an East Anglian? [letter]	East Ang. Mag, vol. 2/8: 360-61
1937, June	Was Shakespeare an East Anglian? [letter]	East Ang. Mag., vol. 2/9: 424

Buckley, Marion
Books and plays
2002	*By Any Other Name.* [A humorous dramatization of the life and times of Edward de Vere]	

Shorter pieces
2004, Fall	The Shakespeare Authorship Debate and the Proper Standard of Proof	Tennessee Law Review, vol. 72/1: 295-307

Buckley, Jr., William F.
1985	*Firing Line: The Mysterious William Shakespeare* (pamphlet). [transcript of the program with Charlton Ogburn and Prof. Maurice Charney taped on 11 Dec. 1984; Columbia, SC: Southern Educational Communication Association] [See also article by Gordon C. Cyr in SON, vol. 21/1: 7-8 (Winter, 1985)]	

Buckridge, Patrick
1992	The "Oxford/Shakespeare" Debate: Reasons to Believe	Imago, vol. 4/3: 39
1994, Autumn	[review of *The Shakespeare Conspiracy* by Graham Phillips and Martin Ketamen (1994)]	Eliz. Review, vol. 2/2: 4-70
1996, Winter	Authorship Down Under: One-Man Publicity Campaign in Australia	Sh. Ox. Newsl., vol. 32/1: 20
1996, Autumn	What Did John Marston Know About Shakespeare? [repr. in BTC, vol. 8: 255-75] Response by Derran K. Charlton, Spring 1997, p. 4-6.	Eliz. Review, vol. 4/2: 24-40
1997, Spring	[letter: Derran Charlton's response]	Eliz. Review, vol. 5/1: 4
1998, Autumn	Christopher Hatton, Edward Dyer and the "First Adonis"	Eliz. Review, vol. 6/2: 15-30
2000, May	[letter: the 2nd Shakespearean Research Symposium, Oct. 7-8, 2000]	De Vere Soc. Newsl., p. 28
2013	Doubter Response to Question #10: Do writers of Shakespeare's time identify him as an author of specific works?, in *Shakespeare Beyond Doubt?* (Shahan: 168-69)	
2013	Doubter Response to Question #11: Do writers of Shakespeare's time dispraise his works?, in *Sh. Beyond Doubt?* (Shahan: 169-70)	

Buisman, Louise
1973, Summer	The Problems of *Henry VI* and of *King John*	Sh. Authorship Rev. #28: 14-24
1974, Summer	Shakespeare Personal or Impersonal?	Sh. Authorship Rev. #29: 11-16

Bullard, Linda
2019, Summer	Shakespeare Authorship Question Comes to the Texas Hill Country	Sh. Ox. Newsl., vol. 55/3: 8-9
2020, Fall	Faces of the Centennial	Sh. Ox. Newsl., vol. 56/4: 16-17

Bullitt, Russell Thayer
2018, Spring	[letter: Looney gravesite in Saltwell Cemetery]	Sh. Ox. Newsl., vol. 54/2: 3

Bunnett, R. J. A.
1939, July	[letter: authorship issues in the decades after de Vere died in 1604]	SF News-letter (E), no. 15: 8-11

Bünsch, Iris
2005	[review of *Der Fall Shakespeare* by Walter Klier (2004)]	Literatur in Wissenschaft und Unterricht, vol. 28: 252

Burchard, Hank

    1971, July 29   Charlton Ogburn: Spaceship Earth's Happy Prisoner [Very long and   Washington Post, p. G1
        favorable profile of Charlton Ogburn]

    1992, Feb. 14   Uncover Temptation   Wall St. J., p. N67

Burford, Charles – see Charles Beauclerk

Burgess, Anthony

    1977, Oct. 9   [review of *Shakespeare by Hilliard* by Leslie Hotson (1977)]   Observer, p. 26

Burgess, Gelett

    1923, May 25   The Ten Books I havre Enjoyed Most   Courier-Journal, p. 6

    1945, July   Gelett Burgess' Tribute to *"Shakespeare" Identified*   SF Quarterly, vol. VI/3: 34
        [reprint of his May 19, 1920 letter]

    1947, June 8   Modern Research Sheds New Light on Bard of Avon [letter: resp. to   NY Herald Trib., p. A7
        the May 30 editorial] [letters in response to Burgess ran
        through seven Sunday editions] [repr. in SON, vol. 5/4
        (Dec. 1969); and in BTC, vol. 7: xxvii-xxx; and in
        The Inspiration of Shakespeare (pamphlet, p. 4-7)]

    1947, June 22   The Modern Challenge of Shakespearean Authorship   NY Herald Trib., p. A7
        [response to recent letters]

    1948, July 31   Oxford is Shakespeare: A Communication [very long rebuttal to   Washington Post, p. 5
        critics of the idea that Edward de Vere was Shakespeare]
            Response by Mumpsimum, Aug. 8, p. B4.
            Response by E. V. Wilcox, T. M. Kerr, Jr., Aug. 9, p. 6.
            Response by Antonio Spiggonio, Aug. 10, p. 10.

    1948, Oct. 2   Pseudonym, Shakespeare   Sat. Review, p. 22
        [repr. in *Sh. and His Rivals* (McMichael & Glenn 1962): 173-75]

    1949, June 4   An Oxford Tutorial [letter]   Sat. Review, p. 24-25
        [repr. in *Sh. and His Rivals* (McMichael & Glenn 1962): 186-88]

    1949, Dec. 11   Shakespeare a Pen Name [letter]   NY Herald Trib., p. A5

    1950, May 12   The Three Centuries-Old Mystery of Shakespeare Solved   Argonaut

Burghauser, Jeffrey

    2021, July   On Alexander Waugh   New English Review

Burgstahler, Albert

    2004, Fall   [letter: support for PT theory]   Sh. Matters, vol. 4/1: 2

    2009, Fall   News: Collaborative Authorship for *Edward III*?   Sh. Matters, vol. 8/4: 18-19

Burns, Tom

    1993, Feb. 28   The Bard and the Bison [letter: Ch. Champlin's Feb. 21 article]   Los Angeles Times, p. 13
        Champlin's Feb. 21 article]

Burris, Barbara

    2001, Fall   A Golden Book, Bound Richly Up: Comparing Chapman's Words   Sh. Matters, vol. 1/1: 1, 12-17
        with the Ashbourne portrait
        Response by David Roper, Winter 2002, p. 2.
        Response by Virginia J. Renner, Winter 2002, p. 2-3.
            Reply by Barbara Burris, Spring 2002, p. 2. See also:
        Barbara Burris, Winter 2002, p. 17-21; Spring 2002, p. 1, 8.
        Response by Gordon C. Cyr, Spring 2002 p. 9.
            Reply by Burris, Fall 2002, p. 2-3.

    2002, Winter   The Ashbourne Portrait: Part II: Costume Dating Debunks Folger's   Sh. Matters, vol. 1/2: 1, 17-21
        Hamersley Claim

    2002, Spring   Ashbourne Story III: Review of the Painting's Restoration Reveals   Sh. Matters, vol. 1/3: 1, 10-22
        History of Deception [repr. in BTC, vol. 10: 102-138]

    2002, Spring   [letter: reply to responses to her Fall 2001 "Ashbourne" article]   Sh. Matters, vol. 1/3: 2

    2002, Spring   Comparison of the Conclusions of Two Major Published Studies of   Sh. Matters, vol. 1/3: 13
        the Ashbourne Portrait: Barrell in 1940 and Pressly in 1993
        Response by John M. Rollett, vol. 1/4: 2-3 (Summer 2002).
        Response by Gordon C. Cyr, vol. 1/4: 2-3 (Summer 2002).
        Response by Gordon C. Cyr, vol. 2/1: 3-4 (Fall 2002).
        Reply by Barbara Burris, vol. 2/1: 2: (Fall 2002).

Burris, Barbara (continued)

2002, Spring	The Coat of Arms and the Composite Sketch	Sh. Matters, vol. 1/3: 17
2002, Spring	What Did Hamersley Look Like?	Sh. Matters, vol. 1/3: 18
2002, Fall	The Ashbourne Portrait: Part IV [repr. in BTC, vol. 10: 139-176]	Sh. Matters, vol. 2/1: 1, 9-22
2002, Fall	[letter: reply to responses to her Fall 2001 "Ashbourne" article]	Sh. Matters, vol. 2/1: 2-3
2002, Fall	A History of Alterations to the Coat of Arms	Sh. Matters, vol. 2/1: 12-13
2003, Summer	Oxford's New Coat of Arms in 1586	Sh. Matters, vol. 2/4: 20-23
	Response by Robert Brazil, Spring 2006, p. 1, 15-25.	
2004, Fall	Back to the Ashbourne: More Layers of Deception in 2002 Examination of the Portrait	Sh. Matters, vol. 4/1: 1, 15-21
2005, Summer	Ashbourne Portrait [letter]	Sh. Matters, vol. 4/4: 4
2014, Summer	[letter: reply to Lisa Dean's Summer 2014 "Ashbourne" letter]	Sh. Ox. Newsl., vol. 50/3: 4-5

Burrows, Joh

2012	A Second Opinion on "Shakespeare and Authorship Studies in the Twenty-First Century [response to Brian Vickers' 2011 article]	Sh. Quart., vol. 63/3: 355-92

Burt, F. Allen

1938	[feature article on Edward de Vere] [noted in SFA]	Boston Herald
1941, Oct.	[letter: final proof of Oxford's authorship]	SF News-letter (A), vol. 2/6: 72

Burton, J. Anthony

2000, Fall	An Unrecognized These in Hamlet: Lost Inheritance and Claudius's Marriage to Gertrude, Part 1 (repr. in *Shakespeare and the Law* (Stritmatter, 2022): 171-86]	Sh. Newsl. of Claremont McKenna College, vol. 50/3
2000-01, Wntr.	An Unrecognized These in Hamlet: Lost Inheritance and Claudius's Marriage to Gertrude, Part 2 (repr. in *Shakespeare and the Law* (Stritmatter, 2022): 171-86]	Sh. Newsl. of Claremont McKenna College, vol. 50/4

Bush, Douglas

1950, April 24	[review of *"Shakespeare" Identified* by J. Thomas Looney (1949)]	New Republic, issue 24: 20

Bushell, W. F.

1945, Jan. 10	Canon Rendall [letter]	Liverpool Daily Post, p. 2

Butcher, Fanny

1920, June 13	Tabloid Book Review [review of *"Shakespeare" Identified*]	Chicago Tribune, p. 9

Butler, Isaac

2023, May 11	Shakespeare Was Shakespeare [review of *Shakespeare Was a Woman and Other Heresies* by Elizabeth Winkler]	Slate

Butler, Robert

2018	Shakespeare & Co. by Robert Butler [repr. from Independent on Sunday, 31.3.1996] [trans. Heinrich Payr] [eingereicht von Walter Klier" 23. 7. 1997]	Neues Sh. Jou., vol. NS 6: 28-31

Byrne, Ciar

2004, June 25	Devotees of De Vere, "The Real Bard," Mark 400th Anniversary [repr. in SON, vol. 40/3: 9 (Sum., 2004); and in DVN (July 2004), p. 2]	Independent, p. 14

Byrne, Muriel St. Clare

1928, Sept.	Reviews and Notices [review of *The Seventeenth Earl of Oxford* by Capt. Bernard M. Ward]	Library, vol. IX/2: 211-14
1929, March 21	Shakespeare and Chapman [review of *Shakespeare and Chapman as Topical Dramatists* by Percy Allen]	Times Lit. Sup., is. 1416: 229
1929, Sept. 26	Stuart Politics in Chapman [review of *Stuart Politics in Chapman's Tragedy of Chabot* by Norma D. Solve]	Times Lit. Sup., is. 1443: 741
1930, May 22	De Vere and the Sonnets [review of *Shakespeare's Sonnets and Edward de Vere* by Gerald Rendall (1930)] Response by Gerald Rendall, May 29, issue 1478: 457.	Times Lit. Sup., is. 1477: 430
1930, Sept. 11	Oxford as 'Shakespeare' [review of *The Case for Edward de Vere as Shakespeare* by Percy Allen (1930)] Response by Percy Allen, Sept. 18, issue 1494: 735. Response by Gerald Rendall, Sept. 25, issue 1495: 757.	Times Lit. Sup., is. 1493: 712

Author Index

C. B.
    1920, April 23   Shakespeare's Identity: A New Theory of a Very Entertaining Subject   Western Mail, p. 7
         [review of SI]

C. B. D.
    1932, Dec.   Who Wrote Shakespeare? [review of *The Tragic Story of*   Bookman, vol. 83/495: 228
        "Shakespeare:" Disclosed in the Sonnets by G. Phillips (1932)

C. E. L.
    1931, Aug. 24   Was It Shakespeare? [review of *Shake-speare: Handwriting and*   West. Morn. News, p. 2
        Spelling by Gerald H. Rendall]
    1931, Dec. 14   The Shakespeare Controversy: "Crucial Evidence" Just Obtained   Manchester Guardian, p. 15
        [report on lecture by P. Allen at the Gallery First-Nighters' Club]

C. F. A.
    1928, Aug. 23   Elizabethan Borrowers [review of *Borrowers* by Percy Allen   Christian Sci. Monitor, p. 10
    1931, April 25   The Oxford Theory [review of *Corroborated* by Percy Allen   Christian Sci. Monitor, p. 12
        Resp. by Percy Allen, June 5, p. 20.

C. H.
    1928, April 30   17th Earl of Oxford" Political History of Period of Queen Elizabeth   Western Morning News, p. 2
        [review of Ward's book]

C. H. H. [see Charles H. Herford]

C. K. S.
    1923, July 28   A Literary Letter: "Shakspere" or "Shakespeare"? [full page article]   Sphere, p. 118

C. R.
    1920, April 22   Shakespeare: Was He Edward de Vere, Lord Oxford? [review of *"SI"*]   Nottingham J. and E., p. 5

C. R. B.
    1944, April 15   Another Reputed Author: Edward de Vere [review of *SI*]   Age (Melbourne), p. 5

C. W. B.
    1934, Feb. 15   Ducdame, Ducdame [letter]   Times Lit. Sup., is. 1672: 108

Cain, Lincoln S.
    1991, Aug.   Spear Shaker, the Folger, and *The Shakespeare Quarterly* [letter]   Spear-shaker Review, is. 5: 24
    1995, Summer   To the President of Amherst College: The College's Oversight of the   Sh. Ox. Newsl., vol. 31/3: 1-6
        Folger Shakespeare Library [letter] [repr. in BTC, vol. 7: 332-39]
        Response by Richard Whalen, SON, vol. 31/4: 22.

Caines, Michael
    2010, June 25   Unbaken or Shaken: How the Bacon Society Hoped to Unearth a   Times Lit. Sup., is. 5595: 14
        400-Year Old Proof of Authorship

Caink, T.
    1924, Sept.   Shakespearean Metaphor [letter: hawk from a heron]   English Review, p. 318-19

Cairncross, Andrew S.
Books
    1936   *The Problem of Hamlet: A Solution*. London: Macmillan. Repr. in 1970: Folcroft, PA: Folcroft Press. 1975,
        Norwood, PA: Norwood Editions. 1978, Philadelphia: R. West.]
Shorter pieces
    1937, Jan. 9   Hamlet Problems [letter: reply to Percy Allen's Jan. 2 letter]   Times Lit. Sup., is. 1823: 28
        [repr. in SFE, no. 2: 8-9 (March 1937)]
        Response by Hubert Holland, SFE, May 1937, p. 11.

Caldwell, Roland G.
    2002, Nov.   One Man's Overview and Summary [2nd annual studies conference]   Great Ideas Online, no. 203: 3-7
    2022, Summer   [letter: time to declare victory for Oxford]   Sh. Ox. Newsl., vol. 58/3: 3

Cali, Grace
    1994, Winter   Shakespeare's *Tempest* Locale: Cuttyhunk?   Sh. Ox. Newsl., vol. 30/1: 14-18
        See also:
        American Heritage, June-July 2002, p. 9.
        Tim Clark, *Yankee*, vol. 66/3: 18 (2002).
        Richard Romeo, *Yankee*, vol. 62/9: 35 (1997).
    1997, Winter   [letter: Hughes' call to reach academics]   Sh. Ox. Newsl., vol. 33/1: 21

Caruana, Stephanie (continued)

1990, Summer	Of Pen Names, Busy Brains and *Oxford's Revenge*	Sh. Newsl., vol. 40/2: 21, 23
1991, Feb.	Oxford's "Robin Hood" Plays and "Shakespeare's" *King John*	Spear-shaker Rev., is. 1/1: 5-15
1991, May	Six "Signatures" In Search of an Author	Spear-shaker Rev., is. 3/4: 1-3
1991, Aug.	I Hypnotized Dr. Louis Marder . . . and Made Him Believe Oxford Wrote the Plays!	Spear-shaker Rev., is. 5: 14-15
1993, Summer	A New-Coined Word for Oxford's Father	Sh. Ox. Newsl., vol. 29/3a: 8
1996, Winter	An Update on the Controversy Surrounding *A Funeral Elegy*	Ever Reader, vol. 3
1996, Summer	Of "'Em's" and "Them's": Important Clues in the Elegy Debate? [repr. in EVR, vol. 2 (Winter 1996)]	Sh. Ox. Newsl., vol. 32/3: 10-11
1998, Winter	Oxford's Lute Music Manuscript at Folger Shakespeare Library	Spear-shaker Rev., is. 1/2: 37

Caruso, Carl S.
Books

2008	*The Mystery of Hamlet*. PublishAmerica.	

Shorter pieces

2002, Summer	The Maiden and the Mermaid Response by Robert Brazil, Fall 2002, p. 2. Reply by Caruso, Winter 2003, p. 2.	Sh. Matters, vol. 1/4: 12-13
2003, Winter	[letter: "The Maiden and the Mermaid"]	Sh. Matters, vol. 2/2: 2
2004, Spring	Post Mortem on John de Vere, 16th Earl of Oxford [with Nina Green and Christopher Paul]	Sh. Ox. Newsl., vol. 40/2: 8-9
2007	Sacred Pearls in the Machinery of *Hamlet*	Oxfordian, vol. 10: 85-110

Cassidy, Claudio

1949, April 17	On the Aisle [review of *Under the Mask of Shakespeare* by Abel Lefranc, with much to say about Oxford as well as Derby]	Chicago Tribune, p. H2

Casson, John

2018	"Our Shakespeare: Henry Neville 1562-1615" [with William D. Rubinstein & David Ewald], in *My Shakespeare* (Leahy: 113-38)	

Castaldo, A.

2004, March	[review of *Monstrous Adversary: The Life of Edward de Vere* by Alan Nelson (2003)]	Choice, vol. 41/7: 1298

Catlin, Roger

2003, Jan. 3	Who Wrote Works of Shakespeare? [review of *Frontline* programs]	Hartford Courant, p. D8

Caunt, George

1963, June	The De Veres of Castle Hedingham I	Essex Countrys. M., p. 326-27
1963, July	The De Veres of Castle Hedingham II	Essex Countrys. M., p. 378-79
1963, Aug.	The De Veres of Castle Hedingham III [All three articles are review of the book by Verily Anderson. See report by R. Wainewright in SAR, issue 10: 16 (Aut. 1963)]	Essex Countrys. M., p. 420-21

Causey, William F.

2004, Fall	The Burden of Proof and Presumptions in the Sh. Authorship Debate [repr. in BTC, vol. 8: 337-57]	Tennessee Law Review, vol. 72/1: 93-109

Cavanaugh, Gerald J.

1988, Winter	[letter: Messrs. Rowse, Marder, Evans, Levin, etc. remain intransig.]	Sh. Ox. Newsl., vol. 24/1: 13
1999, March 3	[letter: Gregory M. Bouman's Feb. 22 article stating that discussion of alternative authors disgraces a family newspaper]	Cincinnati Enq., p. A15
2006, Nov.	[letter: discussion of the SAQ can now take place]	Smithsonian, vol. 37/8: 10

Cavendish, Dominic

2007, Sept. 5	[review of *The Big Secret Live* by Mark Rylance & Matthew Marchus]	Telegraph
2010, Aug. 11	A New Look at the Man from Stratford	Telegraph, p. 25

Cawardine-Probert, Col. W. G.

1935, Nov. 2	De Vere Monuments [letter]	Essex County Standard

Cecil, Michael (8th Marquess of Exter, Baron Burghley)

2010, Fall	William Cecil and Shakespeare: Revisiting Baron Burghley's "Precepts"	Sh. Matters, vol. 9/3: 1, 21-22
2013	Doubter Response to Question #30: What was the relationship	Sh. Beyond Doubt?, p. 186-87

between the aristocracy and the theatre in Shakespeare's time?

2023, Jan.	Welcoming Speech	De Vere Soc. New., v. 30/1: 9-13

Chaillet, Ned

1977, April 13	The Ballad of Aslomon Pavey [refers to de Vere as Shakespeare]	Times (London), p. 11

Challinor, Arthur M.

Books

1996	*Alternative Shakespeare: A Modern Introduction.* Sussex, England: Book Guild. [excerpt repr. in *Shakespeare Criticism, vol. 41* (Lee & Barnes 1998): 42-48]	

Shorter pieces

1995, May	Bias of the World: Lack of Objectivity in Stratfordian Commentary	De Vere Soc. Newsl., v. 2/1: 3-4
1996	Concerning Prejudice and Pride: Some Observations on the Reception Given to Authorship Doubters	Baconiana, vol. 76/193: 18-29
1996, April	Brief Extracts From *An Imaginary Stratfordian Casebook*	De Vere Soc. Newsl., vol. 2/5: 4
1996, Dec.	Amateurs Versus Professionals	De Vere Soc. New., v. 2/7: 19-20
1997, Autumn	Controversy Among Gentlemen	Eliz. Review, vol. 5/2: 61-78
1998, Feb.	Oxfordian Weaknesses	De Vere Soc. New., v. 2/11: 7-11
1999, Feb.	Further Thoughts on 'Weaknesses'	De Vere Soc. New., v. 3/2: 23-25
2000, May	The Wider Aspects of Authorship Debate	De Vere Soc. Newsl., p. 8-9
2000, July	The De Vere Society Dating Project [editor's observations]	De Vere Soc. Newsl., p. 17-18
2001, Jan.	[review of *Shakespeare's Unorthodox Biography* by Diana Price]	De Vere Soc. Newsl., p. 39-40
2001, Apr./May	Reason and Rigour in Argument – 1 Response by David Roper, Oct. 2001, p. 14-15. Reply by Challinor, Oct. 2001, p. 15.	De Vere Soc. Newsl., p. 12-14
2001, July	Reason and Rigour in Argument – 2 Response by David Roper, Oct. 2001, p. 14-15. Reply by Challinor, Oct. 2001, p. 15.	De Vere Soc. Newsl., p. 17-18
2001, Oct.	[letter: reply to Roper's responses to his Apr. and July *Reason* articles]	De Vere Soc. Newsl., p. 15
2002, April	The Society's Dating Project: report and observations	De Vere Soc. Newsl., p. 32-33

Chambers, E. K.

Books and pamphlets

1923	*The Elizabethan Stage*, vol. I-III. Oxford: The Clarendon Press.	
1924	*The Disintegration of Shakespeare* [The Annual Shakespeare Lecture] [pamphlet]. London: Oxford University Press for The British Academy.	
1925	*A Shakespeare Reference Library.* [pamphlet: prepared with Sir Sidney Lee]	
1932	*The Oxford Book of Sixteenth Century Verse.* London: Oxford University Press. [see p. vi-vii: "The most hopeful of the courtier poets was Edward de Vere." The collection includes three of his poems, selected by "a standard of absolute poetry, rather than one of merely historic interest" (vii).]	

Shorter pieces

1934, Jan. 25	The 'Mortal Moon' Sonnet [letter]	Times Lit. Sup., is. 1669: 60
1934, Feb. 1	The 'Mortal Moon' Sonnet [letter, with correction]	Times Lit. Sup., is. 1670: 76

Chambers, Paul

2022	Employing Mathematics to Identify the Real Shakespeare	Oxfordian, vol. 24: 111-129

Chambers, R. W.

1939, June 3	Shakespeare and "More" [letter]	Times Lit. Sup., is. 1948: 327

Champlin, Charles

1983, Feb. 12	A Bard By Any Other Name . . . [repr. in SON, vol. 19/3: 11-12 (Summer 1983)]	Los Ang. Times, Sec. 5: 1-3
1983, April 23	To Be Or Not To Be the Bard	Los Ang. Times, Sec. 5: 1, 7
1984, Jan. 12	Whomsoever Art Thou, Shaksper?	Los Ang. Times, Sec. 6: 1, 7
1984, Feb. 11	Decoding Stratford's Dark Laddie	Los Angeles Times, p. G1, 6
1984, April 2	Marlovians Resurrect a Kit of Bard Evidence	Los Angeles Times, M1
1984, June 23	Shaksper Has His (Her?) Day in Court	Los Angeles Times, p. F1, 4
1984, July 19	Veil Still Shrouds the Real Bard	Los Angeles Times, Sec. 6: 1
1984, July 19	The Bard By Any Other Name	Los Angeles Times, p. E1
1984, Dec. 30	[review of *The Mysterious William Shakespeare* by Ch. Ogburn, Jr.] Responses by James Bednarz, Celeste Innocenti, David Argall, and Mark Nichols, Jan. 13, p. N6.	Los Angeles Times, p. I1, I5
1986, March 1	Hoffman's Questions About the Bard Live On	Los Angeles Times, p. E1

Champlin, Charles (continued)

1986, Sept. 4	A New Crop of Hedging on the Bard	Los Angeles Times, p. H1
1987, Sept. 29	Shakspere Shaken by Moot Court	Los Angeles Times, p. 2, 3
1987, Sept. 30	What Fools These Mortals Be!	Los Angeles Times, p. C6
1989, April 18	PBS Plays Out the Debate Over the Bard [review of *Frontline*'s "The Shakespeare Mystery" [repr. in SON, vol. 25/2: 4-5 (Spr. 1989)]	Los Angeles Times, p. J1E
1989, April 18	[review of "The Shakespeare Mystery," documentary by Al Austin] [repr. in SON, vol. 25/2: 4-5 (Spring 1989)]	Los Angeles Times
1990, Feb. 8	William Shakespeare Is Still News After Four Centuries [repr. in SON, vol. 26/2: 6 (Spring 1990)]	Los Angeles Times, p. F4
1993, Feb. 21	Displacing Will [rev. of *The 100, Revised Edition* by Michael Hart] Response by Tom Burns, Feb. 28, p. 13.	Los Angeles Times, p. 10
1993, May 8	[letter: response to LaBelle's April 21 article]	Los Ang. Times, p. VCB17

Chandler, David

1987, July 13	Peer-Review System for Scientific Plans Being Reevaluated [excerpt repr. as "Where the Professoriate is Deeply but Wrongly Committed . . ." in SON, vol. 23/3: 12 (Summer 1987)]	Boston Globe, p. 1
1994, Spring	Death Put Off by Cunning and Forc'd Cause	Eliz. Review, vol. 2/1: 15-20
1995, Spring	[review of *Greene's Groatsworth of Wit* ed. by D. Allen Carroll]	Eliz. Review, vol. 3/1: 62-67
1995, Autumn	A Further Reconsideration of Heywood's Allusion	Eliz. Review, vol. 3/2: 15-24
1997, Autumn	Lady Macbeth's Curds and Whey	Eliz. Review, vol. 5/2: 126-27
2000, Spring	Historicizing Difference: Anti-Stratfordianism and the Academy	Eliz. Review, Internet ed.

Chaplin, Alison

1995, May	Changing Minds	De Vere Soc. Newsl., vol. 2/1: 2

Chaplin, Charles

1964	*My Auto-Biography*. New York: Simon and Schuster. [See esp. p. 364]

Chapman, L. Edgar

1993, Jan. 16	Shakespeare: The Pen or the Pen Name Behind the Work? [Burford might have mesmerized some . . .]	St. Louis Post Disp., p. B3

Chapman, Rebecca

2012	[review of *Contested Will* by James Shapiro (2010)]	Sh. Int'l Yearb., vol. 12: 169-94

Chappell, Charles

1994-95	Lawrence Wells of Oxford: An Interview ["massive upheavals" that recognition of de Vere's authorship could cause]	Mississippi Quarterly vol. 48: 319-36

Chard, Costa

2021, Jan.	[review of *The Shakespeare Masterclasses* by Ron Destro]	De Vere Soc. Newsl., v. 28/1: 49
2022, April	Interview with Charles Beauclerk, DVS Founder (1986) and Honorary President (2022)	De Vere Soc. New., v. 29/2: 24-5
2022, April	Interview with Charles Beauclerk, Part 2	De Vere Soc. New., v. 29/3: 5-22

Charles, Ron

2003, June 26	Where's William? [review of *Chasing Shakespeares* by Sarah Smith]	Christian Sci. Monitor, p. 15
2011, Oct. 31	The Playwright's the Thing – No Question About It Response by Jonathan F. Keiler, Nov. 5, p. A13.	Washington Post

Charlton, Derran K.

1991, May	Edward de Vere and the Knights of the Grail	Spear-shaker Rev., is. 3/4: 4-11
1992, Summer	An Eloquence of Light Quenched in Darkness	Sh. Ox. Newsl., vol. 28/3: 4-5
1995, May	The Essentiality of Oxfordian Archival Researches	De Vere Soc. Newsl., v. 2/1: 8-11
1995, Nov.	Archival Research	De Vere Soc. Newsl., v. 2/3: 6-7
1996, Spring	[letter: *Funeral Elegy*]	Sh. Ox. Newsl., vol. 32/2: 21
1997, Spring	[letter: resp. to Pat Buckridge's Autumn 1996 "Marston" article]	Eliz. Review, vol. 5/1: 4-6
1997, Spring	[letter: Diana Price's Autumn 1996 "Rough Winds" article]	Eliz. Review, vol. 5/1: 7
1997, Summer	[letter: resp. to Chiljan's Winter 1997 "Portrait" article]	Sh. Ox. Newsl., vol. 33/3: 23
1997, Dec.	Shakespeare im Archiv	Neues Sh. Journal, vol. 1: 107-10
1998, May	Visit to Southampton [letter]	De Vere Soc. Newsl., v. 2/12: 24
1998, June	Die Diener des Herzogs – William, Richard und Ben	Neues Sh. Journal, vol. 2: 78-80
1999, May	[letter: resp. to Imlay's Feb. 1999 "Country House" article and and Jolly's Feb. 1999 "Dating *Hamlet*" article]	De Vere Soc. Newsl., v. 3/3: 2-3

1999, May	Edward de Vere's 449th Birthday Celebrated at Penshurst Place	De Vere Soc. Newsl., vol. 3/3: 10
1999, July	Zwei Bilddokumente zu Shake-speare	Neues Sh. Journal, vol. 4: 121-25
1999, July 1	[letter: resp. to the April 1 special "authorship" issue]	Harper's Mag., vol. 299: 6-11
1999, Summer	[letter: resp. to Peter Dickson's Fall 1998 "Peacham" article]	Sh. Ox. Newsl., vol. 35/2: 27
2000, Winter	Earl of Oxford's handwriting [letter]	Sh. Ox. Newsl., vol. 35/4: 21
2001, Oct.	John Southworth's *Shakespeare, The Player* [letter]	De Vere Soc. Newsl., p. 15-16
2003, Aug.	Zwei Manuskriptseiten des Herzogs von Rutland	Neues Sh. Journal, vol. 8: 116-25
2003, Summer	[review of *In Search of Shakespeare* by Michael Wood (1985)]	Sh. Ox. Newsl., vol. 39/3: 23-24
2005, Summer	The Grandsire Phrase in *Romeo and Juliet* [with John Barton]	Sh. Ox. Newsl., vol. 41/3: 17-18
2005, Fall	Who Was Emaricdulfe's "E. C. Esquire"? [repr. in RCA, p. 142-145] Response by Robert Prechter, Winter 2006, p. 23.	Sh. Ox. Newsl., vol. 41/4: 3-4
2005, Fall	[review of *Shakespeare: The Biography* by Peter Ackroyd (2005)]	Sh. Ox. Newsl., vol. 41/4: 24, 32
2006, Winter	Pardon by King James I of Henry Wriothesley, the E. of Southampton Response by Christopher Paul, Spring 2006, p. 9.	Sh. Ox. Newsl., vol. 42/1: 12
2006, Spring	[review of "Searching for Shakespeare" Exhib, Nat'l Portrait Gallery] [repr. in NSJ, vol. 11: 128-33 (April 2007)]	Sh. Ox. Newsl., vol. 42/2: 26-27
2006, Spring	[report on the Annual Meeting of the De Vere Society]	Sh. Ox. Newsl., vol. 42/2: 7-9, 32
2006, Fall	[review of *Pseudonymous Shakespeare* by Penny McCarthy (2006)]	Sh. Ox. Newsl., vol. 42/3: 31-32
2007, Winter	The Droeshout Collar	Sh. Ox. Newsl., vol. 43/1: 27-29
2007, Winter	[review of *Behind Shakespeare's Mask* by Charles Murray Willis]	Sh. Ox. Newsl., vol. 43/1: 31-32
2008, March	Death of Member Katherine Eggar	De Vere Soc. Newsl., v. 15/1: 29
2008, Spring	Cambridge University "Implications" of Polimanteia	Sh. Ox. Newsl., vol. 44/2: 5-9
2009, Sept.	Edward de Vere as Henry IV	Sh. Ox. Newsl., vol. 45/2: 11-14
2009, Dec.	Death of Oxfordian Paul Blair in California (1915-2009)	Sh. Ox. Newsl., vol. 45/3: 7
2010	Love's Labour's Lost [with Kevin Gilvary] [in *Dating Shakespeare's Plays* (Gilvary 2010): 101-12]	
2010	*The Lamentable Tragedy of Titus Andronicus* [with Kevin Gilvary] [in *Dating Sh's Plays* (Gilvary 2010): 332-42]	
2010	*Doctor Faustus, Tamburlaine* and *The Taming of the Shrew*	Oxfordian, vol. 12: 108-118
2010	In Memoriam: Verily Anderson (1915-2010) [repr. in NSJ, vol. NS1: 159 (Nov. 2010)]	Oxfordian, vol. 12: 16
2010, Aug.	Fulke Greville	Sh. Ox. Newsl., vol. 46/2: 14
2010, Aug.	Obituaries: Robert Brazil (1955-2010) & Verily Anderson (1915-2010) [with Hank Whittemore]	Sh. Ox. Newsl., vol. 46/2: 16-17
2012	Giordano Bruno: Mad, Bad and Dangerous to Know	Oxfordian, vol. 14: 104-120

Chater, Ezra

2017, Oct.	Shakespeare: The Original Fake News?	De Vere Soc. Newsl., p. 45-49

Chatterly, Albert

2012, Jan. 16	The Tears of Fancie Or Love Disdained by T. W. (1983)	Notes & Q., vol. 59/1: 48-52

Chaunes

2018	*Le Vrai Shakespeare*. Independent Publisher.	

Cheadle, Jane B.

1993, April	Who Was Shakespeare?	Mills Quarterly, vol. 75: 26
1994, Winter	[letter: authorship issues at Mills College]	Sh. Ox. Newsl., vol. 30/1: 5

Cheal, Yvonne

2021, Jan.	[review of *Behind the Name Shakespeare: Power, Lust, Scorn & Scandal*; a documentary by Robin Phillips]	De Vere So. New., v. 28/1: 50-51
2022, Jan.	[commentary on Ian Cole's Edward de Vere, Earl of Oxford: His Relationships with the North Family]	De Vere Soc. Newsl., v. 29/1: 18

Cheney, Alan

1995, Spring	[review of *The Twilight Lords: an Irish Chronicle* by R. Berleth]	Eliz. Review, vol. 3/1: 48-53

Cherubin, Sam

1991, Spring	Vero Nihil Verius	Sh. Ox. Newsl., vol. 27/2: 7

Chevalley, Abel

1931	[review of *Shakespeare's Plays in the Order of Their Writing* by Eva Turner Clark (1931)] [in French]	Mercure de France, vol. 233: 444-46

Chew, Samuel C.

1931, March 15   Who Was W. S.? [review of *Hidden Allusions* by Eva Turner Clark]   NY Herald Tribune, p. J12

Chibi, Andrew A.

2007, Summer   [review of *Edward de Vere: The Crisis and Consequences of Wardship* by Daphne Pearson (2005)]   Sixteenth Cen. J., vol. 38/2: 460-62

Chiklis, Michael

2015, Summer   Actor Michael Chiklis Comes Out as an Oxfordian [with K. Pollak]   Sh. Ox. Newsl., v. 51/3: 24-5

Child, Harold H.

1924, Oct. 30   Shakespeare's Handwriting [review of *The Shakespeare Signatures and Sir Thomas More* by George Greenwood]
Response by G. Greenwood, Nov. 6.   Times Lit. Sup., 1189: 682

1926, June 10   [review of *A Hundreth Sundrie Flowres* by George Gascoigne]   Times Lit. Sup., is. 1271: 391

1933, Aug. 3   History and Plays [review of *The Plays of Shakespeare and Chapman in Relation to French History* by Percy Allen]
Response by Percy Allen, Aug. 10, p. 537.   Times Lit. Sup., is. 1644: 522

1935, March 28   Oxford's Sonnets [review of *Sunlight on Shakespeare's Sonnets* by Gerald Phillips (1935) and *Personal Clues in Shakespeare Poems and Sonnets* by Gerald H. Rendall]   Times Lit. Sup., is. 1730: 203

1935, Oct. 10   What Happens in *Hamlet* [review of the book by J. Dover Wilson]   Times Lit. Sup., is. 1758: 617

Chiljan, Katherine

Books

1994   *Dedication Letters to the Earl of Oxford* [editor]. Northridge, CA: K. Chiljan.

1998   *Letters and Poems of Edward, Earl of Oxford* [editor]. Northridge, CA: K. Chiljan.

2011   *Shakespeare Suppressed: The Uncensored Truth about Shakespeare and His Works: A Book of Evidence and Explanation*. San Francisco: Faire Editions. [excerpt from Chapter 16 repr. in BTC, vol. 10: 321-351; another excerpt repr. as "First Folio Fraud" in BC Special issue, p. 69-87) and in *The First Folio* (Stritmatter 2023): 35-52] [2nd ed., 2016]

Periodicals edited

2001, Fall: *Shakespeare Oxford Newsletter* [with Daphne Pearson], vol. 37/3

2002, Winter; and 2003, Winter-2003, Summer: *Shakespeare Oxford Newsletter*, vol. 38/1; vol. 39/1-39/3

2010, May: *Shakespeare Oxford Newsletter* [with Ramon Jiménez], vol. 46/1

Shorter pieces

1993, Fall   The Shakespeare Authorship Question   Sh. Ox. Newsl., vol. 29/4: 13

1994, Spring   Richard Brome's "The Antipodes" and English Earle   Sh. Ox. Newsl., vol. 30/2a: 6-9

1996, Fall   Reporting His Cause Through Local Chapters [with Randall Sherman]   Sh. Ox. Newsl., vol. 32/4: 3

1997, Feb.   [letter: response to Krass' Dec. 1997 "Hilliard Miniature" article]   De Vere Soc. Newsl., vol. 2/8: 6

1997, Winter   A New Portrait Comes to Light [repr. in BTC, vol. 7: 392-94; and in German in NSJ, vol. 4: 126-30 (July 1999)]
Response by Darren Charlton, Summer 1997, p. 23.   Sh. Ox. Newsl., vol. 33/1: 18

1997, Spring   Oxford Week Spreads the Word [with Walter Hurst]   Sh. Ox. Newsl., vol. 33/2: 8, 13

1998, Summer   By This Hat, Then . . . New Evidence about the 1580s "Portrait of a Gentleman" [repr. in BTC, vol. 7: 392-94; and in German in NSJ, vol. 4: 126-30 (July 1999)]   Sh. Ox. Newsl., vol. 34/2: 2

1999, Spring   Oxford and *Palamon and Arcite*: an early work by Edward de Vere? [repr. in BTC, vol. 8: 75-85; and in EVR, vol. 10 (Spr. 2000)]
Response by Dennis Baron, SON, vol. 35/3: 21.   Sh. Ox. Newsl., vol. 35/1: 10-13

2001, Fall   The Trout De Vere Album: Rare Book Collector Made Rare Find   Sh. Ox. Newsl., vol. 37/3: 6, 23

2002, Spring   Oxford Document Bought by Film Composer   Sh. Ox. Newsl., vol. 38/2: 2

2003, Winter   Dating the Ashbourne Portrait: Oxfordian Evidence and Recent Lab Analysis Suggests 1597   Sh. Ox. Newsl., v. 39/1: 1, 12-14

2003, Winter   CCI Report on Ashbourne Portrait: Scientific Analysis Raises More Questions   Sh. Ox. Newsl., vol. 39/1: 15

2004, Summer   "Tribute to the "Authentic" Shakespeare" [letter] [repr. in SON, vol. 40/3: 9 (Sum. 2004)]   San Francisco Chronicle

2005, Fall   Earl of Oxford's Annuity to Robert Hales (Queen's Favored Musician)   Sh. Ox. Newsl., vol. 41/4: 1, 5-9

2008, Winter   Complaints About *A Lover's Complaint* [repr. in BTC, vol. 9: 308-20]   Sh. Ox. Newsl., vol. 44/1: 1, 5-8

2012   Reclaiming *The Passionate Pilgrim* for Shakespeare [repr. in *Poems of Edward de Vere*, vol. 2 (Stritmatter, 2019): 3-12]   Oxfordian, vol. 14: 74-81

Clark, Eva Turner (continued)

1931	*Hidden Allusions in Shakespeare's Plays*. [published in London as *Shakespeare's Plays in the Order of Their Writing*.] New York: W. F. Payson. [preface and Part III repr. in BTC, vol. 1: 298-313]	
1933	*The Satirical Comedy: Love's Labour's Lost*. New York: W. F. Payson. 2nd ed., edited by Ruth Loyd Miller, pub. inside *Hidden Allusions*, 3rd ed., edited by Ruth Loyd Miller, p. 125-162, 163-238 and 242-251]	
1937	*The Man Who Was Shakespeare*. New York. R. R. Smith. Repr. in 1970: New York: AMS Press. (Intro. and Ch. 1 repr. in BTC, vol. 4: 187-203. Ch. 21 repr. in SFQ, vol. VIII/3: 34-36 (Autumn 1947); in OXV, p. 306-310; and in BTC, vol. 4: 25-29) [another excerpt repr. in TOX, vol. 16: 46]	
1974	*Hidden Allusions in Shakespeare's Plays*. 3rd revised edition. Ruth Loyd Miller, editor. With introduction and additional notes by the editor and others. Port Washington, NY: Kennikat Press. [includes Clark's *The Satirical Comedy*, 2nd ed., p. 125-162, 163-238 and 242-251]	

Periodicals edited

1940, Oct.-Nov. – 1943, Oct.?: *Shakespeare Fellowship News-letter (American)*, vol. 1/6 – vol. 4/6?

[Clark served as editor for at least two years after Charles Barrell was called to duty in the Army in Sept. 1940.]

Shorter pieces

1931	Introduction in *The Shakespeare Garden* by Esther Singleton, p. vii-xv [repr. in BTC, vol. 1: 114-115]	
1939, Dec.	To Members of the Shakespeare Fellowship [repr. in BTC, vol. 2: 68-69]	SF News-letter (A), vol. 1/1: 1
1939, Dec.	Underdowne's Translation Which Shakespeare Had Read	SF News-letter (A), vol. 1/1: 3
1940, Feb.	Shakespeare Read Books Written in Greek [repr. in BTC, vol. 2: 92-95]	SF News-letter (A), vol. 1/2: 9-10
1940, Feb.	The Neapolitan Prince	SF News-letter (A), vol. 1/2: 11
1940, Apr./May	Shakespeare's Birthday: The Calendar Argues For Lord Oxford	SF News-letter (A), vol. 1/3: 1-2
1940, Apr./May	The Date of *Hamlet's* Composition [repr. in BTC, vol. 2: 104-06]	SF News-letter (A), vol. 1/3: 9-10
1940, June/July	He Must Build Churches Then [repr. in BTC, vol. 2: 111-113]	SF News-letter (A), vol. 1/4: 6
1940, Aug./Sept.	Through De Vere Country	SF News-letter (A), vol. 1/5: 1-4
1940, Aug./Sept.	The Painting in *Lucrece* [repr. in BTC, vol. 2: 121-122]	SF News-letter (A), vol. 1/5: 5
1940, Oct./Nov.	Topicalities in the Plays [repr. in BTC, vol. 2: 125-128]	SF News-letter (A), vol. 1/6: 9-10
1940, Oct./Nov.	If We Have Leisure! [repr. in SON, vol. 56/3 (Summer 2020)	SF News-letter (A), v. 1/6: 11-12
1940, Oct./Nov.	Anamos, or A. W. [repr. in BTC, vol. 2: 129-131]	SF News-letter (A), v. 1/6: 10-11
1940, Dec.	Annotations by Shakespeare?	SF News-letter (A), vol. 2/1: 10
1940, Dec.	Gabriel Harvey and *Axiophilus* [repr. in BTC, vol. 2: 132-134]	SF News-letter (A), vol. 2/1: 11-1
1941, Feb.	The Earthquake	SF News-letter (A), vol. 2/2: 20
1941, June	Washington Physicist Speaks (Dr. John Howard Dellinger)	SF News-letter (A), vol. 2/4: 41
1941, June	De Vere Theory Growing in California	SF News-letter (A), vol. 2/4: 43
1941, June	Christopher Marlowe: Certain Perplexing Problems	SF News-letter (A), v. 2/4: 47-50
1941, Aug.	Dr. Sanders and the Miracle	SF News-letter (A), v. 2/5: 55-57
1941, Oct.	Elizabethan Stage Scenery: More Elaborate Than Ordinarily Believed [repr. in EVR, vol. 6 (Wntr. 1998)]	SF News-letter (A), v. 2/6: 72-75
1941, Dec.	The World's Great Letters [letter from Edward Oxenford to his Father-in-law in 1572, following the St. Bartholomew Massacre]	SF News-letter (A), vol. 3/1: 7
1941, Dec.	Horse and Rider	SF News-letter (A), v. 3/1: 11-12
1942, Feb.	War and the Fellowship	SF News-letter (A), vol. 3/2: 18
1942, April	Lord Oxford as Shakespeare [A paper read at the Browning Society of San Francisco (Feb. 13, 1942)] [repr. in BTC, vol. 2: 235-49]	SF News-letter (A), v. 3/3: 38-44
1942, June	The Red Rose [repr. in BTC, vol. 2: 309-311]	SF News-letter (A), vol. 3/4: 53
1942, Oct.	Hand C in *Sir Thomas More* and the Plot of The Seven Deadly Sins	SF News-letter (A), v. 3/6: 79-80
1943, Oct.	Cryptic Passages by Davies of Hereford [repr. in BTC, vol. 2: 416-419]	SF News-letter (A), v. 4/6: 75-76
1943, Aug.	*A Hundreth Sundrie Flowres* [repr. in BTC, vol. 2: 393-404]	SF News-letter (A), v. 4/5: 53-58
1944, Jan.	Stolen and Surreptitious Copies [repr. in BTC, vol. 3: 18-21]	SF Quarterly, vol. V/1: 6-8
1944, April	Some Character Names in Shakespeare's Plays, Part 1 [repr. in BTC, vol. 3: 45-49]	SF Quarterly, vol. V/2: 30-32
1944, July	Some Character Names in Shakespeare's Plays, Part 2 [repr. in BTC, vol. 3: 50-56]	SF Quarterly, vol. V/3: 41-43
1944, Oct.	Some Character Names in Shakespeare's Plays, Part 3 [repr. in BTC, vol. 3: 90-95]	SF Quarterly, vol. V/4: 66-68
1945, Jan.	Lord Oxford's Shakespearean Travels On the European Continent	SF Quarterly, vol. VI/1: 3-10
1945, April	Keep the Light Burning	SF Quarterly, vol. VI/2: 29

1945, Oct.	Lord Oxford's Letters Echoed in Sh.'s Plays: An Early Letter Examined, Part 1 [repr. in BTC, vol. 3: 203-208]	SF Quarterly, vol. VI/4: 51-53
1946, Jan.	Lord Oxford's Letters Echoed in Shakespeare's Plays, Part 2: An Early Letter Examined [repr. in BTC, vol. 3: 209-213]	SF Quarterly, vol. VII/1: 10-11
1946, Oct.	Shakespeare's Strange Silence When James I Succeeded Elizabeth [the last article written by Ms. Clark before her death in April 1947] [repr. in OXV, p. 290-302]	SF Quarterly, vol. VII/4: 55-60
1947, Spring	Alias [repr. in BTC, vol. 4: 78-79]	SF Quarterly, vol. IX/1: 7-8

Clark, Roy B.
1957, July	The Earl of Oxford and the Queen's English	Notes & Q., vol. 4/7: 280-83

Clark, Sally
2023	*The King of Nothing* [a play about Edward de Vere]	Sh. Ox. Newsl., vol. 59/3: 5

Clark, Tim
2002	The Bard on the Cape	Yankee, vol. 66/3: 18

Clarke, A. Walrond
1924, Jan. 18	Edward De Vere 17th Earl of Oxford and His Burial Place in Hackney	Hackney Specator, p. 2
1924, Oct. 24	St. Augustine's Church, Hackney	Hackney Spectator, p. 10

Clarke, Barry R.
2018	My Shakespeare – Francis Bacon, in *My Shakespeare: The Authorship Controversy* (Leahy): 163-87	

Clarke, Danielle
2010, April	Battling About the Bard: Shakespeare	Irish Times (Dublin), p. 10

Clarke, Francis
1920, April 16	[letter: resp. to M.'s review of *"Shakespeare" Identified*]	Athenaeum, p. 521
1921, March 25	[letter: resp. to S.'s review of *The Poems of Edward de Vere*]	Bookman's J., vol. 3/74: 388
1923, Jan. 19	Shakespearean Researches [letter]	Hackney Spectator, p. 2
1923, Oct. 12	An Elizabethan List of Poets [letter]	Hackney Spectator, p. 4
1924, March 7	The Derby Theory [letter]	Hackney Spectator, p. 10
1930, May	A Literary Group [letter]	Sh. Pictorial, no. 27: 16

Clarke, Marilyn Kay
1991, May	[letter: de Vere and the *King James Bible*]	Spear-shaker Rev., is. 3/4: 18

Clary, William W.
1959, July	The Case for the Defense: De Vere, et al. v. Shakespeare [repr. in SC, p. 25-32, 1961; and in *Shakespeare and his Rivals* (McMichael & Glenn 1962): 206-11]	Am. Bar Assoc. Journ., vol. 45/7: 700-03+
1960, Oct.	The Prima Facie Case for Shakespeare [letter]	Am. Bar Assoc. Journ., vol. 46/10: 1044

Clayton, Tom
1996, Oct. 19	Authorship Theorists Do Protest Too Much [letter]	Minneap. Star. Trib., p. 21A

Cleave, Julia
2006, April	The Earls of Oxford's Manor in Wivenhoe	De Vere Soc. Newsl., p. 14
2006, July	[letter: follow up to 'The Earls of Oxford's Manor in Wivenhoe']	De Vere Soc. Newsl., p. 23
2008, March	More a Player Than a Playwright?	De Vere So. New., v. 15/1: 17-19
2014, May	Seeing Double: Early Doubters of Shakespeare's Identity	De Vere So. New., v. 41/2: 32-35
2017, Oct.	[review of *The Great Debate: Who Wrote Shakespeare?*] [w. K. Gilvary]	De Vere S. New., v. 24/4: 38-44
2009, Nov. 28	Reports on Conference: Shakespeare: From Rowe to Shapiro [with Richard Malim & Kevin Gilvary] [repr. in SON, vol. 45/3: 14-17 (Dec. 2009)]	Globe

Clegg, Cyndia S.
1997	*Press Censorship in Elizabethan England*. New York: Cambridge University Press.	

Clement, Rex
Books
1924	*A Gipsy of the Horn: The Narrative of a Voyage Round the World*. [excerpt, "Shakespeare's Amazing Nautical Knowledge," repr. in SON, vol. 47/2: 16 (Spring, 2011)]	

Shorter pieces
1956, Autumn	Shakespeare As Mariner [repr. in BTC, vol. 4, p. 146-156]	SF News-letter (E), p. 4-8

Clement, Richard
  1990, Fall   [letter: top 25 Shakespeare Oxford Clues]   Sh. Ox. Newsl., vol. 26/4: 14

Clending, Logan
  1933, Nov. 22   Good Reading   NY Herald Tribune, p. 15

Clensy, David
  2012, Feb. 18   The Case Against Shakespeare: Retired Solicitor Richard Malim . . .   Evening Post, p. 19
                    To Prove Shakespeare Was Not the Author

Clifford, James
  1956, Jan. 29   Speaking of Books: Biographies   New York Times, p. BR12
                    Response by Dorothy Ogburn, Feb. 19, p. BR17.

Clifford, Richard
  2023, Summer   [letter, with Amanda Hinds: the recent Moot Court Trial at Middle   Sh. Ox. Newsl., vol. 59/3: 4
                    Temple Hall]

Clutton-Brock, Arthur
  1916, April 20   Shakespeare   Times Lit. Sup., is. 744: 181+
  1921, Dec. 15   [letter: review of *Will Shakespeare: An Invention in Four Acts* by   Times Lit. Sup., is. 1039: 841
                    Clemmence Dane]
  1932, June 23   Edward de Vere [review of *The Tragic Story of Shakespeare,*   Times Lit. Sup., is. 1586: 462
                    Disclosed in the Sonnets by Gerald Phillips and
                    The Life Story of Edward de Vere by Percy Allen]

Coale, Sam
  2003, July   A Novel Search for the Real Shakespeare [review of *Chasing*   Providence Journal, p. B5
                    Shakespeares by Sarah Smith]

Coates, George
  2001   *The Crazy Wisdom Sho.* [A musical about Edward de Vere]

Coblante, Stanton A.
  1931, May 31   Shakespeare as the Earl of Oxford [review of *Hidden Allusions* by   New York Times, p. BR17
                    Eva Turner Clark]

Cohen, Alan
  2009, June   The Riddle of the Countess of Pembroke [with Bernice Cohen]   De Vere Soc. New., v. 16/2: 24-9
  2010, Nov.   Susan Vere in Her Own 'Write' [with Bernice Cohen]   De Vere Soc. New., v. 17/3: 22-7

Cohen, Bernice
  2007, Oct.   Geniuses Behaving Badly   De Vere Soc. Newsl., p. 8-10
  2009, June   The Riddle of the Countess of Pembroke [with alan Cohen]   De Vere Soc. New., v. 16/2: 24-9
  2010, Nov.   Susan Vere in Her Own 'Write' [with Alan cohen]   De Vere Soc. New., v. 17/3: 22-7

Cole, Diane
  2004, Dec. 5   Tempest On Avon: Scholars Question and Defend the Identity and   Sun (Baltimore), p. 10E
                    Authorship of Shakespeare

Cole, Jan
Periodicals edited
  2014, May-Oct.   *De Vere Society Newsletter*, vol. 21/2-vol. 21/3 [with Kevin Gilvary and Eddi Jolly]
Shorter pieces
  2011, July   Was Oxford Chapman's Patron?   De Vere So. New., v. 18/2: 30-34
  2011, Nov.   Edward de Vere in France: the French connection, and the Greek   De Vere Soc. New., v. 18/3: 7-14
  2012, March   Davenant, Shakespeare and the de Veres   De Vere Soc. New., v. 19/1: 6-11
  2012, March   [review of *The Shakespeare Guide to Italy; Retracing the Bard's*   De Vere So. New., v. 19/1: 22-24
                    Unknown Travels, by Richard Paul Roe (2011)]
  2012, March   'And you thought it was all over' – Reaction to *Anonymous* in   De Vere Soc. Newsl., v. 19/1: 27
                    de Vere Country
  2012, July   Oxford and Alexander: Another Look at the Spear in "Shake-speare"   De Vere So. New., v. 19/2: 15-17
  2012, July   Oxford, "Alexander" and Lyly's *Campaspe*   De Vere So. New., v. 19/2: 18-25
  2012, July   [letter: R. Detobel's March 2012 "Love is a Discord" article]   De Vere Soc. Newsl., v. 19/2: 34
  2012, Nov.   Oxford in Germany   De Vere Soc. New., v. 19/3: 5-14
  2012, Nov.   Canopy, Cloth and Communion: Jan Cole Shines Light on Sonnet 125   De Vere So. New., v. 19/3: 33-40
  2013, April   Life at Cecil House: Architectural Plan of c. 1565 and What It Tells De Vere So. New., v. 20/1: 15-24
                    Us [talk given at the DVS meeting on April 6, 2013]

Colvin, Ian
 1929, July   Shakespeare Unlocked His Heart: A Key to the Sonnets   Atlantic Monthly, p. 56-62

Comans, Grace P.
 1962, Sept. 2   The Earl's Case [review of *Shake-speare: The Man Behind the Name*   Hartford Courant, p. 14F
                        by Dorothy and Charlton Ogburn, Jr.]

Commanday, Robert
 1985, Oct. 20   The Return of 'Falstaff' [review of *The Mysterious William*   San Fran. Chronicle, p. 1
                        Shakespeare by Charlton Ogburn]

Condon, Joey
 1991, Dec.   Shakespearean Scripture?   Strictly Shakespeare, p. 4

Conlogue, Ray
 1999, March 22   The Ghost of Shakespeare   Globe & Mail, p. C3

Conner, Fran
 1999, Jan. 30   [letter: resp. to Don Oldenburg's Jan. 24 article]   Washington Post, p. A17
                        Response by Peter W. Dickson, Feb. 6, p. A19.
                        Reply to Dickson by Jack Gonzales, Feb. 20, p. A17.

Conner, Lester I.
 1989, May 17   Hardly Unmourned [letter: Warren Hope's April 20 article]   Phil. Inquirer, p. A10
                        Reply by Warren Hope, May 17, p. A10.

Connes, Georges
Books
 1926   *Le Mystere Shakespearien*. Paris: Bovin & Cie.
 1927   *The Shakespeare Mystery, Abridged and Translated into English by a Member of the Shakespeare*
                        Fellowship. London: Cecil Palmer. [Chapter 6 repr. in BTC, vol. 1: 134-146]
Shorter pieces
 1924, Oct.   Une difficulte d'une des methodes anti-stratfordiennes   Rev. Anglo-Am., v. 2: 529-31
 1927, July 28   [letter: resp. to George Greenwood's July 7 review]   Times Lit. Sup., p. 520
 1928, Dec.   Du nouveau sur De Vere, Part 1 [review of *The Seventeenth Earl of*   Revue Anglo-Am., vol. 6/2:
                        Oxford and seven other publications by Capt. Bernard M. Ward]   145-54
 1929, Feb.   Du nouveau sur De Vere, Part 2   Revue Anglo-Am., vol. 6/3:
                                                              241-57
 1930, April   [review of *Shakespeare's Sonnets and Edward de Vere* by G. Rendall]   Rev. Ang.-Am., v. 7/6: 549
 1930, Dec.   [review of *Shakespeare Authorship* by G. Standen] [in French]   Revue Anglo.-Am., v. 8/3:
                                                              253-54
 1931, June   [review of *Shakespeare's Plays in the Order of Their Writing* by Eva   Revue Anglo-Am., vol. 8/5:
                        Turner Clark (1930)] [in French]   439-40
 1931, Aug.   [review of *Shake-speare: Handwriting and Spelling* by G. Rendall]   Revue Anglo-Am., vol. 8/6:
                        [in French]   544
 1932, Dec.   [review of *The Case for Edward de Vere* by Percy Allen (1930)]   Rev. Anglo-Am., v. 10/2: 235
 1933, Oct.   Encore Cinq ans de Travaux Oxoniens [The De Vere-Shakespeare   Revue Anglo-Am., vol. 11:
                        Hypothesis]   193-207
                        Response by Capt. Bernard M. Ward, p. 531-34.
 1935, Oct.   [review of *Sunlight on Shakespeare's Sonnets* by Gerald Phillips]   Rev. Angl.-Am., v. 13/1: 52-3
 1964, Autumn   I Have Changed My Mind [the Earl of Derby was the author]   Sh. Authorship Rev. #12: 2-6

Conrad, Peter
 2010, April 4   The Bard . . . Or Not the Bard? Shakespeare Doubters Reveal More   Observer, p. 46
                        about Themselves than the Poet [review of *Contested Will*
                        by James Shapiro]
 2011, Jan. 9   Contested Will [rev. of paperback ed. of *Contested Will*]   Observer, p. 41

Conroy, Ed
 2004, Dec. 19   Assumptions Damage Book on Authorship [review of *Will in the*   San Antonio Express-News
                        World by Stephen Greenblatt]

Considine, John
 1988, Jan.   The Miller Shakespeare Library of the De Vere Society   De Vere Soc. New., no. 1: 29-30
 1988, April   Concordance to the Poems of Lord Oxford   De Vere Soc. New., no. 2: 41-42

Author Index

Constable, Burt
2006, Aug. 31   Shakespeare By Any Other Name Would Smell as Sweet   Daily Herald (Illinois), p. 11

Cooke, Dorian
1937, April 20   Bacon or Shakespeare? [letter]   Western Morn. News, p. 3
         Response by Percy Allen, April 28, p. 11.

Cooke, Morris Llewellyn
1956, May   To the Editor and Readers of *The Shakespeare Newsletter*   Sh. Newsl., vol. 6/3: 18
         [letter, with 21 other signers]

Cook, Nancy
1991   Shakespeare Comes to the Law School Classroom   Denver U. Law Review, vol. 68: 387-411

Cooksey, T. L.
2010, Feb. 15   [review of *Contested Will* by James Shapiro (2010)]   Library Journal, v. 135/3: 95-96

Cooper, E. R.
1937, Nov.   Shakespeare in Suffolk [letter]   East Angl. Mag., vol. 3/2: 83

Cooper, Susan
1964, April 5   The Great Detective   Sunday Times

Corbin, John
1920, June 27   Who is "Baconian" Now? A Curious Mania That Reaches Its Climax   New York Times, p. 58
         in "Identifying" Shakespeare with an Earl of Oxford [rev. of SI]
1943, Feb. 7   A New Candidate for Shakespeare's Honors [review of *Will*   New York Times, p. BR18
         Shakespeare and the Dyer's Hand by Alden Brooks]

Corby, Herbert
1951, July/Aug.   The Shakespeare Mystery, Part 1   Poetry Review, v. 42: 196-99
1951, Sept./Oct.   The Shakespeare Mystery, Part 2   Poetry Review, v. 42: 255-59
1951, Nov./Dec.   The Shakespeare Mystery, Part 3   Poetry Review, v. 42: 329-33

Corder, Henry
1920, May 20   Who Wrote Shakespeare? [review of SI]   Advocate (Melbourne), p. 3

Cornfield, Robert
2005, Oct. 31   In Search of the Elusive Bard: The Plays Are Still the Thing   New York Observer

Cornwell, Tim
2010, Aug. 19   [review of *The Man Who Was Hamlet* by George Dillon]   Scotsman, p. 6

Corrigan, Michael
2012, July 15   The Shakespeare Controversy: Doubts About Authorship Still Persist   Idaho State Journal, p. C1
         [review of *Anonymous*]

Cossolotto, Lora
2012, Winter   [letter: her donation to the SOS]   Sh. Ox. Newsl., vol. 48/1: 2

Cossolotto, Matthew
2005, Winter   Shakespeare's "Last Will" Sonnets   Sh. Ox. Newsl., vol. 41/1: 8-12
2005, Fall   President's Page   Sh. Ox. Newsl., vol. 41/4: 2, 29
2006, Winter   President's Letter   Sh. Ox. Newsl., vol. 42/1: 2, 28
2006, Spring   President's Page   Sh. Ox. Newsl., vol. 42/2: 2, 25
2006, Fall   President's Page   Sh. Ox. Newsl., vol. 42/3: 2, 31
2006, Fall redux   Dear Fellow SOS Members!   Sh. Ox. Newsl., vol. 42/4: 2, 15
2007   Standing on the Shoulders of Giants, in *Report My Cause Aright*,
         published by the SOS, p. 5-9
2007   [letter: thanks to Stephanie Hopkins Hughes for great work   Oxfordian, vol. 10: 165-165
         as editor of *The Oxfordian*]
2007, Winter   President's Page: Doubling Membership in 2007; Shakespeare   Sh. Ox. Newsl., vol. 43/1: 2, 12
         Authorship Commission
2007, Summer   President's Page   Sh. Ox. Newsl., vol. 43/3: 1-2
2007, Fall   President's Page   Sh. Ox. Newsl., vol. 43/4: 2, 13
2007, Fall   Interview with Allegra Krasznekewicz   Sh. Ox. Newsl., vol. 43/4: 14-15
2008, Winter   President's Page   Sh. Ox. Newsl., vol. 44/1: 2, 12
2008, March   Tribute to Sue Sybersma   De Vere Soc. Newsl., v. 15/1: 28
2008, Spring   President's Page   Sh. Ox. Newsl., vol. 44/2: 2, 12

Cossolotto, Matthew (continued)

2008, Summer	President's Page	Sh. Ox. Newsl., vol. 44/3: 2, 19
2008, Summer	Noted Shakespearean Egan Takes Over *The Oxfordian*	Sh. Ox. Newsl., vol. 44/3: 24
2009	[letter: the *Sonnets* at four hundred]	Oxfordian, vol. 11: 4-10
2009, Feb.	[letter: video clip of his discussion of authorship issues]	De Vere Soc. Newsl., v. 16/1: 27
2009, June	Enchanted April 2009 – Big Mo for the Big O	Sh. Ox. Newsl., v. 45/1: 2, 35-36
2009, Sept.	My Name Be Buried: 400th Ann. of Posthumously Published *Sonnets*	Sh. Ox. Newsl., v. 45/2: 2, 45-47
2009, Dec.	Oxfordian-of-the-year Award Presented to Justice Stevens [with Alex McNeil]	Sh. Ox. Newsl., vol. 45/3: 1
2009, Dec.	Oxfordian Update	Sh. Ox. Newsl., vol. 45/3: 6, 31
2012, Spring	Top Ten Reasons To Doubt that Shakespeare Wrote 'Shakespeare'	Sh. Ox. Newsl., vol. 48/2: 25
2012, Sum./Fall	Top Ten Reasons Why Oxford is Shakespeare	Sh. Ox. Newsl., vol. 48/3: 19

Costello, Daniel

1999, March 26	Poetic License	Wall St. Journal, p. W2

Cottle, Elizabeth

1996, Dec.	Shakespeare & Scriptures: *Merchant of Venice* [with Chr. Dams] [repr. in GO, pp. 159-68]	De Vere Soc. Newsl., vol. 2/7: 8-15

Coulter, Brian

1988, April	Call for a Definitive Chronology	De Vere Soc. New., no. 2: 30-32
1972, Summer	[letter: *Love's Labour's Lost* and *Locrine*]	Sh. Authorship Review, #26: 20

Court, Judith

2003, June 21	Bilton Hall; The Many Chapters of Its History	Coventry Even. Tel., p. 20-21

Courthope, W. J.

1910	*History of English Poetry*, vol. II. New York/London: Macmillan and Co.	

Courtney, W. L.

1920, March 19	Shakespeare Identified [review of SI]	Telegraph, p. 16

Cousins, Peter

2010, Feb.	[letter: response to Goldstein's Nov. 2009 "Native Tongue" article] Reply by Goldstein, Feb. 2010, p. 26.	De Vere Soc. New., vol. 17/1: 26

Cove, Kim

2010, Aug.	[letter: Modernization of spelling on SOS website]	Sh. Ox. Newsl., vol. 46/2: 15

Covert, Colin

2011, Oct. 28	Playwright Theory Lacks Substance [review of *Anonymous*]	Minneapolis Star. Tr., p. E8

Cowen, Dick

1991, Dec. 11	Crusader [Lord Vere] Says His Kin Wrote Shakespeare's Plays	Morning Call, p. B5

Crace, John

2011, June 17	To B-movie or Not to B-movie [review of *Anonymous*]	Guardian, p. 4

Crafts, Daniel Steven

Date not known	*Bury My Name.* [theatrical presentation of the Oxfordian idea, with songs by Will. Sh. and Edward de Vere]	
Date not known	*The Real Shakespeare.* [A song cycle from poems by Edward de Vere]	

Crafts, Fred

1990, April 1	A Midsummer Day's Dream in Shakespeareland [Visitors to Stratford defrauded]	Los Angeles Times, p. 3

Craig, Hardin

1934, Nov.	Hamlet's Book	Huntington Library Bulletin, vol. 6: 17-37
1964, Dec.	The Study of Shakespeare, Part I: Advice	Sh. Newsl., no. 79, v. 14/6: 81
1965, Feb.	The Study of Shakespeare, Part II: Essentials	Sh. Newsl., no. 80, v. 15/1: 6
1965, April	The Study of Shakespeare, Part III: Explanations	Sh. Newsl., no. 81, v. 15/2: 12

Craik, Katherine

2007, Oct. 5	[letter: comments on Bill Bryson's *Shakespeare*]	Times Lit. Sup., is. 5453: 26

Crampin, Alice

2010, Nov.	A Novice Heretic Reads Shapiro	De Vere Soc. Newsl., v. 17/3: 30
2011, March	Following a Cambridge Trail	De Vere Soc. New., v. 18/1: 8-10
2014, May	Earl of Oxford and Dr. John Caius of Cambridge, The	De Vere So. New., v. 21/2: 30-31

2019, Oct.	[review of *Early Shakespeare Authorship Doubts* by Bryan H. Wildenthal]	De Vere Soc. Newsl., vol. 26/4: 30-32
2020, Jan.	[review of *A Question of Will* by Lynne Kositsky]	De Vere S. News., v. 27/1: 44-45
2020, April	[review of *The Case for Edward de Vere* by John Milnes Baker]	De Vere S. News., v. 27/2: 46-47
2009, June	[letter: de Vere's links to the Southwell family]	De Vere Soc. New., vol. 16/2: 29

Crane, Lelia

1989, July 17	Will Real Shakespeare Please Stand! [review of a performance of John Nassivera's play *All the Queen's Men*	Hour (Norwalk, CT)

Crane, Milton

1953, Feb. 15	Authors Say: Author—Not Shakespeare [rev. of *This Star of England*]	Chicago Tribune, p. B10

Cranston, Hoy

1948, Nov. 6	The Shakespeare Confusion [letter: response to Burgess]	Sat. Review, p. 21-22

Creasey, Beverly

2001, Spring	Hamlet Formerly Known as Prince	Sh. Ox. Newsl., vol. 37/1: 3
2000, Summer	[letter: *Power Plays: Shakespeare's Lessons in Leadership and Management* by Tina Packer and John Whitney (2000)]	Sh. Ox. Newsl., vol. 36/2: 22

Crew, Louis

1978	Homosexual Conflict in Shakespeare's *Sonnets*	Bard, vol. 2/1: 1-3

Crewe, Jonathan

1984, Dec. 30	[review of *The Mysterious William Shakespeare*]	Atlantic Mon., vol. 29: 448-50

Crick, Jeremy

2006, Nov.	Elizabeth and Francis Trentham	De Vere Soc. Newsl., p. 16
2007, Feb.	Elizabeth and Francis Trentham, Part 2	De Vere Soc. Newsl., p. 24-35
2007, Feb. 28	Ivy the Terrible [letter]	Times (London), p. 18
2007, June	The Ashbourne Portrait [with Dorna Bewley] Response by Christopher Paul, Oct. 2007, p. 29-30.	De Vere Soc. Newsl., p. 24-35
2007, Sept. 12	Much Ado About Shakespeare [letter: resp. to David Aaronovitch's Sept. 11 article]	Times (London), p. 18
2008, March	[letter: *Earls of Paradise* by Adam Nicolson (2008)]	De Vere Soc. Newsl., v. 15/1: 27
2008, March	News: the DVS website and poster campaign	De Vere Soc. Newsl., vol. 15/1: 3
2008, June	DVS Website Review	De Vere Soc. Newsl., v. 15/2: 10
2008, June	Oxfordian Research – Turning Challenge into Opportunity: Elizabeth Imlay interviews Jeremy Crick	De Vere Soc. Newsl., vol. 15/2: 17-20
2009, Feb.	De Vere Website Review	De Vere S. News., v. 16/1: 31-32
2009, March 14	[letter: the Cobbe portrait] [repr. in DVN, vol. 16/2: 30 (June 2009)]	Times (London)
2009, March 30	[letter: the Cobbe portrait] [repr. in DVN, vol. 16/2: 30 (June 2009)]	Independent
2009, Nov.	[letter: Robert Brazil's marvelous blog]	De Vere Soc. Newsl., v. 16/3: 34
2010, Aug.	The Search for Shakespeare Manuscripts in Fulke Greville's Monument in Warwick	De Vere Soc. Newsl., vol. 17/2: 19-21
2011, July	Viewing Statistics: The DVS Website	De Vere Soc. Newsl., v. 18/2: 39
2015, April	[letter: Shakespeare DNA analysis]	De Vere Soc. Newsl., v. 22/2: 46
2016, July	[letter: stale media reporting on the SAQ]	De Vere Soc. Newsl., v. 22/3: 47

Crider, Andrew

2011, Fall	Shakespeare's Antagonistic Disposition: Personality Trait Approach	Brief Chronicles, vol. III: 201-12
2015, Summer	Is Ben Jonson's *De Shakespeare Nostrati* a Depiction of Edward de Vere? [repr. in *The Oxfordian*, vol. 22 (2020): 131-130]	Sh. Ox. Newsl., vol. 51/3: 19-22
2019, Sept.	Edward de Vere and the Psychology of Creativity	Oxfordian, vol. 21: 215-28
2021, Spring	Will Shakspere as a Successful Psychopath	Sh. Ox. Newsl., vol. 57/2: 28-31

Crinkley, Richmond

1985, Winter	New Perspectives on the Authorship Question [condensed excerpts repr. in *Shakespeare Authorship Sourcebook* (Stritmatter editor (2022): 47-49]	Sh. Quarterly, vol. 36/4: 515-22

Croft, Pauline (editor)

2002	*Patronage, Culture and Power: The Early Cecils, 1558-1612.* New Haven: Yale University Press.	

Crosby, Ernest

1956   *Shakespeare's Attitude Towards the Working Class*. [excerpt, "The Aristocratic Look of Shakespeare," repr. in SFE, p. 4-5 (Spring 1956); and in BTC, vol. 4: 144-45]

Crosse, Gordon

| 1917, April | The Real Shakespeare Problem | Nineteenth Cen., vol. 81:883-94 |
| 1920, Oct. | Yet Another Shakespeare [review of SI] | Commonwealth, p. 288-92 |

Crow, John

| 1964, April 23 | Heretics Observed | Times Lit. Sup.is 3243, p. 358 |

Culligan, Glendy

| 1962, Aug. 26 | Shakespeare (?) Is Back [review of *Shake-speare: The Real Man Behind the Name* by Dorothy Ogburn & Ch. Ogburn, Jr. (1962)] | Washington Post, p. G6 |

Cuningham, Granville C.

1911   *Bacon's Secret Disclosed in Contemporary Books* ["Introduction" repr. in BTC, vol. 1: 200-205]

Cureton, Kevin K.

| 1986, Jan. 25 | [letter: Morse Johnson's Jan. 9 letter] Response by Charlton Ogburn, Feb. 8, p. A26. | New York Times, p. A26 |

Curry, John T.

| 1902, Feb. 8 | Edward de Vere and Thomas Watson | Notes & Queries, S. 9/9: 101-03 |

Curtis, Myra

| 1964, Sept. 24 | Author! Author? [letter: evidence for Shakspere is "slight"] | Times Lit. Sup., is. 3265: 886 |

Curtius, Ernst Robert

| 2016, June | Ernst Robert Curtius über Shakespeare als Buchkenner und -liebhaber | Neues Sh. Jour., v. NS5: 97-112 |

Cushman, Allerton

| 1987, March 11 | Prejudice and Shakespeare [letter to *The American Spectator* (not pub.) | Sh. Ox. Newsl., vol. 27/1: 3 |

Cusick, John

1983, Winter	Cusick Forms Oxford-Shakespeare Group Within Mensa	Sh. Ox. Newsl., vol. 19/1: 7
1988, May 31	[letter: pseudonyms]	Wall St. Journal
1991	[letter] [repr. in SSN, issue 1/1: 3 (Feb. 1991)]	Daily News (Sun City)

Cutler, John

| 1977, May 2 | On the Shakespearean Authorship Question [letter] [resp. to Marjorie Gifford's April 25 letter] | Boston Globe, p. 15 |

Cutler, Keir

Books

2014   *The Shakespeare Authorship Question: A Crackpot's View*. Amazon Digital Services, Inc.

Shorter pieces

2010	The Top Ten Reasons Shakespeare Did Not Write Shakespeare	Oxfordian, vol. 12: 17-20
2011, Oct. 27	There is Method in This Madness; Traditional Scholars Believe Shakespearean Doubters Are an Army of Crazies. Count Me a Soldier in That Army.	Gazette (Montreal), p. A23
2013	Doubter Response to Question #46: Do you agree with Mark Twain that you have to experience something in order to write about it?, in *Shakespeare Beyond Doubt?* (Shahan): 205-06	
2018, Dec.	A Theatre Artist's Path: Questioning Shakespeare's Authorship	Critical Stages, vol. 18
2021, Winter	Banned and Blocked from the "Shakespeare Forum"	Sh. Ox. Newsl., vol. 57/1: 35-36

Cutner, Herbert

1944, May	A Note on John M. Robertson	SF News-letter (E), p. 7
1946, Sept.	The Stratford Monument Again Response by J. Shera Atkinson, same issue, p. 7-8.	SF News-letter (E), p. 7
1947, Sept.	Alias William Shakespeare	SF News-letter (E), p. 4-5
1948, Sept.	Are We Progressing?	SF News-letter (E), p. 6-7
1949, March	The Shakespearean Birthplace	SF News-letter (E), p. 5-6
1949, Sept.	The Stratford Monument Again Response by J. Shera Atkinson, same issue, p. 7-8.	SF News-letter (E), p. 7
1951, April	Provincial Dialect in Shakspere's Day [repr. in BTC, vol. IV: 115-6]	SF News-letter (E), p. 7-8
1951, Sept.	Shakespeare of London	SF News-letter (E), p. 7-8

1953, April	[review of *Life and Times of Edward Alleyn* by G. L. Hosking]	SF News-letter (E), p. 9-10
1953, Nov.	Professor Abel Lefranc on Oxford	SF News-letter (E), p. 6
1953, Nov.	More Proofs for Shakespeare of Stratford?	SF News-letter (E), p. 10
1954, Sept.	Two Books on "Shakespeare:" *Shakespeare Survey 7*, ed. by Allardyce Nicoll and *The Annotator* by Alan Keen and Roger Lubbock	SF News-letter (E), p. 4-5
1955, Autumn	[review of *Ben Jonson of Westminster* by Marchette Chute (1954)]	SF News-letter (E). p. 10
1956, Autumn	[review of *Shakespeare's Magic Circle* by Alfred J. Evans (1956)]	SF News-letter (E), p. 8-9
1958, Spring	[report on Martin Pares' Dec. 7, 1957 talk "Case For Francis Bacon"]	SF News-letter (E), p. 3
1958, Autumn	[review of *A Pictorial Biography* by F. E. Halliday (1956)]	SF News-letter (E), p. 10-11
1958, Autumn	[review of *The Cult of Shakespeare* by F. E. Halliday (1957)]	SF News-letter (E), p. 10-11
1958, Autumn	[letter: H. L. Senior's Autumn 1957 "Omissions" article] Reply by Senior, same issue, p. 12.	SF News-letter (E), p. 11-12
1959, Spring	[review of *Elizabethan Literature* by Helen Morris (1958)]	Sh. Authorship Rev. #1: 12-13
1959, Spring	[letter: *Love's Labour's Lost* and R. C. Churchill]	Sh. Authorship Rev. #1: 23-24
1959, Autumn	[report on L. S. Penrose's Feb. 14, 1959 talk "Statistical Approach to the Authorship Problem"]	Sh. Authorship Rev. #2: 13-14
1960, Spring	On the Poems of Edward de Vere	Sh. Authorship Rev. #3: 4-6
1960, Spring	[report on Jackson's Jan. 9, 1960 talk "Lord Oxford & the Dramatists"]	Sh. Authorship Rev. #3: 19-20
1960, Autumn	Denigrating the Earl of Oxford	Sh. Authorship Rev. #4: 1-2
1960, Autumn	[letter: Rosaline de Vere]	Sh. Authorship Rev. #4: 22
1961, Spring	The Spelling of "Shakespeare"	Sh. Authorship Rev. #5: 6-7
1961, Spring	[letter: Lord Burghley and Queen Elizabeth]	Sh. Authorship Rev. #5: 24
1961, Autumn	Mr. J. B. Priestley and Shakespeare	Sh. Authorship Rev. #6: 1-2
1962, Spring	[review of *Shakespeare Today* by Margaret Webster (1957)]	Sh. Authorship Rev. #7: 13-15
1962, Spring	[report on Sir John Russell's Jan. 13, 1962 talk "The Magic Circle"]	Sh. Authorship Rev. #7: 17-18
1963, Autumn	[review of *The Rise of the Elizabethan Common Player* by M. C. Bradbrook (1962)]	Sh. Authorship Rev. #10: 15-16
1963, Autumn	Obituary: William Kent (1886-1963) [repr. in BTC, vol. 5, p. 130-131]	Sh. Authorship Rev. #10: 21-22
1964, Spring	[review of *How Shakespeare Spent the Day* by Ivor Brown (1963)]	Sh. Authorship Rev. #11: 12-13
1964, Autumn	]letter: the BBC and the "Claimants"]	Sh. Authorship Rev. #12: 21
1965, Spring	[letter: Georges Connes' Afterthoughts]	Sh. Authorship Rev. #13: 21

Cutting, Bonner Miller

Books

2018	*Necessary Mischief: Exploring the Shakespeare Authorship Question*. Jennings, LA: Minos Publish. Co.	

Shorter pieces

2005, Fall	[letter: Anderson's *Shakespeare By Another Name*]	Sh. Matters, vol. 5/1: 2
2006, Summer	The Case of the Missing First Folio [expanded and repr. in NM (2018): 151-172] [repr. in TFF (Stritmatter 2023): 319-36]	Sh. Matters, vol. 5/4: 6-11
2007	[letter: Thanks to Stephanie Hopkins Hughes for great work as editor of *The Oxfordian*]	Oxfordian, vol. 10: 166-166
2007, Spring	Say It With Music	Sh. Matters, vol. 6/3: 25, 30
2007, Summer	11th Annual Shakespeare Authorship Studies Conference Convenes [with Earl Showerman]	Sh. Matters, vol. 6/4: 1, 8-13
2009	Shakespeare's Will . . . Considered Too Curiously [repr. in BTC, vol. 10: 421-52 as "Is Shakespeare's Will Missing the Mind of Shakespeare?"; and in *Necessary Mischief* (2018): 27-57]	Brief Chron., vol. I: 169-191
2009, Spring	The Case of the Wrong Countess	Sh. Matters, vol. 8/2: 1, 13-23+
2009, Nov.	The Time is Out of Joint: Chronological Incongruence in Early Modern English Portraiture	De Vere Soc. Newsl., vol. 16/3: 20-24
2010, Fall	Contest of Wills: Reviewing Shapiro's Reviewers [repr. in *Necessary Mischief* (2018), p. 17-26]	Sh. Matters, vol. 9/3: 12-14+
2011	Alas, Poor Anne: Shakespeare's "Second-Best Bed" in Historical Perspective [repr. in BTC, vol. 10: 65-90; and in *Necessary Mischief* (2018): 59-82]	Oxfordian, vol. 13: 76-93
2011, Summer	[letter: *Studies in English Literature* notices *Brief Chronicles*]	Sh. Matters, vol. 10/3: 2
2011, Fall	[review of *Shakespeare: The Concealed Poet* by Robert Detobel]	Brief Chron., vol. III: 272-274
2011, Fall	She Will Not Be a Mother: Evaluating the Seymour Prince Tudor Hypothesis] [repr. in *Necessary Mischief* (2018): 197-228] Resp. by Paul Streitz, SM, Summer 2012, p. 18-31.	Brief Chron., vol. III: 169-199

Cutting, Bonner Miller (continued)

2012, Winter	[review of *The Shakespeare Guide to Italy: Retracing the Bard's Unknown Travels*, by Richard Paul Roe (2011)]	Sh. Matters, vol. 11/1: 13, 33
2012, Fall	[review of *The Truth About William Shakespeare: Fact, Fiction, and Modern Biographies*, by David Ellis (2012)]	Sh. Matters, vol. 11/4: 7-8
2013	Appendix A: Shakspere's Last Will and Testament, in *Shakespeare Beyond Doubt?* (Shahan): 225-27	
2013	Shakspere's Will: Missing the Mind of Shakespeare, in *Shakespeare Beyond Doubt?* (Shahan): 58-68	
2013	Doubter Response to Question #21: In what ways are the plays revealing about Shakespeare's knowledge of theatrical practice?, in *Shakespeare Beyond Doubt?* (Shahan): 180-81	
2013	Doubter Response to Question #35: Does Shakespeare's will shed any light on his professional practice?, in SBD? (Shahan): 192-93	
2013	Doubter Response to Question #36: Is it suspicious that no books are mentioned in Shakespeare's Will?, in SBD? (Shahan): 193-94	
2013, Spring	A Countess Transformed: How Lady Susan Vere Became Lady Anne Clifford [repr. in *Necessary Mischief* (2018): 173-195]	Brief Chron., vol. IV: 107-134
2013, July	"Let the Punishment Fit the Crime" [Summary by editor] [repr. in *Necessary Mischief* (2018): 83-103]	De Vere Soc. Newsl., v. 20/2: 8+
2013, Summer	2012 Essay Winners Announced	Sh. Matters, vol. 12/3: 1, 11-12
2016	Evermore in Subjection: Wardship and Edward de Vere [repr. in *Necessary Mischief* (2018): 105-131]	Oxfordian, vol. 18: 65-84
2017, Winter	[review of *Summer Storm: A Novel of Ideas* by James A. Warren]	Sh. Ox. Newsl., vol. 53/1: 24-25
2017, Summer	[review of *Shakespeare's Wilderness* by David Rains Wallace (2017)]	Sh. Ox. Newsl., vol. 53/3: 14-15
2017, Oct.	Sufficient Warrant: Censorship, Punishment, and Sh. in Early Modern England [excerpt repr. in *Necessary Mischief* (2018): 133-150]	Oxfordian, vol. 19: 69-100
2020, Winter	The Persistent Mystery of Oxford's Annuity	Sh. Ox. Newsl., vol. 56/1: 20-23
2020, Fall	A Retrospective Look at John Thomas Looney's Discovery of Shakesp.	Sh. Ox. Newsl., v. 56/4: 17, 20+
2021, Fall	Shakespeare Oxford Fellowship Annual Meeting Report	Sh. Ox. Newsl., vol. 57/4: 24
2022, Spring	In Memoriam: Virginia Renner (1933-2022)	Sh. Ox. Newsl., vol. 58/2: 9
2022, Summer	Does the 17th Earl of Oxford "lieth buried in Westminster"? [with Cheryl Eagan-Donovan]	Sh. Ox. Newsl., v. 58/3: 1, 18-21
2022, Fall	In Memoriam: Margaret Robson (1928-2022)	Sh. Ox. Newsl., vol. 58/4: 15
2022, Fall	Shakespeare Oxford Fellowship Annual Meeting Report	Sh. Ox. Newsl., vol. 58/4: 22-23
2023, Winter	Examining the Earl of Oxford's "New" Signature of 1603	Sh. Ox. Newsl., vol. 59/1: 13-14
2023, Spring	[letter: reply to Christopher Paul's letter re Oxford in Westminster] [with Cheryl Eagan-Donovan]	Sh. Ox. Newsl., vol. 59/2: 5
2023, Summer	Shakespeare and Southampton: Blest Be the Tie that Unbinds	J. of Sci. Exploration, vol. 37/2

Cyr, Gordon C.

Pamphlets

1986	*The Shakespeare Identity Crisis: A Reference Guide. Shakespeare Oxford Society.* [author not stated; perhaps by Gordon and/or Dorothy Cyr]	

Periodicals edited

1975, Winter-1978, Summer; 1980, Spring and Summer; and with Helen W. Cyr, 1984, Fall-1986, Summer: *Shakespeare Oxford Newsletter*, vol. 11/1-14/3, vol. 16/2-16/3, and vol. 20/4-22/3

Shorter pieces

1971, March 30	[review of *Rational Belief: An Introduction to Logic* by Albert Frye and Albert Levi (1941) ("de Vere is with a high degree of probability the author")]	Sh. Ox. Newsl., vol. 7/1: 1
1971, Sept. 2	A New Shakespeare Signature [letter] [repr. in SON, vol. 8/1: 5 (Jan. 1972)]	San Francisco Chronicle, p. 35
1972, Jan.	Shaksper's "Genius" – Some Alleged Parallels	Sh. Ox. Newsl., vol. 8/1: 9-10
1974, Wntr./Spr.	The Harvard Case	Sh. Ox. Newsl., vol. 11/1: 4
1975, Wntr./Spr.	Solzhenitsyn Uses Anti-Stratfordian's Arguments	Sh. Ox. Newsl., vol. 11/1: 5-6
1975, Summer	An Oxfordian Reply to Two Harvard Professors [Evans and Levin] [repr. in BTC, vol. 6: 35-54]	Sh. Ox. Newsl., vol. 11/2: 1-19
1975, Fall	Three Oxfordian Classics Are Re-issued	Sh. Ox. Newsl., vol. 11/3: 3-4
1975, Fall	In Memoriam: Charles Wisner Barrell (d. 1975)	Sh. Ox. Newsl., vol. 11/3: 5

1976, March	In Memoriam: Richard C. Horne, Jr. (d. 1976) [repr. in BTC, vol. 6: 82-83]	Sh. Ox. Newsl., Special issue: 1
1976, Spring	[review of *"Shakespeare" Identified* and *The Poems of Edward de Vere*, by J. T. Looney, 3rd ed. edited by Ruth Loyd Miller (1975)]	Sh. Ox. Newsl., vol. 12/1: 5-6
1976, May 10	Student Newspaper Features SOS Member and Oxford Theory [UCLA *Daily Bruin*]	Sh. Ox. Newsl., vol. 12/3: 9
1976, May 10	To Be Or Not To Be? [repr. in SON, vol. 12/3: 9-10 (Fall 1976)]	Daily Bruin
1976, Summer	[review of *Absent Thee From Felicity* by Rhoda Henry Messner]	Sh. Ox. Newsl., vol. 12/2: 4
1976, Fall	Editor's Note: Election of Charlton Ogburn, Jr. as SOS President	Sh. Ox. Newsl., vol. 12/3: 1
1976, Fall	[review of *Hidden Allusions in Shakespeare's Plays* by Eva Turner Clark, 3rd Revised Edition edited by Ruth Loyd Miller (1974)]	Sh. Ox. Newsl., vol. 12/3: 10-11
1976, Winter	[review of *A Hundreth Sundrie Flowres*, with an Intro. by Bernard Mordaunt Ward, 2nd Edition edited by Ruth Loyd Miller (1975)]	Sh. Ox. Newsl., vol. 12/4: 6-7
1976, Winter	[review of *Secrets of Shakespeare* by A. Bronson Feldman (1972)]	Sh. Ox. Newsl., vol. 12/4: 7-8
1977, Summer	A Post Mortem on the Messner-Marder Exchange [repr. in BTC, vol. 6: 107-111]	Sh. Ox. Newsl., vol. 13/2: 1-4
1977, Summer	Noted Stratfordian Objects to Shakespeare's "Imaginary Life"	Sh. Ox. Newsl., vol. 13/2: 4-5
1977, Summer	Overpainting on the "Ashbourne" Portrait: A Conservator's View	Sh. Ox. Newsl., vol. 13/2: 5-8
1977, Summer	Shakespeare Country: Real and Imagined	Sh. Ox. Newsl., vol. 13/2: 10-11
1977, Fall	Shakespeare Oxford Society Second National Conference	Sh. Ox. Newsl., vol. 13/3: 2-5
1978, Winter	Harvard Case, Part II	Sh. Ox. Newsl., vol. 14/1: 5-6
1978, Winter	More on the "Ashbourne" Pedigree	Sh. Ox. Newsl., vol. 14/1: 9-10
1978, Spring	Famous People Comment . . . [repr. in BTC, vol. 6: 85-86, 123-24]	Sh. Ox. Newsl., vol. 14/2: 1-3
1978, Summer	Prejudice and Shakespeare – Continued [Warren Hope and *College English*]	Sh. Ox. Newsl., vol. 14/3: 3-4
1979, May	The Case for Edward de Vere, 17th Earl of Oxford, as "Shakespeare"	Sh. Newsl., vol. 29/2: 22
1979, Summer	Portrait Identified: "Ashbourne" Sitter <u>Not</u> Oxford, New Findings Show	Sh. Ox. Newsl., vol. 15/3: 1-6
1979, Summer	Oxfordian Theory Gets Coverage in Stratfordian Periodical	Sh. Ox. Newsl., vol. 15/3: 7
1979, Sept.	The Case for Edward de Vere, 17th Earl of Oxford as "Shakespeare"	Sh. Newsl., vol. 29/3: 30
1979, Nov.	Why Are There Doubts About "Shakespeare's" Authorship?	Sh. Newsl., vol. 29/4: 38
1979, Dec.	Some Common Replies to the "Authorship Doubters"	Sh. Newsl., vol. 29/5: 47
1980	Oxford's and Shakespeare's "Jacks"	Bard, vol. 2/4: 127-129
1980, Spring	Shakespeare Oxford Society Authors in British and U.S. Journals	Sh. Ox. Newsl., vol. 16/2: 1-3
1980, Spring	*The Shakespeare Newsletter* Uses SOS Newsletter as Source for "Ashbourne" Release	Sh. Ox. Newsl., vol. 16/2: 3-4
1980, Spring	Oxford's Handwriting	Sh. Ox. Newsl., vol. 16/2: 4-5
1980, April	How to Construct a "Shakespeare Biography"	Sh. Newsl., vol. 30/2: 17
1980, May	A Prediction of the Oxford Theory? [examines Greenwood's *The Shakespeare Problem Restated* (1908)]	Sh. Newsl., vol. 30/3: 22
1980, Summer	If Invited to Writ; He Was in Paine [Shaksper's signatures] [with Helen W. Cyr]	Sh. Ox. Newsl., vol. 16/3: 1-12
1980, Summer	Latest *Sir Thomas More* Findings Point to Lord Oxford as "Shakespeare" [repr. in SHNL, vol. 30/4: 35 (Sept. 1980); and in BTC, vol. 6: 131-34]	Sh. Ox. Newsl., v. 16/3: 12-13
1980, Nov.	Oxford's 1604 Death Is No Bar To His Authorship	Sh. Newsl., vol. 30/5: 42
1980, Dec.	Polonius as Lord Burleigh: Oxford's Revenge on His Father-in-law?	Sh. Newsl., vol. 30/6: 48
1981, Feb.	The Latest Shakespearean Mare's Nest: Southampton's "Secretary"	Sh. Newsl., vol. 31/1: 4
1981, May	The Case of the "Alias" Earl!	Sh. Newsl., vol. 31/3: 20
1981, Summer	Mailing of the April/May 1981 issue of the Newsletter	Sh. Ox. Newsl., vol. 17/2: 12
1981, Sept.-Nov.	"Shakespere" vs. Webster as *More*'s Author: A Heretical View	Sh. Newsl., vol. 31/4: 27
1981, Dec.	A Literary Scholar Looks at Lord Oxford's Poetry	Sh. Newsl., vol. 31/5: 38
1982, Feb.	A Literary Scholar Looks at Lord Oxford's Poetry, Part II	Sh. Newsl., vol. 32/1: 6
1982, Apr.-May	Skeptical Thoughts on the "Paper Chase"	Sh. Newsl., vol. 32/2: 11
1982, Summer	[review of *The Search for an Eternal Norm* by Louis J. Halle (1981)] [repr. in BTC, vol. 6: 194-97]	Sh. Ox. Newsl., vol. 18/3: 6-8
1982, Fall	Would It Hold Up In Court?	Sh. Newsl., vol. 32/3: 22
1982, Winter	A Literary Scholar Looks at Lord Oxford's Poetry: Mr. Ramsey's Straw man	Sh. Newsl., vol. 32/4: 32

Cyr, Gordon C. (continued)

Author Index

Cyr, Helen W.
Books and pamphlets
1983	*Lexical Choices and Morphological Variables in the Shakespeare and Oxford Corpora: A Preliminary Study* [pamphlet]. Baltimore: Shakespeare Oxford Society.	
1986	*The Shakespeare Identity Crisis: A Reference Guide. Shakespeare Oxford Society.* [author not names; perhaps by Gordon and/or Dorothy Cyr]	

Periodicals co-edited with Gordon C. Cyr
1984, Fall-1986, Summer: *Shakespeare Oxford Newsletter*, vol. 20/4-22/3
Shorter pieces

1976, Spring	Oxfordians as Scholars	Sh. Ox. Newsl., vol. 12/1: 4
1976, Summer	The Work of the Society: Research or Spectator Sport?	Sh. Ox. Newsl., vol. 12/2: 5-6
1976, Fall	Report on the SOS. National Conference, Sept. 24-26, 1976	Sh. Ox. Newsl., vol. 12/3: 3-5
1977, Fall	Détente With the Orthodox Stratfordians: Possibility of Impossibility?	Sh. Ox. Newsl., vol. 13/3: 1-2
1980, Winter	IRS Regulations and the Shakespeare Oxford Society	Sh. Ox. Newsl., vol. 16/1: 13-14
1980, Summer	If Invited to Writ; He Was in Paine [with. G. Cyr]	Sh. Ox. Newsl., vol. 16/3: 1-12
1985, Winter	A Salute To Our Man in England (Harold W. Patience)	Sh. Ox. Newsl., vol. 21/1: 1
1985, Spring	Debater's Corner: Oxford as Translator of Ovid's *Metamorphoses*	Sh. Ox. Newsl., vol. 21/2: 5-6
1985, Fall	The Work of the Shakespeare Oxford Society	Sh. Ox. Newsl., vol. 21/4: 6-7
1986, Spring	Lord Oxford Said It First!	Sh. Newsl., vol. 36/1: 11
1987, Spring	What's Wrong With Word Studies?	Sh. Ox. Newsl., vol. 23/2: 10-15
1990, Fall	Why Some Word Studies Fail – And Why the Shake. Clinic Misfires	Sh. Newsl., vol. 40/3: 43

D. F.
1959, Spring	[report on Eggar's Jan. 17, 1959 talk "Lord Oxford and His Servants"]	Sh. Authorship Rev. #1: 21-22

D. H.
2003	Der Psychologie von Shakespeares Sonett 117	Neues Sh. Journal, vol. 8: 164-66

D. M. (1)
1933, Nov.	Shake-Spear [review of *Elizabethan Times* by H. H. Holland]	Tablet

D. M. (2)
2011, Oct. 18	Rewriting History and Losing Plots [review of *Anonymous*]	Evening Standard, p. 36

Dabney, Virginius
1991, Winter	[letter: thanks to Charlton Ogburn, Jr. for his masterful book]	Sh. Ox. Newsl., vol. 27/1: 3

Daschlager, Earl L.
1997, June 22	[review of *Alias Shakespeare* by Joseph Sobran (1997)]	Houston Chron., Zest: 23, 31
1994, Winter	What Shakespeare Knew About Baseball	Sh. Ox. Newsl., vol. 30/1: 5

Dalley, Jan
2016, April 23	Steeped in Shakespeare	Financial Times, p. 18

Dalton, Terence
1998, Feb.	Annual General Meeting, 24 January 1998	De Vere Soc. Newsl., v. 2/11: 2-6

Dams, Christopher H.
Pamphlets
1994	*Discovering the True Shake-speare* [pamphlet, with Iris Krass]. Pub. by the De Vere Society. [2nd ed., 1996]	

Periodicals edited
1995, May-2000, Jan.; Feb. 2003: *The De Vere Society Newsletter*   De Vere Soc. Newsl., v. 2/1-3/4a
Shorter pieces

1994, Winter	[review of *De Veres Of Castle Hedingham* by Verily Anderson]	Sh. Ox. Newsl., vol. 30/1: 21
1995, May	Editorial	De Vere Soc. Newsl., vol. 2/1
1995, May	Shakespeare's Education or the Circular Argument [repr. in GO, p. 31-33]	De Vere Soc. Newsl., v. 2/1: 5-7
1995, May	[review of *The Shakespeare Conspiracy* by Graham Phillips and Martin Keatman (1994)]	De Vere Soc. Newsl., vol. 2/1: 12
1996, Jan.	[report on the General Meeting of the De Vere Society (Jan. 2, 1996)]	De Vere Soc. Newsl., v. 2/4: 1-3
1996, April	[review of *The Alternative Shakespeare* by Arthur M. Challinor]	De Vere Soc. Newsl., v. 2/5: 2-4
1996, Sept.	[report on the De Vere Society's Aug. 17 Business Meeting]	De Vere Soc. Newsl., v. 2/6: 2-6
1996, Dec.	The Geneva *Bible* & *The Merchant of Venice* [from Roger Stritmatter's *The Quintessence of Dust*]	De Vere Soc. New., v. 2/7: 16-17
1997	Introduction to *De Vere is Shakespeare: Evidence From the Biography and Wordplay* by Dennis Baron	

Dams, Christopher H. (continued)

1997, Autumn	Defending the Oxfordian Hypothesis [response to David Kathman's Spring 1997 article 'Why I'm Not an Oxfordian," with Kathman's reply.] [repr. in BTC, vol. 8: 300-06]	Eliz. Review, vol. 5/2: 10-15
1997, Oct.	A Reply to David Kathman's "Why I'm Not an Oxfordian" article	De Vere So. New., v. 2/10: 15-18
1997, Oct.	Notes on the Shakespeare Oxford Society Conference in Seattle	De Vere So. New., v. 2/10: 19-24
1998, Feb.	Informal Discussion with Mark Rylance, Artistic Director, Shakespeare's Globe	De Vere Soc. Newsl. v. 2/11: 6-7
1998, Oct.	Shakespearean Dating, An Oxfordian Weakness? A Proposal	De Vere Soc. New., v. 3/1: 14-18
1999, Feb.	News	De Vere Soc. New., vol. 3/2: 1-2
1999, Feb.	The De Vere Society Dating Project: Progress Report	De Vere Soc. New., v. 3/2: 25-31
1999, May	An Invitation	De Vere Soc. Newsl., vol. 3/3: 18
1999, Aug.	The Dates of Composition of "The Plays of William Shake-Speare" by Edward de Vere, 17th Earl of Oxford	De Vere Soc. New., v. 3/4a: 1-44
1999, Aug.	Postscript - Shakspere, A Life	De Vere Soc. New., v. 3/4: 11-12
1999, Dec. 2	[letter: Dennis Kay's article mocking Lord Burford's Oxfordian beliefs [repr. in DVN (Jan. 2000), p. 3-4] Also in same DVN issue: Brian Porter's Dec. 9 response to Christopher Dams. Christopher Dams' reply to Porter, not printed in *The Times*. Kevin Gilvary's response to Porter, not printed in *The Times*.	Times (London)
2000, May	Minutes of the Annual General Meeting Held at Castle Hedingham	De Vere Soc. Newsl., p. 3-6
2000, May	The De Vere Society Dating Project – Stages 2 & 3	De Vere Soc. Newsl., p. 24-26
2000, Oct.	Stratford Meeting – Panel Session	De Vere Soc. Newsl., p. 2-4
2000, Oct.	[letter: resp. to John Rollett's Jan. and July "Southampton as son of the Queen" articles] Reply by Rollett, same issue, p. 22; and Jan. 2001, p. 18-19.	De Vere Soc. Newsl., p. 20
2002, Feb. 24	Avoiding Disgrace [letter: resp. to Niederkorn]	New York Times, p. E6
2002, July	Report on the Annual General Meeting (April 16, 2002)	De Vere Soc. Newsl., vol. 31-33
2003, June	Secretary's Report to AGM (May 10, 2003)	De Vere Soc. Newsl., p. 4
2004	Sh. and the Scriptures [with E. Cottle], in *Great Oxford*, p. 159-68	
2007, Oct.	Rylance the Gladiator! Part 1: *I Am Shakespeare* – an appraisal of the Chichester meeting	De Vere Soc. Newsl., p. 5
2011, July	[review of *The Oxfordian Edition of Othello*]	De Vere So. New., v. 18/2: 35-36
2012, Nov.	[review of *The Shakespeare Guide to Italy*, by Richard Paul Roe]	De Vere So. New., v. 19/3: 15-17
2013, April	Oxford and the Italian Plays	De Vere Soc. Newsl., v. 20/1: 3-5
2014, May	DVS Mourns the Death of Brian Hicks	De Vere Soc. Newsl., vol. 21/2: 3
2015, April	[review of *Such Fruits Out of Italy* by Noemi Magri (2014)]	De Vere Soc. New., v. 22/1: 38-9
2017, April	Christopher Dams Remembers DVS . . .	De Vere Soc. Newsl., v. 24/2: 3-5

Danchin, F. C.

1929, April	[review of *Borrowers* by Percy Allen]	Rev. Ang-Am., v. 6/4: 360-61
1929, April	[review of *The Seventeenth Earl of Oxford* by B. M. Ward] [French]	Les Langues Modernes, vol. 2: 224-27

Daniel, Frank

1962, Oct. 21	New Books [review of *Shake-speare: The Man Behind the Name* by Dorothy Ogburn and Charlton Ogburn, Jr.]	Atlanta Journal-Const., p. 8L

Daniels, Joseph J.

1960, Jan.	[letter: resp. to Bentley	Am. Bar Assoc. J., vol. 46/1: 4

Danler, Hubert

2014, Spring	[letter: resp. to Frank Davis's Spring 2007 article "Leass for Making" Reply by Davis, Fall 2014, p. 3-4.	Sh. Ox. Newsl., vol. 50/2: 5-6

Danner, Bruce

Books

2011	*Edmund Spenser's War on Lord Burghley*. New York: Palgrave Macmillan.	

Shorter pieces

2011	"The Anonymous Shakespeare: Heresy, Authorship, and the Anxiety of Orthodoxy, in *Anonymity in Early Modern England: What's in a Name?* (Starner and Traister 2011): 143-158.	

Dantanus, Ulf

1993	Shakespeare: In Search of a Solid Life	Modera Sprak, vol. 87/1: 6

D'Artagnan, Robert [Randall Barron]
1995	*Against This Rage*. London: 1st Books Library.	
2001	*Oxford Summer: Shakespeare's Dark Lady Tells All*. London: 1st Books Library.	

Daugherty, Leo
2011, Fall	Gary Goldstein Interviews Leo Daugherty	Brief Chron., vol. III: 264-271

Davidoff, Henry
1948, Summer	Some Unusual Words in Shakespeare	SF Quarterly, vol. IX/2: 14-16

Davidson, John
1988, Nov. 27	Where There's a Will There's a Moot Point	Times (London), p. 3

Davidson, Elizabeth R.
1941, June	Unbelief in the Belief	SF News-letter (A), v. 2/4: 45-47
2021, Oct.	[review of *Hamlet* performed at the Theatre Royal, Windsor]	De Vere So. New., v. 28/4: 44-48

Davis, Elrick B.
1949, Oct. 9	Elizabethan Secret Agent [review of *Cloak of Folly* by Burke Boyce]	New York Herald, p. F4

Davis, Frank
2000	Shakespeare's Medical Knowledge: How Did He Acquire It?	Oxfordian, vol. 3: 45-58
2001, Summer	Her Warbling Sting - Music, Not Malady: Refuting Alan Nelson's Thesis on Nathaniel Baxter's 1606 poem [repr. in BTC, vol. 7: 326-31]	Sh. Ox. Newsl., vol. 37/2: 3-4
2002	Poem "Grief of Minde:" Who Wrote It and Why it Is Important	Oxfordian, vol. 5: 159-173
2002, Fall	Revisiting the Dating of *Twelfth Night* [repr. in BTC, vol. 9: 259-71]	Sh. Ox. Newsl., v. 38/4: 8-11, 24
2003, Autumn	President's Letter	Sh. Ox. Newsl., vol. 39/4: 2
2004, Spring	President's Letter	Sh. Ox. Newsl., vol. 40/2: 2
2005, Winter	Obituary: Eric Sams (1926-2004)	Sh. Ox. Newsl., vol. 41/1: 23
2006, Winter	William Shakspere, Oxford, Elizabethan Actors and Playhouses, I	Sh. Ox. Newsl., vol. 42/1: 3-4, 12
2006, Spring	Oxford and the First Blackfriars (Part II)	Sh. Ox. Newsl., vol. 42/2: 1, 5-6+
2007	[letter: ten great years of *The Oxfordian*]	Oxfordian, vol. 10: 166-166
2007, Winter	[letter: new option for Newsletter/Oxfordian writers]	Sh. Ox. Newsl., vol. 43/1: 12
2007, Spring	"Leass for Making": Shakespeare Outed as a Liar? [repr. in BTC, vol. 10: 213-17] Response by Hubert Danler, Spring 2014, p. 5-6. Reply by Davis, Fall 2014, p. 3-4.	Sh. Ox. Newsl., vol. 43/2: 3-5
2009	Greene's Groats-worth of Witte: Shakespeare's Biography? Response by Michael Marcus, 2010, p. 5.	Oxfordian, vol. 11: 137-156
2009, June	Relevance of Shakespeare's Signatures: a comparison of autographs [repr. in BTC, vol. 9: 272-82]	Sh. Ox. Newsl., vol. 45/1: 8-13
2009, Dec.	Rowe's Shakespeare Biography: Some Account of the Life of Mr. Shakespeare	Sh. Ox. Newsl., vol. 45/3: 18-20
2009, Dec.	[letter: Whalen's letter re spelling of Shakespeare's name]	Sh. Ox. Newsl., vol. 45/3: 28-29
2011	[letter: Marcus' 2010 response to his *Groatsworth* article]	Oxfordian, vol. 13: 4
2011	The Learned vs. the Unlearned Shakespeare	Oxfordian, vol. 13: 117-133
2013	Shakespeare's Six Accepted Signatures: A Comparison, in *Sh. Beyond Doubt?* (Shahan): 29-40	
2013	Doubter Response to Question #9: When did Shakespeare first appear on the literary scene?, in *Sh. Beyond Doubt?* (Shahan): 167-68	
2013	Doubter Response to Question #40: When did people start to question Sh.'s authorship of the *Works*?, in *Sh. Beyond Doubt?* (Shahan): 197-99	
2014, Fall	[letter: "Leass for Making;" comments from Hubert Danler in Austria]	Sh. Ox. Newsl., vol. 50/4: 3-4

Dawbarn, C. Y. C.
Books and pamphlets
1938	*Oxford and the Folio Plays. A Supplement*. [pamphlet: Repr. from *Baconiana* (Oct. 1938)]	

Shorter pieces
1938, Oct.	Oxford and the Folio Plays [reissued as a pamphlet]	Baconiana

Dawkins, Peter
2013	Doubter Response to Question #20: Why is it important that actor's names appear in some of the early printed texts of Sh's plays? in *Sh. Beyond Doubt?* (Shahan): 179-80	

Dawkins, Peter (continued)

2013	Doubter Response to Question #38: Does the memorial bust of Shakespere tell us anything about his profession? in *Sh. Beyond Doubt?* (Shahan): 195-96	
2013	Doubter Response to Question #39: What do we learn about Shakespere from Ben Jonson? in *Sh. Beyond Doubt?* (Shahan): 196-97	
2013	Doubter Response to Question #40: When did people start to question Shakespeare's authorship of the *Works*? in *Sh. Beyond Doubt?* (Shahan): p. 197-99	
2013	Doubter Response to Question #45: Is it plausible that Sir Francis Bacon wrote the plays attributed to Shakespeare? in *Sh. Beyond Doubt?* (Shahan): 205	

Dawson, Alexis

1970, Summer	Master Apis Lapis [repr. in BTC, vol. 5: 295-299]	Sh. Authorship Rev. #23: 5-9

Dawson, Anthony

2010, Jan. 19	And the Author is . . . [letter: the man from Stratford]	Globe & Mail, p. A16

Dawson, Giles E.

1950, Aug. 10	Who Wrote Shakespeare? Resp. by Philip Humphreys, *Baconiana*, Oct. 1950, p. 212-16. Resp. by Edward D. Johnson, *Baconiana*, Oct. 1950, p. 217+.	Listener, vol. 44: 195-96
1953, April	[review of *This Star of England* by Dorothy and Charlton Ogburn]	Sh. Quarterly, vol. 4/2: 165-70
1964, May 15	Into Round 401 [letter: resp. to Charlton Ogburn's challenge] Reply by Charlton Ogburn, May 27, p. A24.	Washington Post
1964, June 9	"Will-o'-the-Wisp" [letter: resp. to Ogburn re portraits of Oxford and Shakespeare]	Washington Post, p. A14

Dawson, Jon

2012	[review of *Anonymous*, directed by Roland Emmerich (2011)]	Groats. of Wit, v. 23/1: 17-20

Dawson, Paul

2009, April 25	[letter: Bravin's article on Justice Stevens]	Wall St. Journal, p. A10

Dawtrey, John

1927	*The Falstaff Saga* [pamphlet].	

Day, Stephen

2002, Feb. 24	Shakespeare By Committee [letter: response to Niederkorn]	New York Times, p. A&L: E6

Deacon, William

1956, Jan.	Shakespeare's Identity [reviews of *Who Was Shakespeare?* by Hilda Amphlett and *Shakespeare Unmaksed* by Pierre S. Porohovshikov]	Globe & Mail, p. 28

Dean, Lisa Ochrl

2014, Summer	[letter: Peter E. Michaels and the Ashbourne portrait] Response by Barbara Burris, Summer 2014, p. 4-5.	Sh. Ox. Newsl., vol. 50/3: 3-4

Dean, Paul

2013, Nov.	What's in a Name?	New Criterion, vol. 32/3: 66

De Castro, Mariana Gray

2009, Summer	Fernando Pessoa and the "Shakespeare Problem"	J. Romance St., vol. 9/2: 11+

De Chambrun, Clara Longworth

1949, June 25	Was Shakespeare Really Shakespeare? [letter] [repr. in *Sh. and His Rivals* (McMichael & Glenn 1962): 178-85]	Sat. Review, p. 27-28

Decker, Bill

2005, Sept. 19	Two Truths Are Told: Ruth Miller and the Shakespeare Debate	Daily Advertiser, p. A4

Dederer, Claire

2003, June 15	Will the Real Bard Please Stand Up?	Seattle Times, p. L10

Deer, Terry

2021, Summer	From the Data Preservation Committee: Abstracts and Grief Chronicles [with Renee Euchner]	Sh. Ox. Newsl., vol. 57/3: 21-22
2021, Fall	Tales from the Archives: The Drayton Collection; History of The Evered Foundation [with R. Euchner, K. Sharpe & B. Boyle]	Sh. Ox. Newsl., vol. 57/4: 29-32

Delahoyde, Michael (continued)

2023, Sept.   Shakespeare's First Draft of Richard III [review of *The True Tragedy*   Oxfordian, vol. 25: 299-303
    of Richard the Third by Ramon Jiménez]

Delatte, F.

1928, Oct.   [review of *Borrowers* by Percy Allen]   *Revue Belge de Philologie et*
    d'Historie, vol. 7/3: 1099+

1929, Jan.   [review of *Topical* by Percy Allen]   *Revue Belge de Philologie et*
    d'Historie, vol. 8/4: 1255-57

Dellinger, J. Howard [J. H. D.]

1961, Spring   An 1899 Identification of Shakespeare   Sh. Authorship Review, #5: 1-2

1961, Autumn   Obituary: Professor Louis P. Bénézet (1878-1961)   Sh. Authorship Review, #6: 23
    [repr. in BTC, vol. 5: 80]

Dellinger, Royal S.

2009, April 25   [letter: Bravin's article on Justice Stevens]   Wall St. Journal, p. A10

De Luna, B. N.

1970   *The Queen Declined: An Interpretation of Willobie His Avisa, with the Text of the Original Edition*. Oxford:
    Clarendon Press.

Demaline, Jackie

2002, May 17   In Search of the Real Shakespeare [review of *The Bard of Avon* by   Cincinnati Enq., p. W12
    Amy Freed]

Demant, Rev. Canon V. A. [Chancellor of St. Paul's Cathedral]

1946, Sept.   Personal Recollections of the Late J. T. Looney]

1962, Autumn   John Thomas Looney (1870-1944)   Sh. Authorship Review, #8: 8-9
    [repr. in vol. 46/1: 21 (May 2010); in BTC, vol. 1: 214-217
    and vol. 5: 92-94; and in NSJ, vol. NS1: 37-39 (Nov. 2010)]

Deming, Leonard (Len)

1992, Spring   Iona Deletes Oxford p. from *The Shakespeare Newsletter*   Sh. Ox. Newsl., vol. 28/2: 6

1996, Winter   Invalid Logic and the Slippery Stratfordian   Ever Reader, vol. 2
    [from a presentation given at the SOS conference in Nov. 1993]

De Moret, Nicholas

1987, Winter   Edward de Vere's Tour of Italy in 1575-76 Included Visit to Court   Sh. Ox. Newsl., vol. 23/1: 11-14
    of the Duke of Urbino

DeMott, Benjamin

1970, Nov. 7   Will the Real Shakespeare Please Stand Up? [reviews of recent books]   Saturday Review, p. 31-35+
    [review is quoted in TMWS, p. 378]

Dempsey, Jim

1990, May 21   High Tech Boost for Bard of Avon   Telegram & Gazette, p. D1

Dempster, Nigel

1987, July 3   They're Veering to Vere [Lord Vere]   Daily Mail, p. 19

Denby, David

2011, Oct. 31   All That Glitters [review of *Anonymous*]   New Yorker, 2011, Oct. 31

Dent, Nick

2011, Nov. 13   A Brilliant Play on History [review of *Anonymous*]   Sunday Telegraph, p. 131

Derrickson, Howard

1953   [review of *This Star* by Dorothy and Charlton Ogburn]   St. Louis Post Disp.
    [response by Thomas C. Hennings, May 3]

Des Cognets, Russell

1987, Winter   A Message to *Shakespeare Newsletter* Readers   Sh. Newsl., vol. 37/4: 52

1991, Summer   Stonewalling!   Sh. Ox. Newsl., vol. 27/3: 5

Desper, Richard

Plays

1992   *Star-Crossed Lovers: A Play in Three Acts*. Acton, MA: Published by the Author.

Shorter pieces

1992, Spring   Suns or Stars   Sh. Ox. Newsl., vol. 28/2: 3-4

1993, Fall   The Writing of an Oxfordian Play   Sh. Ox. Newsl., vol. 29/4:

Destro, Ron
Books

Shorter pieces

Detobel, Joseph

Detobel, Robert
Books

Periodicals edited
Shorter pieces

Detobel, Robert (continued)

1998, June	Ist E. L. Oxon identisch mit Edward de Vere? III	Neues Sh. Journal, vol. 2: 144-45
1999, Jan.	Über Shakespeares Authentizität und Tod	Neues Sh. Journal, vol. 3: 26-40
1999, Jan.	Neue Spuren zu Shakespeare	Neues Sh. Journal, vol. 3: 110-50
1999, July	Eine Widmung	Neues Sh. Journal, vol. 4: 72-116
2000, April	Edward de Veres Reiseroute	Neues Sh. Journal, vol. 5: 54-62
2000, April	Shylocks Geheimnis	Neues Sh. Journal, vol. 5: 88-108
2001	Authorial Rights in Shakespeare's Time	Oxfordian, vol. 4: 5-24
2001, Apr./May	Melicertus [repr. in GO, p. 223-236]	De Vere Soc. Newsl., p. 15-26
2001, May	Der 22. Juli 1598: Ein Tag in der Geschichte der Stationers' Company	Neues Sh. Journal, vol. 6: 10-66
2001, May	A. W. Pollard zu Shakespeares Kampf mit den Piraten und den eigenen Ahnungen	Neues Sh. Journal, vol. 6: 67-97
2001, May	Der verliebte Pilger und England's Helicon	Neues Sh. Journal, vol. 6: 108-19
2001, May	Othello als postdeparodierte Präparodie	Neues Sh. Journal, vol. 6: 132-39
2002	Authorial Rights, Part II: early Shakespeare critics and the Shakespeare authorship question [Part I does not discuss Shakespeare]	Oxfordian, vol. 5: 30-46
2002, Jan./Feb.	Portia and Shylock: Just Mercy Against the Law of the Talion?	De Vere Soc. Newsl., p. 9-13
2002, April	[letter: the Lord Chamberlain and the control of the stage]	De Vere Soc. Newsl., p. 36-48
2002, May	Ein historisches Vorbild für Shylock?	Neues Sh. Journal, vol. 7: 125-30
2003, Aug.	Die Veröffentlichung von Sidney's Astrophel und Stella und die Gedichte von "Content"	Neues Sh. Journal, vol. 8: 110-13
2003, Aug.	Postskriptum zu Porohovshikov	Neues Sh. Journal, vol. 8: 126-27
2003, Aug.	Emaricdulfe	Neues Sh. Journal, vol. 8: 156-63
2003, Aug.	[review of Monstrous Adversary by Alan H. Nelson (2003)]	Neues Sh. Journal, vol. 8: 169-72
2004	To Be or Not to Be: The Suicide Hypothesis [repr. in German in NSJ, vol. 9: 83-144 (June 2004)]	Oxfordian, vol. 7: 69-88
2004, Spring	The Testimony of Ben Jonson in Redating The Tempest, Othello, and Timon of Athens [also in DVN (2004 Spring), p. 1]	Sh. Ox. Newsl., v. 40/2: 1, 13-18
2004, June	Schweigen und Sub-Versionen in der höfischen Öffentlichkeit	Neues Sh. Journal, vol. 9: 20-47
2005, Fall	Falstaff in the Low Countries	Sh. Matters, vol. 5/1: 4, 7, 11+
2007, April	1605 – Ben Jonson im Jahr danach	Neues Sh. Journal, vol. 11: 24-44
2007, April	Chronologie des Literaturstreits zwischen Gabriel Harvey und Thomas Nashe / Die hohe Kunst des Wegsehens	Neues Sh. Journal, vol. 11: 45-59
2008, March	Captain Tucca, Captain Hannam, and Falstaff	De Vere So. New., v. 15/1: 20-22
2008, June	An Accident of Note: Chapman and Oxford in Revenge of Bussy d'Amboise? Part 1	De Vere So. New., v. 15/2: 22-26
2008, Oct.	An Accident of Note: Chapman and Oxford in Revenge of Bussy d'Amboise? Part 2	De Vere So. New., v. 15/3: 10-18
2008, Oct.	Unsent Letter [to Peter Moore]	Neues Sh. Journal, vol. 12: 55-83
2008, Oct.	Bill Bryson tanzt in der Reihe	Neues Sh. Journal, v. 12: 116-17
2008, Oct.	Mireille Huchon tanzt aus der Reihe	Neues Sh. Journal, v. 12: 118-28
2008, Oct.	[review of 1599: A Year in the Life of W. Shakespeare by J. Shapiro]	Neues Sh. Journal, v. 12: 140-42
2008, Oct.	[review of Edmund Spenser's "Die Lilienhand" [Übersetzt von Alexander Nitzberg]	Neues Sh. Journal, v. 12: 146-47
2009	Francis Meres and the Earl of Oxford [with K. C. Ligon]	Brief Chron., vol. I: 97-108
2009, Feb.	An Accident of Note: Chapman and Oxford in Revenge of Bussy d'Amboise? Part 3	De Vere So. New., v. 16/1: 15-20
2009, Fall	News: Kreiler in Der Spiegel	Sh. Matters, vol. 8/4: 18
2010	An Accident of Note: Chapman's Hamlet and the Earl of Oxford	Brief Chron., vol. II: 79-107
2010, Nov.	In Memoriam: Joseph Sobran (1946-2010)	Neues Sh. J., vol. NS1: 160-1
2010, Nov.	In Memoriam: K. C. Ligon (1949-2009)	Neues Sh. J., vol. NS1: 161-2
2010, Nov.	In Memoriam: Robert Brazil (1995-2010)	Neues Sh. J., vol. NS1: 163-4
2011, July	An Irreparable Loss: Tributes to Noemi Magri (d. 2011) [with Elizabeth Imlay and Kevin Gilvary]	De Vere So. New., v. 18/2: 22-24
2011, Oct.	Die Prinz-Tudor-Hypothesen - Gesichte statt Geschichte: 1) Die Prinz-Tudor-Apologeten und ihre Hauptkritiker Diana Price und Roger Parisious; 2) Christopher Paul über Paul Streitz	Neues Sh. J., v. NS2: 41-56
2011, Oct.	Kleist und Shakespeare Gedanken zu einem Bericht über eine Tagung	Neues Sh. J., v. NS2: 108-23

Dickson, Peter W.

Books

2011	*Bardgate: Shake-speare and the Royalists Who Stole the Bard*. Mount Vernon, OH: Printing Arts Press.
2016	*Bardgate II: Shakespeare, Catholicism and the Politics of the First Folio of 1623*. Mount Vernon, OH: Arts Press Printing.

Shorter pieces

1997, Aug. 17	[reviews of *Alias Shakespeare* by Joseph Sobran (1997); *Shakespeare – Who Was He?* by Richard F. Whalen (1994; and *Who Wrote Shakespeare?* by John Michell (1996)]	Washington Post, p. 11
1997, Oct. 1	Unmasking Shakespeare	News and Observer
1998, Spring	Washington Researcher Offers New Theory on Folio Publication and the Authorship issue [with William E. Boyle]	Sh. Ox. Newsl., vol. 34/1: 2, 22
1998, Autumn	Henry Peacham and the 1623 *First Folio*	Eliz. Review, vol. 6/2: 55-76
1998, Fall	Henry Peacham on Oxford and Shakespeare [repr. in EVR, vol. 7 (Fall 1998)] Response by John Rollett, vol. 34/4: 21. Response by Noemi Magri, vol. 35/1: 21-22. Response by Derran Charlton, vol. 35/2: 27.	Sh. Ox. Newsl., vol. 34/3: 1, 8-13
1999, Feb. 6	[letter: reply to Fran Conner's Jan. 30 letter] Response to Dickson by Jack Gonzales, Feb. 20, p. A17.	Washington Post, p. A19
1998, Fall	Oxford's Literary Reputation in the 17th and 18th Centuries [repr. in EVR, vol. 7 (Fall 1998)]	Sh. Ox. Newsl., vol. 34/3: 14-15
1999, Winter	The Jaggard-Herbert-De Vere Connections (1619-1623)	Sh. Ox. Newsl., vol. 34/4: 14-15+
1999, Spring	Are British Scholars Erasing Two Heroic Earls From Jacobean History to Protect the Shakespeare Industry? [repr. in EVR, vol. 8 (Spr. 1999)]	Sh. Ox. Newsl., vol. 35/1: 8-9, 24
1999, Spring	So Many Biographies, So Few Henries	Sh. Ox. Newsl., vol. 35/1: 9
1999, Summer	Bacon Begs the Two Henries as *First Folio* Appears	Sh. Ox. Newsl., vol. 35/2: 7, 28
1999, Fall	1622 *Othello* Cracks a Frozen Shakespeare Market	Sh. Ox. Newsl., v. 35/3: 15, 23+
1999, Fall	Was the *Troilus and Cressida* Preface Written in 1602-1603?	Sh. Ox. Newsl., vol. 35/3: 19
1999, Sept. 12	Expert's Picks	Washington Post, p. P7
2000, Summer	An Emerging "Crypto-Catholic" Theory Challenges Stratfordians	Sh. Ox. Newsl., vol. 36/2: 1, 6-8
2000, Summer	[letter: exchange of letters with John Andrews on the Catholic issue]	Sh. Ox. Newsl., vol. 36/2: 7
2001, Winter	Flood of Shakespeare Biographies Since the Ogburn & Honigmann works in 1984-85	Sh. Ox. Newsl., vol. 36/4: 6-7
2001, Winter	[letter: Mark Anderson's discovery of Edmund Bolton's biography]	Sh. Ox. Newsl., vol. 36/4: 24
2003	Bardgate: Was Shakespeare a Secret Catholic?	Oxfordian, vol. 6: 109-132
2003, Autumn	Michael Wood Lectures at the Smithsonian on a Catholic Shakespeare	Sh. Ox. Newsl., vol. 39/4: 7-8
2004, Feb. 16	The Roman Plays [review of Michael Wood's BBC Documentary *In Search of Shakespeare*]	Weekly Standard, p. 37
2004, Summer	[review of *The Age of Shakespeare* by Frank Kermode (2004)]	Sh. Ox. Newsl., vol. 40/3: 22-24
2004, Fall	Connecting the Dots: The Catholic Question and the Shakespeare Authorship Debate	Tennessee Law Review, vol. 72/1: 25-66
2005	[review of *Shadowplay: Hidden Beliefs and Coded Politics of William Shakespeare* by Clare Asquith (2005)]	Oxfordian, vol. 8: 128-136
2006	[review of *Sweet Swan of Avon* by Robin Williams (2006)]	Oxfordian, vol. 9: 132-135
2008, Fall	News: Folger Nabs *First Folio* Thief	Sh. Matters, vol. 7/4: 15
2011, Fall	[review of *The Assassination of Shakespeare's Patron* by Leo Daugherty (2011)]	Brief Chron., vol. III: 258-263
2016, Spring	Flawed British Documentary Film Confirms Tombgate [review of *Shakespeare's Tomb* (2016)]	Sh. Ox. Newsl., vol. 52/2: 19-22
2017, Winter	[review of *Shakespeare Unraveled—Court Plays: The 1623 Deception* by Pauline and Michael Black (2014)]	Sh. Ox. Newsl., vol. 53/1: 20-23
2021, Winter	Bardolatry and Oxford's Literary Reputation in the Seventeenth and Eighteenth Centuries	Sh. Ox. Newsl., vol. 57/1: 19-23
2021, Summer	The Shakespeare Statue in Westminster Abbey	Sh. Ox. Newsl., vol. 57/3: 19-20
2023, Summer	Did Jonson and Shakespeare Really Admire One Another?	Sh. Ox. Newsl., vol. 59/3: 12-15

Digby, Diehl

1997, March	[review of *Alias Shakespeare* by Joe Sobran (1997)]	Modern Maturity, v. 40/2: 28

Dillon, George
Plays
    2009   *The Man Who Was Hamlet.*
Shorter pieces
    2008, Oct.   Swordplay   De Vere Soc. New., v. 15/3: 20-1

DiMatteo, Anthony
    2005, Dec.   [review of *"Shakespeare" by Another Name* by Mark Anderson]   Choice, vol. 43/4: 565

Dirda, Michael
    2023, April 21   As We Honor Shakespeare, Scholars Respond to Questions About Him   Washington Post

Disraeli, Isaac
    1823   *Curiosities of Literature: Consisting of Anecdotes, Characters, Sketches*   London: J. Murray.
        [See esp. "The Secret History of Edward de Vere, Earl of Oxford"]
    1827   *Venetia*. London: H. Colburn.

District Court of the United States for the District of Columbia
    1948   Charles Wisner Barrell, Plaintiff v. Giles E. Dawson, Defendant: Action
        for Damages for Libel. [Civil Action No. 2698-48, filed July 1]

Dixon, Jonathan
    2000, Spring   The Upstart Crow Supposes   Sh. Ox. Newsl., vol. 36/1: 7
        Response by Roger Stritmatter, Summer 2000, p. 21.
        Response by Robert Gruman, Fall 2000, p. 22.
    2001, Winter   [letter: "Supposes" and *Greene's Groatsworth of Wit*]   Sh. Ox. Newsl., vol. 36/4: 24
    2002, Summer   [letter: Gabriel Harvey and *Greene's Groatsworth of Wit*]   Sh. Matters, vol. 1/4: 3
    2004   Determining the Identity of the Bard: William Shaksper or the   Renaiss. Mag., vol. 9/1: 54-59
        Earl of Oxford?
        Resp. by Robert Nott, in *Santa Fe New Mexican*, April 30, p. 30.
    2005, Winter   While Counterfeit Supposes Bleared Thine Eyne: Shakespeare   Sh. Matters, vol. 4/2: 12-18
        as authorship front man

Dixon-Scott, J.
    1930, Nov. 25   A Suffolk Tudor Village – Lavenham's Wattle Walls &   Telegraph, p. 14
        Lovely Tudor Lavenham

Dobbs, Anne
    2002, Winter   Film Review: *Much Ado About Something* Explores Marlowe's Case   Sh. Ox. Newsl., vol. 38/1: 20

Dobrowolski, Jacek
    2011   Szekspir to nie tylko Marlowe [Shakespeare Is Not Only Marlowe]   Teatr [Polish], vol. 4

Dobson, Michael
    2010, March 10   Play Rights: A Shakespeare Scholar Definitively Debunks the So-   Financial Times, p. 16
        called Authorship Controversy [review of *Contested Will* by
        James Shapiro] [calls J. Thomas Looney "a preacher in a cranky,
        proto-fascist sect in Newcastle"]

Dockrell, Cynthia
    1999, April 7   Bard Brawl   Boston Globe, p. D3

Dodd, Alfred
    1947   *Who Was Shake-speare? Was He Francis Bacon, the Earl of Oxford, or William Shaksper?* London:
        G. Lapworth & Co. [reprint of an address given in Stratford during a three day discussion
        (May 20-22, 1947), the chief protagonists being Percy Allen and Alfred Dodd.]

Dodge, Arthur J.
    1933, Aug. 6   The Shakespeare "Mystery"   Washington Post, p. 6
    1933, Oct. 31   More of the Shakespeare "Mystery" – Claim that Edward de Vere   Washington Post, p. 6
        was Author of Plays [letter]

Dominik, Mark
    1992, Winter   The Authorship of *The Birth of Merlin*   Sh. Newsl., vol. 42/4: 53

Domnarsk, William
    1993, Aug.   Shakespeare in the Law [repr. in SON, vol. 30/1: 4 (Winter 1994)]   Conn. Bar J. vol. 67/4

Donalbain
    1923, March 1   Shakespeare and "Fat" [letter]   Bulletin, vol. 44: 3

Donnell, Evans
   2018, Oct.   Shakespeare's Secrets [rev. of *Shakespeare's Secrets* by A. Tatum]   De Vere Soc. New., v. 25/4: 45-7

Donoghue, Denis
   2016, April   The Jacobean Dramatist   New Criterion, v. 24/6: 23-27

Dooley, J. and E.
   1954, Sept.   [letter: translations of the couplet that heads *Venus and Adonis*]   SF News-letter (E), p. 11

Doran, D'Arcy
   2007, Sept. 10   Coalition Aims to Expose Playwright. Derek Jacobi and Mark Rylance Unveil Declaration of Reasonable Doubt.   Charleston Daily Mail, p. 3A
   2007, Sept. 18   Coalition Resurrects Doubts About Bard's Identity   Chicago Tribune, p. 8
   2007, Oct. 2   Et Tu, Shakespeare?   Orlando Sen., p. E13

Doran, Gregory
   2001, Jan.   Unhappy Ever After: Preview of *All's Well That Ends Well*   De Vere Soc. Newsl., p. 26-27

Dorbin, Jerry
   1999, July 1   [letter: the April 1 special "authorship" issue]   Harper's Mag., vol. 299: 6-11

Dorian, Bill
Plays
   2001   *A Rose By Any Other Name*. [a play]
Shorter pieces
   2011, Spring   [letter: *A Rose By Any Other Name* and other authorship issues]   Sh. Ox. Newsl., vol. 47/2: 2-3

Dorschel, Andreas
   2007, April   [review of *Will in der Welt* by Stephen Greenblatt]   Neues Sh. Journal, v. 11: 172-74

Dorward, Lisa L.
   2009   *Whose Worth's Unknown: The Life of Edward de Vere, the Man Who Was Shakespeare: A Novel*. Thesis submitted to Eberly College of Arts. West Virginia University.

Douglas, Lt. Col. Montagu W., C. S. I., C I. E.
Books
   1931   *The Earl of Oxford as "Shakespeare:" An Outline of the Case*. Foreword by Canon Gerald H. Rendall. London: Cecil Palmer.
   1934   *Lord Oxford was "Shakespeare": A Summing Up*. Foreword by Gerald H. Rendall. 2nd edition of *The Earl of Oxford as "Shakespeare."* London: Rich & Cowan, Ltd. [Foreword repr. in SHP, no. 95, 1935; and in BTC, vol. 2: 29-31]
   1952   *Lord Oxford and the Shakespeare Group: A Summary of Evidence Presented by J. T. Looney. Gerald H. Rendall and Gilbert Slater*. Introduction by Gerald H. Rendall. 3rd edition, with additional evidence and amendments. Oxford: Alden Press. [Preface repr. in BTC, vol. 4: 223-224]
Shorter pieces
   1923, March   The Mystery of Mr. W. H.   Royal Engineers' J., p. 154-56
   1923, March 23   The Mystery of Mr. W. H., I [review of the book by Col. B. R. Ward]   Hackney Spectator, p. 8
   1923, March 28   The Mystery of Mr. W. H., II [review of the book by Col. B. R. Ward]   Hackney Spectator, p. 2
   1923, April 27   A Review of Reviews   Hackney Spectator, p. 2
   1923, May 18   The Great Unknown   Hackney Spectator, p. 2
   1923, Oct. 26   *Lee, Shakespeare and Tertium* Quid [review of Greenwood's book]   Hackney Spectator, p. 4
   1924, April 11   The Problem of *Hamlet*   Hackney Spectator, p. 11
   1924, April 25   The Date of *Hamlet*, I   Hackney Spectator, p. 11
   1924, May 9   The Date of *Hamlet*, II   Hackney Spectator, p. 11
   1924, May 16   The Date of *Hamlet*, III   Hackney Spectator, p. 5
   1924, June 20   An Omitted Speech in the First Folio   Hackney Spectator, p. 11
   1924, June 27   Recent Research   Hackney Spectator, p. 2
   1924, Sept. 19   Who was the Sentinel Francisco?   Hackney Spectator, p. 4
   1924, Oct. 17   *Shakespeare's Signatures and "Sir Thomas More,"* I [review of the book by Sir George Greenwood]   Hackney Spectator, p. 4
   1924, Nov. 7   *Shakespeare's Signatures and "Sir Thomas More,"* II [review of the book by Sir George Greenwood]   Hackney Spectator, p. 4
   1925, Jan. 16   *Venus and Adonis* and *Lucrece*: The Case for Bacon and Oxford, I   Hackney Spectator, p. 2
   1925, Jan. 23   *Venus and Adonis* and *Lucrece*: The Case for Bacon and Oxford, II   Hackney Spectator, p. 5
   1925, Jan. 30   *Venus and Adonis* and *Lucrece*: The Case for Bacon and Oxford, III   Hackney Spectator, p. 5
   1925, Feb. 6   *Venus and Adonis* and *Lucrece*: The Case for Bacon and Oxford, IV   Hackney Spectator, p. 5

Dowden, Edward

Dowden, Hester

Dowdey, David

Downs, Gerald E.

Downs, Jerry

Drake, Sylvie
    1992, May 25   Questions Abound in 'Oxford' [review of *Oxford's Will*, a play by   Los Angeles Times, p. SDF8
                  Jerry Fey]

Draper, John W.
    1932, Oct.   Sir John Falstaff [See response in *Shakespeare Pictorial*, Jan. 1933]   Rev. Eng. St., vol. 8/32: 414-24

Draper, Norman
    1996, Oct. 9   'Twixt Much Ado, Group Brings Shakespeare Theories to Twin   Minneapolis Star Trib., p. 1A
                  Cities [Charles Burford/Charles Vere Tour]

Draya, Ren
Books edited with Richard F. Whalen
    2010   *Othello the Moor of Venice by William Shakespeare*. The Oxfordian Shakespeare Series, fully annotated
                  from an Oxfordian perspective. Truro, MA: Llumina Press.
                  [excerpt, "The Music in Othello," repr. in BTC, vol. 9: 321-28]
Shorter pieces
    1999, Spring   Shakespeare's *King John*: A Story of Rightful Identity and Eyes to See   Sh. Ox. Newsl., v. 35/1: 1, 13-15
    2005, Summer   Sixteenth-Century Letter Writing and Its Importance to Oxfordians   Sh. Ox. Newsl., v. 41/3: 3, 10-11
    2006, Spring   *Antony and Cleopatra*: The Women's Voices [repr. in DS, p. 23-28]   Sh. Ox. Newsl., vol. 42/2: 22-25
    2006, Spring   Oxford's Outsiders   Sh. Matters, vol. 5/3: 7-9
                  Response by David P. Gontar, Summer 2006, p. 2.
    2006, Fall   Notes from the Field   Sh. Ox. Newsl., vol. 42/3: 30
    2008, Fall   Edward de Vere's Hand in *Titus Andronicus*: The Play as Primer   Sh. Matters, vol. 7/4: 1-2, 18+
    2009, Summer   Song in Shakespeare's Plays   Sh. Matters, vol. 8/3: 1, 12-15
    2010, May 7   [letter: Charles Nicholl's April 23 review of *Contested Will*]   Times Literary Sup., p. A6
    2011, Fall   Singer and Song: the music in *Twelfth Night*   Sh. Ox. Newsl., v. 47/3: 1, 17-23
    2011, Fall   [letter: Elizabeth I: facts not fantasy] [with Elizabeth Imlay and   Sh. Ox. Newsl., vol. 47/3: 2
                  Stephanie Hopkins Hughes]
    2012-2013   [review of *The Man Who Was Never Shakespeare* by A. J. Pointon]   Brief Chronicles, vol. IV: 135-36
    2013   Doubter Response to Question #48: Why did Henry James doubt
                  Shakespeare's authorship? In SBD? (Shahan): 207-08
    2017, Fall   A New *Shrew* [review of a performance in Chicago of *Shrew*]   Sh. Ox. Newsl., vol. 53/4: 35
    2018, Winter   The Three Queens of *Hamlet*   Sh. Ox. Newsl., vol. 54/1: 32-36
    2022, Spring   Eric Flint's *1632* Mentions Edward de Vere as Shakespeare   Sh. Ox. Newsl., vol. 58/2: 6

Drayton, D. Charles
    1956, April 1   De Vere Theory [letter, with Ch. Ogburn and R. H. Montgomery]   NY Herald Tribune., p. A4
    1956, May   To the Editor and Readers of *The Shakespeare Newsletter*   Sh. Newsletter, vol. 6/3: 18
                  [letter, with 21 other signers]

Dressler, Leslie Anne
    1987, Winter   Was There a Likeness Used for the *First Folio* Portrait?   Sh. Ox. Newsletter, vol. 23/1: 8-9

Drew, Philip
    1953, Nov.   [review of *Lord Oxford and the Shakespeare Group* by Douglas]   SF News-letter (E), p. 2

Drinkwater, John
Books
    1933   *Shakespeare*. London: Duckworth.
Shorter pieces
    1931, April 30   The Immortal Memory   Stage, p. 15

Dromgoole, Dominic
    2010   Interview with William Leahy, in *Sh. and His Authors* (Leahy): 150-57

Drumbolis, Nick
    2003   *The Pseudonym William Shakespeare*. Toronto: Letters Bookshop.

Drusiana, April
    2021, Jan.   [review of *Contested Will* by James Shapiro (2010)]   De Vere So. New., v. 28/1: 26-45

Duckworth-Barker, V.
    1971, Autumn   [letter: lines of research the Society might undertake]   Sh. Authorship Rev., #25: 18-19

Dudley, Colin
    2014, Jan.   [letter: early German member of Royal Court not allowed to publish]   De Vere Soc. Newsl., v. 21/1: 17

Dunn, Michael
    2006, Winter   Dethroning a Deity   Sh. Matters, vol. 5/2: 6-9, 22

Dunne, Stephen
    2001, Oct. 8   Even a Conspiracy Theory Isn't Enough [review of *Shakespeare,*   Sydney Morning Herald, p. 20
                       A Play about the Life of Edward de Vere by Graham Jones
                       & Jepke Goudsmit]

Durgin, Cyrus
    1953, Oct. 25   Were the Shakespearean Plays Written by Earl of Oxford?   Boston Globe, p. A55

Durkee, Lee
    2023   *Stalking Shakespeare: A Memoir of Madness, Murder, and My Search for the Poet Beneath the Paint*. New
                  York: Scribner.

Dutton, Richard
Books
    2016   *Shakespeare, Court Dramatist*. Oxford: Oxford University Press.
Shorter pieces
    1987   [review of *Edward de Vere and the War of Words*   Shake. Survey, vol. 39: 223-36
                      by Elizabeth Appleton (1985)]

Dwyer, J. J.
Periodicals edited
    1946, March-1947, March: *Shakespeare Fellowship News-letter (English)*
Shorter pieces
    1939, April   Had Shakespeare Read Dante?   SF News-letter (E), no. 14: 1-7
    1941, April   Fabian and Sebastian   SF News-letter (E), p. 3
    1941, April   Patines of Bright Gold   SF News-letter (E), p. 3
    1941, June   Shakespeare Had Read Dante: p.t Toynbee's reasoning fallacious   SF News-letter (A), vol. 2/4: 51-
                     52
    1941, Dec.   [letter: excerpts reprinted]   SF News-letter (A), vol. 3/1: 8
    1942, April   The Vere Motto   SF News-letter (E), p. 3
    1942, Oct.   Comment on *Elizabethan Commentary* by Hilaire Belloc   SF News-letter (E), p. 3
    1942, Dec.   [letter: excerpts reprinted]   SF News-letter (A), vol. 4/1: 11
    1943, Feb.   A Note on *Pericles*   SF News-letter (A), vol. 4/2: 23-
                     24
    1943, Oct.   A Note on the Authorship of Lucrece   SF News-letter (E), p. 3-4
    1944, April   Elizabethan Outlook: a restatement   SF Quarterly, vol. V/2: 28-29
    1944, May   Elizabethan Miniatures   SF News-letter (E), p. 5-6
    1945, May   [review of *Shakespeare's History Plays* by E. M. W. Tillyard (1944)]   SF News-letter (E), p. 3
    1946, Jan.   Italian Art in Poems and Plays of Shakespeare [a paper read before
                     the SF in Jan. 1946], in *Building the Case*, vol. 4: 254-69
    1946, Sept.   [review of *A La Decouverte de Shakespeare* by Abel Lefranc (1945)]   SF News-letter (E), p. 4-5
    1946, Sept.   Shakespeare and Politics   SF News-letter (E), p. 5
    1947, March   Queen Elizabeth and Her Turk [repr. in BTC, vol. 4, p. 106]   SF News-letter (E), p. 5
    1947, March   The Portraits of Shakespeare [repr. in BTC, vol. 4, 107-08]   SF News-letter (E), p. 6
    1947, Summer   The Poet Earl of Oxford and Grays Inn [repr. in BTC, vol. 3: 258-68]   SF Quarterly, vol. VIII/2: 21-25
    1955, June 9   Did Shakespeare Read Dante? A Comparative Enquiry   Tablet, vol. 206: 33-34

Dyer, Allen R.
    2020, Dec.   Does It Matter That Freud Thought Sh. was the Earl of Oxford?   Intl J. of APS, vol. 17/4: 369+

E. S.
    1936, Aug.   [letter: "There is not one valid argument in Ernest Allen's article"]   Sh. Pictorial, no. 102: 128
                     Response by Ernest Allen, Sept., p. 136.
    1938, June   Secrets of the Sonnets [review of *The Sonnets of W. Shakespeare*   Sh. Pictorial, no. 124: 91
                     and Henry Wriothesley edited by Walter Thomson (1938)]

Eagan-Donovan, Cheryl A.
Documentaries
    2018   *Nothing Is Truer Than Truth*. [released in the UK in 2022 as *Shakespeare: The Man Behind the Name*]
Shorter pieces
    2009, Sept.   Update on Eagan-Donovan Film Project   Sh. Ox. Newsl., vol. 45/2: 30-31
    2011, Fall   [review of *Anonymous* [a film directed by Roland Emmerich (2011)]   Sh. Ox. Newsl., vol. 47/3: 11-13
    2012, Fall   [letter: Strategic PR plan]   Sh. Matters, vol. 11/4: 2

2015, Spring	Cheryl Eagan-Donovan Responds [to Howard Schumann's review of *Nothing Truer Than Truth*]	Sh. Ox. Newsl., vol. 51/2: 26-27
2022, Summer	Does the 17th Earl of Oxford "lieth buried in Westminster"? [with Bonner Miller Cutting]	Sh. Ox. Newsl., v. 58/3: 1, 18-21
2023, Spring	[letter, with Bonner Miller Cutting: reply to Christopher Paul]	Sh. Ox. Newsl., vol. 59/2: 5
2023, Sept.	Henslowe, Alleyn, Burbage & Shakespeare: Staging the Myth	Oxfordian, vol. 25: 87-108

Eagle, Roderick L.

Books

1930	*Shakespeare: New Views for Old*. London: Cecil Palmer. Repr. in 1943: New York: Rider & So. [Preface repr. in BTC, vol. 1: 153-159]	

Shorter pieces

1920, April 16	Shakespeare Identified [letter: response to M's review of *SI*]	Athenaeum, p. 521
1921, March,	[review of *Shakespeare's Handwriting* by George Greenwood]	Baconiana, vol. XVI/63: 82
1921, March	Shakespeare and the Earl of Oxford [review of SI]	Baconiana, V. XVI/63: 82-85
1922, June	Orage [letter]	Baconiana, vol. XVII/64: 87-8
1923, June	[review of *Baconian Essay* by Smithson and George Greenwood]	Baconiana., V. XVII65: 149-50
1924, March	The Great Shakespeare Find	Baconiana, V. XVII/66: 180-2
1926, April 15	Francis Bacon: The Plays of Shakespeare [letter]	Morning Post, p. 43
1929, May 18	Authorship of the Sonnets and Their Publications Response by Percy Allen, June 5.	Telegraph
1937, March	Heminge and Condell [letter]	Sh. Pictorial, no. 109: 36
1942, Feb. 28	El-Dorado-on-Avon [See comment "Stratford Relics" in SFA, vol. 4/3: 38 (April 1943)]	Everybody's, p. 6
1943, Aug. 26	Shakespearean Signatures [letter]	Telegraph
1943, Aug. 28	Shakespeare's Hand [letter]	Telegraph
1951, May 11	The Personality of Shakespeare [letter]	Truth, p. 508
1951, July-Aug.	Shakespeare or Bacon—or Oxford [section II. Francis Bacon]	Open Forum, vol. 1/1: 52-56
1953, Nov.	Was Shakspere Illiterate?	SF News-letter (E), p. 6-8
1964, Oct.	Literary Concealments	Baconiana, vol. 47: 65

Eagle, Solomon [see John Collings Squire]

Eagleton, Terry

1970, Oct. 30	Books: From Postcard-length Data, a Wealth of Images and Legends	Commonweal, p. 129-31
1988, Dec. 15	[review of *The Mysterious William Shakespeare* by Ch. Ogburn, Jr.]	Listener, p. 33
1991, Nov. 6	The Anon of Avon [review of *William Shakespeare: A Life* by Garry O'Connor (1991)] [repr. in SON, vol. 27/4: 2-3 (Fall 1991); and in BTC, vol. 7: 72-73]	Independent
2004, March 1	Company Man [rev. of *The Age of Shakespeare* by Frank Kermode]	Nation, p. 29-32
2004, Nov. 15	The Stratford Man [rev. of *Will in the World* by Stephen Greenblatt]	New Statesman, p. 48

Earle, Peter G.

1947, June 22	De Vere's Poetry [letter: Burgess's June 8 article]	NY Herald Tribune, p. A7

Eccles, Mark

1934, Feb. 15	The 'Mortal Moon' Sonnet [letter]	Times Lit. Sup., is. 1672: 108

Edblom, Richard W.

1992, Jan.	[letter: the special issue on Shakespeare's authorship]	Atlantic Mon., p. 6-9
1997, Spring	[letter: Diana Price's 1996 article "Rough Winds Do Shake"]	Eliz. Review, vol. 5/1: 6

Edgett, Edwin Francis

1937	[review of books by Louis Bénézet and Eva Turner Clark]	Boston Transcript

Edmonds, Dean S.

1965, June 30	Death of SOS President and Executive Officer Francis T. Carmody	Sh. Ox. Newsl., vol. 1/2: 1-2

Edmondson, Paul

Books with Stanley Wells

2011	*Shakespeare Bites Back: Not So Anonymous* [e-book].	
2013	*Shakespeare Beyond Doubt: Evidence, Argument, Controversy*. Cambridge; New York: Cambridge University Press.	

Shorter pieces

2011	Speak Up for Shakespeare	Around the Globe, vol. 49: 42

Edwards, Francis, S.J.
Books
1968   *Marvellous Chance: Thomas Howard, Fourth Duke of Norfolk, and the Ridolphi Plot, 1570-1572*. London: Hart-Davis. [excerpt (Appendix 5) repr. in SAR, issue #26: 9-13 (Summer 1972)]
1987   *The Strange Case of the Poisoned Pommel: Richard Walpole, S.J., and the Squire Plot, 1597-1598*. [pamphlet, repr. from *Archivum Historicum Societatis Iesu*, vol. LVI (1987)]
Periodicals edited
1975-1983: *The Bard*, vol. 1/1-4/1
Shorter pieces

1971, April 27	[letter: Shakespeare and his contemporaries: "J. T. Looney must be heard."] [repr. in SAR, 25: 16-17 (Aut. 1971)]	Times (London), p. 17
1972, Summer	The Earl of Oxford's Escape Plot [repr. from *Marvellous Chance*]	Sh. Authorship Rev. #26: 9-13
1973, Summer	Oxford and the Duke of Norfolk [repr. in BTC, vol. 5, p. 345-354]	Sh. Authorship Rev. #28: 7-13
1974, Summer	[review of *The Shakespeare Authorship Question* by Craig Huston]	Sh. Authorship Rev. #29: 17-18
1975, July 1	The Bard: A Ghost Refuses to Be Laid	Contemp. Rev., v. 227: 29-33
1975	Topical Allusions in *The Winter's Tale*, Part 1	Bard, vol. 1/1: 29-42
1976	Topical Allusions in *The Winter's Tale*, Part 2	Bard, vol. 1/2: 47-71
1976	William Shakespeare: a documentary life	Bard, Supp. 1-26
1976, Summer	The Bard Again	PEN Broadsheet
1977	History in Fiction	Bard, vol. 1/4: 111-128
1979	Claim for Roger manners, 5th Earl of Rutland, as "W. Shakespeare"	Bard, vol. 2/2: 39-70
1980	Further Thoughts on Bronson Feldman's Paper "Marlowe Mystery"	Bard, vol. 3/1: 52-54
1980	Unpublished or Little-Known Documents	Bard, vol. 3/1: 55-58
1983	[review of *The Green Cockatrice* by Basil Iske (Elizabeth Hickey)]	Bard, vol. 4/1: 26-32
1984	Editorial Note [on the passing of Dr. Eliot Slater]	Bard, vol. 4/2: 34
1984	The Jesuits in Shakespeare's England	Bard, vol. 4/2: 35-52
1984	[review of *The Life, Loves and Achievements of Christopher Marlowe Alias Shakespeare* by William Honey (1982)]	Bard, vol. 4/2: 53-75
1984	Obituary of Dr. Eliot Slater (1904-1983)	Bard, vol. 4/2: 76
1987	The Strange Case of the Poisoned Pommel: Richard Walpole, S.J., and the Squire Plot, 1597-1598 [repr. as a pamphlet, 1987]	Archivum Historicum soc. Iesu, vol. LVI
1993, Autumn	[review of *Invisible Power: The Elizabethan Secret Services* by Alan Haynes (1992)] [repr. in BTC, vol. 8: 153-67]	Eliz. Review, vol. 1/2: 52-64
1994, Autumn	William Shakespeare: Why was his true identity concealed? [repr. in BTC, vol. 8: 177-204]	Eliz. Review, vol. 2/2: 23-48
1995, Autumn	The Divisions Among the English Catholics: 1580-1610	Eliz. Review, vol. 3/2: 25-34
1997, Spring	[letter: response to John Baker's Spring 1996 "*Henry IV*" article] Reply by John Baker, Spring 1997, p. 20-25.	Eliz. Review, vol. 5/1: 4-5
1997, Spring	[letter: Diana Price's 1996 "Rough Winds Do Shake"]	Eliz. Review, vol. 5/1: 6-7
1997, Autumn	[letter: response to David Kathman, followed by Kathman's reply]	Eliz. Review, vol. 5/2: 5-9
1998, Spring	Elizabethan Handwriting and Education	Eliz. Review, vol. 6/1: 3-8
2001	"Preface" to *An Anatomy of the Marprelate Controversy, 1588-1596* by Elizabeth Appleton	

Edwards, Michael T.

2009, April	Who Was the Real William Shakespeare?	Mathematics Teacher, vol. 102/8: 580-85

Edwards, William H.
1900   *Shaksper Not Shakespeare*. Cincinnati: The Robert Clarke Company.

Egan, James Alan

2017, July	Shakespeare and John Dee Co-wrote *The Tempest*	De Vere So. New., v. 24/3: 33-46

Egan, Gabriel (editor, with Gary Taylor)
2017   *The New Oxford Shakespeare Authorship Companion*. Oxford: Oxford University Press.

Egan, Michael
Periodicals edited
2009-14: *The Oxfordian*, vol. 11-16
2010, Aug-2013, Fall: *Shakespeare Oxford Society Newsletter*, vol. 46/2-49/3
Shorter pieces

2007	Did Samuel Rowley Write *Thomas of Woodstock*?	Oxfordian, vol. 10: 35-54

Author Index

Egan, Michael (continued)

2014	The Importance of Oxford's Geneva Bible	Oxfordian, vol. 16: 68-72
2014, Spring	Dr. Y Asdust Resolves the Authorship Question	Sh. Ox. Newsl., vol., 50/2:15

Egbert, Lester D.

1956, May	To the Editor and Readers of *The Shakespeare Newsletter* [letter, with 21 other signers]	Sh. Newsl., vol. 6/3: 18

Eggar, Katherine E.

Pamphlets

1935	*The Seventeenth Earl of Oxford as Musician, Poet and Controller of the Queen's Revels* [pamphlet: repr. from *The Proceedings of the British Musical Association*, vol. LXI (Jan. 17, 1935), pp. 39-59].	
1946	*The Musical Condition of Man* [pamphlet: from the *Proceedings of the Royal Musical Association*, Session LXXIII].	
1951	*Shakespeare In His True Colours* [pamphlet]. London: R. Ridgill Trout.	
1954	*The Unlifted Shadow: Some Misunderstood Features in the Life of Edward de Vere* [pamphlet; Eggar's toast to Edward de Vere at the Annual Dinner of the Sh. Fellowship, 23rd April, 1954].	

Shorter pieces

1920-21	The Subconscious Mind and the Musical Faculty	Proceedings of the Musical Assoc., vol. 47
1923, June 15	Edward De Vere's Lyric Verse—An Unsearched Field of Discovery, I	Hackney Spectator, p. 5
1923, June 22	Edward De Vere's Lyric Verse—An Unsearched Field of Discovery, II	Hackney Spectator, p. 8
1924, Aug. 22	The Players' Version of *Hamlet*	Hackney Spectator, p. 2
1929, Jan. 1	Mr. Byrd's *Battell*	Musical Times, vol. 70: 46-53
1934-35	The Seventeenth Earl of Oxford as Musician, Poet, and Controller of the Queen's Revels [Jan. 17, 1935] [repr. as a pamphlet, and in LC, p. 3-11]	Proceedings of the Musical Assoc., vol. 61: 38-59
1946-47	The Musical Condition of Man [Dec. 10, 1946] [repr. as a pamphlet]	Proceedings of the Musical Assoc., vol. 73
1951	Shakespeare in His True Colours [repr. as a pamphlet]	Proceedings of the British Academy, vol. LXI
1952, Sept.	Earl's Colne and Colne-Kill [letter]	SF News-letter (E), p. 12
1954, April	Turbervile's Tragical Tales	SF News-letter (E), p. 6
1955, Autumn	Anthony Munday's *John A Kent*	SF News-letter (E), p. 6-7
1955, Autumn	Brooke House, Hackney [repr. in BTC, vol. 4, p. 141-143]	SF News-letter (E), p. 8
1955, Spring	[response to Lambin's review of Hotson's *The First Night*]	SF News-letter (E), p. 12
1956, Spring	[review of *The Murder of the Man Who Was Shakespeare* by Calvin Hoffman (1955)]	SF News-letter (E), p. 10
1956, Autumn	[review of *Shakespeare Survey* published by Cambridge University Press (1948)]	SF News-letter (E), p. 10
1957, Autumn	[report on Captain R. Ridgill Trout's March 6, 1957 talk "Shakespeare and the Earl of Southampton"]	SF News-letter (E), p. 2
1957, Autumn	[review of *Elizabethan Quintet* by Denis Meadows (1956)]	SF News-letter (E), p. 11
1958, Sept.	Shakespeare as Musician	Musical Times, vol. 99/1387: 480+
1958, Autumn	[report on T. L. Adamson's May 17, 1958 lecture "Lord Oxford and Plutarch"]	SF News-letter (E), p. 3
1959, Spring	[reports on meetings of the Society]	Sh. Authorship Rev., #1: 18-19
1959, Spring	[report on Gwynneth Bowen's Paper "*Hamlet*, A Mirror of the Time"] [repr. in BTC, vol. 5: 24-25]	Sh. Authorship Rev., #1: 19-20
1959, Autumn	[report on Ruth M. D. Wainewright's Mar. 14, 1959 talk "King Lear and the Authorship Question"]	Sh. Authorship Rev., #2: 14-15
1960, Spring	[report on John MacDonald's Feb. 6, 1960 talk "What a Producer of *Hamlet* Would Like to Know About the Author"]	Sh. Authorship Rev., #3: 20-21
1960, Autumn	Sale of an Alleged Portrait of Edward de Vere	Sh. Authorship Rev. #4: 18-19
1960-61	The Blackfriars Plays and Their Music 1576-1610	Proceedings of the Musical Assoc., vol. 87
1961, Spring	Notes for Newcomers [summary of her Nov. 26, 1960 talk]	Sh. Authorship Rev., #5: 17-18

Eischenberger, Bill

2003, Sept. 14	Playwright's Hidden Life Fuels Speculation About Authorship	Columbus Disp., p. 7C

Author Index

Elb, Julie Harper

2015   "A Mint of Phrases in His Brain": Language, Historiography, and the Authorship Question in *Love's Labour's Lost*   Oxfordian, vol. 17: 131-51

Eldredge, Joseph

Pamphlets

1999   *Tilt Tournai & No Barriers*. West Tisbury, MA: Humility Press.

Shorter pieces

1999   Prospero's Hen   Dukes C. Int., v. 40/4: 179-88

1999, Spr.   *Shakespeare in Love*: A Good Move, and an Authorship Valentine   Ever Reader, vol. 8

2000, Fall   Review of Taymor's *Titus* Illuminates a Troublesome Play   Sh. Ox. Newsl., vol. 36/3: 6-7, 15

2003, Fall   Triumph of (the) Will? New Bio, New Facts - Same Old Propaganda   Sh. Matters, vol. 3/1: 7

Eliot, T. S.

1918, May   Observation   Egoist, p. 69

1928, April 5   Poet's Borrowings [review of *Shakespeare, Jonson, and Wilkins as Borrowers* by Percy Allen]   Times Lit. Sup., is. 1366: 255

1934, July 26   John Marston   Times Lit. Sup., i. 1695: 517+

1962, Sept. 4   [letter: efforts to open Shakespeare's tomb]   Times (London)

1962, Sept. 14   [letter: efforts to open Shakespeare's tomb]   Times (London)

Ellenberger, Leroy

1999, May   [letter: request for information about Ralph L. Tweedale]   De Vere Soc. Newsl., vol. 3/3: 20

Elliott, Ward (from 1991 onwards, all with Robert J. Valenza)

1990, Winter   Glass Houses and Glass Slippers: Shakespeare Clinic and Its Critics   Sh. Newsl., vol. 40/4: 59

1990, Summer   The Shakespeare Clinic Post-Season Update   Sh. Newsl., vol. 40/2: 27

1991, April 26   Pretenders Sound Wrong Chords: We're Pretty Certain Who the Bard Wasn't, Though Not Who He Was   Los Angeles Times, p. VYB11

1991, Aug.   A Touchstone for the Bard   Computers and the Humanities, Vol. 25/4: 199-209

1991, Dec.   Was the Earl of Oxford the True Shakespeare? A Computer-Aided Analysis   Notes & Queries, vol. 38/4: 501

1996   And Then There Were None: Winnowing the Shakespeare Claimants   Computers and the Humanities, Vol. 30/3: 191-245

2000   Can the Oxford Candidacy Be Saved? A Response to W. Ron Hess   Oxfordian, vol. 3: 71-98

2003   [letter: response to John Shahan and W. Ron Hess]   Oxfordian, vol. 6: 154-163

2004, Fall   Oxford By the Numbers: What are the Odds that the Earl of Oxford Could Have Written Shakespeare's Poems and Plays? [revised version repr. in DS, p. 137-42] Response by Richard F. Whalen, TLR, vol. 72/1: 275-76. Response by J. Shahan and R. F. Whalen, TOX, vol. 9: 113-25.   Tennessee Law Review, vol. 72/1: 323-453

2007   My Other Car is a Shakespeare: A Response to Shahan and Whalen   Oxfordian, vol. 10: 142-153

2010   The Shakespeare Clinic and the Oxfordians   Oxfordian, vol. 12: 138-166

2010, May 9   Shakespeare: Playwright or Phantasm? [review of *Contested Will* by James Shapiro]   Los Angeles Times, p. E8

Ellis, A. L.

2004, May   [review of *The Case For Shakespeare* by Scott McCrea (2005)]   Choice, vol. 42: 6346

Ellis, David

Books

2012   *The Truth About William Shakespeare: Fact, Fiction and Modern Biographies*. Edinburgh: Edin. Univ. Pr.

Shorter pieces

2001-02, Winter   Now You See Him, Now . . . [Ellis and Katherine Duncan-Jones discuss challenge of writing a biography of W. Shakespeare] [repr. in DVN (July 2004), p. 22-25]   Around the Globe

2005   Biographical Uncertainty and Shakespeare   Essays in Crit. vol. 55/3: 193-208

2010   [review of *Contested Will: Who Wrote Shakespeare?* by J. Shapiro]   Cambr. Q., vol. 39/3: 297-302

Ellis, Greg

2013, Winter   [letter: Southampton as son of Oxford and Mary Browne]   Sh. Ox. Newsl., vol. 49/1: 3-5

Ellis, Sally

2023, Summer   A Poem   Sh. Ox. Newsl., vol. 59/3: 24

Elmore, David
    2009, April 25   [letter: Bravin's article on Justice Stevens]   Wall St. Journal, p. A10

Elton, Ben
    2020?   *The Upstart Crow.* [a play]

Emch, Arnold F.
    1965   *Uncommon Letters to a Son* [repr. in SON, vol. 24/3: 10 (Summer, 1988)]

EMJ
    1996, Jan.   Shake-speare/Shakspere - a teacher's dilemma   De Vere Soc. Newsl., v. 2/4: 4-8

Emmerich, Roland
Films Directed
    2011   *Anonymous*
Shorter pieces
    2011   "Introduction" in *Anonymous: William Shakespeare Revealed.*
        Designed by Tiomthy Shaner. New York: Newmarket Press.
    2011, Oct. 27   [letter: James Shapiro's Oct. 17 review of *Anonymous*]   New York Times, p. A24
    2013   Doubter's Response to Question #59: Why don't you believe that
        Shakespere wrote Shakespere?, in *Sh. Beyond Doubt?* (Shahan): 415-60

Engle, Lars
    1997   [review of *Who Wrote Shakespeare?* by John Michell (1996)]   Studies in English. Lit. 1500-
        1900, v. 37: 415-60

Epstein, Norrie
    1993   *The Friendly Shakespeare.* [excerpt repr. in SON, vol. 30/2: 9 (Spring 1994)]

Er, Odysseus
    2002   *Paradigm Shift, Shake-speare: Jonson's Introductory Poems to the 1623 Folio, and Oxford as Shake-speare.*
        St. Paul: Nonconformist Press.
    2003   *Hamlet-Christ.* St. Paul, MN: Nonconformist Press.

Erichsen, Marie
    2004, Spring   [letter: Shakespearean essay competition]   Sh. Matters, vol. 3/3: 3

Erickson, Kathleet and Peter Sturrock
    2020, Winter   [letter: Dedication to the Sonnets]   Sh. Ox. Newsl., vol. 56/2: 4
    2020, Summer   [letter: John Hamill re Sonnets Dedication]   Sh. Ox. Newsl., vol. 56/3: 6

Erle, Peter G.
    1947, June 22   De Vere's Poetry   NY Herald Tribune, p. A7

Erné, Nino
    1997, Dec.   Shakespeares fragwürdige Gestalt   Neues Sh. Journal, vol. 1: 6-13
        [repr. from DIE WELT [Sept. 3, 1994]
    2014, Oct.   Der Fall *Othello*   Neues Sh. Journal, v. NS4: 63-82

Ervine, St. John
    1930, Aug. 17   At the Play: Did Shakespeare Despise the Stage? I   Observer, p. 9
    1930, Aug. 24   At the Play: Did Shakespeare Despise the Stage? II   Observer, p. 9

Espinoza, Javier
    2011, Oct. 28   Actor Rafe Spall Stars in a New Role as Dad [review of *Anonymous*]   Wall St. Journal

Esson, Louis
    1922, Feb. 2   Shakespeare?   Bulletin, vol. 43: 25

Euchner, Renee
    2021, Summer   From the Data Preservation Committee: Abstracts and Brief   Sh. Ox. Newsl., vol. 57/3: 21-22
        Chronicles [with Terry Deer]
    2021. Fall   Tales from the Archives: The Drayton Collection; History of The   Sh. Ox. Newsl., vol. 57/4: 29-32
        Evered Foundation [with T. Deer, K. Sharpe & B. Boyle]
    2022, Spring   Tales from the Archives: Kattharine E. Eggar (1874-1961)   Sh. Ox. Newsl., vol. 58/2: 29-31
        [with Kathryn Sharpe]

Evans, Alfred. J.
    1956   *Shakespeare's Magic Circle.* London: A. Barker. Repr. in 1970: Freeport, NY: Books for Libraries Press.
        [excerpt repr. in SFE, p. 5 (Spring 1956)]

Evans, Bergen [B. Ifor Evans]

1949, May 7	Good Friend for Iesvs Sake Forbeare: Was Shakespeare Really Sh.? [repr. in *Sh. and His Rivals* (McMichael & Glenn 1962): 178-85]	Sat. Review, p. 7-8, 29-30
1954, March 19	Shakespearian Mysteries and Shakespearian Critics [review of *This Star of England* by Dorothy and Charlton Ogburn]	Truth, p. 378

Evans, Gwynne

1975, Feb.	Shakespeare as Shakespeare [with Harry Levin] [resp. to Ogburn] Response to Evans and Levin by Charles Dickson III, April 8. Response to Evans and Levin by Gordon Cyr, "An Oxfordian Reply to Two Harvard Professors, SON, vol. 11/2: 1-19 (Summer 1975). Reply to Evans and Levin by Charlton Ogburn, April 8.	Harvard Mag., p. 39-43

Evans, Scott

2010	*First Folio: A Literary Mystery*. AuthorHouse.

Evans, Virginia

2022, Winter	The First Folio [letter]	Sh. Ox. Newsl., vol. 58/1: 4
2022, Spring	Capt. Ward's *The Seventeenth Earl of Oxford* [letter]	Sh. Ox. Newsl., vol. 58/2: 3

Everingham, M. Jane

2005, Sept.	The Tennis Court Affairs: Sidney v. de Vere	De Vere Soc. Newsl., p. 20-25

Everitt, Alastair

2010	*The Tragedie of King Lear* [in *Dating Sh.'s Plays* (Gilvary): 396-405]

Ewald, David

2018	Our Shakespeare: Henry Neville 1562-1615 [with John Casson & William D. Rubinstein], in *My Shakespeare: The Authorship Controversy* (Leahy): 113-38.

Eyre, Geoffrey

Books

2015	*The Case for Edward de Vere as Shakespeare*. Published by Geoffrey Eyre.
2017	*The Shakespeare Authorship Mystery Explained*. Mardle Publications.

Shorter pieces

2017, July	The Parallel Lives of Shakespeare and Beethoven: A Shakespeare Authorship Study	De Vere Soc. Newsl., vol. 24/3: 10-20
2019, July	Our Enduring Authorship Mystery Still Awaiting Academic Breakthrough	De Vere Soc. Newsl., vol. 26/3: 36-43
2022, Oct.	An Appreciation of Richard Malim	De Vere So. New., v. 29/4: 32-34

F. B.

1934, June 13	Brief for the Oxfordians [review of *Anne Cecil* by Percy Allen]	Christian Sci. Monitor, p. WM11

Fair, Shana C.

2003, May	[review of *Shakespeare's Fingerprints* by Michael Brame and Galina Popova (2002)]	Library Journal, vol. 128/6: 88
2005	[review of *Players* by Bertram Fields]	Library Journal, vol. 130/6: 94
2005, Apr.	[review of *The Case For Shakespeare* by Scott McCrea (2005)]	Library Journal, vol. 130/7: 86
2006, March 15	[review of *De Vere as Shakespeare* by William Farina (2006)]	Library Journal, vol. 131/5: 72

Fane, Vernon

1955., May 28	[review of *Who Was Shakespeare?* by Hilda Amphlett]	Sphere, p. 38

Fanger, Iris

2006, July 18	Quick Wit, but Comedy Sheds Little Light on Shakespeare [review of *The Beard of Avon* by Amy Freed]	Patriot Ledger, p. 15

Farey, Peter

2009	Playing Dead: An updated review of the case for Christopher Marlowe	Oxfordian, vol. 11: 83-110
2013	Doubter Response to Question #51: Are there any factual objections to the belief that Christopher Marlowe wrote the work attributed to Shakespeare?, in *Sh. Beyond Doubt?* (Shahan): 208	

Farina, William

Books

2006	*De Vere as Shakespeare: An Oxfordian Reading of the Canon*. Foreword by Felicia Londré. Jefferson, NC: McFarland & Co. [three chapters (*Macbeth, Julius Caesar, Romeo and Juliet*) repr. in *Sh. Authorship Sourcebook* (Stritmatter 2019, 2022): 271-300]

Farina, William (continued)
Shorter pieces

2003, Winter	Twelfth Night in Siena	Sh. Ox. Newsl., vol. 39/1: 5-7
2004, Winter	Edward de Vere and the Courtesan Culture of Venice	Sh. Ox. Newsl., vol. 40/1: 6-8
2004, Summer	[letter: Chicago Oxford Society personnel]	Sh. Matters, vol. 3/4: 2
2008, Fall	*Coriolanus* and Ed. de Vere: Another Good Reason to be an Oxfordian Response by William Ray, Winter 2009, p. 2.	Sh. Matters, vol. 7/4: 1, 22-27
2011, Jan.	Draya and Whalen Triumph with *New Oxfordian Othello* (2010)	Sh. Ox. Newsl., vol. 47/1: 4-6
2011, Summer	Origins of Shylock's Venice: Mermaid Tavern or H. K. U.?	Sh. Mat. vol. 10/3: 5-6, 20+

Farley, Peter

2002, Feb. 24	With Enough Time [letter: response to Niederkorn]	New York Times, p. E6

Farquhar, Michael

1996, Aug. 4	Mysteries of the Millennium SOLVED! Resp. by Charlton Ogburn, SON, Sum. 1996, vol. 32/3: 2.	Washington Post, p. F1

Farrar, E. C.

1938, June	The Shakespeare Controversy [letter]	East Ang. Mag., vol. 3/8: 403-4

Farrell, John

2019, Jan. 13	Why Literature Professors Turned Against Authors—Or Did They?	London Rev. Books

Fearson, George

1939	*The Shakespeare Industry: Amazing Monument* [with Ivor Brown]. New York: Harper & Row. Repr. in 1969: Westport, CT: Greenwood Press.	

Feay, Suzi

2012, May 19	Bard Times: A Poetic Retelling of the Mystery Surrounding Shake- speare's Biggest Rival [review of *The Marlowe Papers* by Ros Barber]	Financial Times, p. 18

Fee, Gayle

1993, Nov. 12	Inside Track [Charles Vere speech]	Boston Herald, p. 8

Feingold, Michael

2010, July 16-22	Farewell, Fair Incredulity! [review of *Contested Will* by J. Shapiro]	Village Voice, p. 34

Feldman, A. (Abraham) Bronson
Books and pamphlets

1953	*The Confessions of William Shakespeare* [pamphlet, repr. from *American Imago*, vol. 10, no. 2 (Summer 1953): 113-166]	
1972	*Secrets of Shakespeare: Four Chapters from a Subversive History*. Philadelphia: Lovelace Press. [privately published in mimeograph. See review by Gordon C. Cyr in SON (Winter 1977), p. 7-8] [Contains early versions of Chapters 4 and 5 of *Early Shakespeare*; and of Chapters 4 and 5 of *Shakespeare, Marlowe, . . .* (2022)]	
1977	*Hamlet Himself*. Philadelphia: Lovelore Press. [privately published in mimeograph. Repr. in 2010: Bloomington: iUniverse.com.] [The "Introduction" is reprinted from "The Man Who Might Have Been Shakespeare," *Critic and Guide*, vol. 5, no. 6 (June 1951)]	
2019	*Early Shakespeare*. Edited by Warren Hope. Buchholz, Germany: Laugwitz Verlfag. [Special issue no. 8 of *Neues Shake-speare Journal*]	
2022	*Shakespeare, Marlowe, and Other Elizabethans*. Edited by Warren Hope. Buchholz, Germany: Laugwitz Verlag. [Special issue no. 9 of *Neues Shake-speare Journal*]	

Shorter pieces

1947, Autumn	Shakespeare's Jester—Oxford's Servant [repr. in SON, vol. 18/2: 3-8 (Spring 1982); in SON, vol. 9/2: 8-12 (Autumn 1973); in BTC, vol. 4: 15-23; and in BTC, vol. 6: 156-64; and in *Sh., Marlowe, and Other Elizabethans*, pp. 8-16]	SF Quarterly, vol. VIII/3: 39-43
1951, April	[letter: *Greene's Groatsworth of Wit*]	SF News-letter (E), p. 6-7
1951, June	The Man Who Might Have Been Shakespeare [repr. as the Introduction to *Hamlet Himself*, pp. v-ix]	Critic and Guide
1952, Summer	Othello's Obsessions [repr. in *Shakespeare, Marlowe . . .*, pp. 83-99]	Am. Imago, vol. 9/2: 147-64
1952, Sept.	Who is Shakespeare? What is He? [repr. in *Shakespeare, Marlowe . . .*, pp. 6-7]	Sh. Newsletter, vol. II
1953, Spring	Shakespeare Worship [repr. in SON, vol. 18/2: 9-17 (Spring 1982); in BTC,	Psychoanalysis, vo. 2/1: 57-72

Ferguson, W. A. (2)

    1965, Spring   The *Sonnets* of Shakespeare: The 'Oxfordian' Solution   Sh. Authorship Rev., #13: 9-12
                  [repr. in BTC, vol. 5: 156-159]
    1965, Autumn   The Marriage of William Hall [letter]   Sh. Authorship Rev., #14: 22
    1971, Spring   Earls Colne [letter]   Sh. Authorship Rev., #24: 23

Ferlita, Ernest

    1988   *The Truth of the Matter: A Play in Two Acts*. New Orleans: Loyola University Drama Department.

Ferna, Tom

    1989, April 18   Shakespeare Dilemma Re-examined [review of *Frontline*]   Plain Dealer (Cleveland)

Feron, James

    1962, Sept. 13   Skeptics of Shakespeare Want to Search Tomb for Writings   New York Times, p. 34

Feste

    1930, March 12   Edward de Vere and Shakespeare [review of *Case* by Percy Allen]   Eastbourne Gazette, p. 27
    1930, April 2   Oxford-Shakespeare [resp.to Allen's letter in same issue]   Eastbourne Gazette, p. 25

Feuillerat, Albert

    1922, Nov. 1   Shakspeare est-il Shakspeare?   Rev. des Deux M., p. 166-200

Fey, Jerry

    1992   *Oxford's Will: A Play*.

Fiehler, Rudolph

Pamphlets
    198?   *The Key to the Great Shake-speare Whodunit* [pamphlet; date is between 1982 and mid 1986]
Shorter pieces
    1981, March 13   Let's Teach Both Sides   Ruston Daily Leader, vol. 91/61

Field, Andrew

Books
    1990   *The Lost Chronicle of Edward de Vere*. London, New York: Viking.
                  [Translated into German by Hans J. Schütz as *Die geheimen Aufzeichnungen des Edward de Vere, Grosskämmerer, Siebzehnter Earl of Oxford, Dichter und Stücheschreiber, genannt Shakespeare*. Stuttgart: Klett-Cotta, 1994]
Shorter pieces
    1992, June 22   Shakespeare Unmasked   Courier-Mail (Queensland), p. 9
    1996, Nov. 16   So Who Was Shakespeare?   Courier-Mail (Queensland), p. 8

Fields, Bertram

Books
    2005   *Players: The Shakespeare Mystery*. New York: Harper Perennial/Regan Books.
Shorter piecves
    2005, Aug. 7   Did Shakespeare Really Write Those Plays?   Edmonton Journal, p. E12

Fiévreux, Solange

    1999, Jan.   [review of *Who Wrote Shakespeare?* by John Michell (1996)]   Neues Sh. Journal, vol. 3: 163-68
    1999, July   [review of *Der Spitzel* by Andreas Höfele (1997)]   Neues Sh. Journal, vol. 4: 154-55
    2001, May   [rev. of *Elisabeth I. – Der Roman ihres Lebens* by Cornelia Wusowski]   Neues Sh. Journal, vol. 6: 162-63

Filby, P. W.

    1960, Autumn   [letter: Peabody Institute exhibitions]   Sh. Authorship Review, #4: 22

Finegold, Oliver

    2005, June 1   To Be or Not To Be? A Fight Over the Bard's ID   Evening Standard, p. 20

Finn, Robert

    1992, March 6   Bard Didn't Write It, Earl Says [Charles Burford]   Plain Dealer (Cleveland)

Fiore, Nora

    2009, Summer   *Hamlet* and *Much Ado About Nothing*: The Keys to Shakespeare   Sh. Matters, vol. 8/3: 21-24

Fish, Seena

    1991, Aug.   [letter: the premise that Oxford was "Shakespeare" is incorrect]   Spear-shaker Review, issue 5: 23

Fish, Stanley

    1993, March 1   Not of an Age, But for All Time   Journal of Legal Education, p. 11

Fisher, Edmund

    1923, March 29   Can't We Let Shakespeare Alone? [letter]   Bulletin, vol. 44: Red Page

Fisher, Edward
  1975, Jan. 5   [letter: Charlton Ogburn Jr.'s Nov. 2 article]   Harvard Mag., vol. 77/5

Fisher, James
  2003, Oct.   [review of *The Beard of Avon* by Amy Freed (2003)]   Theatre J., vol. 55/3: 528-30

Fisher, Trevor
  2011, Feb. 10   Royal Twist to Debate Over Who William Shakespeare Really Was   Birmingham Daily P., p. 28
  2011, Summer   Enter the Tudor Prince   Historian, p. 18-22

Fistori, Art
  1989, April 29 Something Springs Eternal [letter]   Phil. Inquirer, p. A6

Fitch, J. A.
  2007, Sept. 1   [letter: passing of Vice-Admiral Sir Ian McGeoch]   Times (London), p. 65

Fitzgerald, James
  1992, Summer   [letter: Monkeys and typewriters and Shakespere]   Sh. Ox. Newsl., vol. 28/3: 18
  1997, Winter   Shakespeare, Oxford and Du Bartas: Little-Known Story of Edward   Sh. Ox. Newsl., v. 33/1: 1, 10-15
                      De Vere's Revelatory Last Poem
                      [repr. as part of "Know Ye Not This Parable? The Oxford-du
                          Bartas Connection" in TOX, vol. 2: 76-116]
                      [repr. in German in NSJ, vol. 1: 86-98 (Dec. 1997)]
                      Response by Dana Benjamin and Marlene Benjamin, vol. 33/2: 21.
                      Response by Andrew R. Hannas, vol. 34/1: 11.
                          Reply by James Fitzgerald, vol. 34/2: 22.
  1997, Spring   Shakespeare, Oxford and De Bartas: A Follow-up   Sh. Ox. Newsl., vol. 33/2: 18-19
  1997, Fall   Enter Ben Jonson: Did the Key Player in the First Folio Ruse Re-   Sh. Ox. Newsl., v. 33/4: 1, 12-17
                      hearse His Role in the Shakespeare, Oxford, Du Bartas Story?
                      [repr. in TOX 2: 76-116, as part of "Know Ye Not This Parable?
                          The Oxford-du Bartas Connection"]
                      [repr. in German in NSJ, vol. 3: 80-89 (Jan. 1999)]
                      Responses by F. Gidley and R. Detobel, Fall 1997, vol. 34/1: 21.
  1998   Shakespeare, Oxford, and "A Pedlar"   Oxfordian, vol. 1: 27-42
                      [repr. in German in NSJ, vol. 8: 131-50 (Aug. 2003)]
  1998, Spring   E. L. Oxon. [repr. in TOX 2: 76-116, as part of "Know Ye Not This Sh. Ox. Newsl., vol. 34/1: 10-11+
                      Parable? The Oxford-du Bartas Connection"]
  1998, June   Ist E. L. Oxon identisch mit Edward de Vere? II   Neues Sh. Journal, vol. 2: 142-43
  1998, Summer   [letter: the R. R. eulogy]   Sh. Ox. Newsl., vol. 34/2: 22
  1998, Fall   [letter: resp. to R. Whalen's Summer 1998 "Queen's worm" article] Sh. Ox. Newsl., vol. 34/3: 25-26
  1999   Ein Zwinkern, ein Rempler: 'Welcher Autor würde seinen Namen   Neues Sh. Journal, vol. 4: 131-35
                      verbergen?'
  1999   Know Ye Not This Parable? The Oxford-Du Bartas Connection   Oxfordian, vol. 2: 76-116
  1999, Summer   Nudge-Nudge, Wink-Wink: "what author would conceal his name?"   Sh. Ox. Newsl., vol. 35/2: 8-9
                      [repr. in EVR, vol. 10 (Spr. 2000)]
  2001, Winter   [letter: support for Stritmatter's Summer 2000 explication of a phrase Sh. Ox. Newsl., vol. 36/4: 25
                      from Peacham's *Minerva Britanna*]
                      Reply by Roger Stritmatter, Summer 2001, p. 17.

Fitzgerald, W. J. P.
  1922, Dec. 30   Forgotten Celebrity of Elizabeth's Day [review of SI]   Daily Telegraph, p. 14

Flamini, Roland
  2011, Nov. 2   Was Shakespeare a Fraud? To Be or Not To Be [rev. of *Anonymous*] Washington Times, p. B10

Flatter, Richard
  1951, Oct.   Sigmund Freud on Shakespeare   Sh. Quarterly, vol. 2/4: 368-69

Fleet, Preston M.
  1987   *Hue & Cry: Unraveling the Shake-speare Myth*. Templeton, CA: Preston M. Fleet.

Fleischer, Leonore
  1990, May 11   The Bard or Not the Bard? [review of *The Mysterious William   Publisher's Weekly, p. 228
                      Shakespeare* by Charlton Ogburn (1984)]
  1990, Spring   *Talk of the Trade* [excerpt from the 5/14/90 issue]   Sh. Ox. Newsl., vol. 26/2: 6-7

Fleming, John
  2009, April 1   The Show Must Go On [premiere performance of *Elizabeth and*   St. Petersburg Times, p. B2
          Edward, a play by Aubrey Hampton]

Fleming, Thomas F.
  1956, May   To the Editor and Readers of *The Shakespeare Newsletter*   Sh. Newsletter, vol. 6/3: 18
          [letter, with 21 others]

Flint, Eric
  2001   *1632* [A science-fiction novel]. Riverdale, NY: Baen. Dist. by Simon & Schuster.

Fluchere, Henri
  1956   *Shakespere* [excerpt reprinted in DVN (April, 2002), p. 19-20]

Flusfeder, David
  1994, Oct. 22   Whose Canon Is It, Anyway? [review of "Battle of the Wills,"   Times (London), p. 2
          BBC 2: Charles Vere defends Looney's thesis]

Flynn, Rev. R. F.
  1931, Sept.   Arthur Golding and Shakespeare [report on the article in the *Halstead*   Ruri-decanal Magazine
          & Belchamp St. Pauls Colne Valley Gazette, Sept. 11, 1931]
  1931, Nov.   [piece about family into which Edward de Vere was born]   Ruri-decanal Magazine
  1931, Dec.   Arthur Golding and Shakespeare [repr. in the *Belchamp St. Pauls*   Ruri-decanal Magazine
          Halstead & Colne Valley Gazette, Dec. 18, 1931]

Fogan, Lance
  2013, Fall   Will Shaksper's Death: The Coroner's Inquest Hold on May 14, 1616   Sh. Matters, vol. 12/4: 20-21

Foggatt, Tyhler
  2019, Aug. 5-12   Justice Stevens's Dissenting Shakespeare Theory   New Yorker

Folkenflik, Robert
  2011, Dec. 27   Anonymous Was a Writer; Some of the Most Famous Authors in   Los Angeles Times, p. A11
          History Kept Names Off the Title p.

Folliard, Edward T.
  1968, June 23   Shakespeare's Man: Folger Library's Dr. Wright Leaving Behind   Washington Post, p. E1
          Dump-the-Bard Cult [resp. by Ch. Ogburn, Jr., July 3, p. A20]

Fontane, Theodor
  2023   Theodor Fontane: Shakespeares Strumpf   Neues Sh. Journ., v. NS8: 194-95

Foote, G. W.
  1935, March 10   Shakespeare and Jesus Christ   Freethinker, v. 55/10: 156-57

Ford, Gertrude C.
  1965   *A Rose By Any Name*. Intro. by Francis T. Carmody. New York: A. S. Barnes.
  1968   *Shakespeare and Elizabeth Unmasked* [A play].

Ford, Peter
  1997, Dec. 31   Aussian Debunks the Bard [rev. of *The Game of Shakespeare* by Ilya   Christian Sci. Monitor
          Gililov] [Rutland] [excerpt repr. in SON, vol. 34/1: 2 (Spring 1998)]

Fort, J. A.
Books and pamphlets
  1933   *The Order and Chronology of Shakespeare's Sonnets*. [pamphlet: repr. from *Review of English Studies*, vol.
          IX, no. 33 (Jan. 1933)]

Shorter pieces
  1925, Jan. 22   The Shakespeare Signatures [letter]   Times Lit. Sup., is. 1201: 56
  1933, Jan.   The Order and Chronology of Shakespeare's Sonnets [repr. as pamp.]   Rev. Eng. St., vol. 9/33: 19-23
  1934, Feb. 15   The 'Mortal Moon' Sonnet [letter]   Times Lit. Sup., is. 1671: 92
  1934, Feb. 22   The 'Mortal Moon' Sonnet [letter]   Times Lit. Sup., is. 1673: 126
  1934, March 8   The 'Mortal Moon' Sonnet [letter]   Times Lit. Sup., is. 1675: 162
  1934, March 15   The 'Mortal Moon' Sonnet [letter]   Times Lit. Sup., is. 1676: 194
  1934, March 22   The 'Mortal Moon' Sonnet [letter]   Times Lit. Sup., is. 1677: 214
  1934, April 19   The 'Mortal Moon' Sonnet [letter]   Times Lit. Sup., is. 1681: 282

Fort, J. B.
  1964, Oct. 1   Le quatrieme centenaire et le mystere Shakespearien   Etudes Angl., vol. 17/4: 522

Foss, Jonathan

2022, July	[review of *Oxford's Voices: What Shakespeare Wrote Before He was Shakespeare* by Robert Prechter]	De Vere Soc. Newsl., vol. 29/3: 34-42
2023, April.	The Most Powerful Artificial Intelligence Tool is Queried	De Vere Soc. N., v. 30/2: 16-27
2023, April	[review of *Educating Shakespeare* by Stephanie Hopkins Hughes]	De Vere Soc. N., v. 30/2: 42-49

Foster, Donald W.

1996	[letter: Elliot and Valenza's "And Then There Were None"]	Computers and Humanities, vol. 30/3: 247-55
1996, Fall	Shaxicon and Shakespeare's Acting Career [response to Diana Price]	Sh. Newsl., vol. 46/3: 57-58
1998	The Claremont Shakespeare Authorship Clinic: How Severe Are the Problems?	Computers and Humanities, vol. 32/6: 491-510

Foster, Thomas H. (T. Henry)

Books

1946	*Shakespeare—Man of Mystery: An Address Delivered at McCormick Theological Seminary, Chicago, Ill., October 24, 1946.* Cedar Rapids, IA: Torch Press.

Fowler, Alastair

2005, Feb. 4	Shakespeare Fantasies [review of *Will in the World* by Stephen Greenblatt (2004)] [repr. in DVN (May 2005), p. 23-28; excerpt printed in NSJ, vol. 11: 179-81 (2007)]	Times Lit. Sup., is. 5314: 3

Fowler, Richard

2018, Spring	[letter: Richard Whalen's Winter *Hamlet* article]	Sh. Ox. Newsl., vol. 54/2: 4

Fowler, William P.

Books

1986	*Shakespeare Revealed in Oxford's Letters.* Portsmouth, NH: Peter E. Randall.
1986	*Shake-speare's "Phoenix and Turtle": An Interpretation* (pamphlet). With an exegesis by Dorothy Ogburn repr. from *This Star of England*. Portsmouth, NH: Peter E. Randall. [repr. in PR, p. 129-42]

Shorter pieces

1959, June	[letter: articles by Richard Bentley (Feb.) and Ch. Ogburn (March)]	Am. Bar Assoc. J., v. 45/6: 606
1976, Fall	Sonnet CXL: "A Never Writer To An Ever Reader"	Sh. Ox. Newsl., vol. 12/3: 5
1982, Fall	Shake-speare's Heart Unlocked [repr. in BTC, vol. 6: 209-20]	Sh. Ox. Newsl., vol. 18/4: 1-7
1983, Winter	Knyvet's Knife [repr. in BTC, vol. 6: 236]	Sh. Ox. Newsl., vol. 19/1: 12
1986, Summer	Shakespeare's Buried Name Exhumed	Sh. Ox. Newsl., vol. 22/3: 5-11
1988, Fall-Wntr	Oxford's Signatures	Sh. Newsl., vol. 38/3-4: 43
1991, August	[letter: thanks for the *Spear-shaker's* fine articles]	Spear-shaker Rev., is. 5: 24

Fox, Robin

Books

2012	*Shakespeare's Education: Schools, Lawsuits, Theater and the Tudor Miracle* (edited by Gary B. Goldstein). Buchholz, Germany: Verlag Uwe Laugwitz. [Special Editions #5 of *Neues Shake-speare Journal*]

Shorter pieces

2006, Spring	Personal Adventures with the Authorship Question [repr. in SE]	Sh. Ox. Newsl., vol. 42/2: 4-6, 32
2009	Shakespeare, Oxford and the Grammar School Question [repr. in BTC, vol. 9: 196-222; in TOX, vol. 16: 78-96; and expanded in *Shakespeare's Education* (Fox 2012): 7-29]	Oxfordian, vol. 11: 113-136
2010	A Matter of Pronunciation: Shakespeare, Oxford and the Petty-School Question [expanded in *Shakespeare's Education* (Fox 2012): 101-19]	Oxfordian, vol. 12: 56-64
2010, August	Why Is There No History of Henry VII? [repr. in BTC, vol. 9: 223-29; and in SE, p. 33-40]	Sh. Ox. Newsl., vol. 46/2: 1-4
2010, August	Oxford and Evolution	Sh. Ox. Newsl., vol. 46/2: 15
2011	The Black Book, Oedipus and Robin Hood: Oxford's Lawsuits and the Character of Timon [repr. in NSJ, vol. NS3: 85-105 (Mar. 2013); expanded and repr. in *Sh.'s Education* (Fox 2012): 120-63]	Oxfordian, vol. 13: 5-33
2011, Spring	[letter: The Earls Colne database and "Edward Shackespeare"]	Sh. Ox. Newsl., vol. 47/2: 2
2013	Doubter Response to Question #2: Did Shakespeare attend the King Edward VI Grammar School in Stratford-upon-Avon? in *Sh. Beyond Doubt?* (Shahan): 159-60	
2013	Doubter Response to Question #3: Is there anything in the Works which require their author to have been educated at a university? in *Sh. Beyond Doubt?* (Shahan): 160-61	
2013	Doubter Response to Question #4: Do the plays reflect the education the boys in the Stratford grammar school received? in *Sh. Beyond Doubt?* (Shahan): 161-62	

Fox, W. H.
    1937, Sept. 19   The Earls of Oxford [letter: response to last week's article,   Observer, p. 9
                         "Observation," that referred to the 17th Earl of Oxford]

Foyston, John
    2002, April 19   De Vere, Revered [The SARC Conference at Concordia University]   Oregonian, p. 3
    2002, April 26   Readers Talk, We Talk Back: Oxford vs. Stratford   Oregonian, p. 2

Franssen, Paul
    1995   [review of *Shakespeare: Who Was He?* by Richard F. Whalen]   Folio: Sh.-Genoost. van Nederl.
                       en Vl., vol. 2/2: 48-53

Fraser, Stephen
    2006, Feb. 10   Poet or Puppet?   Read, vol. 55/12: 18-22

Frazer, Winifred L.
Plays
    1991   *Truth is Stranger.* [A play/musical about a grad student who is an Oxfordian trying to get a Ph.D. in English
                literature. Songs by David Stryker.]
Shorter pieces
    1990, Summer   [letter: the "twine-like pair" are Philip and Susan]   Sh. Ox. Newsl., vol. 26/3a: 7
    1991, Spring   [letter: handwriting in *The Annotator* by A. Ken and Roger Lubbock]   Sh. Ox. Newsl., vol. 27/2: 10
    1992, April   [transcription of an Oral History interview conducted by the University
                of Florida in which Frazer describes how she became an Oxfordian.
                [from http://ufdc.ufl.edu/UF00006130/00001/]
    1992, Fall   Transvestite Shakespeare [repr. in BTC, vol. 7: 127]   Sh. Ox. Newsl., vol. 28/4a: 7
    1993, Summer   Realistic Look at *Groats-Worth of Wit* [repr. in BTC, vol. 7: 188-200]   Sh. Ox. Newsl., vol. 29/3b: 1-8
    2009   Censorship in the Strange Case of William Shakespeare   Brief Chronicles, vol. I: 9-28

Freed, Amy
Plays
    2004   *The Beard of Avon.* New York: S. French.
Shorter pieces
    2001, May/June   Who Was That Man? Why Amy Freed Can't Stop Thinking About   Am. Theatre, vol. 18/5: 22-23
                Shakespeare [resp. by Christopher Paul, Oct. 2001, vol. 18/8: 7]

Freedley, George
    1949, Oct. 15   [review of *"Shakespeare" Identified*, 2nd ed.]   Library Journal, vol. 74: 1605

Freeman, Don
    1985, Feb. 1   Point of View [Will Buckley's "Firing Line"]   San Diego Union, p. D-17
    1985, Feb. 17   Much Ado About . . . Shakespeare [review of the Dec. 11, 1984   San Diego Union, p. TV-4
                Firing Line episode with guest Charlton Ogburn]
    1999, Feb. 26   If Shakespeare Were Irish, That Would Explain a Lot   San Diego Union, p. E2
    1999, June 21   Shakespeare Again the Draw as Millennium Turns   San Diego Union, p. E2

Freeman, John
    1928, Oct.   [review of *Borrowers* by Percy Allen (1928)]   London Mercury, vol. 18:
                 657-58

Freud, Ernest L. (editor)
    1970   *The Letters of Sigmund Freud & Arnold Zweig.* Translated by Elaine and William Robson-Scott. New York:
                Harcourt Brace Jovanovich.

Freud, Sigmund
Books
    1935   *An Autobiographical Study.* New York: W. W. Norton and Company. [Compare with the 1998 edition
                edited by James Strachey] [repr. in *Sh. and His Rivals* (McMichael & Glenn 1962): 192]
    1949   *An Outline of Psychoanalysis.* [Abriss der Psycho-Analyse] Authorized translated by James
                Strachey (1949). New York: W. W. Norton. [see esp. p. 96, 164, 165, 172]
Shorter pieces
    2010, Nov.   Address Delivered in the Goethe House, Frankfurt (Aug. 28, 1930)   Neues Sh. Journ., vol. NS1: 6-10
                [reprinted as "Ansprache im Frankfurter Goethe-Haus" in *Neues
                Shakespeare Journal*, edited by Uwe Laugwitz]
    1930, Mar. 23   [letter to Theodore Reik, quoted in Norman N. Holland, *Psychoanalysis
                and Shakespeare* (1964), pp. 56-57]
    1932, Sept. 20   [letter to Dr. Richard Flatter, quoted in Richard Flatter, "Sigmund Freud

on Shakespeare," *Sh. Quarterly*, vol. 2, no. 4 (Oct. 1951): 368-69]

1938, June [letter to J. Thomas Looney; excerpt in Feldman, The Confessions of William Shakespeare, *American Imago*, vol. 10/2 (Summer 1953): 165; and in *Oxfordian Vistas*, ed. by Ruth Loyd Miller]

Freudenberg, G. F.
1949, June 4 Was Shakespeare Shakespeare? [letter]   Sat. Review, p. 25
[repr. in *Sh. and His Rivals* (McMichael & Glenn 1962): 188-89]

Friberg, Gösta & Helena Brodin Friberg
2006 *Täcknamn Shakespeare: Edward de Veres hemliga liv*. Stockholm: Albert Bonniers Förlag. [Finnish]

Friedman, Arthur
1993, Nov. 19 Will's Warriors Repel Another Assault on Bard's Authorship   Boston Herald, p. S19
[SOS Conference held in Boston]
1994, April 29 Curtains [Mentions Roger Stritmatter and de Vere's Bible]   Boston Herald, p. S17
1994, Aug. 5 Curtains [Edward de Vere: The Real Shakespeare]   Boston Herald, p. S15

Fripp, Rev. Edgar J.
1920, March 9 The Sonnets of Shakespeare [lecture]   Belfast News-Letter, p. 6

Frisbee, George
Books
1931 *Edward De Vere: A Great Elizabethan*. London: Cecil Palmer.
Shorter pieces
1932, April 7 [Imperiol Throne [letter: North was a pen name de Vere used when   Times Lit. Sup., issue 1575: 18
he translated Plutarch]
1937, Feb. To *Shakespeare Pictorial*: Shakespeare Fellowship [letter]   Sh. Pictorial, vol. 108: 27
1937, July Shame of the Professors [repr. in SFE, no. 5: 8-9 (Sept. 1937);   Reading and Collecting,
in SFA, vol. 1/8: 6-7; vol. 4/6: 69-71 (Oct., 1943);   vol. 1/8: 6-7
in SON, vol. 5/4: 2-4 ; and in BTC, vol. 2: 420-24]
1938, Jan. Admirations and Antipathies [letter: reply to Gekle's Dec. response] Reading & Col., vol. 2/2: 25

Froelich, John F.
1988, Dec. 1 Edward de Vere – The Real Bard   Chicago Sun, p. 52

Frohlich, Newton
2014 *The Shakespeare Mask*. Tucson, AZ: Blue Bird Press.

Fry, Simon
Books – fiction
2008 *Paper Trail*. Pub. by Imprimata.
2011 *The Shakespeare File: A Novel*. Pub. by Imprimata.
Shorter pieces
2009, Nov. [letter: his novel *Paper Trail*]   De Vere Soc. Newsl., vol. 16/3: 8
2016, January [letter: travels to Italy and Oregon; his novel *The Shakespeare File*] De Vere Soc. Newsl., v. 23/1: 44

Frye, Albert Myrton
Books (with Albert William Levi)
1941 *Rational Belief: An Introduction to Logic*. New York: Harcourt, Brace.
[See esp. Chapter XVII, which examines the Shakespeare authorship case]

Fu, Richard
2005, Summer Sidebar: A Review of the Statistical Tests [response to Robert   Sh. Matters, vol. 4/4: 27
Prechter's articles on the Sonnet's Dedication Puzzle

Fuchs, Christian
2018 Zu Shakespeare. Notizen eines Dramaturgen. Lesezirkel, Februar 1994   Neues Sh. Jou., vol. NS6: 26-28
[eingereicht von Walter Klier: 12. 8. 1997]

Furman, Alfred A.
1940, Apr./May Edward de Vere: Accepting Him as Author of Shakespeare   SF News-letter (A), vol. 1/3: 5

Furnas, J. C.
1962, Sept. 2 [letter: efforts to open Shakespeare's tomb]   New York Times, p. 2
1962, Sept. 2 Speaking of Books [the Ogburns and authorship of Sh's works]   New York Times, p. 149

Furner, Jonathan
2004 Conceptual Analysis: A Method for Understanding Information as   Archival Science, vol. 4/3-4: 233
Evidence, and Evidence as Information

Furnival, Jane
    2000, Feb. 12   East Ender Who Says He's an Earl [Aubrey William de Vere]   Daily Mail
        [repr. in DVN (Oct. 2004), p. 21]

Fusini, Nadia
    2012   Shakespeare: Playwright or "Sprachschöpfer"?   Memoria di Sh., vol. 8: 95

G. A. S.
    1933, May 6   Book Reviews [rev. of *Love's Labour's Lost: A Study* by E. T. Clark]   Cincinnati Enquirer, p. 10

G. E. T. S. (G. S.)
    1933, Oct. 24   Books of Today [rev. of *Shakespeare, Oxford, and Elizabethan Times*]   West. Morning News, p. 4
    1937, May 3   [letter: knows who wrote the plays—it wasn't the man from Stratford   West. Morning News, p. 2
        or Oxford—but won't say who us until his research is finished]

G. W. S.
    1936, Jan. 6   Talent and Diligence Combined [letter]   Western Daily Press, p. 5

Gabriel, Helen
    2004, June 25   Would the Real Literary Genius Please Stand Up?   Birmingham Daily P., p. 2

Gage, Carolyn
    1997, Oct. 31   Meeting the Ghost of Hamlet's Father   On the Issues, p. 22
    1998, Oct. 31   The Case for Marlowe as the Bard   Harvard Gay & L. Rev., p. 32

Gale, Gertrude [Gertrude Ford]
    1971   *Masquerade* [a play based on Prince Tudor themes]

Gali, Grace
    1994, Winter   Shakespeare's *Tempest* Locale: Cuttyhunk?   Sh. Ox. Newsl., vol. 30/1: 14-18

Galland, Joseph S.
    1949   *Digesta Anti-Shakespeareana.* [Contains more than 4,500 entries; most are Baconian; edited and completed
        by Burton A. Milligan after Galland's death]. Evanston, Ill: UMI Dissertation Information Service.

Gallup, Elizabeth Wells
    1910   *Bi-literal Cypher of Sir Francis Bacon* [excerpt "Note by the publisher" repr. in BTC, vol. 1: 184-189)

Galston, Sean
    2010   No Biography: Shakespeare, Author, in *Shakespeare and His Authors* (Leahy): 91-103

Galsworthy, John
    1928   *The White Monkey.* New York: Charles Scribner's Sons.

Gannon, Christian H.
    1993, Autumn   [letter: Justice Stevens' "Statutory Construction" article]   Eliz. Review, vol. 1/2: 2-5

Gansecki, Mike
    2019, Spring   [review of *Tyrant: Shakespeare on Politics* by Steven Greenblatt]   Sh. Ox. Newsl., vol. 55/2: 25-26
    2019, Spring   [review of *How Shakespeare Put Politics on the Stage* by Peter Lake]   Sh. Ox. Newsl., vol. 55/2: 25-30
    2021, Winter   [letter: Dedication to Shakespeare's *Sonnets*]   Sh. Ox. Newsl., vol. 57/1: 4

Gantz, Jeffrey
    1989, Aug. 11   "Critical Mass [his weekly column]:" But the Play's the Thing   Boston Phoenix
        [excerpt repr. in SON, vol. 22/4: 12 (Fall 1989)]
        Response by Charles Boyle, Sept. 8 [also repr. in SON, p. 12-13]

Ganz, Charles
    1938, Feb.   [letter: Allen's Jan. article]   East Ang. Mag., vol. 3/5: 219

Garber, Marjorie
Books
    1987   *Shakespeare's Ghost Writers: Literature As Uncanny Causality.* New York and London: Methuen.
    2004   *Shakespeare After All.* New York: Anchor Books.
Shorter pieces
    1994, Nov. 25   The Bard Meets the Undead [excerpt in SON, vol. 30/4 (Aut. 1994)]   New York Times
    1999, April   As They Like It [repr. in LC, p. 57-78]   Harper's Mag., vol. 298: 44-6

Garcia, Emanuel E.
Books
    2008   Sherlock Holmes and the Mystery of *Hamlet*, in *Sherlock Holmes & the Three Poisoned Pawns* edited by
        Antony J. Richards. Cambridge: Breese Books.

Author Index

Shorter pieces
1999, July 31	[letter: the July 24 editorial]	Philadelphia Inquirer, p. A16
2017, Spring	The Two Cinnas: A Covert Allusion to the Two Shakespeares?	Sh. Ox. Newsl., vol. 53/2: 29

Gardner, Jan
2008, Nov. 9 — Doubts About the Bard [Alex McNeil to speak at Boston Pub. Lib.] — Boston Globe, p. K6

Gardner, Lyn
2004, Jan. 8 — The Bard as a Money-Grabbing Yokel [review of *Edward's Presents* by Sally Llewellyn] — Guardian, p. 28

Gardner, Martin
1992, Jan. 19 — William Shakespeare: By Divers Hands [review of *Shakespeare's Lives*, New Edition by S. Schoenbaum] — Washington Post, p. M5
    Response by Thomas Taylor, March 8, p. 14, followed by reply by Gardner.
    Response by Charlton Ogburn, Jr., April 12, p. 14.

Garrett, G. R.
1948, Nov. 20 — Nobody Named Shakespeare [letter] — Sat. Review, p. 24

Garvin, J. L.
1923, April 22 — Who Shakespeare Was: The Comedy of Doubt — Observer, p. 12
    [see response by Looney, *Hackney Spectator*, May 11]
1923, April 29 — Putting William in His Place, II — Observer, p. 12-13

Gay, Peter
1990 — *Reading Freud: Explorations & Entertainments*. New Haven: Yale Univ. Press. [See esp. "Freud and the Man from Stratford," p. 5-53, which was translated by Elisabeth Vorspohl as "Freud, Shakespeare und Looney," in *Psyche: Zeitschrift für Psychoanalyse und ihre Anwendungen* 45 (1991), 649-74]

Gaynor, James
2013 — Foreword "Why Be Shakespeare?" to *A Poet's Rage: Understanding Sh. Through Authorship Studies*, p. vii-x, edited by William E. Boyle

Gazda, Matthew
2023, March 24 — The Right-Wing Crusade Against Shakespeare — Commonwealth

Geikie, Sir Archibald
1916 — *The Birds of Shakespeare* ["Preface" repr. in BTC, vol. 1: 71-72]

Gekle, William F., Jr.
1937, Nov. — A Layman's Lament [response to Frisbee's July 1937 article] — Reading & Col., vol. 1/12: 7-8

Genske, Sylvia S.
1991, Winter — [letter to Charlton Ogburn: thanks for a wonderful book] — Sh. Ox. Newsl., vol. 27/1: 2-3

Geoghegan, Tom
2007, Sept. 11 — Shakespeare: The Dossier — BBC News Mag.

George, W. L.
1920, Spring — [review of *"Shakespeare" Identified*] — World

Gericke, Henryk
2007, April — Ich bin nicht we rich scheinbar bin — Neues Sh. Journal, v. 11: 190-91

Gerrard, Nicci
1994, Oct. 9 — Shakespeare: Not Just William? Who Really Wrote *Hamlet*? — Observer, p. 11

Getchell, Everett L.
1941, Oct. — [letter: Dr. Bénézet's talk (excerpts from letter repr.)] — SF News-letter (A), vol. 2/6: 71

Gibson, Amy L.
2004, Fall — Using Circumstantial Evidence to Discover Shakespeare: The Importance of Good Legal Analysis — Tennessee Law Review, vol. 72/1: 309-21

Gibson, H. N.
1962 — *The Shakespeare Claimants: A Critical Survey of the Four Principal Theories Concerning the Authorship of the Shakespearean Plays*. London: Methuen. New York: Barnes & Noble.
    [excerpt repr. in *Shakespeare Criticism, vol. 41* (Lee & Barnes 1998): 67-76]

Gidley, Fran
1998, Spring — [letter: J. Fitzgerald's Fall 1997 "Ben Jonson" article] — Sh. Ox. Newsl., vol. 34/1: 21
1990, Summer — [letter: *Frontline*'s program convinced her of Oxford's authorship] — Sh. Ox. Newsl., vol. 26/3a: 10-11

Gidley, Fran (continued)

2003	Shakespeare in Composition: Evidence for Oxford's Authorship of *Sir Thomas More* [repr. in RCA, p. 103-125]	Oxfordian, vol. 6: 29-54

Gifford, A. C.

1941, Dec.	[letter: discoveries published in the *News-Letter*]	SF News-letter (A), vol. 3/1: 8
1942, Oct.	[letter: June letter's praise for the Fellowship]	SF News-letter (A), vol. 3/6: 77

Gifford, Marjorie

1977, April 25	It's the Earl of Oxford [letter] [response by John Cutler, May 2]	Boston Globe, p. 17

Gilbert, Matthew

2003, Jan. 2	Much Ado About the Bard [reviews of *Frontline*'s "Much Ado About Something" (1989) and "The Shakespeare Mystery" (2003)]	Boston Globe, p. D5

Gilbert, Sky

Books

2012	*Come Back: A Novel.* Toronto: ECW Press.	
2020	*Shakespeare Beyond Science: When Poetry Was the World.* Toronto: Guernica Editions.	

Shorter pieces

2003, Winter	The Artist as Saint in Freed's *Beard of Avon*	Sh. Matters, vol. 2/2: 1, 14-15
2009	A Sparrow Falls: Olivier's Feminine Hamlet	Brief Chronicles, v. I: 193-204
2010	[review of *Shakespeare and Garrick* by Vanessa Cunningham]	Brief Chronicles, v. II: 227-231
2011, Fall	[review of *Anonymous*]	Brief Chronicles, v. III: 288-293
2014, Summer	Was Shakespeare a Euphuist? Some Ruminations on Oxford, Lyly and Shakespeare	Brief Chronicles, v. V: 171-88
2017, Oct.	*Macbeth*: A Language Obsessed, Heretical Play	Oxfordian, vol. 19: 45-68
2017, Oct.	[review of *Shakespeare, the Man: New Decipherings* edited by R. W. Desai (2014)]	Oxfordian, vol. 19: 215-22
2018, Winter	Exercise in Rhetoric: Let's Learn to Write Like Shakespeare!	Sh. Ox. Newsl., vol. 54/1: 17-18
2020, Sept.	Was Shakespeare Don Quixote (or was He a Jacobean Dramatist)?	Oxfordian, vol. 22: 79-102
2022, Sept.	What is Hamlet's Book? [see Earl Showerman's response, vol. 25: 21-26]	Oxfordian,vol. 24: 193-210
2023, Summer	Shakespeare's Epistemology and the Problem of Truth	J. of Scientific Expl., vol. 37/2
2023, Summer	My New Shakespeare Course on Zoom	Sh. Ox. Newsl., vol. 59/3: 7

Gilfillan, S. Colum

1973, Winter	[letter: authorship issues]	Sh. Ox. Newsl., vol. 9/1: 8-10

Gill, James

1993, Jan. 3	The Play's the Thing, But Is It Mr. Shakespeare's? [repr. in SON, vol. 29/1a: 7-8 (Winter 1993); and in BTC, vol. 7: 150-51]	New Orleans Tr.-Pic., Lag: 8

Gill, John

2009, June	[review of *The Man Who Was Hamlet* by George Dillon, performed at the Hawth Theatre, 8 May 2009]	De Vere Soc. Newsl., v 16/2: 32
2011, March	[review of *Malice Aforethought* by Paul Altrocchi (2010)]	De Vere So. New., v. 18/1: 30-32
2011, March	[review of *Shakespeare's Lost Kingdom* by Charles Beauclerk (2009)] [repr. in NSJ, vol. NS2: 32-40 (Oct. 2011)]	De Vere So. New., v. 18/1: 32-34

Gill, Wally

1950, April	On the Shake-speare Sonnets [a sonnet]	SF News-letter (E), p. 9

Gilvary, Kevin

Books

2010	*Dating Shakespeare's Plays: A Critical Review of the Evidence.* Turnbridge Wells, Kent, UK: Parapress. [2nd ed. Portsea Press, 2022]	
2015	*Shakespearean Biografiction: How Modern Biographers Rely on Context, Conjecture and Inference to Construct a Life of the Bard.* London: Brunel University. [Ph.D. thesis]	
2018	*The Fictional Lives of Shakespeare.* London: Routledge.	

Periodicals edited

2003, June – 2005, Sept; and 2013, April – 2014, Jan.; and 2014, May-2016, April: *The De Vere Society Newsletter*

Shorter pieces

1985, Feb. 3	The Man from Stratford? [letter: reply to Gordon Cyr's Jan. 13 letter]	New York Times, p. BR35
1985, June 9	[letter: reply to Robert Campbell's June 9 letter] Resp. by Morse Johnson, Nov. 9. [repr. in SON, vol. 27/1: 5-6]	New York Times, p. BR38

Author Index

Gilvary, Kevin (continued)

2013, April	Davenant and Shakespeare: The Biographers Dilemma [A talk given at Lincoln College, Oxford (April 6, 2013)]	De Vere So. New., v. 20/1: 25-29
2013, Spring	The *Chronicles* of Hall and Holinshed: Published Under Pseudonyms?	Brief Chronicles, vol. IV: 1-20
2013, July	Exciting Times for Authorship Doubters	De Vere Soc. Newsl., vol. 20/2: 2
2013, July	[review of *Shakespeare Beyond Doubt? Exposing an Industry in Denial*, edited by John M. Shahan and Alexander Waugh]	De Vere Soc. New., vol. 20/2: 18
2013, July	Notice about *The Naked Shakespeare* (2012), a documentary film by Claus Bredenbrock	De Vere Soc. New., vol. 20/2: 29
2013, Oct.	John Shakspere in Public Records (1530?-1601)	De Vere Soc. New., vol. 20/3: 11
2013, Oct.	Royal Shakespeare Company's Psychological Aberration? [Stanley Wells' comments on its website, and responses by Alice Crampin and Danny Evans]	De Vere Soc. New., vol. 20/3: 27
2014, Jan.	Writ in Choice Italian: Shakespeare and Italian Literature	De Vere Soc. New., v. 21/1: 9-14
2014, Oct.	[review of *Shakespeare Suppressed* by Katherine Chiljan (2011)]	De Vere Soc. New., vol. 21/3: 23
2015, April	Richard Malim: Twelve Years' Research	De Vere Soc. Newsl., v. 21/1: 3-4
2015, July	Shakespeare: His True Likeness	De Vere Soc. Newsl., v. 22/3: 3-7
2015, Oct.	The Case for Oxford; FAQs	De Vere So. New., v. 22/4: 21-33
2016, Jan.	Did Shakespeare Know Jonson?	De Vere So. New., v. 23/1: 33-38
2016, April	DVS Welcomes New Chairman: Alexander Waugh	De Vere Soc. Newsl., vol. 23/2: 3
2016, Oct.	Gaps in Our Ignorance: The Limited Biographical Material for William Shakespeare	De Vere So. New., v. 23/4: 26-33
2016, Dec.	Who Wrote the First Biography of Shakespeare? It was not Nicholas Rowe in 1709!	Brief Chronicles, vol. VII: 1-15
2017, Oct.	The De Vere Society and the State of the Sh. Authorship Question	De Vere Soc. New., v. 24/4: 6-10
2017, Oct.	[rev. of *The Great Debate: Who Wrote Shakespeare?*] [with Julia Cleave]	De Vere So. New., v. 24/4: 38-44
2019, Jan.	Towards Oxfordian Chroonology of Shakespeare's Plays	De Vere Soc. NL, v. 26/1: 21-41
2019, July	In Memory of Oxfordian Williard Ron Hess	De Vere Soc. Newsl., v. 26/3: 4-7
2019, Oct.	DVS Mourns Graham Ambridge (d. 2019)	De Vere Soc. Newsl., vol. 26/4: 4
2020, Jan.	A Storm Called Emilia: Was Emilia Bassano the Dark Lady or even the Hidden Author?	De Vere So. New., v. 27/1: 21-30
2020, April	Shakespearean Authorship Trust (in collaboration with Brunel Univ.): Shakespeare and the Essex Rising [with Amanda Hinds]	Sh. Ox. Newsl., vol. 27/2: 13-16
2000, Spring	[letter to *The Times*: response to Porter's Dec. 9 letter [not printed] See also Christopher Dams' response to Porter [also not printed]	De Vere Soc. Newsl., p. 4-5
2020, July	*"Shakespeare" Identified in Edward de Vere the Seventeenth Earl of Oxford* by J. Thomas Looney (1920)	De Vere So. New., v. 27/3: 3-38
2020, Oct.	[review of *The de Vere Papers* by Michael Langford]	De Vere Soc. Newsl., v. 27/4: 32
2020, Oct.	[review of *Who Wrote That? Authorship Controversies from Moses to Sholokhov* by Donald Ostrowski]	De Vere So. New., v. 27/4: 33-6
2020, Oct.	[letter: response to Alan Bodell]	De Vere So. New., v. 27/4: 43-44
2021, Jan.	The Theatres and the Folly: How the 1580 Earthquake Failed to Shake Oxford's Circle	De Vere Soc. Newsl., v. 28/1: 7-9
2021, Jan.	[rev. of *Renaissance Man: World of Thomas Watson* by Ian Johnson]	De Vere So. Nel., v. 28/1: 46-48
2023, April	Tribute to Geoffrey Eyre, RIP	De Vere Soc. Newsl., vol. 30/2: 4
2023, Summer	Demythologizing Shakespeare: What We Really Know About the Man From Stratford	J. of Sci. Exploration, vol. 37/2

Giroux, Robert

1984, Dec. 9	Sweet Swan of Oxford? [rev. of *The Mysterious W. Shakespeare*] Response by Gordon Cyr, Jan. 13, p. BR29. Reply to Gordon Cyr by Robert Giroux, Feb. 3, p. BR35. Response by Robert M. Campbell, June 9, p. BR38. Response by Alden Todd, June 9, p. BR38. Reply to Alden Todd by Robert Giroux, June 9, p. BR38. Response by Morse Johnson, SON, vol. 27/3: 3-4 (Summer 1991).	New York Times, p. BR13

Gilyeat, Dave

2009, Nov. 27	Edward de Vere, Earl of Oxford: The Real Shakespeare?	BBC News Mag.

Author Index

Gittleman, Sharon
  2003, March   Crusader Aims to Prove Shake. Was a Fraud [profile of   Detroit Free Press, p. 3
                     Barbara Burris]

Gladstone, Ryan
  2009   *The Shakespeare Show or How an Illiterate Son of a Glover Became the Greatest Playwright in the World.*
                     Penned by Edward de Vere. [a play] [De Vere, dying, charges horse-holder Will Shakespeare with
                     telling his story . . .]

Glanville, Justin
  2003, Nov. 23   Shakespeare In Another Light [rev. of *Beard of Avon* by A. Freed]   Record (NJ), p. E7

Glaser, Bill
  2022, Winter   [letter: *Midsummer Night's Dream*]   Sh. Ox. Newsl., vol. 58/1: 3

Glawson, Jack
  2007, Summer   The Mysterious Charlton Ogburn: Remembering the Man Behind the   Sh. Matters, vol. 6/4: 7, 17-21
                     Myth-buster

Glazener, Nancy
  2007, Summer   Print Culture as an Archive of Dissent: Or, Delia Bacon and the Case   Am. Lit. History, p. 329-49
                     of the Missing Hamlet

Gleaves, Richard
  2023, April   [letter: Shakespeare's "impossible doublet"]   De Vere Soc. Newsl., v. 30/2: 37

Glenn, Edgar M. (editor)
  1962   *Shakespeare and His Rivals: A Casebook on the Authorship Controversy*
                     [with George L. McMichael] New York: Odyssey Press.

Glore, John
  1986   [review of *The Mysterious William Shakespeare* by Ch. Ogburn, Jr.]   Am. Theatre, vol. 2/10: 30, 32

Goff, Tom
  1987, Sept. 29?   The Oford Shakespeare Scenario [letter]   Sacramento Bee
  1988, Aug.   The Seventeenth Earl of Oxford's Annuity   De Vere Soc. News., no. 3: 74-89
  1988, Fall   [letter to *Sacramento Bee*: Fraser's book *Young Shakespeare* (not pr.)] Sh. Ox. Newsl., vol. 24/4: 11
  1989, Summer   Rumors of Disaster, Premonitions of War [repr. in EVR, vol. 9 (1999)]   Sh. Ox. Newsl., vol. 25/3: 2-6
  1990, Winter   Mark Twain, Shakespeare, and Helen Keller   Sh. Ox. Newsl., vol. 26/1: 3-5
  1990, Winter   For if the Queen Like Not the Comedy   Sh. Ox. Newsl., vol. 26/1: 14-19
  1990, Summer   [review of *The Mysterious William Shakespeare* (1984) and   Sh. Ox. Newsl., vol. 26/3a: 1-2
                     The Mystery of William Shakespeare] [pb. abridged version]
  1990, Summer   [rev. of *Oxford's Revenge: "Shakespeare's" Dramatic   Sh. Ox. Newsl., vol. 26/3a: 3-5
                     Development from Agamemnon to Hamlet* by Stephanie Caruana
                     & Elisabeth Sears (1989)]
  1991, Winter   [letter to the *Sacramento Bee*: Stylometric errors (not printed)] Sh. Ox. Newsl., vol. 27/1: 6-7
  1991, Summer   [review of *The Man Who Was William Shakespeare* by Peter   Sh. Ox. Newsl., vol. 27/3: 6-8
                     Sammartino (1990)] [repr. in BTC, vol. 7: 53-57]
  1991, Fall   "To Calm Contending Kings": Oxfordians receive letter from   Sh. Ox. Newsl., vol. 27/4: 10-11
                     Richard III Society [repr. in BTC, vol. 7: 74-77]
  1992, Winter   [review of *Shakespeare and the Tudor Rose* by Elisabeth Sears] Sh. Ox. Newsl., vol. 28/1: 8-9
  1992, Winter   [review of books edited by Ruth Loyd Miller: *Hidden Allusions in* Sh. Ox. Newsl., vol. 28/1: 10-11
                     Shakespeare's Plays (3rd rev. ed., 1974); *A Hundreth Sundrie*
                     Flowres (1975); *"Shakespeare" Identified and Poems of Ed.*
                     de Vere by J. T. Looney (1975) and *Oxfordian Vistas* (1975)]
  1993, Winter   [review of *The Mysterious William Shakespeare, 2nd Edition*, by Sh. Ox. Newsl., vol. 29/1a: 9-10
                     Charlton Ogburn, Jr.]
  1993, Fall   Charles Van Doren Joins the Stratford-Shakspere Doubters   Sh. Ox. Newsl., vol. 29/4: 9-10
                     Repr. in BTC, vol. 7: 214-16]
  1995, Summer   Lawrence of Arabia and the Shakespeare Mystery   Sh. Ox. Newsl., vol. 31/3: 7-8
  1995, Autumn   A Grand Summation [review of Charlton Ogburn's *The Man Who*   Sh. Ox. Newsl., vol. 31/4: 7-8
                     Was Shakespeare]
  2016, Winter   Two Poems: *And Someday, Maybe the Title*; *Look Under My*   Sh. Ox. Newsl., vol. 52/1: 28
                     Shakespeare Name
  2018, Spring   [letter: Whalen, Sears, Caruana, *Hamlet* and *Horestes*]   Sh. Ox. Newsl., vol. 54/2: 4
  2020, Spring   In Memory of Thomas Regnier, JD, L.L.M., Past President] [a sonnet] Sh. Ox. Newsl., vol. 56/2: 30

101

2020, Spring	[letter: articles by Cutting and Rogers]	Sh. Ox. Newsl., vol. 56/2: 3
2021, Summer	[letter: Moncrieff's article "Falstaff—Unmasked"]	Sh. Ox. Newsl., vol. 57/3: 4-5
2021, Fall	[review of *Shakespeare Revolutionized* by James A. Warren]	Sh. Ox. Newsl., vol. 57/4: 26
2022, Summer	[letter: response to Michael Hyde]	Sh. Ox. Newsl., vol. 58/3: 3
2022, Fall	[letter: Katharine E. Eggar]	Sh. Ox. Newsl., vol. 58/4: 5
2023, Winter	[review of Percy Allen, *Collected Writings on Shakespeare, vol. 5*, edited by James A. Warren (2022)]	Sh. Ox. Newsl., vol. 59/1: 19-20
2023, Spring	[review of *The Seventeenth Earl of Oxford 1550-1604* by B. M. Ward [new hardback edition, James A. Warren, editor]	Sh. Ox. Newsl., vol. 59/2: 29-31

Gohn, Jack B.

| 1982, Feb. 3 | *Richard II*: Shakespeare's Legal Brief on the Royal Prerogative and the Succession to the Throne [repr. in *Sh.and the Law* (Stritmatter 2022), p. 70-102] | George. Law Jour., vol. 70/3: 943 |

Golding, Louis Thorn

| 1937 | *An Elizabethan Puritan: Arthur Golding the Translator of Ovid's Metamorphoses and also of John Calvin's Sermons*. New York: Richard R. Smith. | |

Goldman, David

| 2002, Aug. | The Bard or Not the Bard: Who Wrote Shakespeare's Plays? | Biography Mag., vol. 6/8: 23 |

Goldstein, Gary B.

Broadcasts

| 1992, Sept. 17 | *Frontline: Uncovering Shakespeare: An Update* [an interactive videoconference on VisNet hosted by William F. Buckley, Jr., with 15 guests, including Charles Boyle, Warren Hope, Felicia Londré, Roger Stritmatter and Charles Vere. Produced by John Mucci and Gary Goldstein. See Hope and Holsten (2009) for fuller description] | |

Books

| 2016 | *Reflections on the True Shakespeare*. Buchholz, Germany: Verlag Uwe Laugwitz. [Special Editions #6 of *Neues Shake-speare Journal*] | |

Books edited

2009	*The Lame Storyteller, Poor and Despised,* by Peter R. Moore. Buchholz, Germany: Verlag Uwe Laugwitz	
2012	*Shakespeare's Education: Schools, Lawsuits, Theater and the Tudor Miracle,* by Robin Fox. Buchholz, Germany: Verlag Uwe Laugwitz.	
2014	*Such Fruits Out of Italy: The Italian Renaissance in Shakespeare's Plays and Poems,* by Noemi Magri. Buchholz, Germany: Verlag Uwe Laugwitz.	

Periodicals edited

1993-1999: *The Elizabethan Review*, vol. 1/1-7/1
2003, Autumn-2004, Fall: *Shakespeare Oxford Newsletter*, vol. 39/4-40/4
2018-current: *The Oxfordian*, vol. 20-current

Periodicals edited (managing editor)

| 2009-2013 | *Brief Chronicles: An Interdisciplinary Journal of Authorship Studies*, vol. I-IV | |

Shorter pieces

1989, April	"The Shakespeare Mystery" Unfolds [review of *Frontline* broadcast] [repr. in SON, vol. 25/2: 10-11]	Washington Square News
1989, Spring	News Items of Interest	Sh. Ox. Newsl., vol. 25/2: 22
1989, Summer	News Items of Interest	Sh. Ox. Newsl., vol. 25/3: 18-19
1989, July 21	Shakespeare Sleuths: Will the Real Bard Please Stand Up?	Stamford Advocate
1989, Fall	Hamlet's Art of Falconry [repr. in BTC, vol. 6: 410-13, and in REF, p. 111-17]	Sh. Ox. Newsl., vol. 25/4: 5-8
1990, Winter	Edward de Vere's Hebrew	Sh. Ox. Newsl., vol. 26/1: 6-11
1990, Spring	The Learned and the Lout [repr. in REF, p. 122-129]	Sh. Ox. Newsl., vol. 26/2: 7-10
1990, Spring	News Items of Interest	Sh. Ox. Newsl., vol. 26/2: 15
1990, Fall	Shakespeare's Native Tongue [repr. in DVN, vol. 16/3: 28-31 (Nov. 2009); in BTC, vol. 7: 22-29; and in REF, p. 147-58]	Sh. Ox. Newsl., vol. 26/4: 4-8
1991, May	Who Was Joyce's Shakespeare? [repr. in ER, vol. 5/1: 26-31 (Spr. 1997); and in REF, p. 178-87]	Spear-shaker Rev., is. 3/4: 11-16
1991, Fall	Tudor Theater, the Earls of Oxford, and State Propaganda [repr. in BTC, vol. 7: 78-82; and in REF, p. 101-09]	Sh. Ox. Newsl., vol. 27/4: 13-14
1993, Winter	[review of *The Sh. Controversy* by Warren Hope & Kim Holston]	Sh. Ox. Newsl., vol. 29/1a: 11

Author Index

1993, Spring	From the Editor	Eliz. Review, vol. 1/1: 1
	[repr. in BTC, vol. 8: 125-28]	
1993, Spring	Did Shakespeare Read Dante in Italian?	Eliz. Review, vol. 1/1: 61-62
	[repr. in REF, p. 143-46; and in NSJ, vol. 5: 86-87 (April 2000)]	
1993, Autumn	[review of *Shylock: A Legend and Its Legacy* by John Gross (1994)]	Eliz. Review, vol. 1/2: 78-79
1993, Autumn	[review of *The Essential Shakespeare* by Ted Hughes (1992)]	Eliz. Review, vol. 1/2: 79
1994, Spring	[review of *The Reckoning: Murder of Christopher Marlowe* by	Eliz. Review, vol. 2/1: 29-32
	Charles Nicholl (1992)] [repr. in REF, p. 227-32]	
1995, Spring	[review of *Shakespeare: Who Was He?* by Richard Whalen (1994)]	Eliz. Review, vol. 3/1: 69-69
1995, Autumn	[review of *The Man Who Was Shakespeare* by Charlton Ogburn, Jr.]	Eliz. Review, vol. 3/2: 68-70
1997, Spring	Who was Joyce's Shakespeare?	Eliz. Review, vol. 5/1: 26-31
	[from SSR, issue 3/4: 11-16 (May 1991); repr. in REF, 178-87	
	and in TOX, vol. 19: 173-80 (2017)]	
1997, Spring	[review of *Love's Labor's Lost: Critical Essays* ed. by Felicia H.	Eliz. Review, vol. 5/1: 57
	Londré (1997)]	
1997, Spring	[review of *Texts of Othello and Shakespearean Revision* by	Eliz. Review, vol. 5/1: 57-59
	E. A. J. Honigmann]	
1999, Spring	New Discoveries & Theories	Eliz. Review, vol. 7/1: 3
1999, Spring	Shakespeare's Little Hebrew	Eliz. Review, vol. 7/1: 70-77
	[repr. in DVN, vol. 17/1: 21-25 (Feb. 2010); in BTC, vol. 8:	
	322-30; and in REF, p. 130-42]	
2004	Did Queen Elizabeth Use the Theater for Social and Political	Oxfordian, vol. 7: 152-169
	Propaganda? [repr. in REF, p. 72-100]	
2004, Winter	Oxfordian News	Sh. Ox. Newsl., vol. 40/1: 12-13+
2004, Spring	Oxfordian News [German TV airs program on Oxford, Alan Nelson's	Sh. Ox. Newsl., vol. 40/2: 5
	bio reviewed, etc.]	
2004, Summer	Editor's Column	Sh. Ox. Newsl., vol. 40/3: 2-3
2004, Summer	U.S.-Australian Academics Research Authorship	Sh. Ox. Newsl., vol. 40/3: 3
2004, Summer	International Media Cover Oxford's Quadcentenary	Sh. Ox. Newsl., vol. 40/3: 8
2004, Summer	Two New Biographies of the 17th Earl of Oxford	Sh. Ox. Newsl., vol. 40/3: 10
2004, Fall	Paul Nitze, RIP (1907-2004)	Sh. Ox. Newsl., vol. 40/4: 2-3
2004, Fall	Oxfordian News [De Vere Society book on Oxford]	Sh. Ox. Newsl., vol. 40/4: 4-5
2005	[review of *Shakespeare By Another Name* by Mark Anderson (2005)]	Oxfordian, vol. 8: 124-128
2006	[review of *De Vere as Shakespeare* by William Farina (2006)]	Oxfordian, vol. 9: 135-137
2006	A Cup of Newes	Oxfordian, vol. 9: 144-153
2007	[review of *The Oxfordian Edition of Macbeth* edited by R. Whalen]	Oxfordian, vol. 10: 154-156
2007	Farewell to Peter Moore	Oxfordian, vol. 10: 160-161
2007	A Cup of Newes	Oxfordian, vol. 10: 167-178
2008, March	Peter R. Moore (1948-2007) [obituary]	De Vere Soc. Newsl., v. 15/1: 29
	[repr. in German in NSJ, vol. 12:51-52 (Oct. 2008)]	
2009	Editor's Introduction, in *The Lame Storyteller*, p. ix-xvi	
2009, Spring	News: New Oxfordian Books	Sh. Matters, vol. 8/2: 4
2009, Spring	News: A Cup of Publication News	Sh. Matters, vol. 8/2: 4-5
2009, Summer	[letter: thumbs up for Ian Haste's Spring 2009 "*Merchant*" article]	Sh. Matters, vol. 8/3: 2
2009, Nov.	[letter: Malim's *Great Oxford* mentioned in *Shakespeare Quarterly*	De Vere Soc. Newsl., v. 16/3: 34
2009, Fall	Searchable PDF (of *The Elizabethan Review*)	Sh. Matters, vol. 8/4: 19
2009, Nov.	New Life for Gary Goldstein's *Elizabethan Review*	De Vere Soc. Newsl., v. 16/3: 13
2010, Feb.	[rev. of *The Lame Storyteller: Poor and Despised* by Peter R. Moore]	De Vere Soc. Newsl., v. 17/1: 19
2010, Feb.	[letter: reply to Cousin]	De Vere Soc. New., v. 17/1: 26-7
2010, Spr./Sum.	Portrait of an Oxfordian Scholar: Peter Moore (1949-2007)	Sh. Matters, vol. 9: 22-23, 28
2010, Fall	News: Richard Roe Passes (d. 2010)	Sh. Matters, vol. 9/3: 4-5
2011, Winter	News: In Memoriam, Robert Brazil (1955-2011)	Sh. Matters, vol. 10/1: 5
2011, Jan.	[letter: *Brief Chronicles* publishes second issue online]	Sh. Ox. Newsl., vol. 47/1: 9-10
2011, July	Appeasing the Fringe of the Oxfordian Movement	De Vere S. New., v. 18/2: 29, 38
2011, Fall	[review of *Bardgate: Shake-speare and the Royalists Who Stole	Brief Chronicles, v. III: 285-287
	the Bard* by Peter W. Dickson (2011)] [repr. in REF, p. 221-26]	
2012, Nov.	An Ox on Our Tongues [repr. in REF, p. 118-21]	De Vere Soc. New., v. 19/3: 40-1
2013	Still in Denial: *Shakespeare Beyond Doubt* versus	Oxfordian, vol. 15: 92-99
	Shakespeare Beyond Doubt? [repr. in REF, p. 201-15]	

Gontar, David P.
Books
2013 *Hamlet Made Simple: And other essays*. Nashville: New English Review Press.
2015 *Unreading Shakespeare*. Nashville: New England Review Press.
Shorter pieces
2006, Spring Oxford and Elizabeth [letter: resp. by M. Anderson, same issue, p. 3] Sh. Matters, vol. 5/3: 2-3
2006, Summer [letter: Ren Draya's "Oxford's Outsiders" article (Spring 2006)] Sh. Matters, vol. 5/4: 2
2014, Spring [letter: need for new look at Shakespeare from the Oxfordian viewpoint] Sh. Ox. Newsl., vol. 50/2: 4
2015, Fall [letter: *Hamlet Made Simple* and *Unreading Shakespeare* are the first substantial forays in literary criticism from an Ox. perspective] Sh. Ox. Newsl., vol. 51/4: 3
2019, Summer [letter: *Hamlet Made Simple*] Sh. Ox. Newsl., vol. 55/3: 5

Gonzales, Jack
1999, Feb. 20 [letter: Peter Dickson's Feb. 6 letter] Washington Post, p. A17

Gooch, Steve
2011, Oct. 22 [letter: the Oct. 15 Interview with Mark Rylance] Guardian, p. 45

Goode, Stephen
1994 Literary Class Struggle: The Bard's Identity Crisis [cover story featuring Charles Vere, Lord Burford] Insight on the News, vol. 10/44: 9-11

Goodman, M. Kirsten
1937, July Oxford - Davenant - Shakespeare SF News-letter (E), no. 4: 7-10

Goodman, Walter
1989, April 18 The Shakespeare Mystery: Who Was He? [rev. of *The Shakespeare Mystery*, Al Austin doc.] [repr. in SON, vol. 25/2: 3-4 (Spring 1989); and in BTC, vol. 6: 383-84] New York Times, p. C22

Goodwin, Ken
1991, March 2 Historical Setting for the Looney Theories [review of *The Lost Chronicle of Edward de Vere* by Andrew Field (1990)] Courier-Mail

Gordon, Helen Heightsman
Books
2005 *The Secret Love Story in Shakespeare's Sonnets*. Xlibris Corporation.
Shorter pieces
2002 Alexander Pope: an Oxfordian at heart? Oxfordian, vol. 5: 147-158
2007 Sh.'s Rosicrucian Revelations in the Dedication to the Sonnets Rose+Croix J., vol. 4: 1-20
2009, Summer [review of *Elizabeth and Sh.: Meeting of Two Myths* by H. Hackett] [also in *J. of Social & Psych. Sciences*, vol. 3/1: 25 (Jan. 2010)] Sh. Matters, vol. 8/3: 16-18
2012, Sum./Fall [letter: the Prince Tudor question] Sh. Ox. Newsl., vol. 48/3: 5-8
2014, Summer [letter: Michael Morse's April presentation on anagrams, cryptographs and acrostics in Oxford's works] Sh. Ox. Newsl., vol. 50/3: 5

Gore-Langton, Robert
2007, Sept. 7 Is There a William Shakespeare in the House? [review of *The Big Secret Live* by Mark Rylance and Matthew Warchus (2007)] Daily Mail, p. 1
2014, Oct. 27 Could the Real Mr. Shakespeare Please Stand Up? [repr. in DVN, vol. 21/3: 3-5 (Oct. 2014)] Daily Express, p. 13
2014, Dec. 26 The Campaign to Prove Shakespeare Didn't Exist [online blog] Newsweek,

Gorman, J. T.
1921, March 21 [letter] Montgomery Advertiser

Gottlieb, Jane
1987, Sept. 28 Bard Beats the Rap USA Today, p. 1D

Goudsmit, Jepke
2001 *Shake-speare*. [a play about the life of Ed. de Vere] [with Graham Jones] Sydney Morning Herald, p. 20
2002, Winter [letter, w. Graham Jones: Sydney-based Kinetic Energy Theatre Co.] Sh. Matters, vol. 1/2: 32

Gould, Gordon
1957, Apr. 21 If Shakespeare Didn't Write Shakespeare, Who Did? Chicago Tribune, p. B6

Gould, Rachel
2004, Aug. 4 Shakedown on Shakespeare: Old Debate Reignited About Who Wrote What Spectator (Ontario), p. G11

Gould, Rachel (continued)

2004, Aug. 5	London Debates Authorship of Shakespeare's Plays	Expositor (Ontario), p. C7
2004, Aug. 7	The Shakespeare Enigma Won't Die	Toronto Star, p. J2
2004, Aug. 8	The Playwright's the Thing	Milwaukee Sentinal, p. 7E

Goulding, Captain

1758   *An Essay Against Too Much Reading.* London: Moore.

Gove, John

2002, Fall [letter: Christopher Paul's review of Streitz's book (Summer 2002)] Sh. Matters, vol. 2/1: 4

Grabert, Getraude

2014, Oct.	Karneval in Venedig oder wer war Shakespeare. Ein Maskenspiel.	Neues Sh. Jou., v. NS4: 94-108
2016, Oct.	Gedanken zu einigen Dramen	Neues Sh. Jou., vol. NS5: 180-87
2018	*King John* und *The Troublesome Raign* [review of *The Troublesome Raigne of King John*]	Neues Sh. Jou., vol. NS6: 183-88
2000	Warum ich glaube, dass Oxford der Dichter Shakespeare War	Neues Sh. Jou., vol. NS7: 129-39
2023	Gedanken zu einigen Dramen Teil II	Neues Sh. Jou., vol. NS8: 178-93

Graham, Nicholas

2012, Dec. 1	[review of *Shakespeare's Education* by Robin Fox]	Library Journal, v. 137/20: 82-85
2014, Jan.	The Bard at 450 [resp. by Michael Dudley, Mar. 1, vol. 139/4: 12]	Library Journal., v. 138/14: 48-51
2014	[review of *Contested Will* by James Shapiro (2010)]	Library Journal., v. 139/1: 50
2014	[review of *Who Wrote Shakespeare?* by John Michell (1996)]	Library Journal., v. 139/1: 50

Grames, Roland E.

2013, March In a Labyrinth, Channeling Shakespeare: The Music of Joseph Summer [Sumner explains origin of "The Oxford Songs"] Fanfare, vol. 36/4: 127

Grant, Barry

2010   *Sherlock Holmes and the Shakespeare Letter.* [a novel]

Graves, Charles L.

Books

2014   *27 Essays on Edward de Vere and William Shakespeare.* CreateSpace.

Shorter pieces

2016, October	'Signatures' of Edward de Vere in Anonymous Plays	De Vere So. New., v. 23/4: 19-25
2017, July	The Author of *The Wisdom of Dr. Doddypoll*	De Vere Soc. New., v. 24/3: 21-5
2018, Jan.	How Edward de Vere was Related to William Shakspere Through the Trussell Family of Billesley, Warwickshire]	De Vere Soc. New., vo. 25/1: 3-7
2020, April	Edward de Vere, Euphuism and Bi-Sexuality	De Vere So. New., v. 27/2: 37-46
2020, Oct.	[letter: Gilvary's article on J. Thomas Looney]	De Vere So. New., v. 27/4: 43-44
2021, July	Euphuistic Elements in Edward de Vere's Tragedies	De Vere Sc. New., v. 28/3: 36-44
2021, Oct.	Commentary on Ian Haste's Article "Vere's Rings in *Merchant*]	De Vere So. New., v. 28/4: 24-25
2022, Jan.	Two Gentlemen of Verona: A Euphuistic Story of Edward de Vere	De Vere So. New., v. 29/1: 38-43
2022, April	[letter: Shakespeare and activism]	De Vere Soc. New., vol. 29/2: 42
2023, July	The 1623 Folio Edition of Shakespeare and the Exclusion of the Earl of Oxford as Its Author	De Vere So. New., v. 30/3: 33-38

Graves, Gary

2004   *The Mysterious Mr. Looney* [A dramatic presentation of J. Thomas Looney and Sir Sidney Chambers]

Gray, Austin K.

1924, Sept. The Secret of *Love's Labour's Lost* PMLA, vol. 39/4: 581-611.

Gray, Joshua

2017   *The Life and Death of King Edward.* Forever Press.

Gray, Marilyn Savage

2001	*The Real Shakespeare.* iUniverse.com.
2015	*The Real Shakespeare*, Revised ed. iUniverse.com.

Greatorex, Jane

Books

2022   *Manors, Mills & Manuscripts series: John de Vere, 16th Earl of Oxford.*

Shorter pieces

2023   Conveyance by Edward de Vere of the "Hedingham Honour" to William Cecil De Vere Soc. Newsl., vol. 30/1: 25-26

2023, April	[letter: malfeasance against the Earl of Oxford]	De Vere So. New., v. 30/2: 35-37

Green, Dominic

2019, May 14	Was Shakespeare a Woman? Of Course He Was [response to Winkler's May 10 piece in the *Atlantic*]	Sphere

Green, Nina

Blog: The Oxford Authorship Site – oxford-shakespeare.com

Books edited

1990	*The Marprelate Tracts: Martin's Epistle*. Kelowna, BC, Canada: Devere Press.
1991	*The Langham Letter: A Modern Spelling Edition*. Kelowna, BC, Canada: Devere Press.

Periodicals edited

1989, Mar.-1994, Sept.: *The Edward de Vere Newsletter*, issues 1-67.

Shorter pieces

1989, March	Did Edward de Vere Write the Comedy Known as *The Merry Devil of Edmonton?*	Ed. De Vere Newsl., no. 1
1989, April	What Part Did Edward de Vere Play in the Voyages of Exploration and Trade in the Great Elizabethan Age of Exploration?	Ed. De Vere Newsl., no. 2
1989, May	Who Was the "upstart crow" in *Green's Groats-worth of Witte?*	Ed. De Vere Newsl., no. 3
1989, June	Did Ed. de Vere Write *The Puritan; or the Widow of Watling Street?*	Ed. De Vere Newsl., no. 4
1989, July	Did Edward de Vere Write the *Langham Letter?* (Part 1 of 3)	Ed. De Vere Newsl., no. 5
1989, Aug.	Did Edward de Vere Write the *Langham Letter?* (Part 2 of 3)	Ed. De Vere Newsl., no. 6
1989, Sept.	Did Edward de Vere Write the *Langham Letter?* (Part 3 of 3)	Ed. De Vere Newsl., no. 7
1989, Oct/2001	Did Edward de Vere Know A. Brooke, Author of *Romeus and Juliet?*	Ed. De Vere Newsl., no. 8
1989, Nov.	Did Ben Jonson Write the Inscription for the Sh. Monument at Stratford?	Ed. De Vere Newsl., no. 9
1989, Dec.	Did Edward de Vere Write *The Reign of King Edward the Third?*	Ed. De Vere Newsl., no. 10
1990, Jan.	Did Edward de Vere Write the *Scottish History of James the Fourth, Slaine at Flodden?*	Ed. De Vere Newsl., no. 11
1990, Feb./2001	Did Edward de Vere Write *Sir John Oldcastle?*	Ed. De Vere Newsl., no. 12
1990, March	Did Edward de Vere Write the *Langham Letter?*	Ed. De Vere Newsl., no. 13
1990, April	Did Edward de Vere Write *Sir John Oldcastle* in an Attempt to Save His Cousin, Thomas Howard, From the Headsman's Axe?, Part 1	Ed. De Vere Newsl., no. 14
1990, May	Did Edward de Vere Write *Sir John Oldcastle* in an Attempt to Save His Cousin, Thomas Howard, From the Headsman's Axe?, Part 2	Ed. De Vere Newsl., no. 15
1990, June	Did Edward de Vere Write *Sir John Oldcastle* in an Attempt to Save His Cousin, Thomas Howard, From the Headsman's Axe?, Part 3	Ed. De Vere Newsl., no. 16
1990, July	Did Edward de Vere Write *Sir John Oldcastle* in an Attempt to Save His Cousin, Thomas Howard, From the Headsman's Axe?, Part 4	Ed. De Vere Newsl., no. 17
1990, Aug.	Does the Early Work of Edestf de Vere Reveal That He Wrote Songs?	Ed. De Vere Newsl., no. 18
1990, Sept.	Did Edward de Vere Write the *Ballad of King Arthur* in the *Langham Letter?*	Ed. De Vere Newsl., no. 19
1990, Oct.	Did the Author of the *Langham Letter* Have Pronounced Music Interests and Abilities?	Ed. De Vere Newsl., no. 20
1990, Nov.	Was A Yorkshire Tragedy Written Before Its So-Called "Source"?	Ed. De Vere Newsl., no. 21
1990, Dec.	Was Anne Lyly, Sister of the Poet John Donne, a Promoter of the Ill-Fated Marriage of Walter Calverley and Philippa Brooke?	Ed. De Vere Newsl., no. 22
1991, Jan.	Did Edward de Vere Write *A Yorkshire Tragedy?*	Ed. De Vere Newsl., no. 23
1991, Feb.	Did the Author of the Pamphlet *Two Most Unnaturall and Bloodie Murthers* Make Use of *The Miseries of Enforced Marriage* and *A Yorkshire Tragedy?*	Ed. De Vere Newsl., no. 24
1991, March	Did Ed. de Vere Have a Youthful Love Affair That Was Thwarted?	Ed. De Vere Newsl., no. 25
1991, April	Does the Unusual Orthography of the *Langham Letter* Indicate the Author Was a Proponent of Spelling Reform in the 1570s?	Ed. De Vere Newsl., no. 26
1991, May	To Whom Was Humfrey Martyn Related Through His Mother, Letina Pakington?	Ed. De Vere Newsl., no. 27
1991, June	To Whom Was Humfrey Martyn Related Through His Father, Sir Roger Martyn?	Ed. De Vere Newsl., no. 28
1991, July	What Was William Patten's Involvement in the Publication of the *Langham Letter?*	Ed. De Vere Newsl., no. 29
1991, Aug.	Was the Author of the *Langham Letter* a Mercer and a Merchant-Adventurer?	Ed. De Vere Newsl., no. 30

Green, Nina (continued)

1991, Sept.	Is the *Langham Letter* an Eye-Witness Account of Queen Elizabeth's Entertainment at Kenilworth in 1572, Rather Than 1575?	Ed. De Vere Newsl., no. 31
1991, Oct.	Was Edward de Vere the "Annotator" of a Copy of *Hall's Chronicle*? 1	Ed. De Vere Newsl., no. 32
1991, Nov.	Was Edward de Vere the "Annotator" of a Copy of *Hall's Chronicle*? 2	Ed. De Vere Newsl., no. 33
1991, Dec.	Was Edward de Vere the "Annotator" of a Copy of *Hall's Chronicle*? 3	Ed. De Vere Newsl., no. 34
1992, Jan./2001	Could *The Famous Victories of Henry the Fifth* Have Been Written in 1548?	Ed. De Vere Newsl., no. 35
1992, Feb.	Was the Annotator of *Hall's Chronicle* the Author of *The Famous Victories of Henry the Fifth*?	Ed. De Vere Newsl., no. 36
1992, March	Were the Calverley Murders Entirely Unrelated to the Play *A Yorkshire Tragedy*?	Ed. De Vere Newsl., no. 37
1992, Apr.	Was Edward de Vere Related By Marriage to Thomas Russell, Overseer of the Will of William Shakespeare?	Ed. De Vere Newsl., no. 38
1992, May	Was Sir Ch. Hatton Related By Marriage To Both the Owner of New Place and the Owner of the Annotated Copy of *Hall's Chronicle*?	Ed. De Vere Newsl., no. 39
1992, June	Was Ed. de Vere Contracted to Marry One of the Sisters of Henry, 3rd Earl Of Huntingdon, Because of Their Common Hastings Ancestors?	Ed. De Vere Newsl., no. 40
1992, July	Did Edward de Vere Write the *Verses for Lady Derby's Entertainment*? Part 1	Ed. De Vere Newsl., no. 41
1992, Aug.	Did Edward de Vere Write the *Verses for Lady Derby's Entertainment*? Part 2	Ed. De Vere Newsl., no. 42
1992, Sept.	Did Edward de Vere Write the *Verses for Lady Derby's Entertainment*? Part 3	Ed. De Vere Newsl., no. 43
1992, Oct.	Did Edward de Vere Write the *Verses for Lady Derby's Entertainment*? Part 4	Ed. De Vere Newsl., no. 44
1992, Nov.	Does the *Don Triptych* Portray the Ancestors of Edward de Vere? 1	Ed. De Vere Newsl., no. 45
1992, Dec.	Does the *Don Triptych* Portray the Ancestors of Edward de Vere? 2	Ed. De Vere Newsl., no. 46
1993, Jan.	Does the *Don Triptych* Portray the Ancestors of Edward de Vere? 3	Ed. De Vere Newsl., no. 47
1993, Feb.	Does the *Don Triptych* Portray the Ancestors of Edward de Vere? 4	Ed. De Vere Newsl., no. 48
1993, March	Was Ed. de Vere the "E.K." of Spenser's *Shepheardes Calendar*? 1	Ed. De Vere Newsl., no. 49
1993, April	Was Ed. de Vere the "E.K." of Spenser's *Shepheardes Calendar*? 2	Ed. De Vere Newsl., no. 50
1993, May	Was Ed. de Vere the "E.K." of Spenser's *Shepheardes Calendar*? 3	Ed. De Vere Newsl., no. 51
1993, June	Was Ed. de Vere the "E.K." of Spenser's *Shepheardes Calendar*? 4	Ed. De Vere Newsl., no. 52
1993, July	Was Ed. de Vere the "E.K." of Spenser's *Shepheardes Calendar*? 5	Ed. De Vere Newsl., no. 53
1993, August	Was Ed. de Vere the "E.K." of Spenser's *Shepheardes Calendar*? 6	Ed. De Vere Newsl., no. 54
1993, Sept.	Was Ed. de Vere the "E.K." of Spenser's *Shepheardes Calendar*? 7	Ed. De Vere Newsl., no. 55
1993, Oct.	Was the Annotated Copy of *Hall's Chronicle* in the Library of Robert Worsley a Lineal Descendant of Edward de Vere?	Ed. De Vere Newsl., no. 56
1993, Nov.	Were the Letters and Youthful Poems of Edward de Vere Written in the Lexical Vocabulary of Shakespeare? Part 1 [repr. in SON, vol. 30/2A: 12-15 (1994), and in BTC, vol. 7: 232-36]	Ed. De Vere Newsl., no. 57
1993, Dec.	Were the Letters and Youthful Poems of Edward de Vere Written in the Lexical Vocabulary of Shakespeare? Part 2 [repr. in SON, vol. 30/2A: 12-15 (1994), and in BTC, vol. 7: 232-36]	Ed. De Vere Newsl., no. 58
1994, Jan.	Were the Letters and Youthful Poems of Edward de Vere Written in the Lexical Vocabulary of Shakespeare? Part 3 [repr. in SON, vol. 30/2A: 12-15 (1994), and in BTC, vol. 7: 232-36]	Ed. De Vere Newsl., no. 59
1994, Feb.	Does the Lexical Vocabulary of Edward de Vere's Letters and Youthful Poems Support the Hypothesis of His Authorship of *The Reign of King Edward III*?, Part 1	Ed. De Vere Newsl., no. 60
1994, March	Does the Lexical Vocabulary of Edward de Vere's Letters and Youthful Poems Support the Hypothesis of His Authorship of *The Reign of King Edward III*? Part 2	Ed. De Vere Newsl., no. 61
1994, Apr.	Does the Lexical Vocabulary of Edward de Vere's Letters and Youthful Poems Support the Hypothesis of His Authorship of *The Reign of King Edward III*? Part 3	Ed. De Vere Newsl., no. 62
1994, May	Was an Edition of the *Langham Letter* Published After 1590?	Ed. De Vere Newsl., no. 63

Greenwood, Elsie

1962, Autumn	Obituary of George Greenwood (1850-1928) [repr. in BTC, vol. 1, p. 7 and BTC, vol. 5, p. 89-91]	Sh. Authorship Review, #8: 6-7
1937, March	[letter: thanks to those who supported her new abbreviated edition of her fathers's *The Shakespeare Problem Restated*]	SF News-letter (E), no. 2: 11

Greenwood, George G.

Books

1908   *The Shakespeare Problem Restated*. London, New York: John Lane Company. Repr. in 1970: Westport, CT: Greenwood Press. [excerpts repr. in SON, vol. 24/3: 7 (Summer 1988); SON, vol. 25/1: 12-13 (Winter 1989); SON, vol. 29/2b: 1-7 (Spring 1993); and in BTC, vol. 7: 176-85. Preface repr. in SON, vol. 25/3: 2 (Summer 1989).]

1909   *In re Shakespeare: Beeching v. Greenwood: Rejoinder on Behalf of the Defendant*. London: John Lane.

1911   *The Vindicators of Shakespeare: A Reply to Critics, Together with Some Remarks on Dr. Wallace's "New Shakespeare Discoveries."* London: Sweeting and Co. Repr. in 1970: Port Washington, NY: Kennikat Press. [excerpt repr. in SON, vol. 26/4: 2-4 (Fall 1990), and in BTC, vol. 6: 416-20.] [Another excerpt repr. in SON, vol. 30/4: 14 (Autumn 1994); and in BTC, vol. 7: 287-88; and another excerpt repr. in SON, vol. 31/4: 22 (Autumn, 1995)]

1916   *Is There A Shakespeare Problem?* London, New York: John Lane Company. [Chapter VI: Professor Dryasdust and "Genius" repr. in BTC, vol. 1: 10-23] [Chapter VI: "Shakespeare as a Lawyer" repr. in BTC, vol. 1: 33-42] [Chapter VIII: "Portraits of Shakespeare" repr. in BTC, vol. 1: 24-32] [Notes to Chapter III: Brief Comments on the Sonnets repr. in BTC, vol. 1: 8-9]

1916   *Sir Sidney Lee's New Edition of A Life of William Sh.: Some Words of Criticism*. London: John Lane.

1916   *Shakespeare's Law and Latin—How I was "Exposed" by Mr. J. M. Robertson, M.P.* London: Watts & Co.

1920   *Shakespeare's Law*. London: Cecil Palmer. [excerpts repr. in *Shakespeare and the Law* (2022, Stritmatter), p. 41-62]

1920   *Shakespeare's Handwriting*. London: John Lane.

1921   *Ben Jonson and Shakespeare*. London: Cecil Palmer. [see esp. pp. 45-54] [excerpts repr. in BTC, vol. 1: 43-52; in BC, Special issue, p. 61-68 (Spring, 2016); and in SAS (Stritmatter 2019, 2022): 237-44]

1922   *Baconian Essays (by E. W. Smithson, with an Introduction and two essays by Greenwood)*. London: Cecil Palmer. [repr. in 1970: Port Washington, NY: Kennikat Press]

1923   *Shakespeare and a Tertium Quid*. London: Cecil Palmer.

1924   *Shakespeare's Signatures and Sir Thomas More*. London: Cecil Palmer.

1925   *The Stratford Bust and the Droeshout Engraving*. A monograph. London: Cecil Palmer. [repr. in BTC, vol. 1: 53-58]

Shorter pieces

1917, June	The Real Shakespeare Problem: A Reply to Mr. Gordon Crosse	Nineteenth Cen., v. 81: 1340-54
1920, April 10	Was Shakespeare Uneducated? [letter: response to the review of SI]	Spectator, p. 487
1922, Jan. 12	Mary Fitton [letter: response to Clutton-Brock's review]	Times Lit. Sup., is. 1043: 28
1922, March	Was Shakespeare a Schoolmaster?	National Rev. (UK), vol. 79: 230
1923, Jan. 5	[The Shakespeare Fellowship column no. 11]	Hackney Spectator, no. 1996: 11
1923, Feb. 16	Shakespearean Research	Hackney Spectator, no. 2006: 7
1923, Nov. 9	[Annual General Meeting by Col. Ward includes Greenwood's letter to *The Observer*: A Play in Shakespeare's Handwriting]	Hackney Spectator, no. 2078: 2
1924, Aug. 29	Stratfordian Manners: A Letter to Lord Sydenham	Hackney Spectator, no. 2130: 4
1924, Nov. 6	[letter: response to the Oct. 30 review]	Times Lit. Sup., is. 1190: 709
1924, Nov. 14	[letter: response to Ward's Nov. 7 review]	Spectator
1925, Jan.	The Shakespeare Problem	English Review, p. 52-61
1926, March	A Cambridge Scholar on Schakespeare	National Review, v. 87: 898-910
1926, Oct.	A Reply [letter: reply to Tannenbaum]	Studies in Philology, v. 23: 473-76
1927, March	False Light on Shakespeare	Nat. Rev. (UK), v. 89: 114-24
1927, July 7	[review of *Le Mystere Shakespearien* by Georges Connes (1927)] Response by Georges Connes, 28 July, p. 520.	Times Lit. Sup., is. 1327: 472
1927, Nov. 27	[resp. to "Under the Greenwood Tree"]	Evening Standard
1928, March 21	Shakespeare's Father: Was He Able to Write?	Daily News & Westminster
1928, May 17	Shakespeare's "Purge" of Jonson [letter: critique of Dr. Arthur Gray's book on Shakespeare and Jonson]	Times Lit. Sup., is. 1672: 379

Greer, Jane

1986	[review of *The Mysterious William Shakespeare* by Ch. Ogburn, Jr.]	Choice, vol. 10/2: 18-22

Greg, W. W.
Books and pamphlets
1925   *English Literary Autographs, Part I, Dramatists, 1550-1650.* Oxford University Press.
1928   *A Hundreth Sundry Flowres* edited by Capt Bernard M. Ward. [pamphlet: repr. of Greg's review, from *Transactions of the Bibliographical Society*, New Series, vol. VII, no. 3 (Dec. 1927)]
Shorter pieces

1926, Dec.	[review of *A Hundreth Sundrie Flowres*, ed. by Capt. B. M. Ward] [response by Ward, June 1927] [repr. as a pamphlet]	Library, vol. VII/3: 269-82
1928, Aug. 30	Fulke Greville, Lord Brooke	Times Lit. Sup., is. 1387: 609
1928, Sept. 13	Fulke Greville [letter: response to B. M. Ward]	Times Lit. Sup., is. 1389: 648
1928, Sept. 27	Fulke Greville [letter: response to B. M. Ward]	Times Lit. Sup., is. 1391: 687
1929, Jan.	[review of *The Seventeenth Earl of Oxford, 1550-1604, from Contemporary Documents* by B. M. Ward (1928)] [in resp. to Ward's Aug. 2, 1928 letter to the *Times Literary Supplement*]	Mod. Lang. Rev., vol. 24/2: 216-21
1931, June 4	Tudor Handwriting [rev. of *Shake-speare: Handwriting and Spelling* by Gerald H. Rendall (1931)]	Times Lit. Sup., is. 1531: 446
1936, May 2	Stage or Study [letter: reply to Percy Allen's May 9th response]	Times Lit. Sup., is. 1787: 379

Gregory, Tappan
1961   *Shakespeare Cross-Examination: A Compilation of Articles First Appearing in the American Bar Association Journal.* The American Bar Association. (Foreword by Tappan Gregory repr. in SON, vol. 28/1: 4, Winter, 1992)

Greiling, Margit & Reinhard

2019, Fall	*Mimus*: A Neglected Source of Shakespeare's Plays?	Sh. Ox. Newsl., vol. 55/4: 11-12

Gretton, I.

1955, Autumn	Shakespeare and the General [repr. in Clark, *Hidden Allusions*, 3rd ed., Ruth Lody Miller, editor, p. 671-72 (1974)]	SF News-letter (E), p. 9-10
1957, Spring	The Recusants in *Love's Labour's Lost*	SF News-letter (E), p. 9

Grey, Mike

2014, May	[letter: response to Robert Prechter's Spring and Summer 2005 articles on the Sonnet's Dedication puzzle]	De Vere Soc. Newsl., v. 21/2: 29

Grieveson, P. L.

1937, July	The Droeshout Portrait [letter]	East Anglian Mag., v. 2/10: 469

Griffin, Benjamin

1994	[review of *Shakespeare, In Fact* by Irvin L. Matus (1994)]	Year's Work in Eng. St., vol. 75: 221-27

Griffin, Susan

2011, Oct. 28	Squabbling Scholars Make a Crisis Out of a Dramatist	Western Daily Press, p. 18

Griffin, W. J.

1936, June 6	[letter: Names in *The Winter's Tale*]	Times Lit. Sup., issue 1792: 480

Grillo, Ernesto
1949   *Shakespeare and Italy.* Glasgow: R. Maclehose, University Press. Repr. in 1973: New York: Haskell House. [Preface repr. in BTC, vol. 4: 270-286]

Grimes, John

1991, Spring	[letter: praise for Sobran, Ogburn, Fowler; publicizing the Oxfordian idea	Sh. Ox. Newsl., vol. 27/2: 10-11

Grimes, William

1994, Winter	Erza Stone, 76, Henry Aldrich On the Radio (from the *NY Times*, March 5, 1994)	Sh. Ox. Newsl., vol. 30/1: 18
2010, Oct. 2	Joseph Sobran, 64, Writer Whom Buckley Mentored	New York Times, p. A17

Grimley, Terry

2007, Sept. 12	Author or Just a "Front" [review of *I Am Shakespeare* by Mark Rylance and Matthew Warchus (2007)	Birmingham Daily P., p. 13

Grode, Eric

2007, April 7	The Case for Shakespeare: Words, Words, Words	New York Times, p. C7

Grosart, Alexander B.
1872   *Miscellanies of the Fuller Worthies' Library.* London. [vol. 4 includes a collection of 23 poems by the Earl of Oxford]

Gross, John
    2005, March   Will the Real Shakespeare Please Stand Up?   Commentary, vol. 119/4:
          Response by Jonathan F. Keiler, June 2005, vol. 119/6: 24-25.
          Reply by John Gross, same issue, same page.
    2005, June   [letter: reply to Jonathan Keiler's response to his March article]   Commentary, vol. 119/6: 24
    2010, March   Denying Shakespeare: The 150-year History of Conspiracy Theorists   Commentary, v. 129/3: 38-44
          and Their Efforts to 'Prove' That the Man from Stratford Was
          Not the Author Himself [review of *Contested Will: Who Wrote*
          Shakespeare? by James Shapiro (2010)]
          Response by Samuel Blumenfeld, June 2010, vol. 129/6: 6.
          Response by Rev. Edward T. Oakes, June 2010, vol. 129/6: 6-7
          Reply by John Gross, June 2010, vol. 129/6: 7-8.
    2010, June   [letter: reply to responses to his review of *Contested Will*]   Commentary, vol. 129/6: 7-8

Grotyohann, Walter
    1940   *The Man Who Was Shakespeare* [a play].

Grove, Lee
    1948, July 3   "Shakespeare" Just Pen Name of Oxford Earl, Barrell Says   Washington Post, p. B1

Grumman, Robert
    1991, Aug.   A Stratfordian Objects . . .   Spear-shaker Rev., is. 5: 20-21
    1995, Summer   [letter: how important are parallels between Oxford's life   Sh. Ox. Newsl., vol. 31/3: 12-16
          and event in the plays?]
    1995, Fall   [letter: letters to and from Morse Johnson re parallels between   Sh. Ox. Newsl., vol. 31/4: 1-2
          Oxford's life and the plays]
    1997, Spring   A Groatsworth of Wit [letter]   Elizabethan Review, vol. 5/1: 5
    2000, Fall   [letter: Dixon's Spring 2000 "upstart crow" article and   Sh. Ox. Newsl., vol. 36/3: 22
          Roger Stritmatter's Summer 2000 letter]

Guilfoil, Kelsey
    1949, Oct. 30   [review of the 2nd edition of *"Shakespeare" Identified*]   Chicago Tribune, p. I22

Guiterman, Arthur
    1920, Sept. 30   Rhymed Reviews: "Shakespeare" Identified [review of SI   Life, vol. 76/1978: 590
          by J. Thomas Looney (1920)]

Gumbrecht, Hans Hlrich
    1999, July   [review of *Shakespeare: Invention of the Human* by Harold Bloom]   Neues Sh. Journal, vol. 4: 158-66
          [repr. from FAZ (January 1990)]

Gunning, Dr. C. P.
    1923, May 12   [title not known]   De Massbode
    1923, May 17   [title not known; reprint of excerpts from the May 12 *De Massbode*   De Amsterdammer
          piece, with editorial commentary]
    1923, June 1   Shakespeare and the Netherlands, I   Hackney Spectator, p. 5
    1923, June 8   Shakespeare and the Netherlands, II   Hackney Spectator, p. 8

Gurney, Lawrence S.
    1996, Fall   Jonson and Shakespeare   Sh. Newsletter, vol. 46/3: 71-72
          Response by Richard Whalen, vol. 47, p. 26

Guthrie, Tyronne
    1962, April 22   Threat of Newness to Olde Stratford [NY Times Magazine]   New York Times, p. 12

Gwynn, Stephan
    1930, May 11   Sir Sidney Lee and Others [Short reviews of *Shakespeare's Sonnets*   Observer, p. 7
          and Edward de Vere by Gerard Rendall and *The Case for Ed.*
          de Vere as "Shakespeare" by Percy Allen]

H. D.
    2003, Aug.   Zur Psychologie von Shakespeare's Sonett 117   Neues Sh. Journal, vol. 8: 164-66

H. D. S.
    1920, March   "Shakespeare" Identified? [review of SI]   Bookseller, vol. 19: 147-48

H. H.
    1933, June 17   Oxfordian Rejoinder [letter]   Christian Science Monitor, p. 10

H. R. W.
    1931, Oct. 31   Seven Shakespeares [rev. of the book by Gilbert Slater]   Saturday Review , vol. 152: 560

H. T.
    1932, Oct.   The Shakespeare Authorship Controversy   British Museum Q., v. 7/2: 40-41

H. W. D. C.
    1928, May 22   Books of the Day [rev. of *The Seventeenth Earl of Oxford* by   Manchester Guardian, p. 9
        Bernard M. Ward]

Habgood, Francis E. C.
    1936, Jan. 6   [letter: answer to Messrs. Gill and Severn]   Western Daily Press, p. 5
    1939, Feb. 10   Who Was Shakespeare? [letter]   John O'London's W., p. 750
    1939, Feb. 24   Shakespeare's Signature [letter]   John O'London's W., p. 821

Habsul-Rignyr
    2023, March 16   The Man Who Would Be Shakespeare   Mars Review of Books

Hackett, Helen
Books
    2009   *Elizabeth and Shakespeare: The Meeting of Two Myths*. Princeton: Princeton University Press.
Shorter pieces
    2010, March 11   [review of *Contested Will: Who Wrote Shakespeare?*   Los Angeles Review, p. 21-22
        by James Shapiro (2010)]

Hackney, Orda
    2006, Winter   [letter: response to R. Prechter's 2005 "Sonnets Dedication" articles]   Sh. Matters, vol. 5/2: 2
    2022, Fall   [letter: Mary Sidney opposed to publication of the First Folio?]   Sh. Ox. Newsl., vol. 58/4: 5

Hadfield, Andrew
    2006   [review of *The Case for Shakespeare: The End of the Authorship*   English, vol. 55: 93-101
        Question by Scott McCrea (2004)]

Hadley, Herbert S.
    1920, July 29   Shakespeare: Enter the Legal Element   Reedy's Mirror, v. 29/31: 594-97

Hagger, Nicholas
    1999   *Prince Tudor: A Verse Drama*.

Halfich, Angie
    2016, Oct. 26   Drama Instructor Pens New Play [review of *Truth; Will Out* by Phil   TCA Regional News
        Hoke. Presents Edward de Vere as Shakespeare.]

Hagger, Nicholas
    1998, Feb.   [letter: *The Tempest* written in 1602-3]   De Vere So. New., v. 2/11: 24-25

Hainer, Cathy
    1997, Dec. 9   Solving the Puzzle of Shakespeare's Identity   USA Today, p. 9D

Haines, C. M.
    1924, Oct.   Bacon Legend [letter: resp. to Sydenham & Batchelor]   English Review, p. 564
    1925, Feb.   The Shakespeare Problem   English Review, p. 141-42
    1936, Jan. 6   Possiby Neiter Wrote the Plays [letter]   Western Daily Press, p. 5

Haldeman, Philip
    1997, Summer   [reviews of *Live the Legend*, CD by The New World Renaissance   Sh. Ox. Newsl., vol. 33/3: 13
        Band; and of *Renaissance Music at Princely Courts of Europe*,
        CD by the Rozmberk Consort Prague]

Halio, Jay L.
    1999, Jan. 30   [letter: Don Oldenburg's Jan. 24 article]   Washington Post, p. A17

Hall, Allan
    2009, Nov. 23   William Shakespeare's Plays Were Written by Earl of Oxford,   Telegraph
        Claims German Scholar

Hall, W. E.
    1964, Jan. 31   Anti-Shakespearians and All That   Birmingham Daily P., p. 6

Hall, Zoe Dare

2011, Oct. 8	Was William Shakespeare Literature's Biggest Fraud? [rev. of *Anonymous*] [Charles Beauclerk says yes; Stanley Wells says no]	Telegraph, p. 20
2011, Oct. 15	Lies and Lust in the Snakepit of Tudor England [rev. of *Anonymous*]	Telegraph, p. 62-65

Halle, Louis J.

Books

1981	*The Search for an Eternal Norm: As Represented by Three Classics*. Washington, D.C.: University Press of America. [excerpt repr. in SON, vol. 18/3: 6 (Summer 1992); and in BTC, vol. 6: 193]	

Shorter pieces

1989, Spring	[letter: "It is more important to lose all but the last battle than to win all but the last"; (with addendum by editor)	Sh. Ox. Newsl., vol. 25/2: 20-22
1991, Spring	[letter to Ch. Ogburn, Jr.]	Sh. Ox. Newsl., vol. 27/2: 7-8

Halliburton, Rachel

2004, Jan. 9	Much Ado About Lusting [rev. of *Edward's Presents* by Llewellyn]	Evening Standard, p. 34

Halliday, Frank E.

1949	*Shakespeare and His Critics*. London: Gerald Duckworth.	

Hamblin, Dora Jane

1964, April 23	History's Biggest Literary Whodunit	Life, vol. 56/17

Hamill, John

Books

2022	*The Secret Shakespeare Sex Scandals: Bisexuality and Bastardy*.	

Shorter pieces

2001, Fall	Oxfordian News	Sh. Ox. Newsl., v. 37/3: 7, 18-19
2001, Fall	Who is Buried in Shakespeare's Grave?	Sh. Ox. Newsl., vol. 37/3: 23, 24
2002, Winter	[review of *Sexual Shakespeare* by Michael Keevak (2001)]	Sh. Ox. Newsl., vol. 38/1: 7, 14
2003, Spring	Shakespeare or De Vere? - That is the Question: Authorship Debate at the Smithsonian	Sh. Ox. Newsl., vol. 39/2: 1, 4-5
2003, Summer	The Ten Restless Ghosts of Mantua: Shakespeare's Specter Lingers over the Italian City [repr. in RCA, p. 86-102; and in BTC, vol. 9: 134-48]	Sh. Ox. Newsl., v. 39/3: 1, 12-16
2003, Autumn	The Ten Restless Ghosts of Mantua: Shakespeare's Specter Lingers over the Italian City, Part 2: Castiglione and the Gonzaga Family of Mantua [repr. in RCA, p. 86-102; and in BTC, vol. 9: 149-63]	Sh. Ox. Newsl., vol. 39/4: 3-6
2004, Summer	2nd Annual Shakespearean Authorship Trust Conference	Sh. Ox. Newsl., vol. 40/3: 6-7
2005	Shakespeare's Sexuality and How It Affects the Authorship issue	Oxfordian, vol. 8: 25-59
2005, Summer	The Dark Lady and Her Bastard: An Alternative Scenario	Sh. Ox. Newsl., vol. 41/3: 1, 4-9+
2006, Fall	[letter: Whalen's Summer 2006 "Prince Tudor Hypothesis" article]	Sh. Ox. Newsl., vol. 42/3: 16
2009	Bisexuality and Bastardy: The Reasons for the Shakespeare Cover-up, in DS, p. 29-40 [resp. by Peter Rush, Summer/Fall 2012, p. 11-15]	
2009, June	Publications Committee News	Sh. Ox. Newsl., vol. 45/1: 3
2009, June	Spaniard in the Elizabethan Court: Don Antonio Perez	Sh. Ox. Newsl., vol. 45/1: 14-21
2009, Dec.	Message from SOS President John Hamill	Sh. Ox. Newsl., vol. 45/3: 2
2009, Dec.	Two Shake-speares: The Commoner or the Aristocrat: The Monument vs. the Engraving	Sh. Ox. Newsl., vol. 45/3: 20-24
2009, Dec.	Board of Trustees Approves Changes in Membership Dues [with Susan G. Width]	Sh. Ox. Newsl., vol. 45/3: 4-5
2009, Dec.	[letter: Richard Whalen's letter about the influence of Antonio Perez on *Othello*]	Sh. Ox. Newsl., vol. 45/3: 29-30
2010, May	Notice from SOS President John Hamill	Sh. Ox. Newsl., vol. 46/1: 22
2010, Aug.	From the President of the Shakespeare Oxford Society	Sh. Ox. Newsl., vol. 46/2: 4
2010, Aug.	[letter: Shapiro's *Contested Will* is an embarrassment (not printed)]	Sh. Ox. Newsl., vol. 46/2: 13
2011, Jan.	[letter: authorship question stirs up biblical scholars: summary of "Shakespeare, the Earl of Oxford and Morton Smith," in *Biblical Archaeology Review*, vol. 36/6 (Nov/Dec. 2010)]	Sh. Ox. Newsl., vol. 47/1: 9
2011, Fall	[review of *Shakespeare: The Concealed Poet* by Robert Detobel]	Sh. Ox. Newsl., vol. 47/3: 13-14
2012	New Light on *Willobie His Avisa* and the Authorship Question	Oxfordian, vol. 14: 130-147
2012, Spring	*To Queen Elizabeth* Just a Plea for Mercy Response by Peter Rush, Summer/Fall 2013, p. 11-15.	Sh. Ox. Newsl., vol. 48/2: 13-18

2012, Sum./Fall	President's Message	Sh. Ox. Newsl., vol. 48/3: 3
2013	Doubter's Response to Question #13: Was Shakespeare's name used as a selling point on works we now don't believe he wrote?, in *Sh. Beyond Doubt?* (Shahan): 172	
2013	Doubter's Response to Question #15: Did Shakespeare become famous in his lifetime?, in *Sh. Beyond Doubt?* (Shahan): 74-75	
2013, Winter	A Message From SOS President, John Hamill	Sh. Ox. Newsl., vol. 49/1: 13
2013, Winter	Shakespeare's Bisexuality vs. the Prince Tudor Theory	Sh. Ox. Newsl., vol. 49/1: 7-8
2013, Spring	SOS and SF Propose Unity: Notice of Intent [with Tom Regnier]	Sh. Ox. Newsl., vol. 49/2: 2-4
2013, Fall	Marriage of True Minds	Sh. Ox. Newsl., vol. 49/3: 1-3
2014, Jan.	Shakespeare Oxford Fellowship: Shakespeare Oxford Society to Merge with Shakespeare Fellowship	De Vere So. NL, v. 21/1: 15-16
2014, Jan.	[letter: cooperation between the Fellowship and the DVS]	De Vere Soc. NL, vol. 21/1: 17
2014, Winter	From the Shakespeare Oxford Fellowship President's Office	Sh. Ox. Newsl., vol. 50/1: 2
2014, Winter	From the Shakespeare Oxford Fellowship President's Office [with Tom Regnier]	Sh. Ox. Newsl., vol. 50/1: 2
2014, Spring	From the President's Office: New Research Grant Program Establ'd	Sh. Ox. Newsl., vol. 50/2: 2-3
2014, Summer	From the President's Office [with Tom Regnier]	Sh. Ox. Newsl., vol. 50/3: 2-3
2016, October	SOF Announces Winners of 2016 Research Grant Program	De Vere Soc. Newsl., v. 23/4: 6-7
2017, Spring	Announcing the SOF 2017 Research Grant Program	Sh. Ox. Newsl., vol. 53/2: 10-11
2018, Fall	From the President: Everyone is Tired of Fake News, and We are Tired of Fake Shakespeare!	Sh. Ox. Newsl., vol. 54/4: 2-4
2019, Winter	From the President: Donations and Podcasts	Sh. Ox. Newsl., vol. 55/1: 2
2019, Spring	From the President: This is a Good Time to Be an Oxfordian	Sh. Ox. Newsl., vol. 55/2: 2-3
2019, Summer	From the President	Sh. Ox. Newsl., vol. 55/3: 2-3
2019, Fall	From the President	Sh. Ox. Newsl., vol. 55/4: 2-3
2020, Winter	From the President	Sh. Ox. Newsl., vol. 56/1: 2
2020, Spring	From the President	Sh. Ox. Newsl., vol. 56/2: 2
2020, Summer	From the President	Sh. Ox. Newsl., vol. 56/3: 2-3
2020, Summer	Looney and Mythmaking	Sh. Ox. Newsl., vol. 56/3: 11-13
2020, Summer	[letter: resp. to Peter Sturrock re Dedication to Sonnets]	Sh. Ox. Newsl., vol. 56/3: 5-6
2020, Fall	From the President	Sh. Ox. Newsl., vol. 56/4: 2
2020, Fall	A Note from John Hamill	Sh. Ox. Newsl., vol. 56/4: 29
2021, Winter	From the President	Sh. Ox. Newsl., vol. 57/1: 2
2021, Winter	Unfortunately, Mythmaking Continues	Sh. Ox. Newsl., vol. 57/1: 28-29
2021, Spring	From the President	Sh. Ox. Newsl., vol. 57/2: 4-5
2021, Summer	From the President	Sh. Ox. Newsl., vol. 57/3: 2-3
2023, Sept.	James Warren's article on the First Folio [letter, with John Shahan, followed by Warren's reply]	Oxfordian, vol. 25: 9-15

Hamilton, James

2007, Sept. 9	Actors Aim To Unmask the Bard	Sunday Herald (Glasc.), p. 20

Hamilton, Tina N.

2000, Winter	[letter: her activities to promote awareness of Oxford's authorship]	Sh. Ox. Newsl., vol. 35/4: 21

Hammer, Paul

1994, Spring	The Earl of Essex, Fulke Greville, and the Employment of Scholars	Studies in Philology, vol. 91/2: 167
2008, Spring	Shakespeare's *Richard II*: The Play of 7 Feb. 1601 & the Essex Rising	Sh. Quarterly, vol. 59/1

Hammersmith, Mary Louise

1996, Spring	[letter: praise for the Shakespeare Oxford Newsletter]	Sh. Ox. Newsl., vol. 32/2: 21

Hammond, L. James

1998, Feb.	Why Stratfordians Are So Stubborn	De Vere Soc. Nel., v. 2/11: 25-28

Hampton, Aubrey

2009	*Elizabeth and Edward*. [A play about you-know-who as the real author of Shakespeare's plays.]	

Hampton, Wilborn

1988, April 26	Shakespeare and Freud: Bard is Analyzed on the Academic Couch Response by Charles Boyle, April 28. [Both repr. in SON, vol. 24/2: 8 (Spring 1988)]	New York Times, p. C13

Hanaway, Joseph & John Milnes Baker
2022, Fall	John Shakspere's Grant of Arms: Three Curious Aspects, I	Sh. Ox. Newsl., vol. 58/4: 24-27
2023, Winter	John Shakspere's Grant of Arms: Three Curious Aspects, II	Sh. Ox. Newsl., vol. 59/1: 26-36

Hanifin, Ada
1939, Dec. 24	Forceful Clew on Real Shakespeare	San Francisco Examiner

Hannan, Daniel
2010, March 16	Who Wrote Shakespeare's Plays? [rev. of *Contested Will* by J. Shapiro]	Telegraph

Hannas, Andrew R.
1988, Winter	Is Oxford Pictured in "Arts of Falconry" Prints?	Spear-shaker Rev., is. 1/2: 28-30
1998, Spring	Iosua Silvester Anagram: Vere Os Salustii: by Edward de Vere or Edward Lapworth? [letter: J. Fitzgerald's article, vol. 33/1: 10-15] Reply by James Fitzgerald, vol. 34/2: 22.	Sh. Ox. Newsl., vol. 34/1: 11
1998, June	Ist E. L. Oxon identisch mit Edward de Vere? I	Neues Sh. Journal, vol. 2: 139-42
1993, Winter	In Defense of Edith Duffey: Which Nowell Tutored Oxford?	Sh. Ox. Newsl., vol. 29/1a: 3
1993, Winter	Gabriel Harvey and the Genesis of "William Shakespeare" [repr. in BTC, vol. 7: 164-71]	Sh. Ox. Newsl., vol. 29/1b: 1-8
1996, Summer	"The Rest" is Not Silence [Terry Ross' essay "What George Puttenham Really Said in *The Art of English Poesie*"]	Ever Reader, vol. 3

Hansen, Harry
1944, March 5	"Who's Looney Now?"	Chicago Tribune, p. D9

Hansen, Matthew C.
2007	[review of *The Case For Shakespeare* by Scott McCrea (2005)]	Year's Work in Eng. Studies, vol. 86: 382-83

Hanson, David J.
Books
1992	*"Shake-speare's" Treatise on Verse*. Mill Valley, CA: De Vere Foundation.	

Shorter pieces
1990, Summer	[review of *Oxford's Revenge* by Stephanie Caruana and E. Sears]	Sh. Newsletter, v. 40/2: 24-25
1987	The Shakespeare Conspiracy [excerpted as 'Who Cares Who Wrote Them?' in SON, vol. 23/3: 10-11 (Summer, 1987)]	Ventura County Mag.
1989, Spr./Sum.	A Wildcatter Reports on the London Moot Court Hearing	Sh. Newsl., vol. 38/1-2: 14-16

Harayda, Janice
1988, Apr. 17	Court Rules in Bard's Favor	Plain Dealer (Cleve.), p. 12H
1993, May 23	The Most Influential People in History? [review of *The 100*, 2nd ed., by Michael Hart]	Plain Dealer (Cleve.), p. 11H

Harbage, Alfred
Books
1966	*Conceptions of Shakespeare*. Cambridge, MA: Harvard University Press.	

Shorter pieces
1955, June 12	Sweet Will and Gentle Marlowe [review of *The Murder of the Man Who Was Shakespeare* by Calvin Hoffman]	New York Times, p. BR1
1958, Oct. 19	Author, Author! [review of *The Poacher From Stratford: A Partial Account of the Controversy Over the Authorship of Shakespeare's Plays* by Frank W. Wadsworth]	New York Times

Hardigg, James S.
1997, Fall	Why I Support Inquiry into Authorship of Shakespeare's Works	Sh. Ox. Newsl., vol. 33/4: 6

Harding, Earl
1956, May	To the Editor and Readers of *The Shakespeare Newsletter*] [letter, with 21 others]	Sh. Newsl., vol. 6/3: 18

Harding, John
1988, Jan.	The Vexed Question of Shakespeare's Relationship with John Florio	De Vere Soc. Newsl., no. 1: 8-22

Hardison, O. B., Jr.
1972, Dec. 17	[letter: Day Thorpe's Dec. 3 article "Does the Folger Want the Truth about Shakespeare?" [Both repr. in SON, vol. 9/1: 3 (Winter 1973)]	Washington Star, p. S3
1974, Dec. 8	Shakespeare: Was He Shakespeare? [Charlton Ogburn's Nov. 24 article]	Washington Post, p. B3

Hardy, Thomas
1961, Autumn   To Shakespeare   Sh. Authorship Rev., #6: 18-19

Harman, Charles E.
2001, Summer   [letter: praise for Paul H. Altrocchi's *Most Greatly Lived* (2000)]   Sh. Ox. Newsl., vol. 37/2: 19

Harman, Edward G.
1925   *The "Impersonality" of Shakespeare Examined and Discussed*. London: Cecil Palmer.
    [2nd ed., 1971. New York: Haskell House Pub.]

Harms, Linda
1987, Fall   Waiting for the Assassination   Spear-shaker Rev., is. 1/1: 22-23

Harner, James L.
1991, Aug.   [letter: request for materials for the World Shakespeare Bibliography]   Spear-shaker Rev., is. 5: 22

Harper, William (editor)
1927   *Life, Diary, & Correspondence of Sir William Dugdale*
    [excerpt repr. in SON, vol. 30/2a: 16 (Spring, 1994)]

Harrigan, Tom
2023, Winter   ChatGPT: Can Artificial Intelligence Reshape the Authorship Question?   Sh. Ox. Newsl., vol. 59/1: 22-23
2023, Summer   Leigh Light, *The Which of Shakespeare's Why* [review]   Sh. Ox. Newsl., vol. 59/3: 27-28

Harris, Frank
1909   *The Man Shakespeare and His Tragic Life-story*. New York: Mitchell Kennerley.
    [2nd ed., 1921. Girard, KS: Haldeman-Julius Co. 3rd ed, 1969. New York: Horizon Press.]

Harris, Jonathan G.
2011, Spring   Recent Studies in Tudor and Stuart Drama [has notice of   Studies in English Literature,
    Brief Chronicles]   vol. 51: 465

Harris, M.
1993, Aug. 22   Best Bet [SOS Member Katherine Chiljan to speak]   Los Angeles Times, p. 2

Harris, Sydney J.
1974, July 16   Some Knotty Questions for Shakespeare Fans   Detroit Free Press, p. 9
1978, Sept. 3 or 4   Can You Spot This Famed Englishman?   New Orleans Trib.-Pic.

Harrison, David
2009, Aug. 9   Tomb's Secrets That Could Solve Mystery of the Real Shakespeare   Telegraph
2009, Aug. 10   Stone Tomb May Hold Secret to Shakespeare   Vancouver Sun, p. B3

Harrison, G. B.
1928, Nov. 29   The Mortal Moon [letter]   Times Lit. Sup., is. 1400: 938
1929, April   [review of *The Shakespeare Mystery* by Georges Connes]   Rev. Eng. St., vol. 5/18: 246-47
1929, Aug.   Shakespeare and Chapman as Topical Dramatists [review of Allen's   London Mercury, vol. 20: 118
    book] Response by Allen in Sept.
1930, Jan.   [reviews of *Shakespeare, Jonson, and Wilkins as Borrowers* (1928)   Rev. Eng. Studies, vol. 6/21:
    and *Topical Dramatists* (1929) by Percy Allen]   98-100
1930, April   [letter: reply to Percy Allen's letter, same issue]   Rev. Eng. St., vol. 6/22: 198
1930, June   [review of Lee's posthumous *Elizabethan and Other Essays*]   London Mercury, vol. 21: 185
1930, Nov. 13   Shakespeare's Topical Significances I: King John   Times Lit. Sup., is. 1502: 939
1930, Nov. 20   Shakespeare's Topical Significances II: The Earl of Essex   Times Lit. Sup., is. 1503: 974
1931, Oct. 15   Shakespeare, Essex and *Richard II* [letter]   Times Lit. Sup., is. 1550: 802
1933, Nov. 30   These Late Eclipses [letter]   Times Lit. Sup., is. 1661: 856
1933, Dec. 14   These Late Eclipses [letter]   Times Lit. Sup., is. 1663: 896
1934, Jan. 4   These Late Eclipses [letter]   Times Lit. Sup., is. 1666: 12
1934, Feb. 1   The 'Mortal Moon' Sonnet [letter]   Times Lit. Sup., is. 1670: 76
1939, July   [letter: reply to William Kent's letter, same issue]   SF News-letter (E), no. 15: 7-8
1953, Oct. 10   [review of *This Star of England* by Dorothy and Charlton Ogburn]   Saturday Review, p. 38

Harrison, G. R.
1962, Aug.   Shakespeare, or a Man Known as Shakespeare? [review of *Shake-*   NY Herald Tribune, p. F6
    speare: The Man Behind the Name by Do. and Ch. Ogburn, Jr.]

Harrison, John E.
1993   [review of *The Mysterious William Shakespeare* by Ch. Ogburn, Jr.]   Virginia Lawyer, vol. 42/1: 54
1993, Summer   Does it Matter?   Sh. Ox. Newsl., vol. 29/3a: 8

Hart, Alfred
  1934   *Shakespeare and the Homilies, and Other Pieces of Research into the Elizabethan drama*. Melbourne: Melbourne Univ. Press. [2nd ed, 1970. New York: Continuum. 3rd ed. 1971. New York: AMS Press.]
  1942   *Stolne and Surreptitious Copies: A Comparative Study of Shakespeare's Bad Quartos*. Melbourne: Melbourne University Press.

Hart, Christopher
  2011, Oct. 27   Why Does Hollywood Hate the English? [review of *Anonymous*]   Daily Mail, p. 15

Hart, Jeffrey
  1997, June 10   [review of *Alias Shakespeare* by Joseph Sobran (1997)]   National Review (NY), p. 48-49

Hart, Joseph C.
  1848   *The Romance of Yachting*. New York: Harper.

Hart, Michael H.
Books
  1992   *The 100: A Ranking of the Most Influential Persons in History, Revised and Updated for the Nineties*. New York: Citadel Press.

Shorter pieces
  1996, Spring   [letter: Joseph Sobran]   Sh. Ox. Newsl., vol. 32/2: 22

Hartmann, Kurt
  2002, July 14   Debate Plays On: Oxford vs. Stratford [repr. fr. *Santa Cruz Sentinel*)   Santa Cruz Sentinal
             [repr. in SON, vol. 38/3:3 (Summer, 2002)]

Hartnig, James Edmund
  1864   *Ornithology of Shakespeare Critically Examined* [cxcerpt from Ch. 1 repr. in BTC, vol. 1: 62-70]

Harvey, Charles
  1989, Spring   [letter: "one is at a loss to know how it is possible for the academe   Sh. Ox. Newsl., vol. 25/2: 19-20
             to keep up the charade"]

Haskins, David
  2017, Oct.   [review of *The Shakespeare Authorship Mystery Explained* by   Oxfordian, vol. 19: 209-14
             Geoffrey Eyre (2017)]   Oxfordian, vol. 19:

Hassler, Evalyn
  1991, May   [letter: de Vere's lineage]   Spear-shaker Rev., is. 3/4: 18

Haste, Ian
  2009, Spring   The Name Within the Ring: Edward de Vere's "Musical" Signature   Sh. Matters, vol. 8/2: 1, 23-26+
             in *Merchant of Venice*
                  Response by Gary Goldstein, Summer 2009, p. 2.
  2006, Winter   Reading Secretary Hand   Sh. Matters, vol. 5/2: 23
  2006, Summer   The Secretary Hand - Part 2   Sh. Matters, vol. 5/4: 21
  2006, Fall   [Sonnet dedication puzzle]   Sh. Matters, vol. 6/1: 2
  2021, Oct.   Vere's Rings in *The Merchant of Venice*   De Vere So. New., v. 28/4: 26-35
  2022, April   The Play on the Eve of the Essex Rebellion   De Vere So. New., v. 29/2: 32-39
  2022, July   [letter: reply to responses by Whittemore and Malim]   De Vere So. New., v. 29/3: 30-31

Hastings, Chris
  2014, April 27   Bard Blood at the Palace as Princes Split Over Shakespeare   Daily Mail
             [Summary repr. in DVN, vol. 21/2: 37 (May 2014)]

Hastings, Robe
  2011, Oct. 26   Shakespeare Movie Has Lost the Plot, Lament Loyal Fans of the   Independent, p. 14
             Bard [review of *Anonymous*]

Hastings, William T.
  1959, Autumn   Shakspere Was Shakespeare   Amer. Scholar, v. 28/4: 479-88
             Resp. by Dorothy and Ch. Ogburn, Spring 1960, p. 271, 290-95.
             See commentary on this exchange of views in *The English Journal*, vol. 49/6: 430 (Sept. 1960).
  1960, Spring   [reply to Ogburn's letter]   Amer. Scholar, v. 29/2: 295-96
  1963, Autumn   [review of *The Shakespeare Claimants* by Harry N. Gibson (1962)]   Sh. Quarterly, vol. 14/4: 465-66

Hatinguais, Catherine
  2016   The Sycamore Grove, Revisited   Oxfordian, vol. 18: 85-99

Heller, Scott
    1999, June 4   Illustrator of *Titus Andronicus* also Figures in Authorship Controversy   Chronicle of Higher Ed., vol. 45/39: A19
    1999, June 4   In a Centuries-old Debate, Shakespeare Doubters Point to New Evidence   Chronicle of Higher Ed., vol. 45/39: A22-23

Helsloot, Pieter N.
Books
    2004   *Edward de Vere: Onvermijdelijk Shakespeare.* [Edward de Vere: Inevitably Shakespeare] Zaltbommel: Aprilis. [Dutch]
Shorter pieces
    2004, April   [letter: Dutch language biography of Edward de Vere]   De Vere Soc. Newsl., p. 31
    2004, April   Portrait of Pembroke Family at Wilton House [letter]   De Vere Soc. Newsl., p. 32
                [followed by editor's response]

Moore, Harvey T.
    1948, Aug. 3   Memos to Mr. Burgess   Washington Post, p. 10

Hendle, Pauline
    2001, Oct.   Queen Elizabeth and the Watchers   De Vere Soc. Newsl., p. 18-27
    2001, Apr./May   [letter: resp. to the March 15 program [with Kevin Gilvary, Philip   De Vere Soc. Newsl., p. 49-50
                Johnson and Eddi Jolly]

Hennings, Thomas H.
    1953, May 3   A Bard by Any Other Name [letter: Derrickson's reviw of   St. Louis Post Disp., p. 4B
                the Ogburns' *This Star*]
    1956, May   To the Editor and Readers of *The Shakespeare Newsletter*   Sh. Newsl., vol. 6/3: 18
                [letter, with 21 other signers]

Henriot, Emile
    1938, March 1   [review of Abel Lefranc's article in the Feb. issue of *Revue Bleue*,   Temps
                "La Question Shakespearienne au XVIII Siècle"]

Henry, Calvin
    1999   Bacon and Oxford [letter]   Oxfordian, vol. 2: 163-163

Hensher, Philip
    2010, April 3   [review of *Contested Will* by James Shapiro]   Spectator
                Response by Richard Malim, April 10.

Herberger, Charles F.
    1994, Winter   Oxford and Rare Manuscript Sources   Sh. Ox. Newsl., vol. 30/1: 1-2
                [repr. in RCA, p. 21-22 (1994); and in BTC, vol. 7: 222-24]
    2007, Summer   [Sonnet dedication puzzle]   Sh. Matters, vol. 6/4: 2, 31
    2013, Spring   William Shakespeare: The Makings of a Pseudonym   Sh. Mat., vol. 12/2: 1, 22-23
    2013, Summer   Oxford's Death: Suicide or Multiple Coincidences?   Sh. Matters, vol. 12/3: 13, 36
    2014, Winter   For Edward de Vere [a sonnet]   Sh. Ox. Newsl., vol. 50/1: 4

Herbert, James
    1999, March 29   Heavens Above, Is Shakespeare an Imposture?   San Diego Union, p. A1

Herbert, Tony
    2019, July   [rev. of *Nothing is Truer than Truth*; film by Cheryl Eagan-Donovan]   De Vere So. New., v. 26/3: 36-43
    2020, April   [review of *Shakespeare and the Resistance* by Clare Asquith]   De Vere So. New., v. 27/2: 48-49
    2020, April   [review of *The Upstart Crow*, a play by Ben Elton]   De Vere So. New., v. 27/2: 50-51
    2020, Oct.   [letter: Gilvary's article on J. Thomas Looney]   De Vere So. New., v. 27/4: 43-44
    2022, July   Shakespeare in the Squares [review of *The Tempest*]   De Vere So. New., v. 29/3: 33-34

Herford, Charles H. [C. H. H.]
    1920, March 19   Shakespeare Deposed Again [review of SI]   Manchester Guardian, p. 7
    1923, June 5   New Books: Mr. W. H. [review of the book by Col. B. R. Ward]   Manchester Guardian, p. 7

Herford, Oliver
Books
    1899   *An Alphabet of Celebrities*. Boston: Small, Maynard.
Shorter pieces
    1920, July 24   Pen and Inklings: *Shakespeare Identified*   Leslie's Weekly, vol. 131: 3379
    1932, Aug. 27   Oliver Herford Adopts "William Shakespeare"   Literary Digest, vol. 114/9: 14

1933, Aug. 19	A Great Peradventure	San Francisco Examiner

Herman, Jan
1991, Dec. 31	Bard Boom on the Boards	Los Angeles Times, p. 2
1992, April 14	Small Pay but Great Change? [Notes Lord Vere's lecture]	Los Angeles Times, p. F2

Hernandez, Romel
1999, March 21	Shakespeare in Doubt; Portland Prof. Backs Rival [Daniel Wright at 3rd Annual De Vere Studies Conference]	Oregonian, p. A1
1999, March 26	Shakespeare in Doubt; Skeptics Label Bard a Fraud [repr. Mar. 31, p. E1]	Newhouse New Service, p. 1
1999, April 4	Scholar [Daniel Wright] Stands By Theory of Sh. as a Fraud	Seattle Times, p. B4
1999, April 5	Fraud of Avon? Scholar Pays Price for Dissent [Dan Wright]	Minneapolis Star Trib., p. 4E

Heron, Flodden W.
Booklets and pamphlets
1942, April	*Who Wrote Shakespeare?* [compilation of his lectures, published by the Literary Anniversary Club of San Francisco]	
1945, April 23	April 23 Birthday of a Genius [pamphlet]	

Shorter pieces
1939, April 21	The Shakespeare Anniversary: Literature's Greatest Mystery	Argonaut
1939, Dec.	[lengthy piece on Barrell's article in *Scientific American*]	Argonaut
1941, Sept. 13	[letter: famous pen names]	Saturday Review
1941, Oct.	Shakspere-Shakespeare	SF News-letter (A), v. 2/6: 67-69
1941, Dec.	Folger Shakespeare Library Suggestion	SF News-letter (A), v. 3/1: 9
1942, April	Bacon Was Not Shakespeare [repr. in BTC, vol. 2: 229-34]	SF News-letter (A), v. 3/3: 36-38

Heron, G. Allan
1929, Sept. 11	Shakespeare and Richard III: Historians Agree [letter]	Morning Post, p. 6

Hershenson, Roberta
2005, Dec. 25	Brush Up Your De Vere? [Matthew Cossolotto and the Shakespeare Oxford Society]	New York Times, p. 6

Hervier, Paul-Louis
1920, Nov-Dec	Shakespeare, Bacon, Rutland & Compagnie	Revue Mondiale, v. 100: 419-28

Hess, W. Ron
Books
2002	*The Dark Side of Shakespeare, vol. 1: An Iron-Fisted Romantic in England's Most Perilous Times*. New York: Writers Club Press. [Appendix A is an English translation of Georges Lambin's *Voyages de Shakespeare en France et en Italie*]
2003	*The Dark Side of Shakespeare, vol. 2: An Elizabethan Courtier, Diplomat, Spymaster & Epic Hero*. Foreword by Gordon C. Cyr. New York: Writers Club Press.

Shorter pieces
1993, Fall	An Excursion to the Latest (Maybe the Last) Baconian Conference [repr. in BTC, vol. 7: 217-20]	Sh. Ox. Newsl., vol. 29/4: 14-16
1993, Summer	Certain European Researches Into Sh's French and Italian Connections	Sh. Ox. Newsl., vol. 29/3a: 1-4
1996, Autumn	Robert Greene's Wit Re-evaluated	Eliz. Review, vol. 4/2: 41-48
1998	Hotwiring the Bard into Cyberspace	Oxfordian, vol. 1: 88-101
1999	Shakespeare's Dates: Their Effects on Stylistic Analysis	Oxfordian, vol. 2: 25-59
	Response by Ward Elliott and Robert J. Valenza, vol. 3: 71-97	
	Response by Winston C. Chow, vol. 3: 119-23	
	Response by Howard Bloch, vol. 3: 119-23	
	Response by John M. Shahan, vol. 4: 154-65	
	Reply to Shahan by Elliott and Valenza, vol. 6: 154-63	
2002, Winter	Obituary: Vincent J. Mooney, Jr. (1944-2001)	Sh. Ox. Newsl., vol. 38/1: 21
2003, Sept.	[letter: Lambin's "Derbyite" views]	De Vere Soc. Newsl., p. 24
2003, Autumn	Stanley Wells at the Smithsonian	Sh. Ox. Newsl., v. 39/4: 16, 18+
2004, Summer	[letter: update on *Greene's Groats-Worth*]	Sh. Ox. Newsl., vol. 40/3: 10
2004, Oct.	When Shakespeare 'Originated' His *Sonnets*, Did They Have a 'Euphues' Meaning?	De Vere Soc. Newsl., p. 9-15
2005	Another Rare Dreame: Is This an "Authentic" Oxford poem?	Oxfordian, vol. 8: 60-75
2006, April	Who Was the Honoured Lady of Oxford's 'Knight of the Tree of the Sunne'?	De Vere Soc. Newsl., p. 12

Hess, W. Ron (continued)

2006, Spring	Did Shakespeare Read from 17th Earl of Oxford's Personal Library, 1 [with assistance from Alan Tarica]	Sh. Ox. Newsl., v. 42/2: 1, 13-26
2006, July	Were Oxford's and Sidney's Poetry Groups Really One and the Same	De Vere Soc. Newsl., p. 26-27
2006, Fall	Did Shakespeare Read from 17th Earl of Oxford's Personal Library, 2 [with assistance from Alan Tarica]	Sh. Ox. Newsl., vol. 42/3: 25-28
2006, Fall redux	[letter: Bolbec crest]	Sh. Ox. Newsl., vol. 42/4: 31-32
2007, Winter	Did Thomas Heywood List "Will Sh." as an Imitator or Front?	Sh. Matters, vol. 6/2: 21-27+
2007, Spring	Searching Under the Lamp-posts for Dating Shakespeare's *Sonnets* [See update in letter to the SON, vol. 43/3: 12-14]	Sh. Ox. Newsl., vol. 43/2: 14-20
2007, Summer	[letter: recent articles]	Sh. Ox. Newsl., vol. 43/3: 12-14
2007, Fall	Recollections of Peter Moore on the Occasion of His Passing [repr. in German in NSJ, vol. 12: 49-50 (Oct. 2008)]	Sh. Ox. Newsl., vol. 43/4: 24
2009, Feb.	Did Oxford Travel Abroad as a Teenager? Response by Richard Malim, June 2009, p. 30.	De Vere So. New., v. 16/1: 29-31
2009, June	The Speare-shaker and the Dragon: Oxford, *Beowulf* and *Hamlet*	De Vere So. New., v. 16/2: 15-22
2011	Did Shakespeare Have a Literary Mentor? Response by Sabrina Feldman, *The Oxfordian*, vol. 13: 152.	Oxfordian, vol. 13: 146-152
2011, March	Did Thomas Sackville Influence *Shake-speare's Sonnets*?	De Vere So. New., v. 18/1: 21-30
2011, Spring	Gilvary: new bricks in the wall of evidence	Sh. Ox. Newsl., vol. 47/2: 1, 8
2011, Spring	In Memoriam: Noemi Magri (d. 2011)	Sh. Ox. Newsl., vol. 47/3: 5
2011, Spring	In Memoriam: Joseph Sobran (1946-2011)	Sh. Ox. Newsl., vol. 47/2: 11-13
2012, Winter	[review of *The Apocryphal William Shakespeare*, by Sabrina Feldman]	Sh. Ox. Newsl., vol. 48/1: 17-18
2012, March	Did Shakespeare Have a Literary Mentor?	De Vere So. New., v. 19/1: 16-21
2012, July	Why Anti-Stratfordians Should Reject 1592's *Groatsworth of Wit*	De Vere So. New., v. 19/2: 26-31
2014, Nov.	Hypothetical Earlier Dating for *Passionate Pilgrim* and *First Folio*	J. of Romance Studies, vol. 4/11: 916-40
2015, April	[review of *An Index to Oxfordian Publications, Third Edition*, edited by James A. Warren]	De Vere So. New., v. 22/2: 42-43
2016, Winter	[review of *William Stanley as Shakespeare: Evidence of Authorship by the Sixth Earl of Derby* by John M. Rollett (2015)]	Sh. Ox. Newsl., vol. 52/1: 11-14
2016, Spring	[review of *Shakespeare Re-Invented: Challenging 400 Years of Shakespeare Fantasy!!* by Keith Browning (2016)]	Sh. Ox. Newsl., vol. 52/2: 29-30
2016, Summer	[review of *Shakespeare and Venice* by Graham Holderness (2010)]	Sh. Ox. Newsl., vol. 52/3: 32-33
2016, Fall	[review of *The Masters of the Revels and Elizabeth I's Court Theatre* by W. R. Streitberger (2016)]	Sh. Ox. Newsl., vol. 52/4: 8-11
2016, October	Shakespeare's *Sonnets*: Half of Them Dated, Part 1	De Vere So. New., v. 23/4: 37-43
2017, January	Shakespeare's *Sonnets*: Half of Them Dated, Part 2	De Vere So. New., v. 24/1: 22-35
2017, Fall	Sh. Dictionaries: A Marching Forest of Sources and Opportunities	Sh. Ox. Newsl., vol. 53/4: 20-23
2018, Spring	[review of *The Fictional Lives of Shakespeare* by Kevin Gilvary]	Sh. Ox. Newsl., vol. 54/2: 30-31
2018, Summer	A Wedding Joust in Trebizond: Commedia Erudita and Sinister Politics in 1575 [with assistance from Jan Scheffer, A. Colin Wright & Concetta Thibideaux]	Sh. Ox. Newsl., vol. 54/3: 9-20
2019, Spring	[rev. of *A Brief Discourse of Rebellion and Rebels* by George North]	Sh. Ox. Newsl., vol. 55/2: 21-24

Heston, Charlton

1991, June 10	[letter: Joseph Sobran's April column] Reply by Joseph Sobran, same issue and page.	National Review, vol. 43/10: 34

Hewett, G. Nele

1971, Spring	[letter: the original *Venus and Adonis*]	Sh. Authorship Rev., #24: 23-24

Heydt, Bruce

1991	The Many Shakespeares	British Heritage, vol. 12/6: 53-58

Hicks, Brian

2000, May 13	Oxford in Italy [letter]	Spectator, p. 26
2001, Jan.	Edward de Vere – Facts, Myths and Probabilities	De Vere Soc. Newsl., p. 35-38
2002, July	Notice about the De Vere Society's upcoming July 20 meeting	De Vere Soc. Newsl., p. 37-38
2003, Feb.	[report on the plans for the July conference]	De Vere Soc. Newsl., p. 3-4
2003, June	Chairman's Report from the May 10 AGM	De Vere Soc. Newsl., p. 2-3
2006, July	[letter] [excerpt repr. in DVN (July 2006), p. 2]	Guardian

Hildebrandt, Peter
    2012   *The Rest is Silence: a novel.* CreateSpace.

Hill, Carl
    1989, June 3   Was Will's Will Wilful?   Toronto Star, p. M23

Hill, H. W.
    1907, Oct. 12   Edward de Vere [letter: H. Pemberton, Jr.'s May 25 Query]   Notes & Q., issue 198: 297-98

Hill, Tracey
    2009   *Anthony Munday and Civic Culture: Theatre, History and Power in Early Modern London 1580-1633.*
                  Manchester University Press.

Hinds, Amanda

2018, July	Shakespeare Week: 23 April to 26 April 2018, Brunel University	De Vere S. New., v. 25/3: 34-42
2018, Oct.	[letter to *Prospect* Magazine]	De Vere Soc. Newsl., v. 25/4: 41
2018, Oct.	[response to recent media reports]	De Vere So. New., v. 25/4: 39-40
2019, Jan.	[review of *Shakespeare's Apprenticeship: Identifying the Real Playwright's Earliest Works* by Ramon Jiménez]	De Vere So. New., v. 26/1: 45-47
2019, July	Who was "Our English Terence Will: Shake-speare? Could it have been William Stanley, 6th Earl of Derby? [with Alex. Waugh]	De Vere So. New., v. 26/3: 13-29
2020, April	Shakespearean Authorship Trust (in collaboration with Brunel Univ.): Shakespeare and the Essex Rising [with Kevin Gilvary]	Sh. Ox. Newsl., vol. 27/2: 13-16
2021, Jan.	Band of Brothers: Ed. de Vere and His Literary Circle in the 1580s	De Vere Soc. Newsl., vol. 28/1: 1-3, 46+
2021, April	Tribute to Tom Bethell: Author, investigative journalist—and Oxfordian	De Vere Soc. Newsl., v. 28/2:5-6
2022, Jan.	The Food of Love: Edward de Vere and the Music of the Spheres	De Vere Soc. New., v. 29/1: 6-10
2022, Jan.	Shakespearean Authorship Trust Conference, 13th-14th Nov. 2021	De Vere So. New., v. 29/1: 44-49
2022, April	[review of *The Merchant of Venice* directed by Abigail Graham at the Sam Wanamaker Playhouse]	De Vere So. New., v. 29/2: 48-49
2022, Oct.	[review of the one-woman play *A Rose by Any Other Name* by Rosemary Loughlin]	De Vere Soc. New., vol. 29/4: 45 29/4: 45
2022, Oct.	[review of *Much Ado About Nothing* produced by the National Theatre]	De Vere Soc. New., vol. 29/4: 48
2022, Oct.	[review of *The Taming of the Shrew* produced by the Cambridge Shakespeare Festival]	De Vere Soc. Newsl., vol. 29/4: 49-52
2023, July	The Seventeenth Earl of Oxford 1550-1604 [review of the book by Bernard M. Ward, new edition edited by James A. Warren	De Vere Soc. Newsl., vol. 30/3: 41-42
2023, Summer	[letter, with Richard Clifford: the recent Moot Court Trial at Middle Temple Hall]	Sh. Ox. Newsl., vol. 59/3: 4

Hinton, Harold C.
    1975, April 8   [letter: resp. to Charlton Ogburn's Nov. 1974 article]   Harvard Mag., vol. 77/8

Hipperson, Mary
    1939, July   The Other View-point   East Ang. Mag., vol. 4/8: 439-40
                  Resp. by Douglas in September; reply by Hipperson in October.
    1939, Oct.   The Other Viewpoint [[letter: resp. to Douglas]   East Ang. Mag., v. 4/11: 627-28

Hirst, W. A.
    1928, Nov. 4   Sir George Greenwood [letter]   Sunday Times

Hobart-Hampden, A. K.
    1923, July 20   Professor Lefranc at Oxford [letter]   Hackney Spectator, p. 4

Hobson, Harold
    1951, March 4   Blood and Tears   Sunday Times

Hochberg, Sandy
    2000, Spring   [letter: resp. to Stephanie Hughes' "Prince Tudor" letter]   Sh. Ox. Newsl., vol. 36/1: 29

Hocking, Bree
    2006, March 20   Getting to the Root of the Bard [profile of Matthew Cossolotto]   Roll Call, p. 1

Hodge, Megan
    2010, April   [review of *Shakespeare's Lost Kingdom* by Charles Beauclerk]   Library Journ., vol. 135/6: 75

Hodgins, Paul
    2001, May 29   Searching for Shakespeare [rev. of *The Beard of Avon* by Amy Freed]   Orange Co. Reg., p. 1

Hodgson, Geoffrey M.

1995, Aug.	A Countenance More in Sorrow Than in Anger	De Vere So. Newsl., v. 2/2: 8-10
1996, Jan.	[letter: comments on the six points]	De Vere So. Newsl., vol. 2/4: 3-4
2008, March	Early Support for the Oxfordian Case by a Famous British Economist [Joan V. Robinson] [resp. by Chris. Paul, June 2008, p. 31-32]	De Vere So. New., v. 15/1:12-13

Hoepfner, T. C.

1948, Nov. 6	The Shakespeare Confusion [letter: resp. to Burgess]	Saturday Review, p. 21-22

Hoffmann, Calvin
Books

1960	*The Murder of the Man Who Was Shakespeare*. New York: Grosset & Dunlap. [excerpt repr. in SAS (Stritmatter, 2019, 2022): p. 157-60]	

Shorter pieces

1962, Sept. 1	[letter: efforts to open Shakespeare's tomb]	Times (London), p. 11

Hogan, Martha Kurtz

2009, April 25	[letter: resp. to Bravin's article on Justice Stevens]	Wall St. Journal, p. A10

Hogg, J. A.

1938, Jan. 13	The Bard of Stratord [letter]	Northern Whig., Belfast Pst, p. 3
1938, Jan. 18	Bacon-Shakespeare Theory [letter]	Northern Whig., Belfast Pst, p. 3
1938, Jan. 24	Bacon-Shakespeare Theory [letter]	Northern Whig., Belfast Pst, p. 3
1938, Jan. 27	Further Speculation in the Bacon-Shakespeare Theory [letter]	Northern Whig., Belfast Pst, p. 9

Hoke, Phil

2016	*Truth; Will Out.* [A play presenting Edward de Vere as Shakespeare.]

Holden, Anthony

2000, Jan. 11	The Avon Man	Globe & Mail, p. R3

Holden, Constance

1987, Oct. 24	No One Knows if Sh. Wrote the Plays [resp. to A. Schwartz's Oct. 14 article [repr. in SON, vol. 23/4: 8-9 (Fall 1987)]	Washington Post, p. A19
1989, Fall	[review of *Horses in Shakespeare's England* by Anthony Dent] [with Isabel Holden]	Sh. Ox. Newsl., vol. 25/4: 5-6
1990, May 4	Did Queen Write Shakespeare's *Sonnets*? [Elliott and Claremont]	Science., vol. 248, p. 548
1998, Nov. 13	Cosmic Clue to Bard's Identity	Science, vol. 282

Holden, Isabel

1989, Fall	[review of *Horses in Shakespeare's England* by Anthony Dent] [with Constance Holden]	Sh. Ox. Newsl., vol. 25/4: 5-6
1989, Winter	For a Vere and Herbert's Wife	Sh. Ox. Newsl., vol. 25/1: 11-12
1991, Spring	[review of *Lost Chronicle of Edward de Vere* by Andrew Field]	Sh. Ox. Newsl., vol. 27/2: 6-7
1989, Fall	[review of *Horses in Shakespeare's England* by Anthony Dent] [with Constance Holden]	Sh. Ox. Newsl., vol. 25/4: 5-6
1994, Winter	Edward de Vere's Will [letter]	Sh. Ox. Newsl., vol. 30/1: 3
1998, Spring	[letter: Warren Hope's Autumn 1997 "Lady Susan Vere" article]	Eliz. Review, vol. 6/1: 3
1998, Fall	Ida Hughes-Standon at Hedingham Castle [letter]	Sh. Ox. Newsl., vol. 34/3: 27

Holderness, Graham

2010	Shakespearean Selves, in *Shakespeare and His Authors* (Leahy): 104-113	
2010, Fall	The Road to Oxford	Sh. Matters, vol. 9/3: 1, 19-20

Holland, Admiral Hubert H.
Books

1923	*Shakespeare Through Oxford Glasses: Topical Allusions in Shakespeare's Plays*. London: Cecil Palmer. [excerpt repr. in BTC, vol. 1: 248-255]	
1933	*Shakespeare, Oxford, and Elizabethan Times*. London: Denis Archer. [2nd ed., 1974. Folcroft, PA: Folcroft Library Editions.]	

Shorter pieces

1931, July 28	Speght's Chaucer [letter re Gabriel Harvey's Copy]	Morning Post, p. 6
1931, July 29	The Trussell Family [letter]	Morning Post, p. 6
1933, June 17	Oxfordian Rejoinder [review of *Lord Oxford and Shakespeare: A Reply to John Drinkwater* by Percy and Ernest Allen]	Christian Science Monitor, p. 10
1933, Sept.	The Four Continental Suitors in *Merchant of Venice*	Sh. Pictorial, no. 66: 128
1934, Jan.	Shakespeare and Oxford [letter: resp. to review]	John O'London's Weekly

Holston, Kim
Books co-authored with Warren Hope
1992   *The Shakespeare Controversy: An Analysis of the Claimants to Authorship, and Their Champions and Detractors* [with Warren Hope]. Jefferson, NC: McFarland.
2009   *The Shakespeare Controversy: An Analysis of the Authorship Theories, 2nd ed* [with Kim Holston]. Jefferson, NC: McFarland & Co. [excerpts repr. in SAS (Stritmatter 2019, 2022): 51-67]
Shorter pieces
1983, Winter   Grand Master Tackles Shakespeare Question   Sh. Ox. Newsl., vol. 19/1: 11

Holston, Noel
1998, April 18   *Frontline* Makes Much Ado Over Shakespeare [rev. of "The Sh. Mystery" Minneapolis Star Trib., p. 1E-2E [repr. in SON., v. 25/2: 7-8 (Spr. 1989); and in BTC, v. 6: 388-90]

Holt, Felix
1938, Jan. 17   Bacon-Shakespeare Theory [letter]   Northern Whig/Belfast Post, p. 9
1938, Jan. 19   Bacon-Shakespeare Theory [letter]   Northern Whig/Belfast Pst, p. 11
1938, Jan. 25   Bacon-Shakespeare Theory [letter]   Northern Whig/Belfast Post, p. 3
1938, May 12   Shakespeare's Plays [letter]   Northern Whig/Belfast Pst, p. 11

Holton, E. Gibbs
1951, May 18   Mr. Brophy and Shakespeare [letter]   Truth, p. 533

Holtz, Nancy A.
1997, May 15   [letter: resp. to Jonathan Bate's May 1 review of *Alias Shakespeare*]   Wall St. Journal, p. 23A
1999, Fall   [letter: Oxfordian presentation at a New England college]   Sh. Ox. Newsl., vol. 35/3: 21

Honan, Park
1990   *Authors' Lives: On Literary Biography and the Arts of Language.* New York: St. Martin's Press.

Honey, T. H. L.
1937, April 20   Bacon or Shakesppeare? [letter]   Western Morning News, p. 3
1937, May 8   "Shakespeare" Fellowship? [name is a misnomer.]
1939, July 15   Oxford or Bacon? [letter]   Western Morning News, p. 13

Honigmann, E. A. J.
1985, Jan. 17   Sweet Swan of Oxford? [review of *The Mysterious William Shakespeare* by Charlton Ogburn, Jr.]   New York Review, p. 23-26
1991, Nov. 7   The Second-Best Bed   New York Review, p. 27-30
     Response by Charlton Ogburn, April 9, 1992.
     Reply by Honigmann, same date.
       Additional response by Charlton Ogburn, April 25.
       Additional reply by Honigmann, same date.
         [Selections from all responses and replies repr. in SON, vol. 28/2: 16-17; and in BTC, vol. 7: 107-08]

Hony, T. H. L.
1939   Oxford or Bacon? *Western Morning News*, July 15, p. 13.

Hookham, George
Books
1922   *Will o' the Wisp, or The Elusive Shakespeare.* Oxford: B. Blackwell. [J. T. Looney and Edward de Vere mentioned on page 60.]
Shorter pieces
1922, March   Edward de Vere and the Shakespeare Plays   National Review, vol. 79: 94-96
1922, Nov. 25   The Elusive Image [letter]   Spectator, vol. 129: 759-60

Hope, Warren
Books
1992   *The Shakespeare Controversy: An Analysis of the Claimants to Authorship, and Their Champions and Detractors* [with Kim Holston]. Jefferson, NC: McFarland.
2009   *The Shakespeare Controversy: An Analysis of the Authorship Theories, 2nd ed* [with Kim Holston]. Jefferson, NC: McFarland & Co. [excerpts repr. in *Sh. Authorship Sourcebook* (Stritmatter 2019, 2022): 51-67]
2019   *Early Shakespeare* by A. Bronson Feldman. Edited by Warren Hope. Laugwitz Verlag. [Special issue no. 8 of *Neues Shake-speare Journal*]
2022   *Shakespeare, Marlowe, and Other Elizabethans* by A. Bronson Feldman. Edited by Warren Hope. Laugwitz Verlag. [Special issue no. 9 of *Neues Shake-speare Journal*]

Author Index

Hope, Warren (continued)

2010	[review of *The Lame Storyteller* by Peter Moore (2009)]	Brief Chronicles, vol. II: 233-236
2018, Sept.	Geoffrey Fenton	Oxfordian, vol. 20: 157-58
2018, Sept.	The Quest for the Historical Shakspere [review of *The Fictional Lives of Shakespeare* by Kevin Gilvary]	Oxfordian, vol. 20: 191-94
2019, Summer	Oxford's Reputation: A Note [repr. in NSJ, vol. NS7: 126-27]	Sh. Ox. Newsl., vol. 55/4: 31
2019, Sept.	Who was the Model for the Butcher of Ashford in *2 Henry VI*?	Oxfordian, vol. 21: 191-98
2020	Oxford's Reputation: A Note [repr. from SON, vol. 55/4: 31]	Neues Sh. Jou., vol. NS7: 126-27
2020	A Celebration [poem]	Neues Sh. Jou., vol. NS7: 128
2020, Sept.	[review of *Shakespeare Beyond Science* by Sky Gilbert (2020)]	Oxfordian, vol. 22: 141-144
2021, Sept.	The English Petrarch: review of *Renaissance Man: The World of Thomas Watson* by Ian Johnson	Oxfordian, vol. 23: 247-352
2022, Sept.	Some Autobiographical Aspects of *Timon of Athens*	Oxfordian, vol. 24: 69-72
2023	Abraham Bronson Feldman (1914-1982)	Neues Sh. Jou., vol. NS8: 141-46

Hopkins, Keith

2014, Feb.	William Shakespeare, Edward de Vere, Seventeenth Earl of Oxford, and the Still-Vexed Bermoothes	New English Review

Hopkins, Vivian C.

1961, April	The Baconian Theory: An Enchanted Wood	Sh. Newsl., vol. 11/2: 13

Hopper, C. W.

1926, March 20	Was Bacon Queen Elizabeth's Son?	Graphic, p. 506-07
1926, March 26	Queen Elizabeth's Guilty Secret	Graphic, p. 552
1926, April 3	The Missing Manuscripts	Graphic, p. 599
1926, April 10	The Enigma of the Elizabethan Age	Graphic, p. 631

Hoppner, Francis

1953, Dec. 26	Bacon and Oxford [letter]	NY Herald Trib.T, p. 6

Horne, Francis Gregg

1995, Summer	[letter: Nelson's "Oxford in Venice:" Oxford had Malaria.]	Sh. Ox. Newsl., vol. 31/3: 11-12

Horne, Richard C., Jr.

Periodicals edited

1966, Mar 30-1974, Sum/Fall: *Shakespeare Oxford Newsletter*, vol. 2/1-10/1

Shorter pieces

1965, May 28	Shakespeare Portrait X-rayed [repr. in SON, vol. 28/2: 3 (June 1966); excerpts repr. in BTC, vol. 6: 72-74]	Times (London)
1966, March 30	Oxfordian Business and Recent News	Sh. Ox. Newsl., vol. 2/1: 1, 3
1966, Oct. 30	Southampton MS in Library of St. John's College, Cambridge U.	Sh. Ox. Newsl., vol. 2-3: 1-2
1966, Oct. 30	Edmund Spenser and William Shakespeare	Sh. Ox. Newsl., vol. 2/3: 3-5
1966, Dec. 15	SOS Business and Newsletter	Sh. Ox. Newsl., vol. 2/4: 1-2
1968, May 25	Recent Oxfordian Developments	Sh. Ox. Newsl., vol. 4/1: 2-4
1969, Feb. 28	Letter to SOS Members [recent Oxfordian developments]	Sh. Ox. Newsl., vol. 5/1: 1-6, 8-9
1969, Feb. 28	Provincial Dialect in Shakesper's Day	Sh. Ox. Newsl., vol. 5/1: 6-8
1970, March 31	Meanwhile, Back at the "Shrine" . . .	Sh. Ox. Newsl., vol. 6/1: 1-5
1970, March 31	Progress Report: recent Oxfordian news [repr. in BTC, vol. 6: 8-34]	Sh. Ox. Newsl., vol. 6/1: 1-17
1970, March 31	[review of *The Authorship of Shakespeare*, Folger Library Booklet by James G. McManaway, edited by Louis B. Wright (1962)]	Sh. Ox. Newsl., vol. 6/1: 6-8
1970, March 31	[review of *The Folger Library General Reader's Shakespeare*, edited by Louis B. Wright and Virginia A. Lamar (1969)]	Sh. Ox. Newsl., vol. 6/1: 8-11
1970, March 31	[review of *The Author* by Dr. Louis Wright, in *Plays & Poems*]	Sh. Ox. Newsl., vol. 6/1: 12
1970, March 31	The Earl of Oxford and the Privy Council	Sh. Ox. Newsl., vol. 6/1: 13-15
1970, March 31	The Folger Shakespeare Library	Sh. Ox. Newsl., vol. 6/1: 16-17
1970, June 30	More Comments on *Folger Library General Reader's Shakespeare*, and *Shakespeare's Poems*, both edited by Louis B. Wright	Sh. Ox. Newsl., vol. 6/2: 1-2
1970, June 30	The Earl of Hertford	Sh. Ox. Newsl., vol. 6/2: 3
1970, June 30	Is a Search for Original "Shakespeare" Manuscripts Worthwhile?	Sh. Ox. Newsl., vol. 6/2: 4
1970, June 30	J. Thomas Looney's Anniversaries	Sh. Ox. Newsl., vol. 6/2: 4
1971, March 30	[review of *Shakespeare's Lives* by S. Schoenbaum (1970)]	Sh. Ox. Newsl.,vol. 7/1: 4-12
1971, June 1	*Newsweek* Article on the Authorship issue quoting A. L. Rowse	Sh. Ox. Newsl., vol. 7/2: 1-3
1971, June 1	The Earl of Northampton (Henry Howard, 1540-1614)	Sh. Ox. Newsl., vol. 7/2: 4

Howard, Shafter
    1920, Aug. 23   Scholarship and the Baconian Controversy   San Francisco Chronicle, p. 16

Howe, Norma
    2000   *Blue Avenger Cracks the Code*. New York: Holt. Repr. in 2002: New York: Harper Tempest.

Howell, Peter
    2011, Oct. 28   To Be Or Not To Believe [review of *Anonymous*]   Toronto Star, p. E5

Howerton, Jr., Philip F.
    1990, Winter   Vladimir Nabokov and William Shakespeare   Sh. Ox. Newsl., vol. 26/1: 1-3
            [repr. in EVR, vol. 9 (Fall 1999)]
    1992, Fall   Shakspere as Shakespeare Is a Myth [open letter to Th. Pendleton]   Sh. Ox. Newsl., vol. 28/4a: 9
            [repr. in BTC, vol. 7: 129-30]

Hoyt, Richard
    1983   *The Siskiyou Two-Step*. New York: William Morrow and Company, Inc.

Hudson, Alexandra
    2004, Summer   De Vere Anniversary Revives Shakespeare Debate [reprint from Reuters] Sh. Ox. Newsl., vol. 40/3: 8-9

Hudson, John
Books
    2014   *Shakespeare's Dark Lady: Amelia Bassano Lanier: The Woman Behind Shakespeare's Plays*. Amberley
            Publishing.
Shorter pieces
    2009   Amelia Bassano Lanier: A New Paradigm   Oxfordian, vol. 11: 65-82

Hughes, Jacob
    2014, Summer   Comparative Caricatures in *King John* and *Troublesome Raigne*   Brief Chronicles, vol. V: 101-12
    2015, Summer   Chaucer Lost and Found in Shakespeare's Histories   Brief Chronicles, vol. VI: 83-105

Hughes, R. C.
    1997, June 10   From Nowhere, A Genius For All Time [letter]   Wall Street Journal, p. A19

Hughes, Stephanie Hopkins
Websites and blogs: Politicworm – politicworm.com
Books and booklets
    1993   *Oxford & Byron*. Portland, OR: Paradigm Press.
    1997   *The Great Reckoning: Who Killed Christopher Marlowe, and Why*. Portland, OR: Paradigm Press.
            [repr. in TOX, vol. 18: 101-132 (2016)]
    1998   *The Relevance of Robert Greene to the Oxfordian Thesis*. Portland, OR.: Paradigm Press.
    2009   *Robert Greene, King of the Paper Stage* [pamphlet].
    2022   *Educating Shakespeare: What he knew and how and where he learned it*. Cary, NC: Veritas Publications.
Periodicals edited
    1998-2007: *The Oxfordian*, vol. 1-10
Shorter pieces
    1996, Fall   First issue of *The Oxfordian* Scheduled for Next Spring   Sh. Ox. Newsl., vol. 32/4: 3
    1996, Fall   Oxford as Shakespeare: Belief or Hypothesis? [letter]   Sh. Ox. Newsl., vol. 32/4: 21-22
    1997, Winter   Of Standins, Pseudonyms, Mummings and Disguisings   Sh. Ox. Newsl., vol. 33/1: 4-5, 23
            [repr. in BTC, vol. 7: 385-91; and in EVR, vol. 6 (Winter 1998)]
    1997, Spring   First Ever: Concordia Univ. Opens the Academic Door to Oxford   Sh. Ox. Newsl., vol. 33/2: 9
    1998   In Memoriam: Morse Johnson, Editor of the *Shakespeare Oxford*   Oxfordian, vol. 1: 0
            Newsletter (1986-1995)
    1998   Editorial: The Curious Incident of the Shakespeare Paper Trail   Oxfordian, vol. 1: 1-3
    1998   Sonnet XXXIII, and Much, Much Less   Oxfordian, vol. 1: 102-103
    1998   Note from the Editor   Oxfordian, vol. 1: 104-105
    1998, Spring   Society of Secrets: How the Elizabethan Era Still Confounds Us   Sh. Ox. Newsl., vol. 34/1: 1, 6-8+
            Today [repr. in BTC, vol. 7: 421-30]
    1999   In Memoriam: Charlton Ogburn, Jr., Founding Member of the   Oxfordian, vol. 2: 0
            Shakespeare-Oxford Society, Author, Board Member,
            Newsletter Editor (1911-98)
    1999   To the Reader   Oxfordian, vol. 2: 1-2
    1999, Summer   [letter: Hank Whittemore's Summer "Prince Tudor" article]   Sh. Ox. Newsl., vol. 35/2: 25-26
            Response to Hughes by Sandy Hochberg, vol. 36/1: 29.
            Response to Hughes by Richard Whalen, vol. 36/1: 29.

Hughes, Stephanie Hopkins (continued)

2012, July	[letter: doodles in Smith's notebook]	De Vere So. New., v. 19/2: 32-33
2013	Storm Over *The Tempest* [review of *On the Date, Sources and Design of Shakespeare's "The Tempest"* by Roger Stritmatter and Lynne Kositsky (2013)]	Oxfordian, vol. 15: 149-154
2013, Winter	The Big Six Candidates for Shakespeare's Crown	Sh. Ox. Newsl., vol. 49/1: 18-19
2017, Spring	Oxford's Authorship in a Nutshell	Sh. Ox. Newsl., vol. 53/2: 18-22
2021, April	Who Was Sir Thomas Smith?	De Vere So. New., v. 28/2: 17-33
2022, Winter	Oxford and Plutarch [letter]	Sh. Ox. Newsl., vol. 58/1: 3
2022, Sept.	Shake-speare's Sonnets: Their Dates, Their History, and the Story They Tell	Oxfordian, vol. 24: 149-70

Hughes-Stanton, Ida

1963, Spring	The Hare-Brained Escapade	Sh. Authorship Review, #9: 6-7
1999, Summer	[letter: Whittemore and the Prince Tudor thesis]	Sh. Ox. Newsl., vol. 35/2: 25-26
2001, July	[letter: compliments on an excellent newsletter]	De Vere Soc. Newsl., p. 24-28
2002, Fall	[letter: age of King Edward VI on Oxford's birthday]	Sh. Ox. Newsl., vol. 38/4: 23
2013, Winter	[letter: Oxford's childhood with Sir Thomas Smith; medical issues]	Sh. Matters, vol. 12/1: 2, 28

Hughley, Marty

2008, Jan. 21	The World's a State, No Matter Who Created Plays [Stratfordians vs. Oxfordians]	Oregonian, p. C4

Humphreys, Christmas

1955	"Introduction" to *Who Was Shakespeare? a new enquiry* by Hilda Amphlett [2nd ed. 1970]	
1962, Aug. 30	[letter: efforts to open Shakespeare's tomb]	Times (London), p. 11
1962, Autumn	[review of *Shakespeare Cross-Examination* published by *The American Bar Association Journal* (1961)]	Sh. Authorship Rev., #8: 17-19
1968, Autumn	"A Cross Examination of Oxfordians" [summary of his Dec. 6, 1967 Lecture] [repr. in BTC, vol. 5: 261-263]	Sh. Authorship Rev., #19: 16-18
1970, Summer	[report on David W. T. C. Vessey's Jan. 21 lecture "Some Allusions to Shakespeare in Elizabethan Literature"]	Sh. Authorship Rev., #23: 17-18

Humphreys, Henry Sigurd

1948, Nov. 6	Shakespeare Confusion [letter: resp. to Burgess]	Saturday Review, p. 21-22

Humphreys, Philip

1950, Oct.	Who Wrote Shakespeare? A Controversy and a Challenge [response to Giles E. Dawson, *The Listener*, Aug. 10, 1950] [See also: Edward Johnson, "Can We Educate Dr. Giles E. Dawson?", in same issue]	Baconiana, vol. 34: 212-16

Hunt, Douglas

1991	*The Riverside Guide to Writing*. Boston: Houghton Mifflin. [2nd edition: 1995] [See chapter "Arguing When the Facts are Disputed"]	

Hunt, Marvin

2010, July 11	A Readable Look Into the Debate Over Who Penned Shakespeare [review of *Contested Will* by James Shapiro]	News & Observer (Raeigh)

Hunt, Paula

2006, Feb. 19	Shakespeare: The Man	San Antonio Express-News

Hunter, Major Newsl. B.

1949, Sept.	The Earls and Shakespeare	SF News-letter (E), p. 5-6

Hunter, Mark

1929, Sept. 5	Shakespeare and Richard III: Inefficient Propagandist [letter]	Morning Post, p. 5
1929, Sept. 12	Shakespeare and Richard III: A Modern Parallel [letter]	Morning Post, p. 9

Hunter, R. Cetus

2006, Summer	[letter: the essential truth]	Sh. Matters, vol. 5/4: 2-3

Hunter, R. Thomas

2003, Spring	Every Word in Shakespeare: Textual Signatures by the True Author	Sh. Matters, vol. 2/3: 6-7, 32
2003, Autumn	Mark Rylance Addresses Oxfordian Students at Univ. of Michigan	Sh. Ox. Newsl., vol. 39/4: 24
2004, Winter	Mark Rylance Featured Guest in Michigan	Sh. Matters, vol. 3/2: 6

Hutchison, Matt

2021, Sept.	The Slippery Slope of Shakspere's "Signatures"	Oxfordian, vol. 23: 81-166
2022, Sept.	A Companion for a King: "Shakespeare . . . THOU HADST BIN]	Oxfordian, vol. 24: 57-61
2022, Sept.	"Sogliardo" and Green's Upstart Crow	Oxfordian, vol. 24: 63-68
2023, Spring	Was Thomas North a Secretary to the Earl of Oxford	Sh. Ox. Newsl., vol. 59/2: 22-24
2023, Sept.	When did Shakespeare Die?	Oxfordian, vol. 25: 127-68

Hutsching, Ed

1984, Sept. 3	For This Section, Seven Is a Lucky Number [brief review of *The Mysterious William Shakespeare*]	San Diego Union, p. Books-2

Hyde, Michael

2009, Winter	Who Was Spenser's E.K.? Another Look at the Evidence	Sh. Matters, vol. 08/1: 5, 23-6
2010	[letter: Richard Waugaman's Fall 2010 "*English Posie*" article] Reply by Richard Waugaman.	Brief Chronicles, vol. II: 258-259
2019, Spring	[review of *Shakespearian Fantasias* by Esther Singleton, modern ed. edited by James A. Warren]	Sh. Ox. Newsl., vol. 55/2: 30-31
2020, Winter	Rereading Shakespeare's *King John* and *The Troublesome Reign*	Sh. Ox. Newsl., vol. 56/1: 10-15
2020, Sept.	Calgreyhounds and the First Folios of Jonson and Shakespeare [repr. in *The First Folio* (Stritmatter 2023): 233-48]	Oxfordian, vol. 22: 49-63
2021, Winter	The Great Seamark at Wivenhoe	Sh. Ox. Newsl., vol. 57/1: 25-26
2021, Spring	[review of *North by Shakespeare: A Rogue Scholar's Quest for the Truth Behind the Bard's Work* by Michael Blanding (2021)]	Sh. Ox. Newsl., vol. 57/2: 12-18
2021, Summer	The Badge of the Blue Boar and Edward de Vere	Sh. Ox. Newsl., vol. 57/3: 25-28
2021, Sept.	Additional Evidence for Edward de Vere's Authorship of Shakespeare's *Troilus and Cressida*	Oxfordian, vol. 23: 15-24
2021, Sept.	[review of *North by Shakespeare* by Michael Blanding]	Oxfordian,vol. 23: 353-363
2022, Winter	My Kindle Told Me It Was Edward de Vere (Part One)	Sh. Ox. Newsl., vol. 58/1: 20-25
2022, Spring	My Kindle Told Me It Was Edward de Vere (Part Two)	Sh. Ox. Newsl., vol. 58/2: 20-26
2022, Summer	[review of *The Famous Victories of Henry the Fifth: An Earl Play by the Real William Sh., Ed. de Vere* by Ramon Jiménez]	Sh. Ox. Newsl., vol. 58/3: 11-12
2023, Winter	[review of *The True Tragedy of Richard the Third*, ed. by Ramon Jiménez (2022)]	Sh. Ox. Newsl., vol. 59/1: 20-22
2023, Spring	[rev. of *Shakespeare and the Law* by Roger Stritmatter (2022)]	Sh. Ox. Newsl., vol. 59/2: 27
2023, Sept.	How the Romance of *Leir* Became the Tragedy of *King Lear*	Oxfordian, vol. 25: 69-86

I. B.

1933, May 17	The Oxfordians [review of *A Reply to John Drinkwater* by Percy and Ernest Allen]	Manchester Guardian, p. 5

I. C. Q.

2016, Oct.	£1,000 and the Beginning of England's National Theater	De Vere So. New., v. 23/4:34-36

Iacovou, Andreas

2005	*Shakespeare Unparadised: Defining Shakespeare: An Essay Concerning Human Stupidity* [Text selected and edited by Antonios Iacovou]. Victoria, BC, Canada: Trafford Publishing.

Ide, Wendy

2011, Oct. 28	Not Half Bard, But Nothing Like the Truth [review of *Anonymous*]	Times (London), p. 11

Idle, Eric

2011, Nov.	Who Wrote Shakespeare?	New Yorker, vol. 87/37: 65

Ignatius, David

1999, March 21	Honor the True Bard [Edward de Vere] Response by Irene Vartanoff, April 3, p. A13.	Washington Post, p. B7

Ignoto

1990, Spring	Beowulf, Hamlet, and Edward de Vere	Sh. Ox. Newsl., vol. 26/2: 3-6
2003, Spring	[letter: authorship issues in bookstores]	Sh. Matters, vol. 2/3: 2

Illig, Heribert

2004, June	[review of *Freispruch - für CO2* by Wolfgang Thüne (2002)]	Neues Sh. Jou., vol. 9: 177-80
2023	Issachar ben Mordecai ibn Susan oder vier Lilien	Neues Sh. Jou., vol. NS8: 125-34

Author Index

Imlay, Elizabeth (continued)

2011, Fall	[letter: Elizabeth I: facts not fantasy] [with Stephanie Hopkins Hughes and Ren Draya]	Sh. Ox. Newsl., vol. 47/3: 2
2011, Nov.	Breakfast Television Transcript: BBC Programme with Stanley Wells and Elizabeth Imlay [Broadcast Sept. 2, 2011]	De Vere Soc. Newsl., vol. 18/3: 6
2011, Nov.	DVS Meeting in London (Sept. 24, 2011)	De Vere Soc. Newsl., v. 18/3: 4-5
2011, Nov.	Drawings by Edward de Vere? – Possibly – A Cambridge Discovery	De Vere So. New., v. 18/3: 15-17
2011, Nov.	*Anonymous* Passes: The Film Reviewed	De Vere So. New., v. 18/3: 22-25
2011, Nov.	Untapped Potential of Phaeton	De Vere So. New., v. 18/3: 30-31
2012, March	*Time* Team at Colne Priory	De Vere Soc. Newsl., vol. 19/1: 4
2012, March	A Possible Portrait of Anne Cecil Considered	De Vere So. New., v. 19/1: 12-14
2012, March	Monsters of the 16-17th Century no. 5: de Vere Easily Surpassed in 'Monstrousness' By Many of His Contemporaries	De Vere So. New., v. 19/1: 30-31
2012, July	Meeting at Clarance House, Thaxted, and at Horham Hall	De Vere Soc. Newsl., vol. 19/2: 5
2012, Nov.	Meeting of The De Vere Society, 29th September 2012	De Vere Soc. Newsl., vol. 19/3: 4
2013, Oct.	Elizabeth Imlay Steps Down from the De Vere Society	De Vere Soc. Newsl., vol. 20/3: 3
2022, July	[review of *Shakespeare's Revolution* by Richard Malim]	De Vere So. New., v. 29/3: 47-48

Inskeep, Steve
Radio programs hosted

2016, April 25	Two Shakespearean Actors Revive Debate Over the Bard's Identity [trans. of "Morning Edition" with Mark Rylance and Derek Jacobi]	National Public Radio

Iota

1920, June 5	A New Shakespeare	Southland Times (New Zealand), issue 18840

Irwin, Anna

1997, June 10	From Nowhere, A Genius For All Time [letter: response to Sobran]	Wall St. Journal, p. A19

Irwin, Wallace

1940, March 17	[Short story mentions de Vere as author]	Minneapolis Star-Jou., p. 73

Ish-Kishor, Sulamith

1953, Dec. 26	Oxford Theory [letter]	NY Herald Tribune, p. 6

Itzkoff, Dave

2011, Oct. 26	Shakespeare Birthplace Trust Slams New Film . . . Or Does It?; No, It Really Does [review of *Anonymous*]	National Post, p. A3
2011, Oct. 26	Covering Up Shakespeare's Name to Protest a Film [*Anonymous*]	New York Times, p. C3

Ives, Eric

2001, Oct.	[letter: William Rubinstein's Aug. article] Reply by William Rubinstein, same issue and page.	History Today, vol. 51: 28-35

J. B. D.

1932, May 17	Why There is a Shakespeare Problem	Christian Sci. Monitor, p. 16

J. B. S.

1937, June	Follow the Bacon Myth [letter]	East Ang. Mag., vol. 2/9: 425

J. H. D. [see J. Howard Dellinger]

J. H. R.

1910	"Vere," in *Encyclopedia Britannica, 11th ed.*, vol. 27: 1019-1020.	

J. R.

1923, June,	The Search for a Substitute	Baconiana, vol. xviii: 126-32

J. S. A.

1947, Sept.	Oxfordians Debate With Miss Neill	SF News-letter (E), p. 5-6
1947, Sept.	Heretics' Week, Stratford-on-Avon	SF News-letter (E), p. 6-7
1958, Spring	[review of *Shakespearean Ciphers* by William F. Friedman (1957)]	SF News-letter (E), p. 7-9

J. S. L. M.

1927, Nov. 21	The Bishop of Durham and Shakespeare [letter]	Scotsman, p. 11

Jackson, Joseph Henry

1939, Dec. 29	Science Takes a Hand in the Shakespearean Controversy [response to	San Francisco Chronicle, p. 13

Barrell's *Scientific American* article]

Jannsch, Heidi (continued)

2020, Jan.	Sogliardo & Co.	De Vere So. New., v. 27/1: 35-43
2020, Fall	The First Online Shakespeare Authorship Symposium: A Milestone for Oxfordian Research	Sh. Ox. Newsl., v. 56/4: 1, 30-31
2020, Fall	Behind the Scenes at the Shakespeare Authorship Symposium	Sh. Ox. Newsl., vol. 56/4: 32-33
2020, Oct.	John Davies of Hereford Identifies W.S. as Oxford in *Microcosmos*	De Vere Soc. New., v. 27/4: 5-18
2022, Sept.	Are the Paratexts of *Sejanus His Fall* an Homage to Edward de Vere?	Oxfordian, vol. 24: 131-148
2022, Fall	SOF Conf. in Ashland, Oregon, Combines In-Person Attendance with Live-Streaming [with D. Dickerman & A. McNeil]	Sh. Ox. Newsl., v. 58/4: 1, 28-36
2023, Spring	Moot Court Trial of William of Stratford Held in London	Sh. Ox. Newsl., vol. 59/2: 8-9

Jansen, W.

2006	Authorship Clues in *Henry VI, Part 3* [with Eric L. Atlschuler]	Oxfordian, vol. 9: 126-131

Jaroff, Leon

2002, July 16	By Yonder Blessed Moon, Sleuths Decode Life/Art	New York Times

Jarrett, Thomas D.

1960, Sept.	Language and Literature: Was Shakespeare Really Shakespeare [The Ogburns vs. Hastings]	English Journal, vol. 49/6: 430

Jaszi, Peter A.

1988, Winter	"We Still Know Virtually Nothing About Shakespeare . . ." [remarks at the debate before 3 U.S. Supr. Court Justices, 25 Sept. 1987]	Sh. Ox. Newsl., vol. 24/1: 1-2
1988, Spring	Who Cares Who Wrote 'Shakespeare'?	Am U. Law Rev., vol. 37/3: 617-24
1988, Spring	Brief of Appellant Edward de Vere, Seventeenth Earl of Oxford	Am U. Law Rev., vol. 37/3: 647-724
1988, Spring	Reply Brief of Appellant Edward de Vere, Seventeenth Earl of Oxford	Am U. Law Rev., vol. 37/3: 799-807

Jaynes, Dwight

1997, Sept. 18	[Sometimes you think you know something . . .]	Oregonian, p. C1

Jensen, Elizabeth
Radio programs hosted

2016, April 29	To Be Or Not to Be Falsely Equivalent [listener responses to the April 25 interview with Mark Rylance and Derek Jacobi]	National Public Radio

Jensen, Michael P.

2003, Fall	Finding Shakespeare: Brian Vickers vs. the Attributers	Sh. Newsl., vol. 53/3: 67-68

Jensen, Mike

1995, Winter	[review of *Shakespeare, In Fact* by Irvin Matus]	Small Press, vol. 13: 59

Jessup, John K.

1962, Sept. 7	Fresh Troops Join the Battle of the Bard [review of *Shake-speare: The Man Behind the Name* by Dorothy and Charlton (Jr.) Ogburn]	Life, p. 4

Jewell, Keith D.

1998, Spring	A London Visitor's Homage to Edward de Vere	Sh. Ox. Newsl., vol. 34/1: 12-13

Jiménez, Ramon
Books

2018	*Shakespeare's Apprenticeship: Identifying the Real Playwright's Earliest Works.* Jefferson, NC: McFarland & Co., Inc.
2022	*The Famous Victories of Henry V*, an early play by the real William Shakespeare, Edward de Vere, Seventeenth Earl of Oxford. [introduced, edited and fully annotated from an Oxfordian perspective]

Periodicals co-edited with James Brooks
2005, Winter-2005, Fall: *Shakespeare Oxford Newsletter*, vol. 41/1-41/4
Periodicals co-edited with Katherine Chiljan
2010, May: *Shakespeare Oxford Newsletter*, vol. 46/1
Shorter pieces

1999, Spring	[review of *Shakespeare's Sonnets and the Court of Navarre* by D. Honneyman (1997)] [repr. in EVR, vol. 8 (Spr. 1999)]	Sh. Ox. Newsl., vol. 35/1: 18
2000, Fall	[letter: Oxford's ancestors in *The Famous Victories*]	Sh. Ox. Newsl., vol. 36/3: 21
2001, Summer	*Famous Victories of Henry the Fifth* – Key to the Authorship Question? [repr. in GO, p. 201-207]	Sh. Ox. Newsl., v. 37/2: 7-10

Author Index

Jiménez, Ramon (continued)

2013	Appendix B: Stylometrics: How Reliable is it Really? in *Sh. Beyond Doubt?* (Shahan): 228-36	
2013	The Two *Lear* Plays: How Shakespeare Transformed His First Romance into His Last Tragedy	Oxfordian, vol. 15: 27-73
2013, Fall	Oxford's Fifty-Play Canon and When It Was Written, Part 1	Sh. Ox. Newsl., vol. 39/3: 10-18
2014, Winter	Oxford's Fifty-Play Canon and When It Was Written, Part 2	Sh. Ox. Newsl., v. 50/1: 1, 12-17
2014, Fall	[review of *William Shakespeare & Others: Collaborative Plays* ed. by Jonathan Bate and Eric Rasmussen (2013)]	Sh. Ox. Newsl., vol. 50/4: 13-15
2015, Winter	Six Characters in Search of an Author	Sh. Ox. Newsl., v. 51/1: 1, 14-18
2015, Summer	[review of *John de Vere: Thirteenth Earl of Oxford* by James Ross]	Sh. Ox. Newsl., vol. 51/3: 11-14
2016, October	An Evening at the Cockpit: Further Evidence of an Early Date for *Henry V*	Oxfordian, vol. 18: 9-22
2016, Spring	[review of *The First Two Quartos of Hamlet, A New View of the Origins and Relationship of the Texts* by Margrethe Jolly]	Sh. Ox. Newsl., vol. 52/3: 29-32
2018, Winter	*Vero Nihil Verius*—Nothing Truer than What?	Sh. Ox. Newsl., vol. 54/1: 16-17
2018, Spring	An Oxfordian Looks into Henslowe's Diary	Sh. Ox. Newsl., vol. 54/2: 15-18
2019, Sept.	[review of *Shakespeare, Court Dramatist* by Richard Dutton]	Oxfordian, vol. 21: 237-42
2020, Sept.	Was *The Famous Victories of Henry the Fifth* Sh.'s First Play?	Oxfordian, vol. 22:15-47
2020, Sept.	[review of *Who Wrote That?* by Donald Ostrowski (2020)]	Oxfordian, vol. 22:145-153
2021, Summer	[letter: Blanding's *North by Shakespeare*]	Sh. Ox. Newsl., vol. 57/3: 5
2022, Sept.	TO.THE.ONLIE.BEGETTER. Making Sense of the Dedication	Oxfordian, vol. 24: 167-193
2023, Summer	The Shakespeare Authorship Question: A Forensic Examination	Jou. of Sci. Exploration, vol. 37/2
2023, Sept.	Heresies, Certainties, Conspiracies and Shadows [review of *Shakespeare Was a Woman and Other Heresies* by Elizabeth Winkler]	Oxfordian, vol. 25: 273-78

Johnson, Barry

1999, April 25	Talk About a Dead Poets Society	Oregonian, vol. F1

Johnson, David

2007, Sept. 8	[letter: M. Billington's false claim that no major actors are Oxfordians	Guardian, p. 39

Johnson, Edward D.

Books

1947	*The Shakespeare Illusion, 3rd ed.* London: Mitre Press.	
1964	*The Shakespeare Quiz: 100 Questions for Stratfordians to Answer*. Pamphlet. [perhaps a revision of a first edition in 1950]	

Shorter pieces

1939, Feb. 24	The Notes in the First Folio [letter]	John O'London's Weekly, p. 821
1950, Oct.	Can We Educate Dr. Giles E. Dawson?	Baconiana, vol. 34: 217-20

Johnson, Ian

Books

2020	*Renaissance Man: The World of Thomas Watson*. New Generation Publishing.	
2021, Jan.	Edward de Vere and Thomas Watson	De Vere Soc. Newsl., v. 28/1: 10

Shorter pieces

1991, Aug.	[letter: delight with *Spear-shaker*]	Sh. Review, issue 5: 25
2000, Jan.	[letter: resp. to Milner-Gulland re canals in Italy] [repr. in DVN (Jan. 2000), p. 14] Response by Nick Milner-Gulland, vol. 128. Reply by Johnson, DVN (Jan. 2000), p. 14.	Oldie, issue 127
2010, Nov.	[letter: photo in *The Guardian* shows *The Mystery of William Shakespeare* by Charlton Ogburn]	De Vere Soc. Newsl., v. 17/3: 21

Johnson, John

1920, April 11	Shakespeare Identified [letter]	Sunday Times, p. 5

Johnson, Morse

Periodicals edited

1986, Fall-1995, Autumn: *Shakespeare Oxford Newsletter*, vol. 22/4-31/4

Shorter pieces

1977, Feb. 13	The Man Who Wasn't Shakespeare [review of SI]	Cincinnati Enq., vol. 136/309: D5

Johnson, Morse (continued)

1992, Summer	Traditional Portraits of William Shakespeare	Sh. Ox. Newsl., vol. 28/3: 11-12
1992, Winter	[letter to the Writing Company: lack of books about de Vere [repr. in BTC, vol. 7: 95-98]	Sh. Ox. Newsl., vol. 28/1: 7-8
1992, Summer	[letter to *Sh. Newsletter*: cancellation of Oxfordian page deprives readers of information	Sh. Ox. Newsl., vol. 28/3: 13-14
1992, Fall	Signs of a Turning Tide [repr. in BTC, vol. 7: 128]	Sh. Ox. Newsl., vol. 28/4a-b: 7-8
1993, Winter	Shake-speare Could Only Have Been a Pseudonym [repr. in BTC: vol. 7: 148-49]	Sh. Ox. Newsl.. vol. 29/1a: 5-6
1993, Winter	Peregrine Bertie's Startling Report [repr. in BTC, vol. 7: 148-49]	Sh. Ox. Newsl., vol. 29/1a: 18
1993, Winter	[letter: 43 Distinguished Stratfordian Scholars: Oxford's Authorship]	Sh. Ox. Newsl., vol. 29/1a: 19
1993, Spring	[letter to Rebecca Flynn: Dugdale drawings [Feb. 9, 1993] [repr. in BTC, vol. 7: 172-73]	Sh. Ox. Newsl., vol. 29/2a: 13
1993, Spring	List of 62 Prominent People Who Have Rejected Shaksper	Sh. Ox. Newsl., vol. 29/2b: 8
1993, Spring	[responses to Gary Taylor's *Reinventing Shakespeare* (1991)] [repr. in BTC, vol. 7: 159-63]	Sh. Ox. Newsl., vol. 29/2a: 9-11
1993, Spring	Lord Burford [Charles Beauclerk] Reaches 15,000 With the Case For Oxford [repr. in BTC, vol. 7: 174-75]	Sh. Ox. Newsl., vol. 29/2a: 14
1993, Summer	Contradictory Factual Evidence is Unearthed [repr. in BTC, vol. 7: 186-87]	Sh. Ox. Newsl., vol. 29/3a: 12-13
1993, Fall	Acclaim for Johnny Price's Accomplishments as Chairman of the Board	Sh. Ox. Newsl., vol. 29/4: 23
1994, Winter	[letter: Louis Marder's distortions of authorship evidence in "Bard, Marder Best in Boston" (27 Jan. 1994)] [repr. in BTC, vol. 7: 225-29]	Sh. Ox. Newsl., vol. 30/1: 6-10
1994, Spring	Schoenbaum and Twain [repr. in BTC, vol. 7: 253-54]	Sh. Ox. Newsl., vol. 30/2b: 8
1994, Summer	Cumulative Facts that Conclusively Prove Will Shakspere Was Not the Playwright "William Sh." [repr. in BTC, vol. 7: 264-80]	Sh. Ox. Newsl., vol. 30/3b: 1-12
1994, Autumn	Lord Burford [Charles Beauclerk] Speaks at the Smithsonian; BBC Program is Broadcast]	Sh. Ox. Newsl., vol. 30/4: 9-10
1994, Autumn	Faultfinding Expositions of the First Two Paragraphs in Thomas A. Pendleton's Review of Irvin Matus' *Shakespeare in Fact* [in *The Shakespeare Newsletter*]	Sh. Ox. Newsl., vol. 30/4: 11
1995, Winter	The Way to Avoid the Ill-suited is to Keep it From Being Communicated [repr. in BTC, vol. 7: 292-94]	Sh. Ox. Newsl., vol. 31/1a: 1-2
1995, Winter	[review of *Shakespeare, In Fact* by Irvin Matus (1994)] [repr. in BTC, vol. 7: 295-304]	Sh. Ox. Newsl., vol. 31/1b: 1-7
1995, Spring	A Quotation [from Charles W. Barrell, in the *Saturday Review*, May 1, 1937] [repr. in BTC, vol. 7: 305]	Sh. Ox. Newsl., vol. 31/2a: 5
1995, Spring	*Smithsonian Magazine* Gets the Facts Wrong: Stritmatter and Anderson Reply [repr. in BTC, vol. 7: 308-10]	Sh. Ox. Newsl., vol. 31/2a: 7-8
1995, Summer	[response to Bob Grumman's letters] [repr. in BTC, vol. 7: 344-46]	Sh. Ox. Newsl., vol. 31/3: 12-16
1995, Autumn	Letters and Responses [parallels between Oxford's life and the plays] [repr. in BTC, vol. 7: 347-48]	Sh. Ox. Newsl., vol. 31/4: 1-2
1995, Autumn	The World's Most Baffling Literary Mystery [repr. from SON, vol. 9/4: 1-2; repr. in BTC, vol. 6: 248-53 and vol. 7: 350-52]	Sh. Ox. Newsl., vol. 31/4: 9-10

Johnson, Philip

2000, July	Thomas Smith letter to Burghley, April 25, 1576 [with Eddi Jolly]	De Vere Soc. Newsl., p. 28-29
2000, Oct.	Shakespeare's Education and Stratford Grammar School [repr. in GO, p. 34-37]	De Vere Soc. Newsl., p. 8-11
2001, Apr./May	[letter: the BBC Radio 4's March 15 program] [with Kevin Gilvary, Pauline Hendle and Eddi Jolly]	De Vere Soc. Newsl., p. 49-50
2001, July	John Lyly's Endimion and William Shakespeare's *Much Ado About Nothing* [repr. in GO, p. 151-158]	De Vere Soc. Newsl., p. 12-16
2001, July	[review of *Ungentle Shakespeare* by Katherine Duncan-Jones (2000)] [with Eddi Jolly]	De Vere Soc. Newsl., p. 30-31
2001, Oct.	The Third Earl of Southampton and a Gentleman of Stratford [repr. in GO, p. 267-275]	De Vere Soc. Newsl., p. 9-14
2002, July	*Measure for Measure* and the French Connection [repr. in GO, p. 196-200] Response by Sally Hazelton, Oct. 2002, p. 20.	De Vere Soc. Newsl., p. 22-25

Jolly, Margrethe/Emma (Eddi) (continued)

2002, April	Matching the Man to His Works	De Vere Soc. Newsl., p. 27-32
2002, Oct.	Note about Tindall's *The Man Who Drew London*	De Vere Soc. Newsl., p. 24
2002, Fall	New Place [letter]	Sh. Ox. Newsl., vol. 38/4: 23
2003, Aug.	Ein Vorbild für Sonett CXXX? [repr. from DVN (June 2003)] [Sonnet 130 parodies a poem in Watson's *Hekotompathia* and is evidence for de Vere's authorship]	De Vere Soc. New., v. 8: 128-30
2003, June	My Mistress' Eyes . . . An Original For Sonnet CXXX?	De Vere Soc. Newsl., p. 15
2003, June	[review of *Voyages de Shakespeare en France et en Italie*, by Georges Lambin (1962)]	De Vere Soc. Newsl., p. 16-17
2004	Dating the Plays: *Hamlet*, in *Great Oxford*, p. 169-79	
2004, Jan.	[review of *Monstrous Adversity* by Alan Nelson (2003)] [with Philip Johnson and Kevin Gilvary]	De Vere Soc. Newsl., p. 6-7
2004, July	The Life of William Shaksper in the Documentary Records [with Kevin Gilvary]	De Vere Soc. Newsl., p. 12-13
2004, Oct.	[review of *The Late Mr. Shakespeare: a novel* by Robert Nye (1999)]	De Vere Soc. Newsl., p. 25
2006, April	[review of a Lecture at the University of Southampton: 'Six Weeks in the Life of Shakespeare' by James Shapiro]	De Vere Soc. Newsl., p. 23-24
2006, Nov.	Creation of the *Ur-Hamlet*	De Vere Soc. Newsl., p. 9
2006, Nov.	[report on the Dating Project] [with Philip Johnson]	De Vere Soc. Newsl., p. 14-15
2007, Oct.	Obituary: Philip Johnson	De Vere Soc. Newsl., p. 4
2007, Oct.	Meres - His Usefulness and His Limitations	De Vere Soc. Newsl., p. 13-18
2008, March	News: the dating project	De Vere Soc. Newsl., vol. 15/1: 3
2008, March	[review of *The Shakespeare Secret* by Jennifer L. Carrell (2008)]	De Vere Soc. Newsl., v. 15/1: 30
2009, Nov.	Analogies and Cliches	De Vere So. New., v. 16/3: 25-27
2009, Nov.	[review of *Paper Trail* by Simon Fry (2008)]	De Vere Soc. New., vol. 16/3: 32
2009, Nov.	Monsteriana	De Vere Soc. New., vol. 16/3: 33
2010	The Uses and Limits of Francis Meres, in *Dating Sh.'s Plays*, p. 19-27	
2010	*The Winter's Tale* [in *Dating Shakespeare's Plays* (Gilvary): 177-86]	
2010	*The Tragedy of Hamlet* [in *Dating Shakespeare's Plays* (Gilvary): 379-95]	
2010, Aug.	Thomas Nashe's Preface: Toward a New Reading	De Vere So. New., v. 17/2: 13-18
2010, Nov.	Which Came First: Q1 or Q2 *Hamlet*?: The Evidence of Belleforest	De Vere So. New., v. 17/3: 17-21
2012, July	Memorial Reconstruction and *Hamlet*	De Vere Soc. Newsl., vol. 19/2: 8
2011, July	Shakespeare's Debt to Hall and Holinshed	De Vere Soc. New., vol. 18/2: 13
2012, March	[review of *Proving Shakespeare: In Ben Jonson's Own Words, "I Vow He Is E. De Vere"*, by David Roper (2011)]	De Vere So. New., v. 19/1: 28-29
2013, October	Newington Butts, Drains, and the Nature of Evidence	De Vere So. New., v. 20/3: 20-21
2014, May	Mommsen's Legacy?	De Vere So. New., v. 21/2: 16-23
2015, April	Shakespeare: the French Connection: *Love's Labour's Lost*	De Vere So. New., v. 22/2: 13-21
2016, January	In Memoriam: Marion Peel (d. 2015); Michael Le Gassick (d. 2016); John Rollett (d. 2015)	De Vere So. New., v. 23/1: 42-43
2016, July	Summary of her paper "A Tale of Three Juliets"	De Vere Soc. New., vol. 23/3: 13
2016, October	Sc(e)acan, Shack, and Shakespeare	Oxfordian, vol. 18: 41-53
2017, Fall	Alexander Waugh vs. Sir Jonathan Bate: "Who Wrote Shakespeare?"	Sh. Ox. Newsl., vol. 53/4: 9-12
2018, Jan.	[letter from Robert Bertie to Edward de Vere]	De Vere So. New., v. 25/1: 45-46
2018, April	[review of *The Fictional Lives of Shakespeare* by Dr. Kevin Gilvary]	De Vere So. New., v. 25/2: 44-46
2018, Summer	Researching de Vere in Paris	Sh. Ox. Newsl., vol. 54/3: 20-25
2018, Oct.	Shakespeare's Knowledge of French	De Vere Soc. New., v. 25/4: 6-11
2019, April	John Casson, the Source for *Hamlet*, and *The Guardian*	De Vere So. New., v. 26/2: 16-17
2019, April	[rev. of *Hamlet's Elsinore Revisited* by Sten F. Vedi & Ger. Wagner] [repr. in NSJ, vol. NS7 (2020): 140-41]	De Vere So. New., v. 26/2: 29-30
2019, April	[rev. of *Francis Bacon's Contribution to Shakespeare* by Barry Clarke]	De Vere So. New., v. 26/2: 36-37
2019, Oct.	[review of *Nothing Truer than Truth* by Darrol Blake]	De Vere So. New., v. 26/4: 33-34
2021, Spring	SOF Spring Symposium [letter]	Sh. Ox. Newsl., vol. 57/2: 6
2021, Winter	Research Grant Report: The "Flemingii" Manuscript	Sh. Ox. Newsl., vol. 57/1: 16-18
2021, Jan.	Abraham Fleming—Another "Grand Possessor?"	De Vere Soc. Newsl., vol. 28/1: 9
2021, Summer	"A Pleasant Conceit" and a Coincidence?	Sh. Ox. Newsl., vol. 57/3: 16-17
2021, Summer	In Pursuit of "A Pleasant Conceit"	Sh. Ox. Newsl., vol. 57/3: 18
2022, Spring	Shakespeare's Beehive?	Sh. Ox. Newsl., vol. 58/2: 12-19

Junior, Junius (continued)

1926, April 3	Bacon—Queen Elizabeth's Son, III	Gentlew. & Mod. Life, p. 511-13
1926, April 10	Bacon—Queen Elizabeth's Son, IV	Gentlew. & Mod. Life, p. 573-74
1926, April 17	Bacon—Queen Elizabeth's Son, V	Gentlew. & Mod. Life, p. 617
1926, April 24	Bacon—Queen Elizabeth's Son, VI	Gentlew. & Mod. Life, p. 662

Jury, Louise

2004, Sept. 17	Director Who Gave Shakespeare Back to Masses Quits Globe [repr. in DVN (Oct. 2004), p. 23]	Independent
2006, April 21	Was Shakespeare the Love Child of Queen Elizabeth?	Independent, p. 28

K. C. T.

1937, Feb.	Ingenuity and Acumen [review of *Lord Burghley in Shakespeare* by Gerald W. Phillips] [response by Phillips, March issue]	Sh. Pictorial, no. 108: 28

Kakutani, Michiko

1990, March 23	Of Freud and His Obsession With the Enigmatic [review of *Reading Freud: Exploration and Entertainment* by Peter Gay] [repr. in *Sun Sentinel*, 1 April, p. 13F]	New York Times, p. C33

Kamm, Oliver

2010, March 16	A Rediscovered Play Adds to the Bard's Shifting Reputation	Times (London), p. 20
2011, June 11	The Pendant [Commentary on *Anonymous*]	Times (London), p. p. 93
2011, Oct. 19	This Mix of Crank Conspiracy Theories Should Be Dismissed [review of *Anonymous*]	Times (London), p. 19
2011, Nov. 5	The Pendant	Times (London), p. 105
2012, April 20	Good Will Hunter: Profile of James Shapiro	Times (London), p. 4
2012, May 19	"Wherever She Went, Including Here, . . ." [review of *The Marlowe Papers* by Ros Barber]	Times (London), p. 83
2015, Winter	[letter: misquoted by Alexander Waugh?]	Sh. Ox. Newsl., vol. 51/1: 3
2016, April 23	Where There's a Will, There's a Wacky Conspiracy Theory	Times (London), p. 40
2016, April 27	We Published a Story Last Week	Times (London), p. 79
2019, May 14	Conspiracism at the *Atlantic* [response to Winkler's May 10 piece]	Quillette

Kanter, Victor

1969, Feb. 27	[letter: the Jan. 30 review of his paper on Freud and Shakespeare]	Times Lit. Sup., is. 3496: 210

Karasek, Hellmuth

2009, Nov. 16	Seins oder nicht seins?	Hamburger Abendblatt, p. 1

Karpel, Ari

2011, Oct. 11	Will's Quill as a Deadly Weapon [review of *Anonymous*]	Int'l Herald Tribune
2011, Oct. 23	Brush Up Your Shakespeare, or Whomever [review of *Anonymous*]	NY Times, Arts: p. 14, 16

Karr, Merilee

2001, Winter	Semiotics and the Shakespeare Authorship Debate Response by Edward H. Sisson, vol. 37/1: 21.	Sh. Ox. Newsl., vol. 36/4: 1, 8-14
2001, Winter	A Brief History of Interpretation	Sh. Ox. Newsl., vol. 36/4: 8-9

Kastan, David Scott

2008	'To think these trifles something': Shakespearean Playbooks and the Claims of Authorship	Sh. Studies (Japan), vol. 36: 37

Kathman, David

1997, Spring	Why I'm Not an Oxfordian [repr. in DVN, vol. 2/10: 7-15; and in BTC, vol. 8: 279-97 (1997)] Response by Richard F. Whalen, Autumn 1997, p. 4-5. Response by Francis Edwards, Autumn 1997, p. 5-9. Reply to Whalen and Edwards by David Kathman, Autumn 1997, 9-10. Response by Christopher H. Dams, Autumn 1997, p. 10-15. Response by Christopher H. Dams, *De Vere Society Newsletter*, Oct. 1997, p. 15-18. Reply to Christopher H. Dams by David Kathman, ER, Autumn 1997, p. 15-16. Response by Charlton Ogburn, Autumn 1997, p. 16-21. Comment on Charlton Ogburn's response by Warren Hope, Autumn 1997, p. 5/2: 23. Reply to Charlton Ogburn by David Kathman, Autumn 1997, p. 21-24.	Eliz. Review, vol. 5/1: 32-48
1997, Autumn	[letter: response to Messrs. Whalen and Edwards]	Eliz. Review, vol. 5/2: 9-10

Kelly, Kevin (continued)

1989, April 18	The Shakespeare Mystery Persists [rev. of *Frontline*'s "The Shakespeare Mystery," (1989)] [repr. in SON, vol. 25/2: 10 (Spring 1989)]	Boston Globe, p. 32
1990, March	[article notes 440th anniversary of Edward de Vere's birth]	Boston Globe
1991, April 19	Packer Sets *Hamlet* a Continent Apart [mentions the annual SOS conf.]	Boston Globe
1991, April 26	[recommendation to look into *The Mysterious William Shakespeare*]	Boston Globe
1992, March 27	[article mentions the SOS, Charles Boyle, and the 442nd anniversary of de Vere's birth]	Boston Globe, p. 27
1992, July 24	Shakespeare, Buckley and Interactive TV	Boston Globe
1992, Oct. 16	[article mentions Looney and doubts about Shakespeare]	Boston Globe, p. 35
1993, Jan. 22	Looking Ahead [Kristin Linklater's intent to open closed minds]	Boston Globe, p. 27
1993, April 9	[article notes the 443rd anniversary of de Vere's birth]	Boston Globe, p. 43
1993, Nov. 5	[Authorship debate featuring Allan van Gestel and Charles Vere, Earl of Burford, pressing the Oxfordian case]	Boston Globe, p. 35
1994, April 8	After Limping Through Winter, Theater Spring to Life [Charles Vere's speech]	Boston Globe, p. 47
1994, Oct. 7	Who Really Wrote Brecht's Plays?	Boston Globe, p. 55
2010, April 15	Much Ado About Shakespeare	Boston Globe

Kelly, Walt

1992, Fall	[*Pogo* comic strip about spellings of Shaksper]	Sh. Ox. Newsl., vol. 28/4a: 10

Kempling, W. Bailey

1923, April 21	The Shakespeare First Folio Tercentenary	Graphic, p. 554
1928, June	[review of *The Shakespeare Mystery* by Georges Connes]	Sh, Review, vol. 1/2: 121-22
1928, July	[review of *The Seventeenth Earl of Oxford* by B. M. Ward]	Sh. Review, vol. 1/3: 200-01

Kennedy, Dick [Richard J. Kennedy?]

1994, Autumn	Subject: Negative Evidence	Sh. Ox. Newsl., vol. 30/4: 13

Kennedy, Louise

1991, Sept. 18	Would Shakespeare By Any Other Name Be As Sweet?	Boston Globe
2006, July 7	"The Beard" Tries Too Hard With the Bard [rev. of *The Beard of Avon* by Amy Freed]	Boston Globe, p. D5

Kennedy, Richard J. [see also Dick Kennedy?]
Books and pamphlets

1993	*Between the Lines* [pamphlet]	

Shorter pieces

2006, Winter	Woolpack Man: John Shakspere's Monument in Holy Trinity Church	Sh. Matters, vol. 5/2: 4-5, 27+
2022, Summer	The Worth of Wriothesley	Sh. Ox. Newsl., vol. 58/3: 28-29
2023, Summer	The Holy Hyphen	Sh. Ox. Newsl., vol. 59/3: 31

Kennedy-Skipton, Horace K.

1931, July 10	The Trussell Family [letter]	Morning Post, p. 6
1931, July 22	The Trussell Family: [letter: probable Meaning of Shakespeare's 'Candle-Holder' Pun]	Morning Post, p. 7
1932, Sept.	[review of *The Tragic Story of Shakespeare* by G. W. Phillips (1932)]	Sh. Pictorial, no. 54: 132
1954, April	Seal of the Journal of the Royal Society of Arts [letter]	SF News-letter (E), p. 15
1969, Christmas	[letter: meaning of "ever-living"]	Sh. Authorship Rev. #22: 19-20

Kenney, Patricia

2016, Spring	What's the News?: Report from Academe: de Vere Wins Again	Sh. Ox. Newsl., vol. 52/2: 4-5

Kenseth, Lar

2022, Oct. 31	[cartoon referencing Edward de Vere] [repr. in SON, vol. 58/4 (Fall 2022): 7]	New Yorker, p. 28

Kent, William
Books

1947	*The Lost Treasures of London*. London: Phoenix House.
1947	*Edward de Vere, the Seventeenth Earl of Oxford: The Real Shakespeare*. Shakespeare Fellowship. [A 40-page pamphlet. Two chapters by William Kent, a third by "Another"] [excerpt repr. in SON, vol. 31/3: 22-24 (Sum. 2005); and in BTC, vol. 5: 379-385] [See commentary on the pamphlet in *The Inspiration of Shakespeare* [a pamphlet edited by T. M. Atiken and Sir H. S. Lawrence]

Kingsmill, Hugh

    1931, Feb. 10   Who Was Shakespeare? [review of *Shakespeare's Plays in the Order*   Yorkshire Post & LI, p. 6
                     of Their Writing by Eva Turner Clark]

    1933, June   Shakespeare Criticism [mentions Shakespeare Fellowship's tenth   English Review, p. 692-94
                     annual dinner]

Kinnaird, Clark

    1948, Nov. 6   The Shakespeare Confusion [letter: response to Burgess]   Saturday Review, p. 21-22
                     [repr. in *Sh. and His Rivals* (McMichael & Glenn 1962): 175-78]

Kinney, Arthur F.

    1978   [review of *Shakespeare By Hilliard* by Leslie Hotson (1977)]   Study of Eng. Lit., v. 18: 361-418

Kinsey, Oliver

    2020, Jan.   Nothing Truer than Truth [with Darrol Blakley]   De Vere So. New., v. 27/1: 18-20

Kinsman, Robert

    1962, Aug. 31   The Bard – Man or Myth [review of *Shake-speare: The Real Man*   Los Angeles Times, p. C7
                     Behind the Name by Dorothy and Charlton Ogburn]

Kirsch, Hans-Christian

    2002   *Oxford oder der Mann, der Shakespeares Stücke schrieb*. Mit Bildern von Christina Nagel. Blieskastel:
                     Gollenstein. [German]

Kirwin, Peter

    2014, March   "You Have No Voice!" Constructing Reputation Through   Sh. Bulletin, vol. 32/1: 11-26
                     Contemporaries in the Shakespeare Biopic

Kittle, Christy Ann

    1953, April   [letter: her husband's book, *George Gascoigne or Edward de Vere*]   SF News-letter (E), p. 12

Kittle, William

    1930   *G. Gascoigne or Edward De Vere, Seventeenth Earl of Oxford*. Washington, D. C.: W. F. Roberts Company.

    1935   *Edward de Vere, Seventeenth Earl of Oxford, 1550-1604*. Washington, D. C.: The Buchanan Company.
                     Baltimore: Monumental Printing.

    1942   Edward de Vere, 17th Earl of Oxford and Shakespeare: External and contemporary evidence connecting the
                     seventeenth Earl of Oxford and the writer named Shakespeare. Monumental Printing Co., Baltimore
                     (edited and published by Christy Ann Kittle after his death)

Klay, Andor

    1974, Nov. 30   [letter: Charlton Ogburn's Nov. 24 article]   Washington Post, p. A11

Klein, David

    1962, Oct. 1   Did Shakespeare Produce His Own Plays?   Modern Lang. Rev., v.57/4: 556

Klier, Walter

Books

    2004   *Der Fall Shakespeare – Die Autorschaftsdebatte und der 17. Graf von Oxford als der wahre*
                     Shakespeare: Bisher bekannt als Das Shakespeare-Komplott [*The Case of Shakespeare – The Author's*
                     Edition and the 17th Earl of Oxford as the True Shakespeare: So Far Known as The Shakespeare Plot.
                     Buchholz: Verlag Uwe Laugwitz. [German]

Shorter pieces

    1997, Spring   [letter: Shakespeare in Germany and Austria]   Eliz. Review, vol. 5/1: 3

    1997, June   Report from Austria: Austria Discovers Ogburn   De Vere Soc. Newsl., v. 2/9: 6-8

    1997, Dec.   Die Hand aus den Wolken   Neues Sh. Jou., vol. 1: 76-83

    1997, Dec.   Augsteins Hammer [repr. from GEGENWART, July 30, 1996]   Neues Sh. Jou., vol. 1: 117-31

    1999, Jan.   [review of Shakespeare – Wie er euch gefällt. Gie Geschichte einer   Neues Sh. Jou., vol. 3: 162-63
                     Plünderung durch vier Jahrhunderte by Gary Taylor (1992)]
                     [Translated by Helga Schwalm]

    1999, Jan.   [reviews of several books: Shakespeare. Aus dem Italienischen von   Neues Sh. Jou., vol. 3: 169-75
                     von Maja Pflug by Giuseppe Tomasi di Lampedusa (1994)
                     Shakespeares Sonette Deutsch. Eine Übersetzung von Wolfgang
                     Kausen (1993) and *Shakespeare, Sonette. English und deutsch.*
                     Hrsg.und mit einem Vorwort von Hanno Helbling (1994)
                     William Shakespeare: Sämtliche Sonette. Zweisprachige Ausgabe.Aus
                     dem Englischen übertragen von Simone Katrin Paul. Mit einem
                     Nachwort Von Ernst Piper (1998)

	Die geheimen Aufzeichnungen Des Edward de Vere [*Lost Chronicle of Edward de Vere*] by Andrew Field (1990)] [repr. from *Gegenwart* (January 1993 and October 1994)]	
1999, July	Shakespeare? Oder doch de Vere? Neue Erkenntnisse in einer alten Streitfrage [review of *Alias Shakespeare* by Joseph Sobran] [repr. from *Wiener Zeitung* 7.3 (1998)]	Neues Sh. Jou., vol. 4: 138-44
1999, July	[review of *William Shakespeare im dtv. Zweisprachige Ausgaben.* Neuübersetzung von Frank Günther]	Neues Sh. Jou., vol. 4: 155-58
2000, April	Variation auf ein Thema von Ovid: Venus und Adonis von Sh. nach Titian [Influence of Titian's Venus and Adonis on Sh.'s poem is evidence of de Vere's authorship]	Neues Sh. Jou., vol. 5: 12-18
2001, May	Überlieferungskritik und Erkenntniskritik	Neues Sh. Jou., vol. 6: 98-107
2001, May	[reviews of two works by Christopher Marlowe: *Sämtliche Dramen.* Ins Deutsche übertragen und berausgegeben von Wolfgang Schlüter (1999); and *Das Massaker von Paris.* Die Historie von Doktor Faustus. Deutsch von Dietrich Schamp (1999)]	Neues Sh. Jou., vol. 6: 159-61
2002, May	Ein Gespräch im Hause Detobel über den abwesenden Herrn Sh. [Walter Klier im Gespräch mit Robert Detobel]	Neues Sh. Jou., vol. 7: 131-46
2002, May	[review of *Wer schrieb Shakespeare?* [Who Wrote Shakespeare?] by John Michell (2001)] [deutsche Ausgabe von Reinhard Kaiser]	Neues Sh. Jou., vol. 7: 152-54
2003, Aug.	Edward de Veres Lyrik: *A Hundreth Sundrie Flowres*	Neues Sh. Jou., vol. 8: 30-33
2003, Aug.	Das "Sanders Portrait" – der "kanadische Shakespeare"	Neues Sh. Jou., vol. 8: 167-68
2003, Aug.	[review of *Genannt Shakespeare* [*Alias Shakespeare*] by J. Sobran]	Neues Sh. Jou., vol. 8: 173-76
2004, June	Oxford als Shakespeare, romanhaft betrachtet [Zwei Romane von Mary Lavater-Sloman und Hans-Christian Kirsch]	Neues Sh. Jou., vol. 9: 174-76
2004, June	[reviews of *Inglaterra* by Leop. Brizuela (2004). *Sansibar* by Giles Foden (2003), and *Belles Lettres* by Charles Simmons (2003)]	Neues Sh. Jou., vol. 9: 181-82
2009	[review of *The Man Who Invented Shakespeare* by Kurt Kreiler]	Brief Chr., vol. I: 285-7
2016, Oct.	Von den Sagenhaften [revs. of *Odipus und Echmaton* by Immanuel Velikovsky and *Ist Shakespeare tot?* by Mark Twain]	Neues Sh. Jou., vol. NS5: 197-99
2020	Ein Gespräch im Hause Detobel über den abwesenden Herm Shakespeare [ungekürzte Fassung, unabridged version] [with Robert Detobel]	Neues Sh. Jou., vol. NS7:23-47

Kline, Syril Levin

2013	*Shakespeare's Changeling: A Fault Against the Dead.* CreateSpace.	

Klinkenberg, Jeff

2003, April 14	Or Was It Marlowe?	St. Petersburg Times, p. 1D

Klomp, Louis

1997, Fall	Acrostic Poem on Edward de Vere	Sh. Ox. Newsl., vol. 33/4: 27

Kloepfer, Deborah Kelly

1978, Spring	The Case for Edward de Vere in the Classroom	Sh. Ox. Newsl., vol. 14/2: 3-4

Kloepfer, John G.

1976, Fall	Monument Vs. Moniment	Sh. Ox. Newsl., vol. 12/3: 12

Klutts, William A.

1949, June 4	Was Shakespeare Shakespeare? [letter] [repr. in *Sh. and His Rivals* (McMichael & Glenn 1962): 185]	Sat. Review, p. 24

Knapp, Margaret L.

1924, June 13	Oxford Theory Coincidences	Hackney Spectator, p. 10
1924, Sept. 26	[letter: the office of the Lord Great Chamberlain]	Hackney Spectator, p. 4
1925, Feb. 20	[letter: notes on the Oxford Players]	Hackney Spectator, p. 2
1940, Apr./May	Only a Smock: But It Covers a Famous Rivalry	SF News-letter (A), vol. 1/3: 3
1941, Feb.	Shakespeare and Mark Twain	SF News-letter (A), v. 2/2: 22-23
1941, Oct.	[letter: keeping alive the free spirit]	SF News-letter (A), vol. 2/6: 72

Knight, Alfred

1940, Jan. 28	William Shakespeare's Authorship Defended by Phoenix Expert on Old England's Bard	Arizona Republic, p. 12

Knight. G. Wilson
    1930, May 3   Shakespeare and the Earl of Oxford [review of *The Case for Edward*   Nation & Athena.., vol. 46/4: 150
                  de Vere as "William Shakespeare" by Percy Allen]

Knutson, Roslyn L.
    1994   The Oldcastle Controversy and *The Famous Victories of Henry V*   Sh. Review, vol. 22: 340-44
    2007   [review of *Monstrous Adversary* by Alan Nelson (2003)]   SMAN, vol. 27/1: 7

Kolker, Jeanne
    2014, Aug. 31   Shakespeare Skeptics Make Much Ado in Madison [The SOF conf.,   Wisconsin State Journal, p. E5
                  and an interview with Eddie Nix]

Kolker, Jeanne (continued)
    2017   Just Read It [Eddie Nix recommends Anderson's *"Shakespeare"*   TCA Regional News
                  By Another Name, Richard Roe's *Shakespeare Guide to Italy*,
                  and *Shakespeare Beyond Doubt?* ed. J. Shahan and A. Waugh]

Koning, Christina
    1988, Dec. 9   New Paperbacks [short review of *The Mystery of William*   Guardian, p. 26
                  Shakespeare by Charlton Ogburn]

Kornstein, Daniel J.
    1995, Summer   *Kill All the Lawyers* (1994) (excerpt) [repr. in BTC, vol. 7: 349]   Sh. Ox. Newsl., vol. 31/4: 2
    2004, Fall   Mark Twain's Evidence: The Never-Ending Riverboat Debate   Tennessee Law Review, vol.
                                                  72/1, 1-23

Korr, David
    2007, Spring   Hamlet's First Soliloquy: Imagery Beyond the Language   Sh. Matters, vol. 6/3: 1, 6-12

Kositsky, Lynne
Books
    2000   *A Question of Will*. Montreal: Roussan Publishers, Inc.
    2013   *On the Date, Sources and Design of Shakespeare's The Tempest* [with Roger Stritmatter]. Jefferson, NC:
                  McFarland & Co. [excerpt repr. in *Sh. Authorship Sourcebook* (Stritmatter 2022): 429-49]
Shorter pieces
    2002, Winter   First Fellowship Meeting Held   Sh. Matters, vol. 1/2: 1, 4
    2003, Winter   Fellowship in Cambridge: Conference Brings Together Cross-section   Sh. Matters, vol. 2/2: 1, 6
                  of Shakespeareans [with Richard Whalen and W. Boyle]
    2004, Fall   A Critique of *The Monument* Theory (2005) [with Roger Stritmatter]   Sh. Matters, vol. 4/1: 1, 10-14
                  Response by Hank Whittemore, vol. 4/1: 1, 10-14.
    2005, Winter   President's Letter   Sh. Matters, vol. 4/2: 3
    2005, Fall   University of Miami to Offer Course in Shakespeare's Law   Sh. Matters, vol. 5/1: 6
    2007   *The Spanish Maze* and the Dates of *The Tempest* [with R. Stritmatter]   Oxfordian, vol. 10: 9-19
                  [repr. in BTC, vol. 10: 273-87]
    2007, Sept.   Shakespeare and the Voyagers Revisited [with Roger Stritmatter]   Rev. of En. St., v. 58/236: 447-72
    2008   A Movable Feast: *The Tempest* as Shrovetide Revelry [with R. Strit.]   Sh. Yearbook, vol. XVII: 365
    2009   How Shakespeare Got His *Tempest*: Another "Just So" Story   Brief Chronicles, vol. I: 205-267
                  [with Roger Stritmatter]
    2009   Pale as Death: Fictionalizing Influence of Erasmus's "Naufragium"
                  on the Renaissance Travel Narrative, in *Discovering Shakespeare*,
                  p. 143-153 [with R. Stritmatter]
    2009, Summer   'O Brave New World': *The Tempest* and P. Martyr's *De Orbe Novo*   Critical Survey, vol. 21/2: 7-42
                  [with Roger Stritmatter]
    2014, Summer   Pattern of Parody in *Eastward Ho*, and a New Date for *King Lear*   Critical Survey, vol. 26/2: 21-52
                  [with Roger Stritmatter]
    2016   A Note on Dating the Plays, in *Contested Year*

Kositsky, Michael
Plays
    2011, Summer   *Detective Superintendent Blattshap Gets His Man* [A play in one act]   Sh. Matters, vol. 10/3: 7, 18-20
Shorter pieces
    2019, Winter   [review of *Nutshell* by Ian McEwan]   Sh. Ox. Newsl., vol. 55/1: 28-29
    2021, Summer   [letter: the authorship "question" has been answered]   Sh. Ox. Newsl., vol. 57/3: 5

Kostanczuk, Bob
    2003, April 18   Where There's a Will, There's a Sway   Post-Tribune (Gary), p. D9

Kreiler, Kurt (continued)

2013	Doubter Response to Question #31: How has the Shakespeare authorship discussion been presented in fiction?, in *Sh. Beyond Doubt?*, p. 188-89	

Kruh, Louis

2000, Jan.	Who Wrote Shakespeare? [review of John Michell's book]	Cryptologia, vol. 24/1: 81
2002, Oct.	Blue Avenger Code Cracker [review of *Blue Avenger Cracks the Code* by Norma Howe]	Cryptologia, vol. 26/4: 311
2005, April	Shakespeare Enigma	Cryptologia, vol. 29/2: 179-81

Krusche, Friedemann

2018	Grosser Zeh im Ozean: Auf der Suche nach Gewissheiten bei Klassikern: die europäishe Theater-Avantgarde und Shakespeare	Neues Sh. Jour., vol. NS6:31-34

Krutch, Joseph W.

1920, Aug. 28	Shakespeare Unidentified [review of *"Shakespeare" Identified*]	Nat'l Post, vol. III, p. 248-49
1953, Jan. 11	Meet *Hamlet*'s New Author [review of *This Star of England* by Dorothy and Charlton Ogburn (1952)	NY Herald Tribune, p. BR13

Kunin, Carolyn

1996, Summer	[review of CD: *William Byrd: Songs, Dances, Battles, Games*]	Sh. Ox. Newsl., vol. 32/3: 18

L. H.

1955, March 13	Oxford or Shakespeare? [review of *The Renaissance Man of England* by Dorothy and Charlton Ogburn]	Nashville Tennessean

L. S. P.

1934	Was Shakespeare a Johnian? [St. John's College, Cambridge]	Eagle (St. John's College, Cam.), vol. 48/218: 83-7

L. T. G.

1928, Nov. 4	The Late Sir George Greenwood [letter]	Sunday Times

La Greca, Donald

1984, Spring	Dynasticide: A Note on *Macbeth*	Sh. Ox. Newsl., vol. 20/1+2: 7-8
1986, Spring	Character of Kent in *King Lear* [repr. in EVR, vol. 6 (Wntr. 1998)]	Sh. Ox. Newsl., vol. 22/2: 8-12

LaBelle, Jenijoy

1991	The Authorship Question, or Will the Real William Shakespeare Please Stand Up?	Eng. & Science, v. 45/1: 22-9
1993, April 21	Happy Birthday, Dear William [repr. in SON, vol. 30/4: 5 (Autumn, 1994)] Response by Al Alu: May 2, 1993, p. VCB17 Response by Charles Champlin: May 2, 1993, p. VCB17	Los Angeles Times, p. B7
1993, May 8	Shakespeare	Los Angeles Times, p. 7

Labeo

1943, May	Bacon and "The Group"	SF News-letter (E), p. 4

Lafew, Edmonn

1984, Spring	The Veriest Nonsense	Sh. Ox. Newsl., vol. 20/1+2: 3-5
1984, Spring	Notes on d'Hiver	Sh. Ox. Newsl., vol. 20/1+2: 10
1985, Fall	Make Thee Another Self For Love Of Me	Sh. Ox. Newsl., vol. 21/4: 4-6

Lagerros, Jacob K.

2013, Summer	Bringing Truth to Light: Why It Matters Who Wrote William's Words [The 2012 Student Essay Contest winning essay] [Also in SON, vol. 49/3: 19-24]	Sh. Matters, vol. 12/3: 1, 8-11

Lague, Jeffrey

1998, Oct.	[letter: Dennis Baron's May 1998 article on Sonnet 20]	De Vere Soc. Newsl., vol. 3/1: 2

Lake, James H.

1983, Nov.	Psychobiography and Pseudo-Shakespeare	English Journal, vol. 72/7: 70-72

Lake, Peter

2016	*How Shakespeare Put Politics on the Stage: Power and Succession in the History Plays*. New Haven: Yale University Press.	

Lamb, George M.
　1999, April 23　　Seeking the Real Bard of Stratford　　　　　　　　　Christian Science Monitor, p. 13

Lamb, V. B.
　1952, Sept. 19　　Cecil Palmer [letter]　　　　　　　　　　　　　　　Truth, p. 292

Lambin, Georges
Books and pamphlets
　1954　　*Shakespeare et Tournon.* [pamphlet]
　1956　　*Explorations Sur la Trace d'un Shakespeare inconnu.* [pamphlet]
　1962　　*Voyages de Shakespeare en France et en Italie.* Geneve: E. Droz. [English translation by Talmadge
　　　　　Gartley Wilson (completed by Wendy G. and Vance E. Adams, Beorn S. Hall, Anne Lander;
　　　　　W. Ron Hess, general editor) in *The Dark Side of Shakespeare*, vol. 1, Appendix A, p. 355-535]
　　　　　[excerpt reprinted in Clark, *Hidden Allusions*, 3rd ed., Ruth Loyd Miller, editor (1974) , p. 120-24]

Shorter pieces
　1953, April　　Professor Abel Lefranc (1863-1952)　　　　　　　　　SF News-letter (E), p. 10
　1955, Spring　[review of *The First Night of Twelfth Night* by Leslie Hotson]　　SF News-letter (E), p. 11-12
　　　　　　　　　Response by Katherine E. Eggar, same issue, p. 12.
　1957, Autumn　Shakespeare in Milan　　　　　　　　　　　　　　　SF News-letter (E), p. 5
　1958, Spring　[letter: Did Oxford go to Milan?]　　　　　　　　　　SF News-letter (E), p. 11
　1959, Autumn　The Heir of Alanson, Katharine Her Name　　　　　　Sh. Authorship Review, #2: 5-6
　1960, Spring　Did Oxford Go to Milan?　　　　　　　　　　　　　Sh. Authorship Review, #3: 23
　1961, Spring　Did Oxford Go North-East of Milan? [repr. in BTC, vol. 5, p. 56-59]　Sh. Authorship Review, #5: 9-11
　1961, Autumn　[letter: Friar Patrick in Milan: 1575 or 1576?]　　　Sh. Authorship Review, #6: 24
　1962, Autumn　Professor Abel Lefranc, (1863-1952) [repr. in BTC, vol. 5, p. 95-97]　Sh. Authorship Rev. #8: 10-13

Landsbury, Edgar
　2000, Winter　[letter: "the true author deserves better from academics"]　Sh. Ox. Newsl., vol. 35/4: 21

Lang, Andrew
　1910, Dec. 22　A New Theory of Shakespeare　　　　　　　　　　Independent, p. 1,373

Laker, J. J. H. C.
　1948, Jan. 3　[review of *Talks With Elizabethans* by Percy Allen (1947)]　Fifeshire Advertiser, p. 3

Langford, Michael
　2008　　*The de Vere Papers.* Turnbridge, Wells, Kent, UK: Parapress.

Langley, William
　2012, Dec.　Ready for the Toughest Role . . . Whoever Wrote It, Derek Jacobi is　　Telegraph, p. 24
　　　　　　　Ready For It

Lapham, Lewis H.
　1999, April　Full Fathom Five [repr. in SAS (Stritmatter): 39-44]　　Harper's Mag., v. 298: 10-12

Larcen, Donna
　1992, June 11　Why We Love a Mystery　　　　　　　　　　　　San Francisco Chronicle, p. D3
　1992, June 13　Everybody Loves a Mystery　　　　　　　　　　　Orlando Sentinal, p. E3
　1992, June 13　Some Things Never Die – Right, Elvis?　　　　　　St. Petersburg Times, p. 3D
　1992, June 16　Ah, Sweet mystery of Life . . . Do UFOs Really Exist? Is Elvis Really　Ottawa Citizen, p. D4
　　　　　　　　　Dead? Who Really Knows?
　1992, June 28　Mysteries Range from Entertaining Curiosities to Vexing Riddles　Minneapolis Star Trib., p. 3E
　1992, Aug. 2　The Three Categories of Mysteries　　　　　　　　Oregonian, p. L12

Lardner, James
　1988, April 11　Onward and Upward with the Arts: The Authorship Question　New Yorker, p. 87-106
　　　　　　　　　[1987 Moot Court Trial] [repr. in SON, vol. 24/2: 10 (Spr. 1988)]

LaSalle, Mick
　2002, Aug. 14　A Witty Case Against the Stratford Bard [review of Mike Rubbio's　San Francisco Chronicle., p. D1
　　　　　　　　　"Much Ado About Something"]

Lasar, Theodore
　1986, Jan. 19　[letter: Morse Johnson's Jan. 9 letter]　　　　　New York Times, p. E22

Lasocki, David
　1995　　*The Bassanos: Venetian Musicians and Instrument Makers in England* [with Roger Prior]. Aldershot,
　　　　　England: Scolar Press. Brookfield, VT: Ashgate Pub. Co. [Chapter 8 repr. in DVN, vol. 2/2: 1-4]

Laugwitz, Uwe
Periodicals edited

1997-2008	*Neues Shake-speare Journal* [with Robert Detobel]	
2010-2008	*Neues Shake-speare Journal*	

Shorter pieces

1997, Dec.	Zu dieser Veröffentlichung	Neues Sh. Journal, vol. 1: 14-20
1997, Dec.	Shake-speare im Spiegel der Press	Neues Sh. Journal, vol. 1: 132-42
1998, June	Zum zweiten Band des *Neuen Shake-speare Journals*	Neues Sh. Journal, vol. 2: 15-24
1998, June	Die acht Zeugen des Alan H. Nelson	Neues Sh. Journal, vol. 2: 146-54
1998, June	Shake-speare im Spiegel der Presse	Neues Sh. Journal, vol. 2: 155-77
1999, Jan.	Zum dritten Band des *Neuen Shake-speare Journals*	Neues Sh. Journal, vol. 3: 18-25
1999, Jan.	Literaturbericht: Oxfordianische Studien zur First Folio	Neues Sh. Journal, vol. 3: 66-79
	1) Miller, Ruth L.: Die First Folio – eine Familienangelegenheit ["The First Folio. A Family Affair." Repr. from *Ox. Vistas*]	
	2) Dickson, Peter: Henry de Vere und die First Folio	
1999, Jan.	[review of Das erfundene Mittelalter by Heribert Illig (1996)]	Neues Sh. Journal, vol. 3: 175-79
1999, Jan.	Shake-speare im Spiegel der Presse (Fortsetzung aus dem NSJ, vol. 2	Neues Sh. Journal, vol. 3: 180-86
1999, July	Zum vierten Band des *Neuen Shake-speare Journals*	Neues Sh. Journal , vol. 4: 4-9
1999, July	*Edward III*. Im Spiegel nicht nur der Presse	Neues Sh. Journal, vol. 4: 167-81
2000, April	Zum fünften Band des *Neuen Shake-speare Journals*	Neues Sh. Journal, vol. 5: 4-9
2000, April	[review of *Das Shylock-Syndrom oder die Dramaturgie der Barbarei* by Dietrich Schwanitz (1997)]	Neues Sh. Journal, vol. 5: 152-57
2001, May	Zum sechsten Band des *Neuen Shake-speare Journals*	Neues Sh. Journal, vol. 6: 8-9
2001, May	Notizen	Neues Sh. Journal, vol. 6: 164-74
2002, May	Zum siebenten Band des *Neuen Shake-speare Journals*	Neues Sh. Journal, vol. 7: 8-12
2002, May	Was zeichnet einen Oxfordinaer aus? Nachruf auf James Fitzgerald	Neues Sh. Journal, vol. 7: 121-24
2002, May	Notizen	Neues Sh. Journal, vol. 7: 155-68
2003, Aug.	Zum achten Shake-speare Journal	Neues Sh. Journal, vol. 8: 4-8
2003, Aug.	Edward de Veres Lyrik: *A Hundreth Sundrie Flowres*	Neues Sh. Journal, vol. 8: 34-35
2003, Aug.	Thomas Watsun und de Vere	Neues Sh. Journal, vol. 8: 60-61
2003, Aug.	*The Paradise of Dainty Devices*	Neues Sh. Journal, vol. 8: 64-66
2003, Aug.	Notizen	Neues Sh. Journal, vol. 8: 177-83
2004, June	Zum neunten Shake-speare Journal	Neues Sh. Journal, vol. 9: 4-7
2004, June	[review of *Shakespeare: Der Dichter und seine Zeit*. Text von Peter Chrisp. (2002)]	Neues Sh. Journal, vol. 9: 182-83
2007, April	Zum Shake-speare Journal Nr. 11	Neues Sh. Journal, vol. 11: 7-17
2007, April	Vier Nachrufe [four obituaries]: Michael Peer (d. 2004), Eric Sams 1926-2004), Dietrich Schwanitz, Ruth L. Miller (1922-2005)/ Minos D. Miller (1921-2006)	Neues Sh. Journ., vol. 11: 140-49
2007, April	Notizen	Neues Sh. Journ., vol. 11: 150-70
2008, Oct.	Zum Neuen Shake-speare Journal Nr. 12	Neues Sh. Journal, vol. 12: 4-6
2008, Oct.	Peter Moore Bibliographie	Neues Sh. Journal, vol. 12: 84-89
2008, Oct.	Nachruf auf George Blume [obituary]	Neues Sh. Journ., vol. 12: 129-31
2008, Oct.	[review of Edward De Vere's "Echoverse"] [Übersetzt von Henryk Gericke und Andreas Koziol]	Neues Sh. Journ., vol. 12: 143-45
2008, Oct.	Notizen	Neues Sh. Journ., vol. 12: 148-75
2010, Nov.	Zur Gründung der *Neuen Shake-speare Gesellschaft*	Neues Sh. Journal, v. NS1: 10-13
2010, Nov.	Zu dieser Veröffentlichung	Neues Sh. Journal, v. NS1: 14-23
2010, Nov.	I. Hamlet und Ödipus / Freuds Shakespeare-Studien bis (1910)	Neues Sh. Journal, vol. NS1: 43
2010, Nov.	IV. "Da sind dunkle Mächte im Spiel" – Freuds Abkehr von Stratford	Neues Sh. Journal, v. NS1: 83-94
2010, Nov.	V. "Eine ungeheure Taktlosigkeit" / Sigmund Freud, Ernest Jones, Thomas Looney und Peter Gay	Neues Sh. Journ., v. NS1: 95-106
2010, Nov.	VI. Freud als Oxfordianer [Freud's letters mention Looney and Oxford]	Neues Sh. Journ., v. NS1: 107-23
2010, Nov.	Ludwig Wittgenstein über Shakespeare	Neues Sh. Journ., v. NS1: 132-35
2010, Nov.	Notizen	Neues Sh. Jou., vol. NS1: 143-58
2010, Nov.	In Memoriam: William Paul Blair (1915-2009)	Neues Sh. Journ., vol. NS1: 160
2010, Nov.	In Memoriam: Andrew Hannas (1951-2009)	Neues Sh. Journ., vol. NS1: 162
2011, Oct.	Klassiker-Lektüre	Neues Sh. Journ., vol. NS2: 6-8
2011, Oct.	Zu dieser Veröffentlichung	Neues Sh. Journ., vol. NS2: 9-12
2011, Oct.	Über Noemi Magri (ca. 1940-5 Sept. 2011)	Neues Sh. Jou., vol. NS2: 79-80

Lawrence, W. J.
    1935, Sept. 19   The Original Staging of *Romeo and Juliet*, Act III, Scene V   Times Lit. Sup., is. 1775: 580

Lawson, Mark
    2011, April 23   Should We Care Who Wrote William Shakespeare's Plays?   Guardian, p. 32

Lay, C. H.
    1937, May   Shakespeare, a Suffolk Man [letter]   East Ang. Mag., vol. 2/8: 362

Leach, W. Barton
    1960, Aug.   Folger Library Director on Our Shakespeare Series [letter]   Am. Bar Assoc. Journal,
        [SOS Trustee Leach's letter repr. in Louis B. Wright's   vol. 46/8: 810-12
        "Lawyer's Amusement," repr. from *Folger Library*, vol. 9/1: 5
        (May 20, 1960)] [repr. in SC]

Leahy, William
Books
    2010   *Shakespeare and His Authors: Critical Perspectives on the Authorship Question*. London and New York:
        Continuum.
    2018   *My Shakespeare: The Authorship Controversy: Experts Examine the Arguments for Bacon, Neville, Oxford,*
        Marlowe, Mary Sidney, Shakspere, and Shakespeare (Edward Everett Root, Publishers).
Shorter pieces
    2000   A Stranger Ladies Thrall: Elizabeth I, Henry Lee and the Ditchley   Eliz. Review, online ed.
        Progress of 1592
    2005, June 20   Business of Bill: Who Was Shakespeare? And Why Does it Matter?   New Statesman, v. 134: 42-44
    2005, July 22   Bard, By Any Name, Is Still Sweet   Times Higher Ed. Sup., p. 14
    2006, Summer   Brunel University to Offer Master's Degree in Authorship Studies   Sh. Matters, vol. 5/4: 1, 14-17
        [interview with William Leahy]
    2007, Feb.   'Two households, both alike in dignity': The Authorship Question   Guardian
        and Academia [repr. in DVN, vol. 20/1: 9-10 (April 2013); and
        in NSJ, vol. 12: 90-106 (Oct. 2008)]
    2009, Summer   The Shakespeare Question: A Suitable Subject for Academia? in DS, p. 5-11
    2009, Summer   Introduction to the 'Questioning Shakespeare' Special Section   Critical Survey, vol. 21/2: 1-6
    2013, April 23   On Shakespeare's Birthday . . . [excerpt repr. in DVN, vol. 20/1: 9]   Guardian

Lederer, Richard
    1995, May 1   Who Was the Real Shakespeare? [Burford and the SOS]   Patriot Ledger, p. 11
    1995, Dec. 23   Much Ado Over Shakespeare   Patriot Ledger, p. 33

Lee, Chris
    2011, Oct. 17   Was Shakespeare a Fraud? [review of *Anonymous*]   Newsweek

Lee, Sir Sidney
Books and pamphlets
    1898   *A Life of William Shakespeare*. London: Macmillan & Co.
    1910   *Dictionary of National Biography, 11th edition* [editor]. London: Smith, Elder & Co.
    1925   *A Shakespeare Reference Library* [pamphlet; prepared with Dir Edmond Chambers]
Shorter pieces
    1898, 1910   "Shakespeare, William (1564-1616)," in *Dictionary of National Biography*, vol. 51: 348-97
    1898, 1910   "Vere, Edward (1550-1604)," in *Dictionary of National Biography*, vol. 58: 225-29
    1919, Jan. 25   Shakespeare Dethroned Again   Illustrated London News, p. 8
    1919, July 19   More Doubts About Shakespeare [review of *Sous le Masque de*   Quarterly Review, vol. 231:
        'William Shakespeare' by Abel Lefranc]   194-206
    1920, May 21   The Identity of Shakespeare [letter: resp. to review of SI]   Bookman's J., vol. 2/30: 58
        Response by J. Thomas Looney, May 28, p. 68.
    1923, Feb. 6   Shakespeare and Wren [referrred to in SF colum in the HS, Feb. 6]   Times (London)
    1926, Jan. 18   Shakespeare's Will: Sir Sidney Lee's Comments   Times (London)

Leech, Clifford
    1949   Hall's Chronicle and Shakespeare [repr. in SFE, p. 6 (Sept. 1951)]   Sh. Survey
    1962   [review of *The Shakespeare Claimants* by Harry N. Gibson (1962)]   Study of Eng. Lit., vol. 3: 282

Lefait, Sebastien
    2015   Irreverence as Fidelity? Adapting Shakespearean Reflexivity in   Int. Lit. St., vol. 17/2: 241-63
        Anonymous [review of *Anonymous*]

Lefranc, Abel
Books
1918-19   *Sous le Masque de "William Shakespeare": William Stanley, Vle Comte de Derby*. Paris: Payot & Cie.
            1988 ed. *Under the Mask of William Sh.* Trans. by Cecil Cragg. Braunton, Devon: Merlin Books, Ltd.
            2022 ed. *Behind the Mask of William Shakespeare, a new translation by Frank Lawler*. Cary, NC:
            Veritas Publications.
1923   *Le Secret de William Stanley*. Bruxelles: L'Edition du Flambeaux
1945   *A la Découverte de Shakespeare*. Paris: Michel.
Shorter pieces
1920, Oct. 16   Du nouveau sur Shakespeare: Le secret du Songre d'une nuit d'ete, I   L'Opinion, no. 42: 423-25
                [*Midsummer Night's Dream*]
1920, Oct. 23   Du nouveau sur Shakespeare: Le secret du Songre d'une nuit d'ete, II   L'Opinion, no. 43: 451-52
                [*Midsummer Night's Dream*]
1921, Feb. 12   Du nouveau sur Shakespeare: Le secret du Songre d'une nuit d'ete, III   L'Opinion
                [*Midsummer Night's Dream*]
1921, Feb. 21   Du nouveau sur Shakespeare: A propos des 'Joyeuses Commeres du   L'Opinion
                Windsor' [*Merry Wives of Windsor*]
1922, Nov. 24   [letter: acceptance of position of Vice President of the newly-   Hackney Spectator, p. 14
                formed Shakespeare Fellowship] [repr. in the *Hackney Spectator*]
1929, Feb.   [letter in French]   Sh. Pictorial, no. 12: 16
1936   Les Elements Francais de *Peines d'Amour Perdues* [French Elements   Revue Historique
                in *Love's Labour's Lost*]
1937, March   [letter in French]   SF News-letter (E), no. 2: 1-2
1938, Feb.   La Question Shakespearienne au XVIII Siècle [see also review   Revue Bleue
                of the article in *Le Temps*, March 1, 1938]
1945   [long piece on *Midsummer Night's Dream*]

Lefranc, P.
1964, Oct. 1   Les études anti-stratfordiennes en France   Etudes Anglaises, vol. 13: 293

Le Gassick, Michael
2014, Winter   [letter: *Nobody and Somebody* and other anonymous plays]   Sh. Ox. Newsl., vol. 50/1: 3, 27-8
2014, Oct.   The Playwright Who Never Was . . .: Who Wrote the Anonymous   De Vere So. New., v. 21/3: 12-22
                Plays of the Second Half of the 16th Century?
2015, April   [letter: why he avoids mainstream publications]   De Vere Soc. New., vol. 22/2: 46
2015, July   Who Wrote The Wisdome of Doctor Dodypoll?   De Vere Soc. New., v. 22/3: 8-18
2016, January   'Newly set foorth, ouerseene an corrected, By V.V.S.'   De Vere So. New., v. 23/1: 23-32
2016, January   [letter: Sonnet XVI, in *The Passionate Pilgrim* by W. Shakespeare]   De Vere Soc. New., vol. 23/1: 41

Leiding, Dietrich
2023   "ies, wenn du kannst": Die Inschrift auf Shaksperes Grabdenkmal   Neues Sh. Jou., v. NS8: 196-203

Leighton, George A.
1933, March 26 Poor Bill! Shakespeare, Surviving the Baconian Racket for Lo These   Cincinnati Enquirer., p. 43
                Many Years, Now Beset with Another Attack on His Identity

Leith, Isabel May
2008, March   [letter: bearers of the coronation canopy of George V in 1911]   De Vere So. New., v. 15/1: 25-26

Leith, Sam
1999, Oct. 30   Theatricals in the Lords Put Bard's Reputation On Line [The Earl of   Telegraph, p. 14
                Burford and the authorship societies]

Lemmon, Aaron
2004, Spring   [letter: Shakespearean essay competition]   Sh. Matters, vol. 3/3: 3

Lennon, Troy
2000, April 26 Bard in the Shadows   Daily Tel. (Surry H.), p. 43
2004, April 27 Shakespeare   Daily Tel. (Surry H.), p. 32
2007, Sept. 11 No Holes Bard As Old Debate Flares Again   Daily Tel. (Surry H.), p. 29
2010, May 27   [review of *Contested Will* by James Shapiro]   Daily Tel. (Surry H.), p. 36

Lenz, Bonnie
2023, Winter   Margo Anderson [letter]   Sh. Ox. Newsl., vol. 59/1: 3

Leon, Joan

2019, Spring	SOF Research Grant Program: Donations Requested for New Grants	Sh. Ox. Newsl., vol. 55/2: 10
2019, Spring	Mark Twain's Manuscript of *Is Shakespeare Dead?* at the UC-Berkeley Bancroft Library	Sh. Ox. Newsl., vol. 55/2: 11
2019, Spring	Marketing Ourselves to the Public [with Julie Sandys Bianchi, Shelley Maycock & Kathryn Sharpe]	Sh. Ox. Newsl., vol. 55/2: 20

Leonard, Edwin S.

1953, March 5	Still the Query: Who Wrote Shakespeare's Works? [review of *This Star of England* by Dorothy and Charlton Ogburn]	Christian Science Monitor, p. 13

LeRiche, Kathleen
Books and pamphlets

1961	*Shakespeare in Essex* [pamphlet]. London: Printed privately. [repr. from *Essex Review* 61 (October 1952)]	

Shorter pieces

1951, May 11	The Personality of Shakespeare [letter]	Truth, p. 509-10
1951, June 29	The Personality of Shakespeare [letter]	Truth, p. 695-96
1952, March	[letter: poem by Sir Walter Raleigh really authored by Oxford?]	SF News-letter (E), p. 8
1952, Sept.	Shakespeare's Farewell [letter]	SF News-letter (E), p. 10-11
1952, Sept.	Nicholas Hilliard and Edward de Vere [letter]	SF News-letter (E), p. 10
1952, Sept.	The Shakespeare Country	SF News-letter (E), p. 9
1952, Oct.	Shakespeare in Essex [repr. as a pamphlet]	Essex Review, vol. 61: 187
1953, April	A Portrait of Shake-speare? [repr. in BTC, vol. 4: 119-122]	SF News-letter (E), p. 5-6
1953, Sept.	The Third Earl of Southampton	SF News-letter (E), p. 4-5
1954, Feb. 12	Hackney Tudor [letter]	Telegraph
1954, April	Shakespeare's Anniversary	SF News-letter (E), p. 8
1954, April	Oxford Junior Encyclopedia	SF News-letter (E), p. 11
1954, April	[letter] *This Star of England*	SF News-letter (E), p. 13-14
1954, Sept.	Arthur Golding – No Puritan [letter]	SF News-letter (E), p. 11-12
1954, Sept.	Portrait of John De Vere, Sixteenth Earl of Oxford	SF News-letter (E), p. 8-9
1956, Autumn	Shakespeare and the Palazzo del Te [letter]	SF News-letter (E), p. 11
1957, Spring	[report on T. L. Adamson's Nov. 1 talk "Plays of Ch. Marlowe"]	SF News-letter (E), p. 2
1957, Spring	Marlowe and the Sonnets	SF News-letter (E), p. 8-9
	Resp. by R. C. Churchill and J. Shera Atkinson, Autumn 1957, p. 12.	

Lerner, Maura

1995, April 21	Could a Man With Handwriting Like This Really Construct the Greatest Literature in the English Language? [full page review of *The Mysterious William Shakespeare* by Charlton Ogburn]	Minneapolis Star Tribune, p. 16A
2005, Sept. 4	The Bard By Another Name? [review of *"Shakespeare" By Another Name* by Mark Anderson]	Minneapolis Star Tribune, p. 1F

Lerud, T. K.

1994-95	[review of *Shakespeare, In Fact* by Irvin L. Matus (1994)]	Choice, vol. 32: 783

Lester, Richard

1998, Spring	Why was *Venus and Adonis* Published?	Eliz. Review, vol. 6/1: 67-72
	Response by Elizabeth Imlay, Autumn 1998, p. 3.	
	[repr. in German in NSJ, vol. 3: 90-97 (Jan. 1999)]	
1998, Autumn	Shakespeare's Name	Eliz. Review, vol. 6/2: 4-14
1999, Spring	An Alternative Theory of the Oxford Cover-Up [repr. in LC, p. 50-57]	Eliz. Review, vol. 7/1: 33-46

Levandoski, John

2012, Spring	[review *of Shakespeare Suppressed: The Uncensored Truth About Shakespeare and His Works* by Katherine Chiljan (2011)]	Sh. Matters, vol. 11/2: 20, 28+

Leventon, Annabel

2020, Oct.	[letter: Gilvary's article on J. Thomas Looney]	De Vere So. New., v. 27/4: 43-44
2023, Jan.	[Video Masterlasses on "Shakespeare's Women" (summary)] [letter]	De Vere So. New., v. 30/1: 20-24

Levesque, John

1998, March 21	Shakespeare's Ghost: Who Was the 'Real' Bard of Avon?	Spectator, p. W5

Levin, Bernard

1966, Feb. 18	The Stratford Frauds [repr. Nov. 30]	Daily Mail

Levin, Bernard
 1996, Nov. 1   A Heretic at the Globe   Times (London), p. 20

Levin, Harry
 1975, Feb.   Shakespeare as Shakespeare [with Gywnne Evans] [resp. to Charlton Harvard Mag., p. 39-43
           Ogburn's Nov. 1974 article "The Man Who Shakespeare Was
           Not (and Who He Was)"]
           Response to Evans and Levin by Charles Dickson III, April 8.
           Response to Evans and Levin by Gordon Cyr, "An Oxfordian Reply
            to Two Harvard Professors, SON, vol. 11/2: 1-19 (Summer 1975).
           Reply to Evans and Levin by Charlton Ogburn, April 8.

Levin, Mikhail
 1979   Fortinbras   Bard, vol. 2/2: 71-74

Levitt, Cyril
 2010, Spring   Freud, Smith, and Feuerebach on Sacrifice   Canadian Journal of Psycho-
                          analysis, v. 18/1: 20-42+

Lewis, George L.
 1962, May-Oct. [review of *Shake-speare: The Man Behind the Name* by Dorothy PLMA, vol. 39: 215-16
           Ogburn and Charlton Ogburn, Jr. (1962)]

Lewis, Rhodri
 2019, April 29 Vanilla of Magical Thinking [review of *How the Classics Made* London Review of Books,
           Shakespeare by Jonathan Bate]   vol. 18/1: 20-42+

Li, Liexun; Rong Heng; Hsinchun Chen
 2006, April   From Fingerprint to Writeprint: Identifying the Key Features to Help Communications of the ACH,
           Identify and Trace Online Authorship   vol. 49/4: 76-82

Lichtmesz, Martin
 2023   Oxfordianische Lektionen   Neues Sh. Jou., vol. NS8: 147-77

Lifton, Barbara
 2005, Spring   Shakespeare in the World [letter: resp. to Diana   Skeptic, , vol. 12/1: 33
           Price's Fall 2005 article]

Light, Leigh
 2023   *The Which of Shakespeare's Why: A Novel of the Authorship Mystery Near Solution Today*. City Point Pr.

Ligneus
 2020, Sept.   [review of *Honour Killing in Shakespeare* by Loraine Fletcher (2019)] Oxfordian, vol. 22: 187-189

Ligon, K. C.
Plays
 Not known   *Isle of Dogs* [about Edward de Vere, Earl of Oxford]
Shorter pieces
 2003, Fall   Who's an Amateur?   Sh. Matters, vol. 3/1: 21
 2004, Winter   Do Oxford's Letters Spell Shakespeare?   Sh. Matters, vol. 3/2: 1, 15-19
 2004, Winter   [review of *In Search of Shakespeare* by Michael Wood (1985)] Sh. Matters, vol. 3/2: 20-21
 2005, Fall   New Book Identifies Sir Henry Neville as the True Bard: *The Truth* Sh. Matters, vol. 5/1: 5-6
           Will Out by Brenda James and William Rubinstein (2005)
 2005, Fall   Ruth Loyd Miller, Oxfordian Pioneer, Honored (1922-2005) Sh. Matters, vol. 5/1: 6
 2005, Fall   [review of *Players: Mysterious Identify of William Shakespeare* by Sh. Matters, vol. 5/1: 12-13+
           Bertram Fields (2005)]
 2006, Fall   In Loving Memory: Ruth Loyd Miller (1922-2005) and   Sh. Matters, vol. 6/1: 5-7
           Minos D. (1921-2006)
 2006, Fall   Elizabeth I: Did She or Didn't She?   Sh. Matters, vol. 6/1: 14-16
 2006   One Last Gift   Oxfordian, vol. 9: 33-34
 2009   Francis Meres and the Earl of Oxford [with Robert Detobel] Brief Chronicles, vol. I: 97-108

Limons, L.
 1932, Jan.   Reply from Holland [letter]   Sh. Pictorial, no. 47: 14-15

Lindquist, Eric Newsl.
 2006, Summer [review of *Edward de Vere: The Crisis and Consequences of* Renaisance Qt., vol. 59/2: 612
           Wardship by Daphne Pearson (2005)]

Lindsay, Jack
    1923, April 19   Shakespeare and Shylock   Bulletin, Red page

Linklater, Kristen
Books
    1992   *Freeing Shakespeare's Voice* [excerpt repr. in SON, vol. 29/3a: 14 (Summer, 1993)]
Shorter works
    2013   Doubter Response to Question #23: How do you respond as an actor and
                                director to the Shakespere authorship conspiracy theory? (Shahan): 182
    2014, Winter   Edward's Sonnet [a sonnet]   Sh. Ox. Newsl., vol. 51/1: 4

Linnett, Peter
    1992, May   [letter: resp. to special issue on Shakespeare's authorship]   Atlantic Monthly, p. 21
    1992, Spring   [letter: Tom Bethel and Oxford win battle hands down in *The Atlantic*]   Sh. Ox. Newsl., vol. 28/2: 18

Linscott, Roger B.
    1947, June 1   On the Books: The Bard   NY Herald Tribune, p. VII-8

Lipman, Carole S.
    1987, Winter   The Origins of the Shakespeare Authorship Roundtable   Sh. Newsletter, vol. 37/4: 54
    1987, Fall   Profile: The Shakespeare Authorship Roundtable   Spear-shaker Rev., is. 1/1: 38-39
    1989, Winter   Tribute To Dr. S. Colum Gilfillan (1921-1978)   Sh. Ox. Newsl., vol. 25/1: 10-11
    1996, Fall   [review of *The Shakespeare Folio Handbook and Census* compiled   Sh. Ox. Newsl., vol. 32/4: 19, 24
                                  by H. Otness (1990)]
    1999, Fall   Oxfordian News: Authorship Roundtable Hosts Lectures; Oxford and   Sh. Ox. Newsl., vol. 35/3: 16-18
                                  Bruno' in England; An Oxfordian Theater Debuts in London
    2003, Spring   A Tribute to Delia Bacon   Sh. Ox. Newsl., v. 39/2: 3, 16-17
    2012, Fall   News: The Roundtable Remembers Barbara Crowley (1924-2012)   Sh. Matters, vol. 11/4: 6, 14
    2013   Doubter Response to Question 44: What part did Delia Bacon play in
                                the Shakespeare authorship discussion?, in SBD? (Shahan): 204-05
    2013, Winter   Barbara Crowley, 1924-2012   Sh. Ox. Newsl., vol. 49/1: 5-6

Livacari, Gary L.
    1993, Winter   [letter: Rose Bowl parade float of Shakespeare]   Sh. Ox. Newsl., vol. 29/1a: 8
                                [repr. in BTC, vol. 7: 152]
    1996, Spring   Joseph Sobran [letter]   Sh. Ox. Newsl., vol. 32/2: 22
    2001, Summer   [letter: thumbs Up for Price's *Shakespeare's Unorthodox Biography*]   Sh. Ox. Newsl., vol. 37/2: 17-19
    2001, Fall   [letter: remembrance of Charlton Ogburn, Jr.]   Sh. Ox. Newsl., vol. 37/3: 22
    2004, Spring   Time to Declare Victory   Sh. Ox. Newsl., vol. 40/2: 7
    2010   [letter: Paul Altrocchi's *Malice Aforethought* (2010)]   Sh Matters, vol. 12: 4-5
    2017, Winter   The Mystery of *Emaricdulfe*   Sh. Ox. Newsl., vol. 53/1: 1, 9-11

Livas, Javier
    1999, April 5   Shakespeare en duda   El Norte (Monterrey), p. 7

Llewellyn, Michael
    1995, Nov.   My Lord of Oxenford's Maske   De Vere Soc. Newsl., v. 2/3: 5-6
    1997, Feb.   [review of *De Vere is Shakespeare* by Dennis Baron (1997)]   De Vere Soc. New., v. 2/8: 12-13
    2003, Feb.   The Death of Edward de Vere [repr. in GO, p. 276-283]   De Vere Soc. Newsl., p. 5-11
    2005, May   Collaboration   De Vere Soc. Newsl., p. 14-18

Llewellyn, Sally Hazelton
Plays
    2004   *Edward Presents: A Play.*
    2004   *Return to a Forbidden Planet.* [a play]
Shorter pieces
    1995, Nov.   Shakespeare Oxford Society Conference, October 1995   De Vere Soc. Newsl., v. 2/3: 1-5
    1996, Jan.   Freud and Oxford [repr. in GO, p. 307-311]   De Vere Soc. Newsl., v. 2/4: 8-12
    1997, Feb.   Phantasies of Shakespeare [repr. in GO, p. 312-316]   De Vere Soc. Newsl., v. 2/8: 8-12
    2001   Such Shaping Fantasies? Psychology & the Authorship Debate   Oxfordian, vol. 4: 143-53
                                [from DVN, vol. 2/5: 8-12 (Feb. 1997). Revised version
                                "Phantasies of Shakespeare" repr. in *Great Oxford*, p. 312-16]
    2001, Feb.   Shakespeare's 'Will' Sonnets   De Vere Soc. Newsl., p. 30-31
    2002, Oct.   [letter: Johnson's July "*Measure for Measure*" article]   De Vere Soc. Newsl., 20
    2003, June   [letter: Globe Shakespeare Authorship Conference]   De Vere Soc. Newsl., p. 5

Looney, J. Thomas (continued)

1920, March 25	Shakespeare Identified [letter: resp. to Alfred Pollard's March 4 rev.]	Times Lit. Sup., is. 949: 201
1920, April 1	Shakespeare Identified [letter: excerpts, in resp. to the March 19 rev.]	Daily Telegraph
1920, April 1	Shakespeare Identified: A Reply to Critics and Some New Facts	Yorkshire Post & LI, p. 8
1920, April 9	Is "Shakespeare Identified?" [letter: resp. to the March 19 review] [repr. in TOX, vol. 20: 131-56] Reviewer's reply on April 16.	Bookman's J., v. 1/24: 452-53
1920, April 10	Edward de Vere and Shakespeare [letter: resp. to its March 27 rev.]	Spectator, p. 487
1920, April 17	Edward de Vere and Shakespeare [letter: resp. to the March 27 rev.]	Saturday Review, vol. 129: 370
1920, April 23	To *The Bookman's Journal*: The Shakespeare Controversy [further resp. to the March 19 rev. and to other revs. repr. in the April 9 issue] [repr. in TOX, vol. 20: 131-56]	Bookman's J., vol. 1/26: 484
1920, April 30	Edward de Vere and Shakespeare [letter: resp. to M's April 2 review]	Athenaeum, 4696: 585
1920, May 6	Shakespeare's Identity: Case for Lord Oxford [resp. to the April 23 rev.]	Western Mail, p. 7
1920, May 8	Query: Edward de Vere's Mother	Notes & Q., vol. 138/208: 190
1920, May 8	Query: Henry de Vere's Sponsors	Notes & Q., vol. 138/208: 190
1920, May 21	The Identity of Shakespeare Resp. by Sir Sidney Lee in the same issue. Resp. by Rt. Hon. J. M. Robertson in the same issue. Reply by Looney in TOX, vol. 20: 131-56]	Bookman's J., v. 2/30: 58-59
1920, May 28	The Identity of Shakespeare [letter: reply to Robertson] [repr. in TOX, vol. 20: 131-56]	Bookman's J., v. 2/31: 68
1920, Dec. 23	Readers and Writers [letter: response to R. H. C.'s Dec. 2 review] See R. H. C.'s reply, same date, p. 91-92. [repr. in TOX, vol. 22 (2020): 103-20]	New Age, vol. 28/8: 91
1921, Jan. 20	Readers and Writers [letter: resp. to R. H. C.] See R. H. C.'s reply, same date, p. 139. See R.H. C.'s further reply, Jan. 27, 1921, p. 155-56. [repr. in TOX, vol. 22 (2020): 103-20]	New Age, vol. 28/12: 138-39
1921, Feb. 17	Shakespeare Identified [letter: resp. to R. H. C.] [repr. in TOX, vol. 22 (2020): 103-20]	New Age, vol. 28/16: 192.
1921, March 25	Stratford and Stony Stratford [letter: resp. to the March 4 review] See reviewer's reply, same issue] [repr. in TOX, vol. 20: 131-56]	Bookman's J., vol. 3/74: 388
1921, June 25	Shakespeare, Lord Oxford, Solomon Eagle and Mr. Looney [letter: resp. to Eagle's March 12 review] See R. H. C.'s reply, July 2, 1921, p. 15. [repr. in TOX, vol. 22 (2020): 103-20]	Outlook, p. 543-44
1921, July 15	"Shakespare's" Identity [letter: resp. to mention of SI on April 23] [repr. in SON, vol. 56/4 (Fall 2020): 21-22]	Sydney Morning Herald
1921, July 16	Mr. Looney Replies [letter: resp. to Eagle's July 2 reply] [repr. in TOX, vol. 22 (2020): 103-20]	Outlook, p. 58-59.
1922, Feb.	'Shakespeare': Lord Oxford or Lord Derby? [letter: resp. to R. Macdonald Lucas' Nov. 1921 article] [repr. in SON, vol. 53/2: 1, 12-16 (Spring 2017)]	National Review, v. 78: 801-09
1922, Oct.	The Earl of Oxford as "Shakespeare:" New Evidence [repr. in part in OXV, pp. 168-76; and in full in TOX, vol. 17: 82-93 (2015)]	Golden Hind, vol. 1/1
1922, Nov. 24	"Shakespeare at Hackney" [repr. of letter accepting position of Vice President of the Shakespeare Fellowship]	Hackney Spectator, no. 1990: 14
1923, April 13	The Oxford Movement	Hackney Spectator, no. 2020: 8
1923, April 20	Who Wrote *Hamlet*?	Hackney Spectator, no. 2022: 4
1923, May 11	How the *The Observer* Observes	Hackney Spectator, no. 2028: 2
1923, May 25	The Tracking of Margery Gryffyn [three letters to Col. B. R. Ward]	Hackney Spectator, no. 2031: 2
1923, June 10	The Shakespeare Problem [excerpt repr. in SFE, Sept., 1952, p. 2-3]	Freethinker, vol. 43/23: 364-5
1923, July 1	"Shakespeare"; Was it Oxford, Bacon, or Derby, Part 1 [excerpts repr. in SFE, Sept., 1952, p. 2-3]	Freethinker, vol. 43/26: 412-3
1923, July 8	"Shakespeare"; Was it Oxford, Bacon, or Derby, Part 2 [excerpts repr. in SFE, Sept., 1952, p. 2-3]	Freethinker, vol. 43/27: 428-9

Love, Harold
2002   *Attributing Authorship: An Introduction*. Cambridge: ambridge University Press.

Lovell, Stanley P.
1965, June   A Mystery Beyond Words [a paper distributed to all SOS members,
        see SON, (June 30, 1965), p. 2 for details]
1992, Spring   Lyly and Shakespeare [letter; repr. in BTC, vol. 7: 109]   Sh. Ox. Newsl., vol. 28/2: 17

Low, I. S.
1972, Summer *Two Gentlemen of Verona* and *Diana Enamorada*   Sh. Authorship Review, #26: 21

Low, Richard H.
2002, Feb. 24 Read the Poetry [letter: response to Niederkorn]   New York Times, p. A&L: E6

Lowell, Stanley P.
Books and pamphlets
1956   *A Mystery Beyond Words*. [pamphlet]
Shorter pieces
1956, May   To the Editor and Readers of *The Shakespeare Newsletter* Sh. Newsl., vol. 6/3: 18
        [letter, with 21 other signers]

Lubow, Sid
2013, Spring   [letter: the *Sonnets*]   Sh. Ox. Newsl., vol. 49/2: 7-8
2013, Fall   [letter: similarities between Oxford's and Shakespeare's styles] Sh. Ox. Newsl., vol. 49/3: 8-9

Lucas, Edward V.
1937   *All of a Piece: New Essays*. Philadelphia, New York: J. B. Lippincott Company.

Lucas, R. Macdonald
1921, Nov.   Did Lord Derby Write Shakespeare?   National Review, v. 78: 359-69
        Response by J. Thomas Looney, Feb. 1922, p. 801-09.
1924, Feb. 29 The Derby Theory   Hackney Spectator, p. 4-5
        Response by Col. B. R. Ward on March 7, p. 10.
1924, March 21 The Character of Oxford, I   Hackney Spectator, p. 4-5
1936, Sept. 20 A Wanderer's Note-Book: Lavenham [letter]   Sunday Times
1938, Jan.   Shakespeare's Vital Secret [letter: response to review] National Rev., vol. 110: 532-33

Lucchese, Sam F.
1952, Dec. 7 Was the 17th Earl of Oxford the Man Who Did Shakespeare's Work? Atlanta Journal-Const., p. 6F
        [review of *This Star of England* by Ch. and Dorothy Ogburn]

Lund, Thomas A.
1991, Feb.   [letter: poem about authorship issue]   Spear-shaker Newsl., is. 1/1:3

Lundskkow, Alice Newsl.
1991, Aug.   [letter: praise for *Spear Shaker's* article "The Man Behind the Name"] Spear-shaker Rev., issue 5: 25

Lynch, Jack
2011, March 18 This Our Life [reviews of *Shakespeare and Biography* by David Times Lit. Sup., is. 5602: 12
        Bevington, *Shakespeare as a Challenge for Literary Biography* by
        Arthur Maltby, and *Sidney Lee* by Marvin Spevack]

Lynch, Lucy
2016, July 12 Shakespeare Doubters Dismiss Bard's Output   Coventry Evening Tel., p. 11

Lynd, Robert
1939, Jan. 14 Robert Lynd's Saturday Essay [has image of Edward de Vere New Witness, p. 1
        labelled Shakespeare]

Lyons, Bridget G.
2003, Summer [review of *Shakespeare's Unorthodox Biography* by Diana Price] Renais. Quarterly, vol. 53/2: 553

Lyons, Donald
2003, Nov. 19 Good Will Fronting [review of *The Beard of Avon* by Amy Freed] New York Post, p. 56

M.
1920, April 2 Another Shakespeare [review of *"Shakespeare" Identified*] Athenaeum, p. 450
        Response by Francis Clarke, April 16, 1920, p. 521.
        Response by R. L. Eagle, April 16, 1920, p. 521.
         Reply by Editor, April 16, 1920, p. 521.
        Response by J. Thomas Looney, April 30, 1920.

M. H. L.
   1959, Spring   [rev. of John Russell's Dec. 6, 1958 talk "Shakespeare and the Law"]   Sh. Authorship Rev., #1: 20-21

M. H. M.
   1937, June 12   Elizabethan Translator [rev. of *An Elizabethan Puritan* by L. Golding]   Cincinnati Enq., p. 5

M. M. P.
   1921, Dec.   Shakespeare Identified? [letter]   Bulletin, vol. 42: Red Page
   1922, Feb. 9   De Vere Identified [letter]   Bulletin, vol. 43: 25

Maar, Michael
   1997, Dec.   Sture Vögel auf der Stratford   Neues Sh. Journal, vol. 1: 111-16

MacDonald, John
   1961, Spring   [review of *Shakespeare's Wooden O* by Leslie Hotson (1960)]   Sh. Authorship Rev., #5: 12-14

MacDonald, Russ
   2012, Aug. 10   A Re-fitted Stage   Times Lit. Sup., is. 5706: 11

MacDonald, Sandy
   2006, Aug. 8   Provocative and Fresh, This 'Beard' Is a Charmer [review of   Boston Globe
            The Beard f Avon by Amy Freed]

Machen, Arthur
   1926, April 17   The B in Baconian Bonnets   Graphicp. 36

MacIntyre, Ben
   2005, Oct. 7   Help, Lasagne's Out To Get Me [conspiracy theories]   Times (London), p. 24

MacIntyre, John P.
   1976   The Shepheardes Calendar: Poet's Progress   Bard, vol. 1/3: 73-86

Mackail, J. W.
   1930   Sir E. K. Chambers's Shakespeare   Periodical, vol. 15/157: 134-8

Mackey, Aurora
   1989, March 6   Shakespeare's 'Outstanding' Medical Knowledge   Washington Post
            [repr. in SON, vol. 25/2: 17-19 (Spring 1989)]

MacKillop, James
   2008, April 16   Free Willy [review of *The Beard of Avon* by Amy Freed]   Syracuse New Times, p. 13

MacMahon, Sean
   2014, May   [letter: *Tuscany Now's* blog on the authorship question]   De Vere Soc. Newsl., v. 21/2: 29

Macrone, Michael
   2003, Winter   Household Words: Common & uncommon words coined by Sh.   Sh. Ox. Newsl., vol. 39/1: 10-11+
   2003, Spring   Household Words: Part II   Sh. Ox. Newsl., vol. 39/2: 10-11
            Response by Verily Anderson (p.t), Fall 2003, p. 20.

Madigan, Patrick
   2013, Nov.   [review of *The Earl of Oxford and the Making of "Sh."* by R. Malim   Heythorp Journ., v. 54/6: 1047-8

Magri, Noemi
Books
   2014   *Such Fruits Out of Italy: The Italian Renaissance in Shakespeare's Plays and Poems.* Edited by Gary B.
            Goldstein. Buchholz, Germany: Verlag Uwe Laugwitz. [Special Editions #3 of *Neues Shake. Journal*]

Shorter pieces
   1997, Winter   Testimony of Orazio Cogno Before the Venice Inquisition of   Ever Reader, vol. 5
            Aug. 27, 1577 [a new translation]
   1997, Feb.   [letter: Krass' Dec. 1997 "Hilliard's Miniature" article]   De Vere Soc. Newsl., v. 2/8: 6-7
   1997, June   Report from Italy   De Vere Soc. Newsl., v. 2/9: 9-10
   1998, May   No Errors in Shakespeare: Historical Truth and the *Two Gentlemen*   De Vere Soc. New., v. 2/12: 9-22
            of Verona [repr. in GO, p. 66-78; in SF, p. 93-118; and in
            German in NSJ, vol. 5: 63-75 (April 2000)]
   1998, Summer   [letter: Latin motto: attici amois ergo]   Sh. Ox. Newsl., vol. 34/2: 21
   1998, Oct.   [letter: spelling of name of Venetian choirboy sh. be Orazio Cuoco]   De Vere Soc. Newsl., v. 3/1: 2-3
   1999, Spring   The Latin Mottoes on the Title p. of Henry Peacham's *Minerva*   Eliz. Review, vol. 7/1: 65-69
            Britanna [repr. in DVN, vol. 3/3: 4-6, (May 1999); in BTC,
            vol. 8: 317-21; in SF, p. 237-240; and in NSJ, vol. NS2 (Oct. 2011)]

Magri, Noemi (continued)

1999, Spring	[letter: Peter Dickson's Fall 1998 "Peacham" article]	Sh. Ox. Newsl., vol. 35/1: 21-22
1999, Aug.	Names in Shakespeare: Ophelia and Othello [repr. in SF, p. 241-45; and in German in NSJ, vol. NS4: 54-58 (Oct. 2014)]	De Vere Soc. Newsl., v. 3/4: 9-11
2000	Giulio Romano und *Das Wintermarchen* [*Winter's Tale* points to de Vere's authorship]	Neues Sh. Journal, vol. 5: 19-43
2000	Keine Irrtumer bei Shakespeare: Die historische Wahrheit und *Zwei Herren aus Verona* [Knowledge of Italian Society in *Two Gentlemen of Vernoa* points to de Vere's authorship]	Neues Sh. Journal, vol. 5: 63-75
2000, April	Das Inquisitionsverhör des Orazio Cuoco	Neues Sh. Journal, vol. 5: 44-49
2000, July	Italian Renaissance Art in Shakespeare: Guilio Romano and *The Winter's Tale* [repr. in GO, p. 50-65; and in SF, p. 37-66; repr. in German in NSJ, vol. 5: 19-43 (2000)]	De Vere Soc. Newsl., p. 2-16
2000, July	[letter: Canaidos and Cyned]	De Vere Soc. Newsl., p. 28
2001, Jan.	The Influence of Italian Renaissance Art on Shakespeare's Works: Titan's Barberini Painting: The Pictorial Source of *Venus and Adonis* [repr. in GO, p. 79-90; in SF, p. 13-36; and in NSJ, vol. NS2: 60-78 (Oct. 2011)]	De Vere Soc. Newsl., p. 2-11
2001, Spring	[letter: Oxford's choir-boy Cogno]	Sh. Ox. Newsl., vol. 37/1: 21
2002, Jan./Feb.	The Venetian Inquisition Inquiry into Orazio Cuoco (1577) [repr. in GO, p. 45-49; and in SF, 199-222]	De Vere Soc. Newsl., p. 2-8
2003, June	Places in Shakespeare: Belmont and Thereabouts [repr. in GO, p. 91-106, and in SF, p. 119-144]	De Vere Soc. Newsl., p. 6-14
2003, Sept.	[letter: Oxford and Greek church in Venice] [repr. in SF, p. 214-15)]	De Vere Soc. Newsl., p. 27
2004, April	Italianismos in Shakespeare [repr. in SF, p. 246-49; and in German in NSJ, vol. NS4: 59-62 (Oct. 2014)]	De Vere Soc. Newsl., p. 23
2005, May	Shakespeare and Italian Renaissance Painting: 3 wanton pictures in *Taming of Shrew* [repr. in SF, p. 67-92]	De Vere Soc. Newsl., p. 4-12
2005, Dec.	"The Three Sisters of Mantua": A Known History and an Unknown Play [repr. in SF, p. 250-261]	De Vere Soc. Newsl., p. 13-17
2006, April	Puntarvolo or Puntaruolo?	De Vere Soc. Newsl., p. 4
2006, April	Orazio v. Nelson [repr. in SF, p. 216-222]	De Vere Soc. Newsl., p. 6
2006, July	[letter: the 'Monsters of the 16th Century' proposal]	De Vere Soc. Newsl., p. 23
2007, Feb.	Geographical Exactness in *All's Well That Ends Well* [repr. in SF, p. 145-150]	De Vere Soc. Newsl., p. 16-17
2007, June	Shakespeare's Illyria and Bohemia: Oxford's Journey in the Adriatic [repr. in SF, p. 151-165]	De Vere Soc. Newsl., p. 6-11
2007, Oct.	[letter: Rollett's June "canopy" article] Reply by Rollett, March 2008, p. 24-25. See also Rollett's further thoughts, Oct. 2008, p. 27.	De Vere Soc. Newsl., p. 20
2007, Oct.	[letter: Puttenham's treatise as unreliable dating tool]	De Vere Soc. Newsl., p. 30
2007, Oct.	Shakespeare's Illyria and Bohemia - notes to the June 2007 issue [repr. in SF, p. 151-165]	De Vere Soc. Newsl., p. 31-32
2008, March	Shakespeare's Knowledge of Illrian Rulers: Duke Orsino and *Twelfth Night* [repr. in 166-183]	De Vere Soc. New., v. 15/1: 5-11
2008, June	Edward de Vere Did Not Build Himself a House in Venice [repr. in SF, p. 223-236]	De Vere So. New., v. 15/2: 11-16
2008, Oct.	[letter: Malim's June 2008 "*Winter's Tale*" article]	De Vere So. New., v. 15/3: 27-28
2009, Feb.	The Italian Legal System in *The Merchant of Venice*: the single bond [repr. in SF, p. 262-274]	De Vere Soc. Newsl., v. 16/1: 5-9
2009, June	Hamlet's 'The Murder of Gonzago' in Contemporary Documents [repr. in SF, p. 275-299]	De Vere So. New., v. 16/2: 8-14+
2010	*The Two Gentlemen of Verona* [in *Dating Shakespeare's Plays* (Gilvary): 56-64]	
2010	*All's Well That Ends Well* [in *Dating Shakespeare's Plays* (Gilvary): 155-66]	
2010	*The Tragedy of Othello, the Moore of Venice* [in *Dating Sh's Plays* (Gilvary): 407-14]	

2010	*The Merchant of Venice* [with Joe Peel] [in *Dating Shakespeare's Plays* (Gilvary): 123-39]	
2010, Feb.	Othello's House on the Sagittary; Shakespeare's Familiarity With the Streets of Venice [repr. in SF, p. 184-190; and in German in NSJ, vol. NS4: 39-45 (Oct. 2014)]	De Vere Soc. New., v. 17/1: 8-10
2010, Feb.	[letter: her enjoyment of *The De Vere Papers* by Michael Langford]	De Vere Soc. Newsl., v. 17/1: 26
2011, March	Shakespeare and the Ships of the Venetian Republic [repr. in SF, p. 191-98; and in German in NSJ, vol. NS4: 46-53 (Oct. 2014)]	De Vere So. New., v. 18/1: 11-13

Mahar, Ted

2003, Jan. 2	Was It Shakespeare or Marlowe? [*Frontline*'s "Much Ado About Something"]	Oregonian, p. E10

Mahon, John W.

1994, Fall	Irvin Matus: Beyond the Authorship Question [review of *Shakespeare, In Fact* by Irvin Matus (1993)]	Sh. Newsletter, vol. 44/2: 42
2004, Summer	[letter: *Monstrous Adversary* by Alan Nelson]	Sh. Matters, vol. 3/4: 8
2011, Spr-Sum	Irvin Leigh Matus, RIP	Sh. Newsl., vol. 61/1: 33

Mahoney, Jeff

2016, April 11	Much Ado About Shakespeare's Authenticity [Chris Pannell and Sky Sky Gilbert at Toronto Oxfordian Event (April 24)]	Spectator (Ontario), p. A3

Mair, G. H.

1923, Nov.	The First Folio Shakespeare	Standard

Majauskas, Alan S.

2001, May 14	Our Bard [letter: *Globe* owes its readers an objective look] Response by J. Kelly Nestruck, May 16, 2001, p. A14. Response by Martin Wallace, May 16, 2001, p. A14.	Globe & Mail, p. A14

Majendie, Lewis

1796	*An Account of Hedingham Castle in the County of Essex.*

Majendie, Severne Andrew Ashhurst

1904	*Some Account of the Family of De Vere, the Earls of Oxford, and of Hedingham Castle in Essex.* London: H. T. Smith & Son.

Malcolm, Sundra G.

2007, Fall	M.O.A.I. Unriddled: Anatomy of an Oxfordian Reading Response by David Roper, Winter 2008, p. 2. Response by Kathryn Sharpe, Spring 2008, p. 2, 9.	Sh. Matters, vol. 7/1: 24-25

Maley, Willy

2010	Malfolio: Foul Papers on the Shakespeare Authorship Question, in *Shakespeare and His Authors*, ed. by William Leahy, p. 23-40

Malim, Richard C. W.

Books

2004	*Great Oxford: Essays on the Life and Work of Edward de Vere, 17th Earl of Oxford, 1550-1604* (editor). Tunbridge, Wells, Kent, UK: Parapress.
2012	*The Earl of Oxford and the Making of "Shakespeare": The Literary Life of Edward de Vere in Context.* London: McFarland & Co.
2022	*Shakespeare's Revolution.* London: Austin Macauley Publishers.

Shorter pieces

1996, Dec.	Eric Sams	De Vere Soc. New., v. 2/7: 17-18
1997, Oct.	Wolf, Cormorant or Headless Pig: Shakspere's London Career from 1599	De Vere Soc. Newsl., v. 2/10: 4-7
1998, May	More on EVER THE FORTH	De Vere Soc. Newsl., v. 2/12: 2-4
1998, Summer	[letter: Sisson's article and Mr. Shaksper]	Sh. Ox. Newsl., vol. 34/2: 21
1999, Jan. 9	They Haven't the Necessary Will	Spectator, p. 20
2000, Jan.	Some Thoughts on the Shakespeare Apocrypha	De Vere Soc. Newsl., p. 12-13
2000, Oct.	Shake-speare the Actyor	De Vere Soc. Newsl., p. 24-28
2000, Oct.	[letter: Brookmans Old Farm]	De Vere Soc. Newsl., p. 21
2000, Oct.	[letter: interpreting Greek words in Shakespeare]	De Vere Soc. Newsl., p. 20
2001, Jan.	Deconstructing Groatsworth	De Vere Soc. Newsl., p. 12-16
2001, Apr./May	[letter: Price's *Shakespeare's Unorthodox biography*] Response by Price, April/May 2001, p. 36.	De Vere Soc. Newsl., 34-35

Malim, Richard C. W. (continued)

2001, Apr./May	Shakespeare: Man and Pseudonym	De Vere Soc. Newsl., p. 27-32
2001, Apr./May	[review of *Shakespeare's Unorthodox Biography* by Diana Price] Response by Diana Price, same issue, p. 36.	De Vere Soc. Newsl., p. 35-36
2001, July	Criticism: Giordano Bruno [repr. in GO]	De Vere Soc. Newsl., p. 25-27
2001, July	1588-1591: When Shakespeare Did Not Write	De Vere Soc. Newsl., p. 31-35
2002, July	*The Spanish Maze* [repr. in GO, p. 284-288]	De Vere Soc. Newsl., p. 9-11
2002, July	[letter: *Henry VIII*]	De Vere Soc. Newsl., p. 28
2003, Sept.	[letter: *Henry VIII*]	De Vere Soc. Newsl., p. 25
2003, Sept.	Did Oxford Know Ronsard? [repr. in GO, p. 16-21]	De Vere Soc. Newsl., p. 11-13
2003, Autumn	Professor Wells and the Silver Bullet Question	Sh. Ox. Newsl., vol. 39/4: 17, 20
2004	Giordano Bruno, in *Great Oxford*, p. 208-11	
2004	Oxford's View of Shakespeare, in *Great Oxford*, p. 247-52	
2004	Blackfriars Theatre, 1608, in *Great Oxford*, p. 296-98	
2004, Jan.	Oxford the Actor [repr. in GO, p. 212-22; and in LC, p. 112-21]	De Vere Soc. Newsl., p. 14-19
2004, April	[review of *Shakespeare's Melancholics* by W. I. D. Scott (1962)]	De Vere Soc. Newsl., p. 23
2004, April	The Coast of Bohemia – Did Oxford Err?	De Vere Soc. Newsl., p. 14
2004, April	[letter: critique of 'solid literary analysis']	De Vere Soc. Newsl., p. 31
2004, Nov. 2	[letter: Paul Nitze was supporter of de Vere's authorship]	Times (London), p. 66
2005, Jan.	[review of *Will in the World* by Stephen Greenblatt (2004)]	De Vere Soc. Newsl., p. 21-22
2005, Dec.	The Fallacy of Selectivity in Caricature	De Vere Soc. Newsl., p. 6-17
2005, Dec.	[review of *Shakespeare, the Biography* by Peter Ackroyd (2006)]	De Vere Soc. Newsl., p. 18-19
2006, April	Malim Represents DVS at Shakespeare Authorship Event at the National Portrait Gallery (March 23, 2006)	De Vere Soc. Newsl., p. 2
2006, April	[review of *1599: A Year in the Life of William Shakespeare* by James Shapiro (2005)]	De Vere Soc. Newsl., p. 22
2006, July	[review of *Pseudonymous Shakespeare* by Penny McCarthy (2006)]	De Vere Soc. Newsl., p. 19
2006, Nov.	[letter: postscript to his review of Shapiro's lecture by Pole and Jolly]	De Vere Soc. Newsl., p. 30-31
2006, Nov.	[review of *Shadowplay* by Asquith (2005)]	De Vere Soc. Newsl., p. 29
2007, Feb.	[review of *Shakespeare and Company* by Stanley Wells (2006)]	De Vere Soc. Newsl., p. 23
2007, Oct.	[letter: resp. to Rollett's June 2007 "canopy" article] Reply by Rollett, March 2008, p. 24-25. See also Rollett's further thoughts, Oct. 2008, p. 27.	De Vere Soc. Newsl., p. 20-21
2007, Oct.	[letter: refuting Vickers' contention from *Coriolanus*]	De Vere Soc. Newsl., p. 29
2007, June	*The Arte of English Poetry* as a Dating Tool	De Vere Soc. Newsl., p. 11-16
2007, Oct.	[review of *Shakespeare the Thinker* by Anthony D. Nuttall (2007)]	De Vere Soc. Newsl., p. 33-34
2007, Oct.	[review of *Shakespeare, Marlowe, Jonson*, ed. by Kozuka and Mulryne (2006)]	De Vere Soc. Newsl., p. 35-36
2008, March	[review of *Shakespeare Revealed* by Rene Weis (2007)]	De Vere So. New., v. 15/1: 30-31
2008, April 21	[letter: asks why Shakspere was residing with hatmaker when his plays were being performed at court, Christmas 1594] [repr. in DVN, vol. 15/3: 28 (Oct. 2008)]	Daily Telegraph (Surry Hills)
2008, June	No Mistakes in Shakespeare: A Return to Bohemia Response by Noemi Magri, Oct. 2008, p. 27-28.	De Vere So. New., v. 15/2: 29-31
2008, Aug. 8	Shakspere the actor at The Theatre [letter] [repr. in DVN, vol. 15/3: 28 (Oct. 2008)]	Times (London)
2008, Oct.	[letter: the *Daily Telegraph's* review of *Love's Labour's Lost*] [repr. in DVN, vol. 15/3: 27 (Oct. 2008)]	De Vere Soc. New., vol. 15/3: 27
2008, Oct.	Summary of the Stratford-upon-Avon Conference (June 28, 2008)	De Vere Soc. Newsl., v. 15/3: 7-9
2009, Feb.	[review of *Soul of the Age* by Jonathan Bate (2008)]	De Vere Soc. New., v. 16/1: 24-6
2009, Feb.	[letter: Rubinstein/James art. in *Folio Book of Historical Mysteries*]	De Vere Soc. New., vol. 16/1: 27
2009, June	[letter: Ron Hess' Feb. 2009 "Oxford traveled abroad" article]	De Vere Soc. New., vol. 16/2: 30
2009, June	Two Rival Venues for the Theater; Press release from the Tower Theatre Company; Letter from Richard Malim; TTC response	De Vere Soc. Newsl., vol. 16/2: 5
2009, June	How Sidney Helps Date Shakespeare's Plays	De Vere Soc. Nel., vol. 16/2: 34
2009, Nov.	Martin South of The Theatre Comes to DVS Meeting	De Vere Soc. Newsl., v. 16/3: 7-8
2009, Dec.	[reports on Conference: "Shakespeare: From Rowe to Shapiro"] [with Kevin Gilvary and Julia Cleve]	Sh. Ox. Newsl., vol. 45/3: 14-17
2010	*Edward III* [in *Dating Shakespeare's Plays* (Gilvary): 454-60]	

Malim, Richard C. W. (continued)

2017, Oct.	The Mystery of Willy: Oxford, Spenser, and Theocritus' *Six Idilla*	Oxfordian, vol. 19: 129-52
2017, Oct.	Sir George Buc's Copy of George A' Green	De Vere So. New., v. 24/4: 12-14
2018, Jan.	[letter: reprint of his Dec. 11 letter to *The Times*]	De Vere Soc. New., vol. 25/1: 46
2018, Jan.	Scholarship and Professor Gary Taylor [letter]	De Vere So. New., v. 25/1: 14-17
2018, April	Lawyers and the Shakespeare Authorship Question	De Vere Soc. Newsl., v. 25/2: 3-6
2018, July	The 'Latten Spoons'	De Vere So. New., v. 25/3: 30-32
2018, Oct.	Oxford the Comedian	De Vere So. New., v. 25/4: 15-29
2019, Jan.	Shakespeare: Seventeenth Century Biographical References to Shakespeare as Author	De Vere Soc. New., v. 26/1: 4-20
2019, April	Beaumont's Letter to Jonson	De Vere So. New., v. 26/2: 25-28
2019, April	[review of *Necessary Mischief: Exploring the Shakespeare Authorship Question* by Bonner Miller Cutting]	De Vere So. New., v. 26/2: 31-35
2019, July	[letter: Vere effigies miniature is anti-Oxford-is-Shakespeare Propaganda	De Vere Soc. New., vol. 26/3: 47
2019, Sept.	The Politics of Edward de Vere, 17th Earl of Oxford [with R. Detobel]	Oxfordian, vol. 21: 177-90
2019, Oct.	The Shakespeare Bastard	De Vere So. New., v. 26/4: 10-17
2019, Oct.	Oxford, the Last Years	De Vere So. New., v. 26/4: 18-23
2020, Oct.	The Dating of *The Rape of Lucrece*	De Vere So. New., v. 27/4: 25-27
2020, Oct.	EK and *The Shepheard's Calendar* [letter]	De Vere Soc. New., vol. 27/4: 46
2021, April	Jonson: Oxford's Chief Admirer	De Vere So. New., v. 28/2: 34-45
2022, July	[letter: Ian Haste's April 2022 article on Hayward's *Henry the Fourth*]	De Vere Soc. New., vol. 29/3: 30
2022, Sept.	The 17th Earl of Oxford and the Occult	Oxfordian, vol. 24: 211-236
2022, April	[review of *The Famous Victories of Henry the Fifth* edited by Ramon Jiménez]	De Vere So. New., v. 29/2: 45-48
2023, April	More and *More*	De Vere So. New., v. 30/2: 28-34

Maltby, Arthur

2009   *Shakespeare As a Challenge for Literary Biography: A History of Biographies of Shakespeare Since 1898.* Lewiston: The Edwin Mellen Press. [See esp. p. 180, 190-192]

Malvern, Jack

2001, June 6	Where There's No Will, Is There a Way? Hollywood is Stage for Battle Over Who Wrote Shakespeare	Times (London), p. 12
2005, June 1	Class War Over Shakespeare's Identity	Times (London), p. 20
2013, April 19	Shakespeare Defenders Decide Who Is to Be, and Not to Be [review of *Sh. Beyond Doubt* by Paul Edmondson and Stanley Wells]	Times (London), p. 22

Mander, Rosalie

1983, May 28	They Kept Their Heads [review of *Eminent Elizabethans* by A. L. Rowse (1983)	Financial Times, p. 16

Mankoff, Bob

2000, June 19	[cartoon: "I'm confused now. Was Shakespeare somebody else or was somebody else Shakespeare?" [repr. in DVN (July 2000): p. 30]	

Mann, Bert

1981, Jan. 15	Plays Not by Shakespeare, Writer Claims [Ruth Loyd Miller]	Los Angeles Times, p. SG1

Mantel, Hilary

2010, March 20	Only a Warwickshire Glover's Son: A Look at the Wilder Shores of Anti-Shakespeare Conspiracy Theory [review of *Contested Will* by James Shapiro]	Guardian, p. 6
	[reprint of blog commentary on Mantel's article, March 27, p. 19.]	Guardian, blog

Manwell, Margaret K.

1969, Dec. 10	An Unconsidered Trifle Snapped Up	Sh. Ox. Newsl., vol. 5/4: 6-9

Manzo, Fred W.

1992, Summer	Never Be Certain of Anything, It's a Sign of Weakness	Sh. Ox. Newsl., vol. 28/3: 1-3
1995, Autumn	Who Was Joseph Hall's Labeo	Eliz. Review, vol. 3/2: 53-59

Marche, Stephen

2011, Oct. 23	Wouldn't It Be Cool if Shakespeare Wasn't Shakespeare? [review of *Anonymous*] [*NY Times Magazine*]	New York Times, p. 60-61

Marchione, Margherita
 1992, Spring [rev. of *The Man Who Was William Shakespeare* by P. Sammartino] Italica vol. 69/1: 92-94

Marcus, David
 2019, May 13 No, Shakespeare was Not a Jewish Woman. He Was Just a Genius Federalist
    [response to Winkler]

Marcus, Leah S.
Books
 1988 *Puzzling Shakespeare: Local Reading and Its Discontents*. Berkeley: University of California Press.
Shorter pieces
 2012 [review of *Contested Will* by James Shapiro (2010)] Sh. Jahrbuch, vol. 148: 215-20
 2014 [review article: includes rev. of *The Earl of Oxford and the Making* Studies in Eng. Lit., vol. 54/1:
    of "Shakespeare" by Richard Malim] 193-242

Marcus, Michael
 2010 [letter: Frank Davis' 2009 "Groats-worth" article] Oxfordian, vol. 12: 5
    Reply by Frank Davis, 2011, p. 4.

Marder, Louis
Books
 1963 *His Exits and His Entrances: The Story of Shakespeare's Reputation*. Philadelphia: Lippincott.
    [excerpts (p. 156-188) repr. in *Shakespearean Criticism*, vol. 41 (Lee & Barnes, 1998): 5-18]
Periodical editor
 1951-1991: Founder and editor of *The Shakespeare Newsletter*, issue 1, vol. 1/1 – issue 210, vol. 41/3.
Shorter pieces
 1956, May Who Wrote Shakespeare? Sh. Newsl., vol. 6/3: 18
 1962, Sept. Shakespeare's Bones, Birthplace and Burial, Part 1 Sh. Newsl., vol. 11/4: 28-29+
    [response to a *NY Times'* Sept. 21 editorial]
 1962, Nov. Shakespeare's Bones, Birthplace and Burial, Part 2 Sh. Newsl., vol. 11/5: 35-36
    [response to the same *NY Times'* Sept. 21 editorial]
 1963, Feb. Quest for Shakespeare Manuscripts and Exposure of "Sham Sh. Newsl., vol. 13/1: 1
    Shakespeare" Continues Among "Heretics"
 1963, April Authorship Question Still Inspiring Research Among Disbelievers Sh. Newsl., vol. 13/2: 1
 1963, April Questions and Answers on the Authorship of Shakespeare Sh. Newsl., vol. 13/2: 16-17
 1963, May Authorship Controversy Continues: No Solution Yet Sh. Newsl., vol. 13/3: 1
 1963, Sept. Shakespeare Debate Continues: Oxfordians Submit More Questions Sh. Newsl., vol. 13/4: 1
 1964, Dec. The Computer and Shakespearean Scholarship Sh. Newsl., vol. 14/6: 77
 1973, Feb. [review of *Wasn't Shakespeare Someone Else?* by Ralph Tweedale] Sh. Newsl., vol. 23/1: 6
 1975, May Authorship Problem: Stretching Credulity Sh. Newsl., vol. 25/3: 27
 1977, May Imaginary Life of Shakespeare for TV Sh. Newsl., vol. 27/3: 1, 26
 1978, Nov./Dec. Shakespeare By Hilliard? Sh. Newsl., vol. 28/5-6: 38
 1979, April Shakespeareans: Who are They Sh. Newsl., vol. 29/1: 10
 1979, April The Oxfordian Movement: News/scholarship in Oxfordian periodicals Sh. Newsl.,vol. 29/1: 10
 1979, Dec. Stylometrics: The New Authorship Weapon Sh. Newsl., vol. 29/5: 41-42
 1980, Feb. Famous People Comment on the Shakespearean Authorship Sh. Newsl., vol. 31/1: 9
 1980, Sept. Stylometry "Proves" Entire Sir Thomas More is All Shakespeare's Sh. Newsl., vol. 30/4: 29
 1983, Spring Authorship and the Oxfordians Sh. Newsl., vol. 33/1: 6
 1984, Spring Anti-Stratfordians Active in Los Angeles Sh. Newsl., vol. 34/1: 9
 1984, Winter The Mysterious William Shakespeare: A Myth of Double Identity Sh. Newsl., vol. 34/4: 37-38
    [review of *The Mysterious William Shakespeare* by Ch. Ogburn]
 1985, Spring Is the Real Shakespeare Mysterious? Sh. Newsl., vol. 35/1: 2
 1985, Summer Editor's Resp. [to Cyr's "What Does It Mean To 'Argue in a Circle?'] Sh. Newsl., vol. 35/2: 22
 1985, Summer Oxford, the War of Words & Shakespeare: Review of *Edward de* Sh. Newsl., vol. 35/2: 22
    Vere and the War of Words by Elizabeth Appleton (1985)
 1985, Fall Pro-Shakespeare – An Orthodox Reply Sh. Newsl., vol. 35/3: 34
 1985, Fall Shakespeare Authorship Roundtable Meetings and Tour Sh. Newsl., vol. 35/3: 34
 1986, Spring Notice: Marlowe as Marprelate Sh. Newsl., vol. 36/1: 10
 1986, Fall Shakespeare Authorship Round Table Annual Meeting Sh. Newsl., vol. 36/3: 38
 1986, Fall Appleton's Continued Search for True Bard Sh. Newsl., vol. 36/3: 40
 1986, Fall E VER[e] More on the Authorship Question Sh. Newsl., vol. 36/3: 40
 1986, Fall [review of *Shakespeare Revealed in Oxford's Letters* by W. P. Fowler] Sh. Newsl., vol. 36/3: 40, 57
 1986, Winter Oxford as Author? Sh. Newsl., vol. 36/4: 57

Marder, Louis (continued)

1986, Winter	An Oxfordian Challenge	Sh. Newsl., vol. 36/4: 56
1987, Spring	Lord Charles Vere in the U.S.A.	Sh. Newsl., vol. 37/1: 11
1987, Summer	Anti-Stratfordian Resources List	Sh. Newsl., vol. 37/2: 26
1987, Summer	New De Vere Society Challenges Authorship	Sh. Newsl., vol. 37/2: 26
1987, Summer	[review of *The Shakespeare Identity Crisis: A Reference Guide*]	Sh. Newsl., vol. 37/2: 26
1987, Fall	Shakespeare Wins Verdict in Moot Court Authorship Debate	Sh. Newsl., vol. 37/3: 1, 30
1987, Fall	Shakespeare/Oxford in *The Smithsonian*	Sh. Newsl., vol. 37/3: 37
1987, Fall	*The Spear-shaker Review* Published by Stephanie Caruana	Sh. Newsl., vol. 37/3: 37
1987, Winter	Shakespeare/Oxford Society News	Sh. Newsl., vol. 37/4: 56
1988, Spring	More Oxfordian Activities for the Anti-Stratfordian Supplement	Sh. Newsl., vol. 38/1: 10
1988, Spring	An Anti-Stratfordian Supplement: Middle Temple "Trial" Seeks Authorship Solution; Shakespeare/Oxford Debate Continues; Shakespeare Wins in Detroit; Shakespeare Loses in Florida; Commemorative Poster Available; *The Spear-shaker Review* – Number 2; *De Vere Society Newsletter* Off to Auspicious Start	Sh. Newsl., vol. 38/1: 11
1988, Spring	The Sakespeare-Oxford Debate	Sh. Newsl., vol. 38/1: 13
1988, Summer	The Shakespeare Oxford Society	Sh. Newsl., vol. 38/2: 29
1988, Fall/Wntr	Middle Temple Moot Court Decides in Favor of Shakespeare	Sh. Newsl., vol. 38/3-4: 33, 35
1988, Fall/Wntr	Shakespeare Authorship Clinic Eliminates Marlowe as Shakespeare Claimant: Further Testing Planned	Sh. Newsl., vol. 38/3-4: 1, 35
1988, Fall-Wntr.	Anti-Stratfordian Activities	Sh. Newsl., vol. 38/3-4: 43
1989, Spr./Sum.	News: An Anti-Shakespearean Museum Proposed; Authorship Roundtable Programs; McPherson's Pyrrhic Victory	Sh. Newsl., vol. 39/1-2: 16
1989, Spr./Sum.	[reply to a Letter from Charlton Ogburn]	Sh. Newsl., vol. 39/1-2: 16
1989, Spr/Sum	[review of *Shakespeare, Man of Mystery* by Thomas H. Foster]	Sh. Newsl., vol. 39/1-2: 40-42
1989, Fall./Wntr	News from the Oxfordians; Oxford Society Annual Meeting; Shakespeare Authorship Roundtable Activities	Sh. Newsl., vol. 39/3-4: 37, 44
1989, Fall/Wntr	*The Phoenix and the Turtle*: Another Unsolved Mystery	Sh. Newsl., vol. 39/3-4: 40-2
1990, Spr.	New Computer Study Wreaks Havoc with Disputed Author. Theories	Sh. Newsl., vol. 40/1: 1
1990, Summer	A "Slight Difference of Opinion:" Oxford vs. Shakespeare	Sh. Newsl., vol. 40/2: 23, 39
1990, Summer	California Computer Authorship Study Raises Controversy	Sh. Newsl., vol. 40/2: 26
1990, Fall	The Shakespeare Authorship Roundtable	Sh. Newsl., vol. 40/3: 42
1991, Fall	Oxford's Descendant Speaks at Folger and the Harvard Club [Charles Vere, Lord Burford, April 24 and 26]	Sh. Newsl., vol. 41/3: 19
1991, Fall	Oxfordian Publications: The Cold War	Sh. Newsl., vol. 41/3: 41
1991, Fall	*The Spear-shaker Review* Reviewed	Sh. Newsl., vol. 41/3: 41
1993, Fall	Bard, Marder Best in Boston [repr. in Sh. Newsl., vol. 59/2: 57+) [Account of mock trial; jury voted for Shakespeare] Response by Morse Johnson, SON, vol. 30/1: 6-10.	Sh. Newsl., vol. 43/3: 1, 42+
2009, Fall	Bard, Marder Best in Boston [repr. from SHNL, vol. 43/3: 1, 42+]	Sh. Newsl., vol. 59/2: 57+

Markham, Clements R.

1888	*The Fighting Veres*. Boston and New York: Houghton, Mifflin and Co.	

Marks, Jim

1997	[review of *Alias Shakespeare* by Joseph Sobran (1997)]	Lambda Book Report, vol. 6/3: 9-10

Marlow, Stuart

2005, Summer	Bringing Oxford in Fom the Margins/Marshes: New Stratfordianism	Sh. Ox. Newsl., vol. 41/3: 19-20+
2005, Summer	Insights on Sh.'s Sources Fuel Lively Debate at Concordia Sem.	Sh. Matters, vol. 4/4: 34-36

Marquard, Bryan

2011, Jan. 12	Elliott Stone, 79, Lover of Art, Including Art of Conversation [Obit.]	Boston Globe, p. B12

Martin, Milward W.

Books

1965	*Was Shakespeare Shakespeare? A Lawyer Reviews the Evidence*. New York: Cooper Square.	

Shorter pieces

1959, June	[letter: resp. to articles by Richard Bentley (Feb.) and Charlton Ogburn, Sr. (March)	Am. Bar Assoc. Journal, p. 605

Martin, Samuel
    2009, Nov. 27   Sorry, It's True. The Bard Was a Mere Brummie.   Daily Mail, p. 18

Martyn, Kathleen
    1958, Spring   Thomas Aitken: A Memoir (d. 1958)   SF News-letter (E), p. 4

Mason, David
    1914   *Shakespeare Personally*. London: Smith, Elder & Co. [see p. 17: states that Shakspere left London in 1604]

Mason, Hugh L.
    2005, Sept.   The Problem of a Stratford-Born Shakespeare [with A. Pointon]   De Vere Soc. Newsl., p. 26-29

Mason, Jacquelyn L.
    1987, Fall   Collage: Oxford Peering Out From Behind a Mask of Shaksper   Spear-shaker Rev., is. 1/1: bk cvr.
    1987, Fall   Shall I Die? Shall I Fly?: An Early Poem by Oxford?   Spear-shaker Rev., is. 1/1: 2-5
    1995, Autumn   [letter: Richard Desper's article on *Twelfth Night* in ER, Spring 1995]   Eliz. Review, vol. 3/2: 3
    2008, March   [letter: word usage in *Axiochus*]   De Vere S. New., v. 15/1: 23-24
    2015, Summer   [letter: Richard Waugaman's Spring 2015 "1578 poem" article]   Sh. Ox. Newsl., vol. 51/3: 3
        See also response by Robert Prechter, same issue, p. 3.

Mason, M. S.
    2002, Dec. 27   What's on TV [review of *Frontline*'s "Much Ado About Something"]   Christian Sci. Monitor, p. 19

Mason, Una
    2002, Winter   [letter: correspondence with Charlton Ogburn]   Sh. Ox. Newsl., vol. 38/1: 22

Mason, William
    1956, May   To the Editor and Readers of *The Shakespeare Newsletter*   Sh. Newsl., vol. 6/3: 18
        [letter, with 21 other signers]

Massey, Gerald
    1946, Jan.   Shakespeare [a tribute to the bard from about 1866]   SF Quarterly, vol. VII/1: 19

Massie, Alan
    2011, Oct. 26   Only Foolish Snobs Don't Believe in Sh. [rev. of *Anonymous*]   Telegraph, p. 22

Masters, Ryan
    2005, Sept. 22   Conspiracy Theory; Beard Dramatizes Dispute Over the Dramatist's   Monterey County Weekly, p. 51
        Identity [review of *The Beard of Avon* by Amy Freed]

Matchett, Robin
    2002   *The Lion Bats the Bvtterfly, or, the True and Tragicke Historie of Shake-speare*. Toronto: J. Piercemore.

Matthias, Laura Wilson
    2012   *Last Will. & Testament*. [An 84-minute film documenting the life of Edward de Vere] [with Lisa Wilson]

Mattix, Micah
    2014, March 17   Bard of Honor [review of *Shakespeare Beyond Doubt* edited by Paul   Weekly Standard, p. 38-39
        Edmondson and Stanley Wells

Matus, Irvin L.
Books
    1994   *Shakespeare, In Fact*. New York: Continuum.
        Repr. in 1999. New edition in 2012 with a new intro. by Thomas Mann. Mineola: Dover Publications.
Shorter pieces
    1991, Oct.   The Case for Shakespeare [repr. in *Shakespearean Criticism*, vol. 41]   Atlantic Mon., v. 268/4: 62-73
        [repr. in *Sh. Criticism, vol. 41* (Lee & Barnes 1998): 57-61]
    1991, Oct.   Reply by Matus [repr. in *Shakespearean Criticism*, vol. 41]   Atlantic Mon., v. 268/4: 78-81
        [repr. in *Sh. Criticism, vol. 41* (Lee & Barnes 1998): 63-66]
    1992, Jan.   [reply to letters re the special issue on Sh's authorship]   Atlantic Monthly, p. 6-9
    1999, April   The Reproof Valiant [repr. in LC, p. 57-78]   Harper's Mag., v. 298: 49-53
    2003, Dec. 4   Good Will Hunting: A Biography and a Novel Wrestle with Some   Washington Post, WBK4
        Big Questions about the Bard [reviews of *Shakespeare* by M.
        Wood and *Chasing Shakespeares* by Sarah Smith]

Maude, Francis C.
    1895   *Bacon or Shakespeare? Enquiries as to the Authorship of the Plays of Shake-speare*. [pamphlet]

Maupin, Elizabeth
    1989, Nov. 12   The Mysteries of Shakespeare Legend is Clear, but Facts are Lost in   Orlando Sentinel, p. F1
        History's Fog

Maxse, L. J.
 1922, Nov. 24 [letter: acceptance of position of VP with the Sh. Fellowship] Hackney Spectator, p. 14

Maxwell, Baldwin
 1929, Jan. 1 [review of *The Seventeenth Earl of Oxford* by B. M. Ward] Sh. Quarterly, vol. 8: 223-24
 1959, Summer [review of *Shakespeare and His Betters: A Criticism of the Attempts* Sh. Quarterly, vol. 10/3: 435-37
  Made to Prove that Shakespeare's Works Were Written By Others
  by R. C. Churchill, Maurice Hussey and Ivor Brown (1958)]
 1959, Summer [review of *The Poacher From Stratford* by Frank W. Wadsworth] Sh. Quarterly, vol. 10/3: 435-37

Maxwell, J. C.
 1963, Sept. [review of *The Shakespeare Claimants* by Harry N. Gibson (1962)] Notes & Q., vol. 10: 352-54

May, Steven W.
Books
 1991 *The Elizabethan Courtier Poets: The Poems and Their Contexts*. Columbia: University of Missouri Press
  [2nd edition, 1999. Asheville, NC: Pegasus Press.] [excerpt repr. in LC, p. 11-15

Shorter pieces
 1975, Nov. The Authorship of "My Mind to Me a Kingdom Is" Rev. Eng. St., vol. 26/104: 385+
 1980 Tudor Aristocrats and the Mystical 'Stigma of Print' Renaiss. Papers, vol. 10: 11-18
 1980, Winter The Poems of Edward de Vere, Seventeenth Earl of Oxford and of Studies in Philology
  Robert Devereux, 2nd Earl of Essex vol. 77/5: 1, 3, 5+
 1985, Fall Lord Oxford Sues for a Patent of Monopoly Sh. Ox. Newsl., vol. 21/4: 1-2
  Response by Charlton Ogburn, Jr., SON, vol. 22/2, p. 7-8.
 1992, March The Countess of Oxford's Sonnets: A Caveat Eng. Lang. Notes, vol. 29: 9-19
 2004, Fall The Seventeenth Earl of Oxford as Poet and Playwright Tennessee Law Review, vol.
  72/1: 221-254
 2005, Summer [rev. of *Monstrous Adversary: Life of Edward de Vere* by A. Nelson] Sh. Quarterly, vol. 56/2: 214-26
 2007 Early Courtier Verse: Oxford, Dyer, and Gascoigne, in Cheney,
  Patrick; et al. *Early Modern English Poetry*, p. 60-69

May, T.
 1923, Sept. 21 Tthe Mystery of Shakespeare: Is He a Myth? [letter] Hackney Spectator, p. 2

Maycock, Shelly
 2013, Spring News: Oxfordians Hear James Shapiro at the Folger Sh. Matters, vol. 12/2: 4, 18
 2013, Spring Studying de Vere [a poem] Sh. Matters, vol. 23
 2016, Winter Oxfordians Meet Folger Director at First Folio Tour Kickoff Event Sh. Ox. Newsl., vol. 52/1: 5
 2016, Spring Branding the Author: Feigned Neutrality and the Folger Folio Tour Brief Chronicles, Sp. issue: 5-29
 2017, Oct. All That is Shakespeare Melts into Air [review of *The Shakespeare* Oxfordian, vol. 19: 195-208
  Authorship Companion [with Michael Dudley and Gary Goldstein]
  [exc. repr. in *Sh. Authorship Sourcebook* (Stritmatter 2022): 173-88]
 2019, 2022 "What's in a Name"? "No Fear" Shakespeare Authorship for the
  Secondary and College Classroom [with Roger Stritmatter], in
  The Sh. Authorship Sourcebook (Stritmatter 2019, 2022): 25-33]
 2019, Spring Marketing Ourselves to the Public [with Julie Sandys Bianchi, Joan Sh. Ox. Newsl., vol. 55/2: 20
  Leon & Kathryn Sharpe]
 2023 The Book that Shakespeare Gave Us or "The Book that Gave Us
  Shakespeare"? in *The First Folio—A Shakespearean Enigma*
  [*Brief Chronicles*, vol. VIII] (Stritmatter): 3-34

Mayer, Susanne
 2004 [review of *Will in der Welt* by Stephen Greenblatt] Die Zeit (Germany), issue 51
  [excerpt repr. in NSJ, vol. 11 (April 2011)]

McAree, J. V.
 1937, Aug. 2 Makes Shakespeare Look Dubious Globe & Mail, p. 6
 1937, Aug. 7 Shakespeare Fans Read the Column Globe & Mail, p. 6
 1937, Sept. 8 Another Claimant for Poet's Crown Globe & Mail, p. 6
  Response in SFE, no. 6: 2-5 (Nov. 1937).
 1940, Jan. 5 Barrell Rolls Out Some Rich Stuff Globe & Mail, p. 6
 1940, Jan. 13 Not a Controversy But a Good Imitation Globe & Mail, p. 6
 1955, June 27 It's Shakespeare, After All Globe & Mail, p. 6

McCabe, John
    1959, April 4   The Talk of the Town: Carmody's Torch   New Yorker, p. 29-31
    1959, June 20   The Talk of the Town: Straightforward Stratfordian [See comment   New Yorker, p. 23-24
            by Charlton Ogburn, SON, vol. 2/1: 2 (March 1996).

McCarter, Jeremy
    2002, April 23   What's In a Date?   New York Sun
    2010, May 2   A Question of Authorship [reviews of *Contested Will* by J. Shapiro   New York Times, p. 10-11
            and *Shakespeare's Lost Kingdom* by Charles Beauclerk]

McCarthy, Andrew D.
    1992, April   [review of *Profiling Shakespeare* by Marjorie Garber (2008)]   Rocky M. Rev., v. 62/2: 107-110

McCarthy, Dennis
    2018   *A Brief Discourse of Rebellion and Rebels by George North: A Newly Uncovered Manuscript Source for Shakespeare's Plays*. Cambridge: D. S. Brewer.

McCarthy, Patrick
    2012, Winter   [letter: mental contortions of orthodox critics such as Harold Bloom]   Sh. Matters, vol. 11/1: 2
    2017, Winter   Hamlet's Intent: A Comment and Query   Sh. Ox. Newsl., vol. 53/1: 11-14
            Response by Allan Shickman, Spring 2017, p. 5.
            Reply by McCarthy, same issue, p. 5-6.
    2017, Spring   [letter: response to Allan Shickman's letter and legal issues in *Hamlet*]   Sh. Ox. Newsl., vol. 53/2: 5-6

McCarthy, Penny
Books
    2006   *Pseudonymous Shakespeare*. Burlington: Ashgate Publishing Company.
Shorter pieces
    2009, Summer   *Cymbeline*: 'The First Essay of a New Brytish Poet'?   Critical Survey, v. 21/2: 43-59

McCauley, Mary C.
    2003, Jan. 2   Forever Bound: Books in a Folger Library Exhibit [. . . Highlight   Sun (Baltimore), p. 1C
            de Vere's Geneva Bible]
    2004, Oct. 9   By the Bard? Who Wrote All Those Shakespeare Plays?   Sun (Baltimore), p. 1D

McClarran, Steven [See Steven Steinburg]

McClinton, Brian
    2008   *The Shakespeare Conspiracies: Untangling a 400-Year Web of Myth and Deceit*. Belfast: Shanway Press.

McCombe, John P.
    2010   Henry James, Sh. Biography, and the Question of National Identity   Harry James Review, vol.
            in 'The Birthplace' and the 'Introduction' to *The Tempest*   31/2: 169-87

McConnaughey, Janet
    1988, Feb. 7   Two Lousianians Say Shakespeare Wasn't the One   New Orleans T-P, p. J2

McCormick, A. D.
    1934, Dec.   The Prince of Wales Christmas Card [shows Queen Elizabeth   Sh. Pictorial, no. 82: 190
            giving an audience to Shaespeare.]

McCray, Nancy
    2001, June   *The Shakespeare Conspiracy* [review of the *Frontline* documentary]   Booklist, p. 1903

McCrea, Scott
Books
    2005   *The Case for Shakespeare: The End of the Authorship Question*. Westport, CT and London: Praeger/Greenwood Publishing Group.

Shorter pieces
    2002, Winter   Two Shakespeares: A Skeptical Analysis of Shakespeare and His Works   Skeptic Mag., vol. 9/4: 70
            Reveals the Real Author
            Response by Diana Price, vol. 10/1: 22 (Spring 2003).
            See also Price's article, vol. 11/3: 10 (Fall 2004).
                Reply to Price by McCrea, vol. 12/1: 31-33 (Spring 2005).
                Response to Price by Barbara Lifton, vol. 12/1: 33 (Spring 2005).
    2005, Spring   [letter: response to Diana Price's Fall 2005 article]   Skeptic Mag., vol. 12/1: 31-33

McCrum, Robert
    1997, June 29   McCrum on Shakespeare   Observer, p. 9
    1997, July 19   Shakespeare's Genius the Key to the Mystery   Cincinnati Post, p. 11C

McCrum, Robert (continued)

1997, Nov. 2	McCrum on the Genius of Shakespeare	Observer, p. 15
2010, March 14	Who Wrote Shakespeare? Was It Really That 'Illiterate Third-Rate Actor' From the Provinces" [rev. of *Contested Will* by James Shapiro]	Observer, p. 18
2011, Oct. 23	Shakespeare or Anonymous [review of *Anonymous*]	Observer, p. 37
2011, Nov. 6	Where There's a Will . . . [review of *Anonymous*]	Observer, p. 42

McCullough, David

1984	Foreword to *The Mysterious William Shakespeare* by Charlton Ogburn, Jr. (and in 2nd edition, 1992). [repr. in SON, vol. 20/3: 2-3 (Summer 1984); and in BTC, vol. 6: 264-70]	

McDonnell, Tom

2016	*Sweete Wittie Soules: Shakespeare's Connections to Oxford, Town, Gown & Shire.* Oxford: Autolycus.	

McFarlane, Brian

2012, Autumn	Is This an Author I See Before Me? *Anonymous* and the Interminable Shakespeare Question	Screen Ed., issue 65: 30-37

McFee, William

1949	Introduction to *"Shakespeare" Identified* by J. T. Looney. [2nd ed.]	
1956, Jan. 10	Shakespeare and Stratford [letter] [repr. in SFE, p. 12 (Spring, 1956)]	NY Herald Trib., p. 22
1956, May	To the Editor and Readers of *The Shakespeare Newsletter* [with 21 other signatories]	Sh. Newsl., vol. 6/3: 18

McGeoch, Sir Ian L. M.

Books and pamphlets

Date not known	*Aspects of the Truth* [A pamphlet printed privately]	

Shorter pieces

1965, Autumn	[review of *Shakespeare and the Sea* by A. F. Falconer (1964)] [repr. in BTC, vol. 5, p. 170-172]	Sh. Authorship Rev. #14: 10-11

McGeoch, Ian

2000, Jan.	*Macbeth* Produced by the United Spirits Theatre	De Vere Soc. Newsl., p. 16
2001, Jan.	[letter: Southampton as son of Edward de Vere and Mary Browne]	De Vere Soc. Newsl., p. 19
2006, July	'In Loco Parentis' – An Heir and an Invention	De Vere Soc. Newsl., p. 5-7
2006, July	Note: Proposal to reprint several key texts in 3 volumes	De Vere Soc. Newsl., p. 23
2006, Nov. 17	[letter: de Vere as another Shakespeare Collaborator? [repr. in DVN (Feb. 2007), p. 22]	Times Lit. Sup.

McGlinchee, Claire

1930, Aug. 31	Esther Singleton [letter]	New York Times, p. X7

McGoogan, Ken

1997, May 10	Say Goodbye to . . . Shakespeare [review of *Alias Shakespeare* by Joseph Sobran (1997)	Calgary Herald, p. 1B

McGrath, Charles

2005, Oct. 29	Looking at Shakespeare, in 3 Different Ways	New York Times, p. B7

McGrath, Craig

2002, Winter	Orson the Oxfordian: Orson Welles's Shakespearean pursuits	Sh. Ox. Newsl., vol. 38/1: 8, 24

McGrath, William J.

1990, April 8	Freudian Pursuit	Newsday (Long Island), p. 24

McHenry, Robert

2011, Spring	Shakespeare and Biography [review of *Shakespeare and Biography* by David Bevington	Biograhy (Honolulu), vol. 34/2: 334+

McHugh, F. D.

1962	'Curst Be He That Moves My Bones' [letter]	Washington Star

McIntosh, P. D.

Books

2003	*Shakespeare's Sonnets: An Elizabethan Love Story.* Tasmania, Australia: Otakou Press.	

Shorter pieces

2010	The Fable of the Belly: A Reassessment of the Date of Composition of *Coriolanus*	Oxfordian, vol. 12: 65-74

McNeil, Alex (continued)

2010	*As You Like It* in *Dating Shakespeare's Plays* (Gilvary): 140-48	
2011, Winter	Wait Till They See This	Sh. Matters, vol. 10/1: 2-3
2011, Winter	Elliott Stone (1931-2010)	Sh. Matters, vol. 10/1: 6
2011, Winter	Joseph Sobran (1946-2010)	Sh. Matters, vol. 10/1: 28
2011, Spring	. . . But Not Shakespeare: Absence of Evidence or Evidence of Absence?	Sh. Matters, vol. 10/2: 1, 21-3
2011, Fall	*Anonymous* Dramatizes the Authorship Question	Sh. Matters, vol. 10/4: 3, 32
2011, Fall	*Anonymous* Generates Publishing Tsunami	Sh. Matters, vol. 10/4: 6
2012, Winter	Seventh Annual Joint Conference Held – *Anonymous* Screened	Sh. Matters, vol. 11/1: 1, 23-6
2012, Winter	Survey Says (2011)	Sh. Matters, vol. 11/1: 29-33
2012, Spring	Flabbergasted at the Academic Ring of Silence: Interview with Don Rubin [repr. in SAS (Stritmatter 2019, 2022): 93-95]	Sh. Matters, vol. 11/2: 25, 29
2012, Spring	*Last Will. & Testament* Screened at Shakespeare Authorship Studies [with Howard Schumann]	Sh. Matters, vol. 11/2: 1, 14-9
2012, Summer	From the Editor	Sh. Matters, vol. 11/3: 2, 28
2013	Doubter Response to Question #60: What do you think about Sh.'s reputation being stolen and passed off as someone else's? in *Sh. Beyond Doubt?* (Shahan): 215-16	
2013, Winter	From the Editor: Shakespeare in Prison	Sh. Matters, vol. 12/1: 3, 27
2013, Spring	From the Editor: Five Easy Pieces	Sh. Matters, vol. 12/2: 5, 27
2013, Summer	*Shakespeare Beyond Doubt* or *Sh. Beyond Doubt?* You Decide	Sh. Mat., vol. 12/3: 1, 19, 36
2013, Summer	From the Editors: A Brief History of Anonymity [repr. in BTC, vol. 9: 192-95]	Sh. Matters, vol. 12/3: 3, 35
2013, Fall	From the Editor: Goodbye and Hello!	Sh. Matters, vol. 12/4: 2
2014, Winter	From the Editor	Sh. Ox. Newsl., vol. 50/1: 3
2014, Summer	Shakespeare's Five "Outlier" Sonnets	Brief Chronicles, vol. V: 31-45
2014, Summer	From the Editor: Alvearie Interesting	Sh. Ox. Newsl., vol. 50/2: 16
2014, Summer	From the Editor: What's This "Genius" Thing, Anyway?	Sh. Ox. Newsl., vol. 50/3: 19-21
2014, Fall	"Authorship Appeal" Held at Stratford, Ontario, in Oct.: Presumption in Favor of Shakspere "Not Rebutted"	Sh. Ox. Newsl., vol. 50/4: 8-10
2014, Fall	Survey Says (2014)	Sh. Ox. Newsl., vol. 50/4: 16-19
2015, Spring	From the Editor: Professor Manfred Weidhorn	Sh. Ox. Newsl., vol. 51/2: 4
2015, Summer	From the Editor: Don Rubin's Interview with Wells and Edmondson	Sh. Ox. Newsl., vol. 51/3: 4
2015, Fall	In Memoriam: Charles Kellogg (1940-2015); Norman Robson (1925-2015); Patricia Urquhart (1946-2015)	Sh. Ox. Newsl., vol. 51/4: 7
2015, Fall	Record Attendance at 2015 SOF Conference in Ashland [with others]	Sh. Ox. Newsl., v. 51/4: 1, 22-30
2016, Spring	Jacobi and Rylance Go Public	Sh. Ox. Newsl., v. 52/2: 1, 27-29
2016, Spring	Shakespeare in Italy 2016: The Tour [with Ann Zakelj]	Sh. Ox. Newsl., v. 52/3: 1, 19-27
2016, Spring	Non-Stratfordians Observe Anniversary Worldwide [with J. Shahan]	Sh. Ox. Newsl., v. 52/2: 1, 24-26
2016, Fall	2016 SOF Conference Comes to Boston [with others]	Sh. Ox. Newsl., v. 52/4: 1, 18-30
2017, Winter	After "Thought Exercise," Folger is Even More Certain Shakspere is Shakespeare	Sh. Ox. Newsl., vol. 53/1: 15-16
2017, Spring	From the Editor	Sh. Ox. Newsl., vol. 53/2: 3-4
2017, Spring	A Late Summer Daydream [with Eliza. J. Rosenthal & Stanley Shur]	Sh. Ox. Newsl., vol. 52/3: 30
2017, Summer	From the Editor	Sh. Ox. Newsl., vol. 53/3: 4
2017, Summer	Acrostic	Sh. Ox. Newsl., vol. 53/3: 26-27
2017, Fall	SOF 2017 Conference Held in Chicago [with others]	Sh. Ox. Newsl., v. 53/4: 1, 27-36
2018, Winter	2017 SOF Conference Survey Results	Sh. Ox. Newsl., vol. 54/1: 12-15
2018, Spring	Sir Brian Vickers Looking for Publisher	Sh. Ox. Newsl., vol. 54/2: 31-32
2018, Fall	*Hamnet*: The Play's Not the Thing	Sh. Ox. Newsl., vol. 54/4: 21
2018, Fall	2018 SOF Conf. Report: Successful Interactions, Added Distractions 31 [with contributions by Bob Meyers, Earl Showerman, James Warren and Hank Whittemore]	Sh. Ox. Newsl., vol. 54/4: 1, 22-
2019, Winter	From the Editor: Authorial Identity	Sh. Ox. Newsl., vol. 55/1: 3-4
2019, Summer	Authorship Question Gets Major Media Coverage: Oxfordians Quoted in *New Yorker* Article	Sh. Ox. Newsl., vol. 55/3: 1, 13
2019, Summer	Authorship Question Gets Major Media Coverage: *The Atlantic*:	Sh. Ox. Newsl., v. 55/3: 1, 15-17
2019, Fall	*New Yorker* Article on Justice Stevens Generates Blowback "Was Shakespeare a Woman?"	Sh. Ox. Newsl., vol. 55/4: 9

Mermelstein, David
    2002, Feb. 10   Splitting the Credit Between a Bad Bard and a Gentle Will   New York Times, Sec. 2: 10

Merriam, Thomas
    1979   What Shakespeare Wrote in *Henry VIII*: Part One   Bard, vol. 2/3: 39-70
    1980   What Shakespeare Wrote in *Henry VIII*: Part Two   Bard, vol. 2/4: 111-118
    1981   *Henry VIII* and the Integrity of the *First Folio*   Bard, vol. 3/2: 69-73
    2001, Spring   Campion's Accuser and Sir Thomas More   Eliz. Review, online ed.

Merritt, Stephanie
    2023, June 18   In Search of a Bard [review of *Shakespeare Was a Woman and Other*   Guardian
                Heresies by Elizabeth Winkler]

Messner, Rhoda   H.
Books – fiction
    1975   *Absent Thee From Felicity: The Story of Edward de Vere, Seventeenth Earl of Oxford, a Biographical*
                Novel. Shaker Heights, OH: The Corinthian Press.
Shorter pieces
    1976, Fall   Rhoda Messner Answers Dr. Marder, Part 1   Sh. Ox. Newsl., vol. 12/3: 6-8
                [repr. in BTC, vol. 6: 94-106]
    1976, Winter   Rhoda Messner Answers Dr. Marder, Part 2   Sh. Ox. Newsl., vol. 12/4: 3-6
                [repr. in BTC, vol. 6: 94-106]
    1977, Spring   Rhoda Messner Answers Dr. Marder, Part 3   Sh. Ox. Newsl., vol. 13/1: 8-10
                [repr. in BTC, vol. 6: 94-106]
    1981, Spring   Notes on Two Noteworthy Books: *The Annotator* by Alan Keen and   Sh. Ox. Newsl., vol. 17/1: 4-5
                Roger Lubbock (1954) and *Case for Shakespeare's Authorship*
                of "The Famous Victories" by Seymour Pitcher (1961)
    1983, Spring   How I Became an Oxfordian [repr. in BTC, vol. 6: 240-41]   Sh. Ox. Newsl., vol. 19/2: 2-3

Metcalfe, Luisa
    2004, June 27   Shakespeare or Not Shakespeare? That Is the Question . . .   Daily Express, p. 63

Metcalfe, W. Day
    1938, Oct. 31   Shakespeare Plays: Several People Had Hand in Composition [letter]   Yorkshire Post & LI, p. 3

Metternich, Hilary Roe
    2011, Jan.   In Memory of Richard Roe (d. 2010)   Sh. Ox. Newsl., vol. 47/1: 22-23
    2012, Spring   [letter: Roe's *Shakespeare Guide to Italy*]   Sh. Ox. Newsl., vol. 48/2: 2

Meyers, Bob
Columns edited
    2016-current: How I Became an Oxfordian [SOF website]
Shorter pieces
    2018, Fall   [contributions to the SOF Conference Report]   Sh. Ox. Newsl., v. 54/4: 1, 22-31
    2019, Winter   Q & A with Steven Sabel   Sh. Ox. Newsl., v. 55/1: 1, 30-32
    2021, Fall   President's Column   Sh. Ox. Newsl., vol. 57/4: 2
    2022, Winter   President's Column   Sh. Ox. Newsl., vol. 58/1: 2
    2022, Spring   President's Column: SOF and Podcaster Part Company   Sh. Ox. Newsl., vol. 58/2: 2-3
    2022, Summer   Special Section: SOF Election   Sh. Ox. Newsl., vol. 58/3: 15-18
    2022, Fall   In Memoriam: Warren Hope (1944-2022)   Sh. Ox. Newsl., vol. 58/4: 15
    2023, Summer   Prophets Without Honor: From Galileo to Looney   J. of Scientific Expl., vol. 37/2

Mez, John R.
Books
    1952   *Edward de Vere – or "Shakespeare": A Bibliography Compiled by J. R. Mez.* Ruvigliana, Switzerland:
                Printed privately.
    1950   *Der Wahre Shakespeare, XVII. Earl of Oxford.* Stuttgart: Origo-Verlag Zurich [translation of Charlton and
                Dorothy's *The Renaissance Man of England*]
Shorter pieces
    1952, March   News From Switzerland   SF News-letter (E), p. 9
    1952, March   [review of *Shakespeare's Farewell*, a pamphlet by Gw. Bowen]   SF News-letter (E), p. 10
    1952, Sept.   [review of *George Gascoigne, or Edward de Vere* by Wil. Kittle]   SF News-letter (E), p. 3-4
    1953, April   [review of *This Star of England* by Dorothy and Charlton Ogburn]   SF News-letter (E), p. 7-8
    1953, Nov.   Informative Booklets   SF News-letter (E), p. 10-11.
    1954, April   [letter: books by William Kittle]   SF News-letter (E), p. 15
    1954, Sept.   Gascoigne and De Vere [repr. in BTC, vol. 4, p. 135-137]   SF News-letter (E), p. 9-10

1955, July 10	[letter: Alfred Harbage's June 12 article]	New York Times, p. BR12
1955, Autumn	The Poet With a Speare [letter] [repr. in BTC, vol. 4, p. 138-140]	SF News-letter (E), p. 7-8
1956, Autumn	[letter: kingdom and grave]	SF News-letter (E), p. 11
1955, Autumn	[letter: Hilda Amphlett's book *Who Was Shakespeare?*]	SF News-letter (E), p. 11-12
1956, Spring	[letter: correction]	SF News-letter (E), p. 12

Michalopoulos, Andre

1956, May	To the Editor and Readers of *The Shakespeare Newsletter* [letter, with 21 other signers]	Sh. Newsl., vol. 6/3: 18

Michel, Roer

1999, June 6	Good Question! Did He Or Didn't He?	Boston Herald, p. 48

Michell, John

Books

1996	*Who Wrote Shakespeare?* New York: Thames and Hudson. [Translated into German by Reinhard Kaiser as *Wer schrieb Shakespeare?* Frankfurt am Main: Aweitausendeins, 2001.] [Japanese tr. by Kenji Takahashi as *Sheikusupia wa Dokoniiru?* Tokyo: Bungei Shunju, 2000.] [excerpt repr. in *Shakespeare Criticism, vol. 41* (Lee & Barnes 1998): 2-5]	

Shorter pieces

1995	[review of *The Alternative Shakespeare: A Modern Introduction* by A. M. Challinor (1996)]	Baconiana, vol. 77/194: 102+
1995, Nov.	[excerpt from an article in *Oldie Magazine*]	De Vere Soc. Newsl., vol. 2/3: 7
1998, Fall	[letter: anagrams and the authorship issue] Response by Richard Whalen, same issue, page.	Sh. Ox. Newsl., vol. 34/3: 25

Millar, J. S. L.

1934, April	The Shakespeare Group	Sh. Pictorial, no. 74: 63
1934, Dec.	Shakespeare and *Sir Thomas More*	Sh. Pictorial, no. 82: 192
1936, Jan.	Falstaff's Last Utterance	Sh. Pictorial, no. 95: 8

Miller, Darren W.

2008	*Web of Conspiracy: A Guide to Conspiracy Theory Sites on the Internet* [with James F. Broderick]. Medford, NJ: Information Today.	

Miller, Eric

2006	Dating Sonnet 107: Shakespeare and the "Mortal Moone"	Oxfordian, vol. 9: 67-80

Miller, J. Valcour

1975	Corambis, Polonius, and the Great Lord Burghley in *Hamlet*	Oxfordian Vistas, p. 430-447

Miller, Michael

1990, April 21	Computer Test Authenticates Shakespeare	Washington Post, p. C3

Miller, Jr., Judge Minos D.

1972, Winter	Address on the Shakespearean Authorship Society's 50th Anniversary [repr. in BTC, vol. 5, p. 322-331]	Sh. Authorship Rev., #27: 1-8
1988, Spring	The Dating of *The Tempest* and "Ostler v. Hemings"	Sh. Ox. Newsl., vol. 24/2: 6-8

Miller, Nathan L.

1952	*A Lawyer's Evaluation of the Evidence Related to the Authorship of the Shakespeare Literature*. New York: Nathan Miller.	

Miller, Ruth Loyd

Books edited

1974	*Hidden Allusions in Shakespeare's Plays: A Study of the Early Court Revels and Personality of the Times,* by Eva Turner Clark. Third revised edition, with introduction and additional notes by the editor and others. Port Washington, NY: Kennikat Press.
1975	*"Shakespeare" Identified in Edward de Vere, Seventeenth Earl of Oxford* [by J. Thomas Looney], 3rd revised, annotated ed.; *The Poems of Edward de Vere* [with biographical notes] by J. Thomas Looney [2nd ed.] Published in one volume, along with a second volume of articles, *Oxfordian Vistas*. Port Washington, NY: Kennikat Press for Minos Pub. Co.
1975	*A Hundreth Sundrie Flowres: From the Original Edition of 1573, by George Gascoigne, with an introduction by Bernard Mordaunt Ward.* 2nd edition. Additional notes by the editor and others. Port Washington, NY: Printed by Kennikat Press for Minos Pub. Co.
1979	*The Seventeenth Earl of Oxford, 1550-1604, From Contemporary Documents, by Bernard M. Ward.* [made available in an authorized photocopy]

Miller, Ruth Loyd (continued)

Shorter pieces

1974	[five-page letter to the *American Bar Association Journal*, dated December 6, 1974, in response to "Who Wrote Shakespeare?" in the October 1974 issue; unpublished, but is item DVS129 in the De Vere Society Archives at Brunel University]	
1975	The First Folio: A Family Affair	Oxfordian Vistas, p. 1-31
1975	The Elliptical Suggestions by William Basse, Ben Jonson, and Percival Golding That Lord Oxford Was Buried at Westminster Abbey	Oxfordian Vistas, p. 31-43
1975	Ben Jonson and the Arms of Sogliardo	Oxfordian Vistas, p. 44-51
1975	The Two Annes and Their Sons	Oxfordian Vist., p. 53-85, 94-105
1975	Contemporary Documents Show Lord Oxford Was Referred to As "The Lord Chamberlain"	Oxfordian Vistas, p. 106-161
1975	The Sidney-Cecil-Oxford Triangle and *The Merry Wives of Windsor*	Oxfordian Vistas, p. 161-168
1975	Cecil Plays the Marriage Game: The "Engagement" of Elizabeth de Vere and the Earl of Southampton	Oxfordian Vistas, p. 177-186
1975	Shake-Speare's Sonnets: 1909	Oxfordian Vistas, p. 206-237
1975	Some Pleas for Common Sense	Oxfordian Vistas, p. 244-273
1975	An Authorship Lawsuit: *Re Hopkins' Will and Trust*, 1964	Oxfordian Vistas, p. 273-280
1975	The Uncontradicted Testimony . . . That William Shakespeare . . . Was Dead in 1615	Oxfordian Vistas, p. 280-283
1975	Strange Silences	Oxf. Vistas, p. 283-86, 303-5
1975	The Forgeries	Oxfordian vistas, p. 324-340
1975	A Computer-Aided Stylistic Analysis	Oxfordian Vistas, p. 340-355
1975	The Cornwallis-Lysons Manuscript	Oxfordian Vistas, p. 369-394
1975	Rowland Yorke: Oxford's Receiver – Othello's Iago: 1576-1581	Oxfordian Vistas, p. 395-404
1975	Lord Oxford and the "Shakespeare" Portraits	Oxfordian Vistas, p. 405-429
1975	Lord Oxford's Office	Oxfordian Vistas, p. 448-483
1975	A Contemporary Notes Shakespeare's Strange Silence on the Passing of Elizabeth	Oxfordian Vistas, p. 484-486
1975	The Earl of Oxford – Patron of the English Renaissance	Oxfordian Vistas, p. 486-533
1990, Spr.	On Dating *The Tempest*	Sh. Newsl., vol. 40/1: 12
1990, Sum.	Three Shakspere Signatures Down the Drain	Sh. Newsl., vol. 40/2: 22-23
1990, Sum.	Notes on Claremont McKenna Shakespeare Project	Sh. Newsl., vol. 40/2:26
1996, Spr.	Letter from the Millers to SON Members	Sh. Ox. Newsl., vol. 32/2: 21
2005, Fall	The Crown Signature: an enigma awaiting time's solution [printed from an unpublished manuscript written in 1988]	Sh. Matters, vol. 5/1: 9, 28-29
2006	Oaths Foresworn in *Love's Labour's Lost* [previously unpublished]	Oxfordian, vol. 9: 35-50

Milligan, Burton A.

1949	*Digesta Anti-Shakespeareana* by Joseph S. Galland. Edited and compmleted by Milligan after Galland's death. [has more than 4,500 entries]. UMI Dissertation Information Service.	

Milmo, Cahal

2005, Sept. 14	Revealed: The Rape Trial That Inspired Shakespeare [repr. in DVN (Sept. 2005), p. 46]	Independent

Milner-Gulland, Nick

2000	[letter: Ian Johnson's vol. 127 letter re canals in Italy] Reply by Johnson in DVN (Jan. 2000), p. 14.	Oldie, vol. 128

Milward, Peter

1979, Spring	[review of *Shakespeare By Hilliard* by Leslie Hotson (1977)]	Sh. Ox. Newsl., vol. 28: 88-92
1976	Shakespeare and the Religious Controversies of His Time	Bard, vol. 1/2: 65-72
1983	[rev. of *Catholic Loyalism in Elizabethan England* by A. Pritchard]	Bard, vol. 4/1: 22-25
2013, Nov.	[review of *The Assassination of Shakespeare's Patron* by L. Daugherty	Heythorp Jour., v. 54/6: 1048-50

Mimmermus

1935, March 10	Shakespeare's Secularism	Freethinker, vol. 55/10: 147-8

Minchin, H. C.

1920, April 4	Who Was Shakespeare? [review of SI]	Sunday Times, p. 5

Miss Manners
2014, March 6	Dear Miss Manners: Must an English Department Secretary Defend Shakespearean Authorship to Conspiracy Theorists?	Washington Post
2014, March 15	Crank Letters Need No Response	Times (London), p. E7

Mitchell, Henry
1989, April 21	Shakespeare and the Will of the World	Washington Post, p. C2

Mitchell, John
Books
1996	*Who Wrote Shakespeare?* New York: Thames and Hudson.	

Shorter pieces
1998, Fall	[letter: anagrams and the authorship issue]	Sh. Ox. Newsl., vol. 34/3: 25

Mitgang, Herbert
1985, Feb. 9	'Blood!' Still Feuding Over the Bard	New York Times, p. 9

Mithoff, H. W.
1962, Sept. 23	Shakespeare's Tomb	Chicago Tribune, p. 20

Mixter, Clara
1993, Winter	"Flights of Angels sing thee to thy rest" [excerpts from obituary of William P. Fowler by his daughter] [repr. in BTC, vol. 7: 146-47)	Sh. Ox. Newsl., vol. 29/1a: 4

Moffat, David
2005, Summer	[letter: resp. to Hank Whittemore's Winter 2005 "*Monument*" letter]	Sh. Matters, vol. 4/4: 2-4
2006, Summer	Some Principles of Sonnet Dedication Solutions	Sh. Matters, vol. 5/4: 18-20
2009, Summer	[letter: lack of evidence for the Stratford man]	Sh. Matters, vol. 8/3: 2
2013, Spring	The Shakespearean Trajectory	Sh. Matters, vol. 1, 23-24
2016, Fall	Problems with Matrix Ciphers	Sh. Ox. Newsl., vol. 52/4: 31-32

Mollow, Benjamin R.
1988, Summer	Knyvet, King of Cats	Sh. Ox. Newsl., vol. 24/4: 14

Molnar, Michael
2012, Spring	Freud in the National Portrait Gallery	Am. Imago, vol. 69/1: 107-33

Molotsky, Irvin
1987, Sept. 26	You-Know-Who Wrote the Plays, Judges Say	New York Times, p. 1, 13
1987, Sept. 27	Justices Find All's Well for Shakespeare	Chicago Tribune, p. 3

Moncrief, Earnest
2019, Winter	Edward de Vere, an Insinuator like Hamlet	Sh. Ox. Newsl., vol. 55/1: 21-24
2021, Winter	Falstaff—Unmasked	Sh. Ox. Newsl., v. 57/1: 1, 11-14
2022, Winter	[letter: *Venus and Adonis* and *Lucrece*]	Sh. Ox. Newsl., vol. 58/1: 3

Mongillo, Peter
2011, Oct. 28	Shakespeare Not Playwright? [review of *Anonymous*]	Austin Am.-Statesman, p. D1

Monk, Linda R.
1999, Jan. 30	[letter: Don Oldenburg's Jan. 24 article]	Washington Post, p. A17

Montagne, Renee
Radio programs hosted
2008, July 3	Who Wrote Shakespeare's Plays? Debate goes on [transcript of "Morning Edition" broadcast with Daniel Wright, Diana Price and Stephen Greenblatt]	National Public Radio
2008, July 4	The Real Shakespeare? Evidence Points to Earl [transcript of "Morning Edition" broadcast with J. Shapiro, Mark Rylance, Ch. Beauclerk, Mark Anderson, Daniel Wright, and Ken. Branagh]	National Public Radio

Montee, David
2014	*Translating Shakespeare: A Guide for Young Actors*. Hanover, NH: Smith and Kraus. [excerpt repr. in *Sh. Authorship Sourcebook* (Stritmatter 2019, 2022): 99-115]	

Montgomery, Robert H.
1956, April 1	De Vere Theory [letter, with Charles D. Drayton and Ch. Ogburn]	NY Herald Tribune, p. A4
1956, May	To the Editor and Readers of *The Shakespeare Newsletter* [letter, with 21 other signers]	Sh. Newsl., vol. 6/3: 18
1956, Dec. 30	Who Wrote Shakespeare? A Boston Scholar Considers the Evidence	Boston Globe, p. A9

Montgomery, Robert H. (continued)

1957, Jan. 6	More on Shakespeare Controversy From an Oxfordian Scholar	Boston Globe, p. A13
1957, Jan. 13	*Romeo and Juliet* from an Oxfordian Point of View	Boston Globe, p. A13
1965, Aug. 23	Was Shakespeare Shakespeare? Maybe . . . [review of *Was Shakespeare Shakespeare* by Milward W. Martin (1965)]	Boston Globe, p. 16

Articles about Robert H. Montgomery

1953, Oct. 25	Durgin, Cyrus: Were the Sh. Plays Written by Earl of Oxford? [resp. to Montgomery's Oxfordian speech given in Spring 1953]	Boston Globe, p. A55

Moody, Ellen

1989, Spring	Six Elegiac Poems, Possibly by Anne Cecil de Vere, Countess of Oxford [see also her response to critiques, at http://www.jimandellen.org/anne.cecil.poems.html]	Eng. Lit. Ren., v. 19/2: 152-70

Moody, Patrick

1988, Jan.	[report on El. Appleton's Oct. 14, 1987 lecture "Edward de Vere: Man of Mystery"]	De Vere Soc. Newsl., vol. 1: 4-6

Moore, Cynthia

2023, Winter	[letter: Shakespeare authorship question]	Sh. Ox. Newsl., vol. 59/1: 3-4

Moore, Harvey T.

1948, Aug. 3	Memo to Mr. Burgess [letter]	Washington Post, p. 10

Moore, Peter R.

Books

2009	*The Lame Storyteller, Poor and Despised.* Edited by Gary B. Goldstein. Buchholz, Germany: Verlag Uwe Laugwitz. [Special Editions #1 of *Neues Shake-speare Journal*]

Shorter pieces

1988, Winter	A Theory on the Rival Poet of Shakespeare's Sonnets	Sh. Ox. Newsl., vol. 24/1: 3
1988, Winter	A Theory on *The Two Noble Kinsmen* [repr. in LS, p. 203-07]	Sh. Ox. Newsl., vol. 24/1: 9-11
1988, Summer	Shakespeare's Astronomy [repr. in LS, p. 244-245, and in German in NSJ, vol. 5: 10-11]	Sh. Ox. Newsl., vol. 24/3: 5
1988, Summer	Ben Jonson's "On Poet-Ape" [repr. in LS, p. 200-02]	Sh. Ox. Newsl., vol. 24/3: 7-9
1988, Fall	Neglected Praise of the Earl of Oxford [repr. in LS, p. 231-233]	Sh. Ox. Newsl., vol. 24/4: 7-8
1989, Winter	Suffolk's Head and Royal Behavior [repr. in LS, p. 246-247]	Sh. Ox. Newsl., vol. 25/1: 4-5
1989, Summer	Masked Adonis and Stained Purple Robes [repr. in LS, p. 224-230]	Sh. Ox. Newsl., vol. 25/3: 9-12
1989, Fall	The Rival Poet of Shakespeare's *Sonnets* [repr. in RCA, p. 15-20; in LS, p. 2-11; in TOX, vol. 18: 133-140; and in German in NSJ, vol. 5: 130-41 (2000)]	Sh. Ox. Newsl., vol. 25/4: 8-11
1990, Winter	Dating Shakespeare's Sonnets 78 to 100 [repr. in LS, p. 12-17; and in German in NSJ, vol. 12: 23-30 (2008)]	Sh. Ox. Newsl., vol. 26/1: 11-13
1990, Spring	The Symbolism of Iago's Name [repr. in BTC, vol. 6: 414]	Sh. Ox. Newsl., vol. 26/2: 2-3
1990, Spring	Every Word Doth Almost Tell My Name [repr. in LS, p. 18-23; and in German in NSJ, vol. 12: 31-41 (2008)]	Sh. Ox. Newsl., vol. 26/2: 12-15
1990, Summer	Claremont McKenna College's Shakespeare Clinic [repr. in LS, p. 282-287; and in German in NSJ, vol. 12: 42-48 (2008)]	Sh. Ox. Newsl., vol. 26/3: 7-10
1990, Fall	The Order of Shakespeare's *Sonnets* [repr. in LS, p. 24-32; and in RCA, p. 23-29]	Sh. Ox. Newsl., vol. 26/4: 9-13
1991, Summer	The Fable of the World, Twice Told (Part 1) [repr. in LS, p. 248-262; and in BTC, vol. 7: 58-62]	Sh. Ox. Newsl., vol. 27/3: 8-10
1991, Fall	The Fable of the World, Twice Told (Part 2) [repr. in LS, p. 248-262; and in BTC, vol. 7: 62-68]	Sh. Ox. Newsl., vol. 27/4: 5-9
1991, Fall	The Dates of Shakespeare's Plays [repr. in EVR, vol. 3 (Sum. 1996)]	Sh. Newsl., vol. 41/3: 40
1991, Winter	*Groatsworth* and Shake-scene [repr. in LS, p. 219-223]	Sh. Newsl., vol. 41/4: 56
1993, Spring	Shake-hyphen-speare [repr. in LS, p. 208-210] Response by Johanna Tabin, Autumn 1993, p. 6.	Eliz. Review, vol. 1/1: 58-60
1993, Winter	The Stella Cover-Up [repr. in DVN, vol. 17/1: 14-18 (Feb. 2010); in LS, p. 312-321 (2009); in EVR, vol. 9 (Fall 1999); and in	Sh. Ox. Newsl., vol. 29/1a: 12-17

German in NSJ, vol. 9: 8-19 (2004)]

1994, Spring	The Demolition of Shakspere's Signatures [repr. in LS, p. 211-213]	Sh. Ox. Newsl., vol. 30/2a: 1-2
1994, Autumn	Kill, Kill, Kill (repr. in LS, p. 152-154)	Eliz. Review, vol. 2/2: 19-22
1994, Autumn	Stratfordians Prove the Bard Had a University Degree [repr. in LS, p. 214-18; in BTC, vol. 7: 281-84; and in *Lame Storyteller* (2009): 214-218]	Sh. Ox. Newsl., vol. 30/4: 1-3
1994, Dec.	Did Raleigh Try to Kill Essex? [repr. in German in NSJ, vol. NS4: 109-17 (Oct. 2014)]	Notes & Q., vol. 41/4: 463-67
1994, Dec.	Ophelia's False Steward [repr. in LS, p. 44-45]	Notes & Q., vol. 41/4: 488-89
1995, Spring	[response to Alan Nelson's "Oxford in Venice"] [repr. in BTC, vol. 7: 320-25; repr. as "Oxford in Venice: New Light on an Old Question,: in LS (2009): 275-281]	Sh. Ox. Newsl., vol. 31/2b: 7-10
1995, Summer	The Lame Storyteller, Poor and Despised [repr. in ER, vol. 3/2: 4-10; and in LS, p. 234-43; and in German in NSJ, vol. 8: 9-20 (Aug. 2003)]	Sh. Ox. Newsl., vol. 31/3: 17-22
1995, Sept.	The Date of F.B.'s Verse Letter to Ben Jonson	Notes & Q., vol. 42/3: 347-52
1996, Spring	Oxford, the Order of the Garter, and Shame [repr. in RCA p. 23-29; in LS, p. 263-74; in LC, p. 45-50; in EVR, vol. 5 (Winter 1997); and in German in NSJ, vol. 12: 7-22 (2008)]	Sh. Ox. Newsl., vol. 32/2: 1, 8-11
1996, June	Shakespeare's Iago and Santiago Matamoros [repr. in LS, p. 147-48]	Notes & Q., vol. 43/2: 162-63
1996, Summer	*The Tempest* and the Bermuda Shipwreck of 1609 [repr. in BTC, vol. 7: 355-58; and in EVR, vol. 3 (Sum. 1996)]	Sh. Ox. Newsl., vol. 32/3: 6
1997, Winter	Recent Developments in the Case for Oxford as Shakespeare [from a paper given at the SOS Conference in October 1996]	Ever Reader, vol. 4
1997, Autumn	The Abysm of Time: The Chronology of Shakespeare's plays [repr. in LS, p. 159-199 (2009); and in German in NSJ, vol. 4: 10-59 (July 1999)]	Eliz. Rev., vol. 5/2: 24-60
1997, Dec.	Hamlet and the Two Witness Rule [repr. in LS, p. 33-43]	Notes & Q., vol. 44/4: 498
1998, Summer	[letter: praise for Ogburn's reticence about expressing political opinions in his work]	Sh. Ox. Newsl., vol. 34/2: 21
2001	The Heraldic Charge Against the Earl of Surrey, 1546-47	Eng. Historical Rev., vol. 116/467: 557
2003	The Irony of Marvell's Horatian Ode	English Studies, v. 84/1: 33-56
2003, Dec.	The Earl of Surrey's Quarrel with George Blage	Notes & Q., v. 248/4: 386-90
2004, Winter	Demonography 101: Alan Nelson's *Monstrous Adversary* (2003) [repr. in LS, p. 288-311]	Sh. Ox. Newsl., v. 40/1: 1, 15-22
2004, Spring	*Hamlet* and *Piers Plowman*: A Matter of Conscience [repr. in LS, p. 61-96]	Cashiers Elis., p. 11-24
2004, June	Neuere Entwicklungen in der Frage von Oxfords Verfasserschaft [repr. from *Ever Reader* 4 (October 1996)] [Übersetzt, kommentiert und ergänzt von Robert Detobel]	Neues Sh. Journal, vol. 9: 48-82
2009, Sept.	A Biblical Echo in *Romeo and Juliet* [repr. in LS, p. 149-151]	Notes & Q., vol. 51/3: 278-79
2009	Epicurean Time in *Macbeth*	Brief Chronicles, vol. I: 141-154
2009	*Hamlet* and Surrey's Psalm 8, in *Lame Storyteller*, p. 46-60	
2009	The Nature of *King Lear*, in *Lame Storyteller*, p. 97-127	
2009	The Role of Time in *Macbeth*, in *Lame Storyteller*, p. 128-146 [repr. in NSJ, Vol, NS3: 57-84 (March 2013)]	
2009	Developments in the Case for Oxford as Shakespeare, in *Lame Storyteller*, p. 322-343	

Morfey, Mr.

1938, Jan.	Shakespeare, Suffolk Poets, and Others [letter: Ward's Oct. article]	East Angl. Mag., vol. 3/4: 177-78
1938, April	[letter: further response to Ward]	East Angl. Mag., vol. 3/6: 291-92

Morgan, Appleton

1881	*The Shakespearean Myth: William Shakespeare and Circumstantial Evidence*. Cincinnati: R. Charles & Co.

Morgan, E.

1938, Jan.	[letter: Shakespeare's remarkable knowledge of Italy]	SF News-letter (E), no. 7: 9-10

Morgenstern, Joe
    2011, Oct. 28   *Anonymous* Is Much Ado About Nothing   Wall St. Journal, p. D3

Moriarty, Coleen (with Michael Delahoyde)
    2016, Winter   New Evidence of Oxford in Venice   Sh. Ox. Newsl., v. 52/1: 1, 29-32
    2017, Spring   Vanishing Vere in Venice   Sh. Ox. Newsl., vol. 52/3: 26-28
    2018, Sept.   The 17th Earl of Oxford in Italian Archives: Love's Labours Found   Oxfordian, vol. 20: 27-48

Morris, Carolyn
    2013   Did Joseph Hall and Ben Jonson Identify Oxford as Shakespeare?   Oxfordian, vol. 15: 5-26
    2016, December   An Arrogant Joseph Hall and an Angry Ed. de Vere in *Virgidemiarum*   Brief Chronicles, vol. VII: 33-82

Morris, James W.
    1941, Oct.   [letter]   SF News-letter (A), vol. 2/6: 72

Morris, Nigel
    1999, Oct. 27   Descendant of Nell Gwynne's Wacky Campaigns [Burford]   Daily Record (Glasgow), p. 4

Morris, Steve
    1989, May 10   Detective Story: Who Wrote Shakespeare?   Philadel. Welcomat, p. 3, 28-32

Morris, Wesley
    2011, Oct. 28   Blow Up Your Shakespeare: Director Emmerich Blasts the Bard   Boston Globe
            in *Anonymous*

Morrison, Patt
    2011, Oct. 29   Who Wrote Shakespeare? [review of *Anonymous*]   Los Angeles Times, p. A19

Morrison, Richard
    2002, March 14   Shakespeare – Genius, Blackmailer and All-Round Clever Chap   Times (London), p. 7
            [notes Roger Stritmatter's work tying annotated passages in
            de Vere's Geneva Bible to Shakespeare's plays]

Morton, Peter
    1998, Autumn   [review of *De Vere is Shakespeare* by Dennis Baron (1997)]   Eliz. Review, vol. 6/2: 84-87
    1999, Sept.   Novel Oxfords [reviews of *The Lost Chronicles of Edward de Vere*   Early Mod. Lit. Studies,
            by Andrew Fields (1990) and *Absent Thee From Felicity*   vol. 5/2: 6-19
            by Rhoda Henry Messner (1975)]

Moser, Franz
    2016   *Shakespere ist nicht Shake-speare? Uber den wahren Autor des Shakespeare-Kanons Edward de Vere, Earl*
            of Oxford [*Shakespeare is Not Shake-speare?: About the True Author of Shakespeare's Canon, Edward*
            de Vere, Earl of Oxford]. Uwe Laugwitz. [German]

Mosher, Sally
    1995, Spring   Was William Byrd's *The Battell* Composed for the Theatre?   Eliz. Review, vol. 3/1: 32-36
    1996, Summer   Music Named for Edward de Vere   Sh. Ox. Newsl., vol. 32/3: 18, 23
    1998   William Byrd's *Battle* and the Earl of Oxford   Oxfordian, vol. 1: 43-52
    2006, Spring   [reply: Hughes's Winter 2006 "Oxford's Childhood" article]   Sh. Ox. Newsl., vol. 42/2: 9
            Reply by Stephanie Hopkins Hughes, same issue, p. 9.
    2007   [letter: Shahan-Elliott debate at Shakespeare Authorship Roundtable]   Oxfordian, vol. 10: 162-163
    2008, Spring   Dueling Stylometricians: Shahan vs. Elliott   Sh. Matters, vol. 7/3: 5, 14, 32

Moskovich, Irina
    2007, Fall   [letter: Shakespeare and the 6th Earl of Derby and Mary Sidney]   Sh. Matters, vol. 7/1: 2, 31

Moss, Stephen
    2000, Oct. 9   The Doubters' Arguments Against Shakespeare   Guardian, p. 9

Mott, Agnes
    1931, July 6   Shakespeare's Friend [letter]   Morning Post, p. 5

Mucci, John
Broadcasts
    1992, Sept. 17   *Frontline: Uncovering Shakespeare: An Update* [an interacctive videoconference on VisNet hosted by
            William F. Buckley, Jr., with 15 guests, including Charles Boyle, Warren Hope, Felicia Londré, Roger
            Stritmatter an Charles Vere. Produced by John Mucci and Gary Goldstein. See Hope and Holsten
            (2009) for fuller description]
Shorter pieces
    1997, Spring   [review of *Alias Shakespeare* by Joseph Sobran (1997)]   Eliz. Review. vol. 5/1: 59-61

| 1998, Autumn | [review of *Rogues, Vagabonds and Sturdy Beggars*, edited by Arthur F. Kinney (1990)] | Eliz. Review, vol. 6/2: 79-84 |
| 1998, Autumn | [review of CD: *The Food of Love: Words and Music for Sh.'s Theater* by the Gesualdo Consort (1996)] | Eliz. Review, vol. 6/2: 88-89 |

Mudge, G. O.
| 1933, March 19 | New Questioning of Shakespeare [review of *The Satirical Comedy: Love's Labour's Lost* by Eva Turner Clark] | News & Obs. (Raleigh), p. 5 |

Muir, Kenneth
| 1953, June 12 | [review of *This Star of England* by Dorothy and Charlton Ogburn] | Spectator, vol. 190: 768 |
| 1962, July 19 | [review of *The Shakespeare Claimants* by Harry N. Gibson (1962)] | Listener, vol. 68: 109 |

Mukherjee, Tapan Kumar
| 2015, April | [letter: I am what I am] | De Vere Soc. Newsl., v. 22/2: 47 |

Mullan, John
| 2007 | *Anonymity: A Secret History of English Literature*. London: Faber and Faber; and Princeton: Princeton University Press. PR121 M85 2007 | |

Mullinix, Donna
| 1995, April 2 | [Charles Vere, Earl of Burford, to speak] | Indianapolis News, p. J4 |

Mumpsimum
| 1948, Aug. 8 | Who Was Shakespeare? [letter: Burgess's July 31 article] | Washington Post, p. B4 |

Munsell, Warren P., Jr.
| 1940 | *By Any Other Name* [dramatization of the life of Edward Earl of Oxford] | |

Murray, Geoffrey
| 1969, Sept. 25 | Stratford on Edge Over Bard Doubters | Los Angeles Times, p. G21 |

Murry, John M.
| 1920, May 13 | The Function of Criticism | Times Lit. Sup., is. 956: 289 |
| 1921, June 2 | Hamlet and History | Times Lit. Sup., 1011: 345+ |

Müller, Burkhard
| 2007, April | [review of *Fortunatus im Unglück* by Ed. de Vere, Earl of Oxford] | Neues Sh. Journal, v. 11: 183-85 |

Musel, Robert
| 1948, Jan. 12 | Spiritual Talks: Shakespeare Breaks Long Silence; Mysteries Solved? [review of *Talks with Elizabethans* by Percy Allen] | South China Morning Post, p. 6 |

Mutschmann, M.
| 1934, March 1 | The 'Mortal Moon' Sonnet [letter] | Times Lit. Sup., is. 1674: 144 |

Myers, Alan
| 1995 | *Myers' Literary Guide: The North East* (Lives & Letters). Mid Northumberland Arts Group. Careanet Press. | |

Myers, Marc
| 2014, April 19 | Photographer William Wegman on Composer William Byrd | Wall Street Journal, p. C13 |

Mysak, Joe
| 1984, Nov. 2 | Random Notes [brief review of *The Mysterious William Shakespeare*] | National Review, p. 49 |

Newsl. U. J.
| 1960, Autumn | [report on Gwynneth Bowen's March 5, 1960 talk "Towards an Oxfordian Chronology"] | Sh. Authorship Review, #4: 14 |

Nabokov, Vladimir
| 2013, March | Vladimir Nabokov über Shakespeare (1924) (Nachdichtung von Frank-Patrick Steckel) | Neues Sh. Journal, v. NS3: 38-39 |

Nash, Paul Newsl.
| 1996, Summer | [letter: Joseph Sobran] | Sh. Ox. Newsl., vol. 32/3: 21 |
| 1999, Summer | [letter: Caesar and Brutus – father and son] | Sh. Ox. Newsl., vol. 35/2: 26-27 |

Nashe, T.
| 1956, June 3 | The Sands of Time [letter: Ogburn's May 11 letter] | Washington Post, p. E4 |

Nashe, Tom, Jr.
| 1940, Aug./Sept. | First Play Presenting Oxford as "Shakespeare" | SF News-letter (A), vol. 1/5: 12 |

Nassivera, John
  1988   *All the Queen's Men*. [a two-act play; unpublished].

Navarre, Alan
  2009   *The Crown Signature*. [a three-act play based on the life of Edward de Vere]

Neale, J. W.
  1938, Oct. 27   An Exponent of the De Vere Theory [letter]   Yorkshire Post & Leeds Int., p. 4

Neihardt, John G.
  1934, Dec. 30   Of Making Many Books [review of *Lord Oxford was Shakespeare*   St. Louis Post Dispatch, p. 14
                 by Col. Montagu W. Douglas]

Neilson, Francis
  1951, June 1   Mr. Brophy and Shakespeare [letter]   Truth, p. 589

Nelson, Alan H.
Books
  2003   *Monstrous Adversary: The Life of Edward de Vere, 17th Earl of Oxford*. Liverpool: Liverpool University
                 Press. [rxcerpt repr. in LC, p. 83-106]
Shorter pieces
  1995, Spring   Oxford in Venice: new light on an old question   Sh. Ox. Newsl., vol. 31/2b: 1-6
                 [repr. in BTC, vol. 7: 311-19]
  1999   [review of *Alias Shakespeare* by Joseph Sobran (1997)]   Sh. Quarterly, vol. 50: 376-82
                 [Nelson laments that "Establishment Shakespeareans . . . are
                 losing the public debate over the 'authorship question."]
                 Response by Joseph Sobran, SON, vol. 36/1: 12-13+.
  2004, July   [review of *Shakespeare's Unorthodox Biography* by Diana Price]   De Vere Soc. Newsl., p. 18-21
                 [With rebuttal by Diana Price]
  2004, Fall   Stratford Si! Essex No! (An Open-and-Shut Case)   Tennessee Law Review, vol.
                 72/1: 149-169
                 [repr. in BTC, vol. 8: 358-84]
  2005, Jan.   [reprint of 'Vere, Edward de' Listing in *The Dictionary of National*   De Vere Soc. Newsl., p. 8-13
                 Biography, O.U.P. (2004)] [annotated; by Kevin Gilvary?]
  2005, Nov. 25   [review of *The Truth Will Out: Unmasking the Real Shakespeare* by   Times Literary Sup., is. 5355: 28
                 Brenda James and William D. Rubenstein]
  2006, Jan. 27   Variations on Looney Tunes [review of *"Shakespeare" by*   Times Literary Sup., is. 5365: 30
                 Another Name by Mark Anderson (2005)]
  2007, Spring   Roscius Annotation Revisited: Epicurean Discovery or Ambiguous   Sh. Ox. Newsl., vol. 43/2: 2, 9-13
                 Tidbit? [with Paul H. Altrocchi]
  2009, Winter   William Shakespeare, "Our Roscius" [with Paul H. Altrocchi]   Sh. Quarterly, vol. 60/4: 460-69
  2013   The Life and Theatrical Interests of Edward de Vere, in *Shakespeare*
                 Beyond Doubt (Edmondson & Wells): 39-48]
  2018   William Shakespeare of Stratford-upon-Avon and London, in
                 My Shakespeare (Leahy): 1-24
  2020, Dec.   Orthodoxy Affirmed   Int'l J. of App. Psychoanalytic
                                                                    Studies, v. 17/4: 372-75

Nelson, B. Wayne
  2013, Oct. 19   [letter: J. Kelly Nestruck's Oct. 17 article]   Globe & Mail, p. F8

Nelson, Donald F.
  2008, Spring   Schurink's Discovery of a Century   Sh. Ox. Newsl., vol. 44/2: 10-11
  2013, Spring   [review of *The Apocryphal William Shakespeare* by Sabrina Feldman]   Sh. Matters, vol. 12/2: 7, 20-2

Nelson, Jane E.
Books
  2022   *Shakespeare and religio mentis: A Study of Christian Hermetism in Four Plays*. Brill.
Shorter pieces
  2022, Oct.   Christian Hermetism and Shakespeare   De Vere Soc. New., v. 29/4: 6-14
  2020, Oct.   [letter: Gilvary's long piece on J. Thomas Looney]   De Vere Soc. New., v. 27/4: 43-4

Nelson, Paul A.
  1991, Aug.   The Only Portrait of William Shakspere of Stratford Published During   Spear-shaker Rev., issue 5: 1-14
                 His Lifetime: In Henry Peacham's *Minerva Britanna* (1612)
  1992, Fall   Walt Whitman [and others] On Shakespeare [repr. in BTC 7: 119-24]   Sh. Ox. Newsl., vol. 28/4a: 1-4

Nichols, Dudley
 1956, May   To the Editor and Readers of *The Shakespeare Newsletter*   Sh. Newsletter, vol. 6/3: 18
                    [letter, with 21 others]

Nichols, Francis L.
 1953, Nov.   [letter: the virgin queen]   SF News-letter (E), p. 12
 1954, April   [letter: *This Star of England*]   SF News-letter (E), p. 12-13

Nichols, Herbert B.
 1993, Dec. 21   Wonders of Research: Three Portraits of Shakespeare X-rayed;   Christian Science Monitor, p. 9
                    Seeing Through Paint

Nicholson, A. P.
 1951, Sept. 5   A Good Playwright [review of *Thomas Heywood: Playwright and*   Saturday Review, p. 303
                    Miscellanist by Arthur M. Clark]

Nicolson, Adam
 2008   *Earls of Paradise: England and the Dream of Perfection*. New York: HarperCollins.

Nickell, Joe
 2011, Nov-Dec   Did Sh. Write 'Shakespeare'? Much Ado About Nothing [cover story]   Skeptical Enquirer, p. 38
                    Response by Bryan H. Wildenthal, March-April, p. 62.

Nickson, Horace
 1929, July   [letter: Shakespeare Fellowship's good fellowship]   Sh. Pictorial, no. 17: 19

Niederkorn, William S.
 2002, Feb. 10   A Historic Whodunit: If Shakespeare Didn't, Who Did?   New York Times
                    Resp. by Christopher Dams repr. in DVN (April 2002), p. 20.
                    Resp. by Wayne Shore repr. in DVN (April 2002), p. 20
                    See also Editor's Note, DVN (April 2002), p. 20.
 2002, Feb. 24   Much Ado About the Bard: What's In a Name? One Theory is   Edmonton Journal, p. D6
                    Gaining Ground – That the Real Bard Was Ed. de Vere, E. of Ox.
 2002, June 20   A Scholar Recants His 'Shakespeare' Discovery   New York Times
 2002, June 26   Beyond the Briefly Inflated Canon: Legacy of the Mysterious 'W.S.' New York Times
 2003, Aug. 19   All Is True? Naye, Not If Thy Name Be Shakespeare   New York Times, p. E1
 2003, Sept. 2   Seeing the Fingerprints of Other Hands in Shakespeare   New York Times, A&L: 1
 2003, Nov. 16   Where There's a Will, or Two, or Maybe Quite a Few [interview with New York Times, A&L: 5
                    Amy Freed and review of her play *The Beard of Avon*]
 2004, Aug. 21   To Be or Not to Be . . . Shakespeare   New York Times, p. D3
 2004, Aug. 25   Re-Imagining the Man from Stratford   Int'l Herald Tribune, p. 10
 2004, Fall   Jumping o'er Times: The Importance of Lawyers and Judges in the   Tennessee Law Review, vol.
                    Controversy Over the Identity of Shakespeare, as Reflected in   72/1: 67-92
                    the pages of the *New York Times*
 2005, Aug. 30   The Shakespeare Code, and Other Fanciful Ideas From the Traditional New York Times, p. 32
                    Camp [review of *1599: A Year in the Life of William Shakespeare*
                    by James Shapiro (2005); and *"Shakespeare" By Another Name* by
                    Mark Anderson (2005)] [repr. in German in NSJ, vol. 11: 18-22]
                    Response by Steven Greenblatt, Sept. 5, p. C9.
                    Response by Ron Rosenbaum, *New York Observer*, Sept. 19, p. 1.
                    Reply by Rosenbaum to Anderson, *New York Observer*, Sept. 26, p. 4.
 2005, Sept. 2   To Be Or Not to Be Shakespeare   Int'l Herald Tribune, p. 9
 2007, April 22   Shakespeare Reaffirmed   New York Times, p. 4A
 2008, Oct.   [review of *Shakespeare, Co-Author* by Brian Vickers]   Neues Sh. Journal, v. 12: 132-34
 2009, May 20   The Sonnets at 400 [in Paper Cuts, blog of the editors of the *NY Times Book Review*]
 2010, April   Absolute Will [review of *Contested Will: Who Wrote Shakespeare?*   Brooklyn Rail
                    by James Shapiro (2010)]
 2011, March   The Bard's Evangelist [review of *Shakespeare's Freedom*   Brooklyn Rail
                    by Stephen Greenblatt (2010)]
 2011, April   The Shakespeare Chronology Recalibrated [review of   Brooklyn Rail
                    Dating Shakespeare's Plays by Kevin Gilvary (2010)]
                    [repr. in DVN, vol. 18/3: 26-27 (Nov. 2011); and in *Sh. Authorship
                    Sourcebook* (Stritmatter 2022): 421-28]
 2011, July   Canonizer's Feast [review of *The Anatomy of Influence: Literature* Brooklyn Rail, p. 74

Oakes, Rev. Edward T.

2010, June	[John Gross's March review of *Contested Will* [reply by John Gross, same issue, p. 7-8]	Commentary, vol. 129/6: 6-7

O'Brien, Conor Cruise

1985, Jan. 17	The Charms of Certitude [rev. of *Mysterious William Shakespeare* by Charlton Ogburn]	NY Review, p. 21

O'Brien, Patrick

2001, July	Shakespeare's Sources and Sir Thomas Smith's Library [with Eddi Jolly] [repr. in GO, p. 22-25]	De Vere Soc. Newsl., p. 19
2004	Shakespeare's Sources Continued: Lord Burghley's Library [with Eddi Jolly]	Great Oxford, p. 26-30
2009, Nov.	Shakespeare and Cambridge	De Vere Soc. New., v. 16/3: 9-13
2012, July	Did Edward de Vere Visit Horham Hall in September 1571?	De Vere Soc. New., v. 19/2: 9-10
2014, May	De Vere, Shakespeare and Queen's College Cambridge	De Vere Soc. New., v. 21/2: 8-11
2021, July	[review of *North by Shakespeare* by Michael Blanding]	De Vere S. New., v. 28/3: 45-50

O'Brien, Robert

1991, Feb.	[letter: misc. issues]	Spear-shaker Newsl., is. 1/1: 2-3

O'Brien, Thomas W.

1985, May 19	The Philosophizing Hamlet and His Creator [rev. of *The Mysterious William Shakespeare* by Charlton Ogburn]	Philadelphia Inquirer, p. G5
1995/96, Winter	Class and Classic [review of *Shakespeare, In Fact* by Irvin Matus]	Cross Currents, p. 558

O'Connor, Hon. T. P.

1928, Nov. 4	[letter: Sir George Greenwood]	Sunday Times, p. 14

O'Connor, Thomas

1992, April 19	Shakespeare [report on Charles Vere's talk]	Orange County. Reg., p. F20

O'Connor, William Douglas

1860	*Harrington: A Story of True Love*. Boston: Thayer & Eldridge.
1886	*Hamlet's Notebook*. Boston: Houghton, Mifflin.
1889	*Mr. Donnelly's Reviewers*. Chicago: Belford, Clarke.

O'Dea, Rosemary

2003, Sept.	[letter: praise for the Newsletter]	De Vere Soc. Newsl., p. 24

Ofield, Jack and Helen

2020, Oct.	[letter: Gilvary's long piece on J. Thomas Looney] 43-44	De Vere Soc. Newsl., vol. 27/4:

Ogburn, Charlton (Jr.)

Books and pamphlets

1962	*Shake-speare: The Man Behind the Name* [subtitle on dust jacket is "The Real Man Behind the Name"] [with Dorothy Ogburn]. New York: Morrow.
1964	*Shakespeare and the Man of Stratford* (pamphlet published by the Shakespeare-Oxford Society).
1984	*The Mysterious William Shakespeare: The Myth and the Reality*. Foreword by David McCullough. New York: Dodd, Mead.
1987	*The Man Who Was Shakespeare* [pamphlet: "an extremely abbreviated version of the case presented in *The Mysterious William Shakespeare*"]
1988	*The Mystery of William Shakespeare* [abridged version of TMWS pub. in the UK] Foreword by Lord Vere. London: Cardinal Books.
1992	*The Mysterious William Shakespeare: The Myth and the Reality*. 2nd edition. Foreword by David McCullough. McLean, VA: EPM Publications. [excerpts repr. in SON, vol. 30/1: 12 (Winter 1994); in SON, vol. 31/1a, vol. 31/1a: 1-2 (Winter 1995) and in *Sh. Criticism, vol. 41* (Lee & Barnes 1998): 2-5]
1992	*Shakespeare's Self-Portrait: A Summary* [pamphlet]. Northampton, MA: Oxenford Press.
1995	*The Man Who Was Shakespeare: A Summary of the Case Unfolded in The Mysterious William Shakespeare: The Myth and the Reality*. McLean, VA: EPM Publications.

Periodicals edited

1978, Fall-1980, Winter, and 1980, Fall: *Shakespeare Oxford Newsletter*, vol. 14/4-16/1.

Shorter pieces

1952	Foreword to *This Star of England* by Dorothy and Charlton Ogburn. [repr. in SON, vol. 24/3: 1-5 (Summer 1988); and in BC, vol. III: 1-7 (Fall 2011)]

1953, Mar. 1	[letter: response to Oscar Campbell's Feb. 8 article]	New York Times, p. BR23
1956, May 11	The Sands of Time [letter: response to the May 4 article]	Washington Post, p. 26
	See also T. Nashe's response to Ogburn's letter, June 3, p. E4.	
1956, May 16	[letter: response to Louis B. Wright's April 26 article]	Washington Post, p. 10
	Response by Louis B. Wright, May 20, p. A16.	
	Response to Wright by Joseph Borkin, May 31, p. E4.	
1959, June 20	Interviewed by John McCabe	New Yorker
1964, May 3	Challenge to Giles E. Dawson [letter]	Washington Post, p. E6
1964, May 27	Will-o'-the-Wisp [letter: resp. to Dawson's May 27 letter]	Washington Post, p. A24
1966	[review of *Was Shakespeare Shakespeare?* by Milward W. Martin]	Washington Star
	[comments by Ogburn in SON, vol. 2/1: 2-3 (March 30, 1966)]	
1966, March 30	Comments on John McCabe's June 20, 1959 *New Yorker* article	Sh. Ox. Newsl., vol. 2/1: 2
	and other publication issues	
1968, July 3	Who Wrote These Plays? [letter: response to Edward Folliard's	Washington Post, p. E1
	June 23 article on Louis B. Wright]	
1970, Sept. 6	Shakespeare, Who He? [letter: challenge to Edward Quinn]	Washington Post, p. 9
	Response by Edward Quinn, Sept. 6, p. 9.	
	Reply by Ogburn, Dec. 13, p. 12.	
1970, Dec. 13	[letter: reply to Edward Quinn's 6 Sept. letter]	Washington Post, p. 12
1972, June	Shakespeare's Missing Manuscripts	Harper's Mag., v. 244: 94-96+
	Responses by Peter Sammartino, Welles Irwin Price, Goodhue	
	Livingston, Joseph R. Surface, in the August issue, p. 4.	
	Reply by Ogburn, same issue.	
1972, Aug. 1	[letter: reply to responses to his June article]	Harper's Mag., p. 4
1973, Aug. 5	What's in a Name [review of *Shakespeare the Man* by A. L. Rowse]	Washington Post, p. BW8
1973, Oct. 19	A Shakespeare Who Never Comes to Life [review of *You, My Brother*	Washington Post, p. B10
	by Philip Burton]	
1974, Nov.	The Man Who Shakespeare Was Not . . . (And Who He Was)	Harvard Mag., p. 21-29
	More than 30 responses were printed over six issues.	
	Response by Edward Fisher, Jan. 5, 1975.	
	Response by Peter Wirth, Jan. 5, 1975.	
	Response by Harold C. Hinton, April 8, 1975.	
	Response by Harry Levin and G. Blakemore Evans, "Shakespeare	
	as Shakespeare," Feb. 1975, p. 39-43.	
	Response to Evans and Levin by Charles C. Dickinson, III, April. 8.	
	Response to Levin and Evans by Gordon Cyr, SON, Summer 1975, p. 1-19.	
	Reply by Ogburn to Evans and Levin, April 8, 1975. [He proposes	
	a trial and notes Weld's offer to finance it.]	
	See also:	
	Gordon C. Cyr, "The Harvard Case," SON, vol. 11/1: 4 (Winter-Spring	
	1974); and Gordon C. Cyr, The Harvard Case, Part II," SON,	
	vol. 14/1: 5-6 (Winter 1978).	
1974, Nov. 24	The Man Shakespeare Was Not . . . And Who He Was	Washington Post, p. B1
	[repr. from *Harvard Magazine*, Nov. 1974]	
	Response by Andor Klay, Nov. 30, p. A11.	
1974, Nov. 24	The Man Who Shakespeare Was Not . . . (And Who He Was)	Outlook (Am.)
	[repr. from *Harvard Magazine*, Nov. 1974]	
	Response by O. B. Hardison, Jr., Dec. 8, p. B3.	
1976, Fall	President's Message [repr. in BTC, vol. 6: 90-93]	Sh. Ox. Newsl., vol. 12/3: 1-3
1978, Summer	The Quest for Shakespeare's Manuscripts	Sh. Ox. Newsl., vol. 14/3: 1-3
1978, Fall	SOS Third Annual Conference	Sh. Ox. Newsl., vol. 14/4: 3-5
1979, Winter	Shakespeare on Television	Sh. Ox. Newsl., vol. 15/1: 1-3
1979, Spring	Henry Clay Folger's Memorial [repr. in BTC, vol. 6: 55-64]	Sh. Ox. Newsl., vol. 15/2: 1-7
1979, Fall	The How Many Guises of Edward de Vere	Sh. Ox. Newsl., vol. 15/4: 1-5
	[repr. in BTC. Vol. 6: 125-30]	
1979, Fall	More on the Portrait [Ashbourne Portrait]	Sh. Ox. Newsl., vol. 15/4: 5-7
1980, Winter	*A Hundreth Sundrie Flowres* Revisited	Sh. Ox. Newsl., vol. 16/1: 1
1980, Winter	The Missing Link [similarity between Oxford's "Echo" Verses and	Sh. Ox. Newsl., vol. 16/1: 2-4
	Shakespeare's *A Lovers' Complaint*]	

Ogburn, Charlton (Jr.) (continued)

1980, Winter	Locating Mount Oxford [findings of Helen Kerfoot]	Sh. Ox. Newsl., vol. 16/1: 5-10
1980, Fall	Future of Castle Hedingham in Doubt	Sh. Ox. Newsl., vol. 16/4: 1
1980, Fall	A Crack in the Dike at the BBC	Sh. Ox. Newsl., vol. 16/4: 5-6
1980, Fall	In Memoriam: Sol Feinstone (d. 1980)	Sh. Ox. Newsl., vol. 16/4: 7
1982, Winter	A New Edition of Oxford's Poems [review of *The Poems of Robert Devereux and of Edward de Vere* by Steven W. May]	Sh. Ox. Newsl., vol. 18/1: 13-15
1983, Fall	Oxford and the Avon [repr. in BTC, vol. 6: 258-61]	Sh. Ox. Newsl., vol. 19/4: 5-7
1984, Summer	If Thou Read This . . . [repr. in BTC, vol. 6: 264-70]	Sh. Ox. Newsl., vol. 20/3: 3-6
1984, Dec. 11	Transcript of *Firing Line* Episode: "The Mysterious William Sh." [host: William F. Buckley, Jr.]	
1985, Sept/Oct.	[letter: resp. to Paul Bertram's review]	Sh. Bulletin, vol. 3/5: 27
1986, Feb. 8	Stratford's Undistinguished Will Shakspere [letter: reply to Kevin Cureton's Jan. 25 letter]	New York Times, p. A26
1986, Spring	Professor May on Oxford's Annuity: A Response by Charleton Ogburn [repr. in BTC, vol. 6: 296-97]	Sh. Ox. Newsl., vol. 22/2: 7-8
1986, Summer	Folger Library Forfeits $10,000 Rather Than Assist in Trial of Shakespeare's Identity	Sh. Ox. Newsl., vol. 22/3: 1-3
1986, Fall	[letter to *Reader's Digest* [Leo Rosten's "The Sh. Nobody Knows]	Sh. Ox. Newsl., vol. 22/4: 11-12
1987, Spring	Emerson, Delia Bacon and the Shakespeare Problem	Sh. Ox. Newsl., vol. 23/2: 1-4
1987, Winter	Oxford Makes It To Prime Time!	Sh. Ox. Newsl., vol. 23/1: 4
1988, Jan.	Costly Consequences of the Moot Court at American University	De Vere Soc. New., no. 1: 23-29
1988, Spring	Some "Facts" and Fancies Invented by Professor James A. D. Boyle for His Brief as Counsel for William Shakspere in the Debate Sept. 15, 1987 Before Three United States Supreme Court Justices [repr. in BTC, vol. 6: 330-37]	Sh. Ox. Newsl., vol. 24/2: 1-5
1988, Summer	The Apotheosis of William Shakespeare	Sh. Newsl., vol. 38/2: 28-29
1989, Winter	Television Documentary on Shakespeare Controversy to be Broadcast	Sh. Ox. Newsl., vol. 25/1: 5-6
1989, Summer	[letter: thanks to Judge Wheaton for his most valued support]	Sh. Ox. Newsl., vol. 25/3: 7
1990, Summer	[letter: recent articles by Stritmatter and Goldstein]	Sh. Ox. Newsl., vol. 26/3a: 5-6
1991, May	[letter: correction; Umberto Ecco is writing a book on Ed. de Vere]	Sp.-Sh. Rev, issue 3/4: 17
1991, Fall	Excerpts From a Paper Read at the 1991 Annual Meeting at Palm Springs [repr. in BTC, vol. 7: 69-71]	Sh. Ox. Newsl., vol. 27/4: 1-2
1992, Jan.	[letter: resp. to special issue on Shakespeare's authorship]	Atlantic Monthly, p. 6-9
1992, April 9	[letter: resp. to Honigmann's Nov. 1991 "Bed" article, with reply by Honigmann [repr. in SON, vol. 28/2: 16; and in BTC, vol. 7: 106-07] Additional response and reply, June 25 (see below).	NY Rev. of Books, p. 27
1992, April 12	More On the Stratford Man [Gardner's Jan. 19 article]	Washington Post, p. 14
1992, June 25	[letter: Honigmann's April 9 reply, followed by reply] [Both repr. in SON, vol. 28/2: 16; and in BTC, vol. 7: 106-07]	NY Rev. of Books, p. 27
1992, Fall	Shakespeare's Self-Portrait [Summary of the case presented in *The Mysterious William Shakespeare*] [repr. in BTC, vol. 7: 131-45)	Sh. Ox. Newsl., vol. 28/4b: 1-11
1993, Summer	The Piquant Genealogy of Sir John Falstaff	Sh. Ox. Newsl., vol. 29/3a: 7
1994, Summer	Turning of the Tide in the Shakespeare Authorship Controversy?	Sh. Ox. Newsl., vol. 30/3a: 2-6
1994, Autumn	[letter: errors made by Werner Gundersheimer	Sh. Ox. Newsl., vol. 30/4: 8
1996, Winter	[letter: appreciation for Florence Sheppard's review of *This Star*	Sh. Ox. Newsl., vol. 32/1: 23
1996, Spr./Sum.	Interview with *Apostrophe Magazine* [conducted by Sheila Tombe] [repr. in EVR, vol. 3 (Summer 1996)]	Apostrophe
1996, Summer	*This Star of England*: Some Historical Notes on its Publication & and Authors	Sh. Ox. Newsl., vol. 32/3: 3, 24
1996, Summer	[letter to *Washington Post*: resp. to Michael Farquhar's Aug. 4 article]	Sh. Ox. Newsl., vol. 32/3: 2
1996, Summer	[letter: Oxfordian articles in *Das Shakespeare-Komplott*; Oxford taught in Geneva]	Sh. Ox. Newsl., vol. 32/3: 21
1996, Fall	[letter: excerpts from his letter to the SOS about Sobran's new book and Southampton's parentage] [repr. in BTC, vol. 7: 376-77]	Sh. Ox. Newsl., vol. 32/4: 7
1997, Winter	[letter: Anderson and Stritmatter's terrific article on Sh.'s Bible]	Sh. Ox. Newsl., vol. 33/1: 21
1997, Spring	[letter: Diana Price's Autumn 1996 "Rough Winds" article] [repr. in BTC, vol. 8: 276-78] Response by Diana Price, Spring 1997, p. 9-11.	Eliz. Review, vol. 5/1: 6-9

Ogburn, Dorothy (continued)

| 1952 | *This Star of England: "William Shake-speare," Man of the Renaissance*. New York: Coward-McCann, Inc. Repr. in 1972: Westport, CT: Greenwood Press. [excerpt repr. in BTC, vol. 4: 383-414; and in TOX, vol. 16: 55-67] | |
| 1955 | *The Renaissance Man of England, Newly Corrected and Augmented*. New York: Coward-McCann, Inc. | |

Books (with Charlton Ogburn, Jr.)

| 1962 | *Shake-speare: The Man Behind the Name* [subtitle on dust jacket is "The Real Man Behind the Name"] New York: Morrow. | |

Shorter pieces

1945, Jan.	[letter: literary sleuthing of the highest order in the *Quarterly*'s articles]	SF Quarterly, vol. VI/1: 2
1945, Oct.	The Wounded Name of Truth	SF Quarterly, vol. VI/4: 61-62
1947, June 29	Oxford's Literary Genius: Shakespeare's Background [letter: resp. to letters by Collins and Earle]	NY Herald Trib, p. A7
1954, April	[letter: reply to reviews of *This Star of England*] Resps. by Francis Nichols, Gwynneth Bowen, Kathleen le Riche and G. W. Phillips, same pub. and issue, p. 12-14.	SF News-letter (E), p. 12
1955, July 10	[letter, with Ch. Ogburn: most spectatular literary hoax of all time]	New York Times, p. BR13
1956, Feb. 19	[letter, with Ch. Ogburn: resp. to J. Clifford's article on biographies]	New York Times, p. BR17
1959, Sept.	The True Shakespeare: England's "Great and Complete Man" [with Charlton Ogburn, Sr.] [repr. in SC, p. 43-57, 1961; in BTC, vol. 4: 360-382; and in *Shakespeare and His Rivals* (McMichael & Glenn 1962): 218-24]	Am. Bar Assoc. Journ., vol. 45/9: 941-43+
1960, Spring	Shakespeare or Shaksper? [with Charlton Ogburn, Sr.]	Am. Scholar, vol. 29/2: 271+
1960, July	Shakespeare Was Oxford, Not Christopher Marlowe [letter, with Charlton Ogburn: resp. to Benjamin Wham]	Am. Bar Assoc. Journ., vol. 46/7: 696, 698
1967, Autumn	Authorship of *True Tragedie of Edward the Second* [repr. in BTC, vol. 5: 245-49]	Sh. Authorship Rev. #18: 8-11
1969, Christmas	[letter: Sonnets' dedication]	Sh. Authorship Rev. #22: 20-21
1971, Spring	[letter: Stratfordian difficulties in seeing that intro. to *FF* is a hoax]	Sh. Authorship Rev. #24: 22-23

Ogburn, Vera

| 1999, Fall | In Memory of Charlton Ogburn, Jr. [letter] | Sh. Ox. Newsl., vol. 35/3: 4 |

Ogilvie, John

| 1998, Feb. | [letter: resp. to J. Rollett's 1997 "Sonnets Dedication" article] | De Vere Soc. Newsl., v. 2/11: 23 |

O'Gorman, Rochelle

| 2006, April 23 | There's Much Ado About Life and Works of Shakespeare | Plain Dealer (Cleve.), p. J4 |

O'Hagan, Thomas

| 1936 | *What Shakespeare is Not*. Toronto: The Hunter-Rose Co., Ltd. [Chapter 2 is titled "Shakespeare Identified" and is a response to Looney's book, though neither he nor it are mentioned directly.] | |

O'Hara, Mary

| 1984/85? | [review of TMWS, quoted on dust jacket of 1992 edition] | Pittsburgh Press |

Ohmann, Richard

| 1991, Winter | [letter: Oxfordian article not suitable for *College English*] Response by Warren Hope, SON, vol. 27/1: 2. | Sh. Ox. Newsl., vol. 27/1: 1 |

Oldenburg, Don

1990, April 17	Shakespeare, By Any Other Name? Professor Samuel Schoenbaum Recants [repr. in SON, vol. 26/4: 8-9 (Fall 1990)]	Washington Post, p. D5
1990, Dec. 18	Sequel; Beating Up on the Bard; Oxfordians: Out, Out Damned Will	Washington Post. p. B5
1990, Dec. 28	Pretenders to the Bard's Throne Fail 'Line-ender' Test	Minneap. Star. Tr., p. 8E
1990, Dec. 30	Who Was the Bard? Was He the Stratford Man or a Powerful Earl?	Houston Chronicle, p. 18
1994, May 17	Shakespeare's Raging Identity Crisis [repr. in SON, vol. 30/2a: 2 (Spr. 1994)]	Washington Post
1994, Oct. 30	A Lingering Shakespearean Drama [double page spread with coverage of Charles Vere's lecture at the Smithsonian]	Washington Post, p. G2
1999, Jun. 24	Shakespeare in Trouble: Who Was Will Shakespeare? And Why is Peter Dickson Saying Such Terrible Things About Him? Response by Linda R. Monk, Jan. 30, p. A17. Response by Fran Conner, Jan. 30, p. A17. Response by Jay L. Halio, Jan. 30, p. A17.	Washington Post, p. F1, 4

Author Index

Response to Fran Conner by Peter Dickson, Feb. 6, p. A19.
Response to Peter Dickson by Jack Gonzales, Feb. 20, p. A17.

Olds, Nathaniel S.
    1945   Revisions May Have to be Made in English Literature Textbooks   Villager
         [repr. in SFQ, vol. VII/1: 13 (Jan. 1946)]

O'Loughlin, Rosemary
Plays
    2022?   *A Rose by Any Other Name.* [a play]
Shorter pieces
    2020, Jan.   Presentation of Her Winning Video "With the Mind I Will Be Seen"   De Vere Soc. New., v. 27/1: 9-15
    2021, July   Brian Friel: Was One of Ireland's Best-Known Playwrights a Secret   De Vere S. New., v. 28/3: 19-35
         Oxfordian?

Olson, Ray
    2010, April 1   Contested Will: Who Wrote Shakespeare? [rev. of J. Shapiro's book]   Booklist, vol. 106/15: 12

Oman, Charles
    1929, Sept. 6   Shakespeare and *Richard III*: Sir Charles Oman Discredits the   Morning Post, p. 5
         Propaganda Theory [letter]

O'Morrison, Kevin
    2002, Feb. 24   Any Actor Knows [letter]   New York Times, p. E6

O'Neal, Cothburn
    1954   *The Dark Lady: A Novel.* New York: Crown Publishers, Inc.

O'Neill, Frank
    1997, June 15   Did Shakespeare Author the Plays?   Greensboro News-Rec., p. F5

Orage, Alfred [r. H. C.]
    1920, Dec. 2   Readers and Writers [review of *"Shakespeare" Indentified*]   New Age, vol. 28/5: 55-56
    1920, Dec. 23   Readers and Writers [reply to Looney's response to the Dec. 2 rev.]   New Age, vol. 28/8: 92
    1921, Jan. 20   Readers and Writers [reply to Looney's Jan. 20 response]   New Age, vol. 28/12: 139
    1921, Jan. 27   Readers and Writers [further reply to Looney's Jan. 20 response]   New Age, vol. 28/13: 155-56

Orloff, John
    2010, April 19   [letter: James Shapiro's April 11 article]   Los Angeles Times
    2011, Oct. 29   Why I Played With Shakespeare's Story [in *Anonymous*]   Wall Street Journal

Orodenker, M. H.
    1940, Aug.   Legitimate Summer Theater Reviews: "By Any Other Name"   Billboard

Orr, John M.
    1960, Sept.   'Machevil' a Clue About Marlowe? [letter]   Am. Bar Assoc. Journ., vol.
         46/9: 942

Ostrowski, Donald
Books
    2020   *Who Wrote That? Authorship Controversies from Moses to Sholokhov.* Ithica: Northern Illinois Univ. Press.
Shorter pieces
    2011, Fall   [review of *Dating Shakespeare's Plays: A Critical Review of the*   Brief Chronicle, vol. III: 246-257
         Evidence edited by Kevin Gilvary (2010)]

O'Shea, Daphne
    2018, Jan.   Edward de Vere's Amanuensis: The Artifacts of Abraham Fleming   De Vere Soc. New., v. 25/1: 7-13
         and the Lost Play of Edward de Vere

O'Sullivan, Charlotte
    1996, April 28   Did Aliens Write *Macbeth*? [review of *Who Wrote Shakespeare?* by   Observer, p. 9
         John Michell]

O'Toole, Fintan
    2011, Nov. 5   Why was William Shakespeare So Hard to Pin Down?   Irish Times (Dublin), p. A19
    2014, April 26   Shakespeare Conspiracy Theories Are a Comedy of Errors   Irish Times (Dublin), p. 8

Ouzounian, Richard
    2002, Nov. 22   Rotten Fruit Hurled at Poor Will [rev. of *The Beard of Avon* by Freed]   Toronto Star, p. E13

Oxenforde

2000, Oct.	Sene and Hearde: A Regular Column Devoted to Sh. in the News	De Vere Soc. Newsl., p. 19
2001, Jan.	Sene and Hearde: A Regular Column Devoted to Sh. in the News	De Vere Soc. Newsl., p. 41-42
2001, Apr./May	Sene and Hearde: A Regular Column Devoted to Sh. in the News	De Vere Soc. Newsl., p. 10-11
2001, July	Sene and Hearde: A Regular Column Devoted to Sh. in the News	De Vere Soc. Newsl., p. 35-36
2001, Oct.	Sene and Hearde: A Regular Column Devoted to Sh. in the News	De Vere Soc. Newsl., p. 29-31
2002, Jan./Feb.	Sene and Hearde: A Regular Column Devoted to Sh. in the News	De Vere Soc. Newsl., p. 18-20
2002, July	Sene and Hearde: A Regular Column Devoted to Sh. in the News	De Vere Soc. Newsl., p. 29-30
2003, June	[review of *In Search of Shakespeare*, by Michael Wood (2003)]	De Vere Soc. Newsl., p. 27
2003, June	Shakespeare's Globe	De Vere Soc. Newsl., p. 28
2003, Sept.	Sene and Hearde	De Vere Soc. Newsl., p. 20
2003, Sept.	Three Cheers for the Marlovians	De Vere Soc. Newsl., p. 21
2004, Jan.	Sene and Hearde	De Vere Soc. Newsl., p. 28-29

Padel, John

1976, July 4	An Analyst at Elsinore [review of *Hamlet's Enemy* by Theodore Lidz [mentions all three editions of *"Shakespeare" Identified*]	Times Lit. Sup., is. 3873: 667

Page, Martin R.

1968, Autumn	[letter: request for information for a life of J. M. Robertson]	Sh. Authorship Rev. is. #20: 21

Paget (Anderson), Verily – see Anderson, Verily (Paget)

Palk, Robert

1931, Dec. 10	Shakespeare, Essex and *Richard II* [letter]	Times Lit. Sup., 1558: 1006

Palmer, Cecil

1920, March 6	"Shakespeare" Identified in Edward de Vere [letter]	Publishers' Circular, p. 237
1930, July	John Lyly and the Office of the Revels [letter]	Sh. Pictorial, no. 29: 16

Palmer, Martyn

2011, Oct. 16	Playing to the Crowd [review of *Anonymous*]	Sunday Times, p. 14

Pannell, Chris
Periodicals edited
2015-2017: *The Oxfordian*, vol. 17-19.
Shorter pieces

2015	My Oxfordian Bookshelf: A review of *A Question of Will* by Lynne Kositsky (2000)	Oxfordian, vol. 17: 222-25
2016, Winter	[review of *The Case for Edward de Vere* by Geoffrey Eyre (2015)]	Sh. Ox. Newsl., vol. 52/1: 15-17
2016, Spring	Toronto Anti-Stratfordians Stage Rebuttal to the 400th Anniversary	Sh. Ox. Newsl., vol. 52/2: 24-25
2017, Sept.	In Conversation with Hank Whittemore: *100 Reasons Shake-speare was the Earl of Oxford*	Oxfordian, vol. 19: 181-94
2020, Sept.	[rev. of *Early Shakespeare Authorship Doubts* by Bryan Wildenthal]	Oxfordian, vol. 22: 181-186

Pares, Commander Martin

1960, April	Francis Bacon and the Knights of the Helmet [repr. in SC, p. 79-92]	Am. Bar Assoc. Journal, vol. 46/4: 402-09

Parisious, Roger N.

1998, Spring	Occultist Influence on the Authorship Controversy [Tudor Rose/PT/Southampton/Dynastic Succession Theory]	Eliz. Review, vol. 6/1: 9-43
1998, Autumn	Postscript to the Tudor Rose Theory	Eliz. Review, vol. 6/2: 90-93
2001, Oct.	Accusing Voices Beyond the Grave: the evidence of Robert Greene and George Buc	De Vere Soc. Newsl., p. 2-8
2010, Nov.	[letter: correct spelling of his name]	De Vere Soc. Newsl., v. 17/3: 21

Parsons, I. M.

1932, Jan. 30	Shakespeare's Ghost [reviews of *Exit Shakespeare* by Bertram G. Theobold (1931) and *Edward de Vere* by George Frisbee (1931)]	Spectator, vol. 148: 149

Parsons, J. Denham
Books and pamphlets
1930   *Report on the Poet Shakespeare's Identity Submitted to the Trustees of the British Museum.* [pamphlet]
Shorter pieces

1924, June 6	Who was Labeo? [letter]	Hackney Spectator, p. 2
1931	Sir Edward Clark, P.C., on Shakespeare's Identity	Baconiana
1933, May	"Son of Elizabeth" letter: Bayley's April 1933 article]	Sh. Pictorial, no. 63: 68

1985, Summer	A Significant Eulogy [repr. in BTC, vol. 6: 274-75]	Sh. Ox. Newsl., vol. 21/3: 1
1986, Winter	A Call For Action	Sh. Ox. Newsl., vol. 22/1: 6-8
1988, Aut.	Oxfordian Echoes	De Vere Soc. New., no. 3: 70-73
1991, Summer	Lord Oxford's Son-in-Law	Sh. Ox. Newsl., vol. 17/2: 2-5

Paton, Graeme

2014, Sept. 12	Holocaust Jibe Angers Sh. Scholar [*Memoria de Shakespeare* editor's unprofessional conduct irks Prof. Dr. Richard Waugaman]	Telegraph, p. 11

Patterson, Annabel M.

1984	*Censorship and Interpretation: The Conditions of Writing and Reading in Early Modern England*. Madison, WI: University of Wisconsin Press.

Patterson, Donald

1995, Sept, 28	A Literary Whodunit – Was Shakespeare Up to the Task? [SOS conference and Charles Burford]	Greensboro News-Rec., p. D1

Pattison, J. P.

1939, Aug.	Shakespearean Chronology [letter]	East Angl. Mag., vol. 4/9: 533-34

Paul, Christopher

2001, Oct.	[letter: response to Amy Freed (vol. 18/5: 22 (May/June 2001)]	Am. Theatre, vol. 18/8: 7
2002	Prince Tudor Dilemma: Hip Thesis, Hypothesis, or Old Wives' Tale?	Oxfordian, vol. 5: 47-69
2002, Summer	This Strange Eventful History: Oxford, Shakespeare, and the Seven Ages of Man [repr. in RCA, p. 66-73; in LC, p. 78-83; and in German in NSJ, vol. NS4: 20-34 (Oct. 2014)]	Sh. Ox. Newsl., v. 38/3: 1, 12-5+
2002, Summer	[review of *Oxford, Son of Queen Elizabeth* by Paul Streitz (2001)] Responses by John Grove and Paul Streitz, Fall 2002, p. 4-5. Reply by Christopher Paul, Winter 2003, p. 2-4.	Sh. Matters, vol. 1/4: 17-20
2003, Sept.	[letter: response to Robinson's June 2003 "Lion and spear" article Response to Robinson and Paul by J. Holmes, Jan. 2004, p. 24-25.	De Vere Soc. Newsl., p. 25
2003, Winter	[letter: Paul Streitz's book *Oxford, Son of Queen Elizabeth 1* (2001)]	Sh. Matters, vol. 2/2: 2-4
2003, Autumn	[letter: resp. to Gerit Quealy's Summer 2003 "Wilton shrine" article]	Sh. Ox. Newsl., vol. 39/4: 20
2004	A Monument Without a Tomb: The Mystery of Oxford's Death Response by Richard Whalen, 2006, p. 140-41. Reply by Christopher Paul, 2006, p. 141-43.	Oxfordian, vol. 7: 6-68
2004, Winter	Oxford, Hamlet, and the Pirates: The Naked Truth	Sh. Ox. Newsl., vol. 40/1: 1-5
2004, Spring	Post Mortem on John de Vere, 16th Earl of Oxford [with Carl Caruso and Nina Green]	Sh. Ox. Newsl., vol. 40/2: 8-9
2006	A Crisis of Scholarship: Misreading the Earl of Oxford	Oxfordian, vol. 9: 91-112
2006	[letter: response to Richard Whalen's comments on de Vere's death]	Oxfordian, vol. 9: 141-143
2006, Spring	[letter: response to Derran Charlton's Winter 2006 "Pardon" article]	Sh. Ox. Newsl., vol. 42/2: 9
2006, Summer	[letter: response to Paul Altrocchi's Spr. 2006 "Bermoothes" article]	Sh. Matters, vol. 5/4: 30-32
2006, Fall redux	[letter: response to Richard Whalen's Summer 2006 "Prince Tudor Hypothesis" article: The PT theory and the 1st Earl of Oxford] Response by Hank Whittemore, spring 2007, p. 21.	Sh. Ox. Newsl., vol. 42/4: 32
2006, Sept.	[review of *Edward de Vere: Crisis and Consequences of Wardship* by Daphne Pearson (2005)]	Eng. Historical Rev., vol. 121/493: 1173
2006, Fall	R.I.P.: Bulbeck Bites the Dust	Sh. Ox. Newsl., v. 42/3: 1, 17-20
2006, Fall	A First Blast of the Trumpet Against [Nelson's] *Monstrous Adversary* Response by Hank Whittemore, SON, 43/2: 21.	Sh. Matters, vol. 6/1: 22-27
2006, Fall redux	Trailing Elizabeth Trentham	Sh. Ox. Newsl., vol. 42/4: 9-15
2007, Summer	A New Letter by J. T. Looney Brought to Light	Sh. Ox. Newsl., vol. 43/3: 8-9
2007, Oct.	[letter: response to Crick and Bewley's June "Ashbourne" article]	De Vere Soc. Newsl., p. 29-30
2008, June	[letter: response to Hodgson's March "Robinson-Looney" article]	De Vere S. New., v. 15/2: 31-32
2010, Fall	The Earl of Oxford's Office . . . Illuminated Response by Hank Whittemore, same issue, p. 266-68.	Brief Chronicles, vol. II: 171-211
2010, Fall	[review of *Shakespeare's Lost Kingdom* by Charles Beauclerk] [repr. in NSJ, vol. NS2: 13-31 (2011)]	Brief Chronicles, vol. II: 244-257
2023, Winter	Does the 17th Earl of Oxford 'lieth buried in Westminster'? [letter]	Sh. Ox. Newsl., vol. 59/2: 4

Paulina

1934, Jan.	[letter: Holland's *Elizabethan Times*]	Sh. Pictorial, no. 71: p. D1

Pendleton, Thomas A. (continued)

1992, Summer	Correspondence with Morse Johnson re the Oxford Page in *The Shakespeare Newsletter* [repr. in BTC, vol. 7: 110-18]	Sh. Ox. Newsl., vol. 28/3: 14
1994, Summer	Irvin Matus' Shakespeare, In Fact [review] Response by Morse Johnson, SON, vol. 30/4: 11. Response by Richard F. Whalen, vol. 44/3: 42. Reply by Thomas Pendleton, vol. 44/3: 42.	Sh. Newsl., vol. 44/2: 21
1994, Fall	Reply to Responses to his review of *Shakespeare, In Fact*	Sh. Newsl., vol. 44/3: 42
1995, Summer	From the editors [laments academe's growing interest in hearing the Oxford story from Charles Burford]	Sh. Newsl., vol. 45/2: 26
2001-02, Sept.	Veering Away: a play	Sh. Newsl., vol. 51/2: 54, 62+
2003, Summer	[review of *Chasing Shakespeares* by Sarah Smith (2003)]	Sh. Newsl., vol. 53/2: 33-34+
2003, Fall	Alan Nelson's *Monstrous Adversary* [review]	Sh. Newsl., vol. 53/3: 65, 69
2003/04, Winter	[letter: reply to Whalen's resp. to his review of *Monstrous Adversary*]	Sh. Newsl., vol. 53/4: 104
2007, Spring	[response to Richard F. Whalen's letter in vol. 57/1: 57 (Spring 2007)]	
2009, Winter	[review of *Contested Will: Who Wrote Shakespeare?* by James Shapiro (2010)]	Sh. Newsl., vol. 58/3: 81, 103
2011, Fall	[review of *Anonymous*, directed by Roland Emmerich (2011)]	Sh. Newsl., vol. 61/2: 41, 72+

Penrose, L. S.

1960, Spring	Annual General Meeting of the Shakespearean Authorship Society [with R. N.]	Sh. Authorship Rev. #3: 17
1962, Spring	[report, with R. N., on G. Bowen's talk "Shakespeare Portraits in Color Transparencies"]	Sh. Authorship Rev. #7: 16-17
1972, Winter	Statistical Approaches to the Authorship Problem [with R. N.]	Sh. Authorship Rev. #27: 9-19

Perplexed

1923, Sept. 23	Authorship of the 'Plays of Shakespeare' [letter]	Sheffield Daily Tel., p. 4

Perry, Tony

2001, Aug. 27	A Doctor by Day and Detective in Spare Time [Eric Alruschler]	Los Angeles Times, p. E2.

Perrett, A. J.

1950, Aug. 24	Who Wrote Shakespeare?	Listener, vol. 44: 273

Person, James E., Jr.

1997, July 16	Writer Got the Wrong Answer From Right Books Unsigned response in July 30 issue, p. A10.	Detroit News, p. A11

Peshov, Igor

2010	Opechatka, ili Kliuch k imeni avtora	Novoe Literaturnoe Obozrenie, vol. 105/5

Pfennig, Hazel

1941, Sept. 1	Edward de Vere as Patron, 1550-1604	Teacher's College Jo., v. 13/1: 14

Phillips, Gerald W.

Books and pamphlets

1932	*The Tragic Story of "Shakespeare: Disclosed in the Sonnets*. London: Cecil Palmer.	
1934	*Shakespeare's Sonnets*. Oxford: Shakespeare Head Press.	
1935	*Sunlight on Shakespeare's Sonnets*. London: T. Butterworth, Ltd.	
1936	*Lord Burghley in Shakespeare: Falstaff, Sly and Others*. London: T. Butterworth,	
1954	*Shake Spears Sonnets* [sic] (pamphlet). London: W. Heffer and Sons.	

Shorter pieces

1937, March	[letter: response to K. C. T.'s Feb. review]	Sh. Pictorial, no. 109: 36
1948, April	The Importance of the *Sonnets*	SF News-letter (E), p. 7-8
1949, March	Did Edward de Vere Make a Private Marriage?	SF News-letter (E), p. 6-7
1951, April	Defense of Dr. Hotson's Dating of Sonnet 107	SF News-letter (E), p. 4-5
1952, March	Shakespeare's *Sonnets* [letter]	SF News-letter (E), p. 8
1953, April	[review of *This Star of England* by Dorothy and Charlton Ogburn]	SF News-letter (E), p. 8-9
1954, April	[letter: *This Star of England*]	SF News-letter (E), p. 14
1955, Spring	[letter: resp. to Ruth Wainewright's Spring 1954 "Sonnets" article]	SF News-letter (E), p. 13

Phillips, Graham

1994	*The Shakespeare Conspiracy* [with Martin Keatman]. London: Century. [excerpt repr. in *Shakespeare Criticism, vol. 41* (Lee & Barnes 1998): 67-76]	

Phillips, Michael
   2001, May 4   Amy Freed Toys With the Mystery of Shakespeare's Identity   Los Angeles Times, p. F2
   2002, Oct. 6   Where There's a Will [review of *The Beard of Avon* by Amy Freed]   Chicago Tribune, p. 7
   2011, Oct. 28   *Anonymous* Debate Rages Here and Abroad   Chicago Tribune, p. 4.1

Phillips, Robin
Film/Documentary
   2020   *SHAKESPEARE: The Truth Behind the Name.* [film/documentary]
Shorter pieces
   2020, Fall   *Behind the Name SHAKESPEARE: Power, Lust, Scorn & Scandal –*   Sh. Ox. Newsl., vol. 56/4: 12-14
       My New Film Makes Splashes

Phoenix, Eleanor
   1991, Fall   [letter: promoting Oxford in her classroom in Boulder City]   Sh. Ox. Newsl., vol. 27/4: 15

Pier, Arthur Stanwood
   1956, May   To the Editor and Readers of *The Shakespeare Newsletter*   Sh. Newsletter, vol. 6/3: 18
       [letter, with 21 other signers]

Pierce, Annie
   1999, April 8   Was Shakespeare a Fraud? Conference Looks Into the Question   Columbian (Vancouver), p. F5
       [Third Annual De Vere Studies Conference]

Pigman III, G. W.
   2012, Nov.   [review of *Fortunatus im Ungluck: Die Aventiuren des Master F. I.*   Modern Philology, vol. 110/2:
       Edward de Vere, Earl of Oxford translated by Chris Hirte]   E82-88

Pizzichini, Lilian
   1999, April 25   [review of *Who Wrote Shakespeare?* by John Michell (1996)]   Independent, p. 12

Pirè, Luciana
   2012   [review of *Contested Will* by James Shapiro (2010)]   Memoria di Sh., NS 8: 464

Pitcher, Seymour
   1961   *The Case for Shakespeare's Authorship of "The Famous Victories of Henry V."* New York: State University
       of New York. [See esp. de Vere material not SAQ-related]

Plank, James A.
   1989, April 29   These Doubts on Shakespeare Are, Well, Loony [letter: resp. to   Philadelphia Inquirer, p. A6
       Warren Hope's April 20 article]
       Reply by Warren Hope, May 17, p. A10.

Plummer, Christopher
   2014   *Nothing Truer Than Truth* (Vero Nihil Verius) [MA Thesis: Oxfordian story in the form of a drama]. Regent
       University.

Plummer, John
   2013   Doubter Response to Question #22: As an actor, what is your sense
       of Shakespeare's personality?, in *Sh. Beyond Doubt?* (Shahan): 181

Plunkett, Paul M.
   1994   *Shacksper of Stratford: A Monumental Deception.* NY: Vantage Press.

Pluto, Anne E.
   1997, Spring   The Oxford Street Players: Lesley College students are learning   Sh. Ox. Newsl., vol. 33/2: 14-15
       a New Shakespeare [repr. in BTC, vol. 7: 399-403]

Poel, William
   1922, Jan. 26   Shakespeare: A Standard Text [letter]   Times Lit. Sup., is. 1045: 60

Pogson, Reuben
   1930, Dec. 24   [letter: Percy Allen's Oct. 18 article]   Christian Science Monitor, p. 20
       Reply by Percy Allen, Feb. 9, p. 14.

Pointon, Anthony J.
Books
   2011   *The Man Who Was Never Shakespeare: The Theft of William Shakspere's Identity.* Turnbridge Wells, Kent,
       UK: Parapress.
Shorter pieces
   2005, Sept.   The Problem of a Stratford-Born Shakespeare [with Hugh Mason]   De Vere Soc. Newsl., p. 26-29
   2012, March   Problems of the 'Front-Man' Theory   De Vere Soc. Newsl., v. 19/1: 15

Pointon, Anthony J. (continued)

2012, Nov.	Shakespeare, Shakspere and Jonson: Tony Pointon Questions Some Oxfordian Assumptions [with the editor]	De Vere S. New., v. 19/3: 30-32
2012, Nov.	[letter: Hayward's *Life of Henry IV*]	De Vere Soc. Newsl., v. 19/3: 44
2013	The Man Who Was Never Shakespeare (in SBD? (Shahan): 14-28	
2013	The Rest is Silence: The Absence of Tributes to the Author in *Sh. Beyond Doubt?* (Shahan): 69-70	
2013	Doubter Response to Question #29: Did Shakespeare have an aristocratic patron? in *Sh. Beyond doubt?* (Shahan): 186-87	
2013	Doubter Response to Question #54: What is the attitude of Mainstream Shakespeare scholars toward the authorship discussion? in *Sh. Beyond Doubt?* (Shahan): 211	
2013, July	The Unnecessary, the Helpful, and the Untenable: Six Arguments Which Oxfordians Should Avoid	De Vere S. New., v. 20/3: 22-24
2015, Oct.	The Case Against William of Stratford	De Vere S. New., v. 22/4: 15-20
2016, January	[letter: Benson's questioning of Shakspere's authorship]	De Vere Soc. New., vol. 23/1: 45
2018, Oct.	Comment on the So-called "Pregnancy Portrait"	De Vere S. New., v. 25/4: 12-14

Pollak, Kevin

2015, Summer	Actor Michael Chiklis Comes Out as an Oxfordian [with M. Chiklis]	Sh. Ox. Newsl., vol. 51/3: 24-25

Pollard, Alfred W.

1920, March 4	"Another 'Identification' of Shakespeare" [review of SI] [response by Looney on March 25]	Times Lit. Sup., is. 946: 149

Pommer, Jennifer

2020, Oct.	[review of *"Shakespeare" Revealed: The Collected Articles and Published Letters of J. Thomas Looney*, edited by James Warren]	De Vere So. New., v. 27/4: 37-40
2021, April	[review of *In the Shadow of Shakespeare* by Richard V. Davies]	De Vere So. New., v. 28/2: 47-49
2022, July	[review of *The Living Record: Shakespeare, Succession, and the Sonnets* by Hank Whittemore]	De Vere So. New., v. 29/3: 43-47

Pope, James S.

1960, Jan.	[letter: response to Bentley]	Am. Bar Assoc. J., v. 46/1: 4

Pope, Russell

1988, April	Myths of Stratford and St. George	De Vere Soc. New., no. 2: 28-30
1988, Summer	Stratford and the Sidney Circle [repr. with title ". . . the silence defies all excuses" in SON, vol. 24/4: 3-7, Fall, 1988; and in BTC, vol. 6: 357-65)	Sh. Newsl., vol. 38/2: 22
1988, Winter	The Will, the Swan, and the Moniment	Spear-shaker Rev., is. 1/2: 40-41

Popova, Galina – See Michael Brame for books, articles and letters co-authored with him.

Porohovshikov, Peter S. [Petr Sergeevich Porokhovshchikov]
Books

1940	*Shakespeare Unmasked*. Brooklyn, NY: Polygon Press, Inc.	

Shorter pieces

1939, Jan. 27	Who Was Shakespeare? A New Examination I	John O'London's Weekly, p. 657-58+
1939, Feb. 3	Who Was Shakespeare? II: The Case for the Earl of Rutland	John O'London's Weekly, p. 389-90+
1941, Oct.	[letter: orthodoxy cannot survive much longer]	SF News-letter (A), vol. 2/6: 72
1952, March	[letter: thanks for the Newsletter]	SF News-letter (E), p. 8

Porter, Brian

2000, Jan.	[letter: reprint of his Dec. 9 response to Ch. Dams' Dec. 2 letter] Also reprinted: Christopher Dams' Dec. 2 resp. to Dennis Kay's Nov. 25 article Christopher Dams' resp. to Porter's Dec. 9 letter [not printed in *The Times*] Kevin Gilvary's resp. to Porter's Dec. 9 letter [not printed in *The Times*]	De Vere Soc. Newsl., p. 3-6

Posener, Alan

1997, Dec.	Ansatz zu einem Dialog zwischen Stratford und Oxford	Neues Sh. Journal, vol. 1: 143-53
2010, Jan. 30	Der mit der Honigzunge [review of *Der Mann, der Shakespeare erfand, Edward de Vere, Earl of Oxford* by Kurt Kreiler]	Die Welt (Berlin), p. 1

Posner, Michael

Potter, Gillie

Poullain, Patricia

Powell, Rt. Hon. J. Enoch

Prechter, Robert R., Jr.

Books, online

Shorter pieces

Prechter, Robert R., Jr. (continued)

2014, Fall	Harvey as Dogberry	Sh. Ox. Newsl., vol. 50/4: 7
2015, Winter	Reply to Michael Morse's Critique of the Sonnets Dedication Puzzle	Sh. Ox. Newsl., vol. 51/1: 19-22
2015	Is Greene's Groats-worth of Wit About Shakespeare, or By Him?	Oxfordian, vol. 17: 95-132
2015, Winter	[letter: Middle Temple Hall]	Sh. Ox. Newsl., vol. 51/1: 5
2015, Summer	[letter: Waugaman's Spring 2015 "1578 poem" article]	Sh. Ox. Newsl., vol. 51/3: 3
	See also Jacquelyn Mason's resp. to Waugaman, p. 3.	
2015, Summer	Oxford's Final Love Letters to Queen Elizabeth	Sh. Ox. Newsl., vol. 51/3: 25-30
2018, Spring	In the Footsteps of Vere and Roe (Part One)	Sh. Ox. Newsl., v. 54/2: 1, 24-28
2018, Summer	In the Footsteps of Vere and Roe (Part Two)	Sh. Ox. Newsl., v. 54/3: 1, 27-29
2019, Summer	A Clear Declaration in 1606 that Prince Tudor Existed	Sh. Ox. Newsl., vol. 55/3: 12
2021, Fall	Oxford's Voices: What Shakespeare Wrote Before He was Sh.	Sh. Ox. Newsl., vol. 57/4: 21-24
2022, Winter	Who Wrote George Peele's "Only Extant Letter"?	Sh. Ox. Newsl., vol. 58/1: 12-16
2022, Summer	George Peele's Personal Note from Shakespeare	Sh. Ox. Newsl., vol. 58/3: 22-26
2022, Fall	[letter: two upcoming Shakespeare performances, including Douglas Post's *By My Will*, a play on the SAQ]	Sh. Ox. Newsl., vol. 58/4: 6
2022, Fall	Robert Prechter Replies to Roger Stritmatter	Sh. Ox. Newsl., vol. 58/4: 21-22
2023, Jan.	The Author Behind the Allonym "Richard Lichfield"	De Vere So. New., v. 30/1: 39-41
2023, Spring	Who Translated "Shakespeare's Favorite Novel"?	Sh. Ox. Newsl., vol. 59/2: 10-13
2023, Spring	[review of *By My Will* by Douglas Post]	Sh. Ox. Newsl., vol. 59/2: 24
2023, July	The Earl of Oxford Contributed to John Gerarde's *The Herball* (1587)	De Vere So. New., v. 30/3: 30-31
2023, Summer	[letter: Prince Tudor]	Sh. Ox. Newsl., vol. 59/3: 4
2023, Summer	The Young Oxfordians	Sh. Ox. Newsl., vol. 59/3: 6
2023, Summer	A Smoking Gun: George Peele's *Anglorum Feriae* Manuscript	Sh. Ox. Newsl., vol. 59/3: 30-31
2023, Sept.	Avisa: Queen Elizabeth or Penelope Rich?	Oxfordian, vol. 25: 233-39

Prener, Nan

2007	[review of *Hamlet's Universe* by Peter Usher (2006)]	Oxfordian, vol. 10: 157-158

Prescott, W. S.

1950, Aug. 31	Who Wrote Shakespeare?	Listener, vol. 44: 309

Pressly, William L.

1993, Spring	The Ashbourne Portrait of Shakespeare: Through the Looking Glass	Sh. Quarterly, v. 44/1: 54-72

Preston, Ernest D.

1955, July 29	Who Was the Author of Shakespeare's Plays? [letter]	Yorkshire Post & Leeds Int., p. 4

Price, Diana

Books

2001	*Shakespeare's Unorthodox Biography: New Evidence of an Authorship Problem.* Westport, CT: Greenwood Press.	
2013	*Shakespeare's Unorthodox Biography: New Evidence of an Authorship Problem.* Published with corrections, revisions, and additions. Cleveland: Shakespeare-authorship.com. [excerpt repr. in *Sh. Authorship Sourcebook* (*Stritmatter* 2019, 2022): 192-95]	

Shorter pieces

1991, Fall	Re: Drayton's *Elegies Upon Sundry Occasions*, 1627	Sh. Ox. Newsl., vol. 27/4: 3-5
1992, Winter	The Boar in the Induction Scene [repr. in BTC, vol. 7: 90-94]	Sh. Ox. Newsl., vol. 28/1: 4-7
1994, Autumn	Westward Ho! The Shakespeare Oxford Society 18ᵗʰ Annual Conf.	Sh. Ox. Newsl., vol. 30/4: 16-17
1995, Summer	Oxford's Coronet Signature [repr. in BTC, vol. 7: 340-43]	Sh. Ox. Newsl., vol. 31/3: 9-10
1996, Spring	[letter: Joseph Sobran]	Sh. Ox. Newsl., vol. 32/2: 22
1996, Summer	Shaxicon and Shakespeare's Acting Career	Sh. Newsl., vol. 46/2: 27-28+
	Response by Donald W. Foster, Fall 1996, p. 57-58.	
	Reply by Price, Spring 1997, p. 11, 14.	
1996, Spring	Shakespeare, Shake-scene and the Clayton Loan	Eliz. Review, vol. 4/1: 3-13
1996, Autumn	Rough Winds Do Shake: A Fresh Look at the Tudor Rose Theory	Eliz. Review, vol. 4/2: 4-23
	Response by Richard W. Edbloom in vol. 5/1: 6-17.	
	Response by Martha N. Walker in vol. 5/1: 6-17.	
	Response by Verily Anderson in vol. 5/1: 6-17.	
	Response by Francis Edwards in vol. 5/1: 6-17.	
	Response by Derran K. Charlton in vol. 5/1: 6-17.	

Propson, David
    2006, Feb.   Shakespiracy Theory [review of *"Shakespeare" By Another Name*   New Criterion, v. 24/6: 23-27
             by Mark Anderson (2005)]

Proulx, Phillip
    1983, Fall   How I Became an Oxfordian [repr. in BTC, vol. 6: 254-56]   Sh. Ox. Newsl., vol. 19/4: 4-5
    1985, Winter   When One and One and One Equals One   Sh. Ox. Newsl., vol. 21/1: 3-5
    1985, Winter   The Dark Lady Ain't No Lady   Sh. Ox. Newsl., vol. 21/1: 5-6
    1995, Spring   [review of *Shakespeare, In Fact* by Irvin Matus (1994)]   Eliz. Review, vol. 3/1: 67-69

Pruvost, Rene
    1923, Oct.   Une nouvelle hypothèse anti-stratfordienne   Revue Anglo-Am., vol. 1: 148-53

    1928, Dec.   [review of *Le Mystere Shakespearien* by Georges Connes]   Revue Anglo-Am., vol. 6/2: 170-72

    1930, Dec.   [review of *Topical Dramatists* by Percy Allen]   Revue Anglo-Am., vol. 8/2: 149-50

Publiatti, Paola
    2012   The Burden of Proof: From New Biographism to New Disintegration   Memoria di Sh., vol. 8: 133

Publius
    1995, Summer   [review of Shakespeare IN FACT by Irvin Matus]   Eliz. Review, vol. 3/1: 67-69
             [repr. in EVR, vol. 1 (Fall 1995)]

Puente, Maria
    2011, Oct. 27   Who Wrote Shakespeare?   USA Today

Pugh, Tom
    2007, Dec. 10   To Be Or Not To Be: Actors Cast Doubt Over Identity of the Bard   Teelegraph
             [Declaration of Reasonable Doubt]

Puig, Claudia
    2011, Oct. 27   *Anonymous* is Shakespeare, writ small   USA Today

Pulford, Angie
    2007   [rev. of *The Big Secret Live* by Mark Rylance & Matthew Warchus]   Groatsworth of Wit, v. 18/4: 23-6

Purdy, Gilbert W.
    2013   *Edward de Vere Was Shake-speare: At Long Last, the Proof.* CreateSpace.

Quealy, Gerit
Books
    2017   *Botanical Shakespeare*. Harper Design.
Shorter pieces
    1999, Winter   Hollywood's the Thing . . . [review of *Elizabeth* and *Shakespeare*   Sh. Ox. Newsl., vol. 34/4: 4-5
             in Love] [repr. in EVR, vol. 8 (Spr. 1999)]
    2001, Winter   News: Authorship play in California, Oxfordian Weekend in Chicago   Sh. Ox. Newsl., vol. 36/4: 18-19
    2002, Winter   Oxford Makes *NY Times*: Authorship Q. is News Fit to Print, Finally   Sh. Ox. Newsl., v. 38/1: 1, 19, 23
    2002, Winter   A Duel in D.C.: The Smithsonian Hosts an Authorship Debate   Sh. Ox. Newsl., vol. 38/1: 12-13
    2002, Spring   The Sixth Annual Edward de Vere Studies Conference   Sh. Ox. Newsl., vol. 38/2: 4-5, 20
    2002, Fall   Gheeraerts Exhibit Featured at the Tate   Sh. Ox. Newsl., vol. 38/4: 2
    2003, Winter   Shakespeare's Globe in London to Host Authorship Conference   Sh. Ox. Newsl., vol. 39/1: 1, 3
    2003, Summer   Globe's Authorship Conference Roundly Successful   Sh. Ox. Newsl., vol. 39/3: 1, 14-5
    2003, Summer   The Temple in Lord Pembroke's Garden: The Truth about Wilton's   Sh. Ox. Newsl., vol. 39/3: 6-8
             Shakespeare Shrine
             Response by Christopher Paul, Fall 2003, p. 20.
    2003, Summer   Elizabeth Exhibited: Maritime Museum Exhibit Honors Tudor Queen   Sh. Ox. Newsl., vol. 39/3: 10-11
    2004, Spring   In Memoriam: Leonard Hansen, Avid Antiquarian and Oxfordian   Sh. Ox. Newsl., vol. 40/2: 6
    2007, Feb.   Notes from the Front: World Shakespeare Congress   De Vere Soc. Newsl., p. 3
    2008, Summer   *The Oxfordian's* New Editor Is Up For the Challenge [with M. Egan]   Sh. Ox. Newsl., vol. 44/3: 14-15
    2008, Oct.   *Oxfordian's* New Editor Is Up For the Challenge: Prof. Michael   De Vere So. New., v. 15/3: 22-23
             Egan Maintains an Objective Eye at the Helm
    2009, Nov.   [letter: need for an open mind; and Editor's note]   De Vere Soc. Newsl., v. 16/3: 6-7

Quinn, Edward
    1970, Sept. 6   Shakespeare, Who He? [letter: Ogburn's Sept. 6 letter]   Washington Post, p. 9

Quirke, Kieron
    2007, Sept. 3   So Whodunit, Will? [review of *The Big Secret Live* by Mark Rylance   Evening Standard, p. 1
        and Matthew Warchus]

R. D. R.
    1959, June 1   Bard and Bar [letter: support for Wright, criticism of Ogburn]   Washington Post, p. A14

R. H. C. [see Alfred Orage]

R. S.
    1919, May 9   The Shakespeare Problem [review of *Sous Le Masque De 'William*   *Athenaeum, p. 301*
        Shakespeare' by Abel Lefranc]

Radford, Ceri
    2007, Sept. 12   RIP William Shakespeare? [Declaration of Reasonable Doubt]   Telegraph

Radford, Tim
    1977, June 2   Nothing Truer Than Truth [review of *Nothing Truer Than Truth*, a   Guardian, p. 10
        play about Edward de Vere by Darrol Blake]
    2004, Dec. 2   What Can the Way This is Written Tell You About the Author?   Guardian, p. 2

Radney, Elaine M.
    2002, Spring   [letter: Prechter's Winter 2002 "Veres and De Vere" article]   Sh. Ox. Newsl., vol. 38/2: 23

Radz, Matt
    2003, Jan. 11   Seeking Shakespeare's Ghostwriter   Gazette (Montreal), p. D5

Raidy, William A.
    1988, Feb. 7   Shakespeare Still Arousing Passions After 400 Years   New Orleans T-P, page J2

Raithel, John (1)
    1937, April   Editor's Comments: Shakespeare and East Anglia   East Angl. M., vol. 2/7: 290
    1937, May   Editor's Comments: Was "Shakespeare" an East Anglian?   East Angl. M., vol. 2/8: 338
    1937, June   Editor's Comments: "Rambler" and "Shakespeare!". Francis Bacon.   East Angl. M., vol. 2/9: 385
    1937, Aug.   Lord Oxford and "Shakespeare" [launching of the "Shakespearean   East Angl. M., vol. 2/11: 518
        Page to be edited by F. Lingard Ranson
    1938, Feb.   Shakespeare Fellowship [donations to the Ipswich Public Library]   East Angl. M., vol. 3/5: 235
    1940, Jan.   Note: Shakespearean Fellowship in America   East Angl. M., vol. 5/1: 11
    1938, Nov.   Editor's Comments: The Opening of Spenser's Tomb   East Angl. M., vol. 4/1: 2-3

Raithel, John (2)
    2009   The Other William Shakespeare: Will. Stanley, Sixth Earl of Derby   Oxfordian, vol. 11: 29-44

Rambler (1)
    1920, May 22   Out and About [review of *"Shakespeare" Identified*]   Avon Gazette (Australia), p. 2

Rambler (2)
    Websites and blogs: Quake-speare Shorterly – lookingforshakespeare.globspot.com

Ramey, Paul
    1982, Fall   A Skeptical Thought about the "Skeptical Thoughts" of Oxfordians   Sh. Newsl., vol. 32/3: 22

Ranson, F. Lingard
Books
    1937   *Lavenham, Suffolk*. Printed privately. ["Foreword" by Lt. Col. Montagu W. Douglas]
Columns edited
    1937, Aug.-1941, April: The Shakespearean Page of the *East Anglian Magazine*, vol. 2/11-vol. 5/6
Shorter pieces
    1937, April   Shakespeare Was an East Anglian [repr. in BTC, vol. 2: 42-55]   East Angl. M., vol. 2/7: 292-300
        Responses in the May issue; Ranson's reply in the June issue.
    1937, June   Correspondence [replies to letters]   E. Angl. M., vol. 2/9: 421-23
    1937, July   Notes on the Stokes's June article 'Bacon and 'Shakespeare'   E. Angl. M., vol. 2/10: 467-68
    1937, Dec.   Shakespearean Page   E. Angl. M., vol. 3/3: 148
    1937, Sept.   Lord Oxford and Shakespeare [reply to Stokes's July letter]   E. Angl. M., vol. 2/12: 530-32
    1938, Jan.   [letter: de Vere as author by Lucas in *All of a Piece*]   SF News-letter (E), no. 7: 10-11
    1938, May   Chronology of the Oxford Theory   E. Angl. M., vol. 3/7: 351-52
    1938, Sept.   The Trend of Shakespearean Thought Today   E. Angl. M., vol. 3/11: 520-21
    1939, Jan   Hamlet   E. Angl. M., vol. 4/3: 156-57

Ranson, F. Lingard (continued)

1939, June	Chronology [based on notes sent by SF President Col. Douglas]	E. Angl. M., vol. 4/7: 412-13
1940, Feb.	Death of Ernest Allen (1875-1940) [repr. in BTC, vol. 1: 381]	E. Angl. M., vol. 5/2: 63: 63
1940, Sept.	The Case for the July	E. Angl. M., vol. 5/5: 186-87
1941, April	[letter to Charles Barrell, dated October 31, 1940 (excerpts)]	SF News-letter (A), no. 2/1: 21

Raphael, Frederic

1993, April 25	Fifteen Success Stories [review of Michael Hart's *The 100*]	Sunday Times, p. 5

Rapport, Evie

1992, April 20	The Genius Mystery: Hundreds of Questions Surround the Works of Shakespeare [reports on Charles Vere talk]	Daily New (Halifax), p. 22

Rascoe, Burton

1945, July 31	[letter: battle still rages over who Shakespeare was] [repr. in SFQ, vol. VI/4: 57-59, Oct. 1945]	New York World-Telegram

Rathburn, Stephen

1930, Feb. 17	Champion of Earl of Oxford as Claimant to Shakespeare's Fame [review of *Case for Edward de Vere* by Percy Allen]	New York Sun

Rathvon, Newsl. Peter, Jr.

1960, Oct.	[letter: praise for its Shakespeare authorship articles]	Am. Bar Assoc. Journal, vol. 46/10: 1044

Ravenshaw, John

1929, Sept. 13	Royal Writs [letter]	Morning Post, p. 9

Ray, William J.

2009, Winter	[letter: response to William Farina's Fall 2008 *Coriolanus* article]	Sh. Matters, vol. 8/1: 2
2009, Sept.	Proofs of Oxfordian Authorship in the Shakespearean Apocrypha	Sh. Ox. Newsl., vol. 45/2: 22-27
2011, Winter	Proving Oxfordian Authorship of "Sweet Cytherea"	Sh. Mat., vol. 10/1: 1, 15-27
2011, Summer	News: I Know Why the Caged Stratfordian Mutters [John Crace's article about Roland Emmerich's film *Anonymous*]	Sh. Matters, vol. 10/3: 4, 32
2011, Fall	Two Years After *Contested Will* or, How Are the Stratfordians Doing?	Sh. Matters, vol. 10/4: 24-31
2011, Fall	[review of *Shakespeare Suppressed* by Katherine Chiljan (2011)]	Brief Chronicles, v. III: 235-245
2012, Fall	[review of *Shakespeare's Education: Schools, Lawsuits, Theater and the Tudor Miracle*, by Robin Fox (2012)]	Sh. Matters, vol. 11/4: 20-21
2012, Fall	[review of *The Man Who Was Never Shakespeare: The Theft of William Shakespeare's Identity*, by Anthony J. Pointon (2011)]	Sh. Matters, vol. 11/4: 21-23
2012, Fall	[review of *Shakespeare's Shrine: The Bard's Birthplace and the Invention of Stratford-upon-Avon*, by Julia Thomas (2012)]	Sh. Matters, vol. 11/4: 23
2013, Winter	[review of *Elsinore Revisited – 'This Ientleman of Polonia': Polonius, A Character in Disguise'* by Sten F. Vedi (2012)]	Sh. Matters, vol. 12/1: 26-27
2013, Spring	[review of *The Fully Annotated Macbeth, Second Edition with Commentary by Richard F. Whalen*, by Richard F. Whalen]	Sh. Matters, vol. 12/2: 6, 17
2014, Summer	[review of *Edward de Vere Was Shake-speare: At Long Last, The Proof* by Gilbert Wesley Purdy (2013)]	Sh. Ox. Newsl., vol. 50/3: 22-24
2013, Fall	Albert Burgstahler Remembrance (1928-2013)	Sh. Matters, vol. 12/4: 9, 33+
2013, Fall	[review of *On the Date, Sources and Design of Shakespeare's The Tempest* by Roger A. Stritmatter and Lynne Kositsky]	Sh. Matters, vol. 12/4: 27-28
2014, Winter	[review of *A Poet's Rage: Understanding Shakespeare Through Authorship Studies* edited by Bill Boyle (2013)]	Sh. Ox. Newsl., vol. 50/1: 20-24+
2014, Fall	[review of *Such Fruits Out of Italy* by Noemi Magri; edited by Gary Goldstein (2014)]	Sh. Ox. Newsl., vol. 50/4: 11-12
2015, Summer	Dr. Magri's Bow and Quiver [review of *Such Fruits Out of Italy: The Italian Renaissance in Shakespeare's Plays and Poems* by Noemi Magri (2014) [repr. in NSJ, vol. NS5: 188-96]	Brief Chronicles, vol. VI: 179-85
2015, Summer	[review of *Unreading Shakespeare* by David P. Gontar (2015)]	Sh. Ox. Newsl., vol. 51/3: 14-16
2015, Summer	[review of *Ver, Begin* by Ricardo Mena (2015)]	Sh. Ox. Newsl., vol. 51/3: 16-18

Read, Conyers

1955	*Mr. Secretary Cecil and Queen Elizabeth*. London: Cape.	
1960	*Lord Burghley and Queen Elizabeth*. New York: Knopf.	

Ready, Gabriel A.

2015	Honest Ben and the Two Tribes He Hath Left Us	Oxfordian, vol. 17: 7-26
2018, Sept.	"The Knotty Wrong-Side": Another Spanish Connection to the FF [repr. in *The First Folio* (Stritmatter 2023): 119-50]	Oxfordian, vol. 20: 49-82
2021, Summer	A Prologue Arm'd: The Printing of *Troilus and Cressida* in the FF	Sh. Ox. Newsl., vol. 57/3: 14-15
2021, Sept.	The Production of the First Folio Reconsidered [repr. in *The First Folio* (Stritmatter 2023): 53-78]	Oxfordian, vol. 23: 49-76
2023, Aug.	History of Fixing: on the 400th Anniversary of Shakespeare's First Folio, in *The First Folio* (Stritmatter): 337-374	
2023, Sept.	Shakespeare's Book: The Story Behind the First Folio and the Making of Shakespeare [review of the book by Chris Laoutaris] [repr. in *The First Folio* (Stritmatter 2023): 383-404]	Oxfordian, vol. 25: 283-92

Reardon, John

| 2013, Oct. 19 | [letter: J. Kelly Nestruck's Oct. 17 article | Globe & Mail, p. F8 |

Redding, D. C.

| 1993, March | [review of *The Shakespeare Controversy* by Warren Hope and Kim Holston] | Choice, vol. 30/7: 1146 |

Redman, Ben Ray

| 1948, June 5 | New Reviews Response by Gelett Burgess, Oct. 2, p. 22. | Saturday Review, p. 46 |

Redstone, V. B.

| 1937, May | Was Shakespeare an East Anglian? [letter] | East Angl. M., vol. 2/8: 362-63 |

Reed, Arthuryes

| 1928, June 21 | Edward de Vere, Earl of Oxford [rev. of *The Seventeenth Earl of Oxford* by B. M. Ward] | Times Lit. Sup., is. 1377: 461 |

Reed, J. D.

| 1964, April | Some Ado About Who Was, or Was Not, Shakespeare | Life, p. 155-60 |
| 1987, Sept. | Some Ado About Who Was, Or Was Not, Shakespeare [excerpt repr. in SON, vol. 23/3 (Sum. 1987): 12] [responses in the Nov. 1987 issue] Response by Scott S. Smith, SON, vol. 23/3 (Winter. 1988): 13-14. | Smithsonian, p. 155-76 |

Reeder, Jackie

| 2006, April 2 | Was Earl of Oxford the Real Bard? | Sunday Mercury, p. 11 |

Reedy, Tom

| 2010 | Dating William Strachey's 'A True Repertory of the Wracke and Redemption of Sir Thomas Gates': A Comparative Textual Study | Rev. of Eng. St., vol. 61: 529-52 |

Reedy, William M.

| 1920, June 10 | Another Shakespeare [review of SI] Response by Henry Watterson and Reedy's reply, June 17. [response and reply repr. in *The Montgomery Advertiser* on June 27 and *The New York Times* on July 18.] | Reedy's Mirror, vol. 29/24: 474-76 |
| 1920, June 17 | Reflections: The Shakespeare Myth [reply to Hatterson's letter] | Reedy's Mirror, vol. 29/25: 493 |

Rees, Jasper

| 2007, Aug. 4 | Call the Real Shakespeare [review of *The Big Secret Live* by Mark Rylance and Matthew Warchus] | Telegraph |

Reeves, James

| 1958, Aug. 24 | The Anti-Shakespeare Industry [review *of Shakespeare and his Betters*, by R. C. Churchill] | Observer, p. 12 |

Reul, Paul de

| 1922, Sept.-Dec. | M. Lefranc et William Stanley | Flambeau, p. 419-25 |

Regnier, John

| 2015, Winter | *How the Authorship Question First Came to Light* [cartoon] | Sh. Ox. Newsl., vol. 51/1: 22 |

Regnier, Thomas

2003, Jan.	Could Shakespeare Think Like a Lawyer? How Inheritance Law issues in *Hamlet* May Shed Light on the Authorship Question [repr. in *Sh. and the Law* (Stritmatter, 2022): 187-230]	Univ. of Miami Law Review, vol. 57/2
2006, Fall	Teaching Shakespeare and the Law [repr. in *Shakespeare Authorship Sourcebook* (Stritmatter 2019, 2022): 87-91]	Sh. Matters, vol. 6/1: 1, 11-13
2011, Fall	The Law in *Hamlet*: Death, Property, and the Pursuit of Justice [repr. in BTC, vol. 10: 241-72; and in *Sh. and the Law* (Stritmatter, 2022): 231-52]]	Brief Chronicles, v. III: 109-134
2012, Fall	From the President: Reinventing Ourselves	Sh. Matters, vol. 11/4: 3
2013	Could Shakespeare Think Like a Lawyer, in SBD? (Shahan): 86-98	
2013	Doubter Response to Question #60: What do you think about Shake-speare's reputation being stolen and passed off as someone else's?, in *Sh. Beyond Doubt?* (Shahan): 215-16	
2013, Winter	From the President: "Shakespeare in a Year:" Why It Matters Who Wrote the Works	Sh. Matters, vol. 12/1: 4
2013, Spring	Did Tudor Succession Law Permit Royal Bastards to Inherit the Crown? [repr. in *Sh. and the Law* (Stritmatter, 2022): 293-308]	Brief Chronicles, vol. IV: 37-55
2013, Spring	From the President: "Let Me Not to the Marriage of True Minds Admit Impediments"	Sh Matters, vol. 12/3: 1, 36
2013, Spring	From the President: Wherever the Evidence Leads . . .	Sh. Matters, vol. 12/2: 3, 24
2013, Spring	SOS and SF Propose Unity: Notice of Intent [with John Hamill]	Sh. Ox. Newsl., vol. 49/2: 2-4
2013, Summer	[review of *Shakespeare Beyond Doubt: Evidence, Argument, Controversy* edited by Paul Edmondson and Stanley Wells]	Sh. Matters, vol. 28-33
2013, Fall	From the [Lame Duck] President: An End . . . And a New Beginning	Sh. Matters, vol. 12/4: 3
2014, Winter	From the Shakespeare Oxford Fellowship President's Office [with John Hamill]	Sh. Ox. Newsl., vol. 50/1: 2
2014, Summer	From the President's Office [with John Hamill]	Sh. Ox. Newsl., vol. 50/3: 2-3
2014, Summer	Further review of *Shakespeare Beyond Doubt: Evidence, Argument, Controversy* edited by Paul Edmondson and Stanley Wells (2013)	Brief Chronicles, vol. V: 193-204
2014, Fall	From the President's Office [membership and publication news]	Sh. Ox. Newsl., vol. 50/4: 2-3
2015, Winter	From the President: Nous Sommes Charlie	Sh. Ox. Newsl., vol. 51/1: 2-3
2015, Spring	From the President: The Future of the Oxfordian Movement	Sh. Ox. Newsl., vol. 51/2: 2-3
2015, Summer	From the President: A Tale of Two Journals	Sh. Ox. Newsl., vol. 51/3: 2-3
2015, Fall	From the President: After Ashland	Sh. Ox. Newsl., vol. 51/4: 2-3
2016	Chapter 9: Equivocation, in Contested Year	
2016, Winter	From the President: Matching Funds Support Oxfordian Research	Sh. Ox. Newsl., vol. 52/1: 2-3
2016, Spring	From the President: Research Grant Fundraising Nears Its Goal	Sh. Ox. Newsl., vol. 52/2: 2-3
2016, July	Alexander Waugh Named 'Oxfordian of the Year'	De Vere Soc. Newsl., vol. 23/3: 4
2016, Summer	From the President: Taking the SOF to Greater Heights	Sh. Ox. Newsl., vol. 52/3: 2-3
2016, Fall	From the President: State of the Organization	Sh. Ox. Newsl., vol. 52/4: 2-4
2017, Winter	From the President: An Oxfordian Consensus	Sh. Ox. Newsl., vol. 53/1: 2-4
2017, Spring	From the President: Headstone for J. T. & Elizabeth Looney; SOF Launches Video Contest; Research Grant Program for 2017; Chicago Conference; SCOTUS Committee	Sh. Ox. Newsl., vol. 53/2: 2-3
2017, Summer	From the President: Be Sure to Ask for *Is Shakespeare Dead?* at the Mark Twain House in Hartford	Sh. Ox. Newsl., vol. 53/3: 2-3
2017, Fall	From the President: State of the Organization	Sh. Ox. Newsl., vol. 53/4: 2-4
2018, Winter	From the President: The SOF Making Waves	Sh. Ox. Newsl., vol. 54/1: 2-3
2018, Spring	From the President: Oxfordians in Action	Sh. Ox. Newsl., vol. 54/2: 2-3
2018, Summer	From the President: Evaluating Unification Five Years Later	Sh. Ox. Newsl., vol. 54/3: 2-3
2018, Summer	Making a Planned Gift to the SOF	Sh. Ox. Newsl., vol. 54/3: 31-32
2018, Dec.	Shakespeare as Lawyer: *Hamlet*, Death, Property and the Pursuit of Justice	Critical Stages, vol. 18
2019, Summer	In Memoriam: Justice John Paul Stevens	Sh. Ox. Newsl., vol. 55/3: 13-14
2019, Fall	Justice Stevens v. James Shapiro: The Law of Evidence and the Shakespeare Authorship Question	Sh. Ox. Newsl., vol. 55/4: 10-11

Rehder, Ernie

2021, Winter	[letter: Shakespeare's biographers and the need for proof]	Sh. Ox. Newsl., vol. 57/1: 5

Rendell, Brian
2004, Jan.   [letter: his growing interest in the Earl of Oxford]   De Vere Soc. Newsl., p. 30

Renner, Virginia J.
2002, Winter   [letter: response to Barbara Burris' Fall 2001 "Ashbourne" article]   Sh. Matters, vol. 1/2: 2-3, 32
2004, Spring   Lilies that Fester: A Tale of Two Queens   Sh. Matters, vol. 3/3: 18-21
2011, Fall   [review of *The Shakespeare Guide to Italy* by Richard Roe (2011)]   Brief Chronicles, v. III: 279-284
2013   "Doubter Response to Question #1: How would Shakespeare have had access to books growing up in Stratford-upon-Avon?" in *Sh. Beyond Doubt?* (Shahan): 158-59

Reno, Jamie
1999, April 21   Shakespeare in Doubt   Newsweek

Repass, Larry
1992, Dec. 27   [letter: Richard Whalen's article]   Greensboro News-Rec., p. F2

Reschke, Annette
2014, Oct.   Laudatio auf Frank-Patrick Steckel   Neues Sh. Journal, v. NS4: 6-11

Reuters
2005, Winter   Soul of the Age to Begin Filming in UK this Fall   Sh. Matters, vol. 4/2: 5

Rever, G. Hammond
1990, Spring   [letter: program notes for a performance of *Twelfth Night* in 1941]   Sh. Ox. Newsl., vol. 26/2: 11

Rhys, Ernest
1949, Sept.   The Birthplace [the origin of Henry James's story]   SF News-letter (E), p. 2-4

Rice, Patricia
1992, Dec. 27   Identity Crisis; Will the Truth Come to Light: Who Was Shakespeare? [debate between Lord Burford and Patrick Spottiswoods]   St. Louis Post Dispatch., p. 4C

Richard, Robert
2011   L'homme qui était Shakespeare   Libertè (Montreal), vol. 52/3: 90-100

Richards, Allison
2023, Summer   [review of *Who Wrote That: Authorship Controversies from Moses to Sholokov* by Donald Ostrowski]   Jou. of Sci. Exploration, vol. 37/2

Richardson, Friend W. [former governor of California; president, Publishers Assoc. of California]
1943, March 16   Fighting a Man of Straw [repr. in SFA. vol. 4/5: 58 (August 1943)]   Hemet News

Richardson, Hannah
2004, May 15   Shakespeare 'may have been a humble schoolmaster' [repr. in DVN, vol. 20/2: 25 (July 2013)]   BBC News Mag.

Riche, Kathleen L.
1952, Oct.   Shakespeare in Essex   Essex Review, vol. 61: 187

Riches, Hester
1989, April 18   Much Ado About Shakespeare   Vancouver Sun, p. B5

Rickert, Edith
Books and pamphlets
1923   *Political Propaganda and Satire in A Midsummer Night's Dream*. [pamphlet]: repr. from *Modern Philology*]
Shorter pieces
1923, Aug.   Political Propaganda and Satire in *A Midsummer Night's Dream*, I   Modern Philology, vol. 21/1
1923, Nov.   Political Propaganda and Satire in *A Midsummer Night's Dream*, II   Modern Philology, vol. 21/2

Rickey, George
1989, May 11   Shakespeare Wrote Shakespeare. Believe It Response by Burton Brody, 3 June, p. 14 [Earl of Oxford Preferred]   New York Times, p. 26

Richmond, Peter
1992, June   Shakespeare at Au Bar   Gentleman's Mag., p. 113

Ridden, Geoff
1998   [review of *Who Wrote Shakespeare?* by John Michell (1996)]   Spectator, vol. 47/2: 44
2014, Fall   [rev. of *The Nine Lives of William Shakespeare* by Gr. Holderness]   Sh. Newsl., vol. 64/2: 57

Rodriguez, Theresa

    2015, Spring   Two Sonnets: *The Earl of Oxenford's Sonnet*; *A Sonnet for the*   Sh. Ox. Newsl., vol. 51/2: 17
                      Sonnet-Maker, E. O.

Roe, Richard P.

Books

    2011   *The Shakespeare Guide to Italy: Retracing the Bard's Unknown Travels.* New York: Harper Perennial.
        [excerpts repr. in TOX, vol. 16: 73-77 and in German in NSJ, vol. NS4: 83-93]

Shorter pieces

    1989, Fall-Wntr.   The Perils of *The Tempest*   Sh. Newsl., vol. 39/3-4: 36-37
    2000, April   Aus einem vergessenen Brief [letter to Professor Alan H. Nelson]   Neues Sh. Journal, vol. 5: 50-53
    2008, Winter   Italian Directions for English Merchants [repr. in BTC, vol. 9: 164-75]   Sh. Matters, vol. 7/2: 12-17, 20

Roffel, Ron

    2022, Winter   "Sweet Swan" of Stratford? Not Necessarily So!   Sh. Ox. Newsl., vol. 58/1: 17-19
    2023, Summer   The How and Why of the Coverup: My Two Cents   Sh. Ox. Newsl., vol. 59/3: 21-22

Rogers, Byron

    1973, April 1   What's Behind Shakespeare's Bust? [Ogburn's quest to open Sh.'s tomb]   Chicago Tribune, p. J74
                      Response by Donald R. Yabush, 29 April, p. I6.
    1973, May 20   Once More in Quest of Shakespeare: Endless Dispute About the Bard   Boston Globe, p. E4
                      [Ogburn's quest to open the grave]
    1973, Jan. 26   Bard Thou Never Wert?   Telegraph

Rogers, Hudson

    1958, Aug.   [review of *The Six Loves of "Shakespeare"* by Louis Bénézet (1958)]   English Journal, v. 47/8: 527-28

Rogers, Peter

    2020, Winter   The First Seventeen Sonnets   Sh. Ox. Newsl., vol. 56/1: 16-19

Rolland, Romain

    1920, Aug.   Shakespeare the Truthteller   Dial, p. 108-21

Rollett, John M.

Books

    2014   *William Stanley as Shakespeare: Evidence of Authorship by the Sixth Earl of Derby.* McFarland & Co., Inc.

Shorter pieces

    1996, April   APIS LAPIS, or, Why Was Shakespeare Called Mellifluous?   De Vere Soc. Newsl., v. 2/5: 5-15
    1997, Autumn   The Dedication to Shakespeare's *Sonnets*   Eliz. Review, vol. 5/2: 93-122
                      See also his further thoughts, Feb. and Autumn 1998.
                      Response by Kathryn Sharpe, SM, vol. 6/2: 30 (Winter 2007).
    1997, Fall   Master F. W. D., R.I.P. . . . A Logical Answer is Not Necessarily   Sh. Ox. Newsl., vol. 33/4: 8-9
                      the Correct Answer [repr. in EVR, vol. 5 (Winter 1997)]
    1998, Feb.   Secrets of the Dedication to Shakespeare's *Sonnets*   De Vere So. New., v. 2/11: 13-23
                      [repr. in GO, p. 60-75]
                      Response by John Ogilvie, same issue, p. 23.
                      Response by Kathryn Sharpe, SM vol. 6/2: 3, 30 (Winter 2007).
    1998, Autumn   [letter: dedication to Shakespeare's Sonnets]   Eliza. Review, vol. 6/2: 3
    1999   Secrets of the Dedication to Shakespeare's *Sonnets*   Oxfordian, vol. 2: 60-75
    1999, Winter   [letter: response to Peter Dickson's Fall 1998 "Peacham" article]   Sh. Ox. Newsl., vol. 34/4: 21
    1999, May   Recent U.S. Press Coverage of the Authorship Question   De Vere Soc. New., vol. 3/3: 6-7
    1999, May   Oxfordian Myths   De Vere Soc. New., v. 3/3: 10-14
    1999, May   Not 'Wherefore', But Who Art Thou, Will?   De Vere Soc. New., v. 3/3: 14-15
    1999, June   'Repel these rebel powers': Shakespeare's Sonnet 146 emended   Notes & Q., vol. 46/2: 228
    2000, Jan.   Was Southampton Regarded as the Son of the Queen? Part 1   De Vere Soc. Newsl., p. 8-12
                      Response by Christopher Dams, Oct. p. 20.
                        Reply by Rollett, Oct. p. 22.
                      Response by Ian McGeoch, Jan. 2001, p. 19.

    2000, July   Was Southampton Regarded as the Son of the Queen? Part 2   De Vere Soc. Newsl., p. 19-27
                      Response by Christopher Dams, Oct. p. 20.
                        Reply by Rollett, Jan. 2001, p. 18-19.
                      Response by Ian McGeoch, Jan. 2001, p. 19.
    2000, Oct.   The First Oxfordian   De Vere Soc. Newsl., p. 5-8
    2000, Oct.   [letter: reply to Dams]   De Vere Soc. Newsl., p. 22

2001, Jan.	[letter: reply to Dam's Oct. 2000 response]	De Vere Soc. Newsl., p. 18
2001, Jan.	Oxford Blue, or Possible Clues in Ben Jonson's Eulogy in the First Folio [repr. in GO, p. 289-295]	De Vere Soc. Newsl., p. 43-48
2001, Sept.	The Compositor's Reader: Shakespeare's Sonnet 146 revisited	Notes & Q., vol. 48/3: 275
2002, Summer	[letter: Barbara Burris' 2001-2002 "Ashbourne" articles]	Sh. Matters, vol. 1/4: 2-3
2002, July	Master W. H. Restored	De Vere Soc. Newsl., p. 2-5
	Response by Jeffrey Jague, Oct. 2002, p. 20.	
2002, Fall	Welsh New Year [letter]	Sh. Ox. Newsl., vol. 38/4: 23
2005, Fall	Oxfordian News: Rollout of The Truth Will Out at The Globe	Sh. Ox. Newsl., vol. 41/4: 29, 32
2007, June	Evidence Against Oxford as Shakespeare I: Certain Sonnets	De Vere Soc. Newsl., p. 17-22
	Response by Noemi Magri, Oct. 2007, p. 20.	
	Response by Richard Malim, Oct. 2007, p. 20-21.	
	Reply by Rollett, March 2008, p. 24-25.	
	Response by Isabel M. Leith, March 2008, p. 25-26.	
	See also Paul's further thoughts, Oct. 2008, p. 27.	
2007, Oct.	Evidence Against Oxford as Shakespeare II: Writing Habits [repr. in NSJ, vol. 12: 162-65 (Oct. 2008)]	De Vere Soc. Newsl., p. 22-28
2007, Oct.	[letter: comments re annotation in the Glasgow First Folio]	De Vere Soc. Newsl., p. 30
2008, March	[letter: reply to Noemi Magri and Richard Malim]	De Vere So. New., v. 15/1: 24-25
2008, Oct.	[letter: more canopy issues]	De Vere Soc. New., vol. 15/3: 27
2010	[letter: Wayne Shore's method for dating Shakespeare's plays]	Oxfordian, vol. 12: 5-6
2010	The Tragedie of Antonie and Cleopatra, in Dating Sh's Plays, p. 415-22	
2010	Shakespeare's Impossible Doublet: Engraving Anatomized [repr. in SBD?, p. 113-25 (2013); in BC, Special issue, p. 31-46 (Spring, 2016); and in TFF (Stritmatter 2023): 219-232)]	Brief Chronicles, vol. II: 9-24
2013, Sept.	Shakespeare's Sonnet 125: Who Bore the Canopy?	Notes & Q., vol. 60/3: 438-41
2015, Spring	Shakespeare and the Theater of the Self	Raritan (Rutgers), vol. 34/4: 108+

Rollins, Hyder E. (editor)

1926	Gorgeous Gallery of Gallant Inventions by Thomas Proctor. Cambridge: Harvard University Press. [1578] [see 3 poems by Edward de Vere]	
1927	Paradise of Dainty Devices. Cambridge: Harvard University Press. [1576-1606] [see p. lviii-liv, lx, 244-46]	
1931	The Phoenix Nest. Cambridge: Harvard University Press. [1593] [see p. 161-62, 194-95, 200]	
1933	Brittons Bowre of Delights. Cambridge: Harvard University Press. [1591] [see p. 95, 105]	
1935	England's Helicon. Cambridge, MA: Harvard University Press. [1600, 1614] [in vol. 1, see p. 120, 130-32, 166; in vol. 2, see 239 and index, in which Edward de Vere is listed as "Alias Shakespeare"]	

Romeo, Richard

1997	The Bard of Cuttyhunk?	Yankee, vol. 62/9: 35

Roof, Marcia M.

1949, June 4	Was Shakespeare Shakespeare? [letter]	Sat. Review, p. 24
	[repr. in Sh. and His Rivals (McMichael & Glenn 1962): 185]	

Roper, David L.

Books

2008	Proving Shakespeare: The Looming Identity Crisis. Cornwall, UK: Orvid Books.	
2010	Shakespeare: To Be or Not To Be? Cornwall, UK: Orvid Books.	
2011	Proving Shakespeare: Verifying Ben Jonson's Vow That Edward de Vere was William Shakespeare (revised and updated paperback edition). Cornwall, UK: Orvid Books.	
2018	How Science Proved Edward de Vere was William Shakespeare. Cornwall, UK: Orvid Editions. [2nd ed., First Proofs, 2020]	

Shorter pieces

1995, Nov.	Matus, in Fact? A Personal View of the Anti-Oxfordian Position Adopted in Shakespeare, In Fact by Irwin Leigh Matus	De Vere Soc. Newsl., v. 2/3: 8-11
1996, Sept.	A Monograph Concerning the Cryptography Found on the Shakespeare Monument of 1623	De Vere Soc. Newsl., v. 2/6: 8-12
2001, Apr./May	The Stratford Monument: Proof or Probability?	De Vere Soc. Newsl., p. 2-10
2001, July	Henry Peacham's Chronogram: The Dating of Shakespeare's Titus Andronicus [repr. in GO, p. 140-150]	De Vere Soc. Newsl., p. 7-11

Roper, David L. (continued)

2001, Fall	The Peacham Chronogram [repr. in RCA, p. 55-65] 7+	Sh. Ox. Newsl., vol. 37/3: 1, 14-
2001, Oct.	[letter: resp. to Challinor's April and July "Reason/Rigour" articles] Reply by Challinor, Oct. 2001, p. 15.	De Vere Soc. Newsl., p. 14-15
2002, Winter	[letter: response to Barbara Burris' Fall 2001 "Ashbourne" article]	Sh. Matters, vol. 1/2: 2
2002, Winter	The Peacham Document Revisited	Sh. Ox. Newsl., vol. 38/1: 9, 17
2003, Spring	We Have the Man Sh.: Edward de Vere and the lost letter of Wilton [repr. as "By Shakespeare's Other Avon," in GO, p. 299-303] See also letter by David Roper, SM 3/1: 2-3 (2003).	Sh. Matters, vol. 2/3: 1, 8-13
2003, Fall	Wilton and the Shakespeare House [letter]	Sh. Matters, vol. 3/1: 2-3
2004, April	By Shakespeare's Other Avon [repr. in GO, p. 299-303]	De Vere Soc. Newsl., p. 18-21
2004, April	[letter: Breakfast TV programme supporting Oxford's authorship]	De Vere Soc. Newsl., p. 31
2008, Winter	[letter: response to Sundra Malcolm's Fall 2007 "M.O.A.I." letter]	Sh. Matters, vol. 7/2: 2
2012, July	Proving Shakespeare	De Vere Soc. Newsl., vol. 19/2: 6
2012, Fall	[review of *Shakespeare Suppressed* by Katherine Chiljan]	J. of Scientific Exploration, vol. 26/3: 679-84
2017, Dec.	[title not known]	J. of Scientific Expl., vol. 31/4
2020, Summer	A Scientific Approach to the Restoration of Oxford's Identity as William Shake-speare	Sh. Ox. Newsl., vol. 56/3: 14-24
2020, Fall	Sonnets Dedication [letter]	Sh. Ox. Newsl., vol. 56/4: 7-9
2023, Summer	[review of *Shakespeare's Knowledge of Astronomy and the Birth of Modern Cosmology* by Peter Usher]	J. of Scientific Expl., vol. 37/2

Rose, Jacqueline

1962, Nov. 13	The Bard of Hackney	Hackney Gazette

Rose, Lloyd

2010, June 6	Pretenders to the Playwright's Pen [rev. of *Contested Will* by J. Shapiro]	Washington Post, p. B6

Rosen, Nick

1988, Jan.	TV or Not TV	De Vere Soc. Newsl., no. 1: 33

Rosenbaum, Ron

Books

2006	*The Shakespeare Wars: Clashing Scholars, Public Fiascoes, Palace Coups*. New York: Random House.	

Shorter pieces

2005, Sept. 19	The Shakespeare Code: Is Times Guy Some Kind of Bard 'Creationist'? [response to William Niederkorn's Aug. 30 NYT article] Response by Mark K. Anderson, Sept. 26, p. 4.	New York Observer. p. 1
2005, Sept. 26	Reply to Mark Anderson [letter]	New York Observer, p. 4

Rosenbaum, Sidney

2004, Fall	[letter: Malvolio's yellow stockings]	Sh. Ox. Newsl., vol. 40/4: 5

Rosenberg, James

1989, Aug. 6	Flat Earthers [letters: response by Morse Johnson] [both pieces repr. in SON, vol. 25/3: 14 (Summer 1989)]	New York Times, p. H3, 17

Rosenberg, Saul

2010, April 8	About an Author Much Ado [review of *Contested Will* by J. Shapiro]	Wall Street Journal, p. A19

Rosenblum, Joseph (editor)

2017	*The Definitive Shakespeare Companion*, edited by Joseph Rosenblum. Santa Barbara: Greenwood. See esp. "The Authorship Question"]	

Rosenthal, Daniel

1999, Jan. 27	Twelve Great Shakespeare Myths	Times (London), p. 34
1999, Jan. 27	Shakespeare Myths: A Comedy of Errors?	Ottawa Citizen, p. A10

Rosenthal, Elizabeth J.

2017, Spring	A Late Summer Daydream [with Alex McNeil and Stanley Shur]	Sh. Ox. Newsl., vol. 52/3: 30

Rosten, Leo

1986, Oct.	The Shakespeare Nobody Knows Resp. by Charlton Ogburn, Jr., SON, vol. 22/4: 11-12 (Fall 1986).	Reader's Digest, p. 35-42

Author Index

Rousuck, J. Wynn
2004, Oct. 9   Calling the Bard Into Question   Sun (Baltimore), p. 3E

Rowe, Charles J.
1946, Aug. 5   The Road to Stratford [letter]   Irish Times (Dublin), p. 5

Rowe, Stephen D.
2000, Spring   *Tamburlaine the Great*: A Ten-act Renaissance Play?   Elizabethan Review, online ed.

Rowse, A. L.
Books
1983   *Eminent Elizabethans*. Athens: University of Georgia Press. [See esp. Chapter 3: "Edward de Vere, 17th Earl of Oxford," p. 75-106]

Shorter pieces
1971, April 24   Shakespeare, the Sexiest Writer in the Language   Times (London), p. 12
1975, April 19   Answering the Scepitcal   Spectator, p. 467-68

Roy, Amitava
2002, May 3   Dialogues: Fitting the Bill

Royle, Nicholas
2010   The Distraction of 'Freud': Literature, Psychoanalysis and the Bacon-Shakespeare Controversy, in *Shakespeare and His Authors* (Leahy): 58-90

Rubbo, Mike
2013   Doubter Response to Question 16: Should we be concerned that there are gaps in the historical record? in *SBD?* (Shahan): 175-76

Rubin, Don
2012, Spring   Flabbergasted at the Academic Ring of Silence: An Interview with   Sh. Matters, vol. 11/2: 25, 29
                      Theater Historian Don Rubin [by Alex McNeil]
                      [repr. in *Sh. Authorship Sourcebook* (Stritmatter, 2022), p. 93-95]
2013, Oct. 21   Bard Basics [letter: response to J. Kelly Nestruck's Oct. 17 article]   Globe & Mail, p. A10
2014, Feb.   [review of *Shakespeare Beyond Doubt* edited by Paul Edmondson   Critical Stages, no. 9
                      and Stanley Wells (2013) and *Shakespeare Beyond Doubt?* ed.
                      by J. Shahan and A. Waugh (2013)]
2014, Summer   [review of *Shakespeare's Changeling: A Fault Against the Dead*   Sh. Ox. Newsl., vol. 50/3: 25-26
                      by Syril Levin Kline (2014)]
2014, Summer   [review of *Shakespeare Beyond Doubt* edited by Paul Edmondson   Brief Chronicles, vol. V: 189-92
                      and Stanley Wells (2013) and *Shakespeare Beyond Doubt?* ed.
                      by J. Shahan and A. Waugh (2013)] [with A. McNeil]
                      [repr. from *Critical Stages 9*; www.critical-stages.org]
2015   Spinning Shakespeare   Oxfordian, vol. 17: 63-77
2015, Summer   Sisyphus and the Globe: Turning (on) the Media   Brief Chronicles, vol. VI: 9-22
2015, Summer   An Hour with Stanley Wells and Paul Edmondson [with Pat Kenney]   Sh. Ox. Newsl., vol. 1, 30-32
2017, Oct.   Methinks the Man: Peter Brook and the Authorship Question   Oxfordian, vol. 19: 101-14
2018, Dec.   An Introduction to "The Question that Won't Go Away: Did the Man   Critical Stages, no. 9
                      from Stratford Really Write the Plays?" [Special Topics II,
                      edited by Don Rubin]
2018, Dec.   Reasonable Doubt about the Identity of William Shakespeare   Critical Stages, no. 9
                      [an interview with Derek Jacobi and Mark Rylance]
2019, Winter   SOF Conference in Hartford: The Inside Scoop   Sh. Ox. Newsl., vol. 55/2: 12-13
2019, Summer   Oct. at the Mark Twain House: Hartford Conf. May be a Big One   Sh. Ox. Newsl., vol. 55/3: 18
2020, Sept.   [reviews of *My Shakespeare* edited by William Leahy (2018),   Oxfordian, vol. 22: 165-79
                      The New Oxford Shakespeare edited by Gary Taylor, et. al. (2018),
                      John Florio: The Man Who Was Shakespeare by Lamberto
                      Tassinari (2009), and *Le Vrai Shakespeare* by Chaunes (2018)]
                      [with Alex McNeil]
2022, Sept.   [review of *Educating Shakespeare* by Stephanie Hopkins Hughes]   Oxfordian, vol. 24: 289-293
2023, Summer   The Shakespeare Authorship Question: Alternative Mappings   J. of Scientific Expl., vol. 37/2
                      [Guest Editor for this special section]
2023, Summer   Further Reading on the Authorship   J. of Scientific Expl., vol. 37/2
2023, Sept.   Percy Allen: Collected Writings on Shakespeare, Volume 5 [review of   Oxfordian, vol. 25: 305-10
                      the book edited by James A. Warren]

Rubinstein, William D.
Books
2005   *The Truth Will Out: Unmasking the Real Shakespeare* [with Brenda James]. Harlow, England; New York: Longman/Pearson Education. [New edition in 2006: New York: Regan]
2012   *Who Wrote Shakespeare's Plays?* Stroud: Amberley.
Shorter pieces

2001, August	Who Was Shakespeare? [responses in vol. 51/10: 10 (Oct. 2001)]	History Today, vol. 51: 28-35
	Resp. by Eric Ives and reply by Rubinstein, Oct. 1, p. 61.	
	Resp. by Richard F. Whalen in SON, vol. 37/2: 20.	
2004, July	The Authorship Debate – The Way Forward	De Vere Soc. Newsl., p. 16-17
2005, Nov.	Mystery Identities	History Today, vol. 55/11: 28-29
2006, Fall	[letter: Sir Henry Neville as Shakespeare]	Sh. Matters, vol. 6/1: 2
2008, Summer	[letter: Authorship issue and Thomas Vicars]	Sh. Ox. Newsl., vol. 44/3: 21
2010	The Authorship Question: An Historian's Perspective, in *Shakespeare and His Authors*, ed. by William Leahy, p. 41-57.	
2012	The Case for Sir Henry Neville as the Real Shakespeare	Oxfordian, vol. 14: 121-129
2013	Doubter Response to Question #6: Did any of Shakespeare's boyhood contemporaries achieve intellectual and professional distinction?, in *Sh. Beyond Doubt?* (Shahan): 163-64	
2013	Doubter Response to Question #17: Where did Shakespeare get his get his money? in *Sh. Beyond Doubt?* (Shahan): 176-77	
2018	"Our Shakespeare: Henry Neville 1562-1615" [with John Casson & David Ewald], in *My Shakespeare: The Authorship Controversy* (Leahy): 113-38	

Rudyerd, G. W.

1956, Autumn	Editorial Notes: The Opening of the Tomb	SF News-letter (E), p. 3

Rush, D. E. A.

1937, June	Shakespeare was an East Anglian [letter]	East Anglian M., v. 2/9: 423-24

Rush, Peter
Books
2015   *Hidden In Plain Sight: The True History Revealed in Shake-speares Sonnets*. Leesburg, VA: Real Deal Publications. [Foreword by Hank Whittemore] 2nd edition, revised, 2016.
Shorter pieces

2003, Summer	Shakespeare Question Debated at Smithsonian	Sh. Matters, vol. 2/4: 1, 12-15
2004, Fall	Shakespeare's Sonnets and the Aesopian Method	Sh. Matters, vol. 4/1: 6-7
2012, Sum./Fall	Answering Hamill: Southampton poem confirms Southampton's Relationship with Oxford, *Sonnets* [resp. to Hamill]	Sh. Ox. Newsl., vol. 48/3: 11-15
2016, Winter	[resp. to J. Norwood's Fall 2015 review of *Hidden in Plain Sight*]	Sh. Ox. Newsl., vol. 52/1: 25-27
2020, Spring	The First Seventeen Sonnets—Their True Hidden Meaning	Sh. Ox. Newsl., vol. 56/2: 20-23
2020, Fall	The PT Theory: Let the Real Debate Begin	Sh. Ox. Newsl., vol. 56/4: 26-29
2021, Winter	[letter: response to John Hamill]	Sh. Ox. Newsl., vol. 57/1: 31-32

Rushton, Ray

1973, July 20	The Oxfordian Case in the Essex Press [repr. in SON, vol. 11/1: 6-7]	Braintree & Witham Times

Russell, Clifford W

1982, May	[Russell served as editor of *Touchstone: A Chronicle published in cooperation with the Shakespearean Authorship Trust*, launched in May 1982] [not yet indexed]

Russell, Sir John W.

1957, Spring	[report on the Jan. 16, 1957 Debate: Oxford (Wainewright) v. Derby (Evans)]	SF News-letter (E), p. 3-4
1958, Autumn	[report on H. S. Shield's April 12, 1958 lecture "Classical Clues in Shakespeare's Plays"]	SF News-letter (E), p. 2
1960, Spring	[review of *The Queen's Wards* by Joel Hurstfield (1973)] [repr. in BTC, vol. 5: 38-42]	Sh. Authorship Rev. #3: 9-10
1960, Spring	The Court of Chivalry	SF News-letter (E), p. 8
1960, Autumn	In Piam Memoriam: A. J. Evans (d. 1960)	Sh. Authorship Rev. #4: 19
1963, Spring	[review of *Voyages de Shakespeare en France et en Italie* by G. Lambin (1962)] [repr. in BTC, vol. 5, p. 107-111]	Sh. Authorship Rev. #9: 11-15
1966, Spring	[report on F. W. Sternfeld's Nov. 16, 1966 Lecture "The Use of Song in Shakespeare's Plays"]	Sh. Authorship Rev. #15: 16-17

Sabel, Steven
Podcasts: Don't Quill the Messenger – dragonwagonradio.com/dontquillthemessenger
Shorter pieces

2005, Dec. 15	On the Trail of the Real Shakespeare [profile of Elwood Miller]	Redlands Daily Facts
2019, Winter	Q & A with Steven Sabel [with Bob Meyers]	Sh. Ox. Newsl., v. 55/1: 1, 30-32
2019, Spring	SOF PR Update	Sh. Ox. Newsl., vol. 55/2: 3-4
2019, Summer	SOF PR & Marketing Update	Sh. Ox. Newsl., vol. 55/3: 3-4
2020, Winter	SOF PR & Marketing Update	Sh. Ox. Newsl., vol. 56/1: 27
2021, Winter	From the Director of Podcasts and Community Outreach	Sh. Ox. Newsl., vol. 57/1: 8

Sabin, Stefana

2008, Oct.	[reviews of *Shakespeare & Co.* by Stanley Wells and *Geheimagent Marlowe* by Dieter Kühn]	Neues Sh. Journal, v. 12: 135-36

Sacks, Sam

2011, April 16	Out of the Miasma of Bardolatry, a Masterpiece	Wall Street Journal

Saintsbury, George
Books edited

1928	*The Cambridge History of Elizabethan Literature* (1928) [excerpt on the authorship question repr. in DVN (July 2001), p. 22-23]	

Shorter pieces

1926, June 12	The Hundred Flowres [review of *A Hundredth Sundrie Flowres* ed. by Capt. B. M. Ward]	Nation & Athenaeum., vol. 39/10: 295

Saliani, Dom

1989, Spring	None of Them Give the Age Old Introduction to Shakespeare That So Many Young People Have Been Exposed To	Sh. Ox. Newsl., vol. 25/2: 15-16
1991, Aug.	[letter: Oxford in the Canadian schools]	Spear-shaker Rev., vol. 5: 24
1993, Spring	[letter: Stratfordian name calling and Oxfordian progress] [repr. in BTC, vol. 7: 154-58]	Sh. Ox. Newsl., vol. 29/2a: 7-9

Salusbury, F. G. H.

1937, Oct. 16	Are You Looking for Something To Do? [brief reference to *"Shakespeare" Identified*]	Daily Herald, p. 10

Sammartino, Peter
Books

1990	*The Man Who Was William Shakespeare.* New York: Cornwall Books.	

Shorter pieces

1991, March	Who Was the Real William Shakespeare?	Illuminator, p. 91-96
1972. Aug. 1	[letter: response to Charlton Ogburn's June 1972 article]	Harper's Mag., p. 4
1956, May	To the Editor and Readers of *The Shakespeare Newsletter* [letter, with 21 other signers]	Sh. Newsletter, vol. 6/3: 18

Sampson, George

1923, June 21	Shakespeare Half-Truths [reviews of *The Mystery of "Mr. W.H."* by Col. B. R. Ward & *Shakespeare Through Oxford Glasses* by H. Holland] [see Looney's critique in HAK, Aug. 31, 1923]	Daily News, p. 18
1928, May	More About Shakespeare [rev. of *Borrowers* by Percy Allen]	Bookman, vol. 75: 113-15

Sams, Eric

1999, Jan.	Zur Geschichte der Ansichten über Edward III [repr. *Shakespeare's "Edward III"* edited by Eric Sams, Yale Univ. Press, 1996]	Neues Sh. Journal, vol. 3: 41-55
1999, July	Der Name Hamlet als Indiz [excerpt]	Neues Sh. Journal, vol. 4: 153

Sams, Richard

2008, Oct.	[letter: online publication of *Real Shakespeare II*]	De Vere Soc. Newsl., v. 15/3: 28

Sanchez, Jorge

1997, July 25	No Question of Quality of Bard's Plays – Whoever He Is	St. Petersburg Times, p. 5

Sanchez, Rene

1987, Sept. 26	All's Well in Shakespeare's Day in Court	Washington Post, p. B1

Sanderson, James L.

1963, April	Three Unpublished Elizabethan Wedding Poems	Modern Lang. Rev. vol. 58/2: 217-19

Sands Film Studio
2011, Spring [letter: its activities, including its production of the film *Anonymous*] Sh. Ox. Newsl., vol. 47/2: 3

Sanford, John
2002, Jan. 9 Panel Featuring Shakespeare Scholars Discusses Whether the Bard Stanford Report
Was a Beard

Saporta, Maria
1997, Aug. 13 Where There's a Will . . . [Oxfordian Gertrude Ford left an estate Atlanta Journ.-Const., p. E2-3
worth $60 million]

Sapryguina, Nina
2015, April Shakespearean *Sonnets*: The True Order? De Vere Soc. Newsl., v. 22/2: 48

Sarasohn, David
1999, April 9 Shakespeare in Doubt: Demand for a Share of the Will Oregonian, p. B9
1999, April 12 The Sequel: Shakespeare in Doubt Newhouse News Service, p. 1

Sasse, E.
1967, Spring [letter: portrait of Anne Vavasour] Sh. Authorship Rev. #17: 23

Satchell, Michael
2000, July 24-31 Hunting For Good Will: Will the Real Shakespeare Please Stand Up? U.S. News & World Rep., vol.
129/4: 71-72

Saunders, Alan
2009 [letter: the case for Fulke Greville] Oxfordian, vol. 11: 11-12

Saunders, B. R.
1945, Nov. A Note on the Origin of *Venus and Adonis* SF News-letter (E), p. 6
1951, Sept. The Scales of Justice [repr. in Clark, *Hidden Allusions*, SF News-letter (E), p. 8-9
3rd ed., Ruth Loyd Miller, editor (1974), p. 570-72]
1957, Spring [letter: Edward Bonaventure] SF News-letter (E), p. 12
1957, Autumn [letter: *Cardan's Comforte*] SF News-letter (E), p. 12

Saunders, Sam C.
2005, Summer Arthur Golding's First Decade of Translating: A Brief Examination Sh. Ox. Newsl., v. 41/3: 1, 21-22
2006, Winter The Case of the Mad Mathematicians Sh. Ox. Newsl., vol. 42/1: 23
2006, Spring A Sharp Blade, a Tall Man and a Good Whore? Sh. Ox. Newsl., vol. 42/2: 19-21
2007 Could Shakespeare Have Calculated the Odds in Hamlet's Wager? Oxfordian, vol. 10: 20-34

Savage, David G.
1987, Sept. 26 Zounds! Much Ado About Poetic Justice Los Angeles Times, p. 2
1987, Sept. 26 Author! Author! Justices Uphold Stratford Bard's Byline Sacramento Bee, A1, A22

Saville, Kirk
1991, Sept. 28 Authorship of Works Debated by Scholars Las Vegas Review-Jou., p. 1C

Schama, Simon
2011, Oct. 24 The Shakespeare Shakedown [review of *Anonymous*] Newsweek, vol. 158/17: 24

Schamp, Dietrich
2002, May Rückblick und Ausblick Neues Sh. Journal, vol. 7: 147-51

Scheffer, Jan H.
1997, June Oxfordianism in the Netherlands De Vere Soc. Newsl., v. 2/9: 8-9
2004, Fall First Dutch Shakespeare Authorship Conf. [with Sandra Schruijer] Sh. Ox. Newsl., vol. 40/4: 10-12
2011, July Das Neue Shake-speare Gesellschaft (A New Sh. Society in Germany) De Vere Soc. Newsl., v. 18/2: 21
2011, July [review of *Shakespeare: The Concealed Poet* by Robert Detobel] De Vere So. New., v. 18/2: 36-38
[with Elke Brachmann]
2013 Doubter Response to Question #47: Why did Sigmund Freud doubt
Shakespeare's authorship? In SBD? (Shahan): 206-07
2015, Oct. Oxford's Capture by Pirates, April 10/11, 1576 De Vere Soc. New., v. 22/4: 4-14
2020, April A Tirade About a Joust in Trebizond: How Was Edward de Vere De Vere So. New., v. 27/2: 27-36
Involved in This Example of Commedia Erudita in 1575?
2020, Oct. [letter: Kevin Gilvary's article on J. Thomas Looney] De Vere So. New., v. 27/4: 43-44
2021, Jan. Introduction of April Drusiana De Vere Soc. New., vol. 28/1: 25
2022, Oct. Veere on the Zeeland Island of Walcheren De Vere So. New., v. 29/4: 15-17
2023 Oxfords Gefangennahme durch Piraten am 10./11. April 1576 Neue Sh. Jou., vol. NS8: 107-17

Schelling, F. E.
 1920, Sept. 9   Who Wrote Shakespeare? [a poem] [repr. in *The Argonaut*, Nov. 13]   Life, vol. 76:442

Schlosser, Jim
 1993, Aug. 22   To Be or Not To Be . . . Shakespearean   Greensboro News-Rec., p. D1

Schmidt, Arno
 2017, Dec.   Dichtergespräche im Elysium   Neues Sh. Jou., vol. 1: 5

Schmidt, Hanjo
 2013, Mar.   Gedanken zum Droeshout-Porträt   Neues Sh. Jou., vol. NS3: 20-9
 2018   Briefe zur *Stum*-Diskussion   Neues Sh. Jou., vol. NS6: 96-103

Schmitt, Juli
 2006   [review of *The Case for Shakespeare: The End of the Authorship Question* by Scott McCrea (2004)]   Theatre History Studies, vol. 26: 152-54

Schneider, Wolfgang
 2008, Oct.   [review of *Shakespeare: Die Biographie* by Peter Ackroyd]   Neues Sh. Journal, v. 12: 137-39

Schoell, Frank L.
 1952, Sept.   T[letter: Saggiatore]   SF News-letter (E), p. 12
 1953, April   The Sense of Shakespeare's Sonnets   SF News-letter (E), p. 10-11

Schoenbaum, S.
Books
 1991   *Shakespeare's Lives*. New York: Clarendon Press. [see especially "Deviations," p. 385-451] [excerpt repr. in SON, vol. 30/2a: 11 (Spring 1994); and in *Shakespeare Criticism, vol. 41* (Lee & Barnes 1998): 8-32]

Shorter pieces
 1977, Oct. 28   [review of *Shakespeare By Hilliard* by Leslie Hotson (1977)]   Times Lit. Sup., p. 1261

Schoenrich, Otto
 1959, July   [letter: Shylock v. Antonio]   Am. Bar Assoc. J., vol. 45/7: 654

Schruijer, Sandra
 2004, Fall   First Dutch Shakespeare Authorship Conference [with Jan Scheffer]   Sh. Ox. Newsl., vol. 40/4: 10-12
 2010   Fighting Over Shakespeare's Authorship: Identity, Power and Academic Debate [with Jan H. Scheffer], in *Shakespeare and His Authors*, ed. by William Leahy, p. 125-41

Schucking, Levin L.
Books
 1897   *The Meaning of Hamlet*. Translated from the German by Graham Rawson. Oxford: The Clarendon Press. [reprintings in 1966: New York: Barnes & Noble; London: Allen & Unwin.]

Shorter pieces
 1936, May 16   Stage or Study? [letter]   Times Lit. Sup., is. 1789: 420

Schudel, Matt
 2011, March 6   Unpaid Shakespeare Scholar Lived by His Own Design [Irvin Matus]   Washington Post, p. C7

Schuessler, Raymond
 1994, Oct.   The Shakespeare Puzzle   Games, p. 12-14+

Schumach, Murray
 1948, Sept. 6   Speech Knocking Mr. Shakespeare Almost Reconciles Puzzle Groups   New York Times

Schumann, Howard
 2003, Winter   [review of *The Lion Bats the Butterfly* by Robin Matchett (2002)]   Sh. Ox. Newsl., vol. 39/1: 22
 2005, Fall   SF and SON Join Forces in Historic Conference   Sh. Matters, vol. 5/1: 1, 10, 26+
 2006, Winter   Anderson Named "Oxfordian of the Year" at Ashland Conference   Sh. Matters, vol. 5/2: 1, 12-15
 2006, Winter   [review of *Taming of the Shrew*, Directed by Sam Taylor (1929)]   Sh. Matters, vol. 5/2: 10
 2006, Spring   Concordia Proposes Shakespeare Authorship Studies Center   Sh. Matters, vol. 5/3: 1, 26-31
 2008, Spring   Groundbreaking! Authorship Studies Research Centre Arrives at Concordia University   Sh. Matters, vol. 7/3: 1, 21-27
 2009, Winter   Fourth Annual Joint Conference: de Vere Bio Series Prepared to Rock Cable TV?   Sh. Matters, vol. 8/1: 1, 6-12+
 2009, Spring   Concordia Authorship Research Center Set to Open . . .   Sh. Matters, vol. 8/2: 1, 6-11
 2010, Spr./Sum.   Authorship in Cyberspace   Sh. Matters, vol. 9: 1, 6-11
 2010, Spr./Sum.   Authorship Research Centre Dedicated; Beauclerk Launches New Book   Sh. Matters, vol. 9: 1, 13-21+

Sears, Elisabeth (Betty) (continued)

1992, Spring	Message From the President: increase in members from *The Atlantic Monthly article* and Beauclerk tour	Sh. Ox. Newsl., vol. 28/2: 18
1994, Winter	Information and Commentaries from Betty Sears, Our Past President	Sh. Ox. Newsl., vol. 30/1: 19-21
1997, Spring	[letter: Diana Price's Autumn 1996 "Rough Winds Do Shake"] Reply by Price, Spring 1997, p. 15-17.	Eliz. Review, vol. 5/1: 11-15
1997, Summer	[letter: Sobran's Spring 1997 "Sonnets" article]	Sh. Ox. Newsl., vol. 33/3: 22-23
2003, Spring	Oxford's Revenge [letter]	Sh. Matters, vol. 2/3: 2

Sears, Florence W.

1947, Sept. 7	[letter: Gelett Burgess's June 8 article]	NY Herald Trib., p. A7

Seeker for the Truth

1923, Sept. 23	[letter: Authorship of the 'Plays of Shakespeare']	Sheffield Daily Tel., p. 4

Seifert, Siegfried

2001, May	*Hamlet*: Indiz kontra Shakspere	Neues Sh. Journal, vol. 6: 140-46
2007, April	Schrieb Shakespeares Sonette ein anderer?	Neues Sh. Journal, v. 11: 136-39
2011, Oct.	The Queen and Mr. *He!*	Neues Sh. Journal, v. NS2: 160-2

Seiler, John

1997, Dec.	The Riddle of the Bard Revisited [review of *Alias Shakespeare* by Joe Sobran (1997)]	Orange County Register, p. G1

Senior, H. L.

1957, Autumn	Strange Omissions	SF News-letter (E), p. 6-8
1958, Autumn	[letter: reply to Herbert Cutner]	SF News-letter (E), p. 12

Sen, Mark A.

2013, Spring	Shakespeare and Land Law in His Life and Works	Real Prop. J. v. 48/1: 111-216

Sennett, M.

1944, July	[letter: Ivor Brown]	Baconiana, no. 112: 118-19

Seto, Chris

2013, Oct.19	To Thine Own Self Be True	Record (Ontario), p. D5
2013, Oct. 19	Local Professors Troubled Over Shakespeare Authorship Debate [coverage of SOF conference at York University]	Guelph Mercury, p. A1

Seymour, Henry

1925, Sept. 28	The Shakespeare Puzzle [letter]	Sheffield Daily Tel., p. 6

Sexton, David

2008, Jan. 14	In Praise of Secret Scribes [review of *Anonymity: A Secret History of English Literature* by John Mullan	Evening Standard, p. 37
2010, March 18	The Dodgy Reasons People Have for Doubting Shakespeare [review of *Contested Will* by James Shapiro]	Evening Standard, p. 36

Sexton, Mildred B. (Pidge)

Books

1999	*As You Like It* (part of the "What Shakespeare's Audiences Knew" pamphlet series). St. Louis: Mildred B. Sexton [written from an Oxfordian perspective]
1999	*Hamlet* (part of the "What Shakespeare's Audiences Knew" pamphlet series). St. Louis: Mildred B. Sexton [written from an Oxfordian perspective]
1999	*Much Ado About Nothing* (part of the "What Shakespeare's Audiences Knew" pamphlet series). St. Louis: Mildred B. Sexton [written from an Oxfordian perspective]
1999	*Twelfth Night* (part of the "What Shakespeare's Audiences Knew" pamphlet series). St. Louis: Mildred B. Sexton [written from an Oxfordian perspective]
1999	*The Winter's Tale* (part of the "What Shakespeare's Audiences Knew" pamphlet series). St. Louis: Mildred B. Sexton [written from an Oxfordian perspective]

Shorter pieces

1993, July 12	Who's the Bard? [letter] [repr. in SON, vol. 29/3a: 5 (Summer 1993)]	St. Louis Post Disp., p. 2B
2004, Summer	[letter: building blocks metaphor]	Sh. Matters, vol. 3/4: 2
2004, Fall	Shakespeare Authorship Trust in London	Sh. Matters, vol. 4/1: 7
2008, Spring	letter: puns in *A Lover's Complaint* and *Julius Caesar*]	Sh. Ox. Newsl., vol. 44/2: 16

Author Index

Shahan, John (continued)

2013	Doubter Response to Question #31: How has the Shakespeare authorship discussion been presented in fiction?, in SBD?, p. 188-89	
2013	Doubter Response to Question #55: What other theories might be compared to the Sh. authorship conspiracy theory and why?, in SBD, p. 212-13	
2013	Conclusion and Request to read/sign the Declaration of Reasonable Doubt, in SBD?, p. 224	
2013	Appendix D: Heminge and Condell Letters in First Folio, in SBD?, p. 249-50	
2014	[resp. to R. Charles's blog post in the *Washington Post* "The Justice Doth Protest Too Much, Methinks" (April 6, 2014)]	
2014, May	Shakespeare Birthplace Trust Declines £40K Donation [letter to SBT trustees]	De Vere Soc. New., vol. 21/2: 38
2015, Winter	The Stratford Festival's "Authorship Appeal:" Another view, and the SAC's "full-blown trial"	Sh. Ox. Newsl., vol. 51/1: 25-29
2015, April	Death of Charles Champlin, Aged 88 (d. 2014)	De Vere Soc. New., vol. 22/1: 18
2015, Spring	[letter: support for Robert Prechter's cryptographic solutions]	Sh. Ox. Newsl., vol. 51/2: 3-4
2015, Fall	[letter: the Shakespeare Authorship Coalition (SAC) challenge to the Shakespeare Birthplace Trust: a mock trial, not a debate]	Sh. Ox. Newsl., vol. 51/4: 3-4
2016	Chapter 4: Possession, in *Contested Year*	
2016	Appendix A: A Second Look at James Shapiro's *Contested Will*, in *Contested Year*	
2016, April	Reaffirming the Declaration of Reasonable Doubt	De Vere Soc. New., vol. 23/2: 14
2016, April	Beyond Reasonable Doubt: Shakspere Was Not Shakespeare!	De Vere So. New., v. 23/2: 15-24
2016, Spring	Non-Stratfordians Observe Anniversary Worldwide [with A. McNeil]	Sh. Ox. Newsl., v. 52/2: 1, 24-26
2016, July	SAC Celebrates its Tenth Anniversary	De Vere Sc. New., v. 23/3: 35-36
2016, Fall	A Question of Will at SOF Conference	Sh. Ox. Newsl., vol. 52/4: 30
2016, December	[letter: response to James Warren's 2015 "State Power" article] Reply by Warren, same issue, p. 182-84.	Brief Chronicles, v. VII: 179-81
2017, Spring	[letter: exchange of letters with Folger Director Michael Witmore]	Sh. Ox. Newsl., vol. 53/2: 4-5
2020, Fall	[letter: Sonnets Dedication]	Sh. Ox. Newsl., vol. 56/4: 5-6
2022, Spring	In Memoriam: Virginia Renner (1933-2022)	Sh. Ox. Newsl., vol. 58/2: 9
2022, Sept.	The Strange Case of "Mr. W. H.": How we know the dedication of Shakespeare's Sonnets is a cryptogram, and what it reveals	Oxfordian, vol. 24: 195-241
2023, Sept.	James Warren's Article on the First Folio [letter, with John Hamill, followed by Warren's reply]	Oxfordian, vol. 25: 9-15

Shakespeare Authorship Coalition (SAC)

Website: doubtaboutwill.org
Books

2011	*Exposing an Industry in Denial: Authorship Doubters Respond to "60 Minutes with Shakespeare.* Claremont, CA: Shakespeare Authorship Coalition (SAC). [77-page PDF download at SAC website: https://doubtaboutwill.org/pd fs/sbt_rebuttal.pdf]	
2013	*Shakespeare Beyond Doubt? Exposing an Industry in Denial.* Edited by John Shahan and Alexander Waugh. Organized and published by The Shakespeare Authorship Coalition. Tamarac, FL: Llumina Press.	

Articles, advertisements, declarations

2007	Declaration of Reasonable Doubt About the Identity of W. Shakespeare	Oxfordian, vol. 10: 179
2007, Fall	Declaration of Reasonable Doubt About the Identity of W. Shakespeare	Sh. Ox. Newsl., vol. 43/4: 21-23
2013, Dec. 6	[full page advertisement challenging The Shakespeare Birthplace Trust to prove before "a panel of neutral judges" that Shakspere wrote Shakespeare's plays] Response by Brian Vickers, Dec. 13, 2013. [repr. in DVS, vol. 21/2L 41 (May 2014)]	Times Lit. Sup., issue 5775: 23
2013, Dec. 6	[full pge ad for Shakespeare Beyond Doubt?	Times Lit sup., issue 5775: 25

Shakespeare, Geoffrey

1937, June	Shakespeare was an East Anglian [letter]	East Ang. Mag., vol. 2/9: 424

Shakespeare Oxford Society (SOS) [later the Shakespeare Oxford Fellowship (SOF)]

Website: shakespeareoxfordfellowship.org
YouTube channel: @shakespeareoxfordfellowship
Books and pamphlets

1980s	*An Inquirer's Guide to the Shakespearean Authorship Problem and the Case for Edward de Vere.* Baltimore: Shakespeare Oxford Society. [probably written by Gordon and/or Helen Cyr]	

Author Index

2007	*Report My Cause Aright: Fiftieth Anniversary Anthology, 1957-2007.* Shakespeare Oxford Society.	

Shakespeare Oxford Society Board of Trustees (SOS)

1994, Summer	Tribute to Charlton Ogburn on the Occasion of the Tenth Anniversary of *The Mysterious William Shakespeare* [repr. in BTC, vol. 7: 255-56]	Sh. Ox. Newsl., vol. 30/ 3a: 1

Shakespearean Authorship Trust (with Brunel University)

2007, Summer	2007 John Silberrad Memorial Lectures, Shakespeare's Globe, Nov. 2007	Sh. Ox. Newsl., vol. 43/3: 22-23

Shanks, Edward

1923, July	[review of *Shakespeare Through Oxford Glasses* by Hubert Holland]	London Mercury, vol. 8: 322

Shapiro, Ari

Radio programs hosted

2011, Oct. 28	For *Anonymous* Scribe, a Shakespearean Speculation [transcript of Broadcast with John Orloff, Derek Jacobi, Rhys Ifans]	National Public Radio

Shapiro, James

Books

2010	*Contested Will: Who Wrote Shakespeare?* New York: Simon & Schuster. [long excerpt repr. in *National Post*, April 19, 2010]	

Shorter pieces

2006, April 23	Happy Birthday, Whoever You Were	Sunday Times, p. 16
2010, March 27	Just William? New Readings Have Cracked Shakespeare's Works Wide Open Response by John Orloff, 19 April 2010.	Financial Times, p. 1
2010, April 11	Alas, Poor Shakespeare: Conspiracy Theories About the Authorship of His Plays Have Gone Mainstream [review of *Anonymous*]	Los Angeles Times, p. A29
2011, Oct. 17	Hollywood Dishonors the Bard [repr. in Int'l Herald Trib., Oct. 17] Response by Mark Anderson, Oct. 27, p. A24. Response by Roland Emmerich, Oct. 27, p. A24. Response by Daniel M. Blank, Oct. 27, p. A24. Response by Andree A. Brooks, Oct. 27, p. A24. Response by Julia Newton, Oct. 27, p. A24.	New York Times, p. A23
2011, Oct. 29	Looney Tune of a Film Plays with Truth Over Bard [review of *Anonymous*]	Irish Times (Dublin), p. 15
2011, Nov. 5	Anonymous? Ridiculous [review of *Anonymous*]	Guardian, p. 16
2019, June 8	Shakespeare Wrote Insightfully about Women. That Doesn't Mean He was One [response to Winkler]	Atlantic Monthly
2019, Aug. 6	An Unexpected Letter from John Paul Stevens, Shakespeare Skeptic	New Yorker

Sharkey, Michael

2012	*Apollo in George Street: The Life of David McKee Wright.* Glebe, NSW, Australia: Puncher & Wattmann.	

Sharpe, Kathryn

2007, Winter	[letter: John Rollet's "Sonnet Dedication puzzle" articles]	Sh. Matters, vol. 6/2: 3, 30
2008, Spring	[letter: Sundra Malcolm's Fall 2007 "M.O.A.I." letter]	Sh. Matters, vol. 7/3: 2, 9
2010, Winter	2009 Joint Shakespeare Authorship Conference	Sh. Matters, vol. 9/1: 1, 7-13+
2017, Winter	In Memoriam: Wenonah Finch Sharpe (1926-2017)	Sh. Ox. Newsl., vol. 53/1: 7
2017, Summer	Abstracting Oxford: Catherine Hatinguais and SOAR	Sh. Ox. Newsl., v. 53/3: 1, 28-32
2018, Winter	*"Shakespeare" Identified* Centennial Progress Update	Sh. Ox. Newsl., vol. 54/1: 9-11
2019, Spring	*"Shakespeare" Identified* Centennial Progress Update	Sh. Ox. Newsl., vol. 55/2: 17-19
2019, Spring	Marketing Ourselves to the Public [with Julie Sandys Bianchi, Joan Leon & Shelly Maycock]	Sh. Ox. Newsl., vol. 55/2: 20
2020, Summer	A Mystery Solved [with Bryan Wildenthal]	Sh. Ox. Newsl., vol. 56/3: 8
2020, Oct.	[letter: Gilvary's piece on J. Thomas Looney]	De Vere S. New., v. 27/4: 43-44
2021, Spring	Have You Written a Book? Make Sure It's Available in the Future!	Sh. Ox. Newsl., vol. 57/2: 32
2021, Fall	Tales from the Archives: The Drayton Collection; History of The Evered Foundation [with Renee Euchner, Terry Deer & B. Boyle]	Sh. Ox. Newsl., vol. 57/4: 29-32
2022, Spring	Tales from the Archives" Kattharine E. Eggar (1874-1961) [with Renee Euchner]	Sh. Ox. Newsl., vol. 58/2: 29-31
2022, Fall	Unpublished (but Unforgettable) Authorship Letters	Sh. Ox. Newsl., vol. 58/4: 13

Sharpe, Will

2010	[review of *Contested Will* by James Shapiro (2010)]	Sh. Bookshop Newsl., v. 16: 1-2

Sharratt, Mary
    2016   *The Dark Lady's Mask*. Marriner Books.

Shaw, Jonathan
    2004, Sept./Oct.   The Mysterious Mr. Shakespeare: Stephen Greenblatt conjures a life   Harvard Magazine, p. 56-59

Sheed, Wilfrid
    1993, July 12   [review of *Shylock* by John Gross] [asks whether a lord might have   New Yorker
              written Shakespeare's works]

Shepard, Florence C.
    1995, Autumn   *This Star of England*: Written Forty Years Ago and Still a Goldmine   Sh. Ox. Newsl., vol. 31/4: 10-11
              of Information [repr. in BTC, vol. 7: 353-54]

Shepard, Odell (O. S.)
    1931, May 22   Hide and Go Seek   Christian Science Monitor

Sheppard, Alfred T.
    1929, Sept. 13   Shakespeare and *Richard III*: A Footnote by R. L. S. [LETTER]   Morning Post, p. 9

Sheppard, Philippa
    1997, Dec. 13   Books Scrutinizing the Bard Continue to Pour Off the Presses   Globe & Mail, p. D11
              [review of *Alias Shakespeare* by Joseph Sobran (1997)]
    2001, Feb. 17   Queen Was No Virgin [interview w/David Starkey;   Globe & Mail
              updated Apr. 10, 2018]

Sherman, Donovan
    2013, April   Stages of Revision: Textuality, Performance, and History in   Lit/Film, Quart., v. 41/2: 129-42
              Anonymous

Sherman, Randall
    1996, Summer   The Marketing of a Paradigm Shift   Sh. Ox. Newsl., vol. 32/3: 8-9
    1996, Fall   Reporting His Cause Through Local Chapters [with Kath. Chiljan]   Sh. Ox. Newsl., vol. 32/4: 3
    1997, Spring   President's Letter   Sh. Ox. Newsl., vol. 33/2: 3, 13
    1997, Fall   The Cause Is In My Will [repr. in BTC, vol. 7: 411-15]   Sh. Ox. Newsl., vol. 33/4: 7, 28

Shermer, Michael
    2009   Shakespeare, Interrupted   Scientific Am., vol. 301/2: 30

Sherwood, James (Jaz)
Books
    2002   *Shakespeare's Ghost: An Historical Mystery Novel*. New York: Opus Books. 2002.
Shorter pieces
    2002, Summer   [review of *Oxford, Son of Queen Elizabeth* by Paul Streitz (2001)]   Sh. Ox. Newsl., vol. 38/3: 17
    2003, Spring   Interview with *Chasing Shakespeares* Author Sarah Smith   Sh. Ox. Newsl., vol. 39/2: 18-19
    2003, Spring   [review of *Chasing Shakespeares* by Sarah Smith (2008)]   Sh. Ox. Newsl., vol. 39/2: 19
    2003, Fall   [review of *Counterfeiting Shakespeare* by Brian Vickers]   Sh. Matters, vol. 3/1: 18-19
    2004, Winter   [letter: Stritmatter and Ogburn's *The Mysterious William Shakespeare*]   Sh. Matters, vol. 3/2: 2
    2004, Winter   What's in a Name, a Parody   Sh. Ox. Newsl., vol. 40/1: 14
    2004, Spring   Interview with *Beard of Avon* Author Amy Freed   Sh. Matters, vol. 3/3: 30-32
    2004, Fall   Shakespeare Fellowship Conference Held in Baltimore, Oct. 7-10   Sh. Ox. Newsl., vol. 40/4: 06
    2005, Winter   President's Letter   Sh. Ox. Newsl., vol. 41/1: 2, 7
    2005, Spring   President's Letter   Sh. Ox. Newsl., vol. 41/2: 9
    2005, Spring   Interview with Hank Whittemore: Author, Actor, Scholar   Sh. Ox. Newsl., v. 41/2: 2, 18-20
    2008, March   Tribute to Sue Sybersma   De Vere Soc. Newsl., v. 15/1: 28
    2008, Spring   News: Dig Reveals The Theatre; Times Archive, 1909;   Sh. Ox. Newsl., vol. 44/2: 3-4
              Oxford on NAP

Shickman, Allan R.
    2004, Spring   [letter: Alan Nelson's *Monstrous Adversary* (2003)]   Sh. Ox. Newsl., vol. 40/2: 6
    2017, Spring   [letter: Pat. McCarthy's Winter 2017 "Hamlet's Intent" article   Sh. Ox. Newsl., vol. 53/2: 5
              Reply by McCarthy, Spring 2017, p. 5-6.
    2023, Winter   [letter: Margo Anderson]   Sh. Ox. Newsl., vol. 59/1: 3

Shield, H. S.
    1954, April   De Shakespeare Nostrati   SF News-letter (E), p. 6-7
    1956, Spring   Names of the King and Queen in A Midsummer-Night's Dream   SF News-letter (E), p. 9
    1956, Spring   Lord Oxford's Settlement [letter]   SF News-letter (E), p. 12

Simak, Clifford D.
1968   *The Goblin Reservation*. New York: Putnam.
1976   *Shakespeare's Planet*. New York: Berkley.

Simmons, Roger D.
1971   *The Non-Psychoanalytic Literature in Sigmund Freud's Library*. Chicago: Univ. of Chicago Dissertations.

Simon, Clea
2003, June 9   *Shakespeares'* Plays Well as a Mystery [review of *Chasing Shakespeares*, a stage production based on her novel]   Boston Globe

Simon, John
2010, Aug. 23   No Mystery Here [review of *Contested Will* by James Shapiro]   Weekly Standard, p. 30-32

Simonton, Dean Keith
Date not known   Shakespeare's 'small Latin and less Greek'   Mensa Research J., vol. 40/2
2004   Thematic Content and Political Context in Shakespeare's Dramatic Output, with Implications for Authorship and Chronology Controversies   Empirical Studies of the Arts, vol. 22/2: 201-13

Simpson, H. B.
1917, Dec.   Shakespeare, Bacon and a "Tertium Quid"   Nineteenth Century and After, pp. 1248-53
1935, Feb.   Shakespeare's Sonnets [reviews of *Personal Clues in Shakespeare Poems and Sonnets* by Gerald H. Rendall (1934) and *Shakespeare's Sonnets* by Gerald W. Phillips (1934)]   Sh. Pictorial, no. 84: 32

Simpson, H. Derwernt
1925, Jan. 22   The Shakespeare Signatures [letter]   Times Lit. Sup., is. 1201: 56

Simpson, Kevin
2004, August   The Psychology of Creativity and Genius: Reflections on Shakespeare and the Oxfordian Challenge   Journal of . Evolutionary Psych., vol. 25/3: 146-53

Simpson, Mary-Helen
1991   [review of *The Mysterious William Shakespeare* by Ch. Ogburn, Jr.]   Unisa Eng. St., vol. 29/1: 62-3

Simpson, Richard
1874, July 10   The Political Use of the Stage in Shakespeare's Time   New Sh. Society Transactions, p. 371-439

Singleton, Esther
Books
1931   *The Shakespeare Garden*. With an Introduction by Eva Turner Clark. New York: A. F. Payson. [Clark's Introduction repr. in BTC, vol. 1: 114-115] [1st ed., without Clark's Intro., was 1922]
1929   *Shakespearian Fantasias, Adventures in the Fourth Dimension*. Norwood, MA: Private printing. Modern edition, edited by James A. Warren. Cary, NC: Veritas Publications, 2019.
Shorter pieces
1928, July 21   A Great Courtier [review of *The Seventeenth Earl of Oxford* by Capt. B. M. Ward (1928)] [Quoted inside Ward's book]   Saturday Review, p. 1049
1940, June/July Was Edward de Vere Shakespeare? [repr. in SON, vol. 9/2: 14-15 (Autumn 1973); and in BTC, vol. 2: 114-117]   SF News-letter (A), vol. 1/4: 9-10

Sinkevich, Ekaterina
2003   *Razvitie Shekspirovskogo voprosa v sovremennom literaturovedenii Anglii I SShA* [*The Development of the Shakespearean Question in the Contemporary Literary Studies of Great Britain and the USA*]. [Russian] Kherson: Vyd-vo KhDU.

Sinnett, A. P.
1901, Aug.   New Light on Shakespeare   National Review, vol. 5/9: 72-82

Sisson, Edward H.
1998, Spring   [letter: Sobran's book *Alias Shakespeare*]   Sh. Ox. Newsl., vol. 34/1: 21-22
2001, Spring   [letter: Shakespeare icon]   Sh. Ox. Newsl., vol. 37/1: 21
2002, Winter   [letter: spelling of Shakespeare's name on Anne Hathaway's tomb]   Sh. Ox. Newsl., vol. 38/1: 22
2002, Summer   [letter: citation issues]   Sh. Matters, vol. 1/4: 3, 28

Skinner-young, S.
1996, Sept.   New Live Theatre at Hedingham Castle, and a Performance of *Dream*   De Vere Soc. Newsl., vol. 2/6: 7

Slater, Eliot

1963	The Color Imagery of Poets	Archives Suisses de Neorologie, vol. 91
1966, Autumn	[report on M. Kendall's March 15, 1966 talk on "The Possibility of Determining Elizabethan Authorship by Statistical Analysis"]	Sh. Authorship Rev. #16: 19-20
1968, Autumn	Terms of Art in *Hamlet*	Sh. Authorship Rev. #20: 1-4
1969, Spring	Terms of Art in *King Lear*	Sh. Authorship Review #21: 4-7
1969, Dec.	A Psychiatric View of Shakespeare's *Sonnets* [repr. in TOX, vol. 18: 155-174]	Anais Portugueses de Psiquia- tria, vol. 21/18: 545-72
1975	Some Psychological Aspects of the *Sonnets*	Bard, vol. 1/1: 1-8
1976	A Reading of Sonnet 120	Bard, vol. 1/2: 43-46
1978	Word Links from *Troilus* to *Othello* and *Macbeth*	Bard, vol. 2/1: 4-22
1982	The Problem of *The Raigne of King Edward the Third*: 1596: A Statistical Approach, Part 1	Bard, vol. 3/4: 133-142
1983	The Problem of *The Raigne of King Edward the Third*: 1596, Part 2	Bard, vol. 4/1: 2-14

Slater, Gilbert
Books

1931	*Seven Shakespeares: A Discussion of the Evidence for Various Theories with Regard to Shakespere's Identity*. London: Cecil Palmer. [excerpt repr. in BTC, vol. 1: 206-210] [reissued in 1972: Folcroft, PA: Folcroft Library Editions; and in 1977: Philadelphia: R. West.] [Modern edition edited by James A. Warren, Veritas Publications, 2023]	

Shorter pieces

1934, May	Shakespeare's Literary Executor	Sh. Pictorial, no. 75: 80
1934, Aug.	Can We Agree?	Sh. Pictorial, no. 78: 128
1934, Oct.	[letter: reply to J. T. Dewhurst's letter] [repr. in BTC, vol. 2: 25-28]	Sh. Pictorial, no. 80: 157
1938, Jan.	[letter: authorship of Shakespeare's plays by Bacon, Ralegh, others]	SF News-letter (E), no. 7: 5-6
1938, March	The Rival Poet of the Sonnets	SF News-letter (E), no. 8: 1-5
1938, March	[letter: correction to his recent article]	SF News-letter (E), no. 8: 12

Smiley, Richard

2007, Spring	Concordia Summary [Richard Joyrich]	Sh. Ox. Newsl., vol. 43/2: 1, 7-8

Smith, Allen A.

1989, May 17	Till Burnham Wood Doth March to Havertown? [letter: Warren Hope's April 20 article] Reply by Hope, May 17, p. A10.	Philadelphia Inquirer, p. A10

Smith, Dave

2023, June 27	"It Was Shocking": The Author Under Attack for Doubting Shakespeare [rev. of *Shakespeare Was a Woman and Other Heresies* by Elizabeth Winkler}	Guardian

Smith, Emma

2008, May	The Shakespeare Authorship Debate Revisited	Literature Compass, vol. 5/3: 618
2023, June 3	Shakespeare Sceptics are the New Literary Heroes	Spectator

Smith, G. C. Moore

1929, Jan.	The Seventeenth Earl of Oxford [rev. of the book by Capt. Ward]	Rev. of Eng. St., v. 5/17: 92-103.
1932, Oct.	Taking Lodgings in 1591 [Resp. by Col. Ward in SP, Jan. 1933]	Rev. of Eng. St., v. 8/32: 447-50

Smith, Gordon Ross

1959, Fall	Shakespeare and Freudian Interpretations	Am. Imago, vol. 16/3: 225

Smith, M. W. A.

1982	A Stylometric Analysis of *Hero and Leander*	Bard, vol. 3/3: 105-132
1982	The Authorship of *Pericles*: An Initial Investigation	Bard, vol. 3/4: 143-176
1983	The Authorship of *Pericles*: Collocations Investigated Again	Bard, vol. 4/1: 15-21
1988, Fall/Wntr	*Edward Ironside* and Principles of Authorship Attribution	Sh. Newsl., vol. 38/3-4: 50
1989, Spr./Sum.	Linkages of Rare Words to Deduce Sh. Chronology and Authorship	Sh. Newsl., vol. 39/1-2: 6
1991, Spr./Sum.	Stylometry: Will the Computer Finally End Authorship Controversies?	Sh. Newsl., vol. 41/1-2: 14+

Smith, Marilyn

1988, Winter	Shakespeare as Nobody: Thoughts on the Attraction of the Stratford Myth	Spear-shaker Rev., 1/2: 5-7

Smith, Rosalind

1994, Dec.	The Sonnets of the Countess of Oxford and Elizabeth I: Translations from Desportes [not by Anne Cecil or Elizabeth]	Notes & Q., vol. 41/4: 446-50

Smith, Sarah
Books and plays
2003	*Chasing Shakespeares*. New York: Atria Books.	
2007	*Chasing Shakespeares: The Play*.	

Shorter pieces
2002	The Reattribution of Munday's "The Paine of Pleasure"	Oxfordian, vol. 5: 70-99
2005	[comment on back cover of Anderson's book]	
2011, Winter	News: Joanna and Bob Wexler: A Remembrance	Sh. Matters, vol. 10/1: 5-6

Smith, Scott C.
1991, Fall	[letter: Stratford tour guide promotes Edward de Vere as true author]	Sh. Ox. Newsl., vol. 27/4: 12

Smith, Scott S.
1988, Winter	[letter: inadequacies in J. D. Reed's Sept. 1987 *Smithsonian's* article]	Sh. Ox. Newsl., vol. 24/1: 13-14
1992, Dec.	Will the Real Shakespeare Stand Up?	Sky (Delta), p. 96, 98+
1999, April 23	Playwright William Shakespeare	Investors Bus. Daily, p. A6
2011, Oct. 29	[letter: response to Rebecca Keegan's Oct. 27 article]	Los Angeles Times, p. D2
2011, Nov. 27	[letter: response to Charles McNulty's Nov. 27 article]	Los Angeles Times, p. D2

Smith, Shepherd
2008, March	A Tribute to Peter Moore [repr. in NSJ, vol. 12: 53-54 (Oct. 2008)]	De Vere Soc. Newsl., v. 15/1: 29

Smithers, Ursula
1924, Feb. 29	Oxford and Jonson, I	Hackney Spectator, p. 4
1924, March 14	Oxford and Jonson, II	Hackney Spectator, p. 4

Smithies, Sandy
1989, July 4	Television and Radio [British TV: "A Midsummer Night's Mystery"]	Guardian, p. 40

Smithson, Edward W.
Books
1922	*Baconian Essays (with an Introduction and two essays by George Greenwood)*. London: Cecil Palmer.	

Shorter pieces
1913	Ben Jonson's Pious Fraud	Nineteenth Century & After

Sobran, Joseph
Books
1997	*Alias Shakespeare: Solving the Greatest Literary Mystery of All Time*. New York: Free Press. [translated into German as *Genannt Shakespeare: die Lösung des grössten literarischen Rätsels*. Cologne: Dumont, 202.] [translated into *Japanese by Yushi Odashima and Noriko Odashima as Sheikusupia Misuteri*. Toyko: Asahi Shinbun Sha, 2000.]	

Shorter pieces
1985, Feb. 21	[review of *The Mysterious William Shakespeare*]	Washington Times
1985, April 5	Not Set Down in Malice [rev. of *The Mysterious William Shakespeare*]	National Review, v. 37/6: 51-52
1986, May 1	Was Earl of Oxford the Real Shakespeare?	Chicago Sun, p. 52
1987, Oct. 5	BARD, Beyond a Reasonable Doubt	National Review
1987, Nov. 6	A Fair Shake for Oxford/Shakespeare Revealed in Oxford's Letters [review of *Shakespeare Revealed in Oxford's Letters* by W. P. Fowler (1986); discussion of the Sept. 25 Supreme Court justices' mock trial and Charlton Ogburn's response to it]	National Review, vol. 39/6: 54-56
1988, Dec. 30	Shakespeare's Aristocratic Origins [repr. in SON, vol. 25/1: 6-7 (1989)]	Washington Times
1990, Nov. 20	Against Funding Odds [repr. in SON, vol. 27/1: 4 (Winter 1991)]	Washington Times
1991, April 29	Bard Thou Never Wert: Fooled by a Folio [repr. in SON, vol. 27/2: 2-5 (Spring 1991); and in BTC. Vol. 7: 36-42) Response by Charlton Heston, June 10, 1991, p. 34-35.	Nat. Review. (NY), vol. 43/7: 44-46
1992	This is a Case of Wishful Thinking [syndicated column]	
1992, Jan.	[letter: response to special issue on Sh's Authorship]	Atlantic Monthly, p. 6-9
1992, Summer	The Orthodox Shakespeare Faces Death (doggerel)	Sh. Ox. Newsl., vol. 28/3: 3
1993	More Light on Real Shakespeare [syndicated column]	
1993, Jan. 2	The Wish Is Often Father To the Thought	Las Vegas Review-Jou., p. 2C
1993, July 31	Bible Holds Proof of Shakespeare's Identity [repr. in SON, vol. 29/4: HER, 8-9 (Fall 1993); in EVR, vol. 1 (Fall 1995); and in BTC, vol. 7: 212-3]	Herald [Universal Press column]
1993, Aug. 2	Shakespeare Authorship Now Turns on Biblical Evidence	Greensboro News-Rec., p. A5

Sobran, Joseph (continued)

1993, Aug. 15	New Light on Shakespeare's Identity	Las Vegas Review-Journal, p. 2C
1994, May 31	Shakespeare and the Faccts [syndicated column]	
1996, Winter	Problem of the *Funeral Elegy* [repr. in ERV, vol. 2 (Winter 1996)]	Sh. Ox. Newsl., vol. 32/1: 1, 8-11
1996, Winter	[letter: open letter to members of the Shakespeare Oxford Society]	Sh. Ox. Newsl., vol. 32/1: 6-7
1996, Jan.	Shakespeare and Fascism	Sobran's
1996, Jan.	Shakespeare Revealed in Oxford's Poetry [repr. in GO, p. 129-39; and in LC, p. 106-112]	De Vere Soc. New., v. 2/4: 13-21
1996, Feb.	The Shakespeare Mystery	Sobran's
1996, Spring	[letter: response to previous letters]	Sh. Ox. Newsl., vol. 32/2: 22
1996, May	Shakespeare's Lives	Sobran's
1996, Summer	The Phaeton Sonnet [repr. in NSJ, vol. 5: 76-85 (April 2000); and in EVR, vol. 4 (Winter 1997)]	Sh. Ox. Newsl., vol. 32/3: 12-14
1996, July	Shakespeare Without Ideas	Sobran's
1996, Nov.	Shakespeare for the Tube	Sobran's
1996, Nov.	Shakespeare and the Official Language	Sobran's
1997, Feb.	Shakespeare's Time Capsule	Sobran's
1997, Spring	Shakespeare's Disgrace: Is This the Key to Identifying and Understanding the Poet? [repr. in EVR, vol. 5 (Winter 1997)] Response by Charlton Ogburn, vol. 33/3: 4, 12 (Spring 1997) Response by Elliott Stone, vol. 33/3: 21 (Spring 1997). Response by Elisabeth Sears, vol. 33/3: 21 (Spring 1997).	Sh. Ox. Newsl., v. 33/2: 1, 4-6
1997, May 15	[letter: response to Jonathan Bate's May 1 review]	Wall St. Journal, p. A23
1997, May 15	The Shakespeare Riddles [syndicated column]	
1997, Aug.	The Stratford Response	Sobran's
1997, Sept.	The Debate Rages On [syndicated column]	
1997, Oct.	The Shakespeare Party Line	Sobran's
1997, Dec.	Meeting Shakespeare	Sobran's
1998, Jan.	Introduction to *Emaricdulfe*	Sobrans, vol. 5/1
1998, Jan.	The Mystery of *Emaricdulfe*	Sobran's, vol. 5/1
1998	David Kathman and the "Historical Record" [reply to David Kathman's review of *Alias Shakespeare*]	[unpublished]
1998, Spring	Shake-speare's Sonnets are Stratfordian Achilles' Heel [repr. in EVR, vol. 8 (1999)]	Sh. Ox. Newsl., vol. 34/1: 15, 22
1999, Jan.	Shakespeare of Christendom	Sobran's
1999, Feb.	Shakespeare's Missing Links	Sobran's
1999, March 23	So, Who Really Done Shakespeare? [Shakespeare in Disguise]	Las Vegas Review-Journal, p. 9B
1999, March 18	Who Done Shakespeare?	Sobran's
1999, April	Every Word Doth Almost Tell My Name [repr. in LC, p. 57-78]	Harper's Mag., p. 54-55
1999, Summer	[review of *Shakespeare: A Life* by Park Honan (1998)]	Sh. Ox. Newsl., vol. 35/2: 21-22
1999, July 8	Debating Shakespeare	Sobran's
1999	How Old was Oxford's Daughter, and When Did William Lose His Hair? [reply to Alan Nelson]	[unpublished]
1999, Nov. 25	Giving Away the Game [syndicated column]	
2000, Feb. 24	Honoring the True Bard [syndicated column]	
2000, Feb. 29	Who are the Snobs? [syndicated column]	
2000, March	Shakespeare's Folks	Sobran's, vol.7/3
2000, Spring	The End of Stratfordianism [reply to Alan Nelson] [repr. in EVR, vol. 10 (Spring 2000)]	Sh. Ox. Newsl., vol. 36/1: 12-13+
2000, April 13	Happy Birthday, 'Shakespeare'! [syndicated column]	
2000, May 23	The Rivals [Syndicated column]	
2000, July 27	Making Sense of Shakespeare [syndicated column]	
2000, Oct.	Oxford and his 'Lovely Boy'	Sobran's
2000, Dec.	The Spirit of Falstaff	Sobran's, vol. 7/12
2001, March 8	Shakespeare and DNA [syndicated column]	
2001, April 17	Whose Testiony? [syndicated column]	
2001, May	Shakespearean Odds and Ends	Sobran's
2002, Winter	Oxford's Uncle Henry: *Sir Thomas More* Considered in Oxfordian Light	Sh. Ox. Newsl., vol. 38/1: 3, 6

2002, April 9	Shakespeare and the Snobs [syndicated column]	
2002, June 20	Rejoice! [Syndicated column]	
2002, Nov. 12	Shakespeare and the Directors [syndicated column]	
2003, April	The Bard's Orphans	Sobran's, vol. 10/4
2003, April 17	Shakespeare's Social Life [syndicated column]	
2003, May 1	Olivier and His Successors [syndicated column]	
2003, May 1	Titus and Lucrece [syndicated column]	
2003, Autumn	Nelson's Flawed Life of Oxford	Sh. Ox. Newsl., vol. 39/4: 1, 9-10
2004, Jan. 22	Burton's Lost *Hamlet* [syndicated column]	
2004, Jan.	A Flawed Life of Oxford	Sobran's
2004, June 24	The Death of Shakespeare [syndicated column]	
2005, Jan.	Shakespeare's 'Early' Poems	Sobran's, vol. 12/1
2005, Feb. 10	The Baker Street Shakespeareans [Syndicated column]	
2005, Winter	Before He Was Shakespeare, Part One	Sh. Ox. Newsl., v. 41/1: 1, 13-16
2005, Spring	Before He Was Shakespeare, Part Two	Sh. Ox. Newsl., v. 41/2: 1, 12-14
2005, May 12	Kyd Stuff [syndicated column]	
2005, May	Old Man Shakespeare	Sobran's
2005, June 16	The Language of Lear [syndicated column]	
2005, Aug. 18	Lear's Fool	Sobran's
2005, Aug. 30	The Queer Bard?	Sobran's
2005, Sept. 13	Hamnet's Father	Sobran's
2005, Sept. 29	Shakespeare, and the Catholic Question	Wanderer
2005, Dec. 8	What's in the Pronoun?	Sobran's
2005, Dec. 15	Reflections of a Conspirator	Sobran's
2006, Jan. 3	The Bard in Retirement	Sobran's
2006, Jan. 17	How to Handle a Woman	Sobran's
2006, April 13	Shakespearean Masterpiece	Sobran's
2006, June 1	Shakespeare and Ms. Grundy	Sobran's
2006, June 22	The Hamlet That Never Was	Sobran's
2006, June 29	My Ilk and I	Sobran's
2006, Oct. 3	Hamlet's Lame Creator	Sobran's
2007, Feb. 22	Fine-Filed Phrases	Sobran's
2007, Feb. 22	The Fun of Falstaff	Sobran's
2007, March 8	A Coriolanus in Our Future?	Sobran's
2007, March 22	The Shakespeare Bigots	Sobran's
2007, April 3	You Be the Judge	Sobran's
2007, April 19	The Time for Digression	Sobran's
2007, May 3	The Sobran Method: A True Story	Sobran's
2007, May 22	Special Edition	Sobran's
2007, Aug. 28	The Lady is the Man	Sobran's

Sokolowski, Peter
1993, Autumn	[review of *Montaigne: Complete Essays*, tr. by M. A. Screech (1991)]	Eliz. Review, vol. 1/2: 43-51
	Response by Roger Stritmatter, Spring 1994, p. 5.	

Somerset, Janetta
1948, Jan. 12	Drama Critic and Spirits Give New Identity to Shakespeare	Sun (Baltimore), p. 1

Souday, Paul
1925, Oct. 4	A French History of English Letters	New York Times, p. BR6

Southern, Richard
1956, Spring	Elizabethan Theatre	SF News-letter (E), p. 6

Sprague, Mrs. Frank J.
1941, Oct.	[letter: the latest *News-Letter*]	SF News-letter (A), vol. 2/6: 72

Spark, Muriel
1998	*A Far Cry from Kensington*. New York: New Dimensions Books. [A character in a publishing firm is sure that Shakspere was not the author, and that he, in the next world, must be laughing up his sleeve at what is going on in Stratford today.]

Sparrow, Andrew
1999, Oct. 27 Yesterday in Parliament: Earl [Burford] Defends this Sceptered Isle Telegraph, p. 16
     Against the Wolves

Spencer, Benjamin T.
1938, Jan. [review of *The Man Who Was Shakespeare* by Eva Turner Clark] Sewanee Review, vol. 47/1: 294

Spencer, Charles
2011, Nov. 7 Geeks, Snobs and a Spurious Controversy [review of *Anonymous*] Telegraph, p. 30
2012, May 7 Peter Brook Debunks Loony Shakespeare Theory Telegraph, p. 22

Spencer, John Bew
2010 "Shakespeare, William," in *Encyclopedia Britannica, 15th ed.: Macropaedia: Knowledge in Depth*, vol. 27:
     253-72 [with John Russell Brown & David Bevington; repeats many points rebutted by Oxfordian
     many times since 1920, with no notice of the rebuttals]

Spiggonio, Antonio
1948, Aug. 10 Shakespeare Solved [letter: Gelett Burgess' July 31 article] Washington Post, p. 10

Spindel, Christine
2015, Spring [letter: her conversion to belief in Oxford's authorship] Sh. Ox. Newsl., vol. 51/2: 3

Spittle, Bruce
2014, Winter [review of *AKA Shakespeare: A Scientific Approach to the* J. of Scientific Exploration
     Authorship Question by Peter A. Sturrock] v. 27/4: 705-10

Sprague, Mrs. H. C.
1947, June 15 [letter: Burgess's June 8 article] NY Herald Tribune, p. A7

Sprengnether, Madelon
2020, Dec. Who Wrote Shakespeare? A Response to Richard Waugaman Int'l Jou. of Applied Psycho-
     analytic Studies, vol.
     17/4: 365-68

Spring-Rice, D.
1933, Aug. 31 Founders of Lavenham Church [letter] Times (London)
     Response by Percy Allen, Sept. 5.

Spurgeon, Caroline
1935 *Shakespeare's Imagery and What It Tells Us.* Cambridge, UK: Cambridge University Press.

Squire, John C.
Books [published under pseud. Solomon Eagle]
1922 *Essays at Large.* New York: H. Doran Company. [see esp. "Shakespeare and the Second Chamber," p. 130-
     134]
Shorter pieces
1921, Jan. 9 Shakespeare and the Skeleton Observer, p. 4
1921, Jan. 21 Books of the Day [*SI* is mentioned in an essay on new books on S.] Observer, p. 4
1921, March 12 Mr. Looney and Lord Oxford [pub. under pseud. Solomon Eagle] Outlook, vol. 47: 231
1921, July 2 The Critic at Large: A Voice from the Past [reply to Looney's Outlook, vol. 47: 15
     July 25 response]
1922, March 18 Shakespeare's Master [Chaucer] Outlook, vol. 221-22
1923, March 25 The Oxford Movement [review of *The Mystery of "Mr. W. H."* by Observer, p. 4
     Col. B. R. Ward [long review]
1928, May 6 Lord Oxford [review of *The Seventeenth Earl of Oxford* by Capt. Observer, p. 6
     Bernard M. Ward]

St. Clair, F. Y.
1949, Sept. 3 A Look at the Register [letter: response to Burgess] Saturday Review, p. 26
     [repr. in *Sh. and His Rivals* (McMichael & Glenn 1962): 192]

St. Clair, Michael
2013, Fall [rev. of *Sh. Beyond Doubt?* edited by John Shahan & Alexander Waugh] Sh. Matters, vol. 12/4: 26, 35
2018, Summer [review of *Shakespeare Confidential* by C. V. Berney] Sh. Ox. Newsl., vol. 54/3: 30
2019, Winter [review of *Necessary Mischief: Exploring the Shakespeare Authorship* Sh. Ox. Newsl., vol. 55/1: 26-27
     Question by Bonner Miller Cutting]
2019, Spring [review of *"Shakespeare" Revealed: The Collected Articles and* Sh. Ox. Newsl., vol. 55/1: 26-27
     Published Letters of J. Thomas Looney, edited by James A. Warren]
2020, Summer [review of *Who Wrote That? Authorship Controversies from Moses to* Sh. Ox. Newsl., vol. 56/3: 32-33

Shokokhov by Donald Ostrowski (2020)]

| 2021, Fall | [review of *Shakespeare Revolutionized* by James A. Warren] | Sh. Ox. Newsl., vol. 57/4: 27-29 |
| 2022, Summer | [review of *Aspects of the Shakespeare Authorship Question* by Richard J. Wallace] | Sh. Ox. Newsl., vol. 58/3: 13-14 |

Standen, Gilbert
Unpublished albums
1927?	[an album with hundreds of articles Baconian in content]	
1929	[the first of two Oxfordian albums; contents of the first are from 1922 to 1929, and include a wealth of Oxfordian items not known to exist anywhere else, including letters, SF Circulars, published articles, and invitations to SF annual dinners. Morethan 470 items are pasted into the two Oxfordian albums]	
1936	[the second of the two Oxfordian albums, with ephemera from 1929 to 1936]	

Books
| 1930 | *Shakespeare Authorship: A Summary of Evidence*. London: Cecil Palmer. | |

Shorter pieces
| 1924, March 21 | A Rosicrucian Group, I | Hackney Spectator, p. 4 |
| 1924, April 4 | A Rosicrucian Group, II | Hackney Spectator, p. 4 |

Starkey, David
| 2001, Feb. 17 | Queen Was No Virgin interview with Philip Sheppard [revised Apr. 10, 2018] | Globe & Mail |

Starkey, Marion
| 1962, Sept. | Mother and Son Champion Earl of Oxford [review of *Shake-speare: The Man Behind the Name* by Dorothy and Charlton, Jr., Ogburn] | Boston Globe, p. 25 |

Starner, Janet W.
| 2011 | *Anonymity in Early Modern England: "What's In a Name?"* [with B. H. Traister]. Burlington, VT: Ashgate. | |

Starr, Carol
| 1976, April 14 | Author Denies Shakespeare Wrote Plays [profile of SOS member and VP S. Colum Gilfillan] | Daily Bruin (UCLA) |

Starrett, Vincent
| 1947, Jan. 5 | [review of *Shakespeare, Man of Mystery* by Thomas Henry Foster] | Chicago Tribune, p. G2 |

Stasio, Marilyn
| 2003, Nov. 24-30 | The Beard of Avon [review of Amy Freed's play] | Variety (Los Angeles), p. 43 |

Stasukevich, Lain
| 2011, Sept. | A Mighty Pen [review of *Anonymous* (2011] | Am. Cinematographer, vol. 92/9: 28-43 |

Steadman, Edmund Clarence
| 1901 | Advice to English Schoolboys Who Want to Become Shakespeare [repr. in BTC, vol. 1: 133] | Literary World, vol. 63: 327 |

Stechow, W.
| 1941, April | The Ashbourne Portrait | SF News-letter (E), p. 4 |

Steckel, Frank-Patrick
| 2013, March | Notizen zu Ben Jonson's Gedicht (mit einer eigenen Übersetzung) | Neues Sh. Journal, v. NS3: 17-19 |
| 2014, Oct. | Brief aus der Werkstatt | Neues Sh. Journal, v. NS4: 35-38 |

Stedman, Nina
| 2000, April | Prinzessin Shakespeare [repr. from *University Players News*, no. 28, (Winter 1999/2000)] | Neues Sh. Journal, vol. 5: 142-49 |

Steed, Wickham
| 1930, Nov. 26 | Protecting the Old Church [in Lavenham] [letter] | Telegraph, p. 14 |

Steele, Mary Susan
| 1926 | *Plays and Masques at Court During the Reigns of Elizabeth, James and Charles*. New Haven: Yale Un. Pr. | |

Steelman, Ben
| 2011, Oct. 23 | [review of *Anonymous*] | Star-News (Wilmington) |

Steer, Francis W.
| 1955, Spring | English History in the Saleroom | SF News-letter (E), p. 3-5 |

Steger, Pat
| 2002, May 5 | [report on the Earl of Burford's Talk] | San Francisco Chronicle, p. C4 |

Stein, E. Jimmee

1987, Fall   To Believe or Not To Believe [repr. in SSR, issue 1/1: 6-9]   Emphasis

Stein, Hannas

2010, April 19   Vulkanasche stört auch das Konzertleben   Die Tageszeitung, p. 16

Steinburg, Steven (Steven McClarran)

Books

2011   *I Come To Bury Shaksper: A Deconstruction of the Fable of the Stratfordian Shake-speare and the Supporting Scholarship: An Oxfordian Perspective.*

2013   *I Come to Bury Shakespeare II: A Deconstruction of the Fable of the Stratfordian Shake-speare and the Supporting Scholarship. An Oxfordian Perspective.* CreateSpace.

2015   *The Shakespeare Puzzles: The Hidden Autobiography of Edward de Vere.* CreateSpace.

2018   *Renaissance of Lies: Part 2 of the Autobiography of Edward de Vere, 17th Earl of Oxford.*

2019   *I Come to Bury Shakspere* (Fifth edition) [first two editions published under the name Steven McClarran]

2021   *A Lover's Complaint: Part 3 of the Autobiography of Edward de Vere, 17th Earl of Oxford.*

2022   *Amoretti: Children of the Virgiin Queen: Part 4 of the Autobiography of Edward de Vere, 17th Earl of Oxford.*

Shorter pieces

2016   Chapter 10: Another Hell Above the Ground, in *Contested Year*

2019   The Rainbow Portrait & A Lover's Complaint—More Evidence of the Catastrophic Failure of "Professional" Elizabethan Scholarship [from the SOF website]

--   Fake Truth & the Language of "Professional Shakespeare Scholarship" [from the SOF website] [repr. in *Sh. Authorship Sourcebook* (Stritmatter 2019, 2022): 327-38]

Stelting, Michelle

2015   *Redating Pericles: A Re-examination of Shakespeare's Pericles as an Elizabethan Play.* University of Missouri at Kansas City, Department of Theatre, Masters Thesis.

Stemle, Lisa

1991, Oct. 20   Just Who Really Wrote Shakespeare's Stuff? [rev. of *All the Queen's Men*, a play by John Nassivere]   Sun Sentinal (Fort Lauderdale), p. 27

Stephens, Jane

1991   [review of *The Lost Chronicle of Edward de Vere* by Andrew Field]   Australian Society, vol. 10/1-2: 59-60

Stepniewski, Michael and Spenser

2021   *Shakespeare's Will . . . In what he hath left us.*

Sterling, Carleton W.

2005, Spring   *Hamlet* in Time and Space   Sh. Ox. Newsl., vol. 41/2: 3-5

2006, Winter   Shakespeare's Monarchs and Mark Anderson   Sh. Ox. Newsl., vol. 42/1: 20-22
                Response by Mark Anderson, same issue.

2008. Winter   Hypothetical Tudor Princes   Sh. Ox. Newsl., vol. 44/1: 3

2008, Winter   *Hamlet* in 1603: A Quick-and-Dirty Quarto   Sh. Ox. Newsl., vol. 44/1: 9-11

2008, Summer   Shakespeare as Brand Name   Sh. Ox. Newsl., vol. 44/3: 23

2009, Dec.   [letter: *Hamlet*]   Sh. Ox. Newsl., vol. 45/3: 30

2012, Winter   Shakespeare's Actors   Sh. Ox. Newsl., v. 48/1: 18, 20+

2013, Spring   [letter: *Richard III* and the eve of the Essex Rebellion]   Sh. Ox. Newsl., vol. 49/2: 8

Stern, Micah

1999, Spring   [review of The *Late Mr. Shakespeare: A Novel* by Robert Nye]   Eliz. Review, vol. 7/1: 82-84

Stevens, Justice John Paul

1988, Spring   Opinions of the Justices [with Justices William J. Brennan and Harry A. Blackmun]   Am U. Law Rev., vol. 37/3: 819-26

1992, April   The Shakespeare Canon of Statutory Construction   Univ. of Penn Law Review, vol. 140/4: 1373+
                [repr. in ER, vol. 1/1: 4-20 (Spring 1993); in BTC, vol. 8: 129-44; in EVR, vol. 1 (Fall 1995); and in SAL (Strit., 2022): 103-13]
                Summarized by Morse Johnson, SOS, vol. 27/2: 1-2 (1991).
                Response to ER reprint by Ch. H. Gannon, Autumn 1993, p. 2-5.

2014, April 6   By the Book: An Interview   NY Times, p. 10

Stewart, Doug

2006, Sept.   To Be or Not to Be Shakespeare   Smithsonian, p. 62-66, 68-71
                Response by *Shakespeare Newsletter*, vol. 56/2: 43

Still, Colin
    1921   *Shakespeare's Mystery Play: A Study of The Tempest*. London: Cecil Palmer.

Stohr, Otto K.
    1993, Feb. 22   Shakespeare Inquiry Sheds Valuable Light [letter]   Greensboro News-Rec., p. A4

Stokes, Roy
    1937, June   Bacon and "Shakespeare"   East Anglian M., vol. 2/9: 392-6
                    Many responses in July; see Stokes's reply in Aug.
    1937, July   [letter: slight correction to his June article]   East Anglian M., vol. 2/10: 468
    1937, Aug.   Bacon and "Shakespeare"   East Ang. M., vol. 2/11: 506-8
    1937, Nov.   "Shakespeare" and Bacon: Reply to Ranson   East Ang.. A., vol. 3/2: 79-80

Stoll, Elmer E.
    1937, May 8   The Detective Spirit in Criticism [rebuttal to Barrell's May 1 article]   Saturday Rev., p. 12, 14, 16-17
                    Reply by Barrell, May 22.

Stoll, Ray
    2021, Winter   [letter: 500th birthday of Edward de Vere]   Sh. Ox. Newsl., vol. 57/1: 5-6

Stone, Elliott
    1997, Summer   [letter: response to Sobran's Spring 1997 "Sonnets" article]   Sh. Ox. Newsl., vol. 33/3: 21
    2009, Fall   [letter: academics' private doubts]   Sh. Matters, vol. 8/4: 2
    2015   Melville's *Billy Budd* and the Disguises of Authorship [with Mark   New England Review, vol.
                    Anderson and Roger A. Stritmatter]   36/1: 100-31

Stone, Lawrence
    1967   *Crisis of the Aristocracy, 1558-1641*. London: Oxford University Press.

Storr, Anthony
    1990, July 2   Freudian Clips   Sunday Times, p. 2
                    Response by Bernard Kaukas, Aug. 12, p. 2.

Story, Ted
Books
    2016   *The Shakespeare Fraud: The Politics Behind the Pen*. Somerville, MA: Forever Press.
Plays co-authored with Hank Whittemore
    2010   *Shake-speare's Treason: The True Story of King Henry IX, Last of the Tudors* [a one-man show based on
                    The Monument]
Shorter pieces
    2007, Winter   President's Blog . . .   Sh. Matters, vol. 6/2: 3, 31
    2011, Winter   Ben Jonson Made Me Laugh   Sh. Matters, v. 10/1: 1, 13-14

Stotsenburg, John H.
    1904   *An Impartial Study of the Shakespeare Title*. Louisville, KY: J. P. Morton & Co.
                    [repr. in 1970: Port Washington, NY: Kennikat Press]
                    [Chapter 4 "William Shaksper Has No Place in Henslow's Diary" repr. in BTC, vol. 1: 190-199]

Stott, Alan
    2007, Summer   Shakespeare – Who Held the Pen: Insights Meets Research   Sh. Matters, vol. 6/4: 1, 24-31
    2007, Fall   [review of *Number and Geometry in Shakespeare's Macbeth* by   Sh. Matters, vol. 7/1: 19-20
                    Sylvia Eckersley, edited by Alan Thewless (2007)]
    2011, Fall   Shakespeare: Treason or Transformation?   Sh. Matters, vol. 10/4: 1, 7-15+
    2013, Winter   Did Rudolf Steiner Name the Bard, 100 Years Ago?   Sh. Matters, vol. 12/1: 1, 11-14

Streitz, Paul
Books
    2001   *Oxford, Son of Queen Elizabeth I*. Darien, CT: Oxford Institute Press.
    2014   *Shakespeare and the Courtesan*. CreateSpace.
Shorter pieces
    2011, Spring   Oxford and the *King James Bible*   Sh. Matters, vol. 10/2: 9-16, 32

    2002, Fall   [letter: resp. to Christopher Paul's review]   Sh. Matters, vol. 2/1: 4-5
                    Reply by Paul, Winter 2003, p. 2-4.
    2007, Fall   Prince Tudor Theory and Stratfordians [letter]   Sh. Matters, vol. 43/4: 20
    2012, Summer   [letter: resp. to Bonner Cutting's BC vol. 3 "Mother" article]   Sh. Matters, vol. 11/3: 28-29+
    2012, Sum./Fall   [letter: seventeen reasons to believe Oxford was Elizabeth's son]   Sh. Ox. Newsl., vol. 48/3: 9-10
    2013, Spring   [letter: newsletter coverage of PT issues]   Sh. Ox. Newsl., vol. 49/2: 5-6

Stritmatter, Roger A.

Websites and blogs: Shake-speare's Bible – shake-speares-bible.com

Books

1993	*A Quintessence of Dust: An Interim Report on the Marginalia of the Geneva Bible of Edward de Vere.* Northampton, MA. [excerpts repr. in SON, vol. 29/2a: 1-2 (Spring 1993); in DVN, vol. 2/7: 16-17 (Dec. 1996); and in EVR, vol. 1 (Fall 1995)] [review by Mark K, Anderson, SOS, vol. 32/4: 8-10 (1996)]
1996	*There's Not the Smallest Orb, But in His Motion Like an Angel Sings.* Northampton, MA: Roger Stritmatter.
2001	*The Marginalia of Edward de Vere's Geneva Bible: Providential Discovery, Literary Reasoning, and Historical Consequence.* University of Massachusetts PhD Dissertation. Northampton, MA: Oxenford Press. Reprinted in 2003, 2015.
2013	*On the Date, Sources and Design of Shakespeare's "The Tempest"* [with Lynne Kositsky]. Foreword by William S. Niederkorn. Jefferson, NC: McFarland & Co. [excerpt repr. in *Sh. Authorship Sourcebook* (Stritmatter 2022): 429-49]
2016	*The 1623 Shakespeare First Folio: A Minority Report,* a special issue of *Brief Chronicles*]. Shakespeare Oxford Fellowship.
2019	*The Poems of Edward de Vere, 17th Earl of Oxford . . . and the Shakespeare Question. Volume I: He that Takes the Pain to Pen the Book . . . . .*
2019	*The Shakespeare Authorship Sourcebook: A Workbook for Educators and Students.* Shakespeare Oxford Fellowship.
2022	*The Shakespeare Authorship Sourcebook: A Workbook for Educators and Students, 2ND Edition.* Shakespeare Oxford Fellowship.
2022	*Shakespeare and the Law: How the Bard's Legal Knowledge Affects the Authorship Question.* Shakespeare Oxford Fellowship.
2023	*The Poems of Edward de Vere, 17th Earl of Oxford, vol. 1, 2nd edition: He that Takes the Pain to Pen the book. Earliest "Canonical" Poems, c. 1566-1580* [general editor]. Shakespeare Oxford Fellowship.
2023	*The Poems of Edward de Vere, 17th Earl of Oxford, vol. 2: As it Fell Upon a Day. Poems from The Passionate Pilgrim* [general editor]. Shakespeare Oxford Fellowship. [includes "Reclaiming The Passionate Pilgrim," pp. 3-11, by Katherine Chiljan, repr. from *Oxfordian 14* (2012)]
2023	*The First Folio: A Shakespearean Enigma. The 1623 First Folio and the Authorship Question* [editor]. Shakespeare Oxford Fellowship.

Periodicals edited

2009-2016: *Brief Chronicles: An Interdisciplinary Journal of Authorship Studies*, vol. I-VII

2005, Fall-2010, Fall: *Shakespeare Matters*, vol. 5/1-9/3

Periodicals edited (co-editor)

2001, Fall-2002, Summer: *Shakespeare Matters*, vol. 1/1-1

Periodicals edited (design editor)

2011, Winter-2013, Fall: *Shakespeare Matters*, vol. 10/1-12/4

Periodicals edited with Mark Anderson

1994-1995: *Oxenford Reader* [a copy of vol. II/1 is in the Oxfordian archives at Brunel University]

Shorter pieces

1990, Spring	[letter: Jaggard's 1619 publication]	Sh. Ox. Newsl., vol. 26/2: 1
1990, Summer	[letter: resp. to Charlton Ogburn]	Sh. Ox. Newsl., vol. 26/3a: 6-7
1991, Winter	[letter: need informal assoc. to critically examine Stratford legend]	Sh. Ox. Newsl., vol. 27/1: 6
1991, Aug.	[letter: the *Spear Shaker*]	Spear-shaker Rev., vol. 5: 23
1991, Fall	[letter: Malcolm X's skepticism about Shaksper]	Sh. Ox. Newsl., vol. 27/4: 12
1992, Spring	[letter: Edward de Vere's *Geneva Bible* and authorship]	Sh. Ox. Newsl., vol. 28/2: 1-2
1993, Spring	A Quintessence of Dusk [excerpts]	Sh. Ox. Newsl., vol. 29/2A: 1-2
1993, Spring	[letter: Shakespearean Association of America Meeting]	Sh. Ox. Newsl., vol. 29/2a: 12
1993, Autumn	[review of *Shakespeare's Personality* ed. by Norman Holland]	Eliz. Review, vol. 1/2: 65-74
1994, May 7	The Bard and the Nonbelievers [repr. in SON, vol. 30/3a: 6 (1994)]	Washington Post
1994, Spring	[letter: Peter Sokolowski's Autumn 1993 "Montaigne" review]	Eliz. Review, vol. 2/1: 5
1995, Spring	[review of *Censorship and Interpretation* by Annabel Patterson]	Eliz. Review, vol. 3/1: 56-62
1995, Spring	Smithsonian Gets the Facts Wrong [about de Vere's Geneva Bible] [letter, with Mark Anderson, to the *Smithsonian*] [repr. in EVR (vol. 1 (Fall 1995); and in BTC, vol. 7: 308-10]	Sh. Ox. Newsl., vol. 31/2a: 8-9
1995, Autumn	[review of *Biblical References in Shakespeare's Comedies* by Naseeb Shaheen] [repr. in EVR, vol. 4 (Fall 1996/Wntr. 1997)]	Eliz. Review, vol. 3/2: 60-68
1996, Winter	[letter to *New York Times* (19 Jan. 1996): *Funeral Elegy* (not printed)]	Sh. Ox. Newsl., vol. 32/1: 23

Stritmatter, Roger (continued)

2002, Spring	[review of *The Marprelate Controversy* 1588-1596 by Elizabeth Appleton (2001)]	Sh. Matters, v. 1/3: 25-27, 36
2002, Summer	From the Editors: Oxford is Shakespeare: Any Questions? [with William Boyle]	Sh. Matters, vol. 1/1: 1, 3, 20
2002, Summer	Swan Song for *Funeral Elegy*: Prof. Donald Foster Concedes It's Not Shakespeare [with William Boyle]	Sh. Matters, vol. 1/4: 1, 4
2002, Summer	Why the Ashbourne Portrait Matters [with William Boyle]	Sh. Matters, vol. 1/4: 3
2003, Fall	Monstrous Animosity: Nelson's Oxford Bio Distorts Both Oxford and Oxfordians (2003)	Sh. Matters, vol. 3/1: 8-9
2003, Spring	[review of *Shakespeare's Fingerprints* by Michael Brame and Galina Popova (2002)]	Sh. Matters, v. 2/3: 24-25, 32
2003, Winter	Scenes From the Death of a Myth: Jonathan Bate and the God of Our Idolatry	Sh. Matters, vol. 2/2: 12-13
2004, Fall	A Critique of *The Monument* Theory (2005) [with Lynne Kositsky] Response by Hank Whittemore, vol. 4/1: 1, 10-14	Sh. Matters, vol. 4/1: 1, 10-14
2004, Fall	A Law Case in Verse: *Venus and Adonis* and the Authorship Question [repr. in BTC, vol. 8: 385-446; and in *Sh. and the Law* (Stritmatter, 2022): 253-91]	Tennessee Law Review, vol. 72/1: 171-219
2006	What's In a Name? Everything, Apparently . . .	Rocky M. R., vol. 60/2: 37-49
2006	On Chronology and Performance Venue of *A Mids. Night's Dream*	Oxfordian, vol. 9: 81-90
2006, Autumn	'Tilting Under Frieries': Narcissus (1595) and the Affair at the Blackfriars [repr. in SM, vol. 6/2: 1, 18-20+ (Winter 2007)]	Cashiers Elis., vol. 70: 39-42
2006, Fall	Shakespeare's Language—and *Our* Education	Sh. Matters, vol. 6/1: 3-4, 7-8
2006, Spring	From the Editor: Fear and Loathing on the Oxford Trail: A Cameo at the SAA	Sh. Matters, vol. 5/3: 3-4, 25+
2006, Summer	Something Rich and Strange: Emerging World Of Authorship Studies	Sh. Matters, vol. 5/4: 3, 22-24
2006, Summer	Brunel University to Offer Master's Degree in Authorship Studies: Interview with William Leahy	Sh. Matters, vol. 5/4: 1, 14-17
2006, Winter	From the Editor: 1604 and Other Red Herrings	Sh. Matters, vol. 5/2: 3, 11+
2007	*The Spanish Maze* and the Dates of *The Tempest* [with L.Kositsky] [repr. in BTC, vol. 10: 273-287]	Oxfordian , vol. 10: 9-19
2007, March 18	Is This the Bard We See Before Us? Or Someone Else? [repr. in *Sh. Authorship Sourcebook* (Stritmatter 2019, 2022): 215-19]	Wash. Post, Outlook, p. B1, 5
2007, Spring	Why *Richard II, Part 1* is Even More Important Than You Think	Sh. Mat., vol. 6/3: 3, 26-29+
2007, Summer	Fencing with Dr. Wells . . . and Clues From My Mailbox	Sh. Matters, vol. 6/4: 3, 22-24
2007, Sept.	Shakespeare and the Voyagers Revisited [with Lynne Kositsky]	Review of Eng. Studies., vol., 58/236: 447-72
2007, Sept.	A Companion to Shakespeare's Sonnets	Choice, vol. 45/1: 96
2007, Fall	Joint SF-SON Conference in Carmel: New Voices, Declaration of Reasonable Doubt	Sh. Matters, vol. 7/1: 1, 26-29+
2007, Winter	2nd Annual Joint Conference in Ann Arbor a Success	Sh. Matters, vol. 6/2: 1, 13-17+
2008	A Movable Feast: *The Tempest* as Shrovetide Revelry [with Lynne Kositsky]	Sh. Yearbook, vol. XVII: 365
2008, Fall	In Praise of Amateurism [review of *Kenneth Burke on Shakespeare*]	Sh. Matters, vol. vol. 7/4: 3, 9+
2008, Feb.	Shakespeare's Sonnets	Choice, vol. 45/6: 979
2008, July	English Renaissance Literature and Contemporary Theory: Sublime Objects of Theology	Choice, vol. 45/11: 1945
2008, May	Religion In the Age of Shakespeare	Choice, vol. 45/9: 1536
2008, Sept.	Shakespeare's Modern Collaborators	Choice, vol. 46/1: 91
2008, Spring	New York's Shakespearean Tragedy: Authorship & the Astor Place Riots	Sh. Matters, vol. 7/3: 3, 17-18
2009	Welcome to Brief Chronicles [with Gary Goldstein]	Brief Chronicles, vol. 1: 1-7
2009	Who Was 'William Shakespeare?' We Propose He Was Edward de Vere [with Richard Waugaman]	Scandinavian Psychoanalytic Review, vol. 32: 105-15
2009	How Shakespeare Got His *Tempest*: Another "Just So" Story [with Lynne Kositsky]	Brief Chronicles, vol. I: 205-267
2009	Pale as Death: Fictionalizing Influence of Erasmus's "Naufragium" on the Renaissance Travel Narrative, in *Discovering Shakespeare*, p. 143-53 [with Lynne Kositsky]	

Author Index

Stritmatter, Roger (continued)

2022	"What's in a Name"? "No Fear" Sh. Authorship for the Secondary and College Classroom [with Shelly Maycock], in *Sh. Authorship Sourcebook* (Stritmatter 2019, 2022): 25-33]	
2022, Sept.	Triumphal Numbers and the "Stigma of Print": Michael Drayton's Encomium to Shakespeare in *Agincourt*	Oxfordian, vol. 24: 73-110
2022, Fall	George Peele's Letter: Who Wrote It?	Sh. Ox. Newsl., vol. 58/4: 17-20
2023, Jan.	Keynote Speech: Every Syllable Fact, Fiction and Fancy in the Shakespeare Question	De Vere S. New., v. 30/1: 13-20
2023, Jan.	Breaking News: De Vere Annotated Books from Audley End	De Vere S. New., v. 30/1: 30-38
2023, Spring	Breaking News: De Vere Annotated Books from Audley End	Sh. Ox. Newsl., vol. 59/2:14-18
2023, Aug.	The First Folio Paratexts, in *The First Folio* (Stritmatter): 189-204	
2023, Autumn	Francis Meres Revisited: Wit, Design and Authorship in *Palladis Tamia* (1598)	Critical Survey, vol. 35/3: 17-61

Stroman, B.

1962	Shakespeare = Francis Bacon = Edward de Vere = The Earl of Derby = Christopher Marlowe, etc.	Algemeen Handelsblad (Swedish), vol. 13: 3

Stromenger, Lela

2009, April 25	[letter: Bravin's article on Justice Stevens]	Wall Street Journal, p. A10

Stuewe, Paul

1989, April 8	Is He or Is he Ain't Our One and Only [review of *The Mystery of William Shakespeare* by Charlton Ogburn]	Toronto Star, p. M6

Sturrock, Peter A.

Books

2013	*AKA Shakespere: A Scientific Approach to the Authorship Question*. Palo Alto: Exoscience.	
2015	*Late Night Thoughts About Science*. Exoscience Publishing.	

Shorter pieces

2014, Spring	Roger Stritmatter Interviews Peter Sturrock	Sh. Ox. Newsl., vol. 50/2: 21-22
2014, Fall	[letter: assigning probabilities to subjective judgments; two typos]	Sh. Ox. Newsl., vol. 50/4: 4-5
2020, Winter	Dedication to the Sonnets [letter, with Kathleen Erickson]	Sh. Ox. Newsl., vol. 56/2: 4
2020, Summer	[letter, with Kathleen Erickson: resp. Hamill re Dedic. to the Sonnets]	Sh. Ox. Newsl., vol. 56/3: 6

Stuttaford, Genevieve

1993, Dec. 13	[review of *Shakespeare, In Fact* by Irvin L. Matus (1994)]	Publisher's Weekly, p. 55-56
1996, July 22	[review of *Who Wrote Shakespeare?* by John Michell (1996)]	Publisher's Weekly, p. 223
1997, March	[review of *Alias Shakespeare* by Joseph Sobran (1997)]	Publisher's Weekly, p. 66

Sullivan, Leo

1956, Jan. 9	Expert Hits Shakespeare Conjecture [Louis B. Wright]	Washington Post, p. 18

Sullivan, Patrick R.

1997, May 15	[letter: resp. to Bate's May 1 review of Sobran's *Alias Shakespeare*]	Washington Post, p. A23
2021, Spring	[review of *Images in an Antique Book: Dante in Shakespeare* by Vivienne Robertson (2019)]	Sh. Ox. Newsl., vol. 57/2: 21-23
2023, Spring	Is Shakespeare Bigger Than a Breadbox?	Sh. Ox. Newsl., vol. 59/2: 19-21
2023, Summer	How Shakespeare Made the Classics into His Own	Sh. Ox. Newsl., vol. 59/3: 23-24

Sullivan, Robert

1994, March	No Holds Bard: Obituary of William Fowler (repr. in SON, vol. 30/2a: 5)	Dartmouth Alumni Magazine p. 14-21

Summers, Andrew

2011, Nov. 10	[letter: praise for Matt Abbott's review of *Anonymous*]	Essex Chronicle, p. 18

Sutton, Graham

1931, Nov.	Another Theory About Shakespeare [review of *The Earl of Oxford as "Shakespeare"* by Montagu W. Douglas]	Bookman, vol. 81: 132

Swan, George S.

2007	*The Woman's Prize*: A Sequel to *The Taming of the Shrew*	Oxfordian, vol. 10: 121-141
2014, June	The Proximate Source of *A Midsummer Night's Dream*: Anthony Munday's *John A Kent and John A Cumber*	Quint, vol. 6.3: 48-113
2016, Fall	[letter: C. V. Berney's article on *Cymbeline*]	Sh. Ox. Newsl., vol. 52/4: 5

Tannenbaum, Samuel A.

1925, April	Shakspere's Unquestioned Autographs and the Addition to Sir Thomas More	Studies in Philology, v. 22/2: 133-60
1926	A New Study of Shakspere's Will [resp. by Greenwood, Oct. p. 276]	Studies in Philology, v. 23: 117
1931, Jan. 1	The Copy for Shakespeare's Sonnets	Philological Quart., v. 10: 393-95

Tappan, Gregory

1961	Foreword to *Shakespeare Cross-Examination*. Richard Bentley, editor. American Bar Association, p. iv. Repr. in SON, vol. 28/1: 4 (Winter 1992); and in BTC, vol. 7: 89]

Tarica, Alan

2006, Spring	Did Shakespeare Read from 17th Earl of Oxford's Personal Library, Part 1 [with W. Ron Hess]	Sh. Ox. Newsl., v. 42/2: 1, 13-26
2006, Fall	Did Shakespeare Read from 17th Earl of Oxford's Personal Library, Part 2 [with W. Ron Hess]	Sh. Ox. Newsl., vol. 42/3: 25-28
2006, Fall	[letter: understanding the sonnets]	Sh. Ox. Newsl., vol. 42/3: 16
2007, Winter	[letter: resp. to Altrocchi's 2006 "Ideational Change" article]	Sh. Ox. Newsl., vol. 43/1: 30
2007, Summer	An Argument for Less Literalism and More Metaphor, Symbolism, and Other Rhetorical Devices in *Shakespeare's Sonnets*	Sh. Ox. Newsl., vol. 43/3: 3-7
2013, Spring	[letter: the *Sonnets*]	Sh. Matters, vol. 12/2: 2, 27-28
2015, Fall	A Collision of Cultural and Ethics with Scholarly Correction [Ethics and the Authorship Question]	J. Info. Ethics, v. 24/2: 105-12

Tassinari, Lamberto
Books

2009	*John Florio: The Man Who Was Shakespeare*. Giano Books.

Shorter pieces

2009, Fall	The Italian Connection: an introduction	Sh. Matters, vol. 8/4: 10-15
2011	John Florio: the Anglified Italian who invented Shakespeare	Oxfordian, vol. 13: 135-145
2012, Sum./Fall	[letter: review of his book *John Florio* is "partisan and unfair"]	Sh. Ox. Newsl., vol. 48/3: 4-5
2013, Winter	A Comparison of Shakespeare's and Florio's Wills	Sh. Ox. Newsl., vol. 49/1: 14-17

Tate, Lew
Periodicals edited
2006, Winter-2008, Summer: *Shakespeare Oxford Newsletter*, vol. 42/1-44/3
Shorter pieces

2006, Winter	Editorial Greeting	Sh. Ox. Newsl., vol. 42/1: 2
2006, Winter	SON Interview Richard Whalen (Richard Whalen and the Professors)	Sh. Ox. Newsl., vol. 42/1: 15-17
2006, Fall redux	Ann Arbor Conference	Sh. Ox. Newsl., vol. 42/4: 1, 5-8
2006, Fall redux	RSC at Ann Arbor	Sh. Ox. Newsl., vol. 42/4: 30
2007, Fall	Nine / Eleven, Iraq, and *Henry V*: Shakespeare in the classroom	Sh. Ox. Newsl., vol. 43/4: 16-18
2008, Winter	[review of *Macbeth: Fully Annotated from an Ox. Perspective*, edited by Richard F. Whalen (2007)]	Sh. Ox. Newsl., vol. 44/1: 25-26

Tatum, Aaron F.
Books

2018	*Shakespeare's Secrets*. WaveCloud Corporation.

Shorter pieces

1998, Summer	Justice Stevens Casts Deciding Vote for Oxford in an Oxfordian Victory at D.C. Authorship Trial [repr. in BTC, vol. 8: 16-21]	Sh. Ox. Newsl., vol. 34/2: 8-9
2002, Winter	[letter: Charlton and Vera Ogburn]	Sh. Ox. Newsl., vol. 38/1: 22
2011, July	[letter: response to the De Vere Society Statement on *Anonymous*]	De Vere Soc. Newsl., v. 18/2: 28
2019, Oct.	[letter: meeting at Hedingham Castle]	De Vere Soc. Newsl., v. 26/4: 43
2022, April	[letter: Alexander Waugh's important articles and broadcasts]	De Vere Soc. New., v. 29/2: 40-1

Taube, Michael

1999, Sept. 15	Boarding the Bard: Debate Still Rages	Record (Ontario), p. E7
2002, Aug. 10	Was He or Was He Not Shakespeare?	Windsor Star, p. F1

Taylor, Gary
Books edited

2017	*The New Oxford Shakespeare Authorship Companion* [with Gabriel Egan]. Oxford: Oxford Univ. Press.

Shorter pieces

1993	Introduction, in *Reinventing Shakespeare* (1989) [repr. in BTC, vol. 7]	Sh. Ox. Newsl., vol. 29/4: 19

Author Index

Taylor, Gilbert
 1993, Nov. 15 [review of *Shakespeare, In Fact* by Irvin L. Matus (1994)] Booklist, vol. 90/6: 597
 1994, Nov. 1 [review of Shakespeare—*Who Was He? The Oxford Challenge to the* Booklist, vol. 91/5: 476
  Bard of Avon by Richard F. Whalen (1994)]

Taylor, Kate
 2002, Nov. 23 The Beard's the Thing [review of *The Bard of Avon* by Amy Freed] Globe & Mail, p. R6
 2005, Oct. 12 Courtier or Son of a Glover. Does it Matter? [review of *The Truth* Globe & Mail, p. R1
  Will Out by Brenda James and William Rubinstein]

Taylor, Lynda
 2012 *Or Not To Be.*

Taylor, Michael
 2006 [review of *The Case For Shakespeare* by Scott McCrea (2005)] Sh. Survey, vol. 59: 358-59

Taylor, Nicole E.
 2011, Dec. [review of *The Shakespeare Guide to Italy* by Richard P. Roe] Am. Theatre, vol. 28/10: 62

Taylor, Paul
 2007, Sept. 4 [rev. of *The Big Secret Live* by Mark Rylance & Matthew Warchus] Independent

Taylor, Robert
 1983, June 1 Gallery of Elizabethan Portraits Boston Globe, p. 1
 1989, Sept, 20 [review of *Reinventing Shakespeare* by Gary Taylor] Boston Globe, p. 98
 1995, March 8 The Real Shakespeare: A closeted Catholic? [review of *Shakespeare:* Boston Globe, p. 34
  The Evidence by Ian Wilson]

Taylor, Thomas
 1992, March 8 [letter: response to Martin Gardner's Jan. 19 article] Washington Post, p. 14
  Reply by Martin Gardner, same issue and page.

Taylor, Welford D.
 1997, July 20 Who Was Shakespeare" [review of *Alias Shakespeare* by J. Sobran] Richmond Times, p. F4

Taymor, Julie
 2000, Fall Julie Taymor's Press Release Comments on *Titus* (excerpts) Sh. Ox. Newsl., vol. 36/3: 7

Teachout, Terry
 2010, April 17 Sightings: Denying Shakespeare Wall St. Journal, p. W14
  Response by James Blair, May 6, 2010.

Tehan, Arline B.
 1984, Dec. A Bard by Any Other Name [review of *The Mysterious William* Hartford Courant, p. G3
  Shakespeare by Charlton Ogburn, Jr.]

Tekastiaks
 2003, Fall Burghley's Bribe; de Vere's Dower? [with Mark K. Anderson] Sh. Matters, vol. 3/1: 25-27

Terzian, Philip
 1989, April 23 Who Wrote Them and Who Cares [review of *Frontline*] Province Journal, p. B18

Tharp, Louise Hall
 1959, Oct. 18 Delia and Sweet Will [review of *Prodigal Puritan: A Life of Delia* New York Times, p. BR22
  Bacon by Vivian C. Hopkins

Theil, Linda
Periodicals edited
 2009, June-Dec.: *Shakespeare Oxford Newsletter*, vol. 45/1-45/3
Shorter pieces
 2009, Fall Justice Stevens and O'Connor Sign *Declaration of Reasonable Doubt* Sh. Matters, vol. 8/4: 17-18
  [with John Shahan]
 2010, May An Interview with Stephanie Hughes, Founding Editor of Sh. Ox. Newsl., vol. 46/1: 16-18
  The Oxfordian
 2015, Spring Crowdsourcing *Hamlet* Sh. Ox. Newsl., vol. 51/2: 8-9
 2016, Spring Reasonable Doubt About Shakespeare in Michigan Sh. Ox. Newsl., vol. 52/2: 25-26
 2023, Winter Frank Lawler Translates Lefranc's Study of Shakespeare Sh. Ox. Newsl., vol. 59/1: 8-9
  [Lawler interviewed by Linda Theil]

Theobald, Bertram G.
Books
1931   *Exit Shakspere*. London: Cecil Palmer.
Shorter pieces

1935, Jan.	Who Was the First Baconian?	Baconiana, vol. 22: 1-9
1936, Jan. 6	Exact Motives of Writing [letter]	Western Daily Pr. (Bristol), p. 5
1937, Jan. 26	[letter: Lane's lecture on Edward de Vere]	Stratfordshire Evening Sentinal, p. 6
1938, Jan. 21	Bacon-Shakespeare Theory [letter]	Northern Whig., Bel. Post, p. 14
1939, Feb. 24	Unreliable Witness [letter]	John O'London's W., p. 821

Thomas, Bill
1999, May 9   The Book's the Thing for Scholar of the Bard and the Bible   Commercial Appeal, p. F1

Thomas, H.
1932, Oct.   The Shakespeare Authorship Controversy   British Musm. Qua., v. 7/2: 40-41

Thomas, Henry
1933, May 4   Shakespeare Emendations [letter]   Times Lit. Sup., is. 1631: 312

Thomas, Sidney
1998, Sum.   On the Dating of Shakespeare's Early Plays   Sh. Quarterly, v. 49/2: 187-94

Thompson, Martin
2013, July   The Rise and Fall of Brooke House, Hackney   London Historians NL
                    [repr. in DVN, vol. 20/3: 26 (Oct. 2013)]

Thompson, Sydney
1947, June 29   Asks Photographic Proof [Barrell's X-rays] [letter]   NY Herald Trib., p. II-7

Thomson, Sir St. Clair, MD
1916   Shakespeare and Medicine [repr. in BTC, vol. 1: 93-113]   Med. Society London, vol. 39

Thornley, H. E.
1920, March 11 Shakespeare Identified [letter] ["I hope Mr. Looney's book will be   Yorkshire Post & Leeds In, p. 4
                    widely read, and his claim discussed by competent critics."]

Thornton, James
1931, Feb. 14   Bacon and Shakespeare [review of *Shakespeare Authorship* by   Nation & Athenaeum, p. 635-6
                    Gilbert Standen

Thorpe, Day

1962, Aug. 26	New Shakespeare Controversy	Washington Star
1972, Dec. 3	Does the Folger Want the Truth About Shakespeare?	Washington Star
	[repr. in SON, vol. 9/1: 1-2 (Winter 1973)]	
	Response by O. B. Hardison, Jr.'s, Dec. 17, also repr. in SON.	

Thorpe, Vanessa
2004, Oct. 24   Sufi or Not Sufi? That Is the Question: Islam week at the Globe   Observer
                 Theatre Will Link Shakespeare With a Mystic Muslim Sect
                    Reprinted in DVN (Oct. 2004), p. 22]
2007, Sept. 9   Who Was He? That Is (Still) the Question   Observer, p. 24

Thurston, Herbert
1930, Nov. 1   The Mr. W. H. of Shakespeare's Sonnets   Month, p. 425-37

Tieck, Ludwig
2018   Fünfter Entwurf: Chronologisches Verzeichnis der Stücke Shakespeares   Neues Sh. Jou., vol. NS6: 22-26
              (1821) [15. 12. 1999]

Tierney, J. W.
1945, Spring   In the Country and Out of It [repr. in SFE, May 1945, p. 4]   Countryman, p. 46

Tiffany, Grace
2011, Spr./Sum. Everyone and No One   Sh. Newsl., vol. 61/1: 21-22+

Tilghman, Harrison
1948, July 14   [letter: response to unsigned July 10 article]   Washington Post, p. 10

Tillyard, E. M. W.
1942   *The Elizabethan World Picture*. New York: Vintage.

Author Index

Tilton, Patrick Michael
2020, Jan.   Athena's "Ox"   De Vere So. New., v. 27/1: 31-35

Timpane, John
2010, June 30   *Contested Will* [by James Shapiro] Proves Shakespeare Wrote It All   Philadelphia Inquirer

Titherley, A. W.
Books
1952   *Shakespeare's Identity: William Stanley, 6th Earl of Derby.* Winchester, England: Warren & Son.
Shorter works
1953, Nov.   [letter: *Two Gentlemen of Verona*]   SF News-letter (E), p. 12-13
1956, Spring   [letter: patience perforce]   SF News-letter (E), p. 12
1958, Autumn   On the Poem Signed I.M.S. (Second Folio)   SF News-letter (E), p. 7-8
1960, Spring   The Two Hours Traffic of Our Stage   Sh. Authorship Rev. #3: 3-4
1961, Spring   Speake of My Lamenesse   Sh. Authorship Rev. #5: 7-9
1961, Autumn   [letter: William Barksted (1577-1620)]   Sh. Authorship Rev. #12: 22

Todd, Alden
1985, June 9   Who Wrote *Hamlet*? [letter: resp. to Robert Giroux's Dec. 9 review]   NY Times, Sec. 7, p. 38

Todd, Eliza
2017   *Bethy* [a novel].

Toksvig, Sandi
2007, Sept. 16   Must Do Better, Mr. Shakespeare   Telegraph

Tombe, Sheila
1996, Spr./Sum.   Interview with Charlton Ogburn   Apostrophe

Tomlinson, Philip
1934, May 3   Bottom's Dream [review of *Anne Cecil* by Percy Allen (1934)]   Times Lit. Sup., p. 321

Tonkin, Boyd
2011, Oct. 28   The Confederacy of Dunces Returns   Independent, p. 22

Took, Barry
1982   *All's Well That Ends Well*   Sh. Perspective, vol. 1: 222-7

Torkut, Nataliya
2005   Antystretfordians'ki hipotezy: Pro et contra [Anti-Stratfordian Hypotheses: Pro and Con] [Ukranian]   Renesansni Studii (Ukraine), vol. 10: 8-22

Torretta, Laura
1934, June 1   L'Italofobia di John Lyly e I rapporti dell' "Euphues" col Rinascimento Italiano   Giornale Storico, p. 205-54

Tower Theater Company
2009, June   Two Rival Venues for the Theater: Press Release from the Tower Theatre Company; Letter from Richard Malim; TTC response   De Vere Soc. Newsl., vol. 16/2: 5

Towns, Vincent
1937, Dec. 30   Human Riddles That Have Vexed the World: The Mystery of Sh.   Boston Globe, p. 14

Townsend, Thomas L.
2021, Summer   Thomas Vicars Shows Us "Shakespeare" is a Pseudonym   Sh. Ox. Newsl., vol. 57/3: 23-24

Townshend, S. R.
1999, July   Shaksperes Tod: eine soziale Genealogie [passages from the English Note-Books of Nathaniel Hawthorne]   Neues Sh. Journal, vol. 4: 136-37

Tracy, Reverend John
1976   Jonson and Shakespeare: A Contrast in Dramatic Theory and Practice   Bard, vol. 1/3: 87-97

Traister, Barbara H.
2011   *Anonymity in Early Modern England: "what's in a name?"* [edited with Janet Starner]. Burlington, VT: Ashgate.

Traister, D.
2001, May   [review of *Shakespeare's Unorthodox Biography* by Diana Price]   Choice, vol. 38/9: 1630

Trevor-Roper, Hugh
1962, Nov.	What's in a Name? [repr. in BC, Vol II: 1-8, 2010]	Réalitiés
1963, April	[letter: critique of Francis Carr's interpretation of his position]	Sh. Newsl., issue 98, vol. 18/2
1963. Dec./Jan.	The Real Character of Shakespeare [reprint of *Realities* piece]	Past & Future, p. 20-21

Trewin, J. C.
1956, Jan. 25	Vex Not His Ghost	Birmingham Daily P., p. 4

Trimbath, Janet
2008, Oct.	[letter: marriage of Anne Neville]	De Vere Soc. Newsl., v. 15/3: 27

Trosman, Harry
1965	Freud and the Controversy Over Shakespearean Authorship	J. Am Psych A., v. 13: 145-98

Trout, R. Ridgill
Albums compiled
1958	*Twenty Earls and Shakespeare.* [a large album with hundreds of pages of notes and clippings on the lives of the de Veres, Earls of Oxford, collected from various sources between 1938 and 1958] [unpublished]	

Shorter pieces
1950, Sept.	A Pound of Flesh	SF News-letter (E), p. 9
1951, April	[letter: Oxford's debts]	SF News-letter (E), p. 8
1957, Spring	Bees and Honey	SF News-letter (E), p. 7
1958, Spring	Elizabeth and the Catholics	SF News-letter (E), p. 5-6
1959, Autumn	Chris-Cross	Sh. Authorship Rev. #2: 6-8
1961, Autumn	Clifford Bax Portrait of W. Shakespeare [repr. in BTC, vol. 5: 70-2]	Sh. Authorship Rev. #6: 8-10
1962, Spring	[letter: the family of Quickly]	Sh. Authorship Rev. #7: 22
1967, Spring	Edward de Vere to Robert Cecil: commentary from his unpublished album *Twenty Earls and Sh.* [repr. in BTC, vol. 5, p. 225-29]	Sh. Authorship Rev. #17: 13-16
1968, Autumn	[letter: questionnaire]	Sh. Authorship Rev. #20: 20-21

Troxell, Edward L.
1965	*Scientists Search For Shakespeare.* Winter Park, FL: Rollins Press.	

Trucco, Terry
1988, Nov. 28	Bard on Trial Again, And Again He Wins [excerpts repr. in SON, vol. 24/4: 10-11 (Summer 1988)]	New York Times, p. C21
1988, Nov. 29	Shakespeare v. 17th Earl: The Verdict	Int'l Herald Trib.
1998, Dec. 4	All's Well That Ends Well in Tempest Over Shakespeare [mock trial]	Orange Co. Reg., p. G10

Trudeau, Lawrence J.
2011	*Literature Criticism 1400 to 1800*, vol. 193 [edited]. Gale Cengage Learning. [collection of essays, mostly Oxfordian in nature]	

Truss, Lynne
1994, Oct. 17	Shakespeare, Bard by Appointment To All	Times (London)., p. 43

Trussell, H. A.
1931, July 25	The Trussell Family [letter]	Morning Post, p. 9

Trussell, Robert
2001, June 17	A Contest of Wills: Oxfordians Insist Their Man Was the Pen Behind Shakespeare's Name	Kansas City Star, p. 11, 14

Tu, Janet I-Chin
1997, Oct. 10	Alas! Poor Shakespeare: Society Debates Authorship	Seattle Times, p. F1

Tudor-Pole, Lesley (Lee)
2010	*The Life of King Henry the Eight* [in *Dating Shakespeare's Plays* (Gilvary 2010): 303-12]	
2010, Aug.	Statutes of Apparel	De Vere S. Newsl., v. 17/2: 8-12
2013, April	The Stationers' Register [talk given at the DVS' Apr. 6 meeting]	De Vere S. News., v. 20/1: 10-14

Turner, Helen
2011, Oct. 19	Prince Joins Campaign Over Shakespeare Literary 'Scam' [review of *Anonymous*] [Prince Charles supports Shakspere]	Western Mail, p. 3

Turrentine, Jeff
2003, July 20	Repossession [review of *Chasing Shakespeares* by Sarah Smith]	New York Times, p. A22

Author Index

Tuxworth, Newsl. C.
   1938, Oct. 31   Shakespeare-Bacon [letter]   Yorkshire Post & Leeds Int., p. 3

Twain, Mark
   1909   *Is Shakespeare Dead?* New York: Harper & Bros.
         [excerpt repr. in SSR, issue 1/1: 31-35; repr. in BTC, vol. 7: 242-52]
         [Another excerpt repr. in TOX, vol. 16: 19-28, 2014]
         ["Facts" repr. in German (Übersetzt von Walter Klier) in NSJ, vol. 7: 4-7 (May 2002)]

Tweedale, Ralph L.
   1971   *Wasn't Shakespeare Someone Else? New Evidence In the Very Words of the Bard Himself About His True Identity.* Southfield, MI: Verity Press. Repr. in 1971. [propounds the PT/Dynastic Succession idea]

Twitchett, E. G.
   1928, May   [review of *The Shakespeare Mystery* by Georges Connes]   London Mercury, v. 1/6: 766

Twyne, Thomas
   2019, April   Another of Hamlet's Books?: Petrach's *De Remediis Utriusque Fortunae*   De Vere Soc. New., v. 26/2: 4-15

Tynan, Kenneth
   1954   *Persona Grata* [with Cecil Beaton]. New York: G. P. Putnam's Sons. [quotes Orson Welles on Oxford]
         [excerpt repr. in SON, vol. 24/4: 11 (Summer 1988)]

Uncle Dudley
   1938, July 10   A Mystery-Tale of Shakespeare   Boston Globe, p. C4

Underwood, Anne
   2004, June 28   Was the Bard a Woman? [review of *Sweet Swan of Avon* by Robin Williams]   Newsweek, p. 58

Underwood, George
   1923, May 20   Readers and Writers: Dethroning Shakespeare—Anti-Stratfordian Scepticism   Freethinker, vol. 43/20: 316-7

Ungerer, Gustav
   1997, April   The Earl of Southampton's Donation to the Bodleian Library in 1605   Bodleian Lib. R., p. 1, 17-41

Upton, Chris
   2006, April 22   Desperately Seeking Will; The Man—and Men—Who Could Well Be Shakespeare   Birmingham Daily P., p. 47

Usher, Peter
Books
   2006   *Hamlet's Universe.* Aventine Press.
   2021   *Shakespeare's Knowledge of Astronomy and the Birth of Modern Cosmology.* Peter Lang.
Shorter pieces
   1999, Spring   Hamlet's Transformation   Eliz. Review, vol. 7/1: 48-64
   2001   Advances in the Hamlet Cosmic Allegory   Oxfordian, vol. 4: 25-50
   2002   Shakespeare's Support for the New Astronomy   Oxfordian, vol. 5: 132-146
   2005   Hamlet's Love Letter and the New Philosophy   Oxfordian, vol. 8: 93-109

Usherwood, E. C.
   1937, July   The Droeshout Portrait [letter]   East Ang., M., vol. 2/10: 469

V.
   1932, Nov. 17   Shakespearean Controversy [review of *The Tragic Story of Shakespeare* by Gerald Phillips]   Belfast News-Letter, p. 15

V. R.
   1928, March   [review of *The Shakespeare Mystery* by Georges Connes]   English Review, p. 363-54
   1928, June   Biography [review of *The Seventeenth Earl* by Capt. B. M. Ward]   English Review, p. 735-36

Vaïs, Michel
   2018, Dec.   Pourquois John Florio alias Shakespeare   Critical Stages, vol. 18

Valenza, Robert J. [all with Ward E. Elliott]

1991, April 26	Pretenders Sound Wrong Chords: We're Pretty Certain Who the Bard Wasn't, Though Not Who He Was	Los Angeles Times, p. VYB11
1991, Aug.	A Touchstone for the Bard	Computers & Humanities, vol. 25/4: 199-09
1991, Dec.	Was the Earl of Oxford the True Shakespeare? A Computer-Aided Analysis	Notes & Q., vol. 38/4: 501
1996	And Then There Were None: Winnowing the Shakespeare Claimants	Computers & Humanities, vol. 30/3: 191-245
2000	Can the Oxford Candidacy Be Saved? A Response to W. Ron Hess	Oxfordian, vol. 3: 71-98
2003	[letter: response to criticism by John Shahan and W. Ron Hess]	Oxfordian, vol. 6: 154-163
2004, Fall	Oxford By the Numbers: What are the Odds that the Earl of Oxford Could Have Written Shakespeare's Poems and Plays?	Tennessee Law Review, vol. 72/1: 323-453
2007	My Other Car is a Shakespeare: A Response to Shahan and Whalen	Oxfordian, vol. 10: 142-153
2010	The Shakespeare Clinic and the Oxfordians	Oxfordian, vol. 12: 138-166

Valeo, Tom

1992, Jan. 23	The Case Against Shakespeare [repr. in SON, vol. 28/1: 1-3 (Winter 1992); and in BTC, vol. 7: 83-88]	Daily Herald (Illinois)
1992, April 9	A Shadow Over Shakespeare [review of *The Mysterious William Shakespeare* by Charlton Ogburn]	St. Petersburg Times, p. 7D

Van Cleve, Charles F.

1941, Dec.	[letter: Campbell's Harper's article]	SF News-letter (A), vol. 3/1: 8

Van Doren, Charles

1980	*Shakespeare: Reading and Talking*. Minos Publishing.
	[presents David Hasen's theory that de Vere did not die in 1604 but instead came to the New World and buried his manuscripts in a trunk in a pit on Oak Island off Newfoundland]

Van Druenen, Elizabeth Appleton – see Elizabeth Appleton

Van Gelder, Lawrence

2007, Sept. 10	Alas, Poor Shakespeare	New York Times, p. 2

Van Lunteren, S. A.

1952, Sept.	Earl's Colne and Colme-Kill [letter]	SF News-letter (E), p. 11-12
1953, Nov.	[review of *Acter het Mombakkes (Behind the Mask)* P. H. Van Moerkkerten (1950)]	SF News-letter (E), p. 8
1953, Nov.	Lord Macaulay and Looney's Methods	SF News-letter (E), p. 11
1954, Sept.	Shakespeare in Paris and *Measure for Measure*	SF News-letter (E), p. 6
1955, Spring	Translation of Horace by Edward de Vere	SF News-letter (E), p. 8
1955, Autumn	[letter: Edward de Vere as translator of Horace]	SF News-letter (E), p. 11

Van Moorkorkan, P. H.

1950	*Achtar hot Monbakhus* [*Behind the Mask*]. Ansterden: G. A. Van Oorschoot, Uitgovor.

Van Valkenburgh, Philip

1941, Oct.	[letter: Lord Oxford's genius]	SF News-letter (A), vol. 2/6: 72

Varney, John

1956, May	To the Editor and Readers of *The Shakespeare Newsletter* [letter, with 21 other signers]	Sh. Newsl., vol. 6/3: 18

Vartanoff, Irene

1999, April 3	[letter: David Ignatius' March 21 article]	Washington Post, p. A13

Vaughan, Alden T.

2008, Fall	William Strachey's "True Repertory" and Shakespeare: A Closer Look at the Evidence [resp. to R. Stritmatter and L. Kositsky's *On the Date, Sources and Design of Shakespeare's "Tempest"*]	Sh. Quarterly, vol. 59/3: 245-73

Vaughan, Virginia M.

1984-85	[review of *The Mysterious William Shakespeare* by Ch. Ogburn, Jr.]	Choice, vol. 22: 992

Vaughan-Davies, Richard

2021	*In the Shadow of Shakespeare*. Mitford Oak Press. [a novel]

Vedi, Sten F.

2012   *Elsinore Revisited – "This Ientleman of Polonia": Polonius, A Character in Disguise* (2012)

2018   *Hamlet's Elsinore Revisited: The Author's Sources of Knowledge about Elsinore and Denmark* [2nd edition, enlarged] [with Gerold Wagner] [*Neues Shakespeare Journal* special issue Book 7.] Buchholz, Germany: Laugwitz Verlag.

Vere, Charles, Earl of Burford – See Charles Beauclerk

Vessey, David W. T. C.

1961, Spring	Freud and the Authorship Question [repr. in BTC, vol. 5: 51-55]	Sh. Authorship Rev. #5: 3-6
1962, Spring	Aspects of Shakespeare's Classics	Sh. Authorship Rev. #7: 8-10
1962, Spring	Queen Elizabeth as "Shakespeare"	Sh. Authorship Rev. #7: 22
1963, Spring	Some Stratfordian Fantasies	Sh. Authorship Rev. #9: 3-5
1964, Spring	Some Early References to Shakespeare [repr. in BTC, vol. 5: 134-40]	Sh. Authorship Rev. #11: 4-9
1965, Spring	After the Pageant: A Meditation for 1965 [repr. in BTC, vol. 5: 150-52]	Sh. Authorship Rev. #13: 1-3
1965, Spring	[letter: BBC broadcast]	Sh. Authorship Rev. #13: 21-22
1966, Spring	Southampton, Essex and Shake-speare: some notes	Sh. Authorship Rev. #15: 7-13
1966, Autumn	[letter: Stratfordians condescending attitude]	Sh. Authorship Rev. #16: 27-28
1967, Spring	Notes on the Dating of Macbeth	Sh. Authorship Rev. #17: 1-5
1967, Spring	"Shakespeare's Classical Learning" [summary of his Jan. 5, 1967 talk] [repr. in BTC, vol. 5: 232-33]	Sh. Authorship Rev. #17: 18-19
1968, Autumn	An Early Allusion to Shakespeare	Sh. Authorship Rev. #19: 4-11
1968, Autumn	"Some Problems in Shakespearean Chronology" [summary of his March 22, 1968 lecture]	Sh. Authorship Rev. #19: 14-15
1968, Autumn	[report on T. D. Bokenham's Feb. 21 lecture "Ben Jonson and Sh.]	Sh. Authorship Rev. #19: 20-21
1969, Spring	[review of *Was Shakespeare Shakespeare?* by Milward W. Martin]	Sh. Authorship Rev. #21: 7-10
1969, Spring	A Discussion on "The Northumberland Manuscript [Jan. 28, 1969]	Sh. Authorship Rev. #21: 12-15
1969, Christmas	[letter: E. R. Curtius and Shakespeare]	Sh. Authorship Rev. #22: 18
1970, Summer	Nashe's Dedication of *Strange News* (McKerrow's Edition)	Sh. Authorship Rev. #23: 9-11
1970, Summer	[rev. of *Shakespeare and the Earl of Southampton* by G.P.V. Akrigg] [repr. in BTC, vol. 5: 300-303]	Sh. Authorship Rev. #23: 12-15
1970, Summer	[report on Sir John Russell's Nov. 18, 1969 lecture "For and Against William of Stratford"] [repr. in BTC, vol. 5, p. 304-06]	Sh. Authorship Rev. #23: 15-17
1977	Thomas Watson's Meliboeus	Bard, vol. 4/1: 162-168
1980	The Singing Swallow: A Note	Bard, vol. 2/4: 130-132
1981	Venery and Sophistication: Shakespeare's *Venus and Adonis* and Marlowe's *Hero and Leander*	Bard, vol. 3/2: 74-91
1988, Aug.	Variant Shakespeares and Shakespearean Variants	De Vere Soc. Newsl., no. 3: 8-34

Unpublished MSS

1961	The Shakespeare Enigma: "Comprimising the Maiden Phoenix," "Queen Elizabeth and *Macbeth*," and "Queen Shakespeare"	

Vezzoli, Gary

1993, Autumn	A Statistical Approach to the Shakespeare Authorship Question [with Richard Desper] [repr. in BTC, vol. 8: 145-52]	Eliz. Review, vol. 1/2: 36-42

Vickers, Brian

Books

2004	*Shakespeare, Co-Author: A Historical Study of Five Collaborative Plays*. Oxford: Oxford University Press.	

Shorter pieces

2001	Shakespeare and Authorship Studies in the Twenty-First Century Response by John Burrows in vol. 63/3: 355-92.	Sh. Quarterly, vol. 62: 106-42
2005, Aug. 9	Idle Worship [reviews of *Great Oxford edited* by Richard Malim, *The Shakespeare Enigma* by Peter Dawkins; *Hamlet by Ch. Marlowe and William Shakespeare* edited by Alex Jack; and *The Case for Shakespeare* by Scott McCrea [repr. in DVN (Sept. 2003), p. 40-43]	Times Lit. Sup., is. 5342: 6-8
2006, Aug. 18	The Face of the Bard?	Times Lit. Sup., is. 5394: 16
2013, Dec. 13	[letter: response to the Shakespeare Authorship Coalition's Dec. 6 challenge [repr.in DVN, vol. 21/2: 41-42 (May 2014)]	Times Lit. Sup., is. 5776: 6

Vinciguerra, Mario

1920, Sept. 15	Shakespeariana	Rivista di Cultvra, p. 247-60

Violen, W. R.

2011, Nov. 11	Will o' the Wisp [letter: doubts about Will]	Daily Mail, p. 68
2016, May 3	Shakespeare Fact or Fiction [letter]	Daily Mail, p. 50

von Koppenfels, Werner

2013, March	So sollst du dir ein Bild machen	Neues Sh. Journal, v. NS3: 30-37

Von Ost, Count Anthony

1988, April	The De Vere Society Charity Ball	De Vere Soc. Newsl., no. 2: 40
1988, Aug.	The De Vere Society Charity Ball	De Vere S. New., no. 3: 108-110

W. G. S.

1937, Sept. 19	Shakespeare and the "Canopy" [letter]	Observer, p. 9

W. R. R. [see Robinson, W. Ringland]

W. W.

1937, July	Five Signatures of Six [letter]	East Angl. Mag., vol. 2/10: 468

W. W. H.

1921, April 15	Who Wrote the Plays Which We Call Shakespeare's?	Northampton Mercury, p. 8

Wadsworth, Frank

Books

1958	*The Poacher from Stratford*. Berkeley: University of California Press.	

Shorter pieces

1964, Apr./May	The Authorship Question	Sh. Newsl., vol. 14/2-3: 46
1993, Spring	The Poacher Revisited	Sh. Newsl., vol. 43/1: 3

Wagner, Gerold

Books

2018	*Hamlet's Elsinore Revisited: The Author's Sources of Knowledge about Elsinore and Denmark* [2nd edition, enlarged and with new subtitle, of Sten F. Vedi's book] [*Neues Shakespeare Journal* special issue Book 7.] Buchholz, Germany: Laugwitz Verlag.	

Shorter pieces

2001, May	Hinweis auf Ludwig Berger	Neues Sh. Jou., vol. 6: 147-58
2007, April	Die blinden Seher	Neues Sh. Jou., vol. 11: 113-27
2013, March	Gedanken eines klassischen Philologen zu Shakespeare (I) Argall, she drowned herself wittingly	Neues Sh. Jou., vol. NS3: 113-23
2016, June	Rocco Bonetti, the Butcher of a Silk Button. Rapier, Fechten, Duell und Ehrenkodex bei Shakespeare	Neues Sh. Jou., vol. NS5: 16-32
2016, June	Shakespeares medizinische Kenntnisse	Neues Sh. Jou., vol. NS5: 33-38
2016, June	Wie kommt Dr. Caius in die Merry Wives of Windsor?	Neues Sh. Jou., vol. NS5: 39-45
2016, June	Latein bei Marlowe und Shakespeare (mit Originaltexten und Übersetzungen von Frank-Patrick Steckel, Ludwig Tieck und Dietrich Schamp, kommentiert von Gerold Wagner)	Neues Sh. Jou., vol. NS5: 46-96
2016, June	Curriculum Vitae mit Teletexts	Neues Sh. Jou., vol. NS5: 113-37
2018	Fremde Hände im *Tempest*?	Neues Sh. Jou., vol. NS6: 67-95
2018	*Cymbeline* – ein sehr frühes Spätwerk?	Neues Sh. Jou., vol. NS6:104-64
2020	The actors are come hither, My Lord: Der Schauspilcluster in Shakespeare's *Hamlet*	Neues Sh. Jou., vol. NS7: 48-114
2020	Why tribute? Why should we pay tribute? Cloten und die Verweigerung von Tributzahlungen	Neues Sh. Jou., vol. NS7: 115-20
2020	Zwei Marginalien zu *Richard II*	Neues Sh. Jou., vol. NS7:121-25
2023	Gerold Wagner: Othello – 1588: Der Jahr des Edward de Vere	Neues Sh. Jou., vol. NS8: 15-62
2023	Blendung und Verblendung	Neues Sh. Jou., vol. NS8:63-103

Wainwright, Michael

2018	*The Rational Shakespeare: Peter Ramus, Edward de Vere, and the Question of Authorship*. Palgrave Macmillan.	
2011, Fall	Veering Toward an Evolutionary Realignment of Freud's *Hamlet*	Brief Chronicles, vol. III: 9-35
2014, Summer	The Logical Basis of Oxford's *Troilus and Cressida*	Brief Chronicles, vol. V: 139-69

Wainewright, Ruth M. D.

Pamphlets

1966	*On the Poems of Edward de Vere.* [pamphlet pub. by the SAS]	

Periodicals edited (co-editor)

1959, Spring-1974, Summer: *Shakespearean Authorship Review*, issue 1-29

Shorter pieces

1954, April	Some Comments on an Early Dedication to De Vere	SF News-letter (E), p. 10-11
1954, Sept.	Shake Spears Sonnets	SF News-letter (E), p. 3
	Response by G. W. Phillips, SFE, Spring 1955, p. 13.	
1955, Autumn	Work of the Study Group	SF News-letter (E), p. 3
1955, Autumn	The Study Group	SF News-letter (E), p. 4
1955, Autumn	The Spanish Romances and "The Tempest"	SF News-letter (E), p. 9
1956, Spring	Shakespeare: Lord Oxford or Lord Derby?	SF News-letter (E), p. 10-11
1957, Autumn	Have a Go: Group Discussion on Authorship issues [April 6, 1957]	SF News-letter (E), p. 3
1957, Autumn	[review of *The Songs and Sonnets of the Earl of Surrey*, edited by Douglas Geary]	SF News-letter (E), p. 10
1957, Spring	[report on Gwynneth Bowen's Dec. 8, 1956 talk "The Upstart Crow"]	SF News-letter (E), p. 2-3
1957, Spring	Psychological Relationships in Hamlet and the Authorship Question	SF News-letter (E), p. 6-7
1958, Spring	[report on David Freedman's Feb. 15, 1958 lecture "Astrology in Shakespeare's Plays"]	SF News-letter (E), p. 4
1959, Autumn	[replies to Criticism of "Who Was Shakespeare?"]	Sh. Authorship Rev. #2: 20-23
1959, Spring	The Elizabethan Noblemen and the Literary Profession [repr. in BTC, vol. 5: 16-18]	Sh. Authorship Rev. #1: 6-7
1959, Spring	Lecture at Newlands Training College for Teachers	Sh. Authorship Rev. #1: 13
1960, Spring	[replies to Mr. Mendl's Criticisms of "Who Was Shakespeare?"] [repr. in BTC, vol. 5: 42-47]	Sh. Authorship Rev. #3: 11-15
1960, Autumn	[review of *Shakespeare and the Elizabethans* by Henri Fluchere]	Sh. Authorship Rev. #4: 10-13
1961, Autumn	[review of *Shakespeare's Public* by Martin Holmes (1960)] [repr. in BTC, vol. 5:73-4]	Sh. Authorship Rev. #6: 10-13
1961, Autumn	[report on L. S. Penrose's March 11, 1961 talk "Shakespeare Portraits"] [repr. in BTC, vol. 5: 75-76]	Sh. Authorship Rev. #6: 13-14
1961, Autumn	[review of *William Shakespeare's Conspiracy,* a play by N. Baker]	Sh. Authorship Rev. #6: 20
1961, Autumn	Miss Katharine Eggar (1873-1961) [obituary]	Sh. Authorship Rev. #6: 23
1962, Autumn	Forty Winters [repr. in BTC, vol. 5: 98-99]	Sh. Authorship Rev. #8: 13-14
1963, Spring	[review of *Shake-speare: The Real Man Behind the Name* by Dorothy Ogburn and Charlton Ogburn, Jr. (1962)] [repr. in BTC, vol. 5: 103-06]	Sh. Authorship Rev. #9: 8-10
1963, Autumn	[re 3 articles on *The De Veres of Castle Hedingham* by George Caunt in the *Essex Countryside Magazine* (June-July, 1963)]	Sh. Authorship Rev. #10: 16
1964, Spring	[report on Gwynneth Bowen's Nov. 21, 1963 lecture: "New Evidence for Dating the Plays"] [repr. in BTC, vol. 5: 141-43]	Sh. Authorship Rev. #11: 14-16
1964, Autumn	[review of *Paging Mr. Shakespeare* by Walter Blumenthal (1961)]	Sh. Authorship Rev. #12: 13-14
1964, Autumn	[report on Dr. Eliot Slater's Feb. 13, 1964 lecture "Shakespeare's Colour Imagery"]	Sh. Authorship Rev. #12: 14
1964, Autumn	[review of *Shakespeare: A Portrait Restored* by Clara L. de Chambrun]	SF News-letter (E), p. 9-11
1965, Autumn	The S.A.S. Library	Sh. Authorship Rev. #14: 9
1965, Autumn	[review of Oxford: *Courtier to the Queen* by Eleanor Brewster] [repr. in BTC, vol. 5: 173]	Sh. Authorship Rev. #14: 11-12
1965, Autumn	[report on Gwynneth Bowen's Feb. 17, 1965 lecture "The Merchant and the Jew"] [repr. in BTC, vol. 5: 174-5]	Sh. Authorship Rev. #14: 12-13
1965, Spring	Annual General Meeting	Sh. Authorship Rev. #13: 17
1965, Spring	[report on Geoffrey Ashe's Dec. 11, 1964 lecture "Mr. W. H.: Another Suggestion"]	Sh. Authorship Rev. #13: 18-19
1966, Spring	[review of *Shakespeare's Southampton—Patron of Virginia* by A. L. Rowse (1965)]	Sh. Authorship Rev. #15: 14-15
1966, Autumn	On the Poems of Edward de Vere [repr. in BTC, vol. 5: 193-212]	Sh. Authorship Rev. #16: 1-18
1966, Autumn	Professor A. W. Titherley (d. 1966) [obituary]	Sh. Authorship Rev. #16: 26
1967, Spring	"Shakespeare and Marlowe" [summary of her Mar. 9, 1967 lecture]	Sh. Authorship Rev. #17: 21-22
1967, Autumn	[review of *Sir Thomas Smith: Tudor Intellectual in Office* by Mary Dewar (1964)] [repr. in BTC, vol. 5: 250-252]	Sh. Authorship Rev. #18: 12-13

Wainewright, Ruth M. D. (continued)

1968, Autumn	[review of *Great Shakespeare Forgery* by Bernard Grebanier (1965)] [repr. in BTC, vol. 5: 274-277]	Sh. Authorship Rev. #20: 12-13
1968, Autumn	[review of *The Herberts of Wilton* by Tresham Lever (1967)] [repr. in BTC, vol. 5: 259-60]	Sh. Authorship Rev. #19: 13-14
1969, Spring	[report on Glenn Black's Nov. 26, 1968 lecture "Poems by Lord Oxford and Others in Elizabethan Manuscripts"]	Sh. Authorship Rev. #21: 11
1969, Spring	[report on Father Francis Edwards' Feb. 19, 1969 lecture "A Sidelight on Robert Cecil's Spy System"]	Sh. Authorship Rev. #21: 15-16
1969, Christmas	[review of *The Man Behind Macbeth and Other Studies* by Sir James Fergusson (1969)]	Sh. Authorship Rev. #22: 13-15
1970, Summer	[report on Arthur Brown's Feb. 25, 1970 lecture "Printing of Plays in Elizabethan England"]	Sh. Authorship Rev. #23: 18-19
1970, Summer	[report on V. Kanter's Mar. 25, 1970 lecture "Shakespeare's Imagery and Identity"]	Sh. Authorship Rev. #23: 19-21
1971, Spring	[review of *Thomas Kyd: Facts and Problems* by Arthur Freedman]	Sh. Authorship Rev. #24: 12-13
1971, Spring	[review of *Who Was Shakespeare?* by Hilda Amphlett, with an Introduction by Christmas Humphreys (1955)]	Sh. Authorship Rev. #24: 13-14
1971, Spring	[report on Alexis Dawson's Jan. 14 lecture "They Tried to Tell Us"] [repr. in BTC, vol. 5: 310-11]	Sh. Authorship Rev. #24: 21-22
1979	[review of *"Shakespeare" Identified* by J. Thomas Looney, 3rd Ed., edited by Ruth Loyd Miller]	Bard, vol. 2/2: 75-79

Walcott, John

1909, August	Delia Bacon and After	Putnam's Mag., p. 619-24

Waldron, John

1937, Dec. 10	"Flying Trapeze: Shakespeare" vs. "Shakespeare" [review of *WThe Man Who Was Shakespeare* by Eva Turner Clark	Washington Post, p. 13

Walker, James

1965, Spring	The Pregnant Silence [repr. in BTC, vol. 5: 153-55]	Sh. Authorship Rev. #13: 7-9
1964, Spring	[letter: the very curious punctuation of the dedication to the sonnets]	Sh. Authorship Rev. #11: 21

Walker, Joan

2006	*The Letters of Edward de Vere* [a CD read by Sir Derek Jacobi, narrated by Joan Walker and edited by Stephanie Hopkins Hughes]	

Walker, John

1814	A Selection of Curious Articles (unlikeness of Shakespeare's busts) [excerpt repr. in SON, vol. 31/2a: 10-11 (Spring 1995)]	Gentleman's Magazine

Walker, Martha N.

1997, Spring	[letter: Diana Price's Autumn 1996 "Rough Winds Do Shake"]	Eliz. Review, vol. 5/1: 6

Walker, Michael

2002, Jan./Feb.	[review of *Recent Oxfordian Thinking in Germany: Literaturen*]	De Vere Soc. Newsl., p. 15-17

Walker, Roosevelt

1952, Nov. 24	Another Claimant to Throne of Shakespeare in Offing [advance short review of *This Star of England* by Charlton and Dorothy Ogburn]	Atlanta Journal-Constit.., p. 4

Walker, William

1955, Aug. 4	Alias Shakespeare [letter]	Yorkshire Post & Leeds Int., p. 4

Wall, Alan

2002	*School of Night: A Novel*. New York: Thomas Dunne Books/St. Martin's Press.	

Wallace, David Rains

Books

2017	*Shakespeare's Wilderness*. Self-published.	

Shorter pieces

2019, Summer	[review of *Shakespeare and Ecocritical Theory* by Gabrield Egan and *Shakespeare and Ecofeminist Theory* by Rebecca Loroche and Jennifer Munroe (2017)]	Sh. Ox. Newsl., vol. 55/3: 28-31

Wallace, Martin

2001, May 16	[letter: Alan Majauskas' May 14 letter]	Globe & Mail, p. A14

Author Index

Wallace, Richard J.
2022   *Aspects of the Shakespeare Authorship Question*. Charleston: Palmetto.

Wallach, Janet
1984, April 29   The Art, Music and Money of David Lloyd Kreeger   Washington Post, p. SM22

Waller, Gary
2007, Spring   Pseudonymous Shakespeare: Rioting Language in the Sidney Circle   Comparative Drama, vol.
     [review of the book by Penny McCarthy]   41/1: 119

Wallis, J. B.
1925, Oct. 1   Shakespeare's Land [letter]   Sheffield Daily Tel., p. 4

Walmsley, D. M.
1957, April 1   Shakespeare's Links with Virginia   History Today, vol. 7/4: 229

Walpole, Horace
1958   *A Catalogue of the Royal and Noble Authors of England, With Lists of Their Works*. London: Strawberry-
     hill. [see esp. "Life of Lord Oxford"]

Walsh, Felicity D.
2005, July   [review of *"Shakespeare" By Another Name* by Mark Anderson]   Library Jour., vol. 130/12: 79

Walsh, John
2006, April 22   The Legends of Shakespeare   Independent, p. 12

Walshe, W.
1965, March 27   Seaman Shakespeare? [letter: Edward de Vere and the Armada]   Times (London), p. 9

Walters, J. Cuming
1916, April   Dickens and the Shakespeare Mystery   Dickensian, p. 89-91
1924, Oct. 11   Shakespeare's Signatures and *Sir Thomas More*   Manchester City News

Walters, J. Cuming
1903, Sept. 8   The Shakespeare Relics at Stratford [letter: quotes Joseph Skipsey]   Times (London), p. 5

Walton, Sara
1937, April   What Rosalind Said [letter]   Sh. Pictorial, no. 110: 61

Wanamaker, Melissa C.
Book excerpts
1994, Spring   [excerpt from *The Dread Voice is Past*]   Sh. Ox. Newsl., vol. 30/2a: 4

Wanamaker, Sam
1988, April   International Shakespeare Globe Centre International Moot Court   De Vere Soc. New., no. 2: 36-37

Wang, Christopher
2007, April   Musicological Research: *Ever Trvely a Mvusician—Connections*   Triangle (Mu Phi Epsilon),
     Between Ed. de Vere and the Development of English Madrigals   vol. 101/1: 6

Ward, Captain Bernard Mordaunt
Books and pamphlets
1925   *The Authorship of The Arte of English Poesie, A Suggestion*. [pamphlet: repr. from *The Review of English
     Studies*, vol. 1, no. 3 (July 1925)]
1926   *George Gascoigne and His Circle*. [pamphlet: repr. from *The Review of English Studies*, vol. II, no. 5
     (Jan. 1926)]
1928   *The Seventeenth Earl of Oxford, 1550-1604, From Contemporary Documents*. London: J. Murray.0
     [excerpt, pages 84-129, repr. in BTC, vol. 4: 160-186]
     2nd edition. London: J. Murray.
     3rd edition, edited by James A. Warren, Veritas Publications, 2023.
1928   *The Famous Victories of Henry V*. [pamphlet: repr. from *The Review of English Studies*, vol. IV, no. 15
     (July 1928)]
1936   *An Enquiry into the Relations Between Lord Oxford as "Shakespeare," Queen Elizabeth and the Fair Youth*
     [pamphlet, with Percy Allen]. London: Percy Allen. [repr. in BTC, vol. 3: 407-27; and in *The Complete
     Shakespeare Writing of Percy Allen*, vol. 6, edited by James A. Warren, 2022]
Books edited
1926   *A Hundreth Sundrie Flowres; From the Original Edition of 1573, by George Gascoigne*. With an
     introduction by the editor. London: L F. Etchells and H. Macdonald.
     2nd edition. Ruth Loyd Miller, editor, with additional notes by the editor and others. Port Washington,
     NY: Published by Kennikat Press for Minos Pub. Co.

Ward, Captain Bernard Mordaunt (continued)

Periodicals edited

1933-1935: *Shakespeare Fellowship Circulars and Notices* [not listed below; see p. 508-510]

1933-1936: Shakespeare Fellowship Page in the *Shakespeare Pictorial*

1937, Jan.-1939, July: *Shakespeare Fellowship News-letter* (English), vol. 1-15

Shorter pieces

1923, Oct. 5	*Love's Labour's Lost* and *Cymbeline*	Hackney Spectator, p. 2
1924, Feb. 8	Elizabethan Dancing	Hackney Spectator, p. 2
1925, July	The Authorship of *The Arte of English Poesie: A Suggestion*	Rev. of Eng. St., v. 1/3: 284-308
1926, Jan.	George Gascoigne and His Circle Response by Genevieve Ambrose, April, 1926.	Rev. of Eng. St., vol. 2/5: 32-41
1926, April	The Death of George Gascoigne	Rev. of Eng. St., vol. 2/6: 169-72
1927, June	[letter to *Library*: resp. to W. W. Greg's review of *A Hundreth Sundrie Flowres*]	Library
1927, Oct.	The Will of John Bacon	Rev. of Eng. St., vol. 3/4: 446-49
1928	*Seventeenth Earl of Oxford* [excerpt from the book], in *Building the Case*, vol. 1: 280-293	
1928, Jan.	Further Research on *A Hundreth Sundrie Flowres*	Rev. of Eng. Studies
1928, June 2	[letter: resp. to the May 19 review of *The Seventeenth Earl of Oxford* in *Transactions of the Biblographical Society*]	Saturday Review, vol. 145: 697
1928, June 28	Edward de Vere [letter to *Times Literary Supplement*: response to its review of *The Seventeenth Earl of Oxford*]	Times Lit. Sup., is. 1289: 486
1928, July	[letter: resp. to the June 11 review, with reviewer's reply]	London Mercury
1928, July	*The Famous Victories of Henry V*: Its Place in Elizabethan Dramatic Literature	Rev. of Eng. St., v. 4/15: 270-94
1928, Aug. 2	[letter: resp. to the reviewer's reply; see also W. W. Greg's resp. to Ward's letter in the Jan. 1929 *Modern Language Review*]	Times Lit. Sup., is. 1383: 568
1928, Sept. 6	Fulke Greville [letter: resp. to Greg, Aug. 30 letter]	Times Lit. Sup., is. 1388: 632
1928, Sept. 20	Fulke Greville [letter: response to Greg, Sept. 13]	Times Lit. Sup., is. 1390: 667
1928, Oct. 4	Fulke Greville [letter: response to Greg, Sept. 27]	Times Lit. Sup., is. 1392: 710
1929, Jan.	Queen Elizabeth and William Davison	Eng. Historical Rev., vol. 44: 104-06
1929, Jan.	John Lyly and the Office of the Revels [repr. in OXV, p. 450-52]	Rev. of Eng. St., vol. 5/17: 57-59
1929, April	Shakespeare and the Anglo-Spanish War, 1585-1604, Part 1 [repr. in OXV, p. 454-69]	Revue Anglo-Am., vol. 6/4: 297-311
1930, April	Shakespeare and the Anglo-Spanish War, 1585-1604, Part 2 [repr. in OXV, p. 454-69]	Revue Anglo-Am., vol. 7/4: 298-311
1931, Oct. 31	Shakespeare [letter: response to H.R.W.'s Oct. 31 review of *Seven Shakespeares* by Gilbert Slater]	Saturday Review, vol. 152: 624
1931, Dec. 31	Shakespeare, Essex and *Richard II* [letter]	Times Lit. Sup., 1561: 1053
1932	"Introduction" to Percy Allen's *Life Story of Edward de Vere as "William Shakespeare,"* p. xi-xv.	
1932, Feb.	*The Merry Wives of Windsor* and The Order of the Garter	Sh. Pictorial, no. 48: 32.
1932, Feb.	The Swan Theatre [letter]	Sh. Pictorial, no. 48: 30
1932, March	L. J. Maxse [obituary]	Sh. Pictorial, no. 49: 48.
1932, April	Alphonso Ferrabosco	Rev. of Eng. St., v. 8/2/30: 201-2
1932, April	The Will of . . .	Rev. of Eng. St., vol. 8/30:
1932, April	The Three Williams of Shakespeare	Sh. Pictorial, no. 50: 68
1932, Sept.	[review of *The Date of Love's Labour's Lost* by Rupert Taylor]	Sh. Pictorial, no. 55: 148
1932, Nov.	Annual General Meeting	Sh. Pictorial, no. 57: 180
1933, Jan.	The Chamberlain's Men in 1597	Rev. of Eng. St., v. 9/1/33: 55-58
1933, June	Annual Dinner	Sh. Pictorial, no. 64: 92-93
1933, July	The Shakespeare Family in Contemporary Satire	Sh. Pictorial, no. 65: 112
1933, Aug.	[letter: reps. to Georges Connes' article, same issue, p. 193-207]	Revue Anglo-Am., no. 11/6: 531-34
1933, Oct.	The Virginia Company and *The Tempest*	Sh. Pictorial, no. 68: 160
1933, Dec.	[review of *Shakespeare, Oxford, and Elizabethan Times* by Admiral H. H. Holland (1933)]	Sh. Pictorial, no. 70: 192
1933, Dec. 7	These Late Eclipses [letter]	Times Lit. Sup., is. 1662: 878
1933, Dec. 21	These Late Eclipses [letter]	Times Lit. Sup., is. 1664: 909

Ward, Colonel Bernard Rowland

Books and pamphlets

Columns, Pages and Circulars edited

Shorter pieces

Ward, Colonel Bernard Rowland (continued)

1923, Jan. 19	[The Shakespeare Fellowship column no. 13]	Hackney Spectator, no. 1998: 3
1923, Jan. 26	[The Shakespeare Fellowship column no. 14]	Hackney Spectator, no. 2000: 8
1923, Feb. 2	[The Shakespeare Fellowship column no. 15]	Hackney Spectator, no. 2002: 6
1923, Feb. 9	[The Shakespeare Fellowship column no. 16]	Hackney Spectator, no. 2004: 7
1923, Feb. 23	[The Shakespeare Fellowship column no. 18]	Hackney Spectator, no. 2008: 7
1923, March 2	*Hamlet* and the Veres	Hackney Spectator, no. 2010: 6
1923, March 9	The Veres in *Hamlet*, I	Hackney Spectator, no. 2012: 7
1923, March 16	The Veres in *Hamlet*, II	Hackney Spectator, no. 2014: 8
1923, April 6	Shakespeare and Chapman—A Suggestion	Hackney Spectator, no. 2018: 5
1923, May 24	[letter: The Mystery of Mr. W. H.]	Times Lit. Sup., is. 1114: 355
1923, June 29	A Dinner at the Lyceum Club	Hackney Spectator, no. 2041: 4-5
1923, July 6	Oxford and Bacon, I	Hackney Spectator, no. 2043: 8
1923, July 13	Oxford and Bacon, II	Hackney Spectator, no. 2045: 3
1923, July 20	Professor Lefranc at Oxford	Hackney Spectator, no. 2047: 4
1923, July 27	Oxford and Bacon, III	Hackney Spectator, no. 2049: 4
1923, Sept. 21	*Shakespeare Through Oxford Glasses*, I [review of the book by Capt. H. H. Holland]	Hackney Spectator, no. 2064: 2
1923, Sept. 28	*Shakespeare Through Oxford Glasses*, II [review of the book by Capt. H. H. Holland]	Hackney Spectator, no. 2066: 4
1923, Oct. 19	*Shakespeare Through Oxford Glasses*, III [review of the book by Capt. H. H. Holland]	Hackney Spectator, no. 2072: 4
1923, Nov. 9	Annual General Meeting	Hackney Spectator, no. 2078: 2
1923, Nov. 16	*Shakespeare's Hand in the Plays of Sir Thomas More* [review of the book by Alfred W. Pollard]	Hackney Spectator, no. 2080: 3
1923, Dec. 14	Report of Our First Year's Work	Hackney Spect., no. 2087: 8, 18
1924, Jan.	The Shakespeare Fellowship [letter]	Galleon, vol. 1/1: 24-25
1924, Feb. 8	The Galleon [Note]	Hackney Spectator, no. 2101: 2
1924, Feb. 22	A Rosicrucian Group	Hackney Spectator, no. 2103: 5
1924, March 7	The Derby Theory	Hackney Spectator, no. 2105: 10
1924, March 21	Fellowship Notes	Hackney Spectator, no. 2107: 4
1924, March 28	The Character of Oxford, II	Hackney Spectator, no. 2108: 4
1924, March 28	Mr. Francis Clarke & Mr. Lucas	Hackney Spectator, no. 2108: 4
1924, April 4	The Shakespeare Good-Fellowship	Hackney Spectator, no. 2109: 4
1924, April 25	Fellowship Notes	Hackney Spectator, no. 2112: 11
1924, May 23	The Date of *Hamlet*	Hackney Spectator, no. 2116: 2
1924, May 30	Oxford and Sir Horace Vere	Hackney Spectator, no. 2117: 2
1924, July	Shakespearean Heterodoxy [letter]	Galleon, vol. 1/3: 89-90
1924, July 4	Oxford and Burghley	Hackney Spectator, no. 2122: 2
1924, July 11	Shakespeare's Signatures	Hackney Spectator, no. 2123: 5
1924, July 18	The Text of *Hamlet*	Hackney Spectator, no. 2124: 11
1924, July 25	Recent Progress	Hackney Spectator, no. 2125: 11
1924, Aug. 1	Recent Progress	Hackney Spectator, no. 2126: 9
1924, Aug. 8	Concerning William Hall, I	Hackney Spectator, no. 2127: 2
1924, Aug. 15	The "Shakespeare" Myth	Hackney Spectator, no. 2128: 11
1924, Sept. 5	Facts Relating to William Hall and His Circle, II	Hackney Spectator, no. 2131: 4
1924, Sept. 12	Facts Relating to William Hall and His Circle, III	Hackney Spectator, no. 2132: 4
1924, Sept. 19	Fellowship Notes	Hackney Spectator, no. 2133: 4
1924, Sept. 26	[response to Margaret Knapp]	Hackney Spectator, no. 2134: 4
1924, Oct. 3	*A Midsummer Night's Dream*, I	Hackney Spectator, no. 2135: 4
1924, Oct. 10	*A Midsummer Night's Dream*, II	Hackney Spectator, no. 2136: 4
1924, Oct. 31	Annual General Meeting	Hackney Spectator, no. 2139: 9
1924, Nov. 7	[review of *The Shakespeare Signatures and Sir Thomas More* by Sir George Greenwood [response by G. Greenwood on Nov. 14]	Spectator
1924, Nov. 14	The Shakespeare Signatures and *Sir Thomas More*	Hackney Spectator, no. 2141: 7
1924, Nov. 21	The Annual Report, 1923-24: Membership	Hackney Spectator, no. 2142: 2
1924, Nov. 28	The Annual Report, 1923-24: *A Midsummer Night's Dream*	Hackney Spectator, no. 2143: 10
1924, Dec. 5	The Annual Report, 1923-24, George Gascoigne	Hackney Spectator, no. 2144: 4
1924, Dec. 12	The Annual Report, 1923-24, Publications	Hackney Spectator, no. 2145: 9

Ward, Colonel Bernard Rowland (continued)

1931, Jan.	Facts Collected. Problems Unsolved [rev.of *William Shakespeare: a Study of Facts and Problems* by Sir Edmund Chambers]	Sh. Pictorial, no. 35: 16
1931, Feb.	A New Shakespeare Chronology [review of *Shakespeare's Plays in the Order of Their Writing* by Eva Turner Clark (1931)]	Sh. Pictorial, no. 36: 32
1931, March	[review of *The Oxford-Shakespeare Case Corroborated* by P. Allen]	Sh. Pictorial, no. 37: 48
1931, April	Oxford's Handwriting [review of *Shake-Speare: Handwriting and Spelling* by Gerald H. Rendall (1931)]	Sh. Pictorial, no. 38: 63
1931, May	Marlowe and His Circle [review of *Marlowe and His Circle* by Frederich S. Boas (1931)	Sh. Pictorial, no. 39: 80
1931, June	The Annual Dinner	Sh. Pictorial, no. 40: 96
1931, July	Sir Edmund Chambers in America	Sh. Pictorial, no. 41: 116
1931, July 28	The Trussell Family: Probable meaning of Shakespeare's 'Candle-Holder' Pun [letter]	Morning Post, p. 6
1931, Aug.	The Records of the Court Revels	Sh. Pictorial, no. 42: 132
1931, Sept.	The Shining Possibilities of Anne Vavasour [resp. to Willoughby]	Sh. Pictorial, no. 43: 148
1931, Oct.	The Original Venus and Adonis [review of *The Original Venus and Adonis* by H. T. S. Forrest	Sh. Pictorial, no. 44: 164
1931, Nov.	[reviews of *The Earl of Oxford as Shakespeare* by Colonel Montagu W. Douglas (1931) and *Seven Shakespeares* by Gilbert Slater]	Sh. Pictorial, no. 45: 180
1931, Dec.	A Great Shakespeare Discovery	Sh. Pictorial, no. 46: 196
1932, Jan.	Mr. Justice Shallow	Sh. Pictorial, no. 47: 16
1933, Jan.	A Protest Addressed to the Editor of the *Review of English Studies* [in response to G. C. Moore Smith's October 1932 article]	Sh. Pictorial, no. 59: 12-13

Ward, Robert P.

1927	*De Vere, or, The Man of Independence*. London: H. Colburn.	

Ward, Victoria

1994, Dec. 16	Outside Edge: An Earl in Search of the Real Bard [Charles Burford and the Shakespeare Oxford Society]	Independent, p. 25

Wardell, Jane

2004, June 25	Society Marks Death of 'True Shakespeare' [repr. in SON, vol. 40/3: 8 (Summer 2004)	Washington Post, p. C8

Ware, Susan

2002, March 3	What's in a Name? Scholar [Richard Desper] Argues Another Man Was Behind the Works of Shakespeare [from Boston Globe Online; repr. in DVN (April 2002), p. 21-22]	Boston Globe, p. 9

Warren, George

2003	The Proof is in the Pembroke: A Stylometric Comparison of the Works of Shakespeare with 12 Works by 8 Elizabethan Authors	Oxfordian, vol. 6: 133-149

Warren, James A.

Books written

2016   *Summer Storm: A Novel of Ideas*. CreateSpace. Reissued by Veritas Publication, 2019.

2021   *Shakespeare Revolutionized: The First Hundred Years of J. Thomas Looney's "Shakespeare" Identified*. Cary, NC: Veritas Publications.

Books edited (all published by Veritas Publications, Cary, NC, unless otherwise noted)

2018   *"Shakespeare" Identified* (1920) by J. Thomas Looney [Centenary Edition]. Somerville, MA: Forever Press. Reissued by Veritas Publications, 2019.

2019   *"Shakespeare" Revealed: The Collected Articles and Published Letters of J. Thomas Looney*.

2019   *Shakespearian Fantasias: Adventures in the Fourth Dimension* (1929) by Esther Singleton.

2021   *Shakespeare Investigated: Publications of the Shakespeare Fellowship, 1922-1936*.

2022   *Complete Writings on Shakespeare, 1923-1953 by Percy Allen* [in seven volumes].

        Vol. 1: Borrowings and Topicality in Elizabethan Drama, 1928-1929.

        Vol. 2: The Case for Edward de Vere as "Shakespeare," 1923-0930.

        Vol. 3: The Oxford-Shakespeare Case Corroborated, 1930-1932.

        Vol. 4: The Life Story of Edward de Vere as "William Shakespeare," 1932-1933.

        Vol. 5: The Plays of Shakespeare in Relation to French History, 1933-1936.

        Vol. 6: Anne Cecil & the Dynastic Successioin Theory, 1934-1943.

        Vol. 7: Later Writings on Shakespeare, 1937-1953.

Warren, James A. (continued)

2022, Sept.	[review of *Shakespeare, Marlowe and Other Elizabethans* by A. Bronson Feldman and edited by Warren Hope]	Oxfordian, vol. 24: 275-82
2023, Jan.	Edward de Vere and William Cecil: Conflicts Between the Documentary and Literary Evidence [extensive summary]	De Vere S. New., v. 30/1: 26-29
2023, Summer	In Memoriam: Roland George Caldwell (1933-2023)	Sh. Ox. Newsl., vol. 59/3: 9
2023, Sept.	[letter: reply to John Hamill and John Shahan]	Oxfordian, vol. 25: 15-19
2023, Sept.	Anne Cecil and the Crisis in Edward de Vere's 26ᵗʰ Year	Oxfordian, vol. 25: 169-226

Wasserman, Jerry

1998, March 7	Shakespeare, Our Contemporary [reviews of *The Genius of Sh.* by Jonathan Bate and *Alias Shakespeare* by Joseph Sobran (1997)	Vancouver Sun, p. C11

Watson, Jean

1920, July 8	Woman's Advocate [letter]	Reedy's Mirror, v. 29/28: 546

Watson, Timothy

2004, Jan.	[letter: comparison of portraits]	De Vere Soc. Newsl., p. 31icles

Watson, W.

1937, May	Shakespeare was a Welshman! [letter]	East Angl. M., vol. 2/8: 362

Watterson, Henry

1920, June 17	The Shakespeare Myth [letter: resp. to Reedy's review of SI] [Reedy's reply is on page 483; both are repr. in *The Montgomery Advertiser* (June 27) and *NY Times* (July 18).]	Reedy's Mirror, vol. 29/25: 498

Watts, Kathryn A.

2012	Justice Stevens's Black Leather Arm Chair	Northwestern Univ. Law Review, vol. 106/2: 845-49

Waugaman, Elisabeth

2019, Sept.	A Reassessment of the French Influence in Shakespeare	Oxfordian, vol. 21: 155-76
2019, Sept.	[review of *Early Shakespeare* by Bronson Feldman and edited by Warren Hope] [with Richard Waugaman]	Oxfordian, vol. 21: 261-66
2021, Winter	[letter: praise for diplomatic finesse of Bill Leahy and the SAT]	Sh. Ox. Newsl., vol. 57/1: 3-4
2021, Sept.	Analyzing the Chiljan Portrait	Oxfordian, vol. 23: 315-340
2023	*Love's Labour's Lost*: Lived Experience, A Pan-European Play	Psychoanalytic Inquiry, vol. 43/5: 355-63
2023, Summer	Shakespeare and the French Lens	J. of Scientific Explor., vol. 37/2
2023, Sept.	The French Influence in *Hamlet*	Oxfordian, vol. 25: 45-68
2023, Sept.	Behind the Mask of William Shakespeare [review of the book by Abel Lefranc, translation by Frank Lawler]	Oxfordian, vol. 25: 311-17

Waugaman, Richard M.

Books

2014	*It's Time to Re-Vere "Shakespeare": A Psychoanalyst Reads the Works of Edward de Vere, Earl of Oxford.* Oxfreudian Press. [2ⁿᵈ ed. pub. in 2020]	
2014	*Newly Discovered Works by "William Shake-speare," a.k.a. Edward de Vere, Earl of Oxford.* Oxfreudian Press. [2ⁿᵈ ed. pub. in 2017]	

Shorter pieces

2003, Fall	Unconscious Communication and Literature: Commentary on "Hamlet" as Process. A Novel Approach to Using Literature in Teaching Psychiatry	Psychiatry, vol. 66: 214-21
2006, Oct.	Shakespeare's Mothers [letters]	Psychiatric News, Pub. online
2007	[review of *"Shakespeare" By Another Name* by Mark Anderson]	Psychoanalytic Quarterly, vol. 76: 1397-1403
2007	Unconscious Communication in Shakespeare: 'Et tu, Brute?' Echoes 'Eloi, Eloi, Lama Sabbachthani?'	Psychiatry, vol. 70: 52-58
2007, Fall	A Wanderlust Poem, Newly Attributed to Edward de Vere	Sh. Matters, vol. 7/1: 1, 21-23
2007, Fall	DC's Shakespeare Theatre Company Acknowledges Authorship Controversy	Sh. Matters, vol. 7/1: 5
2008	[review of *The Mind According to Shakespeare: Psychoanalysis in the Bard's Writings* by Marvin B. Krims (2006)]	Psychoanalytic Quarterly, vol. 77: 1298-1305
2008, Winter	A Shakespearean "Snail Poem," Newly Attributed to Edward de Vere	Sh. Matters, vol. 7/2: 1, 6-11+

Author Index

Waugaman, Richard M. (continued)

2012, Winter	[review of *Shakespeare and His Authors: Critical Perspectives on the Authorship Question*, edited by William Leahy (2010)]	Sh. Matters, vol. 11/1: 9-10, 12
2012, Winter	[review of *Anonymity in Early Modern England: What's In a Name?*, edited by Janet W. Starner and Barbara H. Traister (2011)]	Sh. Matters, vol. 11/1: 14-15+
2012, Spring	Did Sir Walter Ralegh Have Access to an Early Draft of *Venus and Adonis*?	Sh. Matters, vol. 11/2: 5, 26
2012, Spring	*Psalms* Help Confirm de Vere Was Shakespeare: Psalm 77 echoed in Sonnet 28 and in *Hamlet*	Sh. Ox. Newsl., vol. 48/2: 19-24
2012, Summer	A Biblical Source for "Ignoto"?	Sh. Matters, vol. 11/3: 6
2012, Summer	Dispark'd in Shakespeare and Disparking in a 1572 Letter of Edward de Vere	Sh. Ox. Newsl., vol. 48/3: 8-9
2012, Sum./Fall	Shakespeare, Oxford and *The Book of Common Prayer*	Sh. Ox. Newsl., vol. 48/3: 16-18
2012, Sum./Fall	[letter: "Dispark'd" in Shakespeare and "Disparking" in a 1572 letter of Edward de Vere]	Sh. Ox. Newsl., vol. 48/3: 8-9
2013	The Theme of Betrayal in the Works of "William Shakespeare." [in *Betrayal: Developmental, Clinical, and Literary Realms* (Akhtar): 83-87]	
2013	New Discoveries About the Authorship of Shakespeare's Works	Oxfordian, vol. 15: 74-91
2013	[review of *Shakespeare and the Apocalypse: Visions of Doom From Early Modern Tragedy to Popular Culture* by R. Christofides]	Renaisssance Quarterly, vol. 66/3: 1134-35
2013	Doubter Response to Question #47: Why did Sigmund Freud doubt Shakespeare's authorship?, in *Sh. Beyond Doubt?* (Shahan): 206-07	
2013, Winter	A Source for "Remembrance of Things Past" in Sh.'s Sonnet 30	Sh. Matters, vol. 12/1: 1, 15-17
2013, Winter	A New 1569 Poem by Arthur Golding Re-attributed to Edward de Vere	Sh. Ox. Newsl., vol. 49/1: 9-10
2013, Spring	Our Man in Washington	Sh. Matters, vol. 12/2: 26-27
2013, Spring	Dating *Macbeth*: A 1603 Source for 'Equivocation' as an Alleged Gunpowder Plot Allusion in *Macbeth*	Sh. Ox. Newsl., vol. 49/2: 9-10
2013, Spring	Dating Macbeth: a 1603 source for 'equivocation' as an alleged Gunpowder Plot allusion in *Macbeth* [letter]	Sh. Ox. Newsl., vol. 49/2: 9-10
2013, Summer	Biblical Sources for Sonnets 24, 33, and *Henry VIII*: Implications for de Vere's Authorship	Brief Chronicles, vol. IV: 71-85
2013, Oct.	[review of *Shakespeare's Education* by Robin Fox (2012)]	Social Sciences, vol. 50/5: 522
2014	The 1574 *Mirror for Magistrates* is a Possible Source for "Feath'red King" in Shakespeare's *The Phoenix and the Turtle*	Cashiers Elisa., v. 85/1: 67-72
2014, March 7	[review of *Shakespeare Beyond Doubt* by Paul Edmundson and Stanley Wells (eds.) (2014)]	J. of the Am. Psychoanalytic Association
2014	[review of *The Unconscious in Shakespeare's Plays* by Martin S. Bergmann (2013)]	Psychoanalytic Quarterly, vol. 83: 737-42
2014, Winter	[review of *Hamlet Made Simple and Other Essays* by David P. Gontar (2013)]	Sh. Ox. Newsl., vol. 50/1: 18-20
2014, Summer	Betrayal in the Life of Edward de Vere, in the Plays of Shakespeare, and in Sonnet 121	Brief Chronicles., vol. V: 47-60
2014, Summer	News: '*Hamlet* and the Law of Homicide' at the Cosmos Club in Washington, D.C.: A Presentation by Tom Regnier	Sh. Ox. Newsl., vol. 50/3: 10-11
2015	Greed in the Life of William Shakspere—And Generosity in the Life of Edward de Vere, a.k.a. "Shakespeare" [in *Greed: Developmental, Cultural, and Clinical Realms* (Akhtar): 69-86]	
2015	The Psychology of Shakespearean Biography: An Update	Memoria di Sh.
2015, March 5	[reviews of films *Anonymous* and *Last Will. and Testament*]	Int'l Jou. of Applied Psycho-analytic St., vol. 12/1: 81-87
2015, Spring	A 1578 Poem About de Vere's Trip to Italy Responses by J. Mason and R. Prechter, Summer 2015, p. 3.	Sh. Ox. Newsl., v. 51/2: 1, 27-32
2015	[review of *What Shakespeare Teaches Us about Psychoanalysis* by Dorothy and Jerome Grunes]	Renaissance Qu., v. 68/2: 787-88
2015, Summer	Was William Scott a Plagiarist? [review of *The Model of Poesie* (an unpublished manuscript) by William Scott) (1599)]	Brief Chronicles, vol. VI: 173-78
2016	[review of *Anecdotal Shakespeare: A New Performance History* By Paul Menzer (2015)]	Renaissance. Q., v. 69/4: 1598-99

Author Index

Waugh, Alexander

YouTube channel: @alexanderwaugh7036

Books

2014   *Shakespeare in Court*. Amazon Kindle Single. Reissued as a Radio Play in 2017.

Books edited with John Shahan

2013   *Shakespeare Beyond Doubt? Exposing an Industry in Denial.* Tamarac, FL: Llumina Press.

Books edited with Mark Anderson and Alexander McNeil

2016   *Contested Year: Errors, Omissions and Unsupported Statements in James Shapiro's "The Year of Lear: Shakespeare in 1606."* Kindle.

Shorter pieces

2007, Sept.	The Name's the Thing [letter]	Sunday Herald (Glasg.), p. 40
2013	Keeping Shakespeare Out of Italy, in SBD? (Shahan and Waugh): 72-85 [repr. in *Sh. Authorship Sourcebook* (Stritmatter 2022): 383-401]	
2013, Oct.	A Secret Revealed: William Covell and his *Polimanteia* (1595)	De Vere Soc. New., v. 20/3: 7-10
2013, Nov.	Alexander Waugh's Diary: Shakespeare Was a Non de Plume – Get Over It [summary in DVN, vol. 21/1: 18-19 (Jan. 2014)]	Spectator, p. 13
2013, Nov. 2	Alexander Waugh's Diary: Shakespeare Was a Nom de Plume – Get Over It [William Covell's revelations] Response by Samuel Johnson, Nov. 9, p. 32.	Spectator, p. 11
2014	The True Meaning of Ben Jonson's Phrase: 'Sweet Swan of Avon!' [repr. in *The First Folio* (Stritmatter 2023): 271-80]	Oxfordian, vol. 16: 97-103
2014, May	John Weever – Another Anti-Stratfordian	De Vere Soc. New., v. 21/2: 12-5
2014, Summer	[letter: response to Michael Morse on anagrams]	Sh. Ox. Newsl., vol. 50/3: 5-6
2014, Oct.	"Thy Stratford Moniment" – Revisited	De Vere S. New., v. 21/3: 28-39
2015, Spring	[letter: response to letter from Oliver Kamm]	Sh. Ox. Newsl., vol. 51/1: 3-4
2015, Summer	From the Pulpit: A Few Home Truths – A British Introduction	Brief Chronicles, vol. VI: 1-8
2015, July	[letter: picture of Shakespeare in *Gerard's Herball* (1597)]	De Vere Soc. Newsl., vol. 22/3: 4
2016, Spring	BBC Documentary Only Deepens the Mystery [rev.of *Shakespeare's Tomb* (2016)]	Sh. Ox. Newsl., v. 52/2: 19, 22+
2016, July	Shakespeare's Missing Connections	De Vere S. New., v. 23/3: 23-27
2016, Oct.	Shakespeare's Pole: Oxford, Burghley, and Coryat and Polonius	De Vere Soc. New., v. 23/4: 9-13
2017, Jan.	[review of *Reflections on the True Shakespeare* by Gary Goldstein	De Vere S. New., v. 24/1: 42-43
2017, Jan.	Professor Alan Nelson's Blunders (Part 1)	De Vere S. New., v. 24/1: 43-44
2017, Oct.	Hidden Truths (Part II)	De Vere S. New., v. 24/4: 22-37
2018, Jan.	[letter: Youtube channel videos]	De Vere Soc. New., vol. 25/1: 46
2018, April	Oxford as Shakespeare	De Vere Soc. New., v. 25/2: 8-42
2018	My Shakespeare Rise!, in *My Shakespeare: the Authorship Controversy* (Leahy): 47-83.	
2018	Praise for Edward de Vere, 17th Earl of Oxford	Neues Sh. Jou., vol. NS6: 45-66
2018	[review of *Reflections on the True Shakespeare* by Gary Goldstein]	Neues Sh. Jou., vol. NS6: 181-82
2019, 2022	Chart A: Observable Influence Patterns for Twenty-Two Elizabethan Dramatic Writers, in *Sh. Authorship Sourcebook* (Stritmatter 2019, 2020): 190]	
2019, July	Who was "Our English Terence Will: Shake-speare? Could it have been William Stanley, 6th Earl of Derby? [with Amanda Hinds]	De Vere S. New., v. 26/3: 13-29
2020, Spring	That "Famous Persecutor of Priscian": Oxford, Shakespeare and the Repurification of English	Sh. Ox. Newsl., vol. 56/2: 24-28
2020, April	That 'Famous Persecutor of Priscian': Oxford, Shakespeare and the Repurification of English	De Vere S. New., v. 27/2: 17-26
2020, Spring	[letter: letter printed by the TLS]	Sh. Ox. Newsl., vol. 56/2: 14-15
2020, Fall	letter: Sonnets Dedication]	Sh. Ox. Newsl., vol. 56/4: 4-5
2020, Oct.	[letter: EK and *The Shepheard's Calendar*]	De Vere Soc. Newsl., v. 27/4: 46
2021, Jan.	Edward de Vere and Marlowe, Lyly and Kyd	De Vere S. New., v. 28/1: 11-12
2021, July	1581—A Watershed Year for Oxford and the English Theatre	De Vere Soc. New., v. 28/3: 4-18
2021, Summer	"Real Progress" in 1740	Sh. Ox. Newsl., vol. 57/3: 20-21
2022, April	[letter: Jan Cole's excellent article on de Vere and the North family]	De Vere Soc. New., v. 29/2: 43-4
2022, July	Service of Thanksgiving for Lord Burghley	De Vere Soc. New., v. 29/3: 26-8
2023, Jan.	Presentation: Shakespeare and the Cecils [summary]	De Vere Soc. Newsl., v. 30/1: 24
2023, Summer	My Beloved the Author: The Subtext of Ben Jonson's First Folio Encomium to William Shakespeare	Journal of Scientific Exploration, vol. 37/2

Wayland
    2012, May 6   Obituary: Elisabeth Sears   Boston Globe

Waymark, Peter
    1989, July 4   In Search of the Bard [Enoch Powell Leads Case for Doubters in   Times (London), p. 23
          TV Show]

Weber, Bruce
    2003, Nov. 19   Cutting Shakespeare down to Size [review of *The Beard of Avon* by   New York Times, , p. E5
          Amy Freed]

Weber, Tom
    1993, Nov. 1   Debunking of Shakespeare Is Much Ado About Nothing   Bangor Daily News
          [review of Charles Vere speech]

Webster, Lewis H.
    1946, Jan. 30   Those Authorities [repr. in SFQ, vol. VII/1: 12 (Jan. 30, 1946);   Warwick Valley Dispatch
          and in BTC, vol. 3: 238-40]

Weales, Gerald
    2010, Oct.   Two For the Bard: Whoever Wrote Shakespeare's Plays, There's a   Am. Theatre, v. 27/8: 146-47
          Raft of Autobiographical Content to Contend With

Weidhorn, Manfred
    2015, Spring   The Real Shakespeare Mystery   Sh. Ox. Newsl., vol. 51/2: 12-17

Weinberg, Steve
    2005, Aug. 7   Shakespeare's Secret [review of *"Shakespeare" By Another Name*   Atlanta Journal-Const., p. 8L
          by Mark Anderson

Weingartner, Gabriele
    2007   [review of *Der Fall Shakespeare* by Walter Klier (2004)]   Neues Sh. Journal, v. 11: 171-72

Weismann, Max
    2002, Nov.   The Great Shakespeare Hoax: Introduction   Great Ides Online, n. 203: 1-8

Weiss, Hedy
    2002, Oct. 8   The Beard of Avon [review of Amy Freed's play]   Chicago Sun, p. 37

Weiss, Larry
    2006, Fall   [review of *The Shakespeare Wars* by Ron Posenbaum]   Sh. Newsl., vol. 56/2: 47

Welch, Colin
    1990, June 23   Freud's Jungle Book [review of *Reading Freud* by Peter Gay]   Spectator, p. 26

Wellman, Wade
    1991, May 3   Shakespeare, By any Other Name . . . [review of *Alias Shakespeare*   Milwaukee Sentinal, p. I6
          by Joe Sobran]

Wells, Carolyn
Books
    1937   *The Rest of My Life*. New York: J. B. Lippincott Co.
Shorter pieces
    1932, Nov. 24   [title not known; article referred to in Eva Turner Clark's Nov. 24   [presumably the *NY Times*, but
          letter to J. T. Looney as "in this morning's paper"]   article not yet found]
    1937, June 5   The Oxford Theory [letter: re Barrell and Stoll]   Saturday Review, p. 9, 16
    1941, ???   The Shakespeare Title-page Mystery   Dolphin, vol. 4/2: 158
    1941, Oct.   Oxford's Pseudonym   SF News-letter (A), vol. 2/6: 71

Wells, Lawrence
    1992, Dec. 1   Shakespeare Slept Here [Castle Hedingham]   American Way, p. 60-66, 103
    2002, Winter   Obituary: Olga Ironside-Wood (1912-2001)   Sh. Ox. Newsl., vol. 38/1: 21
    2002, Jan./Feb.   Obituary: Olga Ironside-Wood (1912-2001)   De Vere Soc. Newsl., p. 14-15

Wells, Stanley
Books
    2001   *Oxford Companion to Shakespeare* [with M. Dobson] [excerpt repr. in DVN (April 2002), p. 17-19]
    2011   *Shakespeare Bites Back: Not So Anonymous* [e-book]. [with Paul Edmondson]
    2013   *Shakespeare Beyond Doubt: Evidence, Argument, Controversy* [with Paul Edmondson]. Cambridge; New
          York: Cambridge University Press.

Wells, Stanley (continued)
Shorter pieces

1994, April 17	Alias Bacon, Marlowe or the 17th Earl of Oxford? [review of *The Shakespeare Conspiracy* by Graham Phillips and Martin Keatman]	Sunday Times, p. 4
2003, Sept. 25	Shakespeare's First Critic [William Scott (1579-?)] [repr. in DVN (Sept. 2003), p. 16-17]	Times Lit. Sup., issue 5243: 14
2007, March 18	There's No Doubt It's Will [repr. in *Shakespeare Authorship Sourcebook* (Stritmatter 2019, 2022): 221-26]	Wash. Post, Outlook B1, 5
2008	[title not known; attack on the Declaration of Reasonable Doubt] [rebuttal by Mark Rylance in the June 2008 issue]	Stage
2010, May 27	Plotting Against the Stratford Man [review of *Contested Will* by James Shapiro]	NY Review, vol. 57/9: 31
2010, Aug. 13	Poured Over Again [review of *Shakespeare and His Critics* edited by William Leahy]	Times Lit. Sup., is. 5602: 12
2013	Allusions to Shakespeare to 1642, in SBD (Edmondson and Wells): 73-87	
2013	[comments on Royal Shakespeare Company website Authorship Debate page describing disbelief in Shakespeare's authorship as "a psychological aberration . . ."] [responses by Alice Crampin and Danny Evans in DVN, vol. 20/3: 27 (Oct. 2013)]	

Wember, Hanno
Books co-edited with Robert Detobel

2012	*Stratford's Fragestunde*. Introduction by Michael York. Buchholz, Germany: Verlag Uwe Laugwitz. [Translation of *Exposing an Industry in Denial* (Shahan & the Shakespeare Authorship Coalition] [Special Editions #4 of *Neues Shake-speare Journal*]	

Shorter works

2008, Oct.	Erhellende Finsternisse [Dating *Lear* by allusions to an eclipse]	Neues Sh. Journal, v. 12: 107-15
2010	Illuminating Eclipses: Astronomy and Chronology in King Lear	Brief Chronicles, vol. II: 33-43
2012, Spring	[letter: German Oxfordians score coup against German Stratfordians]	Sh. Ox. Newsl., vol. 48/2: 3
2014, Summer	[review of *AKA Shakespeare* by Peter A. Sturrock (2013)]	Brief Chronicles, vol. V: 205-13

Wembridge, Harry A.

1956, May	"To the Editor and Readers of *The Shakespeare Newsletter*" [letter with 22 signers]	Sh. Newsl., vol. 6/3: 18

Wennerstrom, Jack

2005, Winter	[letter: Nabokov, nobility and the Nobel Prize]	Sh. Matters, vol. 4/2: 2

Werlin, Joella

2022, Oct.	Shakespeare Follery, 1623: The First Folio and the Countess of Montgomery's Disappearance	De Vere S. New., v. 29/4: 19-28
2023, July	Shakespeare Foolery (1623-2023): A Tragical-Comical-Historical Family Drama Divulged in "The Dyer's Hand"	De Vere Soc. Newsl., vol. 30/3: 4-29

Werner, Hans

2010, May 9	Will the Real Will Please Stand Up? [review of *Contested Will* by J. Shapiro]	Toronto Star, p. 6

Werth, Andrew

1999	Opinion: Reading by the Lamp of Biography: How Knowledge of the Artist Illuminates Our Understanding of the Art [repr. in EVR, vol. 9 (Fall 1999)]	Oxfordian, vol. 2: 145-151
2000, Spring	Virginia Woolf's Shakespeare: Stratford lad in *A Room of One's Own*	Sh. Ox. Newsl., vol. 36/1: 26-27+
2002	Shakespeare's "Lesse Greek" [repr. in RCA, p. 30-43]	Oxfordian, vol. 5: 11-29
2004, Jan./Feb.	[letter: Ch. Hitchens' Oct. '03 article [repr. in SM, vol. 3/2: 2-3]	Atlantic Mon., vol. 293/1: 18

West, Robert H.

1953, Summer	[review of *This Star of England* by Dorothy and Charlton Ogburn]	Georgia Review, vol. 7/2: 228-31

West, Thomas G. and John Alvis (editors)

1981	*Shakespeare as Political Thinker*. Durham, NC: Carolina Academic Press.	
2000	*Shakespeare as Political Thinker, 2nd edition, Revised and Expanded*. Wilmington, DE: ISI Books.	

Westerfield, Barbara

1987, Summer	A Light on Wivenhoe [repr. in BTC, vol. 6: 300]	Sh. Ox. Newsl., vol. 23/3: 3-4

Author Index

Whalen, Richard F.

Books

1994   *Shakespeare—Who Was He? The Oxford Challenge to the Bard of Avon*. Foreword by Paul H. Nitze. Westport, CT: Praeger. [excerpt (p. 62-102) repr. in LC, p. 19-36] [Translated into Japanese (by Jim'ichi Isoyama, Akinori Sakaguchi, and Yukio Oshima) as *Sheikusupia wa dare data ka: Eeivon no shijin ni taisuru okkusufodo haku no chosen* (Tokyo: Hosei Daigaku Shuppankyoku, 1998)

2007   *Macbeth, fully annotated from an Oxfordian Perspective*. Coral Springs, FL.

2010   *Othello the Moor of Venice by William Shakespeare*. The Oxfordian Shakespeare Series, fully annotated from an Oxfordian perspective by Richard Whalen and Ren Draya. Truro, MA: Llumina Press.

2013   *Macbeth by William Shakespeare*. The Oxfordian Shakespeare Series, fully annotated from an Oxfordian Perspective by Richard Whalen. Second Edition, revised and expanded. With an Essay on "Acting Macbeth" by Derek Jacobi. Truro, MA: Llumina Press.

2018   *Hamlet: Fully Annotated from an Oxfordian Perspective by Richard Whalen*. Santa Fe: Horatio Editions.

Shorter pieces

1992, Spring	A Proposal for Scholarly Cooperation	Sh. Newsl., vol. 42/1: 12
1992, Dec. 27	It's Not Shakespeare, but Edward de Vere, Who Deserves the Credit Response by L. Repass, Dec. 27. Reply to Repass by Otto K. Stohr, Feb. 22, 1993.	Greensboro News-Rec., p. F2
1993, Winter	[review of *The Friendly Shakespeare* by Norrie Epstein (1993)]	Sh. Ox. Newsl., vol. 29/1a: 1-3
1993, Spring	[review of *Shakespeare: His Life, Work and Era* by Dennis Kay]	Sh. Ox. Newsl., vol. 29/2a: 3
1993, Spring	[review of *Shakespeare: The Later Years* by Russell Fraser (1993)]	Sh. Ox. Newsl., vol. 29/2a: 3-4
1993, Spring	[review of *Shakespeare: An Annotated Bibliography* by Joseph Rosenblum (1992)]	Sh. Ox. Newsl., vol. 29/2a: 4
1993, Spring	[review of *Shakespeare's Professional Career* by Peter Thomson]	Sh. Ox. Newsl., vol. 29/2a: 4
1993, Spring	[review of *The Complete Works of Shakespeare*, edited by David M. Bevington (2008)]	Sh. Ox. Newsl., vol. 29/2a: 4
1993, Spring	[review of *The Friendly Shakespeare* by Norrie Epstein (1993)]	Sh. Ox. Newsl., vol. 29/2a: 4-5
1993, Spring	[review of *Shakespeare: The Living Record*: Irwin Matus]	Sh. Ox. Newsl., vol. 29/2a: 5
1993, Spring	[review of *Shakespeare's Lives* by S. Schoenbaum (1993)]	Sh. Ox. Newsl., vol. 29/2a: 5-6
1993, Spring	[report from the Shakespearean Association of America meeting]	Sh. Ox. Newsl., vol. 29/2a: 12
1993, Summer	A *New Yorker* Reviewer Suggests a "Closet Lord"	Sh. Ox. Newsl., vol. 29/3a: 6
1993, Fall	Mock Trial in Fanueil Hall Is Centerpiece of 17th Annual Conference	Sh. Ox. Newsl., vol. 29/4: 18-19
1994, Winter	[review of *Shakespeare: In Fact* by Irvin Matus (1994)] [repr. in EVR, vol. 1 (Fall 1995)]	Sh. Ox. Newsl., vol. 30/1: 11-12
1994, Spring	Folger 'Roasts' the Swan of Avon, But Not Really; Exhibit Errs on Date of Bible	Sh. Ox. Newsl., vol. 30/2a: 3-4
1994, Spring	From the President	Sh. Ox. Newsl., vol. 30/2a: 17-18
1994, Summer	BBC-TV is Making an Hour-Long Special on the Authorship Question and Oxford	Sh. Ox. Newsl., vol. 30/3a: 7
1994, Summer	Cyberspace Embraces Shakespeare	Sh. Ox. Newsl., vol. 30/3a: 8
1994, Summer	Oxfordians in the Theater Bring Oxfordian Readings to Shakespeare's Plays	Sh. Ox. Newsl., vol. 30/3a: 9-10
1994, Summer	From the President	Sh. Ox. Newsl., vol. 30/3a: 10
1994, Fall	[letter: resp. to Thomas Pendleton's review of *Shakespeare, in Fact*] Reply by Thomas Pendleton, same issue and page.	Sh. Newsl., vol. 44/3: 42
1994, Autumn	[review of *Kill All the Lawyers? Shakespeare's Legal Appeal* by Daniel J. Kornstein (1994)]	Sh. Ox. Newsl., vol. 30/4: 4-5
1994, Autumn	Stratford Man Among the Undead in *The New York Times*	Sh. Ox. Newsl., vol. 30/4: 14-15
1994, Autumn	Mock Trial at U.S. Supreme Court: Hamlet Not Insane in Stabbing Death of Polonius	Sh. Ox. Newsl., vol. 30/4: 19
1995, Winter	Oxfordian Productions in Shakespeare Summer Stock	Sh. Ox. Newsl., vol. 31/1a: 8
1995, Winter	From the President	Sh. Ox. Newsl., vol. 31/1a: 10
1995, Winter	[review of *The Reckoning: The Murder of Christopher Marlowe* by Charles Nicholl (1992)]	Sh. Ox. Newsl., vol. 31/1a: 11
1995, Spring	Shakespeare/Oxford in "Jeopardy"	Sh. Ox. Newsl., vol. 31/2a: 12
1995, Autumn	Before Looney, Did Anyone Know Oxford Was Shakespeare? A Novel, A Song, and A Portrait Inventory Suggest So [repr. in BTC, vol. 9: 126-33; and in EVR, vol. 2 (Winter 1996)]	Sh. Ox. Newsl., vol. 31/4: 12-16
1995, Autumn	From the Past President: Congratulations to New President Charles Vere Lord Burford [Charles Beauclerk]	Sh. Ox. Newsl., vol. 31/4: 17

Whalen, Richard F. (continued)

1995, Autumn	[letter: Lincoln Cain's letter: Folger Library open to all]	Sh. Ox. Newsl., vol. 31/4: 22
1996, Winter	[review of *Shakespeare: A Life in Drama* by Stanley Wells (1995)]	Sh. Ox. Newsl., vol. 32/1: 21
1996, Winter	[review of *Shakespeare: The King's Playwright, 1603-1613* by Alvin Kernan (1995)]	Sh. Ox. Newsl., vol. 32/1: 21
1996, Winter	[review of *Vice Versa: Bisexuality and Eroticism of Everyday Life* by Marjorie Garber (1995)]	Sh. Ox. Newsl., vol. 32/1: 21
1996, Spring	Samuel Schoenbaum (1927-1996)	Sh. Ox. Newsl., vol. 32/2: 2
1996, Spring	[review of *Edmond Malone, Shakespearean Scholar* by P. Martin]	Sh. Ox. Newsl., vol. 32/2: 19
1996, Spring	[review of *The Shakespeare Conspiracy* by Graham Phillips and M. Keatman (1994)]	Sh. Ox. Newsl., vol. 32/2: 19
1996, Summer	[review of *The Bedford Companion to Shakespeare* by R. McDonald (1996)]	Sh. Ox. Newsl., vol. 32/3: 19
1996, Spring	[review of *The Sonnets*, A Volume in *The New Cambridge Shake-speare*, ed. by C. Blakemore Evans, intro. by A. Hecht (1996)]	Sh. Ox. Newsl., vol. 32/2: 19
1996, Summer	[review of *The Riverside Guide to Writing* by Douglas Hunt (1995)]	Sh. Ox. Newsl., vol. 32/3: 19, 23
1996, Spring	[review of *Cultural Selection* by Gary Taylor (1996)]	Sh. Ox. Newsl., vol. 32/2: 19, 24
1996, Autumn	[letter: Bloom's support for Sh's "aristocratic sense of culture"]	Elizabethan Review, vol. 4/2: 3
1997, Spring	[letter: comments on "Writing History"]	Sh. Ox. Newsl., vol. 33/2: 21
1997, Spring	[review of *Love's Labour's Lost: Critical Essays*, edited by Felicia Londré (1997)]	Sh. Ox. Newsl., vol. 33/2: 19
1997, Summer	[review of *The Norton Shakespeare*, edited by Stephen Greenblatt]	Sh. Ox. Newsl., vol. 33/3: 17, 24
1997, Sum/Fall	[letter: Gurney's recent article "Jonson and Shakespeare"	Sh. Newsl., vol. 7/2+3: 26
1997, Fall	Morse Johnson (1915-1997) [repr. in BTC, vol. 7: 408-09]	Sh. Ox. Newsl., vol. 33/4: 2
1997, Fall	A Monumental Problem	Sh. Ox. Newsl., vol. 33/4: 10-11
1997, Fall	[review of *Global Shakespeare Series*, ed. by Dom Saliani (1996-97)]	Sh. Ox. Newsl., vol. 33/4: 21
1997, Autumn	Oxfordian Case Defended [letter: resp. to Kathman's "Why I'm Not an Oxfordian," with Kathman's reply] [repr. in BTC, vol. 8: 298-99]	Elizabethan Review, vol. 5/2: 4-5
1998, Spring	English Oxfordian Finds Southampton, De Vere in the Sonnets	Sh. Ox. Newsl., vol. 34/1: 3
1998, Spring	[review of *Shakespeare's Sonnets* edited by K Duncan-Jones (1997)] [repr. in EVR, vol. 8 (Spring 1999)]	Sh. Ox. Newsl., vol. 34/1: 18-19
1998, Spring	[review of *The Art of Shakespeare's Sonnets* by Helen Vendler] [repr. in EVR, vol. 8 (Spring 1999)]	Sh. Ox. Newsl., vol. 34/1: 18-19
1998, Spring	[review of *The Sonnets* edited by G. Blakemore Evans (1996)] [repr. in EVR, vol. 8 (Spring 1999)]	Sh. Ox. Newsl., vol. 34/1: 18-19
1998, Summer	The Queen's Worm, in *Antony and Cleopatra: Does Another of Shakespeare/Oxford's Word Games Clarify an Enigmatic Scene?* [repr. in EVR, vol. 7 (1998)] Response by James Fitzgerald, Fall 1998, p. 25-26. Response by Dennis Baron, Fall 1998, p. 26.	Sh. Ox. Newsl., vol. 34/2: 12-13
1998, Summer	[review of *Creating Literature Out of Life* by Doris Alexander]	Sh. Ox. Newsl., vol. 34/2: 19
1998, Fall	Charlton Ogburn (1911-1998) [repr. in SHNL, vol. 48/3: 63; BTC, vol. 8: 22-25; and in NSJ, vol. 3: 12-14]	Sh. Ox. Newsl., vol. 34/3: 1, 5
1998, Fall	[review of *Genius of Shakespeare* by Jonathan Bate (1998)]	Sh. Ox. Newsl., vol. 34/3: 23, 28
1998, Fall	[letter: resp. to John Mitchell]	Sh. Ox. Newsl., vol. 34/3: 25
1999, Winter	Yes, But is Authorship Dead?: The Folger Reports on George Greenwood vs. Mark Twain	Sh. Ox. Newsl., vol. 34/4: 3, 23
1999, Winter	Authorship and Orthodoxy: Ogburn's Legacy Can Be Found in How Institutions Such as the Folger Now Treat Authorship [repr. in BTC, vol. 8: 43-45]	Sh. Ox. Newsl., vol. 34/4: 9
1999, Winter	[review of *Shakespeare: The Invention of the Human* by Harold Bloom (1998)]	Sh. Ox. Newsl., vol. 34/4: 18, 24
1999, April	Curst Be He Yt Moves My Bones [repr. in LC, p. 57-78]	Harper's Mag., vol. 298: 57-59
1999, Spring	*Harper*'s Shakespeare Folio Articles: a Summary	Sh. Ox. Newsl., vol. 35/1: 4
1999, Spring	[review of *Symptoms of Culture* by Marjorie Garber (1998)]	Sh. Ox. Newsl., vol. 35/1: 19, 23
1999, Summer	[review of *The Late Mr. Shakespeare: A Novel* by Robert Nye]	Sh. Ox. Newsl., vol. 35/2: 20-21
1999, Fall	[review of *Bloody Constraint: War and Chivalry in Shakespeare* by Theodor Meron (1988)]	Sh. Ox. Newsl., vol. 35/3: 18
1999, Fall	[review of *Inscribing the Time* by Eric Mallin (1995)]	Sh. Ox. Newsl., vol. 35/3: 18

Whalen, Richard F. (continued)

2004, Summer	Book Notes: *Never and For Ever, Adventures of Freeman Jones* by Brame and Popova; *Chasing Shakespeares* by Sarah Smith; *Shakespeare and George Puttenham's Art of English Poesie* by Charles Willis; *The Dark Side of Shakespeare* by W. Ron Hess; and *The Shakespeare Question* by Kateryna Sinkevych	Sh. Matters, vol. 3/4: 31
2004, Summer	[letter: *Monstrous Adversary* by Alan Nelson]	Sh. Matters, vol. 3/4: 7-8
2004, Summer	University of Tennessee Law School Hosts Authorship Conference	Sh. Ox. Newsl., vol. 40/3: 1, 4-5
2004, Summer	Shakespeare and the Law	Sh. Ox. Newsl., vol. 40/3: 5
2004, Fall	A Response to Burden of Proof and Presumptions in the Shakespeare 72/1: 273-274 Authorship Debate	Tennessee Law Review, vol.
2004, Fall	Response to Elliott/Valenza's Fall 2004 Article "Oxford by the Numbers"	Tennessee Law Review, vol. 72/1: 275-276
2004, Fall	Who Wrote Shakespeare? The Preponderance of Evidence 72/1: 255-271	Tennessee Law Review, vol.
2004, Fall	Shakespeare's Audience: A Reassessment of the Stratfordian View [repr. in RCA, p. 135-42]	Sh. Ox. Newsl., vol. 40/4: 1, 7-9+
2005	The Stratford Bust: A Monumental Fraud [repr. in RCA, p. 145-61; and in SBD?, p. 136-51 (2013)]	Oxfordian, vol. 8: 7-24
2005, Winter	Math Professor Leads New Seattle Chapter	Sh. Ox. Newsl., vol. 41/1: 24
2005, Winter	[review of *Will in the World: How Shakespeare Became Shakespeare* by Stephen Greenblatt (2004)]	Sh. Matters, vol. 4/2: 22-23
2005, Spring	Monstrous Errors Infect [Nelson's] *Monstrous Adversary* (2003)	Sh. Ox. Newsl., vol. 41/2: 21-22
2005, Spring	[review of *Shakespeare After All* by Marjorie Garber (2004)]	Sh. Ox. Newsl., vol. 41/2: 23
2005, Fall	[review of *The Case for Shakespeare* by Scott McCrea (2005)]	Sh. Ox. Newsl., vol. 41/4: 30
2005, Fall	[review of *Players: The Mysterious Identity of William Shakespeare* by Bertram Fields (2005)]	Sh. Ox. Newsl., vol. 41/4: 31-32
2006	Apples to Oranges in Bard Stylometrics: Elliott & Valenza Fail to Eliminate Oxford [with John Shahan] [response to Elliott and Valenza's Fall 2004 article "Oxford by the Numbers"] [repr. in DC, p. 137-42]	Oxfordian, vol. 9: 13-125
2006	[letter: Christopher Paul's 2004 "Oxford's Death" article] Reply by Christopher Paul, 2006, p. 141-43.	Oxfordian, vol. 9: 140-141
2006, Winter	Richard Whalen and the Professors [with Lew Tate] [repr. in NSJ, vol. 12: 156-59 (Oct. 2008)]	Sh. Ox. Newsl., vol. 42/1: 15-17
2006, Fall	[review of *The Shakespeare Wars* by Ron Rosenbaum (2006)	Sh. Matters, vol. 6/1: 8, 30, 32
2006, Spring	The Prince Tudor Hypothesis: A Brief Survey of the Pros and Cons Response by John Hamill, Fall 2006, p. 16. Response by Christopher Paul, Fall redux 2006, p. 32.	Sh. Ox. Newsl., vol. 42/2: 10-11+
2007	A Dozen Shakespeare Plays Written After Oxford Died? Not Proven!	Oxfordian, vol. 10: 75-84
2007	[letter: Stratfordian scholar affirms bust fraud]	Oxfordian, vol. 10: 163-164
2007, Winter	Don't Overlook the Endnotes	Sh. Matters, vol. 6/2: 29-30
2007, Winter	That Wild and Crazy Shakspere	Sh. Ox. Newsl., vol. 43/1: 30
2007, Spring	[letter: resp. to the editorial in vol. 56/3: 118] Rebuttal by Thomas A. Pendleton in vol. 57/1: 57	Sh. Newsl., vol. 57/1: 57
2007, Summer	Brian Vickers on the Stratford Monument	Sh. Ox. Newsl., vol. 43/3: 10-11
2007, Summer	[review of *The RSC Shakespeare*, edited by Jonathan Bate and Eric Rasmussen (2007)]	Sh. Ox. Newsl., vol. 43/3: 14, 24
2007, Summer	17% of Shakespeare Professors See at Least Possibly Good Reason to Question Shakspere as the Bard [repr. in NSJ, vol. 12: 160-61]	Sh. Ox. Newsl., vol. 43/3: 15
2007, Fall	News: Authorship Spoofs Stratford, Ontario	Sh. Matters, vol. 7/1: 4
2007, Fall	[letter: progress among Stratfordians]	Sh. Ox. Newsl., vol. 43/4: 19-20
2008, Winter	[review of *Shakespeare: The World as Stage* by Bill Bryson (2007)]	Sh. Matters, vol. 7/2: 3, 20
2008, Winter	[report on Oxfordian Activity in Seattle, Washington]	Sh. Ox. Newsl., vol. 44/1: 28
2008, Winter	[letter: doubts about Shakspere in the academy]	Sh. Matters, vol. 7/2: 2, 30-32
2008, Spring	An Overlooked Sub-Plot in *Macbeth* Reveals Oxford's Hand	Sh. Matters, vol. 7/3: 6, 28-31
2008, Spring	Columbia Professor Writing a Book-Length Study of the Authorship issue: *Contested Will* by James Shapiro (2010)	Sh. Ox. Newsl., vol. 44/2: 13-15

Whetstone, David
1995, Feb. 21	Was It Just a Looney Idea	Newcastle Journal, p. 9
2011, Dec. 7	Film Puts Bard in Spotlight [review of Anonymous]	Journal.: Newcastle-upon-Tyne, p. 58
2016, April 16	Why We Should Never Be Bored by the Bard [Keith Jewett to speak at Newcastle's Lit & Phil, where J. Thomas Looney researched *"Shakespeare" Identified*]	Journal: Newcastle-upon-Tyne, p. 54

White, Diana
1997, June 2	A New Volley in the Battle of the Bard [review of *Alias Shakespeare* By Joe Sobran (1997)]	Boston Globe

White, G. H.
1909, Oct. 2	Query: Edward de Vere, 17th Earl of Oxford	Notes and Q., Ser. 0/11: 266

White, Michael
1987, Sept. 26	The U.S. Versus the Man From Stratford: Supreme Court Hears the Case Against Shakespeare	Guardian, p. 36

Whitestone, Deanna R.
2012, Winter	[letter: Rollett's "solution" to the dedication of the *Sonnets*]	Sh. Matters, vol. 11/1: 2, 27+

Whiting, B. J.
1951, April	Historical Novels 1949-1950 [Burke Boyce's Oxfordian *Cloak of Folly*, and C. Brahms's and S. J. Simon's Baconian *No Bed for Bacon*]	Speculum, vol. 26/2: 337-67

Whitney, Star
1999, July 31	[letter: re the July 24 editorial]	Philadelphia Inquirer, p. A16

Whittemore, Hank
Blog: https://hankwhittemore.com
Books
2005	*The Monument*. Marshfield Hills, MA: Meadow Geese Press.
2005	*The Monument: An Abridged Introduction to the 918-page First Reference Edition.* [repr. in BTC, vol. 10: 91-101]
2010	*Shakespeare's Son and His Sonnets*. Groton, MA: Martin and Lawrence Press.
2010	*Shake-speare's Treason: The True Story of King Henry IX, Last of the Tudors* [with Ted Story] [a one-man show based on *The Monument*].
2012	*Twelve Years in the Life of Shakespeare*. Edited by William E. Boyle. Somerville, MA: Forever Press.
2016	*100 Reasons Shake-speare was the Earl of Oxford*. Somerville, MA: Forever Press. 2nd edition, with a new Introduction by the author, 2021: GMJ Global Media. [excerpts repr. in *Sh. Authorship Sourcebook* (Stritmatter 2019, 2022): 315-324]
2022	*The Living Record: Shakespeare, Succession, and the Sonnets*. GMJ Global Media.

Books edited with Paul H. Altrocchi
2009	*Building the Case for Edward de Vere as Shakespeare, vol. 1: The Great Shakespeare Hoax*. iUniverse.com.
2009	*Building the Case for Edward de Vere as Shakespeare, vol. 2: Nothing Truer Than Truth*. iUniverse.com.
2009	*Building the Case for Edward de Vere as Shakespeare, vol. 3: Shine Forth. iUniverse*.com.
2009	*Building the Case for Edward de Vere as Shakespeare, vol. 4: My Name Be Buried*. iUniverse.com.
2009	*Building the Case for Edward de Vere as Shakespeare, vol. 5: So Richly Spun*. iUniverse.com.

Shorter pieces
1994, Summer	[review of *Shakespeare: Who Was He?* by Richard F. Whalen]	Sh. Ox. Newsl., vol. 30/3a: 11-12
1996, Fall	Oxford's *Metamorphoses* [repr. in EVR, vol. 6 (Winter 1998); in BTC, vol. 7: 363-75; and in TYLS, p. 86-99]	Sh. Ox. Newsl., v. 32/4: 1, 11-15
1999, Summer	Abstract & Brief Chronicles: The Sonnets Seen as Shakespeare's True Testimony About the End of the Tudor Era (repr. in BTC, vol. 8: 55-72) Response by Stephanie Hopkins Hughes, vol. 35/2: 25-26. Response to Hughes by Sandy Hochberg, vol. 36/1: 29. Response to Hughes by Richard Whalen, vol. 36/1: 29.	Sh. Ox. Newsl., v. 35/2: 1, 10-14
2001, Spring	Prince Hamlet, the "Spear-shaker" of Elsinore	Sh. Ox. Newsl., vol. 37/1: 8-12
2001, Fall	The Politics of Massacres, the Need for Intelligence: Sh.'s Role in an Elizabethan England Under siege [repr. in TYLS, p. 7-19]	Sh. Matters, vol. 1/1: 4-7, 19
2001, Fall	[letter: re Hughes' Fall 2000 article: The Dark Lady is a metaphor]	Sh. Ox. Newsl., vol. 36/4: 23
2002	"Introduction" in *Shakespeare & the Tudor Rose* by Elisabeth Sears	

Whittemore, Hank (continued)

2016, Fall	2016 SOF Conference Comes to Boston [contributor]	Sh. Ox. Newsl., v. 52/4: 1, 18-30
2017, January	Man of the Theatre [reasons #1 and #2 repr. from *100 Reasons Why Shake-speare was Oxford*]	De Vere So. New., v. 24/1: 36-41
2017, April	Specialized Knowledge: [reasons #59 and #61 repr. from *100 Reasons Why Shake-speare was Oxford*]	De Vere Soc. New., v. 24/2: 7-13
2017, July	Sea and Seamanship, and *The Tempest* [reasons #60 and #80 repr. from *100 Reasons Why Shake-speare was Oxford*]	De Vere So. New., v. 24/3: 26-32
2017, Summer	[review of *The Ashbourne Saga: A Cinematic Epic in Fourteen Episodes* by Mike A'Dair (2017)]	De Vere So. New., v. 53/3: 19-23
2017, Sept.	In Conversation with Hank Whittemore: *100 Reasons Shake-speare was the Earl of Oxford* [with TOX Editor Chris Pannell]	Oxfordian, vol. 19: 181-94
2017, Fall	SOF 2017 Conference Held in Chicago [contributor]	Sh. Ox. Newsl., v. 53/4: 1, 27-36
2017, Oct.	Oxtober in the Sonnets and Oxford and Southampton [reasons #52 & #53 from *100 Reasons Why Shake-speare was Oxford*]	De Vere So. New., v. 24/4: 15-21
2018, April	Oxford Seen in the Plays 'Reasons #7 and #91 repr. from *100 Reasons Why Shake-speare was Oxford*]	De Vere So. New., v. 25/1: 18-22
2018, Fall	SOF Conference Report [contributor]	Sh. Ox. Newsl., v. 54/4: 1, 22-31
2018, Dec.	The Argument for Edward de Vere: Shakespeare Was a Man of the Theatre	Critical Stages, vol. 18
2019, Fall	SOF Annual Conference Sets New Attendance Record [contributor]	Sh. Ox. Newsl., v. 55/4: 1, 18-32
2021, Winter	[review of *All the Sonnets of Shakespeare* by Paul Edmondson and Stanley Wells (2020)]	Sh. Ox. Newsl., vol. 57/1: 33-35
2021, Winter	[letter: response to John Hamill]	Sh. Ox. Newsl., vol. 57/1: 31
2022, Summer	[letter: response to Michael Hyde]	Sh. Ox. Newsl., vol. 58/3: 3
2022, July	[letter: Ian Haste's April article on Hayward's *Henry the Fourth*]	De Vere Soc. Newsl., v. 29/3: 29
2022, Fall	The de Vere Ball Held in New York City	Sh. Ox. Newsl., vol. 58/4: 9
2023, Summer	To Be or Not To Be a Genius: The Argument for Acquired Knowledge and Life Experience	J. of Scientific Expl., vol. 37/27

Whyte, Gordon

1922, Dec. 2	Another "Shakespeare" [brief review of SI]	Billboard, p. 35

Width, Susan G.

2011, Spring	Board Positions Open	Sh. Ox. Newsl., vol. 47/2: 6

Width, Susan G.; John Hamill

2009, Dec.	Board of Trustees Approves Changes in Membership Dues	Sh. Ox. Newsl., vol. 45/3: 4-5

Wilbert, Doris M.

1990, Winter	The Authorship Controversy & Christopher Marlowe	Sh. Newsl., vol. 40/4: 59

Wilcock, Albert

1999, Aug.	Templewood Event, June 13, 1999	De Vere Soc. Newsl., vol. 3/4: 2

Wilcox, E. V.

1948, Aug. 9	Who Was Shakespeare? [letter: Gelett Burgess's July 31 article]	Washington Post, p. 6

Wilcox, Stewart

2021, Summer	Edward de Vere's Lost Playscript	Sh. Ox. Newsl., vol. 57/3: 16

Wildenthal, Bryan H.
Books

2019	*Early Shakespeare Authorship Doubts*. San Diego: Zindabad Press.	

Shorter pieces

2012, Mar-Apr	[letter: Joe Nickell's sneering ad hominem ridicule of doubters in his Nov-Dec cover story]	Skeptic Mag., p. 62
2016, Summer	End of an Oxfordian Era on the Supreme Court?	Sh. Ox. Newsl., vol. 52/3: 9-13
2018, Summer	Shapiro "On the Media": Name-Calling and Bullying Students and Doubters	Sh. Ox. Newsl., vol. 54/3: 25-27
2018, Fall	Summary of SOF Annual Meeting	Sh. Ox. Newsl., vol. 54/4: 14-16
2019, 2023	Oxford'S Poems and the Authorship Question [with Roger Stritmatter] [in *The Poems of Edward de Vere, vol. 1*, Roger Stritmatter, editor, p. 1-28]	

Williamson, Gene (continued)

1991, Aug.	[letter: thanks for the *Spear-shaker*]	Sp. Sh. Rev., issue 5: 25
1991, Aug.	Night Flight	Sp. Sh. Rev., issue 5: 17-18
1992, Spring	When the Search For Shakespeare Got Spooky	Sh. Ox. Newsl., vol. 28/2: 7-11

Williamson, Hugh R.

1933, July	Poor Will	Bookman, vol. 84: 83-84

Willis, Charles M.

Books

2003	*Shakespeare and George Puttenham's Art of English Poesie*. Upso.
2005	*George Puttenham and the Authorship of Shakespeare's Sonnets*. Upso.
2006	*Behind Shakespeare's Mask*. Upso.

Shorter pieces

2002, Fan./Feb.	George Puttenham, the Earl of Oxford and Shakespeare, Part I	De Vere Soc. Newsl., p. 29-31
2002, April	Identification of George Puttenham as the Author of *The Arte of English Poesie* and the *Justification Document*	De Vere Soc. Newsl., p. 34-36
2002, Oct.	George Puttenham's Legal Background, Sir James Dyer and *Hamlet*	De Vere Soc. Newsl., p. 21-24
2003, Sept.	Shakespeare and George Puttenham's *Arte of English Poesie*	De Vere Soc. Newsl., p. 14-15
2004, Jan.	Was Edward de Vere Legitimate?	De Vere Soc. Newsl., p. 20-23
2004, April	The Printing of *The Arte of English Poesie* and the Earl of Oxford [repr. in GO, p. 38-42]	De Vere Soc. Newsl., p. 24-26
2004, Oct.	George Puttenham and *Venus and Adonis*	De Vere Soc. Newsl., p. 16-19
2007, Feb.	Stratford, 'that Ungodly town'	De Vere Soc. Newsl., p. 18-20

Willis, Marie

1992, Spring	[letter: Oxford as Shakespeare is well-known in France]	Sh. Ox. Newsl., vol. 28/2: 2

Willoughby, D.

1931, May 2	[reviews of *Shakespeare's Plays in the Order of Their Writing* by Eva Turner Clark (1930) and *Corroborated* by Percy Allen (1931)]	Saturday Review, vol. 151: 652-3

Wilson, John Dover

Books

1932	*The Essential Shakespeare: A Biographical Adventure*. Cambridge: Cambridge University Press.

Shorter pieces

1962, Sept. 1	[letter: efforts to open Shakespeare's tomb]	Times (London)
1962, Sept. 14	[letter: second letter about Shakespeare's tomb]	Times (London)

Wilson, Larry

2011, Oct. 28	Will of Any Other Name as Sweet? [mentions two Oxfordians: Barbara Crowley and S. Colum Gilfillan]	Pasadena Star-News

Wilson, Lisa [with Laura Wilson Matthias]

2012	*Last Will. & Testament*. [An 84-minute film documenting the life of Edward de Vere]

Winchell, Walter

1939/40	Column responding to Charles Barrell's piece in *Scientific American*	New York Times [not yet found]

Winer, Linda

2003, Nov. 25	A Satire that Fires at Will [rev. of *The Beard of Avon* by Amy Freed]	Newport Daily Express, p. B8

Wingate, Janet

2020, Summer	Another Look at the Dediation to the Sonnets	Sh. Ox. Newsl., vol. 56/3: 25-30
2020, Fall	Sonnets Dedication [letter]	Sh. Ox. Newsl., vol. 56/4: 6

Winkler, Claudia

1983, April 11	William Who? [repr. in SON, vol. 19/2 (Spr. 1983); and BTC, vol. 6]	Cincinnati Post

Winkler, Elizabeth

Books

2023	*Shakespeare Was a Woman and Other Heresies: How Doubting the Bard Became the Biggest Taboo in Literature*. New York: Simon and Schuster.

Shorter pieces

2019, May 10	In Shakespeare's Life Story, Not All is True. In Fact, Much is Invented.	Atlantic Monthly
2019, June???	Was Shakespeare a Woman?	Atlantic Monthly
2023, May 27	To Question, or Not to Question? There is No Question	Washington Post
2023, May 28	[letter: response to the review by Jonathan Bate]	Telegraph

Woods, Michael
    1994, Nov. 23   Key to 'Real' Shakespeare Lies in the Stars, Physicist Says   Milwaukee Sen., p. 2
    1998, Nov. 20   Stars Betray Shakespeare   Daily News (Halifax), p. 34
    1998, Nov. 20   Bard's Genius Is Not Universally Accepted   Philadelphia Daily News

Woods, Richard
    2005, Oct. 5   Is This an Imposter I See Before Me?   Sunday Times, p. 18

Woodward, H. M. M.
    1938, Sept.   The Stratford Monument   SF News-letter (E), no. 11: 6-8

Woodward, Mark
    1999, July 1   [letter: the April 1 special "authorship" issue]   Harper's Mag., vol. 299: 6-11

Woody, Cynthia
    1976, April 23   Was the Bard Shakespeare or de Vere? [highlights Ruth Loyd Miller   State-Times (Baton-Rouge),
        and Minos D. Miller]   p. 3B-4B

Wooley, Robert W.
    1948, July 14   [letter: response to unsigned July 10 article]   Washington Post, p. 10

Woosnam, Tom
    2023, Summer   [review of *Shakespeare Was a Woman and Other Heresies* by   J. of Scientific Expl., vol. 37/2
        Elizabeth Winkler]

Worlen, Joella
    2013, Oct.   On the trail of de Vere in June 2013 [letter]   De Vere Soc. Newsl., v. 20/3: 27

Woudhuysen, H. R.
    1990, April 20   A Freudian Oxfordian [repr. in SON, vol. 26/2: 7 (Spring 1990)]   Times Lit. Sup., p. 418

Wright, Alice W.
    1989, Spring   [letter: Charlton Ogburn, Jr.: her experience teaching about Oxford]   Sh. Ox. Newsl., vol. 25/2: 14-15

Wright, B. D.
    1930, Sept. 5   "Shakespeare" Myth Theories That Fail to Impress [review of *The*   Western Morning News, p. 6
        Case for Edward de Vere as Shakespeare by Percy Allen (1930)

Wright, Daniel L.
Institutions: Shakespeare Authorship Research Centre – authorshipstudies.org
Books
    1993   *The Anglican Shakespeare: Elizabethan Orthodoxy in the Great Histories*. Vancouver, WA: Pacific-
        Columbia Books.
    2009   *Discovering Shakespeare: A Festschrift in Honor of Isabel Holden* (editor). Portland, OR: Concordia
        University Bookstore.
Shorter pieces
    1997, Spring   [review of *Shakespeare's Edward III* edited by Eric Sams]   Elizab. Rev., vol. 5/1: 54-56
        [repr. in BTC, vol. 8: 313-16]
    1998   He Was a Scholar and a Ripe and Good One: Oxford's Education,   Oxfordian, vol. 1: 64-87
        Mirrored in the Sh. Canon [repr. in BTC, vol. 10: 352-81]
    1998   [review of *Shakespeare – Who Was He?* by Richard F. Whalen]   Cresset, vol. 61/4: 35-36
    1998, Spring   [review of *Who Wrote Shakespeare?* by John Michell (1996)]   Sh. Bulletin, vol. 16/2: 46
    1998, Summer   Shaking the Spear at Court: Oxford as "Knight of the Tree of the   Sh. Ox. Newsl., v. 34/2: 1, 14-5+
        Sunne" [repr. in BTC, vol. 8: 5-12; and in EVR, vol. 8 (1999)]
    1999   [review of *Alias Shakespeare* by Joseph Sobran (1997)]   Oxfordian, vol. 2: 152-154
    1999, April   The Lie With Circumstance [repr. in LC, p. 57-78]   Harper's Mag., v. 298: 41-43
    1999, Fall   [excerpts from reviews of *William Shakespeare* by A. Holden]   Sh. Ox. Newsl., vol. 35/3: 18-19
    1999, Fall   Shakespeare and Religion: Conference Panel Highlights Sticking   Sh. Ox. Newsl., vol. 35/3: 8-9
        Points for Scholars [with Roger Stritmatter & William E. Boyle]
    1999, Fall   Shakespeare's Religion   Sh. Ox. Newsl., vol. 35/3: 9
    2000   [review of *Shakespeare and the Christian Tradition* edited by   Oxfordian, vol. 3: 116-18
        E. Beatrice Batson (1994)]
    2000, Spring   Vere-y Interesting: Shakespeare's Treatment of the Earls of Oxford   Sh. Ox. Newsl., v. 36/1: 1, 14-21
        in the History Plays [repr. in BTC, vol. 9: 1-22]
        See also letter by Ramon Jimenez, vol. 36/3: 21 (2000).
    2000, Spring   Preface to his Examination of Roger Stritmatter [Doctoral Diss.   Sh. Ox. Newsl., vol. 36/1: 8
        Committee, University of Mass., Amherst, April 21, 2000]

Wyatt, Neal
2000, Nov. 15   [review of *Shakespeare's Unorthodox Biography* by Diana Price]   Library Jour., vol. 125/19: 68

Wyneken, Warren W.
1991, Spring   [letter: praise for the Newsletter and for Charlton Ogburn, Jr.'s book]   Sh. Ox. Newsl., vol. 27/2: 8
1991, May   Rules of Evidence [letter]   Spear-shaker Rev., issue 3/4: 18

X.Y.Z.
1929, Sept. 12   A Modified View [letter]   Morning Post, p. 9

Yabush, Donald R.
1973, April 29   [letter: Byron Rogers' 1 April article]   Chicago Tribune, p. I6

Yewlett, Hilary Lloyd
2000, Spring   *Macbeth* and Its Celtic Connections   Elizabethan Rev., online ed.

York, Michael
1996, Fall   [letter: regrets not being able to attend Conference]   Sh. Ox. Newsl., vol. 32/4: 18
2003, Summer   Michael York on *Shrew*   Sh. Matters, vol. 2/4: 35-36

Young, John
1977, May 25   Is There a New Bard in the House? [Edward de Vere is doubters'   Times (London), p. 17
    "least far-fetched candidate"]

Young, Louise
2004?   [A Play about Oxford; title not known.]

Yuhas, David
2004   *The Shakespeare-Cervantes Code*. Boulder: Columbine Paperbacks.

Zacharias, Margaret
2007, Winter   [letter: the SF/SON Annual Conference]   Sh. Matters, vol. 6/2: 2

Zacharias, Peter
2006, Winter   Oxford's Years at Cecil House [the creation of a divided mind]   Sh. Matters, vol. 5/2: 1, 15+
2007, Winter   A Boar Among the Flowers: A closer look at *Adventures Passed*   Sh. Matters, vol. 6/2: 7-12
    by F. I.

Zachrisson, Anders
2011   Who Wrote the Works of Shakespeare? Notes on a Matter of   Scandinavian Psychoanalytic
    Curiosity in Freud's Intellectual Biography   Review, v. 34/2: 134-38
    Response by R. Waugaman and R. Stritmatter, vol. 34: 120-22.

Zakarison, Leda
2012, Summer   O-philia   Sh. Matters, vol. 11/3: 1, 26+

Zakelj, Ann
2013, Fall   On the Trail of Edward de Vere: June 18-28, 2013   Sh. Matters, vol. 12/4: 1, 21+
2016, Spring   Shakespeare in Italy 2016: The Tour [with Alex McNeil]   Sh. Ox. Newsl., v. 52/3: 1, 19-27

Zijl, Piet-Hein
2020, Oct.   How I Became a Member of the DVS   De Vere S. New., v. 27/4: 28-30

Zenith, Richard
2014, Spr./Sum   [letter: Waugaman's message on Pessoa and Shakespeare]   Sh. Matters, vol. 9: 2
    Response by Waugaman, same issue, page.

Zwick, Jochen
1999, July   Hamlet als Wittenberger Student – That is the Questio   Neues Sh. Journal, vol. 4: 150-52
    [repr. from FAZ (Sept. 1998)]

* * * * *

IB. INDEX OF REVIEWS OF BOOKS OF SPECIAL INTEREST

Ackroyd, Peter – *Shakespeare, the Biography* **(2005)**

Charlton, Derran K.	Shakespeare Oxford Newsletter	vol. 41/4: 24, 32	2005, Fall
Malim, Richard C. W.	De Vere Society Newsletter	p. 18-19	2005, Dec.
Schneider, Wolfgang	Neues Shake-speare Journal	vol. 12: 137-39	2008, Oct.

A'Dair, Mike – *The Ashbourne Saga: A Cinematic Epic in Fourteen Episodes* **(2017)**

Whittemore, Hank	Shakespeare Oxford Newsletter	vol. 53/3: 19-23	2017, Summer

A'Dair, Mike – *Four Essays on the Shakespeare Question* **(2012)**

Egan, Michael (editor)	Shakespeare Oxford Newsletter	vol. 49/2: 21-23	2013, Spring

Aitken, T. M. & H. S. Lawrence – *The Inspiration of Shakespeare* **(1948)**

--	Truth	p. 312	1948, Sept. 24

Akrigg, G. P. V. – *Shakespeare and the Earl of Southampton* **(1968)**

Vessey, David W. T.	Shakespearean Authorship Review	no. 23: 12-15	1970, Summer
	[repr. in BTC, vol. 5: 300-303]		

Alexander, Doris – *Creating Literature Out of Life* **(1996)**

Whalen, Richard F.	Shakespeare Oxford Newsletter	vol. 34/2: 19	1998, Summer

Alexander, Peter – *Shakespeare* **(1964)**

Bowen, Gwynneth M.	Shakespearean Authorship Review	issue #13: 12-17	1965, Spring

Allen, Ernest – *When Shakespeare Died* **(pamphlet) (1937)**

--	Shakespeare Fellowship Newsletter (Eng.)	no. 5: 5-8	1937, Sept.
Ward, Bernard M.	East Anglian Magazine	vol. 3, no. 1	1937, Oct.
	[repr. in BTC, vol. 2: 40-41]		

Allen, Percy – *Anne Cecil, Elizabeth and Oxford* **(1934)**

--	Aberdeen Press and Journal	p. 6	1934, April 3
Bowen, Marjorie	Shakespeare Pictorial	no. 73: 48	1934, March
F. B.	Christian Science Monitor	p. WM11	1934, June 13
Tomlinson, Philip	Times Literary Supplement	p. 321	1934, May 3
	Response by Percy Allen, 10 May 1934, issue 1684: 342		

Allen, Percy – *The Case For Edward de Vere, 17ᵗʰ Earl of Oxford, as "William Shakespeare"* **[pamphlet] (1930)**

--	Dundee Courier and Advertiser	p. 9	1930, April 2
--	Stage, The	p. 6	1930, Feb. 27
--	Times Literary Supplement	issue 1464: 146	1930, Feb. 20
Feste	Eastbourne Gazette	p. 27	1930, March 12
	Response by Percy Allen and reply by reviewer, April 2, p. 25.		
	Reply by editor to Percy Allen, April 30, p. 20.		

Allen, Percy – *The Case For Edward de Vere, 17ᵗʰ Earl of Oxford, as "Shakespeare"* **(1930)**

--	Bath Chronicle and Weekly Gazette		1930, Nov. 15
--	Belfast News-Letter	p. 10	1930, May 3
--	Christian Science Monitor	p. 6	1930, July 19
--	Dundee Courier and Advertiser		1930, May 8
--	Nation and Athenaeum		1930
--	Saturday Review (London)	vol. 149: 592	1930, May 10
	Response by Percy Allen, May 17, vol. 149: 619.		
	Reply by reviewer, May 24, vol. 149: 654-55.		
--	Scotsman, The	p. 2	1930, April 10
--	Shakespeare Pictorial	no. 25: 13	1930, March
--	Shakespeare Pictorial	no. 27: 8	1930, May
--	Sunday Times (London)	p. 10	1930, May 4
--	Times of India	p. 25	1931, Feb. 25
A. P. W.	Manchester Guardian	p. 7	1930, May 5
Boas, F. S.	Listener	vol. 23: 1041	1930, June 11
Bowen, Marjorie	Shakespeare Pictorial	no. 51: 82-83	1932, May

Allen, Percy – *The Case for Edward de Vere as "Shakespeare"* **(continued)**

Byrne, Muriel C.	Times Literary Supplement	issue 1493: 712	1930, Sept. 11

Response by Allen, Sept. 18, issue 1494: 735.
Response by Gerard Rendall, Sept. 25, issue 1495: 757-58.

Connes, Georges	Revue Anglo-Americaine	vol. 10/2: 235	1932, Dec.
Gwynn, Stephan	Observer, The	p. 7	1930, May 11
Knight, G. Wilson	Nation & Athenaeum	vol. 46/4: 150	1930, May 3
Medicus	Saturday Review (London)	vol. 149: 688	1930, May 31
Rathburn, Stephen	New York Sun		1930, Feb. 17
Ward, Colonel B. R.	Shakespeare Pictorial	no. 31: 16	1930, Sept.
Wright, B. D.	Western Morning News	p. 6	1930, Sept. 5

Allen, Percy – *Collected Writings on Shakespeare, vol. 5: The Plays of Shakespeare and Chapman in Relation to French History,* **edited by James A. Warren (2022)**

Goff, Tom	Shakespeare Oxford Newsletter	vol. 59/1: 19-20	2023, Winter
Rubin, Don	Oxfordian	vol. 25: 305-10	2023, Sept.

Allen, Percy and Captain Bernard M. Ward – *An Enquiry Into the Relations Between Lord Oxford as 'Shakespeare,' Queen Elizabeth, and the Fair Youth of Shakespeare's Sonnets* **(pamphlet) (1936)**

Aitken, T. M.	Shakespeare Fellowship Newsletter (Eng)	vol. 14, Sup. p. 5-9	1939, April
Rendall, Canon Gerald	Shakespeare Fellowship Newsletter (Eng)	vol. 14, Sup. p. 1-5	1939, April

Response by Percy Allen, same pub., p. 9-20.
Response by Bernard M. Ward, same pub., p. 20-24.
T. M. Aitken's reply to Allen's and Ward's responses, Sup. 2, p. 1-4.

Allen, Percy – *The Life Story of Edward de Vere as "William Shakespeare"* **(1932)**

--	Edinburgh Evening News	p. 8	1932, May 17
--	Saturday Review (London)	no. 152: 569	1932, June 4

Response by Percy Allen, June 11, vol. 153: 591.

Bowen, Marjorie	Shakespeare Pictorial	no. 51: 82-83	1932, May
Clutton-Brock, Arthur	Times Literary Supplement	issue 1586: 462	1932, June 23

Response by Percy Allen, June 30, p. 480.

Douglas, Lt. Col. M. W.	Shakespeare Pictorial	no. 49: 48	1932, March
Rendall, Gerald H.	Everyman		1932, Aug. 25

Allen, Percy and Ernest – *Lord Oxford and Shakespeare: A Reply to John Drinkwater* **(1933)**

--	Birmingham Daily Gazette	p. 8	1933, May 25
I. B.	Manchester Guardian	p. 5	1933, May 17
--	Observer, The	p. 5	1933, July 9
H. H. [Hubert H. Holland]	Christian Science Monitor	p. 10	1933, June 17

Allen, Percy – *The Oxford-Shakespeare Case Corroborated* **(1931)**

--	Aberdeen Press and Journal	p. 2	1931, March 19
--	Belfast News-Letter	p. 14	1931, March 19
--	Dundee Courier	p. 10	1931, March 13
--	Notes and Queries	vol. 160/10: 180	1931, March 7

Response by Percy Allen, March 28, vol. 160/13: 230-31.
Reply to Allen by Edward Bensley, April 18, vol. 160/16: 283.

--	Scotsman, The	p. 2	1931, June 8
--	Scotsman, The	p. 2	1932, May 12
--	Times Literary Supplement	p. 30	1932, Jan. 14
--	Western Morning News	p. 6	1931, March 26
C. F. A.	Christian Science Monitor	p. 12	1931, April 25

Response by Percy Allen, June 5, p. 20.

Ward, Colonel B. R.	Shakespeare Pictorial	no. 37: 48	1931, March
Willoughby, D.	Saturday Review (London)	vol. 151: 652-53	1931, May 2

Response by Percy Allen, May 9, vol. 151: 682.

Allen, Percy – *The Plays of Shakespeare and Chapman in Relation to French History* **(1933)**

--	Aberdeen Press and Journal	p. 2	1933, July 18
--	Christian Science Monitor	p. 8	1933, Aug. 19
--	Gloucestershire Echo	p. 4	1933, Oct. 13
--	Observer, The	p. 5	1933, July 9

Child, Harold H.	Times Literary Supplement	p. 522	1933, Aug. 3
	Response by Percy Allen, Aug. 10, p. 537.		
Douglas, Montagu W.	Shakespeare Pictorial	no. 67: 144	1933, Sept.

Allen, Percy – *Shakespeare and Chapman as Topical Dramatists* (1929)

--	Belfast News-Letter	p. 10	1929, May 25
--	Bookman, The	vol. 76: 118	1929, May
--	Era	p. 10	1929, March 20
--	Christian Science Monitor	p. 17	1929, May 14
--	Life and Letters	p. 401	1929, May
--	Scotsman, The	p. 2	1929, Feb. 25
--	Stage, The	p. 17	1929, May 23
	Response by Percy Allen, May 30, p. 15.		
--	Western Morning News	p. 3	1929, March 25
Brown, Ivor	Saturday Review	vol. 147: 251-52	1929, Feb. 23
	Response by Percy Allen, March 2, vol. 147: 281.		
	Reply by Ivor Brown, March 2, vol. 147: 281.		
Byrne, Muriel St. Clare	Times Literary Supplement	issue 1416: 229	1929, March 21
	Response by Percy Allen, March 28, p. 260.		
	Additional response by Percy Allen, April 4, p. 276.		
Delatte, F.	Revue Belge de Philologie et d'Historie	vol. 8/4: 1255-57	1929, Jan.
Harrison, G. B.	Review of English Studies	vol. 6/21: 98-100	1930, Jan.
	Response by Allen, April, vol. 6/21: 196-98.		
	Reply by Harrison, April, vol. 6/22: 196-98.		
Harrison, G. B.	London Mercury	vol. XX/118	1929, Aug.
	Response by Percy Allen, Sept. 1929		
Keller, Wolfgang	Jahrbuch der Deutschen Sh.-Gensellschaft	p. 220+	1930
Newdigate, B. H.	Shakespeare Pictorial	no. 13: 8	1929, March
Pruvost, Rene	Revue Anglo-Américaine	vol. 8/2: 149-50	1930, Dec.
Ward, Colonel B. R.	Shakespeare Pictorial	no. 15: 24	1929, May

Allen, Percy – *Shakespeare, Jonson, and Wilkins as Borrowers* (1928)

--	Belfast News-Letter	p. 14	1928, May 10
--	Illustrated London News	p. 20-21	1928, April 14
--	Leeds Mercury	p. 4	1928, April 13
--	Manchester Guardian	p. 7	1928, March 20
	Response by Percy Allen, April 4, p. 5.		
--	Nation & Athenaeum	vol. 43: 50-51	1928, April 14
--	New Statesman	p. 236	1928, May 26
--	Notes and Queries	vol. 154: 215-16	1928, March 24
Brown, Ivor	Saturday Review (London)		1928, March 24
	Response by Percy Allen, March 31.		
	Reply by Ivor Brown, April 7.		
	Response by Percy Allen, April 14.		
C. F. A.	Christian Science Monitor	p. 10	1928, Aiug. 23
Danchin, F. C.	Revue Anglo-Américaine	vol. 6/4: 360-61	1929, Apr.
Delatte, F.	Revue Belge de Philolgie et d'Historie	vol. 7/3: 1099-00	1928, Oct.
Eliot, T. S.	Times Literary Supplement	issue 1366: 255	1928, April 5
Freeman, John	London Mercury	vol. 18: 657-58	1928, Oct.
Harrison, G. B.	Review of English Studies	vol. 6/21: 98-100	1930, Jan.
	Response by Percy Allen, April, vol. 6/22: 196-98.		
	Reply by G. B. Harrison, April, vol. 6/22: 196-98.		
Jaggard, Geoffrey W.	Shakespeare Review (Seoul)	vol. 1/1: 49-52	1928, May
Keller, Wolfgang	Jahrbuch der Deutschen Sh.-Gensellschaft	p. 223	1930
Sampson, George	Bookman, The	p. 113-15	1928, May

Allen, Ron – *Who Were Shakespeare* (1998)

Boyle, Charles	Shakespeare Oxford Newsletter	vol. 34/3: 22	1998, Fall
	Response by Ron Allen, Winter 1999, vol. 35/1: 22.		

Altrocchi, Paul H. and Hank Whittemore – *Building the Case: The Great Shakespeare Hoax* (2009)

Jiménez, Ramon	Shakespeare Oxford Newsletter	vol. 48/1: 15-17	2012, Winter

Altrocchi, Paul H. – *Malice Aforethought* **(2010)**

Gill, John	De Vere Society Newsletter	vol. 18/1: 30-32	2011, March
Livacari, Gary L.	The Oxfordian	vol. 12: 4-5	2010

Altrocchi, Paul H. – *Most Greatly Lived* **(2000)**

Harman, Charles E.	Shakespeare Oxford Newsletter	vol. 37/2: 19	2001, Summer
Whalen, Richard F.	Shakespeare Oxford Newsletter	vol. 37/1: 18	2001, Spring

American Bar Association Journal – *Shakespeare Cross-Examination* **(1961)**

--	Shakespeare Oxford Newsletter	vol. 12/4: 2	1976, Winter
Humphreys, Christmas	Shakespearean Authorship Review	issue #8: 17-19	1962, Autumn

Amphlett, Hilda – *Who Was Shakespeare?* **(1955)**

--	Shakespeare Fellowship Newsletter (Eng)	p. 11	1955, Spring
--	Yorkshire Post and Leeds Intelligencer	p. 4	1955, July 25
Atkinson, J. Shera	Shakespeare Fellowship Newsletter (Eng)	p. 11	1956, Spring
Browning, Olive H.	Shakespeare Fellowship Newsletter (Eng)	p. 10-11	1955, Spring
Deacon, William	Globe and Mail	p. 28	1956, Jan. 14
Fane, Vernon	Sphere, The	p. 38	1955, May 28
Mez, John R.	Shakespeare Fellowship Newsletter (Eng)	p. 11-12	1955, Autumn
Stewart, J. I. M.	New Statesman and Nation	p. 50	1955, Aug. 27
Wainewright, Ruth M. D.	Shakespearean Authorship Review	issue #24: 13-14	1971, Spring

Anderson, Mark K. – *"Shakespeare" by Another Name* **(2005)**

--	Kirkus Reviews	vol. 73/10: 569	2005, May 15
--	Publishers Weekly	p. 71	2005, June 20
Boyle, William E.	Shakespeare Matters	vol. 4/4: 33	2005, Summer
Cutting, Bonner Miller	Shakespeare Matters	vol. 5/1: 2	2005, Fall
Delahoyde, Michael	Rocky Mountain E-Review of Lang. & Lit.	vol. 60/2: 52-59	2006
DiMatteo, Anthony	Choice	vol. 43/4: 565	2005, Dec.
Goldstein, Gary B.	The Oxfordian	vol. 8:124-128	2005
Gollob, Herman	Minneapolis Star Tribune	p. 12F	2005, Aug. 25
Gontar, David P.	Shakespeare Matters	vol. 5/3: 2-3	2006, Spring

Reply by Mark Anderson, same issue, p. 3.

Hughes, Stephanie H.	Shakespeare Oxford Newsletter	vol. 41/3: 2, 12+	2005, Summer

See correction in vol. 41/4: 32.

Imlay, Elizabeth	De Vere Society Newsletter	p. 24-26	2006, April
Lerner, Maura	Minneapolis Star Tribune	p. 1F	2005, Sept. 4
Nelson, Alan H.	Times Literary Supplement	issue 5365: 30	2006, Jan. 27
Niederkorn, William S.	New York Times		2005, Aug. 30

Response by Steven Greenblatt, Sept. 5, p. C9.
Response by Ron Rosenbaum, *NY Observer*, Sept. 19, p. 1.
Reply by Mark Anderson to Ron Rosenbaum, *NY Observer*, Sept. 26, p. 4.

Propson, David	The New Criterion	vol. 24/6: 23-27	2006, Feb.
Riley, John	Against the Grain (interview w/Anderson)	vol. 4: 48-51	2005
Sterling, Carleton	Shakespeare Oxford Newsletter	vol. 42/1: 20-22	2006

Response by Mark Anderson, same issue and page number.

Swift, Daniel	The Nation	vol. 13: 23-26	2006, March 13
Walsch, Felicity D.	Library Journal	vol. 130/12: 79	2005
Waugaman, Richard M.	Psychoanalytic Quarterly	vol. 76: 1,397-403	2007
Waugaman, Richard M.	Shakespeare Matters	vol. 7/3: 7, 15+	2008, Spring
Whalen, Richard F.	Shakespeare Matters	vol. 6/2: 29-30	2006

Anderson (Paget), Verily – *The De Veres of Castle Hedingham* **(1993)**

Caunt, George	Essex Countryside Magazine	p. 326-7, 378-9+	1963, Jun/Jul/Ag.

Comments by Ruth Wainewright in SAR, issue 10: 16 (Autumn 1963).

Dalton, Terence	Shakespeare Oxford Newsletter	vol. 30/1: 21	1994, Winter

Appleton, Elizabeth – *An Anatomy of the Marprelate Controversy 1588-1596* **(2001)**

Stritmatter, Roger	Shakespeare Matters	vol. 1/3: 25-27+	2002, Spring

Appleton, Elizabeth – *Edward de Vere and the War of Words* **(1985)**

Dutton, Richard	Shakespeare Survey	vol. 39: 223-36	1987
Marder, Louis	Shakespeare Newsletter	vol. 35/2: 22, 36	1985, Summer

Marder, Louis	Shakespeare Newsletter	vol. 36/3: 40	1986, Fall

Arnauld, Andreas von & Christian Klein – *Weil Bücher unsere Welt verdändern* (2019)

Laugwitz, Uwe	Neue Shakespeare Journal	vol. NS7: 141-45	2020

Asquith, Clare – *Shadowplay: The Hidden Beliefs and Coded Politics of William Shakespeare* (2005)

Dickson, Peter W.	The Oxfordian	vol. 8: 128-136	2005
Malim, Richard C. W.	De Vere Society Newsletter	p. 28-29	2006, Nov.

Asquith, Clare – *Shakespeare and the Resistance* (2018)

Herbert Tony	De Vere Society Newsletter	vol. 27/2: 48-49	2020, April

Babik, Peter E. S. – *Shakespeare Films: A Re-evaluation of 100 Years of Adaptations* (2018)

Boyle, William	The Oxfordian	vol. 20: 183-190	2018, Sept.

Bacon, Delia – *The Philosophy of the Plays of Shakespeare Unfolded* (1857)

--	National Review (London)	vol. 5/9: 72-82	1857, July

Baker, H. Kendra – *Elizabeth and Sixtus* (1938)

Allen, Percy	Shakespeare Fellowship Newsletter (Eng.)	no. 11: 8-9	1938, Sept.

Baker, John Milnes – The Case for Edward de Vere as the Real William Shakespeare (2019)

Crampin, Alice	De Vere Society Newsletter	vol. 27/2: 46-47	2020, April

Baker, Norman – *William Shakespeare's Conspiracy* (a play) (1961)

Wainewright, Ruth M. D.	Shakespearean Authorship Review	issue #6: 20	1961, Autumn

Barber, Ros – *The Marlowe Papers* (dissertation, written in blank verse about Shakespeare and Marlowe) (2012)

Collins, Robert	Sunday Times (London)	p. 12	2013, June 30
	[repr. in DVN, vol. 20/2: 30 (July 2013)]		
Feay, Suzi	Financial Times	p. 18	2012, May 19
Kamm, Oliver	New York Times	p. 83	2012, May 19
Nicholl, Charles	New York Times Book Review	p. A15	2013, Jan. 27
Rigden, Kealey	Telegraph (London)		2013, June 27
Sutherland, John	Times, The (London)	p. 45	2012, May 19

Barbour, Reid – *Deciphering Elizabethan Fiction* (1993)

Hope, Warren	Elizabethan Review	vol. 2/2: 61-64	1994, Autumn

Baron, Dennis – *De Vere is Shakespeare: Evidence from the Biography and Wordplay* (1997)

Baron, Dennis	De Vere Society Newsletter	vol. 2/9: 10-11	1997, June
Llewellyn, Michael	De Vere Society Newsletter	vol. 2/8: 12-13	1997, Feb.
Morton, Peter	Elizabethan Review	vol. 6/2: 84-87	1998, Autumn

Bate, Jonathan – *The Genius of Shakespeare* (1998)

Wasserman, Jerry	Vancouver Sun	p. C11	1998, March 7
Whalen, Richard F.	Shakespeare Oxford Newsletter	vol. 34/3: 23, 28	1998, Fall

Bate, Jonathan – *How the Classics Made Shakespeare* (????)

Showerman, Earl	The Oxfordian	vol. 21: 243-48	2019, Sept.

Bate, Jonathan – *Soul of the Age* (2009)

Malim, Richard C. W.	De Vere Society Newsletter	vol. 16/1: 24-26	2009, Feb.
Whalen, Richard F.	Shakespeare Oxford Newsletter	vol. 45/2: 28-29	2009, Sept.
Whalen, Richard F.	Shakespeare Oxford Newsletter	vol. 45/3: 25-26	2009, Dec.

Bate, Jonathan and Eric Rasmussen – *The RSC Shakespeare: Complete Works* (2007)

Whalen, Richard F.	Shakespeare Oxford Newsletter	vol. 43/3: 14, 24	2007, Summer

Bate, Jonathan and Eric Rasmussen (editors) – *William Shakespeare & Others: Collaborative Plays* (2013)

Jiménez, Ramon	Shakespeare Oxford Newsletter	vol. 50/4: 13-15	2014, Fall

Bates, Laura – *Shakespeare Saved My Life—Ten Years in Solitary with the Bard* (2013)

Campbell, Harry	Shakespeare Oxford Newsletter	vol. 57/2: 23-26	2021, Spring

Bateson, F. W. (editor) – *The Cambridge Bibliography of English Literature* (1940)

Douglas, Montagu W.	Shakespeare Fellowship Newsletter (Am)	vol. 1/2: 8	1940, Feb.

Batson, E. Beatrice – *Shakespeare and the Christian Tradition* (1994)

Wright, Daniel L.	The Oxfordian	vol. 3: 116-118	2000

Bearman, Robert – *Shakespeare's Money* (2016)

Waugaman, Richard	The Oxfordian	vol. 18: 183-86	2016

Beauclerk, Charles – *Shakespeare's Lost Kingdom* (2010)

Delahoyde, Michael	Brief Chronicles	vol. II: 237-244	2010
Gill, John	De Vere Society Newsletter	vol. 18/1: 32-34	2011, March
	[repr. in NSJ, vol. NS2: 32-40 (Oct. 2011)]		
Hodge, Megan	Library Journal	vol. 135/6: 75	2010, April
Imlay, Elizabeth	De Vere Society Newsletter	vol. 18/2: 25-28, 39	2011, July
McCarter, Jeremy	New York Times Review of Books	p. 10-11	2010, May 2
Niederkorn, William S.	Brooklyn Rail	p. 66	2011, October
Paul, Christopher	Brief Chronicles	vol. II: 244-257	2010, Fall
	[repr. in NSJ, vol. NS2: 13-31 (Oct. 2011)]		

Bénézet, Louis P. – *Shakspere, Shakespeare and de Vere* (1937)

Douglas, Col. Montagu W.	Shakespeare Fellowship Newsletter (Eng.)	no. 8: 6-8	1938, March
Uncle Dudley	Boston Globe	p. C4	1938, July 10

Bénézet, Louis P. – *The Six Loves of Shake-speare* (1958)

--	Shakespeare Newsletter	no. 48, vol. 9/2: 12	1959, April
Arnold, Frazer	American Bar Association Journal	vol. 45/7: 738-9	1959, July
Bowen, Gwynneth M.	Shakespearean Authorship Review	no. 2: 9-12	1959, Autumn
	[repr. in BTC, vol. 5: 31-35]		
Rogers, Hudson	English Journal	vol. 47/8: 527-28	1958, August

Benson, Jon – *The Death of Shakespeare: As it was Accomplisht in 1616 & the Causes Thereof (Part One)* (2016)

Goldstein, Gary	Shakespeare Oxford Newsletter	vol. 52/3: 28-29	2016, Summer

Bergman, Martin S. – *The Unconscious in Shakespeare's Plays* (2013)

Waugaman, Richard M.	Psychoanalytic Quarterly	vol. 83: 737-42	2014
Waugaman, Richard M.	Shakespeare Oxford Newsletter	vol. 52/2: 31-34	2016, Spring

Berleth, Richard – *The Twilight Lords: An Irish Chronicle* (1978)

Cheney, Alan	Elizabethan Review	vol. 3/1: 48-53	1995, Spring

Berney, C. V. – *Shakespeare Confidential* (2017)

St. Clair, Michael	Shakespeare Oxford Newsletter	vol. 54/3: 30	2018, Summer

Bevington, David M. – *The Complete Works of Shakespeare* (2008)

Whalen, Richard F.	Shakespeare Oxford Newsletter	vol. 29/2a: 4	1993, Spring

Bevington, David M. – *Shakespeare and Biography* (2010)

Lynch, Jack	Times Literary Supplement	issue 5633: 11	2011, March 18
McHenry, Robert	Biography (Honolulu)	vol. 34/2: 334	2011, Spring
Whalen, Richard F.	Shakespeare Oxford Newsletter	vol. 47/2: 9-11	2011, Spring

Black, Pauline and Michael – *Shakespeare Unraveled—Court Plays: The 1623 Deception* (2014)

Dickson, Peter W.	Shakespeare Oxford Newsletter	vol. 53/1: 20-23	2017, Winter

Blake, Darrol – *Nothing Truer Than Truth: The Life and Times of Edward de Vere, Sometimes Known as William Shakespeare* [A Play] (1977/2019)

--	Stage, The	p. 9	1977, June 10
--	Times [Notice for upcoming performance]	p. 14	1977, May 26
Jolly, Eddi	De Vere Society Newsletter	vol. 26/4: 33-34	2019, Oct.
Radford, Tim	Guardian, The (London)	p. 10	1977, June 2

Blanding, Michael – *North by Shakespeare: A Rogue Scholar's Quest for the Truth Behind the Bard's Work* (2021)

Hyde, Michael	Shakespeare Oxford Newsletter	vol. 57/2: 12-18	2021, Spring
Hyde, Michael	The Oxfordian	vol. 23: 353-363	2021, Sept.
McNeil, Alex	Shakespeare Oxford Newsletter	vol. 57/2: 19-20	2021, Spring
O'Brien, H. H. Patrick	De Vere Society Newsletter	vol. 28/3: 45-50	2021, July

Bloom, Harold – *The Anatomy of Influence: Literature as a Way of Life* (2011)

Niederkorn, William S.	Brooklyn Rail	p. 74	2011, July

Bloom, Harold – *Hamlet: Poem Unlimited* (2003)

Jiménez, Ramon	Shakespeare Oxford Newsletter	vol. 39/4: 22	2003, Autumn

Bloom, Harold – *Shakespeare: The Invention of the Human* (1999)

Gumbrecht, Hans Ulrich	Neues Shakespeare Journal	vol. 4: 158-66	1999, July
Malim, Richard C. W.	De Vere Society Newsletter	p. 31	2006, Nov.
Whalen, Richard F.	Shakespeare Oxford Newsletter	vol. 34/4: 18, 24	1999, Winter

Reviews of Books of Special Interest

Bloom, Harold – *The Western Canon: Books and Schools of the Ages* **(1994)**
Hope, Warren	Elizabethan Review	vol. 4/1: 47-48	1996, Spring

Blumenfeld, Samuel L. – *The Marlowe-Shakespeare Connection* **(2008)**
--	Shakespeare Matters	vol. 7/4: 16	2008, Fall

Blumenthal, Walter – *Paging Mr. Shakespeare* **(1961)**
Wainewright, Ruth M. D.	Shakespearean Authorship Review	issue #12: 13-14	1964, Autumn

Boas, Frederick S. (editor) – *Elizabethan and Other Essays* **(posthumous, compiled from Sidney Lee's papers) (1930)**
Harrison, G. B.	London Mercury	vol. 21: 185	1930, June

Boas, Frederich S. – *Marlowe and His Circle* **(1931)**
Ward, Colonel B. R.	Shakespeare Pictorial	no. 39: 80	1931, May

Bond, Jonathan – *The De Vere Code* **(2009)**
Malim, Richard C. W.	De Vere Society Newsletter	vol. 17/1: 29-30	2010, Feb.

Bowen, Gwynneth M. – *Shakespeare's Farewell* **(pamphlet) (1951)**
Mez, R. J.	Shakespeare Fellowship Newsletter (Eng)	p. 10	1952, March

Bowen, Marjorie – *Dickson* **(1929)**
--	Times Literary Supplement	issue 1438: 650	1929, Aug. 22
	Response by Bowen, Sept. 5.		

Boyce, Burke – *Cloak of Folly* **(1949)**
Atkinson, J. Shera	Shakespeare Fellowship Newsletter (Eng)	p. 8-9	1952, Sept.
Davis, Elrick B.	New York Herald Tribune	p. F4	1949, Oct. 9
Whiting, B. J.	Speculum	vol. 26/2: 364-66	1951, April

Boyle, Bill – *A Poet's Rage* **(2013)**
Ray, William	Shakespeare Oxford Fellowship Newsletter	vol. 50/1: 20-24+	2014, Winter

Bradebrook, M. C. – *The Rise of the Elizabethan Common Player* **(1962)**
Cutner, Herbert	Shakespearean Authorship Review	issue #10: 15-16	1963, Autumn

Brahms, C. and S. J. Simon – *No Bed for Bacon* **(1941)**
Whiting, B. J.	Speculum	vol. 26/2: 264-66	1951, April

Brame, Michael and Galina Popova (eds.) – *Shakespeare's Fingerprints* **(2002)**
--	Reference and Research Book News	vol. 18/2	2003, May
--	Shakespeare Matters	vol. 2/2: 31	2003, Winter
Fair, Shana, C.	Library Journal	vol. 128/9: 88	2003
Stritmatter, Roger	Shakespeare Matters	vol. 2/3: 24-25+	2003, Spring
Whalen, Richard F.	Shakespeare Oxford Newsletter	vol. 40/1: 23-24	2004, Winter

Brewster, Eleanor – *Oxford and His Elizabethan Ladies* **(1972)**
Horne, Jr., Richard C.	Shakespeare Oxford Newsletter	vol. 9/1: 14	1973, Winter

Brewster, Eleanor – *Oxford: Courtier to the Queen* **(1964)**
Wainewright, Ruth M. D.	Shakespearean Authorship Review	no. 14: 11-12	1965, Autumn
	[repr. in BTC, vol. 5: 173]		

Bridgers, Sue Ellen – *Keeping Christina* **(1993)**
Whalen, Richard F.	Shakespeare Oxford Newsletter	vol. 36/3: 19, 24	2000, Fall

Briton, Dennis and Melissa Walter (editors) – *Rethinking Shakespeare Source Study* **(2017)**
Waugaman, Richard M.	Renaissance Quarterly		2017

Brizuela, Leopoldo – *Inglaterra* **(2004)**
Klier, Walter	Neues Shake-speare Journal	vol. 9: 181-82	2004, June

Brook, Peter – *The Quality of Mercy* **(2014)**
Heilpern, John	Washington Post	p. C14	2013, Oct. 5

Brooks, Alden – *Will Shakspere and the Dyer's Hand* **(1943)**
--	Los Angeles Times	p. C4	1943, Feb. 7
Barrell, Charles Wisner	Shakespeare Fellowship Newsletter (Am)	vol. 4/5: 59-66	1943, Aug.

Brown, Carolyn (editor) – *Shakespeare and Psychoanalytic Theory* **(2015)**
Waugaman, Richard M.	Psychoanalytic Quarterly		2017
Waugaman, Richard M.	The Oxfordian	vol. 19: 223-30	2017, Oct.

Brown, Ivor – *How Shakespeare Spent the Day* **(1963)**
Cutner, Herbert	Shakespearean Authorship Review	issue #11: 12-13	1964, Spring

Browning, Keith – *Shakespeare Re-Invented: Challenging 400 Years of Shakespeare Fantasy!!* **(2016)**
Hess, W. Ron	Shakespeare Oxford Newsletter	vol. 52/2: 29-30	2016, Spring

Bryson, Bill – *Shakespeare: The World As Stage* **(2007)**
Anderson, Mark K.	Shakespeare Matters	vol. 7/2: 4	2008, Winter
Baker, Simon	Spectator, The	p. 200	2007, Sept.
Whalen, Richard F.	Shakespeare Matters	vol. 7/2: 3, 20	2008, Winter

Burke, Kenneth – *Kenneth Burke on Shakespeare* **(edited by Scott L. Newstock) (2007)**
Stritmatter, Roger	Shakespeare Matters	vol. 7/4: 3, 9, 12	2008, Fall

Burrow, Colin – *Shakespeare and Classical Antiquity*) **(2013)**
Showerman, Earl	Shakespeare Oxford Newsletter	vol. 51/4: 10-12	2015, Fall

Burton, Philip – *You, My Brother* **(1973)**
Ogburn, Charlton, Jr.	Washington Post	p. B10	1973, Oct. 19

Cairncross, A. S. – *The Problem of Hamlet – A Solution* **(1936)**
--	Times Literary Supplement	issue 1820: 1053	1936, Dec. 19
	Response by Percy Allen, Jan. 2, 1937.		
Allen, Percy	Shakespeare Pictorial	no. 104: 164	1936, Oct.

Cambridge University Press – *Shakespeare Survey* **(1948)**
Eggar, Katharine E.	Shakespeare Fellowship Newsletter (Eng)	p. 10	1956, Autumn

Carrell, Jennifer Lee – *Interred With Their Bones* **(2007)**
--	Shakespeare Matters	vol. 7/1: 5	2007, Fall
--	Shakespeare Newsletter	vol. 57/3: 101	2007, Winter

Carrell, Jennifer Lee – *The Shakespeare Secret* **(2008)**
Jolly, Eddi	De Vere Society Newsletter	vol. 15/1: 30	2008, March

Carroll, D. Allen (ed.) – *Greene's Groatsworth of Wit* **(1994)**
Chandler, David	Elizabethan Review	vol. 3/1: 62-67	1995, Spring

Caruana, Stephanie and Elisabeth Sears – *Oxford's Revenge: "Shakespeare's" Dramatic Development from Agamemnon to Hamlet* **(1989)**
Goff, Tom	Shakespeare Oxford Newsletter	vol. 26/3a: 3-5	1990, Summer
Hanson, David J.	The Shakespeare Newsletter	vol. 40/2: 24-25	1990, Summer

Challinor, Arthur M. – *The Alternative Shakespeare: A Modern Introduction* **(1996)**
Dams, Christopher H.	De Vere Society Newsletter	vol. 2/5: 2-4	1996, April
Michell, John	Baconiana	vol. 77/194: 102-03	1995

Chambers, Sir Edmund – *William Shakespeare: a Study of Facts and Problems* **(1930)**
Ward, Colonel B. R.	Shakespeare Pictorial	no. 35: 16	1931, January

Chaunes – *Le Vrai Shakespeare* **(2018)**
Rubin, Don	The Oxfordian	vol. 22: 165-179	2020, Sept.

Chiljan, Katherine – *Shakespeare Suppressed* **(2011)**
Egan, Michael	Shakespeare Oxford Newsletter	vol. 48/1: 13-14	2012, Winter
Gilvary, Kevin	De Vere Society Newsletter	vol. 21/3: 23	2014, Oct.
Levandoski, John	Shakespeare Matters	vol. 11/2: 20, 28-29	2012, Spring
Ray, William J.	Brief Chronicles	vol. III: 235-245	2011, Fall
Roper, David L.	Journal of Scientific Exploration	vol. 26/3: 679-84	2012, Fall

Chrisp, Peter – *Shakespeare: Der dichter und seine Zeit* **(2002)**
Laugwitz, Uwe	Neues Shake-speare Journal	vol. 9: 182-83	2004, June

Christofides, R. M. – *Shakespeare and the Apocalypse* **(2013)**
Waugaman, Richard M.	Renaissance Quarterly	vol. 66/3: 1134-35	2013

Churchill, R. C. – *Shakespeare and His Betters* **(1958)**
Kent, William	Shakespeare Fellowship Newsletter (Eng)	p. 9-10	1958, Autumn
Maxwell, Baldwin	Shakespeare Quarterly	vol. 10/3: 435-37	1959, Summer
McManaway, James G.	New York Times	p. BR4	1959, March 15
Reeves, James	Observer	p. 12	1958, Aug. 24

Reviews of Books of Special Interest

Chute, Marchette – ***Ben Jonson of Westminster*** **(1954)**

Cutner, Herbert	Shakespeare Fellowship Newsletter (Eng)	p. 10	1955, Autumn

Clark, Eva Turner – ***Axiophilus, or Oxord Wrote Shakespeare*** **(1926)**

--	New York Herald Tribune	p. F23	1927, May 22

Clark, Eva Turner – ***Hidden Allusions in Shakespeare's Plays*** **(1931) [See also *Shakespeare's Plays in the Order of Their Writing*, the title when first released in England in 1930 and of the third edition in 1975]**

--	Boston Globe	p. 17	1931, Feb. 7
--	Chicago Daily Tribune	p. 14	1931, March 4
--	Evening Union [Springfield, MA]		1931,
--	Monthly Bulletin of the Carnegie Library	p. 51	1931, June
--	News and Observer (Raleigh)	p. 2	1931, March 29
--	News Leader [richmond, VA]		1931,
--	Philadelphia Public Ledger		1931,
--	Springfield Republican	p. 7E	1931, April 12
--	Times Literary Supplement	issue 1530: 440	1931, May 28
Allen, Percy	Christian Science Monitor	p. 6	1931, Feb. 28
Brooke, Tucker	Yale Review	vol. 21: 215	1931, Autumn
Chew, Samuel C.	New York Herald Tribune	p. J12	1931, March 15
Coblante, Stanton A.	New York Times	p. 17	1931, May 31
Williams, Sidney	Philadelphia Enquirer	p. 14	1931, April 25

Clark, Eva Turner – ***Hidden Allusions in Shakespeare's Plays*** **(3rd revised ed., edited by *Ruth Loyd Miller*) (1975)**

--	Evening News [Springfield, MA]	--	1931
--	News Leader (Richmond, VA)	--	1931
Cyr, Gordon C.	Shakespeare Oxford Newsletter	vol. 12/3: 10-11	1976, Fall
Goff, Tom	Shakespeare Oxford Newsletter	vol. 28/1: 10-11	1992, Winter

Clark, Eva Turner – ***The Man Who Was Shakespeare*** **(1937)**

--	New York Herald Tribune	p. G11	1938, Feb. 13
Barrell, Charles Wisner	Shakespeare Fellowship Newsletter (Am)	vol. 1/1: 8	1939, Dec.
Barrell, Charles Wisner	New York Sun		1937, Dec. 11
Barrell, Charles Wisner	East Anglian Magazine	vol. 3/5: 236-37	1938, Feb.
	[repr. from The Sun York Sun, Dec. 11, 1937]		
	[repr. in BTC, vol. 2: 14-16]		
Brooke, Tucker	Journal of English and Germanic Philology	vol. 37/2: 311-12	1938, April
Spencer, Benjamin T.	Sewanee Review	vol. 47/1: 294	1939, Jan.-Mar.
Waldron, John	Washington Post	p. 13	1937, Dec. 10
Ward, Bernard M.	Shakespeare Fellowship Newsletter (Eng.)	vol. 7: 1-3	1938, Jan.
Withington, R.	MLN: Modern Language Notes	vol. 53/8: 621	1938, Dec.

Clark, Eva Turner – ***The Satirical Comedy, Love's Labour's Lost*** **(1933)**

--	New York Herald Tribune	p. H16	1933, May
--	New York Times	p. BR15	1933, May 28
Allen, Percy	Christian Science Monitor	p. 10	1933, April 22
Allen, Percy	Shakespeare Pictorial	no. 71: 16	1934, Jan.
G.A.S.	Cincinnati Enquirer	p. 10	1933, May 6

Clark, Eva Turner – ***Shakespeare's Plays in the Order of Their Writing*** **(1930) [See Also *Hidden Allusions*, the title of the American edition of Clark's book]**

--	Northern Whig and Belfast Times	p. 11	1931, Feb. 7
--	Scotsman, The	p. 2	1931, March 9
--	Times Literary Supplement	issue 1530: 440	1931, May 28
Alexander, Peter	Review of English Studies	vol. 8/29: 102	1932, Jan.
Chevalley, Abel	Mercure de France [in French]	vol. 233: 444-46	1931
Connes, Georges	Revue Anglo-Américaine [in French]	vol. 8/5: 439-40	1931, June
Kingsmill, Hugh	Yorkshire Post and Leeds Intelligencer	p. 6	1931, Feb. 10
Ward, Colonel B. R.	Shakespeare Pictorial	no. 36: 32	1931, February
Willoughby, D.	Saturday Review (London)	vol. 151: 652-53	1931, May 2
	Response by Percy Allen, May 9, vol. 151: 682.		

Clarke, Barry R. – ***Francis Bacon's Contribution to Shakespeare*** **(2019)**

Jolly, Eddi	De Vere Society Newsletter	vol. 26/2: 36-37	2019, April

Clubb, Louise George – *Italian Drama in Shakespeare's Time* **(1989)**

| Londré, Felicia | Elizabethan Review | vol. 2/2: 55-61 | 1994, Autumn |

Coates, George – *The Crazy Wisdom Sho* **(2001)**

| 2001, Dec. 14 | San Francisco Chronicle | p. D4 | 2001, Dec. |

Connes, Georges – *Le mystere Shakespearien* **(1926)** – *The Shakespeare Mystery* **(1927)**

--	Northern Whig and Belfast Post	p. 9	1928, Jan. 21
--	Nottingham Journal	p. 3	1927, Nov. 25
--	Times Literary Supplement	issue 1275: 464	1926, July 8
--	Western Morning News	p. 11	1928, Jan. 2
Greenwood, George	Times Literary Supplement	p. 472	1927, July 7

Response by Georges Connes, July 28, p. 520.

Harrison, G. B.	Review of English Studies	vol. 5: 246-47	1929, April
Jaggard, Captain William	Shakespeare Pictorial	no. 11: 4	1929, Jan.
Kempling, W. B.	Shakespeare Review	vol. 1/2: 121-22	1928, June
Pruvost, Rene	Revue Anglo-Américaine	vol. 6/2: 170-72	1928, Dec.
Twitchett, E. G.	London Mercury	vol. 1/6: 100	1928, May
V. R.	The English Review	p.s 363-34	1928, March

Cornwell, Bernard – *Agincourt: A Novel* **(2008)**

| Desper, Richard | Shakespeare Matters | vol. 11/4: 15-16, 32 | 2012, Fall |

Costello, Priscilla – *Shakespeare and the Stars: The Hidden Astrological Keys to Understanding the World's Greatest Playwright* **(2016)**

| Adams, R. | Shakespeare Oxford Newsletter | vol. 52/3: 27 | 2016, Spring |

Crystal, David and Ben Crystal – *The Shakespeare Miscellany* **(2005)**

| Anderson, Verily | De Vere Society Newsletter | p. 2-3 | 2006, April |

Cunningham, Vanessa – *Shakespeare and Garrick* **(2008)**

| Gilbert, Sky | Brief Chronicles | vol. II: 227-231 | 2010 |

Cutting, Bonner Miller – *Necessary Mischief: Exploring the Shakespeare Authorship Question* **(2018)**

| Malim, Richard | De Vere Society Newsletter | vol. 26/2: 31-35 | 2019, April |
| St. Clair, Michael | Shakespeare Oxford Newsletter | vol. 55/1: 26-27 | 2019, Winter |

Cyr, Helen W. – *The Shakespeare Identity Crisis: A Reference Guide* **(1986)**

| Marder, Louis | The Shakespeare Newsletter | vol. 37/2: 26 | 1987, Summer |

Daniell, David – *William Tyndale: A Biography* **(1994)**

| Hope, Warren | Elizabethan Review | vol. 3/1: 53-55 | 1995, Spring |

Daugherty, Leo – *The Assassination of Shakespeare's Patron* **(2011)**

| Dickson, Peter | Brief Chronicles | vol. III: 264-271 | 2011, Fall |

Dawkins, Peter – *The Shakespeare Enigma* **(2005)**

| Vickers, Brian | The Times (London) | issue 5342: 6-8 | 2005, Aug. 9 |

[repr. in DVN (Sept. 2005), p. 40-43]

Dawtrey, John – *The Falstaff Saga* **(1927)**

| ----- | Times Literary Supplement | issue 1322: 388 | 1927, June 2 |

De Chambrun, Clara Longworth – *Shakespeare: A Portrait Restored* **(1954)**

| Wainewright, Ruth M. D. | Shakespeare Fellowship Newsletter (Eng) | p. 9-11 | 1958, Spring |

De Chambrun, Clara Longworth – *Shakespeare Rediscovered* **(1938)**

| Allen, Percy | Shakespeare Fellowship Newsletter (Eng.) | no. 9: 7-9 | 1938, May |

Delahoyde, Michael (editor) – *Twelfth Night, Annotated from an Oxfordian Perspective* **(2022)**

| Londré, Felicia | The Oxfordian | vol. 24: 271-273 | 2022, Sept. |

Dent, Anthony – *Horses in Shakespeare's England* **(1988)**

| Holden, Isabel and Constance | Shakespeare Oxford Newsletter | vol. 25/4: 5-6 | 1989, Fall |

Desai, R. W. (editor) – *Shakespeare, the Man: New Decipherings* **(2014)**

| Gilbert, Sky | The Oxfordian | vol. 19: 215-22 | 2017, Oct. |

Destro, Ron – *The Shakespeare Masterclasses* **(2020)**

| Chard, Costa | De Vere Society Newsletter | vol. 28/1: 49 | 2021, Jan. |

Detobel, Robert – *Shakespeare: The Concealed Poet* **(2010)**

| Cutting, Bonner Miller | Brief Chronicles | vol. III: 272-274 | 2011, Fall |

Hamill, John	Shakespeare Oxford Newsletter	vol. 47/3: 13-14	2011, Fall
Scheffer, Jan; Elke Brachmann	De Vere Society Newsletter	vol. 18/2: 36-38	2011, July

Dewar, Mary – *Sir Thomas Smith: A Tudor Intellectual in Office* (1964)

Wainewright, Ruth M. D.	Shakespearean Authorship Review [repr. in BTC, vol. 5: 250-252]	no. 17:12-13	1967, Spring

Di Lampedusa, Giuseppe Tomasi – *Shakespeare. Aus dem Italienischen von Maja Pflug* (1994)

Klier, Walter	Neues Shake-speare Journal	vol. 3: 169-70	1999, Jan.

Dickson, Peter W. – *Bardgate: Shake-speare and the Royalists Who Stole the Bard (2011)*

Goldstein, Gary	Brief Chronicles	vol. III: 285-287	2011, Fall

Dillon, George – *The Man Who Was Hamlet* (unpublished)

--	Essex Chronicle (Chelmsford)	p. 8	2009, Sept. 17
--	Hull Daily Mail	p. 20	2010, Oct. 20
Cornwell, Tim	Scotsman (Edinburgh)	p. 6	2010, Aug. 19
Gill, John	De Vere Society Newsletter	vol. 16/2: 32	2009, June

Dobson, Michael and Stanley Wells (eds.) – *The Oxford Companion to Shakespeare* (2001)

Jiménez, Ramon	Shakespeare Oxford Newsletter	vol. 39/4: 23-24	2003, Autumn
Whalen, Richard F.	Shakespeare Matters	vol. 1/3: 23-24	2002, Spring

Douglas, Lt. Colonel Montagu W. – *The Earl of Oxford as "Shakespeare"* (1931)

--	Belfast News-Letter	p. 12	1931, Oct. 8
--	Times Literary Supplement	p. 30	1932, Jan. 14
P. A. [Percy Allen]	Christian Science Monitor	p. 7	1932, Jan. 9
Sutton, Graham	Bookman, The	p. 132	1931, Nov.
Ward, Colonel B. R.	Shakespeare Pictorial	no. 45: 180	1931, Nov.

Douglas, Lt. Colonel Montagu W. – *Lord Oxford Was "Shakespeare:" A Summing Up* (1934)

--	Aberdeen Journal		1935, Jan. 1
--	Times Literary Supplement	issue 1721: 50	1935, Jan. 24
Neihardt, John G.	St. Louis Post-Dispatch	p. 14	1934, Dec. 30
--	Truth	p. 224	1935, Feb. 6

Douglas, Lt. Colonel Montagu W. – *Lord Oxford and the Shakespeare Group* (1952)

--	Morning Post		1952
--	Truth	p. 708-09	1952, June 27
Aitken, T. M.	Shakespeare Fellowship Newsletter (Eng)	p. 9	1953, April
Drew, Philip	Shakespeare Fellowship Newsletter (Eng)	p. 2	1953, Nov.
Ward, Captain B. M.	Shakespeare Pictorial	no. 83: 16	1935, Jan.

Dowden, Hester (with Percy Allen) – *Talks With Elizabethans* (1947)

--	Boston Globe	p. 1, 8	1948, Jan. 5
--	Los Angeles Times	p. 1	1948, Jan. 5
--	Atlanta Constitution	p. 8	1948, Jan. 8
--	Washington Post	p. 9	1948, Jan. 5
Laker, J. J. H. C.	Fifeshire Advertiser	p. 3	1948, Jan. 3
Musel, Robert	South China Morning Post	p. 6	1948, Jan. 12

Dowdey, David – *Secret Whispers: Searching for the Truth of Shakespeare* (2017)

Cutting, Bonner Miller	Shakespeare Oxford Newsletter	vol. 53/3: 14-15	2017, Summer

Doyle, John and Ray Lischner – *Shakespeare for Dummies* (1999)

Whalen, Richard F.	Shakespeare Oxford Newsletter	vol. 35/4: 16, 23	2000, Winter

Draya, Ren and Richard F. Whalen (editors) – *Oxfordian Edition of Othello* (2011)

Dams, Christopher	De Vere Society Newsletter	vol. 18/2: 35-36	2011, July
Egan, Michael	Shakespeare Oxford Newsletter	vol. 48/1: 10-11	2012
Londré, Felicia	Brief Chronicles	vol. 2: 224-26	2010

Drinkwater, John – *Shakespeare* (1933)

--	Saturday Review Response by Percy Allen, Feb. 18.	vol. 155: 121	1933, Feb. 4
Allen, Percy	Shakespeare Pictorial	no. 61: 37	1933, March
Bowen, Marjorie	Shakespeare Pictorial	no. 63: 64	1933, May

Drury, P. J. – *Hill Hall: A Singular House Devised by a Tudor Intellectual* **(2009)**
Hughes, Stephanie H.   De Vere Society Newsletter   vol. 17/1: 11-13   2010, Feb.

Duffin, Ross W. – *Shakespeare's Songbook* **(2004)**
Cyr, Gordon C.   Shakespeare Oxford Newsletter   vol. 40/3: 18-19   2004, Summer

Duncan-Jones, Katherine (editor) – *Shakespeare's Sonnets* **(1997)**
Whalen, Richard F.   Shakespeare Oxford Newsletter   vol. 34/1: 18-19   1998, Summer

Duncan-Jones, Katherine – *Ungentle Shakespeare – Scenes From His Life* **(2001)**
Ellis, David   Around the Globe   2001-02, Wntr.
                                 [repr. in DVN (July 2004), p. 22-25]
Johnson, Philip and Edi Jolly   De Vere Society Newsletter   p. 30-31   2001, July
Whalen, Richard F.   Shakespeare Oxford Newsletter   vol. 37/2: 15   2001, Summer
Whalen, Richard F.   Shakespeare Oxford Newsletter   vol. 47/2: 9-11   2011, Spring

Dutton, Richard – *Shakespeare, Court Dramatist* **(2016)**
Jimenez, Ramon   The Oxfordian   vol. 21: 237-42   2019, Sept.
Showerman, Earl   Shakespeare Oxford Newsletter   vol. 53/3: 17-19   2017, Summer

Eagle, Roderick L. - *Shakespere – New Views For Old* **(1930, 1943)**
Agate, James   Sunday Times   issue 6275: 2   1943, July 18
Brown, Ivor   Observer   p. 2   1944, April 30
Douglas, Lt. Col. Montagu W.   Shakespeare Fellowship Newsletter (Eng.)   p. 2-3   1943, Oct.

Eckersley, Sylvia – *Number and Geometry in Shakespeare's Macbeth* **(ed. By Alan Thewless) (2007)**
Stott, Alan   Shakespeare Matters   vol. 7/1: 19-20   2007, Fall

Edmondson, Paul and Stanley Wells – *All the Sonnets of Shakespeare* **(2020)**
Whittemore, Hank   Shakespeare Oxford Newsletter   vol. 57/1: 33-35   2021, Winter

Edmondson, Paul and Stanley Wells (editors) – *Shakespeare Beyond Doubt: Evidence, Argument, Controversy* **(2013)**
--   Shakespeare Matters   vol. 12/3: 1, 19, 36   2013, Summer
--   Shakespeare Newsletter   vol. 63/1: 25   2013, Summer
--   Times Literary Supplement   issue 5754: 24   2013, July 12
Alberge, Dalya   Observer   p. 23   2013, March 31
Bate, Jonathan   New Statesman (London)   vol. 142: 44   2013, April 26
Egan, Michael   Shakespeare Oxford Newsletter   vol. 49/3: 25-32   2013, Fall
Goldstein, Gary   The Oxfordian   vol. 15: 92-99   2013
Malim, Richard C. W.   De Vere Society Newsletter   vol. 20/2: 11-15   2013, July
Malvern, Jack   The Times (London)   p. 22   2013, April
Mattix, Micah   Weekly Standard   p. 38-39   2014, March 17
Regnier, Tom   Shakespeare Matters   vol. 12/3: 28-33   2013, Summer
Regnier, Tom   Brief Chronicles   vol. V: 193-204   2014, Summer
Rubin, Don   Critical Stages   no, 14   2014, Feb.
Rubin, Don   Brief Chronicles   vol. V: 189-92   2014, Summer
Waugaman, Richard M.   Journal of the American Psychoanalytic Assoc.2014, March 7

Egan, Gabrield – *Shakespeare and Ecocritical Theory* **(2015)**
Wallace, David Rains   Shakespeare Oxford Newsletter   vol. 55/3: 28-31   2019, Summer

Egan, Michael (ed.) – *The Tragedy of Richard II, Part One* **(2006)**
Jiménez, Ramon   Shakespeare Oxford Newsletter   vol. 42/1: 18-20   2006, Winter

Eggar, Katharine E. – *Shakespeare in His True Colors* **(pamphlet) (1951)**
--   Shakespeare Newsletter (Eng)   p. 10   1952, March

Ellis, David – *The Truth About William Shakespeare: Fact, Fiction, and Modern Biographies* **(2012)**
Cutting, Bonner Miller   Shakespeare Matters   vol. 11/4: 7-8   2012, Fall

Elton, Ben – *The Upstart Crow* **[a play] (2020?)**
Herbert, Tony   De Vere Society Newsletter   vol. 27/2: 50-51   2020, April

Emmison, F. G. – *Elizabethan Life: Wills of Essex Gentry and Merchants* **(1978)**
Patience, Harold W.   Shakespeare Oxford Newsletter   vol. 14/4: 2-3   1978, Fall

Epstein, Norrie – *The Friendly Shakespeare* **(1993)**
Whalen, Richard F.   Shakespeare Oxford Newsletter   vol. 29/1a: 1-3   1993, Winter
Whalen, Richard F.   Shakespeare Oxford Newsletter   vol. 29/2a: 4-5   1993, Spring

Evans, A. J. – *Shakespeare's Magic Circle* **(1956)**

--	Times Literary Supplement	issue 2836: 410	1956, July 6
Cutner, Herbert	Shakespeare Oxford Newsletter (Eng)	p. 8-9	1956, Autumn

Evans, G. Blackmore (editor) – *The Sonnets* **[part of the** *New Cambridge Shakespeare***] (1996)**

Whalen, Richard F.	Shakespeare Oxford Newsletter	vol. 32/2: 19	1996, Spring
Whalen, Richard F.	Shakespeare Oxford Newsletter	vol. 34/1: 18-19	1998, Spring

Eyre, Geoffrey – *The Case for Edward de Vere* **(2015)**

Malim, Richard	De Vere Society Newsletter	vol. 23/1: 46	2016, January
Malim, Richard	De Vere Society Newsletter	vol. 23/3: 39	2016, July
Pannell, Chris	Shakespeare Oxford Newsletter	vol. 52/1: 15-17	2016, Winter

Eyre, Geoffrey – *The Shakespeare Authorship Mystery Explained* **(2017)**

Haskins, David	The Oxfordian	vol. 19: 209-14	2017, Oct.

Falconer, Alexander F. – *Shakespeare and the Sea* **(1964)**

McGeoch, I. L.	Shakespearean Authorship Review	no. 14: 10-11	1965, Autumn
	[repr. in BTC, vol. 5: 170-172]		

Farina, William – *De Vere as Shakespeare* **(2006)**

--	Reference and Research Book News	vol. 18/2	2003, May
Delahoyde, Michael	Rocky Mountain E-Review of Lang. & Lit.	vol. 61/1: 112-20	2007
Fair, Shana C.	Library Journal	vol. 131/5: 72	2006, March
Goldstein, Gary B.	The Oxfordian	vol. 9: 135-137	2006

Feldman, A. Bronson – *Early Shakespeare* **(Edited by Warren Hope) (2019)**

Waugaman, Richard & Elisabeth	The Oxfordian	vol. 21: 261-66	

Feldman, A. Bronson – *Hamlet Himself* **(2006)**

Hope, Warren	Shakespeare Oxford Newsletter	vol. 15/1: 5-7	1979, Winter
Hope, Warren	Bard, The	vol. 2/4: 133-136	1980
Waugaman, Richard M.	Shakespeare Matters	vol. 9/3: 7-11+	2010, Fall

Feldman, A. Bronson – *Secrets of Shakespeare* **(1972)**

Cyr, Gordon C.	Shakespeare Oxford Newsletter	vol. 12/4: 7-8	1976, Winter

Feldman, A. Bronson – *Shakespeare, Marlowe and Other Elizabthans* **(edited by Warren Hope) (2022)**

Warren, James A.	The Oxfordian	vol. 24: 275-282	2022, Sept.

Feldman, Sabrina – *The Apocryphal William Shakespeare* **(2011)**

Hess, W. Ron	Shakespeare Oxford Newsletter	vol. 48/1: 17-18	2012, Winter
Nelson, Donald F.	Shakespeare Matters	vol. 12/2: 7, 20-22	2013, Spring

Fergusson, Sir James – *The Man Behind Macbeth and Other Studies* **(1969)**

Wainewright, Ruth M. D.	Shakespearean Authorship Review	issue #22: 13-15	1969, Dec.

Ferington, Esther – *Infinite Variety: Exploring the Folger Shakespeare Library* **(2002)**

Brazil, Robert	Shakespeare Oxford Newsletter	vol. 38/4: 21	2002, Fall

Fey, Jerry – *Oxford's Will: A Play* **(unpublished)**

Drake, Sylvie	Los Angeles Times	p. SDF8	1992, May 25

Field, Andrew – *The Lost Chronicle of Edward de Vere* **(1990)**

Goodwin, Ken	Courier-Mail		1991, March 2
Holden, Isabel	Shakespeare Oxford Newsletter	vol. 27/2: 6-7	1991, Spring
Klier, Walter	Neues Shake-speare Journal (German)	vol. 3: 173-75	1999, Jan.
Morton, Peter	Early Modern Literary Studies	vol. 5/2	1999, Sept.
Powell, J. Enoch	The Spectator	p. 39-40	1990, Sept. 29
Stephens, Jane	Australian Society	vol. 10/1-2: 59-60	1991

Fields, Bertram – *Players: The Mysterious Identity of William Shakespeare* **(2005)**

--	Kirkus Review	vol. 73/3: 163	2005
--	Publishers Weekly	vol. 21: 171	2005, Feb.
--	Shakespeare Matters	vol. 4/3: 23	2005, Spring
Fair, Shana C.	Library Journal	vol. 130/6: 94	2005
Hunter-Tilney, Ludovic	Financial Times	p. 33	2006, April 1
Imlay, Elizabeth	De Vere Society Newsletter	p. 26-27	2006, April
Ligon, K. C.	Shakespeare Matters	vol. 5/1: 12-13+	2005, Fall
Whalen, Richard F.	Shakespeare Oxford Newsletter	vol. 41/4: 31-32	2005, Fall

Findlay, Alison & Vassiliki Markidou (editors) – *Shakespeare and Greece* **(2017)**

Showerman, Earl	The Oxfordian	vol. 20: 171-76	2018, Sept.

Flint, Eric – *1632* **[a science-fiction novel (2000)**

Dreya, Ren	Shakespeare Oxford Newsletter	vol. 58/2: 6	2022, Spring

Fluchere, Henri – *Shakespeare and the Elizabethans* **(1956)**

Wainewright, Ruth M. D.	Shakespearean Authorship Review	issue #4: 10-13	1960, Autumn

Flynn, Brian – *The Shaking Spear* **(unpublished)**

Loosely, Newsl.	Shakespeare Fellowship Newsletter	p. 10	1956, Spring

Foden, Giles – *Sansibar* **(2003)**

Klier, Walter	Neues Shake-speare Journal	vol. 9: 181-82	2004, June

Forrest, H. T. S. – *The Original Venus and Adonis* **(1930)**

Ward, Colonel B. R.	Shakespeare Pictorial	no. 44: 144	1931, Nov.

Foster, Thomas Henry – *Shakespeare, Man of Mystery* **(1946)**

Marder, Louis	Shakespeare Newsletter	vol. 39/1-2: 40-42	1989, Spr/Sum
Starrett, Vincent	Chicago Daily Tribune	p. G2	1947, Jan. 5

Fowler, William Plumer – *Shakespeare Revealed in Oxford's Letters* **(1986)**

Johnson, Morse	Shakespeare Oxford Newsletter	vol. 23/1: 1-3	1987, Winter
Marder, Louis	Shakespeare Newsletter	vol. 36/3: 40, 57	1986, Fall
Sobran, Joseph	National Review	vol. 39/6: 54-56	1987, Nov. 6

Fox, Alistair – *The English Renaissance: Identity and Representation in Elizabethan England* **(1997)**

Imlay, Elizabeth	De Vere Society Newsletter	vol. 3/1: 12-13	1998, Oct.

Fox, Levi – *The Borough Town of Stratford-upon-Avon* **(1953)**

Editor	Shakespeare Fellowship Newsletter (Eng)	p. 3-4	1954, April

Fox, Robin – *Shakespeare's Education: Schools, Lawsuits, Theater and the Tudor Miracle* **(2012)**

Egan, Michael	Shakespeare Oxford Newsletter	vol. 49/1: 11-13	2013, Winter
Graham, Nicholas	Library Journal	vol. 137/20: 82-85	2012, Dec. 1
Ray, William J.	Shakespeare Matters	vol. 11/4: 20-21	2012, Fall
Waugaman, Richard M.	Shakespeare Oxford Newsletter	vol. 50/5: 522	2013, Oct.
Waugaman, Richard M.	Social Science and Modern Society		2013, Oct.

Fraser, Russell – *Shakespeare: The Later Years* **(1993)**

Whalen, Richard F.	Shakespeare Oxford Newsletter	vol. 29/2a: 3-4	1993, Spring

Freed, Amy – *The Beard of Avon* **(2004)**

--	New York Times	p. 5	2003, Nov. 28
--	Shakespeare Matters	vol. 1/3: 5	2002, Spring
--	Shakespeare Matters	vol. 7/4: 15-16	2008, Fall
--	Shakespeare Oxford Newsletter	vol. 37/2: 2	2001, Summer
--	Star-News (Wilmington, NC)		2008, Aug. 12
Berson, Misha	Seattle Times	p. E8	2001, June 14
Boehm, Mike	Los Angeles Times	p. 1	2001, May 27
Demaline, Jackie	Cincinnati Enquirer	p. W12	2002, May 17
Fanger, Iris	Patriot Ledger (Quincy, Mass.)	p. 15	2006, July 18
Fisher, James	Theatre Journal	vol. 55/3: 528-30	1999
Gilbert, Sky	Shakespeare Matters	vol. 2/2: 1, 14+	2003, Winter
Glanville, Justin	Record, The	p. E7	2003, Nov. 23
Hodgins, Paul	Orange County Register	p. 1	2001, May 29
Hurwitt, Robert	San Francisco Chronicle		2002, Jan. 18
Kennedy, Louise	Boston Globe	p. D5	2006, July 7
Lyons, Donald	New York Post	p. 56	2003, Nov. 19
MacDonald, Nancy	Boston Globe		2006, Aug. 8
MacKillop, James	Syracuse New Times	p. 13	2008, April 16
Marks, Peter	Washington Post	p. C1	2005, Oct. 25
Masters, Ryan	Monterey County Weekly	p. 51	2005, Sept. 22
Niederkorn, William S.	New York Times	vol. 153, A&L: 5	2003, Nov. 16
Ouzounian, Richard	Toronto Star	p. E13	2002, Nov. 22
Phillips, Michael	Los Angeles Times	p. F2	2001, June 4
Phillips, Michael	Chicago Tribune	p. 7	2002, Oct. 6

Stasio, Marilyn	Variety (Los Angeles)	p. 43	2003, Nov. 24
Talcott, Christina	Washington Post	p. R26	2005, Oct. 21
Taylor, Kate	Globe and Mail	p. R6	2002, Nov. 23
Weber, Bruce	New York Times	p. E5	2003, Nov. 19
Weiss, Hedy	Chicago Sun-Times	p. 37	2002, Oct. 8
Whalen, Richard F.	Shakespeare Matters	vol. 3/2: 4	2004, Winter
Winer, Linda	Newsday, Long Island	p. B8	2003, Nov. 25
Winn, Steven	San Francisco Chronicle		2002, Jan. 8

Freedman, Arthur – *Thomas Kyd: Facts and Problems* (1967)

Wainewright, Ruth M. D.	Shakespearean Authorship Review	issue #24: 12-13	1971, Spring

Friedman, William F. – *Shakespearean Ciphers* (1957)

J. S. A.	Shakespeare Fellowship Newsletter (Eng)	p. 7-9	1958, Spring

Frisbee, George – *Edward De Vere: A Great Elizabethan* (1931)

--	Times Literary Supplement	p. 30	1932, Jan. 14
--	Western Morning News	p. 3	1931, Dec. 16
Parsons, I. M.	Spectator	vol. 148: 149-50	1932, Jan. 30

Fry, Simon – *Paper Trail* (2008)

Jolly, Eddi	De Vere Society Newsletter	vol. 16/3: 32	2009, Nov.

Frye, Albert and Albert Levi – *Rational Belief: An Introduction to Logic* (1941)

Cyr, Gordon C.	Shakespeare Oxford Newsletter	vol. 7/1: 1	1971, March 30

Gale, Gertrude – *Masquerade* (1971) [A play based on Prince Tudor themes]

Barnes, Clive	New York Times	p. 57	1971, Nov. 29

Galland, Joseph S. – *Digesta Anti-Shakespearea: A Historical and Analytical Bibliography of the Shakespeare Authorship and Identity Controversy*

Linscott, Roger B.	New York Herald Tribune	p. VII-8	1947, June 1

Garber, Marjorie – *Profiling Shakespeare* (2008)

McCarthy, Andrew D.	Rocky Mountain E-Review of Lang. & Lit.	vol. 62/2: 107-110	1992, April

Garber, Marjorie – *Shakespeare After All* (2004)

Whalen, Richard F.	Shakespeare Oxford Newsletter	vol. 41/2: 23	2005, Spring

Garber, Marjorie – *Shakespeare's Ghost Writers* (2010)

Whalen, Richard F.	Shakespeare Oxford Newsletter	vol. 47/2: 9-11	2011, Spring

Garber, Marjorie – *Symptoms of Culture* (1998)

Whalen, Richard F.	Shakespeare Oxford Newsletter	vol. 35/1: 19, 23	1999, Spring

Garber, Marjorie – *Vice Versa: Bisexuality and Eroticism of Everyday Life* (1995)

Whalen, Richard F.	Shakespeare Oxford Newsletter	vol. 32/1: 21	1996, Winter

Garcia, Emanuel E. – *Sherlock Holmes & the Three Poisoned Pawns* (2008)

Goldstein, Gary B.	Shakespeare Matters	vol. 8/2: 5	2009, Spring

Gascoigne, George – *A Hundreth Sundrie Flowres, revised edition)* (edited by Ruth Loyd Miller) (1975)

Child, Harold H.	Times Literary Supplement	p. 391	1926, June 10
Goff, Tom	Shakespeare Oxford Newsletter	vol. 28/1: 10-11	1992, Winter

Gay, Peter – *Reading Freud: Explorations and Entertainments* (1990)

Kakutani, Michiko	New York Times	p. C33	1990, March 23
Rycroft, Charles	Times Literary Supplement	p. 725	1990, July 6-12
Welch, Colin	Spectator, The	p. 26	1990, June 23

Geary, Douglas (editor) – *Songs and Sonnets of the Earl of Surrey* (1957)

Wainewright, Ruth M. D.	Shakespeare Fellowship Newsletter (Eng)	page 10	1957, Autumn

Gibson, Harry N. – *The Shakespeare Claimants* (1962)

--	Times Literary Supplement	vol. 28: 345	1962, Sept.
Alexander, Peter	Times Literary Supplement	issue 3152: 542	1962, July 27
Bayley, John	South Notts Echo	p. 7	1962, July 20
Bowen, Gwynneth M.	Shakespearean Authorship Review	issue #8: 15-17	1962, Autumn
Brown, Ivor	Observer	p. 24	1962, June 24
Hastings, William T.	Shakespeare Quarterly	vol. 14: 465-66	1962
Leech, Clifford	Studies in English Literature 1500-1900	vol. 3: 282	1962

Maxwell, J. C.	Notes and Queries	vol. 10: 352-54	1962, Sept.
Muir, Kenneth	Listener	vol. 68: 109	1962, July 19

Gilbert, Sky – *Shakespeare Beyond Science* (2020)

Hope, Warren	The Oxfordian	vol. 22: 141-144	2020, Sept.

Gililov, Ilya – *The Shakespeare Game, or The Mystery of the Great Phoenix* (2003)

Ford, Peter	Christian Science Monitor		1997, Dec. 31
	[excerpt repr. in SON, vol. 34/1: 2 (Spring 1998)]		

Gilvary, Kevin – *Dating Shakespeare's Plays: A Critical Review of the Evidence* (2010)

--	Shakespeare Matters	vol. 10/3: 4	2011, Summer
Hess, W. Ron	Shakespeare Oxford Newsletter	vol. 47/2: 1, 8	2011, Spring
Niederkorn, William S.	Brooklyn Rail		2011, April
	[repr. in DVN, vol. 18/3: 26-27 (Nov. 2011)]		
Ostrowski, Don	Brief Chronicles	vol. III: 246-257	2011, Fall
Showerman, Earl	Shakespeare Matters	vol. 11/2: 21, 29	2012, Spring

Gilvary, Kevin – *The Fictional Lives of Shakespeare* (2017)

Hess, W. Ron	Shakespeare Oxford Newsletter	vol. 54/2: 30-31	2018, Spring
Hope, Warren	The Oxfordian	vol. 20: 191-94	2018, Sept.
Jolly, Eddi	De Vere Society Newsletter	vol. 25/2: 44-46	2018, April
Waugaman, Richard	Shakespeare Oxford Newsletter	vol. 57/1: 32-33	2021, Winter

Girard, Rene – *Theater of Envy: William Shakespeare* (1991, 2004)

Wilkinson, Heward	Brief Chronicles	vol. III: 275-278	2011, Fall

Gladstone, Ryan – *The Shakespeare Show* (2009)

--	Maple Ridge, Pitt Meadows Times	p. 17	2009, Oct. 9

Golding, Louis T. – *An Elizabethan Puritan: The Life of Arthur Golding* (1939)

Barrell, Charles, Wisner	East Anglian Magazine	vol. 4/10: 590-93	1939, Sept.
	Continued in the Oct. and Nov. issues, vol. 4/11: 631-33 and vol. 4/12: 688-92.		
M.H.M.	Cincinnati Enquirer	p. 5	1937, June 12

Goldstein, Gary – *Reflections on the True Shakespeare* (2016)

--	Kirkus Reviews	vol. 85/3: 252	2017, Feb. 1
Warren, James A.	Shakespeare Oxford Newsletter	vol. 52/4: 11-12	2016, Fall
Waugh, Alexander	De Vere Society Newsletter	vol. 24/1: 42-43	2017, January
	[repr. in NSJ, vol. NS6 (2018): 181-82]		

Gollob, Herman – *Me and Shakespeare: Adventures With the Bard* (2002)

Whalen, Richard F.	Shakespeare Matters	vol. 2/2: 21	2003, Winter

Gontar, David P. – *Hamlet Made Simple and Other Essays* (2013)

Waugaman, Richard M.	Shakespere Oxford Newsletter	vol. 50/1: 18-20	2014, Winter

Gontar, David P. – *Unreading Shakespeare* (2015)

Ray, William J.	Shakespere Oxford Newsletter	vol. 51/3: 14-16	2015, Summer

Gordon, Helen Heightsman – *The Secret Love Story in Shakespeare's Sonnets* (2005)

Delahoyde, Michael	Rocky Mountain E-Review of Lang. & Lit.	vol. 61/1: 112-20	2007

Grant, Barry – *Sherlock Holmes and the Shakespeare Letter* [A novel] (2011)

--	Publisher's Weekly	vol. 43/20: 2	2010, Nov.

Grant, Stephen H. – *Collecting Shakespeare: The Story of Henry and Emily Folger* (2014)

Dudley, Michael	Brief Chronicles	Sp. Edition: 133-38	2016, Spring

Graves, Gary – *The Mysterious Mr. Looney* (2004) [A dramatic presentation of a fictional confrontation between J. Thomas Looney and Sir Sidney Chambers]

Hurwitt, Robert	San Francisco Chronicle	p. D2	2004, Aug. 10

Gray, Marilyn Savage – *The Real Shakespeare* (2001; Revised ed., 2015)

Aucella, Steven M.	Shakespeare Matters	vol. 2/1: 30	2002, Fall
Brazil, Robert	Shakespeare Oxford Newsletter	vol. 38/4: 21	2002, Fall
Dickerman, Dorothea	Shakespeare Oxford Newsletter	vol. 53/3: 15-16	2017, Summer

Grebanier, Bernard – *The Great Shakespeare Forgery* (1965)

Wainewright, Ruth M. D.	Shakespearean Authorship Review	no. 20: 12-13	1968, Autumn
	[repr. in BTC, vol. 5: 274-276]		

Green, Allan William – *I, Shakespeare: Unanimous or Anonymous?* **(2011)**
Egan, Michael (Editor)   Shakespeare Oxford Newsletter   vol. 49/2: 16-18   2013, Spring

Greenblatt, Stephen (editor) – *The Norton Shakespeare* **(2015)**
Whalen, Richard F.   Shakespeare Oxford Newsletter   vol. 33/3: 17, 24   1997, Summer

Greenblatt, Stephen – *Shakespeare's Freedom* **(2010)**
Niederkorn, William S.   Brooklyn Rail   2011, March

Greenblatt, Stephen – *Tyrant: Shakespeare on Politics* **(2018)**
Gansecki, Mike   Shakespeare Oxford Newsletter   vol. 55/2: 25-26   2019, Spring

Greenblatt, Stephen – *Will in the World: How Shakespeare Became Shakespeare* **(2004)**
--   Shakespeare Matters   vol. 4/1: 3   2004, Fall
Boyle, William E.   Shakespeare Matters   vol. 4/2: 6-7   2005, Winter
Conroy, Ed   San Antonio Express-News   2004, Dec. 19
Dorschel, Andreas   Neues Shake-speare Journal   vol. 11: 172-74   2007, April
Fowler, Alastair   Times Literary Supplement   issue 5314: 3   2005, Feb. 4
       [repr. in DVN (May 2005), p. 23-28]
Gilvary, Kevin   De Vere Society Newsletter   p. 22   2005, Jan.
Malim, Richard C. W.   De Vere Society Newsletter   p. 21-22   2005, Jan.
Mayer, Susanne   Die Zeit   issue 51   2004
Whalen, Richard F.   Shakespeare Oxford Newsletter   vol. 40/2: 18   2004, Spring
Whalen, Richard F.   Shakespeare Matters   vol. 4/2: 22-23   2005, Winter
Wright, Daniel L.   Shakespeare Matters   vol. 4/1: 4, 32   2004, Fall

Greenhill, Rima – *Shakespeare, Elizabeth and Ivan: The Role of English-Russian Relations in Love's Labour's Lost* **(2023)**
Delahoyde, Michael   Shakespeare Oxford Newsletter   vol. 59/2: 25-26   2023, Spr.
Johnston, Bruce   Oxfordian   vol. 25: 279-81   2023, Sept.

Greenwood, Sir George G. & Smithson – *Baconian Essays* **(1922)**
Eagle, Roderick L.   Baconiana   v. XVII/65: 149-50   1923, June

Greenwood, Sir George G. – *Lee, Shakespeare and Tertium Quid* **(1923)**
Douglas, Col. Montagu W.   Hackney Spectator   p. 4   1923, Oct. 26

Greenwood, Sir George G. – *Shakespeare's Handwriting* **(1920)**
--   New Age   --   1920, Dec. 2
Eagle, Roderick L.   Baconiana   vol. XVI/63: 82   1921, March

Greenwood, Sir George G. – *The Shakespeare Problem Restated* **(condensed version by Elsie Greenwood) (1937)**
Cyr, Gordon C.   Shakespeare Newsletter   no. 30: 22   1980
Douglas, Col. Montagu W.   Shakespeare Fellowship Newsletter (Eng.)   no. 3: 9   1937, May
Keller, Helen   Matilda Ziegeler Magazine   --   1909?

Greenwood, Sir George G. – *Shakespeare's Signatures and "Sir Thomas More* **(1924)**
Childs, Harold H.   Times Literary Supplement   issue 1189: 682   1924, Oct. 30
       Response by Sir George Greenwood, Nov. 9.
Douglas, Col. Montagu W.   Hackney Spectator   p. 4   1923, Oct. 24 and Nov. 7

Gregg, W. W. – *The Shakespeare First Folio* **(1955)**
Bowen, Gwynneth M.   Shakespeare Fellowship Newsletter   p. 10-11   1957, Spring

Gross, John – *Shylock: A Legend and Its Legacy* **(1994)**
Goldstein, Gary B.   Elizabethan Review   vol. 1/2: 78-79   1993, Autumn
Sheed, Wilfrid   New Yorker   1993, July 12

Grunes, Dorothy and Jerome – *What Shakespeare Teaches Us About Psychoanalysis* **(2014)**
Waugaman, Richard M.   Renaissance Quarterly   vol. 68/2: 787-88   2015

Günther, Frank – *Neuübersetzung* – *William Shakespeare im dtv. Zweisprachige Ausgaben.* **(2000)**
Klier, Walter   Neues Shake-speare Journal   vol. 4: 155-58   1999, July

Hackett, Helen – *Elizabeth and Shakespeare: The Meeting of Two Myths* **(2009)**
Gordon, Helen H.   Shakespeare Matters   vol. 8/3: 16-18   2009, Summer

Halle, Louis J. – *The Search for an Eternal Norm: As Represented by Three Classics* **(1981)**
Cyr, Gordon C.   Shakespeare Oxford Newsletter   vol. 18/3: 6-8   1982, Summer
       [repr. in BTC, vol. 6: 194-97]

Halliday, F. E. – *Cult of Shakespeare* **(1957)**
Cutner, Herbert	Shakespeare Fellowship Newsletter (Eng)	p. 10-11	1958, Autumn

Halliday, F. E. – *Shakespeare: A Pictorial Biography* **(1956)**
Cutner, Herbert	Shakespeare Fellowship Newsletter (Eng)	p. 10-11	1958, Autumn

Hamill, John – *The Secret Shakespeare Sex Scandals* **(2022)**
Showerman, Earl	Shakespeare Oxford Fellowship Newsletter	vol. 59/1: 16-19	2023, Win.

Hamlin, Hannibal – *The Bible in Shakespeare* **(2013)**
Waugaman, Richard M.	Shakespeare Oxford Newsletter	p. 18-19	2017, Fall

Hampton, Aubrey – *Elizabeth and Edward: A Play* **(2009)**
Fleming, John	St. Petersburg Times	p. B2	2009, April 1

Hancock, Peter – *Hoax Springs Eternal: The Psychology of Cognitive Deception* **(2015)**
Campbell, Harry	Shakespeare Oxford Newsletter	vol. 55/3: 22-27	2019, Summer

Harrison, G. B. – *A Companion to Shakespeare Studies* **(1934)**
Ward, Captain B. M.	Shakespeare Pictorial	no. 79: 144	1934, Sept.

Harrison, G. B. – *Elizabethan Plays and Players* **(1945)**
Allen, Percy	Shakespeare Fellowship News-letter (Eng)	p. 4-5	1946, March

Harrison, G. B. – *Introducing Shakespeare* **(1939)**
Kent, William	Shakespeare Fellowship News-letter (Eng.)	no. 15: 4-7	1939, July

Harrison, G. B. – *Shakespere At Work* **(1933)**
Allen, Percy	Shakespeare Pictorial	no. 69: 176	1933, Nov.
	Response by Frederic Perry Noble, Dec. 1933, p. 14.		

Hart, Alfred – *A Comparative Study of Shakespeare's Bad Quartos* **(1942)**
Allen, Percy	Shakespeare Fellowship News-letter	page 2	1943, Oct.

Hart, Alfred – *Shakespeare and the Homilies* **(1934)**
Ward, Captain B. M.	Shakespeare Pictorial	no. 103: 148	1936, Sept.

Hart, Col. Joseph C. – *The Romance of Yachting* **(1848)**
Horne, Jr., Richard C.	Shakespeare Oxford Newsletter	vol. 8/2: 3-5	1972, May

Hart, Michael – *The 100: A Ranking of the Most Influential Persons in History, Revised for the Nineties* **(1992)**
Champlin, Charles	Los Angeles Times	p. 10	1993, Feb. 21
Harayda, Janice	Plain Dealer	p. 11H	1993, May 23

Haynes, Alan – *Invisible Power: The Elizabethan Secret Services, 1570-1603* **(1992)**
Edwards, Francis	Elizabethan Review	vol. 1/2: 52-64	1993, Autumn
	[repr. in BTC, vol. 8: 153-67]		

Hess, W. Ron – *The Dark Side of Shakespeare, vol. 1* **(2002),** *vol. 2* **(2003)**
Cyr, Gordon C.	Shakespeare Oxford Newsletter	vol. 39/1: 19	2003, Winter
Desper, Richard	Shakespeare Matters	vol. 2/4: 25-26	2003, Summer
Whalen, Richard F.	Shakespeare Matters	vol. 3/4: 31	2004, Summer

Hirte, Chris (translator) – *Fortunatus im Ungluck: Die Adventiuren des Master F. I. Edward de Vere, Earl of Oxford* **(2006)**
Pigman III, G. W.	Modern Philology	vol. 110/2: E82-88	2012, Nov.

Höfele, Andreas – *Der Spitzel* **(1997)**
Fiéreux, Solange	Neues Shake-speare Journal	vol. 4: 154-55	1999, July

Hoffman, Calvin – *The Murder of the Man Who Was Shakespeare* **(1955)**
Eggar, Katharine E.	Shakespeare Fellowship Newsletter (Eng)	p. 10	1956, Spring
Harbage, Alfred	New York Times	p. BR1	1955, June 12

Hoke, Phil – *Truth; Will Out* **(2016)**
Halfich, Angie	TCA Regional News		2016, Oct. 26

Holden, Anthony – *William Shakespeare* **(1999)**
Editor (excerpts from reviews)	Shakespeare Oxford Newsletter	vol. 35/3: 18-19	1999, Fall

Holderness, Graham – *Nine Lives of William Shakespeare* **(2011)**
Niederkorn, William S.	Brooklyn Rail	p. 62	2012, Feb.
Ridden, Geoff	Shakespeare Newsletter	vol. 64/2: 57	2014, Fall

Reviews of Books of Special Interest

Holderness, Graham – *Shakespeare and Venice* **(2010)**

Hess, W. Ron	Shakespeare Oxford Newsletter	vol. 52/3: 32-33	2016, Spring

Holland, Hubert H. – *Shakespeare, Oxford and Elizabethan Times* **(1933)**

--	Aberdeen Press and Journal	p. 2	1933, Nov. 21
--	Books of Today		1933, Nov.
--	Bromley Parish Magazine		1933, Nov.
--	John O'London's Weekly	p. 520	1933, Dec. 30
	Response by Holland, Jan. date not known.		
--	New York Herald Tribune		1933, Nov. ??
--	Times Literary Supplement	issue 1659: 798	1933, Nov. 16
--	Universe		1933, Nov.
Allen, Percy	Christian Science Monitor	p. 10	1934, Oct. 3
Boas, F. S.	Observer, The	p. 3	1933, Dec. 3
D. M.	Tablet, The		1933, Nov.
G. S.	Western Morning News	p. 4	1933, Oct. 24

Holland, Hubert H. – *Shakespeare Through Oxford Glasses* **(1923)**

--	Aberdeen Press and Journal	p. 2	1923, June 5
--	Scotsman, The	p. 2	1923, May 14
--	Times Literary Supplement	issue 1116: 389	1923, June 7
Sampson, George	Daily News		1923, June 21
	[See response by Looney, *Hackney Spectator*, Aug. 31]		
Shanks, Edward	London Mercury	vol. 8: 322	1923, July
Ward, Col. Bernard R.	Hackney Spectator	p. 2	1923, Sept. 21
		Cont. on Sept. 28 and Oct. 19	

Holland, Norman N. – *Shakespeare's Missing Personality* **(1989)**

Stritmatter, Roger	Elizabethan Review	vol. 1/2: 65-74	1993, Autumn

Holmes, Edward – *Discovering Shakespeare: A Handbook for Heretics* **(2001)**

Jiménez, Ramon	Shakespeare Oxford Newsletter	vol. 38/2: 11, 22	2002, Spring
Whalen, Richard F.	Shakespeare Matters	vol. 2/1: 30	2002, Fall

Holmes, Martin R. – *Shakespeare's Public* **(1960)**

Wainewright, Ruth M. D.	Shakespearean Authorship Review	no. 6: 10-13	1961, Autumn
	[repr. in BTC, vol. 5: 73-74]		

Holmes, Nathaniel – *The Authorship of Shakespeare* **(1867)**

--	Athenaeum, The	p. 249	1867, Feb. 2

Honan, Park – *Shakespeare: A Life* **(1998)**

Sobran, Joseph	Shakespeare Oxford Newsletter	vol. 35/2: 21-22	1999, Summer

Honey, William – *The Life, Loves and Achievements of Christopher Marlowe Alias Shakespeare* **(1982)**

Edwards, Francis	Bard, The	vol. 4/2: 68-75	1984

Honneyman, David – *Shakespeare's Sonnets and the Court of Navarre* **(1996)**

Jiménez, Ramon	Shakespeare Oxford Newsletter	vol. 35/1: 18	1999, Spring

Hookham, George – *Will o' the Wisp: The Elusive Shakespeare* **(1922)**

Priestley, J. B.	London Mercury	vol. 7: 215	1922, Dec.

Hope, Warren and Kim Holston – *The Shakespeare Controversy, 1ˢᵗ Edition* **(1992)**

Goldstein, Gary B.	Shakespeare Oxford Newsletter	vol. 29/1a: 11	1993, Winter
Redding, D. C.	Choice	vol. 30/7: 1146	1993, March

Hope, Warren and Kim Holston – *The Shakespeare Controversy, 2ⁿᵈ Edition* **(2009)**

Egan, Michael (editor)	Shakespeare Oxford Newsletter	vol. 49/2: 18-21	2013, Spring
Hunter, R. Thomas	Brief Chronicles	vol. I: 277-283	2009
Waugaman, Richard M.	Int'l Journal of Applied Psychoanalytic Studies	p. 1-16	2020, Aug. 31

Hopkins, Vivian C. – *Prodigal Puritan: A Life of Delia Bacon* **(1959)**

Tharp, Louise Hall	New York Times	p. BR22	1959, Oct. 18

Hosking, G. L. – *The Life and Times of Edward Alleyn* **(1952)**

Cutner, Herbert	Shakespeare Fellowship Newsletter (Eng)	p. 9-10	1953, April

Hosking, Tony – *Shakespeare as Philosopher and the Shakespearean Tragedy of Edward de Vere* **(2016)**

Goldstein, Gary	Shakespeare Oxford Newsletter	vol. 52/2: 30-31	2016, Spring

Hotson, Leslie – *The First Night of Twelfth Night* (1973)
Lambin, Georges	Shakespeare Fellowship Newsletter (Eng)	p. 11-12	1955, Spring

Hotson, Leslie – *I, William Shakespeare* (1970)
Allen, Percy	Shakespeare Fellowship Newsletter (Eng.)	no. 7: 3-5	1938, Jan.

Hotson, Leslie – *Shakespeare By Hilliard* (1977)
Akrigg, G. P. V.	Modern Philology	vol. 77: 427-29	1980
Berry, Ralph	Times Educational Supplement	p. 23	1977, Dec. 30
Bertram, Paul	Shakespeare Quarterly	vol. 33: 121-23	1982
Burgess, Anthony	Observer, The	p. 26	1977, Oct. 9
Kinney, Arthur F.	Studies in English Literature	vol. 18: 361-418	1978
Marder, Lois	Shakespeare News Letter	vol. 28/5-6: 38	1978
Milward, Peter	Sophia	vol. 28: 88-92	1979, Spring
Schoenbaum, S.	Times Literary Supplement	p. 1,261	1977, Oct. 28

Hotson, Leslie – *Shakespeare Versus Shallow* (1931)
Atkinson, J. Shera	Shakespeare Fellowship Newsletter (Eng.)	Supp.: 1-8	1938, July

Hotson, Leslie – *Shakespeare's Wooden O* (1960)
MacDonald, John	Shakespearean Authorship Review	issue #5: 12-14	1961, Spring

Hovey, Jr., J. Allan – *Aye, Shakespeare* (a one-man play)
Editor	Shakespeare Oxford Newsletter	vol. 35/2: 2	1999, Summer

Howe, Norma – *Blue Avenger Cracks the Code* (2002)
Kruh, Louis	Cryptologia	vol. 26/4: 311	2002, Oct.
Roback, Diane	Publishers Weekly	p. 92	2000, Sept. 11
Whalen, Richard F.	Shakespeare Oxford Newsletter	vol. 36/3: 19, 24	2000, Fall

Hudson, John – *Shakespeare's Dark Lady: Amelia Bassano Lanier* (2014)
--	Kirkus Reviews	vol. 82/5	2014, March 1
Alexander, James	De Vere Society Newsletter	vol. 26/1: 42-44	2019, Jan.

Hughes, Stephanie Hopkins – *Educating Shakespeare* (2022)
Foss, Jonathan	De Vere Society Newsletter	vol. 30/2: 42-49	2023, April
Rubin, Don	The Oxfordian	vol. 24: 289-293	2022, Sept.

Hughes, Ted – *The Essential Shakespeare* (1992)
Goldstein, Gary B. (Editor)	Elizabethan Review	vol. 1/2: 79-79	1993, Autumn

Hume, Robert D. – *Reconstructing Contexts: Principles of Archaeo-Historicism* (1999)
Hurst, Wally	The Oxfordian	vol. 19: 231-36	2017, Oct.

Hunt, Douglas – *The Riverside Guide to Writing* (1995)
Ogburn, Charlton, Jr.	Shakespeare Oxford Newsletter	vol. 27/4: 1-2	1991, Fall
Whalen, Richard F.	Shakespeare Oxford Newsletter	vol. 32/3: 19, 23	1996, Summer

Hurstfield, Joel – *The Queen's Wards: Wardship and Marriage Under Elizabeth I* (1973)
Russell, Sir John	Shakespearean Authorship Review	no. 3: 9-10	1960, Spring
	[repr. in BTC, vol. 5: 38-42]		

Huston, Craig – *The Shakespeare Authorship Question* (1971)
Edwards, Reverend Francis	Shakespearean Authorship Review	issue #29: 17-18	1974, Summer
Horne, Jr., Richard C.	Shakespeare Oxford Newsletter	vol. 8/1: 8	1972, Jan.

Illig, Heribert – *Das erfundene Mittelalter* (1996)
Laugwitz, Uwe	Neues Shake-speare Journal	vol. 3: 175-79	1999, Jan.

Illig, Heribert – *Das Kaisers leeres Bücherbrett. Wer beahrte das antike Erbe?* (????)
Laugwitz, Uwe	Neues Shake-speare Journal	vol. NS7: 145-49	2020

Imlay, Elizabeth – *Edward de Vere, Part I* [A play] (unpublished)
Krass, Iris	De Vere Society Newsletter	vol. 2/11: 11-12	1998, Feb.

Iske, Basil (Elizabeth Hickey) – *The Green Cockatrice* (1978)
Edwards, Francis	The Bard	vol. 4/1: 26-32	1983

James, Brenda and William D. Rubinstein – *The Truth Will Out: Unmasking the Real Shakespeare* (2005)
--	Shakespeare Matters	vol. 5/1: 5-6	2005, Fall
Beauclerk, Charles	The Oxfordian	vol. 8: 140-145	2005
Jackson, MacDonald P.	Shakespeare Newsletter	vol. 55/2: 35	2005, Summer

Jiménez, Ramon	Shakespeare Oxford Newsletter	vol. 41/4: 25-28	2005, Fall
Ligon, K. C.	Shakespeare Matters	vol. 5/1: 5-6	2005, Fall
Nelson, Alan H.	Times Literary Supplement	p. 28	2005, Nov. 25
Taylor, Kate	Globe and Mail (Toronto)	p. R1	2005, Oct. 12

Jiménez, Ramon – *The Famous Victories of Henry the Fifth: An Early Play by the Real William Shakespeare, Edward de Vere* **(2022)**

Delahoyde, Michael	The Oxfordian	vol. 24: 382-287	2022, Sept.
Hyde, Michael	Shakespeare Oxford Newsletter	vol. 58/3: 11-12	2022, Summer
Malim, Richard	De Vere Society Newsletter	vol. 29/2: 45-48	2022, April

Jiménez, Ramon – *Shakespeare's Apprenticeship* **(2018)**

Hinds, Amanda	De Vere Society Newsletter	vol. 26/1: 45-47	2019, Jan.
Londré, Felicia Hardison	The Oxfordian	vol. 20: 167-70	2018, Sept.

Jiménez, Ramon – *The True Tragedy of Richard the Third* **(2022)**

Delahoyde, Michael	Oxfordian	vol. 25: 295-98	2023, Sept.
Hyde, Michael	Shakespeare Oxford Newsletter	vol. 59/1: 20-22	2023, Winter

Johnson, Edward D. – *The Fictitious Shakespeare Exposed* **(1949)**

Kent, William	Shakespeare Fellowship Newsletter (Eng)	p. 5-6	1946, March

Johnson, Ian – *Renaissance Man: the World of Thomas Watson* **(2021)**

Gilvary, Kevin	De Vere Society Newsletter	vol. 28/1: 46-48	2021, Jan.
Hope, Warren	The Oxfordian	vol. 23: 347-352	2021, Sept.

Jolly, Margrette (Eddi) – *The First Two Quartos of Hamlet, A New View of the Origins and Relationship of the Texts* **(2014)**

Jiménez, Ramon	Shakespeare Oxford Newsletter	vol. 52/3: 29-32	2016, Spring

Jones, Graham and Jepke Goudsmit – *Shake-speare* **(2001)**

2001, Oct. 8, p. 20	Sydney Morning Herald	p. 20	2001, Oct. 8

Kausen, Wolfgang – Shakespeares *Sonette Deutsch. Eine Übersetzung von Wolfgang Kausen* (1993) and *William Shakespeare, Sonette. English und deutsch.* **[Hrsg. und mit einem Vorwort von Hanno Helbling] (1994)**

Klier, Walter	Neues Shake-speare Journal	vol. 3: 170-72	1999, Jan.

Kay, Dennis – *Shakespeare: His Life, Work and Era* **(1994)**

Whalen, Richard F.	Shakespeare Oxford Newsletter	vol. 29/2a: 3	1993, Spring

Keen, Alan and Roger Lubbock – *The Annotator* **(1954)**

Cutner, Herbert	Shakespeare Fellowship News-letter (Eng)	p. 4-5	1954, Sept.
Messner, Rhoda	Shakespeare Oxford Newsletter	vol. 17/1: 4-5	1981, Spring

Keevak, Michael – *Sexual Shakespeare* **(2001)**

Hamill, John	Shakespeare Oxford Newsletter	vol. 38/1: 7, 14	2002, Winter

Kent, William – *Edward de Vere, the Real Shakespeare* **(1947)**

--	Times Literary Supplement	issue 27, p. 498	1947

Kent, William – *London Worthies* **(1937)**

--	Shakespeare Fellowship News-letter (Eng).	No. 14: 7-8	1939, April

Kermode, Frank – *The Age of Shakespeare* **(2004)**

Dickson, Peter W.	Shakespeare Oxford Newsletter	vol. 40/3: 22-24	2004, Summer
Eagleton, Frank	The Nation	p. 29-32	2004, March 1

Kernan, Alvin – *Shakespeare, the King's Playwright, 1603-1613* **(1995)**

Whalen, Richard F.	Shakespeare Oxford Newsletter	vol. 32/1: 21	1996, Winter

Kinney, Arthur F. – *Rogues, Vagabonds and Sturdy Beggars* **(1990)**

Mucci, John	Elizabethan Review	vol. 6/2: 79-84	1998, Autumn

Kirwan, Peter (editor) – *Shakespeare and the Digital World: Redefining Scholarship and Practice* **(2015)**

Dudley, Michael	Brief Chronicles	vol. VI	2015, Summer

Kittle, William – *George Gascoigne, or Edward de Vere* **(1930)**

Mez, J. R.	Shakespeare Fellowship Newsletter (Eng)	p. 3-4	1952, Sept.

Klein, Christian & Andreas von Arnauld – *Weil Bücher unsere Welt verdändern*

Laugwitz, Uwe	Neue Shakespeare Journal	vol. NS7: 141-45	2020

Klier, Walter – *Der Fall Shakespeare – Die Autorschaftsdebatte und der 17. Graf von Oxford als der wahre Shakespeare: Bisher bekannt als Das Shakespeare-Komplott [The Case of Shakespeare – The Author's Edition and the 17th Earl of Oxford as the True Shakespeare: So Far Known as The Shakespeare Plot] (2004)*

Bünsch, Iris	Literatur in Wissenschaft und Unterricht	vol. 28: 252	2005
Weingartner, Gabriele	Neues Shake-Speare Journal	vol. 11: 171-72	2007

Kline, Syril Levin – *Shakespeare's Changeling: A Fault Against the Dead (2014)*

--	Kirkus Reviews	vol. 82/4	2014, Feb. 15
Rubin, Don	Shakespeare Oxford Newsletter	vol. 50/3: 25-26	2014, Summer

Kornstein, Daniel – *Kill All the Lawyers?: Shakespeare's Legal Appeal (1994)*

Stritmatter, Roger	Shakespeare Oxford Newsletter	vol. 33/3: 18-19+	1997, Summer
Whalen, Richard F.	Shakespeare Oxford Newsletter	vol. 30/4: 4-5	1994, Autumn

Kositsky, Lynne – *A Question of Will (2000)*

Crampin, Alice	De Vere Society Newsletter	vol. 27/1: 44-45	2020, Jan.
Whalen, Richard F.	Shakespeare Oxford Newsletter	vol. 36/3: 19, 24	2000, Fall
Pannell, Chris	The Oxfordian	vol. 17	2015

Kositsky, Lynne – *The Thought of High Windows (2004)*

--	Shakespeare Matters	vol. 3/3: 24	2004, Spring

Kreiler, Kurt – *Der Mann, der Schakespeare erfand: Edward de Vere, Earl of Oxford [The Man Who Invented Shakespeare] (2009)*

Colombo, Rosy	Memoria di Shakespeare New Series	vol. 8: 456	2012
Klier, Walter	Brief Chronicles	vol. 1: 279-82	2009
Posener, Alan	Die Welt (Ausgabe Berlin)	p. 1	2010, Jan. 30

Krims, Marvin B. – *The Mind According to Shakespeare: Psychoanalysis in the Bard's Writings (2006)*

Waugaman, Richard M.	Psychoanalytic Quarterly	vol. 77: 1298-1305 2008	

Kühn, Dieter – *Geheimagent Marlowe (2007)*

Sabin, Stefana	Neues Shake-speare Journal	vol. 12: 135-36	2008, Oct.

Kuzoka and Mulryne (eds.) – *Shakespeare, Marlowe, Jonson (2006)*

Malim, Richard C. W.	De Vere Society Newsletter	p. 35-36	2007, Oct.

Lake, Peter – *How Shakespeare Put Politics on the Stage (2018)*

Gansecki, Mike	Shakespeare Oxford Newsletter	vol. 55/2: 25-30	2019, Spring

Lambin, Georges – *Voyages de Shakespeare en France et en Italie (1962)*

Jolly, Eddi	De Vere Society Newsletter	p. 16	2003, June
Russell, Sir John	Shakespearean Authorship Review [repr. in BTC: vol. 5: 107-111]	no. 9: 11-15	1963, Spring

Langford, Michael – *The de Vere Papers (2008)*

Magri, Noemi	De Vere Society Newsletter	vol. 17/1: 26	2010, Feb.
Gilvary, Kevin	De Vere Society Newsletter	vol. 27/4: 32	2020, Oct.

Laoutaris, Chris – *Shakespeare's Book: The Story Behind the First Folio and the Making of Shakespeare (2023)*

Ready, Gabriel	Oxfordian	vol. 25: 283-92	2023, Sept.

Lawler, Frank (translator) – *Abel Lefranc's Behind the Mask of William Shakespeare (1918/2022)*

Delahoyde, Michael	De Vere Society Newsletter	vol. 30/3: 43-49	2023, July
Waugaman, Elisabeth	Oxfordian	vol. 25: 311-17	2023, Sept.

Lawrence, Herbert – *Life and Adventures of Common Sense (1769)*

Allen, Percy	Shakespeare Fellowship Newsletter (Eng.)	no. 11:1-5	1938, Sept.
Allen, Percy	Shakespeare Fellowship Newsletter (Eng.)	no. 12: 2-16	1938, Nov.
Allen, Percy	East Anglian Magazine	vol. 4/1: 13-14	1938, Nov.

Leahy, William – *My Shakespeare (2018)*

Dudley, Michael	The Oxfordian	vol. 20: 177-82	2018, Sept.
Rubin, Don	The Oxfordian	vol. 22: 165-179	2020, Sept.

Leahy, William – *Shakespeare and His Authors: Critical Perspectives on the Authorship Question (2010)*

Imlay, Elizabeth	De Vere Society Newsletter	vol. 17/3: 6-7	2010, Nov.
Malim, Richard C. W.	De Vere Society Newsletter	vol. 17/2: 26-27	2010, Aug.
Waugaman, Richard M.	Shakespeare Matters	vol. 11/1: 9-10, 12	2012, Winter
Wells, Stanley	Times Literary Supplement	issue 5602: 12	2010, Aug. 13
Whalen, Richard F.	Shakespeare Oxford Newsletter	vol. 47/2: 9-11	2011, Spring

Lee, Michelle and Dana Ramel Barnes (eds.) – *Shakespearean Criticism*, **vol. 41 of 68 (1998)**

Whalen, Richard F.	Shakespeare Oxford Newsletter	vol. 39/1: 20-21	2003, Winter

Lefranc, Abel –*Behind the Mask of William Shakespeare* **[a new translation of** *Sous Le Masque De "William Shakespeare"* **by Frank Lawler] (1918/2022)**

Delahoyde, Michael	De Vere Society Newsletter	vol. 30/3: 43-49	2023, July
Waugaman, Elisabeth	Oxfordian	vol. 25: 305-12	2023, Sept.

Lefranc, Abel – *A La Decouverte de Shakespeare* **(1945)**

Dwyer, J. J.	Shakespeare Fellowship Newsletter (Eng)	p. 4-5	1946, Sept.

Lefranc, Abel – Les *Elements Francais de 'Peines D'Amour Perdues [french Elements in Love's Labour's Lost]* **(1936)**

Douglas, Col. Montagu W.	Shakespeare Fellowship Newsletter (Eng.)	no. 3: 7-9	1937, May

Lefranc, Abel – *Sous Le Masque De "William Shakespeare"* **(Under the Mask of "William Shakespeare") (1918)**

--	Washington Post	p. 6	1924, March 10
Cassidy, Claudio	Chicago Tribune	p. H2	1949, April 17
Lee, Sidney	Quarterly Review	vol. 231: 194-206	1919, July
R.S.	Athenaeum, The	p. 301	1919, May 9
Ward, Col. Bernard R.	Hackney Spectator	p. 12	1922, Dec. 22

Lever, Tresham – *The Herberts of Wilton* **(1967)**

Wainewright, Ruth M. D.	Shakespearean Authorship Review	no. 19: 13-14	1968, Autumn
	[repr. in BTC, vol. 5: 259-260]		

Levin, Carole – *The Heart and Stomach of a King: Elizabeth I and the Politics of Sex and Power* **(1994)**

Whalen, Richard F.	Shakespeare Oxford Newsletter	vol. 35/3: 18	1999, Fall

Light, Leigh – *The Which of Shakespeare's Why: A Novel of the Authorship Mystery Near Solution Today* **(2023)**

Harrigan, Tom	Shakespeare Oxford Newsletter	vol. 59/3: 27-28	2023, Summer

Llewellyn, Sally H. – *Edward's Presents: An Oxfordian Play on London's Bankside* **(2004)**

--	De Vere Society Newsletter	p. 28	2004, July
--	Shakespeare Matters	vol. 3/2: 4	2004, Winter
Gardner, Lyn	Guardian, The	p. 28	2004, Jan. 8
Halliburton, Rachel	Evening Standard, The	p. 34	2004, Jan. 9

Llewellyn, Sally H. – *Return to The Forbidden Planet*

--	Stage, The	p. 11	2004, Jan. 15

Londré, Felicia H. (ed.) – *Love's Labor's Lost: Critical Essays* **(1997)**

Goldstein, Gary B.	Elizabethan Review	vol. 5/1: 57-57	1997, Spring
Whalen, Richard F.	Shakespeare Oxford Newsletter	vol. 33/2: 19	1997, Spring

Looney, J. Thomas (editor) – *The Poems of Edward de Vere* **(1921)**

--	Bookman, The	vol. 60/356: 78-79	1921, May
--	Irish Times	p. 2	1921, April 1
--	New Statesman	p. 252	1921, June 4
--	Saturday Review (London)	vol. 131/3408	1921, Feb.
--	Scotsman, The	p. 2	1921, Feb. 17
--	Spectator, The	p. 277-78	1921, Aug. 27
--	Times Literary Supplement	issue 997: 128	1921, Feb. 24
--	Yorkshire Post and Leeds Intelligencer	p. 4	1921, Feb. 16
Eagle, Solomon	Outlook	p. 231	1921, March 12
S.	Bookman's Journal, The	vol. 3/71: 335	1921, March 4
	Response by J. Thomas Looney, March 25, vol. 3/74: 388.		
	Reply by S. in the same issue.		

Looney, J. Thomas – *"Shakespeare" Identified* **(1920, London and New York editions)**
   [See also reviews of later editions]

--	Aberdeen Daily Journal	p. 2	1920, April 5
--	Age, The	p. 4	1930, March 15
--	American Review of Reviews	p. 112	1920, July-Dec.
--	Bookman's Journal	vol. 1/21: 408	1920, March 19
	Response by J. Thomas Looney, April 9, vol. 1/24: 452-53.		
	Reply by reviewer, April 16, vol. 1/25: 468.		
	Further response by J. Thomas Looney, vol. 1/26: 484.		
	Further comments by J. Thomas Looney, vol. 1/2/30: 58-59.		

Looney, J. Thomas – *"Shakespeare" Identified* (1920, London and New York editions) (continued)

--	Billboard, The	p. 10-11	1920, July 17
--	Boston Guardian	p. 10	1920, April 17
--	Chicago Tribune	p. 8	1920, March 24
--	Christian Science Monitor	p. 64	1923, Aug. 25
--	Courier-Journal (Louisville, KY)	p. A4	1920, June 27
--	Daily News	p. 7	1920, March 4
--	Daily Telegraph (Sydney, Australia)	p. 8	1920, May 1
--	Derbyshire Advertiser and Journal	p. 2	1920, March 13
	Field	vol. 135/3505: 302	1920, Feb. 28
--	Frankfurt State Journal (U.S.)		1920, Summer
--	Freeman's Journal (Sydney)	p. 11	1920, Nov. 11
--	Globe and Mail [Toronto]	p. 13	1920, May 1
--	Halifax Evening Courier	p. 4	1920, March 4
--	Irish Times	p. 7	1920, May 7
--	Literary Digest	p. 32-33	1920, Aug. 14
--	Liverpool Echo	p. 4	1920, March 4
--	London Star		1920, before May 12
--	Morning Post	p. 8	1920, April 1
--	New Forest Magazine	vol. XXXV: 20	1920, Oct.
--	New Statesman	p. 712-13	1920, March 20
--	New York Times [brief comment]	p. X5	1920, April 4
--	New York Times [brief description]	p. 56	1920, June 13
--	New York Times	p. 16	1939, Dec. 16
--	New Yorker		1945
--	Nottingham Evening Post	p. 2	1920, April 12
--	Oamaru Mail (New Zealand)	vol. XLIV/14819	1920, Oct. 19
--	Otago Daily Times (New Zealand)	issue 18738	1922, Dec. 16
--	Outlook (American)	vol. 125: 615	1920, Aug. 4
--	Pall Mall Gazette	p. 6-7	1920, March 4
--	Publishers' Circular	p. 233-34	1920, March 6
--	San Francisco Chronicle	p. E2	1920, Aug. 29
--	Saturday Review (London)	p. 308-09	1920, March 27
	Response by J. Thomas Looney, April 17, p. 370.		
	Reply by reviewer, April 24, p. 389.		
--	Saturday Westminster Gazette	p. 18	1820, March 20
--	Scotsman, The	p. 2	1920, March 4
	Response by J. Thomas Looney, March 20, p. 11.		
--	Sheffield Evening Telegraph	p. 4	1920, March 6
--	Spectator, The	p. 425-46	1920, March 27
	Response by J. Thomas Looney, April 10, p. 487.		
	Response by George G. Greenwood, April 10, p. 487.		
--	Sun (Sydney, Australia)	p. 6	1920, May 12
--	Sun (Sydney, Australia)	p. 22	1920, Dec. 5
--	Sunday Dispatch		1920
--	Sydney Morning Herald	p. 12	1921, April 23
	Response by J. Thomas Looney, July 15, 1921, p. 12.		
--	Telegraph (Brisbane, Australia)	p. 13	1920, May 15
	(Reprint of Charles H. Herford's review; see below)		
--	Times of India	p. 11	1920, May 26
--	Town Talk	p. 8	1920, Sept. 4
--	Yorkshire Post and Leeds Intelligencer	p. 6	1920, March 4
	Response by J. Thomas Looney, March 11, p. 4.		
--	Yorkshire Post and Leeds Intelligencer	p. 10	1920, March 6
--	Yorkshire Post and Leeds Intelligencer	p. 11	1920, April 13
	Response by Francis Clarke	p. 521	1920, April 16
	Response by R. L. Eagle	p. 521	1920, April 16
	Response by Editor	p. 521	1920, April 16
A. Sr. J. A.	Bookman, The	p. 84	1920, May

Reviews of Books of Special Interest

Athos.	Bulletin, The	vol. 42: 25	1921, Oct. 27
Barrell, Charles Wisner	Shakespeare Fellowship Newsletter (Am)	vol. 1/1: 8	1939, Dec.
Beauclerk, Charles Sidney De Vere	Accrington Observer and Times		1931, July 18
Benham, W. Gurney	Essex Review	vol. 29: 95-100	1920, April 1
Butcher, Fanny	Chicago Tribune	p. 9	1920, June 13
Björkman, Edwin	Bookman, The	vol. 51/6, p. 677	1920, August
C. B.	Western Mail	p. 7	1920, April 23

Response by J. Thomas Looney, May 6.

C. R.	Nottingham Journal	p. 4	1920, April 22
C. R. B.	Age (Melbourne, Australia)	p. 5	1944, April 15
Courtney, W. L.	Daily Telegraph	p. 16	1920, March 19

Response by J. Thomas Looney, April 1.

Corbin, John	New York Times	p. 58	1920, June 27
Corder, Henry	Advocate (Melbourne)	p. 3	1920, May 20
Crosse, Gordon	Commonwealth	p. 288-92	1920, Oct.
Eagle, Roderick L.	Baconiana	vol. XVI/63: 82-85	1921, March
Fitzgerald, W. J. P.	Daily Telegraph (Sydney)	p. 14	1922, Dec. 30
George, W. L.	World		1920, Spring
Guiterman, Arthur	Life	vol. 76, p. 590	1920, Sept. 30
H. D. S.	Bookseller	vol. 19: 147-48	1920, Marh
Herford, Charles H.	Manchester Guardian	p. 7	1920, March 19

Repr. in *The Telegraph* (Brisbane, Australia), May 15, p. 13.
Repr. in *The Sun* (Sydney, Australia), June 17, 1920, p. 8.

Herford, Oliver	Leslie's Weekly	vol. cxxxi: 3379	July 24
Howard, Keble	Sketch, The	p. 4	1920, March 17
Iota	Southland Times (New Zealand)	issue 18840	1920, June 5
J. R.	Baconiana	vol. XVII/64: 74-7	1920, June
Krutch, Joseph	Nation (USA)	vol. III, p. 248-49	1920, Aug. 28
L. S. P.	Eagle [St. John's College, Cambridge]	vol. 48/218: 83-87	1934
Lee, Sir Sidney	The Bookman's Journal	p. 58	1920, May 21

Response by J. Thomas Looney, May 28, p. 28.

Lucas, R. Macdonald	National Review	vol. 78: 359-69	1921, Nov.

Response by J. Thomas Looney, Feb. 1922, p. 801-09.

M.	Athenaeum, The	p. 450	1920, April 2

Response by J. Thomas Looney, April 30, p. 585.

McQuilland, Louis J.	Oamaru Mail (New Zealand)	vol. XLIV/14055	1920, May 12
Minchin, H. C.	Sunday Times	p. 5	1920, April 4
Pollard, Alfred W.	Times Literary Supplement	issue 946: 149	1920, March 4

Response by J. Thomas Looney, March 25, p. 201.

R. H. C.	New Age	vol. 28/5: 55-56	1920, Dec. 2

Response by J. Thomas Looney, Dec. 23, p. 91.
Reply by R.H.C. same date, p. 91-92.
Response by Looney, Jan. 20, 1921, p. 138-39.
Reply by R. H. C., same date, p. 139.
Further reply by R. H. C., Jan. 27, p. 155-56.
Response by Looney, Feb. 17, p. 192.

Rambler, The	Avon Gazette and York Times	p. 2	1920, May 22
Reedy, William M.	Reedy's Mirror	vol. 29/24: 474-76	1920, June 10
Robertson, J. M.	The Bookman's Journal	p. 58	1920, May 21

Response by J. Thomas Looney, May 28, p. 68.

Robertson, J. M.	Yorkshire Post and Leeds Intelligencer	p. 8	1920, March 5

Response by J. Thomas Looney, March 11, p. 4.
Response by J. Thomas Looney to all Yorkshire Post reviews, April 1, p. 8.

Squire, John C.	Land and Water		
Squire, John C.	Observer, The (British)	p. 4	1921, Jan. 21
Underwood, George	Freethinker, The	p. 316-17	1923, May 20

Responses by Looney on June 10, July 1 and 8.

Whyte, Gordon	Billboard, The	p. 35	1922, Dec. 2
Wood, Clement	New Leader	p. 9	1925, Sept. 26

Wright, David McKee	Bulletin	vol. 41: Red Page	1920, May 6

Looney, J. Thomas – *"Shakespeare" Identified*, 2nd edition (1949)

--	New York Herald Tribune	p. BR31	1949, Nov. 6
--	San Francisco Chronicle	p. 30	1949, Nov. 6
--	Shakespearean Authorship Review	issue #22: 1	1969, Dec.
Basso, Hamilton	The New Yorker	p. 113-4, 117-9	1950, April 8
Bush, Douglas	New Republic	issue 24, p. 20	1950, April 24
Freedley, George	Library Journal	vol. 74: 1605	1949, Oct. 15
Guilfoil, Kelsey	Chicago Tribune	p. I22	1949, Oct. 30

Looney, J. Thomas – *"Shakespeare" Identified and The Poems of Edward de Vere, 3rd revised edition* edited by Ruth Loyd Miller, 1975)

Cyr, Gordon C.	Shakespeare Oxford Newsletter	vol. 12/1: 5-6	1976, Spring
Goff, Tom	Shakespeare Oxford Newsletter	vol. 28/1: 10-11	1992, Winter
Johnson, Morse	Cincinnati Enquirer	vol. 136/309: 39	1977, Feb. 13
Padel, John	Times [London] [mentions all 3 editions of *"Shakespeare" Identified*]	issue 3873: 667	1976, July 4
Wainewright, Ruth M. D.	Bard, The	vol. 2/2: 75-79	1979

Looney, J. Thomas – *"Shakespeare" Revealed: The Collected Articles and Published Letters of J. Thomas Looney,* edited by James A. Warren (2019)

St. Clair, Michael	Shakespeare Oxford Newsletter	vol. 55/4: 24-25	2019, Spring

Loroche, Rebecca & Jennifer Munroe – *Shakespeare and Ecofeminist Theory* (2017)

Wallace, David Rains	Shakespeare Oxford Newsletter	vol. 55/3: 28-31	2019, Summer

Love, Harold – *Attributing Authorship: An Introduction* (2002)

Jiménez, Ramon	Shakespeare Oxford Newsletter	vol. 39/3: 21-22	2003, Summer

Lucas, R. M. – *Shakespeare's Vital Secret Known to His Queen* (1937)

Douglas, Col. Montagu W.	Shakespeare Fellowship Newsletter (Eng.)	no. 8: 8-12	1938, March

MacKail, J. W. – *A Companion to Shakespeare Studies* (1934)

Douglas, Lt. Col. M. W.	Shakespeare Pictorial	no. 81: 176	1934, Nov.

Magri, Noemi – *Such Fruits Out of Italy: The Italian Renaissance in Shakespeare's Plays and Poems.* Edited by Gary B. Goldstein. (2014)

Dams, Christopher	De Vere Society Newsletter	vol. 22/1: 38-39	2015, January
Ray, William	Shakespeare Oxford Newsletter	vol. 50/4: 11-12	2014, Fall
Ray, William	Brief Chronicles	vol. VI	2015, Summer

Malim, Richard C. W. – *The Earl of Oxford and the Making of "Shakespeare:" The Literary Life of Edward de Vere in Context* (2012)

Egan, Michael	Shakespeare Oxford Newsletter	vol. 48/1: 11-12	2012, Winter
Madigan, Patrick	Heythorp Journal	vol. 54/6: 1047-48	2013, Nov.
Marcus, Leah S.	Studies in English Literature 1500-1900	vol. 54/1: 193-242	2014
Showerman, Earl	Shakespeare Matters	vol. 11/4: 17-19	2012, Fall

Malim, Richard C. W.; Kevin Gilvary; Elizabeth Imlay; Eddi Jolly (eds.) – *Great Oxford: Essays on the Life and Work of Edward de Vere* (2004)

---	Shakespeare Matters	vol. 4/3: 23	2005, Spring
Delahoyde, Michael	Rocky Mountain E-Review of Lang. & Lit.	vol. 60/2: 52-59	2006
Delahoyde, Michael	De Vere Society Newsletter	p. 36	2007, June
Vickers, Brian	Times Literary Supplement [repr. in DVN (Sept. 2005), p. 40-43]	issue 5342: 6-8	2005, Aug. 9
Whittemore, Hank	Oxfordian, The	vol. 8: 137-139	2005

Malim, Richard – *Shakespeare's Revolution* (2022)

Goldstein, Gary	The Oxfordian	vol. 24: 301-302	2022, Sept.
Imlay, Elizabeth	De Vere Society Newsletter	vol. 29/3: 47-48	2022, July

Mallin, Eric – *Inscribing the Time* (1995)

Whalen, Richard F.	Shakespeare Oxford Newsletter	vol. 35/3: 18	1999, Fall

Maltby, Arthur – *Shakespeare as a Challenge for Literary Biography* (2009)

Lynch, Jack	Times Literary Supplement	issue 5633: 11	2011, March 18

Marcus, Leah S. – *Puzzling Shakespeare: Local Reading and Its Discontents* (1988)

Stritmatter, Roger	Brief Chronicles	Sp. issue: 103-109	2016, Spring
Stritmatter, Roger	Oxfordian, The	vol. 2: 154-161	1999

Markham, Clements R. – *The Fighting Veres* (1888)

Patience, Harold W.	Shakespeare Oxford Newsletter	vol. 15/2: 8	1979, Spring

Martin, Milward W. – *Shakespeare? A Lawyer Reviews the Evidence* (1965)

--	Shakespeare Newsletter		1965, Sept.
Montgomery, Robert H.	Boston Globe	p. 16	1965, Aug. 23
Ogburn, Charlton, Jr.	Washington Star		1966
Vessey, David W. T. C.	Shakespearean Authorship Review	issue #21: 7-10	1969, Spring

Martin, Peter – *Edmond Malone, Shakespearean Scholar* (1995)

Whalen, Richard F.	Shakespeare Oxford Newsletter	vol. 32/2: 19	1996, Spring

Matchett, Robin – *The Lion Bats the Butterfly* (2002)

Schumann, Howard	Shakespeare Oxford Newsletter	vol. 39/1: 22	2003, Winter

Matus, Irvin S. – *Shakespeare, In Fact* (1994)

--	Kirkus Reviews	vol. 51/21: 1372	1993, Nov.
--	Shakespeare Oxford Newsletter	vol. 30/4: 11	1994, Autumn
Ashey, L. R. Newsl.	Bibliothèque d'Humanisme et Renaissance	vol. 59: 365-409	1997
Bryant, J. A., Jr.	Sewanee Review	vol. 105: 96-105	1997
Griffin, Benjamin	Year's Work in English Studies	vol. 75: 221-27	1994
Jensen, Mike	Small Press	vol. 13: 59	1995, Winter
Johnson, Morse	Shakespeare Oxford Newsletter	vol. 31/1b: 1-7	1995, Winter
	[repr. in BTC, vol. 7: 295-304]		
Lerud, T. K.	Choice	vol. 32: 783	1994-95
Mahon, John W.	Shakespeare Newsletter	vol. 44/3: 42	1994, Fall
O'Brien, Thomas	Cross Currents	vol. 45: 558-60	1995/96, Winter
Pendleton, Thomas A.	Shakespeare Newsletter	vol. 44/2: 21+	1994, Summer
	Resp. by Richard F. Whalen, vol. 44/3: 42.		
	Reply by Thomas Pendleton, vol. 44/3: 42.		
	Response by Morse Johnson, SON, vol. 30/4: 11.		
Publius	Elizabethan Review	vol. 3/1: 67-69	1995, Spring
Roper, David L.	De Vere Society Newsletter	vol. 2/3: 8-11	1995, Nov.
Stuttaford, Genevieve	Publishers Weekly	p. 55-56	1993, Dec. 13
Taylor, Gilbert	Booklist	vol. 90/6: 597	1993, Nov. 15
Whalen, Richard F.	Shakespeare Oxford Newsletter	vol. 29/2a: 5	1993, Spring
Whalen, Richard F.	Shakespeare Oxford Newsletter	vol. 30/1: 11-12	1994, Winter

May, Steven W. – *The Poems of Robert Devereux and Edward de Vere* (new edition, 1981)

Cyr, Gordon	Shakespeare Newsletter	vol. 31/5: 38	1981, Dec.
Cyr, Gordon	Shakespeare Newsletter	vol. 32/1: 6	1982, Feb.
Feldman, A. Bronson	Bard, The	vol. 3/3: 94-104	1982
Ogburn, Jr., Charlton	Shakespeare Oxford Newsletter	vol. 18/1: 13-15	1982, Winter

Mays, Andrea E. – *The Millionaire and the Bard: Henry Folger's Obsessive Hunt for Shakespeare's First Folio* (2015)

Dudley, Michael	Brief Chronicles	Sp. issue: 133-138	2016, Spring

McCarthy, Dennis (editor) – *A Brief Discourse of Rebellion and Rebels by George North*

Hess, W. Ron	Shakespeare Oxford Newsletter	vol. 55/2: 21-24	2019, Spring

McCarthy, Penny – *Pseudonymous Shakespeare* (2006)

Charlton, Derran K.	Shakespeare Oxford Newsletter	vol. 42/3: 31-32	2006, Fall
Malim, Richard C. W.	De Vere Society Newsletter	p. 19-21	2006, July
Waller, Gary	Comparative Drama	vol. 41/1: 119	2007, Spring

McClarran, Steven – *I Come to Bury Shaksper: A Deconstruction of the Fable of the Stratfordian Shake-speare and the Supporting Scholarship* (2012)

Stritmatter, Roger	Shakespeare Matters	vol. 12/1: 17-18	2013, Winter

McClure, Norman (editor) – *The Letters of John Chamberlain* (1939)

Editor	Shakespeare Fellowship Newsletter (Am)	vol. 3/4: 55	1942, June

McCrea, Scott – *The Case for Shakespeare: The End of the Authorship Question* **(2004)**

--	Shakespeare Matters	vol. 3/4: 23	2005, Spring
--	Reference and Research Book News	vol. 20/2	2005, May
Ellis, A. L.	Choice	vol. 42: 6,346	2004, May
Fair, Shana C.	Library Journal	vol. 130/7: 86-87	2005, April
Hadfield, Andrew	English [in review article]	vol. 55: 93-101	2006
Hansen, Matthew C.	Year's Work in English Studies	vol. 86: 381	2007
Schmitt, Juli	Theatre History Studies	vol. 26: 152-54	2006
Taylor, Michael	Shakespeare Survey	vol. 59: 358-59	2007, Sept. 4
Vickers, Brian	Times Literary Supplement	issue 5342: 6-8	2005, Aug. 9
	[repr. in DVN (Sept. 2005), p. 40-43]		
Whalen, Richard F.	Shakespeare Oxford Newsletter	vol. 41/4: 30	2005, Fall

McDonald, Russ – *The Bedford Companion to Shakespeare* **(1996)**

Whalen, Richard F.	Shakespeare Oxford Newsletter	vol. 32/3: 19	1996, Summer

McEwan, Ian – *Nutshell* **(2016)**

Kositsky, Michael	Shakespeare Oxford Newsletter	vol. 55/1: 28-29	2019, Winter

McManaway, James G. – *The Authorship of Shakespeare* **(Folger Library Booklet, edited by Louis B. Wright) (1962)**

Alexander, Peter	Times Literary Supplement	issue 3152: 542	1962, July 27
Horne, Jr., Richard C.	Shakespeare Oxford Newsletter	vol. 6/1: 6-8	1970, Mar. 31
	See Also Craig Huston's *The Shakespeare Authorship Question* (1971), a book written to counter McManaway's]		

Meadows, Denis – *Elizabethan Quintet* **(1956)**

Eggar, Katharine E.	Shakespeare Fellowship Newsletter (Eng)	p. 11	1957, Autumn

Meagher, John C. – *Shakespeare's Shakespeare: How the Plays Were Made* **(1997)**

Whalen, Richard F.	Shakespeare Oxford Newsletter	vol. 35/3: 18	1999, Fall

Mena, Richard – *Ver, Begin* **(2015)**

Ray, William J.	Shakespere Oxford Fellowship Newsletter	vol. 51/3: 16-18	2015, Summer

Meron, Theodor – *Bloody Constraint: War and Chivalry in Shakespeare* **(1988)**

Whalen, Richard F.	Shakespeare Oxford Newsletter	vol. 35/3: 18	1999, Fall

Messner, Rhoda Henry – *Absent Thee From Felicity* **(1976)**

Cyr, Gordon C.	Shakespeare Oxford Newsletter	vol. 12/2: 4	1976, Summer
Morton, Peter	Early Modern Literary Studies	vol. 5/2:	1999, Sept.

Michell, John – *Who Wrote Shakespeare?* **(1996)**

--	Irish Times (Dublin)	p. 70	1999, May 29
Dickson, Peter W.	Washington Post Book World	p. 11	1997, Aug. 17
Engle, Lars	Studies in English Literature 1500-1900	vol. 37: 415-60	1997
Fiéveux, Solange	Neues Shake-speare Journal (German)	vol. 3: 163-68	1999
Graham, Nicholas	Library Journal	vol. 139/1: 50	2014
Klier, Walter	Neues Shake-speare Journal (German)	vol. 7: 152-53	2002, May
Kruh, Louis	Cryptologia	vol. 24/1: 81	2000, Jan.
Nicholl, Charles	Around the Globe	p. 21	1996, Winter
O'Sullivan, Charlotte	Observer	p. 9	1996, April 28
Pizzichini, Lilian	Independent on Sunday	"Culture," p. 12	1999, April 25
Ridden, Geoff	Spectator	vol. 47/2: 44	1998
Stritmatter, Roger	Shakespeare Oxford Newsletter	vol. 33/1: 19	1997, Winter
Stuttaford, Genevieve	Publishers Weekly	p. 223	1996, July 22
Wright, Daniel L.	Shakespeare Bulletin	vol. 16/2: 46	1998, Spring

Miller, Ruth Loyd (editor) – *Hidden Allusions in Shakespeare's Plays, 3rd revised edition* **(1974)**

Cyr, Gordon C.	Shakespeare Oxford Newsletter	vol. 12/3: 10-11	1976, Fall
Goff, Tom	Shakespeare Oxford Newsletter	vol. 28/1: 10-11	1992, Winter

Miller, Ruth Loyd (editor) – *A Hundreth Sundrie Flowres, revised edition* **(1975)**

Cyr, Gordon C.	Shakespeare Oxford Newsletter	vol. 12/4: 6-7	1976, Winter
Goff, Tom	Shakespeare Oxford Newsletter	vol. 28/1: 10-11	1992, Winter

Miller, Ruth Loyd (editor) – *"Shakespeare" Identified and the Poems of Edward de Vere by J. Thomas Looney, and Oxfordian Vistas* **(1975)**

Cyr, Gordon C.	Shakespeare Oxford Newsletter	vol. 12/1: 5-6	1976, Spring

Goff, Tom	Shakespeare Oxford Newsletter	vol. 28/1: 10-11	1992, Winter

Moore, Peter R. – *The Lame Storyteller, Poor and Despised* **(2009)**

--	Shakespeare Matters	vol. 9/1: 5	2010, Winter
--	Shakespeare Oxford Newsletter	vol. 46/1: 2	2010, May
Goldstein, Gary B.	De Vere Society Newsletter	vol. 17/1: 19	2010, Feb.
Hope, Warren	Brief Chronicles	vol. II: 233-236	2010
Malim, Richard C. W.	De Vere Society Newsletter	vol. 17/1: 13-14	2010, Feb.
Whalen, Richard F.	Shakespeare Matters	vol. 9/2: 5, 25	2010, Spr/Sum

Morhardt, M. Mathias – *A La Recontre de 'William Shakespeare'*

Douglas, Col. Montagu W.	Shakespeare Fellowship Newsletter (Eng.)	no. 10: 5-8	1938, July

Morris, Helen – *Elizabethan Literature* **(1958)**

Cutner, Herbert	Shakespearean Authorship Review	issue #1: 12-13	1959, spring

Muir, Kenneth – *Shakespeare's Sources* **(1957)**

Bowen, Gwynneth M.	Shakespeare Fellowship Newsletter (Eng)	p. 9	1957, Autumn

Mullan, John – *Anonymity: A Secret History of English Literature* **(2007)**

Sexton, David	Evening Standard	p. 37	2008, Jan. 14
Waugaman, Richard M.	Shakespeare Matters	vol. 7/3: 10-14	2008, Spring

Nassivera, John – *All the Queen's Men*

Banner, Bennington Vermont	Shakespeare Oxford Newsletter	vol. 24/4: 13-14	1988, Summer
Stemle, Lisa	Sun Sentinel (Fort Lauderdale)	p. 27	1991, Oct. 20

Nelson, Alan H. – *Monstrous Adversary* **(2003)**

--	De Vere Society Newsletter	p. 28	2003, Sept.
Barnaby, Andrew	Renaissance Quarterly	vol. 57/4: 1,529	2004, Winter
Boyle, William E.	Shakespeare Matters	vol. 3/4: 7	2004, Summer
Brame, Michael; G. Popova	Shakespeare Matters	vol. 3/3: 2	2004, Spring
Canino, Catherine G.	Sixteenth Century Journal	vol. 36/3: 908	2005, Fall
Castaldo, A.	Choice	vol. 41/7: 1,298	2004, March
Cyr, Gordon C.	Shakespeare Matters	vol. 3/1: 2	2003, Fall
Detobel, Robert	Neues Shake-speare Journal	vol. 8: 169-72	2003, Aug.
Gilvary, Kevin; Kevin Johnson; Eddi Jolly	De Vere Society Newsletter	p. 6-7	2004, Jan.
Guibbory, Achsah	Studies in English Literature	vol. 45/1: 268	2005, Winter
Hughes, Stephanie H.	Shakespeare Oxford Newsletter	vol. 40/2: 19-23	2004, Spring
Hunter, R. Thomas	Shakespeare Matters	vol. 3/4: 5-6	2004, Summer
Knutson, Roslyn	SMAN	vol. 27/1: 7-8	2007
Mahon, John W.	Shakespeare Matters	vol. 3/4: 8	2004, Summer
May, Steven W.	Shakespeare Quarterly	vol. 56/2: 214-26	2005, Summer
Moore, Peter R.	Shakespeare Oxford Newsletter [repr. in LS, p. 288-311]	vol. 40/1: 1, 15+	2004, Winter
Paul, Christopher	Shakespeare Matters Response by Hank Whittemore, SON 43/2: 21.	vol. 6/1: 22-27	2006, Fall
Pendleton, Thomas	Shakespeare Newsletter	vol. 53/3: 65, 69	2003, Fall
Shickman, Allan R.	Shakespeare Oxford Newsletter	vol. 40/2: 6	2004, Spring
Sobran, Joseph	Shakespeare Oxford Newsletter	vol. 39/4: 01, 9+	2003, Autumn
Stritmatter, Roger	Shakespeare Matters	vol. 3/1: 8-9	2003, Fall
Waugh, Alexander	De Vere Society Newsletter	vol. 24/1: 43-44	2017, January
Whalen, Richard F.	Shakespeare Matters	vol. 3/1: 1, 20+	2003, Fall
Whalen, Richard F.	Shakespeare Matters	vol. 3/2: 22-23	2004, Winter
Whalen, Richard F.	Shakespeare Matters	vol. 3/4: 7-8	2004, Summer
Whalen, Richard F.	Shakespeare Oxford Newsletter	vol. 41/2: 21-22	2005, Spring

Nicholl, Charles – *The Reckoning: The Murder of Christopher Marlowe* **(1992)**

Goldstein, Gary B.	Elizabethan Review	vol. 2/1: 29-32	1994, Spring
Whalen, Richard F.	Shakespeare Oxford Newsletter	vol. 31/1a: 11	1995, Winter

Nicoll, Allardyce (editor) – *Shakespeare: Shakespeare Survey 7* **(1954)**

Cutner, Herbert	Shakespeare Fellowship Newsletter (Eng)	p. 4-5	1954, Sept.

Nicolson, Adam – *Earls of Paradise: England and the Dream of Perfection (2008)*

Crick, Jeremy	De Vere Society Newsletter	vol. 15/1: 27	2008, March

North, George (edited by Dennnis McCarthy) – *A Brief Discourse of Rebellion and Rebels by George North*

Hess, W. Ron	Shakespeare Oxford Newsletter	vol. 55/2: 21-24	2019, Spring

North, Marcy L. – *The Anonymous Renaissance* (2003)

Waugaman, Richard M.	Shakespeare Matters	vol. 8/3: 20, 25+	2009, Summer

Nuttall, A. D. – *Shakespeare the Thinker* (2007)

Malim, Richard C. W.	De Vere Society Newsletter	p. 33-34	2007, October
Waugaman, Richard M.	Shakespeare Matters	vol. 7/4: 8, 10+	2008, Fall

Nye, Robert – *The Late Mr. Shakespeare: A Novel* (1998)

Jolly, Eddi	De Vere Society Newsletter	p. 25	2004, Oct.
McMahon, Daniel	Washington Post	p. M9	1999, June 13
Stern, Micah	Elizabethan Review	vol. 7/1: 82-84	1999, Spring
Whalen, Richard F.	Shakespeare Oxford Newsletter	vol. 35/2: 20-21	1999, Summer

Nye, Robert – *Paging Mrs. Shakespeare* (2000)

Hope, Warren	Elizabethan Review	vol. 1/2: 75-78	1993, Autumn

O'Connor, Frank – *Shakespeare's Progress* (1960)

McManaway, James G.	New York Times	p. BR62	1960, Nov. 20

O'Connor, Garry – *William Shakespeare: A Popular Life* (2000)

Eagleton, Terry	The Independent	1991, Nov. 6	
	[repr. in SON, vol. 27/4: 2-3 (Fall 1991)]		
	[repr. in BTC, vol. 7: 72-73]		
Whalen, Richard F.	Shakespeare Oxford Newsletter	vol. 36/1: 24-25	2000, Spring

Ogburn, Jr., Charlton – *The Man Who Was Shakespeare* (1995)

Goff, Tom	Shakespeare Oxford Newsletter	vol. 31/4: 7-8	1995, Summer
Goldstein, Gary B.	Elizabethan Review	vol. 3/2: 68-70	1995, Autumn

Ogburn, Jr., Charlton – *The Mysterious William Shakespeare* (1984)

--	Shakespeare Oxford Newsletter	vol. 20/4: 4-8	1984, Fall
--	Shakespeare Oxford Newsletter	vol. 21/2: 1-2	1985, Spring
Ashley, L. R. N.	Bibliothèque d'Humanisme et Renaissance	vol. 48: 125-209	1986
Barr, Robert	New Orleans Times-Picayune	LAG: 8	1985, Apr. 26
Bertram, Paul	Shakespeare Bulletin	vol. 3/2: 26	1985, Mar/Apr.
	Response by Charlton Ogburn, Sept./Oct., vol. 3/5: 27.		
Champlin, Charles	Los Angeles Times Book Review	p. I1, I5	1984, Dec. 30
	Response by James P. Bednarz, Jan. 13, p. N6.		
	Response by Celeste Innocenti, Jan. 13, p. N6.		
	Response by David Argall, Jan. 13, p. N6.		
	Response by Mark Nichols, Jan. 13, p. N6.		
Commanday, Robert	San Francisco Chronicle	p. 1	1985, Oct. 20
Crewe, Jonathan	Atlantic Monthly	vol. 29: 448-50	1984, Dec. 29
Crinkley, Richmond	Shakespeare Quarterly	vol. 36/4: 515-22	1985, Winter
Cyr, Gordon C.	Shakespeare Oxford Newsletter	vol. 20/4: 3-4	1984, Fall
Cyr, Gordon C.	Shakespeare Newsletter	vol. 34/4: 42	1984, Winter
Eagleton, Terry	Listener	p. 33	1988, Dec. 15
Fleischer, Leonore	Publishers Weekly	p. 228	1990, May 11
Giroux, Robert	New York Times	p. 13	1984, Dec. 9
	Response by Gordon Cyr, Jan. 13, p. BR29.		
	Reply by Giroux to Cyr, Feb. 3, p. BR35.		
	[See also "'An Hundreth Sundrie Flaws in the *[New York] Times'*		
	Review," in SON, vol. 20/4: 5-8 (Fall 1984)]		
Glore, John	American Theatre	vol. 2/10: 30, 32	1986
Goff, Tom	Shakespeare Oxford Newsletter	vol. 26/3a: 1-2	1990, Summer
Greer, Jane	Chronicles of Culture	vol. 10/2: 18-22	1986
Harrison, John E.	Virginia Lawyer	vol. 42/1: 54	1993
Honigmann, E. A. J.	New York Times Review of Books	p. 23-26	1985, Jan. 17
Hope, Warren	Shakespeare Oxford Newsletter	vol. 20/3: 1-2	1984, Summer
	[repr. in BTC, vol. 6: 264-70]		

Hutshing, Ed	San Diego Union	p. Books-2	1984, Sept. 23
Jonas, Larry	West Coast Review of Books	vol. 11/2: 33	1985
Kelly, Kevin	Boston Globe	p. B1	1984, Oct. 21
Lerner, Maura	Minneapolis Star-Tribune	p. 16A	1995, April 21
Lochte, Dick	Los Angeles Times	p. J10	1984, Sept. 30
Marder, Louis	Shakespeare Newsletter	vol. 34/4: 37-38	1984. Winter
Marder, Louis	Shakespeare Newsletter	vol. 35/1: 2	1985, Spring
Mysack, Joe	National Review (New York)	p. 49	1984, Nov. 2
O'Brien, Conor Cruise	New York Review of Books	p. 21	1985, Jan. 17
O'Brien, Thomas W.	Philadelphia Inquirer	p. G5	1985, May 19
Simpson, Mary-Helen	Unisa English Studies	vol. 29/1: 62-63	1991
Sobran, Joseph	National Review	vol. 37/6: 51-52	1985, April 5
Sobran, Joseph	Washington Times		1985, Feb. 21
Swindell, Larry	Commercial Appeal	p. A12	1997, Sept. 25
Swindell, Larry	Fort Worth Star-Telegram	p. 6	1997, Aug. 31
Swindell, Larry	Fort Worth Star-Telegram	p. 6	1999, Jan. 24
Tehan, Arline B.	Hartford Courant	p. G3	1984, Dec.
Valeo, Tom	St. Petersburg Times	p. 7D	1992. Jan. 23
Vaughan, Virginia M.	Choice	vol. 22/1: 992	1984-85

Ogburn, Jr., Charlton – *The Mysterious William Shakespeare, 2ⁿᵈ Edition* (1992)

Goff, Tom	Shakespeare Oxford Newsletter	vol. 29/1a: 9-10	1993, Winter
Harrison, John E.	Virginia Lawyer	vol. 42/1: 54	1993
Scully, Frank	Variety (Los Angeles)	p. 69	1950, Nov. 8

Ogburn, Jr., Charlton – *The Mystery of William Shakespeare* (pap. abridgment of TMWS issued in England) (1998)

Goff, Tom	Shakespeare Oxford Newsletter	vol. 26/3a: 1-2	1990, Summer
Solal, Annie	Guardian	p. 26	1988, Dec. 9
Stuewe, Paul	Toronto Star	p. M6	1989, April 8

Ogburn, Dorothy and Charlton Ogburn – *The Renaissance Man of England*, (1947), *Revised Edition* (1955)

--	Shakespeare Fellowship Quarterly	vol. VIII/4: 49-50	1947-48, Win.
Adamson, T. L.	Shakespeare Fellowship Newsletter (Eng)	p. 12	1955, Spring
L. H.	Nashville Tennessean		1955, March 13

Ogburn, Dorothy and Charlton – *Der wahre Shakespeare* [translation of *The Renaissance Man of England* by John Mez] (1950)

Brunner, Karl	Shakespeare Jahrbuch	band 87/88: 211-13	1952

Ogburn, Dorothy and Charlton Ogburn, Jr. – *Shakespeare: The [Real] Man Behind the Name* (1962)

--	Booklist	vol. 59: 66-67	1962, Aug.
--	Library Journal	vol. 87: 4295	1962, Nov. 15
--	School Library Journal	vol. 9/3: 75	1962, Nov.
Arnold, Frazer	American Bar Association Journal	vol. 48/11: 1070	1962, Nov.
Comans, Grace P.	Hartford Courant	p. 14F	1962, Sept. 2
Daniel, Frank	Atlanta Journal-Constitution	p. 9D	1962, Oct. 21
Harrison, G. R.	New York Herald Tribune	p. F6	1962, Aug.
Jessup, John K.	Life	p. 4	1962, Sept. 7
Kinsman, Robert	Los Angeles Times	p. C7	1962, Aug. 31
Lewis, George L.	Player Magazine	vol. 39: 215-16	1962, May-Oct.
Robie, Burton A.	Library Journal	vol. 87: 2381	1962, June 15
Starkey, Marion	Boston Globe	p. 25	1962, Sept. 25
Wainewright, Ruth M. D.	Shakespearean Authorship Review [repr. in BTC, vol. 5: 103-106]	no. 9: 8-10	1963, Spring

Ogburn, Dorothy and Charlton Ogburn – *This Star of England* (1952)

--	New York Times	p. 29	1952, Nov. 18
--	New York Times	p. 25	1953, Feb. 10
--	New Statesman (London)	p. 266-67	1954, Feb. 27
--	Virginia Quarterly	vol. 29/2	1953, Spring
--	Wall Street Journal [editorial]	page 12	1953, Feb. 11
Allen, Percy	Shakespeare Fellowship Newsletter (Eng) [repr. in BTC, vol. 4: 117-118]	p. 2	1953, April
Campbell, Oscar James	New York Times	p. BR7, 32	1952, Feb. 8

Crane, Milton	Chicago Tribune	p. B10	1953, Feb. 15
Dawson, Giles E.	Shakespeare Quarterly	vol. 42: 165-70	1953, April
Derrickson, Howard	St. Louis Post Dispatch		1953
Evans, B. Ifor	Truth	p. 378	1954, March 19

Ogburn, Dorothy and Charlton Ogburn – *This Star of England* (1952) (continued)

Harrison, G. B.	Saturday Review of Literature	p. 38	1953, Oct. 10
Krutch, Joseph W.	New York Herald Tribune Book Review	p. 13	1953, Jan. 11
Leonard, Edwin S., Jr.	Christian Science Monitor	p. 13	1953, March 5
Lucchese, Sam F.	Atlanta Journal-Constitution	p. 6F	1952, Dec. 7
Merlin, Milton	Los Angeles Times	p. D6	1953, Jan. 4
Mez, J. R.	Shakespeare Fellowship Newsletter (Eng)	p. 7-8	1953, April
Muir, Kenneth	Spectator	vol. 190: 768	1953, June 12
Phillips, G. W.	Shakespeare Fellowship Newsletter (Eng)	p. 8-9	1953, April
Shepard, Florence C.	Shakespeare Oxford Newsletter	vol. 31/4: 10-11	1995, Summer
Walker, Roosevelt	Atlanta Journal-Constitution	p. 4	1952, Nov. 24
West, Robert H.	Georgia Review, The	vol. 7/2: 228-31	1953, Summer
Wilkin, Robert Newsl.	American Bar Association Journal	vol. 39/4: 314	1953, April

Excerpts from Dorothy Ogburn's reply to reviews in SFE
repr. in SFE, April 1954, followed by responses by Francis Nichols,
Gwynneth Bowen, Kathleen Le Riche, and G. W. Phillips, p. 12-14.

O'Loughlin, Rosemary – *A Rose by Any Other Name* (2022)

Hinds, Amanda	De Vere Society Newsletter	vol. 29/4: 45	2022, Oct.

O'Neal, Cothburn – *The Dark Lady: A Novel* (1954)

Dunn, Esther	New York Times	p. BR36	1954, Nov. 21

Ostrowski, Donald – *Who Wrote That? Authorship Controversies from Moses to Sholokhov* (2020)

Gilvary, Kevin	De Vere Society Newsletter	vol. 27/4: 33-36	2020, Oct.
Jiménez, Ramon	The Oxfordian	p. 145-153	2020, Sept.
Richards, Allison	Journal of Scientific Exploration	vol. 37/2	2023, Summer
St. Clair, Michael	Shakespeare Oxford Newsletter	vol. 56/3: 32-33	2020, Summer

Otness, Harold M. – *The Shakespeare Folio Handbook and Census* (1990)

Lipman, Carole S.	Shakespeare Oxford Newsletter	vol. 32/4: 19, 24	1996. Fall

Oxford University Press (publisher) – *The Shakespeare Authorship Companion* (2017) [See also reviews of *The New Oxford Shakespeare* edited by Gary Taylor, et. al.]

Dudley, Michael, Gary Goldstein, and Shelley Maycock	Oxfordian, The	vol. 19: 195-208	2017, Oct.

Packer, Tina and John Whitney – *Power Plays: Shakespeare's Lessons in Leadership and Management* (2000)

Creasey, Beverly	Shakespeare Oxford Newsletter	vol. 36/2: 22	2000, Summer

Patterson, Annabel – *Censorship and Interpretation: Writing and Reading in Early Modern England* (1984)

Stritmatter, Roger	Elizabethan Review	vol. 3/1: 56-62	1995, Spring

Paul, Simone Katrin – *William Shakespeare: Sämtliche Sonette. Zweisprachige Ausgabe*. Aus dem Englischen übertragen von Simone Katrin Paul. Mit einem Nachwort Von Ernst Piper (1998)

Klier, Walter	Neues Shake-speare Journal	vol. 2: 172-73	1999, Jan.

Pearson, Daphne – *Edward de Vere: The Crisis and Consequence of Wardship* (2005)

Bowen, Lloyd	Economic History Review	vol. 59/3: 638	2006, August
Chibi, Andrew A.	Sixteenth Century Journal	vol. 38/2: 460-62	2007, Summer
Gilvary, Kevin	De Vere Society Newsletter	p. 31-33	2005, Sept.
Lindquist, Eric Newsl.	Renaissance Quarterly	vol. 59/2: 612	2006, summer
Paul, Christopher	English Historical Review	vol. 121/493: 1,173	2006, Sept.

Phillips, Gerald W. – *Lord Burghley in Shakespeare* (1937)

K. C. T.	Shakespeare Pictorial	no. 108: 28	1937, Feb.

Response by Phillips, March 1937, p. 36.

Phillips, Gerald W. – *Shakespeare's Sonnets* (1934)

Simpson. H. B.	Shakespeare Pictorial	no. 84: 32	1935, Feb.

Phillips, Gerald W. – *Sunlight On Shakespeare's Sonnets* (1935)

Allen, Percy	Shakespeare Pictorial	no. 89: 112	1935, July
Child, Harold H.	Times Literary Supplement	p. 203	1935, March 28

| Connes, Georges | Revue Anglo-Américaine | vol. 13/1: 52-53 | 1935, Oct. |

Phillips, Gerald W. – *The Tragic Story of "Shakespeare," Disclosed in the Sonnets* (1932)

--	Belfast News-Letter	p. 5	1932, Nov. 17
C. B. D.	Bookman	vol. 83/495: 228	1932, Dec.
Clutton-Brock, Arthur	Times Literary Supplement	issue 1586: 462	1932, June 23
Kennedy-Skipton, H. K.	Shakespeare Pictorial	no. 54: 132	1932, August

Phillips, Graham and Martin Keatman – *The Shakespeare Conspiracy* (1994)

Buckridge, Patrick	Elizabethan Review	vol. 2/2: 64-70	1994, Autumn
Dams, Christopher H.	De Vere Society Newsletter	vol. 2/1: 12	1995, May
Wells, Stanley	Sunday Times	p. 4	1994, April 17
Whalen, Richard F.	Shakespeare Oxford Newsletter	vol. 32/2: 19	1996, Spring

Pitcher, Seymour M. – *The Case for Shakespeare's Authorship of "The Famous Victories"* (1961)

Bowen, Gwynneth M.	Shakespearean Authorship Review	no. 10	1963, Autumn
	[repr. in BTC, vol. 5: 124-129]		
Messner, Rhoda	Shakespeare Oxford Newsletter	vol. 17/1: 4-5	1981, Spring

Pointon, A. J. – *The Man Who Was Never Shakespeare: The Theft of William Shakespeare's Identity* (2011)

Draya, Ren	Brief Chronicles	vol. IV: 135-136	2012-2013
Egan, Michael	Shakespeare Oxford Newsletter	vol. 48/1: 12-13	2012, Winter
Gilvary, Kevin	De Vere Society Newsletter	vol. 19/3: 41-42	2012, Nov.
Ray, William J.	Shakespeare Matters	vol. 11/4: 21-23	2012, Fall

Porohovshikov, Pierre S. – *Shakespeare Unmasked* (1940)

| Atkinson, J. Shera | Shakespeare Fellowship Newsletter | p. 10-11 | 1955, Autumn |
| Deacon, William | Globe and Mail | p. 28 | 1956, Jan. 14 |

Post, Douglas – *By My Will* [a play] (2023)

| Prechter, Robert P. | Shakespeare Oxford Newsletter | vol. 59/2: 24 | 2023, Spring |

Prechter, Robert – *Oxford's Voices: What Shakespeare Wrote Before He Was Shakespeare* (2022)

| Foss, Jonathan | De Vere Society Newsletter | vol. 29/3: 34-42 | 2022, July |
| Nir, Phoebe | The Oxfordian | vol. 24: 295-300 | 2022, Sept. |

Price, Diana – *Shakespeare's Unorthodox Biography* (2001)

Bauer, Henry	Journal of Scientific Exploration	vol. 18: 149	2004
Challinor, Arthur M.	De Vere Society Newsletter	p. 39-40	2001, Jan.
Livacari, Gary L.	Shakespeare Oxford Newsletter	vol. 37/2: 17-19	2001, Summer
Lyons, Bridget G.	Renaissance Quarterly	vol. 56/2: 553	2003, Summer
Malim, Richard C. W.	De Vere Society Newsletter	p. 34-35	2001, April
	Response by Diana Price, same issue, p. 35-36.		
Nelson, Alan H.	De Vere Society Newsletter	p. 18-21	2004, July
	With rebuttal by Diana Price.		
Traister, D.	Choice	vol. 38/9: 1630	2001, May
Whalen, Richard F.	Shakespeare Oxford Newsletter	vol. 36/3: 18, 23	2000, Fall
Wyatt, Neal	Library Journal	vol. 125/19: 68	2000, Nov. 15

Pritchard, Arnold – *Catholic Loyalism in Elizabethan England* (1979)

| Milward, Peter | Bard, The | vol. 4/1: 22-25 | 1983 |

Purdy, Gilbert Wesley – *Edward de Vere Was Shake-speare: At Long Last, The Proof* (2013)

| Ray, William J. | Shakespeare Oxford Newsletter | vol. 50/3: 22-24 | 2014, Summer |

Rendall, Gerald H. – *The "Ashbourne" Portrait of Shakespeare* (1940)

--	Derby Evening Telegraph	p. 2	1940, July 31
Allen, Percy	East Anglian Magazine	vol. 5/6: 229-30	1941, April
Bénézet, Louis P.	Shakespeare Fellowship News-Letter (Am.)	vol. 2/1: 41	1940, Dec.

Rendall, Gerald H. – *Ben Jonson and the First Folio of Shakespeare's Plays* (1939)

Douglas, Col. Montagu W.	East Anglian Magazine	vol. 5/2: 62-63	1940, Feb.
	[repr. in SFA, vol. 1/2: 8 (Feb. 1940)]		
	[repr. in BTC, vol. 2: 59-61]		

Rendall, Gerald H. – *Personal Clues in Shakespere Poems and Sonnets* (1934)

--	Irish Times	p. 5	1934, Dec. 1
--	Western Morning News	p. 2	1935, Feb. 18
Child, Harold H.	Times Literary Supplement	issue 1730: 203	1935, Mar. 28

Simpson. H. B.	Shakespeare Pictorial	no. 84: 32	1935, Feb.

Rendall, Gerald H. – *Shake-speare: Handwriting and Spelling* (1931)

--	Belfast News-Letter	p. 12	1931, May 21
--	Saturday Review	vol. 151: 839	1931, June 6
C. E. L.	Western Morning News	p. 2	1931, Aug. 24
Connes, Georges	Revue Américaine	vol. 8/6: 544	1931, Aug.
Greg, W. W.	Times Literary Supplement	p. 446	1931, June 4
Ward, Colonel B. R.	Shakespeare Pictorial	no. 38: 63	1931, April

Rendall, Gerald H. – *Shakespeare in Essex and East Anglia* (pamphlet)

Douglas, Col. Montague W.	Shakespeare Fellowship Newsletter (Eng)	p. 6-7	1944, May

Rendall, Gerald H. – *Shakespeare Sonnets and Edward de Vere* (1930)

--	Aberdeen Press and Journa	p. 2	1930, March 24
--	Christian Science Monitor	p. 6	1930, July 14
--	Dundee Courier and Advertiser	p. 10	1930, Feb. 27
--	English Review	p. 520-21	1930, April
--	Essex Review	vol. 44	1935, Jan.
--	Morning Post		1930, March
--	Scotsman, The	p. 2	1930, March 6
A. P. W.	Manchester Guardian Weekly	p. 7	1930, May 5
Brock, H. I.	New York Times	p. 56	1930, April 20
Byrne, Muriel C.	Times Literary Supplement	p. 430	1930, May 22

Response by Rendall, May 29, issue 1478: 457.

Connes, Georges	Revue Anglo-Américaine	vol. 7/6: 549-50	1930, Aug.
Connes, Georges	Revue Anglo-Americaine [in French]	vol. 8: 544	1930, Oct.
Douglas, Col. Montague W.	Shakespeare Fellowship Newsletter (Eng)	vol. 2/1: 4-5	1949, Sept.

[repr. in BTC vol. 4:109-111]

Gwynn, Stephan	Observer, The	p. 7	1930, May 11
Hayward, John D.	Times Literary Supplement	issue 1452: 996	1929, Nov. 28
Ward, Colonel B. R.	Shakespeare Pictorial	no. 26: 16	1930, April

Riley, Dick and Pam McAllister – *The Bedside, Bathtub & Armchair Companion to Shakespeare* (2001)

Brazil, Robert	Shakespeare Oxford Newsletter	vol. 38/4: 21	2002, Fall

Robertson, Vivienne – *Images in an Antique Book: Dante in Shakespeare* (2019)

Sullivan, Patrick	Shakespeare Oxford Newsletter	vol. 57/2: 21-23	2021, Spring

Roe, Richard P. – *The Shakespeare Guide to Italy: Retracing the Bard's Unknown Travels* (2011)

Cole, Jan	De Vere Society Newsletter	vol. 19/1: 22-24	2012, March
Cutting, Bonner Miller	Shakespeare Matters	vol. 11/1: 13, 33	2012, Winter
Dams, Christopher H.	De Vere Society Newsletter	vol. 19/3: 15-17	2012, Nov.
Egan, Michael	Shakespeare Oxford Newsletter	vol. 48/1: 4-8	2012, Winter
Niederkorn, William S.	Brooklyn Rail	p. 54	2011, Dec.
Renner, Virginia J.	Brief Chronicles	vol. III: 279-284	2011, Fall
Taylor, Nicole E.	American Theatre	vol. 28/10: 62	2011, Dec.

Rohde, Eleanor S. – *Shakespeare's Wild Flowers, Fairy Lore, Gardens and Herbs* (1935)

Rendall, Gerald H.	Shakespeare Pictorial	no. 98: 68	1936, April

Rollett, John – *William Stanley as Shakespeare: Evidence of Authorship by the Sixth Earl of Derby* (2015)

Hess, W. Rom	Shakespeare Oxford Newsletter	vol. 52/1: 11-14	2016, Winter
Malim, Richard	De Vere Society Newsletter	vol. 23/1: 42-43	2016, January

Roper, David – *Proving Shakespeare: In Ben Jonson's Own Words, "I Vow He Is E. De Vere"* (2011)

Jolly, Eddi	De Vere Society Newsletter	vol. 19/1: 28-29	2012, March

Rosenbaum, Ron – *The Shakespeare Wars* (2006)

Weiss, Larry	Shakespeare Newsletter	vol. 56/2: 43	2006, Fall
Whalen, Richard F.	Shakespeare Matters	vol. 6/1: 8, 30+	2006, Fall

Rosenblum, Joseph (editor) – *The Definitive Shakespeare Companion* (2017)

Dudley, Michael	Shakespeare Oxford Newsletter	vol. 54/4: 17-20	2018, Fall

Rosenblum, Joseph – *Shakespeare: An Annotated Bibliography* (1992)

Whalen, Richard F.	Shakespeare Oxford Newsletter	vol. 29/2a: 4	1993, Spring

Ross, James – *John de Vere: Thirteenth Earl of Oxford* **(2015)**
Jiménez, Ramon	Shakespeare Oxford Newsletter	vol. 51/3: 11-14	2015, Summer

Rowse, A. L. – *Eminent Elizabethans* **(1983)**
Collinson, Patrick	Times Literary Supplement	p. 484	1983, May 13
Mander, Rosalie	Financial Times	p. 16	1983, May 28

Rowse, A. L. – *Shakespeare the Man* **(1973)**
Ogburn, Charlton, Jr.	Washington Post	p. BW8	1973, Aug. 5

Rowse, A. L. – *Shakespeare's Southampton—Patron of Virginia* **(1965)**
Wainewright, Ruth M. D.	Shakespearean Authorship Review	issue #15: 14-15	1966, spring

Rubinstein, William D. – *Who Wrote Shakespeare's Plays?* **(2012)**
Gilvary, Kevin	De Vere Society Newsletter	vol. 19/3: 42-43	2012, Nov.

Rudenstine, Neil L. – *Ideas of Order: A Close Reading of Shakespeare's Sonnets* **(2014)**
Whittemore, Hank	Shakespeare Oxford Newsletter	vol. 51/4: 12-14	2015, Fall

Rush, Peter – *Hidden in Plain Sight—The True History Revealed in Shake-speares Sonnets* **(2015)**
Norwood, James	Shakespeare Oxford Newsletter	vol. 51/4: 15-17	2015, Fall
Rush, Peter	Response to Norwood's review (SON)	vol. 52/1: 25-27	2016, Winter

Rylance, Mark and Matthew Warchus – *The Big Secret Live: I Am Shakespeare* **(2007)**
--	Coventry Evening Telegraph	p. 35	2007, Sept. 28
Arendt, Paul	Guardian	p. 25	2007, Sept. 10
Bassett, Kate	Independent on Sunday		2007, Sept. 9
Billington, Michael	Guardian		2007, Sept. 3
Cavendish, Dominic	Daily Telegraph (London)		2007, Sept. 5
Clapp, Susannah	Observer		2007, Sept. 9
Gore-Langston, Robert	Daily Mail (London)	p. 1	2007, Sept. 7
Gilvary, Kevin	The Oxfordian	vol. 10: 159-159	2007
Grimley, Terry	Birmingham Daily Post	p. 13	2007, Sept. 12
Nightengale, Benedict	The Times (London)		2007, Sept. 4
Pulford, Angie	Groatsworth of Wit	vol. 18/4: 23-26	2007
Quirke, Kieron	Evening Standard (London)	p. 1	2007, Sept. 3
Rees, Jasper	Telegraph (London)		2007, Aug. 4
Taylor, Paul	Independent, The		2007, Sept. 4

Salgado, Gamini – *The Elizabethan Underworld* **(2005)**
Hope, Warren	Elizabethan Review	vol. 2/1: 26-28	1994, Spring

Saliani, Dom (editor) – *Global Shakespeare Series* **(1996-97)**
Whalen, Richard F.	Shakespeare Oxford Newsletter	vol. 33/4: 21	1997, Fall

Sammartino, Peter – *The Man Who Was William Shakespeare* **(1990)**
--	Italian Voice	p. 6	1990, July 12
Goff, Tom	Shakespeare Oxford Newsletter	vol. 27/3: 6-8	1991, Summer
	[repr. in BTC, vol. 7: 53-57]		
Marchione, Margherita	Italica	vol. 69/1: 92-94	1992, Spring

Sams, Eric (ed.) – *Shakespeare's Edward III* **(1996)**
Wright, Daniel L.	Elizabethan Review	vol. 5/1: 54-5	1997, Spring
	[repr. in BTC, vol. 8: 313-16]		

Schoenbaum, S. – *A Documentary Life of Shakespeare* **(1975)**
Horne, Jr., Richard C.	Shakespeare Oxford Newsletter	vol. 11/2: 23-28	1975, Summer

Schoenbaum, S. – *Shakespeare's Lives* **(1993)**
Cyr, Gordon C.	Shakespeare Oxford Newsletter	vol. 28/3: 6-10	1992, Summer
Horne, Jr., Richard C.	Shakespeare Oxford Newsletter	vol. 7/1: 4-12	1971, March 30
Whalen, Richard F.	Shakespeare Oxford Newsletter	vol. 29/2a: 5-6	1993, Spring

Scott, W. I. D. – *Shakespeare's Melancholics* **(1962)**
Malim, Richard C. W.	De Vere Society Newsletter	p. 23	2004, April

Schutte, Kimberly – *A Biography of Margaret Douglas, Countess of Lennox* **(2002)**
Whalen, Richard F.	Shakespeare Matters	vol. 3/3: 24	2004, Spring

Screech, M. A. (translator and editor) – *Montaigne: The Complete Essays* **(1991)**
Sokolowski, Peter	Elizabethan Review	vol. 1/2: 43-51	1993, Autumn

Sears, Elisabeth – *Shakespeare and the Tudor Rose* (1992)

Goff, Tom	Shakespeare Oxford Newsletter	vol. 28/1: 8-9	1992, Winter

Shahan, John and Alexander Waugh (editors) – *Shakespeare Beyond Doubt? Exposing an Industry in Denial* (2013)

--	Shakespeare Matters	vol. 12/3: 1, 19, 36	2013, Summer
Dean, Paul	New Criterion, The	vol. 32/3: 66	2013, Nov.
Gilvary, Kevin	De Vere Society Newsletter	vol. 20/2: 18	2013, July
Goldstein, Gary	The Oxfordian	vol. 15: 92-99	2013
Malim, Richard	Heythorp Journal	vol. 56/2: 321-22	2015, March
Rubin, Don	Brief Chronicles	vol. V: 189-92	2014, Summer
Rubin, Don	Critical Stages	no. 14	2014, Feb.
St. Clair, Michael	Shakespeare Matters	vol. 12/4: 26, 35	2013, Fall

Shaheen, Naseeb – *Biblical References in Shakespeare's Comedies* (1993)

Stritmatter, Roger	Elizabethan Review	vol. 3/2: 60-68	1995, Autumn

Shakespeare, William – *Macbeth* (The Oxfordian Shakespeare Series, edited by Richard F. Whalen) (2007)

Goldstein, Gary B.	Oxfordian, The	vol. 10: 154-156	2007
Tate, Lew	Shakespeare Oxford Newsletter	vol. 44/1: 25-26	2008, Winter

Shakespeare, William – *The Fully Annotated Macbeth, Second Edition with Commentary by Richard F. Whalen* (2013)

Egan, Michael	Shakespeare Oxford Newsletter	vol. 49/2: 14-16	2013, Spring
Ray, William	Shakespeare Matters	vol. 12/2: 6, 17	2013, Spring

Shakespeare, William – *Othello the Moor of Venice* (Oxfordian Shakespeare Series, edited by Ren Draya and Richard F. Whalen) (2010)

--	Shakespeare Oxford Newsletter	vol. 46/1: 15	2010, May
Egan, Michael	Shakespeare Oxford Newsletter	vol. 48/1: 10-11	2012, Winter
Farina, William	Shakespeare Oxford Newsletter	vol. 47/1: 4-6	2011, Jan.
Londré, Felicia	Brief Chronicles	vol. II: 225-226	2010

Shakespeare, William and Christopher Marlowe – *Hamlet* (edited by Alex Jack) (2005)

Vickers, Brian	Times Literary Supplement		2005, Aug. 17
	[repr. in DVN (Sept. 2005), p. 40-43]		

Shapiro, James – *1599: A Year In the Life of William Shakespeare* (2005)

Detobel, Robert	Neues Shakespeare Journal	vol. 12: 140-42	2008, Oct.
Malim, Richard C. W.	De Vere Society Newsletter	p. 22	2006, April
Niederkorn, William S.	New York Times	p. 32	2005, Aug. 30

Shapiro, James – *Contested Will: Who Wrote Shakespeare?* (2010)

--	Economist	p. 93	2010, March 27
--	Folger Magazine	vol. 4/1: 16-23	2010
--	Kirkus Review	vol. 78: 1	2010, Jan. 1
--	Sunday Business Post		2010, April 25
--	Times (London)	p. 2	2010, April 5
--	Tehelka (New Delhi)		2010, June 19
--	Wall Street Journal	Online	2010, April 2
Alter, Alexandra	Wall Street Journal	p. W12	2010, April 2
Bate, Jonathan	Sunday Telegraph	p. 25	2010, April 4
Berry, Ralph	Contemporary Review	issue 292: 518-19	2010, Winter
Bethune, Brian	MacLean's (Toronto)	p. 60	2010, April
Brandt, Bruce E.	Choice	vol. 48	2010-11
Brown, Craig	Mail on Sunday	p. 11	2010, April 11
Brown, Tom	Around the Globe	vol. 45: 42-43	2010
Carey, John	Sunday Times	p. 44	2010, March 21
Chapman, Rebecca	Shakespearean International Yearbook	vol. 12: 169-94	2012
Conrad, Peter	Observer	p. 46	2010, April 4
Conrad, Peter	Observer	p. 41	2011, Jan. 9
Cooksey, T. L.	Library Journal	vol. 135/3: 95-96	2010, Feb. 15
Crystal, Ben	Independent	p. 34	2010, March 28
Cutting, Bonner Miller	Shakespeare Matters	vol. 9/3: 12-14+	2010, Fall
Dobson, Michael	Financial Times	p. 16	2010, March 20
Draya, Ren	Times Literary Supplement	issue 5588: 6	2010, May 7
Drusiana, April	De Vere Society Newsletter	vol. 28/1: 26-45	2021, Jan.

Dudley, Michael	Winnipeg Free Press	p. H7	2010, May 15
Elliott, Ward	Los Angeles Times	p. E8	2010, May 9
Ellis, David	Cambridge Quarterly	vol. 39/3: 297-302	2010
Feingold, Michael	Village Voice	p. 34	2010, June 16-22
Graham, Nicholas	Library Journal	vol. 139/1: 50	2014
Gross, John	Commentary	vol. 129/3: 38-44	2010, March

               Response by Samuel Blumenfeld, June 2010, p. 6.
               Response by Rev. Edward T. Oakes, June 2010. p. 6-7.
                    Reply to both by John Gross, June 2010, p. 7-8.

Hackett, Helen	London Review of Books	p. 21-22	2010, Mar. 11
Hannan, Daniel	Telegraph, The (London)		2010, March 16
Hensher, Philip	Spectator, The (London)		2010, April 3

               Response by Richard Malim, April 10.

Hope, Warren	Brief Chronicles	vol. II: 212-223	2010
Howard, Jennifer	Chronicle of Higher Education	vol. 56/29: B11-2	2010, March 28
Hunter, R. Thomas	Shakespeare Matters	vol. 8/4: 2, 26	2009, Fall
Hunter, R. Thomas	Shakespeare Oxford Newsletter	vol. 46/1: 12-3, 23	2010, May
Kamm, Oliver	The Times (London)	p. 4	2012, April 20
Lennon, Troy	Daily Telegraph (Surry Hills, Australia)	p. 36	2010, May 27
Malim, Richard C. W.	De Vere Society Newsletter	p. 22	2006, April
Malim, Richard C. W.	De Vere Society Newsletter	vol. 17/2: 22-26	2010, Aug.
Malim, Richard C. W.	De Vere Society Newsletter	vol. 17/3: 28-29	2010, Nov.
Mantel, Hilary	Guardian	p. 6	2010, March 20
Marcus, Leah	Shakespeare Johrbuch	vol. 148: 215-20	2012
McCarter, Jeremy	New York Times Book Review	p. 10-11	2010, May 2
McCrum, Robert	Observer	p. 18	2010, March 14
Miola, Robert	First Things	p. 63-64	2010, Aug/Sept
Nicholl, Charles	Times Literary Supplement	issue 5586: 3-4	2010, April 23

               Response by Ren Draya, issue 5588, 7 May, p. 6.

Niederkorn, William S.	Brooklyn Rail		2010, April
Noel-Tod, Jeremy	Telegraph (London)	p. 20	2010, March 20
Olson, Ray	Booklist (Chicago)	vol. 106/15: 12	2010, April
Pendleton, Thomas A.	The Shakespeare Newsletter	vol. 58/3: 81, 103	2009, Winter
Pirè, Luciana	Memoria di Shakespeare	New Series 8: 464+	2012
Ray, William	Shakespeare Matters	vol. 10/4: 24-30	2011
Reid, Nicholas	Sunday Star-Times (Wellington)	p. C7	2010, April 25
Rose, Lloyd	Washington Post	p. B6	2010, June 6
Rosenberg, Saul	Wall Street Journal	p. A19	2010, April 8
Sexton, David	Evening Standard	p. 36	2010, March 18
Shahan, John	Contested Year	Appendix A	2016
Sharpe, Will	Shakespeare Bookshop Newsletter	vol. 16: 1-2	2010
Simon, John	Weekly Standard	p. 30-32	2010, Aug. 23
Stritmatter, Roger	Shakespeare Matters	vol. 10/2: 1, 17-23	2011
Timpane, John	Philadelphia Inquirer		2010, June 30
Waugaman, Richard M.	Psychoanalytic Quarterly	vol. 80: 225-31	2011
Wells, Stanley	New York Review of Books	vol. 57/9: 31-33	2010, May 27
Werner, Hans	Toronto Star	p. 6	2010, May 9
Whalen, Richard F.	Shakespeare Oxford Newsletter	vol. 44/2: 13-15	2008, Spring
Whalen, Richard F.	Shakespeare Oxford Newsletter	vol. 46/1: 7-11	2010, May
Whalen, Richard F.	Shakespeare Oxford Newsletter	vol. 47/2: 09-11	2011, Spring
Wilkinson, Heward	Shakespeare Matters	vol. 10/2: 1, 24-26	2011

Shapiro, James – *Shakespeare in a Divided America* **(2020)**

Dudley, Michael	Shakespeare Oxford Newsletter	vol. 56/3: 31	2020, Summer

Shapiro, James – *The Year of Lear: Shakespeare in 1606* **(2015)**

Boyle, William E.	Shakespeare Oxford Newsletter	vol. 52/1: 8-11	2016, Winter

Simmons, Charles – *Belles Lettres* **(2003)**

Klier, Walter	Neues Shakespeare Journal	vol. 9: 181-82	2004, June

Simonton, Dean Keith – *Origins of Genius: Darwinian Perspectives on Creativity* **(1999)**

Shahan, John M.	Shakespeare Oxford Newsletter	vol. 37/3: 13, 20	2001, Fall

Singleton, Esther – *The Shakespeare Garden* **(1922, 1931)**

--	Los Angeles Times	p. 17	1931, April 5

Singleton, Esther – *Shakespearian Fantasias: Adventures in the Fourth Dimension* **(1929)**

Ward, Colonel B. R.	Shakespeare Pictorial (Part 1)	no. 24: 20	1930, Feb.
Ward, Colonel B. R.	Shakespeare Pictorial (Part 2)	no. 25: 16	1930, Mar.

Singleton, Esther – *Shakespearian Fantasias: Adventures in the Fourth Dimension.* **Modern edition edited by James A. Warren (2019)**

Hyde, Mike	Shakespeare Oxford Newsletter	vol. 55/2: 30-31	2019, Spring

Sisson, Charles. J. – *The Boar's Head Theatre: An Inn-Yard Theatre of the Elizabethan Age* **(1972)**

Bowen, Gwynneth M.	Shakespearean Authorship Review	no. 26: 19-23	1972, Summer
	[repr. in BTC, vol. 5: 332-336]		

Sisson, Charles J. – *Shakespeare* **(1956)**

Adamson, T. L.	Shakespeare Fellowship Newsletter (Eng)	p. 9-10	1956, Spring

Skinner, Quentin – *Forensic Shakespeare* **(2014)**

Waugaman, Richard	The Oxfordian	vol. 18: 175-82	2016

Slater, Gilbert – *Seven Shakespeares* **(1931)**

--	Dundee Courier and Advertiser	p. 4	1931, Dec. 3
--	Manchester City News		1931, Nov. 28
--	Times Literary Supplement	p. 30	1932, Jan. 14
--	Western Morning News		1932, Jan. 11
P.A. [Percy Allen]	Christian Science Monitor	p. 7	1932, Jan. 9
H. R. W.	Saturday Review	vol. 152: 560	1931, Oct. 31
	Response by Bernard M. Ward, Nov. 14, p. 624.		
Ward, Colonel B. R.	Shakespeare Pictorial	no. 45: 180	1931, Nov.

Smith, Sara – *Chasing Shakespeares* **(2008)**

--	Shakespeare Newsletter	vol. 53/2: 33	2003, Summer
Anable, Stephen	Publishers Weekly (Review and interview)	p. 51	2003, May 19
Charles, Ron	Christian Science Monitor	p. 15	2003, June 26
Coale, Sam	Providence Journal	p. B5	2003, July 6
Matus, Irvin	Washington Post	p. WBK4	2003, Dec. 4
Pate, Nancy	Orlando Sentinal	p. F10	2003, July 27
Pendleton, Thomas A.	Shakespeare Newsletter	vol. 53/2: 33-34+	2003, Summer
Sherwood, James	Shakespeare Oxford Newsletter	vol. 39/2: 19	2003, Spring
Turrentine, Jeff	New York Times	p. A22	2003, July 20
Whalen, Richard F.	Shakespeare Matters	vol. 2/4: 24	2003, Summer
Whalen, Richard F.	Shakespeare Matters	vol. 4/3: 31	2004, Summer

Sobran, Joseph – *Alias Shakespeare* **(1997)**

--	Calgary Herald		1997, May
--	South China Morning Post	p. 38	1997, Sept. 27
Bate, Jonathan	Wall Street Journal		1997, May 1
	Response by Patrick R. Sullivan, May 15, p. A23.		
	Response by Nancy A. Holtz, May 15, p. A23.		
	Response by Joseph Sobran, May 15, p. A23.		
Bauer, Henry	Journal of Scientific Exploration	vol. 18: 149	2004
Bethell, Tom	American Spectator	p. 22-23	1997, May
Boyle, Charles	Shakespeare Oxford Newsletter	vol. 33/3: 16	1997, Summer
Brownlow, Frank	Chronicles	vol. 21/8: 5	1997
Cantor, Paul A.	Weekly Standard	p. 31-34	1997, Apr. 28
Daschlager, Earl L.	Houston Chronicle	Zest: 23, 31	1997, June 22
Dickerson, D. O.	Choice	vol. 35/3: 485	1997-98
Dickson, Peter W.	Washington Post Book World	p. 11	1997, Aug. 17
Digby, Diehl	Modern Maturity	vol. 40/2: 28	1997, March
Hart, Jeffrey	National Review	p. 48-49	1997, June 30
Holtz, Nancy A.	Wall Street Journal (letter)	p. 23A	1997, May 15
Kathman, David	[not known]		

	Sobran reply to Kathman [unpublished, but available at: http://sobran.com/oxfordlibrary.shtml]		
Klier, Walter	Neues Shake-speare Journal (German) [Also in *Viener Zeitung* 7.3 (1998)]	vol. 4: 138-44	1999, July
Klier, Walter	Neues Shake-speare Journal (German)	vol. 8: 173-76	2003, Aug.
Marks, Jim	Lambda Book Report	vol. 6/3: 9-10	1997
McGoogan, Ken	Calgary Herald	page 1B	1997, May 10
Mucci, John	Elizabethan Review	vol. 5/1: 59-61	1997, Spring
Nelson, Alan H.	Shakespeare Quarterly	vol. 50: 376-82	1999
	Response by Sobran, SON, vol. 36/1: 12-13, 25, 31.		
	Additional response by Sobran, 1999, unpublished, "How Old was Oxford's Daughter, and When Did William Lose His Hair?" [can be found at http://sobran.com/oxfordlibrary.shtml]		
Rodi, Robert	Harvard Gay and Lesbian Review	vol. 5/1: 36-37	1998
Sheppard, Philippa	Globe and Mail (Toronto)	p. D11	1997, Dec. 13
Seiler, John	Orange County Register		1997, Dec.
Sisson, Edward H.	Shakespeare Oxford Newsletter	vol. 34/1: 21-22	1998, Spring
Stritmatter, Roger	Shakespeare Oxford Newsletter	vol. 33/2: 6-7, 28	1997, Spring
Stuttaford, Genevieve	Publishers Weekly	vol. 244/11: 66	1997, March
Stone, Elliott	Shakespeare Oxford Newsletter	vol. 33/3: 21	1997, Summer
Taylor, Welford D.	Richmond Times	p. F4	1997, July 20
Wasserman, Jerry	Vancouver Sun	p. C11	1998, March 7
Wellman, Wade	Milwaukee Sentinal	p. I6	1991, May 3
White, Diana	Boston Globe		1997, June 2
Wright, Daniel L.	The Oxfordian	vol. 2: 152-154	1999

Sohmer, Steve – *Reading Shakespeare's Mind* (2017)

Waugaman, Richard M.	Renaissance Quarterly		2017

Sperack, Marvin – *The Harvard Concordance to Shakespeare* (1973)

Cyr, Helen W.	Shakespeare Oxford Newsletter	vol. 11/3: 6	1975, Fall

Spevack, Marvin – *Sidney Lee: Biographer, Shakespearean, Comparatist, Educator* (2009)

Lynch, Jack	Times Literary Supplement	issue 5633: 11	2011, March 18

Spurgeon, Caroline – *Shakespeare's Imagery and What It Tells Us* (1935)

Allen, Percy	Shakespeare Pictorial	no. 99: 84	1936, May

Standen, Gilbert – *Shakespeare Authorship: A Summary of Evidence* (1930)

--	Age (Melbourne, Australia)	p. 6	1930, Nov. 22
--	Christian Science Monitor	p. 6	1930, Nov. 4
--	Times Literary Supplement	p. 30	1932, Jan. 14
--	Times of India	p. 15	1931, Jan. 21
Connes, Georges	Revue Anglo-Americaine [in French]	vol. 8/3: 253-54	1931, Feb.
Thornton, James	Nation and Athenaeum	p. 635	1931, Feb. 14
Ward, Colonel B. R.	Shakespeare Pictorial	no. 32: 16	1930, Oct.

Starner, Janet Wright; Barbara Howard Traister – *Anonymity in Early Modern England: What's In a Name?* (2011)

Waugaman, Richard M.	Shakespeare Matters	vol. 11/1: 14-15, 33	2012, Winter

Story, Ted – *The Shakespeare Fraud: The Politics Behind the Pen* (2016)

Hurst, Walter	Shakespeare Oxford Newsletter	vol. 53/1: 26-27	2017, Winter

Streitberger, W. R. – *The Masters of the Revels and Elizabeth I's Court Theatre* (2016)

Hess, W. Ron	Shakespeare Oxford Newsletter	vol. 52/4: 8-11	2016, Fall

Streitz, Paul – *Oxford, Son of Queen Elizabeth I* (2001)

Paul, Christopher	Shakespeare Matters	vol. 1/4: 17-20	2002, Summer
	Resp. by John Gove, Fall 2002, p. 4.		
	Resp. by Paul Streitz, Fall 2002, p. 4-5.		
	Reply to Streitz by Paul, Winter 2003, p. 2-4.		
Sherwood, James	Shakespeare Oxford Newsletter	vol. 38/3: 17	2002, Summer
	Response by Paul Streitz Fall, vol. 2/1: 3-4.		

Stritmatter, Roger – *Shakespeare and the Law: How the Bard's Legal Knowledge Affects the Authorship Question* **(2022)**

Hyde, Michael	Shakespeare Oxford Newsletter	vol. 59/2: 27	2023, Spring

Stritmatter, Roger – *The Poems of Edward de Vere, 17th Earl of Oxford . . . and the Shakespeare Question, vol. 1* **(2019)**

Boyle, William	The Oxfordian	vol. 21: 249-54	2019, Sept.

Stritmatter, Roger and Lynne Kositsky – *On the Date, Sources and Design of Shakespeare's The Tempest* **(2013)**

--	Reference and Research Book News	vol. 28/5	2013, Oct.
Hughes, Stephanie H.	The Oxfordian	vol. 15: 149-154	2013
Ray, William J.	Shakespeare Matters	vol. 12/4: 27-28	2013, Fall
Vaughan, Alden T.	Shakespeare Quarterly	vol. 59/3: 245-73	2008, Fall

Sturrock, Peter A. – *AKA Shakespeare: A Scientific Approach to the Shakespeare Authorship Question* **(2013)**

--	Kirkus Reviews	vol. 81/13: 336	2013, July 1
Spittle, Bruce	Journal of Scientific Exploration	vol. 27/4: 705-10	2014, Winter
Stritmatter, Roger	Shakespeare Oxford Newsletter	vol. 50/2: 19-21	2014, Sprint
Wember, Hanno	Brief Chronicles	vol. V: 205-13	2014, Summer

Sturrock, Peter A. – *Late Night Thoughts About Science* **(2015)**

Schumann, Howard	Shakespeare Oxford Newsletter	vol. 52/2: 34-36	2016, Spring

Sulloway, Frank J. – *Born to Rebel: Birth Order, Family Dynamics and Creative Lives* **(1997)**

Shahan, John	Oxfordian, The	vol. 6: 150-153	2003

Tamerl, Alfred – *Hrotsvith von Gandersheim* **(1999)**

Dickenburger, Udo	Neues Shake-speare Journal	vol. 5: 150-52	2000, April

Tassinari, Lamberto – *John Florio: The Man Who Was Shakespeare* **(2009)**

Egan, Michael	Shakespeare Oxford Newsletter	vol. 48/1: 8-10	2012, Winter
	Response by L. Tassinari, Summer 2012, p. 4-5.		
Rubin, Don	The Oxfordian	vol. 22: 165-179	2020, Sept.

Tatum, Aaron F. – *Shakespeare's Secrets*

Donnell, Evans	De Vere Society Newsletter	vol. 25/4: 45-47	2018, Oct.

Taylor, Gary – *Cultural Selection* **(1996)**

Whalen, Richard F.	Shakespeare Oxford Newsletter	vol. 32/2: 19, 24	1996, Spring

Taylor, Gary, et. al. (editors) – *The New Oxford Shakespeare* **(2018) [See also Oxford University Press (publisher),** *The Shakespeare Authorship Companion* **(2017)]**

Rubin, Don	Oxfordian, The	vol. 22: 165-179	2020, Sept.

Taylor, Gary – *Reinventing Shakespeare* **(1991)**

--	Shakespeare Oxford Newsletter	vol. 29/2a: 9-11	1993, Spring
Taylor, Robert	Boston Globe	p. 98	1989, Sept. 20

Taylor, Rupert – *The Date of Love's Labour's Lost* **(1932)**

Ward, Captain B. M.	Shakespeare Pictorial	issue 55: 148	1932, Sept.

Theobald, Bertram G. – *Exit Shakspere* **(1931)**

--	Times Literary Supplement	p. 30	1932, Jan. 14
Parsons, I. M.	Spectator	p. 149	1932, Jan. 30

Thomas, Julia – *Shakespeare's Shrine: The Bard's Birthplace and the Invention of Stratford-upon-Avon* **(2012)**

Ray, William J.	Shakespeare Matters	vol. 11/4: 23	2012, Fall

Thomson, Peter – *Shakespeare's Professional Career* **(1999)**

Whalen, Richard F.	Shakespeare Oxford Newsletter	vol. 29/2a: 4	1993, Spring

Thomson, Walter – *The Sonnets of William Shakespeare and Henry Wriothesley, Third Earl of Southampton, Together With A Lover's Complaint and The Phoenix and Turtle* **(1938)**

E. S.	Shakespeare Pictorial	no. 124: 91	1938, June

Thüne, Wolfgang – *Freispruch - für CO2* **(2002)**

Illig, Heribert	Neues Shake-speare Journal	vol. 9: 177-80	2004, June

Tillyard, E. M. W. – *The Elizabethan World Picture* **(1942)**

Allen, Percy	Shakespeare Fellowship News-letter (Eng.)	p. 6	1943, May

Tillyard, E. M. W. – *Shakespeare's History Plays* **(1944)**

Brown, Ivor	John O'London's Weekly		1945, Jan. 26

Dwyer, J. J.	Shakespeare Fellowship News-letter (Eng)	p. 3	1945, May

Titherley, A. W. – *Shakespeare's Identity: William Stanley, 6th Earl of Derby* **(1952)**

Bowen, Gwynneth M.	Shakespeare Fellowship Newsletter (Eng)	p. 6-7	1952, Sept.
Caranti, Elio	Genus	vol. 12/1/4: 285+	1956

Trow, M. J., and Talieson Trow – *Who Killed Kit Marlowe?* **(2001)**

Hughes, Stephanie H.	The Oxfordian	vol. 5: 174-182	2002

Tweedale, R. L. – *Wasn't Shakespeare Someone Else?* **(1971)**

Horne, Jr., Richard C.	Shakespeare Oxford Newsletter	vol. 7/2: 7	1971, June 1
Marder, Louis	Shakespeare Newsletter	vol. 23/1: 6	1973, Feb.

Usher, Peter – *Hamlet's Universe* **(2006)**

Prener, Nan	Oxfordian, The	vol. 10: 157-158	2007

Usher, Peter – *Shakespeare's Knowledge of Astronomy and the Birth of Modern Cosmology* **(2021)**

Roper, D. L.	Journal of Scientific Exploration	vol. 37/2	2023, Summer

Van Moerkerten – *Acter Het Mombakkes* **(Behind the Mask) (1950)**

Van Lunteren, S. A.	Shakespeare Fellowship Newsletter	p. 8	1953, Nov.

Vaughan-Davies, Richard – *In the Shadow of Shakespeare* **[a novel] (2020)**

Pommer, Jennifer	De Vere Society Newsletter	vol. 28/2: 47-49	2021, April

Vedi, Sten F. – *'This Ientleman of Polonia': Polonius, A Character in Disguise* **(2012)**

Ray, William	Shakespeare Matters	vol. 12/1: 26-27	2013, Winter

Vedi, Sten F. & Gerold Wagner – *Elsinore Revisited – The author's sources of knowledge about Elsinore and Denmark* **(2018)**
[2nd edition, enlarged, with new subtitle, of Vedi's 2012 book]

Jolly, Eddi	De Vere Society Newsletter [repr. in NSJ, vol. NS7 (2020): 140-41)]	vol. 26/2: 29-30	2019, April

Vendler, Helen – *The Art of Shakespeare's Sonnets* **(1997)**

Anderson, Mark K.	Shakespeare Oxford Newsletter	vol. 34/1: 16-17	1998, Spring
Hope, Warren	Elizabethan Review	vol. 7/1: 78-82	1999, Spring
Whalen, Richard F.	Shakespeare Oxford Newsletter	vol. 34/1: 18-19	1998, Spring

Vickers, Brian – *Counterfeiting Shakespeare* **(2002)**

Sherwood, James	Shakespeare Matters	vol. 3/1: 18-19	2003, Fall

Vickers, Brian – *Shakespeare, Co-Author* **(2004)**

Brown, Jayson B.	Early Theater	vol. 9/1: 168	2006, Jan.
Niederkorn, William S.	Neues Shake-speare Journal	vol. 12: 132-34	2008, Oct.

Wadsworth, Frank W. – *The Poacher From Stratford* **(1958)**

Brown, Ivor	Times Literary Supplement	issue 3004: 547	1959, Sept. 25
Harbage, Alfred	New York Times		1958, Oct. 19
Maxwell, Baldwin	Shakespeare Quarterly	vol. 10/3: 435-37	1959, Summer

Wainwright, Michael – *The Rational Shakespeare* **(2018)**

Dudley, Michael	The Oxfordian	vol. 22: 155-163	2020, Sept.

Wallace, David Rains – *Shakespeare's Wilderness* **(2017)**

Anderson, Mark	Shakespeare Oxford Newsletter	vol. 53/3: 13-14	2017, Summer
Keeney, Patricia	De Vere Society Newsletter	vol. 25/3: 43-47	2018, July

Wallace, Rihard J. – *Aspects of the Shakespeare Authorship Question* **(2022)**

St. Clair, Michael	Shakespeare Oxford Newsletter	vol. 58-3: 13-14	2022, Summer

Ward, Capt. Bernard M. (editor) *A Hundreth Sundrie Flowres by George Gascoigne* **(1926)**

--	New Statesman	vol. 27: 266	1926, June 19
Ambrose, Genevieve	Modern Language Review	vol. 22: 214-20	1927, Jan. 1
Bowers, Fredson T.	Modern Language Notes	vol. 52/3: 183-86	1937, March
Child, Harold H.	Times Literary Supplement	issue 1271: 391	1926, June 10
Greg, W. W.	Transactions of the Bibliographical Society [repr. as a pamphlet]	vol. VII/3: 269-82	1927, Dec.
Saintsbury, George	Nation and Anthenaeum	vol. 39/10: 295	1926, June 12

Ward, Capt. Bernard M. – *The Seventeenth Earl of Oxford 1550-1604* **(1928)**

--	Birmingham Daily Post		1928, April 27
--	Guardian	p. 258	1928, April 27

--	New Statesman	p. 268-69	1928, June 2
--	New York Sun	???	1928, May 23
--	Saturday Review (London)	vol. 145: 636	1928, May 19

Response by Bernard M. Ward, June 2, p. 697.

--	Scotsman, The	p. 2	1928, May 10

Ward, Capt. Bernard M. – *The Seventeenth Earl of Oxford 1550-1604* **(1928) (continued)**

--	T. P.'s and Cassel's Weekly		1928, June 23

[review is quoted in the front of Ward's book]

--	Washington Post	p. S9	1928, July 1
A. W.	Telegraph, The [The Daily Telegraph]	p. 6	1928, May 4

[review is quoted in the front of Ward's book]

Allen, Percy	Christian Science Monitor	p. 11	1928, June 15
Allen, Percy	Christian Science Monitor	p. 12	1928, July 3
Barrell, Charles Wisner	Shakespeare Fellowship Newsletter (Am.)	vol. 1/1: 8	1939, Dec.
Bettany, F. G.	Sunday Times	p. 8	1928, May 6
Byrne, Muriel St. Clare	Library, The	vol. IX/2: 211-214	1928, Sept.
C. H.	Western Morning News	p. 2	1928, April 30
Connes, Georges	Revue Anglo-Américaine	vol. 6/2: 145-54	1928, Dec.
Danchin, F. C.	Les Langues Modernes	vol. 2: 224-27	1929, April
Feldman, A. Bronson	Bard, The	vol. 4/2: 53-67	1984
Greenlaw, Edwin	Modern Language Notes	vol. 44/3: 202	1929, March
Greg, W. W.	Modern Language Review	vol. 24/2: 216-21	1929, Jan.

Response by Capt. B. M. Ward, *The Library*, June 1929.

H. W. C. D.	Manchester Guardian	p. 9	1928, May 22
Keller, Wolfgang	Shakespeare Jarbuch	vol. 64: 198-99	1929, Jan.
Kempling, W. B.	Shakespeare Review	vol. 1/3: 200-01	1928, July
Maxwell, Baldwin	Philological Quarterly	p. 233	1929, Jan. 1
Reed, Arthuryes	Times Literary Supplement	issue ???, p. 461	1928, June 21

Response by Capt. Ward, June 28, issue 1289: 486.
Reply to Ward by reviewer, July 5, issue 1379: 504.
Response to reviewer by Ward, Aug. 2, issue 1383: 568.

Sampson, George	Daily News		1923, June 21

Response by Looney, *Hackney Spectator*, Aug. 31.

Singleton, Esther	Saturday Review of Literature [New York]	p. 1049	1928, July 21
Smith, G. C. Moore	Review of English Studies	vol. 5/17: 92-103	1929, Jan.
Squire, J. C.	Observer, The	p. 6	1928, May 6
V. R.	English Review, The	p. 735-36	1928, June
Wilkinson, Clennell	London Mercury	vol. 6/1: 217	1928, June 11

Response by B. M. Ward in July, with reply by reviewer.

Ward, Capt. Bernard M. – *The Seventeenth Earl of Oxford 1550-1604*, **2nd edition, hardback, edited by James A. Warren (1928/2023)**

Anderson, Mark/Margo	Oxfordian	vol. 25: 293-98	2023, Sept.
Goff, Tom	Shakespeare Oxford Newsletter	vol. 59/2: 29-31	2023, Spring
Hinds, Amanda	De Vere Society Newsletter	vol. 30/3: 41-42	2023, July

Ward, Col. Bernard R. – *The Mystery of "Mr. W. H."* **(1923)**

--	Aberdeen Press and Journal	p. 2	1923, March 26
--	Church Times	p. 276	1923, June 29
--	Glasgow Herald		1923, Mar./Apr.
--	Saturday Review	vol. 135: 570-71	1923, April 28
--	Scotsman, The	p. 2	1923, March 19
--	Spectator, The	vol. 130: 1049	1923, June 23
--	Times Literary Supplement	issue 1108: 248-50	1923, Apr. 12
Astrea	Baconiana	vol. XVII/65: 155	1923, June
Douglas, Col. Montagu W.	Hackney Spectator	p. 10	1923, March 23 and on Mar. 28
Douglas, Col. Montagu W.	Royal Engineers Journal	p.s 154-56	1923, March
Herford, Charles H.	Manchester Guardian	p. 7	1923, June 5
Squire, John C.	Observer, The	p. 4	1923, March 25

Warren, James A. (editor) – *The Complete Writings on Shakespeare by Percy Allen, vol. 5: The Plays of Shakespeare and Chapman in Relation to French History* **(2022)**

Goff, Tom	Shakespeare Oxford Newsletter	vol. 59/1: 19-20	2023, Sept.
Rubin, Don	Oxfordian	vol. 25: 305-10	2023, Sept.

Warren, James A. (editor) – *An Index to Oxfordian Publications, Third Edition* **(2015)**

Hess, W. Ron	De Vere Society Newsletter	vol. 22/2: 42-43	2015, April

Warren, James A. (editor) – *The Seventeenth Earl of Oxford 1550-1604* **by Bernard M. Ward (2023)**

Anderson, Mark/Margo	Oxfordian	vol. 25: 293-98	2023, Sept.
Goff, Tom	Shakespeare Oxford Newsletter	vol. 59/2: 29-31	2023, Spring
Hinds, Amanda	De Vere Society Newsletter	vol. 30/3: 41-42	2023, July

Warren, James A. (editor) – *"Shakespeare" Revealed: The Collected Articles and Published Letters of J. Thomas Looney* **(2019)**

Delahoyde, Michael	The Oxfordian	vol. 21: 255-60	2019, Sept.
Pommer, Jennifer	De Vere Society Newsletter	vol. 27/4: 37-40	2020, Oct.
St. Clair, Michael	Shakespeare Oxford Newsletter	vol. 55/2: 24-25	2019, Spring

Warren, James A. – *Shakespeare Revolutionized: The First Hundred Years of J. Thomas Looney's "Shakespeare" Identified* **(2021)**

Goff, Thomas	Shakespeare Oxford Newsletter	vol. 57/4: 26	2021, Fall
Goldstein, Gary	The Oxfordian	vol. 23: 343-346	2021, Sept.
St. Clair, Michael	Shakespeare Oxford Newsletter	vol. 57/4: 27-29	2021, Fall
Wilkinson, Heward	De Vere Society Newsletter	vol. 28/4: 36-43	2021, Oct.

Warren, James A. (editor) – *Shakespearian Fantasias by Esther Singleton.* **Modern Edition (2019)**

Hyde, Mike	Shakespeare Oxford Newsletter	vol. 55/2: 30-31	2019, Spring

Warren, James A. – *Summer Storm: A Novel of Ideas* **(2016)**

--	Kirkus Reviews		2017, Feb.
Cutting, Bonner Miller	Shakespeare Oxford Newsletter	vol. 53/1: 24-25	2017, Winter

Waugh, Alexander – *Shakespeare in Court* **(2014)**

Gore-Langton, Robert	Daily Express, The	p. 13	2014, Oct. 27

Webster, Margaret – *Shakespeare Today* **(1957)**

Cutner, Herbert	Shakespearean Authorship Review	issue #7: 13-15	1962, Spring

Webster, Margaret – *Shakespeare Without Tears* **(1942)**

Editor	Shakespeare Fellowship Newsletter (Am.)	vol. 3/4: 56	1942, June

Weis, Rene – *Shakespeare Revealed* **(2007)**

Malim, Richard C. W.	De Vere Society Newsletter	vol. 15/1: 30-31	2008, March

Wells, Stanley – *Is It True What They Say About Shakespeare?* **(2007)**

Whalen, Richard F.	Shakespeare Oxford Newsletter	vol. 44/2: 15-16	2008, Spring
Whalen, Richard F.	Shakespeare Oxford Newsletter	vol. 45/1: 24-25	2009, June

Wells, Stanley – *Shakespeare: A Life in Drama* **(1995)**

Whalen, Richard F.	Shakespeare Oxford Newsletter	vol. 32/1: 21	1996, Winter

Wells, Stanley – *Shakespeare & Co.* **(2006)**

Malim, Richard C. W.	De Vere Society Newsletter	p. 23, 36	2007, Feb.
Sabin, Stefana	Neues Shake-speare Journal	vol. 12: 135-36	2008, Oct.

Wells, Stanley – *Shakespeare: For All Time* **(2003)**

Hughes, Stephanie H.	Washington Post	Outlook	2007, March 18
	[repr. in SM, vol. 6/4: 6, 13+ (Summer 2007)]		
Jiménez, Ramon	Shakespeare Oxford Newsletter	vol. 39/4: 22-23	2003, Autumn

Whalen, Richard F. – *Shakespeare: Who Was He?* **(1994)**

Ashley, L. R. Newsl.	Biliothèque d'Humanisme et Renaissance	vol. 57: 643-701	1995
Aubrey, Bryan	Library	vol. 119/18: 78	1964
Beauregard, Sue-Ellen	Booklist	vol. 91/5: 486-87	1994, Nov. 1
Bryan, Aubrey	Library Journal	vol. 119/18: 78	1994, Nov.
Dickson, Peter W.	Washington Post Book World	p. 11	1997, Aug. 17
Franssen, Paul	Folio: Shakespeare-Genootschap van Nederland en Vlaanderen	vol. 2/2: 48-53	1995

Goldstein, Gary B.	Elizabethan Review	vol. 3/1: 69-69	1995, Spring
Sexton, Roy	Journal of Dramatic Theory and Criticism	vol. 10/2: 141-43	1996
Taylor, Gilbert	Booklist	vol. 91/5: 476	1994, Nov. 1
Whittemore, Hank	Shakespeare Oxford Newsletter	vol. 30/3a: 11-12	1994, Summer
Wright, Daniel L.	Cresset	vol. 61/4: 35-36	1998

Whalen, Richard F. (editor) – *Hamlet, Fully Annotated from an Oxfordian Perspective* (2018)

Lauricella, Theresa	Shakespeare Oxford Newsletter	vol. 55/1: 25-26	2019, Winter

Whalen, Richard F. – *The Fully Annotated Macbeth, Second Edition, with Commentary* (2013)

Egan, Michael (editor)	Shakespeare Oxford Newsletter	vol. 49/2: 14-16	2013, Spring
	Response by Whalen, Fall 2013, p. 7-8.		
Londré, Felicia	Brief Chronicles	vol. V: 214-16	2014, Summer
Ray, William	Shakespeare Matters	vol. 12/2: 6, 17	2013, Spring
Whalen, Richard F.	Shakespeare Oxford Newsletter	vol. 49/3: 7-8	2013, Fall

Whittemore, Hank – *100 Reasons Shake-speare Was the Earl of Oxford* (2016)

Hurst, Walter	Shakespeare Oxford Newsletter	vol. 53/1: 25-26	2017, Winter

Whittemore, Hank – *The Living Record: Shakespeare, Succession, and the Sonnets* (2022)

Dickerman, Dorothea	Shakespeare Oxford Newsletter	vol. 58-3: 7-10	2022, Summer
Pommer, Jennifer	De Vere Society Newsletter	vol. 29/3: 43-47	2022, July

Whittemore, Hank – *The Monument* (2005)

--	Shakespeare Matters	vol. 3/4: 3	2004, Summer
--	Shakespeare Matters	vol. 4/2: 3	2005, Winter
Altrocchi, Paul H.	Shakespeare Matters	vol. 4/4: 1, 12-17	2005, Summer
Boyle, William E.	Shakespeare Matters	vol. 3/4: 1, 11-15	2004, Summer
Boyle, William E.	Shakespeare Matters	vol. 4/1: 1, 8+	2004, Fall
Delahoyde, Michael	Rocky Mountain E-Review of La. & Lit.	vol. 60/2: 52-59	2006
Desper, Richard	Shakespeare Matters	vol. 5/1: 14-15	2005, Fall
Hamill, John	Shakespeare Oxford Newsletter	vol. 42/3: 16	2006, Fall
Gilvary, Kevin	De Vere Society Newsletter	p. 34-37	2005, Sept.
Kositsky, Lynne; R. Stritmatter	Shakespeare Matters	vol. 4/1: 1, 10-14	2004, Fall
McNeil, Alex	Shakespeare Matters	vol. 3/4: 3	2004, Summer
Moffat, David	Shakespeare Matters	vol. 4/4: 2-4	2005, Summer
Paul, Christopher	Shakespeare Oxford Newsletter	vol. 4/2: 32	2006
Rush, Peter	Shakespeare Matters	vol. 4/1: 6-7	2004
Tarica, Alan	Shakespeare Oxford Newsletter	vol. 42/3: 16	2006, Fall
Whalen, Richard	Shakespeare Matters	vol. 4/2: 10-11, 17+	2006
Wright, Daniel L.	Shakespeare Matters	vol. 4/1: 9	2004, Fall
See also:			
Sherwood, Jim	Shakespeare Oxford Newsletter	vol. 41/2: 2, 18-20	2005
	[interview with Hank Whittemore]		

Whittemore, Hank – *Shakespeare's Son and His Sonnets* (2010)

Editor	Shakespeare Matters	vol. 10/1: 4	2011, Winter

Wildenthal, Bryan – *Early Shakespeare Authorship Doubts* (2019)

Crampin, Alice	De Vere Society Newsletter	vol. 26/4: 30-32	2019, Oct.
Pannell, Chris	The Oxfordian	vol. 22: 181-186	2020, Sept.
Wilkinson, Heward	Shakespeare Oxford Newsletter	vol. 56/1: 24-27	2020, Winter

Wilkinson, Heward – *The Muse as Therapist* (2009)

Waugaman, Richard M.	Brief Chronicles	vol. I: 283-285	2009

Williams, Robin – *Sweet Swan of Avon* (2006)

--	Shakespeare Matters	vol. 5/4: 24	2006, Summer
Dickson, Peter W.	Oxfordian, The	vol. 9: 132-135	2006
Rutledge, Josh	Washington Times	2006, June 21	
	[repr. in DVN (July 2006), p. 19]		
Underwood, Anne	Newsweek	p. 58	2004, June 28

Williamson, Gene – *Of the Sea and Skies: Historic Hampton* (1993)

Editor	Shakespeare Oxford Newsletter	vol. 31/2b: 11	1995, Spring

Willis, Charles M. – *Behind Shakespeare's Mask* **(2006)**

Charlton, Derran K.	Shakespeare Oxford Newsletter	vol. 43/1: 31-32	2007, Winter
Gilvary, Kevin	De Vere Society Newsletter	p. 39	2007, Feb.

Willis, Charles M. – *George Puttenham and the Authorship of Shakespeare's Sonnets* **(2005)**

Gilvary, Kevin	De Vere Society Newsletter	p. 39	2005, Sept.

Willis, Charles M. – *Shakespeare and George Puttenham's Art of English Poesie* **(2003)**

Gilvary, Kevin	De Vere Society Newsletter	p. 38	2005, Sept.
Whalen, Richard F.	Shakespeare Matters	vol. 3/4: 31	2004, Summer

Wilson, Ian – *Shakespeare: The Evidence* **(1993, 1999)**

Taylor, Robert	The Boston Globe	p. 34	1995, March 8

Wilson, J. Dover – *The Essential Shakespeare* **(1932)**

Allen, Percy	Christian Science Monitor	p. 10	1932, May 21
Allen, Percy	Shakespeare Pictorial	no. 52: 100	1932, June

Wilson, J. Dover (editor) – *Hamlet* **(1934)**

Holland, Admiral H. H.	Shakespeare Pictorial	no. 91: 144	1935, Sept.

Wilson, J. Dover – *What Happens in Hamlet* **(1935)**

Child, Harold H.	Times Literary Supplement	issue 1758: 617	1935, Oct. 10

Winkler, Elizabeth – *Shakespeare Was a Woman and Other Heresies* **(2023)**

Bate, Jonathan	Telegraph		1923, May 28
	Response by Winkler, May 28.		
	Response by Derek Jacobi and Mark Rylance, June 9.		
Butler, Isaac	Slate		1923, May 11
Dudley, Michael	Shakespeare Oxford Newsletter	vol. 59/3: 25-26	2023, Summer
Jiménez, Ramon	Oxfordian	vol. 25: 273-78	2023, Sept.
Londré, Felicia	Village Voice		2023, June 13
McNeil, Alex	Shakespeare Oxford Newsletter	vol. 59/3: 1, 18-21	2023, Summer
Merritt, Stephanie	Guardian		2023, June 18
Shuttleworth, Gen. Jack	De Vere Society Newsletter	vol. 30/3: 39-40	2023, July
Smith, Dave	Guardian		2023, June 27
Smith, Emma	Spectator		1923, June 3
Waugaman, Elizabeth	Washington Post		1923, June 27
Woosnam, Tom	Journal of Scientific Exploration	vol. 37/2	2023, Summer

Wood, Michael – *In Search of Shakespeare* **(1985)**

Charlton, Derran K.	Shakespeare Oxford Newsletter	vol. 39/3: 23-24	2003, Summer
Dickson, Peter	Weekly Standard		2004, Spring
Ligon, K. C.	Shakespeare Matters	vol. 3/2: 20-21	2004, Winter
Matus, Irvin	Shakespeare	p. WBK4	2003, Dec. 4
Oxenforde	De Vere Society Newsletter	p. 28	2003, June

Wood, O. M. Ironside – *Proud Passionate Boy* **(a play) (unpublished)**

--	De Vere Society Newsletter	no. 2: 37-38	1988, April

Woudhuysen, H. R. – *Sir Philip Sidney and the Circulation of Manuscripts: 1558-1640* **(1996)**

Hope, Warren	Elizabethan Review	vol. 5/1: 50-54	1997, Spring

Wusowski, Cornelia – *Elisabeth I. – Der Roman ihres Lebens* **(1997)**

Fièvreux, Solange	Neues Shake-speare Journal	vol. 6: 162-63	2001, May

Wright, Louis B. (editor) – *The Authorship of Shakespeare* **(Folger Library Booklet, by James G. McManaway) (1962)**

Horne, Jr., Richard C.	Shakespeare Oxford Newsletter	vol. 6/1: 6-8	1970, Mar. 31

Wright, Louis B. and Virginia A. Lamar (editors) – *The Folger Library General Reader's Shakespeare* **(1970)**

Horne, Jr., Richard C.	Shakespeare Oxford Newsletter	vol. 6/1: 8-11	1970, March 31
Horne, Jr., Richard C.	Shakespeare Oxford Newsletter	vol. 6/2: 1-2	1970, June 30

Wright, Louis B. – "The Author" Section in *Shakespeare's Plays and Poems* **(1970)**

Horne, Jr., Richard C.	Shakespeare Oxford Newsletter	vol. 6/1: 12	1970, March 31

* * * * *

Ic. INDEX OF REVIEWS OF AUDIO-VISUAL PRODUCTIONS
OF SPECIAL INTEREST

All is True (2018 film directed by Kenneth Branagh)

Schumann, Howard	Shakespeare Oxford Newsletter	p. 31-32	2019, Summer

All's Well that Ends Well – January 21, 1981 BBC Broadcast

Patience, Harold W.	Shakespeare Oxford Newsletter	p. 5-6	1980, Fall
	["Perspective" mentions the Earl of Oxford and the "bed trick"]		

Anonymous (2011 film directed by Roland Emmerich)

--	Belfast Telegraph	p. 18	2011, Nov. 5
--	Birmingham Daily Post	p. 4	1945, Jan. 8
--	Coventry Evening Standard	p. 11	2011, Sept. 1
--	Daily Telegraph (Surrey Hills)	p. 20	2011, Oct. 29
--	De Vere Society Newsletter	vol. 18/2: 5	2011, July
--	Independent		2011, Oct. 31
--	Independent	p. 14	2011, Nov. 5
--	New Indian Express (Chennai, India)		2011, Oct. 28
--	Post-Standard		2011, Nov. 3
--	Shakespeare Matters	vol. 10/4: 6	2011, Fall
--	Shakespeare Matters (SF Board Statement)	vol. 10/4: 6, 31	2011, Fall
--	Sunday Independent		2011, Nov. 6
--	Telegraph (London)	p. 20	2011, Oct. 29
--	Times (London)	p. 2	2011, June 6
Alter, Alexandra	Wall Street Journal	p. W4	2011, April 2
Appleyard, Bryan	Sunday Times	p. 4	2011, Oct. 30
Blakely, Rhys and Ben Hoyle	Times (London)	p. 19	2011, Oct. 18
Berry, Ralph	Contemporary Review	vol. 293: 488	2011, Dec.
Boyle, William E.	Shakespeare Matters	vol. 11/1: 1, 34-36	2012, Winter
Brady, Tara	Irish Times	p. 16	2011, Oct. 28
Brantley, Ben	New York Times	Arts, p. 1, 6	2011, Oct. 29
Brown, Tom	Around the Globe	vol. 50: 40	2012
Cole, Jan	De Vere Society Newsletter	vol. 19/1: 27	2012, March
Corrigan, Michael	Idaho State Journal	p. C1	2012, July 15
Covert, Colin	Minneapolis Star Tribune	p. E8	2011, Oct. 28
Crase, John	Guardian	p. 4	2011, June 17
D. M.	Evening Standard	p. 36	2011, Oct. 18
Dawson, Jon	Groatsworth of Wit	vol. 23/1: 17-20	2012
Denby, David	New Yorker	p. 106	2011, Oct. 31
Dent, Nick	Sunday Telegraph (Sydney)	p. 131	2011, Nov. 13
Eagan-Donovan, Cheryl A.	Shakespeare Oxford Newsletter	vol. 47/3: 11-13	2011, Fall
Espinoza, Javier	Wall Street Journal		2011, Oct. 28
Flamini, Roland	Washington Times	p. B10	2011, Nov. 2
Gilbert, Sky	Brief Chronicles	vol. III: 288-293	2011, Fall
Hall, Zoe Dare	Sunday Telegraph (London)	p. 220	2011, Oct. 8
Hall, Zoe Dare	Daily Telegraph (London)	p. 62-65	2011, Oct. 15
Haresnape, Geoffrey	Shakespeare in Southern Africa	vol. 24: 82-84	2012
Hart, Christopher	Daily Mail	p. 15	2011, Oct. 27
Hastings, Robe	Independent	p. 14	2011, Oct. 26
Howell, Peter	Toronto Star	p. E5	2011, Oct. 28
Ide, Wendy	The Times (London)	p. 11	2011, Oct. 28
Imlay, Elizabeth	De Vere Society Newsletter	vol. 18/3: 22-25	2011, Nov.
Itzkoff, Dave	National Post	p. A3	2011, Oct. 26
Itzkoff, Dave	New York Times	p. C3	2011, Oct. 26
Kamm, Oliver	Times (London)	p. 93	2011, June 11
Kamm, Oliver	Times (London)	p. 19	2011, Oct. 18
Karpel, Ari	New York Times	A&L, p. 14, 16	2011, Oct. 23

Keegan, Rebecca	Los Angeles Times	p. D1	2011, Oct. 29
Lee, Chris	Newsweek		2011, Oct. 17
Lefait, Sebastien	Interdisciplinary Literary Studies	vol. 17/2: 241-63	2015
Lloyd, Christopher	Sarasota Herald Tribune	p. E20	2011, Oct. 27
Marche, Stephen	New York Times Magazine	p. 60-61	2011, Oct. 23
Massie, Alan	Telegraph (London)	p. 22	2011, Oct. 26
McCrum, Robert	Observer	p. 37	2011, Oct. 23
McCrum, Robert	Observer	p. 42	2011, Nov. 6
McFarlane, Brian	Screen Education	issue 65: 30-37	2012, Autumn
McMullen, Marion	Coventry Evening Telegraph	p. 87	2011, Oct. 26
McNeil, Alex	Shakespeare Matters	vol. 10/4: 3, 32	2011, Fall
Mongillo, Peter	Austin American-Statesman	p. D1	2011, Oct. 28
Morgenstern, Joe	Wall Street Journal	p. D3	2011, Oct. 28
Morris, Wesley	Boston Globe		2011, Oct. 28
Morrison, Patt	Los Angeles Times	p. A19	2011, Oct. 29
Newmark, Judith	St. Louis Post Dispatch	p. D1	2011, Nov. 6
Niederkorn, William S.	Brooklyn Rail	p. 66	2011, Oct.
Noveck, Jocelyn	Telegraph Herald (Dubuque, Iowa)	p. C1	2011, Nov. 2
Palmer, Martyn	Sunday Times	p. 14	2011, Oct. 16
Pendleton, Thomas A.	Shakespeare Newsletter	vol. 61/2: 41, 72+	2011, Fall
Puig, Claudia	USA Today		2011, Oct. 27
Schama, Simon	Newsweek	vol. 158/17: 24	2011, Oct. 24
Schumann, Howard	Shakespeare Matters	vol. 11/1: 4-5	2012, Winter
Scott, A. O.	New York Times	Arts: 1, 17	2011, Oct. 28
Shapiro, James	Los Angeles Times	p. A29	2010, April 11
	Response by John Orloff, April 19, p. A14.		
Shapiro, James	New York Times	p. A23	2011, Oct. 17
	Response by Mark Anderson, Oct. 27, p. A24.		
	Response by Roland Emmerich, Oct. 27, p. A24.		
	Response by Daniel M. Blank, Oct. 27, p. A24.		
	Response by Andree A. Brooks, Oct. 27, p. A24.		
	Response by Julia Newton, Oct. 27, p. A24.		
Shapiro, James	International Herald Tribune	p. 8	2011, Oct. 17
Shapiro, James	Irish Times	p. 15	2011, Oct. 29
Shapiro, James	Guardian	p. 16	2011, Nov. 5
Sherman, Donovan	Literature/Film Quarterly	vol. 41/2: 129-42	2013, April
Spencer, Charles	Telegraph (London)	p. 30	2011, Nov. 7
Stasukevich, Lain	American Cinematographer	vol. 92/9: 28-43	2011, Sept.
Steelman, Ben	Star-News (Wilmington)		2011, Oct. 23
Turner, Helen	Western Mail (Cardiff)	p. 3	2011, Oct. 19
Waugaman, Richard M.	Academy Forum	vol. 56: 33-34	2012
Waugaman, Richard M.	International Journal of Applied Psychoanalytic Studies	vol. 12/1: 81-87	2015, March 5
Whetstone, David	Journal (Newcastle-upon-Tyne)	p. 58	2011, Dec. 7

As You Like It: 1936, 1978, 1983 (films)

Berney, Charles V.	Shakespeare Matters	vol. 1/3: 34-36	2002, Spring

Battle of Wills (BBC 2 TV Program _Bard on the Box_) (1994)

Barber, Nicholas	Independent, The	p. 21	1994, Oct. 30
Flusfeder, David	Times (London)	p. 2	1994, Oct. 22
	[Charles De Vere defends Looney's thesis]		

Behind the Name Shakespeare: Power, Lust, Scorn & Scandal] [new name: _SHAKESPEARE: The Truth Behind the Name_] (a documentary by Robin Phillips) (2020)

Cheal, Yvonne	De Vere Society Newsletter	vol. 28/1: 50-51	2021, Jan.

Breakfast Show: Looking for the Real Shake-Speare [WDR TV (Germany), broadcast March 4, 11, 18, 2004)]

--	De Vere Society Newsletter	p. 31	2004, April
--	Shakespeare Oxford Newsletter	vol. 40/2: 5	2004, Spring

Crown, The [British TV series]

McNeil, Alex	Shakespeare Oxford Newsletter	vol. 57/1: 24	2021, Winter

Elizabeth [movie]
    Quealy, Gerit   Shakespeare Oxford Newsletter   vol. 34/4: 4-5   1999, Winter

Fa La La – The Bastardy of Shakespere's Madrigals **(a song cycle for four cellos, three voices, percussion and digital looping by Melora Creager)**
    Editor   Shakespeare Matters   vol. 12/3: 4-5   2013, Summer

Firing Line – "The Mysterious William Shakespeare": **Guests author Charlton Ogburn, Rutgers Professor Maurice Charney (Dec. 11, 1984)**
    --   Washington Post   p. TV11   1985, Feb. 3
    Freeman, Don   San Diego Union   p. D-17   1985, Feb. 1
    Freeman, Don   San Diego Union   p. TV Week-4   1985, Feb. 17

The Food of Love – Words and Music for Shakespeare's Theater **(CD by The Gesualdo Consort) (1996)**
    Mucci, John   Elizabethan Review   vol. 6/2: 88-89   1998, Autumn

Granite Flats **(American TV Sitcom; 2014 season has an Oxfordian character played by Christopher Lloyd)**
    McNeil, Alex   Shakespeare Oxford Newsletter   vol. 50/2: 7   2014, Spring

Hamlet **(film with Kenneth Branagh as Hamlet)**
    Beauclerk, Charles   Shakespeare Oxford Newsletter   vol. 33/1: 2, 14-15 1997, Winter

Head of the Class **(U.S. TV Sitcom – Fall 1986 Episode)**
    Ogburn, Charlton, Jr.   Shakespeare Oxford Newsletter   vol. 23/1: 4   1987 Winter

Henry V **(film)**
    Tabin, Johanna K.   Shakespeare Oxford Newsletter   vol. 46/2: 5-8   2010, Aug.

In Search of the Bard **(First Tuesday TV Program)**
    Waymark, Peter   Times (London)   p. 23   1989, July 4
                            [Enoch Powell presented the case for the doubters]

Jeopardy **(American TV quiz show)** [Oxfordian Alex McNeil participated in the program in 1995 and mentioned the Shakespeare authorship issue. Since then, questions dealing with the authorship issue were asked at least twice. One was on March 22, 2012. And, on April 12, 2012 host Alex Trebeck mentioned the authorship issue in the context of a question on Shakespeare.
    Whalen, Richard F.   Shakespeare Oxford Newsletter   vol. 31/2a: 12   1995, Spring
    McNeil, Alex   Shakespeare Oxford Newsletter   vol. 50/2: 7   2014, Spring

King Lear **(film)**
    Berney, Charles V.   Shakespeare Matters   vol. 2/3: 30-31   2003, Spring

Last Will. & Testament (2012) **[a documentary by Lisa Wilson and Laura Wilson Matthias]**
    Boyle, William E.   Shakespeare Matters   vol. 11/2: 7-8   2012, Spring
    Schumann, Howard   Shakespeare Matters   vol. 11/1: 6, 32   2012, Spring
    Waugaman, Richard M.   International Journal of Applied   vol. 12/1: 81-87   2015, March 5
                              Psychoanalytic Studies

The Letters of Edward de Vere – **Derek Jacobi (reader); Joan Walker (narrator); Stephanie Hopkins Hughes (editor)**
    The Times (3 June 2006)   De Vere Society Newsletter (reprint)   p. 18   2006, July
    Delahoyde, Michael   RMR   vol. 61/1: 112-120 2007

Live the Legend **(a CD by The New World Renaissance Band)**
    Haldeman, Philip   Shakespeare Oxford Newsletter   vol. 33/3: 13   1997, Summer

Love's Labour's Lost: **The BBC vs. Branagh (films)**
    Berney, Charles V.   Shakespeare Matters   vol. 1/1: 18-19   2001, Fall

Malcolm in the Middle **[American TV sitcom in early 2002 WITH regular character who was an Oxfordian]**
    McNeil, Alex   Shakespeare Oxford Newsletter   vol. 50/2: 7   2014, Spring

The Merchant of Venice **(2004 and 1980 films)**
    Berney, Charles V.   Shakespeare Matters   vol. 4/2: 30-32   2005, Winter

Midsummer Night's Dream **(film and opera)**
    Berney, Charles V.   Shakespeare Oxford Newsletter   vol. 37/1: 17, 23+ 2001, Spring
    Berney, Charles V.   Shakespeare Matters   vol. 1/4: 26-27   2002, Summer

Midsummer Night's Mystery **(British TV program)**
    Smithies, Sandy   Guardian   p. 40   1989, July 4

Reviews of Audio-Visual Productions

Mister V (a film by Leslie Howard, titled *Pimpernel Smith* in UK) (1941)

--	Shakespeare Fellowship Newsletter (Am)	vol. 3/4:52	1942, June
Gilvary, Kevin	De Vere Society Newsletter	p. 24	2004, Oct.

Much Ado About Something: Marlowe's Case for Authorship (PBS *Frontline* documentary produced by Mike Rubbio)

--	Shakespeare Matters	vol. 1/3: 5	2002, Spring
--	Times (London)	p. 7	2002, March 14
Boyle, William E.	Shakespeare Matters	vol. 2/2: 30-31	2003, Winter
Catlin, Roger	Hartford Courant	p. D8	2003, Jan. 3
Dobbs, Anne	Shakespeare Oxford Newsletter	vol. 38/1: 20	2002, Winter
Gilbert, Matthew	Boston Globe	p. D5	2003, Jan. 2
Maher, Ted	Oregonian, The	p. E10	2003, Jan. 2
Mason, M. S.	Christian Science Monitor	p. 15	June 26

My Lord of Oxenford's Maske

Imlay, Elizabeth	De Vere Society Newsletter	p. 33	2007, Oct.

The Naked Shakespeare ([*Der Nackte Shakespeare*] (a documentary film by Claus Bredenbrock) (2012)

Gilvary, Kevin (editor)	De Vere Society Newsletter	vol. 20/2: 29	2013, July

Nothing Is Truer Than Truth (a documentary film by Cheryl Eagan-Donovan) (2015)

Brokaw, Leslie	Boston Globe [advance look film's production]	2006, June 25	
Herbert, Tony	De Vere Society Newsletter	vol. 26/3: 44-46	2019, July
Schumann, Howard	Shakespeare Oxford Newsletter	vol. 51/2: 25-26	2015, Spring
	Response by Cheryl Eagan-Donovan, same issue, p. 26-27.		
Waugaman, Richard M.	American Psychoanalyst		2017

Oxford's Letters [see *The Letters of Edward de Vere*]

Pimpernel Smith (a film by Leslie Howard, titled *Mister V* in the U.S.) (1941)

--	Shakespeare Fellowship Newsletter (Am)	vol. 3/4:52	1942, June
Gilvary, Kevin	De Vere Society Newsletter	p. 24	2004, Oct.

Renaissance Music at Princely Courts of Europe (a CD by the Rozmberk Consort Prague)

Haldeman, Philip	Shakespeare Oxford Newsletter	vol. 33/3: 13	1997, Summer

Shakespeare Conspiracy, The (directed by Michael Peer) (2011)

Cantu, Amy	Library Journal	vol. 126/3: 214	2001
McCray, Nancy	Booklist	p. 1903	2001, June

Shakespeare in Love (film)

Quealy, Gerit	Shakespeare Oxford Newsletter	vol. 34/4: 4-5	1999, Winter

"Shakespeare Mystery, The" (*Frontline* program first broadcast April 18, 1989, produced by Al Austin)
[See also Al Austin, "Who Wrote Shakespeare" in Boston's public television magazine]

--	Shakespeare Oxford Newsletter	vol. 25/2: 1	1989, Spring
--	Memoria di Shakespeare		1989, April
	[repr. in SON, vol. 25/2: 1-3]		
Bevington, David M.	Eleven Magazine (Chicago)	p. 14-15	1989, August
Bianculli, David	New York Post		1989, April 18
	[repr. in SON, vol. 25/2: 9]		
Bronte, Lydia	Shakespeare Oxford Newsletter	vol. 25/2: 12-13	1989, Spring
	[repr. in BTC, vol. 6: 393-95]		
Carman, John	San Francisco Chronicle		1989, April 18
	[repr. in SON, vol. 25/2: 8-9]		
Catlin, Roger	Hartford Courant	p. D8	2003, Jan. 3
Champlin, Charles	Los Angeles Times	p. J1E	1989, April 18
	[repr. in SON, vol. 25/2: 4-5]		
Ferna, Tom	Plain Dealer		1989, April 18
Gilbert, Matthew	Boston Globe	p. D5	2003, Jan. 2
Goldstein, Gary B.	Washington Square News		1989, Spring
	[repr. in SON, vol. 25/2: 10-11]		
Goodman, Walter	New York Times	p. C21	1989, April 18
	[repr. in SON, vol. 25/2: 3-4]		
Hope, Warren	Philadelphia Inquirer		1989, April 20
	[repr. in SON, vol. 25/2: 5-6]		

"Shakespeare Mystery, The" (*Frontline* program first broadcast April 18, 1989, produced by Al Austin) (continued)

Holston, Noel	Minneapolis Star Tribune [advance look]	p. 1E	1988, Nov. 19
Holston, Noel	Minneapolis Star Tribune	p. 1-2E	1989, April 18
	[repr. in SON, vol. 25/2: 7-8]		
	[repr. in BTC, vol. 6: 388-90]		
Kelly, Kevin	Boston Globe	p. 32	1989, April 18
	[repr. in SON, vol. 25/2: 10]		
Laurence, Robert P.	San Diego Union	p. E7	1989, April 18
Ogburn, Charlton	Shakespeare Oxford Newsletter	vol. 25/1: 5-6	1989, vol. 25/1: 5-6
Rickey, George	New York Times	p. 26	1989, May 11
	Response by Burton H. Brody, June 3, p. 14.		
Ryan, Desmond	Philadelphia Inquirer	p. D8	2003, Jan. 2
Terzian, Philip	Providence Journal	p. B18	1989, April 23

SHAKESPEARE: The Truth Behind the Name [original title: *Behind the Name Shakespeare: Power, Lust, Scorn & Scandal*] **(a documentary by Robin Phillips) (2020)**

Cheal, Yvonne	De Vere Society Newsletter	vol. 28/1: 50-51	2021, Jan.

Shakespeare Uncovered (PBS, 2013)

Norwood, James	Shakespeare Matters	vol. 12/3: 7, 33-34	2013, Summer

Shakespeare's Tomb (BBC, 2016)

Dickson, Peter W.	Shakespeare Oxford Newsletter	vol. 52/2: 19-22	2016, Spring
Waugh, Alexander	Shakespeare Oxford Newsletter	vol. 52/2: 19, 22-23	2016, Spring

Songs, Dances, Battles, Games by William Byrd (CD)

Kunin, Carolyn	Shakespeare Oxford Newsletter	vol. 32/3: 18	1996, Summer

The Taming of the Shrew (film)

Berney, Charles V.	Shakespeare Matters	vol. 2/4: 34-35	2003, Summer
Schumann, Howard	Shakespeare Matters	vol. 5/2: 10	2006, Winter

Titus Andronicus (film)

Berney, Charles V.	Shakespeare Matters	vol. 2/1: 34-36	2002, Fall
Eldredge, Joseph	Shakespeare Oxford Newsletter	vol. 36/3: 6-7, 15	2000, Fall

The Tragedy of Macbeth (2021) (film)

Schumann, Howard	Shakespeare Oxford Newsletter	vol. 58/2: 10	2022, Spring

Tuesday

--	Sunday Times [Charles Vere and A. L. Rowse clash]	p. 4E	1989, July 2

Will (10-part TNT series)

Norwood, James	Shakespeare Oxford Newsletter	vol. 53/4: 24-26	2017, Fall

*   *   *   *   *

Id. INDEX OF REMEMBRANCES OF NOTED OXFORDIANS

Adamson, T. L. (d. 1969)
Editor — Shakespearean Authorship Review — issue #22: 17-18 — 1969, Dec.

Aitken, Thomas (d. 1958)
Martyn, Kathleen — Shakespeare Fellowship Newsletter (Eng.) — p. 4 — 1958, Spring

Akrigg, G. P. V. (1913-2001)
Editor — Shakespeare Oxford Newsletter — vol. 38/1: 21 — 2002, Winter

Alexander, Ted (1953-2017)
Editor — Shakespeare Oxford Newsletter — vol. 53/2: 8 — 2017, Spring

Alexis, Louis E. M. (1977)
Editor — Shakespeare Oxford Newsletter — vol. 14/1: 9 — 1978, Winter

Allen, Ernest Stirling (1872-1939)
Barrell, Charles Wisner — Shakespearean Fellowship Newsletter (Am) — vol. 1/1, p. 6 — 1939, Dec.
    [repr. in BTC, vol. 2: 77-79]
Editor — Shakespeare Fellowship Newsletter (Eng.) — p. 1 — 1940, April
Ranson, F. Lingard — East Anglian Magazine — vol. 5/2: 63 — 1940, Feb.
    [repr. in BTC, vol. 1: 381]

Allen, Percy (1875-1959)
Adamson, T. L. — Shakespearean Authorship Review — no. 1: 22-23 — 1959, Spring
    [repr. in BTC, vol. 1: 329-330]
Editor — Stage, The — p. 17 — 1959, Feb. 12

Ambridge, Graham (d. 2019)
Gilvary, Kevin — De Vere Society Newsletter — vol. 26/4: 4 — 2019, October

Amphlett, Hilda (1897-1981)
Editor — Shakespeare Oxford Newsletter — vol. 17/2: 9 — 1981, Spring

Anderson, George R. (1934-2021)
Editor — Shakespeare Oxford Newsletter — vol. 58/1: 11 — 2022, Winter.

Anderson (Paget), Verily (1915-2010)
Charlton, Derran K. — Shakespeare Oxford Newsletter — vol. 46/2: 16 — 2010, Aug.
Charlton, Derran K. — Oxfordian [repr. In NSJ, vol. NS1: 159] — vol. 12: 16 — 2010

Editor — Shakespeare Oxford Newsletter — vol. 46/2: 16 — 2010, Aug.
Editor — Times [repr. in DVN, vol. 17/2: 4] — — 2010, June 24

Atkins, Gertrude "Trudy" (1925-2019)
Editor — Shakespeare Oxford Fellowship Newsletter — vol. 55/2: 8-9 — 2019, Spring

Atkinson, Helen (d. 1956)
Editor — Shakespeare Fellowship Newsletter (Eng) — p. 11 — 1956, Spring

Atkinson, J. Shera (d. 1958)
Adamson, T. L. — Shakespeare Fellowship Newsletter (Eng) — p. 8 — 1958, Autumn
Editor — Shakespeare Fellowship Newsletter (Eng) — p. 4 — 1958, Spring

Barrell, Charles Wisner (1885-1974)
-- — Warwick Valley Dispatch — — 1974, June 26
A'Dair, Mike — Shakespeare Matters — vol. 9/1: 1, 14-21 — 2010, Winter
Editor — Shakespeare Oxford Newsletter — vol. 11/3: 5 — 1975, Fall

Beauclerk, Rev. Charles de Vere (d. 1934)
-- — Lancashire Evening Post — p. 5 — 1934, Nov. 29

Bénézet, Louis P. (1878-1961)
Dellinger, J. Howard — Shakespearean Authorship Review — no. 6: 23 — 1961, Autumn
    [repr. in BTC, vol. 5: 80-90]

Bethell, Tom (1936-2021)
Hinds, Amanda — De Vere Society Newsletter — vol. 28/2: 5-6 — 2021, April

Blair, Paul (1915-2009)
Charlton, Derran K.	Shakespeare Oxford Newsletter	vol. 45/3: 7	2009, Dec.
Laugwitz, Uwe	Neues Shake-speare Journal	vol. NS1: 160	2010, Nov.

Bloch, Howard (1937-2000)
Editor	Shakespeare Oxford Newsletter	vol. 35/4: 2	2000, Winter

Blume, Georg
Laugwitz, Uwe	Neues Shake-speare Journal	vol. 12: 129-31	2008, Oct.

Bond, F. Bligh (1864-1945)
Allen, Percy	Shakespeare Fellowship News-Letter (Eng.)	p. 3	May 1945

Bowen, Gwynneth M. (d. 1984)
Editor	Shakespeare Oxford Newsletter	vol. 20/4: 8	1984, Fall

Bowen, Marjorie (Margaret Gabrielle Vere Long) (née Campbell) (d. 1952)
Editor	Shakespeare Fellowship Newsletter (Eng)	p. 2	1953, April

Brazil, Robert (1955-2010)
--	Shakespeare Matters	vol. 9/3: 26	2010, Fall
--	Shakespeare Oxford Newsletter	vol. 46/2: 16-17	2010, Aug.
Detobel, Robert	Neues Shake-speare Journal	vol. NS1: 163-64	2010, Nov.
Egan, Michael (ed.)	The Oxfordian	vol. 12: 8-15	2010
Editor (with tributes by Gerit Quealy, Ron Hess, Gary Goldstein, and Matthew Cossolotto)	De Vere Society Newsletter	vol. 17/2: 5	2010, Aug.
Goldstein, Gary B.	Shakespeare Matters	vol. 10/1: 5	2011, Winter
Whittemore, Hank	Shakespeare Oxford Newsletter	vol. 46/2: 16-17	2010, Aug.

Breitwiser, Ludwig (d. 1966)
Bowen, Gwynneth M.	Shakespearean Authorship Review	issue #16: 27	1966, Autumn

Brewster, Eleanor (d. 1985)
--	Shakespeare Oxford Newsletter	vol. 21/4: 4	1985, Fall

Broadwood, Captain Evelyn (d. 1975)
--	Shakespeare Oxford Newsletter	vol. 11/3: 5	1975, Fall

Brooks, Douglas (1957-2009)
Stritmatter, Roger	Shakespeare Matters	vol. 8/4: 16	2009, Fall

Brown, Patricia Carroll Ann (1931-2014)
Editor	Shakespeare Oxford newsletter	vol. 50/3: 19-21	2014, Summer

Burgstahler, Albert (1928-2013)
Ray, William J.	Shakespeare Matters	vol. 12/4: 9, 33, 35	2013, Fall

Caldwell, Roland George (1933-2023)
Warren, James A.	Shakespeare Oxford Newsletter	vol. 59/3: 9	2023, Summer

Carmody, Francis T. (1909-1965)
--	Wall Street Journal	p. 56	1965, Feb. 16
--	Wall Street Journal	p. B7	1965, Feb. 17
Edmonds, Dean S.	Shakespeare Oxford Newsletter	vol. 1/2: 1-2	1965, June 30

Chambers, Sir Edmund (1866-1954)
Bowen, Gwynneth M.	Shakespeare Fellowship Newsletter (Eng)	p. 6	1954, April

Champlin, Charles (d. 2014)
Editor	Shakespeare Oxford Newsletter	vol. 51/1: 10-11	2015, Winter
Shahan, John	De Vere Society Newsletter	vol. 22/1: 18	2015, January

Clark, Eva Turner (1871-1947)
--	New York Herald Tribune	p. 26A	1947, April 3
--	New York Times	p. 25	1947, April 3
Editor	Shakespeare Fellowship Quarterly	vol. VIII: 1: 1-3	1947, Spring

Craig, Edward Gordon (1872-1966)
Bowen, Gwynneth M.	Shakespearean Authorship Review	issue #16: 27	1966, Autumn

Remembrances of Noted Oxfordians

Crowley, Barbara (1924-2012)

Lipman, Carole Sue	Shakespeare Matters	vol. 11/4: 6, 14	2012, Fall
Lipman, Carole Sue	Shakespeare Oxford Newsletter	vol. 49/1: 5-6	2013, Winter

Cushman, James S. (1872-1952)

--	New York Times	p. 29	1952, March 20

Cutner, Herbert (d. 1969)

Editor	Shakespearean Authorship Review	issue #21: 19	1969, Spring

Cyr, Gordon (1926-2007)

Editor	Shakespeare Matters	vol. 7/1: 4	2007, Fall
Rasmussen, Frederick Newsl.	Baltimore Sun	--	2007, May 15

Cyr, Helen W. (1926-1993)

Editor	Shakespeare Oxford Newsletter	vol. 29/3a: 13	1993, Summer

Davis, Frank (1935-2021)

Editor	Shakespeare Oxford Newsletter	vol. 57/4: 9	2021, Fall

Deller, Anthony William (d. 1976)

Editor	Shakespeare Oxford Newsletter	vol. 12/2: 4	1976, Summer

Dellinger, J. Howard (d. 1962)

Bowen, Gwynneth M.	Shakespearean Authorship Review	issue #9: 20	1963, Spring

Des Cognets, Russell (1923-2014)

Editor	Shakespeare Oxford Newsletter	vol. 50/2: 7	2014, Spring

Desper, C. Richard "Dick" (1937-2020)

Editor	Shakespeare Oxford Newsletter	vol. 57/1: 15	2021, Winter

Detobel, Robert (1939-2018)

Editor	Shakepeare Oxford Newsletter	vol. 54/4: 12-13	2018, Fall

Douglas, Lt. Col. Montagu W. (d. 1957)

Aitken, T. M.	Shakespeare Fellowship Newsletter (Eng)	p. 11	1957, Spring

Duffey, Edith Bell (d. 2004)

--	Lansing State Journal	p. B5	2004, March 7

Eggar, Katharine E. (1873-1961)

Charlton, Derran K.	De Vere Society Newsletter	issue 15/1: 29	2008, March
Euchner, Renee & Kathryn Sharpe	Shakespeare Oxford Newsletter	vol. 58/2: 29-31	2022, Spring
Wainewright, Ruth M. D.	Shakespearean Authorship Review	issue 6: 22-23	1961, Autumn

Erickson, Mrs. Sverre (d. 1939)

Editor	Shakespeare Fellowship Newsletter (Eng.)	p. 1-2	1940, April

Evans, A. J. (d. 1960)

Russell, John	Shakespearean Authorship Review	issue #4: 19	1960, Autumn

Eyre, Geoffrey

Gilvary, Kevin	De Vere Society Newsletter	vol. 30/2: 4	2023, April

Fadiman, Clifton (1904-1999)

Editor	Shakespeare Oxford Newsletter	vol. 35/2: 2	1999, Summer

Feinstone, Rose (d. 1986)

Editor	Shakespeare Oxford Newsletter	vol. 22/3: 12	1986, Summer

Feinstone, Sol (d. 1980)

Editor	Shakespeare Oxford Newsletter	vol. 16/4: 7	1980, Fall

Feldman, Abraham Bronson (1914-1982)

Hope, Warren	Shakespeare Oxford Newsletter [repr. in BTC, vol. 6: 151-55]	vol. 18/2: 1-3	1982, Spring
Hope, Warren	Neue Shakespeare Journal	vol. NS8: 141-46	2023

Ferguson, Mrs. Tess

Editor	De Vere Society Newsletter	p. 10	2002, Oct.

Fitzgerald, James Edmund (1943-2001)

Boyle, William E. (Editor)	Shakespeare Oxford Newsletter	vol. 37/1: 3	2001, Spring
Boyle, William E. (Editor)	Shakespeare Oxford Newsletter	vol. 37/1: 20	2001, Spring
Hughes, Stephanie Hopkins	The Oxfordian	vol. 4: 1-4	2001
Laugwitz, Uwe	Neue Shakespeare Journal	vol. 7: 121-24	2002, May

Fleet, Preston (d. 1994)

NY Times	New York Times (repr. in SON, [repr. in SON, vol. 31/1a: 7 (Winter 1995)]	p. 25	1995, Feb. 4

Ford, E. B. (1902-1988)

The Times	De Vere Society Newsletter	no. 2: 26-27	1988, April

Ford, Gertrude C. (d. 1996)

Editor	Shakespeare Oxford Newsletter	vol. 35/4: 4	2000, Winter

Fowler, William (1901-1992)

Mixter, Clara	Shakespeare Oxford Newsletter	vol. 29/1a: 4	1993, Winter
Sullivan, Robert	Dartmouth Alumni Magazine [repr. in SON, vol. 30/2a: 5 (Spring 1994)]		1994, March

Frazer, Winifred L. (d. 1995)

Editor	Shakespeare Oxford Society	vol. 31/2a: 11	1995, Spring

Furman, Alfred Antoine (1856-1940)

Editor	Shakespeare Fellowship Newsletter (Am)	p. 6	1940, Oct./Nov.

Gielgud, Sir John (1904-2000)

Editor	Shakespeare Oxford Newsletter	vol. 36/1: 2	2000, Spring

Gifford, G. Grant (d. 2003)

Beauclerk, Charles	Shakespeare Oxford Newsletter	vol. 39/2: 20	2003, Spring

Gilfillan, S. Colum (1921-1978)

Lipman, Carol S.	Shakespeare Oxford Newsletter	vol. 25/1: 10-11	1989, Winter

Gordon, Helen Heightsman (1932-1922)

Boyle, William	Shakespeare Oxford Newsletter	vol. 59/3: 10	2023, 10

Greenwood, Sir George (1859-1928)

--	Evening Standard		1928, Oct. 28
Editor	Shakespeare Fellowship Quarterly [repr. in BTC, vol. 3: 379-380]	vol. VIII, no. 2	1947. Summer
Greenwood, Elsie	Shakespearean Authorship Review [repr. in BTC, vol. 1: 7 and vol. 5: 89-91]	no. 8	1962, Autumn
--	Washington Post	p. 6	1928, Nov. 15
O'Connor, Hon. T. P.	Sunday Times	issue 5510: 14	1928, Nov. 4
Hirst, W. A.	Sunday Times [letter]	issue 5510: 14	1928, Nov. 4
L.T.G.	Sunday Times [letter]	issue 5510: 14	1928, Nov. 4
--	The Times		1928, Oct. 29
--	The Times		1928, Oct. 30

Gridley, Fran (1931-2018)

Editor	Shakespeare Oxford Newsletter	vol. 54/3: 7	2018, Summer

Halstead, Ron (1940-2014)

Editor	Shakespeare Oxford Newsletter	vol. 51/1: 10-11	2015, Winter

Hannas, Andrew (1941-2009)

Editor	Shakespeare Matters	vol. 8/4: 5, 15+	2009, Fall
Editor	Shakespeare Oxford Newsletter	vol. 45/3: 7	2009, Dec.
Laugwitz, Uwe	Neues Shake-speare Journal	vol. NS1: 162	2010, Nov.

Hansen, Leonard (d. 2003)

Quealy, Gerit	Shakespeare Oxford Newsletter	vol. 40/2: 06	2004, Spring

Hardigg, James S. (1922-2020)

Boyle William E.	Shakespeare Oxford Newsletter	vol. 59/1: 5	2023, Winter

Hart, T. B. (d. 1963)
Bowen, Gwynneth M.   Shakespearean Authorship Review   issue #9: 20   1963, Spring

Haydon, Mr. J. Martin (d. 1937)
Editor   Shakespeare Fellowship Newsletter (Eng.)   no. 6: 8-9   1937, Nov.

Hayes, Stanley (d. 1984)
Editor   Shakespeare Oxford Newsletter   vol. 20/3: 6   1984, Summer

Hess, Ron (1949-2019)
Boyle, William   Shakespeare Oxford Newsletter   vol. 55/3: 9-11   2019, Summer
Gilvary, W. Ron   De Vere Society Newsletter   vol. 26/3: 4-7   2019, July

Hicks, Brian (d. 2014)
Dams, Christopher   De Vere Society Newsletter   vol. 21/2: 3   2014, May

Hobart-Hampden, Canon A. K.
Ward, Capt. Bernard M.   Shakespeare Pictorial   no. 93: 176   1935, Nov.

Hoffman, Calvin (d. 1986)
Editor   Shakespeare Oxford Newsletter   vol. 22/2: 13   1986, Spring

Holden, Isabel (1915-2007)
Beauclerk, Charles   Shakespeare Matters   vol. 7/2: 1, 18+   2008, Winter
Editor   Shakespeare Matters   vol. 7/1: 4   2007, Fall
Editor   Shakespeare Oxford Newsletter   vol. 43/4: 13   2007, Fall

Holland, Rear-Admiral H. H. (1873-1957)
Editor   Shakespeare Fellowship Newsletter (Eng)   p. 11   1957, Autumn
     [repr. in BTC, vol. 1: 246-247]

Hope, Warren (1944-2022)
Goldstein, Gary   The Oxfordian   vol. 24: 9-10   2022, Sept.
Laugwitz, Uwe   Neue Shakespeare Journal   vol. NS8: 207-   2023
Meyers, Bob   Shakespeare Oxford Newsletter   vol. 58/4: 15   2022, Fall

Horne, Jr., Richard C. (d. 1976)
Cyr, Gordon C.   Shakespeare Oxford Newsletter   Special issue: 1   1976, March
     [repr. in BTC, vol. 6: 82-83]

Howe, Norma Claire (1930-2011)
Wright, Daniel L.   Shakespeare Oxford Newsletter   vol. 47/2: 13-14   2011, Spring
Editor   Shakespeare Matters   vol. 10/3: 33   2011, Summer

Humphrey, Travers Christmas (1901-1983)
Robins, M. H.   Shakespeare Oxford Newsletter   vol. 19/3: 2-5   1983, Summer

Hunt, William O. (d. 1994)
Beauclerk, Charles   Shakespeare Oxford Newsletter   vol. 30/4: 12-13   1994, Autumn

Hunter, Tom (d. 2011)
Joyrich, Richard   Shakespeare Oxford Newsletter   vol. 47/3: 6   2011, Fall

Huston, Craig (d. 1978)
Hope, Warren   Shakespeare Oxford Newsletter   vol. 14/4: 1-2   1978, Fall

Ironside-Wood, Olga (1913-2001)
Wells, Lawrence   De Vere Society Newsletter   p. 14-15   2002, Jan./Feb.
Wells, Lawrence   Shakespeare Oxford Newsletter   vol. 38/1: 21   2002, Winter

Johnson, Morse (1915-1997)
Hughes, Stephanie Hopkins   The Oxfordian   vol. 1: 0   1998
Whalen, Richard F.   Shakespeare Oxford Newsletter   vol. 33/4: 2   1997, Fall
     [repr. in BTC, vol. 7: 408-09]

Johnson, Philip (d. 2007)
Jolly, Eddi   De Vere Society Newsletter   p. 4   2007, Oct.

Kellog, Charles (1940-2015)
McNeil, Alex   Shakespeare Oxford Newsletter   vol. 51/4: 7   2015, Fall

Kelly, Kevin (c. 1930-1994)
--   New York Times   1994, Nov.
     [repr. in SON, vol. 30/4: 15 (Autumn 1994)]

Kent, William (1886-1963)

Cutner, Herbert	Shakespearean Authorship Review [repr. in BTC, vol. 5: 130-131]	no. 10: 21-22	1963, Autumn

Kline, Peter (1936-2020)

--	Shakespeare Oxford Newsletter	vol. 57/1: 14	2021, Winter

Kloepfer, John G. (d. 2000)

--	Buffalo News	p. B17	2000, Jan. 30

Knapp, Margaret

--	Shakespeare Fellowship Quarterly	vol. VIII/4: 54	1946, Oct.

Kreeger, David Lloyd (d. 1991)

Barnes, Bart	Wall Street Journal	p. A1	1990, Nov. 20
Editor	Spear-shaker Newsletter	issue 1/1: 1	1991, Feb.

Langford, Reverend Dr. Michael J. (1931-2020)

Editor	De Vere Society Newsletter	vol. 27/4: 31	2020, Oct.

Lefranc, Abel (1863-1952)

Lambin, Georges	Shakespeare Fellowship Newsletter (Eng)	p. 10	1953, April
Lambin, Georges	Shakespearean Authorship Review [repr. in BTC, vol. 5: 95-97]	no. 8	1962, Autumn

Le Gassick, Michael (d. 2016)

Jolly, Eddi M.	De Vere Society Newsletter	vol. 23/1: 42-43	2016, Jan.
Malim, Richard	De Vere Society Newsletter	vol. 23/1: 42-43	2016, January

Leiding, Dietrich (1938-2023)

Laugwitz, Uwe	Neue Shakespeare Journal	vol. NS8: 204-06	2023

Ligon, Katherine (K. C.) (1948-2009)

Editor	Shakespeare Matters	vol. 8/4: 4-5	2009, Fall
Whittemore, Hank	Shakespeare Oxford Newsletter	vol. 45/2: 4-5	2009, Sept.
Egan, Michael (ed.)	The Oxfordian	vol. 11: 0	2009
Detobel, Robert	Neues Shake-speare Journal	vol. NS1: 161-62	2010, Nov.

Linklater, Kristin (1936-2020)

--	Shakespeare Oxford Newsletter	vol. 9-10	2020, Summer

Looney, John Thomas (1870-1944)

--	New York Times	p. 15	1944, Feb. 21
Allen, Percy	Shakespeare Fellowship Newsletter (Eng)	p. 2-4	1944, May
Bénézet, Louis P.	Shakespeare Fellowship Quarterly [repr. in BTC, vol. 3: 26-36; and in NSJ, vol. NS1: 24-36 (Nov. 2010)]	vol. V/2: 17-23	1944, April
Demant, V. A.	Shakespearean Authorship Review [repr. in BTC, vol. 1: 214-217 and Vol 5: 2-94; and in NSJ, vol. NS1: 37-39 (Nov. 2010)]	no. 8: 8-9	1962, Autumn

Louther, John (1924-2003)

Beauclerk, Charles	Shakespeare Oxford Newsletter	vol. 39/2: 20	2003, Spring
Boyle, William E. (Editor)	Shakespeare Matters	vol. 2/3: 3	2003, Spring

Lovell, Stanley P. (d. 1976)

Editor	Shakespeare Oxford Newsletter	vol. 11/3: 5	1975, Fall

Magri, Noemi (d. 2011)

Anderson, Mark K.	Shakespeare Oxford Newsletter	vol. 47/3: 5	2011, Fall
Editor	Shakespeare Matters	vol. 10/3: 32-33	2011, Summer
Gazzetta de Mantua	Shakespeare Oxford Newsletter	vol. 47/3: 5-6	2011, Fall
Hess, W. Ron	Shakespeare Oxford Newsletter	vol. 47/3: 5	2011, Fall
Imlay, Elizabeth; *Gazetta di* *Mantua*; Kevin Gilvary; Robert Detobel	De Vere Society Newsletter	vol. 18/2: 22-24	2011, July

Mason, Jacquelyn L. (1940-1921)

Editor	Shakespeare Oxford Newsletter	vol. 57/4: 10	2021, Fall

Matus, Irvin Leigh (1941-2011)

Egan, Michael	Shakespeare Oxford Newsletter	vol. 47/2: 14-15	2011, Spring
Mahon, John M.	Shakespeare Newsletter	vol. 61/1: 33	2011, Spr-Sum

Maxse, L. J. (d. 1932)

Ward, Captain B. M.	Shakespeare Pictorial	no. 49: 48	1932, March

McCullough (1933-2022)

Editor	Shakespeare Oxford Newsletter	vol. 58/4: 16	2022, April

McGeoch, Sir Ian (D. 2007)

Fitch, J. A.	The Times (London)	p. 65	2007, Sept. 1
Imlay, Elizabeth	De Vere Society Newsletter	p. 4	2007, Oct.

Messner, Rhoda Henry (d. 1986)

Editor	Shakespeare Oxford Newsletter	vol. 22/2: 13	1986, Spring

Mez, John R. (d. 1959)

Bowen, Gwynneth M.	Shakespearean Authorship Review	issue #2: 23	1959, Autumn

Miller, Ruth Loyd (1922-2005) and/or Minos D. Miller, Jr. (1921-2006)

--	Advocate, The	p. 5D	2005, Sept. 8
--	Shakespeare Oxford Newsletter	vol. 41/4: 13	2005, Fall
--	Daily Advertiser	p. C5	2005, Sept.
--	Advocate, The	p. 9	2006, July 3
Hughes, Stephanie Hopkins	The Oxfordian	vol. 9	2006
Laugwitz, Uwe	Neues Shake-speare Journal	vol. 11: 148-49	2007, April
Ligon, K. C.	Shakespeare Matters	vol. 5/1: 6	2005, Fall
Ligon, K. C.	Shakespeare Matters	vol. 6/1: 5-7	2006, Fall

Monteath, E. R. (d. 1956)

Editor	Shakespeare Oxford Newsletter (Eng)	p. 12	1956, Autumn

Mooney, Jr., Vincent J. (1944-2001)

Hess, W. Ron	Shakespeare Oxford Newsletter	vol. 38/1: 21	2002, Winter

Moore, Peter R. (1948-2007)

Editor	Shakespeare Matters	vol. 7/2: 05	2008, Winter
Goldstein, Gary B.	De Vere Society Newsletter	vol. 15/1: 29	2008, March
	[repr. in NSJ, vol. 12: 51-52 (Oct. 2008)]		
Goldstein, Gary B.	Shakespeare Matters	vol. 9/2: 5, 25	2010, Spr/Sum
Hess, W. Rom	Shakespeare Oxford Newsletter	vol. 43/4: 24	2007, Fall
	[repr. in NSJ, vol. 12: 49-50 (Oct. 2008)]		
Hughes, Stephanie Hopkins	The Oxfordian	vol. 10: 0	2007
Smith, Shepherd	Neue Shakespeare Journal	vol. 12: 53-54	2008, Oct.
	[repr. from DVN, vol. 15/1: 29 (March 2008)]		

Nichols, Francis L. (d. 1956)

Bowen, Gwynneth M.	Shakespeare Fellowship Newsletter (Eng)	p. 12	1956, Autumn

Nitze, Paul (1907-2004)

--	Times, The (London)		2004, Oct. 22
	Response by Richard Malim, Nov. 2, p. 66.		
Editor	Shakespeare Matters	vol. 4/2: 4	2005, Winter
Goldstein, Gary B.	Shakespeare Oxford Newsletter	vol. 40/4: 2-3	2004, Fall

O'Connell, Frank (1914-2008)

Editor	Shakespeare Matters	vol. 7/4: 17	2008, Fall

Ogburn, Sr., Charlton (1882-1962)

--	New York Herald Tribune	p. 16	1962, Feb. 24
Adamson, T. L.	Shakespearean Authorship Review	no. 7: 19	1962, Spring
	[repr. in BTC, vol. 5: 81-82]		
--	New York Times	p. 27	1962, Feb. 24

Ogburn, Jr., Charlton (1911-1998)

--	New York Times	p. D6	1998, Oct. 22
--	New York Times	p. 53	1998, Oct. 25
--	Shakespeare Newsletter	p. 56	1988, Summer
--	Washington Post	p. D6	1998, Oct. 22
Anderson, Mark K.	Shakespeare Oxford Newsletter	vol. 34/3: 6-7	1998, Fall
	[Also in The Valley Advocate (Oct. 29, 1998)]		
Bennett, Tom	Atlanta Journal-Constitution	p. C6	1998, Oct. 22
Editor	Shakespeare Oxford Newsletter	vol. 34/3: 24	1998, Fall
Hughes, Stephanie Hopkins	The Oxfordian	vol. 2: 0	1999, Fall
Livacari, Gary L.	Shakespeare Oxford Newsletter	vol. 37/3: 22	2001, Fall
Norwood, James	De Vere Society Newsletter	vol. 29/2: 26-31	2022, April
Whalen, Richard F.	Shakespeare Oxford Newsletter	vol. 34/3: 1, 5	1998, Fall
	[repr. in SHNL, vol. 48/3: 63 (Fall 1998); in BTC, vol. 8: 22-25; and in NSJ, vol. 3: 12-14 (Jan. 1999)]		

Ogburn, Dorothy Stevens (1890-1981)

Hope, Warren	SON [repr. in BTC, vol. 6: 149-50]	vol. 17/2: 10	1981, Spring

Paget, Verily Anderson (1915-2010) (see Verily Anderson (Paget))

Palmer, Cecil (d. Jan. 1952)

--	Truth	p. 106	1952, Jan. 25
Lamb. V. B.	Truth	p. 292	1952, Sept. 19
Woodhouse, Bruce	Yorkshire Post and Leeds Intelligencer	p. 7	1953, July 24

Patience, Harold William (1921-1992)

Editor	Shakespeare Oxford Newsletter	vol. 28/3: 10	1992, Summer

Peel, Howard (d. 2015)

Editor	De Vere Society Newsletter	vol. 22/4: 2	2015, Oct.

Peel, Marion (d. 2015)

Jolly, Eddi M.	De Vere Society Newsletter	vol. 23/1: 42-43	2016, Jan.

Peer, Michael (d. 2004)

Laugwitz, Uwe	Neues Shake-speare Journal	vol. 11: 140-42	2007, April

Rendall, Canon Gerald H. (1945)

--	The Times (London)	p. 6	1945, Jan. 6

Penrose, Lionel (d. 1972)

Editor	Shakespearean Authorship Review	issue #26: 17-18	1972, Summer

Phillips, Gerald William (d. 1956)

Shield, H. S.	Shakespeare Fellowship Newsletter (Eng)	p. 12	1956, Autumn

Philpot, Mr. Hamlet (1856-1939)

Editor	Shakespeare Fellowship Newsletter (Eng.)	no. 15: 3-4	1939, July

Philpot, Mrs. Theodora (d. 1954)

Editor	Shakespeare Fellowship Newsletter (Eng)	p. 5	1954, April

Regnier, Tom

Editor [Alex McNeil]	Shakespeare Oxford Newsletter	vol. 56/2: 1, 29-30	2020, Spring
Editor [Gary Goldstein]	The Oxfordian	vol. 22	2020, Sept.
Editor and others	Shakespeare Oxford Newsletter	vol. 56/2: 1, 12-13	2020, Spring
Editor and others	De Vere Society Newsletter	vol. 27/3: 39-41	2020, July
Goff, Tom	Shakespeare Oxford Newsletter	vol. 56/2: 30	2020, Spring

Rendall, Reverend Canon Gerald H. (1851-1945)

--	The Times (London)	p. 6	1945, Jan. 6
--	Essex Newsman		1945, Jan. 9
--	Birmingham Daily	p. 4	1945, Jan. 8
--	New York Times	p. 19	1945, Feb. 20
Douglas, Col. Montague W.	Shakespeare Fellowship Newsletter (Eng)	p. 2	1945, May
Editor	Shakespeare Fellowship Quarterly	vol. VI/2: 21	1945, April

Remembrances of Noted Oxfordians

Renner, Virginia (1933-2022)
Cutting, Bonner Miller	Shakespeare Oxford Newsletter	vol. 58/2: 9	2022, Spring
Shahan, John	Shakespeare Oxford Newsletter	vol. 58/2: 9	2022, Spring

Roberts, Shelia (d. 2006)
Anderson, Verily	De Vere Society Newsletter	p. 30	2006, Nov.

Robinson, J. Alan (1925-2005)
Imlay, Elizabeth	De Vere Society Newsletter	p. 3	2005, Dec.

Robson, Margaret (1928-2022)
Cutting, Bonner Miller	Shakespeare Oxford Newsletter	vol. 58/4:15	2022, Fall

Robson, Norman N. (1925-2015)
McNeil, Alex	Shakespeare Oxford Newsletter	vol. 51/4: 7	2015, Fall
Editor	De Vere Society Newsletter	vol. 22/4: 2	2015, Oct.

Roe, Richard P. (d. 2010)
Goldstein, Gary B.	Shakespeare Matters	vol. 9/3: 4-5	2010, Fall
Metternich, Hilary Roe	Shakespeare Oxford Newsletter	vol. 47/1: 22-23	2011, Jan.
Wright, Daniel L.	Shakespeare Oxford Newsletter	vol. 47/1: 1, 22	2011, Jan.

Rollett, Dr. John (d. 2015)
Editor [and Eddi Jolly]	Shakespeare Oxford Newsletter	vol. 52/1: 7	2016, Winter
Jolly, Eddi M.	De Vere Society Newsletter	vol. 23/1: 42-43	2016, Jan.

Sammartino, Peter (d. 1992)
Editor	New York Times [excerpts repr. in SON, vol. 28/2: 4 (Spring 1992)]	p. B9	1992, March 30

Sams, Eric (1926-2004)
Davis, Frank	Shakespeare Oxford Newsletter	vol. 41/1: 23	2005, Winter
Laugwitz, Uwe	Neues shake-speare Journal	vol. 11: 143-45	2007, April

Schoenbaum, Samuel (1927-1996)
Whalen, Richard F.	Shakespeare Oxford Newsletter	vol. 32/2: 2	1996, Spring

Schumann, Howard (1937-2023)
Editor	Shakespeare Oxford Newsletter	vol. 59/1: 4	2023, Winter

Schwanitz, Dietrich
Laugwitz, Uwe	Neues Shake-speare Journal	vol. 11: 145-47	2007, April

Sears, Elisabeth (Betty) (1921-2011)
Boyle, William E.	Shakespeare Matters	vol. 11/1: 6-7	2012, Winter
Wayland	Boston Globe		2012, May 6

Sharpe, Wenonah Finch (1926-2017)
Sharpe, Kathryn	Shakespeare Oxford Newsletter	vol. 53/1: 7	2017, Winter

Sheridan, Susan (d. 2015)
Editor	De Vere Society Newsletter	vol. 22/4: 2	2015, Oct.

Sherwood, James Webster "Jaz" (1936-2014)
Editor	Shakespeare Oxford Newsletter	vol. 51/1: 10-11	2015, Winter

Shield, H. S. (d. 1966)
Adamson, T. L.	Shakespearean Authorship Review	issue #16: 26	1966, Autumn

Singleton, Esther (d. 1930)
McGlinchee, Claire	New York Times	p. X7	1930, Aug. 31
Ward, Colonel B. R.	Shakespeare Pictorial	no. 30: 16	1930, Aug.

Slater, Eliot (1904-1983)
Edwards, Francis	The Bard	vol. 4/2: 76	1984

Slater, Gilbert (1865-1938)
Edwards, Francis	The Bard	vol. 4/2: 34, 76	1984
Ward, Bernard M.	Shakespeare Fellowship Newsletter (Eng.)	no. 9: 1-2	1938, May

Smith, Moore (1859-1941)
    Editor   Shakespeare Fellowship Newsletter (Am)   vol. 2/2: 17   1941, Feb.

Sobran, Joseph (1946-2010)
    Editor   De Vere Society Newsletter   vol. 17/3: 2-3   2010, Nov.
    Detobel, Robert   Neues Shake-speare Journal   vol. NS1: 160-61   2010, Nov.
    Grimes, William   New York Times   p. A17   2010, Oct. 2
    Hess, W. Ron   Shakespeare Oxford Newsletter   vol. 47/2: 11-13   2011, Spring
    McNeil, Alex   Shakespeare Matters   vol. 10/1: 28   2011, Winter
    Scully, Matthew   National Review   p. 35   2010, Nov. 1

Sprague, Harriet Chapman (d. 1876-1969)
    --   New York Times   1969, Pct/ 3

Stevens, Justice John Paul (d. 2019)
    Regnier, Tom   Shakespeare Oxford Newsletter   vol. 55/3: 13-14   2019, Summer

Stone, Elliott (1932-2011)
    Editor   Shakespeare Oxford Newsletter   vol. 47/2: 15   2011, Spring
    Marquard, Bryan   Boston Globe   p. B12   2011, Jan. 12
                       [repr. in SON, vol. 47/2: 15 (Spring 2011)]

Stone, Erza (1918-1994)
    Grimes, William   Shakespeare Oxford Newsletter   vol. 30/1: 18   1994, Winter
                       [from *New York Times*, March 5, 1994]

Sybersma, Sue (d. 2007)
    Cossolotto, Matthew   De Vere Society Newsletter   vol. 15/1: 28   2008, March
    Editor   Shakespeare Matters   vol. 7/2: 5   2008, Winter
    Editor   Shakespeare Matters   vol. 7/3: 19   2008, Spring
    Imlay, Elizabeth; et al.   Shakespeare Oxford Newsletter   vol. 44/1: 04   2008, Winter
    Joyrich, Richard   De Vere Society Newsletter   vol. 15/1: 28   2008, March
    Sherwood, James (Jaz)   De Vere Society Newsletter   vol. 15/1: 28   2008, March

Titherley, A. W. (d. 1966)
    Wainewright, Ruth M. D.   Shakespearean Authorship Review   issue #16: 26   1966, Autumn

Trout, R. Ridgill (d. 1969)
    Editor   Shakespearean Authorship Review   issue #22: 17-18   1969, Dec.

Tweedale, Ralph (d. 1977)
    Editor   Shakespeare Oxford Newsletter   vol. 13/2: 5   1977, Summer

Urquhart, Patricia (1946-2015)
    McNeil, Alex   Shakespeare Oxford Newsletter   vol. 51/4: 7   2015, Fall

Ward, Captain Bernard Mordaunt (1893-Oct., 1945)
    Editor   Shakespeare Fellowship Quarterly   vol. VI/4: 49-50   1945, Oct.
    Editor   Shakespeare Fellowship News-letter   page 1   1945, Nov.

Ward, Colonel Bernard Rowland (1863-1933)
    --   Morning Post   page 5   1933, April 2
    Carrington, Phyllis   Shakespearean Authorship Review   no. 8: 2-5   1962, Autumn
                       [repr. in BTC, vol. 1: 256-59;
                       and in BTC, vol. 5: 85-88]

Weld, Philip S. (d. 1984)
    Editor   Shakespeare Oxford Newsletter   vol. 20/4: 8   1984, Fall

Wells, Carolyn (de. 1942)
    Editor   Shakespeare Fellowship News-Letter   vol. ¾: 56   1942, June

Willis, Marie (1973)
    Editor   Shakespeare Oxford Newsletter   vol. 29/3a: 14   1993, Summer

Wilson, Talmadge Gartley (1919-2000)
    Editor   De Vere Society Newsletter   p. 1-2   2000, July
    Editor   Shakespeare Oxford Newsletter   vol. 35/4: 2   2000, Winter
    Hughes, Stephanie Hopkins The Oxfordian   vol. 3: 0   2000

Remembrances of Noted Oxfordians

Woodward, Dr. H. M. (1875-1948)
 Editor   Shakespeare Fellowship Newsletter (Eng)   p. 1   1948, April

Wright, Daniel L. "Dan" Wright (1954-2018)
 Boyle, Bill   Shakespeare Oxford Newsletter   vol. 54/4: 10-12   2018, Fall

Zakelj, Ann (1947-2019)
 Editor   Shakespeare Oxford Fellowship Newsletter   vol. 55/2: 8   2019, Spring

This Index of Titles includes the main listings for each title in Parts II-IV; Parts I and V are not included. Also not included are titles of films of Shakespeare's plays—or other films or TV broadcasts—reviewed in Oxfordian periodicals unless there is an Oxfordian angle to them.

Oxfordian periodicals and core Oxfordian collections are in bold.

Index of Titles

Index of Titles

Index of Titles

Title	Periodicals	Other Publs.	Pages
Dispatch (Warwick Valley)	1939		603
Dissertation Abstracts International	2001-2002		603
Dolphin	1941		603
Dover Express (Kent, England)	1936		603
Drama	1938		603
Dramatists Guild Quarterly	1990		603
Dukes County Intelligencer	1999		603
Dundee Courier & Advertiser (Angus, Scotland)	1930-1931		603
Dundee Evening Telegraph and Post	1920-1932		603
Eagle (St. John's College, Cambridge)	1934		603
Earl of Oxford and the Making of "Shakespeare," The (Malim)		2012	701
Earl of Oxford as "Shakespeare," The (Douglas)		1952	691
Earl of Oxford as "Shakespeare," The: An Outline of the Case (Douglas)		1931	689
Earls of Paraside: England and the Dream of Perfection (Nicholson)		2008	699
Early Modern English Poetry: A Critical Companion (Cheney)		2007	699
Early Modern Literary Studies	1999-2015		603
Early Shakespeare (ES) (Feldman & Hope)		2019	735
Early Shakespeare Authorship Doubts (Wildenthal)		2019	704
Early Theatre	2006		603
East Anglian Daily Times (Ipswich)	1973-2013		603
East Anglian Magazine	1937-1941		571-73
Eastbourne Gazette	1930-1934		604
Eastern Daily Press	1997?-1999		604
Economic History Review	2006		604
Economist, The	2010		604
Edinburgh Evening News (Midlothian, Scotland)	1932		604
Edinburgh Journal	1852		604
Edmonton Journal (Alberta)	1990-2005		604
Edmund Spenser's War on Lord Burghley (Danner)		2011	701
Educating Shakespeare: What he knew and how and where he learned it (Hughes)		2022	705
Edward de Vere: A Great Elizabethan (Frisbee)		1931	689
Edward de Vere, AKA William Shakespeare: A Life in Two Acts (Brown)		2002	710
Edward de Vere: An Evaluation of the Financial Problems (Pearson)		2000	697
Edward de Vere and the War of Words (Appleton)		1985	695
Edward de Vere: Fortunatus im Unglück. Die Aventiuren des Master F. I. [German] (Kreiler)		2006	699
Edward de Vere Newsletter (EDV)	**1989-1994**		**497-500**
Edward de Vere: Onvermijdelijk Shakespeare [Dutch] (Helsloot)		2004	698
Edward de Vere—or "Shakespeare": A Bibliography (Mez)		1952	692
Edward de Vere, Part 1 [a play] (Imlay)		1997	709
Edward de Vere, Seventeenth Earl of Oxford, 1550-1604 (Kittle)		1935	690
Edward de Vere, Seventeenth Earl of Oxford, and Shakespeare (Kittle)		1942	690
Edward de Vere: The Crisis and Consequence of Wardship (Pearson)		2005	699
Edward de Vere, the Seventeenth Earl of Oxford: The Real Sh. (pamphlet) (Kent)		1947	691
[2nd edition: 1957]		1957	692
Edward de Vere Was Shake-speare: At Long Last, the Proof (Purdy)		2003	698
[2nd eition: 2013]		2013	702
Edward de Veres Gedichte [The Poems of Edward de Vere] (Kreiler)		2005	699
Edward Oxenford: Spear-shaker [a play] (Caruana)			712
Edward's Presents: An Oxfordian Play on London's Bankside (2004)		2004	710
Egoist, The	1918		604
El Norte (Monterrey, Mexico)	1999		604
Eleven Magazine	1989		604
Elizabeth amd Edward [a play] (Hampton)		2009	710
Elizabeth and Ivan: Role of English-Russian Relations in Love's Labour's Lost (Greenhill)		2023	705
Elizabeth and Shakespeare: The Meeting of Two Minds (Hackett)		2009	700
Elizabethan Chronicle Play as War Propaganda, The [pamphlet] (Ward)		1930	689

Index of Titles

Index of Titles

Title	Periodicals	Other Publs.	Pages
My Auto-Biography (Chaplin)		1964	693
My Shakespeare (MS) (Leahy)		2018	758
My Shakespeare: the Authorship Controversy (Leahy)		2018	704
Myers' Literary Guide: The North East (Myers)		1995	696
Mysterious Mr. Looney [dramatic encounter between J. Thomas Looney and Sir Sidney Chambers] (Graves)		2004	710
Mysterious William Shakespeare, The: The Myth and the Reality (Ogburn) [2nd edition: 1992]		1984, 1992	695, 696
Mystery Beyond Words, A (pamphlet) (Lowell)		1956	692
Mystery of "Mr. W. H.", The (Ward)		1923	687
Mystery of Hamlet, the (Caruso)		2008	699
Mystery of William Shakespeare (Ogburn)		1988	695
Nashville Tennessean	1920-1955		628
Nation	1920-2006		628
Nation and Athenaeum	1921-1931		628
National Encyclopedia: A Dictionary of University Knowledge		1884	777
National Observer	1968		628
National Post	2010-2011		628
National Public Radio	1985-2016		628
National Review (American)	1984-2023		628-29
National Review (London)	1857-1938		629
Necessary Mischief: Exploring the Shakespeare Authorship Question (Cutting)		2017	740
Neues Shake-speare Journal (German) (Laugwitz) (NSJ)	1997-current		412-23
New Age	1920-1921		629
New Brunswick Daily Home News	1940		629
New Criterion	2006-2016		629
New England Quarterly	1996		629
New England Review	2015		629
New English Review	2014-2021		629
New Forest Magazine	1922		629
New Indian Express (Chennai, India)	2011		629
New Leader	1925		629
New Orleans Times-Picayune	1978-1999		630
New Oxford Shakespeare Authorship Companion, The (Taylor & Egan)		2017	703
New Psychoanalytic Readings of Shakespeare (Stone & Newlin)		2023	775
New Republic	1950		630
New Shakespeare Society Transactions	1874		630
New Statesman (London)	1920-2013		630
New Statesman and Nation	1955		630
New Witness	1921		630
New York Herald Tribune (NYH)	1927-1962		630-31
New York Magazine	1983		631
New York Observer	2005		631
New York Post	1939-2003		631
New York Review of Books (NYR)	1942-2010		632
New York Sun	1928-2003		632
New York Times and NYT Book Review (NYT)	1920-2022		632-36
New York World-Telegram	1945		636
New Yorker (NYZ)	1945-2022		636-37
Newcastle Daily Chronicle	1920		637
Newcastle Journal	1995		637
Newhouse NewsService	1999		637
Newport Daily Express (Vermont)	1945		637
News and Observer (Raleigh, North Carolina)	1931-2011		637
News Leader (Richmond, VA)	1931		637
News-Chronicle	1939		637
Newsday (Long Island)	1987-2003		637
Newsweek	1939-2014		637-38

Index of Titles

Title	Periodicals	Other Publs.	Pages
Pall Mall Gazette (London)	1920		642
Palm Beach Post	1988		642
Paper Trail [Fry]		2008	710
Paradigm Shift, Shake-speare (Er)		2002	698
Paradise of Dainty Devices (Rollins)		1927	688
Partnership: The Canadian Journal of Library and Information Practice and Research	2013		642
Pasadena Star-News	2011		642
Past and Future	1960-1963		643
Patriot Ledger (Quincy, Mass.)	1995-2006		643
Patronage, Culture and Power: the Early Cecils, 1558-1612 (Croft)		2002	
PEN Broadsheet	1976		643
Peoria Star-Journal	1940		643
Periodical, The	1930-1944		643
Perkins School for the Blind (online)	2020		643
Persona Grata (Beaton & Tyson)		1954	692
Personal Clues in Shakespeare's Poems and Sonnets (Rendall)		1934	689
Perspective [BBC program]		1981	778
Philadelphia Bulletin	1940		643
Philadelphia Daily News	1996-1998		643
Philadelphia Inquirer	1985-2010		643
Philadelphia Inquirer and Public Ledger	1931-1941		643
Philadelphia Welcomat	1989		643
Philological Quarterly	1929-1931		643
Philosophy of the Plays of Shakspere Unfolded, The (Bacon)		1857	685
Phoenix Nest, The (Rollins, editor)		1931	689
Physicsworld.com	1998		643
Pimpernel Smith / Mister V [film by Leslie Howard]		1941	778
Pittsburgh Post-Gazette	1943-1949		644
Pittsburgh Press	1984-1985		644
Plain Dealer (Cleveland)	1939-2006		644
Player Magazine	1962		644
Players: the Shakespeare Mystery (Fields)		2005	699
Plays and Masques at Court During the Reigns of Elizabeth, James and Charles (Steele)		1926	688
Plays of Shakespeare & Chapman in Relation to French History, The (Allen)		1933	689
Plymouth Evening News (Hampshire)	1951		644
PMLA (Publication of the Modern Language Association of America)	1924-1960		644
Poacher from Stratford, The (Wadsworth)		1958	682
Poems of Edward de Vere . . . and the Sh. Authorship Question, vol. 1 (Stritmatter)	2019, 2023		761
Poems of Edward de Vere . . . and the Sh. Authorship Question, vol. 2 (Stritmatter)	2023		761
Poems of Edward de Vere, The (Looney)		1921	687
Poems of Thomas, Lord Vaux; Edward, Earl of Oxford; Robert, Earl of Essex; and Walter, Earl of Essex		1872	685
Poet's Rage, A: Understanding Shakespeare Through Authorship Studies (Boyle)		2013	762
Poetry and the Play	1930		644
Poetry Review	1951		644
Political Propaganda and Satire in A Midsummer Night's Dream (Richert)		1924	688
Post-Standard	2011		644
Post-Tribune (Gary, Ind.)	2003		644
Prensa, La (San Antonio)	1920		644
Press Censorship in Elizabethan England (Clegg)		1997	697
Prince Tudor: A Verse Drama (Hagger)		1999	709
Princeton Alumni Weekly	1938-2008		644
Problem of Hamlet, The (Cairncross)		1936	690
Problem of the Shakespeare Plays, The (Bompas)		1902	686
Proceedings of the British Academy	1951		644
Proceedings of the Royal Musical Association	1920-1961		644-45
Proud Passionate Boy [a play] (Wood)		1988	709
Providence Journal	1989-2003		645

Index of Titles

Title	Periodicals	Other Publs.	Pages
Such Fruits Out of Italy: The Italian Renaissance in Sh's Plays and Poems (Magri & Goldstein)		2014	747
Summer Storm: A Novel of Ideas (Warren)		2016	711
Sun Sentinal (Fort Lauderdale)	1990-1991		661
Sun, The (Baltimore)	1930-2007		661
Sun, The (Sydney, Australia)	1920		661
Sunday Business Post (Cork)	2010		662
Sunday Herald (Glasgow)	2007-2012		662
Sunday Independent (Johannesburg)	2011		662
Sunday Mercury (Birmingham, UK)	2006		662
Sunday Patriot (Harrisburg, PA)	1989		662
Sunday Star-Times (Wellington, New Zealand	2010		662
Sunday Sun (Newcastle)	1920		662
Sunday Telegraph (Sydney)	2011		662
Sunday Times (London)	1920-2019		662-63
Sunderand Daily Echo and Shipping Gazette	1920-1950		663
Sunlight on Shakespeare's Sonnets (Phillips)		1935	690
Sussex Agricultural Express	1931-1952		663
Sussex County Magazine	1930		663
Sweet Swan of Avon: Did a Woman Write Shakespeare? (Williams)		2006	699
Sweete Wittie Soules: Shakespeare's Connections to Oxford, Town, Gown & Shire (McDonnell)		2016	703
Sydney Morning Herald	1921-2001		663
Syracuse New Times	2008		663
T.P.'s and Cassel's Weekly	1928		663
Tablet, The	1933-1955		663
Täckamn Shakespeare: Edward de Veres hemliga liv [Finnish] (Friberg)		2006	699
Take Physic, Pomp! (Beauclerk)		2020	704
Talk of the Trade	1990		663
Talks with Elizabethans: Revealing the Mystery of William Shakespeare (Allen)		1947	691
Tampa Tribune	1997		663
TCA Regional News	2016-2017		664
Teaching and Learning Practices for Academic Freedom (Sengupta & Blessinger)		2021	775
Teacher's College Journal	1941		664
Teatr [Polish]	2011		664
Tehelka (New Delhi)	2010		664
Telegram & Gazette (Worcester, Mass.)	1990-1995		664
Telegraph, The (Brisbane, Australia)	1920		665
Telegraph, The (Calcutta, India)	2014		665
Telegraph, The [and Daily Telegraph and Sunday Telegraph] (London)	1920-2023		664-65
Telegraph-Herald (Dubuque, Iowa)	2004-2011		665
Temps, Le	1938		665
Tennessee Law Review (TLR)		2004	770
Theatre and Stage	1934		666
Theatre History Studies	2006		666
Theatre Journal	2003		666
There's Not the Smallest Orb, But in His Motion Like an Angel Sings (Stritmatter)		1996	697
This Shakespeare Industry: Amazing Monument (Brown)		1939	690
This Star of England: "William Shake-speare," Man of the Renaissance (Ogburns)		1952	692
Thomas Sackville and the Shakespearean Glass Slipper: Book Two of A "Third Way" (Feldman)		2015	702
Tilt Tournai & No Barriers [pamphlet] (Eldredge)		1999	697
TIME Magazine	1960-2007		666
Times, The (London)	1903-2017		666-68
Times Educational Supplement	1977		668
Times Higher Education Supplement	2005-2014		668
Times Literary Supplement (TLS)	1916-2020		668-73
Times of Acadiana	1986		673

Index of Titles

Title	Periodicals	Other Publs.	Pages
Virginia Lawyer	1993		675
Virginia Quarterly	1953-1959		675
Voice of America [broadcast with pro-Ogburn comments by Gordon Cyr on Jan. 7]		1985	778
Voyages de Shakespeare en France et en Italie (Lambin)		1962	692
Wall Street Journal (WSJ)	1953-2014		675-76
Wanderer	2005		676
Warwick and Warwickshire Advertiser	1920		676
Warwick Valley Dispatch	1939-1974		676
Was Shakespeare Shakespeare? A Lawyer Reviews the Evidence (Martin)		1965	693
Washington Monthly	1999		676
Washington Post and WP Book (WAP) Review/World	1924-2023		676-679
Washington Square News	1989		679
Washington Star	1962-1980		679
Washington Times	1985-2011		679-80
Wasn't Shakespeare Someone Else? (Tweedale)		1966	693
Watchers, The: A Secret History of the Reign of Elizabeth I (Alford)		2012	701
Web of Conspiracy: A Guide to Conspiracy Theory Sites on the Internet (Broderick & Miller)		2008	699
Weekend Review	1933		680
Weekly Dispatch	1920		680
Weekly Standard	2004-2014		680
Wer schrieb Shakespeare? [German translation of Michell's Who Wrote Shakespeare? (Michell & Kaiser)		2001	697
West Coast Review of Books	1985		680
Western Canon: The Books and School of the Ages (Bloom)		1994	696
Western Daily Press and Bristol Mirror	1920-2011		680
Western Mail (Cardiff)	1920, 2011		680
Western Morning News and Mercury (Devon)	1928-1947		680-81
Westminster Gazette	1920		681
WGBH Boston Magazine	1989		681
What Shakespeare is Not (O'Hagan)		1936	690
When Shakespeare Died (pamphlet) (Allen)		1937	690
Which of Shakespeare's Why, The: A Novel of the Authorship Mystery		2023	712
White Monkey, The (Galsworthy)		1928	708
Who is Shakespeare? [panel discussion on British TV]		1974	778
Who is Shakespeare? [Roundtable discussion at S. Oregon Univ.]		1994	779
Who Knew Shakespeare? What Was His Reputation in His Lifetime? (Blumenthal)		1965	693
Who Was William Shakespeare? [talk by Charles Burford at the U. of Washington]		1992	779
Who Was Shakespeare? A New Enquiry (Amphlett)		1955	692
Who Was Shake-Speare?: Was He Francis Bacon, the Earl of Oxford, or William Shaksper? (Dodd)		1947	691
Who Were Shake-speare? The Ultimate Who-dunit (Allen)		1998	697
Who Were the Dark Lady and Fair Youth of the Sonnets, The? (Allen)		1943	690
Who Wrote Shakespeare? (Michell)		1996	697
Who Wrote Shakespeare? [Bate and Waugh debate on Sept. 21]		2017	781
Who Wrote Shakespeare's Plays? (Rubinstein)		2012	701
Who Wrote Shakespeare's Plays? The Debate Goes On [NPR Morning Ed. (July 3)]		2008	780
Who Wrote That? Authorship Controversies from Moses to Sholoklov (Ostrowski)		2020	704
Whose Worth's Unknown: The Life of Edward de Vere: A Novel (Dorward)		2009	710
Wie aus William Shaxsper: William Shakespeare wurde (Detobel)		2005	699
Wiener Zeitung (German)	2000		681
Wiley-Blackwell Encyclopedia of Literature		2012	777
Will in der Welt: Wie Shakespeare zu Shakespeare wurde [German translation of Greenblatt's Will in the World]		2004	698
Will in the World: How Shakespeare Became Shakespeare (Greenblatt)		2004	698
Will o' the Wisp, or The Elusive Shakespeare (Hookham)		1922	687
Will Power: Portrait of a National Wit [10-part TNT series]		2017	781
Will Shakespeare: Factotum and Agent (Brooks)		1937	690
Will Shakspere and the Dyer's Hand, The (Brooks)		1943	690

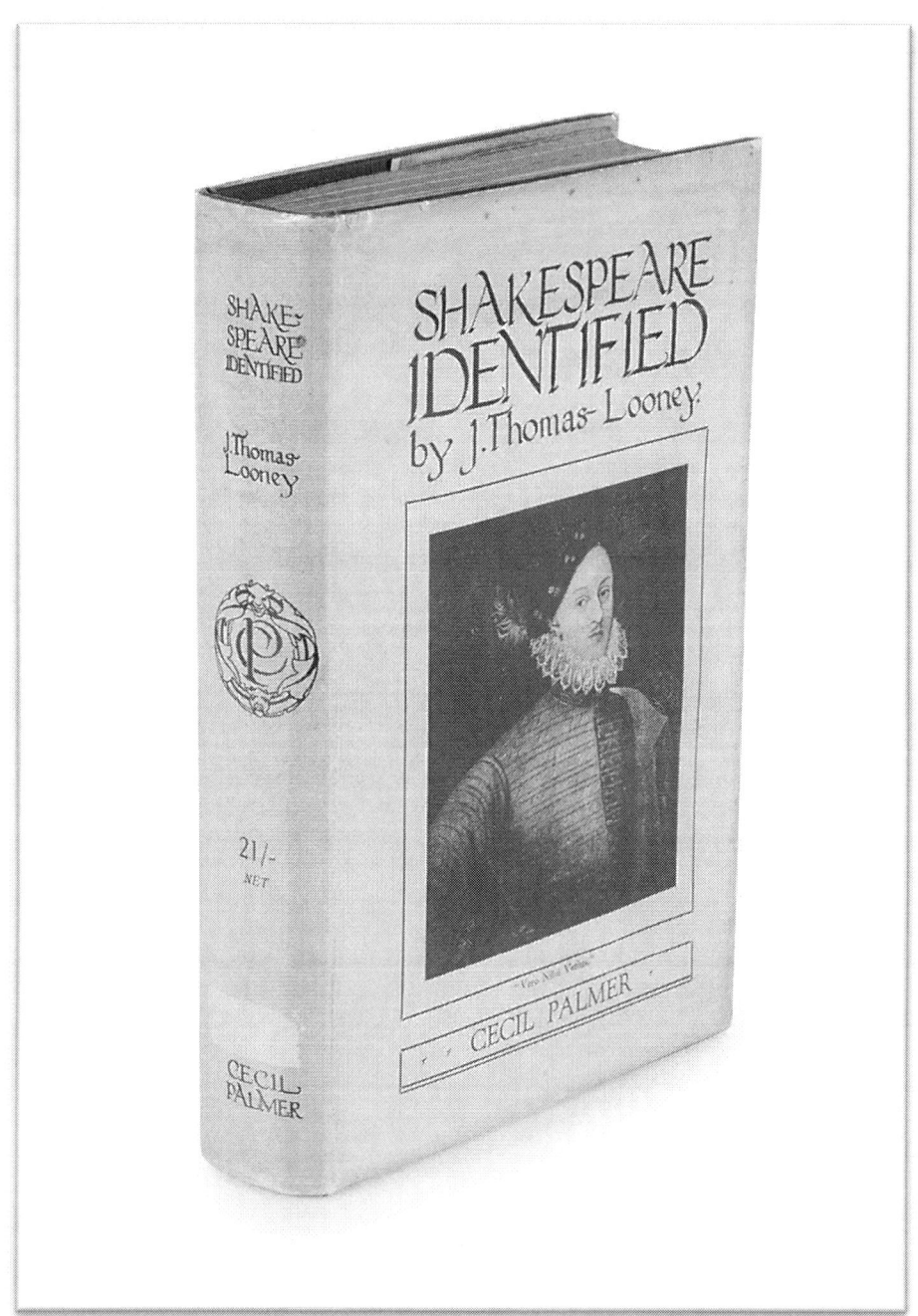

Timeline of Oxfordian Newsletters and Journals

TIMELINE OF OXFORDIAN NEWSLETTERS AND JOURNALS

Section 1 (1930–1960)

Publication	Years of coverage
Hackney Spectator (HS)	22–25
Shakespeare Pictorial (SP)	29 30 31 32 33 34 35 36
Shakespeare Fellowship Newsletter (English) (SFE)	37 38 39 40 41 42 43 44 45 46 47 48 49 50 51 52 53 54 55 56 57 58
Shakespearean Authorship Review (SAR)	59 60
Shakespeare Fellowship Newsletter (American) (SFA)	39 40 41 42 43
Shakespeare Fellowship Quarterly (SFQ)	44 45 46 47 48

Section 2 (1960–1990)

Publication	Years of coverage
Shakespearean Authorship Review (SAR)	60 61 62 63 64 65 66 67 68 69 70 71 72 73 74
Bard (BAR)	75 76 77 78 79 80 81 82 83 84
De Vere Society Newsletter (DVN)	88
Shakespeare Oxford Newsletter (SON)	65 66 67 68 69 70 71 72 73 74 75 76 77 78 79 80 81 82 83 84 85 86 87 88 89 90
Spear-shaker Review and Newsletter (SPN)	87 88 89
Edward de Vere Newsletter (EDN)	89 90

Section 3 (1990–2020)

Publication	Years of coverage
De Vere Society Newsletter (DVN)	90 91 92 93 94 95 96 97 98 99 00 01 02 03 04 05 06 07 08 09 10 11 12 13 14 15 16 17 18 19 20
Shakespeare Oxford Newsletter (SON)	90 91 92 93 94 95 96 97 98 99 00 01 02 03 04 05 06 07 08 09 10 11 12 13 14 15 16 17 18 19 20
Spear-shaker Review and Newsletter (SPN)	90 91
Edward de Vere Newsletter (EDN)	90 91 92 93 94
Elizabethan Review (ER)	93 94 95 96 97 98 99
Oxfordian (TOX)	98 99 00 01 02 03 04 05 06 07 08 09 10 11 12 13 14 15 16 17 18 19 20
Shakespeare Matters (SM)	01 02 03 04 05 06 07 08 09 10 11 12 13
Brief Chronicles (BC)	09 10 11 12 13 14 15 16 17
Neues Shake-speare Journal (Germany)	97 98 99 00 01 02 03 04 05 06 07 08 09 10 11 12 13 14 15 16 17 18 19 20

IIA: CONTENTS OF CURRENT OXFORDIAN PERIODICALS

THE DE VERE SOCIETY NEWSLETTER (DVN)
Publication of The De Vere Society of Great Britain

Complete: January-August, 1988; May 1995-Current

No. 1 (January 1988)   **Editor: Charles Vere**

2	Editor	Officers of the Society
2	Vere, Charles [Ch. Beauclerk]	Introductory Remarks
3	Editor	The Michaelmas Term in Brief
4-6	Moody, Patrick	Summary of Elizabeth Appleton's Oct. 14, 1987 lecture "Edward de Vere; Man of Mystery"
7	Editor	De Vere Society Hunt Shakespeare Authorship Essay Contest
8-22	Harding, John	The Vexed Question of Shakespeare's Relationship with John Florio
23-29	Ogburn, Jr., Charlton	Costly Consequences of the Moot Court at American University
29-30	Considine, John	The Miller Shakespeare Library of the De Vere Society
30-32	Editor	Books Purchased by the De Vere Society in Michaelmas Term 1987
33	Rosen, Nick	TV or Not TV
34-35	Editor	Notices: Talks for Hilary Term 1988; *The Mysterious William Shakespeare* to be Published in the UK This Year; Shakespeare in Court; De Vere Society Charity Ball
36	Editor	Concordance to the Poems of Lord Oxford

No. 2 (April 1988)   **Editor: Charles Vere**

2	Editor	Officers of the Society
2	Vere, Charles [Ch. Beauclerk]	Introductory Remarks
5-14	Lord Dacre of Glanton	Summary of his Jan. 17 talk "Is There a Shakespeare Problem?"
14-15	Vere, Charles [Ch. Beauclerk]	Reply to Lord Dacre
16-26	Powell, Rt. Hon. J. Enoch	Summary of his Feb. 25 talk "Francis Meres and the Authorship Question"
26-27	Editor	Obituary of Professor E. B. Ford (1902-1988) [repr. from *The Times*]
28-30	Pope, Russell	Myths of Stratford and St. George
30-32	Coulter, Brian	Call for a Definitive Chronology
33	Editor	The Miller Library of the De Vere Society
34	Editor	Books Purchased by the De Vere Society in Hilary Term 1988
35	Editor	Books Presented to the De Vere Society by John Spiers
36	Editor	Notices: Talks for Trinity Term 1988; Ogburn's *The Mystery of William Shakespeare*
36-37	Wanamaker, Sam	International Shakespeare Globe Centre International Moot Court
37-38	Editor	[review of *Proud Passionate Boy*, a play by O. M. Ironside Wood]
38-39	Editor	Notices: American Oxfordians Seek English Organizer for Autumn Tour; Anti-Stratfordian Evidence; Publishing; Prizes; Television Documentary
40	Von Ost, Count Anthony	The De Vere Society Charity Ball
41-42	Considine, John	Concordance to the Poems of Lord Oxford
42-43	Editor	Dr. Brian Wilson

No. 3 (August 1988)   **Editor: Charles Vere**

3-4	Vere, Charles [Ch. Beauclerk]	Introductory Remarks
5-7	Editor	The Trinity Term in Brief
8-34	Vessey, David W. T. C.	Summary of his Nov. 13, 1987 talk "Variant Shakespeares and Shakespearean Variants"
35-52	Anderson (p.t), Verily	Summary of her May 5 talk "The De Veres of Castle Hedingham"
53-69	Vere, Charles [Ch. Beauclerk]	A Peculiar Parable [short story]
70-73	Patience, Harold W.	Oxfordian Echoes
74-89	Goff, Tom	The Seventeenth Earl of Oxford's Annuity
90-93	Editor	The Miller Shakespeare Library
94-97	Editor	Books Acquired, Trinity Term 1988

98-108	Editor	The Bowen Bequest to the De Vere Society
108-110	Von Ost, Count Anthony	The De Vere Society Charity Ball
111-112	Editor	Shakespeare Authorship Moot Court [Nov. 26, 1988]
113-115	Editor	Notices: Talks for the Academic Year 1988/89; *The Mysterious William Shakespeare*; *Proud Passionate Boy*; Publishing; Francis Bacon Society

Vol. 2/1 (May 1995)   **Editor: Christopher H. Dams**

1	Dams, Christopher H.	Editorial
2	Chaplin, Alison	Changing Minds
3-4	Challinor, Arthur M.	The Bias of the World: Lack of Objectivity in Stratfordian Commentary
5-7	Dams, Christopher H.	Shakespeare's Education or the Circular Argument [repr. in GO, p. 31]
8-11	Charlton, Derran K.	The Essentiality of Oxfordian Archival Researches
12	Dams, Christopher H.	[review of *The Shakespeare Conspiracy* by Graham Phillips and Martin Keatman]

Vol. 2/2 (August 1995)   **Editor: Christopher H. Dams**

1	Editor	The Society Library
1-4	Lasocki, David & Roger Prior	*The Bassanos: Venetian Musicians and Instrument Makers in England* [excerpt: Chapter 8]
5-7	Vere, Charles [Ch. Beauclerk]	The Shakespeare Authorship Question: Why It Matters [repr. in EVR, vol. 1 (Fall 1995)]
8-10	Hodgson, Geoffrey M.	A Countenance More in Sorrow Than in Anger
11	Choptiak, O. J.	[letter: despair at seeing so many people visiting Stratford]

Vol. 2/3 (November 1995)   **Editor: Christopher H. Dams**

1-5	Hazelton, Sally	Shakespeare Oxford Society Conference, October 1995
5-6	Llewellyn, Michael	My Lord of Oxenford's Maske
6-7	Charlton, Derran K.	Archival Research
7	Michell, John	[excerpt from an article in *The Oldie Magazine*]
8-11	Roper, David L.	Matus, in Fact? A Personal View of the Anti-Oxfordian Position Adopted in *Shakespeare, In Fact* by Irwin Leigh Matus
11-12	Editor	The Six Points

Vol. 2/4 (January 1996)   **Editor: Christopher H. Dams**

1-3	Dams, Christopher H.	[report on the General Meeting of the De Vere Society (Jan. 2, 1996)]
3-4	Hodgson, Geoffrey M.	[letter: the Editor's Nov. 1995 article "The Six Points"]
4-8	EMJ	Shake-speare/Shakspere – A Teacher's Dilemma
8-12	Hazelton, Sally	Freud and Oxford [repr. in GO, p. 307-311]
13-21	Sobran, Joseph	Shakespeare Revealed in Oxford's Poetry [repr. in GO, p. 129-139; and in LC, p. 106-112]

Vol. 2/5 (April 1996)   **Editor: Christopher H. Dams**

1	Editor	Editorial; Recent Oxfordian News
2-4	Dams, Christopher H.	[review of *The Alternative Shakespeare* by Arthur M. Challinor]
4	Challinor, Arthur M.	Brief Extracts From an Imaginary Stratford Casebook
5-15	Rollett, John M.	APIS LAPIS, or, Why Was Shakespeare Called Mellifluous?

Vol. 2/6 (September 1996)   **Editor: Christopher H. Dams**

1	Editor	Editorial
2-6	Dams, Christopher H.	[report on the De Vere Society 's Aug. 17, 1996 Business Meeting]
7	Skinner-Young, S.	New Live Theatre at Hedingham Castle, and a Performance of *A Midsummer Night's Dream*
8-12	Roper, David L.	A Monograph Concerning the Cryptography Found on the Shakespeare Monument of 1623

Vol. 2/7 (December 1996)   **Editor: Christopher H. Dams**

1	Editor	Editorial
2-7	Krass, Iris	A Study of Nicholas Hilliard's Portrait Miniature of an Unknown Man Clasping a Hand From a Cloud (1588): Could This be Lord Oxford/Shakespeare?
8-15	Cottle, Elizabeth	Shakespeare & the Scriptures: *The Merchant of Venice* [repr. in GO, p. 159-168]
16-17	Dams, Christopher H.	The Geneva Bible & *The Merchant of Venice* [from Roger Stritmatter's *The Quintessence of Dust*]
17-18	Malim, Richard C. W.	Eric Sams
19-20	Challinor, Arthur M.	Amateurs Versus Professionals

17	Editor	Note; De Vere Society Winter Meeting
18	Editor	Note about John McEnery

(May 2000) **Editor: Daphne Pearson**

1-2	Editor	Editorial from New Editor Daphne Pearson
2	Editor	The 4th Edward De Vere Conference at Concordia University
3-6	Dams, Christopher H.	Minutes of the Annual General Meeting held at Castle Hedingham House
7	Editor	De Vere Society – Statement of Accounts for 1999
8-9	Challinor, Arthur M.	The Wider Aspects of Authorship Debate
9-13	Malim, Richard C. W.	Most, Most of Me Beloved . . .
14-23	Jolly, Eddi	Shakespeare and Burghley's Library [repr. in GO, p. 26-30]
24-26	Dams, Christopher H.	The De Vere Society Dating Project – Stages 2 & 3
27	Editor	John Galsworthy – Oxfordian [reprint of passage from *The White Monkey*, part of *The Forsyte Saga*]
28	Buckridge, Patrick	[letter: 2nd Shakespearean Research Symposium, Oct. 7-8, 2000]

(July 2000) **Editor: Daphne Pearson**

1-2	Editor	Editorial
1-2	Editor	Obituary – Talmadege Garley Wilson (1919-2000)
2-16	Magri, Noemi	Italian Renaissance Art in Shakespeare: Guilio Romano and *The Winter's Tale* [repr. in SF, p. 37-66; and in German in NSJ, vol. 5: 19-43 (2000)]
17-18	Challinor, Arthur M.	The De Vere Society Dating Project: Editor's Observations
18	Editor	Useful Websites for DVS Members
19-27	Rollett, John M.	Was Southampton Regarded as the Son of the Queen? Part 2
28-29	Johnson, Philip and Eddi Jolly	[letter: Thomas Smith's letter to Lord Burghley, April 25, 1576]
30	Mankoff, Bob	[cartoon repr. from the *New Yorker*, June 19, 2000] ["I'm confused now. Was Shakespeare somebody else or was somebody else Shakespeare?"]
31	Editor	2nd Shakespearean Research Symposium, Detroit, Michigan
32-33	Editor	Notice: International Conference in Summer 2004

(October 2000) **Editor: Daphne Pearson**

1	Editor	Editorial
2-4	Dams, Christopher H.	Stratford Meeting – Panel Session
5-8	Rollett, John M.	The First Oxfordian
5-11	Johnson, Philip	Shakespeare's Education and the Stratford Grammar School [repr. in GO, p. 34-37]
12-18	Jolly, Eddi	Of Shakespeare and Pseudonyms or Halek and ⨉
19	Oxenforde	Sene and Hearde: Shakespeare in the News
19	Bird, Charles	Did You Know? (John de Vere)
20	Malim, Richard C. W.	[letter: Interpreting Greek words in Shakespeare
20	Dams, Christopher H.	[letter: John Rollet's Jan. and July "Southampton as Son of Queen" articles]
21	Malim, Richard C. W.	[letter: Brookmans Old Farm: response to Rollett]
22	Rollett, John M.	[letter: reply to Dam's response to his "Southampton as Son"]
22-23	Bird, Charles	[letter: Jolly's May 2000 "Burghley's Library" article]
24-28	Malim, Richard C. W.	Shake-speare the Actor
29-31	Bird, Charles	Thomas Creede's 'Truth' Motto'
32	Editor	Advertisement and Officers of the De Vere Society

(January 2001) **Editor: Daphne Pearson**

1	Editor	Editorial
2-11	Magri, Noemi	The Influence of Italian Art on Shakespeare's Works: Titian's Barberini Painting: The Pictorial Source of *Venus and Adonis* [repr. in GO, p. 79-90; in SF, p. 13-36; and in German in NSJ, vol. NS2: 60-78 (2011)]
12-16	Malim, Richard C. W.	Destructing *Groatsworth*
16-17	Pearson, Daphne	Records and Copyright
17	Editor	Notice: Lavenham Church Fabric Appeal
18-19	Rollett, John M.	[letter: reply to Dam's Oct. 2000 response to his "Southampton" articles]
19	McGeoch, Ian	[letter: Southampton as son of Edward de Vere and Mary Browne]
20-21	Pendle, Pauline	Letter from Canada
22-33	Jolly, Eddi	The Writing of *Hamlet*
34	Holmes, Robert	His Forthcoming Book – *Discovering Shakespeare*
35-38	Hicks, Brian	Edward de Vere – Facts, Myths and Probabilities

(January/February 2002)   **Editor: Daphne Pearson**

1	Editor	Editorial
2-8	Magri, Noemi	The Venetian Inquisition Inquiry into Orazio Cuoco (1577) [repr. in GO, p. 45-49; and in SF, p. 199-222]
9-13	Detobel, Robert	Portia and Shylock: Just Mercy Against the Law of the Talion?
13	Imlay, Elizabeth	'The Shakespeare Enigma' – A Report
14-15	Wells, Lawrence	Olga Ironside-Wood (1912-2001) [obituary]
15-17	Walker, Michael	Review of Recent Oxfordian Thinking in Germany: Literarturen
18-20	Oxenforde	Sene and Hearde: Regular Column Devoted to Shakespeare in the News
20-24	Hughes, Stephanie Hughes	Shakespeare, Oxford, Astronomy, Medicine and the Law
25-27	Malim, Richard C. W.	Criticism: Giordano Bruno
28	Pearson, Daphne	Sold at Sotheby's
29-31	Willis, Charles M.	George Puttenham, the Earl of Oxford and Shakespeare, Part I
31-32	Anderson, Verily	Verily I say . . . An Occasional Diary

(April 2002)   **Editor: Daphne Pearson**

1	Editor	Editorial
2-12	Jolly, Eddi	Images of 'Old Billy Our Bard'
13-16	Pearson, Daphne	A Tale of Marriage, Spies and Poison: An Analysis of *H.M.C. Salisbury MSS*, vol. XIV, p. 19 [Concerns Anne Cecil]
17-19	Wells, S. and M. Dobson (eds.)	*Oxford Companion to Shakespeare* [edited selection contributed by KG]
19-20	Fluchere, Henri	*Shakespeare and the Elizabethans* (1956) [excerpts translated by RM]
20	Dams, Christopher H.	[letter to *New York Times*: Niederkorn's Feb. 10 article]
20	Shore, Wayne	[letter to *New York Times*: Niederkorn's Feb. 10 article]
20	Editor	Note about William Niederkorn's Feb. 10 *NY Times* article
21-22	Ware, Susan	What's in a Name? [repr. from *Boston Globe*, March 3, 2002]
22-23	--	Did the Bard Hate Lawyers? [editorial fr.*The Independent*, Feb. 19, 2002)]
24-25	Poullain, Patricia	The French Connection
27-32	Jolly, Eddi	Matching the Man to his Works
32-33	Challinor, Arthur M.	The Society's Dating Project: Report and Observations
34-36	Willis, Charles M.	Identification of George Puttenham as the Author of *The Arte of English Poesie* and the *Justification* Document
36-48	Detobel, Robert	[letter: the Lord Chamberlain and the control of the stage]

(July 2002)   **Editor: Daphne Pearson**

1	Editor	Editorial
2-5	Rollett, John M.	Master W. H. Restored
5-6	Bone, James	Poem Not Shakespeare's After All, Scholar Admits [repr. from *The Sunday Times*, June 24, 2002)
6	Greenblatt, Stephen	[letter to *New York Times* re *Funeral Elegy*] [repr. from June 22]
8-9	Mercer, Peter V.	Completely Shakespeare
9-11	Malim, Richard C. W.	*The Spanish Maze* [repr. in GO, p. 284-88]
12-21	Llewellyn, Sally H.	Shakespeare's 'Will' Sonnets
22-25	Johnson, Philip	*Measure for Measure* and the French Connection [repr. in GO, p. 196-200]
26	Whalen, Richard F.	[letter: Jolly's April "Images of 'Old Billy Our Bard'" article]
27	Editor	Editor's Note: Jolly's Images of 'Old Billy Our Bard'
27	Imlay, Elizabeth	[letter: Pearson's April "A Tale of Marriage" article]
28	Pearson, Daphne	[letter: reply to Elizabeth Imply]
28	Malim, Richard C. W.	[letter: *Henry VIII*]
29-30	Oxenforde	Sene and Hearde: Shakespeare in the News
31-33	Dams, Christopher H.	Report of the Annual General Meeting, April 16, 2002
33-35	Editor	Announcements and Statement of Accounts for 2001
36-48	Pearson, Daphne	The Masters Letter

(October 2002)   **Editor: Daphne Pearson**

1	Editor	Editorial
2-10	Sybersma, Sue	*All's Well That Ends Well*: A Reassessment
10	Editor	Obituary: Mrs. Tess Ferguson
11	Editor	Notices
12-18	Gilvary, Kevin	Shakespeare and Italian Comedy I [repr. in GO, p. 107-125]

De Vere Society Newsletter (DVN)

Vol. 15/1 (March 2008)   **Editor: Elizabeth Imlay**

Vol. 15/2 (June 2008)   **Editor: Elizabeth Imlay**

NEUES SHAKE-SPEARE JOURNAL (NSJ)
NEUES SHAKE-SPEARE GESELLSCHAFT
Edited by Uwe Laugwitz and Robert Detobel. Published by Verlag Uwe Laugwitz.

Complete: December 1997 - current

Erste Folge, Band 1 bis 12 (1997 bis 2008)

Band 9: Verschwörungstheorien (Juni 2004)   **Editors: Uwe Laugwitz and Robert Detobel**

(Band 10) (Juli 2005)

Robert Detobel: Wie aus William Shaxsper; William Shakespeare wurde

Neue Folge Band 6 (Jahrgang 2017/2018) (Lfdnr. 24) (Editor: Uwe Laugwitz)
Ochsenfords Art/Manner of Oxenford
20 Jahre Neues Shake-speare Journal 20th year]

Sonderbände 1 bis 10

Sonderband [Special Editions] Book 1 (Oktober 2009) (Lfdnr. 13)
Peter R. Moore: *The Lame Storyteller, Poor and Despised - Studies in Shakespeare*. Edited by Gary B. Goldstein. Buchholz in der Nordheide, Germany: Verlag Uwe Laugwitz.

Sonderband [Special Editions] Book 2 (Oktober 2010) (Lfdnr. 14)
Robert Detobel, *Will – Wunsch und Wirklichkeit* [*Wish and Reality: A Critical Examination of Shapiro's "Contested Will"*] Buchholz in der Nordheide, Germany: Verlag Uwe Laugwitz.

Sonderband [Special Editions] Book 3 (Juli 2014) (Lfdnr. 20)
Noemi Magri: *Such Fruits Out of Italy: The Italian Renaissance in Shakespeare's Plays and Poems*. Edited by Gary B. Goldstein. Buchholz in der Nordheide, Germany: Verlag Uwe Laugwitz.

Sonderband [Special Editions] Book 4 (Januar 2012) (Lfdnr. 17)
Stratford's Fragestunde. Edited by Robert Detobel and Hanno Wember. Introduction by Michael York. Buchholz, Germany: Verlag Uwe Laugwitz (2012). [Translation of *Exposing an Industry in Denial: Authorship Doubters Respond to "60 Minutes with Shakespeare,"* edited by John M. Shahan and published by The Shakespeare Authorship Coalition] Buchholz in der Nordheide, Germany: Verlag Uwe Laugwitz.

Sonderband [Special Editions] Book 5 (August 2012) (Lfdnr. 18)
Robin Fox: *Shakespeare's Education: Schools, Lawsuits, Theater and the Tudor Miracle*. Edited by Gary B. Goldstein. Buchholz in der Nordheide, Germany: Laugwitz, 2012.

Sonderband [Special Editions] Book 6 (September 2016) (Lfdnr. 23)
Gary Goldstein: *Reflections on the True Shakespeare*. Buchholz in der Nordheide, Germany: Laugwitz.

Sonderband [Special Editions] Book 7 (November 2018) (Lfdnr. 25)
Sten F. Vedi and Gerold Wagner: *Hamlet's Elsinore Revisited: The Author's Sources of Knowledge about Elsinore and Denmark*. Buchholz in der Nordheide, Germany: Laugwitz.

Sonderband [Special Editions] Book 8 (February 2019) (Lfdnr. 26)
A. Bronson Feldman, *Early Shakespeare*. Edited by Warren Hope. Buchholz in der Nordheide, Germany: Laugwitz.

Soderband [Special Editions] Book 9 (June 2020) (Lfdnr. 27)
Robert Detobel: *Shakespeare and the Concealed Poet*. English version assisted by K. C. Ligon. Edited by Jan Scheffer. Buchholz in der Nordheide, Germany: Laugwitz.

Sonderband [Special Editions] Book 10 (April 2022) (Lfdnr. 29)
A. Bronson Feldman. *Shakespeare, Marlowe, and Other Elizabethans*. Edited by Warren Hope. Buchholz in der Nordheide, Germany: Laugwitz.

THE OXFORDIAN (TOX)

Published annually each autumn by The Shakespeare Oxford Society / Shakespeare Oxford Fellowship
since 1998

Volume 1 (1998) – Current

Volume 25 (2023, September)   **Editor: Gary Goldstein**

THE SHAKESPEARE OXFORD NEWSLETTER (SON)

Originally titled *The Shakespeare Oxford Society Newsletter*, the name was changed to the *Shakespeare Oxford Newsletter* in 1996. The name remained unchanged when the Shakespeare Oxford Society merged with with the Shakespeare Fellowship to form the Shakespeare Oxford Fellowship at the end of 2013.

Vol. 1/1 (1965) – Current

Vol. 1/1 (1965)

1-3	Carmody, Francis T.	A Legal Case Relevant to the Authorship Question: Trusts and Trustees [legality of Hopkins' legacy for study of the authorship question] [repr. in BTC, vol. 6: 3-7]

Vol. 1/2 (1965, June 30)

1-2	Edmonds, Dean S.	Death of SOS President and Executive Officer Francis T. Carmody

Vol. 2/1 (1966, March 30)   **Editor: Richard C. Horne, Jr.**

1-3	Horne, Jr., Richard C.	SON Business and News Coverage of the Authorship Question
2-3	Ogburn, Jr., Charlton	Comments on John McCabe's June 20, 1959 *New Yorker* article "Charlton Ogburn, Jr. and the Authorship Question" and on the history behind several other publications.

Vol. 2/2 (1966, June 30)   **Editor: Richard C. Horne, Jr.**

1-2	Editor	Oxfordian News and SON Business
3	Editor	Shakespeare Portrait X-Rayed [repr. from *The Times* (May 28, 1966)] [excerpts repr. in BTC, vol. 6: 72-74]

Vol. 2/3 (1966, Oct. 30)   **Editor: Richard C. Horne, Jr.**

1-2	Horne, Jr., Richard C. (Editor)	Southampton Manuscript in Library of St. John's College, Cambridge
3-4	Editor	Bacon Papers in Archbishop of Canterbury Library in Lambeth Palace
3-5	Horne, Jr., Richard C. (Editor)	Edmund Spenser and William Shakespeare
5	Editor	News: Recent talks on Oxford

Vol. 2/4 (1966, Dec. 15)   **Editor: Richard C. Horne, Jr.**

1-2	Horne, Jr., Richard C.	SON Business and Newsletter

Vol. 3/1 (1967, April 15)   **Editor: Richard C. Horne, Jr.**

1-2	Editor	Update on Activities to Promote Oxford

Vol. 3/2 (1967, July 27)   **Editor: Richard C. Horne, Jr.**

1-2	Editor	Recent Activities to Promote Oxford

Vol. 3/3 (1967, Dec. 11)   **Editor: Richard C. Horne, Jr.**

1-2	Editor	SON Business

Vol. 4/1 (1968, May 25)   **Editor: Richard C. Horne, Jr.**

1-4	Horne, Jr., Richard C.	Recent Oxfordian Developments

Vol. 5/1: (1969, Feb. 28)   **Editor: Richard C. Horne, Jr.**

1-6, 8-9	Horne, Jr., Richard C.	Letter to SOS members re recent Oxfordian Developments
6-8	Horne, Jr., Richard C.	Provincial Dialect in Shakesper's Day

Vol. 5/2 (1969, April 7)   **Editor: Richard C. Horne, Jr.**

1	Horne, Jr., Richard C.	Recent Oxfordian News
2-6	Barrell, Charles Wisner	Earliest Authenticated "Shakespeare" Transcript Found with Oxford's Personal Poems [repr. from SAQ (April 1945)]
7	Editor	Editorial Notes on *A. C. Common-Place Book* in Folger Library

Vol. 5/3 (1969, July 31)   **Editor: Richard C. Horne, Jr.**

1-2	Editor	Recent Oxfordian News
3-16	Bénézet, Louis	The Stratford Defendant Compromised By His Own Advocates [repr. from SAQ, 1944, 1945; also in BTC, vol. 3: 79-109; excerpt in BTC, vol. 7: 125-26]

Vol. 5/4 (1969, Dec. 10)   **Editor: Richard C. Horne, Jr.**

1	Editor	Recent Oxfordian News
2-4	Frisbee, George	Shame of the Professors [repr. from REA3, vol. 8/1: 6-7 (July 1937); also in SFE, no. 5: 8-9 (Sept. 1937); in SFA, vol. 4/6: 69-71 (Oct. 1943); and in BTC, vol. 2: 420-24)]
5	Burgess, Gelett	Modern Research Sheds New Light on Bard of Avon [repr. from *NY Herald Tribune* (June 8, 1947); also in BTC, vol. 7: xxvii-xxx]
6-9	Manwell, Margaret K.	An Unconsidered Trifle Snapped Up

Vol. 6/1 (1970, March 31)   **Editor: Richard C. Horne, Jr.**

1, 17	Horne, Jr., Richard C.	Progress Report: Recent Oxfordian News
1-5	Horne, Jr., Richard C.	Meanwhile, Back at the "Shrine" . . .
6-8	Horne, Jr., Richard C.	[review of *The Authorship of Shakespeare*, Folger Library Booklet by James G. McManaway, edited by Louis B. Wright (1962)]
8-11	Horne, Jr., Richard C.	[review of *The Folger Library General Reader's Shakespeare*, edited by Louis B. Wright and Virginia A. Lamar (1969)]
12	Horne, Jr., Richard C.	[review of "The Author" by Dr. Louis B. Wright, in *Plays and Poems*]
13-15	Horne, Jr., Richard C.	The Earl of Oxford and the Privy Council
16-17	Horne, Jr., Richard C.	The Folger Shakespeare Library

Vol. 6/2 (1970, June 30)   **Editor: Richard C. Horne, Jr.**

1-2	Horne, Jr., Richard C.	More Comments on Folger Library *General Reader's Shakespeare*, and *Shakespeare's Poems*, both edited by Louis B. Wright
4	Horne, Jr., Richard C.	The Earl of Hertford
4	Horne, Jr., Richard C.	Is a Search for Original "Shakespeare" Manuscripts Worthwhile?
4	Horne, Jr., Richard C.	J. Thomas Looney's Anniversaries
4-5	Editor	[reprint of a Privie Council Letter from April 8, 1603 with Signature of Edward de Vere As Privie Councilor] [property of the Folger Shakespeare Library]

Vol. 6/3 (1970, Dec. 30)   **Editor: Richard C. Horne, Jr.**

1-2	Horne, Jr., Richard C.	Recent Oxfordian News

Vol. 7/1 (1971, March 30)   **Editor: Richard C. Horne, Jr.**

1-3	Horne, Jr., Richard C.	Recent Oxfordian News
1	Cyr`, Gordon C.	[review of *Rational Belief: An Introduction to Logic* by Albert Frye and Albert Levi (1941) [Concludes that "de Vere is with a high degree of probability the author."]
2	Editor	Discoveries by H. K. Kennedy-Skipton
3	Editor	From Mrs. Julia Cooley Altrocchi
4-12	Horne, Jr. Richard C. (Editor)	[review of *Shakespeare's Lives* by S. Schoenbaum (1970)]

Vol. 7/2 (1971, June 1)   **Editor: Richard C. Horne, Jr.**

1-3	Horne, Jr., Richard C.	*Newsweek* article (May 10) quotes quotes A. L. Rowse on "lunacy of authorship doubters
4	Horne, Jr., Richard C.	The Earl of Northampton [Henry Howard, 1540-1614]
5	Horne, Jr., Richard C.	Professor S. Schoenbaum and Benjamin de Mott
6-7	Altrocchi, Julia Cooley	The Diamond Tablet
7	Horne, Jr., Richard C.	[review of *Wasn't Shakespeare Someone Else* by R. L. Tweedale (1971)]
7-18	Barrell, Charles Wisner	Queen Elizabeth's Master Showman Shakes a Spear in Her Defense [repr. from SAQ (Spring 1947)]

Vol. 8/1 (1972, Jan.)   **Editor: Richard C. Horne, Jr.**

1-3	Horne, Jr., Richard C.	Comments on a talk by S. Schoenbaum at the Folger Library
4	Reinhold, Robert	World Shakespeare Congress, Vancouver, Aug. 21-28, 1971 [repr. from the *New York Times* (Aug. 29, 1971)]
5	Cyr, Gordon C.	[letter to *SF Chronicle*: a new Shakespeare signature, from Sept. 2, 1971, p. 35]
6-7	Editor	[reprint of *Title page* of *Apxaionomia*] [Courtesy of the Folger Library]
8	Horne, Jr., Richard C.	[review of *The Shakespeare Authorship Question* by Craig Huston (1971)]
9-10	Cyr, Gordon C.	Shaksper's "Genius" – Some Alleged Parallels
10-11	Horne, Jr., Richard C.	Recent Oxfordian News

Vol. 11/3 (1975, Fall) | **Editor: Gordon C. Cyr**

1	Cyr, Gordon C.	Editor's Note
2-3	Horne, Jr., Richard C.	James Wilmot, An Early Doubter
3-4	Cyr, Gordon C.	Three Oxfordian Classics Are Re-issued
5	Cyr, Gordon C. (Editor)	In Memoriam: Charles Wisner Barrell (d. 1975)
5	Editor	In Memoriam: Stanley P. Lovell (d. 1976)
5	Editor	In Memoriam: Captain Evelyn Broadwood (d. 1975)
5	Editor	Recent Oxfordian News
6	Cyr, Helen W.	[review of *The Harvard Concordance to Shakespeare* by Marvin Sperack]

Special issue (1976, March) | **Editor: Gordon C. Cyr**

1	Cyr, Gordon C.	In Memoriam: Richard C. Horne, Jr. (d. 1976)
		[repr. in BTC, vol. 6: 82-83]

Vol. 12/1 (1976, Spring) | **Editor: Gordon C. Cyr**

1	Cyr, Gordon C.	Editor's Note
1-2	Editor	SON First National Conference in 1976
2-3, 6	Editor	Recent Oxfordian News
4	Cyr, Helen W.	Oxfordians as Scholars
5-6	Cyr, Gordon C.	[review of *"Shakespeare" Identified and The Poems of Edward de Vere*, 3rd ed. edited by Ruth Loyd Miller (1975)]

Vol. 12/2 (1976, Summer) | **Editor: Gordon C. Cyr**

1	Cyr, Gordon C.	Editor's Note
1-3	Editor	Conference 1976 Plans
4	Cyr, Gordon C.	[review of *Absent Thee From Felicity* by Rhoda Henry Messner (1976)]
4	Editor	In Memoriam: Anthony William Deller (d. 1976)
5-6	Cyr, Helen W.	The Work of the Society: Research or Spectator Sport?

Vol. 12/3 (1976, Fall) | **Editor: Gordon C. Cyr**

1	Cyr, Gordon C.	Editor's Note: Election of Charlton Ogburn, Jr. as SOS President
1-3	Ogburn, Jr., Charlton	President's Message [repr. in BTC, vol. 6: 90-93]
3-5	Cyr, Helen W.	Report on the SON National Conference, Sept. 24-26, 1976
5	Fowler, William Plumer	Sonnet CXL: "A Never Writer To An Ever Reader"
6-8	Marder, Louis; Rhoda Messner	Marder's Responses to Readers' Challenges and Rebuttal by Messner, Part 1 (from *SHNL*, 1963) [repr. in BTC, vol. 6: 94-106]
9	Cyr, Gordon C.	Student Newspaper Features SOS Member [S. Colum Gilfillan] and Oxford Theory (UCLA *Daily Bruin*)
9-10	Cyr, Gordon C.	To Be Or Not To Be? [repr. from *Daily Bruin* [May 10, 1976]]
10-11	Cyr, Gordon C.	[review of *Hidden Allusions in Shakespeare's Plays* by Eva Turner Clark, 3rd revised eition, edited by Ruth Loyd Miller (1974)]
12	Kloepfer, John G.	Monument vs. Moniment

Vol. 12/4 (1976, Winter) | **Editor: Gordon C. Cyr**

1	Editor	Chairman of the Membership Committee Russell des Cognets Promotes Membership
2	Editor	[review of Shakespeare Cross-Examination edited by the *American Bar Association Journal* (1961)]
2-3	Patience, Harold W.	Henslowe's Diary
3-6	Marder, Louis; Rhoda Messner	Marder's Responses to Readers' Challenges and Rebuttal by Messner, Part 2 [from *The Shakespeare Newsletter* (1963)]
6-7	Cyr, Gordon C.	[review of *A Hundreth Sundrie Flowres*, with an Introduction by Captain Bernard M. Ward, 2nd Edition edited by Ruth Loyd Miller]
7-8	Cyr, Gordon C.	[review of *Secrets of Shakespeare* by A. Bronson Feldman (1972)]

Vol. 13/1 (1977, Spring) | **Editor: Gordon C. Cyr**

1	Cyr, Gordon C.	Editor's Note
1-6	Looney, J. Thomas	Shakespeare: A Missing Author [Condensed version, repr. from SFA, vol. II, no. 2 (Feb. 1941); repr. in BTC, vol. 6: 112-18]
6-7	Editor	Shakespearean Authorship Society News
8-10	Marder, Louis; Rhoda Messner	Marder's Responses to Readers' Challenges and Rebuttal by Messner, Part 3 [repr. from *The Shakespeare Newsletter* (1963)]

Vol. 13/2 (1977, Summer)   **Editor: Gordon C. Cyr**

1-4	Cyr, Gordon C. (Editor)	A Post Mortem on the Messner-Marder Exchange [repr. in BTC, vol. 6: 107-111]
4-5	Cyr, Gordon C. (Editor)	Noted Stratfordian [Marder] Objects to Shakespeare's "Imaginary Life"
5	Editor	In Memoriam: Ralph Tweedale
5	Cyr, Gordon C. (Editor)	Overpainting on the "Ashbourne" Portrait: A Conservator's View
5-8	Editor	SON Chapters Take Hold; Activities in England; Sir Horace Vere's Will
8-9	Cyr, Gordon C.	Shakespeare Country: Real and Imagined
11	Editor	More on Ruth Loyd Miller

Vol. 13/3 (1977, Fall)   **Editor: Gordon C. Cyr**

1-2	Cyr, Helen W.	Détente With the Orthodox Stratfordians: Possibility or Impossibility?
2-5	Cyr, Gordon C. (Editor)	Shakespeare Oxford Society Second National Conference
5-7	Cyr, Gordon C. (Editor)	Sept. "Mini-Conference of SON Members at Chevy Chase Library
7-8	Editor	Sol Feinstone Makes Generous Gift to Shakespeare Oxford Society, and Resolution of Appreciation by SON Board of Trustees
8	Editor	And While We Are At It! [Appreciation of Rhoda Messner]
8-10	Patience, Harold W.	Shakespeare and Colchester

Vol. 14/1 (1978, Winter)   **Editor: Gordon C. Cyr**

1-2	Feldman, A. Bronson	Noblesse Oblige
2	Editor	Recent Oxfordian News
3-4	Patience, Harold W.	The Born Descendant [repr. as "The 13th Earl of Oxford in *Henry VI, Part 3*" in BTC, vol. 6: 84]
5-6	Cyr, Gordon C.	Harvard Case, Part II
6-7	Editor	Shakespeare's Gardener ["Stalking the Long Purple" by Jules Janick in *Horticulture Magazine* (Nov. 1977)]
7-8	Editor	IRS Letter Verifying Tax-Exempt Status for SON
9	Editor	In Memoriam: Louis E. M. Alexis
9-10	Cyr, Gordon C. (Editor)	More on the "Ashbourne" Pedigree

Vol. 14/2 (1978, Spring)   **Editor: Gordon C. Cyr**

1-3	Cyr, Gordon C. (Editor)	Famous People Comment . . . [repr. in BTC, vol. 6: 85-86, 123-24]
3-4	Kloepfer, Deborah Kelly	The Case for Edward de Vere in the Classroom
4-6	Hope, Warren	Prejudice and Shakespeare [repr. in BTC, vol. 6: 119-22]
6	Cyr, Gordon C.	Editor's Note

Vol. 14/3 (1978, Summer)   **Editor: Gordon C. Cyr**

1-3	Ogburn, Jr., Charlton	The Quest for Shakespeare's Manuscripts
3	Patience, Harold W.	New Books of Interest to Oxfordians
3-4	Cyr, Gordon C.	Prejudice and Shakespeare – Continued [Warren Hope and *College English*]
5	Editor	Oxfordiana From Mensa [E. Jimmee Stein's article]
5-6	Editor	Look Not On His Picture
6-7	Alexis, Louis E. M.	Common Sense About "Shake-Speare"
8	Editor	Philip Platt's Library
8	Editor	Milleriana

Vol. 14/4 (1978, Fall)   **Editor: Charlton Ogburn, Jr.**

1-2	Hope, Warren	Craig Huston: A Tribute (d. 1978)
2-3	Patience, Harold W.	A Book of Interest to Oxfordians: *Elizabethan Life: Wills of Essex Gentry and Merchant*s by F. G. Emmison (1978)
3	Editor	Stratfordian Theatres to Have an Oxfordian Rival
3-5	Ogburn, Charlton, Jr. (Editor)	SON Third Annual Conference

Vol. 15/1 (1979, Winter)   **Editor: Charlton Ogburn, Jr.**

1-3	Ogburn, Jr., Charlton	Shakespeare on Television
3-4	Editor	Morse Johnson and the Enquirer Again in the Van
4	Editor	De Vere the Subject of Script-Writing Contest
4	Editor	Success of *Shakespeare Cross-Examination*
4-5	Editor	From England [A talk by Harold W. Patience]
5-7	Hope, Warren	[review of *Hamlet Himself* by A. Bronson Feldman (1977)]

Vol. 15/2 (1979, Spring)   **Editor: Charlton Ogburn, Jr.**

1-7	Ogburn, Jr., Charlton	Henry Clay Folger's Memorial [long article about the Ashbourne portrait] [repr.

Vol. 17/2 (1981, Summer) — **Editor: Warren Hope**

1-2	Hope, Warren	The Fruits of Error
2	Feldman, Owen	The Opening of Twelfth Night
2-5	Patience, Harold W.	Lord Oxford's Son-in-Law
5-9	Hope, Warren	John Davies's Sonnets for the Marriage of Elizabeth Vere and William Stanley
9	Editor	Hilda Amphlett: An Obituary (1897-1981)
10	Hope, Warren (Editor)	Dorothy Stevens Ogburn (1890-1981) [repr. in BTC, vol. 6: 149-50]
11-12	Editor	SOS Bulletin Board
12	Cyr, Gordon C.	[the SOS will mail the April/May 1981 issue of *The Shakespeare Newsletter* to all members] [continas an article by the SOS, "The Case of the Alias Earl"]

Vol. 17/4; Vol. 18/1 (1981 Fall; 1982 Winter) — **Editor: Warren Hope**

1-2	Hope, Warren	Poe on Shakespeare Worship
2-13	Hope, Warren (Editor)	Fourth and Fifth SON National Conferences
13-15	Ogburn, Jr., Charlton	New Edition of Oxford's Poems [review of *The Poems of Edward de Vere and of Robert Devereux* by Steven W. May (1981)]
15-16	Editor	SOS Bulletin Board

Vol. 18/2 (1982, Spring) — **Editor: Warren Hope**

1-3	Hope, Warren	Abraham Bronson Feldman (1914-1982) [repr. in BTC, vol. 6: 151]
3-8	Feldman, A. Bronson	Shakespeare's Jester – Oxford's Servant [repr. from SFQ (Aut. 1947); repr. in BTC, vol. 6: 156-64; and in *Shakespeare, Marlowe, . . .* (2022): 8-15]
8-9	Feldman, A. Bronson	Oxford's Sole Acrostic [repr. in BTC, vol. 6: 165-66]
9-17	Feldman, A. Bronson	Shakespeare Worship [repr. from *Psychoanalysis*, vol. 2/1, 1953] [repr. in BTC, vol. 6: 167-81; and in *Sh., Marlowe, . . .* (2022): 16-33]
18	Editor	SOS Bulletin Board

Vol. 18/3 (1982, Summer) — **Editor: Warren Hope**

1-2	Hope, Warren	Morse Johnson: Oxfordian Man of Letters [repr. in BTC, vol. 6: 185]
2-4	Patience, Harold W.	The Water Bearer [repr. in BTC, vol. 6: 188-92]
4-5	Hope, Warren, (Editor)	Did Shakespeare Visit *Saffron Walden*?
6	Halle, Louis J.	*The Search for an Eternal Norm* (excerpts) [repr. in BTC, vol. 6: 193]
6-8	Cyr, Gordon C.	[review of *The Search for an Eternal Norm: As Represented by Three Classics* by Louis J. Halle (1981)] [repr. in BTC, vol. 6: 194-97]
8	Hope, Warren	The Earl of Venice? [repr. in BTC, vol. 6: 198-99]
8-9	Feldman, A. Bronson	A Decalog for Idolaters [repr. in BTC, vol. 6: 182-84]
10-12	Addison, William	"History of de Vere Family" [excerpt from *Essex Worthies*) [repr. in BTC, vol. 6: 200-08]
13	Editor	SOS Bulletin Board

Vol. 18/4 (1982, Fall) — **Editor: Warren Hope**

1-7	Fowler, William Plumer	Shake-speare's Heart Unlocked [repr. in BTC, vol. 6: 209-20]
7-10	Amphlett, Hilda	Sir John Smith
10	Editor	SOS Bulletin Board

Vol. 19/1 (1983, Winter) — **Editor: Warren Hope**

1	Hope, Warren	A Veritable Land of Bleak Bard Fields: Shakespeare, De Vere, and Ireland [repr. in BTC, vol. 6: 221-23]
2-5	Barrell, Charles Wisner	Secret of Shakespeare's Irish Sympathies: Once Again Lord Oxford's Own Personality Speaks Through the Plays [repr. from SFA, vol. 2/4: 37-40 (June 1941); repr. in BTC, vol. 6: 224-31; and in EVR, vol. 6 (Wntr. 1998)]
7	Cusick, John	Cusick Forms Oxford-Shakespeare Group Within Mensa
7	Editor	Scholarly Journals Honor A. Bronson Feldman
7-9	Feldman, A. Bronson	Shakespeare and Patriotism (from his talk in 1969) [repr. in BTC, vol. 6: 232-35]
9-11	Editor	SOS Bulletin Board
11	Holston, Kim	Grand Master Tackles Shakespeare Question
12	Hoffer, Eric	*First Things, Last Things* [excerpts]
12	Patience, Harold W.	Oxford's Holding in Warwickshire
12	Fowler, William P.	Knyvet's Knife [repr. in BTC, vol. 6: 236]

Vol. 19/2 (1983, Spring)   **Editor: Warren Hope**

1-2	Winkler, Claudia	Editorial: William Who? [repr. from *The Cincinnati Post* (April 11, 1983); repr. in BTC, vol. 6: 237-39]
2-3	Messner, Rhoda	How I Became an Oxfordian [repr. in BTC, vol. 6: 240-41]
3	Editor	Mensa Bulletin Announces Formation of Cusick's OSSIG
3-8	Amphlett, Hilda	Oxfordian Background in Pictures [previously unpublished]
8-9	Editor	SOS Bulletin Board

Vol. 19/3 (1983, Summer)   **Editor: Warren Hope**

1	Feldman, Harold	How I Became an Oxfordian [repr. in BTC, vol. 6: 242-43]
1-2	Patience, Harold W.	The Ashbourne Portrait [repr. in BTC, vol. 6: 244-45]
2-5	Robins, M. H.	His Honour Travers Christmas Humphrey: An Obituary (1901-1983)
5-10	Patience, Harold W.	Oxfordian Echoes in *Hamlet*
10-11	Cyr, Gordon C.	SOS in Southern California
11-12	Champlin, Charles	A Bard By Any Other Name . . . [repr. from *LA Times* (Feb. 12, 1983)]
13	Editor	California Hosts First "Shake-speare" Festival
13	Hope, Warren	De Vere Memorials at Wivenhoe [repr. in BTC, vol. 6: 246-47]
13-14	Editor	Stratfordiana: Impressions From Thomas Jefferson and Charlie Chaplin

Vol. 19/4 (1983, Fall)   **Editor: Warren Hope**

1-2	Johnson, Morse	The World's Most Baffling Literary Mystery [repr. in SON, vol. 31/4: 9-10 (Autumn 1995); in BTC, vol. 6: 248-53; and in BTC, vol. 7: 350-52]
2-4	Johnson, Morse	Shakespeare as a Lawyer
4-5	Proulx, Phillip	How I Became an Oxfordian [repr. in BTC, vol. 6: 254-56]
5-7	Ogburn, Jr., Charlton	Oxford and the Avon [repr. in BTC, vol. 6: 258-61]
7-8	Patience, Harold W.	The Second Printing of the Sonnets [repr. in BTC, vol. 6: 262-63]
8	Editor	Highlights of the National Conference

Vol. 20/1 (1984, Winter-Spring)   **Editor: Warren Hope**

1-2	Hope, Warren	Mail Bag: Recent Oxfordian News
2-3	Patience, Harold W.	The Mysterious Swan of Avon [repr. in BTC, vol. 6: 257]
3-5	Lafew, Edmonn	The Veriest Nonsense
6-7	Editor	Lest We Forget
7-8	La Greca, Donald	Dynasticide: a note on Macbeth
8-9	Patience, Harold W.	The Francis Beaumont Poem
9	Editor	Feldman Updates Ward
10	Johnson, Morse	[letter to *New York Magazine*: Prominent Doubters (Ag. 15, 1983, p. 7)]
10	Lafew, Edmonn	Notes on d'Hiver

Vol. 20/3 (1984, Summer)   **Editor: Warren Hope**

1-2	Hope, Warren	Celebration of Charlton Ogburn Jr.'s *The Mysterious William Shakespeare* [repr. in BTC, vol. 6: 65-68 and 264-70]
2-3	McCullough, David	Foreword to Ogburn's *The Mysterious William Shakespeare* [repr. in BTC, vol. 6: 264-70]
3-6	Ogburn, Jr., Charlton	If Thou Read This . . . [repr. in BTC, vol. 6: 264-70]
6	Editor	Stanley Hayes: An Obituary (d. 1984)

Vol. 20/4 (1984, Fall)   **Editors: Gordon C. Cyr and Helen W. Cyr**

1-2	Editors	Eighth Annual Conference Honors Charlton Ogburn
3-4	Cyr, Gordon C.	[review of *The Mysterious William Shakespeare*]
4-8	Editor	*The Mysterious William Shakespeare* in the News
5-8	Editor	'An Hundreth Sundrie Flaws' in the [*New York*] *Times'* Review
8	Editor	In Memoriam: Gwynneth M. Bowen (d. 1984)
8	Editor	In Memoriam: Philip S. Weld (d. 1984)

Vol. 21/1 (1985, Winter)   **Editors: Gordon C. Cyr and Helen W. Cyr**

1	Cyr, Helen W.	A Salute To Our Man in England (Harold W. Patience)
2-3	Patience, Harold W.	Sonnets on Television, The
2	Patience, Harold W.	A Monumental Mystery
3-5	Proulx, Phillip	When One and One and One Equals One
5-6	Proulx, Phillip	The Dark Lady Ain't No Lady
6-8	Editor	*The Mysterious William Shakespeare* In the News – An Update

7-8	Editor	"Firing Line" Debate Between Charlton Ogburn and Professor Charney [repr. in BTC, vol. 6: 271-73; see transcript printed in pamphlet form under author "Buckley, Jr., William F."]

Vol. 21/2 (1985, Spring) — **Editors: Gordon C. Cyr and Helen W. Cyr**

1-2	Editor	Update II: Recent Reviews of Charlton Ogburn Jr.'s Book Keep Authorship issue Alive in the Media
2	Patience Harold W.	Books on Elizabethan Life: *Elizabethan Life: Wills of Essex Gentry and Yeomen* by F. G. Emmison (1980)
2-5	Sears, Elisabeth (Betty)	O'er Green My Bad
5-6	Cyr, Helen W.	Debater's Corner: Oxford as Translator of Ovid's *Metamorphoses*

Vol. 21/3 (1985, Summer) — **Editors: Gordon C. Cyr and Helen W. Cyr**

1	Patience, Harold W.	A Significant Eulogy [repr. in BTC, vol. 6: 274-75]
2-8	Cyr, Gordon C.	Stratfordian Methods of Controversy [repr. in BTC, vol. 6: 276-86]

Vol. 21/4 (1985, Fall) — **Editors: Gordon C. Cyr and Helen W. Cyr**

1-2	May, Steven W.	Lord Oxford Sues for a Patent of Monopoly
2-4	Cyr, Gordon C.	Scholar of Oxford's Poetry Highlights Ninth Annual Conference
4	Editors	In Memoriam: Eleanor Brewster (d. 1985)
4-6	Lafew, Edmonn	Make Thee Another Self For Love Of Me
6-7	Cyr, Helen W.	The Work of the Shakespeare Oxford Society
7-8	Editor	Debater's Corner

Vol. 22/1 (1986, Winter) — **Editors: Gordon C. Cyr and Helen W. Cyr**

1-6	Cyr, Gordon C.	"Historical Fallacies" and Historical Method: A Key to the Authorship Controversy [repr. in RCA, p. 10-14; in LC, p. 15-19; in BTC, vol. 6: 287-95; and in *Sh. Authorship Sourcebook* (Stritmatter 2019, 2022): 227-34]
6-8	Patience, Harold W.	A Call For Action

Vol. 22/2 (1986, Spring) — **Editors: Gordon C. Cyr and Helen W. Cyr**

1-7	Editor	Despite the Society's Pathbreaking Report, the Nonsense About "Shakespeare's Handwriting" Goes On!
7-8	Ogburn, Jr., Charlton	Professor May on Oxford's Annuity: A Response by Charlton Ogburn [repr. in BTC, vol. 6: 296-97]
8-12	La Greca, Donald	The Character of Kent in *King Lear* [repr. in EVR, vol. 6 (Wntr. 1998)]
13	Editor	In Memoriam: Calvin Hoffman (d. 1986) and Rhoda Henry Messner (d. 1986)

Vol. 22/3 (1986, Summer) — **Editors: Gordon C. Cyr and Helen W. Cyr**

1, 4-5	Editor	Will "Shall I Die?" Fly
1-3	Ogburn, Jr., Charlton	Folger Library Forfeits $10,000 Rather Than Assist in Trial of Shakespeare's Identity
5	Editor	New Fowler Book on Oxford's Letters Released
5-11	Fowler, William Plumer	Shakespeare's Buried Name Exhumed
12	Editor	In Memoriam: Rose Feinstone (d. 1986)

Vol. 22/4 (1986, Fall) — **Editor: Morse Johnson**

1	Johnson, Morse	Dedication (to Helen and Gordon Cyr): Thanks For Their Editorship!
1-3	Cyr, Gordon C.	Minutes of the 10th Annual SOS Conference in Boston (Oct. 10-11, 1986) [includes notice that the Boston Book Annex is selling its archive of materials from the collection of Charles Wisner Barrell]
3	Duffin, Ross W.	*The Earle of Oxford's Marche*
4-5	Editor	Recent Oxfordian News: Lord Charles Vere
6	Editor	Front piece of the *First Folio* Engraving by Martin Droeshout [reprint of an article in *Gentlemen's Tailor*, London (1911)]
6-10	Detobel, Robert	[letter: Various authorship issues]
10	Editor	[reprint of article from the *Washington Times* (Nov. 4, 1986)]
11-12	Ogburn, Jr., Charlton	[letter to *Reader's Digest* in response to Leo Rosten's article "The Shakespeare Nobody Knows"]
12-14	Editor	An Improvised Colloquy

10-11	Gidley, Fran	[letter: *Frontline*'s program convinced her Oxford was the author]
11	Editor	Trustee Trudy Atkins Has Arranged for SON to Participate in Shakespeare Festival
11-12	Williamson, Gene	Who Was Shakespeare? [from the *Dramatists Guild Quarterly* (Spring 1990)]

Vol. 26, no. 3A (1990, Summer)

1-11	Johnson, Morse	Quotations Relevant to the Authorship Question [repr. in BTC, vol. 10: 1-21]

Vol. 26, no. 4 (1990, Fall)   **Editor: Morse Johnson**

1	Editor	Obituary of David Lloyd Kreeger [from *Washington Post* (Nov. 20, 1990)]
2-4	Greenwood, George G.	[excerpts from *The Vindicators of Shakespeare: A Reply to Critics*] [repr. in BTC, vol. 6: 416-20]
4-8	Goldstein, Gary B.	Shakespeare's Native Tongue [repr. in BTC, vol. 7: 22-29; and in REF, p. 147-58]
8-9	Oldenburg, Don	Professor Samuel Schoenbaum Recants [repr. from the *Washington Post*, (April 17, 1990)]
9-13	Moore, Peter R.	The Order of Shakespeare's Sonnets [repr. in LS, p. 24-32]
13-14	Johnson, Morse	Stratfordian Self-Delusions [repr. in BTC, vol. 7: 30-32]
14	Clement, Richard	[letter: top 25 Shakespeare Oxford clues]
14-16	Editor	Recent and Future Colloquies on the Authorship Question

Vol. 27, no. 1 (1991, Winter)   **Editor: Morse Johnson**

1	Hope, Warren	Prejudice and Shakespeare [repr. from SON, vol. 14/3]
1	Ohmann, Richard	[letter to Warren Hope]
2	Hope, Warren	[letter to Richard Ohmann: *College English*'s rejection of Oxfordian paper]
2-3	Genske, Sylvia S.	[letter to Charlton Ogburn: thanks for a wonderful and important book]
3	Dabney, Virginius	[letter to Charlton Ogburn: thanks for a masterful and convincing book]
3	Cushman, Allerton	[letter to R. Emmett Tyrell, Jr., editor of the *American Spectator*]
4	Sobran, Joseph	Against Funding Odds [from *The Washington Times* (Nov. 20, 1990)]
5-6	Johnson, Morse	[letter to the *NY Times Book Review*: Mr. Giroux's partisanship] [repr. from July 9, 1985]
5	Levitas, Mitchel	[letter: short response to Morse Johnson's July 9 letter] [not published]
6	Stritmatter, Roger	[letter: proposal for an informal association of academics to critically examine the Stratford legend]
6-7	Goff, Tom	[letter to the *Sacramento Bee*: Stylometric inaccuracies] [not published]
7-9	Louther, John	Ruth Loyd Miller Discusses the Dramatist in Service of the de Veres
9	Johnson, Morse	Telling Passages in Ogburn's *The Mysterious William Shakespeare*
9-10	Johnson, Morse	Michael Drayton, Poet and Dramatist, and Joseph Quincy Adams
10-11	Johnson, Morse	[letter to Barbara Tuchman: what is natural vs. what is true (April 11, 1986)]

Vol. 27/2 (1991, Spring)   **Editor: Morse Johnson**

1-2	Johnson, Morse	U.S. Supreme Court Justices and the Shakespeare Authorship Question [repr. in BTC, vol. 7: 22-35]
2-5	Sobran, Joseph	Fooled by a Folio: Bard Thou Never Wert [repr. from *National Review* (April 29, 1991); repr. in BTC, vol. 7: 36-42]
5-6	Horne, Jr., Richard C.	The Cardiff Giant, Shakespeare and "Modern Scholarship" [repr. in BTC, vol. 7: 43-45]
6-7	Holden, Isabel	[review of *The Lost Chronicle of Edward de Vere* by Andrew Field]
7	Cherubin, Sam	Vero Nihil Verius
7-8	Halle, Louis J.	[letter to Charlton Ogburn, Jr. (excerpts)]
8	Wyneken, Warren W.	[letter: praise for the Newsletter and Charlton Ogburn, Jr.'s book]
8-10	Benson, Jr., Jon	Interview with Professor Cavaliero Academico
10	Frazer, Winifred L.	[letter: handwriting in *The Annotator* by Alan Ken and Roger Lubbock]
10-11	Grimes, John	[letter: praise for Sobran, Ogburn, Fowler; and his efforts to publicize Oxford's authorship]

Vol. 27/3 (1991, Summer)   **Editor: Morse Johnson**

1-3	Johnson, Morse	Reviewing *Palladis Tamia* [adapted by Morse Johnson from J. C. Shepherd's *Shakespeare's Double Image* (1991) [repr. in BTC, vol. 7: 46-51]
3-4	Johnson, Morse	[letter: repr. of his 1984 resp. to Giroux's *NY Times* review of TMWS]

19	Editor	Oxfordian Trip to Italy Set for Oct. 15-29
1-7	Twain, Mark	*Is Shakespeare Dead?* (excerpt) [repr. in BTC, vol. 7: 242-52]
8	Johnson, Morse	Schoenbaum and Twain [repr. in BTC, vol. 7: 253-54]

Vol. 30/3a and 3b (Summer 1994)   **Editor: Morse Johnson**

1	SOS Board of Trustees	Tribute to Charlton Ogburn on the Occasion of the Tenth Anniversary of *The Mysterious William Shakespeare* [repr. in BTC, vol. 7]
2-6	Ogburn, Jr., Charlton	Turning of the Tide in the Shakespeare Authorship Controversy? [repr. in BTC, vol. 7: 257-63]
6	Stritmatter, Roger A.	The Bard and the Nonbelievers [from *Washington Post* (May 7, 1994)]
7	Whalen, Richard F.	BBC-TV is Making an Hour-Long Special on the Authorship Question and Oxford
7	Editor	The Shakespeare Puzzle [*Games Magazine's* "Shakespeare Puzzle" issue (Oct. 1994)]
8	Whalen, Richard F.	Cyberspace Embraces Shakespeare
9-10	Whalen, Richard F.	Oxfordians in the Theater Bring Oxfordian Readings to Sh's Plays
10	Whalen, Richard F.	From the President
11-12	Whittemore, Hank	[review of *Shakespeare: Who Was He?* by Richard F. Whalen]
1-12	Johnson, Morse	Cumulative Facts that Conclusively Prove Will Shakspere of Stratford Was not the Playwright and Poet "William Shakespeare" [repr. in BTC, vol. 7: 264-80]

Vol. 30/4 (Autumn 1994)   **Editor: Morse Johnson**

1-3	Moore, Peter R.	Stratfordians Prove the Bard Had a University Degree [repr. in LS, p. 214-218; and in BTC, vol. 7: 281-84]
4-5	Whalen, Richard F.	[review of *Kill All the Lawyers? Shakespeare's Legal Appeal* by Daniel J. Kornstein (1994)]
5	LaBelle, Jenijoy	Happy Birthday, Dear William [from the *LA Times*, April 21, 1993; repr. in BTC, vol. 7: 285-86]
6-8	Barron, Randall	A New Shakespeare Poem?
8	Ogburn, Jr., Charlton	[letter: errors by Werner Gundersheimer]
9-10	Johnson, Morse (Editor)	Lord Burford [Charles Beauclerk] Speaks at the Smithsonian; BBC Program is Broadcast
11	Johnson, Morse (Editor)	Faultfinding Expositions of the First Two Paragraphs in Thomas A. Pendleton's Review of Irvin Matus' *Shakespeare in Fact* in *The Shakespeare Newsletter*, vol. 44/2: 21
12-13	Beauclerk, Charles	William O. Hunt of Chicago Died Aug. 5th, 1994: A Recollection
13	Kennedy, Dick	Subject: Negative Evidence
14	Greenwood, George G.	*The Vindicators of Shakespeare* (excerpt) [repr. in BTC, vol. 7: 287-88]
14-15	Whalen, Richard F.	Stratford Man Among the Undead in the *New York Times*
15	Editor	Kevin Kelly, *Boston Globe* Theater Critic for 32 Years
16-17	Price, Diana	Westward Ho! The Shakespeare Oxford Society 18th Annual Conference
18	Beauclerk, Charles	What Was the Author's Motivation in Writing This Work?
19	Whalen, Richard F.	Mock Trial at U.S. Supreme Court: *Hamlet* Not Insane in Stabbing Death of Polonius

Vol. 31/1a and 1b (Winter 1995)   **Editor: Morse Johnson**

1-2	Ogburn, Jr., Charlton	*The Mysterious William Shakespeare, 2nd Edition* (excerpts) [repr. in BTC, vol. 7: 289-91]
3-4	Barron, Randall	Shipwreck in the Waters of Orthodoxy [de Vere listed as 'Alias Shakespeare' in index of *England's Helicon*, ed. by Hyder E. Rollins and published by Harvard University Press (1935)] [See Editor's Note, p. 8]
5-6	Editor	Way to Avoid the Ill-Suited is to Keep it from Being Communicated [Schoenbaum's use of selective quotations in *Shakespeare's Lives*] [repr. in BTC, vol. 7: 292-94]
6-7	Editor	Oxfordian Professors Take the issue to College Classes: Professors Londré and Pluto
7	Anon.	[reprint of *NY Times* Obituary of Preston Fleet (Feb. 4, 1995)]
8	Whalen, Richard F.	Oxfordian Productions in Shakespeare Summer Stock
9	Editor	Oxfordian Bulletin Board Posted in Cyberspace

		Burford [Charles Beauclerk]
17-18	Editor	Oxfordians to Participate in World Shakespeare Congress
18-19	Louther, John	John Louther Reports: Effectiveness of Charles Burford's [Charles Beauclerk's] Presentations
21	Editor	Prince Charles Lauds Shakespeare (Thus Oxford?) for Insights Into the Life of the Nobly Born
22	Whalen, Richard F.	[letter: Lincoln Cain's letter: Folger Library is open to all researchers]
22	Greenwood, George G.	*The Vindicators of Shakespeare* (excerpt)

Change in Format
Change in Name, from *The Shakespeare Oxford Society Newsletter* to *The Shakespeare Oxford Newsletter*
Change in Editor, from Morse Johnson to Bill Boyle

Vol. 32/1 (Winter 1996)   **Editor: William E. Boyle**

1, 8-11	Sobran, Joseph	The Problem of the *Funeral Elegy* [repr. in EVR, vol. 2 (Wntr. 1996)]
1, 11	Beauclerk, Charles	To Our Members: From New President Charles Vere
2	Editor	World Shakespeare Congress to be Held in Los Angeles
2, 24	Boettger, Carol	That Way Madness Lies: *Elegy* Conference in LA Still Leaves Questions
2	Editor	*Frontline* to Rebroadcast "The Shakespeare Mystery"
3, 14	Editor	Oxford Prevails in NYC Bar Association Debate
4-5	Boyle, William E.	19th Annual Conference in Greenboro, NC
5	Editor	20th Annual Conference in Minneapolis, Oct. 10-13
6	Beauclerk, Charles	Explanation for Revoking Invitation to Joseph Sobran to Speak at SON Conf.
6-7	Sobran, Joseph	Open Letter to Members of the Shakespeare Oxford Society
7	Beauclerk, Charles	Prince Charles' Views
12-14	Anderson, Mark K.	A Little More than Kuhn, and a Little Less than Kind: Examining the Headlines with *The Structure of Scientific Revolutions* in Mind [repr. in EVR, vol. 2 (Winter 1996); and in German in NSJ, vol. 3: 155-61 (Jan. 1999)]
15	Editor	British Actor Sir Derek Jacobi is Latest to Sign Society Petition on Authorship
16-17	Boyle, William E.	Sh. on the Internet; Discussion Group Grows and Home Page Opened in 1995
18-19	Editor	Oxfordian News: Ruth Loyd Miller Honored in Louisiana
18-19	Editor	Oxfordian News: Horatio Society Founded in San Francisco
19, 24	Louther, John	John Louther Reports: Shakespeare on Sesame Street?
20	Buckridge, Patrick	Authorship Down Under: One-Man Publicity Campaign in Australia
21	Whalen, Richard F.	[review of *Shakespeare, A Life in Drama* by Stanley Wells (1995)]
21	Whalen, Richard F.	[review of *Shakespeare, The King's Playwright*, 1603-1613 by Alvin Kernan]
21	Whalen, Richard F.	[review of *Vice Versa: Bisexuality and Eroticism of Everyday Life* by Marjorie Garber (1995)]
22	Editor	From the Editor: Changes in SON leadership and publications
23	Ogburn, Jr., Charlton	[letter: Appreciation for Florence Sheppard's review of *This Star of England*]
23	Boyle, Charles	The Crown Signature [letter]
23	Stritmatter, Roger	[letter to the *NY Times*: The *Funeral Elegy* (Jan. 19, 1996; not printed)]

Vol. 32/2 (Spring 1996)   **Editor: William E. Boyle**

1, 8-11	Moore, Peter R.	Oxford, the Order of The Garter, and Shame [repr. in RCA, p. 23-29; in LS, p. 263-274; in LC, p. 45-50; in EVR, vol. 5 (Wntr. 1997); and in German in NSJ, vol. 12: 7-22 (Oct. 2008)]
1, 3, 13	Boyle, William E. (Editor)	Authorship Fireworks at the Sixth World Shakespeare Congress
2, 23	Boettger, Carol	Events at the World Sh. Congress: Visions, Revisions and a Premature Death
2	Whalen, Richard F.	Samuel Schoenbaum (1927-1996)
4	Boyle, Charles	Lessons From a Seminar [repr. in PR, p. 1-4; in EVR, vol. 3 (Sum. 1996); and in German in NSJ, vol. 3: 151-54 (Jan. 1999)]
5	Editor	Minneapolis Conference: Full Slate of Events Set
5	Editor	John Price Sues Shakespeare Oxford Society
6-7	Beauclerk, Charles	Board of Trustees Votes in a New Era: Fundraising Now the Key
7	Editor	Action Plan and Mission Statement for the Sh. Oxford Society of the 21st Century
11	Boyle, William E. (Editor)	Some Further Thoughts on Research, Biography and the State of the Debate
12-13	Caruana, Stephanie	*Funeral Elegy*: An Update: Does the Emperor Have Any Clothes Yet? [repr. in EVR, vol. 3 (Sum. 1996)]

An Index to Oxfordian Publications, 5th Edition

An Index to Oxfordian Publications, 5th Edition

Shakespeare Oxford Newsletter (SON)

IIB: CONTENTS OF OLDER OXFORDIAN PERIODICALS

THE BARD (BAR)

The Journal of the Shakespearean Authorship Society (1975-1984)

Vol. 1, no. 1 (1975)   **Chairman of the Editorial Board: Father Francis Edwards**
1-8	Slater, Eliot	Some Psychological Aspects of the *Sonnets*
9-27	Hotine, Margaret	Greene's *Pandosta*: Political Propaganda for the Stuart Succession?
29-42	Edwards, Francis	Topical Allusions in *The Winter's Tale*

Vol. 1, no. 2 (1976)   **Chairman of the Editorial Board: Father Francis Edwards**
43-46	Slater, Eliot	A Reading of Sonnet 120
47-64	Edwards, Francis	Topical Allusions in *The Winter's Tale*, Part 2
65-72	Milward, Peter	Shakespeare and the Religious Controversies of His Time

Vol. 1, no. 3 (1976)   **Chairman of the Editorial Board: Father Francis Edwards**
73-86	MacIntyre, John P.	*The Shepheardes Calendar*: Poet's Progress
87-97	Tracy, Reverend John	Jonson and Shakespeare: a Contrast in dramatic Theory and Practice
98-107	Brand, Alice Blarden	Antony and Cleopatra and the Nature of their Sexuality

Supplement I (1976)   **Chairman of the Editorial Board: Father Francis Edwards**
1-26	Edwards, Francis	William Shakespeare; A Documentary Life: S. Schoenbaum and the Stratford Tradition

Vol. 1, no. 4 (1977)   **Chairman of the Editorial Board: Father Francis Edwards**
111-128	Edwards, Francis	History in Fiction
129-152	Feldman, A. Bronson	Thomas Watson, Dramatist [repr. in *Shakespeare, Marlowe, . . .* (2022): 286-333]
153-161	Hotine, Margaret	*Troylus and Cressida*: Historical Arguments for a 1608 Date
162-168	Vessey, David W. T. C.	Thomas Watson's *Meliboeus*

Vol. 2, no. 1 (1978)   **Chairman of the Editorial Board: Father Francis Edwards**
1-3	Crew, Louie	Homosexual Conflict in Shakespeare's *Sonnets*
4-22	Slater, Eliot	Word Links from *Troilus* to *Othello* and *Macbeth*
23-38	Bowen, Gwynneth M.	The Debatable Date of *King Lear*

Vol. 2, no. 2 (1979)   **Chairman of the Editorial Board: Father Francis Edwards**
39-70	Edwards, Francis	Claim for Roger Manners, 5th Earl of Rutland, as "William Shakespeare"
71-74	Levin, Mikhail	Fortinbras
75-79	Wainewright, Ruth M. D.	[review of *"Shakespeare" Identified* by J. Thomas Looney, 2nd Edition, edited by Ruth Loyd Miller]

Vol. 2, no. 3 (1979)   **Chairman of the Editorial Board: Father Francis Edwards**
81-94	Berriam, Thomas	What Shakespeare Wrote in *Henry VIII*: Part One
95-99	Ashelford, Jane	Shakespeare and the "Dead Indian"
100-109	Feldman, A. Bronson	A Preface to Arden of Feversham [repr. in *Shakespeare, Marlowe, . . .* (2022): 269-83]

Vol. 2, no. 4 (1980)   **Chairman of the Editorial Board: Father Francis Edwards**
111-118	Merriam, Thomas	What Shakespeare Wrote in *Henry VIII*: Part Two
119-126	Feldman, A. Bronson	A Tyrant's Vein [repr. in *Shakespeare, Marlowe, . . .* (2022): 284-95]
127-129	Cyr, Gordon C.	Oxford's and Shakespeare's "Jacks"
130-132	Vessey, David W. T.	The Singing Swallow: A Note
133-136	Hope, Warren	[review of *Hamlet Himself* by A. Bronson Feldman]

Vol. 3, no. 1 (1980)   **Chairman of the Editorial Board: Father Francis Edwards**
1-51	Feldman, A. Bronson	The Marlowe Mystery [repr. in *Shakespeare, Marlowe, . . .* (2022): 182-268]
52-54	Edwards, Francis	Further Thoughts on Dr. Bronson Feldman's Paper 'The Marlowe Mystery"
55-58	Edwards, Francis	Unpublished or Little-Known Documents

An Index to Oxfordian Publications, 5th Edition

Brief Chronicles: *An Interdisciplinary Journal of Authorship Studies* (BC)
Published annually by The Shakespeare Fellowship (2009-13),
and by The Shakespeare Oxford Fellowship (2014-16)
with stand alone volumes published in 2016 and 2023

Volume I (2009) – Volume VII (2016)

Brief Chronicles Stand Alone Volumes (treated as books)

The 1623 Shakespeare First Folio: A Minority Report **(Spring 2016). (SFF)**
Editor: Roger Stritmatter; Managing Editor: Michael Delahoyde. [a Special Issue of *Brief Chronicles*]
[see p. 745 for contents]

The First Folio—A Shakespearean Enigma **(August 2023). (TFF)**
Edited by Roger Stritmatter. [*Brief Chronicles*, vol. VIII]
[see p. 749 for contents]

The Edward de Vere Newsletter (EDV)

Published 1989-1994 by Nina Green

Issue no. 1 (1989, Mar.; rev. 2001)
Green, Nina

Did Edward de Vere Write the Comedy Known as *The Merry Devil of Edmonton*?

Issue no. 2 (1989, May; rev. 2001)
Green, Nina

What Part Did Edward de Vere Play in the Voyages of Exploration and Trade in the Great Elizabethan Age of Exploration?

Issue no. 3 (1989, May; rev. 2001)
Green, Nina

Who was the "upstart crow" in *Green's Groats-worth of Witte*?

Issue no. 4 (1989, June; rev. 2001)
Green, Nina

Did Edward de Vere Write *The Puritan; or The Widow of Watling Street*?

Issue no. 5 (1989, July; rev. 2001)
Green, Nina

Did Edward de Vere Write the *Langham Letter*? Part 1

Issue no. 6 (1989, Aug.; rev. 2001)
Green, Nina

Did Edward de Vere Write the *Langham Letter*? Part 2

Issue no. 7 (1989, Sept.; rev. 2001)
Green, Nina

Did Edward de Vere Write the *Langham Letter*? Part 3

Issue no. 8 (1989, Oct.; rev. 2001)
Green, Nina

Did Edward de Vere Know Arthur Brooke, Author of *Romeus and Juliet*?

Issue no. 9 (1989, Nov.; rev. 2001)
Green, Nina

Did Ben Jonson Write the Inscription for the Shakespeare Monument at Stratford?

Issue no. 10 (1989, Dec.; rev. 2001)
Green, Nina

Did Edward de Vere Write *The Reign of King Edward the Third*?

Issue no. 11 (1990, Jan.; rev. 2001)
Green, Nina

Did Edward de Vere Write the *Scottish History of James the Fourth, Slaine at Flodden?*

Issue no. 12 (1990, Feb.; rev. 2001)
Green, Nina

Did Edward de Vere Write *Sir John Oldcastle*?

Issue no. 13 (1990, Mar.; rev. 2001)
Green, Nina

Did Edward de Vere Write the *Langham Letter*?

Issue no. 14 (1990, Apr.; rev. 2001)
Green, Nina

Did Edward de Vere Write *Sir John Oldcastle* in an Attempt to Save His Cousin, Thomas Howard, from the Headman's Axe?, Part 1

Issue no. 15 (1990, May; rev. 2001)
Green, Nina

Did Edward de Vere Write *Sir John Oldcastle* in an Attempt to Save His Cousin, Thomas Howard, from the Headman's Axe?, Part 2

Issue no. 16 (1990; June; rev. 2001)
Green, Nina

Did Edward de Vere Write *Sir John Oldcastle* in an Attempt to Save His Cousin, Thomas Howard, from the Headman's Axe?, Part 3

Issue no. 17 (1990; July; rev. 2001)
Green, Nina

Did Edward de Vere Write *Sir John Oldcastle* in an Attempt to Save His Cousin, Thomas Howard, from the Headman's Axe?, Part 4

Issue no. 18 (1990, Aug.; rev. 2001)
Green, Nina

Does the Early Work of Edward de Vere Reveal That He Wrote Songs?

Issue no. 19 (1990, Sept.; rev. 2001)
Green, Nina

Did Edward de Vere Write the *Ballad of King Arthur* in the *Langham Letter*?

Issue no. 20 (1990, Oct.; rev. 2001)
Green, Nina

Did the Author of the *Langham Letter* Have Pronounced Music Interests and Abilities?

Issue no. 21 (1990, Nov.; rev. 2001)
   Green, Nina   Was *A Yorkshire Tragedy* Written Before Its So-Called "Source"?

Issue no. 22 (1990; Dec. rev. 2001)
   Green, Nina   Was Anne Lyly, sister of the Poet John Donne, a Promoter of the Ill-Fated Marriage of Walter Calverley and Philippa Brooke?

Issue no. 23 (1991, Jan.; rev. 2001)
   Green, Nina   Did Edward de Vere Write *A Yorkshire Tragedy*?

Issue no. 24 (1991, Feb.; rev. 2001)
   Green, Nina   Did the Author of the Pamphlet *Two Most Unnaturall and Bloodie Murthers* Make Use of *The Miseries of Enforced Marriage* and *A Yorkshire Tragedy*?

Issue no. 25 (1991, Mar.; rev. 2001)
   Green, Nina   Did Edward de Vere Have a Youthful Love Affair That Was Thwarted?

Issue no. 26 (1991, Apr.; rev. 2001)
   Green, NinaDoes the Unusual Orthography of the *Langham Letter* Indicate That the Author Was One of the Proponents of Spelling Reform in the 1570s?

Issue no. 27 (1991, May; rev. 2001)
   Green, Nina   To Whom Was Humfrey Martyn Related Through His Mother, Letitia Pakington?

Issue no. 28 (1991, June; rev. 2001)
   Green, Nina   To Whom Was Humfrey Martyn Related Through his Father, Sir Roger Martyn?

Issue no. 29 (1991, July; rev. 2001)
   Green, Nina   What Was William Patten's Involvement in the Publication of the *Langham Letter*?

Issue no. 30 (1991, Aug.; rev. 2001)
   Green, Nina   Was the Author of the *Langham Letter* a Mercer and a Merchant-Adventurer?

Issue no. 31 (1991, Sept.; rev. 2001)
   Green, Nina   Is the *Langham Letter* an Eye-Witness Account of Queen Elizabeth's Entertainment at Kenilworth in 1572, Rather Than 1575?

Issue no. 32 (1991, Oct.; rev. 2001)
   Green, Nina   Was Edward de Vere the "Annotator" of a Copy of Hall's *Chronicle*? I

Issue no. 33 (1991, Nov.; rev. 2001)
   Green, Nina   Was Edward de Vere the "Annotator" of a Copy of Hall's *Chronicle*? 2

Issue no. 34 (1991, Dec.; rev. 2001)
   Green, Nina   Was Edward de Vere the "Annotator" of a Copy of Hall's *Chronicle*? 3

Issue no. 35 (1992, Jan.; rev. 2001)
   Green, Nina   Could *The Famous Victories of Henry the Fifth* Have Been Written in 1548?

Issue no. 36 (1992, Feb.; rev. 2001)
   Green, Nina   Was the Annotator of Hall's *Chronicle* the Author of *The Famous Victories of Henry the Fifth*?

Issue no. 37 (1992, Mar.; rev. 2001)
   Green, Nina   Were the Calverley Murders Entirely Unrelated to the Play *A Yorkshire Tragedy*?

Issue no. 38 (1992, Apr.; rev. 2001)
   Green, Nina   Was Edward de Vere Related By Marriage to Thomas Russell, Overseer of the Will of William Shakespeare?

Issue no. 39 (1992, May.; rev. 2001)
   Green, Nina   Was Sir Christopher Hatton Related by Marriage To Both the Owner of New Place and the Owner of the Annotated Copy of Hall's *Chronicle*?

Issue no. 40 (1992, June; rev. 2001)
   Green, Nina   Was Edward de Vere Contracted to Marry One of the Sisters of Henry, 3rd Earl of Huntingdon, Because of Their Common Hastings Ancestor?

Issue no. 41 (1992, July; rev. 2001)
   Green, Nina   Did Edward de Vere Write the Verses for Lady Derby's Entertainment? Part 1

Issue no. 42 (1992, Aug.; rev. 2001)
   Green, Nina   Did Edward de Vere Write the Verses for Lady Derby's Entertainment? Part 2

Issue no. 43 (1992, Sept.; rev. 2001)
Green, Nina

Did Edward de Vere Write the Verses for Lady Derby's Entertainment? Part 3

Issue no. 44 (1992, Oct.; rev. 2001)
Green, Nina

Did Edward de Vere Write the Verses for Lady Derby's Entertainment? Part 4

Issue no. 45 (1992, Nov.; rev. 2001)
Green, Nina

Does the *Don Triptych* Portray the Ancestors of Edward de Vere? Part 1

Issue no. 46 (1992, Dec.; rev. 2001)
Green, Nina

Does the *Don Triptych* Portray the Ancestors of Edward de Vere? Part 2

Issue no. 47 (1993, Jan.; rev. 2001)
Green, Nina

Does the *Don Triptych* Portray the Ancestors of Edward de Vere? Part 3

Issue no. 48 (1993, Feb.; rev. 2001)
Green, Nina

Does the *Don Triptych* Portray the Ancestors of Edward de Vere? Part 4

Issue no. 49 (1993, Mar.; rev. 2001)
Green, Nina

Was Edward de Vere the "E.K." of Spenser's *Shepheardes Calendar*? 1

Issue no. 50 (1993, Apr.; rev. 2001)
Green, Nina

Was Edward de Vere the "E.K." of Spenser's *Shepheardes Calendar*? 2

Issue no. 51 (1993, May; rev. 2001)
Green, Nina

Was Edward de Vere the "E.K." of Spenser's *Shepheardes Calendar*? 3

Issue no. 52 (1993, June; rev. 2001)
Green, Nina

Was Edward de Vere the "E.K." of Spenser's *Shepheardes Calendar*? 4

Issue no. 53 (1993, July; rev. 2001)
Green, Nina

Was Edward de Vere the "E.K." of Spenser's *Shepheardes Calendar*? 5

Issue no. 54 (1993, Aug.; rev. 2001)
Green, Nina

Was Edward de Vere the "E.K." of Spenser's *Shepheardes Calendar*? 6

Issue no. 55 (1993, Sept.; rev. 2001)
Green, Nina

Was Edward de Vere the "E.K." of Spenser's *Shepheardes Calendar*? 7

Issue no. 56 (1993, Oct.; rev. 2001)
Green, Nina

Was the Annotated Copy of Hall's *Chronicle* in the Library of Robert Worsley a Lineal Descendant of Edward de Vere?

Issue no. 57 (1993, Nov.; rev. 2001)
Green, Nina

Were the Letters and Youthful Poems of Edward de Vere Written in the Lexical Vocabulary of Shakespeare? Part 1[repr. in SON, vol. 30/2A: 12-15 (1994), and in BTC, vol. 7: 232-36]

Issue no. 58 (1993, Dec.; rev. 2001)
Green, Nina

Were the Letters and Youthful Poems of Edward de Vere Written in the Lexical Vocabulary of Shakespeare? Part 2 [repr. in SON, vol. 30/2A: 12-15 (1994), and in BTC, vol. 7: 232-36]

Issue no. 59 (1994, Jan.; rev. 2001)
Green, Nina

Were the Letters and Youthful Poems of Edward de Vere Written in the Lexical Vocabulary of Shakespeare? Part 3 [repr. in SON, vol. 30/2A: 12-15 (1994), and in BTC, vol. 7: 232-36]

Issue no. 60 (1994, Feb.; rev. 2001)
Green, Nina

Does the Lexical Vocabulary of Edward de Vere's Letters and Youthful Poems Support the Hypothesis of His Authorship of The Reign of King Edward III? Part 1

Issue no. 61 (1994, Mar.; rev. 2001)
Green, Nina

Does the Lexical Vocabulary of Edward de Vere's Letters and Youthful Poems Support the Hypothesis of His Authorship of The Reign of King Edward III? Part 1

Issue no. 62 (1994, Apr.; rev. 2001)
Green, Nina

Does the Lexical Vocabulary of Edward de Vere's Letters and Youthful Poems Support the Hypothesis of His Authorship of The Reign of King Edward III? Part 1

The Elizabethan Review (ER)

A peer-reviewed semi-annual journal edited by Gary B. Goldstein, published 1993-1999.

32-48	Kathman, David	Why I'm Not an Oxfordian [repr. in BTC, vol. 8: 279-97]
50-54	Hope, Warren	[review of *Sir Philip Sidney and the Circulation of Manuscripts* by H. R. Woudhuysen (1996)]
54-56	Wright, Daniel L.	[review of Shakespeare's *Edward III* edited by Eric Sams] [repr. in BTC, vol. 8: 313-16]
57-57	Goldstein, Gary B.	[review of *Love's Labor's Lost: Critical Essays* edited by Felicia Londré]
57-59	Goldstein, Gary B.	[review of *Texts of Othello and Shakespearean Revision* by E. A. J. Honigmann]
59-61	Mucci, John	[review of *Alias Shakespeare* by Joseph Sobran (1997)]

Volume 5/2 (Autumn 1997)

| 3-4 | Baker, John | [letter: reply to responses to his "*Henry IV*" article] |

Responses to David Kathman's Spring 1997 article "Why I'm Not an Oxfordian"

4-5	Whalen, Richard F.	[letter: the Oxfordian case defended [repr. in BTC, vol. 8: 298-99]
5-9	Edwards, Francis	[letter: the Oxfordian case defended]
9-10	Kathman, David	[letter: reply to Messrs. Whalen and Edwards]
10-15	Dams, Christopher	[letter: defending the Oxfordian hypothesis] [repr. in BTC, vol. 8: 300-6]
15-16	Kathman, David	[letter: response to Christopher Dams [repr. in BTC, vol. 8]
16-21	Ogburn, Jr., Charlton	[letter: David Kathman's attack on *The Mysterious William Shakespeare*] [repr. in BTC, vol. 8: 307-12]
21-24	Kathman, David	[letter: reply to Charlton Ogburn]
23-23	Hope, Warren	[letter: response to Charlton Ogburn]

24-60	Moore, Peter R.	The Abysm of Time: The Chronology of Shakespeare's Plays [repr. in LS, p. 156-199, and in German in NSJ, vol. 4: 10-59 (July 1999)]
61-78	Challinor, Arthur M.	Controversy Among Gentlemen
79-92	Desper, Richard	An Alternate Solution to the *Funeral Elegy*
93-122	Rollett, John M.	The Dedication to Shakespeare's *Sonnets* [See his further thoughts, Autumn 1998, p. 3]
123-126	Hope, Warren	Lear's Cordelia, Oxford's Susan, and Manningham's Diary [repr. in German in NSJ, vol. 2: 66-71 (June 1998)]
126-127	Chandler, David	Lady Macbeth's Curds and Whey

Volume 6/1 (Spring 1998)

3	Holden, Isobel	[letter: Warren Hope's vol. 5/2 "Lady Susan Vere" article]
3-8	Edwards, Francis	Elizabethan Handwriting and Education
9-43	Parisious, Roger N.	Occultist Influence on the Authorship Controversy [Tudor Rose] [See also his Autumn 1998 postscript, p. 90-93]
45-66	Bacon, Delia	Book Excerpt: *The Philosophy of the Plays of Shakspere Unfolded* [edited and abridged by Elliott Baker]
67-72	Lester, Richard	Why was *Venus and Adonis* Published? [repr. in German in NSJ, vol. 3: 90-97 (Spring 1998)]

Volume 6/2 (Autumn 1998)

3	Imlay, Elizabeth	[letter: Richard Lester's Spring 1998 "*Venus and Adonis*" article]
3	Rollett, John M.	[letter: further thoughts on the dedication to Shakespeare's *Sonnets*]
4-14	Lester, Richard	Shakespeare's Name
15-30	Buckridge, Patrick	Christopher Hatton, Edward Dyer and the "First Adonis"
31-42	Heil, Leigh Ann	The Use of Renaissance Dance in Shakespearean Productions
44-54	DeFino, Dean	Iago Dilated: Delivering Time in *Othello*
55-76	Dickson, Peter W.	Henry Peacham and the 1623 *First Folio*
77-78	Hope, Warren	William Basse: Who Was He?
79-84	Mucci, John	[review of *Rogues, Vagabonds and Sturdy Beggars*, edited by Arthur F. Kinney]
84-87	Morton, Peter	[review of *De Vere is Shakespeare* by Dennis Baron (1997)]
88-89	Mucci, John	[review of CD: *The Food of Love Words and Music for Shakespeare's Theater* by the Gesualdo Consort (1996)]
90-93	Parisious, Roger N.	Postscript to the Tudor Rose Theory article [Spring 1998]

An Index to Oxfordian Publications, 5th Edition

The Ever Reader (EVR)

Created and edited by William E. Boyle
Published online 1995-2000 by the Shakespeare Oxford Society.

Ever Reader 1 (Fall 1995)

Sobran, Joseph	Bible Holds Proof of Shakespeare's Identity
	[repr. from SON, vol. 29/4: 8-9 (Fall 1993); also in BTC, vol. 7: 212-13]
Stritmatter, Roger	A Quintessence of Dust
	[from SON, vol. 29/2A: 1-2 (Spring 1993)]
Anderson, Mark K. &	*Smithsonian Magazine* Gets the Facts Wrong [in its April 1995 issue]
Roger Stritmatter	[fom SON, vol. 31/2A: 8-9 (Spring 1995)]
Whalen, Richard	[review of *Shakespeare IN FACT* by Irvin Matus]
	[from SON, vol. 30/1: 11-12 (Winter 1994)]
Publius	[review of *Shakespeare IN FACT* by Irvin Matus]
	[from ER, vol. 3/1: 67-69 (Spring 1995)]
Beauclerk, Charles	Why the Authorship of the Shakespeare Canon Matters
(Charles Vere, Lord Burford)	[from DVN, vol. 2/2: 5-7 (Aug. 1995)]
Anderson, Mark	Shakespeare's Good Book
	[from *The Valley Advocate* (March 10, 1994)]
Stevens, Justice John Paul	The Shakespeare Canon of Statutory Construction
	[from *University of Pennsylvania Law Review*, vol. 140/4: 1373+ (April 1992)] [repr. in ER, vol. 1/1: 4-20 (Spring 1993); in BTC, vol. 8: 129-44; and in SAL (Stritmatter, 2022): 103-13]

Ever Reader 2 (Winter 1996)

Boyle, Charles	Notes Towards an Elizabethan *Twelfth Night*
Sobran, Joseph	The Problem of *A Funeral Elegy*
	[from SON, vol. 32/1: 1, 8-11 (Winter 1996)]
Deming, Leonard	Invalid Logic and the Slippery Stratfordian
	[A presentation given at the SOS Conference in Nov. 1993]
Anderson, Mark	A Little More than Kuhn, and Less than Kind
	[from SON, vol. 32/1: 12-14 (Winter 1996)]
Caruana, Stephanie	Shakespeare's Use of Language
	[from SON, vol. 32/3: 10-11 (Summer 1996)]
Caruana, Stephanie	An Update on the Controversy Surrounding *A Funeral Elegy*
Desper, Richard	Allusions to Edmund Campion in *Twelfth Night*
	[from ER, vol. 3/1: 37-47 (Spring/Summer 1995)]
Whalen, Richard	De Vere, Man of Independence
	[from SON, vol. 31/4: 12-16 (Autumn 1995)]

Ever Reader 3 (Spring/Summer 1996)

Boyle, Charles	Lessons From a Seminar
	[from SON, vol. 32/2: 4 (Spring 1996); also in PR, p. 1-4; and in German in NSJ, vol. 2: 151-54 (Jan. 1999)]
Caruana, Stephanie	The Battle Over *A Funeral Elegy*: Does the Emperor Have Any Clothes Yet?
	[from SON, vol. 32/2: 12-13 (Spring 1996)]
Ogburn, Charlton	An Interview with Charlton Ogburn
	[from *Apostrophe* (Spring/Summer 1996)]
Moore, Peter	*The Tempest* and the Bermuda Shipwreck of 1609
	[from SON, vol. 32/3: 6 (Summer 1996)]
Moore, Peter	The Dates of Shakespeare's Plays
	[from SHNL, vol. 41/3: 40 (Fall 1991)]
Stritmatter, Roger	A Matter of Small Consequence [An examination of Terry Ross' essay "What George Puttenham Really Said in *The Arte of English Poesie*"]
Hannas, Andrew	"The Rest" is Not Silence [Another examination of Terry Ross' essay "What George Puttenham Really Said in *The Arte of English Poesie*"]

Ever Reader 4 (Fall 1996/Winter 1997)

Anderson, Mark K. &
Roger Stritmatter

Shakespeare's Bible Brings Truth to Light
[from SON, vol. 32/4: 8-15 (Fall 1996); also in BTC, vol. 7: 378-84;
and in NSJ, vol. 1: 99-106 (Dec. 1997)]

Stritmatter, Roger

Biblical References in Shakespeare's Comedies [rev. of Naseeb Shaheen's book] [from
ER, vol. 3/2: 60-68 (Autumn 1995)]

Moore, Peter

Recent Developments in the Case for Oxford as Shakespeare
[from a paper delivered at the SOS Annual Conference in October 1996]

Sobran, Joseph

The Phaeton Sonnet
[from SON, vol. 32/3: 12-14 (Summer 1996); and in NSJ, vol. 5: 76-85]

Ever Reader 5 (Fall 1996/Winter 1997)

Magri, Noemi

Testimony of Orazio Cogno Before the Venice Inquisition on August 27, 1577
[A new translation]

Rollett, John

Master F. W. D., R.I.P.: A Logical Answer is Not Necessarily Correct
[from SON, vol. 33/4: 8-9 (Fall 1997)]

Sobran, Joseph

Shakespeare's Disgrace
[from SON, vol. 33/2: 1, 4-6 (Spring 1997)]

Ogburn, Charlton

Shakespeare and the Fair Youth [response to Sobran's "Shakespeare's
Disgrace"] [from SON, vol. 33/3: 4, 12 (Summer 1997); also in BTC, vol.
7: 395-98]

Moore, Peter R.

The Earl of Oxford and the Order of the Garter
[from SON, vol. vol. 32/2: 1, 8-11 (Spring 1996); also in RCA, p. 23-29;
in LS, p. 263-74; in LC, p. 45-50; and in German in NSJ, Nov. 12: 7-22
(2008)]

Ever Reader 6 (Fall 1997/Winter 1998)

Anderson, Mark

Beauty and the Paradigm
[from SON, vol. 33/3: 1, 10-12 (Sum. 1997) & vol. 33/4: 19-21 (Wntr.
1998)]

Whittemore, Hank

Oxford's Metamorphoses
[from SON, vol. 32/4: 1, 11-15 (Fall 1996); also in BTC, vol. 7: 363-75;
and in TYLS, p. 86-99]

Barrell, Charles Wisner

The Secret of Shakespeare's Irish Sympathies
[from SFA, vol. 2/4: 37-40 (June 1941); also in SON, vol. 19/1: 2-6
(Winter 1983); in BTC, vol. 2: 156-64; and BTC, vol. 6: 224-31]

La Greca, Donald

The Character of Kent in *King Lear*
[from SON, vol. 22/2: 8-12 (Spring 1986)]

Hughes, Stephanie Hopkins

Of Standins, Pseudonyms, Mummings and Disguisings
[from SON, vol. 33/1: 4-5, 23 (Winter 1997); also in BTC, vol. 7: 385-91]

Clark, Eva Turner

Elizabethan Stage Scenery
[from SFA, vol. 2/6: 72-75 (Oct. 1941)]

Ever Reader 7 (Spring/Summer/Fall 1998)

Boyle, Bill

Shakespeare's Son on Death Row?
[from SON, vol. 34/2: 1, 4-7 (Summer 1998); also in BTC, vol. 7:
433-44; and in BC, Special issue, p. 95-102 (2016)]

Stritmatter, Roger

"Publish We This Peace . . ."
[from SON, vol. 34/3: 16-17 (Fall 1998); also in BTC, vol. 8: 26-31;
and in BC, Special issue, p. 111-15 (2016)

Stritmatter, Roger

"Bestow how, and when you list . . ."
[from SON, vol. 34/3: 18-19 (Fall 1998); also in BC, Special issue,
p. 89-93 (2016)]

Dickson, Peter W.

Henry Peacham on Oxford and Shakespeare
[from SON, vol. 34/3: 1, 8-13 (Fall 1998)]

Dickson, Peter W.

Oxford's Literary Reputation in the 17ᵗʰ and 18ᵗʰ Centuries
[from SON, vol. 34/3: 14-15 (Fall 1998)]

Whalen, Richard

The Queen's Worm
[from SON, vol. 34/2: 12-13 (Summer 1998)]

Ever Reader 8 (Winter/Spring 1999)

Dickson, Peter — Are British Scholars Erasing Two Heroic Earls from Jacobean History to Protect the Shakespeare Industry?
[from SON, vol. 35/1: 8-9, 24 (Spring 1999)]

Wright, Daniel L. — Oxford as "The Knight of the Tree of the Sunne"
[from SON, vol. 34/2: 1, 14-15+ (Sum. 1998); also in BTC, vol. 8: 5-12]

Anderson, Mark K. — The Art of *The Art of Shakespeare's Sonnets*
[review of Helen Vendler's book]
[from SON, vol. 34/1: 16-17 (Spr. 1998)]

Whalen, Richard — *Shake-speare's Sonnets* – Review of recent editions by Helen Vendler, Katherine Duncan-Jones, and G. Blakemore Evans]
[from SON, vol. 34/1: 18-19 (Spring 1998)]

Jiménez, Ramon L. — *Shake-speare's Sonnets* and the Court of Navarre [review of David Honneyman's book with the same title (1996)]
[from SON, vol. 35/1: 18 (Spring 1999)]

Sobran, Joseph — *Shake-speare's Sonnets* are Stratfordians' Achilles' Heel
[from SON, vol. 34/1: 15, 22 (Spring 1998)]

Quealy, Gerit — Hollywood's the Thing . . .
[from SON, vol. 34/4: 4-5 (Winter 1999)]

Eldredge, Joe — *Shakespeare In Love*: A Good Movie, and an Authorship Valentine

Ever Reader 9 (Summer/Fall 1999)

Stritmatter, Roger — Teaching the Next Generation Oxford was Shakespeare
[from SON, vol. 34/4: 1, 10-11 (Winter 1999); and in BTC, vol. 8: 32-36]

Boyle, Bill and Robert Barrett — An Interview with Robert Barrett
[from SON, vol. 34/4: 11-13 (Winter 1999); and in BTC, vol. 8: 43-45]

Werth, Andrew — Reading by the Lamp of Biography
[from TOX II: 145-51 (1999)]

Goff, Tom — Rumors of Disaster, Premonitions of War
[from SON, vol. 25/3: 2-6 (Summer 1989)]

Howerton, Philip F., Jr. — Vladimir Nabokov and William Shakespeare
[from SON, vol. 26/1: 1-3 (Winter 1990)]

Moore, Peter — The Stella Cover-up
[from SON, vol. 29/1a: 12-17 (Winter 1993); also in DVN, vol. 17/1: 14-18 (Feb. 2010); LS, p. 312-21; and in NSJ, vol. 9: 8-19 (2004)]

Ever Reader 10 (Winter/Spring 2000)

Alexander, Mark A. — Shakespeare's Bad Law
[from SON, vol. 35/4: 1, 9-13 (Winter 2000)]

Sobran, Joseph — The End of Stratfordianism
[from SON, vol. 36/1: 12-13, 25+ (Spring 2000)]

Chiljan, Katherine — Palamon and Arcite
[from SON, vol. 35/1: 10-13 (Spring 1999); also in BTC, vol. 8: 75-85]

Anderson, Mark K. — Thomas of Woodstock
[from *Valley Advocate* (July 17, 1999); also in SON, vol. 35/2: 4-6 (Summer 1999); and in BTC, vol. 8: 114-18]

Fitzgerald, James — "What Author Would Conceal His Name?"
[from SON, vol. 35/2: 8-9 (Summer 1999)]

Shakespeare Fellowship Circulars and *Notices* (SFC)

Issued on an irregular basis by The Shakespeare Fellowship (1922-1935)

These pieces have been reprinted in *Shakespeare Investigated: Publications of the Shakespeare Fellowship 1922-1936*, edited by James A. Warren and published by Veritas Publications.

1922, November 22	SF Circular: Report on the foundation meeting
1923, January 1	SF Circular: The origins and objects of the Fellowship
1923, May 15	SF Circular: Oxford and Bacon
1923, November 12	SF Circular: Fellowship officers and members in 1923
1923, December 14	SF Circular: Report of our first year's work [1923]
1924, February 13	SF Circular: Fellowship members and library books in 1924
1925, August 14	SF Circular: Capt. Ward's article on *The Arte of English Poesie*
1925, November 14	SF Circular: Announcements
1925, November 20	SF Circular: Annual Report for 1925
1926, February 1	SF Circular: Capt. Ward's article on George Gascoigne
1926, September 7	SF Circular: Annual meeting to be held September 18
1926, November 1	SF Circular: Fourth Annual Report, 1926
1927, July 1	SF Circular: *Times Literary Supplement* review of Connes' *Le Mystere Shakespearean*
1927, September 7	SF Circular: SF Annual Meeting on October 7
1927, December 21	SF Circular: Fifth Annual Report, 1927
1928, January 5	SF Circular: Capt. Ward's *The Seventeenth Earl of Oxford*
1928, February 3	SF Circular: Recent discoveries
1928, March 27	SF Circular: Translation of Connes's *The Shakespeare Mystery*
1928, April 17	SF Circular: Shakespeare and Ben Jonson
1928, May 16	SF Circular: Professor Abel Lefranc
1928, June 1	SF Circular: Katharine Eggar's *The Earl of Oxford's Marche*
1928, July 5	SF Circular: De Vere Country
1928, July 14	SF Circular: *The Famous Victories of Henry V*
1928, September 12	SF Circular: Sir Denys Bray on the *Sonnets*
1928, September 17	SF Circular: *The Shakespeare Review*; annual general meeting
1928, October 29	SF Circular: Sixth Annual Report, 1928
1928, November 6	SF Circular: Sir George Greenwood
1929, January 1	SF Circular: *The Shakespeare Pictorial*
1929, February 1	SF Circular: *The Revue Anglo-Américaine*
1929, June 14	SF Circular: Percy Allen and the *Sonnets*
1929, June 23	SF Circular: Percy Allen's "Confession of Faith"
1929, November 15	SF Circular: Oxford-Bacon Debate on November 29
1929, December 12	SF Circular: SF VP Sir John Cockburn
1930, January 17	SF Circular: Percy Allen's pamphlet, *The Case for Edward de Vere*
1930, February 26	SF Circular: First Annual Dinner to be held April 12
1930, May? [undated]	SF Circular: Gerald Rendall's Toast at the first Annual Dinner
1930, October 5	SF Circular: Annual Meeting held on September 30
1930, October 5 (2)	SF Circular: *Shakespeare Pictorial*
1930, November 21	SF Circular: Allen's "The de Vere-Shakespeare Controversy Today"
1931, January 7	SF Circular: *The Falstaff Saga*
1931, March 24	SF Circular: Annual Dinner, April 27
1931, September 12	SF Circular: Annual subscriptions
1931, September 12 (2)	SF Circular: Annual Meeting to be held September 30

1931, November 7	SF Circular: Recent Articles
1931, November 11	SF Circular: Meeting re Dr. Hotson's findings to be held November 26
1931, November 22	SF Circular: Dr Hotson and the timing of the plays
1931, December 11	SF Circular: Recent Reviews
1931, Late December	SF Circular: More on Golding
1932, January 21	SF Circular: Percy Allen to speak on February 9 on the three Williams
1932, April 6 [event date]	SF Circular: Marjorie Bowen to speak on connections between the plays and French History
1932, April 22 [date postmarked]	SF Circular: Annual Dinner to be held May 11
1932, June 30 [date postmarked]	SF Circular: Cecil Palmer liquidation
1932, August 1	SF Notice: Annual Meeting to be Held September 8
1932, September 26 [date received]	SF Circular: Percy Allen to Speak October 11 on the inner story of *Two Gentlemen*
1932, November 8 [event date]	SF Circular: Gerald Phillips to Speak on Willy and the gentle spirit
1932, December 13 [event date]	SF Circular: Gerald H. Rendall to Speak on Shakespeare's poems and sonnets
1933, March 28 [event date]	SF Notice: Percy Allen to Speak on "Who were Labeo, Lolio & Lolio's son?"
1933, May 16 [event date]	SF Notice: Annual Dinner to be held May 16
1933, July 7 [event date]	SF Notice: Fellowship meeting following death of Col. Ward
1933, July? [undated]	SF Circular: List of Fellowship members for 1933
1933, July? [undated]	SF Circular: Fellowship Cash Flow Statement for 1932
1933, September 27 [event date]	SF Notice: Annual general meeting will be followed by debate on "Whether there is sufficient evidence to show that Queen Elizabeth had a son by the Earl of Oxford."
1933, September 29 [date received]	SF Notice: Meeting on Oct. 9 to discuss Hampstead district branch
1933, October 17 [event date]	SF Notice: Georges Connes to speak on the Oxfordian movement in France
1933, November	SF Circular: The Shakespeare Fellowship (Douglas)
1933, December 4	SF Notice: Capt. Ward to Speak on political propaganda on December 12
1933, end of year or early in 1934	SF Notice: Dr. Ranjee Shahani to speak on Shakespeare through Eastern eyes [date is not visible]
1934, January 11 [event date]	SF Notice: Meeting to be held January 11
1934, February 21 [event date]	SF Notice: Katharine Eggar to speak on the early work of de Vere
1934, March 9 [event date]	SF Notice: Desmond Shaw to speak on *The Tempest*
1934, April	SF Circular: The Shakespeare Fellowship Library
1934, April 26 [event date]	SF Notice: Capt. Ward to speak on two William Shakespeares
1934, April 21	SF Notice: SF Annual Dinner to be held May 16
1934, May 22 [event date]	SF Notice: Golding dedication event to be held at Belchamps on May 22
1934, July [undated]	SF Circular: Fellowship members for 1934
1934, July 12 [event date]	SF Notice: Discussion by Allen and others on Ben Jonson, Shaksper and "Shakespeare"
1934, September 28 [event date]	SF Notice: Percy & Ernest Allen to speak on Shakespeare's influences
1934, October? [undated]	SF Circular: Annual General Meeting held on September 28
1934, October 29 [event date]	SF Notice: J. S. L. Millar to speak on Bacon's share in the poems and plays
1934, November 1	SF Circular from President Douglas: Gilbert Slater's *Seven Shakespeares*
1934, November 6 [date received]	SF Notice: Col. Douglas to speak on the case for the jury on November 21
1934, December 4	SF Notice: Percy Allen to speak on *Twelfth Night* on December 13
1935, January 25 [event date]	SF Notice: G. F. Holland to speak on the personality of Shakespeare
1935, February 19 [event date]	SF Notice: Katharine Eggar to speak on the Arcadia Circle
1935, March 19	SF Notice: Ernest Allen to speak on the Stratfordian tradition on March 29
1935, April 25	SF Notice: Rev Paxton to speak on Shakespeare from a preacher's viewpoint
1935, April 25 [date received]	SF Notice: *"Shakespeare" Identified.* now available at St. Giles Bookshop
1935, April 28 [date received]	SF Notice: Annual Dinner to be held on May 13
1935, July 12 [event date]	SF Notice: July 12 Dinner to be held to welcome J. Cushman
1935, October 2 [event date]	SF Notice: Annual General Meeting to be held October 2
1935, October 23 [event date]	SF Circular: Rev. Vincent Henson to speak on "What's Hecuba to him?"
1935, October	SF Notice from President Douglas: Meeting on incorporation of the Fellowship

1935, December 6 [event date]   SF Notice: William Kent to speak on the London of the Shakespeare plays
1935? [undated]   SF Notice: The Library

The Shakespeare Fellowship News-letter (English) (SFE)

Published 1937-1958 by the Shakespeare Fellowship (English Branch)
founded by Col. B. R. Ward.

No. 1, January 1937 **Editor: Captain Bernard M. Ward**
1-2	Douglas, Col. Montagu. W.	Editorial: Farewell to *The Shakespeare Pictorial*
2-7	Allen, Percy	Shakespearean Adventures in Canada and the United States
8-9	Editor	Occasional Notes

No. 2, March 1937 **Editor: Captain Bernard M. Ward**
1-2	Lefranc, Abel	[letter to Col. Douglas (in French)]
3-8	Holland, Rear-Admiral H. H.	M. O. A. I. Doth Sway My Life
8-9	Cairncross, A. S.	[letter to TLS (Jan. 9, 1937): response to Percy Allen's Jan. 2 letter]
9-10	Allen, Percy	[letter to TLS (Jan. 2, 1937): re *Hamlet's* dates]
10-11	Editor	Occasional notes
11	Greenwood, Elsie	[letter: thanks to those who supported the new (condensed) edition of her father's *The Shakespeare Problem Restated*]

No. 3, May 1937 **Editor: Captain Bernard M. Ward**
1-4	Ward, Bernard M.	Two New Oxford Discoveries: is Lord Oxford Buried in Westminster Abbey?; Anne Cecil and the Crisis of 1576
4-5	Editor	Our President at Lavenham
5-7	Allen, Percy	Shakespeare and Montaigne
7-9	Douglas, Col. Montagu W.	[review of *Les Elements Francais de 'Peines D'Amour Perdues* by Abel Lefranc (1936) (*French Elements in 'Love's Labour's Lost'*)]
9	Douglas, Col. Montagu W.	[review of *The Shakespeare Problem Restated* by George G. Greenwood, condensed by Elsie Greenwood]
10-11	Editor	Occasional Notes
11	Holland, Rear-Admiral H. H.	[letter: response to Cairncross' Jan. 9 TLS letter (which was repr. in the Fellowship's March 1937 *News-Letter*]

No. 4, July 1937 **Editor: Captain Bernard M. Ward**
1-6	Editor	News from America [Charles Wisner Barrell's article "Elizabethan Mystery Man" in the *Sat. Review*); Carolyn Wells's response)]
6-7	Allen, D. F.	The Annual Dinner
7-10	Goodman, M. Kirsten	Oxford – Davenport – Shakespeare
10	Editor	Occasional Notes

No. 5, September 1937 **Editor: Captain Bernard M. Ward**
1-5	Ward, Bernard M.	The Earl of Oxford and the Succession Question
5-8	Editor	[review of *When Shakespeare Died*, a pamphlet by Ernest Allen]
8	Editor	Occasional Notes
8-9	Frisbee, George	Shame of the Professors (excerpts) [repr. from *Reading and Collection*, vol. 1/8: 6-7 (July 1937)] [Also in SFA, vol. 4/6: 69-71 (Oct. 1943); in SON, vol. 5/4: 2-4 (Dec. 1969); and in BTC, vol. 2: 420-24]

No. 6, November 1937 **Editor: Captain Bernard M. Ward**
1-2	Editor	General Annual Meeting of the Shakespeare Fellowship
2-5	Editor	News from Canada [J. V. McAree's article "Another claimant for Poet's Crown" in the *Toronto Globe and Mail*]
5-6	Editor	News from East Anglia
6-8	Editor	Is Lord Oxford Buried in Westminster Abbey?
8-9	Editor	Death of Mr. J. Martin Haydon (d. 1937) [obituary]

No. 7, January 1938 **Editor: Captain Bernard M. Ward**
1-3	Ward, Bernard M.	[review of *The Man Who Was Shakespeare* by Eva Turner Clark (1937)]
3-5	Allen, Percy	[review of *I, William Shakespeare* by Leslie Hotson]
5-6	Slater, Gilbert	[letter: Authorship of "Shakespeare's" plays by Bacon, Ralegh, Lady] Pembroke, etc. [See correction in no. 8, p. 12]
6-9	Ward, Capt. Bernard M.	[response to Gilbert Slater's letter]
9-10	Morgan, E.	[letter: Shakespeare's remarkable knowledge of Italy]

| 10-11 | Ranson, F. Lingard |]letter: E. V. Lucas mentions de Vere's authorship in *All of a Piece*] |
| 11 | Editor | Occasional Notes |

No. 8, March 1938   **Editor: Captain Bernard M. Ward**
1-3	Slater, Gilbert	The Rival Poet of the *Sonnets*
3-5	Allen, Percy	[response to Gilbert Slater's "The Rival Poet of the *Sonnets*"]
6-8	Douglas, Col. Montagu W.	[review of *Shakspere, Shakespeare and de Vere* by Louis P. Bénézet]
8-12	Douglas, Col. Montagu W.	[review of *Shakespeare's Vital Secret Known to His Queen* by R. M. Lucas]
12	Slater, Gilbert	[letter: correction to his letter in vol. 7]
12-13	Ward, Bernard M.	[letter: Oxford's co-authors]
13	Allen, Ernest	[letter: Sir Christopher Hatton as Malvolio?]
13-14	Editor	Occasional Notes

No. 9, May 1938   **Editor: Captain Bernard M. Ward**
1-2	Ward, Bernard M.	Gilbert Slater: An Appreciation (1865-1938)
2-4	Douglas, Col. Montagu W.	News from France [Professor Lefranc's activities]
4-5	Holland, Rear-Admiral H. H.	Have the Ballads of Tarleton Perished?
6-7	Allen, Percy	Shakespeare's *Coriolanus*
7-9	Allen, Percy	[review of *Shakespeare Rediscovered* by Clara L. de Chambrun (1938)]

No. 10, July 1938   **Editor: Captain Bernard M. Ward**
1-2	Allen, D. F.	The Annual Dinner
2-4	Editor	News from Holland
4-5	Editor	News from America
5-8	Douglas, Col. Montagu W.	[review of *A La Recontre de 'William Shakespeare'* by M. Mathias Morhardt]
8-9	Allen, Percy	Recent Books on the Sonnets
10	Editor	Occasional Notes
10-11	Editor	The Supplement to This News-Letter

Supplement, July 1938   **Editor: Captain Bernard M. Ward**
| 1-8 | Atkinson, J. Shera | Criticism of Dr. Leslie Hotson's *Shakespeare Versus Shallow* (1931) |

No. 11, September 1938   **Editor: Captain Bernard M. Ward**
1-5	Allen, Percy	The First Anti-Stratfordian [review of *The Life and Adventures of Common Sense* by Herbert Lawrence (1769)]
6-8	Woodward, H. M. M.	The Stratford Monument
8-9	Allen, Percy	[review of *Elizabeth and Sixtus* by H. Kendra Baker (1938)]
10	Editor	Occasional Notes

No. 12, November 1938   **Editor: Captain Bernard M. Ward**
1	Editor	Annual General Meeting
2-16	Allen, Percy	Commentary on *Life and Adventures of Common Sense* by Herbert Lawrence
17-18	Allen, Percy	How Lawrence Acquired His Information
18	Editor	Occasional Notes

No. 13 – Missing – January 1939

No. 14, April 1939   **Editor: Captain Bernard M. Ward**
1-7	Dwyer, J. J.	Had Shakespeare Read Dante?
7-8	Editor	Mr. William Kent's New Book *London Worthies*
8-9	Editor	News from America
9-11	Editor	Occasional Notes

No. 14, Supplement and Supplement 2 (April 1939) [responses to Percy Allen's and Captain B. M. Ward's pamphlet *An Enquiry Into the Relations Between Lord Oxford as 'Shakespeare,' Queen Elizabeth, and the Fair Youth of Shakespeare's Sonnets*]   **Editor: Captain Bernard M. Ward**
1-5	Rendall, Canon Gerald	Notes and Comments on "An Enquiry"
5-9	Aitken, T. M.	A Criticism of "An Enquiry"
9-20	Allen, Percy	Mr. Percy Allen's Reply
20-24	Ward, Bernard M.	Reply to the "Refutations" of Canon Rendall and Mr. Aitken
Sup 2: 1-4	Aitken, T. M.	Queen Elizabeth – Oxford – Son Theory: A Reply

No. 15, July 1939   **Editor: Captain Bernard M. Ward**
1	Editor	Annual Dinner
2-3	Editor	News from America
3-4	Editor	Death of Mr. Hamlet Philpot (1856-1939)
4-7	Kent, William	An Open Letter to Dr. G. B. Harrison [review of Harrison's *Introducing*

		Shakespeare]
7-8	Harrison, G. B.	[letter: response to William Kent's letter]
7-8	Editor	Occasional Notes
8-11	Bunnett, R. J. A.	[letter: Authorship issues in the decades after E. de Vere died in 1604]
1940, April		**Editor: Percy Allen**
1	Editor	Minutes of the General Meeting; The Fellowship's New Secretary
1	Editor	Ernest Stirling Allen (d. 1939)
1-2	Editor	Mrs. Sverre Eriksen (d. 1939)
3	Editor	Oxford as "Shakespeare" and the Ashbourne Portrait
4	Holland, Rear-Admiral H. H.	That's the Dog's Name (*Romeo and Juliet*)
5-6	Allen, Ernest	Who Was Cheveril?
6	Allen, Percy	[letter to the *Times Literary Supplement* (not published)]
7-8	Editor	Mr. John Barrymore; Herbert Lawrence's *Life and Adventures of Common Sense*; Shakespeare's Signatures; The Falstaff Cup; Occasional Notes
1941, April		**Editor: Percy Allen**
1-2	Editor	Editorial Notes
3	Editor	Editorial Notes
3	Dwyer, J. J.	Patines of Bright Gold
3	Barrell, Charles Wisner	Another Name for the Dog
3	Holland, Rear-Admiral H. H.	Who Was Cheveril?
4	Stechow, W.	The Ashbourne Portrait
4	Editor	Comments by the Editor
1941, October		**Editor: Percy Allen**
1-2	Editor	Editorial Notes
2-3	Douglas, Col. W. Montagu	The Ashbourne Portrait
3	Allen, Percy	Did Queen Elizabeth Bear a Child?
3-4	Allen, Percy	Actors and the Oxford-Shakespeare Case
4	Editor	Recent References to the Oxford Theory
4	Editor	Romeo and Juliet
1942, April		**Editor: Percy Allen**
1-2	Editor	Important Notice and Editorial Notes
2	Allen, Percy (editor)	How Lord Oxford Paid His Way [includes exceprts from Looney's Dec. 29, 1941 letter to Allen]
2	Holland, Rear-Admiral H. H.	Shake-speare 1573-1593: Latest Research Into Internal Evidence by Topical Allusions
3	Allen, Percy, (editor)	Mr. Charles Barrell and Our American Branch [reprints excerpts from Barrell's Dec. 21, 1941 letter to Allen]
3	Allen, Percy (editor)	Nostradamus
3	Dwyer, J. J.	The Vere Motto
3-4	Allen, Percy	Melford Hall and Shakespeare
4	Allen, Percy (editor)	Mr. Charles Boissevain and Mons. H. R. Lenormand; Mr. Osbert Sitwell on Shakespeare
1942, October		**Editor: Percy Allen**
1-2	Editor	Editorial Notes
2	Allen, Percy	The Vere Motto; Sir Edward Vere and Mr. Barrell's Discovery
2-3	Pearson, Hesketh	[excerpt from *The Life of William Shakespeare* (Penguin Series)]
3	Dwyer, J. J.	Comment on 'Elizabethan Commentary' by Hilaire Belloc
3-4	Allen, Percy (editor)	Peele's Sonnet on Oxford (1590)
4	Allen, Percy	Shake-speare Speaks Again? [letter to the BBC World Service]
1943, May		**Editor: Percy Allen**
1	Editor	Editorial notes [reprints Evelyn Bodell's Oct. 14, 1943 letter to Allen]
2-3	Douglas, Col. Montagu	Comments on Barrell's Shakespeare's Own Secret Drama
3-4	Editor	Oxfordian News: Shakespeare's Sonnet 134; Brooke House, Hackney, Damaged; "Long Melford"
4	Allen, Percy (editor)	Peele's Verses in *Polyhymmus* (II)
4	Labeo	Bacon and "The Group"
1943, October		**Editor: Percy Allen**
1	Editor	Editorial Notes

4-5	Dwyer, J. J.	[review of *A La Decouverte de Shakespeare* by Abel Lefranc (1945)]
5	Dwyer, J. J.	Shakespeare and Politics
6-7	Holland, Rear-Admiral H. H.	Shakespeare and Contemporary Plays, Part 2
7	Cutner, Herbert	The Stratford Monument Again
7-8	Atkinson, J. Shera	[letter: Herbert Cutner's "Stratford Monument" article]
8	Kent, William	Shakespeare's London: A topographical argument

1947, March   Editor: J. J. Dwyer

1	Editor	The Annual General Meeting
1-5	Editor	Editorial Notes: Annual General Meeting; Abstracts and Brief Chron-icles; Correction; Lecture by Miss Marjorie Bowen; Shakespeare in East Anglia; Shakespeare's London; Brains Trust
5	Dwyer, J. J.	Queen Elizabeth and Her Turk [repr. in BTC, vol. 4: 106]
6	Dwyer, J. J. (Editor)	The Portraits of Shakespeare [repr. in BTC, vol. 4: 107-08]
6-8	Holland, Rear-Admiral H. H.	*Much Ado About Nothing* and *The Shepherd's Calendar*
8	Kent, William	Orthodox Ineptitude

1947, September   Editor: William Kent

1-4	Editor	Editorial Notes: Birthplace Celebrations; The Stratfordian Retreat; The Shakespeare Fellowship's Pamphlet
4-5	Cutner, Herbert	Alias William Shakespeare
5-6	J. S. A.	Oxfordians Debate With Miss Neill
6-7	J. S. A.	Heretics' Week, Stratford-on-Avon
7-8	Lawrence, Sir Henry	The Shakespeare Mystery

1948, April   Editor: William Kent

1	Editor	Announcements
1	Editor	Dr. H. M. Woodward (1875-1948)
1	Kent, William	[letter to the *Stratford-on-Avon Herald* and the *Herald's* response]
2-6	Editor	Oxfordian News: Shakespeare Sell-Out; A Libel on Stratford?; The Stratford Monument; Priestley Plays the Priest; A Monument to a Myth; A New Theory of the *Sonnets*; The Shakespeare Fellowship's Pamphlet; Apology to America; Reports of Meetings; Mr. J. B. Priestley Enters the Arena
6	Bowen, Gwynneth M.	[letter to the TLS (not printed): Sir Christopher Hatton as Shallow]
6-7	Lawrence, Henry	The Shakespeare Mystery, Part 2
7-8	Phillips, G. W.	The Importance of the *Sonnets*

1948, September   Editor: William Kent

1-3, 7	Editor	Editorial Notes: Oxfordians—What Of the Night; A Conon Without Courage; The Shakespeare "Birthplace"; Sir William Dugdale; Lavenham; Dickens and Shakespeare; Gems of Mythology
3-4	Holland, Rear-Admiral H. H.	Shakespeare's Topical References to His Own Plays
4-6	Kent, William	The Shakespeare Circle
6-7	Cutner, Herbert	Are We Progressing?
7-8	Editor	Dickens and Shakespeare; Gems of Mythology

1949, March   Editor: William Kent

1-5	Editor	Notices: Shakespeare "Birthplace"; A Battle of Stratford Spurs; The Pusillanimity of the Professors; Baconian Barks; The Stratford Monument; Misapplied Quotations; The Shakespeare Biographers; What of 1950?; The Play's The Thing; Truth
5-6	Cutner, Herbert	The Shakespearean Birthplace
6-7	Phillips, G. W.	Did Edward de Vere Make a Private Marriage?
7-8	Name Not Clear	Methinks I See My Father
8	Editor	Meetings

1949, September   Editor: William Kent

1	Editor	Notices
1-2	Editor	Editorial Notes: Physician Heal Thyself; A Winter's Campaign;
2-4	Rhys, Ernest	The Birthplace [The origin of Henry James's story]
4-5	Douglas, Col. Montague	[review of *Shakespeare's Sonnets and Edward de Vere* by Gerald Rendall (1930)] [repr. in BTC, vol. 4: 109-11]
5-6	Hunter, Major Newsl. B.	The Earls and Shakespeare
6-7	Pages are missing	[Contents not known]

| 7-8 | Aitken, T. M. | [Title not known] |
| 8 | Editor | Salvador de Madariaga on *Hamlet* |

1950, April — **Editor: William Kent**

1-3	Editor	Editorial Notes: The Quatercentenary; Looney Again; Still They Run!; Cambridge for Oxford!; The Enemy Fainteth; A Poet Convert
3	Holland, Rear-Admiral H.H.	April 22nd, 1950 (a sonnet)
3-4	Douglas, Lt.-Colonel M. W.	Praeterita
4-5	Allen, Percy	*Much Ado About Nothing*—A Burlesque of the Oxford-Howard-Arundel Quarrel
6-7	Atkinson, J. Shera	Polonius
7-9	Kent, William	Nothing but Leaves
9	Gill, Wally	On the Shake-speare *Sonnets* (a sonnet)
10	Editor	Editorial Notes: The Debate; Sergeant Shakespeare; Gems of Mythology

1950, September — **Editor: William Kent**

1-5	Editor	Notices: A Real Oxford Movement!; Another Busy Professor; The Plight of the Professors; Popular Fallacies; Dr. Abraham Feldman
5-7	Atkinson, J. Shera	Comments on Dr. Leslie Hotson's *Sh.'s Sonnets Dated, and Other Essays*
7-9	Kent, William	The BBC Talk
9	Trout, R. Ridgill	A Pound of Flesh

1951, April — **Editor: William Kent**

1-3	Editor	Editor's Notes: Shakespeare and the Encyclopaedists; E. E. Kellett; Meetings
3-4	Amphlett, Hilda	Was Shakespeare an Essex Man?
4-5	Phillips, G. W.	Defense of Dr. Hotson's Dating of Sonnet 107
6	Allen, Percy	*King Lear* in Relation to French History [repr. in BTC, vol. 4: 112-14]
6-7	Feldman, A. Bronson	[letter: *Greene's Groatsworth of Wit*]
7-8	Cutner, Herbert	Provincial Dialect in Shakspere's Day [repr. in BTC, vol. 4: 115-16]
8	Trout, R. Ridgill	[letter: Oxford's debts]
8	Robertson, Archibald	[excerpt from his letter to *Literary Guide* (Feb. 1950): Shakspere was the author]

1951, September — **Editor: William Kent**

1-5	Editor	Editorial Notes: More and More Leaves; Progress in the Press; Still Busy!; Dr. J. R. Mez; Stands Stratford Where it Did?; Open Forum
5-6	Editor	The Shakespeare Trial [from *South London Observer* (April 19, 1951)]
6	Leech, Clifford	Hall's *Chronicle* and Shakespeare [from *Shakespeare Survey*]
6-7	Editor	Shakespeare Fellowship Dinner
7-8	Cutner, Herbert	Shakespeare of London
8-9	Saunders, B. R.	The Scales of Justice [repr. in Clark, *Hidden Allusions*, 3rd ed., Ruth Lody Miller, editor, p. 570-72 (1974)]

1952, March — **Editor: William Kent**

1-2	Editor	Meetings
2-5	Editor	Editorial Notes: Abuse No Argument; Why Not Shakespeare?; Oxford/Shaksper Debate at Stratford-on-Avon; Cecil Palmer; Starry Vere; More Mythology; More Anti-Stratfordian Converts; Soowtherne's Tribute; Bearding the Baconians
5-6	Editor	Shots by the Editor: References to Oxford in the *Encyclopedia of London*
6-7	Amphlett, Hilda	Nicholas Hilliard and Edward de Vere
7-8	Editor	The Library
8	Le Riche, Kathleen	[letter: poem by Sir Walter Raleigh really authored by Oxford?]
8	Phillips, G. W.	[letter: Shakespeare's *Sonnets*]
8	Porohovshikov, Peter S.	[letter: thanks for the *Newsletter*]
8-9	Editor	Just a Little Coincidence
9	Mez, J. R.	News From Switzerland
9-10	Amphlett, Hilda	A Suggestion
10	Mez, R. J.	[review of *Shakespeare's Farewell* by Gwynneth Bowen (pamphlet)]
10	Editor	[review of *Shakespeare in His True Colours* by Katharine E. Eggar]
10	Editor	The Fellowship Study Group

1952, Sept. — **Editor: William Kent**

1	Editor	Meetings
2	Editor	Editorial Notes: The Blind Eye; New Recruits
2-3	Editor	Thomas Looney On the Defensive

3-4	Mez, J. R.	[review of *George Gascoigne, or Edward de Vere* by William Kittle]
4-6	Amphlett, Hilda	Oxford and the Faerie Queene
6-7	Bowen, Gwynneth M.	[review of *Sh.'s Identity: William Stanley, 6th Earl of Derby* by A. W. Titherley]
7-8	Atkinson, J. Shera	The Lord Great Chamberlain of England
8-9	Atkinson, J. Shera	[review of *Cloak of Folly* by Burke Boyce (1949)]
9	Le Riche, Kathleen	The Shakespeare Country
10	Le Riche, Kathleen	[letter: Nicholas Hilliard and Edward de Vere]
10-11	Le Riche, Kathleen	[letter: Shakespeare's Farewell]
11	Holland, Rear-Admiral H. H.	[letter: Shakespeare and Montaigne]
11-12	van Lunteren, S. A.	[letter: Earl's Colne and Colme-Kill]
12	Eggar, Katharine E.	[letter: Earl's Colne and Colme-Kill]
12	Schoell, Frank L.	[letter: Saggiatore]
12	Editor	Note [presentation by T. L. Adamson on "Why I Am an Oxfordian" at the City Literary Institute]

1953, April   **Editor: William Kent**

1	Editor	Portraits of Edward de Vere [Welbeck Abbey (1575), Gheeraerts (1586); Hilliard (1588)]
2	Editor	Notices
2	Editor	Death of Marjorie Bowen (Gabrielle Long) (d. 1952)
2-4	Editor	Editorial Notes: The *News Chronicle* and Shakespeare; A Magnus Opus; Notes and Queries; Lord Wakehurst; Shakespeare Bibliographies; Another Shakespeare Portrait!; A New Shakespeare Magazine
4	Editor	Meetings
5-6	Le Riche, Kathleen	A Portrait of Shake-speare? [repr. in BTC, vol. 4: 119-22]
6-7	Allen, Percy	[review of *This Star of England* by Dorothy and Charlton Ogburn (1952)] [repr. in BTC, vol. 4: 117-18]
7-8	Mez, J. R.	[review of *This Star of England* by Dorothy and Charlton Ogburn (1952)]
8-9	Phillips, G. W.	[review of *This Star of England* by Dorothy and Charlton Ogburn (1952)]
9	Aitken, T. M.	[review of *Lord Oxford and the Shakespeare Group* by Lt. Col. M. W. Douglas]
9-10	Cutner, Herbert	[review of *The Life and Times of Edward Alleyn* by G. L. Hosking (1952)]
10	T. C. H.	E. O. (a sonnet)
10	G. L.	Professor Abel Lefranc (1863-1952)
10-11	Schoell, Frank L.	The Sense of Shakespeare's Sonnets
11-12	Bowen, Gwynneth M.	[letter: wishful thinking and the authorship issue]
12	Kittle, Christy Ann	[letter: her husband's book, *George Gascoigne, or Edward de Vere*]

1953, September   **Editor: William Kent**

1-2	Editor	Editorial Notes: Marjorie Bowen; Save Shakespeare's Avon; Miss Diana Neill and Mr. Alan Keen
2	Drew, Philip	[review of *Lord Oxford and the Shakespeare Group* by Lt.-Colonel Douglas]
3-4	Editor	Oxfordian News: A Shakespeare Quiz; A New Member; Another Convert; Shakespeare Statues; Annual Dinner; Other Events
4-5	Le Riche, Kathleen	The Third Earl of Southampton
6	Cutner, Herbert	Professor Abel Lefranc on Oxford
6-8	Eagle, R. L.	Was Shakspere Illiterate?
8	van Lunteren, S. A.	[review of *Acter het Mombakkes (Behind the Mask)* by P. H. Van Moerkkerken]
8-9	Atkinson, J. Shera	The Manor of Billesley
10	Cutner, Herbert	More Proofs for Shakespeare of Stratford?
10-11	Mez, J. R.	Informative Booklets
11	Van Lunteren, S. A.	Lord Macaulay and Looney's Methods
11-12	Amphlett, Hilda	[letter: Nicholas Hilliard's Miniature]
12	Nicholas, F. L.	[letter: the virgin queen]
12-13	Titherley, A. W.	[letter: *Two Gentlemen of Verona*]
13	Holland, Rear-Admiral, H. H.	[letter: Diana in the Fountain]
13	Greenwood, George G.	[excerpt from his Introduction to *Baconian Essays* (1922)]
13	James, Henry	[excerpts from two letters (1902, 1903)]

1954, April   **Editor: Hilda Amphlett**

1-2	Editor	Notices: The Annual Dinner; The Library; Proposed Visit to Hatfield House; Meetings
2	Editor	Editorial Notes: Members' Activities; Overseas Members
3-4	Editor	[review of *The Borough Town of Stratford-upon-Avon* by Levi Fox]
4-5	Crosby, Ernest	The Aristocratic Look (from *Shakespeare's Attitude Towards the Working Classes*) [repr. in BTC, vol. 4: 144-45]
5	Editor	Mrs. Theodora Philpot (d. 1954)
5-6	Amphlett, Hilda (editor)	Brooke House, Hackney [repr. in BTC, vol. 4: 141-43]
6	Le Riche, Kathleen	[letter to the *Daily Telegraph* (Feb. 12, 1954): Hackney Tudor]
6	Bowen, Gwynneth, M.	Sir Edmund Chambers (1866-1954)
6-7	Eggar, Katharine E.	Turbervile's Tragical Tales
8	Shield, H. S.	De Shakespeare Nostrati
9	Le Riche, Kathleen	Shakespeare's Anniversary
10-11	Wainewright, Ruth M. D.	Some Comments on an Early Dedication to De Vere
11	Le Riche, Kathleen	Oxford Junior Encyclopedia
12	Ogburn, Dorothy	[excerpts from her letter to the Fellowship]
12-13	Nichols, Francis L.	[letter: Dorothy Ogburn's letter]
13	Bowen, Gwynneth M.	[letter: Dorothy Ogburn's letter]
13-14	Le Riche, Kathleen	[letter: Dorothy Ogburn's letter]
14	Phillips, G. W.	[letter: Dorothy Ogburn's letter]
15	Kennedy-Skipton, H. K.	[letter: Seal of the *Journal of the Royal Society of Arts*]
15	Mez, John R.	[letter: books by William Kittle]
15	Editor	Addenda: Recent pamphlets

1954, September   **Editor: Gwynneth M. Bowen and T. L. Adamson**

1	Editor	Notices
1-3	Editor	Editorial Notes: Stanley Baron's articles in the *News Chronicle*; Peterborough Again; the Library; Sir Walter Maxwell Scott; The Annual Dinner; Other Meetings
3	Wainewright, Ruth M. D.	Shake Spears *Sonnets*
4-5	Cutner, Herbert	Two Books on "Shakespeare:" [*Shakespeare Survey 7* edited by Allardyce Nicoll (1954) and *The Annotator* by Alan Keen and Roger Lubbock]
6	Van Lunteren, S. A.	Shakespeare a Paris and *Measure for Measure*
7-8	Bowen, Gwynneth M.	The Wounded Name [repr. in BTC, vol. 4: 123-26] [correction, Spr. 1955, p. 14]
8-9	La Riche, Kathleen	Portrait of John De Vere, the Sixteenth Earl of Oxford
9	Atkinson, J. Shera	*The Famous Victories of Henry V* [repr. in BTC, vol. 4: 133-34]
9-10	Mez, John R.	Gascoigne and De Vere [repr. in BTC, vol. 4: 135-37]
10	Editor	Leaves From the Editor's Notebooks
11	Dooley, J. and E.	[letter: translations of the couplet that heads *Venus and Adonis*]
11-12	Le Riche, Kathleen	[letter: Arthur Golding – No Puritan]
12	Bowen, Gwynneth M.	[letter: Shakespeare Fellowship Study Circle]

1955, Spring   **Editors: Gwynneth M. Bowen and T. L. Adamson**

1	Editor	Notices
1-2	Editor	Editorial Notes: Editor William Kent's Ill Health; Meetings
2	Editor	[summary of Gwynneth Bowen's Nov. 13, 1954 talk "Autobiography in *Measure for Measure*"]
2	Editor	[summary of Capt. Ridgill Trout's Dec. 11, 1954 talk "Oxford and His Forebears"]
2	Editor	[summary of William Kent's Jan. 22, 1955 talk "The Stratfordian Case Examined"]
3	Editor	[summary of Ruth Wainewright's Feb. 19, 1955 talk "The Poems of Edward de Vere"]
3	Editor	[summary of Katharine Eggar's March 19, 1953 talk "Our Debt to Ben Jonson"]
3-5	Steer, Francis W.	English History in the Saleroom
5-6	Amphlett, Hilda	Willobie His Avisa
7-8	Adamson, T. L.	Shakespeare and Oxford in the Lecture Room [repr. in BTC, vol. 4: 127-32]
8	Van Lunteren, S. A.	Translation of Horace by Edward de Vere
8	J. W. R.	The Court of Chivalry
9-10	Bowen, Gwynneth M.	Falstaff, Tarlton and *The Famous Victories*

10-11	Browning, Olive H.	[review of *Who Was Shakespeare?* by Hilda Amphlett (1955)]
11-12	Lambin, Georges	[review of *The First Night of Twelfth Night* by Leslie Hotson]
12	Eggar, Katharine E.	[response to Lambin's review of Hotson's *The First Night*]
12	Adamson, T. L.	[review of *The Renaissance Man of England, Revised Edition* by Dorothy and Charlton Ogburn, (1955)]
13	Editor	Notices: Brooke House and St. Augustine's Church
13	Phillips, G. W.	[letter: Ruth Wainewright's Spring 1954 "Sonnets" article]
14	Bowen, Gwynneth M.	[letter: correction of error in her article "The Wounded Name"]
14	Editor	Study Group Meetings

1955, Autumn — **Editors: Gwynneth M. Bowen and T. L. Adamson**

1	Editor	Advance Notices
1-2	Browning, Olive	Annual Dinner
2-3	Bowen, Gwynneth M.	[summary of Christmas Humphreys' April 22, 1955 talk "Who Wrote Shakespeare – A Lawyer Enquires"]
3	Wainewright, Ruth M. D.	Work of the Study Group
4-5	Editor	Editorial Notes
4	Editor	Report on Shakespeare Scholarship
5-6	Bowen, Gwynneth M.	Chronology in the Melting Pot
6-7	Eggar, Katherine E.	Anthony Munday's "John A Kent"
7-8	Mez, John R.	The Poet With a Speare [repr. in BTC, vol. 4: 138-40] [See correction in Spring 1956 issue, p. 12]
8	Eggar, Katharine E.	Brooke House, Hackney [repr. from SFA, Aut. 1955; also in BTC, vol. 4: 141-43]
9	Wainewright, Ruth M. D.	The Spanish Romances and *The Tempest*
9-10	Gretton, I.	Shakespeare and the General [repr. in Clark, *Hidden Allusions*, 3rd ed., Ruth Loyd Miller, editor, p. 671-72 (1974)]
10	Cutner, Herbert	[review of *Ben Jonson of Westminster* by Marchette Chute (1954)]
10-11	Atkinson, J. Shera	[review of *Shakespeare Unmasked* by Pierre S. Porohovshikov (1940)]
11	Van Lunteren, S. A.	[letter: Edward de Vere as translator of Horace]
11	Kent, William	[letter: John Crow's review of Percy Simpson's *Studies in Eliz. Drama*]
11-12	Mez, John R.	[letter: Hilda Amphlett's book *Who Was Shakespeare?*]

1956, Spring — **Editors: Gwynneth M. Bowen and T. L. Adamson**

2	Amphlett, Hilda	Shakespeare and the Palazo Del Te
3	Editor	Notices: Annual Dinner; Debate Postponed
4	Editor	Reports of Meetings
4-5	Editor	Report on The President's Cross-Examination [(Christmas Humphreys) (Nov. 8, 1955)]
5	Evans, A. J.	The Magic Circle
5-6	Bowen, Gwynneth M.	The Banished Duke
6	Southern, Richard	Elizabethan Theatre
6	Editor	Editorial Notes: Kennedy-Skipton Elected; Lecture on Lord Oxford at Leys School; Verses of Kensington; Shakespeare's Italy
7-9	Bowen, Gwynneth M.	Coronation Sonnet
9	Shield, H. S.	Names of the King and Queen in *A Midsummer-Night's Dream*
9-10	Adamson, T. L.	[review of *Shakespeare* by Charles. J. Sisson]
10	Eggar, Katharine E.	[review of *The Man Who Was Shakespeare* by Calvin Hoffman (1955)]
10	Loosely, N.	[review of *The Shaking Spear* by Brian Flynn]
10-11	Wainewright, Ruth M. D.	Shakespeare: Lord Oxford or Lord Derby?
11	Editor	Miss Helen Atkinson [obituary]
11	Atkinson, J. Shera	[letter: *Who Was Shakespeare?* by Hilda Amphlett]
11	Editor	[brief extracts from a few of the many letters received from readers of *Who Was Shakespeare?* by Hilda Amphlett]
11-12	Shield, H. S.	[letter: Lord Oxford's settlement]
12	McFee, William	[letter to the *New York Herald Tribune* (Jan. 1956)] [How ridiculous to search for manuscripts in Marlowe's tomb]
12	Titherley, A. W.	[letter: patience perforce]
12	Mez, John R.	[letter: correction of an error]

1956, Autumn   **Editors: Gwynneth M. Bowen and T. L. Adamson**

1	Editor	Notices; The Annual Dinner
2	Editor	[summary of Ruth Wainewright's March 10, 1956 talk "George Gascoigne, Pioneer of Elizabethan Literature"]
2-3	Editor	[summary of Katharine Eggar's April 14, 1956 talk "Lord Oxford and the Players' Company"]
3	Rudyerd, G. W.	Editorial Notes: The Opening of the Tomb
3-4	Bowen, Gwynneth M.	Freud and Shakespeare [letter not printed in *The Observer*]
4-8	Clement, Rex	Shakespeare as Mariner [repr. in BTC, vol. 4: 146-56]
8	Amphlett, Hilda	Edward II at Stratford-by-Bow
8-9	Cutner, Herbert	[review of *Shakespeare's Magic Circle* by A. J. Evans (1956)]
10	Eggar, Katharine E.	[review of *Shakespeare Survey* published by Cambridge University Press]
10-11	Atkinson, J. Shera	[letter: Gwynneth Bowen's Spr. 1956 "Coronation Sonnet" article] Reply by Bowen, Spring 1957, p. 11-12.
11	Le Riche, Kathleen	[letter: Shakespeare and the Palazzo del Te]
11	Mez, John	[letter: Kingdom and grave]
12	Bowen, Gwenneth M.	Mr. Francis L. Nichols [obituary]
12	Shield, H. S.	Mr. Gerald William Phillips [obituary]
12	Editor	Miss E. R. Monteath [obituary]

1957, Spring   **Editors: Gwynneth M. Bowen and T. L. Adamson**

1	Editor	Notices
1	Editor	Editorial Notes
2	Editor	Reports of Meetings
2	Le Riche, Kathleen	[summary of T. L. Adamson's Nov. 14, 1956 talk "The Plays of Christopher Marlowe"]
2-3	Wainewright, Ruth M. D.	[summary of Gwynneth Bowen's Dec. 8, 1956 talk "The Upstart Crow"]
3-4	Russell, John W.	Report on the Debate [Oxford (Wainewright) v. Derby (Evans) (Jan. 16, 1957)]
4	Amphlett, Hilda	[summary of Kathleen Le Riche's Feb. 16 talk "Journey Through Shakespeare's Italy"]
4-5	Editor	Outside Lectures: South Place Ethical Society; London Society; Marlowe Society; Aberdeen; Dublin Shakespeare Society; Massachusetts Historical Society
6-7	Wainewright, Ruth M. D.	Psychological Relationships in *Hamlet* and the Authorship Question
7	Trout, R. Ridgill	Bees and Honey
8-9	Le Riche, Kathleen	Marlowe and the Sonnets
9	Gretton, I.	The Recusants in Love's Labour's Lost
10-11	Bowen, Gwynneth M.	[review of *The Shakespeare First Folio* by W. W. Greg (1955)]
11	Aitken, T. M.	Lt.- Col. Montagu W. Douglas [obituary]
11-12	Bowen, Gwynneth M.	[letter: reply to J. Shera Atkinson]
12	Saunders, B. R.	[letter: Edward Bonaventure]

1957, Autumn   **Editors: Gwynneth M. Bowen and T. L. Adamson**

1	Editor	Notices
1-2	Editor	News and Notes: Honest Doubt
2	Eggar, Katharine E.	[summary of Captain R. Ridgill Trout's March 6 talk "Shakespeare and the Earl of Southampton"]
3	Wainewright, Ruth M. D.	Have a Go: Group discussion on authorship issues (April 6, 1957)
3	M. H. R.	The Annual Dinner
4	Wainewright, Ruth M. D.	The Study Group
5	Lambin, G.	Shakespeare in Milan
6-8	Senior, H. L.	Strange Omissions
8	Holland, Rear-Admiral H. H.	The Fore-Horse to a Smock
8	Editor	Notice [death of Rear-Admiral H. H. Holland]
9	Bowen, Gwynneth M.	[review of *Shakespeare's Sources* by Kenneth Muir (1957)]
10	Wainewright, Ruth, M. D.	[review of *Songs and Sonnets of the Earl of Surrey*, ed. by Douglas Geary]
11	Eggar, Katharine E.	[review of *Elizabethan Quintet* by Denis Meadows (1956)]
11	Editor	Rear-Admiral H. H. Holland (1873-1957) [obituary] [repr. in BTC, vol. 1: 246-47]
12	Churchill, R. C.	[letter: Kathleen Le Riche's Spr. 1957 "Marlowe" article]
12	Atkinson, J. Shera	[letter: Kathleen Le Riche's Spr. 1957 "Marlowe" article]
12	Saunders, B. R.	[letter: *Cardan's Comforte*]

The Shakespeare Fellowship News-Letter (English) (SFE)

1958, Spring   **Editors: Gwynneth M. Bowen and T. L. Adamson**

1	Editor	Notices
2	Editor	News and Notes: The Shakespeare Fellowship Trust; Reports of Meetings
2	Bowen, Gwynneth M.	[summary of Katharine Eggar's Nov. 9, 1957 talk "What We Learn of de Vere from Shakespeare's Fools and Clowns"]
3	H. C.	[summary of Commander Martin Pares' Dec. 7, 1957 talk "The Case For Francis Bacon"]
3	Adamson, T. L.	[summary of Gwynneth Bowen's Jan. 16 talk "*The Tr. Reign of John*"]
4	Wainewright, Ruth M. D.	[summary of David Freedman's Feb. 15 talk "Astrology in Sh.'s Plays"]
4	Editor	In Memoriam: J. Shera Atkinson (d. 1958)
4	Martyn, Kathleen	Thomas Aitken: A Memoir (d. 1958)
5-6	Trout, R. Ridgill	Elizabeth and the Catholics
6	Bowen, Gwynneth M.	Shakespeare and the Trussells of Billesley
7-9	J. S. A.	[review of *Shakespearean Ciphers* by William F. Friedman (1957)]
9-11	Wainewright, Ruth M. D.	[review of *Sh.: A Portrait Restored* by Clara Longworth de Chambrun (1954)]
11	Lambin, Georges	[letter: Did Oxford go to Milan?]
11	Bowen, Gwynneth M.	[letter: esponse to Lambin's Letter on Shakespeare in Milan]
12	Shield, H. S.	[letter: Is Ignoto Oxford?]

1958, Autumn   **Editors: Gwynneth M. Bowen and T. L. Adamson**

1	Editor	Notices
1	Editor	News and Notes: Sh. Fellowship Study Group; News From America
2	Bowen, Gwynneth M.	[summary of Ruth Wainewright's March 18 talk "All's Well and the Authorship Question"]
2	J. W. R.	[summary of H. S. Shield's April 12 talk "Classical Clues in Sh.'s Plays"]
3	Eggar, Katharine E.	[summary of T. L. Adamson's May 17 talk "Lord Oxford and Plutarch"]
3	Bowen, Gwynneth M.	The Annual Dinner
4-6	Bowen, Gwynneth M.	Shakespeare's Early Style
6-7	Holland, Rear-Admiral H. H.	The Bells of St. Bennet
7-8	Titherley, A. W.	On the Poem Signed I.M.S. (Second Folio)
8	Adamson, T. L.	Memoir of Mr. J. Shera Atkinson (d. 1958)
9-10	Kent, William	[review of *Shakespeare and His Betters* by R. C. Churchill (1958)]
10-11	Cutner, Herbert	[review of *A Pictorial Biography* by F. E. Halliday (1956)]
10-11	Cutner, Herbert	[review of *The Cult of Shakespeare* by F. E. Halliday (1957)]
11-12	Cutner, Herbert	[letter: H.L. Senior's Aut. 1957 "Strange Omissions" article]
12	Senior, H. L.	[letter: H. Cutner's letter]

The Shakespeare Fellowship News-letter (American) (SFA)

Published 1939-1943 by the Shakespeare Fellowship (American Branch)
founded by Eva Turner Clark, Charles Barrell and Louis Bénézet

Vol. 1, no. 1 (1939, December)   **Head of Editorial Committee: Charles Wisner Barrell**

1	Clark, Eva Turner	Introduction to the Shakespeare Fellowship, American Branch [repr. in BTC, vol. 2: 89-91]
2	Bénézet, Louis P.	President Louis Bénézet's Message [repr. in BTC, vol. 2: 70-71]
2-3	Barrell, Charles Wisner	To Pluck the Heart of the Mystery [repr. in BTC, vol. 2: 72-73]
3	Clark, Eva Turner	Underdowne's Translation Which Shakespeare Had Read
4	Bénézet, Louis P.	Youthful Minds Are Open
5	Barrell, Charles Wisner (Ed.)	Origins and Achievements of the Shakespeare Fellowship [repr. in BTC, vol. 2: 74-76]
6	Barrell, Charles Wisner (Ed.)	Ernest Stirling Allen: Noted Oxford Advocate Passes Away in England (1872-1939) [repr. in BTC, vol. 2: 77-79]
7	Barrell, Charles Wisner	Baseless Fabric
7	Barrell, Charles Wisner	Judith the Illiterate
8	Barrell, Charles Wisner (Ed.)	[review of *"Shakespeare" Identified* by J. Thomas Looney (1920)]
8	Barrell, Charles Wisner (Ed.)	[review of *The Seventeenth Earl of Oxford* by B. M. Ward (1928)]
8	Barrell, Charles Wisner (Ed.)	[review of *The Man Who Was Shakespeare* by Eva Turner Clark (1937)]

Vol. 1, no. 2 (1940, February)   **Head of Editorial Committee: Charles Wisner Barrell**

1	Editor	The Secret Personality of "Shakespeare" Brought to Light After Three Centuries
2-5	Editor [Barrell]	Scientific Proof that Lord Oxford Posed for Ancient Portraits of the Bard [repr. in BTC, vol. 2: 80-86]
4-5	New York Sun Editorial	The Roentgen Shakespeare [repr. from the *The New York Sun* (Dec. 16, 1939)] [repr. in BTC, vol. 2: 85-86]
5	Editor [Barrell]	Dean of Literary Detectives on the War [reprints recent letter from Looney to Eva Turner Clark] [repr. in BTC, vol. 2: 87-88]
6	Hansen, Harry	Shakespeare Fellowship business
7	Editor [Barrell]	Rapid Growth of Research Fellowship Means End of Pompous Obstructionists
8	Douglas, Montagu W.	[review of *Ben Jonson and the First Folio Edition of Shakespeare's Plays* by Canon Gerald H. Rendall (1939)]
9-10	Clark, Eva Turner	Shakespeare Read Books Written in Greek [repr. in BTC, vol. 2: 92]
10	Editor	Best Wishes From Abroad
11	Clark, Eva Turner	The Neapolitan Prince
12	Editor	Oxfordian News: Oxfordian Happy Thought; *Earle of Oxford's March*

Vol. 1, no. 3 (1940, April/May)   **Head of Editorial Committee: Charles Wisner Barrell**

1-2	Clark, Eva Turner	A Shakespeare's Birthday: The Calendar Argues For Lord Oxford [repr. in BTC, vol. 2: 96-97]
2	Editor	An Unanswered Query and Its Implications
2	Editor	De Vere's Life In Uncut *Hamlet*
3	Knapp, Margaret L.	Only a Smock: But It Covers a Famous Rivalry
3	Editor	Lecture on "Pictorial Evidence at Club Founded by H. H. Furness"
4-5	Argonaut	Who Was Shakespeare? [reprint of editorial from *The Argonaut* of San Francisco (Jan. 26, 1940] [repr. in BTC, vol. 2: 98-100]
5	Furman, Alfred A.	Edward de Vere: Accepting Him as Author of Shakespeare
6	Editor	Shakespeare Fellowship Business
6	Brooks, Philip	Crime Imitates Fiction [repr. from *The New York Times Book Review* (March 3, 1940)]
7-8	Barrell, Charles Wisner	Mountanous Error [repr. in BTC, vol. 2: 101-103]
8	Editor	Burt of Boston and the Globe
8	Editor	Commendation from Lord Tweedsmuir [The writer John Buchan, who was also the British Governor-General of Canada]
9-10	Clark, Eva Turner	The Date of *Hamlet's* Composition [repr. in BTC, vol. 2: 104-06]
10-11	Editor	Oxfordian News: Translation of Portrait Article to be Published in the Lowlands; Authorship Mystery Classic Available

| 11 | Editor (Barrell) | *Scientific American* Follow-Up |
| 12 | Editor | Oxfordian News: Oxford's Wide Knowledge of Music Reflected in "Shakespeare's" Plays |

Vol. 1, no. 4 (1940, June/July)   **Head of Editorial Committee: Charles Wisner Barrell**

1-3	Barrell, Charles Wisner	Is Not Oxford Here Another Anchor?
4	Editor	Oxfordian News: Oxford-Shakespeare Birthday Party; Letter From France
5	Bénézet, Louis P.	Shakespeare and Ben Jonson [repr. in BTC, vol. 2: 107-08]
5	Barrell, Charles Wisner (editor)	A Master of Double-Talk [repr. in BTC, vol. 2: 110]
6	Editor	Oxfordian News: Invasions; Oxford's Life Dramatized [Warren P. Munsell, Jr.'s play *By Any Other Name*]
7-8	Clark, Eva Turner	He Must Build Churches Then [repr. in BTC, vol. 2: 111-13]
8	Editor	Baltimore Discovers Oxford
9	Editor	*King Lear* in the News
9-10	Editor	*Three Plays of Shakespeare* (1909) [excerpt]
10-11	Singleton, Esther	Was Edward de Vere Shakespeare? [repr. in BTC, vol. 2: 114-117]
12	Editor	The Honor of Authorship

Vol. 1, no. 5 (1940, August/September)   **Head of Editorial Committee: Charles Wisner Barrell**

1-4	Clark, Eva Turner	Through De Vere Country
4-5	Barrell, Charles Wisner	Muddled Miracle: Dr. Phelps Conjugates the Incongruous
5	Clark, Eva Turner	The Painting in Lucrece [repr. in BTC, vol. 2: 121-22]
6	Editor	Oxfordian News: . . . Let No Dog Bark; Under the Stukas' Shadow
7-11	Barrell, Charles Wisner	Had Shakespeare Read Dante?
12	Nashe, Jr., Tom	First Play Presenting Oxford as "Shakespeare"
12	Editor	Eminent Elizabethan Scholar's New Publication: Rev. Dr. Gerald H. Rendall and *The "Ashbourne" Portrait of Shakespeare*

Vol. 1, no. 6 (1940, October/November)   **Head of Editorial Committee: Charles Wisner Barrell**

[Eva Turner Clark took over as editor after Barrell was called to duty in the Army in September, 1940. She served as editor from the Oct.-Nov. 1940 issue (vol. 1/6) through, perhaps, the Oct. 1943 issue [vol. 4/6].]

1-5, 7-8	Barrell, Charles Wisner	Arthur Golding: The Uncle of Edward de Vere [repr. in BTC, vol. 2: 123-24]
6, 8	Editor	Oxfordian News: In the Army Now; Index; Five Thousand New Readers; The Tongues
6	Editor	Poet Passes: Alfred Antoine Furman (1856-1940)
9-10	Clark, Eva Turner	Topicalities in the Plays [repr. in BTC, vol. 2: 125-28]
10-11	Clark, Eva Turner	Anamos, or A. W. [repr. in BTC, vol. 2: 129-31]
11, 12	Editor	Oxfordian News: Resolute and Determined; If We Have Leisure!; Memorial Library
11-12	Clark, Eva Turner	If We Have Leisure! [repr. in SON, vol. 56/3 (Summer 2020)]

Vol. 2, no. 1 (1940, December)   **Head of Editorial Committee: Charles Wisner Barrell**

1-3	Looney, J. Thomas	Author of "Shakespeare" Identified Comments on Professor Campbell's Article in *Harpers*
3	Editor	Sisson's Researches
4	Barrell, Charles Wisner [editor]	Canon Rendall's Pamphlet [on the Ashbourne portrait]
5	Bénézet, Louis P.	Shake-scene and Shake-Rags
6, 12	Editor	Oxfordian News: Some of Our Speakers; Annual Meeting; A New Comedy; Middle Temple Bombed; English Periodicals Keep Coming; *Twelfth Night*; Oxford-Shakespeare Books
7-10	Barrell, Charles Wisner	Arthur Golding: The Uncle of Edward de Vere, Part 2
10	Clark, Eva Turner	Annotations by Shakespeare?
11-12	Clark, Eva Turner	Gabriel Harvey and *Axiophilus* [repr. in BTC, vol. 2: 132]

Vol. 2, no. 2 (1941, February)   **Head of Editorial Committee: Charles Wisner Barrell**

13-17	Looney, J. Thomas	Shakespeare: A Missing Author, Part 1 [repr. in BTC, vol. 2: 135-44; and in BTC, vol. 6: 112-18)
17	Editor	Shakespeare's Will
17	Editor	Death of Professor Moore Smith (1859-1941)
18, 24	Editor	Oxfordian News: Leading Article; *Twelfth Night* Club's Jubilee; Echoes; Influence of Beaumont and Fletcher; Birds of Shakespeare; Letters from England
19-20	Editor	The Annual Meeting

20	Clark, Eva Turner	The Earthquake
21	Editor	A Letter from Lavenham (from F. Lingard Ranson)
21	Ranson, F. Linguard	[letter to Charles Barrell dated October 31, 1940 (excerpts)]
22-23	Knapp, Margaret L.	Shakespeare and Mark Twain

Vol. 2, no. 3 (1941, April) **Head of Editorial Committee: Charles Wisner Barrell**

25-30	Looney, J. Thomas	Shakespeare: A Missing Author, Part 2 [repr. in BTC, vol. 2: 1]
30-31, 36	Editor	Oxfordian News: Growing Interest; Books and Flames; Shakespeare's Birthday; Letters from England; Our New Member
31-32	Editor	Shakespearean Research
32	Allen, Percy	[letter dated March 1941]
33-34	Bone, F. D.	Castle Hedingham
34-36	Editor	Notes of Twelfth Night
36	Bone, Capt. F. D.	[letter dated March 1941]
36a-36c	Editor	Editor's Note [on the "Arms of Sogliardo" in Jonson's Humour]

Vol. 2, no. 4 (1941, June) **Head of Editorial Committee: Charles Wisner Barrell**

37-40	Barrell, Charles Wisner	Shakespeare's Irish Sympathies [repr. in SON, vol. 19/1: 2-6 (Winter 1983); in BTC, vol. 2: 156-64; in EVR, vol. 6 (Wntr. 1998); and in BTC, vol. 6: 224]
41	Clark, Eva Turner	Washington Physicist Speaks (Dr. John Howard Dellinger)
41-42, 43	Editor	Oxfordian News: Westminster Abbey; NY Public Library; Our President's Boston Lecture; Important Books; *Richard II*
43	Clark, Eva Turner	De Vere Theory Growing in California
44	Barrell, Charles Wisner (editor)	Bénézet Versus Campbell
45-47	Davidson, Elizabeth R.	Unbelief in the Belief
47-50	Clark, Eva Turner	Christopher Marlowe: Certain Perplexing Problems
50-52	Editor	Oxfordian News: The Shakespeare Document; Shakespeare in Texas; The Passionate Pilgrim; Old Vic; Interest at West Point; News From England
51-52	Dwyer, J. J.	Shakespeare Had Read Dante: p.t Toynbee's Reasoning Fallacious

Vol. 2, no. 5 (1941, August) **Head of Editorial Committee: Charles Wisner Barrell**

53-55	Bénézet, Louis P.	Nineteenth Century Revolt Against the Stratford Theory, Part 1 [repr. in BTC, vol. 2: 165-170]
55-57	Clark, Eva Turner	Dr. Sanders and the Miracle
57	Editor	[review of *The Cambridge Bibliography of English Literature*, edited by F. W. Bateson (1940)]
58	Editor	Oxfordian News: Hidden Allusions; Re-Ordered; The Book Club of California
59-62	Barrell, Charles Wisner	Shakespeare's "Fluellen" Identified as a Retainer of the Earl of Oxford [repr. in BTC, vol. 2: 177-183]
62-64	Editor	Oxfordian News: Huntington Library; Words for Music; The Genevan Bible; Messaline; San Francisco Interest

Vol. 2, no. 6 (1941, October) **Head of Editorial Committee: Charles Wisner Barrell**

65-67	Bénézet, Louis P.	The Great Debate of 1892-1893: Bacon Versus Shakespeare, Part 2
67-69	Heron, Flodden W.	Shakspere-Shakespeare
69-72	Editor	Oxfordian News:Micro-Films; Enemy Action; Professor Kittredge; Shakspere, Shakespeare and de Vere; Oxford's Pseudonym;
71-72	Editor	Letters from Members [excerpts from letters from Prof. Everett L. Getchell, John L. Astley-cok, James W. Morris, Margaret L. Knapp, Mrs. Frank J. Sprague, Philip Van Valkenburgh, Mrs. George A. Ball, F. Allen Burt, and Prof. Pierre S. Porohovshikov]
72-75	Clark, Eva Turner	Elizabethan Stage Scenery: More Elaborate Than Originally Believed [repr. in EVR, vol. 6 (Wntr. 1998)]
76	Editor	Oxfordian News: Surprising Error; Annals of English Drama

Vol. 3, no. 1 (1941, December) **Head of Editorial Committee: Charles Wisner Barrell**

1-5	Barrell, Charles Wisner	Shake-speare's Own Secret Drama, Part 1 [repr. in BTC, vol. 2: 184]
5-7	Editor	Oxfordian News: De Vere at Newport; Out Third Year; Leading Article; Most Famous Pseudonym (Flodden Heron's letter to the *Saturday Review of Literature*)
7	Clark, Eva Turner	The World's Great Letters (Letter from Edward Oxenford to his Father-in-in law in 1572, following the St. Bartholomew Massacre; Letter presented in full)
8-12	Editor	Oxfordian News: La Vie Intellectuals in Switzerland; Shakespeare on the NY

[After the October 1943 issue *The Shakespeare Fellowship Newsletter* was replaed by *The Shakespeare Fellowship Quarterly*, which was launched in January 1944. The first issue was numbered Volume V, no. 1 and had the same editor, Charles W. Barrell, as the *Newsletter*.]

The Shakespeare Fellowship Quarterly (SFQ)

Published by the Shakespeare Fellowship (American Branch) (1944-1948)
founded by Eva Turner Clark, Charles Barrell and Louis Bénézet.

[The *Shakespeare Fellowship Quarterly* replaced the Shakespeare Fellowship News-letter in January, 1944. It began with Volume V, no. 1, and initially had the same editorial committee as the *Newsletter*.]

Vol. V, no. 1 (1944, Jan.)   **Head of Editorial Committee: Charles Wisner Barrell**

1-2	Barrell, Charles Wisner (ed.)	Introducing the Quarterly (a continuation of the News-Letter) [repr. in BTC, vol. 3: 5-7]
2-6	Bénézet, Louis P.	Frauds and Stealths of Injurious Imposters [repr. in BTC, vol. 3: 8-17]
6-8	Clark, Eva Turner	Stolen and Surreptitious Copies [repr. in BTC, vol. 3: 18-21]
8-9	Barrell, Charles Wisner	Documentary Notes on the Swan Theatre [repr. in BTC, vol. 3: 22-25]
10-15	Barrell, Charles Wisner	Matinee at the Swan: A Topical Interlude in Oxford-Sh. Research
16	Editor	Editorial Policy

Vol. V, no. 2 (1944, April)   **Head of Editorial Committee: Charles Wisner Barrell**

17-23	Barrell, Charles Wisner	Discoverer of the True Shakespeare Passes: John Thomas Looney, 1870-1944 [Includes letters from Looney to Eva Turner Clark (Aug. 10, 1928); Carolyn Wells (Dec. 6, 1932); Charles Wisner Barrell (June 6, 1937 and May 15, 1942); and Will D. Howe (June 2, 1938)] [repr. in BTC, vol. 3: 26-36; and in NSJ, vol. NS1: 24-36 (Nov. 2010)]
30-32	Clark, Eva Turner	Some Character Names in Shakespeare's Plays, Part 1 [repr. in BTC, vol. 3: 45-49]
32	Editor	Oxfordian News: News-Letters Bound; In Facta Non Verba

Vol. V, no. 3 (1944, July)   **Head of Editorial Committee: Charles Wisner Barrell**

33-40	Barrell, Charles Wisner	Lord Oxford as Supervising Patron of Shakespeare's Theatrical Company [repr. in BTC, vol. 3: 61-78]
41-43	Clark, Eva Turner	Some Character Names in Shakespeare Plays, Part 2 [repr. in BTC, vol. 3: 50-56]
44-46	Bénézet, Louis P.	Stratford Defendant Compromised His Own Advocates, Part 1 [repr. in SON, vol. 5/3: 3-16; and in BTC, vol. 3: 79-83]
46-48	Bénézet, Louis P.	The Authorship of Othello [repr. in BTC, vol. 3: 110-15]
48	Editor	Oxfordian News: Progress and a Handicap

Vol. V, no. 4 (1944, Oct.)   **Head of Editorial Committee: Charles Wisner Barrell**

49-66	Barrell, Charles Wisner	New Milestone in Shakespearean Research: "Gentle Master William" [repr. in BTC, vol. 3: 116-54]
66-68	Clark, Eva Turner	Some Character Names in Shakespeare's Plays, Part 3 [repr. in BTC, vol. 3: 90-95]
68	Editor	Oxfordian News: To New Readers of the Quarterly

Vol. VI, no. 1 (1945, Jan.)   **Head of Editorial Committee: Charles Wisner Barrell**

1-2	Editor	Beginning Our Sixth Year
2	Ogburn, Dorothy	[letter: literary sleuthing of the highest order in the *Quarterly*'s articles]
3-10	Clark, Eva Turner	Lord Oxford's Shakespearean Travels On the European Continent [repr. in OXV, p. 187-205; and in BTC, vol. 3: 155-75]
10	Editor	"Shakespeare" Identified
11-12	Barrell, Charles Wisner	Sole Author of Renowned Victorie: Gabriel Harvey Testifies in the Oxford-Shakespeare Case [repr. in BTC, vol. 3: 176-79]
13-15	Bénézet, Louis P.	Stratford Defendant Compromised His Own Advocates, Part 2 [repr. in SON, vol. 5/3: 3-16 (Jy. 1969); and in BTC, vol. 3: 90]
15-16	Editor	Oxfordian News: Oxford-Shakespeare Talks; The Forehorse to a Smock; Did Hals Paint the Bard?

		Shakespearian Fantasias
14-16	Editor	Oxfordian News: U.S.A. Papers Please Copy; Ward's Biography of Oxford is Now Available; Signifying Nothing?; Modern Works Godfathered by the Author of Macbeth; Dr. Sigmund Freud Found Oxford Was the Bard; Agony Column

Vol. VII, no. 2 (1946, April)   **Head of Editorial Committee: Charles Wisner Barrell**

17-19	Bénézet, Louis P.	Another Stratfordian Aids the Oxford Cause [repr. in BTC, vol. 3, p. 241-46]
19	Massey, Gerald	Shakespeare (a tribute to the bard from about 1866)
20-31	Barrell, Charles Wisner	A Literary Pirate's Attempt to Publish *The Winter's Tale* in 1594 [repr. in BTC, vol. 3: 247-72]
31-32	Editor	Oxfordian News: Progress Reported

Vol. VII, no. 3 (1946, July)   **Head of Editorial Committee: Charles Wisner Barrell**

33-34	Editor	Radio Presentation of Oxford-Shakespeare Case Proves Notably Successful: Gelett Burgess and Charles Wisner Barrell Win Acclaim and Important Practical Aid for The Fellowship [WEAF, July 22, 1946 broadcast]
34	Editor	Truth From Texas
35-42	Barrell, Charles Wisner	The Playwright Earl Publishes "*Hamlet*'s Book" [repr. in BTC, vol. 3: 273-88]
43-44	Bénézet, Louis P.	False Shakespeare Chronology Regarding the Date of King Henry VIII [repr. in BTC, vol. 3: 289-92]
44-48	Editor	Oxfordian News: Shakespeare Authorship Fraudulent; Proof of the Pudding . . . and the maker thereof; British Activities; Bound Volume VI Ready; Passing the Word About

Vol. VII, no. 4 (1946, Oct.)   **Head of Editorial Committee: Charles Wisner Barrell**

49-54	Barrell, Charles Wisner	Shakespeare's *Henry V* Can Be Identified As "Harry of Cornwall" in Henslowe's Diary [repr. in BTC, vol. 3: 293-302]
54	Editor	In Memoriam: Margaret L. Knapp, Ruth Mack Brunswick, Mary H. Barrell, Edward Hardy Clark, Rev. E. D. Book, Mrs. James Stewart Cushman
54, 60, 71-72	Editor	Oxfordian News: Lord Oxford Among the Lambs; Flodden in Field Again; Meet Mr. Allvine; Famous Book in Good Hands; Constructive Aid; Oxford Evidence Restated by Marjorie Bowen; Admiral Holland Accepts Presidency of British Fellowship; Our Current Needs
55-60	Clark, Eva Turner	Shakespeare's Strange Silence When James I Succeeded Elizabeth [The last article written by Ms. Clark before her death in April 1947] [repr. in OXV, p. 290-302; and in BTC, vol. 3: 303-15]
61-69	Barrell, Charles Wisner	Proof That Shakespeare's Thought and Imagery Dominate Oxford's Own Statement of Creative Principles [repr. in BTC, vol. 3: 316)
70-71	Editor	Thou Shalt Not Bear False Witness: A Hint to the Editors of the *Encyclopedia Britannica*

Vol. VIII, no. 1 (1947, Spring)   **Head of Editorial Committee: Charles Wisner Barrell**

1-3	Editor	Mrs. Eva Turner Clark, Founder of The Shakespeare Fellowship, USA (1871-1947) [repr. in BTC, vol. 1: 294-97]
3	Editor	Oxfordian News: Shakespeare: Man of Mystery; Oxford Lecture in Texas; Ward Volume Essential For Permanent Reference
4-11	Barrell, Charles Wisner	Queen Elizabeth's Master Showman Shakes a Spear in Her Defense [repr. in BTC, vol. 3: 336-57]
11-13	Editor	Oxford's Shakespearean Hand Apparent in the 1581 Tournament Documents
13-14	Barrell, Charles Wisner	The Arundel-Arundell Mix-Up
15-16	Editor	Philadelphia's New Shakespeare Society Points Way to Truer Understanding of the Dramatist

Vol. VIII, no. 2 (1947, Summer)   **Head of Editorial Committee: Charles Wisner Barrell**

17-20	Editor	The Fellowship's General Meeting Highly Successful
20, 31-32	Editor	Oxfordian News: Authority Admits Failure; Seeing is Disbelieving; What Do You Think?
32	Editor	Physician, Heal Thyself [repr. in BTC, vol. 3: 381-82]
21-25	Dwyer, J. J.	The Poet Earl of Oxford and Grays Inn [repr. in BTC, vol. 3: 358-68]
26	Editor	[review of *The Lost Treasures of London* by William Kent (1947)]

Shakespeare Matters (SM)

Published quarterly 2001-2013 by the Shakespeare Fellowship. Publication ceased when the Fellowship merged with The Shakespeare Oxford Society to form The Shakespeare Oxford Fellowship at the end of 2013.

30-31	Berney, Charles V.	Confidential Video Bard: Three *Lears*: Horden, Holm, and Olivier

Volume 2/4 (Summer 2003)   **Editor: William E. Boyle**

1, 12-15	Rush, Peter	Shakespeare Question Debated at Smithsonian
1, 7, 33	Baca, Nathan	Wilmot Did Not: The "First" Authorship Story Possible Baconian Hoax
1, 8-12	Boyle, William E.	7th Annual De Vere Studies Conference
2-3	Hughes, Stephanie Hopkins	[letter: Alex McNeil's Spring 2003 *"As You Like It"* article]
3	Boyle, William E. (editor)	From the Editor: Jacobi, York to Serve as Honorary Trustees
3	McNeil, Alex	[letter: reply to Stephanie Hopkins. Hughes]
4-6	Editor	16th Annual Oxford Day Banquet at MIT; Shakespeare Authorship Trust Conference in London; Chicago Oxford Society; Katharine Hepburn - a Shakespearean Woman; *Measure for Measure* in real life; Conference update; Shakespeare documentary goes Catholic; Trustee election news
5	Whalen, Richard F.	"Will Writ Wrong:" *New Yorker* Takes a Bite of the Authorship Apple
8	Editor	EDVSC Raises Over $10,000 During Conference for Oxford Memorial
16-19	Altrocchi, Paul H.	Sleuthing an Enigmatic Latin Annotation
20-23	Burris, Barbara	Oxford's New Coat of Arms in 1586
24	Whalen, Richard F.	[review of *Chasing Shakespeares* by Sarah Smith (2008)]
25-26	Desper, Richard	[review of *The Dark Side of Shakespeare* by W. Ron Hess (2002, 2003)]
27-33	Whittemore, Hank	A Year in the Life: 1586, Part I: "Buy a Thousand Pound, Buy a Rope" [repr. in *Twelve Years in the Life of Shakespeare*, p. 50-68]
34-35	Berney, Charles V.	Confidential Video Bard: *Taming of the Shrew*: Zeffirelli and Miller
35-36	York, Michael	Michael York on *Shrew*

Volume 3/1 (Fall 2003)   **Editor: William E. Boyle**

1, 12-16	Altrocchi, Paul H.	William Camden: What Did He Say, and When Did He Say It?
1, 20-21	Whalen, Richard F.	Nelson's New Oxford Biography: F Review of *Monstrous Adversary*
1, 6-7	Boyle, William E.	Drive, They Said: Revised Shakespeare Bios, Authorship Novels & Anti-Oxfordian Tracts
2	Cyr, Gordon C.	[letter: Nelson's *Monstrous Adversary* (2003)]
2-3	Roper, David	[letter: Wilton and the Shakespeare House]
3	Boyle, William E. (editor)	From the Editor: Reality Check; Congratulations, Dr. Stritmatter
4	Boyle, William E.	Folger Displays Ashbourne Portrait in Exhibition on Frauds
4-5	Editor	Authorship talks in Vermont; Roscius annotation debated; Shakeyland Theme Park and Food Court; New computer analysis technique for comparing texts and determining authorship unveiled; Second Annual Oxfordian Seminar Convenes at Concordia University
7	Eldredge, Joseph	Triumph of (the) Will? New Bio, New Facts – Same Old Propaganda
8-9	Stritmatter, Roger	Monstrous Animosity: How Nelson's Oxford Bio Distorts Oxford & Oxfordians
10-11, 17	Wright, Daniel L.	Knocking on Wood [review of *In Search of Shakespeare* by Michael Wood]
18-19	Sherwood, James	[review of *Counterfeiting Shakespeare* by Brian Vickers]
21	Ligon, K. C.	Who's an Amateur?
22-24, 32	Whittemore, Hank	A Year in the Life: 1586, Part II: Preparing For War
25-27	Anderson, Mark K. & Tekastiaks	Burghley's Bribe; de Vere's Dower?
28-29	Brame, Michael & Galina Popova	Ilicit Reversal
30-32	Berney, Charles V.	Sir Walter Scott as Paleo-Oxfordian, Part 2: The Abbot

Volume 3/2 (Winter 2004)   **Editor: William E. Boyle**

1, 12-13	Boyle, William E.	The Play's the Thing . . . Authorship Debate in NYC
1, 15-19	Ligon, K. C.	Do Oxford's Letters Spell Shakespeare?
1, 8-11, 32	Boyle, William E. (editor)	Conference in Carmel: Fellowship's 2nd Annual Gathering
2	Brame, Michael & Galina Popova	[letter: Pushkin and Shakespeare]
2	Sherwood, James	[letter: Stritmatter and Ogburn's *The Mysterious William Shakespeare*]
2-3	Werth, Andrew	[letter to *Atlantic Monthly* (Jan/Feb. 2004 issue)]
3	Boyle, William E. (editor)	From the Editor: Authorship Lesson from *Peter Pan*; "plentiful lack" . . . "irreducible particularity"
3-7	Editor	In the News: *Edward's Presents* Gets Rave Reviews in London; A *Hamlet*-like Falstaff; *Miami Law Review* article questions traditional Stratford story;

Shakespeare Matters (SM)

Shakespeare Matters (SM)

The Shakespearean Authorship Review (SAR)

Published bi-annually 1959-1973 by The Shakespearean Authorship Society.

		[repr. in BTC, vol. 5: 80]
24	Lambin, G.	Letter: Friar Patrick in Milan: 1575 or 1576?

Issue #7 (1962, Spring) — **Editors: Gwynneth M. Bowen and Ruth M. D. Wainewright**

1-6	Bowen, Gwynneth M.	Shakespeare and His Contemporaries
7	Kent, William	De Vere's Poetry
8-10	Vessey, David W. T. C.	Aspects of Shakespeare's Classics
10-12	Bowen, Gwynneth M.	A Shakespeare Allusion Continued?
13-15	Cutner, Herbert	[review of *Shakespeare Today* by Margaret Webster (1957)]
15-16	Editor	The Annual General Meeting
16-17	Penrose, L. S.	[summary of Gwynneth M. Bowen's Dec. 2 talk "The Shakespeare Portraits: In Colour Transparencies"]
17-18	Cutner, Herbert	[summary of Sir John Russell's Jan. 13, 1962 talk "The Magic Circle"]
19	Adamson, T. L.	Charlton Ogburn [1882-1962] [obituary] [repr. in BTC, vol. 5: 81-82]
20-21	Editor	News and Notes: Brooke House, Hackney; Publication of Shakespeare Cross-Examination; *Shakespeare and His Betters* on American Television
21-22	Shield, H. S.	[letter: a Boar – with a difference]
22	Trout, R. Ridgill	[letter: the family of quickly]
22	Vessey, David W. T. C.	Queen Elizabeth as "Shakespeare"

Issue #8 (Autumn 1962) — **Editors: Gwynneth M. Bowen and Ruth M. D. Wainewright**

1	Editor	A Backward Look [repr. in BTC, vol. 5, p. 83-84]
2-5	Carrington, Phyllis	Colonel Bernard Rowland Ward [1863-1933] [obituary] [repr. in BTC, vol. 1: 256-259 and vol. 5: 85-88]
6-7	Greenwood, Elsie	George Greenwood [1850-1928] [obituary] [repr. in BTC, vol. 5: 89-91]
8-9	Demant, Rev. V. A.	John Thomas Looney [1870-1944] [obituary] [repr. in BTC, vol. 5: 92-94; and in NSJ, vol. NS1: 37-39 (Nov. 2010)]
10-12	Lambin, Georges	Abel Lefranc [1863-1952] [obituary] [repr. in BTC, vol. 5: 95-97]
13-14	Wainewright, Ruth M. D.	Forty Winters [repr. in BTC, vol. 5: 98-99]
15-17	Bowen, Gwynneth M.	[review of *The Shakespeare Claimants* by H. N. Gibson (1962)]
17-19	Humphreys, Christmas	[review of *Shakespeare Cross-Examination* published by the *American Bar Association Journal* (1961)]
19-23	Editor	S.A.S. Meetings and Annual Dinner

Issue #9 (1963, Spring) — **Editors: Gwynneth M. Bowen and Ruth M. D. Wainewright**

1-2	Kent, William	Professor Saintbury and Shakespeare [repr. in BTC, vol. 5: 100]
3-5	Vessey, David W. T. C.	Some Stratfordian Fantasies
6-7	Hughes-Stanton, Ida	The Hare-Brained Escapade
8-10	Wainewright, Ruth M. D.	[review of *Shake-speare: The Real Man Behind the Name* by Dorothy Ogburn and Charlton Ogburn, Jr. (1962)] [repr. in BTC, vol. 5: 103-06]
11-15	Russell, Sir John	[review of *Voyages de Shakespeare en France et en Italie* by Georges Lambin (1962)] [repr. in BTC, vol. 5: 107-11]
15-19	Editor	News and Notes: Fortieth Anniversary Party; Appreciation From the Athenaeum; Poor Yorick!; The Shakespeare Dilemma and Christopher Marlowe
20	Bowen, Gwynneth M.	Dr. J. Howard Dellinger (d. 1962) [obituary]
20	Bowen, Gwynneth M.	T. B. Hart (1963) [obituary]
21	Editor	[extracts from letters: Dorothy Ogburn, David Vessey, Louis Marder]
22-24	Editor	The Shakespearean Authorship Society; What is the Shakespeare Fellowship?

Issue #10 (1963, Autumn) — **Editors: Gwynneth M. Bowen and Ruth M. D. Wainewright**

1-9	Editor	Debate with Orthodoxy on "The Authorship Question:" Louis Marder and Francis Carr [repr. in BTC, vol. 5: 114-23]
10-14	Bowen, Gwynneth M.	[review of *The Case for Shakespeare's Authorship of 'The Famous Victories'* by Seymour M. Pitcher (1961)] [repr. in BTC, vol. 5: 124-29]
15-16	Cutner, Herbert	[review of *The Rise of the Elizabethan Common Player* by M. C. Bradbrook]
16	Wainewright, Ruth M. D.	Three articles on *The De Veres of Castle Hedingham* by George Caunt in *Essex Countryside Magazine* (June-July 1963)
17-20	Bowen, Gwynneth M.	[summary of Gwynneth Bowen's March 14, 1963 talk "The Case for Edward de Vere as "Shakespeare"]
21	Bowen, Gwynneth M.	[summary of H. Amphlett's April 30, 1963 talk "The Haunts of Edward de Vere"]
21-22	Cutner, Herbert	William Kent [1886-1963] [obituary] [repr. in BTC, vol. 5: 130-31]

| 22 | Patience, H. W. | [letter: the Northumberland Manuscript] |

Issue #11 (1964, Spring) — **Editors: Gwynneth M. Bowen and Ruth M. D. Wainewright**

3	Bowen, Gwynneth	Stratfordian Quatercentenary [repr. in BTC, vol. 5, p. 132-33]
4-9	Vessey, David W. T.	Some Early References to Shakespeare [repr. in BTC, vol. 5: 134-40]
10-12	Bowen, Gwynneth M.	Book Reviews: The Verdict of History [literary scholars vs. Historians]
12-13	Cutner, Herbert	[review of *How Shakespeare Spent the Day* by Ivor Brown (1963)]
14	Bowen, Gwynneth M.	The Annual General Meeting
14-16	Wainewright, Ruth M. D.	[summary of Gwynneth Bowen's Nov. 21, 1963 lecture: "New Evidence for Dating the Plays"] [repr. in BTC, vol. 5: 141-43]
16-18	Amphlett, Hilda	[summary of G. Cimino's Jan. 16, 1964 lecture "The Golden Age of Padua"] [repr. in BTC, vol. 5: 144-45]
19	Editor	News and Notes: Homes of the Earls of Oxford
20	Editor	Captain R. Ridgill Trout's Books (sale of his books due to his blindness)
21	Patience, H. W.	[letter: First Folio has only one reference to Stratford: are the manuscripts inside the monument?]
21	Walker, James	[letter: the very curious punctuation of the dedication to the sonnets]

Issue #12 (1964, Autumn) — **Editors: Gwynneth M. Bowen and Ruth M. D. Wainewright**

1	Editor	Upcoming Talks by Society Members
2-6	Connes, Georges	I Have Changed My Mind [The Earl of Derby was the author]
7-9	Bowen, Gwynneth M.	Reverberations [repr. in BTC, vol. 5: 146-49]
9-12	Ashe, Geoffrey	Sir John Harington and the Authorship Question
13-14	Wainewright, Ruth M. D.	[review of *Paging Mr. Shakespeare* by Walter Blumenthal (1961)]
14	Wainewright, Ruth M. D.	[summary of Dr. Eliot Slater's Feb. 13, 1964 lecture "Sh.'s Colour Imagery"]
15-16	Bowen, Gwynneth M.	[review of Professor L. S. Penrose's March 12, 1964 lecture "Shakespeare's Knowledge of Medicine"]
16-17	Amphlett, Hilda	The Spring Pilgrimage
17-21	Editor	Annual Dinner and News and Notes: The Welbeck Portrait
21	Cutner, Herbert	[letter: the BBC and the "Claimants"]
22	Titherley, A. W.	[letter: William Barksted (1577-1620)]
22	Patience, H. W.	[letter: a pre-conquest Earl of Oxford]

Issue #13 (1965, Spring) — **Editors: Gwynneth M. Bowen and Ruth M. D. Wainewright**

1-3	Vessey, David W. T. C.	After the Pageant: A Meditation for 1965 [repr. in BTC, vol. 5: 150]
3-6	Amphlett, Hilda	Sir John Smith
7-9	Walker, James	The Pregnant Silence [repr. in BTC, vol. 5: 153-55]
9-12	Ferguson, W. A.	The *Sonnets* of Shakespeare: The 'Oxfordian' Solution [repr. in BTC, vol. 5: 156-59)
12-17	Bowen, Gwynneth M.	[review of *Shakespeare* by Peter Alexander (1964)]
17	Wainewright, Ruth M. D.	Annual General Meeting
18-19	Wainewright, Ruth M. D.	Summary of Geoffrey Ashe's Dec. 11, 1964 lecture "Mr. W. H.: Another Suggestion"
19-20	Editor	News and Notes: Colour transparencies, films and tape-recording; Sir John Russell's lecture at Royal Naval College; Death of Mr. Francis T. Carmody
21	Cutner, Herbert	[letter: Georges Connes' Autumn 1964 Afterthoughts]
21-22	Vessey, David W. T. C.	[letter: BBC broadcast]

Issue #14 (1965, Autumn) — **Editors: Gwynneth M. Bowen and Ruth M. D. Wainewright**

1	Editor	Upcoming Talks by Society Members
2-7	Bowen, Gwynneth M.	Hackney, Harsnett, and the Devils in *King Lear* [repr. in OXV, p. 237-43; and in BTC, vol. 5: 160-67]
8	Patience, Harold W.	Topical Allusions in *King John* [repr. in BTC, vol. 5: 168-69]
9	Wainewright, Ruth M. D.	The S.A.S. Library
10-11	McGeoch, I. L.	[review of *Shakespeare and the Sea* by A. F. Falconer (1964)] [repr. in BTC, vol. 5: 170-72]
11-12	Wainewright, Ruth M. D.	[review of *Oxford: Courtier to the Queen* by Eleanor Brewster (1964)] [repr. in BTC, vol. 5: 173]
12-13	Wainewright, Ruth M. D.	[summary of Gwynneth Bowen's Feb. 17, 1965 lecture "The Merchant and the Jew"] [repr. in BTC, vol. 5: 174-75]
13-15	Bowen, Gwynneth M.	[summary of Ruth Wainewright's March 17, 1965 lecture "Conflicting Dates for Various Candidates"] [repr. in BTC, vol. 5: 176-78]

12-13	Wainewright, Ruth	[review of *Sir Thomas Smith: Tudor Intellectual in Office by Mary Dewar* (1964)] [repr. in BTC, vol. 5: 250-52]
14-18	Editor	The Francis Bacon Society's Legacy [repr. from *All England Law Report*s, 1964]
18-22	Editor	Annual Dinner of the Shakespearean Authorship Society (April 20, 1967)
23	Amphlett, Hilda	A Surrey Reception

Issue #19 (1968, Autumn)   **Editors: Gwynneth M. Bowen and Ruth M. D. Wainewright**

1-3	Huston, Craig	Edward de Vere [repr. in BTC, vol. 5: 153-56]
4-11	Vessey, David W. T. C.	An Early Allusion to Shakespeare
11-12	Amphlett, Hilda	Titchfield Abbey [repr. in BTC, vol. 5: 157-58]
13-14	Wainewright, Ruth M. D.	[review of *The Herberts of Wilton* by Tresham Lever (1967)] [repr. in BTC, vol. 5: 259-60]
15	Editor	S.A.S. Meetings
15-16	Bowen, Gwynneth M.	The Ostler v. Hemminges Case
16-18	Humphreys, Christmas	[summary of his Dec. 6, 1967 talk "A Cross Examination of Oxfordians"] [repr. in BTC, vol. 5, p. 261-63]
19-20	Bowen, Gwynneth M.	[summary of Sir John Russell's Jan. 17, 1969 lecture "The Authorship Problem for Beginners"]
20-21	Vessey, David W. T. C.	[summary of T. D. Bokenham's Feb. 21, 1968 lecture "Ben Jonson and Shakespeare"]
21-22	Patience, H. W.	[letter: mystery of Lord Oxford's grave]

Issue #20 (1968, Autumn)   **Editors: Gwynneth M. Bowen and Ruth M. D. Wainewright**

1-4	Slater, Eliot	Terms of Art in *Hamlet*
5-10	Bowen, Gwynneth M.	More Brabbles and Frays [repr. in BTC, vol. 5: 264-71]
10-11	Patience, Harold W.	Earls Colne and Castle Hedingham [repr. in BTC, vol. 5: 272-3]
12-13	Wainewright, Ruth M. D.	[review of *The Great Shakespeare Forgery* by Bernard Grebanier (1965)] [repr. in BTC, vol. 5: 274-77]
14-15	Vessey, David W. T. C.	[summary of his March 22, 1968 talk "Some Problems in Shakespearean Chronology"]
15-16	Bowen, Gwynneth M.	[summary of his May 15, 1968 lecture "*The Merchant of Venice*: A Living Source"]
16-18	Editor	The Annual Dinner
18	Huston, Craig	[letter: John de Vere's Deed of Covenants]
19	Editor	[Craig Huston's Letter]
19-20	Loosely, Newsl.	[letter: the mystery of Lord Oxford's grave]
20-21	Trout, R. Ridgill	[letter: questionnaire]
21	p., Martin R.	[letter: information wanted for a life of J. M. Robertson]

Issue #21 (Spring 1969)   **Editors: Gwynneth M. Bowen and Ruth M. D. Wainewright**

1-4	Bowen, Gwynneth M.	The Mysterious Mr. W. H.
4-7	Slater, Eliot	Terms of Art in *King Lear*
7-10	Vessey, David W. T. C.	[review of *Was Shakespeare Shakespeare?* by Milward W. Martin (1965)]
10-11	Editor	The Annual General Meeting
11	Wainewright, Ruth M. D.	[summary of Glenn Black's Nov. 26, 1968 lecture "Poems by Lord Oxford and Others in Elizabethan Manuscripts"]
12-15	Vessey, David W. T. C.	[summary of a Jan. 28, 1969 discussion on "The Northumberland Manuscript]
15-16	Wainewright, Ruth M. D.	[summary of Father Francis Edwards' Feb. 19, 1969 lecture "A Sidelight on Robert Cecil's Spy System"]
16-18	Bowen, Gwynneth M.	[summary of of Ruth Wainewright's March 20, 1969 lecture "Oxfordian Views on the *Sonnets*"]
18	Editor	News and Notes: The Shakespeare Fellowship *News-Letter*
19	Editor	Herbert Cutner (d. 1969) [obituary]
20-21	Patience, H. W.	[letter: Shakespearean chronology]
21	Patience, H. W.	[letter: the mystery of Lord Oxford's grave]

Issue #22 (Christmas 1969)   **Editors: Gwynneth M. Bowen and Ruth M. D. Wainewright**

1	Editor	*"Shakespeare" Identified* Fiftieth Anniversary
2-12	Looney, J. Thomas	*"Shakespeare" Identified* [excerpts from Chapters 2, 3, 4; repr. in BTC, vol. 1: 218-38]
13-15	Wainewright, Ruth M. D.	[review of *The Man Behind Macbeth and Other Studies* by Sir James Fergusson]
15	Editor	Annual Dinner 1969, and Annual General Meeting

Issue #27 (1972, Winter)   **Editors: Gwynneth M. Bowen and Ruth M. D. Wainewright**

1-8	Miller, Jr., Minos D.	Address to the Shakespearean Authorship Society at the Conference to Celebrate the Society's 50th Anniversary
		[repr. in BTC, vol. 5: 322-31]
9-19	Penrose, L. S.	Statistical Approaches to the Authorship Problem
19-23	Bowen, Gwynneth M.	[review of *The Boar's Head Theater: An Inn-Yard Theater of the Elizabethan Age* by Charles. J. Sisson (1972)] [repr. in BTC, vol. 5: 332-36]

Issue #28 (1973, Summer)   **Editors: Gwynneth M. Bowen and Ruth M. D. Wainewright**

1-6	Bowen, Gwynneth M.	Oxford's and Worcester's Men and the Boar's Head (1972) [repr. in BTC, vol. 5: 337-44]
7-13	Edwards, Reverend Francis	Oxford and the Duke of Norfolk [repr. in BTC, vol. 5: 345-54]
14-24	Buisman, Louise	The Problems of *Henry VI* and of *King John*
25	Editor	Lecturers of the Shakespearean Authorship Society 1972-1973
25	Loosely, Newsl.	The Annual Dinner

Issue #29 (1974, Summer)   **Editors: Gwynneth M. Bowen and Ruth M. D. Wainewright**

1-10	Bowen, Gwynneth M.	Worchester's Oxford's and The Admiral's
11-16	Buisman, Louise	Shakespeare Personal or Impersonal?
17-18	Edwards, Reverend Francis	[review of *The Shakespeare Authorship Question* by Craig Huston]
19	Editor	Lectures of the Shakespearean Authorship Society 1973-1974
20	Loosely, Newsl.	The Annual Dinner 1974
20-21	Pataki, Ronald	[letter: Oxford dividing his personality between characters in his plays]

The Spear-shaker Review (SSR) and The Spear-shaker Newsletter (SSN)

Published by Stephanie Caruana as *The Spear-shaker Review* (1987-1988)
and as *The Spear-shaker Newsletter* (1991).

Issue 1/1 (1987, Fall)

p.	Author	Title
2-5	Mason, Jacquelyn L.	Shall I Die? Shall I Fly?: An Early Poem by Oxford?
6-9	Stein, E. Jimmee	To Believe or Not To Believe (Repr. from *Emphasis: The Newsletter of Greater New York Mensa* (March 1987)]
10	Assante, Katharine	Letter to the Earl of Oxford: Edward De Vere
11-21	Caruana, Stephanie	The Guy of Warwick: Oxford Knocks Shaksper
22-23	Harms, Linda	Waiting for the Assassination
24-30	Sears, Elisabeth (Betty)	Oxford, Golding, and the Translation of Ovid's *Metamorphoses*
31-35	Twain, Mark	Life of William Shakespeare
36	Beauclerk, Charles	News From the De Vere Society: Lady Diana is Direct Descendant of Edward de Vere
37	Editor	De Vere Society Meeting Schedule
38-39	Lipman, Carole S.	Profile: The Shakespeare Authorship Roundtable
40	De Vere, Rollin	How I Became an Oxfordian
41	Editor	A Modest Proposal: The *Oxford* Oxford Shakespeare
42-43	Editor	Oxford Equations
44	Editor	Cavallery Cobweb's Corner
Back cover	Mason, Jacquelyn L.	Collage: Oxford Peering Out From Behind a Mask of Shaksper

Issue 1/2 (1988, Winter)

p.	Author	Title
1-4	Caruana, Stephanie	Secrets of Michael Drayton's Poly-Olbion
5-7	Smith, Marilyn	Shakespeare as Nobody: The Attraction of the Stratford Myth
8-15	Caruana, Stephanie	Shakespeare/Oxford by Hilliard
16-23	Appleton, Elizabeth	Proving Shakespeare's Identity: Oxford's Role in the War of Words
24-27	Sears, Elisabeth (Betty)	Oxford's Hand in *Thomas of Woodstock* and *Richard II*
28-30	Hannas, Andrew	Is Oxford Pictured in "Arts of Falconry" Prints?
31-32	Editor	Man Bytes Bard
33-36	Editor	Two Lives: Oxford and Shaksper: Which One Was the Poet?
37	Caruana, Stephanie	Oxford's Lute Music Manuscript at Folger Shakespeare Library
38-39	Beauclerk, Charles	News From the De Vere Society
40-41	Pope, Russell	The Will, the Swan, and the Moniment
42	Editor	Shakespeare Authorship Roundtable Schedule
43	Editor	The Shakespeare Oxford Society
44	Editor	Cavallery Cobweb's Corner

New Issue 1/1 (1991, Feb.)

p.	Author	Title
1	Editor	Return of *Spear Shaker*
1	Editor	David Lloyd Kreeger Dies
2	Editor	News: Charles Vere at the Folger; Vere's the Word; De Vere's "Lost Chronicles"
2-3	O'Brien, Robert	[letter: misc. items]
3	Cusick, John	[letter to *Daily News-Sun*, Sun City, Arizona]
3	Lund, Thomas A.	[letter: poem about authorship issue]
3	Winkworth, Tish	[letter: Michel Drayton's *Poly-Olbion*]
3-4	Editor	News From the Societies
5-15	Caruana, Stephanie	Oxford's "Robin Hood" Plays and "Shakespeare's" *King Johnn*

Issue 3/4 (1991, May)

p.	Author	Title
1-3	Caruana, Stephanie	Six "Signatures" In Search of an Author
4-11	Charlton, Derran K.	Edward de Vere and the Knights of the Grail
11-16	Goldstein, Gary B.	Who Was Joyce's Shakespeare?

IIc: REGULAR OXFORDIAN COLUMNS
IN NON-OXFORDIAN PUBLICATIONS

Oxfordian articles in
The Hackney Spectator (HAK)

An independent local journal published every Tuesday and Friday. Henry Nevill, publisher.

These pieces have been reprinted in *Shakespeare Investigated: Publications of the Shakespeare Fellowship 1922-1936*, edited by James A. Warren and published by Veritas Publications.

1922, September 1 (no. 1978)
12	Ward, Col. Bernard R.	Shakespeare's Mysterious "W.H." A Hackney Man?" [letter]

1922, September 8 (no. 1979)
6-7	--	Problems of Past and Present

1922, October 27 (no. 1986)
3	Ward, Col. Bernard R.	"Shakespeare" at Hackney: The Theories of Professor Lefranc and Mr. Looney [Shakespeare Fellowship column no. 1]

1922, November 3 (no. 1987)
11	Ward, Col. Bernard R.	*"Shakespeare" Identified*: A Famous Book [Shakespeare Fellowship Column no. 2]

1922, November 10 (no. 1988)
12	Ward, Col. Bernard R.	Shakespeare Identified: Shakespeare Characteristics [Shakespeare Fellowship column no. 3]

1922, November 17 (no. 1989)
7	—	Report on the inaugural meeting [Shakespeare Fellowship no. 4] [repr. in *The Mystery of Mr. W. H.* by Col. B R. Ward]

1922, November 24 (no. 1990)
14	Ward, Col. Bernard R.	"Shakespeare" at Hackney [Shakespeare Fellowship column no. 5]
14	Maxse, L. J.	[letter accepting position of Vice President]
14	Lefranc, Abel	[letter accepting position of Vice President]
14	Looney, J. Thomas	[letter accepting position of Vice President]

1922, December 1 (no. 1991)
3	Ward, Col. Bernard R.	Objectives of the Fellowship [Shakespeare Fellowship column no. 6]

1922, December 8 (no. 1992)
11	Ward, Col. Bernard R.	A Lecture in the Leyton Taon Hall, Nov. 16, 1922, on *"Shakespeare" Identified* [SF column no. 7]

1922, December 15 (no. 1993)
4	Ward, Col. Bernard R.	A First Skirmish [SF column no. 8]

1922, December 22 (no. 1994)
12	Ward, Col. Bernard R.	The Derby Theory: *Sous le Masque de William Shakespeare* [SF column no. 9]

1922, December 29 (no. 1995)
12	Ward, Col. Bernard R.	The Derby Theory, Part 2 [SF column no. 10]

1923, January 5 (no. 1996)
11	Greenwood, Sir George	[SF column no. 11]

1923, January 12 (no. 1997)
3	Ward, Col. Bernard R.	[SF column no. 12]

1923, January 19 (no. 1998)

2	Clarke, Francis	Letter to Editor [Baconian]
3	Ward, Col. Bernard R.	[SF column no. 13]

1923, January 26 (no. 2000)

8	Ward, Col. Bernard R.	[SF column no. 14]

1923, February 2 (no. 2002)

6	Ward, Col. Bernard R.	[SF column no. 15]

1923, February 9 (no. 2004)

7	Ward, Col. Bernard R.	[SF column no. 16]

1923, February 16 (no. 2006)

7	Greenwood, Sir George	Shakespearean Research [SF column no. 17]

1923, February 23 (no. 2008)

7	Ward, Col. Bernard R.	[SF column no. 18]

1923, March 2 (no. 2010)

6	Ward, Col. Bernard R.	*Hamlet* and the Veres [SF column no. 19]

1923, March 9 (no. 2012)

7	Ward, Col. Bernard R.	The Veres in *Hamlet*, I [SF column no. 20]

1923, March 16 (no. 2014)

8	Ward, Col. Bernard R.	The Veres in *Hamlet*, II [SF column no. 21]

1923, March 23 (no. 2016)

10	Douglas, Col. Montagu W.	*The Mystery of "Mr. W. H.",* I [review of the book by Col. Bernard R. Ward] [SF column no. 22]

1923, March 28 (no. 2017) [March 30 was Good Friday]

2	Douglas, Col. Montagu W.	*The Mystery of "Mr. W. H.",* II [review of the book by Col. Bernard R. Ward] [SF column no. 23]

1923, April 6 (no. 2018)

5	Ward, Col. Bernard R.	Shakespeare and Chapman—A Suggestion [SF column]

1923, April 13 (no. 2020)

8	Looney, J. Thomas	The Oxford Movement [SF column]

1923, April 20 (no. 2022)

4	Looney, J. Thomas	Who Wrote *Hamlet*? [SF column]

1923, April 27 (no. 2024)

2	Douglas, Col. Montagu W.	A Review of Reviews [SF column]

1923, May 4 (no. 2026)

2	Wise, Ernest G.	"To Thine Own Self Be True" [SF column]

1923, May 11 (no. 2028)

2	Looney, J. Thomas	How *The Observer* Observes [SF column]

1923, May 18 (no. 2030)

2	Douglas, Col. Montagu W.	The Great Unknown [SF column]

1923, May 25 (no. 2031)

2	Ward, Col. Bernard R. & J. Thomas Looney	The Tracking of Margery Gryffyn [SF column] [includes column] [excerpts from three letters from Looney to Ward]

1923, June 1 (no. 2033)

5	Gunning, Dr. C. P.	Shakespeare and the Netherlands, I [SF column]

1923, June 8 (no. 2035)

8	Gunning, Dr. C. P.	Shakespeare and the Netherlands, II [SF column]

1923, June 15 (No 2037)

5	Eggar, Katherine E.	Edward De Vere's Lyric Verse – An Unsearched Field of Discovery, I [SF column]

1923, June 22 (no. 2039)

8	Eggar, Katherine E.	Edward De Vere's Lyric Verse – An Unsearched Field of Discovery, II [SF column]

1923, June 29 (no. 2041)
    4-5   Ward, Col. Bernard R.   A Dinner at the Lyceum Club [SF column]

1923, July 6 (no. 2043)
    8   Ward, Col. Bernard R.   Oxford and Bacon, I [SF column]

1923, July 13 (no. 2045)
    3   Ward, Col. Bernard R.   Oxford and Bacon, II [SF column]

1923, July 20 (no. 2047)
    4   Ward, Col. Bernard R.   Professor Lefranc at Oxford [Quotes in full letter from A. K. Hobart-Hampden] [SF column] [and in no. 2048 (July 24)]

1923, July 27 (no. 2049)
    4   Ward, Col. Bernard R.   Oxford and Bacon, III [SF column] [and in no. 2050 (July 27)]

1923, August 3 (no. 2051) (Friday)
    4   Looney, J. Thomas   An Elizabethan Literary Group, I [extracts from a letter in response to Col. Ward's "Oxford and Bacon" articles] [SF column]

1923, August 14 (no. 2053) (Tuesday)
    9   Looney, J. Thomas   An Elizabethan Literary Group, II [further extracts from a letter] [SF col.] [no SF col. in no. 2052 (Aug. 10)] [and in no. 2054 (Aug. 14)]

1923, August 24 (no. 2056) (Friday)
    4   Looney, J. Thomas   An Elizabethan Literary Group, III [Concluding extracts from a letter] [SF column] [and in no. 2057 (Aug. 28)]

1923, August 31 (no. 2058) (Friday)
    4   Looney, J. Thomas   A *Daily News* Critic [SF column] [and in no. 2059 (Sept. 4)]

1923, September 7 (no. 2060)
    2   Looney, J. Thomas   *The Church Times* Critic and a Rejected Letter, I [SF column] [and in no. 2061 (Sept. 11)]

1923, September 14 (no. 2062)
    4   Looney, J. Thomas   *The Church Times* Critic and a Rejected Letter, II [SF column] [and in no. 2063 (Sept. 18)]

1923, September 21 (no. 2064)
    2   Ward, Col. Bernard R.   *Shakespeare Through Oxford Glasses*, I [review of the book by Capt. H. H. Holland] [The Shakespeare Fellowship column]
    2   May, T.   The Mystery of Shakespeare: Is He a Myth? [letter] [SF column] [and in no. 2065 (Sept. 25)]

1923, September 28 (no. 2066)
    4   Ward, Col. Bernard R.   *Shakespeare Through Oxford Glasses*, II [review of the book by Capt. H. H. Holland] [SF column] [and in no. 2067 (Oct. 2)]

1923, October 5 (no. 2068)
    2   Ward, Capt. Bernard M.   *Love's Labour's Lost* and *Cymbeline* [SF col.] [and in no. 2069 (Oct. 9)]

1923, October 12 (no. 2070)
    4   Clarke, Francis   An Elizabethan List of Poets [SF column] [and in no. 2071 (Oct. 16)]

1923, October 19 (no. 2072)
    4   Ward, Col. Bernard R.   *Shakespeare Through Oxford Glasses*, III [review of the book by Capt. H. H. Holland] [SF column] [and in no. 2073 (Oct. 23)]

1923, October 26 (no. 2074)
    4   Douglas, Col. Montagu W.   *Lee, Shakespeare and Tertium Quid* [review of Sir Geoge Greenwood's book] [SF column] [and in no. 2075 (Oct. 30)]

1923, November 2 (no. 2076)
    2   Barley, Annie L.   Alternative Solutions [SF column] [and in no. 2077 (Nov. 6)]

1923, November 9 (no. 2078)
    2   Ward, Col. Bernard R.   Annual General Meeting [SF column]
    2   Looney, J. Thomas   Letter to Col. Ward to be read at the Annual General Meeting [both also in no. 2079 (Nov. 13)]

1923, November 16 (no. 2080)

3   Ward, Col. Bernard R.   *Shakespeare's Hand in the Play of Sir Thomas More* [review of the book edited by Alfred W. Pollard [SF column] [and in no. 2081 (Nov. 20)]

1923, November 23 (no. 2082)

9   Greenwood, Sir George   Rejected Letter to *The Observer*: A Play in Shakespeare's Handwriting [SF column] [and in no. 2083 (Nov. 27)]

1923, November 30 (no. 2084)

4   Looney, J. Thomas   Shakespearean Research in Hackney and Southwark, I [SF column] [and in no. 2085 (Dec. 4)]

1923, December 7 (no. 2086)

2   Looney, J. Thomas   Shakespeare Researches, Etc., II [SF column]

1923, December 14 (no. 2087)

8, 18   Ward, Col. Bernard R.   Report of Our First Year's Work [Includes photo of Sir George Greenwood] [SF column]

1923, December 21 (no. 2089)

4   Looney, J. Thomas   Shakespearean Researches at Hackney and Southwark, III [SF column]

1923, December 28 (no. 2090)

7   Looney, J. Thomas   Shakespearean Researches at Hackney and Southwark, IV [SF column] [and in no. 2091 (Jan. 1, 1924)]

1924, January 4 (no. 2092)

4   Looney, J. Thomas   Shakespearean Researches at Hackney and Southwark, V [SF column] [and in no. 2093 (Jan. 8)]

1924, January 11 (no. 2094)

9   Looney, J. Thomas   Shakespearean Researches at Hackney and Southwark, VI [SF column] [and in no. 2095 (Jan. 15)]

1924, January 18 (no. 2096)

2   Clarke, A. Walrond   Edward De Vere 17th Earl of Oxford and His Burial Place in Hackney [SF column] [and in no. 2097 (Jan. 22)]

1924, January 25 (no. 2098)

9   Looney, J. Thomas   Shakespearean Researches at Hackney and Southwark, VII [SF column] [and in no. 2099 (Jan. 25)]

1924, February 1 (no. 2100)

9   Looney, J. Thomas   Shakespearean Researches at Hackney and Southwark, VIII [SF column]

1924, February 8 no. 2101)

2   Ward, Capt. Bernard M.   Elizabethan Dancing [SF column]
2   Ward, Col. Bernard R.   Fellowship notes: The Galleon

1924, Februray 15 (no. 2102)

5   Looney, J. Thomas   Shakespearean Researches at Hackney and Southwark, IX [SF column] [Looney's 22nd and final appearance in *The Hackney Spectator*]

1924, February 22 (no. 2103)

5   Ward, Col. Bernard R.   A Rosicrucian Group [SF column]

1924, February 29 (no. 2104)

4   Smithers, Ursula   Oxford and Jonson, I [SF column]
4-5   Lucas, R. Macdonald   The Derby Theory [SF column]

1924, March 7 (no. 2105)

10   Ward, Col. Bernard R.   The Derby Theory [SF column]
10   Clarke, Francis   The Derby Theory [letter]

1924, March 14 (no. 2106)

4   Smithers, Ursula   Oxford and Jonson, II [SF column] [not in this issue, but a photocopy of it is in the SF archives at Brunel University – a mystery]

1924, March 21 (no. 2107)

4   Standen, Gilbert   A Rosicrucian Group, I [SF column]
4   Ward, Col. Bernard R.   Fellowship Notes [SF column]
4-5   Lucas, R. Macdonald   The Character of Oxford, I [letter] [SF column]

1924, March 28 (no. 2108)

4	Ward, Col. Bernard R.	The Character of Oxford, II [SF column]
4	Ward, Col. Bernard R.	Mr. Francis Clarke & Mr. Lucas

1924, April 4 (no. 2109)

4	Standen, Gilbert	A Rosicrucian Group, II [SF column]
4	Ward, Col. Bernard R.	Fellowship Notes [SF column]
4	Ward, Col. Bernard R.	The Shakespeare Good-Fellowship [SF column]

1924, April 11 (no. 2110)

4	Douglas, Col. Montagu W.	The Problem of *Hamlet* [SF column]

1924, April 17 (no. 2111)

11	A. S. B.	A Rosicrucian Group, III [SF column]

1924, April 25 (no. 2112)

11	Douglas, Col. Montagu W.	The Date of *Hamlet*, I [SF column]
11	Ward, Col. Bernard R.	Fellowship Notes [SF column]

1924, May 9 (no. 2114)

11	Douglas, Col. Montagu W.	The Date of *Hamlet*, II [SF column] [no SF column in no. 2013 (May 2)]

1924, May 16 (no. 2115)

5	Douglas, Col. Montagu W.	The Date of *Hamlet*, III [SF column]

1924, May 23 (no. 2116)

2	Ward, Col. Bernard R.	The Date of *Hamlet* [fS column]

1924, May 30 (no. 2117)

2	Ward, Col. Bernard R.	Oxford and Sir Horace Vere [SF column]

1924, June 6 (no. 2118)

2	Parsons, J. Denham	Who was Labeo? [letter] [SF column]

1924, June 13 (no. 2019)

10	Knapp, Margaret L.	Oxford Theory Coincidences [SF column]

1924, June 20 (no. 2120)

11	Douglas, Col. Montagu W.	An Omitted Speech in the First Folio [SF column]

1924, June 27 (no. 2121)

2	Douglas, Col. Montagu W.	Recent Research [SF column]

1924, July 4 (no. 2122)

2	Ward, Col. Bernard R.	Oxford and Burghley [SF column]

1924, July 11 (no. 2123)

5	Ward, Col. Bernard R.	Shakespeare's Signatures [SF column]

1924, July 18 (no. 2124)

11	Ward, Col. Bernard R.	The Text of *Hamlet* [SF column]

1924, July 25 (no. 2125)

9	Ward, Col. Bernard R.	Recent Progress [SF column]

1924, August 1 (no. 2126)

10	Ward, Col. Bernard R.	Fellowship Notes [SF column]

1924, August 8 (no. 2127)

2	Ward, Col. Bernard R.	Concerning William Hall, I [SF column]

1924, August 15 (no. 2128)

11	Ward, Col. Bernard R.	The "Shakespeare" Myth [SF column]

1924, August 22 (no. 2129)

2	Eggar, Katherine E.	The Players' Version of *Hamlet* [SF column]

1924, August 29 (no. 2130)

4	Greenwood, Sir George	Stratfordian Manners: A Letter to Lord Sydenham [SF column]

1924, September 5 (no. 2131)

4	Ward, Col. Bernard R.	Facts Relating to William Hall and His Circle, II [SF column]

1924, September 12 (no. 2132)

4	Ward, Col. Bernard R.	Facts Relationg to William Hall and His Circle, III [SF column]

1924, September 19 (no. 2133)
4	Douglas, Col. Montagu W.	Who Was the Sentinel Francisco? [SF column]
4	Ward, Col. Bernard R.	Fellowship Notes [SF column]

1924, September 26 (no. 2134)
4	Knapp, Margaret	[letter: the office of Lord Great Chamberlain] [SF column]
4	Ward, Col. Bernard R.	Response to Knapp

1924, October 3 (no. 2135)
4	Ward, Col. Bernard R.	*A Midsummer Night's Dream*, I [SF column]

1924, October 10 (no. 2136)
4	Ward, Col. Bernard R.	*A Midsummer Night's Dream*, II [SF column]

1924, October 17 (no. 2137)
4	Douglas, Col. Montagu W.	*Shakespeare's Signatures and "Sir Thomas More*, I*"* [review of the book by Sir George Greenwood] [SF column]

1924, October 24 (no. 2138)
10	Clarke, A. Walrond	St. Augustine's Church, Hackney [SF column]

1924, October 31 (no. 2139)
9	Ward, Col. Bernard R.	Annual General Meeting [SF column]

1924, November 7 (no. 2140)
4	Douglas, Col. Montagu W.	*Shakespeare's Signatures and "Sir Thomas More,* II*"* [A review of the book by Sir George Greenwood, II] [SF column]

1924, November 14 (no. 2141)
7	Ward, Col. Bernard R.	The Shakespeare Signatures and *Sir Thomas More* [SF column]

1924, November 21 (no. 2142)
2	Ward, Col. Bernard R.	The Annual Report 1923-24: Membership [SF column]

1924, November 28 (no. 2143)
10	Ward, Col. Bernard R.	The Annual Report 1923-24: *A Misdummer Night's Dream* [SF column]

1924, December 5 (no. 2144)
4	Ward, Col. Bernard R.	The Annual Report 1923-24: George Gascoigne [SF column]

1924, Decembner 12 (no. 2145)
9	Ward, Col. Bernard R.	The Annual Report 1923-24: Publications [SF column]

1924, December 19 (no. 2146)
21	Ward, Col. Bernard R.	The Earl of Derby as Shakespeare [SF column]

1925, January 2 (no. 2147)
2	Ward, Col. Bernard R.	The Annual Report 1923-24, V [SF column]

1925, January 9 (no. 2148)
5	Ward, Col. Bernard R.	The Annual Report 1923-24, VI [SF column]

1925, January 16 (no. 2149)
2	Douglas, Col. Montagu W.	*Venus and Adonis* and *Lucrece*: The Case for Bacon and Oxford, I [SF column]

1925, January 23 (no. 2150)
5	Douglas, Col. Montagu W.	*Venus and Adonis* and *Lucrece*: The Case for Bacon and Oxford, II [SF column]

1925, January 30 (no. 2151)
5	Douglas, Col. Montagu W.	*Venus and Adonis* and *Lucrece*: The Case for Bacon and Oxford, III [SF column]

1925, February 6 (no. 2152)
5	Douglas, Col. Montagu W.	*Venus and Adonis* and *Lucrece*: The Case for Bacon and Oxford, IV [SF column]

1925, February 13 (no. 2153)
5	Ward, Col. Bernard R.	The Initials "W.H." in the Earl Seventeenth Century [SF column]

1925, February 20 (no. 2154)
2	Knapp, Margaret I.	Notes on the Oxford Players [letter] [SF column]

1925, February 27 (no. 2155)
    5   Ward, Col. Bernard R.   *The Review of English Studies*, I [SF column]

1925, March 6 (no. 2156)
    4   Ward, Col. Bernard R.   *The Review of English Studies*, II [SF column]

1925, March 13 (no. 2157)
    5   Ward, Col. Bernard R.   The Trenthams and Castle Hedingham [SF column]

1925, March 20 (no. 2158)
    5   Ward, Col. Bernard R.   *Shakespeare's Mystery Play: A Study of "The Tempest,"* I [review of the book by Colin Still [SF column]

1925, March 27 (no. 2159)
    10   Ward, Col. Bernard R.   *Shakespeare's Mystery Play: A Study of "The Tempest,"* II [review of the book by Colin Still] [SF column]

Oxfordian articles in
The Shakespeare Pictorial (SHP)

A monthly illustrated chronicle of events in Shakespeareland. From January 1929 until December 1936, *The Shakespeare Pictorial* placed one page in each issue at the disposal of the Shakespearean Fellowship. The column on that page highlighted discoveries about Edward de Vere's authorship of the works attributed to Shakespeare and chronicled the degree to which acceptance of his authorship began to spread throughout the world.

These pieces have been reprinted in *Shakespeare Investigated: Publications of the Shakespeare Fellowship 1922-1936*, edited by James A. Warren and published by Veritas Publications.

No. 11 (1929, January)
4	Jaggard, Capt. William	[review of *The Shakespeare Mystery* by Georges Connes (1927)]
16	Ward, Col. Bernard R.	1928: An Important Year [SF page]

No. 12 (1929, February)
16	Ward, Col. Bernard R.	The Shakespeare Mystery; Brief But Lucid; Earlier French Research; Elizabethan Secret Service; Propaganda in Plays [SF page]
16	Looney, J. Thomas	Death of George Greenwood [letter] [SF page]
16	Lefranc, Abel	Colonel B. R. Ward [letter, in French] [SF page]

No. 13 (1929, March)
8	Newdigate, B. H.	[review of *Sh. and Chapman as Topical Dramatists* by Percy Allen]
14	Jaggard, William	The Shakespeare Fellowship and Baconian Blunders [letter]
16	Ward, Col. Bernard R.	Elizabethan Exchequer Figures [SF page]

No. 14 (1929, April)
11	Douglas, Col. Montagu	Baconian Blunders [letter]
11	Ward, Col. Bernard R.	School Fellow of Benson [letter]
16	Ward, Col. Bernard R.	Summary of Reviews of Captain Ward's *Seventeenth Earl of Oxford* (1928) [SF page]

No. 15 (1929, May)
24	Ward, Col. Bernard R.	[review of *Shakespeare and Chapman as Topical Dramatists* by Percy Allen (1929)] [SF page]
24	Jaggard, William	[letter: Oxfordians suffer from the virus of literary rabies]

No. 16 (1929, June)
12	Douglas, Col. Montagu	[letter: Secret Service funded Earl of Oxford 1586-1604]
20	Ward, Col. Bernard R.	Queen Elizabeth's "Parsimony" [SF page]

No. 17 (1929, July)
19	Ward, Col. Bernard R.	Queen Elizabeth and Secretary Davison; Fine of £10,000 Unpaid [SF page]
19	Nickson, Horace	[letter: the Shakespeare Fellowship's good fellowship]

No. 18 (1929, August)
14	Ward, Col. Bernard R.	Presentation to Professor Lefranc [SF page]

No. 19 (1929, September)
6	--	"Book Reviews" [review of *Shake-Speare's Sonnets Unmasked* by Bertram G. Theobald]
16	Ward, Col. Bernard R.	Annual General Meeting; What Lurks Behind Shakespeare's Historical Plays [SF page] [repr. in SON, vol. 56/3 (Summer 2020): 34-35]

No. 20 (1929, October)
16	Ward, Col. Bernard R.	Annual General Meeting [SF page]

No. 21 (1929, November)
20	Ward, Col. Bernard R.	Shakespeare and *Richard III* [SF page]
20	Douglas, Col. Montagu	[letter: reprint of his Sept. 19 letter to the *Morning Post*]

No. 22 (1929, December)
20	Ward, Col. Bernard R.	The Case for Oxford as Shakespeare [SF page]

No. 23 (1930, January)
16	Ward, Col. Bernard R.	The "Oxford Movement" [SF page]
16	--	[Cecil Palmer ad for Allen's *Case for Edward de Vere as Shakespeare*]

No. 24 (1930, February)
20	Ward, Col. Bernard R.	An Introduction to Shakespeare [review of *Shakespearian Fantasias* by Esther Singleton (I) (1929)] [SF page]
20	--	[John Murray ad for Ward's *The Seventeenth Earl of Oxford*]

No. 25 (1930, March)
13	--	Short review of Allen's *Case for Edward de Vere as Shakespeare*
16	Ward, Col. Bernard R.	A Poetical Alice in Wonderland [review of *Shakespearian Fantasias* by Esther Singleton (II) (1929)] [SF page]
16	--	[Cecil Palmer ad for Allen's *Case for Edward de Vere as Shakespeare*]

No. 26 (1930, April)
16	Ward, Col. Bernard R.	A New Study of the Sonnets (I): Review of *Shakespeare Sonnets and Edward de Vere* by Gerald H. Rendall (1930) [SF page]
16	--	[John Murray ad for Rendall's *Shakespeare Sonnets and Edward de Vere*]

No. 27 (1930, May)
8	--	[review of *The Case for Edward de Vere, 17th Earl of Oxford As "Shakespeare"* by Percy Allen (1930)]
16	Ward, Col. Bernard R.	A Government Propaganda Department; A Literary Group; First Annual Dinner [SF page]
16	Clarke, Francis	A Literary Group [letter] [SF page]

No. 28 (1930, June)
16	Ward, Col. Bernard R.	Captain Ward's Researches [SF page]

No. 29 (1930, July)
9	Jacques	Three Famous Shakespeareans: Mr. Henry Cay Folger, Sir Israel Gollancz, Dr. Horace Howard Furness [obituaries]
16	Ward, Col. Bernard R.	Brooke House, Hackney [SF page]
16	Palmer, Cecil	John Lyly and the Office of the Revels [letter to Colonel B. R. Ward praising Captain B. M. Ward's researches] [SF page]

No. 30 (1930, August)
16	Ward, Col. Bernard R.	The Shakespeare Cult [SF page]
16	Ward, Col. Bernard R.	Death of Miss Esther Singleton [obituary] [SF page]
16	--	[Cecil Palmer ad for Gilbert Standen's pamphlet *Shakespeare Authorship: A Summary of Evidence* (1930)] [SF page]

No. 31 (1930, September)
6	--	[review of *Shakespeare Authorship* by Gilbert Standen]
16	Ward, Col. Bernard R.	[review of *The Case for Edward de Vere, 17th Earl of Oxford, as "Shakespeare"* by Percy Allen (1930)] [SF page]
16	Ward, Col. Bernard R.	Forthcoming Lectures; Lavenham Past and Present; Annual General Meeting [SF page]

No. 32 (1930, October)
16	Ward, Col. Bernard R.	Which Was the Earliest Propaganda Play? [SF page]
16	Ward, Col. Bernard R.	[review of *Shakespeare Authorship: A Summary of Evidence* by Gilbert Standen (1930)] [SF page]
16	Ward, Col. Bernard R.	Mr. Allen's Lectures [SF page]

No. 33 (1930, November)
16	Ward, Col. Bernard R.	Henry Wriothesley and Henry De Vere [SF page]
16	Boissevan, K. D. W.	The Farnese Library [letter to Colonel Ward about Oxford in Holland in 1585, citing entries in the Farnese Library] [SF page]

No. 34 (1930, December)
16	Ward, Col. Bernard R.	A Challenge and Its Acceptance [SF page]

No. 35 (1931, January)

| 16 | Ward, Col. Bernard R. | Facts Collected. Problems Unsolved. [review of *William Shakespeare: a Study of Facts and Problems* by Sir Edmund Chambers] [SF page] |

No. 36 (1931, February)

| 32 | Ward, Col. Bernard R. | A New Shakespeare Chronology [review of *Shakespeare's Plays in the Order of Their Writing* by Eva Turner Clark (1931)] [SF page] |

No. 37 (1931, March)

| 42 | Allen, Percy | Historic Identity of Sir Toby Belch [letter] |
| 48 | Ward, Col. Bernard R. | [review of *The Oxford-Shakespeare Case Corroborated* by Percy Allen (1931)] [SF page] |

No. 38 (1931, April)

| 62 | -- | [Payson ad for Singleton's *Shakespearian Fantasias* and Clark's *Hidden Allusions* and Palmer ad for Clark's *Shakespeare's Plays in the Order of Their Writing*] |
| 63 | Ward, Col. Bernard R. | Oxford's Handwriting [review of *Shake-Speare: Handwriting and Spelling* by Gerald H. Rendall (1931)] [response to *TLS.*, Sept. 25, 1930; see also Byrne's Sept. 11, 1930 review of Allen's *Case*] [SF page] |

No. 39 (1931, May)

| 80 | Ward, Col. Bernard R. | Marlowe and His Circle [review of *Marlowe and His Circle* by Frederich S. Boas (1931)] [SF page] |
| 80 | -- | [Palmer ad for *Shakespeare's Plays in the Order of Their Writing* by Eva Turner Clark; *The Oxford-Shakespeare Case Corroborated* by Percy Allen; and *Shake-Speare: Handwriting and Spelling* by G. H. Rendall |

No. 40 (1931, June)

| 96 | Ward, Col. Bernard R. | The Annual Dinner [SF page] |
| 96 | -- | [Palmer ad for *Shakespeare's Plays in the Order of Their Writing* by Eva Turner Clark; *The Oxford-Shakespeare Case Corroborated* by Percy Allen; and *Shake-Speare: Handwriting and Spelling* by G. H. Rendall] |

No. 41 (1931, July)

110	Frisbee, George	[letter]
116	Ward, Col. Bernard R.	Sir Edmund Chambers in America [SF page]
116	--	[Palmer ad for *Shakespeare's Plays in the Order of Their Writing* by Eva Turner Clark; *The Oxford-Shakespeare Case Corroborated* by Percy Allen; and *Shake-Speare: Handwriting and Spelling* by G. H. Rendall]

No. 42 (1931, August)

| 132 | Ward, Col. Bernard R. | The Records of the Court Revels [shows that documents in the records are copies] [SF page] |

No. 43 (1931, September) [cover mistakenly says August]

| 139 | -- | The Churches of Shakespeareland. no. 11: St. John the Baptist, Henley-in-Arden |
| 148 | Ward, Col. Bernard R. | The Shining Possibilities of Anne Vavasour [response to Willoughby's May 2 *Saturday Review* article] [SF page] |

No. 44 (1931, October)

| 164 | Ward, Col. Bernard R. | The Original Venus and Adonis [review of the book by H. T. S. Forrest (1930)] [SF page] |
| 157 | -- | The Folger Shakespeare Library |

No. 45 (1931, November)

| 180 | Ward, Col. Bernard R. | [reviews of *The Earl of Oxford as Shakespeare* by Lt-Colonel Montagu W. Douglas (1931) and *Seven Shakespeares* by Gilbert Slater] [SF page] |
| 181 | -- | [Palmer and Payson joint ad for Clark's book (see April 1931)] |

No. 46 (1931, December)

189	--	*Twelfth Night* Produced by Shakespeare at the Swan Theatre, 1596 [with drawing of stage and scene]
196	Ward, Col. Bernard R.	A Great Shakespeare Discovery [SF page]
197	--	[Palmer and Payson joint ad for Clark's book (see April 1931)]

No. 47 (1932, January)

14-15	Limons, L.	A Reply from Holland [letter]
15	--	Heraldry in *The Merry Wives of Windsor*
16	Ward, Col. Bernard R.	Mr. Justice Shallow [SF page]

No. 48 (1932, February)

30	Ward, Capt. Bernard M.	The Swan Theatre [letter]
32	Ward, Capt. Bernard M.	*The Merry Wives of Windsor* and The Order of the Garter [SF page]

No. 49 (1932, March)

48	Douglas, Col. Montagu	[review of *The Life Story of Edward de Vere as Shakespeare"* by Percy Allen (1932)] [SF page]
48	Ward, Capt. Bernard M.	L. J. Maxse [obituary] [SF page]

No. 50 (1932, April)

68	Ward, Capt. Bernard M.	The Three Williams in Shakespeare [SF page]

No. 51 (1932, May)

82-83	Bowen, Marjorie	The Identity of 'William Shakespeare [review of *The Case for Edward de Vere As 'William Shakespeare'* by Percy Allen (1930)] [SF page]

No. 52 (1932, June)

100	Allen, Percy	[review of *The Essential Shakespeare* by J. Dover Wilson (1932)] [SF page]

No. 53 (1932, July)

116	Allen, Ernest	Annual Dinner [SF page]

No. 54 (1932, August)

132	Kennedy-Skipton, H. K.	[review of *The Tragic Story of Shakespeare* by G. W. Phillips] [SF page]

No. 55 (1932, September)

140-41	--	Folger Shakespeare Library at Washington, U. S. A.: A Munificent Gift to the world in Memory of Shakespeare
144	--	The Shakespeare Garden
148	Ward, Capt. Bernard M.	[review of *The Date of Love's Labour's Lost* by Rupert Taylor] [SF page]

No. 56 (1932, October)

150	--	Lectures on *Twelfth Night* (by Percy Allen)
160	Frisbee, George	De Vere Champion [letter]
164	Allen, Percy	The Inner Story of *Twelfth Night* [SF page]

No. 57 (1932, November)

180	Ward, Capt. Bernard M.	Annual General Meeting [SF page]
180	Douglas, Col. Montagu	Ben Jonson and Shakespeare (Part 1) [SF page]

No. 58 (1932, December)

196	Douglas, Col. Montagu	Ben Jonson and Shakespeare (Part 2) [SF page]

No. 59 (1933, January)

12-13	Ward, Col. Bernard R.	A Protest Addressed to the Editor of the *Review of English Studies* [response to G. C. Moore Smith's October 1932 article.] [SF page]

No. 60 (1933, February)

22-23	Allen, Percy	*King Lear* – The Castle and the Storm: An Adventure in Burgundy [SF page]

No. 61 (1933, March)

37	Allen, Percy	Mr. John Drinkwater's *Shakespeare* [review of *Shakespeare* by John Drinkwater (1933)
37	--	Mr. Bridges Adams Addresses the Stage Society
48	Douglas, Lt. Col. W. M.	Edward de Vere and Academic Scholarship [SF page]

No. 62 (1933, April)

60	Bayley, M. F.	Bacon's and Shakespeare's Manuscripts in One Portfolio Response by J. Denham Parsons in the May issue.
64	Bowen, Marjorie	[review of *Shakespeare* by John Drinkwater (1933)] [SF page]

No. 63 (1933, May)

68	Parsons, J. Denham	Son of Elizabeth [letter: Bayley's April 1933 article.]
80	Allen, Percy	Sir Edmund Chambers and Shakespearean Orthodoxy [SF page]

No. 64 (1933, June)

92	Douglas, Montagu W.	Death of Colonel Ward [letter, with photo of Col. Ward] [SF page]
92-93	Ward, Capt. Bernard M.	Annual Dinner [SF page]

No. 65 (1933, July)

112	Ward, Capt. Bernard M.	The Shakespeare Family in Contemporary Satire [SF page]

No. 66 (1933, August)

128	Holland, Adm. Hubert H.	The Four Continental Suitors in *Merchant of Venice* [SF page]

No. 67 (1933, September)

144	Douglas, Col. Montagu W.	[review of *The Plays of Shakespeare & Chapman in Relation to French History* by Percy Allen (1929)] [SF page]

No. 68 (1933, October)

159	--	Honour for Mr. Percy Allen
160	Ward, Capt. Bernard M.	The Virginia Company and *The Tempest* [SF page]

No. 69 (1933, November)

176	Allen, Percy	[review of *Shakespeare At Work* by G. B. Harrison (1933)] [SF page]

No. 70 (1933, December)

192	Ward, Capt. Bernard M.	[review of *Shakespeare, Oxford, and Elizabethan Times* by Admiral H. H. Holland (1933)] [SF page]

No. 71 (1934, January)

D1	Paulina	[letter: re Holland's *Sh., Oxford and Elizabethan Times*]
14	--	The Other Side of the Atlantic [percy Allen planning speaking tour of North America]
14	--	Lecture on the Elizabethan Drama [by Percy Allen at the Livingstone Hall, Westminster]
14	Noble, Frederic Perry	[letter: re Allen's Nov. 1933 review of Harrison's *Shakespeare at Work*]
16	Allen, Percy	[review of *The Satirical Comedy, Love's Labour's Lost* by Eva Clark (1933)] [SF page]
17	--	Francis Clarke/the Gower Bookshop ad for "Mr. Looney's Pioneer Books. Reduced Price.

No. 72 (1934, February)

30-31	Colson, F. H.	Ben Jonson's "Discoveries" ("Timber") & Shakespeare [SF page]
20	Allen, Percy	[letter: long reply to Perry Noble]
20	Holland, H. H.	[letter: reply to Perry Noble]

No. 73 (1934, March)

48	Bowen, Marjorie	[Review of *Anne Cecil, Elizabeth and Oxford* by Percy Allen (1934)] [SF page]

No. 74 (1934, April)

63	Millar, J. S. L.	The 'Shakespeare' Group [SF page]

No. 75 (1934, May)

80	Slater, Gilbert	Shakespeare's Literary Executor [SF page]

No. 76 (1934, June)

84	--	Arthur Golding Memorial (at which Percy Allen spoke)
84	--	Shakespeare Fellowship Dinner
96	Douglas, Col. Montagu	The "Oxford Movement" in France [SF page]

No. 77 (1934, July)

112	Allen, Percy	A Year's Results Epitomised [SF page]

No. 78 (1934, August)

128	Slater, Gilbert	Can We Agree? [SF page]

No. 79 (1934, September)

144	Ward, Capt. Bernard M.	[review of *A Companion to Sh. Studies* by G. B. Harrison] [SF page]
149	Ward, Capt. Bernard M.	Shakespeare's Plays as Dramatized History [upcoming lectures by Percy Allen]

No. 80 (1934, October)

156-57	Holland, Adm. Hubert	Date Analysis of *The Merchant of Venice*, and the Locality of Belmont [SF page]
157	Dewhurst, J. T.	Can We Agree? [letter: Response to Gilbert Slater's Aug. 1934 article "Can We Agree?"]
157	Slater, Gilbert	Can We Agree? [letter: Reply to J. T. Dewhurst's response]

No. 81 (1934, November)

173	Hipkiss, F. W.	Can We Agree [letter]
173	Greenwood, Elsie	A Response [letter]
173	Blaauw, J. R.	From Holland [letter]
176	Douglas, Col. Montagu	[rev. of *A Companion to Sh. Studies* by J. W. MacKail (1934)] [SF page]

No. 82 (1934, December)

190	McCormick, A. D.	The Prince of Wales Christmas Card [Shows Queen Elizabeth giving an audience to Shakespeare]
192	Millar, J. S. L.	Shakespeare and *Sir Thomas More* [SF page]

No. 83 (1935, January)

16	Ward, Capt. Bernard M.	[review of *Lord Oxford Was Shakespeare* by Lt. Colonel Montagu W. Douglas] [SF page]

No. 84 (1935, February)

32	Simpson, H. B.	[reviews of *Personal Clues in Sh. Poems and Sonnets* by Gerald Rendall, and of *Sh.'s Sonnets* by Gerald Phillips] [SF page]

No. 85 (1935, March)

48	Ward, Capt. Bernard M.	*Hamlet* [SF page]

No. 86 (1935, April)

64	Looney, J. Thomas	Jonson v. Jonson (Part 1) [SF page]

No. 87 (1935, May)

80	Looney, J. Thomas	Jonson v. Jonson (Part 2) [SF page]

No. 88 (1935, June)

93	Allen, Percy	Our Year's Activities [SF page]

No. 89 (1935, July)

102	A. B.	A More Important Christopher Sly [letter]
112	Allen, Percy	[review of *Sunlight On Shakespeare's Sonnets* by G. W. Phillips (1935)] [SF page]

No. 90 (1935, August)

120	Looney, J. Thomas	A More Important Christopher Sly [response to A. B.'s July article]
128	Ward, Capt. Bernard M.	The Trentham Family [SF page]

No. 91 (1935, September)

144	Holland, Adm. Hubert	[review of *Hamlet* edited by John Dover Wilson (1934)] [SF page]

No. 92 (1935, October)

158	Allen, Ernest	The Sonnets [letter: Evidence in the *Sonnets* points to Lord Oxford]
160	Douglas, Col. Montagu	The Shakespearean Group [SF page]

No. 93 (1935, November)

165	Holland, Adm. Hubert	Who was Yorick? [letter]
172	Allen, Percy	Yet Another Contender [letter: The Shakespeare monument at Stratford] [response to George Corlius' October article.]
176	Looney, J. Thomas	Lord Oxford and the Shrew Plays (Part 1) [repr. in BTC, vol. 2: 17-19] [SF page]
176	Ward, Capt. Bernard M.	Notices: The Late Canon A. K. Hobart-Hampden

No. 94 (1935, December)

190-91	Looney, J. Thomas	Lord Oxford and the Shrew Plays (Part 2) [repr. in BTC, vol. 2: 20-24] [SF page]
191	Bridgewater, H.	The Missing Plays of the Earl of Oxford [letter: Response to Looney]

No. 95 (1936, January)

8	Millar, J. S. L.	Falstaff's Last Utterance [SF page]

No. 96 (1936, February)

| 36 | Allen, Percy | More *Hamlet* Problems [review of *The Manuscript of Shakespeare's Hamlet, and The Problems of Its Transmission* by John Dover Wilson] [SF page] |

No. 97 (1936, March)

| 52 | Ward, Capt. Bernard M. | The Original Order of Shakespeare's *Sonnets* [review of Denys Bray's book] SF page] |

No. 98 (1936, April)

| 68 | Rendall, Gerald H. | [review of *Shakespeare's Wild Flowers, Fairy Lore, Gardens and Herbs* by Eleanor S. Rohde (1935)] [SF page] |

No. 99 (1936, May)

| 84 | Allen, Percy | Shakespeare's Imagery [review of the book by Suprgeon] [SF page] |

No. 100 (1936, June)

| 100 | Holland, Adm. Hubert | Date Analysis of *Romeo and Juliet*: Lammas-tide or Summer-tide? [SF page] |

No. 101 (1936, July)

| 116 | Allen, Ernest | Claimants to "Shakespeare" Authorship [See E.S.'s response in the August issue and Allen's reply in September.] [SF page] |

No. 102 (1936, August)

| 128 | E. S. | [letter: resp. to E. Allen's article; see also Allen's reply in the Sept. issue] |
| 132 | Allen, Percy | Topical Events in Drama of Shakespeare's Age [SF page] |

No. 103 (1936, September)

| 136 | Allen, Ernest | [letter: response to E. S.'s Aug. 1936 letter] |
| 148 | Ward, Capt. Bernard M. | [review *of Shakespeare and the Homilies* by Alfred Hart (1934)] [SF page] |

No. 104 (1936, October)

| 164 | Allen, Percy | Another Bombshell for the Orthodox [review of *The Problem of Hamlet – A Solution* by A. S. Cairncross (1936)] [SF page] |

No. 105 (1936, November)

| 180 | Allen, Ernest | Criticism From Australia [SF page] |

No. 106 (1936, December)

| 196 | Douglas, Col. Montagu | Last Words From the Shakespeare Fellowship [final SF] [SF page] |

No. 108 (1937, February)

| 27 | Frisbee, George | Shakespeare Fellowship [letter] |
| 28 | K. C. T. | "Ingenuity and Acumen" [review of *Lord Burghley in Shakespeare* by G. W. Phillips] |

No. 109 (1937, March)

| 36 | Phillips, G. W. | "Lord Burghley in Shakespeare" [letter: resp. to the February review] |
| 36 | Eagle, R. L. | Heminge and Condell [letter] |

No. 110 (1937, April)

| 61 | Walton, Sara | What Rosalind said [letter: Rosalind's reference to her child's father in AYLI, I.iii] |

No. 116 (1937, October)

| 152 | Ward, Capt. Bernard M. | Mr. Percy Allen [letter] |

No. 124 (1938, June)

| 91 | E. S. | Secrets of the Sonnets: Review of *The Sonnets of William Shakespeare and Henry Wriothesley, Third Earl of Southampton, Together With A Lover's Complaint and the Phoenix and Turtle* by Walter Thomson |

No. 125 (1938, July)

| 107 | Allen, Percy | Pirate Publishers [letter: *Macbeth* was abbreviated acting version] |

No. 143 (1939, January)

| 8 | Allen, Percy | Opening Spencer's Grave [long letter: Oxford's remains are at Westminster Abbey |

Oxfordian articles in
The East Anglian Magazine (EAM)

Listed here are the pieces published on the Shakespearean Page edited by F. Lingard Ranson, as well as others addressing the Oxfordian idea. All have been reprinted in *Shakespeare Investigated: Publications of the Shakespeare Fellowship 1922-1936*, edited by James A. Warren and published by Veritas Publications.

Vol. 2/7 (1937, April)

290	Editor [John Raithel]	Comments: Shakespeare and East Anglia
292-300	Ranson, F. Lingard	Shakespeare Was an East Anglian [repr. in BTC, vol. 2: 42-55]

Vol. 2/8 (1937, May)

338	Editor [John Riathel]	Comments [was "Shakespeare" an East Anglian?]
340-45	Allen, Percy	Lord Oxford as Shakespeare [repr. in BTC, vol. 2: 5] [See commentary in *The Bury Free Press*, April 24]
360-61	Buckley, E. R.	Was Shakespeare an East Anglian? [letter: resp. to Ranson]
361-62	Brereton, Cloudesley	"Shakespeare"—A "Stage Manager" [letter: response to Ranson]
362	Lay, C. H.	Shakespeare, a Suffolk Man [letter: resp. to Ranson]
362	Lloyd, S. Massy	Controversy Will Lead to Nothing [letter: resp. to Ranson]
362	Watson, W.	"Shakespeare Was a Welshman!" [letter: resp. to Ranson]
362-63	Redstone, V. B.	Was Shakespeare an East Anglian? [letter: resp. to Ranson]
363	T. R. Newsl.	Arms of the 17th Earl of Oxford [letter: resp. to Ranson]

Vol. 2/9 (1937, June)

385	Editor [John Raithel]	Comment ["Rambler" and "Shakespeare." Francis Bacon.]
392-96	Stokes, Roy	Bacon and "Shakespeare"
421-23	Ranson, F. Lingard	[reply to letters]
423-24	Rash, D. E. A.	Shakespeare was an East Anglian [letter]
424	Shakespeare, Geoffrey	Shakespeare was an East Anglian [letter]
424	Keeble, Ida M. Everett	"Was Shakespeare an East Anglian?" [letter]
424	Buckley, Eric R.	Was Shakespeare an East Anglian? [letter]
425	J. B. S.	"Follow the Bacon Myth" [letter]

[Note: see commentary on this issue in *The Bury Free Press*, June 5, 1937]

Vol. 2/10 (1937, July)

467-68	Ranson, F. Lingard	[letter: "Bacon and 'Shakespeare'" by Mr. Roy Stokes]
468	Stokes, Roy	[letter: correction to his article in the June issue]
468	W. W.	Five Signatures of Six [letter: Stokes's "Bacon" article]
469	Usherwood, E. C.	The Droeshout Portrait of Shakespeare [letter:Stokes's "Bacon" article]
469	Grieveson, P. L.	The Droeshout Portrait of Shakespeare [letter: Stokes's "Bacon" article]

Vol. 2/11 (1937, August)

506-08	Stokes, Roy	Bacon and "Shakespeare" [reply to responses to his "Bacon" article]
518	Editor [John Raithel]	Lord Oxford and "Shakespeare" [launching of the monthly "Shakespearean Page" edited by F. Lingard Ranson]

Vol. 2/12 (1937, September)

530-32	Ranson, F. Kingard	Lord Oxford and Shakespeare [letter: reply to Roy Stokes]
537-38	Allen, Ernest	Shakespearean Page [repr. in BTC, vol. 2: 34 with the title "Shakespeare's Sonnets"]

Vol. 3/1 (1937, October)

40-41	Ward, Capt. Bernard M.	Shakespearean Page [the dating of Shakespeare's plays] [repr. in BTC, vol. 2: 38-39]
41	Ward, Capt. Bernard M.	[review of *When Shakespeare Died* by Ernest Allen] [repr. in BTC, vol. 2: 40-41] Response by Mr. Morfey, Jan. 1938. Reply by Ward, Feb. 1938.

Vol. 4/7 (1939, June)

    412-13   Ranson, F. Lingard   Shakespearean Page: Chronology [Based on notes sent by Col. Montagu W. Douglas, President of the Sh. Fellowship]

Vol. 4/8 (1939, July)

    439-40   Hipperson, Mary   The Shakespearean Page: The Other View-point

Vol. 4/9 (1939, August)

    533-34   Pattinson, J. P.   The Shakespearean Page [letter: Shakespearean chronology

    534-35   Allen, Percy   The Other View-point [letter: Hipperson's article]

Vol. 4/10 (1939, September)

    590-93   Barrell, Charles Wisner   Shakespearean Page: "An Elizabethan Puritan," Part 1 [review of *An Elizabethan Puritan: The Life of Arthur Golding* by Louis T. Golding]

    595-96   Douglas, Col. Montagu W.   Shakespearean Chronology [letter: Pattison's article]

Vol. 4/11 (1939, October)

    627-28   Hipperson, Mary   "Shakespeare" The Other Viewpoint" [letter: reply to Douglas]

    631-33   Barrell, Charles Wisner   Shakespearean Page: "An Elizabethan Puritan," Part 2 [review of *An Elizabethan Puritan: The Life of Arthur Goldingn* by Louis T. Golding]

Vol. 4/12 (1939, November)

    688-92   Barrell, Charles Wisner   Shakespearean Page: "An Elizabethan Puritan," Part 3 [review of *An Elizabethan Puritan: The Life of Arthur Golding* by Louis T. Golding]

Not published: December 1939

Vol. 5/1 (1940, January)

    11   Editor   Shakespearean Fellowship in America

    16-17   Allen, Percy   Shakespearean Page: Moai Doth Sway My Life

Vol. 5/2 (1940, February)

    62-63   Douglas, Col. Montagu W.   Ben Jonson and the First Folio Edition [review of the pamphlet by Gerald H. Rendall] [repr. in BTC, vol. 2: 59-61]

    63   Ranson, F. Lingard   Mr. Ernest Allen [obituary] [repr. in BTC, vol. 2: 59-61]

Not published: March 1940

Vol. 5/3 (1940, April)

    121-22   Douglas, Col. Montagu W.   Shakespearean Page: The American Branch of the Shakespeare Fellowship [repr. in BTC, vol. 2: 62-64]

Vol. 5/4 (1940, May)

    153-54   Allen, Percy   Shakespearean Page: Shakespeare's *Cymbeline* and East Anglia

Not published: June, July, August 1940

Vol. 5/5 (1940, September)

    186-87   Ranson, F. Lingard   Shakespearean Page: The Case for the Jury

Not Published: October 1940-March 1941

Vol. 5/6 (1941, April)

    229-30   Allen, Percy   Shakespearean Page: The "Ashbourne" Portrait of Shakespeare [review of the pamphlet by Gerald H. Rendall]

Oxfordian articles in
The Shakespeare Newsletter (SHNL)

A scholarly journal that began publication in 1951 under the editorship of Louis Marder. The English Department at Iona College became the publisher in 1991. Many of these articles appeared on the monthly page sponsored by the Russell des Cognets Fund, Shakespeare-Oxford Society, from 1979 to 1991.

No. 10?, vol. 2/6 (1952, Sept.)

Feldman, A. Bronson   Who is Shakespeare? What is He? [repr. in *Sh., Marlowe, . . .* (2022): 6-7]

No. 11?, vol. 2/7 (1952, Sept.)

13   --   The "Earl of Oxford's" *Tempest*? [note about *Shakespeare's Farewell* by Gwynneth Bowen (pamphlet)]

No. 14?, vol. 3/1 (1953, Feb.)

2   --   Of Heresies and Heretics

No. 29?, vol. 5/5-6 (1955, Nov.-Dec.)

40   --   Gestation of the Baconian Heresy [report on Louis J. Budd's "The Baconians: Madness Through Method," *So. Atlantic Quart.*, LIV:3 (July 1955), 359-368]

40   --   Critical Reviews [report on an anonymous review in the *Times Lit. Sup.*, No. 2783 (July 1, 55): 371, of Hilda Amphlett's *Who Was Shakespeare?*]

No. 32, vol. 6/3 (1956, May)

18   Montgomery, Robert H. &   To the Editor and Readers of *The Shakespeare Newsletter* [An open
     Arthur Stanwood Pier,   letter signed by 22 distinguished Americans stating that recent
     Stanley P. Lowell,   research proves that Shakespeare was the pseudonym of
     William McFee,   Edward de Vere]
     Peter Sammartino,
     Sidney S. Alderman, Charles D. Drayton, Morris Llewellyn Cooke,
     Thomas F. Fleming, Thomas H. Hennings, David Winton,
     Dudley Nichols, Harry A. Wembridge, Julian Avery,
     Lester D. Egbert, Earl Harding, Alfred Winslow Jones,
     Andre Michalopoulos, Charlton Ogburn, William Mason,
     John Varney, Rudolph von Bernuth

18   Marder, Louis   Who Wrote Shakespeare? [editorial]

No. 34, vol. 6/5-6 (1956, Nov.-Dec.)

38   Editor   Critical Reviews [note on rev. of Evans' *Sh.'s Magic Circle* in *TLS* (July 6): 410]

No. 48, vol. 9/2 (1959, April)

12   --   Critical Reviews [review of *The Six Loves of "Shakespeare"* by Louis P. Bénézet]

No. 51, vol. 9/5 (1959, Nov.)

39   --   Digests of Periodical Reviews [summaries of reviews in *Sh. Quarterly*, summer '59: 435-7, of R. C. Churchill's *Sh. and His Betters: A History of the Attempts Which Have Been Made to Prove that Shakespeare's Works Were Written by Others* and Frank Wadsworth's *The Poacher from Stratford: A Partial Account of the Controversy over the Authorship of Sh's Plays*]

No. 54, vol. 10/3 (1960, May)

29   --   On Shakespearean Heretics [summary of Wright's "The Anti-Shakespearean Industry and the Growth of Cults," in *Virginia Qu. Review*, vol. 35 (Spring 1959): 289-303]

No. 58, vol. 11/2 (1961, April)

13   Hopkins, Vivian C.   The Baconian Theory: An Enchanted Wood

No. 66, vol. 12/4 (1962, Sept.)

28-29   Marder, Louis   Shakespeare's Bones, Birthplace and Burial, Part 1 [response to the editorials and flurry of letters in *The Times* and *The New York Times* Aug. 30-Sept. 21]

No. 67, vol. 12/5 (1962, Nov.)
35-36   Marder, Louis   Shakespeare's Bones, Birthplace and Burial, Part 2 [response to the editorials and flurry of letters in *The Times* and The *New York Times* Aug. 30-Sept. 21]

No. 69, vol. 13/1 (1963, Feb.)
1   Marder, Louis   Quest for Shakespeare Manuscripts and Exposure of "Sham Shakespeare" Continues Among "Heretics"

No. 70, vol. 13/2 (1963, April)
1   Marder, Louis   Authorship Question Still Inspiring Research Among Disbelievers
16-17   Marder, Louis   Questions and Answers on the Authorship of Shakespeare [repr. with commentary by Rhoda Messner in SON, vol. 12/3: 6-8 (Fall, 1976); SON, vol. 12/4: 3-6 (Winter, 1976); and SON, vol. 13/1: 8-10 (Spring, 1977); and in BTC, vol. 6: 94-111]

No. 71, vol. 13/3 (1963, May)
1   Marder, Louis   Authorship Controversy Continues; No Solution Yet

No. 72, vol. 13/4 (1963, Sept.)
1   Marder, Louis   Shakespeare Debate Continues: Oxfordians Submit More Questions

No. 74, vol. 13/6 (1963, Dec.)
55   Feldman, A. Bronson   The March of Hamlet [repr. in *Shakespeare, Marlowe, . . .* (2022): 81-82]

No. 76, vol. 14/2-3 (1964, April-May)
46   Wadsworth, Frank W.   The Authorship Question

No. 78, vol. 14/5 (1964, Nov.)
69, 74   --   Bacon Society Wins Funds for Seeking Shakespeare Manuscripts

No. 79, vol. 14/6 (1964, Dec.)
77   Marder, Louis ,   The Computer and Shakespearean Scholarship
81   Craig, Hardin   The Study of Shakespeare, Part I: Advice

No. 80, vol. 15/1 (1965, Feb.)
6   Craig, Hardin   The Study of Shakespeare, Part II: Essentials

No. 81, vol. 15/2 (1965, April)
12   Craig, Hardin   The Study of Shakespeare, Part III: Explanations

No. 83, vol. 15/4 (1965, Sept.)
31   --   Was Shakespeare Shakespeare? [review of *Was Shakespeare Shakespeare?* by Milward W. Martin]
35   --   Who Was Shakespeare? [advertisement]
38   Freud and the Controversy Over Shakespearean Authorship

No. 88, vol. 16/3 (1966, May)
27   --   The Literary Amateur Detectives [excerpts from the review of Churchill's *Shakespeare and His Betters*, in *Sh.-Jahrbuch*, 1965, 146-60]

No. 98, vol. 18/2 (1968, April)
10   --   The Authorship Controversy
10   Trevor-Roper, H. B.   [letter: disavowal of Francis Carr's interpretation of his position]

No. 107, vol. 20/1-2-3 (1970, Feb. April, May)
17   --   *Shakespearean Authorship Review* Celebrates 50th Anniversary of Book

No. 123, vol. 23/1 (1973, Feb.)
6   Marder, Louis   [review of *Wasn't Shakespeare Someone Else?* by Ralph L. Tweedale]

No. 136, vol. 25/3 (1975, May)
27   Marder, Louis   Authorship Problem: Stretching Credulity

No. 148, vol. 27/3 (1977, May)
1, 26   Marder, Louis   Imaginary Life of Shakespeare for TV

No. 155, vol. 28/5-6 (1978, Nov/Dec)
38   Marder, Louis   Shakespeare by Hilliard?

No. 157, vol. 29/1 (1979, April)
10   Marder, Louis   Shakespeareans: Who are They?
10   Marder, Louis   The Oxfordian Movement [news and scholarship in the Oxfordian Periodicals]
11   --   The Shakespeare-Oxford Society In America [advertisement]

No. 158, vol. 29/2 (1979, May)
22   Cyr, Gordon C.   The Case for Edward de Vere, 17th Earl of Oxford as "Shakespeare"

No. 159, vol. 29/3 (1979, September)
30   Cyr, Gordon C.   The Case for Edward de Vere, 17th Earl of Oxford as "Shakespeare"

No. 160, vol. 29/4 (1979, November)
38   Cyr, Gordon C.   Why Are There Doubts About "Shakespeare's" Authorship?

No. 161, vol. 29/5 (1979, December)
41-42   Marder, Louis   Stylometrics: The New Authorship Weapon
43-44   Jackson, MacDonald   A Hint for Investigators of Authorship
47   Cyr, Gordon C.   Some Common Replies to the "Authorship Doubters"

No. 162, vol. 30/1 (1980, February)
9   Marder, Louis   Famous People Comment on the Shakespearean Authorship

No. 163, vol. 30/2 (1980, April)
17   Cyr, Gordon C.   How to Construct a "Shakespeare Biography"

No. 164, vol. 30/3 (1980, May)
22   Cyr, Gordon C.   A Prediction of the Oxford Theory? [by George G. Greenwood]

No. 165, vol. 30/4 (1980, September)
29   Marder, Louis   Stylometry 'Proves' Entire *Sir Thomas More* is All Shakespeare's
35   Cyr, Gordon C.   Latest *Sir Thomas More* Findings Point to Lord Oxford as "Shakespeare"

No. 166, vol. 30/5 (1980, November)
42   Cyr. Gordon C.   Oxford's 1604 Death Is No Bar To His Authorship

No. 167, vol. 30/6 (1980, December)
48   Cyr, Gordon C.   Polonius as Lord Burleigh: Oxford's Revenge on His Father-in-law?

No. 168, vol. 31/1 (1981, Feb.)
4   Cyr, Gordon C.   The Latest Shakespearean Mare's Nest: Southampton's "Secretary"
7   --   Oxfordian Essay Contest

No. 170, vol. 31/3 (1981, May)
20   Cyr, Gordon C.   The Case of the 'Alias' Earl!

No. 171, vol. 31/4 (1981, September-November)
27   Cyr, Gordon C.   "Shakespere" vs. Webster as *More*'s Author: A Heretical View

No. 172, vol. 31/5 (1981, December)
38   Cyr, Gorgon C.   A Literary Scholar Looks at Lord Oxford's Poetry

No. 173, vol. 32/1 (1982, February)
6   Cyr, Gordon C.   A Literary Scholar Looks at Lord Oxford's Poetry, Part II

No. 174, vol. 32/2 (1982, April-May)
11   Cyr, Gordon C.   Skeptical Thoughts on the "Paper Chase"

No. 175, vol. 32/3 (1982, Fall)
22   Cyr, Gordon C.   Would It Hold Up in Court?
22   Ramey, Paul   A Skeptical Thought about the "Skeptical Thoughts" of Oxfordians

No. 176, vol. 32/4 (1982, Winter)
32   Cyr, Gordon C.   A Literary Scholar Looks at Oxford's Poetry: Mr. Ramsey's Straw Man

No. 177, vol. 33/1 (1983, Spring)
6   Marder, Louis   Authorship and the Oxfordians
6   Cyr, Gordon C.   The Glass House at Stratford

No. 178, vol. 33/2 (1983, Summer)
19   Cyr, Gordon C.   More on the Stratfordians' Glass House

No. 179, vol. 33/3 (1983, Fall)
30   Cyr, Gordon C.   Was Shakespeare Really an Ignoramus?

No. 180, vol. 33/4 (1983, Winter)
41   Cyr, Gordon C.   Was Shakespeare Really an Ignoramus?, Part II

No. 181, vol. 34/1 (1984, Spring)
8-9   Cyr, Gordon C.   What Can We At Least Find Out About the *Sonnets*?
9   Marder, Louis   Anti-Stratfordians Active in Los Angeles

Shakespeare Newsletter (SHNL)

IID: OXFORDIAN ARTICLES IN NON-OXFORDIAN PERIODICALS

Aberdeen Daily Journal (Aberdeen, Scotland)

1919, Dec. 22, p. 3.	--	[notice about upcoming publication of *"Shakespeare" Identified*]
1920, April 5, p. 2	--	"Shakespeare" [long review of *"Shakespeare Identified*]
1922, Oct. 23, p. 2	--	Bacon-Shakespeare Controversy [mentions J. Thomas Looney and Edward de Vere in a review of E. W. Smithson's *Baconian Essays*]

Aberdeen Press and Journal (Aberdeenshire, Scotland)

1920, March 6, p. 5	--	Shakespeare.
1923, March 26. p. 2	--	Yet Another "Shakespeare" [review of *The Mystery of "Mr. W. H."* by Col. B. R. Ward]
1923, June 5, p. 2 ,	--	Shakespeare and Oxford [review of *Shakespeare Through Oxford Glasses* by Hubert H. Holland]
1930, March 24, p. 2	--	Shakespeare's Rival [review of *Shakespeare's Sonnets and Edward de Vere* by Gerald Rendall]
1931, March 19, p. 2	--	Oxford, Shakespeare? [review of *The Oxford-Shakespeare Case Corroborated* by Percy Allen]
1933, July 18, p. 2	--	That Shakespeare Argument [review of *The Plays of Shakespeare & Chapman in Relation to French History* by Percy Allen]
1933, Nov. 21, p. 2	--	A Plea for Oxford [review of *Shakespeare, Oxford and Elizabethan Times* by Hubert H. Holland]
1934, Feb. 26, p. 6	--	A Reading Guide [Percy Allen's *Anne Cecil, Elizabeth and Oxford* is on the list]
1934, April 3, p. 2	--	Writing on Shakespeare [review of *Anne Cecil, Elizabeth and Oxford* by Percy Allen]
1935, Jan. 1, p. 2 ,	--	Who Wrote the Plays? [review of *Lord Oxford Was "Shakespeare:" A Summing Up* by Montagu W. Douglas]

Academy Forum

2010, vol. 54/2: 16-18	Waugaman, Richard M.	Shakespeare's Bible: A Personal Odyssey
2012, vol. 56: 18-19	Waugaman, Richard M.	Trauma in the Life of 'Shakespeare:' Its Impact on His Work
2012, vol. 56: 33-34	Waugaman, Richard M.	Unanimous on *Anonymous*? A Film Essay

Accrington Observer and Times

1931, July 18	Beauclerk, C. S. de Vere	Shakespeare Identified at Last

Advocate, The (Baton Rouge, La.)

2005, Sept. 8, p. 5D	--	Obituary: Ruth Loyd Miller
2006, July 3, p. 9D	--	Obituary: Judge Minos D. Miller, Jr. (c. 1921-2006)

Advocate, The (Melbourne, Australia)

1920, May 20, p. 3	Corder, Henry	Who Wrote Shakespeare?

Against the Grain

2005, Sept., vol. 17/4: 48-51	Riley, John & Mark Anderson	Edward de Vere and the Shakespeare Question Updated [interview with Mark Anderson and review of *"Shakespeare" By Another Name*]

Age, The (Melbourne, Australia)

1930, March 15, p. 4	--	Shakespearian Problems
1930, Nov. 22, p. 6	--	Shakespeariana [review of Standen's *Shakespeare Authorship: A Summary of Evidence*]
1944, April 15, p. 5	C. R. B.	Another Reputed Author: Edward de Vere [review of SI]

Alexandria Daily Town Talk

1986, Sept 21, p. A2	Williams, Sidney	Future Duke Believes Shakespeare was Pseudonym of Edward de Vere [Lord Vere]

Algemeen Handelsblad (Swedish)

1962, issue 13, p. 3	Stroman, B.	Shakespeare = Francis Bacon = Edward de Vere = The Earl of Derby = Christopher Marlowe, etc.

American Bar Association Journal (AMB)

1953, April, vol. 39/4: 314	Wilkin, Robert Newsl.	[review of *This Star of England* by Dorothy Ogburn and Charlton Ogburn (1952)]
1959, Feb., vol. 45/2: 143-46, 204-08	Bentley, Richard	Elizabethan Whodunit: Who Was "William Shakespeare?" [repr. in SC, p. 1-16; in BTC, vol. 7: 240-41; and in *Sh. and His Rivals* (McMichael & Glenn 1962): 193-203]
1959, Mar., vol. 45/3: 237-41	Ogburn, Sr., Charlton	A Mystery Solved: The True Identity of Shakespeare [repr. in SC, p. 17-24 [excerpt repr. in SON, vol. 30/23A: 10-11; and in BTC, vol. 7: 237-39; in SAL (Stritmatter, 2022): 63-69; and in *Sh. and His Rivals* (McMichael & Glenn 1962): 203-06]
1959, June, vol. 45/6: 604-06	--	Shakespeare Arena [The February and March authorship articles produced a "torrent" of letters, including 14 printed in the June issue from: Ivan Light, Everett A. Drake, Henry Stone, Walter C. Frame, William Frost, Norman Nathan, Sherwood E. Silliman, George P. Dike, Robert M. Kaufman, Milward W. Martin, Louis P. Benezet, George B. Parks, and William P. Fowler], *American Bar Association Journal*, vol. 45/6.] [Most letters are repr. in SC, p. 116-125.]
1959, July, vol. 45/7: 700-3+	Clary, William W.	The Case for the Defense: De Vere et al. v. Shakespeare [repr. in SC, p. 23-32]
1959, July, vol. 45/7: 704-7, 765-66	Hauser, John Newsl.	The Shakespearean Controversy: A Stratfordian Rejoinder [repr. in SC, p. 33-42; and in *Sh. and His Rivals* (McMichael & Glenn 1962): 211-18]
1959, July, vol. 45/7: 738-9	Arnold, Frazer	[review of *The Six Loves of "Shakespeare"* by Louis P. Bénézet (1938)]
1959, July, vol. 45/7: 654	Schoenrich, Otto	Shylock v. Antonio [letter: response to Bentley] [repr. in SC]
1959, Sept., vol. 45/9: 941-43, 990-96	Ogburn, Dorothy; Charlton Ogburn	The True Shakespeare: England's Great and Complete Man [repr. in SC, p. 43-57; and in *Sh. and His Rivals* (McMichael & Glenn 1962): 193-203]
1959, Nov., vol. 45/11: 1160-63, 1222-30	Bentley, Richard	Elizabethan Whodunit: Supplementary Notes [repr. in SC, p. 58-78]
1960, Jan., vol. 46/1: 4	Daniels, Joseph J.	[letter: response to Bentley] [repr. in SC]
1960, Jan., vol. 46/1: 4	Pope, James S.	[letter: response to Bentley] [repr. in SC]
1960, April, vol. 46/4: 402-9	Pares, Martin	Francis Bacon and the Knights of the Helmet [repr. in SC, p. 79-92]
1960, April, vol. 46/4: 410-12	Briggs, Arthur E.	Did Shaxper Write Shakespeare? [repr. in SC, p. 93-97]
1960, May, vol. 46/5: 509-13	Wham, Benjamin	"Marlowe's Mighty Line": Was Marlowe Murdered at Twenty-nine? [repr. in SC, p. 98-107]
1960, May, vol. 46/5: 519-22	Bénézet, Louis P.	A Hoax Three Centuries Old [repr. with postscript in SC, p. 108-15]
1960, July, vol. 46/7: 696, 698	Ogburn, Dorothy and Charlton, Sr.	Shakespeare Was Oxford, Not Christopher Marlowe [letter: response to Benjamin Wham]
1960, Aug., vol. 46/8: 810-11	Leach, W. Barton	Folger Library Director on Our Shakespeare Series [letter: SOS Trustee Leach's letter quotes in its entirely Louis B. Wright's response to the ABA's authorship articles, "Lawyers' Amusement" repr. from *Folger Library*, vol. 9/1: 5 (May 20, 1960)] [repr. in SC]
1960, Aug., vol. 46/8: 811	Ogburn, Charlton	Elizabethan Drama at Gray's Inn [letter] [repr. in SC]
1960, Aug., vol. 46/8: 812, 814	Pares, Martin	Addenda to Francis Bacon article [letter] [repr. in SC]
1960, Sept., vol. 46/9: 938, 942	Wham, Benjamin	Marlowe's Mighty Line May Have Been Shakespeare's [letter: resp. to Ogburns' Aug. letter] [repr.in SC]
1960, Sept. vol. 46/9: 942	Orr, John M.	"Machevil" a Clue About Marlowe? [letter] [repr. in SC]
1960, Oct., vol. 46/10: 1044	Rathvon, Newsl. Peter, Jr.	Another Fan of the Shakespeare Articles [letter: response to Bentley] [repr. in SC]
1960, Oct., vol. 46/10: 1044	Clary, William W.	The Prima Facie Case for Shakespeare [letter: resp. to Bentley] [repr. in SC; and in *Sh. and His Rivals* (McMichael & Glenn 1962): 206-11]

1962, Nov., vol. 48/11: 1070	Arnold, Frazer	[review of *Shake-Speare: The Real Man Behind the Name* by Dorothy Ogburn & Charlton Ogburn, Jr.]
1974, Oct., vol. 60/10	--	Who Wrote Shakespeare? [Notice about *Shakespeare Cross-Examination*] [See Ruth Loyd Miller's unpublished five-page response, in the De Vere Society Archives at Brunel University, item DVS129]

American Cinematographer
2011, Sept., vol. 92/9: 28-43	Stasukevich, Lain	A Mighty Pen [review of *Anonymous*]

American Heritage
2002, June-July, p. 9	--	Shakespeare's Tempest Locale: Cuttyhunk?

American Imago
1952, Sum., vol. 9/2: 147-164	Feldman, A. Bronson	Othello's Obsessions [repr. in *Shakespeare, Marlowe, . . .* (2022): 83-99]
1953, Sum., vol. 10/2: 113	Feldman. A. Bronson	The Confessions of William Shakespeare [repr. in *Shakespeare, Marlowe, . . .* (2022): 132-81]
1954, Sum., vol. 11/2: 147	Feldman, A. Bronson	Othello in Reality [repr. in *Shakespeare, Marlowe, . . .* (2022): 100-31]
1955, Sum, vol. 12/2: 117	Feldman, A. Bronson	Imaginary Incest [rev. version pub. in *Early Shakespeare* (Feldman/Hope 2019): 86-122]
1959, Spr., vol. 16/1: 77	Feldman, A. Bronson	Portals of Discovery [rev. version pub. in *Early Shakespeare* (Feldman/Hope 2019): 54-85]
1959, Fall, vol. 16/3: 225	Smith, Gordon Ross	Shakespeare and Freudian Interpretations
2012, Spr., vol. 69/1: 107	Molnar, Michael	Freud in the National Portrait Gallery

American Literary History
2007, Summer, pp. 329-49	Glazener, Nancy	Print Culture as an Archive of Dissent: Or, Delia Bacon and the Case of the Missing Hamlet

American Psychoanalyst
2011, vol. 45: 18	Waugaman, Richard M.	The Tempest
2017, vol. 51: 28-29	Waugaman, Richard M.	[review of Film *Nothing Truer Than Truth*]

American Review of Reviews
1920, July-Dec, p. 112	--	"Shakespeare" Identified [review of Am edition of SI]

American Scholar, The
1959, Aut., vol. 28/4: 479-88	Hastings, William T.	Shakspere Was Shakespeare
1960, Spr., vol. 29/2: 271, 290-5	Ogburn, Dorothy & Charlton Ogburn	Shakespeare or Shaksper?
1960, Spr. vol. 29/2: 295-96	Hastings, William T.	[letter: reply to the Ogburns]

See commentary on this exchange of letters in *The English Journal*, vol. 49/6: 430 (Sept. 1960).

American Spectator
1997, May, p. 22-23	Bethell, Tom	Outing Shakespeare [review of *Alias Shakespeare* by Joe Sobran]

American Theatre
1986, vol. 2/10: 30, 32	Glore, John	[review of *The Mysterious William Shakespeare* by Charlton Ogburn, Jr. (1992)]
2001, May/June, vol. 18/5: 22	Freed, Amy	Who Was That Man? Why Amy Freed Can't Stop Thinking about Shakespeare
2001, Oct., vol. 18/8: 7	Paul, Christopher	[letter: resp. to Amy Freed]
2010, Oct., vol. 27/8: 146-47	Weales, Gerald	Two For the Bard: Whoever Wrote Shakespeare's Plays, There's a Raft of Autobiographical Content to Contend With
2011, Dec., vol. 28/10: 62	Taylor, Nicole E.	[review of *The Shakespeare Guide to Italy* by Richard P. Roe]

American Theatre Review
2005, July	Wolf, Mark	Rylance Exits Stage [repr. in DVN (Sept. 2005), p. 9]

American Thinker
2016, April 26	Keller, Jonathan F.	Finding Shakespeare and Conservatism

American University Law Review
1988, Spr., vol. 37/3: 609-16	Kreeger, David L.	In Re Shakespeare: The Authorship of Shakespeare on Trial
1988, Spr., vol. 37/3: 617-24	Jaszi, Peter A.	Who Cares Who Wrote 'Shakespeare'?
1988, Spr., vol. 37/3: 625-43	Boyle, James D. A.	The Search for an Author: Shakespeare and the Framers

American University Law Review (continued)

1988, Spr., vol. 37/3: 647-724	Jaszi, Peter A.	Brief of Appellant Edward de Vere, Seventeenth Earl of Oxford
1988, Spr., vol. 37/3: 725-97	Boyle, James D. A.	Brief of Appellee William Shakespeare (or Shakspere) of Stratford-Upon-Avon
1988, Spr., vol. 37/3: 799-807	Jaszi, Peter A.	Reply Brief of Appellant Edward de Vere, Seventeenth Earl of Oxford
1988, Spr., vol. 37/3: 809-17	Boyle, James D. A.	Reply Brief of Appellee William Shakespeare (or Shakspere) of Stratford-Upon-Avon
1988, Spr., vol. 37/3: 819-26	Blackmun, Harry A.; & William J. Brennan; & John Paul Stevens	Opinion of the Justices

American Way (American Airlines)

1992, Dec. 1, p. 60-66, 103	Wells, Lawrence	Shakespeare Slept Here [Castle Hedingham]

Amsterdammer, De [the leading weekly Dutch newspaper]

1923, May 17	Gunning, Dr. C. P.	[title not known] [repr. of excerpts from a piece in the May 12 *De Massbode*, with editorial commentary]

Anais Portugueses de Psiquiatria

1969, Dec., vol. XXI/18: 545-72	Slater, Eliot	A Psychiatric View of Shakespeare's Sonnets [repr. in TOX, vol. 18: 155-74]

Apostrophe

1996, Spr./Sum	Tombe, Sheila	[interview with Charlton Ogburn] [repr. in EVR, vol. 3 (Sum. 1996)]

Archival Science (Dordrecht)

2004, vol. 4/3-4: 233-35	Furner, Jonathan	Conceptual Analysis: A Method for Understanding Information as Evidence, and Evidence as Information

Archives Suisses de Neorologie. Neurochirugie et de Psychiatrie

1963, vol. 91	Slater, Eliot	The Color Imagery of Poets – Brunel

Archivum Historicum Societatis Iesu

1987, vol. LVI	Edwards, Francis, S.J.	The Strange case of the Poisoned Pommel: Richard Walpole, J.S., and the Squire Plot, 1597-1598 [repr. as a pam.]

Argonaut (San Francisco)

1920, Nov. 13, p. 317	Schelling, F. E.	Who Wrote Shakespeare [A poem repr. from *Life*]
1939, April 21	Heron, Flodden W.	The Shakespeare Anniversary: Literature's Greatest Mystery
1939, Dec.	Heron, Flodden W.	[lengthy piece on Barrell's findings]
1940, Jan. 26	Editor	Who Was Shakespeare? [repr. in SFA, vol. 1/3: 4-5 (April/May 1940)]
1950, May 12	Burgess, Gelett	The Three Centuries-Old Mystery of Shakespeare Solved

Arizona Republic

1940, Jan. 28	Knight, Alfred	William Shakespeare's Authorship Defended by Phoenix Expert on Old England's Bard

Around the Globe: the Magazine of the International Shakespeare Globe Theatre (ARO)

1996, Winter, p. 21	Nicholl, Charles	[review of *Who Wrote Shakespeare?* by John Michell]
2002, Winter	Ellis, David & Katherine Duncan-Jones	Now You See Him, Now . . . [Ellis and Duncan-Jones discuss the challenge of writing a biography of William Shakespeare] [repr. in DVN (July 2004), p. 22-25]
2010, vol. 45: 42-43	Brown, Tom	[review of *Contested Will* by James Shapiro (2010)]
2011, vol. 49: 42	Edmondson, Paul	Speak Up For Shakespeare
2012, vol. 50: 40	Brown, Tom	[review of *Anonymous*]

Athenaeum, The

1856, Sept. 13, p. 1133	--	[review of *Was Lord Bacon the Author of Shakespeare's Plays? A Letter to Lord Ellesmere* by William Henry Smith]
1867, Feb. 2, p. 249	--	The Authorship of Shakespeare [review of *The Authorship of Shakespeare* by Nathaniel Holmes]
1919, May 9, p. 301	R. S.	The Shakespeare Problem [review of *Sous Le Masque De 'William Shakespeare'* by Abel Lefranc]
1920, April 2, p. 450	M.	Another Shakespeare [review of *"Shakespeare" Identified* by J.

		Thomas Looney (1920)]
1920, April 2, p. 464	Editor	[notice of publication: *"Shakespeare" Identified*]
1920, April 16, p. 521	Clarke, Francis	Shakespeare Identified [letter: response to M]
1920, April 16, p. 521	Eagle, R. L.	Shakespeare Identified [letter: response to M]
1920, April 16, p. 521	Editor	Shakespeare Identified [reply to responses to M]
1920, April 30, p. 585	Looney, J. Thomas	Edward de Vere and Shakespeare [letter: response to M.'s April 2 review of *"Shakespeare" Identified*]

Atlanta Journal-Constitution

1948, Jan. 8, p. 8	--	Another Assignment for Percy [review of *Talks with Elizabethans*]
1952, Nov. 24, p. 4	Walker, Roosevelt	Another Claimant to Throne of Shakespeare in Offing [advance short review of *This Star of England* by Charlton and Dorothy Ogburn]
1952, Dec. 7, p. 6F	Lucchese, Sam F.	Was 17th Earl of Oxford Man Who Did Shakespeare's Work? [review of *This Star of England* by Charlton and Dorothy Ogburn]
1962, Oct. 21, p. 9D	Daniel, Frank	New Books [review of *Shake-speare: The Man Behind the Name* by Dorothy Ogburn and Charlton Ogburn, Jr.]
1963, July 15, p. 5	Atkinson, Brooks	Shakespeare: An Ex-Butcher Boy? [reprint of Brooks's July 12, 1963 *New York Times* article]
1966. Nov. 6, p. 21B	--	Five Georgia Authors Honored by Awards [Charlton Ogburn, Jr., is one of them]
1997, Aug. 13, p. E2-3	Saporta, Maria	Where There's a Will . . . [Oxfordian Gertrude Ford left an estate worth $60 million]
1998, Oct. 22, p. C6	Bennett, Tom	Charlton Ogburn Obituary
2005, Aug. 7, p. 8L	Weinberg, Steve	Shakespeare's Secret [review of *"Shakespeare" by Another Name* by Mark Anderson (2005)]

Atlantic Monthly

1920, June, no page no.	--	[Stokes Books ad for SI. SI listed first, with description]
1929, July, p. 56-62	Colvin, Ian	Shakespeare Unlocked His Heart: A Key to the Sonnets
1984, Dec., vol. 29: 448-50	Crewe, Jonathan	[review of *The Mysterious William Shakespeare* by Charlton Ogburn, Jr., (1992)]
1991, Oct., vol. 268/4: 43-86	Editors	Looking for Shakespeare: Two Partisans Explain and Debate the Authorship Question
1991, Oct., vol. 268/4: 44-61	Bethell, Tom	The Case for Oxford [repr. in SCV (Lee & Barnes 1998): 48-57]
1991, Oct., vol. 268/4: 62-73	Matus, Irvin	The Case for Shakesp. [repr. in SCV (Lee & Barnes 1998): 57-61]
1991, Oct., vol. 268/4: 74-75	Bethell, Tom	Reply by Bethell [repr. in SCV (Lee & Barnes 1998): 61-63]
1991, Oct., vol. 268/4: 78-81	Matus, Irvin	Reply by Matus [repr. in SCV (Lee & Barnes 1998): 63-66]

          Responses to the special issue on Shakespeare authorship question by:
          Richard W. Edbloom, Jan. 1992, p. 6-9.
          Robert Giroux, Jan. 1992, p. 6-9.
          Joseph Sobran, Jan. 1992, p. 6-9.
          Charlton Ogburn, Jan. 1992, p. 6-9.
               Reply by Tom Bethell, Jan. 1992, p. 6-9.
               Reply by Irvin Matus, Jan. 1992, p. 6-9.
          Peter Linnett, May 1992, p. 21.
          Thomas A. Pendleton, *Shakespeare Newsletter*, vol. 41/4: 48 (Winter 1991).
          Bruce Blackadar, *Toronto Star*, Oct. 5, 1991, p. F5
          Shakespeare Newsletter, vol. 63/2: 46 (Fall 2013)
          For other responses, see also *Wilson Quarterly*, Winter 1992, p. 150: "The Plays' the Thing"

2004, Jan., vol. 293/1: 18	Werth, Andrew	[letter: resp. to Christopher Hitchens' Oct. 2003 article] [repr. in SM, vol. 3/2: 2-3 (Winter 2004)]
2019, May 10	Winkler, Elizabeth	In Shakespeare's Life Story, Not All is True. In Fact, Much is Invented.
2019, June, p. 86-95.	Winkler, Elizabeth	Was Shakespeare a Woman?
2019, June 8	Shapiro, James	"Shakespeare Wrote Insightfully about Women. That Doesn't Mean He was One
2019, June 8	Rylance, Mark	Keep Questioning Shakespeare's Identity

Atlantic Monthly (continued)

2019, June 8	Rackin, Phyllis	The Hidden Women Writers of the Elizabethan Theater

For responses to Winkler, see also:

Dominic Green, "Was Shakespeare a Woman? Of Course He Was,"
    Spectator USA, May 13, 2019

David Marcus, "No, Shakespeare Was Not a Jewish Woman, He Was Just a Genius,"
    Federalist, May 13, 2019

Oliver Kamm, "Conspiracism at the Atlantic," *Quilette*, May 14, 2019

"Shakespeare Derangement Syndrome," *Shakespeare Magazine*, May 16, 2019

Noah Millman, "What If Shakespeare Was a Woman?," *Week*, May 19, 2019

Augusta Chronicle

2005, Sept. 17	--	Shakespeare: A Bard by Any Other Name

Austin American-Statesman

1996, April 22, p. 33	--	*Frontline* Investigates Edward de Vere as Real Shakespeare
2011, Oct. 28, p. D1	Mongillo, Peter	Shakespeare Not Playwright? [review of *Anonymous*]

Australasian, The

1920, Feb. 21, p. 40	--	"The 'Identification' of Shakespeare" [Notice]

Australian Society

1991, vol. 10/1-2: 59-60	Stephens, Jane	[review of *The Lost Chronicle of Edward de Vere* by Andrew Field (1990)]

Avon Gazette and York Times (Australia)

1920, May 22, p. 2	Rambler	Out and About [review of SI]

Back Stage West

2004, Sept. 9-15, vol. 11: 13	Schiffman, Jean	[review of *The Mysterious Mr. Looney* by Gary Graves]

Baconiana

1921, March, vol. 16: 62	Eagle, Roderick L.	[review of *Shakespeare's Handwriting* by George Greenwood]
1921, March, vol. 16/63: 82-85	Eagle, Roderick L.	Shakespeare and the Earl of Oxford [review of SI]
1922, June, vol. 17/64: 74-77	--	Baconian Flotsam [Mentions *Shakespeare Identified*]
1922, June, vol. 17/64: 87-88	Eagle, Rogerick L.	Correspondence [letter about Orage]
1923, June, vol. 17/65: 126-31	J.R.	The Search for a Substitute
1923, June, vol. 17/65: 149-50	Eagle, Roderick L.	[review of *Baconian Essays* by Smithson & George Greenwood]
1923, June, vol. 17/65: 150-51	Greenwood, George	[letter]
1923, June, vol. 17/65: 155	Astrea	[review of Col. Ward's *The Mystery of "Mr. W. H."*]
1924, March, vol. 17/66: 180-82	Eagle, Roderick L.	The Great Shakespeare Find
1924, March, vol. 17/66: 223-24	--	Lecture Series 1923-24
1931	Parsons, J. Denham	Sir Edward Clarke, P.C., on Shakespeare's Identity
1935, Jan., vol. 22: 1-9	Theobald, Bertram G.	Who Was the First Baconian?
1938, Oct.	Bridgewater, H.	Shakespeare and Italy [repr. as a pamphlet]
1938, Oct.	Dawbarn, C. Y. C.	Oxford and the Folio Plays [reissued as a pamphlet]
1944, July, no. 112: 118-19	Sennett, M.	Correspondence [letter about Ivor Brown]
1950, Oct., vol. 34: 212-16+	Humphreys, Philip	Who Wrote Shakespeare? A Controversy and a Challenge [response to Giles E. Dawson, "Who Wrote Shakespeare?," in *The Listener*, Aug. 10, 1950]
1950, Oct., vol. 34: 217-20	Johnson, Edward D.	Can We Educate Dr. Giles E. Dawson?
1964, Oct., vol. 47: 65	Eagle, Roderick L.	Literary Concealments
1995, vol. 77/194: 102-03	Michell, John	[review of *The Alternative Shakespeare: A Modern Introduction* by A. M. Challinor (1996)]
1996, vol. 76/193: 18-29	Challinor, Arthur M.	Concerning Prejudice and Pride: Some Observations on the Reception Given to Authorship Doubters

Baltimore Sun – See Sun (Baltimore)

Bangor Daily News

1993, Nov. 1	Weber, Tom	Debunking of Shakespeare Is Much Ado About Nothing [Charles Vere speaking tour]

Bath Weekly Chronicle and Herald

1930, Nov. 8, p. 15	--	Shakespeare Discussion in Bath [debate between Ernest Allen for Oxford and Dr. W. E. Pack for Stratford man]
1930, Nov. 15, p. 15	--	Surprise at Bath Meeting [Debate on "The Case for the 17th Earl of Oxford as Author of the Shakespearean Plays." Ernest Allen set forth the case for Oxford.]
1934, May 12, p. 14	--	One Shakespeare or Two? [recent meeting of the Shakespeare Fellowship]
1935, Nov. 23, p. 12	--	New Light on Shakespeare: Did Earl of Oxford Write *Hamlet*? [report on a talk by Percy Allen]
1941, Feb. 1, p. 18	--	Shakespeare Under the Microscope: *Hamlet*'s Topicalities Discussed [report on lecture by Percy Allen]
1941, Feb. 8, p. 18	--	Don't Marry a Genius: Hint by Dramatic Critic at Bath [report on Percy Allen's talk on *A Winter's Tale* at the Bath branch of the British Empire Shakespeare Society]

BBC

2001	Hendle, Pauline; Kevin Gilvary; Philip Johnson & Eddi Jolly	[letter to the Editor] [repr. in DVN (April/May 2001), p. 49-50]

BBC News Magazine

2007, Sept. 11	Geoghegan, Tom	Shakespeare: The Dossier
2009, Nov. 27	Gilyeat, Dave	Edward de Vere, Earl of Oxford: The Real Shakespeare?

BBC Radio 4

2004, May 15	--	Row Over Shakespeare Name Claim [transcript in DVN (July 2004), p. 26-27] [see also SON, vol. 40/3: 9 (Summer 2004)]

Belchamp St. Pauls Parish Magazine

1931, Nov.	--	Belchamps St. Pauls

Belfast News-Letter (Belfast, Newsl. Ireland)

1920, March 9, p. 6	Fripp, Edgar J.	The Sonnets of Shakespeare [lecture printed]
1928, May 10, p. 14	--	[review of *Shakespeare, Jonson, and Wilkins as Borrowers* by Percy Allen (1928)]
1929, April 13, p. 6	--	Shakespeare Once More: Links Between Shakespeare and the Earls of Derby, Bacon, Oxford, and Rutland
1929, May 25, p. 10	--	[review of *Shakespeare and Chapman as Topical Dramatists* by Percy Allen (1929)]
1930, May 3, p. 10	--	Another "Shakespeare" [review of *The Case for Edward de Vere as Shakespeare* by Percy Allen]
1931, March 19, p. 14	--	Yet Another Immortal! [review of *The Oxford-Shakespeare Case Corroborated* by Percy Allen]
1931, May 21, p. 12	--	Short Notices [review of *Shake-speare: Handwriting and Spelling* by Gerald H. Rendall]
1931, Oct. 8, p. 12	--	Shakespeare Once More [review of *The Earl of Oxford as Shakespeare* by Montagu W. Douglas (1931)]
1932, Nov. 17, p. 15	V.	Shakespearean Controversy [review of *The Tragic Story of Shakespeare* by Gerald Phillips (1932)]
1934, Dec. 27, p. 12	--	Short Notices

Belfast Telegraph (Belfast, Newsl. Ireland)

2006, April 21, p. 1	--	Was Shakespeare the Love Child of Queen Elizabeth?
2011, Nov. 5, p. 18	--	Acting's In My Blood [interview with Joely Richardson] [review of *Anonymous*]

Bennington Vermont Banner

1988, Summer	--	[review of *All The Queen's Men* by John Nassivera] [repr. in SON, vol. 24/4: 13-14]

Biblical Archeology Review

2010, Nov/Dec, vol. 36/6	--	Shakespeare, the Earl of Oxford and Morton Smith [repr. in SON, vol. 47/1: 9 (Jan. 2011)]

Biblio: A Journal for Book Lovers (New Jersey)
1921, Oct., p. 91-92   --   A First Folio Tercentenary

Bibliothèque d'Humanisme et Renaissance
1986, vol. 48: 125-209   Ashley, L. R. Newsl.   [review of *The Mysterious William Shakespeare* by Charlton Ogburn, Jr. (1984)]

1995, vol. 57: 643-701   Ashley, L. R. Newsl.   [review of *Shakespeare: Who Was He?* by Richard F. Whalen]
1997, vol. 59: 365-409   Ashley, L. R. Newsl.   [review of *Shakespeare, In Fact* by Irvin Matus]

Billboard, The (Cincinnati)
1920, July 17, p. 10-11   --   Shakespeare—Identified in Edward de Vere [review of SI]
1922, Dec. 2, p. 1   Whyte, Gordon   Another "Shakespeare" [Brief review of SI]
1923, Aug. 25, p. 64   Allen, Percy   Hamlet's Identity With an Elizabethan [repr. from *The Christian Science Monitor*, May 19, 1923, p. D7]

1940. Aug.   Orodenker, M. H.   Legitimate Summer Theater Reviews: "By Any Other Name"

Biography (Honolulu)
2011, Spring, vol. 34/2: 334+ McHenry, Robert   Shakespeare and Biography [review of *Shakespeare and Biography* by David Bevington]

Biography Magazine
2002, Aug., vol. 6/8: 23   Goldman, David   The Bard or Not the Bard: Who Wrote Shakespeare's Plays?

Birmingham Daily Gazette
1920, April 12, p. 6   --   Sh.'s Plays: Author of New Theory Puts Forward Fresh Clue
1931, Dec. 14, p. 7   --   Who Wrote Shakespeare's Plays? [report on Percy Allen's lecture at the Gallery First Nighter's Club, London]

1933, May 25, p. 8   --   Oxford Wrote Shakespeare [review of *A Response to John Drinkwater* by Percy and Ernest Allen]

Birmingham Daily Post (West Midlands, England)
1928, April 27   --   An Elizabethan Dark Horse [review of *The 17th Earl of Oxford* by B. M. Ward]

1945, Jan. 8, p. 4   --   Obituary: Rev. Canon Gerald H. Rendall
1955, April 23, p. 6   --   Noble Shakespeare
1956, Jan. 25, p. 4   Trewin, J. C.   Vex Not His Ghost
1956, April 24, p. 17   --   Who Wrote Shakespeare? Claim for Edward de Vere
1957, April 13, p. 13   --   The Dreary Old Bore of Stratford
1964, Jan. 1, p. 6   Hall, W. E.   Anti-Shakespeariana and All That
1999, Oct. 27, p. 6   --   Earl's Leap of Protest in Dying Days of Chamber [Burford]
2004, Jan. 15, p. 4   --   Earl Upstages Shakespeare in Theatrical Claim to Fame [review of *Anonymous*]

2004, June 25, p. 2   Gabriel, Helen   Would the Real Literary Genius Please Stand Up?
2006, April 22, p. 3   --   U.S. Theory Says Bard Was Son of Queen
2006, April 22, p. 47   Upton, Chris   Desperately Seeking Will; The Man—and Men—Who Could Well Be Shakespeare

2007, Sept. 10, p. 3   Scotney, Tom   Academic Pours Scorn on Shakespeare's Doubters
2007, Sept. 12, p. 13   Grimley, Terry   Author or just a "Front" [review of *I Am Shakespeare* by Mark Rylance and Matthew Warchus (2007)

2007, Sept. 12, p. 13   Blennerhassett, Leslie   [letter: She joins the doubters]
2009, April 23, p. 11   --   Actors Cast Fresh Doubt Over Shakespeare Authorship
2011, Feb. 10, p. 28   Fisher, Trevor   Royal Twist to Debate Over Who William Shakesp. Really Was

Blackheath Local Guide and District Advertiser
1940, April 6, p. 14-15   --   A Humble Petition [Makes the case for examination of the SAQ.]

Bodleian Library Record
1997, April 16, p. 1, 17-41   Ungerer, Gustav   Earl of Southampton's Donation to the Bodleian Library in 1605

Book Bulletin of the Chicago Public Library
1920, Dec., vol. 11/10: 157   --   [list of new books includes SI, with description]

Book Window
1933, Nov.   --   Shakespeare, Oxford and Elizabethan Times [Notice of publication H. H. Holland's book]

Articles in Non-Oxfordian Periodicals

Booklist (Chicago)

1962, Aug/Sept, vol. 59: 36-37	Anon.	[review of *Shake-speare: The Man Behind the Name* by
1993, Nov. 15, vol. 90/6, p. 597	Taylor, Gilbert	[review of *Shakespeare, In Fact* by Irvin L. Matus]
1994, Nov. 1, vol. 91/5: 476	Taylor, Gilbert	[review of *Shakespeare—Who was He?* by Richard F. Whalen]
1994, Nov. 1, vol. 91/5: 486-87	Beauregard, Sue E.	[review of *Shakespeare—Who Was He?* by Richard F. Whalen]
2001, June 1, p. 1903	McCray, Nancy	*The Shakespeare Conspiracy* [review of the documentary]
2010, April 1, vol. 106/15: 12	Olson, Ray	*Contested Will*: Who Wrote Shakespeare? [review of Shapiro]

Bookman, The: A Review of Literature and Life

1920, May, vol. 51/3: 84	A. Sr. J. A.	Notes on New Books [Shakespeare and the Lilliputians [review of *"Shakespeare" Identified*]
1920, June, vol. 51/4: 499	S. M. R.	Looking Ahead with the Publishers
1920, June, vol. 51/4: 115	--	Advertisement: Mr. Cecil Palmer's Announcements
1920, Aug., vol. 51/6: 677-82	Björkman, Edwin	Shakespeare? [review of *"Shakespeare" Identified*]
1920, Dec., vol. 59/351: 89	--	Advertisement: Mr. Cecil Palmer's Announcements
1921, May, vol. 60/356: 78	--	[review of *The Poems of Edward de Vere* (Looney)]
1923, April, vol. 64: 34-36	A. Sr. J. A.	Shakespeare's Ghosts
1928, May, vol. 75: 113-15	Sampson, George	More About Shakespeare [review of *Borrowers* by Percy Allen]
1929, May, vol. 76: 118	--	Notes on Recent Books [review of *Topical* by Percy Allen]
1930, March, vol. 77: 369	--	[Notice of publication of *Case* by Percy Allen]
1931, Nov. vol. 81: 132	Sutton, Graham	Another Theory About Shakespeare
1932, Dec. vol. 83/495: 228	C. B. D.	Who Wrote Shakespeare? [review of *The Tragic Story of "Shakespeare"* by Gerald Phillips (1932)]
1933, July, vol. 84: 83-84	Williamson, Hugh R.	Poor Will

Bookman's Journal & Print Collector, The

1920, March 19, vol. 1/24: 408	--	A New Mask for Shakespeare [review of SI]
1920, April 9, vol. 1/24: 452-3	Looney, J. Thomas	Is "Shakespeare Identified"? [letter: resp. to the March 19 review] [letter is preceded by editor's introduction and followed by excerpts from reviews in *The Spectator* (March 27), *The Saturday Westminster* (March 20), *The Times Literary Supplement* (March 4), and *The Sunday Times* April 4)] [Banner at top of the cover reads: "IS SHAKESPEARE IDENTIFIED? Mr. Looney's New Clue"]
1920, April 16, vol. 1/25: 468	--	Is "Shakespeare Identified"? [editor's reply to Looney's April 9 response to his March 19 review of SI]
1920, April 23, vol. 1/26: 483	--	Henry James on Shakespeare Theories
1920, April 23, vol. 1/26: 484	Looney, J. Thomas	The Shakespeare Controversy: Mr. Thomas Looney and Oxford's Boys" [letter: response to the reviewer's April 9 reply]
1920, May 21, vol. 2/30: 58	--	The Identity of Shakespeare [advertisement for "The Shakespeare Controversy" section of the May 21 issue of *The Bookman's Journal* ran in the May 20 issue of TLS]
1920, May 21, vol. 2/30: 58	Lee, Sir Sidney	The Identity of Shakespeare [letter]
1920, May 21, vol. 2/30: 58	Robertson, J. M., MP	The Identity of Shakespeare [letter]
1920, May 21, vol. 2/30: 58-59	Looney, J. Thomas	The Identity of Shakespeare [letter]
1920, May 21, vol. 2/30: 59	--	[Cecil Palmer quarter page ad for SI]
1920, May 28, vol. 2/31: 68	Looney, J. Thomas	The Identity of Shakespeare [letter: Robertson's May 21 letter]
1920, May 28, vol. 2/31: 70	--	The Play's the Thing [discussion of authorship issue]
1920, June 4, vol. 2/32: 84	Atkinson, R.	The Identity of Shakespeare [followed by editor's note]
1921, Jan. 21, vol. 3/65: 234	--	This Week's Books [*The Poems of Edward de Vere* edited by J. Thomas Looney is on the list]
1921, March 4, vol. 3/71: 335	S.	Stratford and Stony Stratford [review of *The Poems of Edward de Vere* edited by J. Thomas Looney]
1921, March 25, vol. 3/74: 388	Looney, J. Thomas	Stratford and Stony Stratford [letter: resp. to the March 4 review]
1921, March 25, vol. 3/74: 388	Clarke, Francis	Stratford and Stony Stratford [letter: resp. to the March 4 review]
1921, March 25, vol. 3/74: 388	S.	Stratford and Stony Stratford [letter: reply to Looney and Clarke]
1921, April 22, vol. 3/78: 463	--	Men and Manners [touches on the authorship issue]
1921, July 29, vol. 4/92: 225	--	A Dark Shakespeare [touches on the authorship issue]

Books of Today

1933, Nov.	--	Shakespeare – AND the Earl of Oxford? [review of *Shakespeare, Oxford and Elizabethan Times* by Adm. H. H. Holland]

Bookseller, The

1920, March, vol. 19: 147-48	H. D. S.	"Shakespeare" Identified? [review of SI]
1920, March, vol. 19: 162	--	[Cecil Palmer half-page ad for SI]

Boston Globe (and Daily Boston Globe)

1931, Feb. 7, p. 17	--	Claims Earl of Oxford was Really Shakespeare [review of *Hidden Allusions in Shakespeare's Plays* by Eva Turner Clark]
1937, Dec. 30, p. 14	Towns, Vincent	Human Riddles That Have Vexed the World: The Mystery of Shakespeare
1938, July 10, p. C4	Uncle Dudley	A Mystery-Tale of Shakespeare
1940, Jan.	--	Bard was Noble, Researcher Says [response to Barrell]
1948, Jan. 5, p. 1, 8	--	Shakespeare's Spirit Admits Collaborating with Oxford on Plays [review of *Talks with Elizabethans* by Percy Allen]
1953, Oct. 25, p. A55	Durgin, Cyrus	Were the Shakespearean Plays Written by Earl of Oxford?
1954, Aug. 29, p. A32	Price, Lucien	Shakespeare Never Should Have Written Those Diaries
1956, Dec. 30, p. A9	Montgomery, Robert	Who Wrote Shakespeare? A Boston Scholar Considers the Evidence
1957, Jan. 6, p. A13	Montgomery, Robert	More on Shakespeare Controversy
1957, Jan. 13, p. A13	Montgomery, Robert	Romeo and Juliet Examined from Oxfordian Point of View
1962, Sept, p. 25, p. 25	Starkey, Marion	Mother and Son Champion Earl of Oxford [review of *Shakespeare: The Man Behind the Name* by Dorothy and Charlton Ogburn, Jr.]
1965, Aug. 23, p. 16	Montgomery, Robert	Was Shakespeare Shakespeare? Maybe . . . [review of *Shakespeare? A Lawyer Reviews the Evidence* by Milward W. Martin]
1973, May 20, p. E4	Rogers, Byron	Once More in Quest of Shakespeare: Endless Dispute About the Bard [Ogburn's quest to open the grave]
1977, April 25, p. 17	Gifford, Marjorie	It's the Earl of Oxford [letter]
1977, May 2, p. 15	Cutler, John	On the Shakespearean Authorship Question [letter: response to Gifford's April 25 letter]
1983, June 1, p. 1	Taylor, Robert	Gallery of Elizabethan Portraits
1984, Oct. 21, p. B1	Shirley, Frances	Probably, and Author Hasn't Proved Contrary
1984, Oct. 21, p. B1	Kelly, Kevin	Detective Story, Was It Really Shakespeare?; No, and Now a Book Offers the Proof [review of *The Mysterious William Shakespeare*]
1984, Dec. 30, p. A1	Kelly, Kevin	And Edward de Vere, Earl of Oxford, Makes 11 Territorial
1987, Jan. 18, p. B12	--	Writers [notice about *Shakespeare Revealed in Oxford's Letters* by William Plumer Fowler]
1987, July 23, p. 1 ,	Chandler, David	Peer-Review System for Scientific Plans Being Reevaluated [excerpt repr. as "Where the Professoriate is Deeply but Wrongly Committed" in SON, vol. 23/3: 12 (Summer 1987)]
1989, April 18, p. 32	Kelly, Kevin	Shakespeare's Mystery Persists [review of PBS's "The Shakespeare Mystery"] [repr. in SON, vol. 25/2: 10 (Spring 1989)]
1989, Sept. 20, p. 98	Taylor, Robert	[review of *Reinventing Shakespeare,* Third Edition by Gary Taylor]
1990, March 9	Kelly, Kevin	[article notes 440th anniversary of Edward de Vere's birth]
1991, April 19	Kelly, Kevin	Packer Sets "Hamlet" a Continent Apart [mentions the SOS conf.]
1991, April 26	Kelly, Kevin	[article recommends looking into TMWS]
1991, Sept. 18	Kennedy, Louise	Would Shakespeare By Any Other Name Be As Sweet?
1992, March 27, p. 27	Kelly, Kevin	[article mentions the SOS, Charles Boyle, and the 442nd anniversary of de Vere's birth]
1992, July 24	Kelly, Kevin	Shakespeare, Buckley and Interactive TV
1992, Oct. 16, p. 35	Kelly, Kevin	[article mentions Looney and doubts about Shakespeare]
1993, Jan. 22, p. 27	Kelly, Kevin	Looking a Little Bit Ahead [Kristin Linklater's intent "is to open closed minds"]
1993, April 9, p. 43	Kelly, Kevin	[Article notes the 443rd anniversary of de Vere's birth]

1993, Oct. 28, p. 63	Robinson, John	Nobleman's Bid for the Bard is a Family Affair [Burford tour]
1993, Nov. 5, p. 35	Kelly, Kevin	[Authorship debate, with Allan van Gestel and Charles Vere, Earl of Burford pressing the Oxfordian case]
1994, April 8, p. 47	Kelly, Kevin	After Limping Through Winter, Theater Spring to Life [includes reporting on Charles Vere's talk]
1994, Oct. 7, p. 55	Kelly, Kevin	Who Really Wrote Brecht's Plays?
1995, March 8, p. 34	Taylor, Robert	The Real Shakespeare: A Closeted Catholic? [review of *Shakespeare: The Evidence* by Ian Wilson]
1997, June 2	White, Diana	A New Volley in the Battle of the Bard [review of *Alias Shakespeare* by Joe Sobran (1997)]
1999, April 7, p. D3	Dockrell, Cynthia	Bard Brawl
1999, Nov. 7, Focus 1	Anderson, Mark K.	Who Wrote Shakespeare? Was it the William We Know? [prominent placement: front page upper left of Focus section, with picture of the Ashbourne portrait]
2002, March 3, p. 9	Ware, Susan	What's In a Name?: Scholar [Richard Desper] Argues Another Man Was Behind the Works of Shakespeare (*Boston Globe Online*) [repr. in DVN (April 2002), p. 21-22]
2003, Jan. 2, p. D5	Gilbert, Matthew	Much Ado About the Bard [reviews of *Frontline's* "Much Ado About Something" (1989) and "The Shakespeare Mystery" (2003)]
2003, June 9	Simon, Clea	*Shakespeare's* Plays Well as a Mystery [review of Sarah Smith's stage production *Chasing Shakespeares*]
2006, June 25	Brokaw, Leslie	She's Bringing Shakespeare Controversy to Film [Cheryl Eagan-Donovan]
2006, July 7, p. D5	Kennedy, Louise	'The Beard' Tries Too Hard With the Bard [review of *The Beard of Avon* by Amy Freed]
2006, Aug. 8	MacDonald, Sandy	Provocative and Fresh, This 'Beard' Is a Charmer [review of *The Beard of Avon* by Amy Freed]
2007, May 16	Aucion, Don	Total Television Scribe Alex McNeil is Now Consumed With Proving That Shakespeare Wasn't the Real Bard
2008, Nov. 9, p. K6	Gardner, Jan	Doubts About the Bard [Alex McNeil to speak at Boston Public Library]
2009, Sept. 25	Beam, Alex	The Shakespeare Truthers: Search for the "Real" Shakespeare is Collective Madness
2010, April 15	Kelly, Kevin	Much Ado About Shakespeare
2010, May 2	--	"Who Wrote Shakespeare? [preview of day-long program featuring Charles Beauclerk]
2011, Jan. 12, p. B12	Marquand, Bryan	Elliott Stone, 79, Lover of Art, Including the Art of Conversation
2011, Oct. 28	Morris, Wesley	Blow Up Your Shakespeare: Director Emmerich Blasts the Bard in *Anonymous*
2012, May 6	Wayland	Obituary: Elisabeth Sears

Boston Guardian (Lincolnshire England)

| 1920, April 17, p. 10 | -- | Mr. Looney's Identification of Shakespeare [review of SI] [incorrecty cites *The Bookman*; should *be Saturday Review*] |
| 1920, Dec. 25, p. 12 | -- | Member and Bard [letter: born, not made] |

Boston Herald

1938	Burt, F. Allen	[feature article on Ed de Vere] [noted in SFA]
1993, Nov. 12, p. 8	Fee, Gayle	Inside Track [Charles Vere speech]
1993, Nov. 19, p. S19	Friedman, Arthur	Will's Warriors Repel Another Assault on Bard's Authorship; SOS Conference held in Boston]
1994, April 29, p. S17	Friedman, Arthur	Curtains [mentions Roger Stritmatter and de Vere's Bible]
1994, Aug. 5, p. S15	Friedman, Arthur	Curtains [Edward de Vere, the real Shakespeare?]
1999, June 6, p. 48	Michel, Roer	Good Question! Did He Or Didn't He?

Boston Phoenix, The

| 1989, Aug. 11 | Gantz, Jeffrey | Critical Mass: But the Play's the Thing [excerpt repr. in SON, vol. 22/4: 12 (Fall 1989)] |
| 1989, Sept. 8 | Boyle, Charles | Barring the Bard [response to Gantz's Aug. 11 column] [repr. in SON, vol. 25/4: 12-13 (Fall 1989)] |

Boston Post
1941, April 5 —   --   [editorial re Bénézet's lecture at Boston University]
                                                   [three other Boston newspapers commented soon after]

Boston Transcript
1937   Edgett, Edwin Francis   [reviews of books by Louis Bénézet and Eva Turner Clark]
1937   Bénézet, Louis P.   [response to Edgett's review]

Braintree & Witham Times
1972   --   What'a In a Name?
1973, July 20   Rushton, Ray   Hamlet of Hedingham by the Bard of Braintree?
                                                     [repr. in SON, vol. 11/1: 6-7 (Winter 1975)]
1973, July 27   Patience, Harold W.   Only Oxford Could Have Written These Masterpieces [letter]
                                                     [resp. in SON, vol. 11/1: 7-8 (Winter 1975)]
1976, June 3   Hayes, Stanley   The Two Faces of Good Will Sh. [highlights Ruth Loyd Miller]

Brattleboro Reformer
2012, Oct. 6   --   In Defense of the Bard

Britannia and Eve (London)
1950, Oct., vol. 41/4: 25-28   --   Sir Philip Sidney's Stella

British Heritage
1991, vol. 12/6: 53-58   Heydt, Bruce   The Many Shakespeares [cover asks "Who Was William
                                                     Shakespeare?"

British Museum Quarterly
1932, Oct., vol. 7/2: 40-41   Thomas, H.   The Shakespeare Authorship Controversy

British Weekly
1938, Jan. 20, p. 314.   Aitken, T. M.   A New Shakespeare Candidate [letter]

Bromley Parish Magazine
1933, Nov.   --   [review of *Sh., Oxford and Elizabethan Times* by H. H. Holland]

Brooklyn Rail
2010, April   Niederkorn, William S.   Absolute Will [review of *Contested Will: Who Wrote
                                                     Shakespeare?* by James Shapiro (2010)]
2011, March   Niederkorn, William S.   The Bard's Evangelist: [review of *Shakespeare's Freedom* by
                                                     Stephen Greenblatt (2010)]
2011, April   Niederkorn, William S.   The Shakespeare Chronology Recalibrated [review of *Dating
                                                     Shakespeare's Plays by K. Gilvary] [repr. in DVN, vol. 18/3:
                                                     26-27 (Nov. 2011); and in SAS (Stritmatter 2022): 421-28]
2011, July, p. 74   Niederkorn, William S.   Canonizer's Feast [review of *The Anatomy of Influence: Literature
                                                     as a Way of Life by Harold Bloom]
2011, Oct., p. 66   Niederkorn, William S.   A Binary Star with *Anonymous* [review of Charles Beauclerk's
                                                     Shakespeare's Lost Kingdom (2011)]
2011, Dec., p. 54   Niederkorn, William S.   Beyond the Previously Known Bard [review of *The Shakespeare
                                                     Guide to Italy by Richard Paul Roe]
2012, Feb., p. 62   Niederkorn, William S.   Occupying W. S. [review of *Nine Lives of William Shakespeare*
                                                     by Graham Holderness (2011)]
2013, Feb., p. 60   Niederkorn, William S.   Shake-Speare Fission

Brunswick Daily News
1939-1940   --   Shakespeare Paintings Really Earl of Oxford, Says Student
                                                     [commentary on Barrell's findings]

Buffalo News
1994, Mar. 31, p. B1   Achenbach, Joes   Why Things Are
1999, Feb. 7, p. H5   Kilpatrick, James   After All These Years, Shakespeare's Identity Still a Mystery
2000, Jan. 30, p. B17   --   Obituary of John G. Kloepfer, Oxfordian
2005, Sept. 18, p. H2   Kilpatrick, James   The Bard By Any Other Name Would Sound As Sweet

Bulletin, The (Sydney)
1920, May 6, vol. 41/2099:   Wright, David McKee   William Shakespeare de Vere [review of SI]
    Red Page, 24
1921, Oct. 27, vol. 42/2176: 25   Athos.   The Real Shakespeare [review of SI]
1921, Dec. 8, vol. 42/2182:   M. M. P.   Shakespeare Identified? [letter]

Red Page

1922, Jan. 5, vol. 43/2186: 25	Wright, David McKee	Edward de Vere Identified [response to M.M.P.]
1922, Jan. 19, vol. 43/2188: 44	--	Answers to Correspondents
1922, Feb. 2, vol. 43/2190: 25	Esson, Louis	Shakespeare? [letter]
1922, Feb. 9, vol. 43/2191: 25	M. M. P.	De Vere Identified [letter]
1922, Feb. 16, vol. 43/2192: 27	Wright, David McKee	The Search for Shakespeare
1922, Feb. 23, vol. 43/2193: 25	Wright, David McKee	The Search for Shakespeare
1923, Feb. 22, vol. 44/2245: Red Page	Wright, David McKee	The Elusive Shakespeare
1923, March 1, vol. 44/2246: 3	Donalbain	Shakspeare and "Fat" [letter]
1923, Mar. 29, vol. 44/2250: Red Page	Fisher, Edmund	Can't We Let Shakspeare Alone? [letter]
1923, April 19, vol. 44/2253: 3	Lindsay, Jack	Shakspeare and Shylock

Bulletin of the Faculty of Letters, Hosei University, Tokyo, Japan

1993, May 11, no. 39-1993	Londré, Felicia H.	*Hamlet* as Autobiography: An Oxfordian Analysis [repr. in SAS (Stritmatter 2019, 2022): 303-14]

Bulletin of the Public Library of the City of Boston

1920, Dec., Fourth Series, vol. II,-- p. 340, 357		Newly-Acquired Books [list includes SI under author and subject of "Shakespeare"]

Burnley Express and Advertiser

1920, March 6, p. 7	--	[*"Shakespeare" Identified* mentioned in passing]

Bury Free Press

1937, April 24, p. 16	--	Lavenham [lecture by Col. Montagu Douglas, President of the Shakespeare Fellowship]
1937, May 22, p. 6	--	Was "Shakespeare" Written by East Anglian? [resp. to the May issue of *East Anglian Magazine.*]
1937, June 5, p. 7	--	Was Shakespeare an East Anglian? [resp. to the June issue of *East Anglian Magazine.*]

Business Wire (BUS)

1999, March 22, p. 1	--	Who Really Wrote All Those Plays?
2004, June 22, p. 1	--	The SOS and the 400th Anniversary of Oxford's Death
2004, Oct. 19	--	Shakespeare Oxford Society to Stage 28th Annual Conf. in Atlanta
2006, Jan. 16, p. 1	--	A Monumental Shakespeare Fraud in Stratford? [highlights the latest edition of *The Oxfordian*, mentions the SOS and Matthew Cossolotto]
2006, Feb. 3, p. 1	--	Shakespeare's Standard Biography Could Shatter into "A Million Little Pieces"
2007, Oct. 3	--	The Joint Shakespeare Authorship Conference in Carmel
2008, Feb. 28	--	SOS Appoints Professor Michael Egan, Award-Winning Shakespeare Scholar, as Editor of *The Oxfordian*

Calgary Herald

1989, April 17, p. D2	Blakey, Bob	Was Shakespeare a Fake? Some Scholars Think So
1989, Dec. 2, p. C1	--	Mystery Behind the Bard
1991. Oct. 13, p. C5	--	[resp. to *The Atlantic's* October 1991 issue]
1992, Dec. 22, p. D10	--	Today's Best [mentions Edward de Vere as Shakespeare]
1997, May 10, p. 1B	McGoogan, Ken	Say Goodbye to . . . Shakespeare [review of *Alias Shakespeare* by Joe Sobran (1997)]
2004, Oct. 19, p. 1	--	Shakespeare Oxford Society to Stage 28th Annual Conference

Cambridge Quarterly

2010, vol. 39/3: 297-302	Ellis, David	[review of *Contested Will* by James Shapiro (2010)]

Cambridge Review

1933, May 12, vol. 54: 389	Robinson, Joan	Shakespeare and Mr. Looney [repr. in DVN, vol. 15/1: 14-16 (March 2008)]

Canadian Journal of Psychoanalysis

2010, Spring, vol. 18/1: 20-42+	Levitt, Cyril	Freud, Smith, and Feuerbach on Sacrifice

Cashiers Elisabéthains

2004, Spring, p. 11-24	Moore, Peter R.	*Hamlet* and *Piers Plowman*: A Matter of Conscience [repr. in LA, p. 61-96]
2006, Autumn, vol. 70: 39-42	Stritmatter, Roger	'Tilting Under Frieries': Narcissus (1595) and the Affair at Blackfriars
2010, vol. 77/1: 9-22	Stritmatter Roger	Spenser's 'perfect pattern of a poet' and the 17th Earl of Oxford
2014, vol. 85/1: 67-72	Waugaman, Richard M.	The 1574 *Mirror for Magistrates* is a Possible Source for "Feath'red King" in Shakespeare's *The Phoenix and the Turtle*

Chambers' Edinburgh Journal

1852, Aug. 7, vol. 18/449: 87-9	--	Who Wrote Shakespeare?

Charleston Daily Mail (Charleston, WV)

2007, Sept. 10, p. 3A	Doran, D'Arcy	Coalition Aims to Expose Playwright. Derek Jacobi and Mark Rylance Unveil Declaration of Reasonable Doubt

Charleston News & Courier

1988, Jan. 10	Editorial	Was 'The Bard' Really 'The Earl?' That, As They Say, Is The Question [repr. in SON, vol. 24/1: 11-12 (1988)]

Chelsea News

1966, August 5, p. 8	--	Oxford was "Shakespeare"—Q.E.D.

Chicago Daily Law Bulletin

1987, Sept. 16	--	Three Justices to Decide if Shakespeare Goes By Any Other Name

Chicago Sun-Times

1986, May 1, p. 52	Sobran, Joe	Was the Earl of Oxford the Real Shakespeare?
1987, Sept. 18, p. 9	--	Justices Rule Bard is Not to be Denied
1988, Nov. 27, p. 4	--	Judges Rule that Shakespeare Was for Real
1988, Dec. 1, p. 52	Froelich, John F.	Edward de Vere – The Real Bard
1993, May 30, p. 44	Harayda, Janice	History's Hot 100 [review of *The 100*, rev. ed., by Michael Hart]
1999, Feb. 7, p. 18	Kilpatrick, James	Who's This Fellow Will Shakespeare?
2002, Oct. 8, p. 37	Weiss, Hedy	The Beard of Avon [review of Amy Freed's play]
2005, Sept. 18, p. 9	Kilpatrick, James	What's in a Name? He Whom We Call the Bard / By Another Name Would Read as Well

Chicago Tribune (Chicago Daily Tribune)

1920, March 24, p. 8	--	Shakespeare [Short comment about *"Shakespeare" Identified* by J. Thomas Looney]
1920, June 13, p. 9	Butcher, Fanny	Tabloid Book Reviews [review of SI]
1920, Aug. 8, p. 8	--	And Yet Some Peope Say . . . [rerinted from *Punch*]
1931, March 14, 10	--	Now It Seems De Vere Wrote Shakespeare's Plays [review of *Hidden Allusions* by Eva Turner Clark (1931)]
1940, Jan.		X-Rays Reveal Real Shakespeare
1944, March 5. p. D9	Hansen, Harry	"Who's Looney Now?"
1944, April 24, p. 12	--	A Line o' Type or Two: Shakespeare's Ghosts
1947, Jan. 5, p. G2	Starrett, Vincent	Magazine of Books [review of *Shakespeare, Man of Mystery* by Thomas Henry Fowler (1946)]
1947, May 30, p. 8	Astley-Lock, John	Infra-Red Peers Into Mystery of Shakespeare [Barrell's work on the Hampton court portrait]
1948, May 8, p. 10	--	A Line o' Type or Two: Shakespeare's Ghost
1948, Dec. 27, p. 20	Astley-Lock, John	Check and Mate [letter]
1949, March 23, p. 18	Collins, Charles	Strange Case of Mr. W. S.
1949, April 17, p. H2	Cassidy, Claudio	On the Aisle [review of *Under the Mask of Shakespeare* by Abel Lefranc] [Has much to say about Oxford]
1949, Oct. 30, p. I22	Guilfoil, Kelsey	[review of the Second Edition of *"Shakespeare" Identified*]
1950, May 4, p. 20	--	"Not Without Right"
1953, Feb. 15, p. B10	Crane, Milton	Authors Say: Oxford—Not Shakespeare [review of *This Star of England*]
1957, April 21, p. B6	Gould, Gordon	If Shakespeare Didn't Write Shakespeare. Who Did?
1962, Sept. 23, p. 20	Mithoff, H. W.	Shakespeare's Tomb
1963, August 18, p. G2	Atkinson, Brooks	Shakespeare or Bacon or . . . The Debate Runs On [reprint of

		Brooks's July 12 *New York Times* article]
1973, April 1, p. J74	Rogers, Byron	What's Behind Shakespeare's Bust? [Ogburn's quest to open Shakespeare's tomb]
1973, April 29, p. I6	Yabush, Donald R.	[letter: response to Rogers' April 1 "tomb" article]
1987, Sept. 27, p. 3	Molotsky, Irvin	Justices Find All's Well for Shakespeare
1987, Oct. 2, p. 20	--	A Left-Handed Win for the Bard
1988, May 29, p. D6	Baily, Moira	No Snobs They; 2nd Best is Good Enough
1988, Nov. 27, p. 8	--	Did He or Did He Not Write *Twelfth Night*?
1989, Aug. 7, Sec. 5: 1-2	Boyd, Bentley	Was the Earl the Bard? Defenders of an Oxford NoblemanTake Center Stage in the Long-Running Drama Over Whether Shakspere Really Wrote His Plays
1992, Jan. 17, p. C1	Van Matre, Lyn	Bard Questions [Lord Burford's Speaking Tour]
2002, Oct. 6, p. 7	Phillips, Michael	Where There's a Will [review of *The Beard of Avon* by Amy Freed]
2002, Oct. 20, p. 7	Jones, Chris	The Great Shakespearean Debate: Some Argue the Earl of Oxford Wrote the Plays
2007, Sept. 18, p. 8	Doran, D'Arcy	Coalition Resurrects Doubts About Bard's Identity
2011, Oct. 28, p. 4.1	Phillips, Michael	*Anonymous* Debate Rages Here and Abroad

China Press (Shanghai)

1930, Dec. 4, p. 14	Allen, Percy	The De Vere-Shakespeare Controversy Today [Overview of Oxfordian developments] [repr. from *The Christian Science Monitor*, Oct. 18, 1930]

Choice: Current Reviews for Academic Libraries

1984-85, vol. 22: 992	Vaughan, Virginia M.	[review of *The Mysterious William Shakespeare* by Charlton Ogburn, Jr. (1992)]
1993, March, vol. 30/7: 1146	Redding, D. C.	[review of *The Shakespeare Controversy* by Warren Hope and Kim Holston]
1994-95, vol. 32: 783	Lerud, T. K.	[review of *Shakespeare, In Fact* by Irvin L. Matus]
1997-98, vol. 35/3: 485	Dickerson, D. O.	[review of *Alias Shakespeare* by Joseph Sobran (1997)]
2001, May, vol. 38/9: 1630	Traister, D.	[review of *Shakespeare's Unorthodox Biography* by Diana Price]
2004, March, vol. 41/7: 1298	Castaldo, A.	[review of *Monstrous Adversity: The Life of Edward de Vere* by Alan Nelson (2003)]
2004, May, vol. 42: 6346	Ellis, A. L.	[review of *The Case for Shakespeare* by Scott McCrea]
2005, Dec., vol. 43/4: 565	DiMatteo, Anthony	[review of *"Shakespeare" By Another Name* by Mark Anderson]
2007, Sept., vol. 45/1: 96	Stritmatter, R. A.	A Companion to Shakespeare's Sonnets
2008, Feb., vol. 45/6: 979	Stritmatter, R. A.	Shakespeare's Sonnets
208, May, vol. 45/9: 1536	Stritmatter, R. A.	Religion In the Age of Shakespeare
2008, July, vol. 45/11: 1945	Stritmatter, R. A.	English Renaissance Literature and Contemporary Theory: Sublime Objects of Theology
2008, Sept., vol. 46/1: 91	Stritmatter, R. A.	Shakespeare's Modern Collaborators
2009, Feb., vol. 46/9: 1099	Stritmatter, R. A.	Pogue, Kate Emery, Shakespeare's Family
2010-11, vol. 48	Brandt, Bruce E.	[review of *Contested Will* by James Shapiro (2010)]

Christian Science Monitor (CHM)

1920, March 27, p. 15	Jonson, Ben	Shakespeare
1920, April 10, p. 3	S.	At Random
1920, May 7, p. 3	--	Shakespeare and Bacon Again
1920, May 18, p. 6	--	Is Shakespeare Identified? [review of *SI*]
1923, May 19, p. 17	PA [Percy Allen]	Hamlet's Identify with an Elizabethan [repr. in *Billboard*, Aug. 25, 1923, p. 64]
1928, June 15, p. 11 , PA [Percy Allen]		With Hamlet in Hackney [review of *The 17th Earl of Oxford* by B. M. Ward]
1928, July 3, p. 12	PA [Percy Allen]	Versatile Elizabethan [review of *The 17th Earl of Oxford* by B. M. Ward]
1928, Aug. 18, p. 7	PA [Percy Allen]	Musings Over the Shakespearean First Folio
1928, Aug. 23, p. 10	C. F. A.	Elizabethan Borrowers [review of *Borrowers* by Percy Allen]
1929, Jan. 18, p. 4	PA [Percy Allen]	The Rhyme-Linked Order of Shakespeare's *Sonnets*
1929, May 14, p. 17	--	Shakespeare and Chapman as Popular Dramatists [review of *Topical Dramatists* by Percy Allen (1929)]

Christian Science Monior (continued)

1929, May 24, p. 9	PA [Percy Allen]	One Theory as to the Authorship of Shakespeare's Sonnets
1929, Dec. 27, p. 7	Allen, Percy	How Shakespeare Wrote *King Lear*
1930, July 2, p. 16	--	Shakespeare and the Sheriff
1930, July 19, p. 6	--	De Vere as Shakespeare [reviews of *Shakespeare's Sonnets and Edward de Vere* by Gerard Rendall (1930) and *The Case for Edward de Vere as Shakespeare* by Percy Allen] ["It is, probably, no exaggeration to say that belief in the Stratfordian authorship of the Shakespearean poems and plays, though still accepted by the vast majority, is rapidly being discarded by inquiring and thoughtful scholars throughout the English-speaking world."]
1930, Oct. 18, p. 18	Allen, Percy	The de Vere-Shakespeare Controversy Today
1930, Nov. 4, p. 6	PA [Percy Allen]	Shakespearean Research [reviews of *Shakespearean Authorship: A Summary* by Gilbert Standen and two other books]
1930, Dec. 24, p. 20	Pogson, Reuben	The de Vere-Shakespeare Controversy [letter: Percy Allen's Oct. 18 article]
1931, Feb. 9, p. 14	Allen, Percy	The de Vere-Shakespeare Controversy [letter: reply to Pogson's Dec. 24 letter]
1931, Feb. 28, p. 6	Allen, Percy	The Oxford Theory Again [review of *Hidden Allusions* by Eva Turner Clark]
1931, April 25, p. 12	C. F. A.	The Oxford Theory [review of *Corroborated* by Percy Allen]
1931, May 22	Shepard, Odell (O.S.)	Hide and Go Seek
1931, June 5, p. 20	Allen, Percy	The Oxford-Shakespeare Theory [letter: resp. to C. F. A.'s review of "*Corroborated*"]
1931, Nov. 21, p. 10	Allen, Percy	A Miscast Shallow [review of *Shakespeare Versus Shallow* by Leslie Hotson]
1932, Jan. 9, p. 7	PA [Percy Allen]	As to Shakespearean Authorship [reviews of *Seven Shakespeare* by Gilbert Slater and *The Earl of Oxford as "Shakespeare"* by Lt. Col. Montagu Douglas]
1932, May 17, p. 16	J. B. D.	Why There is a Shakespeare Problem
1932, May 21, p. 10	Allen, Percy	For the Stratfordians
1932, Oct. 1, p. 6	Allen, Percy	Shakespeare in the East
1932, Dec. 3, p. 10	Allen, Percy	As You Like It
1933, Jan. 31, p. 7	Allen, Percy	Shakespearean Adventure in Burgundy, A
1933, April 22, p. 10	Allen, Percy	New Shakespearean Books [review of *The Satirical Comedy* by Eva Turner Clark] ["A satisfactory, yet orthodox, 'Life' of William Shakespeare . . . is manifestly impossible, for almost nothing is known."]
1933, May 27, p. 10	Allen, Percy	Shakespeare's Times [review of two books about Shakespeare's life]
1933, June 17, p. 10	H. H. [Hub. H. Holland]	Oxfordian Rejoinder [review of *Lord Oxford and Shakespeare: A Reply to John Drinkwater* by Percy and Ernest Allen]
1933, Aug. 19, p. 8	--	Shakespeare and Politics [review of *The Plays of Shakespeare and Chapman in Relation to French History* of Percy Allen]
1934, June 13, p. WM11	F. B.	Brief for the Oxfordians [review of *Anne Cecil, Elizabeth and Oxford* by Percy Allen]
1934, Oct. 3, p. WM10	Allen, Percy	Shakespearean Topicalities [review of *Shakespeare, Oxford, and Elizabethan Times* by Adm. Hubert H. Holland]
1935, Dec. 4, p. WM12	Allen, Percy	Hamlet, Topically [review of *What Happens in Hamlet* by J. Dover Wilson]
1938, Feb. 16, p, WM11	Pritchett, V. S.	A Shakespearean Detective at Work Again [review of *I, William Shakespeare, Do Appoint Thomas Russell* by Leslie Hotson]
1939, Dec. 21, p. 9	Nichols, Herbert B.	Wonders of Research: Three Portraits of Shakespeare X-rayed Seeing Through Paint
1953, March 5, p. 13	Leonard, Edwin S., Jr.	Still the Query: Who Wrote Shakespeare's Works? [review of *This Star of England* by Dorothy and Charlton Ogburn]
1980, July 14	Kidder, Rushworth M.	A Play by Another Smells as Sweet
1988, Sept. 28	Sammartino, Peter	Who Wrote the Greatest Plays in the English Language?

1988, Nov. 28	--	British Law Lords Back Shakespeare
1991, April	Johnson, Morse	Who Wrote *Edmund Ironside*? [repr. in SON, vol. 27/3: 5 (Summer, 1991); and in BTC, vol. 7: 52]
1997, Dec. 31	Ford, Peter	Aussian Debunks the Bard [review of *The Game of Shakespeare* by Ilya Gililov] [excerpt repr. in SON, vol. 34/1: 2 (Spring, 1998)]
1999, Apr. 23, p. 13	Lamb, George M.	Seeking the Real Bard of Stratford
2002, Dec. 27, p. 19	Mason, M. S.	What's on TV [review of *Frontline*'s "Much Ado About Something"]
2003, June 26, p. 15	Charles, Ron	Where's William? [rev. of *Chasing Shakespeares* by Sarah Smith]

Chronicle-Herald (Halifax)

| 2015, Oct. 7, p. S19 | King, Jim | Exploring Belief: Skeptics Will Always Be the Underdog |

Chronicle of Culture

| 1986, vol. 10/2: 18-22 | Greer, Jane | [review of *The Mysterious William Shakespeare* by Charlton Ogburn, Jr. (1992)] |

Chronicle of Higher Education

1987, Oct. 7, p. A6	Editor	Footnotes [Summary of Supreme Court mock debate]
1990, May 9, p. A4	--	Footnotes [Summary of Ward Elliot's computer analysis]
1999, June 4, vol. 45/39: A19	Heller, Scott	The Illustrator of *Titus Andronicus* Also Figures in Authorship Controversy
1999, June 4, vol. 45/39: A22	Heller, Scott	In a Centuries-old Debate, Shakespeare Doubters Point to New Evidence
2010, March 28, vol. 56/29	Howard, Jennifer	A Shakespeare Scholar Takes on a 'Taboo' Subject: James Shapiro Explores the Authorship Question – And Why So Few in Academe Will Touch It
2010, April 2, p. B11-12	Howard, Jennifer	[review of *Contested Will: Who Wrote Shakespeare?* by James Shapiro (2010)]

Chronicles

| 1997, vol. 21/8: 26 | Brownlow, Frank | [review of *Alias Shakespeare* by Joe Sobran (1997)] |

Church Times, The

| 1923, June 29, 1923, p. 276 | -- | Shakespeareana [review of *The Mystery of "Mr. W.H."* by Col. Bernard R. Ward] [See resp. by J. T. Looney, Sept. 7 and 14] |

Cincinnati Enquirer

1920, June 12, p. 5	--	New Books [*"Shakespeare" Identified* is on the list.]
1933, March 26, p. 43	Leighton, George A.	Poor Bill! Surviving the Baconian Racket for Lo These Many Years, Now Beset with Another Attack on His Identity
1933, May 6, p. 10	G.A.S.	Book Reviews [review of *Love's Labour's Lost: A Study* by Eva Turner Clark]
1933, Dec. 3, p. 57	--	LeComtesse De Chambrun Defends the Authority of Her Shakespearean Data
1977, Feb. 13, p. D5	Johnson, Morse	The Man Who Wasn't Shakespeare [review of *"Shakespeare" Identified* by J. Thomas Looney]
1937, June 12, p. 5	M.H.M.	Elizabethan Translator [review of *An Elizabethan Puritan* by Louis T. Golding]
1978, Nov. 26, p. 294	--	History's Most Successful Coverup
1987, Sept. 24, p. 45	--	Judges to Decide Who's the Real Shakespeare
1999, Feb. 22	Bouman, Gregory M.	[letter: discussion of alternative authors disgraces a family newsp.]
1999, March 3, p. A15	Cavanaugh, Gerald J.	[letter: SOS Member responds to Bouman]
2002, May 17, p. W12	Demaline, Jackie	In Search of the Real Shakespeare [review of *The Beard of Avon* by Amy Freed]
2004, June 27	Wardell, Jane	Shakespeare a Sham, Society Says [De Vere Society]

Cincinnati Post

| 1983, April 11 | Winkler, Claudia | William Who? [repr. in SON, vol. 19/2: 1-2 (Spring, 1983); and in BTC, vol. 6: 237-39] |
| 1997, July 19, p. 11C | McCrum, Robert | Shakespeare's Genius the Key to the Mystery |

Clark Clarion

| 1946, Feb. 22? | -- | [report on Benezet's talk at Clark School] |

Clearing House, The
 1956, Sept, vol. 31/1: 23-25   Angoff, Charles   Was Shakespeare "Shakespeare"?

Columbian (Vancouver, Wash.)
 1999, April 8, p. F5   Pierce, Annie   Was Shakespeare a Fraud? Conference Looks Into the Question [Third Annual De Vere Studies Conference]

Columbus Dispatch
 2003, Sept. 14, p. 7C   Eichenberger, Bill   Playwright's Hidden Life Fuels Speculation About Authorship

Commentary
 2005, March, vol. 119/4   Gross, John   Will the Real Shakespeare Please Stand Up?
 2005, June, vol. 119/6: 24-25   Keiler, Jonathan F.   The Man from Stratford [letter: resp. to John Gross]
 2005, June, vol. 119/6: 24   Gross, John   The Man from Stratford [letter: reply to Jonathan Keiler]
 2010, March, vol. 129/3: 38-44   Gross, John   Denying Shakespeare: The 150-year History of Conspiracy Theorists and Their Efforts to 'Prove' that the Man from Stratford Wasn't the Author [rev. of *Contested Will: Who Wrote Shakespeare?* by James Shapiro]
 2010, June, vol. 129/6: 6   Blumenfeld, Samuel   [letter: Gross' March review of *Contested Will*]
 2010, June, vol. 129/6: 6-7   Oakes, Rev. Edward T.   [letter: Gross' March review of *Contested Will*]
 2010, June, vol. 129/6: 7-8   Gross, John   [letter: reply to responders]

Commercial Appeal (Memphis)
 1995, March 16, p. TE4   Beggs, Mary   Who What Where [many Believe Earl of Oxford was Shakespeare]
 1997, Sept. 25   Swindell, Larry   Theories of the 'Real' Shakespeare Signify Little [review of *The Mysterious William Shakespeare*]
 1999, May 9, p. F1   Thomas, Bill   The Book's the Thing for Scholar of the Bard and the Bible

Commonweal
 1970, Oct. 30, p. 129-31   Eagleton, Terry   Books: From Postcard-length Data, a Wealth of Images and Legends

Commonwealth
 1920, Oct., p. 288-92   Crosse, Gordon   Yet Another Shakespeare [review of SI]

Communications of the ACH
 2006, April, vol. 49/4: 76-82   Li, Jiexun; Rong Zheng Hsinchun Chen   From Fingerprint to Writeprint: Identifying the Key Features to Help Identify and Trace Online Authorship

Compact Magazine
 2023, March 24   Gasda, Matthew   The Right-Wing Crusade Against Shakespeare

Comparative Drama
 2007, Spring, vol. 41/1: 119   Waller, Gary   Pseudonymous Shakespeare: Rioting Language in the Sidney Circle [review of the book by Penny McCarthy]

Computers and the Humanities
 1991, Aug., vol. 25/4: 199-209   Elliott, Ward E.; & Robert J. Valenza   A Touchstone for the Bard
 1996, vol. 30/3: 191-245   Elliott, Ward E.; Robert J. Valenza   And Then There Were None: Winnowing the Shakespeare Claimants
 1996, vol. 30/3: 247-55   Foster, Donald W.   [response to Elliot and Valenza, "And Then There Were None"]
 1998, vol. 32/6: 491-510   Foster, Donald W.   The Claremont Shakespeare Authority Clinic: How Severe Are the Problems?

Connoisseur
 1910, April-May   Spielmann, M. H.   [piece on the Ashbourne portrait; title not known]

Connecticut Bar Journal
 1993, Aug., vol. 67/4   Domnarsk, William   Shakespeare In the Law [repr. in SON, vol. 30/1: 4 (Winter 1994)]

Contemporary Review
 1975, July 1, vol. 227: 29-33   Edwards, Francis   The Bard: A Ghost Refuses to Be Laid
 2010, Winter, issue 292: 518-19   Berry, Ralph   [review of *Contested Will* by James Shapiro (2010)]
 2011, Dec., vol. 293, p. 488   Berry, Ralph   Anonymous Shakespeare?

Country Life

2015, May 20, p. 103	Hedges, Mark	The Literary Discovery of the Century [resp. by Alexander Waugh in DVN, vol. 22/3: 4 (July 2015)]

Countryman, The (Burford, Oxfordshire)

1945, Spring, p. 46	Tierney, J. W.	In the Country and Out of It [exc. repr. in SFE, p. 4 (May 1945)]

Courier-Journal (Louisville, KY)

1920, June 27, p. A4	--	Mr. Looney's "Loonacy" [short review of SI]
1923, May 25, p. 6	Burgess, Gelett	The Ten Books I Have Enjoyed Most [includes SI]
1953, Feb. 16	--	'Tis Neither Here Nor There [reprinted from the WSJ]
1975, Feb. 15, vol. 240/46: 16	--	[title not known]

Courier-Mail (Queensland, Australia)

1991, March 2	Goodwin, Ken	Historical Setting for the Looney Theories [review of *The Lost Chronicle of Edward de Vere* by Andrew Field (1990)]
1992, June 22, p. 9	Field, Andrew	Shakespeare Unmasked
1995, Nov. 28	Carbon, Deanie	Who Was the Real Bard?
1996, Nov. 16	Field, Andrew	So Who Was Shakespeare?

Coventry Evening Telegraph (Coventry, UK)

1972, March 31, p. 12	Avon, John	Challenge to Stratford
1973, Feb. 1, p. 18	--	Another Bid to Open Shakespeare's Tomb [Charlton Ogburn]
1973, Feb. 1, p. 35	--	American's Plea on Sh.'s Tomb Opening [Charlton Ogburn]
2003, June 21, p. 20-21	Court, Judith	Bilton Hall; The Many Chapters of Its History
2004, June 24, p. 31	--	Who Was Real Shakespeare?
2007, Sept. 28, p. 35	--	Stage Whispers [review of *The Big Secret Live: I Am Shakespeare* by Mark Rylance and Matthew Warchus]
2009, Aug. 13, p. 31	--	Is Tomb Answer to Bard Debate?
2011, Sept. 1, p. 11	--	By Will or Not By Bard Fraud? [review of *Anonymous*]
2011, Oct. 26, p. 87	McMullen, Marion	Film's Much Ado About Nothing [review of *Anonymous*]
2011, Oct. 27, p. 27	McMullen, Marion	More Join Bard Ban Protests
2016, July 12, p. 11	Lynch, Lucy	Shakespeare Doubters Dismiss Bard's Output [25% think Shakspere didn't write the plays; 48% want better jokes; 27% want more sex scenes]

Coventry Herald

1920, March 6, p. 10	--	Who was Shakespeare? Another "Discovery"

Cresset: A Review of Literature, the Arts, and Public Affairs

1998, vol. 61/4: 35-36	Wright, Daniel, L.	[review *of Shakespeare – Who Was He?* by Richard F. Whalen]

Critic and Guide

1951, June	Feldman, A. Bronson	The Man Who Might Have Been Shakespeare [repr. as the introduction to *Hamlet Himself.*]

Critical Stages [www.critical-stages.org]

2014, Feb., no. 14	Rubin, Don	[review of *Shakespeare Beyond Doubt* (Edmondson & Wells 2013), and *Shakespeare Beyond Doubt?* (Shahan and Waugh 2013)] [repr. in BC, vol. V: 189-92)]

2018, Dec. no. 18: Special Topics II: The Question That Won't Go Away, edited by Don Rubin

	Rubin, Don	An Introduction to "The Question that Won't Go Away: Did the Man from Stratford Really Write the Plays?"
	Rubin, Don	Reasonable Doubt about the Identity of William Shakespeare [an interview with Derek Jacobi and Mark Rylance]
	Cutler, Keir	A Theatre Artist's Path: Questioning Shakespeare's Authorship
	Price, Diana	What's the Question in *Shakespeare's Unorthodox Biography*?
	Goldstein, Gary	Transforming Productions of Shakespeare's Plays
	Regnier, Thomas	Shakespeare as Lawyer: *Hamlet,* Death, Property and the Pursuit of Justice
	Whittemore, Hank	The Argument for Edward de Vere: Shakespeare Was a Man of the Theatre
	Vaïs, Michel	Pourquoi John Florio alias Shakespeare
	Editor	It's Important to Know How Great Works of Theatre are Made [BBC interview with Mark Rylance]

Critical Survey

2009, Sum., vol. 21/2: 1-6	Leahy, William	Introduction to 'Questioning Shakespeare' special section
2009, Sum., vol. 21/2: 7-42	Stritmatter, Roger; & Lynne Kositsky	'O Brave New World': *The Tempest* and Peter Martyr's *De Orbe Novo*
2009, Sum., vol. 21/2: 43-59	McCarthy, Penny	*Cymbeline*: 'The First Essay of a New Brytish Poet'?
2009, Sum., vol. 21/2: 60-82	Stritmatter, Roger	The Tortured Signifier: Satire, Censorship, and the Textual History of *Troilus and Cressida*
2009, Sum., vol. 21/2: 83-110	Barber, Rosalind	Shakespeare Authorship Doubt in 1593
2014, Sum., vol. 26/2: 21-52	Stritmatter, Roger & Lynne Kositsky	The Pattern of Parody in *Eastward Ho*, and a New Date for *King Lear*
2023, Autumn, vol. 21/3: 17-61	Stritmatter, Roger	Francis Meres Revisited: Wit, Design and Authorship in *Palladis Tamia* (1598)

Cross Currents

1995/1996, Winter, p. 558	O'Brien, Thomas	Class and Classic [review of *Shakespeare, In Fact* by Irvin Matus]

Cryptologia (West Point)

2000, Jan., vol. 24/1: 81	Kruh, Louis	*Who Wrote Shakespeare?* [review of John Michell's book]
2002, Oct., vol. 26/4: 311	Kruh, Louis	Blue Avenger Code Cracker [review of *Blue Avenger Cracks the Code* by Norma Howe]
2005, April, vol. 29/2: 179-81	Kruh, Louis	Shakespeare Enigma

Daily Advertiser (Lafayette, La.)

2005, Sept. 17, p. C5	--	Obituary: Ruth Loyd Miller
2005, Sept. 19. p. A4	Decker, Bill	Two Truths Are Told. Ruth Miller and the Shakespeare Debate

Daily Bruin (UCLA)

1976, April 14, p. 1, 9	Starr, Carol	Author Denies Shakespeare Wrote Plays [profile of SOS member and VP S. Colum Gilfillan]
1976, May 10	Cyr, Gordon C.	To Be or Not To Be?

Daily Express

2004, June 27	Metcalfe, Luisa	Shakespeare or Not Shakespeare? That Is the Question
2014, Oct. 14, p. 13	Gore-Langton, Robert	Could the Real Mr. Shakespeare Please Stand Up? [repr. in DVN, vol. 21/3: 3-5 (October 2014)]

Daily Herald (UK)

1937, Oct. 16, p. 10	Salusbury, F. G. H.	Are You Looking for Something to Do? [Brief mention of *"Shakeseare" Identified*]

Daily Herald (Arlington Heights, Illinois)

1992, Jan. 23	Valeo, Tom	The Case Against Shakespeare [repr. in SON, vol. 28/1: 1-3 (Winter 1992); and in BTC, vol. 7: 83]
2006, Aug. 31, p. 11	Constable, Burt	Shakespeare By Any Other Name Would Smell as Sweet

Daily Herald (Biloxi, Mississippi)

1939, Dec.	--	[front page story on Charles Barrell]

Daily Mail and Mail on Sunday (London)

1931, Oct.-Dec. and into 1932	Jeffires	[pieces on Beauclerk's portraits analysis]
1962, June 7, p. 12	Allsop, Kenneth	The Day Those Tudor Beatniks Dreamed Up Shaksper
1966, Feb. 18	Levin, Bernard	The Stratford Frauds [repr. Nov. 30]
1987, July 3, p. 19	Dempster, Nigel	They're Veering to Vere [lord Vere]
1987, Sept. 26, p. 10A	--	Bard is Adjudged Bona Fide
1999, Oct. 27, p. 21	--	Making a Play for Shakespeare [Burford]
2000, Feb. 12	Furnival, Jane	East Ender Who Says He's An Earl [Aubrey William de Vere] [repr. in DVN (Oct. 2004), p. 20-21]
2002, April 14, p. 2	Beauclerk, Charles	Don't Call Me Lord – Traitors Have Stolen My Birthright
2006, Feb. 1, p. 55	Black, James	The Bard or Not the Bard: Answers to Correspondents
2007, Sept. 7, p. 1	Gore-Langston, Robert	Is There a William Shakespeare in the House? [review of *The Big Secret Live* by Mark Rylance and Matthew Warchus (2007)]
2009, Nov. 27, p. 18	Martin, Samuel	Sorry, It's True. The Bard Was a Mere Brummie
2010, Feb. 1, p. 36	Price, Richard	Will Opening This Tomb Prove Shakespeare Didn't Write His Plays?
2010, April 11, p. 11	Brown, Craig	The MAD, the SAD & the BARD [review of *Contested Will* by James Shapiro]

2011, Oct. 27, p. 15	Hart, Christopher	Why Does Hollywood Hate the English? [review of *Anonymous*]
2011, Nov. 11, p. 68	Violen, W. R.	[letter: Will o' the Wisp: Doubts about Will]
2013, April 1, p. 21	--	Researchers at Aberystwyth University Say Playwright Had 'Another Life' [repr. in SON, vol. 49/2: 12-13 (2013)]
2013, July 5, p. 41	Kay, Richard	A Waugh of Words Over the Bard
2014, April 27, P. 3	Hastings, Chris	Bard Blood at the Palace as Princes Split Over Shakespeare [Summarized in DVN, vol. 21/2: 37 (May 2014)]
2014, April 30, p. 32	--	The Debate Over Who Wrote Shakespeare
2016, May 3, p. 50	Violen, W. R.	Shakespeare: Fact or Fiction [letter]

Daily News
| 1920, March 4, p. 7 | -- | Hunting the Bard. Mr. T. Looney 'Discovers' the Earl of Oxford |
| 1923, June 21, p. 18 | Sampson, George | Shakespeare Half-Truths [reviews of *The Mystery of "Mr. W.H."* by Col. Bernard R. Ward and *Shakespeare Through Oxford Glasses* by Capt. H. H. Holland] [See Looney's critique of this article in *The Hackney Spectator*, Aug. 31, 1923] |

Daily News (Halifax)
| 1992, April 20, p. 22 | Rapport, Evie | The Genius Mystery: Hundreds of Questions Surround the Works of Shakespeare [reports on Charles Vere address] |
| 1998, Nov. 20, p. 34 | Woods, Michael | Stars Betray Shakespeare |

Daily News and Westminster
| 1928, March 21 | Greenwood, Sir George | Shakespeare's Father: Was He Able to Write? |

Daily News-Sun (Sun City, Arizona)
| 1991 | Cusick, John | [letter] [repr. in SSN, issue 1/1: 3 (Feb. 1991)] |

Daily Post (Liverpool)
| 2009, April 22 | Wright, Jade | To Be Or Not To Be . . . Did Shakespeare Write Sonnets? [Canon Gerald Rendall donated his collection of books and papers to the University of Liverpool Library] |

Daily Record (Glasgow)
| 1999, Oct. 27, p. 4 | Morris, Nigel | Descendant of Nell Gwynne's Wacky Campaigns [Burford] |

Daily Saratogian
| 1948, Jan. | -- | [an account of the Bénézet-Joseph Bolton discussion broadcast live on WGY of Schenectady on Jan. 5. Program resulted from publication of Bénézet's "The Shakespeare Hoax" in the *Dartmouth Quarterly*] |

Daily Sketch (London)
1933, Oct. 28, p. 7	Candidus	The Sense of Things: Lord Oxford & . . .
1934, June	Candidus	[column advises all interested in the authorship issue to read Mr. Looney's *"Shakespeare" Identified*]
1936, April 13, p. 10	--	They Call Him 'The Just Pilate': Judge Meets Witness After Forty Years [Col. Douglas]

Daily Telegraph (London) – See The Telegraph (London)

Daily Telegraph (Surry Hills, Newsl.S.W., Australia)
2000, April 26, p. 43	Lennon, Troy	Bard in the Shadows
2004, April 27, p. 32	Lennon, Troy	Shakespeare
2007, Sept. 11, p. 29	Lennon, Troy	No Holds Bard As Old Debate Flares Again
2010, May 27, p. 36	Lennon, Troy	[review of *Contested Will* by James Shapiro]
2011, Oct. 29, p. 20	--	To Be, or Not To Be, the Bard: *Anonymous* Sparks Fresh Debate Over Authorship of Plays Attributed to Shakespeare

Daily Telegraph (Sydney, Australia)
| 1920, May 1, p. 8 | -- | "Shakespeare Identified" |
| 1930, Dec. 22, p. 14 | Fitzgerald, W. J. P. | Forgotten Celebrity of Elizabeth's Day |

Dallas Morning News
| 1987, Sept. 26, p. 10A | -- | The Bard is Adjudged Bona Fide [The 1987 Moot Court] |

Dartmouth, The (student newspaper)
| 1938, April 21 | -- | Article about Benezet and Edward de Vere |

Dartmouth Alumni Magazine
1994, March, p. 14-21   Sullivan, Robert   No Holds Bard: Obituary of William Fowler (March 1994) [repr. in SON, vol. 30/2a: 5 (Spring 1994)]

Dartmouth Alumni Quarterly
1947, Nov.   Bénézet, Louis P.   The Shakespeare Hoax: An Improbable Narrative [see SFQ, vol. VIII/4: 56 (Winter, 1947-48); and repr. in BTC, vol. 4: 4-11]

Deaney Magazine
1931, Nov.   --   Belchamps St. Pauls

Denver Post
1990, Oct. 30, p. 2A   --   [report on the Shakespeare Oxford Society conference]

Denver University Law Review
1991, vol. 68: 387-411   Cook, Nancy   Shakespeare Comes to the Law School Classroom

Der Spiegel (German)
2007, Dec. 31   --   Über Kochzepte, schwarze Magie, marketing, die klügsten Leute der Welt und Experimente, die nicht gestsestet Warden [repr. in NSJ, vol. 12: 170-73]

Derby Daily/Evening Telegraph (Derbyshire, England)
1920, March 5, p. 6   --   Another "Shakespeare" Discovered
1940, July 31, p. 2   --   A Derby Diary [review of The "Ashbourne" Portrait of Shakespeare by Gerald H. Rendall (1940)]

Derbyshire Advertiser and Journal
1920, March 12, p. 2   --   New Books ["Shakespeare" Identified is on the list]
1920, March 12 & 13, p. 2   --   Shakespeare Demolished Once More: Mr. Looney and The Earl of Oxford [short review of SI]
1924, June 14, p. 2   Feilden, Hermione   A Peakland Heritage [has passing reference to Looney, Oxford]

Des Moines Register
1940, Jan.   --   Is This the Poet I See Before Me? [Barrell in Scientific Am.]

Deseret News (Salt Lake City
2013, April 27   Bennett, Jim   Who Shakespeare Was is Still a Mystery

Detroit Free Press
1939, Dec. 18, p. 3   --   Iffy . . . the Dopester
1974, July 16, p. 9   Harris, Sydney J.   Some Knotty Questions for Shakespeare Fans
2003, March 20, p. 3   Gittleman, Sharon   Crusader Aims to Prove Shakespeare Was a Fraud [profile of Barbara Burris]

Detroit News
1997, July 16, p. A11   Person, James E., Jr.   Writer Got the Wrong Answer From Right Books
1997, July 30, p. A10   --   [letter: James Person's July 16 review]

Dial
1920, Aug., p. 108-21   Rolland, Romain   Shakespeare the Truthteller

Dickensian
1916, April, p. 89-91   Walters, J. Cuming   Dickens and the Shakespeare Mystery

Die Tageszeitung (Berlin)
2010, June 1, p. 25   --   Shakespeare oder nicht Shakespeare, das ist hier die Frage
2011, Nov. 9, p. 16   Schweizerhof, Barbara   Mit Tinte befleckte Finger

Die Welt (Ausgabe Berlin)
1997, Sept. 3   Erné, Nino   Shakespeares fragwürdige Gestalt [repr. in NSJ, vol. 1: 6-13 (Dec. 1997)]
1999, March 2   Schwanitz, Dietrich   Mit aller Liebe: Shakespeare! [repr. in NSJ, vol. 3: 145-49 (July 1999)]
2008, June 20   --   Sogar Beckett ist real [repr. in NSJ, vol. 12: 166-69 (Oct. 2008)]
2010, Jan. 30, p. 1   Posener, Alan   Der mit der Honigzunge [review of Der Mann, der Shakespeare erfand, Edward de Vere, Earl of Oxford by Kurt Kreiler]
2010, April 19, p. 1   Stein, Hannes   Vulkanasche stört auch das Konzertleben
2011, Nov. 9, p. 1   Rodek, Hanns-Georg   Der Mann, der Shakespeare war

Die Zeit (Germany)
2004, issue 51 — Mayer, Susanne — [review of *Will in der Welt* by Stephen Greenblatt] [repr. in NSJ, vol. 11: 175 (April 2007)]

Dispatch (Warwick Valley)
1939, Dec. — -- — [front page story on Barrell]

Dissertation Abstracts International
2001-02, vol. 62: 161A — Stritmatter, Roger — The Marginalia of Edward de Vere's Geneva Bible: Providential Discovery, Literary Reasoning, and Historical Consequence

Dolphin
1941, vol. 4/2: 158 — Wells, Carolyn — The Shakespeare Title-page Mystery

Dover Express (Kent, England)
1936, Feb. 21, p. 8 — -- — Dover Museum Lecture Series [Shakespeare Fellowship to give lecture on Authorship question]

1936, Feb. 28, p. 4 — -- — Shakespeare Authorship [lecture by Col. F. E. G. Skey: many left the hall "thoroughly upset"]

Drama
1938, Feb. — Allen, Percy — Shakespeare Upon a Platform Stage

Dramatists Guild Quarterly
1990, Spring — Williamson, Gene — Who Was Shakes.? [repr. in SON, vol. 26/3: 11-12 (Sum. 1990)]

Dukes County Intelligencer
1999, vol. 40/4: 179-88 — Eldredge, Joseph L. — Prospero's Hen

Dundee Courier and Advertiser (Angus, Scotland)
1930, Jan. 28, p. 4 — -- — Books Received: *The Case for Edward de Vere as "Shakespeare"* by Percy Allen

1930. Feb. 27, p. 10 — -- — Tradition Disturbed [review of *Shakespeare's Sonnets and Edward de Vere* by Gerald H. Rendall (1930)]

1930, April 2, p. 9 — -- — Books Received [*Case* by Percy Allen is on the list]
1930, May 8, p. 8 — -- — Shakespeare and Edward de Vere ["The Baconian theory [is] shattered."]

1931, Mar. 13, p. 10 — -- — Who Wrote Shakespeare? [review of *The Oxford-Shakespeare Case Corroborated* by Percy Allen]

1931, Dec. 3, p. 4 — -- — For the Book Lover [review of *Seven Shakespeares* by Gilbert Slater]

Dundee Evening Telegraph and Post (Angus, Scotland)
1920, March 15, p. 4 — -- — Day by Day [brief note about Looney and SI]
1932, Sept. 19, p. 2 — -- — Shakespeare Plays Controversy: Author 'Clearly an Aristocrat' [review of Oliver Herford's lecture based on *"Shakespeare" Identified*]

Eagle (St. John's College, Cambridge)
1934, Sum., vol. 48/213: 83-87 — L. S. P. — Was Shakespeare a Johnian? [review of SI] [referred to in the *Yorkshire Post*, Aug. 18]

Early Modern Literary Studies
1999, Sept., vol. 5/2: 1-19 — Morton, Peter — Novel Oxfords [reviews of *The Lost Chronicles of Edward de Vere* by Andrew Fields (1990) and *Absent Thee From Felicity* by Rhoda Messner]

2015, vol. 18/1-2 — Ridden, Geoff — [review of *Shakespeare Beyond Doubt* edited by Paul Edmondson and Stanley Wells]

Early Theatre
2006, vol. 9/1: 168 — Brown, Jayson B. — [review of *Shakespeare, Co-Author* by Brian Vickers]

East Anglian Daily Times (Ipswich UK)
1973, July 7 — -- — American Seeks Aid Over Essex Theory on the Bard [repr. in SON, vol. 11/1: 8 (Winter 1975)]

1973, July 10 — -- — Poetry in Motion [repr. in SON, vol. 11/1: 9 (Spr. 1975)]
1973, July 18 — Patience, H. W. — Shakespeare Country [letter: response to recent articles] [repr. in SON, vol. 11/1: 9-10 (Wntr./Spr. 1975)]

2013, March 8 — -- — Conspiracy Theories Have an Uncanny Ability . . .

East Anglian Magazine [see listing in Section IIC: Regular Oxfordian Columns in Non-Oxfordian Publications]

Eastbourne Gazette (East Sussex)

1930, March 12, p. 27	--	Edward de Vere and Shakespeare [review of *Case* by Percy Allen]
1930, April 2, p. 25	Allen, Percy	Oxford-Shakespeare [letter: the March 12 review of his *Case*]
1930, April 2, p. 25	Feste	Oxford-Shakespeare [response by the reviewer]
1930, April 16, p. 27	--	Mr. Percy Allen Replies [editor's note re Allen's reply]
1930, April 30, p. 20	Allen, Percy	Oxford and Mr. Percy Allen's Reply
1930, May 7, p. 15	--	Mr. Percy Allen's Letter: Oxford v. Shakespeare [editor's response to Allen's April 30 letter]
1934, Feb. 7, p. 10	--	Recent Additions to Public Libraries [Gerald Rendall's *Shakespeare: Handwriting and Spelling* is on the list]

Eastern Daily Press

Later 1990s	--	Several articles run on the likelihood of Edward de Vere's authorship [not yet found]
1999, July	--	Rumbling Old Will!

Economic History Review

2006, Aug., vol. 59/3: 638	Bowen, Lloyd	[review of *Edward de Vere: The Crisis and Consequences of Wardship* by Daphne Pearson]

Economist, The

2010, March 27, p. 93	--	Hero or Hoax: William Shakespeare [review of *Contested Will* by James Shapiro (2010)]

Edinburgh Evening News (Midlothian, Scotland)

1932, May 17, p. 8	--	Down With Shakespeare! [review of *Life Story* by Percy Allen]

Edinburgh Journal

1852, Aug. 7, p. 87-89	Jameson, Dr. Robert W.	Who Wrote Shakespeare?

Edmonton Journal (Alberta)

1990, Nov. 2, p. D7	--	Computers Confirm Bard
1993, Sept. 18, p. D6	Nicholls, Liz	Challenging the Shakespeare Mythology; Lord Burford Claims His Ancestor Penned All Those Plays
2002, Feb. 24, p. D6	Niederkorn, William	Much Ado About the Bard: What's in a Name? One Theory is Gaining Ground – That the Real Bard Was Edward de Vere, Earl of Oxford
2003, Sept. 7, p. D10	Carson, Robin	Did He Or Did He Not Write Those Plays?
2005, Aug. 7, p. E12	Fields, Bertram	Did Shakespeare Really Write Those Plays?

Egoist, The

1918, May	Eliot, T. S.	Observation

El Norte (Monterrey, Mexico)

1999, April 5, p. 7	Livas, Javier	Shakespeare en duda

Eleven Magazine

1989, Aug., p. 14-15	Bevington, David M.	[review of "The Shakespeare Mystery" (1989)] [See Judge Bonnie Wheaton's response in SON, vol. 25/3: 6-7 (Summer 1989)]

Emphasis (The Newsletter of Greater New York Mensa

1978, March	Stein, E. Jimmee	To Believe or Not to Believe [repr. in SSR, 1/1: 6-9 (Fall 1987)]

Empirical Studies of the Arts

2004, vol. 22/2: 201-13	Simonton, Dean Keith	Thematic Content and Political Context in Shakespeare's Dramatic Output, with Implications for Authorship and Chronology Controversies

Engineering and Science

1991, vol. 45/1: 22-29	LaBelle, Jenijoy	The Authorship Question, or Will the Real William Shakespeare Please Stand Up

English

2006	Hadfield, Andrew	[review article covers *The Case for Shakespeare* by Scott McCrea]

English Digest

1946, Sept.	Bowen, Marjorie	April 23 Doesn't Impress Me: Why? Because I Don't Believe in Shakespeare [from *Strand Magazine*, vol. CXI (April 1946)]

Articles in Non-Oxfordian Periodicals

English Historical Review

1929, Jan., vol. 44/173: 104-06	Ward, Captain B. M.	Queen Elizabeth and William Davison
2001, vol. 116/467: 557-83	Moore, Peter R.	The Heraldic Charge Against the Earl of Surrey, 1546
2006, Sept., V. 121/493: 1,173+	Paul, Christopher	[review of *Edward de Vere: The Crisis and Consequence of Wardship* by Daphne Pearson]

English Journal

1958, Aug., vol. 47/8: 527-28	Rogers, Hudson	[review of *The Six Loves of "Shakespeare"* by Louis P. Bénézet]
1960, Sept. vol. 49/6: 430	Jarrett, Thomas D.	Language and Literature: Was Sh. Really Sh" [the Ogburn-Hasting letters in *American Scholar*, (Sept. 1960)]
1983, Nov., vol. 72/7: 70-72	Lake, James H.	Psychobiography and Pseudo-Shakespeare

English Language Notes

| 1992, March, vol. 29: 9-19 | May, Steven W. | The Countess of Oxford's Sonnets: A Caveat |

English Literary Renaissance

| 1989, Spring, vol. 19/2: 152-70 | Moody, Ellen | Six Elegiac Poems, Possibly by Anne Cecil de Vere, Countess of Oxford [see also her reply to critiques, at http://www.jimandellen.org/anne.cecil.poems.html] |

English Review, The

1924, Aug., p. 221-29	Sydenham of Combe, Lord & H. Crouch Batchelor	The "Shakespeare" Myth: A Challenge [repr. as a pamphlet]
1924, Sept., p. 318-19	Caink, T.	Shakespearean Metaphor [letter]
1924, Oct., p. 460	Gollancz, I.	Challengers Challenged [resp. to Sydenham & Batchelor]
1924, Oct., p. 461	Sydenham & Batchelor	Challengers Challenged [reply to responses]
1924, Oct., p. 564	Haines, C. M.	Bacon Legend [letter: resp. to Sydenhan & Batchelor]
1924, Nov., p. 603-04	Batchelor, H. Crouch	The "Shakespearean" Myth [letter]
1925, Jan., p. 52-61	Greenwood, George	The Shakespeare Problem: A Reply to Mr. C. M. Haines
1925, Feb., p. 141-42	Haines, C. M.	The Shakespeare Problem [letter]
1928, March, p. 363-64	V. R.	[review of *The Shakespeare Mystery* by Georges Connes]
1928, June, p. 735-36	V. R.	[review of *The Seventeenth Earl of Oxford 1550-1604* by Captain Bernard M. Ward (1928)]
1930, April, p. 520-21	--	[review of *Shakespeare Sonnets and Edward de Vere* by Gerald H. Rendall (1930)]
1933, June, p. 692-94	Kingsmill, Hugh	Shakespeare Criticism [mentions the SF's tenth annual dinner at which one speaker proclaimed "it is now perfectly certain that the young man of the Sonnets was the illegitimate son of Oxford and Queen Elizabeth."]

English Studies .

| 2003 | Moore, Peter R. | The Irony of Marvell's Horatian Ode |

Era, The (London)

1929, March 20, p. 10	--	[review of *Topical Dramatists* by Percy Allen]
1935, May 22, p. 1	--	Talking Shop
1936, March 18, p. 12	--	Percy Allen to speak on "Shakespeare—The Man Behind the Name"

Essays in Criticism

| 2005, vol. 55/3: 193-208 | Ellis, David | Biographical Uncertainty and Shakespeare |

Essex Archaeology and History

| 1974, vol. 6, p. 89- | Powell, J. Enoch | The Riddles of Bures |

Essex Chronicle (Chelmsford)

1922, Dec. 1, p. 3	--	Shakespeare: An Essex Claim [lecturer at Leyton Library discusses de Vere's authorship]
1933, June 16, p. 7	--	Belchamp St. Paul's
1940, April 12, p. 5	--	News in Brief [Mr. F. D. Bone speaks at Southend Rotary Club, says Oxford was real author]
2009, Sept. 17, p. 8	--	Coming Soon . . . [*The Man Who Was Hamlet*, a play by George Dillon about Edward de Vere as Shakespeare]
2011, Nov. 3, p. 8-9	Abbott, Matt	Was Shakespeare an Essex Courtier? We look at the evidence. [review of *Anonymous*]
2011, Nov. 10, p. 18	Summers, Andrew	[letter: Praise for Matt Abbott's article]

Essex Country Standard

1935, Nov. 2	Carwardine-Probert, W.	De Vere Monuments [letter]
1937, Feb. 4	--	Home of the De Vere Monuments
1940, Feb. 17	--	Who was Shakespeare?
1940, Feb. 24	Rendall, Gerald H.	Ashbourne Shakespeare, The [letter]

Essex Countryside Magazine

1963, June, no. 77, p. 326-27	Caunt, George	The De Veres of Castle Hedingham I
1963, July, no. 78, p. 378-79	Caunt, George	The De Veres of Castle Hedingham II
1963, Aug., no. 79, p. 420-21	Caunt, George	The De Veres of Castle Hedingham III[All three articles are reviews of *The De Veres of Castle Hedingham* by Verily Anderson [see comments by Ruth M. D. Wainewright in SAR, issue 10: 16 (Autumn 1963)]

Essex Newsman

1940, April 13, p. 4	--	News in Brief [Mr. F. D. Bone promotes Edward de Vere as the real author at Southend Rotary Club]
1945, Jan. 9	--	Canon Rendall Dies at the Age of 93 [obituary]

Essex Review (Chelmsford, Essex)

1920, April 1, vol. 29: 95-100	Benham, W. Gurney	Edward de Vere, Earl of Oxford "Identified" as Shakespeare
1935, Jan., vol. 44	--	[review of *Sh.'s Sonnets and Edward de Vere* by Gerald Rendall]
1941, April 1, vol. 50:108	Rendall, Canon Gerald	Arthur Golding, Translator – Personal and Literary – Shakespeare and Edward de Vere [repr. as pam.]
1945, July, vol. 54: 116	Douglas, Montagu W.	Canon G. H. Rendall and the Shakespeare Mystery
1952, Oct., vol. 61: 187	Le Riche, Kathleen	Shakespeare in Essex

Etudes Anglaises (Paris)

1960, vol. 13: 293	Lefranc, P.	Les études anti-stratfordiennes en France
1964, Oct. 1, vol. 17/4: 522	Fort. J. B.	Le quatrième centenaire et le mystère Shakespearien

Evening Citizen (Ottawa)

1947, July 7	--	Who Wrote Shakespeare?

Evening Despatch

1920, March 4, p. 2	--	The Real Shakespeare. What do Stratfordians Say?

Evening News [Springfield, MA]

1931	--	[review of *Hidden Allusions* by Eva Turner Clark]

Evening Post (Bristol)

2010, Feb. 25, p. 10	--	Was de Vere the Real Shakespeare?
2012, Feb. 18, p. 19	Clensy, David	The Case Against Shakespeare: Retired Solicitor Richard Malim . . . To Prove Shakespeare Was Not the Author

Evening Standard, The

1922, Nov. 23	--	A Londoner's Diary: The Shakespeare Fellowship
1922, Nov. 25	--	A Londoner's Diary: Under the Greenwood Tree
1927, Nov. 27	Greenwood, George	[response to "Under the Greenwood Tree"]
1928, Oct. 28	--	Sir George Greenwood Dead
1934, April 19 page Gray 38	--	Francis Bacon, Lord Chancellor—and "Broken Reed"
2004, Jan. 9, p. 34	Halliburton, Rachel	Much Ado About Lusting [review of *Edward's Presents* by Sally Llewellyn]
2005, June 1, p. 20	Finegold, Oliver	To Be or Not To Be? A Fight Over the Bard's ID
2007, Sept. 3, p. 1	Quirke, Kieron	So Whodunit, Will? [review of *The Big Secret Live* by Mark Rylance and Matthew Warchus (2007)]
2008, Jan. 14, p. 37	Sexton, David	In Praise of Secret Scribes [review of *Anonymity: A Secret History of English Literature* by John Mullan]
2009, April 23, p. 19	Blunden, Mark	Shakespeare Did Not Write His Own Plays, Claims Jacobi [he is "99.9 percent certain" that the actual author was Edward de Vere, the Earl of Oxford"]
2010, March 18, p. 36	Sexton, David	The Dodgy Reasons People Have for Doubting Shakespeare [review of *Contested Will* by James Shapiro]
2011, Oct. 18, p. 36	D. M.	Rewriting History and Losing Plots [review of *Anonymous*]

Articles in Non-Oxfordian Periodicals

Everybody's
    1942, Feb. 28, p. 6   Eagle, Roderick L.   El-Dorado-on-Avon

Everyman
    1932, Aug. 25   Rendall, Gerald H.   The Earl of Oxford as Shakespeare [review of *The Life-Story of Edward de Vere* by Percy Allen]

Ex Libris
    1924, July or earlier FIND   Greenwood, George   Letter, The Comtesse de Chambrun and the Supposed Shakespeare Manuscript

Expositor (Brantford, Ont.)
    2004, Aug. 5, p. C7   Gould, Rachel   London Debates Authorship of Shakespeare's Plays

Express, The
    2014, Oct. 14, p. 13   Gore-Langton, Robert   Could the Real Mr. Shakespeare Please Stand Up?

Fanfare
    2013, March, vol. 36/4: 127   Grames, Roland E.   In a Labyrinth, Channeling Shakespeare: The Music of Joseph Summer [Sumner explains why he set texts from the Shakespeare canon for his "The Oxford Songs"]

FAZ
    1990, Jan. 14   Gumbrecht, Hans Ulrich   [review of *Shakespeare: The Invention of the Human* by Harold Bloom] [repr. in NSJ, vol. 4: 158-66]
    1999, July   Zwick, Jochen   Hamlet als Wittenberger Student – That is the Questio [repr. in NSJ, vol. 4: 150-52 (July 1999)]

Federalist
    2019, May 13   Marcus, David   No, Shakespeare was Not a Jewish Woman, He was Just a Genius – response to Elizabeth Winkler in the *Atlantic*

Field, The
    1920, Feb. 28, vol. 135: 302   --   Shakespeare Identified [notes review of SI by J. C. Squire in *Land and Water*]

Fifeshire Advertiser
    1948, Jan. 3, p. 3   Laker, J. J. H. C.   [review of *Talks With Elizabethans* by Hester Dowden]

Financial Times
    1983, May 28, p. 16   Mander, Rosalie   They Kept Their Heads [review of *Eminent Elizabethans* by A. L. Rowse (1983)]
    2003, June 28, p. 30   Wood, Michael   Some are Born Great: Shakespeare's Life Embodies the Conflicts of His Time
    2006, April 1, p. 33   Hunter-Tilney, Ludovic   [review of *Players: The Mysterious Identity of William Shakespeare* by Bertram Fields (2005)]
    2010, March 20, p. 16   Dobson, Michael   Play Rights: A Shakespeare Scholar Definitively Debunks the So-called Authorship Controversy [review of *Contested Will* by James Shapiro] [calls J. Thomas Looney "a preacher in a cranky, proto-fascist sect in Newcastle"]
    2010, March 27, p. 1   Shapiro, James   Just William? New Readings Have Cracked Shakespeare's Works Wide Open
    2012, May 19, p. 18   Feay, Suzi   Bard Times: A Poetic Retelling of the Mystery Surrounding Shakespeare's Biggest Rival [review of *The Marlowe Papers* by Ros Barber]
    2016, April 23, p. 18   Dalley, Jan   Steeped in Shakespeare

Firing Line
    1984, Dec. 11   Buckley, William F.   The Firing Line: Guests Charlton Ogburn, Jr. and Maruice Charney [Transcript]

First Things: A Monthly Journal of Religion and Public Life
    2009, June/July, p. 68-72   --   While We're At It [Critique of Justice John Paul Stevens. [See also Jess Bravin's April 18 WSJ article]
    2010, Aug/Sept. p. 63-64   Miola, Robert   Willy-Nilly [review of *Contested Will* by James Shapiro]

Flambeau, Le: Revue Belge des Questions Politiques et Littéraires
    1922, July 3, Aug, 31, Oct 31   Lefranc, Abel   [three articles]
    1922, Sept.-Dec., p. 419-25   Reul, Paul de   M. Lefranc et William Stanley

Folger Magazine

2010, vol. 4/1: 16-23	--	[review of *Contested Will* by James Shapiro (2010)]

Folger Shakespeare Library Online

2021, March 13 [accessed]	--	Shakespeare's handwriting: Hand D in *Sir Thomas More*

Folio: Shakespeare-Genoostchap van Nederland en Vlaanderen

1995	Franssen, Paul	[review of *Shakespeare: Who Was He?* by Richard F. Whalen]

Fort Worth Star-Telegram

1995, Feb. 12, p. 7	Swindell, Larry	Changing of the Bard: Was it Wills' Writing, or Did Someone Else Put Him in His Place?
1997, Aug. 31, p. 6	Swindell, Larry	The Tempest Over the Bard Continues [review of *The Mysterious William Shakespeare*]
1999, Jan. 24, p. 6	Swindell, Larry	The Case for an Alternative Shakespeare [review of *The Mysterious William Shakespeare*]
1999, Jan. 31, p. 6	Swindell, Larry	Much Ado About the Bard's True Identity

Frankfurt State Journal (U.S.)

1920, Summer	--	[positive review of SI]

Freeman's Journal (Sydney)

1920, Nov. 11, p. 11	--	"Shakespeare" Identified [review of SI]

Freethinker

1923, May 20, vol. 43/20: 316-17	Underwood, George	Readers and Writers: Dethroning Shakespeare—Anti-Stratfordian Scepticism
1923, June 10, vol. 43/23: 364-65	Looney, J. Thomas	The Shakespeare Problem [excerpt repr. in SFE, Sept. 1952, p. 2-3]
1923, July 1, vol. 43/26: 412-13	Looney, J. Thomas	"Shakespeare"; Was it Oxford, Bacon, or Derby? Part 1 [excerpt repr. in SFE, Sept. 1952, p. 2-3]
1923, July 8, vol. 43/27: 428-29	Looney, J. Thomas	"Shakespeare"; Was it Oxford, Bacon, or Derby? Part 2 [excerpt repr. in SFE, Sept. 1952, p. 2-3]
1935, March 10, vol. 55/10: 147-48	Mimnermus	Shakespeare's Secularism
1935, March 10, vol. 55/10: 156-57	Foote, G. W.	Shakespeare and Jesus Christ
1935, April 28, vol. 55/17: 268-69	Kent, William	A Plea for Shakespearean Freethinking
1935, Aug. 18, vol. 55/33: 522-23	Douglas, Lt. Col. M.	Shakespeare, The Great Unknown

Galleon, The [The Golden Galleon, edited by Alfred Fowler] [Kansas City, MO]

1924, Jan. vol. 1/1: 24-25	Ward, Col. Bernard R.	The Shakespeare Fellowship [letter]
1924, July, vol. 1/3: 89-90	Ward, Col. Bernard R.	Shakespearean Heterodoxy [letter]

Games

1994, Oct. p. 12-14+	Schuessler, Raymond	The Shakespeare Puzzle

Gathering, The (Library Guild of the University of Cincinnati)

1988, April, vol. 7/1	Applegate, John S.	Report on the 1987 Trial Before Supreme Court Justices
1988, April, vol. 7/1	Johnson, Morse	The Oxfordian Position [repr. in SON, vol. 24/3: 9-10 (Summer 1988); and in BTC, vol. 6: 351-53]

Gazette, The (Montreal)

1986, March 31, p. C7	Ackerman, Marianne	Bard Scholars Not A-Verse to Debate
1988, Nov. 26, p. B8	--	Three British Judges Ponder the Question: De Vere or Not de Vere?
1988, Nov. 27, p. A2	--	Truth Will Come to Light: Lords Back Shakespeare
1990, Nov. 3, p. D6	--	Computer Has No Comfort for Shakespeare Skeptics
2003, Jan. 11, p. D5	Radz, Matt	Seeking Shakespeare's Ghostwriter
2011, Oct. 27, p. A23	Cutler, Keir	There is Method in This Madness; Traditional Scholars Believe Shakespearean Doubters Are an Army of Crazies. Count Me a Soldier in That Army.

Gegenwart

1996, July 30	Klier, Walter	Augsteins Hammer [repr. in NSJ, vol. 1: 117-31 (Dec. 1997)]

Genealogist

1891, July, vol. 7: 205-08	Greenstreet, James	A Hitherto Unknown Noble Writer of Elizabethan Comedies
1892, Jan., vol. 8: 8-15	Greenstreet, James	Further Notices of William Stanley
1892, May, vol. 8: 137-46	Greenstreet, James	Testimony Against the Accepted Authorship of Sh.'s Plays

Gentleman's Magazine

| 1814 | Walker, John | A Selection of Curious Articles [repr. in SON, vol. 31/2a: 10-11 (Spring 1995)] |

Gentlemen's Quarterly (New York)

| 1992, June, p. 113 | Richmond, Peter | Shakespeare at Au Bar |

Gentleman's Tailor

| 1911. April, vol. 46 | -- | A Problem for the Trade |

Gentlewoman & Modern Life

1926, March 20, p. 447-48	Junior, Junius	Bacon—Queen Elizabeth's Son
1926, March 27, p. 505-06	Junior, Junius	Bacon—Queen Elizabeth's Son—II
1926, April 3, p. 511-13	Junior, Junius	Bacon—Queen Elizabeth's Son—III
1926, April 10, p. 573-74	unior, Junius	Bacon—Queen Elizabeth's Son—IV
1926, April 17, p. 617	Junior, Junius	Bacon—Queen Elizabeth's Son—V
1926, April 24, p. 662	Junior, Junius	Bacon—Queen Elizabeth's Son—VI

Genus

| 1956, vol. 12/1/4: 285+ | Caranti, Elio | [review of *Shakespeare's Identity: William Stanley, 6th Earl of Derby* by A. W. Titherley (1952)] |

Georgetown Law Journal

| 1982, Feb. 3, vol. 70/3 | Gohn, Jack Benoit | *Richard II*: Shakespeare's Legal Brief on the Royal Prerogative and the Succession to the Throne [repr. in *Sh. and the Law* (2022, Roger Strimatter, editor), p. 70-102] |

Georgia Review

| 1953, Sum., vol. 7/2: 228-31 | West, Robert H. | [review of *This Star of England* by Dorothy & Charlton Ogburn] |

Giornale Storico della Letterature Italiana

| 1934, June 1, p. 205-54 | Torretta, Laura | L'Italofobia di John Lyly e I rapporti dell' "Euphues" col Rinascimento Italiano |

Glasgow Herald

| 1923, March or April | -- | [review of *The Mystery of "Mr. W. H."* by Col. B. R. Ward] |

Globe, The (International Shakespeare Globe Centre)

| 1989, Spring, p. 1-2 | Anon. | Shakespeare on Trial |
| 2009, Nov. 28 | Gilvary, Kevin, Julia Cleave, Richard C. Malim | Shakespeare: From Rowe to Shapiro [repr. in SON, vol. 45/3: 14-17 (Dec. 2009)] |

Globe and Mail (Toronto)

1920, May 1, p. 13	-----	Life and Letters [review of SI]
1937, Aug. 2, p. 6	McAree, J. V.	Makes Shakespeare Look Dubious
1937, Aug. 7, p. 9	McAree, J. V.	Shakespeare Fans Read the Column
1937, Sept. 8, p. 6	McAree, J. V.	Another Claimant for Poet's Crown [see also comments on article in SFE, no. 6: 2-5 (Nov. 1937)]
1940, Jan. 5, p. 6	McAree, J. V.	Barrell Rolls Out Some Rich Stuff
1940, Jan. 13, p. 6	McAree, J. V.	Not a Controversy But a Good Imitation
1955, June 27, p. 6	McAree, J. V.	It's Shakespeare, After All
1956, Jan. 14, p. 28	Deacon, William	Shakespeare's Identity [reviews of *Who Was Shakespeare?* by Hilda Amphlett and *Shakespeare Unmasked* by Pierre S. Porohovishikov]
1988, April 27, p. A6	--	Shakespeare and Company
1988, Oct. 31, p. D12	--	A Winter's Trial for the Bard
1988, Nov. 28, p. D10	--	British Law Lords Back Shakespeare [lord Vere present]
1991, April 26, p. A14	--	The Bard Decoded
1997, Dec. 13, p. D11	Sheppard, Philippa	Books Scrutinizing the Bard Continue to Pour Off the Presses [review of *Alias Shakespeare* by Joseph Sobran (1997)]
1999, March 22, p. C3	Conlogue, Ray	The Ghost of Shakespeare

Globe and Mail (continued)

1999, April 22, p. C3	Posner, Michael	'E'er a good chap but ne'er a poet' Has the world been celebrating the wrong writer for more than 400 years? [in the form of a letter signed by Edward de Vere]
2000, Jan. 11, p. R3	Holden, Anthony	The Avon Man
2000, June 14, p. R1	Posner, Michael	Back to the Bard [profile of Michael York]
2001, Feb. 17	Sheppard, Philippa	Queen Was no Virgin [interview with David Starkey] [updated April 10, 2018]
2001, May 14, p. A14	Majauskas, Alan S.	Our Bard [letter: *Globe* owes its readers an objective look at the authorship question]
2001, May 16, p. A14	Nestruck, J. Kelly	Edward de Vere, Inevitably [letter]
2001, May 16, p. A14	Wallace, Martin	Edward de Vere, Inevitably [letter: Majauskas' May 14 letter]
2002, Nov. 20, p. R5	Nolen, Stephanie	Face-off Over a Portrait
2002, Nov. 23, p. R6	Taylor, Kate	The Beard's the Thing [rev. *of The Beard of Avon* by Amy Freed]
2002, Nov. 27, p. A22	Alexander, Ted	[letter to the Editor: Defending Oxfordians]
2005, Oct. 12, p. R1	Taylor, Kate	Courtier or Son of a Glover. Does It Matter? [review of *The Truth Will Out* by Brenda James and William Rubinstein]
2010, Jan. 16, p. F4	Posner, Michael	One Bard – Hold the Beard
2010, Jan. 16, p. F4	--	More Contenders for the Quill
2010, Jan. 19, p. A16	Dawson, Anthony	And the Author is . . . [the man from Stratford] [letter]
2011, Nov. 9, p. R2	Posner, Michael	What Will We Believe?: The Evidence Isn't There
2011, Nov. 9, p. R2	Cimolino, Antoni	What Will We Believe?: Does It Matter?
2011, Nov. 9, p. R2	Nestruck, J. Kelly	What Will We Believe?: An Ardent Defender of the Bard
2013, Oct. 17 p. L1	Nestruck, J. Kelly	Is He Or Isn't He: That is the Question: Canadian University Support for Oxfordian Conference Fires Up Debate About Shakespeare's Authorship
2013, Oct. 19, p. F8	Reardon, John	[letter: Oxfordians are flat-earthers]
2013, Oct. 19, p. F8	Dudley, Michael	[letter: Nestruck uses futile rhetorical tricks]
2013, Oct. 19, p. F8	Nelson, B. Wayne	[letter: Nestruck uses *ad hominem* attacks and ignores] Oxfordians' evidence]
2013, Oct. 21, p. A10	Rubin, Don	Bard Basics [letter: Nestruck: A challenge to debate him publicly]
2013, Nov., p. R4	Nestruck, J. Kelly	Shakespeare as Reviser and Collaborator?

Gloucester Journal (Gloucestershire, England)

1923, Feb. 10, p. 7	Kerr, William	Is There a Shakespeare Problem?

Gloucestershire Echo

1933, Oct. 13, p. 4	--	[review of *French History* by Percy Allen (1930)]

Golden Hind, The: A Quarterly of Art and Literature

1922, Oct, vol. 1/1, p. 23-30	Looney, J. Thomas	The Earl of Oxford as "Shakespeare:" New Evidence [excerpt repr./paraphrased in OXV, p. 168-76; repr. in TOX, vol. 17: 79-93 (2015)

Graphic, The

1923, April 21, p. 554	Kempling, W. Bailey	The Shakespeare First Folio Tercentenary
1926, March 20, p. 506-07	Hopper, C. W.	Was Bacon Queen Elizabeth's Son?
1926, March 26, p. 552	Hopper, C. W.	Queen Elizabeth's Guilty Secret
1926, April 3, p. 599	Hopper, C. W.	The Missing Manuscripts
1926, April 10, p. 631	Hopper, C. W.	The Enigma of the Elizabethan Age
1926, April 17, p. 669	Machen, Arthur	The B in Baconian Bonnets
1930, Sept. 27, p. 486	Aitchiff	Week after Week

Great Ideas Online, The

2002, Nov., no. 203, p. 1-8	Weismann, Max	Who Wrote *Hamlet*? The Great Shakespeare Hoax
2002, Nov., no. 203, p. 3-7	Caldwell, Roland G.	One Man's Overview and Summary [of Concordia University's 2nd annual authorship studies conference]
2002, Nov., no. 203, p. 7-8	Adler, Mortimer J.	[lNov. 7, 1997 letter to Max Weismann: states his conviction that Edward de Vere wrote the works of Shakespeare, and recommends Looney's *"Shakespeare" Identified*]
2014, Sept. 23, no. 786	Warren, James A.	The Use of State Power to Hide Edward de Vere's Authorship of the Works Attributed to "William Shake-speare," Part 1
2014, Sept. 30, no. 787	Warren, James A.	The Use of State Power, Part 2

Articles in Non-Oxfordian Periodicals

Greensboro News-Record

1992, Dec. 10, p. A18	Whalen, Richard F.	It's Not Shakespeare, but Edward de Vere, who Deserves the Credit [editorial]
1992, Dec. 27, p. F2	Repass, Larry	Shakespeare Article was Out of Place [letter: Whalen's editorial]
1993, Jan. 13	--	There's Only One Shakespeare [letter]
1993, Feb. 14, p. F2	Hayes, Laura	It Wasn't Shakespeare Who Wrote the Plays [letter]
1993, Feb. 22, p. A4	Stohr, Otto K.	Shakespeare Inquiry Sheds Valuable Light [resp. to Repass's]
1993, Aug. 1	--	"The Playwright Debate – Report on the July 27 Debate"
1993, Aug. 2, p. A5	Sobran, Joseph	Shakespeare Authorship Now Turns on Biblical Evidence
1993, Aug. 22, p. D1	Schlosser, Jim	To Be or Not To Be . . . Shakespearean
1995, Sept. 19, p. D3	--	Scholars Will Debate Identity of Shakespeare [at 19th SOS conf]
1995, Sept. 28, p. D1	Patterson, Donald	A Literary Whodunit – Was Shakespeare Up to the Task? [SOS Conference and Lord Burford]
1997, June 15, p. F5	O'Neill, Frank	Did Shakespeare Author the Plays?
1997, Aug. 1, p. A8	--	The Playwright Debate: Was It Shakespeare? [the July 27 debate]

Groatsworth of Wit: Journal of the Open University Shakespeare Society

2007. vol. 18/4: 23-26	Pulford, Angie	[review of *The Big Secret Live* by Mark Rylance and Matthew Warchus (2007)]
2012, vol. 23/1: 17-20	Dawson, Jon	[review of *Anonymous*, directed by Roland Emmerich]

Guardian, The (See also The Manchester Guardian)

1964, June 17, p. 5	--	Who Wrote Shakespeare? Issue Raised in Court
1977, June 2, p. 10	Radford, Tim	Nothing Truer Than Truth [review of *Nothing Truer Than Truth*, a play about Edward de Vere by Darrol Blake]
1981, April 23, p. 22	--	Television/Radio: BBC-1: Will the Real Shakespeare?
1987, Sept. 26, p. 36	White, Michael	The U.S. Versus the Man From Stratford: Supreme Court Hears the Case Against Shakespeare
1988, Dec. 9, p. 26	Koning, Christina	New Paperbacks [short review of The *Mystery of William Shakespeare* by Charlton Ogburn]
1989, July 4, p. 40	Smithies, Sandy	Television and Radio ["A Midsummer Night's Mystery"]
1989, July 5, p. 46	Banks-Smith, Nancy	Shakespeare and the Loonies
1994, Oct. 9, p. 11	Gerrard, Nicci	Shakespeare: Not Just William? Who Really Wrote *Hamlet*?
2000, Oct. 9, p. 9	Moss, Stephen	The Doubters' Arguments Against Shakespeare
2003, June 23, p. 17	Wood, Michael	Meet Mr. Shakespeare: Do We Need to Know Who the Bard Really Was to Understand His Work?
2004, Jan. 8, p. 28	Gardner, Lyn	The Bard as a Money-Grubbing Yokel [review of *Edward's Presents* by Sally Llewellyn]
2004, Feb. 25	--	Editorial #1: The Search For Shakespeare – Mystery [repr. in DVN (April 2004), p. 2-3]
2004, Feb. 25	--	Editorial #2: The Search For Shakespeare – Explanation [repr. in DVN (April 2004), p. 2-3] See also "An Oxfordian Replies," DVN (April 2004), p. 4.
2004, Dec. 2, p. 2	Radford, Tim	What Can the Way This is Written Tell You About the Author?
2006, July	Hicks, Brian	[letter to the editor] [excerpt repr. in DVN (July 2006), p. 2]
2007, Sept. 3	Billington, Michael	"I Am Shakespeare" [review of *The Big Secret Live* by Mark Rylance and Matthew Warchus (2007)]
2007, Sept. 8, p. 39	Johnson, David	[letter: Billington's Sept. 3 article re major actors who are Oxfordians]
2007, Sept. 10, p. 25	Arendt, Paul	[letter: another View on *I Am Shakespeare* by Mark Rylance and Matthew Warchus]
2007, Oct.	Hunter, R. Thomas	Shakespeare's wife [letter][excerpt repr. in DVN (Oct. 2007), p. 3]
2010, March 20, p. 6	Mantel, Hilary	Only a Warwickshire Glover's Son: A Look at the Wilder Shores of Anti-Shakespeare Conspiracy Theory [review of *Contested Will* by James Shapiro]
2010, March 27, p. 19	--	[reprint of blog commentary on Mantel's review]
2010, April 3, p. 15	--	Critical Eye: Investigation of the Bard
2011, April 23, p. 32	Lawson, Mark	Should We Care Who Wrote William Shakespeare's Plays?
2011, June 17, p. 4	Crace, John	To B-movie or Not to B-movie [review of *Anonymous*]
2011, Oct. 15, p. 44	Nunn, Trevor and Mark Rylance	So, Who Did Write Hamlet? Director Trevor Nunn and Actor Mark Rylance Disagree - Passionately

Guardian (continued)

2011, Oct. 22, p. 45	Gooch, Steve	[letter: response to Nunn and Rylance]
2011, Nov. 5, p. 16	Shapiro, James	Anonymous? Ridiculous [review of *Anonymous*]
2013, April 23	Leahy, William	On William Shakespeare's Birthday [excerpt in DVN, vol. 20/1: 9 (Apr. 2013)]
2017, Oct. 28	--	I Can Prove that 'William Shakespeare' is buried in Westminster Abbey – Scholar [Alexander Waugh]
2020, Feb. 4	Brown, Mark	I Don't Care Who Wrote Shakespeare, Says RSC Artistic Director [online U.S. edition]
2023, June 18	Merritt, Stephanie	In Search of a Bard [review of *Shakespeare Was a Woman* by Elizabeth Winkler]
2023, June 27	Smith, Dave	"It Was Shocking": The Author Under Attack for Doubting Shakespeare [review of *Shakespeare Was a Woman* by Elizabeth Winkler]

Guelph Mercury, The (Guelph, Ontario)

2013, Oct. 19, A1	Seto, Chris	Local Professors Troubled Over Shakespeare Authorship Debate [the SOF Conference at York Univ.)

Haagsch Maandblad (Holland)

1931, September?	Boissevain, K. D. W.	Essay on de Vere

Hackney and Stoke Newington Recorder

1925, Nov. 20, no. 2888	Ward, Col. B. R.	SF Annual Report for 1924-1925

Hackney Gazette

1962, Nov. 13	Rose, Jacqueline	The Bard of Hackney
1964, June 2	Broder, C.	The Real "Shakespeare"? [exc. in SAR, #14: 21 (Autumn 1965)]

Hackney Spectator [see listing in Section IIC: Regular Oxfordian Columns in Non-Oxfordian Publications]

Halifax Evening Courier

1920, March 4, p. 4	--	"The Real Shakespeare" [review of SI]

Halstead Advertiser [Essex, England]

1975, Nov. 26	--	The Continuing Story of Our Great Bard . . . Is It Too Much of a Coincidence?

Halstead and Colne Valley Gazette

1931, Sept. 11	--	Belhamp St. Pauls
1931, Dec. 18	--	Arthur Golding and Shakespeare

Hamburger Abendblatt (Hamburg)

2009, Nov. 16, p. 1	Karasek, Hellmuth	Seins oder nicht seins?

Harper's Magazine

1940, June. vol. 181: 172	Campbell, Oscar James	Shakespeare Himself [repr. in *Shakespeare and His Rivals* (McMichael & Glenn 1962): 159-73] Resp. by J. Thomas Looney, SFA, vol. 2/1: 1-3, Dec. 1940)
1972, June, vol. 244: 94-96+	Ogburn, Charlton, Jr.	Shakespeare's Missing Manuscripts
1972, Aug., vol. 245: 4.	Ogburn, Charlton, Jr. and others	The Missing Manuscripts [responses to Ogburn by Peter Sammartino, Welles, Irwin Price, Goodhue Livingston, and Joseph R. Surface, with reply by Ogburn]
1999, April, vol. 29	--	The Ghost of Shakespeare
p. 10-21	Lapham, Lewis H.	Full Fathom Five [repr. in *Sh. Authorship Sourcebook* (Stritmatter 2019, 2022): 39-44]
p. 35-62	Bethell, Tom (ed.)	The Ghost of Shakespeare: Who, in Fact, Was the Bard: The Usual Suspect from Stratford, or Edward de Vere, 17th Earl of Oxford? [repr. in LC, p. 57-78]
p. 36-38	Bethell, Tom	A Never Writer [repr. in LC, p. 57-78]
p. 38-41	Paster, Gail Kern	The Sweet Swan [repr. in LC, p. 57-78]
p. 41-43	Wright, Daniel L.	The Lie With Circumstance [repr. in LC, p. 57-78]
p. 44-46	Garber, Marjorie	As They Like It [repr. in LC, p. 57-78]
p. 46-49	Anderson, Mark K.	Thy Countenance Shakes Spears [repr. in LC, p. 57-78]
p. 49-53	Matus, Irvin	The Reproof Valiant [repr. in LC, p. 57-78]

p. 54-55	Sobran, Joseph	Every Word Doth Almost Tell My Name [repr. in LC, p. 57-78]
p. 55-57	Bloom, Harold	A Salvo for Lucy Negro [repr. in LC, p. 57-78, and in MEM, vol. 2: 195-96 (2015)]
p. 57-59	Whalen, Richard F.	Curst Be He Yt Moves My Bones [repr. in LC, p. 57-78]
p. 60-62	Bate, Jonathan	Golden Lads and Chimney-Sweepers [repr. in LC, p. 57-78]
1999, July, vol. 299: 6-11	--	[more than a dozen letters printed in response to "The Ghost of Shakespeare," including those by Mark Woodward, Jerry Dorbin, Derran Charlton. Other responses include: Editorial, *Toronto Star*, March 27, 1999, p. 1. Editorial, SON, vol. 35/1: 3 (1999). Editorial, SON, vol. 35/2: 2 (1999) Mark K. Anderson, SON, vol. 35/1: 4-5, 23 Richard F. Whalen, SON, vol. 35/1: 4

Hartford Courant

1962, Sept. 2, p. 14F	Comans, Grace P.	The Earl's Case [review of *Shake-speare: The Man Behind the Name* by Dorothy and Charlton Ogburn]
1984, Dec. p. G3	Tehan, Arline B.	A Bard by Any Other Name [review of *The Mysterious William Shakespeare* by Charlton Ogburn, Jr.]
2003, Jan. 3, p. D8	Catlin, Roger	Who Wrote Works of Shakespeare? [*Frontline* programs]

Harvard Gay and Lesbian Review

1998, vol. 5/1: 36-37	Rodi, Robert	[review of *Alias Shakespeare* by Joseph Sobran (1997)]
1998, Oct. 31, p. 32	Gage, Carolyn	The Case for Marlowe as the Bard

Harvard Magazine (formerly Harvard Alumni Bulletin)

1974, Nov. p. 21-29	Ogburn, Jr., Charlton	The Man Who Shakespeare Was Not (and Who He Was)[repr. in *Washington Post*, Nov. 24, 1974, p. B1] Response by Andor Klay, Nov. 30, p. A11. [repr. in *Outlook*, Nov. 24, 1974] Response by O. B. Hardison, Jr., Dec. 8, p. B3.
1975, Jan. 5, vol. 77/5	Fisher, Edward	[letter: Ogburn's Nov. 2 article]
1975, Jan. 5, vol. 77/5	Wirth, Peter	[letter: Ogburn's Nov. 2 article]
1975, Feb., p. 39-43	Evans, Gwynne, and Harry Levin	Shakespeare as Shakespeare [response to Ogburn] Response to Evans and Levin by Gordon Cyr, "An Oxfordian Reply to Two Harvard Professors, SON, vol. 11/2: 1-19 (Summer 1975).
1975, April 8, vol. 77/8	Dickinson, Charles C. III	[letter: reply to Evans and Levin]
1975, April 8, vol. 77/8	Hinton, Harold C.	[letter: response to Ogburn] [note: more than 30 letters in response to Ogburn's article were printed over 6 issues]
1975, April 8, vol. 77/8	Ogburn, Charlton	[letter: reply to Evans and Levin; he proposes a trial that Philip Weld offered to finance]
2004, Sept./Oct., p. 56-59	Shaw, Jonathan	The Mysterious Mr. Shakespeare: Stephen Greenblatt conjures a life.

Hemet News (California)

1943, March 16	Richardson, Friend W.	Fighting a Man of Straw [Richardson was a former Governor of California and currently President of the Publishers Association of California]

Henry James Review

2010, vol. 31/2: 169-187	McCombe, John P.	Henry James, Shakespeare's Biography, and the Question of National Identity in 'The Birthplace' and the 'Introduction to *The Tempest*'

Herald [Universal Press column]

1993, July 31	Sobran, Joseph	*Bible* Holds Proof of Shakespeare's Identity [repr in SON, vol. 29/4: 8-9 (Fall 1993); in EVR, vol. 1 (Fall 1995); and in BTC, vol. 7: 212-13]

Herald-Sun (Durham)

1995, Nov.	--	[long article on the evidence for Oxford written after interviewing Edith Duffy and Felix Vann]

Heythorp Journal

2013, Nov., vol. 54/6: 1047-48	Madigan, Patrick	[review of *The Earl of Oxford and the Making of "Shakespeare"* by Richard Malim]
2013, Nov., vol. 54/6: 1048-50	Milward, Peter	[review of *The Assassination of Shakespeare's Patron* by Leo Daugherty]
2015, March, vol. 56/2: 321-22	Malim, Richard	[review of *Shakespeare Beyond Doubt?* edited by John Shahan and Alexander Waugh (2013)]
2017, May, vol. 58/3: 413-16	Malim, Richard	Southwell and Oxford

Hindu, The (Chennai, India)

1999, Oct. 3, p. 1	--	Love's Labour Resurrected
1999, Nov. 29, p. 1	--	A Shakespearean Dilemma [editorial]

Hindustan Times, The (New Delhi)

2006, April 21	--	William Shakespeare May Have Been the Virgin Queen's Lovechild!

Historian, The (London)

2011, Summer, vol. 110: 18-22	Fisher, Trevor	Enter the Tudor Prince

History Today

1957, April 1, vol. 7/4: 229	Walmsley, D. M.	Shakespeare's Links with Virginia
2001, Aug., vol. 51: 28-35	Rubinstein, William D.	Who Was Shakespeare? Response by Richard F. Whalen, SON, v01. 37/2: 1, 20 (Summer, 2001).
2001, Oct., vol. 51/10: 61	Ives, Eric	[letter: response to Rubinstein's article]
2001, Oct., vol. 51/10: 61	Rubinstein, William D.	[reply to letters by Eric Ives and others]
2005, Nov., vol. 55/11: 28-29	Rubinstein, William D.	Mystery Identities

Honolulu Advertiser

2005, Jan. 30, p. D3	--	Lit Beat [Paul H. Altrocchi to give presentation "The Shakespeare Hoax"]

Horticulture Magazine

1977, Nov.	Janick, Jules	Stalking the Long Purple

Hour (Norwalk, CT)

1989, July 17	Crane, Lelia	Will Real Shakespeare Please Stand! [review of a performance of John Nassivera's play *All the Queen's Men*

Houston Chronicle

1987, Sept. 27, p. 1	--	Shakespeare – Or Not Shakespeare?
1988, Nov. 27, p. 31	--	World Briefs [Shakespeare, not Edward de Vere]
1990, Dec. 30, p. 18	Oldenburg, Don	Who Was the Bard? The Stratford Man or a Powerful Earl?
1997, June 22, p. 23, 31	Daschlager, Earl L.	[review of *Alias Shakespeare* by Joseph Sobran (1997)]

Hudson Review

1956, Fall, vol. 9/3: 325	Winter, Yvor	Problems for the Modern Critic of Literature

Hull Daily Mail (East Riding of Yorkshire)

1920, March 4, p. 4	--	Mr. J. Thomas Cooney [sic] Almost Proves that Shakespeare's Works Were Written by Edward de Vere [review of *"Shakespeare" Identified*]
1920, March 5, p. 1	--	Short mention of Looney's They
1921, Nov. 2, p. 4	--	Assault on a Demi-God
2010, Oct. 13, p. 20	--	Was de Vere the Author?
2010, Oct. 20, p. 20	--	Was de Vere the Real Genius Behind *Hamlet*? [review of *The Man Who Was Hamlet*, a play by George Dillon]

Huntington Library Bulletin

1934, Nov. no. 6: 17-37	Craig, Hardin	Hamlet's Book

I Libri del Giorno

1920, May, p. 275	--	[list of new books includes Looney's SI, with descr.]

Idaho State Journal

2012, July 15, p. C1	Corrigan, Michael	The Shakespeare Conspiracy: Doubts About Authorship Still Persist [review of *Anonymous*]

IEEE Spectrum

| 2011, July 28 | Anderson, Mark | Wikipedia's Shakespeare Problem: Wikipedia is a little too sure we know who authored *Hamlet* |

Illuminator, The (University Club Library, New York)

| 1991, March, p. 91-96 | Sammartino, Peter | Who Was the Real William Shakespeare? |

Illustrated London News

1919, Jan. 25, p. 8	Lee, Sidney	Shakespeare Dethroned Again
1919, April 26, p. 13	Law, Ernest	Shakespeare in Hampton Court Palace
1920, Oct. 30, p. 5-6	--	Was Lord Derby's Ancestor "Shakespeare"? A French Theory
1928, April 14, p. 20-21 (628)	--	Books of the Day [review of *Shakespeare, Jonson, and Wilkins as Borrowers* by Percy Allen (1928)]
1937, Oct. 9, p. 28	Brown, Ivor	The World of Theatre ["It is possible that we are going to celebrate still further the memory of the wrong man."]
1938, April 23, p. 29-30	Brown, Ivor	The World of Theatre [passing reference to Edward de Vere as Shakespeare]
1939, April 29, p. 740-41	--	["If the Authorship Were Traced to Edward de Vere . . ."]
1975, Dec. 1, p. 130	--	Houses with Histories [Edward de Vere's residence]

Imago (St. Lucia, Queensland)

| 1992 | Buckridge, Patrick | The 'Oxford/Shakespeare' Debate: Reasons to Believe |

Independent, The (and The Independent on Sunday)

1910, Dec. 22, p. 1373	Lang, Andrew	A New Theory of Shakespeare ["The number of people who have lost their belief in Shakespeare of Stratford-on-Avon is rapidly increasing."]
1991, Nov. 6	Eagleton, Terry	[review of *William Shakespeare: A Life* by Garry O'Connor (1991) (repr. in SON, vol. 27/4: 2-3, Fall, 1991)]
1994, Oct. 30, p. 21	Barber, Nicholas	Television [*Bard on the Box* episode "Battle of Wills:" rival groups contest the authorship]
1994, Dec. 16, p. 25	Ward, Victoria	Outside Edge: An Earl in Search of the Real Bard [Charles Burford and the Shakespeare Oxford Society]
1998, Nov. 5, p. 7	Arthur, Charles	Shakespeare's Indemnity 'is in the stars'
1999, Apr. 25	Pizzichini, Lilian	[review of *Who Wrote Shakespeare?* by John Michell]
2002, Feb. 19	Editor	Editorial: Did the Bard Hate Lawyers? [repr. in DVN (April 2002), p. 22-23]
2003, May 3	--	Did Shakespeare See the Wilton Diptych? [repr. in DVN (April 2004), p. 22]
2004, June 25, p. 14	Byrne, Ciar	Devotees of De Vere, 'the real Bard', Mark 400th Anniversary [repr. in DVN (July 2004), p. 2; and in SON, vol. 40/3: 9 (Summer 2004)]
2004, Sept. 17	Jury, Louise	Director Who Gave Shakespeare Back to Masses Quits Globe [repr. in DVN (Oct. 2004), p. 23]
2005, Sept. 14	Milmo, Cahal	Revealed: The Rape Trial That Inspired Shakespeare [repr. in DVN (Sept. 2005), p. 46]
2005, Oct. 5, p. 12-13	Keys, David	Much Ado About Identity As Scholars Claim a Diplomat Was the 'Real' Shakespeare [repr. in DVN (Sept. 2005), p. 44-45]
2006, April 21, p. 28	Jury, Louise	Was Shakespeare the Love Child of Queen Elizabeth?
2006, April 21, p. 42	Nevin, Charles	Bard-Barney [editorial]
2006, April 22, p. 12	Walsh, John	The Legends of Shakespeare
2007, Sept. 4	Taylor, Paul	[review of *The Big Secret Live* by Mark Rylance and Matthew Warchus (2007)]
2007, Sept. 9	Bassett, Kate	[review of *The Big Secret Live* by Mark Rylance and Matthew Warchus (2007)]
2009, March 20	Crick, Jeremy	[letter to the Editor (20 March 2009)][repr. in DVN, vol. 16/2: 30 (June 2009)]
2010, March 28, p. 34	Crystal, Ben	A Rose by Any Other Name [review of *Contested Will* by James Shapiro]
2011, Oct. 26, p. 14	Hastings, Robe	Shakespeare Movie Has Lost the Plot, Lament Loyal Fans of the Bard [review of *Anonymous*]
2011, Oct. 28, p. 22	Tonkin, Boyd	The Confederacy of Dunces Return

Independent (continued)

2011, Oct. 31	--	Rylance Defends Shakespeare Film's right to Question Identity of Bard
2011, Nov. 5, p. 14	--	Was the Bard a Fraud? [review of *Anonymous*]

Indianapolis News, The

1995, April 2, p. J4	Mullinix, Donna	[Charles Vere, Earl of Burford, to Speak]
1995, April 18, p. D1	Price, Nelson	English Earl Says Ancestor Was the Real Shakespeare [Burford speaking tour] [repr. in SON, vol. 31/2a: 1-2 (Spring 1995)]

Insight on the News

1994, Oct. 31, no. 10/44: 9-11	Goode, Stephen	Literary Class Struggle: The Bard's Identity Crisis [cover story featuring Charles Vere, Lord Burford]

Interdisciplinary Literary Studies: A Journal of Criticism and Theory

2015, vol. 17/2: 241-63	Lefait, Sebastien	Irreverence as Fidelity? Adapting Shakespearean Reflexivity in *Anonymous*

International Herald Tribune

1988, Nov. 29	Trucco, Terry	Shakespeare v. 17th Earl: The Verdict
2004, Aug. 25, p. 10	Niederkorn, William S.	Re-Imagining the Man from Stratford
2005, Sept. 2, p. 9	Niederkorn, William S.	To Be Or Not To Be Shakespeare
2011, Oct. 11	Karpel, Ari	Will's Quill as a Deadly Weapon [review of *Anonymous*]
2011, Oct. 17, p. 8	Shapiro, James	Hollywood Dishonors the Bard [repr. from *New York Times*, 17 Oct. 2011]

International Journal of Psycho-analysis

1955, April, vol. xxxvi	Feldman, A. Bronson	Shakespeare's Early Errors [revised version pub. in *Early Shakespeare* (Feldman/Hope 2019): 8-53]

International Journal of Applied Psychoanalytic Studies

2015, March 5, vol. 12/1: 80	Sklarew, Bruce	[editor's intro. to "Reviews of Films" by Richard Waugaman]
2015, March 5, vol. 12/1: 81-87	Waugaman, Richard M.	[reviews of Films *Anonymous* and *Last Will. And Testament]*
2020, Aug. 31, vol. 17/3: 1-16	Waugaman, Richard M.	Friendly Fire: Shakespeare's Accidental Enemies, A Review of *The Shakespeare Authorship Controversy*
2020, Dec., vol. 17/4: 362-64	Menzer, Paul	The Firing Squad: A Comment upon "Friendly Fire"
2020, Dec., vol. 17/4: 365-68	Sprengnether, Madelon	Who Wrote Shakespeare? A Response to Richard Waugaman
2020, Dec., vol. 17/4: 369-71	Dyer, Allen R.	Does It Matter That Freud Thought Shakespeare was the Earl of Oxford?
2020, Dec., vol. 17/4: 372-75	Nelson, Alan	Orthodoxy Affirmed
2020, Dec., vol. 17/4: 376-79	Waugaman, Richard M.	Replies to Commentaries on "Friendly Fire"

International Women's News

1947, Oct.	Aitken, T. M.	Woman's Hand in Shakespeare [letter]

Investor's Business Daily

1999, April 23	Smith, Scott S.	Playwright William Shakespeare

Irish Times, The (Dublin)

1920, May 7, p. 7	--	Books of the Week [review of *Shakespeare" Identified*]
1921, April 1, p. 2	--	Elizabethan Poems [review of *The Poems of Edward de Vere*, edited by J. Thomas Looney]
1934, Dec. 1, p. 5	--	My Name is Will [review of *Personal Clues in Shakespeare's Poems and Sonnets* by Gerald Rendall]
1946, Aug. 5, p. 5	Rowe, Charles J.	The Road to Stratford
1950, April 27, p. 5	--	The Man
1956, Feb. 29, p. 5	--	Concealed Story in *Hamlet*
1958, Feb. 5, p. 3	--	Counsel for Shakespeare
1999, May 29, p. 70	--	*Who Wrote Shakespeare?* [review of John Michell's book by the same title]
2009, April 24, p. 15	McNally, Frank	An Irishman's Diary [The Declaration of Reasonable Doubt and the legitimacy of Shakespeare's authorship]
2010, April, p. 10	Clarke, Danielle	Battling About the Bard: Shakespeare
2011, Oct. 28, p. 16	Brady, Tara	Anonymous [review of *Anonymous*]
2011, Oct. 29, p. 15	Shapiro, James	Looney Tune of a Film Plays with Truth Over Bard [review of *Anonymous*]

| 2011, Nov. 5, p. A19 | O'Tool, Fintan | Why was William Shakespeare So Hard to Pin Down? |
| 2014, April 26 | O'Tool, Fintan | Shakespeare Conspiracy Theories Are a Comedy of Errors |

ISIS: Magazine of Oxford University

| 1975, p. 20-23 | Alexis, Louis E. M. | At Last the Truth about Shakespeare: Every Word Doth Almost Sell His Name |

Italian Voice (Totowa, NJ)

| 1990, July 12, p. 6 | -- | Italy and Shakespeare [review of *The Man Who Was William Shakespeare* by Peter Sammartino] |

Italica

| 1992, Spring, vol. 69/1: 92-94 | Marchione, Margherita | [review of *The Man Who Was William Shakespeare* by Peter Sammartino (1990)] |

Jahrbuch der Deutschen Shakesepeare-Gensellschaft

| 1930, p. 220- | Keller, Wolfgang | [review of Allen's *Topical Dramatists*] |
| 1930, p. 223- | Keller, Wolfgang | [review of Allen's *Borrowers*] |

Jennings Daily News

| 1986, Sept. 18 | -- | British Student Visits Jennings [lord Vere and Ruth Loyd Miller] |

Jerusalem Post

| 1991, April 9, p. 5 | Berlyne, Alex | [Commentary on Channel 2's "Who Was Shakespeare?"] |
| 1992, Jan. 17, p. 4 | Nesvisky, Matt | Reversal of Fortune [Burford's speaking tour] |

John O'London's Weekly

1933, Dec. 30, p. 520 , --		Shake-Speare & Shakspere [review of *Shakespeare, Oxford and Elizabethan Times* by Adm. H. H. Holland]
1934	Holland, H. H.	Shakespeare and Oxford [letter: response to review]
1939, Jan. 27, p. 657-58+	Porohovshikov, P. S.	Who Was Shakespeare? A New Examination I
1939, Feb. 3, p. 689-90+	Porohovshikov, P. S.	Who Was Shakespeare? II: The Case for the Earl of Rutland
1939, Feb. 10, p. 733-34	Barrett, W. P.	Who Was Shakespeare? III: The Traditional View
1939, Feb. 10, p. 750	Habgood, Francis E. C.	Who Was Shakespeare? [letter]
1939, Feb. 24, p. 821	Allen, Percy	Who Was Shakespeare? [letter]
1939, Feb. 24, p. 821	Johnson, Edward D.	The Notes in the First Folio [letter]
1939, Feb. 24, p. 821	Theobald, Bertram G.	Unreliable Witness [letter]
1939, Feb. 24, p. 821-22	Habgood, Francis E.	Shakespeare's Signature [letter]
1939, Feb. 24, p. 821	Hauger, E. G.	Shakespeare and Italy [letter]
1939, Feb. 24, p. 821	Megroz, R. L.	Loosely Spelt Proper Names [letter]
1939, Feb. 24, p. 821-22	Barrett, W. P.	Who was Shakespeare? [reply to letters]
1939, March 10, p. 888-89	Kent, William	Who Was Shakespeare? [letter]
1939, March 10, p. 889	Barrett, W. P.	Reply to Kent
1945, Jan. 26, p. 75	Brown, Ivor	Had Shakespeare Leisure? [review of *Shakespeare's History Plays* by Dr. Tillyard]

Journal de Genève, The

| 1929, Feb. 4 | -- | [report on *The Shakespeare Problem*, a lecture by Charles Boissevain to the Anglo-Genevese Society] |

Journal; Newcastle-upon-Tyne

2011, June 16, p. 37	--	Hats Off to Bard Poet at Speakers' Corner
2011, Dec. 7, p. 58	Whetstone, David	Film Puts Bard in Spotlight [review of *Anonymous*]
2016, April 16, p. 54	Whetstone, David	Why We Should Never Be Bored by the Bard [Keith Jewett to speak at Newcastle's Lit & Phil, where Looney wrote SI]

Journal News, The (White Plains)

| 2008, Oct. 5, p. E1 | Kramer, Peter D. | The Bard by Another Name? Matthew Cossolotto Loves Shakespeare. Make that "Shakespeare." [report on the SOS Conference in White Plains] |

Journal of Dramatic Theory and Criticism

| 1996, vol. 10/2: 141-43 | Sexton, Roy | [review of *Shakespeare – Who Was He?* by Richard F. Whalen] |

Journal of Early Modern Studies

| 2016, no. 5: 91-118 | Barber, Ros | Shakespeare and Warwickshire Dialect [repr. in *Sh. Authorship Sourcebook* (Stritmatter 2022): 351-81] |
| 2016, no. 5: 329-52 | Price, Diana | Hand D and Shakespeare's Unorthodox Literary Paper Trail |

Journal of English and Germanic Philology
1938, April, vol. 37/2: 311-12 Brooke, Tucker [review of *The Man Who Was Shakespeare* by Eva Turner Clark]

Journal of Evolutionary Psychology
2004, Aug., vol. 25/3-4: 146+ Simpson, Kevin The Psychology of Creativity and Genius: Reflections on Shakespeare and the Oxfordian challenge

Journal of Information Ethics
2015, Fall, vol. 24/2: 105-12 Tarica, Alan A Collision of Cultural and Ethics with Scholarly Correction [Ethics and the authorship question]

Journal of Legal Education
1993, March 1, p. 1 Fish, Stanley Not of an Age, But for All Time

Journal of Philosophical Logic
2014, Feb., p. 153-70 Bjerring, Jens-Christian Problems in Epistemic Space [Uses Edward de Vere's authorship in considering "epistemic space"]

Journal of Romance Studies
2009, Summer, vol. 9/2: 11+ de Castro, Mariana Gray Fernando Pessoa and the 'Shakespeare Problem'

Journal of Scientific Exploration
2004 Bauer, Henry [reviews of *Shakespeare's Unorthodox Biography* by Diana Price (2001), & *Alias Shakespeare* by J. Sobran (1996)]
2012, Fall, vol. 26/3: 679-84 Roper, David L. [review of *Shakespeare Suppressed* by Katherine Chiljan]
2014, Winter, vol. 27/4: 705-10 Spittle, Bruce [review of *AKA Shakespeare: A Scientific Approach to the Authorship Question* by Peter A. Sturrock)]
2017, Dec., vol. 31/4 Roper, David L. [title not known]
2023, Summer, vol. 37/2 Rubin, Don The Shakespeare Authorship Question: Alternative Mappings [Guest Editor for this Section]
  Meyers, Bob Prophets Without Honor: From Galileo to Looney
  Gilvary, Kevin Demythologizing Shakespeare: What We Really Know About the Man from Stratford
  Jiménez, Ramon The Shakespeare Authorship Question: A Forensic Examination
  Cutting, Bonner Miller Shakespeare and Southampton: Blest Be the Tie that Unbinds
  Waugaman, Elisabeth Shakespeare and the French Lens
  Showerman, Earl A Century of Neglect: Shakespeare and Greek Drama
  Gilbert, Sky Shakespeare's Epistemology and the Problem of Truth
  Chiljan, Katherine The Queen's Favorite Unknown Dramatist: Were There Other Royal Plays by Shakespeare?
  Waugh, Alexander My Beloved the Author: The Subtext of Ben Jonson's First Folio Encomium to William Shakespeare
  Whittemore, Hank To Be or Not To Be a Genius: The Argument for Acquired Knowledge and Life Experience
  Woosnam, Tom [review of *Shakespeare Was a Woman and Other Heresies* by Elizabeth Winkler]
  Richards, Allison [review of *Who Wrote That: Authorship Controversies from Moses to Sholokov* by Donald Ostrowski]
  Roper, D. L. [review of *Shakespeare's Knowledge of Astronomy and the Birth of Modern Cosmology* by Peter Usher]
  Rubin, Don Further Reading on the Authorship
  Houran, James Editorial [why academics in non-literary fields should help bring attention to the authorship question]

Journal of Social and Psychological Sciences
2010, Jan., vol. 3/1: 25 Gordon, Helen H. [review of *Shakespeare and Elizabeth: Meeting of Two Myths* by Helen Hackett (2009)] [repr. in SM, vol. 8/3: 16-18]

Journal of the American Academy of Psychoanalysis and Dynamic Psychiatry
2009, vol. 37/4: 627-43 Waugaman, Richard M. A Psychoanalytic Study of Edward de Vere's *The Tempest*

Journal of the American Psychoanalytic Association
1965, vol. 13: 145-98 Trosman, Harry Freud and the Controversy Over Shakespearean Authorship
2014, March 7 Waugaman, Richard M. [review of *Shakespeare Beyond Doubt* by Edmundson & Wells]

Judge (New York)
1920, Aug. 7, p. 21 -- Words [Brief mention of Looney and Edward de Vere]

Articles in Non-Oxfordian Periodicals

Kansas City Star

1940, Jan.	--	X-Rays Reveal True Shakespeare [Barrell and Sci Am]
2001, June 17, p. 11, 14	Trussell, Robert	A Contest of Wills: Oxfordians Insist Their Man Was the Pen Behind Shakespeare's Name [front page of "Arts"]
2004, March 17	Martin, Judith	Miss Manners: Dealing With Fools Who Think Themselves Wise

Kensington Post

1965, June 25, p. 8	--	Was Shakespeare Edward de Vere?
1966, Aug. 5, p. 11	--	Lord Oxford and the Shakespeare "Italian" Plays

Kirkus Review

1993, Nov., vol. 61/21: 1372	--	[review of *Shakespeare, In Fact* by Irvin Matus]
2003, April 15, vol. 71: 8	--	[review of *Chasing Shakespeares* by Sarah Smith]
2005, Feb. 1, vol. 73: 3	--	[review of *Players: The Shakespeare Mystery* by Bertram Fields]
2005, May 15, vol. 73/10: 569	--	[review of *Shakespeare by Another Name* (2005) by Mark K. Anderson]
2005, vol. 73/3: 163	--	[review of *Players: The Mysterious Identity of William Shakespeare* by Bertram Fields (2005)]
2010, Jan. 1, vol. 78: 1	--	[review of *Contested Will: Who Wrote Shakespeare?* by James Shapiro]
2013, July 1, vol. 81/13: 336	--	[review of *AKA Shakespeare: A Scientific Approach to the Authorship Question* by Peter A. Sturrock]
2014, Feb. 15, vol. 82/4	--	[review of *Shakespeare's Changeling: A Fault Against the Dead* by Syril Levin Kline]
2014, March 1, vol. 82/5	--	[review of *Shakespeare's Dark Lady: Amelia Bassano Lanier* by John Hudson]
2017, Feb. 1, vol. 85/3: 252	--	[review of *Reflections on the True Shakespeare* by Gary Goldstein]
2017, Feb. 15, online	--	[review of *Summer Storm: A Novel of Ideas* by James A. Warren]

Lamar Journal of the Humanities

2011, vol. 36/1: 5	Priest, Dale	The Shakespeare Authorship Question: A Review and Update

Lambda Book Report

1997, vol. 6/3: 9-10	Marks, Jim	[review of *Alias Shakespeare* by Joseph Sobran (1997)]

Lancashire Evening Post (Lancashire, England)

1934, Nov. 29, p. 5	--	And a Claim [Obituary of Rev. Charles de Vere Beauclerk, "who was a firm believer that Shakespeare was the pen name of Edward de Vere."]

Land and Water

1920	Squire, J. C.	[review of *"Shakespeare" Identified*]

Lansing State Journal

2004, March 7, p. B5	--	Obituary of Oxfordian Edith Bell Duffey

Las Vegas Review-Journal

1991, Sept. 28, p. 1C	Saville, Kirk	Authorship of Works Debated by Scholars
1993, Jan. 3, p. 2C	Sobran, Joseph	The Wish Is Often Father to the Thought
1993, Aug. 15, p. 2C	Sobran, Joseph	New Light on Shakespeare's Identity
1999, Feb. 7, p. 4E	Kilpatrick, James	Willie Who?
1999, March 23, p. 9B	Sobran, Joseph	So, Who Really Done Shakespeare?

Leader, The

1925, Sept. 26, p. 9	Wood, Clement	[review of *"Shakespeare" Identified* by J. Thomas Looney]

Leeds Mercury (West Yorkshire)

1928, April 13, p. 4	--	[review of *Borrowers* by Percy Allen (1928)]
1931, Dec. 14, p. 1	--	Who Wrote the Plays of Shakespeare? Queen Elizabeth or an Earl?
1937, Jan. 16, p. 3	--	Percy Allen to Speak on "Shakespeare, The Man Behind the Playwright"

Les Langues Modernes

1929, April, vol. 2: 224-27	Danchin, F. C.	[review of *The Seventeenth Earl of Oxford* by B. M. Ward] [in French]

Leslie's Weekly [Frank Leslie's Illustrated Weekly]

| 1920, July 24, vol. 131: 3379 | Herford, Oliver | Pen and Inklings: *Shakespeare Identified* |

Library, The

1927, June, p. 123   Ward, Capt. Bernard M.   [letter: response to Greg's review of *A Hundreth Sundrie Flowres* in *Transactions of the Bibliographical Society*]

1928, Sept., vol. IX/2: 211-14   Byrne, Muriel St. Clare   Reviews and Notices [review of *The Seventeenth Earl of Oxford* by Capt. Bernard M. Ward]

Library Journal

1920, June 1, p. 519   --   [Stokes Books ad includes *"Shakespeare" Identified*]

1949, Oct. 15, vol. 74: 1605   Freedley, George   [review of *"Shakespeare" Identified*, 2nd ed.]

1962, June 15, vol. 87: 2381   Robie, Burton A.   [review of *Shake-speare: The Man Behind the Name* by Dorothy Ogburn and Charlton Ogburn, Jr. (1962)]

1962, Nov. 15, vol. 87: 4295   --   [Another review of *Shakes-speare: The Man Behind the Name* by Dorothy Ogburn and Charlton Ogburn, Jr.]

1994, Nov. 1, vol. 119/18: 78   Bryan, Aubrey   [review of *Shakespeare—Who Was He?* by Richard Whalen]

2000, Nov. 15, vol. 125/19: 68   Wyatt, Neal   [review of *Shakespeare's Unorthodox Biography* by Diana Price]

2001, Feb. 15, vol. 126/3: 214   Cantu, Amy   The Shakespeare Conspiracy [review of video *The Shakespeare Conspiracy*, directed by Michael Peer]

2001, June, vol. 126/10: 42   Aycock, Anthony   Shakespeare Authorship [Overview of authorship orgs.]

2003, May, vol. 128/9: 88   Fair, Shana C.   [review of *Shakespeare's Fingerprints* by Michael Brame and Galina Popova (2002)]

2005, April, vol. 130/6: 94   Fair, Shana C.   [review of *Players: The Mysterious Identity of William Shakespeare* by Bertram Fields (2005)]

2005, April, vol. 130/7: 86   Fair, Shana C.   [review of *The Case for Shakespeare: The End of the Authorship Question* by Scott McCrea (2005)]

2005, July, vol. 130/12: 79   Walsh, Felicity D.   [review of *"Shakespeare" By Another Name* by Mark Anderson]

2006, March, vol. 131/5: 72   Fair, Shana C.   [review of *De Vere as Shakespeare: An Oxfordian Reading of the Canon* by William Farina]

2010, Feb. 15, vol. 135/3: 95-96   Cooksey, T. L.   [review of *Contested Will* by James Shapiro (2010)]

2010, April, vol. 135/6: 75   Hodge, Megan   [review of *Shakespeare's Lost Kingdom* by Charles Beauclerk]

2012, Dec. 1, vol. 137/20: 82-5   Graham, Nicholas   [review of *Shakespeare's Education* by Robin Fox]

2014, Jan. 1, vol. 138/14: 48-51   Graham, Nicholas   The Bard at 450]

2014, vol. 139/1: 50   Graham, Nicholas   [review of *Who Wrote Shakespeare?* by John Michell]

2014, vol. 139/1: 50   Graham, Nicholas   [review of *Contested Will* by James Shapiro (2010)]

2014, March 1, vol. 139/4: 12   Dudley, Michael   Author of Shakespeare? [letter: Nicholas Graham's Jan. article]

Life and Letters

1929, May, p. 401   --   [eview of Allen's *Topical Dramatists*]

Life Magazine

1920, July 1, vol. 76: 374   --   [brief mention of Looney and the Earl of Oxford]

1920, Sept. 9, vol. 76: 442   Schelling, F. E.   Who Wrote Shakespeare? [a poem]

1920, Sept. 30, vol. 76, p. 590   Guiterman, Arthur   Rhymed Reviews: "Shakespeare" Identified [review of SI]

1962, Sept. 7, p. 4   Jessup, John K.   Editorial: Fresh Troops Join the Battle of the Bard [review of *Shake-speare: The Man Behind the Name* by Dorothy Ogburn and Charlton Ogburn, Jr]

1964, April, p. 155-60   Reed, J. D.   Some Ado About Who Was, or Was Not, Shakespeare [Reed's piece in the Sept. 1987 issue of *Smithsonian* had the same title]

1964, April 23, vol. 56/17   Hamblin, Dora Jane   History's Biggest Literary Whodunit

Light: The Organ of the London Spiritualist Alliance

1949, June, vol. 69/3350: 155-60   Allen, Percy   Was it Hester Dowden?

Linguistic Analysis

1999, Jan., vol. 29/3-4: 349-68   Brame, Michael   Behind and Beyond Shakespeare's Wordplay

2000, Jan., vol. 30/3-4, 359-96   Brame, Michael   Sweet Will's Big O

2000, Jan., vol. 30/3-4: 397-400   Brame, Michael   Will I Am

Listener

1930, June 11, vol. 23: 1041   Boas, F. S.   Sidelight on Shakespeare [review of Allen's *Case*]

1950, Aug. 10, vol. 44: 195-96   Dawson, Giles E.   Who Wrote Shakespeare?

1950, Aug. 24, vol. 44: 273 Kent, William   Who Wrote Shakespeare?
1950, Aug. 24, vol. 44: 273 Perrett, A. J.   Who Wrote Shakespeare?
1950, Aug. 31, vol. 44: 309 Prescott, W. S.   Who Wrote Shakespeare?
1950, Sept. 21, vol. 44: 384 Kent, William   Who Wrote Shakespeare?
1950, Sept. 28, vol. 44: 425 Kent, William   Who Wrote Shakespeare?
1962, July 19, vol. 68: 109 Muir, Kenneth   [review of *The Shakespeare Claimants* by Harry N. Gibson]
1988, Dec. 15, p. 33   Eagleton, Terry   [review of *The Mysterious William Shakespeare* by Charlton Ogburn, Jr. (1992)]

Literary Digest
1920, Aug. 14, vol. 66/7: 32-33 --   "Shakespeare" Identified Again [reviews of SI]
1932, Aug. 27, vol. 114/9: 14-15 Herford, Oliver   Oliver Herford Adopts "William Shakespeare" [repr. from *The American* or *NY American*; might be vol. 122, July-Sept.; Clark sent copies of both to Looney]

Literary Guide
1950, Feb.   Robertson, Archibald   [letter to the Editor] [repr. in SFE, p. 8 (April 1951)]
1955, Sept., p. 19-20   Adamson, T. L.   Shakespeare, Earl of Rutland?
1994, vol. 119/18: 78   Aubrey, Byran   [review of *Shakespeare—Who Was He?* by Richard Whalen]

Literary World, The
1901, vol. 63: 327   Steadman, Edmund C.   Advice to English Schoolboys Who Want to Become Shakespeare [repr. in BTC, vol. 1: 133]

Literatur in Wissenschaft und Unterricht
2005, vol. 28: 252   Bünsch, Iris   [review of *Der Fall Shakespeare* by Walter Klier]

Literaturblatt fur germanische und romanische Philologie
1920   Neumann, Fritz (editor)   Books published in 1920 [list includes SI]

Literature Compass
2008, May, vol. 5/3: 618   Smith, Emma   The Shakespeare Authorship Debate Revisited

Literature/Film Quarterly
2013, Apr., vol. 41/2: 129-42   Sherman, Donovan   Stages of Revision: Textuality, Performance, and History in *Anonymous*

Liverpool Daily Post
1945, Jan. 10, p. 2   Bushell, W. F.   Canon Rendall [letter]

Liverpool Echo
1920, March 4, p. 4   --   The Real Shakespeare [review of SF]
2009, April 22, p. 18   Wright, Jade   Is This a Blagger I See Before Me? Did Shakespeare Really Write All His Own Work? [states that Gerald Rendall, Univ. of Liverpool's first principal, bequeathed his books and manuscript notes to its library]

Living Age, The
1920, May 8, issue 3957: 368   --   The Arts and Letters [brief memtion of Looney]
1921, June 11, issue 4014: 672   Nesbit, E.   An Iconoclast in Stratford [repr. from *The New Witness* (April 29)]
1921, Sept. 24, p. 795   --   The Tercentenary of the First Folio [mentions Looney]
1923, June 16, vol. 317: 675   --   Life, Letters, and the Arts [brief mention of Looney]

London Historians Newsletter
2013, July   Thompson, Martin   The Rise and Fall of Brooke House, Hackney [repr. in DVN, vol. 20/3: 26]

London Mercury
1920, April, vol. 1/6: 766   --   Select List of Publications [SI is on the list]
1922, March, vol. 5/29: 540   --   Select List of Publications [Looney's *The Poems of Edward de Vere* is on the list]
1922, Dec., vol. 7/38: 118   --   New and Recent Periodicals [*The Golden Hind*]
1922, Dec., vol. 7/38: 215   Priestley, J. B.   Neither Shakespeare Nor Bacon [review of *Will o' theWisp: The Elusive Shakespeare* by George Hookham]
1923, July, vol. 8: 322   Shanks, Edward   [review of *Shakespeare Through Oxford Glasses* by H. H. Holland]
1928, May, p. 100,   Twitchett, E. G.   [review of *The Shakespeare Mystery* by Georges Connes]
1928, June, p. 217   Wilkinson, Clennell   [review of *The Seventeenth Earl of Oxford* by Capt. B. M. Ward]

London Mercury (continued)

1928, July, p. 300	Ward, Capt. Bernard M.	The Seventeenth Earl of Oxford [letter: response to June review; followed by reviewer's reply]
1928, Oct. vol. 18: 657-58	Freeman, John	[review of *Borrowers* by Percy Allen (1928)]
1928, Nov.	--	[article calls for compiling reporting on the authorship issue]
1929, Aug., vol. 20: 118	Harrison, G. B.	Shakespeare and Chapman as Topical Dramatists [review of the book by Percy Allen]
1929, Sept., vol. 20: 119	Allen, Percy	Shakespeare and Chapman [letter: resp. to Harrison's review]
1930, June, vol. 21: 185	Harrison, G. B.	[review of Sir Sidney Lee's posthumous *Elizabethan and Other Essays*, ed. by Frederick S. Boas]

London Review of Books

2010, Mar. 11, p. 21-22	Hackett, Helen	[review of *Contested Will* by James Shapiro (2010)]

London Star

1920, before May 12	--	[review of SI: "Sh. was more than a pseudonym; it was a mask"]

Londonderry Sentinal

1932, May 3, p. 3	Lord Sydenham	Lord Sydenham on Authorship Dispute. [letter repr. from *The Morning Post*]

Long Eaton Advertiser

1962, July 20, p. 8	Bayley, John	The Shakespeare Fringe [review of *The Shakespeare Claimants* by H. M. Gibson]

L'Opinion (France)

1920, Oct. 16, no. 42, p. 423-25	Lefranc, Abel	Du nouveau sur Shakespeare: Le secret du Songre d'une nuit d'ete, I [*Midsummer Night's Dream*]
1920, Oct. 23, no. 43, p. 451-52	Lefranc, Abel	Du nouveau sur Shakespeare: Le secret du Songe d'une nuit d'ete, II [*Midsummer Night's Dream*]
1921, Feb. 12	Lefranc, Abel	Du nouveau sur Shakespeare: Le secret du Songe d'une nuit d'ete, III [*Midsummer Night's Dream*]
1921, Feb. 21	Lefranc, Abel	Du nouveau sur Shakespeare: A propos des 'Joyeuses Commeres du Windsor' [*Merry Wives of Windsor*]

Los Angeles Public Library Monthly Bulletin

1920, Sept., vol. 15/3: 7	--	[list of newly-acquired books includes SI, with description]

Los Angeles Review of Books

2019, Jan. 13	Farrell, John	Why Literature Professors Turned Againt Authors—Or Did They?
2019, April 29	Lewis, Rhodri	Vanilla of Magical Thinking [review of *How the Classics Made Shakespeare* by Jonathan Bate]

Los Angeles Times (includes Los Angeles Times Book Review)

1931, April 5, p. 17	--	Shapshots at Recent Books [short review of *The Shakespeare Garden* by Esther Singleton; notes that Clark's Introduction reveals Singleton's belief in de Vere's authorship]
1936, Jan. 5, p. A6	Bailey, Millard	New Ghost Writer for Shakespeare
1939, Dec. 14, p. 9	--	X-ray Tests Called Proof Shakespeare Earl of Oxford
1940, Jan.		Shakespeare Fraud, Critic Says
1943, Feb. 7, p. C4	--	New Fuel Added to Flame of Shakespeare Argument [review of *Will Shakspere and the Dyer's Hand* by Alden Brooks]
1948, Jan. 5, p. 1	--	'Spirit' of Shakespeare Admits Earl of Oxford Collaborated With Him [says Percy Allen]
1953, Jan. 4, p. D6	Merlin, Milton	Image Breakers Again Tear Into Shakespeare [review of *This Star of England* by Dorothy and Charlton Ogburn]
1954, Sept. 20, p. A4	Adams, Percy F.	A View of Shakespeare
1954, Nov. 14, p. D6	Merlin, Milton	Theories About Bard Spoofed
1959, July 6, p. B4	Baxter, Frank C.	Shakespeare Not Ghost Written
1962, Aug. 31, p. C7	Kinsman, Robert	The Bard—Man or Myth [review of *Shake-speare: The Real Man Behind the Name* by Dorothy and Charlton Ogburn]
1981, Jan. 15, p. SG1	Mann, Bert	Plays Not By Shakespeare, Writer Claims [ruth Loyd Miller]
1983, Feb. 12, Sec. 5: 1-3	Champlin, Charles	A Bard By Any Other Name . . .[repr. in SON, vol. 19/3: 11-12 (Summer 1983)]
1983, April 23, Sec. 5: 1, 7	Champlin, Charles	To Be Or Not To Be the Bard

1984, Jan. 12, Sec. 6: 1, 7	Champlin, Charles	Whomsoever Art Thou, Shaksper?
1984, Feb. 11, p. G1, 6	Champlin, Charles	Decoding Stratford's Dark Laddie
1984, April 2, p. M1	Champlin, Charles	Marlovians Resurrect a Kit of Bard Evidence
1984, June 23, p. F1	Champlin, Charles	Shaksper Has His (Her?) Day in Court
1984, July 19, Sec. 6: 1, 4	Champlin, Charles	Veil Still Shrouds the Real Bard
1984, July 19, p. E1	Champlin, Charles	The Bard By Any Other Name
1984, Sept. 30, p. J10	Lochte, Dick	Book Notes [review of *The Mysterious William Shakespeare* by Charlton Ogburn]
1984, Dec. 30, p. I1, I5	Champlin, Charles	[review of *The Mysterious William Shakespeare*]
1985, Jan. 13, p. N6	Bednarz, James P.	[letter: response to Champlin's review]
1985, Jan. 13, p. N6	Innocenti, Celeste	[letter: response to Champlin's review]
1985, Jan. 13, p. N6	Argall, David Carl	[letter: response to Champlin's review]
1985, Jan. 13, p. N6	Nichols, Mark	[letter: response to Champlin's review]
1986, March 1, p. E1	Champlin, Charles	Hoffman's Questions About the Bard Live On
1986, Sept. 4, p. H1	Champlin, Charles	A New Crop of Hedging on the Bard
1987, Sept. 26, p. 2	Savage, David G.	Zounds! Much Ado About Poetic Justice
1987, Sept. 29, p. 2, 3	Champlin, Charles	Shakspere Shaken by Moot Court
1987, Sept. 30, p. C6	Champlin, Charles	What Fools These Mortals Be!
1988, April 26, p. G1	Champlin, Charles	Putting Bard to Computer Test on Thorny Authorship issue
1989, April 18, p. J1E	Champlin, Charles	PBS Plays Out the Debate Over the Bard [review of *Frontline*'s "The Shakespeare Mystery"] [repr. in SON, vol. 25/2: 4-5 (Spring 1989)]
1990, Feb. 8, p. F4	Champlin, Charles	William Shakespeare Is Still News After Four Centuries [excerpt repr. in SON, vol. 26/2: 6 (Spring 1990)]
1990, April 1, p. 3	Crafts, Fred	A Midsummer Day's Dream in Shakespeareland [visitors to Stratford defrauded]
1990, April 21, p. VCB11	Newton, Edmund	Shakespeare Shakedown: Computer Narrows Field of Claimants to Bard's Throne
1990, Oct. 29, p. B1	Newton, Edmund	Computer Reads Shakespeare, Dismisses Authorship Candidate
1990, Nov. 3, p. 6	--	Computer Reads Shakespeare, Dismisses Authorship Candidate
1991, April 26, p. VYB11	Elliott, Ward; Robert Valenza	Pretenders Sound Wrong Chords: We're Pretty Certain Who the Bard Wasn't, Though Not Who He Was
1991, Dec. 31, p. 2	Herman, Jan	Bard Boom on the Boards
1992, April 14, p. F2	Herman, Jan	Small Pay but Great Change? [notes Lord Vere's lecture]
1992, April 23, p. 8	Biederman, Patricia W.	What Manner of Birthday Gift Be This? The Authorship Question Surrounding Shakespeare Never Ends
1992, April 23, p. WSJ1	Biederman, Patricia W.	For the Bard, Slings and Arrows [presentation by the Earl of Burford]
1992, April 24, p. A1-2	Bravin, Jess	Much Ado About Real Shakespeare: Charles Vere
1992, April 28, p. SDF1	Bravin, Jess	Claiming the Bard's Mantle: Descendants Contend That the Earl of Oxford Was the Author
1992, May 25, p. SDF8	Drake, Sylvie	Questions Abound in 'Oxford' [review of *Oxford's Will*, a play by Jerry Fey]
1993, Feb. 21, p. 10	Champlin, Charles	Displacing Will [review of *The 100*, rev. ed., by Michael Hart]
1993, Feb. 28, p. 13	Burns, Tom	The Bard and the Bison [letter: Champlin's Feb. 21 article]
1993, Apr. 21, p. B7	LaBelle, Jenijoy	Happy Birthday, Dear William [repr. in SON, vol. 30/4: 5 (Aut. 1994); and in BTC, vol. 7: 285-86]
1993, May 8, p. VCB17	Alu, Al	[letter: LaBelle's recent article]
1993, May 8, p. VCB17	Champlin, Charles	[letter: LaBelle's recent article]
1993, Aug. 22, p. 2	Harris, M.	Best Bet [SOS Member Katherine Chiljan to speak]
2001, May 27, p. 1	Boehm, Mike	[review of *The Beard of Avon* by Amy Freed]
2001, June 4, p. F2	Phillips, Michael	Amy Freed Toys With the Mystery of Shakespeare's Identity [review of *The Beard of Avon* by Amy Freed]
2001, Aug. 27, p. E2	Perry, Tony	A Doctor by Day and Detective in Spare Time [profile of Eric Altruschler]
2010, Apr. 11, p. A29	Shapiro, James	Alas, Poor Shakespeare: Conspiracy Theories About the Authorship of His Plays Have Gone Mainstream [review of *Anonymous*]

Los Angeles Times (continued)

2010, April 19, p. A14	Orloff, John	No Denying a Genius at Work [letter: response to Shapiro]
2010, May 9, p. E8	Elliott, Ward	Shakespeare: Playwright or Phantasm? [review of *Contested Will* by James Shapiro]
2011, Oct. 27, p. D1	Keegan, Rebecca	Alas, Poor Will [review of *Anonymous*]
2011, Oct. 29, p. D7	Smith, Scott S.	[letter: Keegan's article: "Scholars should read Ogburn or *Shine Forth* by Altrocchi if they want to educate themselves."]
2011, Oct. 29, p. A19	Morrison, Patt	Who Wrote Shakespeare? [review of *Anonymous*]
2011, Nov. 20, p. E5	McNulty, Charles	A Better Debate: The Bard's Legacy
2011, Nov. 27, p. D2	Smith, Scott S.	[letter: McNulty's Oct. 29 article]
2011, Nov. 27, p. D2	Kreger, D. W.	[letter: McNulty's Oct. 29 article]
2011, Dec. 27, p. A11	Folkenflik, Robert	Anonymous Was a Writer; Some of the Most Famous Authors in History Kept Names Off the Title Page

Love Lore [a journal privately published and circulated by A. Bronson Feldman and Stephen Karpowitz]

1968	Morse, B. Obadiah	Shakespeare's First Tragedy [a pseudonym used by Feldman]

Ma'ariv (Tel Aviv)

1987, Oct. 7	Andrews, Robert	William Shakespeare—Not Guilty

Maclean's (Toronto)

1999, July 5, p. 52	Bethune, Brian	International Man of Mystery
2010, April, p. 60	Bethune, Brian	What's Behind the Shakespeare Wars [review of *Contested Will* by James Shapiro]

Mail on Sunday – See Daily Mail

Manchester City News

1924, Oct. 11	Walters, Cuming	Shakespeare's Signatures and *Sir Thomas More*
1931, Nov. 28	--	The Shakespeare Maze: A Sevenfold Clue [review of *Seven Shakespeares* by Gilbert Slater]

Manchester Evening News

1923, March or April	--	[article referred to in the *Hackney Spectator*]

Manchester Guardian [See also The Guardian]

1920, March 19, p. 7	Herford, Charles H.	Shakespeare Deposed Again [review of SI] ["It is impossible not to like, and even to admire, Mr. Looney."] [repr. in *The Telegraph* (Brisbane), May 15, 1920, p. 13; repr. in *The Sun* (Sydney), June 17, 1920, p. 8]
1920, April 8, p. 5	--	[Ad for the *Bookman's Journal & Print Collector's* issue with Looney's letter]
1923, June 5, p. 7	Herford, Charles H.	Mr. W. H. [review of *The Mystery of "Mr. W. H."* by Col. B. R. Ward]
1928, March 20, p. 7	--	Books of the Day [review of *Borrowers* by Percy Allen]
1928, April 4, p. 5	Allen, Percy	Shakespeare, Jonson and Wilkins [letter: response to the March 20 review, with reviewer's reply: "I have read Mr. Allen's letter. I do not wish to vary a syllable of my review."]
1928, April 27, p. 258	--	[review of *The Seventeenth Earl of Oxford* by Capt. Bernard M. Ward]
1928, May 22, p. 9	H. W. C. D.	Books of the Day [review of *The Seventeenth Earl of Oxford* by Bernard M. Ward (1928)]
1930, Jan. 30, p. 7	--	Books Received [Percy Allen's *The Case for Edward de Vere as "Shakespeare"*]
1930, Feb. 17, p. 5	--	Books Received [Gerald Rendall's *Shakespeare's Sonnets and Edward de Vere*]
1930, April 4, p. 7	--	Books Received [Percy Allen's *The Case for Edward de Vere as Shakespeare*]
1930, May 5, p. 7	A. P. W.	The Case Against Shakespeare [reviews of *The Case for Edward de Vere* by Percy Allen and *Shakespeare Sonnets and Edward de Vere* by G. H. Rendall]
1931, Dec. 14, p. 15	C. E. L.	The Shakespeare Controversy: "Crucial Evidence" Just Obtained [Percy Allen's talk at the Gallery First-Nighters' Club]
1932, March 24, p. 7	--	This Bacon Business

1933, May 17, p. 5	I. B.	The Oxfordians [review of *A Repy to John Drinkwater* by Percy and Ernest Allen]
1941, July 19, p. 6	--	The Theatre in the East End
1948, Sept. 13, p. 3	--	The Higher Criticism
1948, Oct. 1, p. 3	--	Miscellany: Jolly Good Fellows [about J. Thomas Looney]
1949, Jan. 26, p. 3	--	Shakespeare Substitutes
1950, April 20	--	Miscellany: Shakespeare and Others

Manuscripts

1966, vol. 18: 20-31	Blumenthal, Walter	One Cannot Flesh the Shakespeare Figure

Maple Ridge, Pitt Meadows Times (Maple Ridge, B. C.)

2009, Oct. 9, p. 17	--	Was Shakespeare Really Fakespeare? [review of *The Shakespeare Show* by Ryan Gladstone. De Vere charges horse-holder Will Shakespeare with telling his story . . .]

Mars Review of Books

2023, March 16	Habsul-Rignyr	The Man Who Would Be Shakespeare

Massbode, De

1923, May 12	Gunning, Dr. C. P.	[title not known] [excerpts reprinted in *De Amsterdammer* on May 12, with editorial commentary]

Mathematics Teacher, The

2009, April, vol. 102/8: 580-85	Edwards, Michael T.	Who Was the Real William Shakespeare?

Matilda Ziegler Magazine

1909, Jan.	Keller, Helen	The Question Now Remains: Who Was William Shakespeare?
???	Keller, Helen	[review of *The Shakespeare Problem Restated* by G. Greenwood]

Medical Society of London, Transactions

1916, vol. 39	Thomas, Sir St. Clair	Shakespeare and Medicine (repr. in BTC, vol. 1: 93-113)

Memoria di Shakespeare

2012, vol. 8: 95	Fusini, Nadia	Shakespeare: Playwright or 'Sprachschöpfer'?
2012, vol. 8: 133	Publiatti, Paola	The Burden of Proof: From New Biographism to New Disintegration
2012, vol. 8: 313	Colombo, Rosy	*Hamlet*: Authorship Enacted
2012, vol. 8: 464	Pirè, Luciana	[review of *Contested Will* by James Shapiro (2010)]
2012, vol. 8: 456	Colombo, Rosy	[review of *Der Mann, der Schakespeare erfand* by Kurt Kreiler (2009)]
2015	Waugaman, Richard M.	The Psychology of Shakespearean Biography: An Update
2015, vol. 2: 195-96	Bloom, Harold	A Salvo for Lucy Negro [repr. from HAP, vol. 298: 55-57 (April 1999); repr. in LC, p. 57-58]

Mensa Research Journal

vol. 40/2	Simonton, Dean Keith	Shakespeare's 'small Latin and less Greek'

Mercure de France

1931, vol. 233: 444-46	Chevalley, Abel	[review of *Shakespeare's Plays in the Order of Their Writing* by Eva Turner Clark (1931)] [in French]

Middlesex County Times

1924, Feb. 16, p. 8	--	New Volumes [list includes *"Shakespeare" Identified* and *The Mystery of "Mr. W. H."*]

Mills Quarterly

1993, April, vol. 75: 26	Cheadle, Jane B.	Who Was Shakespeare?

Milwaukee Sentinal

1991, May 3, p. I6	Wellman, Wade	Shakespeare, By Any Other Name . . . [review of *Alias Shakespeare* by Joe Sobran]
1998, Nov. 23, p. 2	Woods, Michael	Key to 'Real' Shakespeare Lies in the Stars, Physicist Says
2004, Aug. 8, p. 7E	Gould, Rachel	The Playwright's the Thing

Minneapolis Star-Journal

1940, March 17	Irwin, Wallace	[mention of de Vere as author in a short story]
1940, Aug. 4, p. 37, p. 37	--	[mention of a new play about de Vere by Warren P. Munsell, *By Any Other Name*]

Minneapolis Star Tribune

1987, Oct. 16, p. 19A	Schwartz, Amy E.	Partisans Gather to Debate Identity of the True Bard
1988, Nov. 19, p. 1E	Holston, Noel	Who Wrote Shakespeare's Plays? [Advance look at Al Austin's *Frontline* Program]
1988, Nov. 26, p. 10A	--	The Author of Shakespeare's Works? That is the Question
1988, Nov. 27, p. 28A	--	Who Wrote Shakespeare's Drama? He Did
1989, April 18, p. 1-2E	Holston, Noel	*Frontline* Makes Much Ado Over Shakespeare [review of "The Shakespeare Mystery" (1989)] [repr. in SON, vol. 25/2: 7-8 (Spring 1989)]
1990, Dec. 28, p. 8E	Oldenburg, Don	Pretenders to the Bard's Throne Fail 'Line-ender' Test
1992, June 28, p. 3E	Larcen, Donna	Mysteries Range from Entertaining Curiosities to Vexing Riddles With No Answers
1995, April 21, p. 16A	Lerner, Maura	Could a Man With Handwriting Like This Really Construct the Greatest Literature in the English Language? [full page review of *The Mysterious William Shakespeare*]
1996, Oct. 6, p. 15F	Wood, Dave	Lofty Ideals Come of Age for Literary Center [Charles Burford and the SOS Conference]
1996, Oct. 9, p. 1A	Draper, Norman	'Twixt Much Ado, Group Brings Shakespeare Theories to Twin Cities [Charles Burford/Charles Vere Tour]
1996, Oct. 13, p. 22A	--	Shakespeare: Read Him, Whoever He Was
1996, Oct. 19, p. 21A	Clayton, Tom	Authorship Theorists Do Protest Too Much [letter]
1999, April 5, p. 4E	Hernandez, Romel	Fraud of Avon? Scholar Pays Price for Dissent [Daniel Wright]
2005, Aug. 25, p. 12F	Gollob, Herman	What's in a Name? Did Edward de Vere Really Write the Works Attributed to William Shakespeare? [review of *"Shakespeare" By Another Name* by Mark Anderson]
2005, Sept. 4, p. 1F	Lerner, Maura	The Bard By Another Name? [review of *"Shakespeare" By Another Name* by Mark Anderson]
2011, Oct. 28, p. E8	Covert, Colin	Playwright Theory Lacks Substance [review of *Anonymous*]

Mississippi Quarterly

1994-95, vol. 48: 319-36	Chappell, Charles	Lawrence Wells of Oxford: Interview ["recognition of de Vere as author would case massive upheavals"]

Modera Sprak

1993, vol. 87/1: 6	Dantanus, Ulf	Shakespeare: In Search of a Solid Life

Modern Language Notes

1929, Mar., vol. 44/3: 202	Greenlaw, Edwin	[review of *The Seventeenth Earl of Oxford* by Capt. B. M. Ward]
1937, Mar. vol. 52/3: 183-86	Bowers, Fredson T.	Gascoigne and the Oxford Cipher [review of *A Hundreth Sundrie Flowres* by George Gascoigne, edited by Bernard M. Ward]
1938, Dec., vol. 53/8: 621	Withington, R.	[review of *The Man Who Was Shakespeare* by Eva Turner Clark]

Modern Language Review

1920, April 1, vol. 15, p. 345	--	New Books [*"Shakespeare" Identified* is on the list.]
1921, April 1, vol. 16: 206	--	New Publications [Looney's *The Poems of Edward de Vere*]
1927, Jan. 1, vol. 22, p. 214-20	Ambrose, Genevieve	[review of *A Hundreth Sundrie Flowres* by George Gascoigne, edited by Bernard M. Ward]
1929, Jan., vol. 24/2: 216-21	Gregg, W. W.	[review of *The Seventeenth Earl of Oxford, 1550-1604* by B. M. Ward] [response to Ward's August 2 letter to the *Times Literary Supplement*]
1962, Oct. 1, vol. 57/4: 556	Klein, David	Did Shakespeare Produce His Own Plays?
1963, April, vol. 58/2: 217-19	Sanderson, James L.	Three Unpublished Elizabethan Wedding Poems

Modern Maturity

1997, March, vol. 40/2: 28	Digby, Diehl	[review of *Alias Shakespeare* by Joseph Sobran (1997)]

Modern Philology

1923, Aug., vol. 21/1	Rickert, Edith	Political Propaganda and Satire in *A Midsummer Night's Dream*, Part 1
1923, Nov., vol. 21/2	Rickert, Edith	Political Propaganda and Satire in *A Midsummer Night's Dream*, Part 2
1980, vol. 77: 427-29	Akrigg, G. P. V.	[review of *Shakespeare By Hilliard* by Leslie Hotson]
2012, Nov., vol. 110/2: E82-88	Pigman III, G. W.	[review of *Fortunatus im Ungluck: Die Aventiuren des Master F. I. Edward de Vere, Earl of Oxford*, translated by Chris Hirte]

Monterey County Weekly

| 2005, Sept. 22, p. 51 | Masters, Ryan | Conspiracy Theory; Beard Dramatizes Dispute Over the Dramatist's Identity [review of *The Beard of Avon* by Amy Freed] |

Montgomery Advertiser

| 1920, June 27, p. 1 | Watterson, Henry & William M. Reedy | The "Real" Shakespeare [an exchange between Watterson and Reedy repr. from *Reedy's Mirror* (June 17)] |
| 1921, March 21 | Gorman, J. T. | Who Wrote Shakespeare? [letter] |

Month, The

| 1930, Nov. 1, vol. 156: 425-37 | Thurston, Herbert | The Mr. W. H. of Shakespeare's Sonnets |

Monthly Bulletin of the Carnegie Library of Pittsburgh

| 1931. June, vol. 36: 51 | -- | [review of *Hidden Allusions in Sh.'s Plays* by Eva Turner Clark] |

Morning Call

| 1934, Spring | -- | [article quotes Mr. Shaw Desmond's opinion that the Oxford hypothesis was "steadily undermining orthodoxy."] |
| 1991, Dec. 11, p. B5 | Cowen, Dick | Crusader [lord Vere] Says His Kin Wrote Shakespeare's Plays |

Morning Post, The

1920, April 1, p. 5.	--	A New Round Game [review of SI]
1926, April 15	Eagle, Roderick, L.	Francis Bacon: The Plays of Shakespeare [letter]
1929, Aug. 30, p. 7	Bowen, Marjorie	Shakespeare and *Richard III*: Little Evidence and "A Mass of Legend and Calumny" [letter]
1929, Sept. 3, p. 10	--	The Way of History [editorial]
1929, Sept. 3, p. 5	Ward, Col. Bernard R.	Shakespeare and *Richard III*: A Tudor Government Propaganda Department
1929, Sept. 5, p. 5	Hunter, Mark	Shakespeare and *Richard III*: An Inefficient Propagandist [letter]
1929, Sept. 6, p. 5	Oman, Charles	Shakespeare and *Richard III*: Sir Charles Oman Discredits the Propaganda Theory [letter]
1929, Sept. 7, p. 7	Ward, Col. Bernard R.	Shakespeare and *Richared III*: Queen Elizabeth's Secret Service [letter]
1929, Sept. 9, p. 5	Hearnshaw, F. J. C.	Shakespeare and *Richard III*: Misused Whitewash [letter: response to Ward]
1929, Sept. 10, p. 9	Barnard, Francis P.	Shakespeare and RIII: Destruction of Records and Documents
1929, Sept. 11, p. 6	Beazley, Raymond	Shakespeare and *Richard III*: An Historical Enigma [letter]
1929, Sept. 11, p. 6	Heron, G. Allan	Shakespeare and *Richard III*: Historians Agree [letter]
1929, Sept. 12, p. 9	X.Y.Z.	A Modified View [letter]
1929, Sept. 12, p. 9	Hunter, Mark	Shakespeare and *Richard III*: A Modern Parallel [letter]
1929, Sept. 13, p. 9	Ravenshaw, John	Royal Writs
1929, Sept. 13, p. 9	Sheppard, Alfred T.	Shakespeare and *Richard III*: A Footnote by R. L. S. [letter]
1929, Sept. 14, p. 7	Bowen, Marjorie	Shakespeare and *Richard III*: Miss Marjorie Bowen's Reply [letter]
1929, Sept. 19, p. 9	Douglas, Col. Montagu W.	Elizabeth's war: The First of England's Three Fights Against Famine [letter]
1930, March	--	[review of *Shakespeare's Sonnets and Edward de Vere* by Gerald Rendall]
1930, April 7, p. 9	--	[notice for the SF dinner on April 12]
1930, April 14, p. 5	--	Shakespeare's Plays: Edward de Vere and Their Authorship [report on the SF's first dinner]
1931, June 6	Wilson, S. C.	[letter]
1931, July 6, p. 5	Mott, Agnes	Shakespeare's Friend [letter]
1931, July 10, p. 6	Kennedy-Skipton, H.	A Double Coincidence in *Romeo and Juliet* [letter]
1931, July 22, p. 7	Kennedy-Skipton, H.	The Trussell Family: A Double Coincidence in *Romeo and Juliet* [letter]
1931, July 25, p. 9	Trussell, H. A.	The Trussell Family: A Denial of the 'Candle-Holder: Theory [letter]
1931, July 28, p. 6	Ward, Col. Bernard R.	The Trussell Family: Probable Meaning of Shakespeare's 'Candle-Holder' Pun [letter]

Morning Post, The (continued)

1931, July 28, p. 6	Holland, Adm. H. H.	Speght's Chaucer: Mystery of Review in Gabriel Harvey's Copy
1931, July 29, p. 6	Holland, Adm. H. H.	The Trussell Family [letter]
1931, Dec. 4	--	Shakespeare Play-Dates: *Twelfth Night* and *The Merry Wives*: When Were They Written?
1933, May 2, p. 5	--	Colonel B. Rowland Ward [Obituary]
1933, May 22	--	Shakespeare as Propaganda: "Oxford" Theorists Challenge: A Reply to John Drinkwater
1933, July 11	Allen, Percy	Disputed Shakespeare MSS: 'Shaxberd' for Shakespeare-Oxford [letter]
1933, Sept. 28	--	New Shakespeare Theory: Queen Elizabeth and Oxford
1933, Oct. 18	--	Shakespeare in France: Professor Georges Connes' Lecture
1934, April 27	--	One Shakespeare or Two?
1952	--	[review of *Lord Oxford and the Shakespeare Group* by Col. Montagu Douglas] [quoted in SFE, April 1953]

Musical Times, The

1929, Jan. 1, vol. 70: 46-53	Eggar, Katherine E.	Mr. Bird's *Battell*
1958, Sept., vol. 99/1387: 480+	Eggar, Katherine E.	Shakespeare as Musician

Nashville Tennessean

1920, Aug. 23, p. 4	--	[brief description of *"Shakespeare" Identified*]
1955, March 13	L. H.	Oxford or Shakespeare? [review of the Ogburn's *Renaissance Man of England*]

Nation

1920, March 13, p. 836	--	Books of the Spring Season [SI is on the list]
1920, April 24, vol. 110: 560	--	Notes and News [Brief mention of Looney]
1920, Aug. 28, vol. 111: 248-49	Krutch, Joseph	Shakespeare Unidentified [review of *"Shakespeare" Identified*]
2004, March 1, vol. 11: 29-32	Eagleton, Terry	Company Man [review of *The Age of Shakespeare* by Frank Kermode]
2006, March 13, vol. 13: 23-26	Swift, Daniel	Bad Will Hunting [review of *"Shakespeare" By Another Name* by Mark Anderson (2005)]

Nation and Athenaeum

1921, Feb. 26, vol. 28: 756	--	This Week's Books [Looney's *The Poems of Edward de Vere*]
1926, June 12, vol. 39/10: 32-41	Saintsbury, George	The Hundred Sundrie Flowres [review of *A Hundredth Sundrie Flowres* edited by Capt. B. M. Ward]
1928, April 14, vol. 43: 50-51	--	Literary Borrowings [review of *Borrowers* by Percy Allen (1928)]
1930, May 3, vol. 46/4: p. 150	Knight, G. Wilson	Shakespeare and the Earl of Oxford [review of *he Case for Edward de Vere* by Percy Allen (1930)]
1931, Feb. 14, p. 635-36	Thornton, James	Bacon and Shakespeare [review of of *Shakespeare Authorship* by Gilbert Standen and two other books]

National Observer

1968, April 29, p. 1	Wright, Louis B.	Years of Drollery Amid Shakespeare

National Post (Don Mill, Ontario)

2010, April 19	Shapiro, James	Driven Mad by the Great Bard [long excerpt from *Contested Will*]
2010, April 26, p. A11	Nelson, Virginia Hart	[letter: Shakespeare let de Vere take credit behind the scene]
2011, Oct. 26, p. A3	Itzkoff, Dave	Shakespeare Birthplace Trust Slams New Film . . . Or Does It?; No, It Really Does [rev. of *Anonymous*]

National Review (New York)

1984, Nov. 2, p. 49	Mysak, Joe	Random Notes [Brief review of *The Mysterious William Shakespeare*]
1985, April 5, vol. 37/6: 51-52	Sobran, Joseph	Not Set Down in Malice [review of *The Mysterious William Shakespeare* by Charlton Ogburn, Jr.
1987, Oct. 5	Sobran, Joseph	BARD, Beyond a Reasonable Doubt
1987, Oct. 27, vol. 39/20: 15	--	[Untitled: Three Justices rule in favor of traditional claimant]
1987, Nov. 6, vol. 37/6: 54-56	Sobran, Joseph	A Fair Shake for Oxford/Shakespeare Revealed in Oxford's Letters [the Sept. 25 Supreme Court justices' mock trial and Charlton Ogburn's response to it; and review of *Shakespeare Revealed in Oxford's Letters* by William Fowler (1986)]
1991, April 29, vol. 43/7: 44-46	Sobran, Joseph	Bard Thou Never Wert: Fooled By a Folio [repr. in SON, vol.

		27/2: 2-5 (Spring 1991); and in BTC, vol. 7: 36-42]
1991, June 10, vol. 43/10: 34+	Heston, Charlton	Touch Swords [letter from Charlton Heston and Sobran response]
1997, June 10, vol. 49/10: 48-49	Hart, Jeffrey	Phantom of the Theater [review of *Alias Shakespeare* by Joseph Sobran (1997)]
2010, Nov. 1, p. 35	Scully, Matthew	Bard of the Right: Remembering Joe Sobran
2017, Jan. 21 [online]	Goldstein, Gary	The Nobility of High Politics in Shakespeare [repr. in SON, vol. 53/1: 16-17]
2023, Feb. 12 [online]	Goldstein, Gary	The Mystery of Shakespeare Lingers

National Review (London)

1857, July, vol. 5/9: 72-82	--	The Alleged Non-Existence of Shakespeare [review of *The Philosophy of the Plays of Shakespeare Unfolded* by Delia Bacon; Preface by Nathaniel Hawthorne (1857)]
1901, Aug., p. 913-25	Sinnett, A. P.	New Light on Shakespeare
1921, Nov., vol. 78: 359-69	Lucas, R. Macdonald	Did Lord Derby Write Shakespeare?
1922, Feb., vol. 78: 801-9	Looney, J. Thomas	'Shakespeare': Lord Oxford or Lord Derby?
1922, March, vol. 79: 94-6	Hookham, George	Edward de Vere and the Shakespeare Plays
1922, March, vol. 79: 230	Greenwood, George	Was Shakespeare a Schoolmaster?
1922, Sept., vol. 81: 81-93	Ward, Col. Bernard R.	"Mr. W. H." and "Our Ever-Living Poet"
1922, Oct., vol. 81: 267-76	Ward, Col. Bernard R.	Edward de Vere and William Shakespeare – A Dual Mystery
1926, March, vol. 87: 898-910	Greenwood, George	A Cambridge Scholar on Shakespeare [Arthur Gray]
1927, March, vol. 89: 114-124	Greenwood, George	False Light on Shakespeare
1938, Jan., vol. 110: 532-33	Lucas, R. Macdonald	Shakespeare's Vital Secret [letter: response to review]

New Age, The: A Weekly Review of Politics, Literature and Art

1920, Dec. 2, vol. 28/5: 55-56	R. H. C.	Readers and Writers [review of *"Shakespeare" Identified*]
1920, Dec. 2	--	[rev. of *Shakespeare's Handwriting* by George Greenwood]
1920, Dec. 23, vol. 28/8: 91	Looney, J. Thomas	Readers and Writers [response to the Dec. 2 review]
1920, Dec. 23, vol. 28/8: 91-92	R. H. C.	Readers and Writers [reviewer's reply to Looney]
1921, Jan. 20, vol. 28/12: 138-39	Looney, J. Thomas	Readers and Writers [response to reviewer]
1921, Jan. 20, vol. 28/12: 139	R. H. C.	Readers and Writers [reviewer's reply to Looney]
1921, Jan. 27, vol. 28/13: 155-56	R. H. C.	Readers and Writers. [reviewer's further reply]
1921, Feb. 17, vol. 28/16: 192	Looney, J. Thomas	Shakespeare Identified [looney's response to reviewer]

New Brunswick Daily Home News

1940, Jan., p. 3	--	Shakespeare Paintings Really Earl of Oxford, Says Student

New Criterion, The

2006, Feb., vol. 24/6: 23-27	Propson, David	Shakespiracy Theory [review of *"Shakespeare" By Another Name* by Mark Anderson (2005)]
2013, Nov. vol. 32/3: 66	Dean, Paul	What's in a Name?
2016, April, vol. 34/8: 4-8	Donoghue, Denis	The Jacobean Dramatist

New England Quarterly

1996, June, vol. 69/2: 223-49	Baym, Nina	Delia Bacon, History's Odd Woman Out

New England Review

2015, vol. 36/1: 100-131+	Stritmatter, Roger A., Mark K. Anderson & Elliott Stone	Melville's *Billy Budd* and the Disguises of Authorship

New English Review

2014, Feb.	Hopkins, Keith	William Shakespeare, Edward de Vere, Seventeenth Earl of Oxford, and the still-Vexed Bermoothes
2021, July	Burghauser, Jeffrey	On Alexander Waugh

New Forest Magazine

1922, Oct., vol. XXXV: 20 --	Books to Read	[short review of SI]

New Indian Express (Chennai, India)

2011, Oct. 28	--	Much Ado About Legacy of W. Shakesp. [review of *Anonymous*]

New Leader

1925, Sept. 26, p. 9	Wood, Clement	The Shakespeare Riddle: Has It at Last Been Solved? [rev. of SI]

New Orleans Times-Picayune

1978, Sept. 3 or 4	Harris, Sydney J.	Can You Spot This Famed Englishman?
1980, July 7	--	Play Said the Bard
1985, Apr. 26, Lag: 8	Barr, Robert	[review of *The Mysterious William Shakespeare* by Charlton Ogburn, Jr. (1992)]
1988, Feb. 7, p. J2	Raidy, William A.	Shakespeare Still Arousing Passions After 400 Years
1988, Feb. 7, p. J2	McConnaughey, Janet	Two Louisianians Say Shakespeare Wasn't the One
1989, Oct. 22, p. B1	Eggler, Bruce	Shakespeare Who? The Plot Thickens [SOS conference]
1993, Jan. 3, p. B07	Gill, James	The Play's the Thing, But Is It Mr. Shakespeare's? [repr. in SON, vol. 29/1a: 7-8 (Winter 1993); and in BTC, vol. 7: 150-51]
1999, March 31, p. E1	Hernandez, Romel	Shakespeare in Doubt, Skeptics Label the Bard a Fraud

New Republic

| 1950, April 24, issue 24: 20 | Bush, Douglas | [review of *"Shakespeare" Identified* (2nd ed., 1949)] |

New Shakespeare Society Transactions

| 1874, July 10, p. 371-439 | Simpson, Richard | The Political Use of the Stage in Shakespeare's Time |

New Statesman: Weekly Review of Politics and Literature (London)

1920, March 20, p. 712-13	--	The Latest Shakespeare [review of *"Shakespeare" Identified*]
1921, June 4, p. 252	--	The Poems of Shakespeare [review of *Poems of Edward de Vere* edited by J. Thomas Looney]
1926, June 19, vol. 27: 266+	--	[review of *A Hundredth Sundrie Flowres* edited by B. M. Ward]
1928, May 26, p. 236	--	[review of *Borrowers* by Percy Allen (1928)]
1928, June 2, p. 268-69	--	[review of *The Seventeenth Earl of Oxford* by Bernard M. Ward]
1954, Feb. 27, p. 266-67	--	Shorter Reviews [review of *This Star of England* by Dorothy and Charlton Ogburn]
2004, Nov. 15, p. 48	Eagleton, Terry	The Stratford Man [review of *Will in the World* by Stephen Greenblatt]
2005, June 20, p. 42-44	Leahy, William	The Business of Bill: Who Was Shakespeare? And Why Does it Matter?
2013, April 26, vol. 142: 44	Bate, Jonathan	A Player, Not a Gentleman [review of *Shakespeare Beyond Doubt*, edited by Paul Edmondson and Stanley Wells]

New Statesman and Nation

| 1955, Aug. 27, p. 50 | Stewart, J. I. M. | Romance of Spotting [review of *Who Was Shakespeare?* by H. Amphlett] |

New Witness, The

| 1921, April 29 | Nesbit, E. | An Iconoclast in Stratford [repr. in *The Living Age* (June 11)] |

New York Herald Tribune

1927, May 22, p. F23	--	Who Wrote Shakespeare? [review of *Axiophilus, or Oxford Wrote Shakespeare* by Eva Turner Clark]
1931, March 15, p. J12	Chew, Samuel C.	Who Was W. S.? [review of *Hidden Allusions in Shakespeare's Plays* by Eva Turner Clark
1933, May 21, p. H16	--	*Love's Labour's Lost*: A Study [review of *The Satirical Comedy* by Eva Turner Clark]
1933, Nov.	--	Shakespeare, Oxford and Elizabethan Times [review of the book by Adm. H. H. Holland]
1933, Nov. 22, p. 15	Clending, Logan	Good Reading
1937, Dec. 1, p. 21	--	Books Out Today [Eva Turner Clark's *The Man Who Was Shake.*]
1938, Feb.13, p. G11	--	The Mantle of Shakespeare [review of *The Man Who Was Shakespeare* by Eva Turner Clark]
1947, April 3, p. 26A	--	Mrs. Eva Turner Clark [Obituary]
1947, May 30, p. 17	--	Bacon Has a Rival as Shakespeare; De Vere Supporters Make Post-War Appearance
1947, June 1, p. VII-8	Linscott, Roger Bourne	"On the Books: The Bard" [review of *Digesta Anti-Shakespearea*, a bibliography by Joseph S. Galland]
1947, June 8, p. A7	Burgess, Gelett	Modern Research Sheds New Light on Bard of Avon: Recent Discoveries Strengthen Oxford Theory Concerning Authorship [responses to Burgess ran through seven Sunday editions] [repr. in SON, vol. 5/4: 5 (Dec. 10, 1969); and in BTC, vol. 7: xxvii-xxx]

1947, June 15, p. A7	Ogburn, Charlton, Sr.	Oxford, Poet and Playwright? [letter: Gelett Burgess's June 5 article][excerpt repr. in SFE, April 1948, p. 8]
1947, June 15, p. A7	Peasley, Harriet	Oxford, Poet and Playwright? [letter: response to Burgess]
1947, June 15, p. A7	Sprague, Mrs. H. C.	Oxford, Poet and Playwright? [letter" response to Burgess]
1947, July 20, p. A2	Carter, Joseph	The Shakespeare Controversy: Now it is a Case for the 17th Earl of Oxford
1947, June 22, p. A7	Burgess, Gelett	The Modern Challenge of Shakespearean Authorship [letter: reply to recent letters]
1947, June 22, p. A7	Collins, Edmund	Genius and Lowly Origins [letter: response to Burgess]
1947, June 22, p. A7	Earle, Peter G.	De Vere's Poetry [letter: response to Burgess]
1947, June 29, p. A7	Allvine, Glendon	Oxford's Literary Genius [letter]
1947, June 29, p. A7	Ogburn, Dorothy	Oxford's Literary Genius: Shakespeare's Background [letter: Response to letters by Collins and Earle]
1947, July 29, p. A7	Thompson, Sydney	Asks Photographic Proof [letter: Barrell's X-rays]
1947, Sept. 7, p. A7	Sears, Florence W.	Acclaimed as a Poet [letter: response to Burgess]
1948, Oct. 22, p. 18	--	Shakespearean Authorship Upheld at Amherst Club
1949, Oct. 9, p. F4	Davis, Elrick B.	Elizabethan Secret Agent [review of *Cloak of Folly* by Burke Boyce]
1949, Nov. 6, p. BR31	--	Reprints, New Editions [Short comments on new edition of SI]
1949, Dec. 11, p. A5	Burgess, Gelett	Shakespeare a Pen Name [letter]
1952, May 3, p. 9	--	Shakespeare Series Gets WNYC in Row: Anti-Stratfordians Protest, Receive Air Time
1953, Jan. 11, p. BR13	Krutch, Joseph W.	Meet "Hamlet's New Author" [review of *This Star of England* by Dorothy and Charlton Ogburn (1952)]
1953, Nov. 16, p. 14	--	The Great Literary Hoax [editorial] [not about the SAQ, but Ogburn referred to it in his Dec. 12 letter]
1953, Dec. 12, p. 12	Ogburn, Charlton	The Plays of Shakespeare are Attributed to Oxford [letter: the Nov. 16 editorial]
1953, Dec. 19, p. 8	McFee, William	Shakespeare's Works: Attribution to the Earl of Oxford Supported [letter]
1953, Dec. 26, p. 6	Ish-Kishor, Sulamith	Oxford Theory [letter]
1953m Dec. 26, p. 6	Hoppner, Francis	Bacon and Oxford [letter]
1956, Jan. 10, p. 22	McFee, William	Shakespeare and Stratford [letter]
1956, April 1, p. A4	Montgomery, R. H. & Charles D. Drayton & Charlton Ogburn	De Vere Theory [letter]
1957, Dec.29, p. E7	Winterich, John T.	If Not Shakespeare, Who?
1962, Feb. 24, p. 16	--	Charlton Ogburn Dead, Was AFL Chief Counsel
1962, Aug.26, p. F6	Harrison, G. R.	Shakespeare, or a Man Known as Shakespeare? [review of *Shakespeare: The Man Behind the Name* by Dorothy Ogburn and Charlton Ogburn Jr. (1962)]

New York Magazine

1983, July 18, p. 9	Churcher, Sharon	Shakespeare Authorship: A Secret of the Tomb?
1983, Aug. 15, p. 7	Johnson, Morse	Prominent Doubters [letter] [repr. in SON, vol. 20/1+2: 10 (Winter/Spring, 1984)]

New York Observer

2005, Sept. 19, p. 1	Rosenbaum, Ron	The Shakespeare Code: Is Times Guy Kind of Bard 'Creationist'? [Niederkorn's NYT article, "The Shakespeare Code."]
2005, Sept. 26, p. 4	Anderson, Mark K.	[letter: response to Rosenbaum's Sept. 19 article]
2005, Sept. 26, p. 4	Rosenbaum, Ron	[letter: reply to Anderson's letter]
2005, Oct. 31	Cornfield, Robert	In Search of the Elusive Bard: The Plays Are Still the Thing

New York Post

1989, April 18	Bianculli, David	Noble Test of Shakespeare [review of *Frontline* broadcast] [repr. in SON, vol. 25/2: 9 (Spr. '89)]
2003, Nov. 19, p. 56	Lyons, Donald	Good Will Fronting [review of *The Beard of Avon* by Amy Freed]

New York Review of Books

1942, April 16		Obituary of Carolyn Wells
1985, Jan. 17, p. 21	O'Brien, Conor Cruise	The Charms of Certitude [review of *The Mysterious William Shakespeare* by Charlton Ogburn]
1985, Jan. 17, p. 23-26	Honigmann, E. A. J.	Sweet Swan of Oxford? [review of *The Mysterious William Shakespeare* by Charlton Ogburn, Jr.
1991, Nov. 7, 27-30	Honigmann, E. A. J.	The Second-Best Bed
1992, April 9, p. 27	Ogburn, Charlton, Jr. & Honigmann, E. A. J.	Shakespeare & Co. [letters: Ogburn's response to Honigmann's Nov. 1991 article followed by Honigmann's reply] [repr. in SON, vol. 28/2: 16 (Spr. 1992); and in BTC, vol. 7: 106-07]
1992, June 25, p. 27	Ogburn, Charlton, Jr.	The Second-Best Bed [letter: resp. to Honigmann's April 9 reply] [with new reply by Honigmann] [repr. in SON, vol. 28/2: 16-17 (Spr. 1992); and in BTC, vol. 7: 107-08]
2006, May 11, p. 27	Barton, Anne	The One and Only [reviews of five recent books on Shakespeare biography] [see also comments in SM, vol. 6/3(Spr., 2007)]
2010, May 27, vol. 57/9: 31	Wells, Stanley	Plotting Against the Stratford Man [review of *Contested Will* by James Shapiro (2010)]

New York Sun

1928, May 23	--	[review of Capt. Ward's *Seventeenth Earl of Oxford*] [Col. Ward says "best so far"]
1930, Feb. 17	Rathburn, Stephen	Champion of Earl of Oxford as Claimant to Shakespeare's Fame [review of *The Case for Edward de Vere* by Percy Allen]
1930, Oct. 28	--	Shakespeare Was Not an Earl [referred to in Percy Allen's Feb. 9, 1931 letter to the CSM]
1936, Nov. or Dec.	--	[important interview at end of Percy Allen's speaking tour of eastern United States and Canada]
1937, Dec. 11	Barrell, Charles Wisner	Alias William Shakespeare? The Man Behind the Plays [review of *The Man Who Was Shakespeare* by Eva Turner Clark]
1939, Dec. 16	--	The Roentgen Shakespeare [editorial] [repr. in SFA, vol. 1/2: 4-5 (Feb. 1940); and in BTC, vol. 2: 85-86]
1942, April 23	--	Shakespeare's Day [exc. repr. in SFA, vol. 3/4: 54 (June 1942)]
1947, June or July	--	[long article about Benezet's June 1947 talk at the Wedgwood Club in Boston, some weeks after the event]
2002, April 23	McCarter, Jeremy	What's In a Date?
2003, May 2	--	[article highlights Ron Destro's plans for a non-profit Oxford Shakespeare Centre]

New York Times and New York Times Book Review

1920, April 4, p. X5	--	News of Authors [Brief mention of SI]
1920, May 30, p. 281	--	[Stokes Books ad for three books; SI with descr. is first]
1920, June 6, p. 58	--	Convincing Evidence on the Shakespeare Problem [Advertisement and brief description of *"Shakespeare" Identified*]
1920, June 13, p. 56	--	Latest Books [brief description of *"Shakespeare" Identified*]
1920, June 27, p. 58	Corbin, John	Who Is "Baconian" Now: A Curious Mania That Reaches Its Climax in "Identifying" Shakespeare With an Earl of Oxford [review of *"Shakespeare" Identified*]
1920, July 18, p. 87	Watterson, Henry & William M. Reedy	The "Real" Shakespeare [reprint of an exchange between Watterson and Reedy from *Reedy's Mirror*, (June 17)]
1925, Oct. 4, p. BR6	Souday, Paul	A French History of English Letters
1928, Nov. 25, p. SM6	Brock, H. I.	Seeking a True Shakespeare Portrait
1930, April 20, p. 56	--	News and Views of Literary London [Short description of Gerald Rendall's *Shakespeare's Sonnets*]
1930, Aug. 31, p. X7	McGlinchee, Claire	Esther Singleton [letter: obituary]
1931, May 31, p. 17	Coblante, Stanton A.	Shakespeare as the Earl of Oxford [review of *Hidden Allusions in Shakespeare's Plays* by Eva T. Clark]
1932, Nov. 24	Wells, Carolyn	[article by Wells mentioned in Eva Turner Clark's letter to J. T. Looney as appearing in "this morning's paper;" presumably in the *NY Times*, but article not yet found]

1933, May 28, p. BR15	--	Love's Labour's Lost [review of *The Satirical Comedy: Love's Labour's Lost* by Eva Turner Clark (1933)]
1937, Dec.1, p. BR21	--	Books Published Today [Eva Turner Clark's *The Man Who Was Shakespeare* is on the list]
1939, March 5, p. BR17	Barrell, Charles W.	D'avenant's Life [letter]
1939, Dec. 16, p. 16	--	Alias Shakespeare [editorial on *"Shakespeare" Identified* and on Charles Wisner Barrell and the Ashbourne Portrait]
1939, Dec. 24, p. 45	Barrell, Charles W.	Shakespeare's Portraits: Features and Coloring Similar to Those of Lord Oxford [response to the Dec. 16 editorial]
1939, Dec. or Jan. 1940	Winchell, Walter	[ccolumn responding to Charles Barrell's piece in *Scientific Am.*]
1940, Jan.	--	To Be or Not To Be: A New Shakespeare?
1940, March 3	Brooks, Philip	Crime Imitates Fiction [repr. in SFA, vol. 1/3: 6 (April/May '40)]
1940, Oct. 27, p. 93	Horwill, Herbert W. H.	News and Views of London
1941, Aug. 17, p. BR10	--	Books and Authors [mentions the Shakespeare Fellowship]
1943, Feb. 7, p. BR17	Corbin, John	A New Candidate for Shakespeare's Honors [review of *Will Shakspere and the Dyer's Hand* by Alden Brooks]
1944, Feb. 21, p. 15	--	John T. Looney: Shakespearean Scholar Held that Edward de Vere Wrote the Plays [obituary]
1945, Feb. 20, p. 19	--	Dr. Gerald H. Rendall [obituary]
1947, April 3, p. 25	--	Mrs. E. H. Clark, Author, Succumbs: Leading Proponent of De Vere as Writer of Shakespearean Works Dies on Coast
1947, Nov. 30, p. X1	Atkinson, Brooks	Maurice Schwartz and a Good Company Offer a Reformed Shylock [review of *Shylock and His Daughter*] [repr. with note by editor and letter to Drama Editor of the NYT and followed by letter from Charles W. Barrell in SFQ, vol. VIII/3: 44-45; also repr. in TC, vol. 4: 35-37]
1948, Sept. 6	Schumach, Murray	Speech Knocking Mr. Shakespeare Almost Reconciles Puzzle Groups
1949, Sept. 23, p. 21	--	Books Published Today: SI, 2nd ed., is on the list]
1949, Oct. 23, p. BR23	--	[advertisement for second edition of *"Shakespeare" Identified*]
1952, March 20, p. 29	--	James S. Cushman, Realty Man, Dead
1952, Nov. 18, p. 29	--	[notice and brief advance review of *This Star of England* by Dorothy and Charlton Ogburn]
1952, Nov. 25, p. 27	--	Books Published Today [Ogburn's *This Star of England*]
1953, Feb. 8, p. BR7, 32	Campbell, Oscar James	To Be or Not To Be [review of *This Star of England* by Dorothy and Charlton Ogburn (1952)]
1953, Feb. 10, p. 25	--	Books—Authors [notice about *This Star of England*]
1953, March 1, p. BR23	--	Oxford and Shakespeare [letter from the editor introducing letters from readers; letters from readers not available]
1953, March 1, p. BR23	Ogburn, Charlton, Jr.	[letter: response to Oscar Campbell's Feb. 8 review]
1953, March 22, p. X3	--	Bard at Bar [William Shakespeare to be tried before a jury at Fairleigh Dickinson College: "Did William Shaksper of Stratford really write the plays of Shakespeare? Charlton Ogburn will argue 'no.']
1954, Nov. 21, p. BR36	Dunn, Esther	A Stand-in For the Bard [review of *The Dark Lady* by Cothburn O'Neal]
1955, Feb. 6, p. X1	Atkinson, Brooks	Who Wrote Shaw's Plays? [Charlton Ogburn's Oct. 23 letter]
1955, April 17, p. X2	Nelson, Virginia A.	No New Thing [letter]
1955, June 12, p. BR1	Harbage, Alfred	Sweet Will and Gentle Marlowe [review of *The Murder of the Man Who Was "Shakespeare"* by Calvin Hoffman]
1955, July 10, p. BR12	Mez, John R.	The 'Real' Shakespeare [letter: corrects Alfred Harbage on title of Looney's book]
1955, July 10, p. BR13	Ogburn, Dorothy and Charlton	[letter: "The most spectacular literary hoax of all time."]
1956, Jan. 29, p. BR12	Clifford, James	Speaking of Books: Biographies
1956, Feb. 19, p. BR17	Ogburn, Dorothy & Charlton Ogburn	Shakespeare [letter:James Clifford's Jan. 29 article on writing biographies]
1956, Sept. 9, p. X1	Atkinson, Brooks	Quit Proselytizing: Pleas for Moratorium on Question of Who Wrote Shakespeare's Plays

1958, Oct. 19	Harbage, Alfred	Author, Author! [review of *The Poacher From Stratford. A Partial Account of the Controversy Over the Authorship of Shakespeare's Plays* by Frank W. Wadsworth]
1959, March 15, p. BR4	McManaway, James G.	Who Did It If Not Will? [review of *Shakespeare and His Betters: A History and a Criticism of the Attempts Which Have Been Made to Prove That Shakespeare's Works Were Written by Others* by R. C. Churchill]
1959, Oct. 18, p. BR22	Tharp, Louise Hall	Delia and Sweet Will [review of *Prodigal Puritan: A Life of Delia Bacon* by Vivian C. Hopkins]
1960, Nov. 20, p. BR62	McManaway, James G.	With No Applause for Master Will [review of *Shakespeare's Progress* by Frank O'Connor]
1962, Feb. 24, p. 27	--	Charlton Ogburn is Dead at 79
1962, April 22, p. 12	Guthrie, Tyronne	Threat of Newness to Olde Stratford [*NY Times Magazine*]
1962, Aug. 3, p. 21	--	The Shakespeare Controversy [editorial]
1962, Sept. 2, p. 149	Furnas, J. C.	Speaking of Books [the Ogburns and the authorship of Shakespeare's works]
1962, Sept. 2, p. 149	de Vere, Edward	Poets' Column [two poems by Edward de Vere: "Revenge of Wrong" and "Woman's Changeableness"]
1962, Sept. 13, p. 34	Feron, James	Skeptics of Shakespeare Want to Search Tomb for Writings
1962, Sept. 21, p. 28	Editorial	The Dust Enclosed Here [efforts to open Shakespeare's Tomb] [see responses by Louis Marder, *Shakespeare Newsletter*, vol. 11/4: 28-29 (Sept. 1962) and vol. 11/5: 28-29 (Nov. 1962); other responses in *The Times* (London), Aug. 30-Sept. 15, 1962.
1963, July 12, p. 22	Atkinson, Brooks	Critic at Large: A Shakespearean Replies to a Baconian and Gets Some Unsolicited Support [repr. with different titles in *Atlanta Constitution* (July 15, 1963) and *Chicago Tribune* (Aug. 18, 1963)]
1965, Feb. 16, p. 56	--	Obituary: Francis T. Carmody (1909-1965) [SOS Trustee]
1966, May 11, p. 43	--	Notice about the Association of the Bar of the City of New York's "Stratfordians v. Oxfordians" event that night]
1969, Oct. 3	--	Mrs. Frank J. Sprague is Dead [obituary]
1971, Aug. 29, p. 55.	Reinhold, Robert	Shakespeare's World: A Stage for Study? [World Shakespeare Congress] [repr. in SON, vol. 8/1: 4 (Jan. 1972)]
1971, Nov. 29, p. 57	Barnes, Clive	Earl Who Wrote Shakespeare [review of *Masquerade*, Gertrude Gale's play about Prince Tudor/Dynastic Succession idea]
1984, Dec. 9, p. BR13	Giroux, Robert	Sweet Swan of Oxford? [review of *The Mysterious William Shakespeare* by Charlton Ogburn] [response by Morse Johnson, SON, vol. 27/3: 3-4]
1985, Jan. 13, p. BR29	Cyr, Gordon C.	Mysterious Shakespeare [letter: Giroux's Dec. 9 review of TMWS]
1985. Feb. 3, p. BR35	Giroux, Robert	The Man From Stratford? [letter: reply to Cyr]
1985, Feb. 9, p. 9	Mitgang, Herbert	'Sblood!' Still Feuding Over the Bard
1985, May 5, p. BR19	--	[large ad for *The Mysterious William Shakespeare*]
1985, June 9, p. BR38	Todd, Alden	Who Wrote *Hamlet*? [letter: Robert Giroux's Dec. 9 review: "not once does he address the real issues"]
1985, June 9, p. BR38	Campbell, Robert M.	[letter: Giroux's 9 Dec. review] ["Ogburn cannot be ignored"]
1985, June 9, p. BR38	Giroux, Robert	[letter: reply to Robert Campbell]
1985, Nov. 9	Johnson, Morse	Prejudice and Shakespeare [letter: Robert Giroux's June 9 letter] [repr. in SON, vol. 27/1: 5-6 (Winter 1991)]
1986, Jan. 9, p. A22	Johnson, Morse	Filling in the Gaps in Shakespeare's Life [letter: "Scholars are inventing biographical facts."]
1986, Jan. 19, p. E22	Lasar, Theodore	[letter: Morse Johnson's Jan. 9 letter]
1986, Jan. 25, p. A26	Cureton, Kevin K.	[letter: Morse Johnson's Jan. 9 letter]
1986, Feb. 8, p. A26	Ogburn, Charlton	Stratford's Undistinguished Will. Shakspere [letter: Kevin Cureton's Jan. 25 letter]
1987, Sept. 10, p. B8	--	In Re Shakespeare [three Members of Supreme Court to Adjudicate Debate on Shakespeare]

1987, Sept. 18, p. 12Y	--	In Re Shakespeare
1987, Sept. 26, p. 1, 13	Molotsky, Irvin	You-Know-Who Wrote the Plays, Judges Say
1988, April 26, p. C13	Hampton, Wilborn	Shakespeare and Freud: The Bard is Analyzed on the Academic Couch [repr. in SON, vol. 24/2: 8 (Spr. 1988)]
1988, April 28	Boyle, Charles	[letter: Wilborn Hampton's April 26 article] [repr. in SON, vol. 24/2: 8-9 (Spr. 1988)]
1988, Nov. 28, p. 13	Trucco, Terry	Bard on Trial, Again, And Again He Wins [repr. in SON, vol. 24/4: 10-11 (Summer 1988)]
1989, April 18, p. C21	Goodman, Walter	The Shakespeare Mystery: Who Was He? [review of *Frontline* program] [repr. in SON, vol. 25/2: 3-4 (Spring 1989); and in BTC, vol. 6: 383-84]
1989, May 11, p. 26	Rickey, George	Shakespeare Wrote Shakespeare. Believe It. [review of *Frontline*'s "The Shakespeare Mystery"]
1989, June 3, p. 14	Brody, Burton H.	Earl of Oxford Preferred [letter: G. Rickey's May 11 article]
1989, July 9	Johnson, Morse	Rose Theatre: Something Missing [letter][repr. in SON, vol. 25/3: 13-14 (Summer 1989); and in BTC, vol. 6: 408-09]
1989, Aug. 6, p. H3, 17	Rosenberg, James	Flat Earthers [letter] [repr. in SON, vol. 25/3: 14 (Summer 1989)]
1990, March 23, p. C33	Kakutani, Michiko	Of Freud and His Obsession With the Enigmatic [review of *Reading Freud: Exploration and Entertainment* by Peter Gay] [repr. in *Sun Sentinal*, 1 April, p. 13F]
1992, March 30	--	Obituary of Dr. Peter Sammartino [excerpts repr. in SON, vol. 28/2: 4 (Spring 1992)]
1994, March 5	Grimes, William	Obituary of Erva Stone (1918-1994) [repr. in SON, vol. 30/1: 18 (Winter 1994)]
1994, Nov. 25	Garber, Marjorie	The Bard Meets the Undead [excerpts in SON, vol. 30/4 (Autumn 1994)]
1995, Feb. 4, p. 25	--	Preston Fleet, 60, Creator of Fotomat and Omnimax, Dies [exc. repr. in SON, vol. 31/1a: 7 (Wnt. 1995)]
1998, Oct. 22, p. D6	--	Charlton Ogburn Dies at 87; State Department Official, Writer
1998, Oct. 25, p. 53	--	Charlton Ogburn, 87, Proponent of Earl as the 'Real' Shakespeare
2002, Feb. 10, A&L: 10	Mermelstein, David	Splitting the Credit Between a Bad Bard and a Gentle Will
2002, Feb. 10, A&L: A7	--	Was Marlowe Shakespeare? Much Ado, Indeed
2002, Feb. 10, A&L: A7	Niederkorn, William S.	A Historic Whodunit: If Shakesepeare Didn't, Who Did?
2002, Feb. 24, A&L: E6	Dams, Christopher H.	Avoiding Disgrace [letter: response to Niederkorn]
2002, Feb. 24, A&L: E6	Stritmatter, Roger	American Grain [letter: response to Niederkorn]
2002, Feb. 24, A&L: E6	Barnett, Lori	Sins of Omission [letter: response to Niederkorn]
2002, Feb. 24, A&L: E6	Kathman, David and Terry Ross	No Standards [letter: response to Niederkorn]
2002, Feb. 24, A&L: E6	O'Morrison, Kevin	Any Actor Knows [letter: response to Niederkorn]
2002, Feb. 24, A&L: E6	Low, Richard H.	Read the Poetry [letter: response to Niederkorn
2002, Feb. 24, A&L: E6	Shore, Wayne	The Door's Open [letter: response to Niederkorn]
2002, Feb. 24, A&L: E6	Price, Diana	Lack of Evidence [letter: response to Niederkorn]
2002, Feb. 24, A&L: E6	Norman, Colin	A Megaconspiracy [letter: response to Niederkorn]
2002, Feb. 24, A&L: E6	Day, Stephen M. D.	Shakespeare by Committee [letter: resp. to Niederkorn]
2002, Feb. 24, A&L: E6	Farley, Peter	With Enough Time [letter: response to Niederkorn]
2002, June 20	Niederkorn, William S.	A Scholar Recants His 'Shakespeare' Discovery
2002, June 22	Greenblatt, Stephen	Who Was the Bard? Don't Ask a Computer [letter: *Funeral Elegy*] [repr. in DVN (July 2002), p. 6]
2002, June 26	Niederkorn, William S.	Beyond the Briefly Inflated Canon: Legacy of the Mysterious 'W.S.'
2002, July 16	Jaroff, Leon	By Yonder Blessed Moon, Sleuths Decode Life/Art
2003, July 20, p. A22	Turrentine, Jeff	Repossession [review of *Chasing Shakespeares* by Sarah Smith]
2003, Aug. 19, p. E1	Niederkorn, William S.	All Is True? Naye, Not If Thy Name Be Shakespeare
2003, Sept. 2	Niederkorn, William S.	Seeing the Fingerprints of Other Hands in Shakespeare
2003, Nov. 16, A&L: 5	Niederkorn, William S.	Where There's a Will, or Two, or Maybe Quite a Few [interview with Amy Freed and review of her play *The Beard of Avon*]
2003, Nov. 19, p. E5	Weber, Bruce	Cutting Shakespeare Down to Size [review of *The Beard of Avon* by Amy Freed]
2003, Nov. 28, p. 5	--	Off Broadway [review of *The Beard of Avon* by Amy Freed]

New York Times (continued)

2004, Aug. 21, p. D3	Niederkorn, William S.	To Be or Not to Be . . . Shakespeare
2005, Aug. 30, p. 32	Niederkorn, William S.	The Shakespeare Code, and Other Fanciful Ideas From the Traditional Camp [reviews of *1599* by James Shapiro (2005); and *"Shakespeare" By Another Name* by Mark Anderson (2005)] [repr. in German in NSJ, vol. 11: 18-22 (April 2007)]
2005, Sept. 5, p. C9	Greenblatt, Stephen	Shakespeare Doubters [letter: response to Niederkorn's Aug. 30 article by comparing authorship doubters with Holocaust deniers] [repr. in German in NSJ, vol. 11: 23 (April 2007)]
2005, Oct. 29, p. B7	McGrath, Charles	Looking at Shakespeare, in 3 Different Ways
2005, Dec. 25, p. 6	Hershenson, Roberta	Brush Up Your De Vere? [Matthew Cossolotto and the Shakespeare Oxford Society]
2007, April 7, p. C7	Grode, Eric	The Case for Shakespeare: Words, Words, Words
2007, April 22, p. A4	Niederkorn, William S.	Shakespeare Reaffirmed [English Departments polled] [titled "Did He or Didn't He? That is the Question" in the online edition]
2007, Sept. 10, p. E2	Van Gelder, Lawrence	Alas, Poor Shakespeare
2009, May 20	Niederkorn, William S.	The Sonnets at 400 [in Paper Cuts, blog of the *NY Times Book Review*]
2010, May 2, p. BR10	McCarter, Jeremy	The Question of Authorship [reviews of *Contested Will* by James Shapiro and *Shakespeare's Lost Kingdom* by Charles Beauclerk
2010, Oct. 2, p. A17	Grimes, William	Joseph Sobran, 64, Writer Whom Buckley Mentored
2011, Oct. 17, p. A23	Shapiro, James	Hollywood Dishonors the Bard [review of *Anonymous*] Response by Mark Anderson, Oct. 27, p. A24. Response by Roland Emmerich, Oct. 27, p. A24. Response by Daniel M. Blank, Oct. 27, p. A24. Response by Andree A. Brooks, Oct. 27, p. A24. Response by Julia Newton, Oct. 27, p. A24.
2011, Oct. 23, p. 60-61	Marche, Stephen	Wouldn't It Be Cool if Shakespeare Wasn't Shakespeare? [review of *Anonymous*, directed by Roland Emmerich] [*New York Times Magazine*]
2011, Oct. 23, p. Arts 14, 16	Karpel, Ari	Brush Up Your Shakespeare, Or Whomever [review of *Anonymous* (2011)
2011, Oct. 26, p. C3	Itzkoff, Dave	Covering Up Shakespeare's Name to Protest a Film [*Anonymous*]
2011, Oct. 27, p. A24	Anderson, Mark K.	Whose Plays? That is the Question [letter: James Shapiro's Oct. 17 review]
2011, Oct. 27, p. A24	Emmerich, Roland	Whose Plays? That is the Question [letter: James Shapiro's Oct. 17 review]
2011, Oct. 28, p. Arts 1, 17	Scott, A. O.	How Could a Commoner Write Such Great Plays? [review of *Anonymous*]
2011, Oct. 29, p. Arts 1, 6	Brantley, Ben	Author? Who Cares? The Play's the Thing [review of *Anonymous*]
2012, Feb.	Stritmatter, Roger	[letter: response to William Niederkorn]
2013, Jan. 27, p. BR5	Nicholl, Charles	Exiting the Stage: In Ros Barber's Verse-Novel, Marlowe Fakes His Own Death In Order to Keep Writing
2014, April 6, p. BR10	Stevens, John Paul	By the Book: An Interview with John Paul Stevens

New York World-Telegram

1945, July 31	Rascoe, Burton	The Battle Still Rages Over Who Was Shakespeare[repr. in SFQ, vol. VI/4: 57-59 (Oct. 1945)]

New Yorker

1945	--	[review of the first American edition of J. Thomas Looney's *"Shakespeare" Identified* (1920)]
1950, April 8, p. 113-14, 117-19	Basso, Hamilton	The Big Who-Done-It [review of SI, new edition]
1959, April 4, p. 29-31	McCabe, John	The Talk of the Town: Carmody's Torch [The Ereved Foundation]
1959, June 20, p. 23-24	McCabe, John	The Talk of the Town: Straightforward Stratfordian [se comment by C. Ogburn, SON, v. 2/1: 2, 30 (Mar. 1966)]
1988, Apr. 11, p. 87-94, 96-106	Lardner, James	Onward and Upward with the Arts: The Authorship Question [highlights the 1987 Moot Court Trial] [repr. in SON, vol. 24/2: 10 (Spring 1988)]

1993, July 12	Sheed, Wilfrid	[review of *Shylock* by John Gross] [asks whether a lord might have written Shakespeare's works]
1995	Editor	Martin Luther at Elsinore? [see "*New Yorker* Airs a Bizarre Dispute Over Hamlet" in SON, vol. 31/4: 3 (Autumn 1995)]
2011, Oct. 31, p. 106	Denby, David	All That Glitters [review of *Anonymous*]
2011, Nov., vol. 87/37: 65	Idle, Eric	Who Wrote Shakespeare?
2019, Aug. 5-12	Foggatt, Tyler	Justice Stevens's Dissenting Shakespeare Theory
2019, Aug. 6	Shapiro, James	An Unexpected Letter from John Paul Stevens, Shakespeare Skeptic
2019, Aug. 19	Paster, Gail Kern	By Any Other Name [letter]
2022, Oct. 31, p. 28	Kenseth, Lars	Cartoon [referencing Edward de Vere] [see SON, Vol. 58/4 (Fall 2022): 7]

Newcastle Daily Chronicle

1920, March 5, p. 6	--	The Passing Hour [mentions Looney and Edward de Vere]

Newcastle Journal

1995, Feb. 21, p. 9	Whetstone, David	Was It Just a Looney Idea?

Newhouse News Service

1999, March 26, p. 1	Hernandez, Romel	Shakespeare in Doubt: Skeptics Label Bard a Fraud
1999, April 12, p. 1	Sarasohn, David	The Sequel; Shakespeare in Doubt

Newport Daily Express (Vermont)

1945, Oct. 31	--	[etensive coverage of Benezet's talk at Stanstead College, Quebec]

News and Observer (Raleigh, North Carolina)

1931, March 29, p. 2	--	Was Shakespeare Earl of Oxford? [review of *Hidden Illusions* by Eva Turner Clark]
1933, March 19, p. 5	Mudge, G. O.	New Questioning of Shakespeare [review of *Love's Labour's Lost* by Eva Turner Clark]
1997, Oct. 1	Dickson, Peter W.	Unmasking Shakespeare
1999, Feb. 8, p. A11	Kilpatrick, James	Shakespeare: A Hard Bard to Track Down
2010, July 11	Hunt, Marvin	A Readable Look Into the Debate Over Who Penned Shakespeare [review of *Contested Will* by James Shapiro]
2011, Nov. 3	--	Will Found His Ways

News Leader (Richmond, VA)

1931	--	[excerpt quoted in ad for Clark's *Hidden Allusions* in the Dec. 1931 issue of *Shakespeare Pictorial*]

News-Chronicle

1939, Jan. 14, p. 7	Lynd, Robert	Robert Lynd's Saturday Essay [has image of Edward de Vere labelled "Shakespeare"]
1939, Jan. 18	Kellett, E. E.	Shakespeare [letter]

Newsday, Long Island

1987, Sept. 26, p. 2	--	Forsooth, A High Court Truth; Moot Court at American University Law School]
1988, Nov. 27, p. 13	--	To Be or Not to Be the Bard: Judges Say Shakespeare
1988, Nov. 30, p. 71	Collins, Thomas	One More Time, Who Wrote Shakespeare
1990, April 8, p. 24	McGrath, William J.	Freudian Pursuit
2003, Nov. 25, p. B8	Winer, Linda	A Satire that Fires at Will [review of *The Beard of Avon* by Amy Freed]

Newsweek

1939, Dec. 14, vol. 14/26: 33	--	Was Shakespeare Oxford? Old Row Brought Up to Date by X-Rays of Portraits
1957, Oct. 7, vol. 50/15: 106-07	--	Did the Bard Write It? [review of *The Shakespearean Ciphers Examined* by William F. and Elizabeth S. Friedman]
1959, April, vol. 53/17: 112	--	The Other "Shakespeares"
1971, May 10	--	[article refers to "lunacy" of authorship doubters] [see also Richard Horne, Jr. in SON, vol. 7/2, p. 1-3 (June 1, 1971)]
1999, April 21	Reno, Jamie	Shakespeare in Doubt
2004, June 28, p. 58	Underwood, Anne	Was the Bard a Woman? [review of *Sweet Swan of Avon* by Robin Williams]

Newsweek (continued)

2011, Oct. 17	Lee, Chris	Was Shakespeare a Fraud? [review of *Anonymous*]
2011, Oct. 24, vol. 158/17: 24	Schama, Simon	The Shakespeare Shakedown [review of *Anonymous*]
2014, Dec. 26 (online blog)	Gore-Langton, Robert	The Campaign to Prove Shakespeare Didn't Exist

Nieuwe Rotterdamsche Courant

1938, end of May	--	[article addresses issue of de Vere's authorship, quotes Looney, Rendall, Ward, Allen]

Nineteenth Century and After

1913	Smithson, Edward W.	Ben Jonson's Pious Fraud
1917, April, vol. 81: 883-94	Crosse, Gordon	The Real Shakespeare Problem
1917, June, vol. 81: 1340-54	Greenwood, George G.	The Real Shakespeare: A Reply to Mr. Gordon Crosse
1917, Dec., p. 1248-53	Simpson, H. B.	Shakespeare, Bacon and a 'Tertium Quid'

North Peoria Journal-Star

1939, Dec.	--	Painting Proves Bard Switched

Northampton Mercury

1921, April 15, p. 8	W. W. H.	Who Wrote the Plays Which We Call Shakespeare's?

Northern Whig and Belfast Post (Antrim, N. Ireland)

1923, March 3, p. 10	--	Shakespeare and the Soviet
1928, Jan. 21, p. 9	--	[review of *The Shakespeare Mystery* by Georges Connes]
1931, Feb. 7, p. 11	--	Anti-Shakespeare [review of *Shakespeare's Plays in the Order of Their Writing* by Eva Turner Clark]
1935, June 1, 1935	--	The Shakespeare Plays
1938, Jan. 6, p. 8	Baker, H. Kendra	Bacon-Shakespeare Theory [letter]
1938, Jan. 8, p. 9	Holt, Felix	Bacon-Shakespeare Theory [letter]
1938, Jan. 13, p. 3	Hogg, J. A.	The Bard of Stratford [letter]
1938, Jan. 13, p. 3	W.R.R.	Bacon-Shakespeare Theory [letter: "Don't ignore the great scholars Greenwood, Looney, Ward, Allen, Slater, Douglas"]
1938, Jan. 17, p. 3	Baker, H. Kendra	Bacon-Shakespeare Theory [letter]
1938, Jan. 18, p. 3	Hogg, J. A.	Bacon-Shakespeare Theory [letter]
1938, Jan. 19, p. 11	Holt, Felix	Bacon-Shakespeare Theory [letter]
1938, Jan. 21, p. 14	Theobald, Bertram G.	Bacon-Shakespeare Theory [letter]
1938, Jan. 24, p. 3	Hogg, J. A.	Bacon-Shakespeare Theory [letter]
1938, Jan. 25, p. 3	Baker, H. Kendra	Bacon-Shakespeare Theory [letter]
1938, Jan. 25, p. 3	Holt, Felix	Challenge to Baconians [letter]
1938, Jan. 27, p. 9	W.R.R.	A Group of Authors [letter]
1938, Jan. 27, p. 9	Hogg, J. A.	Bacon-Shakespeare Theory [letter]
1938, Jan. 29, p. 11	Holt, Felix	Bacon-Shakespeare Theory [letter]
1938, May 12, p. 11	Holt, Felix	Shakespeare's Plays [letter]

Northwestern University Law Review

2012, vol. 106/2: 845-49	Watts, Kathryn A.	Justice Stevens's Black Leather Arm Chair

Notes and Queries

1864, March 19, Series 3/5: 232	Swifte, Edmund L.	On Sh.'s Profession [repr. in SON, vol. 39/2: 22 (Spring 2003)]
1902, Feb. 8, Series 9/9: 101-03	Curry, John T.	Edward de Vere and Thomas Watson
1907, May 25, Series 10/7: 409	Pemberton, H., Jr.	Query: Edward de Vere, 17th Earl of Oxford
1907, Oct. 12, Series 10: 297-98	Hill, Newsl. W.	Edward de Vere [response to Pemberton's Query]
1909, Oct. 2, Series 10/11: 266	White, G. H.	Query: Edward de Vere, 17th Earl of Oxford
1920, May 8, vol. 138/208: 190	Looney, J. Thomas	Query: Edward de Vere's Mother
1920, May 8, vol. 138/208: 190	Looney, J. Thomas	Query: Henry de Vere's Sponsors
1920, June 19	--	[Times Book Club advertisement: SI is third on list]
1920, July 31, p. 365	--	Author's Index [looney is on the list]
1928, Mar. 24, vol. 154: 215-16	--	[review of *Borrowers* by Percy Allen]
1931, March 7, vol. 160/10: 180	--	[review of *Corroborated* by Percy Allen (1931)]
1931, March 28, vol. 160/13: 230-31	Allen, Percy	[letter: response to the March 7 review of *Corroborated*] Response by Percy Allen, same issue, same page.
1931, April 18 vol. 160/16: 283	Bensley, Edward	The Oxford-Shakespeare Case Corroborated [letter: Percy Allen's March 28 letter]
1939, Nov. 18, vol. 177/21: 368	--	Edward de Vere, Earl of Oxford, Author of Shakespeare's Plays

1949, Aug. 20	Atkinson, A. D.	Additional Florio-Shakespeare Resemblances
1957, July, vol. 4/7: 280-83	Clark, Roy B.	The Earl of Oxford and the Queen's English
1963, Sept., vol. 10/9: 352-54	Maxwell, J. C.	[review of *The Shakespeare Claimants* by Harry N. Gibson]
1978, Oct., vol. 25: 427-31	Peck, D. C.	Raleigh, Sidney, Oxford, and the Catholics, 1579
1991, Dec., vol. 38/4: 501	Elliott, Ward E. & Robert J. Valenzia	Was the Earl of Oxford the True Shakespeare? A Computer-Aided Analysis
1994, Dec. vol. 41/4: 446-50	Smith, Rosalind	The Sonnets of the Countess of Oxford and Elizabeth I: Translations from Desportes" [not by Anne Cecil]
1994, Dec. vol. 41/4: 463-67	Moore, Peter R.	Did Raleigh Try to Kill Essex? [repr. in NSJ, vol. NS4: 109-17 (Oct. 2014)]
1994, Dec., vol. 41-4: 488-89	Moore, Peter R.	Ophelia's False Steward [repr. in LS, p. 44-45]
1995, Sept., vol. 42/3: 347-52	Moore, Peter R.	The Date of F. B.'s Verse Letter to Ben Jonson
1996, June, vol. 43/2: 162-63	Moore, Peter R.	Shakespeare's Iago & Santiago Matamoros [repr. in LS, p. 147-8]
1997, Dec., vol. 44/4: 498	Moore, Peter R.	Hamlet and the Two Witness rule [repr. in LS, p. 33-43]
1997, Dec., vol. 44/4: 514-16	Stritmatter, Roger	The Influence of a Genevan Note from Romans 7:19 on Shakespeare's Sonnet 151
1999, June, vol. 46/2: 207-09	Stritmatter, Roger	A New Biblical Source for Shakespeare's Concept of "All Seeing Heaven"
1999, June, vol. 46/2: 226-28	Stritmatter, Roger	The Heavenly Treasure of Sonnets 48 and 52
1999, June, vol. 46/2: 228	Rollett, John M.	'Repel these rebel powers': Shakespeare's Sonnet 146 emended
2000, March, vol. 47/1: 70-72	Stritmatter, Roger	'Old' and 'New' Law in *The Merchant of Venice*: A Note on Source of Shylock's Mortality in Deuteronomy 15
2000, March, vol. 47/1: 97-100	Stritmatter, Roger	By Providence Divine: Shakespeare's Awareness of Some Geneva Marginal Notes of "I Samuel"
2001, Sept., vol. 48/3: 275	Rollett, John M.	The Compositor's Reader: Shakespeare's Sonnet 146 Revisited
2001, Sept., vol. 48/3: 280-82	Stritmatter, Roger	The Biblical Source of Harry of Cornwall's Theological Doctrine
2003, Dec., vol. 248/4: 386-90	Moore, Peter R.	The Earl of Surry's Quarrel with George Blage
2009, April 5, vol. 56/1: 67-70	Stritmatter, Roger	Shakespeare's Ecclesiasticus 28.2-5: A Biblical Source for Ariel's Doctrine of Mercy
2009, Sept., vol. 51/3: 278-79	Moore, Peter R.	A Biblical Echo in *Romeo and Juliet* [repr.. in LS, p. 149-51]
2009, Dec., vol. 56: 359-64	Waugaman, Richard M.	Sternhold and Hopkins Whole Book of Psalms is a Major Source For the Works of Shakespeare
2010, Sept., vol. 57: 359-64	Waugaman, Richard M.	Echoes of the Whole Book of Psalms in 1 *Henry VI*, *Richard II* and *Edward III*
2012, Jan. 16, vol. 59/1: 48-52	Chatterley, Albert	The Tears of Fancie Or Love Disdained by T.W. (1593)
2013, March, vol. 60: 415-18	Stritmatter, Roger	Revelations 14:13 and *Hamlet* I.v.91-108: "Write, Blessed are the Dead!"
2013, Sept., vol. 60/3: 438-41	Rollett, John M.	Shakespeare's Sonnet 125: Who Bore the Canopy?
2015, Jan. 15, vol. 62/1: 48-51	Woodcock, Matthew	Thomas Churchyard and Music
2017, June, vol. 64/2: 265-66	Waugaman, Richard M.	A Possible Source for *Richard III's* Prophetic Nightmare in Guicciardini

Nottingham Evening Post (Nottinghamshire, England)

1920, April 12, p. 2	--	"Shakespeare" Identified: Plays Said to Have Been Work of Earl of Oxford [review of *SI*]

Nottingham Guardian

1931, Aug. 10	--	Lord Oxford "Shakespeare"

Nottingham Journal and Express (Nottinghamshire, England)

1920, March 19, p. 5	--	Merchant of Venice: Interesting "Half Hour Talk" at Carrington [presentation introducing Looney's ideas]
1920, April 22, p. 4	C.R.	Shakespeare: Was He Edward de Vere, Lord Oxford? [review of *"Shakespeare" Identified*]
1920, April 26, p. 4	--	Greatness and Gramaphones
1921, April 18, p. 4	Roberts, Cecil	A Star From Indianapolis
1927, Nov. 25, p. 3	--	Books and Bookmen [review of *The Shakespeare Mystery* by Georges Connes]
1930, Nov. 24, p. 4	--	[review of lecture by Percy Allen]

Novoe Literaturnoe Obozrenie

2010, vol. 105/5	Peshkov, Igor	Opechatka, ili Kliunch k imeni avtora

Oamaru Mail (New Zealand)

1920, May 12, vol. XLIV/14055	Quilland, Louis J.	The Mystery of William Shakespeare [review of SI]
1920, Oct. 19, vol. XLIV/14819	--	Shakespeare Identified Again. "Who's Looney Now?"

Observer, The (London)

1919, Aug. 10, p. 7.	--	Shakespeare Hits Back
1921, Jan. 9, p. 4	Squire, John C.	Shakespeare and the Skeleton
1921, Jan. 21, p. 4	Squire, John C.	Books of the Day [mentions *SI* in review essay]
1923, March 25, p. 4	Squire, John C.	The Oxford Movement [long review of *The Mystery of "Mr. W. H."* by Col. Bernard R. Ward]
1923, April 22, p. 12	Garvin, J. L.	Who Shakespeare Was: The Comedy of Doubt [see Looney's resp. in *Hackney Spectator*, May 11]
1923, April 29	Garvin, J. L.	Putting William in His Place, II
1928, May 6, p. 6	Squire, John. C.	Lord Oxford [review of *The Seventeenth Earl of Oxford 1550-1604 by* Capt. Bernard M. Ward (1928)]
1930, March 30, p. 7	--	[ad for Gerald Rendall's *Shakespeare's Sonnets and Edward de Vere* quotes *Morning Post* review]
1930, May 11, p. 7	Gwynn, Stephan	Sir Sidney Lee and Others [short reviews of *Shakespeare's Sonnets and Edward de Vere* by Gerald Rendall and *The Case for Edward de Vere as "Shakespeare"* by Percy Allen]
1930, Aug. 17, p. 9	Ervine, St. John	At the Play: Did Shakespeare Despise the Stage? I
1930, Aug. 24, p. 9	Ervine, St. John	At the Play: Did Shakespeare Despise the Stage? II
1931, April 12, p. 13	Gielgud, John	Leak on the Stage: Interview with Mr. John Gielgud
1931, April 19, p. 10	Allen, Percy	The Shakespeare Plays [letter]
1931, May 10, p. 10	Allen, Percy	Kent in *King Lear* [letter: Oxford was himself banished]
1931, May 19, p. 10	Allen, Percy	Three Shakespeare Plays [letter]
1933, July 9, p. 5	--	The Oxford Case [reviews of *A Reply to John Drinkwater* by Percy and Ernest Allen and *The Plays of Shakespeare and Chapman in Relation to French History* by Percy Allen]
1933, Dec. 3, p. 3	Boas, F. S.	Anthologies With a Purpose [review of *Shakespeare, Oxford and Elizabethan Times* by H. H. Holland]
1937, Sept. 12, p. 15	--	At Random
1937, Sept. 19, p. 9	W. G. S.	Shakespeare and the "Canopy" [letter]
1937, Sept. 19, p. 9	Fox. W. H.	The Earls of Oxford [letter: refers to an article last week, "Observation," that referred to the 17th Earl of Oxford]
1943, July 11, p. 2	Brown, Ivor	Theatre and Life
1944, April 30, p. 2	Brown, Ivor	Theatre and Life [review of *Shakespeare: New Views for Old* by R. W. Eagle]
1958, Aug. 24, p. 12	Reeves, James	The Anti-Shakespeare Industry [review of *Shakespeare and His Betters* by R. C. Churchill]
1962, June 24, p. 24	Brown, Ivor	Shakespeare's Rivals [review of *The Shakespeare Claimants* by H. N. Gibson]
1964, Feb. 2, p. 12	--	Anti-Shakespeare Movement Hots Up
1976, March 14, p. 4	Hawkes, Nigel	Word Detective Proves the Bard Wasn't Bacon
1977, Oct. 9, p. 26	Burgess, Anthony	Where There's a Will . . . [review of *Shakespeare by Hilliard* by Leslie Hotson]
1988, Nov. 27, p. 2	--	Bard Verdict
1994, Oct. 9, p. 15	Gerrard, Nicci	Shakespeare: Not Just William? Who Really Wrote*Hamlet*?
1996, April 28, p. 9	O'Sullivan, Charlotte	Did Aliens Write *Macbeth*? [review of *Who Wrote Shakespeare?* by John Michell]
1997, June 29, p. 15	McCrum, Robert	McCrum on Shakespeare
1997, Nov. 2, p. 15	McCrum, Robert	McCrum on the Genius of Shakespeare
2002, March 31, p. D16	McCrum, Robert	Where There's a Will, There's an Edward
2004, Oct. 24	Thorpe, Vanessa	Sufi or Not Sufi? That is the Question: Islam week at the Globe Theatre will link Shakespeare with a mystic Muslim sect [repr. in DVN (Oct. 2004), p. 22]
2007, Sept. 9, p. 24	Thorpe, Vanessa	Who Was He? That is (Still) the Question
2007, Sept. 9, p. 24	Clapp, Susannah	[review of *The Big Secret Live* by Mark Rylance and Matthew Warchus (2007)]
2010, March 14, p. 18	McCrum, Robert	Who Wrote Shakespeare? Was It Really That 'Illiterate Third-

		Rate Actor' From the Provinces?
2010, April 4, p. 46	Conrad, Peter	The Bard . . . Or Not the Bard? Shakespeare's Doubters Reveal More About Themselves Than the Poet [review of *Contested Will* by James Shapiro]
2011, Jan. 9, p. 41	Conrad, Peter	Contested Will [review of paperback edition of *Contested Will* by James Shapiro]
2011, Oct. 23, p. 37	McCrum, Robert	Shakespeare or Anonymous [review of *Anonymous*]
2011, Nov. 6, p. 42	McCrum, Robert	Where There's a Will . . . [review of *Anonymous*]
2012, Aug. 19	Alberge, Dalya	Suzman 'mad as a snake' With Rylance Over Bard 'Myths'
2013, March 31, p. 23	Alberge, Dalya	National Shakespearean Scholars United to See Off Claims of 'Bard Deniers' [review of *Shakespeare Beyond Doubt* edited by Paul Edmonton and Stanley Wells]
2015, Feb. 1, p. 13	Alberge, Dalya	Has the Mystery of Shakespeare's Sonnets Finally Been Solved?

Observer, The (Sarnia, Ontario)

2005, Oct. 20, p. B7	--	Yes, but Is It Shakespeare?

Oldie, The

2000, vol. 127	Johnson, Ian	[letter: canals from Verona to Milan]
2000, vol. 128	Milner-Gulland, Nick	[letter: Jonson's "Canals" letter] Repr. in DVN (Jan. 2000), p. 14. Reply by Ian Johnson, DVN (Jan. 2000), p. 14.

On the Issues (Long Island)

1997, Oct. 31, p. 22	Gage, Carolyn	Meeting the Ghost of Hamlet's Father

Open Forum

1951, July-Aug., vol. 1/1: 48-52	Allen, Percy	Shakespeare or Bacon—or Oxford? I. The Composite Shakespeare
1951, July-Aug., vol. 1/1: 52-56	Eagle, Roderick K.	Shakespeare or Bacon—or Oxford? II. Francis Bacon Wrote "Sh."

Open Shelf: A Popular Selection of Books Added to the Cleveland Public Library

1928, no. 6-10, Sept./Oct., p. 84	--	[SI, with description, is on the list]

Orange County Register

1988, Dec. 4, p. G10	Trucco, Terry	All's Well That Ends Well in Tempest Over Shakespeare
1989, Aug. 20, p. L22	Boyd, Bentley	A Rose Might Smell as Sweet by Any Other Name
1992, April 19, p. F20	O'Connor, Thomas	Shakespeare [reports on Charles Vere's talk]
1997, Dec. 7, p. G1	Seiler, John	The Riddle of the Bard Revisited [review of *Alias Shakespeare* by Joe Sobran (1997)]
1998, Dec. 4, p. 10	Trucco, Terry	All's Well That Ends Well in Tempest Over Shakespeare [coverage of mock trial]
2001, May 29, p. 1	Hodgins, Paul	Searching for Shakespeare [review of *The Beard of Avon* by Amy Freed]
2014, April 25	Mellen, Greg	Debate Continues About Whether the Bard Was "All That"

Oregonian, The (Portland)

1992, Aug. 2, p. L12	Larcen, Donna	The Three Categories of Mysteries
1997, Sept. 18, p. C1	Jaynes, Dwight	[Sometimes you think you know something . . .]
1999, March 21, p. A1	Hernandez, Romel	Shakespeare in Doubt; Portland Prof Backs Rival [Daniel Wright at 3rd Annual De Vere Studies Conference]
1999, March 30, p. B10	--	Oscar Goes to "De Vere in Love"
1999, April 9, p. B9	Sarasohn, David	Shakespeare in Doubt: Demands for a Share of the Will
1999, April 25, p. F1	Johnson, Barry	Talk About a Dead Poets Society
1999, Nov. 30, p. C1	Boule, Margie	Millennium Is Worth 1,000 Queries
2002, April 19, p. 3	Foyston, John	De Vere, Revered [The SARC Conference at Concordia University]
2002, April 26, p. 2	Foyston, John	Readers Talk, We Talk Back: Oxford vs. Stratford
2003, Jan. 2, p. E10	Mahar, Ted	Was It Shakespeare or Marlowe? [*Frontline's* "Much Ado About Something"]
2008, Jan. 21, p. C4	Hughley, Marty	The World's a Stage, No Matter Who Created Plays [Stratfordians vs. Oxfordians]

Orlando Sentinal

1987, Nov. 27, p. A22	--	Shakespeare Wins
1988, Oct. 28, p. A12	--	Shakespeare Trial: Was Edward de Vere the Real Author?
1988, Nov. 26, p. A8	--	What's in a Name? – Everything To Those in Shakespeare's 'Trial'
1989, Nov. 12, p. F1	Maupin, Elizabeth	The Mysteries of Shakespeare Legend is Clear, but Facts are Lost in History's Fog
1992, June 13, p. E3	Larcen, Donna	Everybody Loves a Mystery
1994, June 12, p. 22	Achenbach, Joel	Was the Bard of Avon Really the Earl of Oxford?
1999, April 25, p. F9	Wolf, Matt	Shakespeare Remains Elusive
2003, July 27, p. F10	Pate, Nancy	Shakespeare in Love and Mystery [review of *Chasing Shakespeares* by Sarah Smith]
2007, Oct. 2, p. E13	Doran, D'Arcy	Et Tu, Shakespeare?

Otago Daily Times (New Zealand)

1922, Dec. 16, issue 18738	--	Shakespeare and Shakspere: Echoes of an Ancient Controversy

Ottawa Citizen

1992, 16 June, p. D4	Larcen, Donna	Ah, Sweet Mystery of Life . . . Do UFO's Really Exist? Is Elvis Really Dead? Who Really Knows?
1993, Sept. 29, p. B8	Nicholls, Liz	Earl Pleads Ancestor's Literary Case [Charles Vere]
1999, Jan. 27, p. A10	Rosenthal, Daniel	Shakespeare Myths: A Comedy of Errors?
2009, Nov. 24, p. A9	Hall, Allan	Shakespeare a Sham, German Scholar Argues [review of *The Man Who Invented Shakespeare* by Kurt Kreiler]

Outlook, The: A Weekly Review of Politics, Art, Literature and Finance (British)

1921, Feb. 11, v. 47/1202: 119	--	[ad for *The National Review* shows Looney's article, "Shakespeare: Lord Oxford or Lord Derby"]
1921, March 12, v. 47/1206: 231	Eagle, Solomon [pseud. of John Collings Squire]	Mr. Looney and Lord Oxford
1921, June 25, v. 47/1221: 543-4	Looney, J. Thomas	Shakespeare, Lord Oxford, Solomon Eagle and Mr. Looney [letter: resp. to the March 12 review]
1921, July 2, vol. 48/1223: 15	Eagle, Solomon [pseud. of John Collings Squire]	The Critic at Large: A Voice from the Past [reply to Looney's June 25 response]
1921, July 16, v. 48/1225: 58-59	Looney, J. Thomas	Mr. Looney Replies [letter: resp. to Eagle's July 2 reply]
1922, March 4, v. 49/1257: 160	--	[ad for *The National Review's* March 1922 issue shows George Hookham's article, "Edward de Vere and Shakespeare's Plays"]
1922, March 18, vol. 49: 221	Eagle, Solomon	Shakespeare's Master [Chaucer]
1922, Sept. 30, v. 50/1287: 282	--	[ad for *The National Review's* October 1922 issue that shows Col. B. R. Ward's article, "Edward de Vere and William Shakespeare – A Dual Mystery"]

Outlook (American)

1920, Aug. 4, p. 615	--	The New Books [review of *"Shakespeare" Identified*]
1974, Nov. 24	Ogburn, Jr., Charlton	The Man Who Shakespeare Was Not (And Who He Was) [repr. from *Harvard Alumni Magazine*]
1974, Dec. 8	Hardison, O. B. Jr.	[letter: Ogburn's Nov. 24 article]

Oxenford Reader [compiled by Roger Stritmatter and Mark Anderson]

1995, vol. II, issue 1	--	[not indexed; this issue can be found in the Oxfordian archives at Brunel University]

Pall Mall Gazette (London)

1920, March 4, p. 6	--	Shakespeare [notice for *"Shakespeare" Identified*]

Palm Beach Post

1988, April 6	Brookman, Belinda	Group Persuades "Jurors" Bard Really Earl, Not Will [repr. in SON, vol. 24/2: 9 (Spring 1988)]

Partnership: The Canadian Journal of Library and Information Practice and Research

2013, July, vol. 8/2: 1	Dudley, Michael	"My Library Was Dukedom Large Enough": Academic Libraries Mediating the Shakespeare Authorship Question

Pasadena Star-News

2011, Oct. 28	Wilson, Larry	Will of Any Other Name as Sweet? [mentions two Oxfordians:

Barbara Crowley and S. Colum Gilfillan]

Past and Future
1960, June-July, vol. 2/3: 4-10 Amphlett, Hilda   Who Was Shakespeare? The Earl of Oxford
1963, Dec.-Jan. 1964, p. 20-21 Trevor-Roper, Hugh   The Real Character of Shakespeare [from *Realities*, Nov. 1962]

Patriot Ledger (Quincy, Mass.)
1995, May 1, p. 11   Lederer, Richard   Who Was the Real Shakespeare? [Burford and the SOS]
1995, Dec. 23, p. 33   Lederer, Richard   Much Ado Over Shakespeare
2006, July 18, p. 15   Fanger, Iris   Quick Wit, but Comedy Sheds Little Light on Shakespeare
                                                      [review of *The Beard of Avon*]

PenBroadsheet
1976, Summer, no. 2   Edwards, Father Francis   The Bard Again

Peoria Journal-Star
1940, Jan.   Painting Proves Bard Switched [Barrell and *Scientific Am.*]

Periodical, The
1930, vol. XV/157: 134-38   Mackail, J. W.   Sir E. K. Chambers's Shakespeare
1944, July, vol. 26/210: 124-25 --   *Coriolanus* and *The Tempest*

Perkins School for the Blind
2020 [online]   --   Helen Keller, Shakespeare Skeptic
                                                      [https://www.perkins.org/helen-keller-shakespeare-skeptic/]

Philadelphia Bulletin
1940, Feb. 3   --   [interview with Charles Barrell]

Philadelphia Daily News
1996, July 5   McKinney, Jack   Shakespeare Couldn't Spell, so Who Tamed the Shrew?
1998, Nov. 20   Woods, Michael   Bard's Genius Is Not Universally Accepted

Philadelphia Inquirer
1985, May 19, p. G5   O'Brien, Thomas W.   The Philosophizing Hamlet and His Creator
                                                      [review of *The Mysterious William Shakespeare*]
1987, Oct. 27   Batiuk, Tom   Funky Winkerbean Cartoon mentions authorship issue
1989, April 20, p. 21A   Hope, Warren   It Was the Bard of Oxford – Not Avon
                                                      [review of *Frontline* program] [repr. in SON, vol. 25/2: 5-6
                                                      (Spring 1989); and in BTC, vol. 6: 385-87]
1989, April 29, p. A6   Fistori, Art   Something Spring Eternal [letter]
1989, April 29, p. A6   Plank, James A.   These Doubts on Shakespeare Are, Well, Loony [letter]
1989, May 17, p. A10   Hope, Warren   Scorned Author is Heard From [letter: reply to letters]
1989, May 17, p. A10   Smith, Allen A.   Till Burnham Wood Doth March to Havertown? [letter]
1989, May 17, p. A10   Conner, Lester I.   Hardly Unmourned [letter]
1999, July 24, p. A10   Editor   Merchants of Venom [editorial]
1999, July 31, p. A16   Hope, Warren   [letter: the July 24 editorial]
1999, July 31, p. A16   Garcia, Emanuel E.   [letter: the July 24 editorial]
1999, July 31, p. A16   Nolan, Michael   [letter: the July 24 editorial]
1999, July 31, p. A16   Whitney, Star   [letter: the July 24 editorial]
2003, Jan. 2, p. D8   Ryan, Desmond   *Frontline* Takes Up the Debate Over Shakespeare's Work
2010, June 30   Timpane, John   *Contested Will* [Shapiro] Proves Shakespeare Wrote It All

Philadelphia Enquirer Public Ledger and Philadelphia Public Ledger
1931, April 25, p. 14   Williams, Sidney   The Earl of Oxford Also a Candidate for Shakespeare's Crown
                                                      [review of *Hidden Allusions in Shakespeare's Plays* by Eva
                                                      Turner Clark]
1941, Jan. 28, p. 101   --   Notice: Bard Lecture at the Shakespeare Club on Feb. 2

Philadelphia Welcomat
1989, May 10, p. 3, 28-32   Morris, Steve   Detective Story: Who Wrote Shakespeare?

Philological Quarterly
1929, Jan. 1, vol. 8, p. 223-24 Maxwell, Baldwin   [review of *The Seventeenth Earl of Oxford* by B. M. Ward]
1931, Jan. 1, vol. 10, p. 393-95 Tannenbaum, Samuel A. The Copy for Shakespeare's Plays

Physicsworld.com
1998, Oct. 23   Altschuler, Eric L.   Searching for Shakespeare in the Stars

[http://atxiv.org/abs/physics/9810042v1]

Pittsburgh Post-Gazette
| 1943, March 15, p. 13 | Kiernan, John | One Small Voice |
| 1949, Nov. 13, p. 18 | -- | Notice of publication of *"Shakespeare" Identified* |

Pittsburgh Press
| 1984/85 | O'Hara, Mary | [review of TMWS, quoted on dust jacket of 1992 edition] |

Plain Dealer (Cleveland)
1939, Dec. 21, 22, 23	--	So Edward de Vere Wrote Shakespeare? [3-part discussion]
1940, Jan.	Hoty, Herlow R.	[coverage of Barrell/*Scientific American* article]
1988, Apr. 17, p. 12H	Harayda, Janice	Court Rules in Bard's Favor
1989, April 18	Ferna, Tom	Shakespeare Dilemma Re-examined [review of *Frontline*]
1992, March 6	Finn, Robert	Bard Didn't Write It, Earl Says [Lord Burford]
1992, Oct. 15	--	Bard Doubters Plan Seminars [SOS 16th Conference]
1992, Oct. 16	--	Shakespeare Unbelievers to Visit Cleveland
1993, May 23, p. 11H	Harayda, Janice	The Most Influential People in History? [review of *The 100*, 2nd edition by Michael Hart]
2006, April 23, p. J4	O'Gorman, Rochelle	There's Much Ado About Life and Works of Shakespeare

Player Magazine
| 1962, May-Oct., vol. 39: 215+ | Lewis, George L. | [review of *Shake-speare: The Man Behind the Name* by Dorothy Ogburn and Charlton Ogburn, Jr. (1962)] |

Plymouth Evening News (Hampshire)
| 1951, Feb. 21, p. 3 | -- | Evidence for Edward de Vere |

PMLA: Publication of the Modern Language Association
1924, Sept., vol. 39/4: 581-611	Gray, Austin K.	The Secret of Love's Labour's Lost
1937, Sept., vol. 52/3: 652-74	Angell, Pauline K.	Light on the Dark Lady: A Study of some Elizabethan Libels
1940, June, vol. 55/2: 598-602	Baldwin, T. W. and	Light on the Dark Lady [An exchange of four letters Pauline K. Angell-Baldwin-Angell-Baldwin-Angell)]
1942, June, vol. 57/2: 354-69	Bennett, Josephine W.	Oxford and *Endimion*
1960, June, vol. 75/3: 163-73	Holland, Norman N.	Freud on Shakespeare [excerpts repr. in *Sh. and His Rivals* (McMichael & Glenn 1962): 193]

Poetry and the Play
| 1929/1930, Winter, p. 10-13 | Ward, Col. Bernard R. | Shakespeare's Sonnets: A Suggested Interpretation [repr. as a pamphlet] |

Poetry Review
1951, July/Aug., v. 42: 196-99	Corby, Herbert	The Shakespeare Mystery, Part 1
1951, Sept./Oct., v. 42: 255-59	Corby, Herbert	The Shakespeare Mystery, Part 2
1951, Nov./Dec., v. 42: 329-33	Corby, Herbert	The Shakespeare Mystery, Part 3

Post-Standard
| 2011, Nov. 3 | -- | [review of *Anonymous*] |

Post-Tribune (Gary, Ind.)
| 2003, April 18, p. D9 | Kostanczuk, Bob | Where There's a Will, There's a Sway |

Prensa, La (San Antonio)
| 1920, Sept. 5, p. 10 | -- | ¿Escribio, Shakespeare Dramas? [Translation of "'Shakespeare' Identified Again" [review of SI], *The Literary Digest*, Aug. 14, 1920, pp. 32-33] |

Princeton Alumni Weekly
| 1938, May 13 | -- | [coverage of James S. Cushman's lecture] |
| 2008, March 19 | Waugaman, Richard M. | The Pseudonymous Author of Shakespeare's Works |

https://www.princeton.edu/~paw/web_exclusives/plus/plus_031908wegeman.html

Proceedings of the British Academy
| 1951, vol. LXI | Eggar, Katharine E. | Shakespeare in His True Colours [repr. as a pamphlet] |

Proceedings of the Royal Musical Association
| 1920-21, vol. 47 | Eggar, Katharine E. | The Subconscious Mind and the Musical Faculty |
| 1934-35, vol. 61: 39-59 | Eggar, Katherine E. | The Seventeenth Earl of Oxford as Musician, Poet and Controller of the Queen's Revels [Jan. 17, 1935][repr. in LC, p. 3-11] |

1946-47, vol. 73	Eggar, Katharine E.	The Musical Condition of Man [Dec. 10, 1946] [repr. as a pamphlet]
1960-61, vol. 87: ????	Eggar, Katharine E.	The Blackfriars Plays and Their Music 1576-1610

Providence Journal

1989, April 23, p. B18	Terzian, Philip	Who Wrote Them and Who Cares [review of *Frontline*]
2003, July 6, p. B5	Coale, Sam	A Novel Search for the Real Shakespeare [review of *Chasing Shakespeares* by Sarah Smith]

Psyche: Zeitschrift für Psychoanalyse und ihre Anwendungen

1991, vol. 45: 649-74	Gay, Peter (translated by Elisabeth Vorspohl)	Freud, Shakespeare und Looney [Translated from "Freud and the Man from Stratford"]

Psychiatric News

2006, Oct. 6	Waugaman, Richard M.	Shakespeare's Mothers [letter]

Psychiatry

2003, Fall, vol. 66/3: 214-21	Waugaman, Richard M.	Unconscious Communication in Literature: Commentary on "Hamlet" as Process. A Novel Approach to Using Literature in Teaching Psychiatry
2007, vol. 70: 52-58	Waugaman, Richard M.	Unconscious Communication in Shakespeare: 'Et tu, Bruté?' echoes 'Eloi, Eloi, Lama Sabbachthani?'

Psychoanalysis

1953, vol. 2/1: 57-72	Feldman, A. Bronson	Shakespeare Worship [repr. in SON, vol. 18/2: 9-17 (Spring 1982); in BTC, vol. 6: 167-81; and in *Shakespeare, Marlowe, . . .* (2022): 16-33]

Psychoanalytic Inquiry

2023, vol. 43/5: 311-314	Waugaman, Richard M.	Psychoanalytic Perspectives on Fictional Characters
2023, vol. 43/5: 355-63	Waugaman, Elisabeth	*Love's Labour's Lost*: Lived Experience, A Pan-European Play
2023, vol. 43/5: 364-382	Waugaman, Richard M.	The Origins of Modern Literary Theory in the Repudiation of Autobiographical Readings of Shakespeare's Sonnets
2023, vol. 43/5: 383-84	Waugaman, Richard M.	Editor's Epilogue [for the issue titles "Psychoanalytic Perspectives on Fictional Characters"

Psychoanalytic Quarterly

2007, vol. 76: 1397-1403	Waugaman, Richard M.	[review of *"Shakespeare" By Another Name* by Mark Anderson]
2008, vol. 77: 1298-1305	Waugaman, Richard M	[review of *The Mind According to Shakespeare: Psychoanalysis in the Bard's Writing* by Marvin B. Krims (2006)]
2010, Oct., vol. 97/5: 857-79	Waugaman, Richard M.	The Bisexuality of Shakespeare's Sonnets and Implications for De Vere's Authorship
2011, vol. 80: 225-31	Waugaman, Richard M.	[review of *Contested Will: Who Wrote Shakespeare?* by James S. Shapiro (2010)]
2014, vol. 83: 737-42	Waugaman, Richard M.	[review of *The Unconscious in Shakespeare's Plays* by Martin S. Bergman (2013)]

Psychoanalytic Review

1966, vol. 53	Feldman, A. Bronson	Psychoanalysis and Shakespeare
2010, May, vol. 97/5: 835-56	Waugaman, Richard M.	Samuel Clemens and Mark Twain: Pseudonym as an Act of Reparation
2010, May, vol. 97/5: 857-79	Waugaman, Richard M.	The Bisexuality of *Shakespeare's Sonnets* and Implications for De Vere's Authorship

Publishers' Circular

1920, Feb. 18, p. 188	--	[Cecil Palmer 3/4 page ad for *"Shakespeare" Identified*]
1920, March 6, p. 236-37	--	"Shakespeare" Identified in Edward de Vere, the 17th Earl of Oxford [review]
1920, May 8, p. 488	--	Cecil Palmer advertisement [SI is listed first]
1920, Aug. 14, p. 160	--	Cecil Palmer advertisement

Publishers Weekly: The American Book Trade Journal

1920, April 17, p. 1236	--	[brief memtion of Looney and SI]
1920, May 8, p. 1437	--	[Stokes Books ad [SI with description is second on list of five]
1920, June 5, p. 1833	--	[list of new books has SI, with brief description]
1973, April 23, p. 70	--	[review of *Shakespeare the Man* by Alfred L. Rowse]

Publishers Weekly (continued)

Punch, or the London Charivari

Putnam's Monthly Magazine of American Literature, Science, and Art

Quarterly Review

Queen's Quarterly

Quillette

Quint, The: An Interdisciplinary Quarterly From the North

Rapid City Journal

Raritan: A Quarterly Review (Rutgers University)

Read (Stamford

Reader's Digest

Reading and Collecting

Real Property, Trust and Estate Law Journal

Réalitiés
 1962, Nov.   Trevor-Roper, Hugh   What's in a Name? The Real Character of Shakespeare [repr. in BC, vol. II: 1-8 (2010)

Record, The (Bergen County, NJ)
 2000, April 23, p. L1   Brewer, Caroline   Book Value Between Elegant Covers [profile of Oxfordian Leonard Hansen]

 2003, Nov. 23, p. E7   Glanville, Justin   Shakespeare In Another Light [review of *The Beard of Avon* by Amy Freed]

Record, The (Kitchener-Waterloo, Ontario)
 1999, Sept. 15, p. A11   Taube, Michael   Boarding the Bard; Debate Still Rages
 2013, Oct. 19, p. D5   Seto, Chris   To Thine Own Self Be True: Guelph professors troubled by debate over authorship of Shakespeare work

Redlands Daily Facts
 2005, Dec. 15   Sabel, Steven   On the Trail of the Real Shakespeare [profile of Oxfordian Elwood Miller]

Reedy's Mirror
 1920, June 10, vol. 29/24: 474-6 Reedy, William M.   Another Shakespeare [review of SI]
 1920, June 17, vol. 29/25: 493   Reedy, William M.   Reflections: The Shakespeare Myth
 1920, June 17, vol. 29/25: 498   Watterson, Henry &   The Shakespeare Myth [letter] [Watterson's and Reedy's June 17 exchange was repr. in *The Montgomery Advertiser* on June 27 and *The New York Times* on July 18]

 1920, July 8, vol. 29/28: 546   Watson, Jean   Woman's Advocate [letter]
 1920, July 29, vol. 29/31: 594-7 Hadley, Herbert S.   Shakespeare: Enter the Legal Element

Reference and Research Book News (Portland)
 2003, May, vol. 18/2   --   Shakespeare's Fingerprints [review of the book by Michael Brame and Galina Popova]

 2005, May, vol. 20/2   --   The Case for Shakespeare [rev. of Scott McCrea's book]
 2006, May, vol. 21/2   --   De Vere as Shakespeare: An Oxfordian Reading of the Canon [review of the book by William Farina]

 2013, Oct., vol. 28/5   --   On the Date, Sources and Design of Shakespeare's The Tempest [review of the book by Roger Stritmatter & Lynne Kositsky]

Renaissance Magazine
 2004, vol. 9/1: 54-59   Dixon, Jonathan   Determining the Identity of the Bard: William Shaksper or the Earl of Oxford?

Renaissance Papers
 1980, vol. 10: 11-18   May, Steven W.   Tudor Aristocrats and the Mythical 'Stigma of Print'

Renaissance Quarterly (Before 1967, was Renaissance News)
 2003, Summer, vol. 56/2:553   Lyons, Bridget G.   [review of *Shakespeare's Unorthodox Biography* by Diana Price]
 2004, Winter, vol. 57/4: 1529   Barnaby, Andrew   [review of *Monstrous Adversary: The Life of Edward de Vere* by Alan Nelson (2003)]

 2006, Summer, vol. 59/2: 612   Lindquist, Eric Newsl. [review of *Edward de Vere: The Crisis and Consequences of Wardship* by Daphne Pearson]

 2013   Waugaman, Richard M. [review of *Shakespeare and the Apocalypse: Visions of Doom From Early Modern Tragedy to Popular Culture* by R. M. Christofides (2013)]

 2015, vol. 68/2: 787-88   Waugaman, Richard M. [review of *What Shakespeare Teaches Us About Psychoanalysis* by Dorothy and Jerome Grunes]

 2016, vol. 69/4: 1598-66   Waugaman, Richard M. [review of *Anecdotal Shakespeare: A New Performance History* by Paul Menzer (2015)]

 2017, vol. 70/1: 420-22   Waugaman, Richard M. Shakespeare in Hate: Emotions, Passions, Selfhood
Renesansni Studii [Ukranian]
 2005, vol. 10: 8-22   Torkut, Nataliya   Antystretfordians'ki hipotezy: Pro et contra [Anti-Stratfordian Hypotheses: Pro and Con]

Rethinking History: The Journal of Theory and Practice
 2010, vol. 14/2: 165-87   Barber, Rosalind   Exploring Biographical Fictions: The Role of Imagination in Writing and Reading Narrative

Review, The

| 1920, May 1, vol. 2/51: 464 | -- | [Brief mention of Looney and Edward de Vere] |
| 1920, May 28, vol. 3/2: 551 | -- | [Stokes Books ad; SI with desc. is listed fourth] |

Review of English Studies

1925, July, vol. 1/3: 284-308	Ward, Capt. Bernard M.	The Authorship of *The Arte of English Poesie: A Suggestion* [repr. as a pamphlet]
1926, Jan., vol. 2/5: 32-41	Ward, Capt. Bernard M.	George Gascoigne and His Circle [repr. as a pamphlet]
1926, April, vol. 2/6: 163-68	Ambrose, Genevieve	George Gascoigne [letter]
1926, April, vol. 2/6: 169-72	Ward, Capt. Bernard M.	The Death of George Gascoigne
1927, Oct., vol. 3/4: 446-49	Ward, Capt. Bernard M.	The Will of John Bacon
1928, Jan., vol. 4/13: 35-48	Ward, Capt. Bernard M.	Further Research on *A Hundreth Sundrie Flowres*
1928, July, vol. 4/15: 270-94	Ward, Capt. Bernard M.	*The Famous Victories of Henry V: Its Place in Elizabethan Dramatic Literature* [repr. as a pamphlet]
1929, Jan., vol. 5/17: 57-59	Ward, Capt. Bernard M.	John Lyly and the Office of the Revels [repr. in OXV, p. 450-52]
1929, Jan., vol. 5/17: 92-103	Smith, G. C. Moore	[review of *The Seventeenth Earl of Oxford* by B. M. Ward]
1929, April, vol. 5/18: 246-47	Harrison, G. B.	[review of *The Shakespeare Mystery* by Georges Connes]
1930, Jan., vol. 6/21: 98-100	Harrison, G. B.	[reviews of *Borrowers*, and of *Topical Dramatists* by Percy Allen]
1930, April, vol. 6/22: 196-8	Allen, Percy	[letter: G. B. Harrison's Jan. reviews]
1930, April, vol. 6/22: 198	Harrison, G. B.	[letter: reply to Percy Allen's letter]
1932, Jan., vol. 8/29: 102	Alexander, Peter	[review of *Shakespeare's Plays in the Order of Their Writing* by Eva Turner Clark (1930)]
1932, April, vol. 8/2/30: 202-02	Ward, Capt. Bernard M.	Alphonse Ferrabosco
1932, Apr. vol. 8/30	Ward, Capt. Bernard M.	The Will of . . .
1932, Oct., vol. 8/32: 447-50	Smith, G. C. Moore	Taking Lodgings in 1591 [response in *Sh. Pictorial*, January 1933]
1932, Oct., vol. 8/32: 414-424	Draper, John W.	Sir John Falstaff – [response in *Sh. Pictorial*, January 1933]
1933, Jan., vol. 9/1/33: 55-58	Ward, B. M.	The Chamberlain's Men in 1597
1933, Jan., 9/33: 19-23	Fort, J. A.	The Order and Chronology of Shakespeare's Sonnets [repr. as a pamphlet]
1975, Nov., vol. 26/104: 385-94	May, Steven W.	The Authorship of 'My Mind to Me a Kingdom Is'
1989, VOL. 40/157: 48-71	Hume, Anthea	Love's Martyr, The Phoenix and Turtle, and the Aftermath of the Essex Rebellion
1997, May, vol. 48: 168-82	Price, Diana	Reconsidering Shakespeare's Monument
2007, Sept. vol. 58/236: 447-72	Stritmatter, Roger & Lynne Kositsky	Shakespeare and the Voyagers Revisited
2009, May, vol. 21/2: 7	Stritmatter, Roger & Lynne Kositsky	'O Brave New World': *The Tempest* and Peter Martyr's *De Orbe Novo*
2010, vol. 61 (251): 529-52	Reedy, Tom	Dating William Strachey's 'A True Reparatory of the Wracke and Redemption of Sir Thomas Gates': a comparative textual study

Revue Anglo-Américaine: Annual Bibliography of English Language and Literature

1923, Oct., vol. 1: 148-53	Pruvost, Rene	Une nouvelle hypothèse anti-stratfordienne
1924, Oct., vol. 2: 529-31	Connes, Georges	Une difficulte d'une des methodes anti-stratfordiennes
1928, Dec., vol. 6/2: 145-54	Connes, Georges	Du nouveau sur De Vere, Part 1 [review of *The Seventeenth Earl of Oxford* and seven other publications by B. M. Ward]
1928, Dec., vol. 6/2: 170-72	Pruvost, Rene	[review of *Le Mystere Shakespearien* by Georges Connes]
1929, Feb., vol. 6/3: 241-57	Connes, Georges	Du nouveau sur De Vere, Part 2 [Overview of SF activities]
1929, April, vol. 6/4: 297-311	Ward, Bernard M.	Shakespeare and the Anglo-Spanish War (1585-1604), Part 1 [repr. in OXV, p. 454-69]
1929, April, vol. 6/4: 360-61	Danchin, F. C.	[review of *Borrowers* by Percy Allen]
1930, April, vol. 7/4: 298-311	Ward, Bernard M.	Shakespeare and the Anglo-Spanish War (1585-1604), Part 2 [repr. in OXV, p. 454-69]
1930, August, vol. 7/6: 549-50	Connes, Georges	[review of *Shakespeare's Sonnets and Edward de Vere* by Gerald Rendall]
1930, Dec., vol. 8/2: 149-50	Pruvost, Rene	[review of *Shakespeare and Chapman as Topical Dramatists* by Percy Allen] [in French]
1931, Feb., vol. 8/3: 253-54	Connes, Georges	[review of *Shakespeare Authorship* by G. Standen] [in French]
1931, June, vol. 8/5: 439-40	Connes, Georges	[review of *Shakespeare's Plays in the Order of Their Writing* by Eva Turner Clark (1930)] [in French]

1931, Aug., vol. 8/6: 544	Connes, Georges	[review of *Shake-speare: Handwriting and Spelling by Gerald Rendall*] [in French]
1932, Dec., vol. 10/2: 235	Connes, Georges	[review of *The Case for Edward de Vere* by Percy Allen]
1933, Dec., vol. 11/2: 193-207	Connes, Georges	Encore Cinq ans de Travaux Oxoniens [Five Years of Oxfordian Work]
1933, Aug., vol. 11/6: 531-34	Ward, Capt. Bernard M.	[letter: George Connes' article in same issue, p. 193-207]
1935, Oct., vol. 13/1: 52-53	Connes, Georges	[review of *Sunlight on Sh.'s Sonnets* by Gerald Phillips (1935)

Revue Belge de Philologie et d'Historie

| 1928, Oct., vol. 7/3: 1099-00 | Delatte, F. | [review of Allen's *Borrowers*] |
| 1929, Jan., vol. 8/4: 1255-57 | Delatte, F. | [review of Allen's *Topical*] |

Revue Bleue

| 1938, Feb. | Lefranc, Abel | La Question Shakespearienne au XVIII Siècle [Article is reviewed in *Le Temps*, March 1, 1938, and in SFE, May 1938] |

Revue des Deux Mondes

| 1922, Nov. 1, vol. 12/1: 166-200 | Feuillerat, Albert | Shakspeare est-il Shakspeare? |

Revue Historique

| 1936 | Lefranc, Abel | Les Elements Francais de *Peines d'Amour Perdues* [French Elements in *Love's Labour's Lost*] |

Revue Mondiale (Paris)

| 1920, Nov. 1-Dec. 15, vol. CXXIX, p. 419-28 | Hervier, Paul-Louis | Shakespeare, Bacon, Rutland &Compagnie |

Richmond Herald

| 1929, Nov. 9, p. 7 | -- | Mr. Percy Allen on the Drama [report on his talk "The Drama as an Expression of Life"] |

Richmond Times

| 1997, July 20, p. F4 | Taylor, Welford D. | Who Was Shakespeare" [review of *Alias Shakespeare* by Joseph Sobran] |

Rivista di Cvltvra (Rome)

| 1920, Sept. 15, p. 257-60 | Vinciguerra, Mario | Shakespeariana |

Rocky Mountain E-Review of Languages and Literature

1992, Apr., vol. 62/2: 107-10	McCarthy, Andrew D.	[review of *Profiling Shakespeare* by Marjorie Garber]
2003, Fall, vol. 60/2	Delahoyde, Michael	Recent Publications in Oxfordian Studies [*Great Oxford*, edited by Richard Malim]
2004, Spring, vol. 58/1: 60-62	Delahoyde, Michael	The Shakespeare Enigma
2006, Fall, vol. 60/2: 37-49	Stritmatter, Roger	What's In a Name? Everything, Apparently . . .
2006, Fall, vol. 60/2: 52-59	Delahoyde, Michael	[review of *"Shakespeare" By Another Name* by Mark Anderson]
2006, Fall, vol. 60/2: 52-59	Delahoyde, Michael	[review of *The Monument* by Hank Whittemore (2005)]
2006, Fall, vol. 60/2: 52-59	Delahoyde, Michael	[review of *Great Oxford: Essays on the Life and Work of Edward de Vere*, ed. by Richard C. W. Malim]
2007, Spring, vol. 61/1: 112-20	Delahoyde, Michael	[review of *The Secret Love Story in Shakespeare's Sonnets* by Helen Heightsman Gordon (2005)]
2007, Spring, vol. 61/1: 112-20	Delahoyde, Michael	[review of *Oxford's Letters: The Letters of Edward de Vere, 17th Earl of Oxford Read by Derek Jacobi*]
2007, Spring, vol. 61/1: 112-20	Delahoyde, Michael	[review of *De Vere as Shakespeare* by William Farina]

Roll Call (Washington, D.C.)

| 2006, March 20, p. 1 | Hocking, Bree | Getting to the Root of the Bard [profile of Matthew Cossolotto] |

Rose+Croix Journal

| 2007 | Gordon, Helen H. | Shakespeare's Rosicrucian Revelations in the Dedication to the Sonnets |

Royal Engineers' Journal

1923, Mar. p. 154-56	Douglas, Col. Montagu W.	*The Mystery of Mr. W. H.* [review of the book by Col. B. R. Ward]
1928, Dec., vol. 42/4: 658-68	Ward, Col. Bernard R.	Shakespeare and Elizabethan War Propaganda [repr. in OXV, p. 469-81, and as a pamphlet]
1930, March, p. 14-16	Ward, Col. Bernard R.	The Elizabethan Chronicle Plays as War Propaganda [repr. as a pamphlet]

Ruri-decanal Magazine

1931, Sept.   Flynn, Rev. R. F.   Arthur Golding and Shakespeare [report on the article in the *Halstead & Belchamp St. Pauls Colne Valley Gazette*, Sept. 11, 1931]

1931, Nov.   Flynn, Rev. R. F.   [piece about the family into which EDV was born]
1931, Dec.   Flynn, Rev. R. F.   Arthur Golding and Shakespeare [repr. in the *Belchamp St. Pauls Halstead & Colne Valley Gazette*, Dec. 18, 1931]

Ruston Daily Leader

1981, March 13, vol. 91/6   Fiehler, Rudolph   Let's Teach Both Sides

Sacramento Bee

1987, Sept. 26, p. A1, A22   Savage, David G.   Author! Author! Justices Uphold Stratford Bard's Byline
1987, Sept.   Goff, Thomas A.   The Oxford Shakespeare Scenario [letter]
1997, April 20, p. EN16   Haugen, Peter   Who Wrote *Hamlet*? The Heirs of the Earl of Oxford Keep Alive the Controversy Over Sh.'s Authorship [Charles Vere]

1997, April 26, p. E11   Haugen, Peter   Shaksper vs. De Vere
1999, April 18, p. EN21   Wolf, Matt   "A Life" Chases the Man Behind the Quill Pen

Salt Lake Tribune

1992, June 14, p. F8   --   To Figure Out the Mystery, Decide In Which Category It Belongs

San Antonio Express-News

2004, Dec. 19   Conroy, Ed   Assumptions Damage Book on Authorship [review of *Will in the World* by Stephen Greenblatt]

2006, Feb. 19   Hunt, Paula   Shakespeare: The Man

San Diego Union

1984, Sept. 23, p. Books-2   Hutshing, Ed   For This Section, Seven Is a Lucky Number [Brief review of *The Mysterious William Shakespeare*]

1985, Feb. 1, p. D-17   Freeman, Don   Point of View [Will Buckley's "Firing Line"]
1985, Feb. 17, TV Week-4   Freeman, Don   Much Ado About . . . Shakespeare [review of the Dec. 11, 1984 *Firing Line* episode with guest Charlton Ogburn]

1989, April 18, p. E7   Laurence, Robert P.   Did Bard Do the Writing? [review of *Frontline*]
1999, Feb. 26, p. E2   Freeman, Don   If Shakespeare Were Irish, That Would Explain a Lot
1999, March 29, p. A1   Hebert, James   Heavens Above, Is Shakespeare an Imposture?
1999, June 21, p. E2   Freeman, Don   Shakespeare Again the Draw as Millennium Turns

San Francisco Chronicle

1920, Aug. 23, p. 16   Shafter, Howard   Scholarship and the Baconian Controversy [letter]
1920, Aug. 29, p. E2   --   Shakespeare is Again Unmasked: The Earl of Oxford Enters as Author of Shakespeare's Plays [review of SI]

1939, Dec. 29, p. 13   Jackson, Joseph Henry   Science Takes a Hand in the Shakespearean Controversy [Barrell and his *Scientific American* article]

1949, Nov. 6, p. 30   --   [review of *"Shakespeare" Identified*, 2ⁿᵈ ed.]
1971, Sept. 2, p. 35   Cyr, Gordon   A new Shakespeare signature [letter] [repr. in SON, vol. 8/1: 5 (Jan. 1972)]

1985, Oct. 20, p. 1   Commanday, Robert   The Return of 'Falstaff' [review of *The Mysterious William Shakespeare* by Charlton Ogburn]

1987, Sept. 26, p. A9   --   Justices Back Shakespeare/The Trial's the Thing
1987, Sept. 30, p. A22   --   Bard in Tempest
1988, Nov. 26, p. C6   --   Mock Trial Seeks the 'Real' William
1988, Nov. 28   --   Verdict Is In: Shakespeare Wrote Plays
1989, April 18   Carman, John   Was Shakespeare the Real Thing? [review of *Frontline*'s "The Shakespeare Mystery"] [repr. in SON, vol. 25/2: 8-9 (Spring 1989); and in BTC, vol. 6: 391-92]

1992, June 11, p. D3   Larcen, Donna   Why We Love a Mystery
1994, April 3, p. 14   Achenbach, Joel   Alas Poor William, We Know Him Not
1994, May 29, p. Z7   Achenbach, Joel   The Spaceship in Your Bedroom
1997, April 26, p. E11   Carroll, Jerry   To Be or Not to Be the Bard: Vere Claims Earl of Oxford Wrote Oeuvre

2001, Dec. 14, p. D4   Hurwitt, Robert   Sara Moore Showcased in Crazy Wisdom [review of *The Crazy Wisdom Sho*, a musical about Ed. de Vere by George Coates]

2002, Jan. 8   Winn, Steven   Bard or "Beard"? [review of *The Beard of Avon* by Amy Freed]

2002, Jan. 18	Hurwitt, Robert	Whose Lines Were Those Anyway? [review of *The Beard of Avon* by Amy Freed]
2002, May 5, p. C4	Steger, Pat	[report on a talk by the Earl of Burford]
2002, Aug. 14, p. D1	LaSalle, Mick	A Witty Case Against the Stratford Bard [review of Mike Rubbio's "Much Ado About Something"]
2004, June 25, p. E4	--	Datebook [400th Anniversary of Edward de Vere's death]
2004, Summer	Chiljan, Katherine	Tribute to the "Authentic" Shakespeare [letter to Datebook" [repr. in SON, vol. 40/3: 9 (2004)]
2004, Aug. 10, p. D2	Hurwitt, Robert	A Scholarly Shakespearean Showdown [review of *The Mysterious Mr. Looney*, a play by Gary Graves [dramatizes a confrontation between Sir Sidney Chambers & J. T. Looney]

San Francisco Examiner

1933, Aug. 19	Herford, Oliver	A Great Peradventure
1939, Dec. 24	Hanifin, Ada	Forceful Clew on Real Shakespeare

Santa Cruz Sentinal

2002, July 14	Hartmann, Kurt	Debate Plays on: Oxford vs. Stratford [repr. in SON, vol. 38/3: 3 (Summer 2002)]

Santa Fe New Mexican

2004, April 30, p. 30	Nott, Robert	Toying With the Bard [response to Jonathan Dixon's article in *Renaissance Magazine*, vol. 9/1: 54-59]

Sarasota Herald Tribune

2011, Oct. 27, p. E20	Lloyd, Christopher	Delicious Historical Fiction [review of *Anonymous*]

Saturday Review of Literature (New York)

1928, July 21, p. 1049	Singleton, Esther	[review of *The Seventeenth Earl of Oxford* by Bernard M. Ward]
1937, May 1, p. 11	Editor	Prefatory Note
1937, May 1, p. 11-12, 14-15	Barrell, Charles Wisner	Elizabethan Mystery Man [published as a pamphlet (1940) [repr. in BTC, vol. 3: 386-95; excerpt repr. in SON, vol. 31/2a: 5 (Spring 1995); and in BTC, vol. 7: 305]
1937, May 8, 12, 14, 16-17	Stoll, Elmer Edgar	The Detective Spirit in Criticism [response to Barrell]
1937, May 22, 16: 9	Barrell, Charles Wisner	The Oxford Theory [letter: reply to Stoll]
1937, June 5, p. 9, 16	Wells, Carolyn	The Oxford Theory [letter]
1941, Sept. 13	Heron, Flodden W.	[letter: famous pen names]
1948, June 5, p. 46	Redman, Ben Ray	New Reviews
1948, Oct. 2, p. 22	Burgess, Gelett	Pseudonym, Shakespeare [The Earl of Oxford "had every possible qualification for authorship, while the dummy of Stratford had not one."] [repr. in *Shakespeare and His Rivals* (McMichael & Glenn 1962): 159-73]
1948, Nov. 6, p. 21-22	Hoepfner, T. C., & Cranston, Theodore H. Kenworth, and Henry Sigurd Humphreys	The Shakespeare Confusion [five letters in response to Gelett Burgess's Oct. 2 article]
1948, Nov. 6, p. 21-2	Kinnaird, Clark	The Shakespeare Confusion [letter] [repr. in *Shakespeare and His Rivals* (McMichael & Glenn 1962): 175-78]
1948, Nov. 20, p. 24	Garrett, G. R.	Nobody Named Shakespeare [letter]
1949, May 7, p. 7-8, 39-40	Evans, Bergen	Good Friend for Iesvs Sake Forbeare: Was Shakespeare Really Shakespeare? [repr. in *Shakespeare and His Rivals* (McMichael & Glenn 1962): 178-85]
1949, June 4, p. 24	Aycock, John L & Freudenberg, G. F., Marcia M. Roof, and William A. Klutts	Was Shakespeare Shakespeare? [four letters] [Freudenberg, Roof and Klutts letters repr. in *Sh. and His Rivals* (McMichael & Glenn 1962): 185, 188-89]
1949, June 4, p. 24-25	Burgess, Gelett	The Oxford Primer [letter: reply to responses] [repr. in *Sh. and His Rivals* (McMichael & Glenn 1962): 186-88]
1949, June 25, p. 27-28	de Chambrun, Clara L.	Was Shakespeare Really Shakespeare? [letter] [repr. in *Sh. and His Rivals* (McMichael & Glenn 1962): 189-90]
1949, Sept. 3, p. 26	Brooks, Alden	A Look at the Register [letter: response to Burgess] [repr. in *Sh. & His Rivals* (McMichael & Glenn 1962): 1190-92]

Saturday Review of Literature (New York) (continued)

1949, Sept. 3, p. 26	St. Clair, F. Y.	A Look at the Register [letter: response to Burgess] [repr. in *Shakespeare and His Rivals* (McMichael & Glenn 1962): 192]
1953, Oct. 10, p. 38	Harrison, G. B.	[review of *This Star of England* by Dorothy and Charlton Ogburn]
1970, Nov. 7, p. 31-35+	DeMott, Benjamin	Will the Real Shakespeare Please Stand Up? [reviews of several recent books on Shakespeare] [review is quoted in TMWS, p. 378]

Saturday Review of Politics, Literature, Science, and Art (London)

1920, Mar. 27, vol. 129: 308	--	Shakespeare: A New Folly [review of SI]
1920, April 17, vol. 129: 370	Looney, J. Thomas	Edward de Vere and Shakespeare [letter: the March 27 review]
1920, April 24, vol. 129: 389	--	Edward de Vere and Shakespeare [reviewer's reply to Looney]
1920, May 8, vol. 129: 434	Devey, H. B.	Shakespeare [letters from Devey and others]
1921, Feb 11, vol. 131: 340	--	[review of Looney's *The Poems of Edward de Vere*]
1921, Feb. 19, vol. 131: 159	--	Books of the Week [*The Poems of Edward de Vere*]
1922, Feb. 4, vol. 133: 123	--	The Magazines [commentary on Looney's letter in the February issue of *National Review*]
1922, March 11, v.. 133: 260-61	--	Shakespeare's Patron [mention of the Earl of Oxford in a review of Stopes's *The Life of Henry, Third Earl of Southampton*]
1923, April 28, vol. 135: 570-71	--	*The Mystery of 'Mr. W. H.'* [review of Col. B. R. Ward's book]
1928, March 24, v. 145: 215-16	Brown, Ivor	The Theatre: Merchandise Marks [review of *Borrowers* Allen]
1928, March 31, vol. 145: 388	Allen, Percy	Shakespeare, Jonson and Wilkins [letter: resp. to the March 24 review]
1928, April 7, vol. 145: 432-33	Brown, Ivor	Shakespeare, Jonson and Wilkins [letter: reply to Allen]
1928, April 14, vol. 145: 462-63	Allen, Percy	Shakespeare, Jonson and Wilkins [letter: response to Ivor Brown's April 7 review, reply by editor and Brown]
1928, May 19, vol. 145: 634-36	--	The Elizabethan Earl of Oxford [review of *The Seventeenth Earl of Oxford 1550-1604* by Captain Bernard M. Ward (1928) [quoted in front of Ward's book (Miller edition)]
1928, June 2, vol. 145: 697	Ward, Capt. Bernard M.	[letter: response to the May 19 review]
1929, Feb. 23, vol. 147: 251-52	Brown, Ivor	Shakespeare and Chapman as Topical Dramatists [review of Percy Allen's book]
1929, March 2, vol. 147: 281	Allen, Percy	Shakespeare and Chapman as Topical Dramatists [response to Ivor Brown's Feb. 23 review]
1929, March 2, vol. 147: 281	Brown, Ivor	[reply to Percy Allen's response]
1930, May 10, vol. 149: 592	--	Fiddlesticks [review of *Case* by Percy Allen (1930)]
1930, May 17, vol. 149: 619	Allen, Percy	Fiddlesticks [response to the May 10 review]
1930, May 24, vol. 149: 654-55	--	Fiddlesticks [reviewer's reply to Percy Allen's May 17 letter]
1930, May 31, vol. 149: 688	Medicus	Fiddlesticks and Physiognomy [letter: Allen's *Case*]
1931, May 2, vol. 151: 652-53	Willoughby, D.	Who was Shakespeare? [review of Clark's *Sh.'s Plays in the Order of Their Writing* & Allen's *The Oxford-Sh. Case Corroborated* (1931)] ["Assuming [Oxford's] authorship, half the most baffling Sh. riddles can be answered."]
1931, May 9, vol. 151: 682	Allen, Percy	Who was Shakespeare? [letter: resp. to Willoughby's review]
1931, June 6, vol. 151: 839	--	Shorter Notices [review of *Shakespeare: Handwriting and Spelling* by Gerald H. Rendall]
1931, Sept. 5, vol. 152: 303	Nicholson, A. P.	A Good Playwright [review of *Thomas Heywood, Playwright and Miscellanist* by Arthur M. Clark]
1931, Sept. 12, vol. 152: 327	Allen, Percy	The Shakespeare-Oxford Problem [letter: Critics should study 'the ever-accumulating mass of evidence pointing ruthlessly toward Edward de Vere as "Shakespeare"]
1931, Oct. 31, vol. 152: 560	H. R. W.	Seven Shakespeares [review of the book by Gilbert Slater]
1931, Nov. 14, vol. 152: 624	Ward, Bernard M.	[letter: response to H.R.W.'s Oct. 31 review]
1932, June 4, vol. 152: 569	--	[review of *Life Story* by Percy Allen (1932)]
1932, June 11, vol. 153: 591	Allen, Percy	De Vere and Shakespeare [letter: response to the June 4 review]
1933, Feb. 4, vol. 155: 121	--	Great Lives [review of *Shakespeare* by John Drinkwater]
1933, Feb. 18, vol. 155: 173	Allen, Percy	Understanding Reason [letter: response to recent review of Drinkwater's *Shakespeare*]

Saturday Westminster Gazette
    1920, March 20, p. 18   --   Another Shakespeare Claimant [review of SI]

Scandinavian Psychoanalytic Review
    2009, vol. 32/1: 105-15   Waugaman, Richard M.;   Who Was "William Shakespeare?": we propose he was
                 & Roger Stritmatter   Edward de Vere
    2011, vol. 34/2: 134-38   Zachrisson, Anders   Who Wrote the Works of Shakespeare? Notes on a Matter of
                                      Curiosity in Freud's Intellectual Biography
    2011, vol. 34/1: 120-22   Waugaman, Richard M.;   The Significance of Anonymous Authorship in
                  & Roger Stritmatter   Elizabethan England [A reply to Anders Zacchrison]
    2016, vol. 39/1: 148-51   Waugaman, Richard M.   An Unpublished Letter by Sigmund Freud on the Shakespeare
                                        Authorship Question

School Library Journal
    1962, Nov., vol. 9/3: 75   --   [review of *Shake-speare* by D. Ogburn and Charlton Ogburn, Jr.]

Science
    1990, May 4, p. 548   --   Did Queen Write Shakespeare's Sonnets? [review of Ward
                                         Elliott's and and Robert Valenza's Stylometrics approach]
    1998, Nov. 13, vol. 282/5392   Holden, Constance   Cosmic Clue to Bard's Identity

Scientific American
    1940, Jan., vol. 162/1: 5-8, 43-5   Barrell, Charles   Identifying 'Shakespeare'
    1940, May, vol. 162/5: 299   Editor   Who Was Shakespeare [editor's intro. to reader responses]
    1940, May, vol. 162/5: 264+   Barrell, Charles   Who Was Shakespeare: Reader Responses [and Barrell reply]
    2009, vol. 301/2: 30   Shermer, Michael   Shakespeare, Interrupted

Scotland on Sunday (Edinburgh)
    2010, Aug. 22, p. 3   --   If You Like . . . Shakespeare [review of *The Man Who Was
                                         Hamlet* by George Dillon]

Scotsman (Edinburgh)
    2010, Aug. 19, p. 6   Cornwell, Tim   [review of *The Man Who Was Hamlet* by George Dillon]

Scotsman, The (Midlothian, Scotland)
    1920, March 4, p. 2   --   Shakespeare Identified [review of *"Shakespeare" Identified*]
    1920, Mar. 20, p. 11   Looney, J. Thomas   Shakespeare Identified [letter: response to the March 4 review]
                                           [states pub. date was March 4]
    1921, Feb. 17, p. 2   --   Poetry [review of Looney's *Poems of Edward de Vere*: "Adverse
                                         criticism and neglect has not discouraged Mr. Looney"]
    1923, March 19, p. 2   --   [review of *The Mystery of "Mr. W. H."* by Col. B. R. Ward]
    1923, May 14, p. 2   --   "Minor Notions" [review of *Shakespeare Through Oxford Glasses*
                                         by Hubert H. Holland]
    1927, Nov. 21, p. 11   J. S. L. M.   The Bishop of Durham and Shakespeare [letter]
    1928, May 10, p. 2   --   A Misjudged Elizabethan [review of *The Seventeenth Earl of
                                         Oxford* by Col. Bernard M. Ward (1928)]
    1929, Feb. 25, p. 8   --   [review of *Topical Dramatists* by Percy Allen]
    1930, March 6, p. 2   --   Shakespearean Mysteries [review of *Shakespeare Sonnets and
                                         Edward de Vere* by Gerald Rendall]
    1930, April 10, p. 2   --   Shakespeare Condemned [review of *Case* by Percy Allen]
    1931, March 9, p. 2   --   Bacon or Oxford? [review of *Shakespeare's Plays in the Order of
                                         Their Writing* by Eva Turner Clark]
    1931, June 8, p. 2   --   Shakespearean Research [reviews of *Case Corroborated* by Percy
                                         Allen; *Shakespeare's Tragic Heroes* by Lily Campbell; and
                                         Sh., Chapman, and "Sir Thomas More" by Arthur Aceson]
    1931, Oct. 26, p. 2   --   Books Received
    1932, May 5, p. 2   --   Books Received [Percy Allen's *Life Story* is on the list]
    1932, May 12, p. 2   --   [review of *Life Story* by Percy Allen (1932)]

Screen Education
    2012, Autumn, issue 65: 30-37   McFarlane, Brian   Is This an Author I See Before Me? *Anonymous* and the
                                         Interminable Shakespeare Question

Seattle Times

1988, Nov. 27, p. B6	--	Shakespeare Really Was the Author, Judges Rule
1997, Oct. 10, p. F1	Tu, Janet I-Chin	Alas! Poor Shakespeare: Society Debates Authorship
1999, April 4, p. B4	Hernandez, Romel	Scholar [Daniel Wright] Stands By Theory of Sh. As a Fraud
2001, Nov. 9, p. E1	Berson, Misha	Seattle Rep Delights in Tempest Over Shakespeare's Real Identity
2001, Nov. 14, p. E8	Berson, Misha	*Beard of Avon* an Entertaining, Literate Fantasy [review of Amy Freed's play]
2003, June 15, p. L10	Dederer, Claire	Will the Real Bard Please Stand Up?

Sewanee Review

1939, Jan-Feb	Spencer, Benjamin T.	[review of *The Man Who Was Shakespeare* by Eva Turner Clark]
1976, Fall, V. 84/4: 657-68	Berman, Ronald	The Shakespeare Industry
1997	Bryant, J. A., Jr.	[review of *Shakespeare, In Fact* by Irvin Matus]

Shakespeare Association Bulletin

1931, Jan., vol. VI, no. 1	--	Ocford – Shakespeare Question [reviews 9 Oxfordian texts]
1941, Oct., vol. 16/4: 195-214	Holstein, Mark	The Shakespeare-Bacon-Oxford-Whoozis Mixup

Shakespeare Bookshop Newsletter

2010, vol. 16: 1-2	Sharpe, Will	[review of *Contested Will* by James Shapiro (2010)]

Shakespeare Bulletin

1985, Mar/Apr. 1, vol. 3/2: 26	Bertram, Paul	[review of *The Mysterious William Sh.* by Charlton Ogburn, Jr.]
1985, Sept/Oct., vol. 3/5: 27	Ogburn, Charlton, Jr.	[letter: response to Paul Bertram's review]
1998, Spring, vol. 16/2: 46	Wright, Daniel L.	[review of *Who Wrote Shakespeare?* by John Michell]
2014, March, vol. 32/1: 11-26	Kirwan, Peter	'You Have No Voice!': Constructing Reputation Through Contemporaries in the Shakespeare Biopic

Shakespeare in Perspective

1982, vol. 1: 222-27	Took, Barry	All's Well That Ends Well

Shakespeare in Southern Africa

2012, vol. 24: 82-84+	Haresnape, Geoffrey	Shakespeare Through the Looking Glass [review of *Anonymous*]

Shakespeare Jahrbuch

1928, Jan., band 64: 198-99	Keller, Wolfgang	[rev. of *Seventeenth Earl of Oxford* by B. M. Ward (in German)]
1952, band 87/88: 211-13	Brunner, Karl	[review of *Der wahre Shakespeare*, John Mez's translation of Ch. and Dorothy Ogburn' *Renaissance Man of England*]
1965, band 101: 146-60	--	The Noble Candidates: A Study in Ermine [review of *Shakespeare and His Betters* by R. C. Churchill] [West]
1997, band 133: 158-65	Meller, Horst	Reprisen aus wurmstichiger Schublade: zum neuesten Plädoyer für den siebzehntsen Earl
2012, band 148: 215-20	Marcus, Leah	[review of *Contested Will* by James Shapiro (2010)]

Shakespeare Newsletter [see listing in Section IIC: Regular Oxfordian Columns in Non-Oxfordian Publications]

Shakespeare Newsletter of Claremont McKenna College

2000, Fall, vol. 50/3	Burton, J. Anthony	An Unrecognized Theme in *Hamlet*: Lost Inheritance and Claudius's Marriage to Gertrude, Part 1 [repr. in *Shakespeare and the Law* (Stritmatter, 2022): 171-86]
2000-01, Winter, vol. 50/4	Burton, J. Anthony	An Unrecognized Theme in *Hamlet*: Lost Inheritance and Claudius's Marriage to Gertrude, Part 1 [repr. in *Shakespeare and the Law* (Stritmatter, 2022): 171-86]

Shakespeare Pictorial [see listing in Section IIC: Regular Oxfordian Columns in Non-Oxfordian Publications]

Shakespeare Quarterly

1951, Oct., vol. 2/4: 368-69	Flatter, Richard	Sigmund Freud on Shakespeare [reprints Freud's letter to Dr. Richard Flatter dated Sept. 20, 1932]
1953, April, vol. 4/2: 165-70	Dawson, Giles E.	[review of *This Star of England* by Dorothy & Charlton Ogburn]
1959, Sum., vol. 10/3: 435-37	Maxwell, Baldwin	[reviews of *S. and His Betters* by R. C. Churchill and *The Poacher From Stratford* by Frank W. Wadsworth]
1963, Spr., vol. 14/2: 170-71	Wadsworth, Frank W.	[review of *Shakespeare and His Rivals* by George McMichael and Edgar M. Glenn]
1963, Aut., vol. 14/4: 465-66	Hastings, William T.	[review of *The Shakespeare Claimants* by Harry N. Gibson]
1982, vol. 33: 121-23	Bertram, Paul	[review of *Shakespeare By Hilliard* by Leslie Hotson]
1985, Winter, vol. 36/4: 515-22	Crinkley, Richmond	New Perspectives on the Authorship Question [excerpts repr. in

		Sh. Authorship Sourcebook (Stritmatter 2019, 2022): 47-49]
1993, Spring, vol. 44/1: 54-72	Pressly, William L.	The Ashbourne Portrait of Shakesp.: Through the Looking Glass
1998, vol. 49: 74-83	Nelson, Alan H.	George Buc, William Shakesp., and the Folger George a Greene
1998, Sum., vol. 49/2: 187-94	Thomas, Sidney	On the Dating of Shakespeare's Early Plays
1999, Fall, vol. 50/3: iii-iv	Paster, Gail Kern	From the Editor [cites Nelson's quote in next entry]
1999, Fall, vol. 50/3: 376-82	Nelson, Alan H.	[review of *Alias Shakespeare* by Joseph Sobran (1997)] [Nelson laments that "Establishment Shakespeareans . . . are losing the public debate over the 'authorship question."]
2000, Jan., vol. 51: 610	--	Authorship Controversy: Bibliographic Information
2002, Jan., vol. 53: 649-51	--	Biography and Milieu
2002, Jan., vol. 53: 680-724	--	General Studies
2003, Jan., vol. 54: 571-74	--	Shakespeare in Literature
2003, Jan., vol. 54/5: 584-87	--	Authorship Controversy
2005, Sum., vol. 56/2: 214-26	May, Steven W.	[review of *Monstrous Adversary* by Alan Nelson (2003)]
2008, Spring, vol. 59/1	Hammer, Paul	Shakespeare's *Richard II*: The Play of 7 February 1601 and the Essex Rising
2008, Fall, vol. 59/3: 245-73	Vaughan, Alden T.	William Strachey's "True Repertory" and Shakespeare: a closer look at the evidence [response to Stritmatter & Kositsky's *On the Date, Sources and Design of Sh.'s "The Tempest"*]
2009, Winter, vol. 60/4: 460-69	Nelson, Alan H.; and Paul H. Altrocchi	William Shakespeare, "Our Roscius"
2011, vol. 62: 106-42	Vickers, Brian	Shakespeare and Authorship Studies in the Twenty-First Century
2012, vol. 63/3: 355-92	Burrows, John	A Second Opinion on "Shakespeare and Authorship Studies in the Twenty-First Century"

Shakespeare Review

1928, May, vol. 1/1: 49-52	Jaggard, Geoffrey W.	The Elizabethans as Borrowers [review of *Shakepeare, Jonson, and Wilkins as Borrowers* by Percy Allen]
1928, June, vol. 1/2: 121-22	Kempling, W. B.	[review of *The Shakespeare Mystery* by Georges Connes]
1928, July, vol. 1/3: 166-71	Allen, Percy	The Historic Originals of Ophelia
1928, July, vol. 1/3: 200-01	Kempling, W. B.	[review of *The Seventeenth Earl of Oxford* by B. M. Ward]

Shakespeare Studies (Shakespeare Society of Japan)

1975, vol. 8: 241-53,	Hays, Michael	Shakespeare Hand in *Sir Thomas More*: Some Aspects of the Paleographic Argument
1994, vol. 22: 340-44+	Knutson, Roslyn L.	The Oldcastle Controversy and *The Famous Victories of Henry V* [response to recent articles in SON]
2008, vol. 36: 37	Kastan, David Scott	'To think these trifles something': Shakespearean playbooks and the claims of authorship

Shakespeare Survey

1949, issue #2	Leech, Clifford	Hall's *Chronicle* and Shakespeare [repr. in SFE (Sept. 1951), p. 6]
1987, vol. 39: 223-36	Dutton, Richard	[review of *Edward de Vere and the War of Words* by Elizabeth Appleton (1985)]
2006, vol. 59: 358-59	Taylor, Michael	[review of *The Case For Shakespeare* by Scott McCrea]

Shakespeare Yearbook

2008, vol. XVII: 365-404	Stritmatter, Roger & Lynne Kositsky	A Movable Feast: *The Tempest* as Shrovetide revelry

Shakespearean International Yearbook

2012, vol. 12: 169-94	Chapman, Rebecca	[review of *Contested Will* by James Shapiro (2010)]

Sheffield Daily Telegraph

1920, April 12, p. 3	--	Is Shakespeare Identified? Author of the New Theory and the Discovery of Important Papers
1920, May 24, p. 6	--	Bad Faith and Bad Scholarship
1922, Feb. 8, p. 6	--	The National Review
1925, Sept. 19, p. 6	Anti-Shagspere	Shakespeare's Land [letter]
1925, Sept. 22, p. 6	Collis, Whitaker	Shakespeare Plays [letter]
1925, Sept. 23, p. 4	Perplexed	The Authorship of the "Plays of Shakespeare" [letter]
1925, Sept. 25, p. 4	A Seeker for the Truth	The Authorship of the "Plays of Shakespeare" [letter]
1925, Sept. 28, p. 6	Seymour, Henry	The Shakespeare Puzzle [letter]
1925, Oct. 1, p. 4	Wallis, J. B.	The Shakespeare Puzzle [letter]

Sheffield Evening Telegraph (South Yorkshire)

1920, March 6, p. 4	--	Workshop [short summary of ideas from SI]

Sixteenth Century Journal

1990, Spring, vol. 21: 548	Holden, Constance	Did Queen Write Shakespeare's *Sonnets*? [Elliott and Claremont]
2005, Fall, vol. 36-3: 908	Canino, Catherine G.	[review of *Monstrous Adversary* by Alan Nelson (2003)]
2007, Summer, vol. 38/2: 460	Chibi, Andrew A.	[review of *Edward de Vere: The Crisis and Consequences of Wardship* by Daphne Pearson

Skeptic Magazine

2002, Winter, vol. 9/4, p. 70	McCrea, Scott	Two Shakespeares: A Skeptical Analysis of Shakespeare and His Works Reveals the Real Author
2003, Spring, vol. 10/1: 22	Price, Diana	Not Skeptical Enough [response to McCrea]
2004, Fall, vol. 11/3: 10	Price, Diana	Shakespeare's Authorship and Questions of Evidence
2005, Spring, vol. 12/1: 31-33	McCrea, Scott	How Do We Know Shakespeare? Let Me Count The Ways [response to Diana Price's article]
2005, Spring, vol. 12/1: 33	Lifton, Barbara	Shakespeare in the World [letter: resp. to Diana Price]

Skeptical Enquirer

2011, Nov-Dec, p. 38	Nickell, Joe	Cover Story: Did Shakespeare Write 'Shakespeare'? Much Ado About Nothing
2012, March-April, p. 62	[various writers]	Did Shakespeare Write Shakespeare? [all letters sneeringly support the Stratford line—except one (see next listing)]
2012, March-April, p. 62	Wildenthal, Bryan H.	[letter: Wildenthal is the lone defender of Edward de Vere as "Shakespeare" against Joe Nichell's sneering ad hominem ridicule of doubters]

Sketch, The (London)

1920, March 17, p. 410	Howard, Keble	Mr. Looney on Shakespeare [review of SI: "Looney, it seems, has smashed Shake-speare to atoms."]

SKY (Delta Airlines)

1992, Dec., p. 96, 98+	Smith, Scott S.	Will the Real Shakespeare Stand Up?

Slate

2023, May 11	Butler, Isaac	Shakespeare Was Shakespeare

Small Press

1995, Winter	Jensen, Mike	[review of *Shakespeare, In Fact* by Irvin Matus (1994)]

SMAN (Newsletter of the Marlowe Society of America)

2007, vol. 27/1: 7	Knutson, Roslyn	[review of *Monstrous Adversary* by Alan Nelson (2003)]

Smithsonian, The

1987, Sept. vol. 18/6, p. 155-76	Reed, J. D.	Some Ado About Who Was, Or Who Was Not, Shakespeare [Reed's piece in *Life* in April 1964 had the same title] [excerpt repr. in SON, vol. 23/3: 12 (Sum. '87)] See comments by Scott S. Smith, SON, vol. 24/1: 13-14 (Winter 1988).
1987, Nov.	--	[letters commenting on Reed's article]
1995, April, vol. 26/1: 40	--	Smithsonian Updates [repr. in SON, vol. 31/2a: 7 (Spring 1995); and in BTC, vol. 7: 308-09] Response by R. Stritmatter and M. Anderson, SON, vol. 31/2a: 8-9 (Spr. 1995).
2006, Sept., p. 62-66, 68-71	Stewart, Doug	To Be or Not to Be Shakespeare Response by *Shakespeare Newsletter*, vol. 56/2: 43.
2006, Nov., vol. 37/8: 10	Cavanaugh, Gerald J.	[letter: discussion of the SAQ]
2006, Nov., vol. 37/8: 10	Joyner, Janice Faye	[letter: Marlowe was the author]

Sobran's [available at http://sobran.com/oxfordlibrary.shtml]

1996, Jan.	Sobran, Joseph	Shakespeare and Fascism
1996, Feb.	Sobran, Joseph	The Shakespeare Mystery
1996, May	Sobran, Joseph	Shakespeare's Lives
1996, July	Sobran, Joseph	Shakespeare Without Ideas
1996, Nov.	Sobran, Joseph	Shakespeare for the Tube
1996, Nov.	Sobran, Joseph	Shakespeare and the Official Language

1997, Feb.	Sobran, Joseph	Shakespeare's time Capsule
1997, Aug.	Sobran, Joseph	The Stratford Response
1997, Oct.	Sobran, Joseph	The Shakespeare Party Line
1997, Dec.	Sobran, Joseph	Meeting Shakespeare
1998, Jan., vol. 5/1	Sobran, Joseph	Introduction to *Emaricdulfe*
1998, Jan., vol. 5/1	Sobran, Joseph	The Mystery of *Emaricudlfe*
1999, Jan.	Sobran, Joseph	Shakespeare of Christendom
1999, Feb.	Sobran, Joseph	Shakespeare's Missing Links
1999, March 18	Sobran, Joseph	Who Done Shakespeare?
1999, July 8	Sobran, Joseph	Debating Shakespeare
2000, March, vol. 7/3	Sobran, Joseph	Shakespeare's Folks
2000, Oct.	Sobran, Joseph	Oxford and his 'Lovely Boy'
2000, Dec., vol. 7/12	Sobran, Joseph	The Spirit of Falstaff
2001, May	Sobran, Joseph	Shakespearean Odds and Ends
2003, April, vol. 10/4	Sobran, Joseph	The Bard's Orphans
2004, Jan.	Sobran, Joseph	A Flawed Life of Oxford
2005, Jan., vol. 12/1	Sobran, Joseph	Shakespeare's "Early" Poems
2005, May	Sobran, Joseph	Old Man Shakespeare
2005, Aug. 18	Sobran, Joseph	Lear's Fool
2005, Aug. 30	Sobran, Joseph	The Queer Bard?
2005, Sept. 13	Sobran, Joseph	Hamnet/s Father
2005, Dec. 8	Sobran, Joseph	What's in the Pronoun?
2005, Dec. 15	Sobran, Joseph	Reflections of a Conspirator
2006, Jan. 3	Sobran, Joseph	The Bard in Retirement
2006, Jan. 17	Sobran, Joseph	How to Handle a Woman
2006, April 13	Sobran, Joseph	Shakespearean Masterpiece
2006, June 1	Sobran, Joseph	Shakespeare and Ms. Grundy
2006, June 22	Sobran, Joseph	The Hamlet That Never Was
2006, June 29	Sobran, Joseph	My Ilk and I
2006, Oct. 3	Sobran, Joseph	Hamlet's Lame Creator
2006, Feb. 22	Sobran, Joseph	Fine-Filed Phrases
2007, Feb. 22	Sobran, Joseph	The Fun of Falstaff
2007, March 8	Sobran, Joseph	A Coriolanus in Our Future?
2007, March 22	Sobran, Joseph	The Shakespeare Bigots
2007, April 3	Sobran, Joseph	You Be the Judge
2007, April 19	Sobran, Joseph	The Time for Digression
2007, May 3	Sobran, Joseph	The Sobran Method: A True Story
2007, May 22	Sobran, Joseph	Special Edition
2007, Aug. 28	Sobran, Joseph	The Lady is the Man

Social Science and Modern Society

2013, Oct.	Waugaman, Richard M.	[review of *Shakespeare's Education* by Robin Fox]

Social Sciences

2015, vol. 4/3: 758-99	Aljumily, Refat	Applying Hierarchical and Non-Hierarchical Linear and Non-Linear Clustering Methods to the "Shakespeare Authorship Question"

Society

2013, Oct., vol. 50/5: 522	Waugaman, Richard	[review of *Shakespeare's Education* by Robin Fox]

Sophia

1979, Spring, vol. 28: 88-92	Milward, Peter	[review of *Shakespeare by Hilliard* by Leslie Hotson]

South China Morning Post

1948, Jan. 12, p. 6	Musel, Robert	Spiritual Talks: Shakespeare Breaks Long Silence: Mystery Solved? [review of *Talks with Elizabethans* by Percy Allen]
1997, Sept. 27, p. 38	--	[review of *Alias Shakespeare* by Joe Sobran]

South London Observer

1951, April 19	--	The Shakespeare Trial ["Librarian Shouted Down in Shakespeare Debate"] [coverage of an April 14 lecture by Dr. J. R. Mez and a Shakespeare trial]

South Notts Echo

1962, July 20, p. 7	Bayley, John	The Shakespearean Fringe [review of *The Shakespeare Claimants* by H. M. Gibson]

Southend Standard

1940, May	--	[coverage of talks by F. D. Bone at the southend Business Luncheon Club]

Southland Times (New Zealand)

1920, June 5, issue 18840	Iota	A New Shakespeare [review of SI]

Spectator, The (London)

1920, March 27, p. 416	--	A Sleepless Shakespeare
1920, March 27, p. 425-26	--	Shakespeare Identified [review of *"Shakespeare" Identified*]
1920, April 10, p. 487	Looney, J. Thomas	Edward de Vere and Shakespeare [letter: resp. to the March 27 review of SI]
1920, April 10, p. 487	Greenwood, George G.	Was Shakespeare Uneducated? [letter: resp. to the March 27 review]
1921, Aug. 27, p. 277-78	--	The Poems of Edward de Vere [short review of Looney's book]
1922, Nov. 25, vol. 129: 759-60	Hookham, George	The Elusive Image [letter]
1923, June 23, vol. 130: 1049	--	The Mystery of "Mr. W. H." [review of the book by Col. Ward]
1924, Nov. 7	Ward, Col. Bernard R	.[review of *Shakespeare's Signatures and Sir Thomas More* by Sir George Greenwood]
1924, Nov. 14	Greenwood, George	[letter: response to review]
1932, Jan. 30, vol. 148: 149	Parsons, I. M.	Shakespeare's Ghost [reviews of *Exit Shakespeare* by Bertram G. Theobold (1931) and *Edward de Vere* by George Frisbee]
1937, Dec. 10	Rowse, A. L.	[review of *Shakespeare versus Shallow* by Leslie Hotson]
1953, June 12, vol. 190: 768	Muir, Kenneth	The Oxford Case [review of *This Star of England* by Dorothy and Charlton Ogburn (1952)]
1975, April 19, p. 466-68	Carr, Francis	Shakespeare and Stratford: 20 questions for believers
1975, April 19, p. 467-68	Rowse, A. L.	Answering the Sceptical
1988, vol. 47/2: 44	Ridden, Geoff	[review of *Who Wrote Shakespeare* by John Michell]
1989, Feb. 4, p. 33	Hillier, Bevis	Someone Who Fits the Bill [review of *The Mystery of William Shakespeare* by Charlton Ogburn]
1990, June 23, p. 26	Welch, Colin	Freud's Jungle Book [rev. of *Reading Freud* by Peter Gay]
1990, Sept. 29, p. 39-40	Powell, J. Enoch	[review of *The Lost Chronicle of Edward de Vere* by Andrew Field (1990)]
1994, May 17, p. C5	Anon.	Shakespeare's Raging Identity Crisis
1998, March 21, p. W5	Levesque, John	Shakespeare's Ghost: Who Was the 'Real' Bard of Avon?
1999, Jan. 9, p. 20	Malim, Richard	They Haven't the Necessary Will
1999, Jan. 16, p. 24	Meredith, Neal	The True Will [letter: Agrees with Malim's Jan. 9 article]
2000, May 13, p. 26	Hicks, Brian	Oxford in Italy [letter]
2007, Sept. 22, p. 200	Baker, Simon	Where There's a Will [review of *Shakespeare* by Bill Bryson (2007)
2010, April 3	Hensher, Philip	[review of *Contested Will* by James Shapiro]
2010, April 10	Malim, Richard	The Master of Venice [letter: resp. to Philip Hensher's April 3 review of *Contested Will*]
2013, Nov. 2, p. 13	Waugh, Alexander	Alexander Waugh's Diary: Shakespeare Was a Nom de Plume – Get Over It [William Covell's revelations] [Summary in DVN, vol. 21/1: 18-19 (Jan. 2014)]
2013, Nov. 9	Johnson, Samuel	[letter: response to Alexander Waugh's Nov. 2 Diary]
2023, June 3	Smith, Emma	Shakespeare Sceptics are the New Literary Heroes [review of *Shakespeare Was a Woman* by Elizabeth Winkler]

Spectator, The (Hamilton, Ontario)

2004, Aug. 4, p. G11	Gould, Rachel	Shakedown on Shakespeare: Old Debate Reignited About Who Wrote What
2016, April 11, p. A3	Mahoney, Jeff	Much Ado About Shakespeare's Authenticity [Chris Pannell and Sky Gilbert at Shakespeare's Unorthodox Biography: A Celebration, in Toronto, April 24]

Articles in Non-Oxfordian Periodicals

Spectator USA

2019, May 14	Dominic Green	Was Shakespeare a Woman? Of Course He Was. [resp. to Elizabeth Winkler May 10 piece in the Atlantic]

Speculum

1951, April, vol. 26/2: 364-66	Whiting, B. J.	Historical Novels 1949-1950 [reviews of two authorship novels: Burke Boyce's Oxfordian *Cloak of Folly*, and C. Brahms's & J. Simon's Baconian *No Bed for Bacon*]

Sphere, The (London)

1922, Feb. 25, p. viii	Spalding, Anthony	In Good Queen Bess's Glorious Days"
1923, July 28, p. 118	C. K. S.	"A Literary Letter: "Shakspere" or "Shakespeare"? [full page]
1933, Feb. 4, p. 20-21	--	Elizabethan England Revealed in a Loan Exhibition [portraits loaned by the Duke of Beaufort show Edward de Vere as the Beau Brummel of his age]
1936, April 23, p. 152-53	--	Shakespeare's Handwriting
1954, March 6, p. 327	--	Hackney's Tudor Mansion to be Demolished? [Oxford's residence until his death in 1604]
1955, May 28, p. 38	Fane, Vernon	The World of Books [review of *Who is Shakespeare?* by Hilda Amphlett]
1956, Jan. 28, p. 150	--	New Views on the Bard: Brooke House Could Become Shrine for Newly-Crowned Bard

Spokesman Review

1940, Jan.	--	Painting Hints at Shake-Fraud [re Barrell's *Sci. Am.* piece]

Springfield Republican

1931, April 12, p. 7E	--	[review of *Hidden allusions in Shakespeare's Plays* by Eva Turner Clark]

St. Louis Post Dispatch

1934, Dec. 30, p. 14	Neihardt, John G.	Of Making Many Books [review of *Lord Oxford was Shakespeare* by Col. Montagu W. Douglas]
1939, Dec. 13, p. 23	--	X-Ray Expert Says Shakespeare Portraits are of Earl of Oxford
1953	Derrickson, Howard	[review of *This Star* by Dorothy and Charlton Ogburn]
1953, May 3, p. 4B	Hennings, Thomas C.	A Bard by Any Other Name [letter re *This Star*]
1992, June 29, p. 1D	--	Sorting Out Mysteries Into Three Categories
1992, Dec. 27, p. C4	Rice, Patricia	Identity Crisis; Will the Truth Come to Light? Who Was Shakespeare?
1993, Jan. 16, p. B3	Chapman, L. Edgar	Shakespeare: The Pen or the Pen Name Behind the Work? [letter: Response to Pat. Rice's Dec. 27 article]
1993, July 12, p. 2B	Sexton, Mildred B.	Who's the Bard? [letter: resp. to Patricia Rice's Dec. 27 article] [repr. in SON, vol. 29/3a: 5 (1993)]
2011, Nov. 5	--	St. Louis Experts Don't Consider William Shakespeare Anonymous
2011, Nov. 6, p. D1	Newmark, Judith	Doth the Movie Protest Too Much? St. Louisans Defend Shakespeare Against *Anonymous*

St. Louis Public Library Monthly Bulletin

1920, Oct., vol. 18/10: 248	--	[list of newly acquired books includes *"Shakespeare" Identified*]

St. Petersburg Times

1987, Sept. 26, p. 8A	--	Supreme Court Justices Back the Bard in Authorship 'Trial'
1988, Nov. 27, p. 34A	Wolf, Matt	Judges rule on the Bard: Yes, the Play's His Thing
1992, April 19, p. 7D	Valeo, Tom	A Shadow Shakespeare [review of *The Mysterious William Shakespeare* by Charlton Ogburn]
1992, June 13, p. 3D	Larcen, Donna	Some Things Never Die – Right, Elvis?
1997, July 25, p. 5	Sanchez, Jorge	No Question of Quality of Bard's Plays – Whoever He Is
2003, April 14, p. 1D	Klinkenberg, Jeff	Or Was It Marlowe?
2009, April 1, p. B2	Fleming, John	The Show Must Go On [premiere performance of *Elizabeth and Edward* by Aubrey Hampton, which presentts Edward de Vere as the real author of Shakespeare's plays]

Stage, The (London)

1928, Oct. 11, p. 17	B. E. S. S.	Shakespeare and Chapman [review of a lecture by Percy Allen]
1929, May 23, p. 17	--	Book Chat: "Topical Dramatists" [review of *Shakespeare and Chapman as Topical Dramatists* by Percy Allen (1929)]
1929, May 30, p. 15	Allen, Percy	Topical Dramatists [letter: resp. to May 23 review of *Topical*]
1930, Feb. 27, p. 6	--	Book Chat: De Vere, Not Shakespeare [review of *The Case for Edward de Vere as "Shakespeare"* by Percy Allen]
1931, April 30, p. 15	--	Shakespeare Fellowship [Gerald Rendall proposes toasts to Edward de Vere and William Shakspere at Shakespeare Fellowship dinner. P. Allen and Col. B. R. Ward also spoke.]
1931, April 30, p. 15	Drinkwater, John	The Immortal Memory [letter]
1931, July 16, p. 15	--	Autobiographical Drama [review of talk by Percy Allen]
1952, May 1, p. 13	--	Shakespeare Fellowship [Christmas Humphreys presides over annual dinner]
1959, Feb. 12, p. 17	--	Percy Allen [obituary]
1962, April 19, p. 14	--	Shakespeare Authorship [Authorship Society holds dinner to commemorate 412th anniversary of de Vere's birth]
1977, June 10, p. 9	--	Nothing Truer Than Truth [review of Darrol Blake's play]
2004, Jan. 15, p. 11	--	[review of the play *Return to a Forbidden Planet* by Sally Lewellyn]
2007	Wells, Stanley	[title not known; attack on the the Declaration of Reasonable Doubt]
2008, June	Rylance, Mark	letter: rebuttal to Wells' 2007 article]

Stagebill (Chicago)

1994, Nov. p. 14	Adler, Tony	The Big Whodunnit

Stamford Advocate

1989, July 21	Goldstein, Gary	Shakespeare Sleuths: Will the Real Bard Please Stand Up?

Standard

1911, Feb. 26	--	Fantastic Baconian Treasure Hunt. "Cypher" Hunt
1911, Feb. 27	--	The Bacon Claims
1923, Jan. 25	--	The First Folio: Sir I. Gollancz on The Baconian Theory
1923, Nov. 8	Mair, G. H.	The First Folio Shakespeare

Stanford Report (Stanford University)

2002, Jan. 9	Sanford, John	Panel Featuring Shakespeare Scholars Discusses Whether the Bard Was a Beard

Star-News (Wilmington, NC)

2008, Aug. 12	--	Will the Real William Shakespeare Please Stand Up? [review of *The Beard of Avon* by Amy Freed]
2011, Oct. 23	Steelman, Ben	[review of *Anonymous*]

Star-Tribune – see Minneapolis Star-Tribune

State-Times (Baton-Rouge)

1976, April 23, p. 3B-4B	Woody, Cynthia	Was the Bard Shakespeare or de Vere? [highlights Ruth Loyd Miller and Minos D. Miller]

Statesman, The (New Delhi)

2002, May 3, p. 1	Roy, Amitava	Dialogues: Fitting the Bill
2006, April 22, p. 1	--	The Bastard, Shakespeare!

Strand Magazine

1946, April, vol. 111: 26	Bowen, Marjorie	April 23 Doesn't Impress Me: Why? Because I Don't Believe in Shakespeare [short version repr. in *English Digest*, Sept. 1946] [report in SFQ, vol. 7/4: 71 (October 1946)]

Stratfordshire Evening Sentinal

1937, Jan. 9, p. 5	--	Works of Shakespeare: Newcastle Speaker's Views on Authorship Question
1937, Jan. 26, p. 6	Theobald, Bertram G.	The Authorship of Shakespeare [letter]
1938, Jan. 8, p. 5	--	Shakespeare's Work: Authorship Discussed by Newcastle Speaker

Articles in Non-Oxfordian Periodicals

Strictly Shakespeare: A Newsletter of the Shakespeare Festival of Greater Kansas City

1991, Dec., p. 4	Condon, Joey	Shakespearean Scripture?

Studies in English Literature 1500-1900

1962, vol. 3: 282	Leech, Clifford	[review of *The Shakespeare Claimants* by Harry N. Gibson]
1978, vol. 18: 361-418	Kinney, Arthur F.	[review of *Shakespeare by Hilliard* by Leslie Hotson]
1997, vol. 37: 415-60	Engle, Lars	[review of *Who Wrote Shakespeare?* by John Michell]
1998, vol. 41	Editors, Tom Bethel, and Irvin Matus	Looking for Shakespeare: Two Partisans Explain and Debate the Authorship Question
2005, Winter, vol. 45/1: 268	Guibbory, Achsah	[review of *Monstrous Adversary* by Alan H. Nelson]
2011, Spring, vol. 51: 465	Harris, Jonathan G.	Recent Studies in Tudor and Stuart Drama [notes existence of *Brief Chronicles*]
2014, vol. 54/1: 193-242	Marcus, Leah S.	[review article: includes review of *The Earl of Oxford and the Making of "Shakespeare"* by Richard Malim]

Studies in Philology (Chapel Hill)

1925, April, vol. 22/2: 133-60	Tannenbaum, Samuel A.	Shakspere's Unquestioned Autographs and the Addition to *Sir Thomas More*
1926, vol. 23: 117	Tannenbaum, Samuel A.	A New Study of Shakspere's Will
1926, Oct., vol. 23: 473-76	Greenwood, George	A Reply [to Tannenbaum]
1980, Winter, vol. 77/5: 1-128	May, Steven W.	The Poems of Edward de Vere, Seventeenth Earl of Oxford and of Robert Devereux, Second Earl of Essex
1994, Spring, vol. 91/2: 167	Hammer, Paul	The Earl of Essex, Fulke Greville, and the Employment of Scholars

Sun, The (and Evening Sun) (Baltimore)

1930, July 6, p. H10	--	Shakespeare Plays Credited to Another [reports on the Sh. Fellowship's first annual dinner; mentions remarks by Percy Allen and Canon G. H. Rendall] [perhaps a different *Sun*?]
1939, Dec. 14, p. 14	--	Fuel for a Fresh Shakespearean Squabble
1940, Jan.	--	X-Rays Find Hamlet's Ghost [Barrell's piece in *Scientific Am.*]
1947, June 30, p. 10	--	Again the Question, Who Wrote Shakespeare?
1948, Jan. 12, p. 1	Somerset, Janetta	Drama Critic and Spirits Give New Identity to Shakespeare
1948, July 3, p. 7	Ruth, Robert W.	Libel Suit Rises Out of Who Wrote Shakespeare's Plays
1962, Oct. 11, p. 17	--	Two English Churchmen Reject Bid to Exhume Shakespeare
1987, Sept. 25, p. 3B	--	Justices to Weigh Shakespearean Debate
1987, Sept. 25, p. 11A	Berry, Jason	Sicklied o'er with Contumely [three Supreme Court Justices will hear arguments . . .]
1989, May 30, p. 6A	Cyr, Gordon C.	Shakespeare Never Played the Rose [letter] [repr. in SON, vol. 25/3: 12-13 (Summer, 1989); and in BTC, vol. 6: 406-07]
1990, Nov. 7, p. E13	--	Computer Test Defends Shakespeare
2003, Jan. 2, p. 1C	McCauley, Mary C.	Forever Bound: Books in a Folger Library Exhibit [Highlights de Vere's Geneva Bible]
2004, Oct. 7, p. 3E	Rousuck, J. Wynn	Calling the Bard Into Question
2004, Oct. 9, p. 1D	McCauley, Mary C.	By the Bard? Who Wrote All Those Shakespeare Plays?
2004, Dec. 5, p. 10E	Cole, Diane	Tempest On Avon: Scholars Question and Defend the Identity and Authorship of Shakespeare
2007, May 15	Rasmussen, Frederick N.	Composer, Townson University Professor Took Long, Unconventional Path [Gordon Cyr obituary]

Sun (Sydney, Australia)

1920, May 12, p. 6	--	Hunting for the Bard: Mask of Shakespeare
1920, June 17, p. 8	Herford, Charles H.	Deposed Again: A New "Shakespeare:" Mr. Looney's Discovery [repr. from *Manchester Guardian*, March 19, 1920, p. 7]
1920, June 17	--	[Notice of an Australian edition of SI published by Angus and Robertson]
1920, Dec. 5, p. 22	--	Alias Shakespeare: De Vere Writes *Hamlet*

Sun Sentinel (Fort Lauderdale)

1990, April 1, p. 13F	Kakutani, Michiko	Author Tries to Resolve 'Mystery that was Freud' [repr. from *New York Times* (March 23), p. C33]
1991, Oct. 20, p. 27	Stemle, Lisa	Just Who Really Wrote Shakespeare's Stuff? [review of *All the Queen's Men*, a play by John Nassivere]

Sunday Business Post (Cork)

2010, April 25 — Just Who Was William Shakespeare? [review of *Contested Will* by James Shapiro]

Sunday Herald (Glasgow, Scotland)

2007, Sept. 9, p. 20	Hamilton, James	Actors Aim To Unmask the Bard
2007, Sept. 23, p. 40	Waugh, Alexander	The Name's the Thing [letter: "There is little doubt that 'William Shakespeare' was a pseudonym."]
2012, Nov. 25, p. 3	Duffy, Judith	Shakespeare Was Just a Businessman, Not a Bard

Sunday Independent (Johannesburg)

2011, Nov. 6 — Glorious Fun With Shakespeare [review of *Anonymous*]

Sunday Mercury (Birmingham, UK)

2006, April 2, p. 11 — Reeder, Jackie — Was Earl of Oxford the Real Bard?

Sunday Patriot (Harrisburg, Pa.)

1989, April 16, p. G1 — Johnson, Sharon — Shakespeare Work Still Draws Interest

Sunday Star-Times (Wellington, New Zealand)

2010, April 25, p. C7 — Reid, Nicholas — The Best Will In the World [review of Shapiro's *Contested Will*]

Sunday Sun (Newcastle)

1920-03-07, p. 7 — A Low Fell Author

Sunday Telegraph (London) – see The Telegraph (London)

Sunday Telegraph (Sydney)

2011, Nov. 13, p. 131 — Dent, Nick — A Brilliant Play on History [review of *Anonymous*]

Sunday Times, The (London) (see also The Times)

1920, April 4, p. 5	Minchin, H. C.	Who Was Shakespeare? [review of *SI*]
1920, April 11, p. 5	Johnson, John	"Shakespeare Identified" [letter]
1920, May 7, p. 9	--	Books of the Week [has short description of SI]
1924, July 13	Powell, Dilys	[review of *The Text of Sh.'s Hamlet* by B. A. P. Van Dam]
1928, May 6, p. 8.	Bettany, F. G.	A Favourite of Elizabeth [review of *The Seventeenth Earl of Oxford* by Capt. Bernard M. Ward]
1928, Nov. 4, issue 5510: 14	O'Connor, Hon. T. P.	Sir George Greenwood
1928, Nov. 4, issue 5510: 14	Hirst, W. A.	Sir George Greenwood [letter]
1928, Nov. 4, issue 5510: 14	L.T.G.	The Late Sir George Greenwood [letter]
1930, Feb. 16, p. 11	John Murray (publisher)	Advertisement for *Shakespeare's Sonnets and Edward de Vere* by Gerald Rendall [repeated March 30]
1930, May 4, p. 10	--	The Shakespeare-De Vere Controversy [review of *The Case for Edward de Vere, 17th Earl of Oxford as "Shakespeare"* by Percy Allen (1930)
1930, May 4, p. 10	--	[ad for Rendall's *Shakespeare's Sonnets and Edward de Vere*]
1931, July 12, issue 5648: 16	--	A Beautiful English Village: Lavenham, Suffolk
1932, Sept. 18, p. 21	--	Shakespeare's Rivals: Claims of the 17th Earl of Oxford
1936, Sept. 20	Lucas, Edward V.	A Wanderer's Note-Book: Lavenham
1937, Sept. 12	--	Dr. Hotson's Discovery
1937, Nov. 21, p. 16	Allen, Percy	The 17th Earl of Oxford [letter]
1938, July 31, p. 10	Allen, Percy	Shakespeare and Herbert Lawrence, 1769
1943, July 18, issue 6275: 2	Agate, James	Shakespeare, Bacon, or Both? [review of *Shakespeare: New Views for Old* by R. s. Eagle]
1951, March 4 DVS 030	Hobson, Harold	Blood and Tears
1964, April 5 DVS 064	Cooper, Susan	The Great Detective
1964, April 12	Hotson, Leslie	The Shakespeare Mystery Solved [Sun. Times Mag. cover story]
1964. April 26 DVS 073	--	Hatcliffe Arms: From the Portcullis Pursulvant of Arms
1988. March 6, p. 14	--	Between the Lines [recent Oxfordian news]
1988, Nov. 27, p. 3	Davidson, John	Where There's a Will There's a Moot Point
1989, July 2, p. 2	--	Tuesday [A. L. Rowse and Charles Vere clash on a TV program]
1990, April 22, p. 4E	Bakewell, Joan	Much Ado About Nothing
1990, July 29, p. 2	Storr, Anthony	Freudian Clips
1990, Aug. 12, p. 2	Kaukas, Bernard	What You Will [letter: resp. to Storr's July 29 article]
1992, Jan. 5, p. 5	--	Diary [Charles Vere speaking tour in the U.S.]

1993, April 25, p. 5	Raphael, Frederic	Fifteen Success Stories [review of Michael Hart's *The 100*]
1994, April 17, p. 4	Wells, Stanley	Alias Bacon, Marlowe or the 17th Earl of Oxford? [review of *The Sh. Conspiracy* by Graham Phillips and Martin Keatman]
2000, April 23, p. 39	--	Where There's a Will There's a Website
2002, June 24	Bone, James	Poem Not Shakespeare's After All, Scholar Admits [repr. in DVN (July 2002), p. 5-6]
2003, March 30, p. 41	Wood, Michael	A Whole New Bard Game
2005, Oct. 9, p. 18	Woods, Richard	Is This an Imposter I see Before Me?
2006, April 23, p. 16	Shapiro, James	Happy Birthday, Whoever You Were
2007, August 26, p. 18	Campbell, Jarlath	Doubting the Bard [letter]
2010, March 21, p. 44	Carey, John	Who Was the Real Bard? [review of *Contested Will* by James Shapiro]
2011, Oct. 16, p. 14	Palmer, Martyn	Playing to the Crowd [review of *Anonymous*]
2011, Oct. 30, p. 4	Appleyard, Bryan	Tragedy of Errors [review of *Anonymous*]
2012, Oct. 13	Alberge, Dalya	Zounds! He's Cracked the de Vere Code
2013, June 30, p. 12	Collins, Robert	Love's Labour's Not Lost [review of Ros Barber's dissertation, *The Marlowe Papers*)
2013, Oct. 13, p. 17	--	Zounds! He's Cracked the de Vere Code [Alexander Waugh]
2013, Nov. 13, p. 17	--	Writer [Alexander Waugh] Finds Cryptic Clue to "Real Bard" [summary in DVN, vol. 21/1: 18-19]
2019, Feb. 3	Rylance, Mark	Did Shakespeare Write His Own Plays? That Is the Question

Sunderand Daily Echo and Shipping Gazette (Tyne and Wear, Engand)

| 1920, March 4, p. 4, 5 -- | Who is Shakespeare? | |
| 1950, Dec. 6, p. 5 | -- | It Wasn't the Bard [report on Dorothy Giles Dec. 5 lecture at the Sunderland Literary Club] |

Sussex Agricultural Express (East Sussex, England)

| 1931, Sept. 4, p. 9 | -- | Nonfiction Added in August [P. Allen's *Corroborated* noted] |
| 1952, Dec. 19, p. 9 | -- | Shakespeare or Earl of Oxford? [SF VP T. L. Adamson's lecture ties incidents in Oxford's life to Shakespeare's Plays] |

Sussex County Magazine

| 1930, May | -- | Oxford v. Shakespeare |

Sydney Morning Herald

1921, April 23, p. 12	--	Shakespeare's Birthday [has notice of SI]
1921, July 15, p. 12	Looney, J. Thomas	"Shakespeare's" Identity [response to April 23 article]
1939, June 17, p. 13	Carter, M. J.	Shakespeare [letter]
2001, Oct. 8, p. 20	Dunne, Stephen	Even a Conspiracy Theory Isn't Enough [review of *Shake-speare*, a play about the life of Edward de Vere by Graham Jones and Jepke Goudsmit]

Syracuse New Times

| 2008, April 16, p. 13 | MacKillop, James | Free Willy [review of *The Beard of Avon* by Amy Freed] |

T. P.'s and Cassel's Weekly

| 1928, June 23 | -- | Renaissance Courtier and Patron of Letters [review of *The Seventeenth Earl of Oxford 1550-1604* by Capt. Bernard M. Ward (1928)] [review is quoted in the front of Ward's book] |

Tablet, The

| 1933, Nov. | D. M. | Shake-Spear [review of *Shakespeare, Oxford and Elizabethan Times* by H. H. Holland] |
| 1955, July 9, vol. 206: 33-34 | Dwyer, J. J. | Did Shakespeare Read Dante? A Comparative Enquiry |

Talk of the Trade

| 1990, May 14 | Fleischer, Leonore | [title not known; excerpt repr. in SON, vol. 26/2: 7 (Spring, 1990)] |

Tampa Tribune

| 1997, May 1, p. 1 | Roberts, Edwin A., Jr. | In Search of the Real Shakespeare |

TCA Regional News

2016, Oct. 26	Haflich, Angie	Drama Instructor Pens New Play [review of *Truth; Will Out* by Phil Hoke, which presents Edward de Vere as Shakespeare]
2017, Sept. 7	Kolker, Jeanne	Just Read It [Eddie Nix recommends Mark Anderson's *Shakespeare by Another Name*, Richard Roe's *The Shakespeare Guide to Italy*, and *Shakespeare Beyond Doubt?* edited by John Shahan and Alexander Waugh]

Teacher's College Journal

1941, Sept. 1, vol. 13/1, p. 14	Pfennig, Hazel	Edward de Vere as Patron, 1550-1604

Teatr (Polish)

2011, vol. 4	Dobrowolski, Jacek	Szekspir to nie tylko Marlowe [Sh. Is Not Only Marlowe]

Tehelka (New Delhi)

2010, June 19	--	The Naming of the Bard [review of Shapiro's *Contested Will*]

Telegram & Gazette (Worchester, Mass)

1990, May 21, p. D1	Dempsey, Jim	High Tech Boost for Bard of Avon
1995, Oct. 4, p. 1	Bisol, Anna L.	Was Shakespeare Really Shakespeare? – Lecturer [Grace Cali, SOS Member] Asks Who Wrote Classic Literature]

Telegraph, The (Brisbane, Australia)

1920, May 15, p. 13	Herford, Charles H.	The New Shakespeare [review of SI] [repr. from *Manchester Guardian*, March 19, 1920, p. 7]

Telegraph, The (London) (Includes Daily Telegraph and Sunday Telegraph)

1920, March 19, p. 16.	Courtney, W. L.	Shakespeare Identified [review of Looney's book]
1920, April 1	Looney. J. Thomas	"Shakespeare Identified" [letter]
1928, May 4, p. 6	A. W.	A Forgotten Elizabethan [review of *The Seventeenth Earl of Oxford 1550-1604* by Capt. Bernard M. Ward] [review is quoted in the front of Ward's book]
1929, May 18	Eagle, Roderick	Authorship of the Sonnets and Their Publication
1929, June 5	Allen, Percy	Authorship of the Sonnets [letter: resp. to Eagle]
1930, Nov. 25, p. 14	Dixon-Scott, J.	A Suffolk Tudor Village – Lavenham's Wattle Walls & Lovely Tudor Lavenham
1930, Nov. 26, p. 14	Steed, Wickham	Protecting the Old Church [letter]
1939, June 2	--	New Interest in Old MS
1943, Aug. 24	--	Shakespeare's Signature: Chance Discovery Made in U.S.
1943, Aug. 26	Eagle, Roderick L.	Shakespearean Signatures [letter]
1943, Aug. 28	Eagle, Roderick L.	Shakespeare's Hand [letter]
1950	Holland, Adm. H. H.	The Babington Plot [letter]
1950	Holland, Adm. H. H.	Sgt. Shakespeare [letter]
1950	--	Shakespeare's Rivals: Claims of Earl of Oxford
1950, April	Holland, Adm. H. H.	Shakespeare's Rival [letter]
1950, April,	--	Perturbed Spirit
1954, Feb. 12	Le Riche, Kathleen	Hackney Tudor [letter]
1973, January 26	Rogers, Byron	Bard Thou Never Wert?
1979, Aug. page	Atkins, Harold	Who was the Bard of Avon? [Brunel – SAT 023]
1995, April 9, p. 11	Bate, Jonathan	Snobbish About Shakespeare
1999, Jan. 3, p. 25	--	A Man For All Ages: William Shakespeare
1999, Oct. 27, p. 16	Sparrow, Andrew	Yesterday in Parliament: Earl [Burford] Defends This Sceptered Isle Against the Wolves
1999, Oct. 30, p. 14	Leith, Sam	Theatricals in the Lords Put Bard's Reputation On Line [The Earl of Burford and the authorship societies]
2000, June 7	--	Much Ado as Branagh Sniffs an Interloper
2006, April 23	Shapiro, James	Happy Birthday, whoever You Were
2007, Aug. 4	Rees, Jasper	Call the Real Shakespeare [review of *The Big Secret Live* by Mark Rylance and Matthew Warchus]
2007, Sept. 6, p. 29	Cavendish, Dominic	[review of *The Big Secret Live* by Mark Rylance and Matthew Warchus (2007)]
2007, Sept. 12	Radford, Ceri	RIP William Shakespeare? [Declaration of Reasonable Doubt]
2007, Sept. 16	Toksvig, Sandi	Must Do Better, Mr. Shakespeare
2007, Dec. 10	Pugh, Tom	To Be Or Not To Be: Actors Cast Doubt Over Identity of the Bard

		[Declaration of Reasonable Doubt]
2008, April 21	Malim, Richard C. W.	[letter: Shakspere resided with hatmaker while plays being performed at court, Christmas 1604]
		[repr. in DVN, vol. 15/3: 28 (Oct. 2008)]
2009, June 9	--	Oxford Brag [letter]
2009, Aug. 9	Harrison, David	Tomb's Secrets That Could Solve Mystery of the Real Shakespeare
2009, Nov. 23, p. 3	Hall, Allan	"Strongest Evidence Yet" That Shakespeare is a Sham [review of *The Man Who Invented Shakespeare* by Kurt Kreiler]
2010, March 16	Hannan, Daniel	Who Wrote Shakespeare's Plays? [review of *Contested Will* by James Shapiro]
2010, March 20, p. 20	Noel-Tod, Jeremy	James Shapiro Sheds New Light on Who Wrote Shakespeare's Plays and Makes the Intrigue Irresistible [review of *Contested Will* by James Shapiro]
2010, April 4, p. 25	Bate, Jonathan	The Question of Who Wrote Shakespeare's Plays is Easy to Answer [review of *Contested Will* by James Shapiro]
2010, Aug. 11, p. 25	Cavendish, Dominic	A New Look at the Man from Stratford
2011, Oct. 8, p. 20	Hall, Zoe Dare	Was William Shakespeare Literature's Biggest Fraud? [Charles Beauclerk says yes, Stanley Wells says no] [review of *Anonymous*]
2011, Oct. 15, p. 62-65	Hall, Zoe Dare	Lies and Lust in the Snakepit of Tudor England [review of *Anonymous*]
2011, Oct. 26, p. 22	Massie, Alan	Only Foolish Snobs Don't Believe in Shakespeare [review of *Anonymous*]
2011, Oct. 29, p. 20	--	To Be, or Not To Be, the Bard: Sony's film *Anonymous* Has Sparked Fresh Debate
2011, Nov. 7, p. 30	Spencer, Charles	Geeks, Snobs and a Spurious Controversy [review of *Anonymous*]
2012, May 7, p. 22	Spencer, Charles	Peter Brook Debunks Loony Shakespeare Theory
2012, Dec. 12, p. 24	Langley, William	Ready for the Toughest Role . . . Whoever Wrote It, Derek Jacobi is Ready For It
2013, June 27	Rigden, Kealey	Desmond Elliot Prize 2013: Ros Barber's *The Marlowe Papers*
2014, Sept. 11	--	Shakespearean Academics Clash Over 'Conspiracy Theories' [*Memoria de Shakespeare's* reversal on Richard Waugaman's paper]
2014, Sept. 12, p. 11	Paton, Graeme	Holocaust Jibe Angers Shakespeare Scholar [*Memoria de Shakespeare* editor's unprofessional conduct irks Professor Dr. Richard Waugaman]
2023, May 28	Bate, Jonathan	Was Shakespeare Really a Woman? And Does Taylor Swift Know Him Best?
2023, June 9	Jacobi, Derek & Mark Rylance	The Shakespearean Taboo that Must be Broken [response to Bate's review]
2023.	Winkler, Elizabeth	[letter: response to Bate's review]

Telegraph, The (Calcutta, India)

2014, May 11	--	Talk, Tempest and Tribute

Telegraph Herald (Dubuque, Iowa)

2004, April 18, p. E3	Kauffmann, Bruce	Shakespeare By Any Other Name . . . Most Say He Was Edward de Vere
2011, Nov. 2, p. C1	Noveck, Jocelyn	New Shakespeare Film Ruffles Academic Feathers [review of *Anonymous*]

Temps, Le

1938, March 1	Henriot, Emile	[review of Abel Lefranc's article in the February issue of *Revue Bleue*, "La Question Shakespearienne au XVIII Siècle"]

Tennessee Law Review

2004, Fall, vol. 72/1, p. 1-453	--	Symposium: Who Wrote Shakespeare? An Evidentiary Puzzle [for full contents, see Section IIID]

Theatre and Stage

1934, April, vol. 13: 585-86	Allen, Percy	Topicalities in Shakespeare

Theatre History Studies

2006, vol. 26: 152-54   Schmitt, Juli   [review of *The Case for Shakespeare: The End of the Authorship Question* (2004)]

Theatre Journal

2003, Oct., vol. 55/3: 528-30   Fisher, James   [review of *The Beard of Avon* by Amy Freed (2003)]

TIME Magazine

1960, July 4, p. 60-68, 70-72   --   The Stage: To Man from Mankind's Heart

1999, Feb. 15, vol. 153/6: 74-5   Chua-Eoan, Howard   The Bard's Beard? He's Hot Again, and So Is That Nagging Question: Who Really Wrote Shakespeare?

1999, March 8, p. 16   --   Contenders in the Shakespeare Shake-Out [readers responses to Chua-Eoan's Feb. 15 article]

2007, Sept. 13 Online   Farouky, Jumanta   The Mystery of Shakespeare's Identity

Times, The (London) (see also The Sunday Times

1903, Sept. 8, p. 5   Walters, J. Cuming   The Shakespeare Relics at Stratford

1923, Feb. 6   Lee, Sir Sidney   Shakespeare and Wren

1926, Jan. 18   Lee, Sir Sidney   Shakespeare's Will: Sir Sidney Lee's Comments

1928, Oct. 29   --   Sir George Greenwood

1928, Oct. 30   --   The Late Sir George Greenwood

1930, Sept. 25, p. 757-58   Rendall, Gerald H.   Shakespeare's Handwriting and Orhtography

1931, July 3   --   Shakespeare and a Plagiarist

1931, July 9   --   Notes on Sales

1932, Aug. 26, p. 15   --   Shorter Notices [Clark's introduction to *Shakespeare's Garden* states that "it was through the eyes of Edward de Vere that she [Singleton] visualized the scenes"]

1933, Aug. 31   Spring-Rice, D.   Founders of Lavenham Church [letter]

1933, Sept. 5   Allen, Percy   Founders of Lavenham Church [letter]

1945, Jan 6, p. 6   --   Canon G. H. Rendall [obituary] [notes his vigorous plea for Edward de Vere as Shakespeare]

1954, Jan. 29, p. 3   --   Attempt to Save Brooke House, Hackney [home of Edward de Vere, by the Shakespeare Fellowship]

1962, Aug. 30, p. 11   Carr, Frances   [letter: opening Shakespeare's tomb and the SAQ]

1962, Aug. 30, p. 11   Humphreys, Christmas   [letter: opening Shakespeare's tomb and the SAQ]

1962, Sept. 1, p. 11   Wilson, J. Dover   [letter: opening Shakespeare's tomb and the SAQ]

1962. Sept. 1, p. 11   Hoffmann, Calvin   [letter: opening Shakespeare's tomb and the SAQ]

1962, Sept. 4, p. 11   Eliot, T. S.   [letter: opening Shakespeare's tomb and the SAQ]

1962, Sept. 8, p. 9   Potter, Gillie   [letter: opening Shakespeare's tomb and the SAQ]

1962, Sept. 13, p. 12   --   Open Tomb Action Group Formed

1962, Sept. 14, p. 11   Eliot, T. S.   [letter: opening Shakespeare's tomb and the SAQ]

1962, Sept. 14, p. 11   Wilson, J. Dover   [letter: opening Shakespeare's tomb and the SAQ]

1962, Sept. 15, p. 16   --   Stratford Folk Say: "Leave Him Be"

1962, Sept. 15, p. 11   --   Editorial [closing statement after lengthy exchange of letters]

1964, April 23, p. 6   --   The Poetry Remains

1964, June 17, p. 15   --   Bacon-Shakespeare Manuscripts [search for Shakespeare's manuscripts; de Vere mentioned as possible author] [repr. on July 9, p. 6]

1965, March 27, p. 9   Walshe, W.   Seaman Shakespeare? [letter: Edward de Vere saw action against the Armada]

1965, May 28   Horne, Richard C., Jr.   Shakespeare Portrait X-rayed [repr. in SON, vol. 2/2: 3, 30 (June 1966); and in BTC, vol. 6: 72-74]

1967, April 21, p. 1   Howard, Philip   Silent Guest Among Much Ado [Oxfordians, the St. Albans portrait, and the Shakespearean Authorship Society]

1971, April 24, p. 12   Rowse, A. L.   Shakespeare, the Sexiest Writer in the Language [Shakespeare was "highly, devotedly, passionately heterosexual. . . . In what a marked contrast he stands with those contemporaries of his, Fr. Bacon, Ch. Marlowe, [&] Ed. de Vere, Earl of Oxford"]

1971, April 27, 17   Edwards, Francis   Sh. and His Contemporaries [letter: "Looney must be heard."]

1977, April 13, p. 11   Chaillet, Ned   The Ballad of Aslomon Pavey [passing reference to those viewing

		de Vere as Shakespeare]
1977, May 25, p. 16	Young, John	Is There a New Bard in the House? [Edward de Vere is doubters "least far-fetched candidate"]
1977, May 26, p. 14	--	Entertainments [Notice for *Nothing Truer Than Truth: The Life and Times of Edward de Vere, Sometimes Known as William Sh.* at the Overground Theatre [a play by Darrol Blake]
1983, March 18, p. 14	Howard, Philip	No Mr. Honey, I Am Still Unconvinced
1986, Sept. 24 DVS 009	Berry, Jason	A Playwright by Any Other Name
1987, Sept. 26, p. 5	Binyon, Michael	All's Well That Ends Well as Judges Back Bard
1988, April 21	--	Obituary of E. B. Ford [repr. in DVN, no. 2: 26-27 (April 1988)]
1989, July 4, p. 23	Waymark, Peter	In Search of the Bard [first Tuesday TV program, Enoch Powell leads the case for the doubters]
1991, May 23	--	Whose Shrew? [the Rose Theatre is marketing *The Taming of the Shrew* as by "Edward de Vere"]
1992, March 31, p. 15	--	Bess Unmasked [editorial: analysts have shown first folio portrait resembles Queen Elizabeth more than Shakespeare, de Vere, or other authorship candidates]
1994, Oct. 17, p. 43	Truss, Lynne	Shakespeare, Bard by Appointment To All
1994, Oct. 22, p. 2	Flusfeder, David	Whose Canon Is It Anyway? [review of *Battle of Wills*, BBC 2; Charles De Vere defends Looney's thesis]
1996, April 23, p. 4	Alberge, Dalya	McKellen Scorns Much Literary Ado About Nothing
1996, Nov. 1, p. 20	Levin, Bernard	A Heretic at the Globe
1999, Jan. 27, p. 34	Rosenthal, Daniel	Twelve Great Shakespeare Myths
1999, Nov. 25, p. 28	Kay, Dennis	Comment [mocks Charles Beauclerk's Oxfordian beliefs]
1999, Dec. 2	Dams, Christopher	[letter: resp. to Dennis Kay's article] [repr. in DVN (Jan. 2000), p. 3-6]
1999, Dec. 9	Porter, Brian	[letter: resp. to Christopher Dams' Dec. 2 letter] [repr. in DVN (Jan. 2000), p. 3-6]
2002, March 14, p. 7	Morrison, Richard	Shakespeare – Genius, Blackmailer and All-Round Clever Chap [notes Roger Stritmatter's work tying annotated passages in de Vere's Bible to Shakespeare's plays]
2002, Apr. 26	Nightingale, Benedict	The Bard or Not, Someone Clever Wrote This Play
2003, Sept. 17	--	How Elizabeth's Lover Laid On a Feast Fit for a Queen [repr. in DVN (Sept. 2003), p. 17]
2004, April 25	Rylance, Mark; Bryan	Theatre: Global Domination [interview with Mark Rylance] [repr. in DVN (April 2004), p. 28]
2004, Oct. 22	--	Obituary: Paul Nitze
2004, Nov. 2, p. 66	Malim, Richard	[letter: Paul Nitze was supporter of de Vere's authorship]
2005, June 1, p. 17	--	Smoked Bacon: Shakespeare's Plays Were Written By Another Chap With the Same Name
2005, June 1, p. 20	Malvern, Jack	Class War Over Shakespeare's Identity
2005, June 11, p. 27	Betts, Hannah	Who Says that Rylance is Golden?
2005, Oct. 5, p. 35	--	Academics Split Over Evidence to Suggest New Bard
2005, Oct. 7, p. 24	MacIntyre, Ben	Help, Lasagne's Out To Get Me [Conspiracy theories]
2007, Feb. 28, p. 18	Crick, Jeremy	Ivy the Terrible [letter]
2007, Sept. 1, p. 65	Fitch, Canon J. A.	[letter: passing of Vice-Admiral Sir Ian McGeoch]
2007, Sept. 4, p. 21	Nightengale, Benedict	Stratford Pretender Exposed as Playwright. Should Be Bard; I Am Shakespeare [review of *The Big Secret Live* by Mark Rylance and Matthew Warchus
2007, Sept. 11, p. 17	Aaronovitch, David	What Links Shakespeare and the McCanns? [300 signatories of the 'Declaration of Reasonable Doubt"]
2007, Sept. 12, p. 18	Crick, Jerely	Much Ado About Shakespeare [letter: resp. to David Aaronovitch's Sept. 12 article]
2008, Aug. 8	Malim, Richard C. W.	Shakesper the actor at The Theatre [letter][repr. in DVN, vol. 15/3: 28 (Oct. 2008)]
2009, March 14	Crick, Jeremy	[letter] [repr. in DVN, vol. 16/2: 30 (June 2009)]
2009, Nov. 21	Aaronovitch, David	The Hunting of the Bard—A Fruitless Act
2010, March 16, p. 20	Kamm, Oliver	A Rediscovered Play Adds to the Bard's Shifting Reputation

Times, The (London) (continued)

2010, April 5, p. 2	--	Will Uncontested [editorial: review of *Contested Will* by James Shapiro]
2010, June 24	--	Obituary of Verily Anderson p.t (2015-2010)
2011, June 6	--	Not Anonymous: The True Author of Shakespeare Was the Actor From Stratford [editorial: review of *Anonymous*]
2011, June 6, p. 12	Malvern, Jack	Where There's No Will, Is There a Way? Hollywood is Stage for Battle Over Who Wrote Shakespeare
2011, June 11, p. 93	Kamm, Oliver	The Pendant [review of *Anonymous*]
2011, Oct. 18, p. 19	Blakely Rhys & Ben Hoyle	Shakespeare as U.S. Likes It: Film Credits New Leading Man [review of *Anonymous*]
2011, Oct. 19, p. 19	Kamm, Oliver	This Mix of Crank Conspiracy Theories Should Be Dismissed [Commentary on *Anonymous*]
2011, Oct. 28	Ide, Wendy	Not Half Bard, But Nothing Like the Truth `[review of *Anonymous*]
2011, Nov. 5, p. 105	Kamm, Oliver	The Pendant
2012, April 20, p. 4	Kamm, Oliver	Good Will Hunter [profile of James Shapiro]
2012, May 19, p. 45	Sutherland, John	Was Marlowe the Bard? [review of *The Marlowe Papers: A Novel in Verse* by Ros Barber]
2012, May 19, p. 83	Kamm, Oliver	"Wherever She Went, Including Here . . ." [review of *The Marlowe Papers* by Ros Barber]
2013, April 19, p. 22	Malvern, Jack	Shakespeare Defenders Decide Who Is to Be, and Not To Be [review of *Shakespeare Beyond Doubt* by Paul Edmondson and Stanley Wells]
2014, March 15, p. E7	Miss Manners	Crank Letters Need No Response
2014, Sept. 12, p. 33	Hurst, Greg	Much Ado as Shakespeare Scholars Feud Over Authorship [*Memoria di Shakespeare* rejects paper it had earlier called "absolutely pertinent"]
2016, April 23, p. 40	Kamm, Oliver	Where There's a Will, There's a Wacky Conspiracy Theory
2016, April 27, p. 79	Kamm, Oliver	We Published a Story Last Week
2017, Jan. 2, p. 22	Bate, Jonathan	Shakespeare Study Turns Into a Comedy of Errors

Times Educational Supplement, The

1977, Dec. 30, p. 23	Berry, Ralph	[review of *Shakespeare by Hilliard* by Leslie Hotson]

Times Higher Education Supplement, The

2005, July 22, p. 14	Leahy, William	Bard, By Any Name, Is Still Sweet
2011, Sept 29, issue 2016: 7	Reisz, Matthew	Will's Quill or Not Will's Quill
2014, Sept. 11, issue 2169: 10	Reisz, Matthew	Much Taboo, But Not About Nothing [*Memoria di Shakespeare* rejects a paper by Richard Waugaman that it had previously described as "absolutely pertinent."] See also Comment by Richard Malim, DVN, vol. 2283, p. 41-43 (July 2015).

Times Literary Supplement, The

1916, April 20, issue 744: 181+	Clutton-Brock, Arthur	Shakespeare
1919, Dec. 11, issue 934: 735	--	"Sidelight on Shakespeare and Others" [notes upcoming pub. of SI; first mention of the book in any publication]
1920, March 4, issue 946: 157	--	New Books [list includes *"Shakespeare" Identified*]
1920, March 4, issue 946: 149	Pollard, Alfred W.	"Another 'Identification' of Shakespeare" [review of *"Shakespeare" Identified*] [repr. on March 20, 2020]
1920, March 11, issue 947: 13	--	[Cecil Palmer Ad for *'Shakespeare" Identified*]
1920, March 25, issue 949: 201	Looney, J. Thomas	*"Shakespeare" Identified* [letter: resp. to Pollard's March 4 rev.]
1920, May 13, issue 956: 289	Murry, John Middleton	The Function of Criticism
1920, May 20, issue 957: 322	--	[ad for *The Bookman's Journal* states that "this week's contents include "Shakespeare's Identity' with articles by Sir Sidney Lee, Rt. Hon. J. M. Robertson, and Mr. J. T. Looney]
1920, Dec. 9, issue 986: 832	--	[Cecil Palmer Ad for *"Shakespeare" Identified*]
1921, Feb. 24, issue 997: 128	--	[review of *The Poems of Edward de Vere* edited by Looney]
1921, June 2, issue 1011: 345+	Murry, John M.	Hamlet and History
1921, Dec. 15, issue 1039: 841	Clutton-Brock, Arthur	[review of *Will Shakespeare: An Invention in Four Acts* by Clemmence Dane]

1922, Jan. 12, issue 1043: 28	Greenwood, Sir George	Mary Fitton [letter responding to Clutton Brock's Dec. 15 review]
1922, Jan. 26, issue 1045: 60	Poel, William	Shakespeare: A Standard Text [letter]
1923, April 12, is. 1108: 248-50	--	[review of *The Mystery of "Mr. W. H".* by Col. B. R. Ward]
1923, May 24, issue 1114: 355	Ward, B. R.	[letter: The Mystery of Mr. W. H.]
1923, June 7, issue 1116: 389	--	[review of *Shakespeare Through Oxford Glasses* by Hubert Holland]
1924, Oct. 30, issue 1189: 682	Child, Harold H.	Shakespeare's Handwriting [review of *The Shakespeare Signatures and "Sir Thomas More"* by George Greenwood]
1924, Nov. 6, issue 1190: 709	Greenwood, Sir George	The Shakspere Signatures and "Sir Thomas More [letter: Greenwood response to the Oct. 30 review]
1925, Jan. 22, issue 1201: 56	Fort, J. A.	The Shakespeare Signatures [letter]
1925, Jan. 22, issue 1201: 56	Simpson, H. Derwernt	The Shakespeare Signatures [letter]
1926, June 10, issue 1271: 391	Child, Harold H.	[review of *A Hundreth Sundrie Flowres* by George Gascoigne, edited by Bernard M. Ward]
1926, July 8, issue 1275: 464	--	Le Mystere Shakespearien [review of *Le Mystere Shakespearien*] by Georges Connes]
1927, June 2, issue 1322: 388	--	The Real Falstaff? [review of *The Falstaff Saga* by John Dawtrey]
1927, July 7. issue 1327: 472	Greenwood, George	Le Mystere Sakespearien [review of *Le Mystere Shakespearien* by Georges Connes]
1927, July 28, issue 1330: 520	Connes, Georges	Le Mystere Shakespearien [letter: resp. to Greenwood, July 7 rev.]
1927, Nov. 20	--	[review of *The Shakespeare Mystery* by Georges Connes]
1928, April 5, issue 1366: 255	Eliot, T. S.	Poet's Borrowings [review of *Shakespeare, Jonson, and Wilkins as Borrowers* by Percy Allen (1928)
1928, May 17, issue 1372: 379	Greenwood, Sir George	Shakespeare's "purge" of Jonson [letter]
1928, June 21, issue 1377: 461	Reed, Arthuryes	Edward de Vere, Earl of Oxford [review of *The Seventeenth Earl of Oxford* by Bernard. M. Ward]
1928, June 28, issue: 1378: 486	Ward, Capt. Bernard M.	Edward de Vere [letter: response to Arthur Reed's review of *The Seventeenth Earl of Oxford*]
1928, July 5, issue 1379: 504	--	Edward de Vere [letter: Reviewer's reply to Ward's response to his review]
1928, Aug. 2, issue 1383: 568	Ward, Capt. Bernard M.	Edward de Vere [letter: response to Arthur Reed] [See W. W. Gregg's response to Ward's letter in the Jan. 1929 *Modern Language Review*.]
1928, Aug. 30, issue 1387: 609	Greg, W. W.	Fulke Greville, Lord Brooke
1928, Sept. 6, issue 1388: 632	Ward, Capt. Bernard M.	Fulke Greville, Lord Brooke [letter: response to Greg]
1928, Sept. 13, issue 1388: 648	Greg, W. W.	Fulke Greville, Lord Brooke [letter: reply to Ward]
1928, Sept. 20, issue 1390: 667	Ward, Capt. Bernard M.	Fulke Greville, Lord Brooke [letter: response to Greg]
1928, Sept. 27, issue 1391: 687	Greg, W. W.	Fulke Greville, Lord Brooke [letter: reply to Ward]
1928, Oct. 4, issue 1392: 710	Ward, Capt. Bernard M.	Fulke Greville, Lord Brooke [letter: response to Greg]
1928, Nov. 29, issue 1400: 938	Harrison, G. B.	The Mortal Moon [letter]
1929, Feb. 7, issue 1410: 98	Allen, Percy	Elizabeth and Essex [letter]
1929, Mar. 21, issue 1416: 229	Byrne, Muriel St. Clare	Shakespeare and Chapman [review of *Shakespeare and Chapman as Topical Dramatists* by Percy Allen
1929, Mar. 28, issue 1417: 260	Allen, Percy	Shakespeare and Chapman [letter: long response to the March 21 review]
1929, April 4, issue 1418: 276	Allen, Percy	Shakespeare and Chapman [letter: additional comments on the March 21 review]
1929, Aug. 22, issue 1468: 650	--	Dickson [review of Marjorie Bowen's novel]
1929, Sept. 5, issue 1440: 684	Bowen, Marjorie	Dickson [letter: response to the review]
1929, Sept. 12, issue 1441: 705	Allen, Percy	Shakespeare and Chapman [comments on a review of Chapman's play *The Tragedy of Byron*]
1929, Sept. 19, issue 1442: 723	Ferguson, A. S.	Shakespeare and Chapman [reply to Allen's Sept. 12 letter]
1929, Sept. 26, issue 1443: 741	Byrne, Muriel C.	Stuart Politics in Chapman [review of *Stuart Politics in Chapman's Tragedy of Chabot* by Norma D. Solve]
1929, Sept. 26, issue 1443: 746	Allen, Percy	Shakespeare and Chapman [letter: response to A. S. Ferguson's Sept. 19 review of "*Borrowers*"]
1929, Nov. 28, issue 1452: 996	Hawyard, John D.	The Symbolists [brief review of *Shakespeare's Sonnets and Edward de Vere* by Gerald Rendall (1930)

Times Literary Supplement, The (continued)

1930, Feb. 20, issue 1464: 146 --		[review of *The Case for Edward de Vere as 'Shakespeare'* by Percy Allen (1930)] [the review is of the booklet, not the book; ad for it is nearby]
1930, Feb. 27, issue 1465: 158 --		[John Murray Company ad includes Rendall's *Shakespeare's Sonnets and Edward de Vere*]
1930, Mar. 20, issue 1468: 253 --		Cecil Palmer New non-Fiction [ad for *The Case for Edward de Vere as Shakespeare* by Percy Allen]
1930, May 22, issue 1477:430	Byrne, Muriel C.	De Vere and the Sonnets [review of *Shakespeare's Sonnets and Edward de Vere* by Gerald Rendall
1930, May 29, issue 1478: 457+	Rendall, Gerald H.	Shakespeare Sonnets and Edward de Vere [letter: response to Muriel Byrne's review of "*Shakespeare's Sonnets*"]
1930, Sept. 11, issue 1493: 712	Byrne, Muriel C.	Oxford as Shakespeare [review of *The Case for Edward de Vere as "Shakespeare"* by Percy Allen (1930)]
1930, Sept. 18, issue 1494: 735	Allen, Percy	Oxford as 'Shakespeare' [letter: response to Muriel Byrne's Sept. 11 review of "*The Case*"]
1930, Sept. 25, issue 1495: 757	Rendall, Gerald	Shakespeare's Handwriting and Orthography [response to Muriel Byrne's Sept. 11 review of "*The Case*"]
1930, Nov. 13, issue 1502: 939	Harrison, G. B.	Shakespeare's Topical Significances I: King John
1930, Nov. 20, issue 1503: 974	Harrison, G. B.	Shakespeare's Topical Significances II: Earl of Essex
1931, March 19, issue 1520: 233 --		Cecil Palmer Spring 1931 [ad includes title and brief description of Eva Turner Clark's *Shakespeare's Plays in the Order of Their Writing*; Percy Allen's *The Oxford-Shakespeare Case Corroborated*; Gerald Rendall's *Shakespeare—Handwriting & Spelling*; and W. Lansdown Goldsworthy's *Ben Jonson and the First Folio*]
1931, May 28, issue 1530: 440 --		Shakespeare's Plays [review of *Shakespeare's Plays in the Order of Their Writing* by Eva Turner Clark]
1931, June 4, issue 1531: 446	Gregg. W. W.	Tudor Handwriting [review of *Shake-speare: Handwriting and Spelling* by Gerald Rendall]
1931, Oct. 15, issue 1550: 802	Harrison, G. B.	Shakespeare, Essex and *Richard the Second* [letter]
1931, Dec. 10, issue 1558: 1006	Palk, Robert	Shakespeare, Essex and *Richard the Second* [letter]
1931, Dec. 31, issue 1561: 1053	Ward, Col. Bernard R.	Shakespeare, Essex and Richard II
1932, Jan. 14, issue 1563: 29 --		[reviews of *Exit Shakspere* by BertramTheobald (1931); *The Earl of Oxford as Shakespeare* by Montagu Douglas (1931); *Seven Shakespeares* by Gilbert Slater (1931); *Edward De Vere* by George Frisbee (1931); *The Oxford-Shakespeare Case Corroborated* by Percy Allen (1931); and *Shakespeare Authorship* by Gilbert Standen (1930)]
1932, April 7, issue: 1575: 18	Frisbee, George	The Imperial Throne [letter: North was a pen name adopted by de Vere translated Plutarch]
1932, June 23, i. 1586: 462, 492	Clutton-Brock, Arthur	Edward de Vere [review of *The Tragic Story of Shakespeare* by Gerard Phillips (1932) and *The Life Story of Edward de Vere as "William Shakespeare"* by Percy Allen (1932)]
1932, June 23, issue 1586: 465 --		New Books [incl. two books that Clutton-Brock reviews nearby]
1932, June 30, issue 1587: 480	Allen, Percy	Edward de Vere [letter: resp. to Clutton-Brock's June 23 reviews]
1933, May 4, issue 1631: 312	Thomas, Henry	Shakespeare Emendations [letter]
1933, Aug. 3, issue 1644: 522	Child, Harold H.	History and Plays [review of *French History* by Percy Allen]
1933, Aug. 10, issue 1645: 537	Allen, Percy	History and Plays [letter: resp. to Harold Child's Aug. 3 review]
1933, Nov. 16, issue 1659: 798 --		[review of *Elizabethan Times* by Hubert Holland (1933)]
1933, Nov. 30, issue 1661: 856	Harrison, G. B.	These Late Eclipses [letter]
1933, Dec. 7, issue 1662: 878	Ward, Capt. Bernard M.	These Late Eclipses [letter]
1933, Dec. 14, issue 1663: 896	Collins, D. C.	These Late Eclipses [letter]
1933, Dec. 14, issue 1663: 896	Harrison, G. B.	These Late Eclipses [letter]
1933, Dec. 21, issue 1664: 909	Ward, Capt. Bernard M.	These Late Eclipses [letter]
1934, Jan. 4, issue 1666: 12	Collins, D. C.	These Late Eclipses [letter]
1934, Jan. 4, issue 1666: 12	Ward, Capt. Bernard M.	These Late Eclipses [letter]
1934, Jan. 4, issue 1666: 12	Holland, H. H.	These Late Eclipses [letter]
1934, Jan. 4, issue 1666: 12	Harrison, G. B.	These Late Eclipses [letter]

1934, Jan. 4, issue 1666: 12	Editor	Editor's Note: These Late Eclipses
1934, Jan. 25, issue 1669: 60	Chambers, E. K.	The 'Mortal Moon' Sonnet [letter]
1934, Feb. 1, issue 1670: 76	Harrison, G. B.	The 'Mortal Moon' Sonnet [letter]
1934, Feb. 1, issue 1670: 76	Chambers, E. K.	The 'Mortal Moon' Sonnet [letter: correction]
1934, Feb. 8, issue 1671: 92	Ward, Capt. Bernard M.	The 'Mortal Moon' Sonnet [letter]
1934, Feb. 15, issue 1672: 108	Fort, J. A.	The 'Mortal Moon' Sonnet [letter]
1934, Feb. 15, issue 1672: 108	C. W. B.	Ducdame, Ducdame [letter]
1934, Feb. 15, issue 1672: 108	Eccles, Mark	The 'Mortal Moon' Sonnet [letter]
1934, Feb. 22, issue 1673: 126	Fort, J. A.	The 'Mortal Moon' Sonnet [letter]
1934, Feb. 22, issue 1673: 126	Allen, Percy	Ducdame, Ducdame [letter]
1934, March 1, issue 1674: 144	Mutschmann, M.	The 'Mortal Moon' Sonnet [letter]
1934, March 1, issue 1674: 144	Ward, Capt. Bernard M.	The 'Mortal Moon' Sonnet [letter]
1934, March 8, issue 1675: 162	Fort, J. A.	The 'Mortal Moon' Sonnet [letter]
1934, March 8, issue 1675: 162	Allen, Percy	The "Mortal Moon" Sonnet [letter: Cleopatra and the Dark Lady, "both are Elizabeth"]
1934, March 15, issue 1676: 194	Fort, J. A.	The 'Mortal Moon' Sonnet [letter]
1934, March 15, issue 1676: 194	Rendall, Gerald	The 'Mortal Moon' Sonnet [letter]
1934, March 22, issue 1677: 214	Fort, J. A.	The 'Mortal Moon' Sonnet [letter]
1934, April 19, issue 1681: 282	Ward, Bernard M.	The Mortal Moon Sonnet [letters]
1934, April 19, issue 1681: 282	Fort, J. A.	The Mortal Moon Sonnet [letters]
1934, April 19, issue 1681: 282	Rendall, Gerald	The Mortal Moon Sonnet [letters]
1934, April 19, issue 1681: 282:	Editor	Editor's Note: The 'Mortal Moon' Sonnet
1934, May 3, issue 1683: 321	Tomlinson, Philip	Bottom's Dream [review of *Anne Cecil, Elizabeth and Oxford* by Percy Allen (1934)]
1934, May 10, issue 1684: 342	Allen, Percy	Elizabeth, Anne Cecil, and Oxford [letter: resp. to Philip Tomlinson's May 3 review of *Anne Cecil*]
1934, July 26, iss. 1695: 517-18	Eliot, T. S.	John Marston
1935, Jan. 24, issue 1721: 50	--	[review of *Lord Oxford Was "Shakespeare"* rev. ed., by Col. Montagu Douglas]
1935, Mar. 28, issue 1730: 203	Child, Harold H.	Oxford's Sonnets [review of *Personal Clues in Shakespeare Poems and Sonnets* by Gerald H. Rendall and *Sunlight on Shakespeare's Sonnets* by Gerald Phillips (1935)]
1935, Sept. 19, issue 1775: 580	Lawrence, W. J.	The Original Staging of *Romeo and Juliet*, Act III, Sc. V
1935, Oct. 3, issue 1757: 612	Allen, Percy	Lord Oxford as Shakespeare [letter: response to W. J. Lawrence
1935, Oct. 10, issue 1758: 617	Child, Harold H.	What Happens in *Hamlet* [review of the book by J. Dover Wilson]
1936, Feb. 8, issue 1775: 116	Allen, Percy	Thomas Sackville [letter]
1936, May 2, issue 1787: 379	Greg, W. W.	Stage or Study? [letter]
1936, May 9, issue 1788: 400	Allen, Percy	Stage or Study? [letter: response to Greg: *Hamlet*, Q2, supports de Vere's authorship"]
1936, May 16, issue 1789: 420	Schucking, Levin L.	Stage of Study? [letter]
1936, June 6, issue 1792: 480	Griffin, W. J.	Names in *The Winter's Tale* [letter]
1936, July 18, issue 1798: 600	Allen, Percy	Names in *The Winter's Tale* [letter: response to W. J. Griffin's June 6 letter]
1936, Dec. 19, issue 1820: 1053	--	[review of *The Problem of Hamlet* by Dr. A. S. Cairncross]
1937, Jan. 2, issue 1822: 12	Allen, Percy	The Date of *Hamlet* [letter: response to review of Cairncross] [repr. in SFE, no. 2 (March 1937): 9-10]
1937, Jan. 9, issue 1823: 28	Cairncross, A. S.	Hamlet Problems [letter: response to a Percy Allen's Jan. 2 letter] [repr. in SFE, no. 2 (March 1937): 8-9]
1937, Sept. 18, issue 1859: 675	Allen, Percy	Montaigne and *Twelfth Night* [letter]
1939, June 3, issue 1948: 327	Chambers, R. W.	Shakespeare and "More" [letter]
1947, Sept. 27, issue 2382: 498	--	[review of *Edward de Vere, The Real Shakespeare* by William Kent (1947)]
1951, Dec. 7, issue 2601: 793	--	[review of *Shakespeare's Farewell* by G. Bowen]
1956, July 6, issue 2836: 410	--	[review of *Shakespeare's Magic Circle* by A. J. Evans]
1959, Sept. 25, issue 3004: 547	Brown, Ivor	Borrowed Plumes [review of *The Poacher from Stratford* by Frank W. Wadsworth] [temperate overview of doubters]
1962, July 27, issue 3152: 542	Alexander, Peter	Who Was Shakespeare? [reviews of *The Shakespeare Claimants* by Harry N. Gibson and *The Authorship of Shakespeare* by James McManaway]

Times Literary Supplement, The (continued)

1964, April 23, issue 3243: 358	Crow, John	Heretics Observed
1964, Sept. 24, issue 3265: 886	Curtis, Myra	Author! Author? [letter: evidence is "quantitatively slight"]
1969, Jan. 30., issue 3492: 108	--	Commentary [Freud's Oxfordian views]
1969, Feb. 27, issue 3496: 210	Kanter, Victor	Freud and Shakespeare [letter: resp. to Jan. 30 review of his paper]
1976, July 4, issue 3873: 667	Padel, John	An Analyst at Elsinore [review of *Hamlet's Enemy* by Theodore Lidz] [mentions all three editions of *"Shakespeare" Identified* by J. T. Looney]
1977, Oct. 28, issue 3944: 1261	Schoenbaum, S.	[review of *Shakespeare By Hilliard* by Leslie Hotson]
1983, May 13, issue 4180: 484	Collinson, Patrick	Outsize Egos [review of *Eminent Elizabethans* by A. L. Rowse (1983)
1990, April 20, issue 4542: 418	Woudhuysen, H. R.	A Freudian Oxfordian [repr. in SON, vol. 26/2: 7 (Spring 1990)]
1990, July 6, issue 4553: 725	Rycroft, Charles	Freud's Best Face [review of *Reading Freud: Explorations and Entertainments* by Peter Gay]
1993, Feb. 12, issue 4689: 12	Bate, Jonathan	The Bard for All Causes
2003, Sept. 26, issue 5243: 14	Wells, Stanley	Shakespeare's First Critic [William Scott [1579-?)] [repr. in DVN (Sept. 2003), p. 16-17]
2004, May 28, issue 5278: 32	--	Shakespearean Authorship Trust [notice for event chaired by Mark Rylance, with Charles Beauclerk and others]
2005, Feb. 4, issue 5314: 3	Fowler, Alastair	Enter Speed [Shakespeare Fantasies] [review of *Will in the World: How Shakespeare Became Shakespeare* by Stephen Greenblatt (2004)] [repr. in DVN (May 2005), p. 23-38; excerpt repr. in NSJ, vol. 11: 179-81 (April 2007)]]
2005, Aug. 19, issue 5342: 6-8	Vickers, Brian	Idle Worship [review of *Great Oxford* edited by Richard Malim, *The Case for Shakespeare* by Scott McCrea, *Hamlet by Christopher Marlowe and William Shakespeare* edited by Alex Jack, and *The Shakespeare Enigma* by Peter Dawkins][repr. in DVN (Sept. 2005), p. 40-43]
2005, Nov. 25, issue 5355: 28	Nelson, Alan H.	[review of *The Truth Will Out* by Brenda James and William D. Rubenstein]
2006, Jan. 27, issue 5365: 30	Nelson, Alan H.	Variations on Looney Tunes [review of *"Shakespeare" by Another Name* by Mark Anderson (2005)]
2006, June 2, issue 5383: 17	Bewley, Dorna	Hamlets vs. hamlettes [letter] [repr. in DVN (Feb. 2007), p. 22-23]
2006, Aug. 18, issue 5394: 16	Vickers, Brian	The Face of the Bard?
2007, Oct. 5, issue 5453: 26	Craik, Katherine	[letter: review of Bill Bryson's *Shakespeare*]
2007, Nov. 17, issue 5407: 17	McGeoch, Ian	[letter: de Vere as another Shakespeare collaborator?] [repr. in DVN (Feb. 2007), p. 22]
2010, April 23, issue 5586: 3-4	Nicholl, Charles	Full Circle [review of *Contested Will: Who Wrote Shakespeare?* by James Shapiro (2010)]
2010, May 7, issue 5588: 6	Draya, Ren	[letter: response to Charles Nicholl's review of*Contested Will* by James Shapiro (2010)]
2010, June 25, issue 5595: 14	Caines, Michael	Unbaken or Shaken: How the Bacon Society Hoped to Unearth a 400-Year Old Proof of Authorship
2010, Aug. 13, issue 5602: 12	Wells, Stanley	Poured Over Again [review of *Shakespeare and His Authors* edited by William Leahy]
2011, Mar. 18, issue 5633: 11	Lynch, Jack	This Our Life [reviews of *Shakespeare and Biography* by David Bevington, *Shakespeare as a Challenge for Literary Biography* by Arthur Maltby, and *Sidney Lee* by Marvin Spevack]
2012, Aug. 10, issue 5706: 11	MacDonald, Russ	A Refitted Stage
2013, July 12, issue 5754: 24	--	[review of *Shakespeare Beyond Doubt* edited by Paul Edmonson and Stanley Wells]
2013, Dec. 6, issue 5775: 23	Shakespeare Authorship Coalition (SAC)	[full page advertisement challenging The Shakespeare Birthplace Trust to prove before "a panel of neutral judges" that Shakspere wrote Shakespeare's plays]
2013, Dec. 6, issue 5775: 25	Shakespeare Authorship Coalition (SAC)	[full page ad for *Shakespeare Beyond Doubt?*, ed. by John Shahan]
2013, Dec. 13, issue 5776: 6	Vickers, Brian	[letter: response to the SAC's challenge] [repr. in DVS, vol. 21/2: 41 (May 2014)]

2020, March 20, issue 6103	Pollard, Alfred W.	Another "Identification" of Shakespeare [review of *"Shakespeare" Identified*] [repr. from March 4, 1920]

Times of Acadiana
1986, Sept. 24, p. 20-22	Berry, Jason	A Playwright by Any Other Name [Lord Vere & Ruth L. Miller]

Times of India (Bombay)
1920, May 26, p. 11	--	The Latest Shakespeare [review of *"Shakespeare" Identified*]
1931, Jan. 21, p. 15	--	That Old Topic [review of *Shakespeare Authorship* by Gilbert Standen]
1931, Feb. 25, p. 5	--	Who Wrote Shakespeare? [review of *The Case for Edward de Vere as Shakespeare* by Percy Allen]

Times Picayune – see New Orleans Times Picayune

Tomorrow
1946, Feb.	Barrell, Charles Wisner	Verifying the Secret History of *Shake-speare's Sonnets*, Part 1 [prospectus for his book about Anne Vavasour and her son, Edward Vere, slated for publication in 1946 but never published; see SFQ, Oct. 1945] [repr. in BTC, vol. 4: 345-59]
1946, March	Barrell, Charles Wisner	Verifying the Secret History of *Shake-speare's Sonnets*,Part 2 [repr. in BTC, vol. 4: 345-59]

Topičův Sbornik Literárni Aumělecky
1921, Dec., vol. 9: 138-39	--	Shakespeare, Bacon, Rutland et Co! [in Czech]

Toronto Star
1986, April 2, p. F3	--	Scholars Question Bard's Real Identity
1987, Oct. 4, p. A23	--	Justices Rule that Shakespeare Did Write the Plays
1988, Nov. 1, p. F2	--	TV Trial Looks at Bard's Authenticity [three Law Lords in London to preside]
1988, Nov. 26, p. A23	--	What's In a Name, as Bard Goes on Trial
1988, Nov. 27, p. F5	--	Judges to Decide Whether Nobleman Was Immortal Bard
1988, Nov. 28, p. C4	--	U.K. Judges Decide in Favor of Shakespeare
1989, April 8, p. M6	Stuewe, Paul	Is He or Is He Ain't Our One and Only [review of *The Mystery of William Shakespeare* by Charlton Ogburn]
1989, June 3, p. M23	Hill, Carl	Was Will's Will Wilful?
1991, Oct. 5, p. F5	Blackadar, Bruce	[refers to Tom Bethel and *The Atlantic*]
1999, March 27, p. 1	--	This Much Ado Adds More to Harper's
2002, Nov. 22, p. E13	Ouzounian, Richard	Rotten Fruit Hurled at Poor Will [review of *The Beard of Avon* by Amy Freed]
2004, Aug. 7, p. J2	Gould, Rachel	The Shakespeare Enigma Won't Die
2007, Sept. 16, p. D1	Hurst, Lynda	We Have Nothing Against the Man from Stratford, But . . .
2010, May 9, p. 6	Werner, Hans	Will the Real Will Please Stand Up? [review of *Contested Will* by James Shapiro]
2011, Oct. 28, p. E5	Howell, Peter	To Be Or Not To Believe [review of *Anonymous*]

Touchstone [A Chronicle published in cooperation with the Shakespearean Authorship Trust]
1982, May, vol. 1/1	Russell, Clifford W. [editor][not yet indexed]	

Town Talk
1920, Sept. 4, p. 8	--	Another Shakespearean Claimant [review of SI]

Transactions of the Bibliographical Society, New Series [see The Library]
1926, Dec. vol. VII, no. 3: 269-82Greg, W. W.		[review of *A Hundreth Sundry Flowres* edited by Capt. Bernard M. Ward] [repr. as a pamphlet]]SAT 053]

Transactions of the Royal Historical Society
1949	Hurstfield, Joel	Lord Burghley as Master of the Court of Wards (1949) [repr. in TOX, vol. 3: 99-115 (2000)]

Triad (Australia)
1920, Oct. 11, p. 37	--	Shakespeare, Bacon, Oxford [repr. from *Literary Digest*]

The Triangle of Mu Phi Epsilon
2007, April, vol. 101/1: 6	Christopher Wang	Musicological Research: *Ever Trvely a Mvsician—Connections Between Edward de Vere and the Development of English Madrigals*

Tribune, The (San Diego)

1987, Sept. 26, p. A3	Meinert, Don	Bard at Center Stage in Debate; Justices 'Rule' Shakespeare's Work Authentic

Tribune de Geneva, La

1938, Feb. 1	--	Report on a lecture of SF member Charles Boissevain at the Lyceum de Suisse, Geneva

Truth, The

1935, Feb. 6, p. 234	--	In Vere Veritas [review of Douglas's *Lord Oxford was Shakespeare*]
1948, Sept. 24, p. 312	--	Wilhelmina Shakespeare [review of *The Inspiration of Shakespeare* by H. S. Lawrence and T. M. Aitken]
1949, April 29	Kent, William	My War with the Professors
1951, April 27, p. 432	Brophy, John	The Personality of Shakespeare
1951, May 4, p. 477	Kent, William	Mr. John Brophy and Shakespeare [letter]
1951, May 11, p. 508	Eagle, Roderick L.	The Personality of Shakespeare [letter]
1951, May 11, p. 509-09	Le Riche, Kathleen	The Personality of Shakespeare [letter]
1951, May 18, p. 533	Holton, E. Gibbs	Mr. Brophy and Shakespeare [letter]
1951, May 18, p. 533	Beesley, F.	Mr. Brophy and Shakespeare [letter]
1951, May 25, p. 559	Brophy, John	Mr. Brophy and Shakespeare [letter]
1951, June 1, p. 589	Neilson, Francis	Mr. Brophy and Shakespeare [letter]
1951, June 1, p. 589-90	Kent, William	Mr. Brophy and Shakespeare [letter]
1951, June 8, p. 620	Kent, William	Mr. Brophy and Shakespeare [letter]
1951, June 8, p. 620	Beesley, F.	Mr. Brophy and Shakespeare [letter]
1951, June 29, p. 695-96	Le Riche, Kathleen	The Personality of Shakespeare [letter]
1951, Oct. 5, p. 365	Editor and Kent	Who Was Shakespeare?
1952, Jan. 25, p. 106	--	Cecil Palmer [obituary]
1952, June 27, p. 708-09	--	The Identity of Shakespeare [review of *Lord Oxford and the Shakespeare Group* by Col. Montagu Douglas]
1952, Sept. 19, p. 292	Lamb, V. B.	Cecil Palmer [letter]
1954, March 19, p. 378	Evans, B. Ifor	Shakespearian Mysteries and Shakespearian Critics [review of *This Star of England* by Dorothy & Charlton Ogburn]

Unisa English Studies

1991, vol. 29/1: 62-63	Simpson, Mary-Helen	[review of *The Mysterious William Shakespeare* by Charlton Ogburn, Jr. (1992)]

Universe

1933, Nov.	--	Shakespeare, Oxford & Elizabethan Times [review of the book by Adm. H. H. Holland]

University of Miami Law Review

2003, Jan., vol. 57/3	Regnier, Thomas	Could Shakespeare Think Like a Lawyer? How Inheritance Law issues in *Hamlet* May Shed Light on the Authorship Question [repr. in *Sh. and the Law* (Stritmatter, 2022): 187-230]

University of Pennsylvania Law Review

1992, April, vol. 140/4: 1373+	Stevens, John Paul	The Shakespeare Canon of Statutory Construction [repr. in ER, vol. 1: 4-20 (Spring 1993); in EVR, vol. 1 (Fall 1995); in BTC, vol. 8: 129-44; and in SAL (Stritmatter, 2022): 103-13]

University Players News

1999/2000 Winter, no. 28	Stedman, Nina	Prinzessin Shakespeare [repr. in NSJ, vol. 5: 142-49]

US Fed News Service

2007, Sept. 17	--	Washington State University Professor Takes 'Heretical' View of Shakespeare Authorship Question [profile of Michael Delahoyde]
2010, March 4	--	New York Actor and Author to Uncover *Shake-speare's Treason* at Flathead Valley Community College [Hank Whittemore to perform his one-man play]

U.S. News & World Report

2000, July 24, vol. 129/4: 71-72	Satchell, Michael	Hunting for Good Will: Will the Real Shakespeare Please Stand Up?

USA Today

1987, Sept. 28, p. 1D	Gottlieb, Jane	Bard Beats the Rap
1997, Dec. 9, page 9D	Hainer, Cathy	Solving the Puzzle of Shakespeare's Identity
2011, Oct. 27	Puente, Maria	Who Wrote Shakespeare?
2011, Oct. 27	Puig, Claudia	'Anonymous' is Shakespeare, Writ Small

Valley Advocate (Springfield, MA

1994, March 10	Anderson, Mark K.	Editorial [the case for Edward de Vere] [repr. in EVR, vol. 1 (Fall 1995)]
1999, July 17	Anderson, Mark K.	*Thomas of Woodstock*—Prequel to *Richard II*?[repr. in SON, vol. 35/2: 4 (Sum. 1999); in EVR, vol. 10 (Spr. 2000); and in BTC, vol. 8: 114]

Vancouver Sun

1940, July 28, p. 4	Carter, Joseph	Shakespeare Identified as Earl of Oxford
1987, Sept. 26, p. A1	--	Doubts Over Bard Ruled Much Ado About Nothing
1988, Nov. 26, p. E9	Wolf, Matt	Mock Trial to Settle Dispute Over Shakespeare
1989, April 18, p. B5	Riches, Hester	Much Ado About Shakespeare
1998, March 7, page C11	Wasserman, Jerry	Shakespeare, Our Contemporary [reviews of *The Genius of Shakespeare* by Jonathan Bate (1998) and *Alias Shakespeare* by Joseph Sobran (1997)]
2009, Aug. 10, p. B3	Harrison, David	Stone Tomb May Hold Secret to Shakespeare
2011, Oct. 29, p. C5	Wogan, Terry	Why Do They Keep Trotting Out This Looney Idea About the Bard?

Variety (Los Angeles)

1950, Nov. 8, V. 196: 69	Scully, Frank	Scully's Scrapbook [Notice of second edition of SI]
2003, Nov. 24-30, p. 43	Stasio, Marilyn	The Beard of Avon [review of Amy Freed's play]

Ventura Country Magazine

1987	Hanson, David J.	The Shakespearean Conspiracy [exc. repr. as 'Who Cares Who Wrote Them?' in SON, vol. 23/3: 10-11 (Summer 1987)]

Village

1948, May 27	--	Authority Talks on Shakespeare [Barrell lawsuit]

Village Voice

2001, Jan. 23	Winter, Jessica	Scrawler I.D.: A Literary Detective Shakes Speares at Hidden Authors
2010, June 16-22, p. 34	Feingold, Michael	Farewell, Fair Incredulity! [review of *Contested Will* by James Shapiro]
2023, June 13	Londré, Felicia	The Lady Doth Protest Too Much for Traditionalists [review of *Shakespeare Was a Woman* by Elizabeth Winkler]

Villager, The

Winter 1945-46	Olds, Nathaniel S.	Revisions May Have to be Made in English Literature Textbooks [repr. in SFQ, vol. VII/1: 13 (1946)]

Virginia Lawyer

1993, vol. 42/1: 54	Harrison, John E.	[review of *The Mysterious William Shakespeare*]

Virginia Quarterly

1953, Spring, vol. 29/2	--	[review of *This Star of England* by Dorothy and Charlton Ogburn]
1959, Spring, vol. 35/2: 289-303		Wright, Louis B.The Anti-Shakespeare Industry and the Growth of Cults [repr. in *We Write for Our Own Time* edited by Alexander Burnham. Charlottesville: University of Virginia Press, 2000, p. 105-15.]

Wall Street Journal

1953, Feb. 11, p. 12	Editorial	Tis Neither Here Nor There [review of *This Star of England* by Dorothy and Charlton Ogburn]
1988, May 31	Cusick, John	[letter: Cynthia Crossen omitted Samuel Clemens and Edward de Vere]
1997, April 28, p. 31-34	Cantor, Paul A.	[review of *Alias Shakespeare* by Joseph Sobran (1997)]
1997, May 1, p. A16	Bate, Jonathan	Bard Beyond Belief [review of *Alias Shakespeare* by Joseph Sobran (1997)]

Wall Street Journal (continued)

1997, May 15, p. A23	Holtz, Nancy Ann	A Shakespeare by Any Other Name . . . [letter: response to Bate]
1997, May 15, p. A23	Sullivan, Patrick R.	A Shakespeare by Any Other Name . . . [letter: response to Bate]
1997, May 15, p. A23	Sobran, Joseph	A Shakespeare by Any Other Name . . . [letter: response to Bate; The sonnets are "an eerily accurate description of Oxford, the fate of his works, and his centuries of oblivion"]
1997, June 10, p. A19	Hughes, R. C.	From Nowhere, A Genius For All Time [letter]
1997, June 10, p. A19	Irwin, Anna	From Nowhere, A Genius For All Time [letter: resp. to Sobran]]
1999, March 26, p. W2	Costello, Daniel	Poetic License
2009, Apr. 18, p. A1-2	Bravin, Jess	Justice Stevens Renders an Opinion on Who Wrote Shakespeare's Plays
2009, April 25, p. A10	Elmore, David	A Word in Your Ear: Was the Bard an Oxford Man? [letter: response to Justice Stevens]
2009, April 25, p. A10	Dawson, Paul	A Word in Your Ear: Was the Bard an Oxford Man? [letter: response to Justice Stevens]
2009, April 25, p. A10	Hogan, Martha Kurtz	A Word in Your Ear: Was the Bard an Oxford Man? [letter: response to Justice Stevens]
2009, April 25, p. A10	Dellinger, Royal S.	A Word in Your Ear: Was the Bard an Oxford Man? [letter: response to Justice Stevens]
2009, April 25, p. A10	Stromenger, Lela	A Word in Your Ear: Was the Bard an Oxford Man? [letter: response to Justice Stevens]
2010, April 1 (Online)	--	[review of *Contested Will* by James Shapiro]
2010, April 2, p. W4	Alter, Alexandra	The Shakespeare Whodunit: A Scholar Tackles Doubters on Who Wrote the Plays [Interview with James Shapiro]
2010, April 8, p. A19	Rosenberg, Saul	About an Author Much Ado [review of *Contested Will* by James Shapiro
2010, April 9, p. W12	Alexandra, Alter	The Plays the Thing – Shakespeare Still Has His Doubters [review of *Contested Will: Who Wrote Shakespeare?* by James Shapiro]
2010, April 17, p. W14	Teachout, Terry	Sightings: Denying Shakespeare
2010, May 6, p. A18	Blair, James	[letter: response to Teachout's article]
2011, April 2, p. W4	Alter, Alexandra	Just Asking: Hollywood Weighs In [review of *Anonymous*]
2011, April 16	Sacks, Sam	Out of the Miasma of Bardolatry, a Masterpiece
2011, Oct. 28, p. D3	Morgenstern, Joe	*Anonymous* Is Much Ado About Nothing
2011, Oct. 28, p. D3	Espinoza, Javier	Actor Rafe Spall Stars in a New Role as Dad [review of *Anonymous*]
2011, Oct. 29, p. C2	Orloff, John	Why I Played With Shakespeare's Story: *Anonymous*
2014, April 19, p. C13	Myers, Marc	Photographer William Wegman on Composer William Byrd

Wanderer

2005, Sept. 29	Sobran, Joseph	Shakespeare, and the Catholic Question

Warwick and Warwickshire Advertiser

1920, April 24, p. 7	--	Shakespeare Festival [Notes and dismisses authorship challenges from Derby and Oxford]

Warwick Valley Dispatch

1946, Jan. 30	Webster, Lewis H.	Those Authorities [repr. in SFQ, vol. VII/1: 12 (Jan. 1946); and in BTC, vol. 3: 238-240]
1974, June 26	--	[obituary of Charles Barrell]

Washington Monthly

1999, May	--	Tilting at Windmills
1999, Sept., p. 3	Hovey, J. Allan	False Bard [letter: response to May article]

Washington Post (includes Washington Post Book World)

1924, March 10, p. 6	--	A New Rival to Shakespeare [review of *The Mask of Shakespeare* by Abel Lefranc]
1928, July 1, p. S9	--	Terse Reviews of Latest Books [review of *The Seventeenth Earl of Oxford* by Bernard M. Ward]
1928, Nov. 15, p. 6	--	A Noted Baconian [Obituary of Sir George Greenwood]
1933, Aug. 6, p. 6	Dodge, Arthur J.	The Shakespeare "Mystery"
1933, Oct. 31, p. 6	Dodge, Arthur J.	More of the Shakespeare "Mystery" – Claim that Edward de Vere

		Was Author of Plays [letter]
1934, April 24, p. 8	--	By Any Other Name
1937, Dec. 10, p. 13	Waldron, John	"Shakspeare" vs. "Shakespeare" [review of *The Man Who Was Shakespeare* by Eva Turner Clark]
1948, Jan. 5, p. 9	--	Shakespeare Had Aides, 'Spirits' Say
1948, July 2, p. 1	--	Shakespeare Plays Basis of Libel Suit: $50,000 Libel Suit Filed [By Charles Barrell]
1948, July 3, p. B1	Grove, Lee	"Shakespeare" Just Pen Name of Oxford Earl, Barrell Says
1948, July 10, p. 4	--	Who Wrote That?
1948, July 14, p. 10	Tilghman, Harrison	[letter: response to "Who Wrote That?"]
1948, July 15, p. 10	Wooley, Robert W.	[letter: response to "Who Wrote That?"]
1948, July 25, p. B4	Puck	Who Was Shakespeare? A Communication
1948, July 31, p. 5	Burgess, Gelett	Oxford Is Shakespeare: A Communication [long rebuttal to critics of idea de Vere was Shakespeare]
1948, Aug. 3, p. 10	Moore, Harvey T.; Barbara Joe Henderson	Memos to Mr. Burgess
1948, Aug. 4, p. 12	Skovar, I.P.	Shakespeareski [letter]
1948, Aug. 8, p. B4	Mumpsimum	Who Was Shakespeare? [letter: resp. to Gelett Burgess]
1948, Aug. 9, p. 6	Wilcox, E. V.	Who Was Shakespeare? [letter: response to Gelett Burgess]
1948, Aug. 9, p. 6	Kerr, T. M., Jr.	Who Was Shakespeare? [letter: response to Gelett Burgess]
1948, Aug. 10, p. 10	Spiggonio, Antonio	Shakespeare Solved [letter: response to Gelett Burgess]
1949, June 22, p. B1	--	Shakespeare Dispute Letter Studied by Judge for Libel
1956, Jan. 9, p. 18	Sullivan, Leo	Expert Hits Shakespeare Conjecture [Louis B. Wright]
1956, May 4, p. 20	--	The Sands of Time
1956, May 11, p. 26	Ogburn, Charlton, Jr.	The Sands of Time [letter: resp. to the May 4 article]
1956, June 3, p. E4	Nashe, T.	Sands of Time [letter: support for Ogburn's May 11 letter]
1959, Apr. 26, p. E1	Wright, Louis B.	Never Say Die Is Anti-Avon Watchword
1959, May 16, p. 10	Ogburn, Charlton, Sr.	[letter: response to Louis B. Wright]
1959, May 20, p. A16	Wright, Louis B.	[letter: reply to responses to his article]
1959, May 21, p. 22	Ogburn, Charlton	Was it Shakespeare? [letter]
1959, May 31, p. E4	Borkin, Joseph	Humbug at Avon? [letter: criticism of Wright]
1959, June 1, p. A14	R. D. R.	Bard and Bar [letter: Support for Wright, criticism of Ogburn]
1959, June 8, p. A12	Greenleaf, Marian Y.	[letter: doubts about Will are justified]
1962, May 27, p. E4	--	Sheik of Stratford [editorial]
1962, Aug. 26, p. G6	Culligan, Glendy	Shakespeare (?) Is Back [review of *Shake-speare: The Real Man Behind the Name* by Charlton Ogburn, Jr.
1962, Sept. 14, p. A14	Brooks, Helen E.	The Truth Is Out! [letter: regrets that the *Post* wasted space to review Ogburn's book]
1964, Apr. 26, p. B9	--	No Mystery About Bard, Expert [Giles E. Dawson] Says
1964, May 3, p. E6	Ogburn, Charlton, Jr.	[letter: Challenge to Giles E. Dawson]
1964, May 15	Dawson, Giles E.	Into Round 401 [letter: response to Ogburn's letter]
1964, May 27, p. A24	Ogburn, Charlton, Jr.	"Will-o'-the-Wisp" [letter: response to Dawson's May 27 letter]
1964, June 9, p. A14	Dawson, Giles E.	"Will-o'-the-Wisp" [letter: reply to Ogburn; portraits of Oxford and Shakespeare]
1965, Feb. 17, p. B7	--	Shakespeare Disputant [obit. of Francis T. Carmody (1909-1965)]
1966, Apr. 22, p. B18	--	Oxfordian Author [Gertrude C. Ford] To Speak
1968, June 23, p. E1	Folliard, Edward T.	Shakespeare's Man: Folger Library's Dr. Wright Leaving Behind Dump-the-Bard Cult
1968, July 3, p. A20	Ogburn, Charlton, Jr.	Who Wrote Those Plays? [letter: response to Folliard's June 23 article on Louis B. Wright]
1970, Sept. 6, p. 9	Ogburn, Charlton, Jr.	Shakespeare, Who He? [letter: challenges Quinn's June 21 assertion that "a creative writer's life need have little to do with his work"]
1970, Sept. 6, p. 9	Quinn, Edward	Shakespeare, Who He? [letter: response to Ogburn's Sept. 6 letter]
1970, Dec. 13, p. 12	Ogburn, Charlton, Jr.	Shaksper [letter: response to Edward Quinn's letter]
1971, July 29, p. G1	Burchard, Hank	Charlton Ogburn: Spaceship Earth's Happy Prisoner [very long and favorable profile of Charlton Ogburn]
1973, Aug. 5, p. BW8	Ogburn, Charlton, Jr.	What's in a Name [review of *Shakespeare the Man* by A. L. Rowse]

1973, Oct. 19, p. B10	Ogburn, Charlton, Jr.	A Shakespeare Who Never Comes to Life [review of *You, My Brother* by Philip Burton]
1974, Nov. 24, p. B1	Ogburn, Charlton, Jr.	The Man Shakespeare Was Not . . . And Who He Was [repr. from *Harvard Magazine* (Nov. 1974)]
1974, Nov. 30, p. A11	Klay, Andor	Something From Nothing [letter: Ogburn's Nov. 24 article]
1974, Dec. 8, p. B3	Hardison, O. B., Jr.	Shakespeare: Was He Shakespeare?
1984, April 29, p. SM22	Wallah, Janet	The Art, Music and Money of David Lloyd Kreeger
1985, Feb. 3, p. TV11	--	Notice about *Firing Line*: "The Mysterious William Shakespeare" [Guests are author Charlton Ogburn and Rutgers Professor Maurice Charney]
1987, May	Johnson, Morse	[letter: Droeshout engraving]
1987, Sept. 26, p. B1	Sanchez, Rene	All's Well in Shakespeare's Day in Court
1987, Oct. 14, p. A19	Schwartz, Amy E.	Three Justices, a Poetry-Starved Crowd and Shakespeare
1987, Oct. 24, p. A19	Holden, Constance	No One Knows if Shakespeare Wrote the Plays [response to Amy Schwartz's Oct. 14 article][repr. in SON, vol. 23/4: 8-9 (Fall 1987)]
1988, June 3, p. D8	Baily, Moira	When Only no. 2 Will Do
1988, Nov. 23, p. A1	Conroy, Sarah B.	[David L. Kreeger, Oxfordian, to attend debate in London]
1989, March 6	Mackey, Aurora	Shakespeare's 'Outstanding' Medical Knowledge[repr. in SON, vol. 25/2: 17-19 (Spring 1989)]
1989, Apr. 21, p. C2	Mitchell, Henry	Shakespeare and the Will of the World
1989, Sept. 18, p. B4	Boyd, Bentley	The Bard: Oxford Earl or 'the Stratford Man'?
1990, April 17, p. D5	Oldenburg, Don	Shakespeare, By Any Other Name? Professor Samuel Schoenbaum Recants [repr. in SON, v. 26/4: 8-9 (Fall 1990)]
1990, April 21, p. C3	Miller, Michael	Computer Test Authenticates Shakespeare
1990, Nov. 20, p. A1	Barnes, Bart	Geico Chairman David L. Kreeger Dies
1990, Dec. 18, p. B5	Oldenburg, Don	Sequel; Beating Up on the Bard; Oxfordians: Out, Out Damned Will
1992, Jan. 19, p. M5	Gardner, Martin	William Shakespeare: by Divers Hands [review of *Shakespeare's Lives, New Edition* by S. Schoenbaum]
1992, Feb. 14, p. N67	Burchard, Hank	Undercover Temptation
1992, March 8, p. 14	Taylor, Thomas	Will the Real . . . [letter: response to Gardner]
1992, March 8, p. 14	Gardner, Martin	[letter: reply to Thomas Taylor]
1992, April 12, p. 14	Ogburn, Charlton, Jr.	More on the Stratford Man [letter: response to Martin Gardner]
1994, April 1, p. D5	Achenbach, Joel	The Hole Thingy? Go Figure
1994, May 7	Stritmatter, Roger	The Bard and the Nonbelievers [repr. in SON, vol. 30/3a: 6 (Summer 1994)]
1994, May 17	Oldenburg, Don	Shakespeare's Raging Identity Crisis [repr. in SON, vol. 30/2a: 2 (Spring 1994)]
1994, May 27, p. D5	Achenbach, Joel	The Alien Notion: Why Do Some People Think They've Been Abducted by Aliens From Space?
1994, Oct. 30, p. G2	Oldenburg, Don	A Lingering Shakespearean Drama [Double page spread with favorable coverage of Charles Vere lecture at the Smithsonian that evening]
1996, Aug. 4, p. F1	Farquhar, Michael	Mysteries of the Millennium SOLVED!
1997, Aug. 17, p. I11	Dickson, Peter W.	Unmaking the Bard [reviews of *Who Wrote Shakespeare?* by John Michell; *Shakespeare – Who Was He?* and *Alias Shakespeare* by Joseph Sobran
1997, Aug. 23, p. TV36	Brennan, Patricia	On Shakespeare and Cadfael [profile of Derek Jacobi]
1998, Oct. 22, p. D6	--	Charlton Ogburn Dies at 87; State Department Official, Writer
1999, Jan. 24, p. F1, F4	Oldenburg, Don	Shakespeare in Trouble: Who Was Will Shakespeare? And Why is Peter Dickson Saying Such Terrible Things About Him?
1999, Jan. 30, p. A17	--	Op-Ed: A Bard, By Any Other Name
1999, Jan. 30, p. A17	Monk, Linda R.	A Bard By Any Other Name [letter: response to Don Oldenburg]
1999, Jan. 30, p. A17	Conner, Fran	A Bard By Any Other Name [letter: response to Don Oldenburg]
1999, Jan. 30, p. A17	Halio, Jay L.	A Bard By Any Other Name [letter: response to Don Oldenburg]
1999, Feb. 6, p. A19	Dickson, Peter W.	The Man Behind the Curtain [letter: response to Fran Conner]
1999, Feb. 20, p. A17	Gonzales, Jack	Tips for 'The Tempest' [letter: response to Peter Dickson]

1999, March 21, p. B7	Ignatius, David	Honor the True Bard [Edward de Vere]
1999, April 3, p. A13	Vartanoff, Irene	Working-Class Wit [letter: response to David Ignatius]
1999, April 10, p. A19	Bethell, Tom	Studious, Not Snobbish
1999, June 13, p. M9	McMahon, Daniel	Bard Watching [rev. of *The Late Mr. Shakespeare* by Robert Nye]
1999, Sept. 12, p. P7	Dickson, Peter W.	Expert's Picks
2003, Dec. 4, p. WBK4	Matus, Irvin	Good Will Hunting: A Biography and a Novel Wrestle With Some Big Questions About the Bard [reviews of *Shakespeare* by Michael Wood and *Chasing Shakespeares* by Sarah Smith
2004, June 25, p. C8	Wardell, Jane	Society Marks Death of 'True Shakespeare' [repr. in SON, vol. 40/3: 8 (Summer 2004)
2005, Oct. 21, p. T26	Talcott, Christina	Will the Real 'Beard of Avon' Please Stand Up? [review of *The Beard of Avon* by Amy Freed]
2005, Oct. 25, p. C1	Marks, Peter	Rorschach's 'Beard' Playfully Tweaks the Bard
2007, March 18, Outlook B1, 5	Wells, Stanley	There's No Doubt It's Will [repr. in SAS (Stritmatter 2019, 2022): 221-26]
2007, March 18, Outlook B1, 5	Stritmatter, Roger	Is This the Bard We See Before Us? Or Someone Else? [repr. in SAS (Stritmatter 2019, 2022): 221-26]
2007, March 18, Outlook	Hughes, Stephanie H.	Four Hundred Years of Stonewalling [response to Stanley Wells] [repr. in SM, vol. 6/4: 6, 13-17 (Sum. 2007)]
2009, April 18	--	Justice Stevens Renders an Opinion on Who Wrote Shakespeare's Plays
2010, June 6, p. B6	Rose, Lloyd	Pretenders to the Playwright's Pen [review of *Contested Will: Who Wrote Shakespeare?* by James Shapiro]
2010, Oct. 3, p. C6	Schudel, Matt	Hard-line Commentator [Obituary of Joseph Sobran]
2011, March 6, p. C7	Schudel, Matt	Unpaid Shakespeare Scholar Lived by His Own Design [Irvin Matus]
2011, Oct. 31	Charles, Ron	The Playwright's the Thing – No Question About It
2011, Nov. 5, p. A13	Keiler, Jonathan F.	[letter: response to Ron Charles]
2013, Oct. 5, p. C14	Heilpern, John	Thoughts on Shakespeare from the Most Influential Living Director [review of *The Quality of Mercy* by Peter Brook]
2014, March 6	Miss Manners	Crank Letters need No Response [Dear Miss Manners: Must an English Department Secretary Defend Shakespearean Authorship to Conspiracy Theorists?]
2014, April 6, blog post	Charles, Ron	The Justice doth Protest too Much, Methinks [reply to John Shahan's response)
2023, April 21	Dirda, Michael	As We Honor Shake., Scholars Respond to Questions About Him
2023, May 27	Waugaman, Elisabeth	To Question, or Not to Question? There is No Question [letters]

Washington Square News

1989	Goldstein, Gary B.	"The Shakespeare Mystery" Unfolds [review of the *Frontline* Broadcast] [repr. in SON, vol. 25/2: 10-11 (Spring, 1989)]

Washington Star, The (and Washington Sunday Star and Daily News)

1962	McHugh, F. D.	'Curst Be He That Moves My Bones' [letter]
1962, Aug. 26	Thorpe, Day	New Shakespeare Controversy
1966	Ogburn, Charlton, Jr.	[review of *Was Shakespeare Shakespeare?* by Milward W. Martin[[See comments by Charlton Ogburn in SON, Vol, 2/1: 2-3 (March 30, 1966)]
1972, Dec. 3, p. 3	Thorpe, Day	Does the Folger Want the Truth About Shakespeare? [repr. in SON, vol. 9/1: 1-2 (Winter 1973)]
1972, Dec. 17	Hardison, O. B., Jr.	[letter: response to Day Thorpe's Dec. 3 question] [repr. in SON, vol. 9/1: 3, Winter 1973)]
1980, April 11	Bell, James H.	Orwell and Oxford [letter][repr. in SON, vol. 16/1: 12, Winter 1980)

Washington Times

1985, Feb. 21	Sobran, Joseph	[review of *The Mysterious William Shakespeare*]
1986, Nov. 4	Editor	Mr. Keegor Is More Likely to Pull it Off than Most People [Upcoming mock trial at American University] [repr. in SON, vol. 22/4: 10]
1988, Dec. 30	Sobran, Joseph	Shakespeare's Aristocratic Origin

Washington Times (continued)

1990, Nov. 20	Sobran, Joseph	Against Funding Odds [repr. in SON, vol. 27/1: 4 (Winter 1991)]
1997, April 25, p. 12	Arnold, Gary	Much Ado About Shakespearean Actor [Derek Jacobi is "very beguiled by the Earl of Oxford theory."]
2006, June 21	Rutledge, Josh	A Bard by Any Other Sex . . . [review of *Sweet Swan of Avon: Did a Woman Write Shakespeare?* by Robin P. Williams (2006)] [repr. in DVN (July 2006)]
2011, Nov. 2, p. B10	Flamini, Roland	Was Shakespeare a Fraud? To Be or Not To Be . . . [review of *Anonymous*]

Weekend Review

1933, Nov.	--	Shakespeare, Oxford and Elizabethan [sum. of Holland's book]

Weekly Dispatch [In 1928, became the Sunday Disatch, which in 1961 merged with the Sunday Express]

1920	--	[Cecil Palmer says (in SFE (March 1952, p. 4) that the first review of SI appeared here]
1920, March 14, p. 16	--	[picture of Edward de Vere and notice of publication of SI]

Weekly Standard

2004, Feb. 16, p. 37	Dickson, Peter	The Roman Plays [review of Michael Wood's BBC Documentary *In Search of Shakespeare*]
2010, Aug. 23, p. 30-32	Simon, John	No Mystery Here [review of *Contested Will* by James Shapiro]
2014, March 17, p. 38-39	Mattix, Micah	Bard of Honor [review of *Shakespeare Beyond Doubt* by Paul Edmondson and Stanley Wells]

West Coast Review of Books

1985, vol. 11/2: 33	Jonas, Larry	[review of *The Mysterious William Shakespeare* by Charlton Ogburn, Jr. (1992)]

Western Daily Press and Bristol Mirror (Bristol)

1920, Sept. 2, p. 6	--	Books Worth Reading [*SI* is on the list]
1936, Jan. 6, p. 5	--	Shakespeare v. Bacon. Desire of Fame or Money? Unlikely that Either Wrote the Masterpieces!
1936, Jan. 6, p. 5	Theobald, Bertram C.	Exact Motives of Writing [letter]
1936, Jan. 6, p. 5	Haines, C. M.	Possibly Neither Wrote the Plays [letter]
1936, Jan. 6, p. 5	G. W. S.	Talent and Diligence [letter]
1936, Jan. 6, p. 5	Habgood, Francis E. C.	Answer to Messrs. Gill and Severn [letter]
2011, Oct. 28, p. 18	Griffin, Susan	Squabbling Scholars Make a Crisis Out of a Dramatist

Western Mail (Cardiff)

1920, April 23, p. 7	C.B.	Shakespeare's Identity: A New Theory of a Very Entertaining Subject [review of SI]
1920, May 6, p. 7	Looney, J. Thomas	Shakespeare's Identity: Case for Lord Oxford [letter: response to the April 23 review]
2011, Oct. 19, p. 3	Turner, Helen	Prince [Charles] Joins Campaign Over Shakespeare Literary 'Scam' [review of *Anonymous*]

Western Morning News and Mercury (Devon, England)

1928, Jan. 2, p. 11	--	The Shakespeare Mystery [review of *The Shakespeare Mystery* by Georges Connes]
1928, April 30, p. 2	C. H.	17th Earl of Oxford: Political History of Period of Queen Eliabeth [review of Ward's book]
1929, Feb. 16, p. 6	--	New Books [Allen's *Shakespeare and Chapman* is on the list]
1929, March 25, p. 3	--	[review of *Topical Dramatists* by Percy Allen (1929)]
1929, Dec. 12, p. 1	--	Playgoers' Circle for Plymouth [Percy Allen listed first on Inaugural Meeting list of speakers]
1929, Dec. 16, p. 5	--	Playgoers' Circle for Plymouth [Summary of a lecture by Percy Allen: "The Old Drama and the New." First mention of Allen's *Case,* to be published early in 1930.]
1930, April 10, p. 8	--	New Book List [On the list is Percy Allen's *The Case for Edward de Vere, 17th Earl of Oxford, as Shakespeare*]
1930, Sept. 5, p. 6	Wright, B. D.	"Shakespeare" Myth Theories That Fail to Impress (review of *The Case for Edward de Vere, Seventeenth Earl of Oxford, as Shakespeare* by Percy Allen (1930)

1930, Oct. 8, p. 4	--	Playgoers' Circle Plymouth [Percy Allen to speak in upcoming lecture series; mentions *The Case for Edward de Vere*]
1931, Jan. 5, p. 4	--	Playgoer's Circle at Plymouth [Mr. Allen's Address Last Night]
1931, Jan. 28, p. 8	--	Community Drama [Percy Allen will serve as Adjudicator of performances]
1931, Jan. 30, p. 1	--	Notice [Percy Allen to Give Feb. 3 Lecture on Edward de Vere, Earl of Oxford, as Shakespeare]
1931, Feb. 2, p. 3	--	High Praise for Amateurs [from Adjudicator Percy Allen]
1931, Feb. 4, p. 5	--	Who Was William Shakespeare? [report on Percy Allen's lecture "The Case for Edward de Vere as Shakespeare"]
1931, March 26, p. 6	--	New Books [Percy Allen's *Corroborated* is on the list]
1931, Aug. 24, p. 2	C. E. L.	Was It Shakespeare? (review of *Shake-speare; Handwriting and Spelling* by Gerald H. Rendall
1931, Sept. 26, p. 8	--	[review of *The Earl of Oxford as "Shakespeare"* by Montagu W. Douglas (1931)]
1931, Dec. 16, p. 3	--	An Elizabethan Colossus [review of *Edward de Vere* by George Frisbee (1931)]
1932, Jan. 11, p. 2	--	The Stratford Maze: Was 'Shakespeare' A Group of Writers? [review of *Seven Shakespeares* by Gilbert Slater (1931) and *The Earl of Oxford as Shakespeare* by Montagu W. Douglas]
1932, Oct. 31, p. 3	--	Who was Shakespeare? [review of a lecture by Percy Allen]
1933, Oct. 20, p. 4	--	Books Received [Holland's *Shakespeare, Oxford and Elizabethan Times* is on the list]
1933, Oct. 24, p. 4	G. S. (G. E. T. S.)	Books of Today [review of *Shakespeare, Oxford, and Elizabethan Times* by Hubert H. Holland (1933)]
1935, Feb. 18, p. 2	--	Blue-Blooded Poet? Did Shakespeare Write Shakespeare? [review of *Personal Clues in Shakespeares Poems and Sonnets* by Gerald Rendall]
1937, April 20, p. 3	Hony, T. H. L.	Bacon or Shakespeare? [letter: Will Percy Allen reply to Mr. Theobald?]
1937, April 20, p. 3	Cooke, Dorian	Bacon or Shakespeare? [letter] [see Percy Allen's response on April 28]
1937, April 28, p. 11	Allen, Percy	Was Oxford Shakespeare? [letter: response to Dorian Cook]
1937, May 3, p. 2	G. E. T. S.	[letter: He knows he wrote the plays—it wasn't the man from Stratford or Lord Oxford—but won't tell us until his research is finished]
1937, May 8, p. 13	Hony, T. H. L.	"Shakespeare" Fellowship? [letter: Shakespeare Fellowship is a misnomer.]
1938, Oct. 6, p. 1	--	Huquenot Society of London [Percy Allen to speak in upcoming lecture series]
1939, July 15, p. 13	Hony, T. H. L.	Oxford or Bacon? [letter: Percy Allen is "the great protagonist of the Oxfordian cause"]
1947, May 1, p. 2	--	Shakespeare Claim [*The Real Shakespeare*, an interesting booklet, published by The Shakespeare Fellowship]

Westminster Gazette

1920, May 22, p. 6	--	[ad for the *Bookman's Journal & Print Collector's* special "Shakespeare's Identity" May 20th issue]

WGBH Magazine (Boston)

1989, April, p. 8-9	Austin, Al	Who Wrote Shakespeare?

Wiener Zeitung

2000, Feb. 25	Dickenburger, Udo	[review of *Hrotsvith von Gandersheim* by Alfred Tamerl (1999)] [repr. in NSJ, vol. 5: 150-52 (April 2000)]

Wilson Quarterly

1992, Winter, p. 150	--	The Plays' the Thing [response to "Looking For Shake- speare" articles in the *Atlantic Monthly* (Oct. 1991)]

Windsor Star (Windsor, Ont.)

1944, April 28	--	Shakespeare's Ghosts
1990, Nov. 3, p. C12	--	[Stylometrics supports Shakespeare]
2002, Aug. 10, p. F1	Taube, Michael	Was He or Was He Not Shakespeare?

Winnipeg Free Press

2010, April 21, p. A11	Dudley, Michael	Goodbye, Bard of Avon [letter: response to James Shapiro's April 20 op-ed "Alas, Poor Shakespeare"]
2010, May 15, p. H7	Dudley, Michael	Out, Damned Skeptics, Author Fills in Blanks with Stratfordian Doctrine [review of *Contested Will* by James Shapiro]

Wisconsin State Journal

2014, Aug. 31, p. E5	Kolker, Jeanne	Shakespeare Skeptics Make Much Ado in Madison [The SOF Conference & an interview with Eddie Nix]

World, The

1920	George, W. L.	[review of *"Shakespeare" Identified*]

Yale Review (YAL)

1931, Autumn, vol. 21: 215	Tucker, Brooke	[review of *Hidden Allusions in Sh.'s Plays* by Eva Turner Clark]

Yankee

1997, vol. 62/9: 35	Romeo, Richard	The Bard of Cuttyhunk?
2002, vol. 66/3: 18	Clark, Tim	The Bard on the Cape

Yarmouth Independent (Norfolk)

1937, April 10, p. 9	--	Who was Shakespeare? [an East Anglian courtier]

Year's Work in English Studies

1994, vol. 75: 2221-27	Griffin, Benjamin	[review of *Shakespeare, In Fact* by Irvin L. Matus]
2007, vol. 86: 382-83	Hansen, Matthew C.	[review of *The Case for Shakespeare* by Scott McCrea]

Yorkshire Evening Post (West Yorkshire)

1920, March 4, p. 6	--	Shakespeare Again

Yorkshire Post and Leeds Intelligencer (West Yorkshire, England)

1920, March 4, p. 6	--	The Real Shakespeare! Edward de Vere, Earl of Oxford [long review of *"Shakespeare" Identified*]
1920, March 4, p. 6	--	"Shakespeare Identified"
1920, March 5, p. 8	Robertson, J. M.	Shakespeare and Other Peers [review of *"Shakespeare" Identified* by J. Thomas Looney (1920)]
1920, March 6, p. 10	--	The New Shakespeare Claim [review of *"Shakespeare" Identified"* by J. Thomas Looney]
1920, March 11, p. 4	Looney, J. Thomas	Shakespeare Identified [letter: response to J. M. Robertson's March 5 review of *"Shakespeare" Identified*]
1920, March 11, p. 4.	Thornley, H. E.	Shakespeare Identified [letter: "I hope Mr. Looney's book will be widely read, and his claim discussed by competent critics."]
1920, March 4-10?	Metcalfe, W. Day	[both Metcalf and Looney later refer to a letter that Metcalf wrote around this time; not yet found]
1920, April 1, p. 8	Looney, J. Thomas	*"Shakespeare" Identified*: A Reply to Critics and Some New Facts [letter]
1920, April 13, p. 11	--	Mr. Looney's Identification of Shakespeare [review of *"Shakespeare" Identified* by J. Thomas Looney]
1921, Feb. 16, p. 4	--	Mr. Looney's Solution of "Shakespeare": Edward de Vere's Poems [review of Looney's *The Poems of Edward de Vere*]
1921, Feb. 18, p. 3	--	*Yorkshire Weekky Post* Advertisement [ad for its current issue mentions "Mr. Looney's new book on the Shakespeare controversy"]
1922, June 21, p. 4	--	Shakespeare: Sir Sidney Lee's "Life" [And a new edition of Shakespeare's works]
1923, April 25, p. 4	--	Shakespeare "Discoveries" [Summary of the ideas of J.Thomas Looney]
1931, Feb. 10, p. 6	Kingsmill, Hugh	Who Was Shakespeare? [review of *Shakespeare's Plays in the Order of Their Writing* by Eva Turner Clark]
1932, Jan. 22, p. 6	--	This World of Ours [Mentions J. Thomas Looney, *Shakespeare" Identified*, and Edward de Vere in passing]

Articles in Non-Oxfordian Periodicals

1934, Aug. 18, p. 8	--	A Late Starter
1938, Oct. 27, p. 4	Neale, J. W.	An Exponent of the De Vere Theory [letter]
1938, Oct. 31, p. 3	Metcalf, W. Day	Several People Had Hand in Composition [letter]
1938, Oct. 31, p. 3	Tuxworth, Newsl. C.	Shakespeare-Bacon [letter]
1953, July 24, p. 7	Woodhouse, Bruce	Cecil Palmer [letter]
1955, July 25, p. 4	--	Who *Did* Write Shakespeare's Works? [review off *Who Wrote Shakespeare?* by Hilda Amphlett]
1955, July 29, p. 4	Preston, Ernest D.	Who Was the Author of "Shakespeare's" Works? [letter: Shake Spear was a pen name]
1955, Aug. 4, p. 4	Walker, William	Alias Shakespeare [letter]
1955, Aug. 27, p. 7	--	Not To Be Missed: Talk by Shakespeare Fellowship

THE SEVENTEENTH EARL OF OXFORD

as the Author

"William Shakespeare"

Mr. Percy Allen's studies of Shakespeare and other Elizabethan writers, resulting in the publication by him of two books,

"Shakespeare, Jonson, and Wilkins as Borrowers" (1928)
and
"Shakespeare and Chapman as Topical Dramatists" (1929)
have convinced him that Mr. J. T. Looney was right when in "Shakespeare Identified" he argued that Edward de Vere 17th Earl of Oxford was the actual author of writings usually attributed to "William Shakespeare."

Mr. Allen further pursues that line of research in his forthcoming book, which seems to establish a very powerful case,

The Case for Edward de Vere

(SEVENTEENTH EARL OF OXFORD)

AS SHAKESPEARE

By Percy Allen.

Crown 8vo.	7/6 Net.	Cloth.

CONTENTS.

Chapter.
- I. Introductory.
- II. Oxford's Poems and Shakespeare.
- III. Shakespeare in the Lyrics of Lyly's Plays.
- IV. Oxford in "Venus and Adonis" and "Lucrece."
- V. Oxford in Chapman's Poems.
- VI. Oxford in the Shakespearean Sonnets.
- VII. Oxford's connection with Elizabethan Drama.
- VIII. & IX. Oxford in Some Shakespearean Comedies.
- X. & XI. Oxford in Some Shakespearean Tragedies.
- XII. Oxford in the Folio and Summary.

CECIL PALMER, 49, Chandos Street, LONDON, W.C.2.

THE SEVENTEENTH EARL OF OXFORD 1550 — 1604.

BY

B. M. WARD.

With portraits, maps, and genealogical tables, 21s. net.

"A contribution to Elizabethan biography of first-rate importance."

The English Review.

"Such a sound and scholarly piece of work . . . puts to shame the easy exercises of the bookmakers."

The Daily Telegraph.

"It has been Mr. Ward's pleasant task to restore to favour Edward de Vere Lord Great Chamberlain of England in the reign of Queen Elizabeth, and one of the outstanding figures in that age of famous men."

The Guardian.

"An extremely able study . . . . an excellent picture both of the man and of his times . . . . a book full of entertainment."

T.P.'s and Cassell's Weekly.

"It is here that the reader must look for whatever information he wants about one of the most brilliant and fascinating figures of the English Renaissance."

J. C. Squire in *The Observer.*

"The format is entirely praiseworthy ; and the book, notwithstanding its illustrations and maps is light in weight and pleasant to handle. The binding is dark old rose with the de Vere arms in gold and the motto' "Vero nihil verius." Happily the truth regarding this most distinguished member of a most distinguished race has at last triumphed over calumny and has been put forward in a book that will rank high both as a biography and as a picture of the Elizabethan peiod."

Esther Singleton in *The Saturday Review of Literature*, New York.

JOHN MURRAY, Albemarle St., LONDON, W.

Advertisements from *Shakespeare Pictorial*.
The Cecil Palmer ad is from the January and March 1930 issues.
The John Murray ad is from the February 1930 issue.

PART III: SOURCES – BOOKS

IIIa. NON-FICTION BOOKS AND PAMPHLETS OF SPECIAL INTEREST
IN CHRONOLOGICAL ORDER
(Alphabetical listings by author and by title—and a list of reviews of most books listed below—can be found in Part I.)

1752

Collins, Arthur. *Historical Collections of the Noble Families of Cavendishe, Holles, Vere, Harley, and Ogle, with the Lives of the Most Remarkable Persons . . . the Lives of the Earls of Oxford*. London: E. Withers.

1758

Walpole, Horace. *A Catalogue of the Royal and Noble Authors of England, With Lists of Their Works*. London: Strawberry-hill. [see esp. "Life of Lord Oxford"]

1791/1823

Disraeli, Isaac. *Curiosities of Literature: Consisting of Anecdotes, Characters, Sketches . . .* London: J. Murray.
[see esp. "The Secret History of Edward de Vere, Earl of Oxford"]

1796

Majendie, Lewis. *An Account of Hedingham Castle in the County of Essex*. [see also Severne Andrew Ashhurst Majendie. *Some Account of the Family of De Vere, the Earls of Oxford, and of Hedingham Castle in Essex*. London: H. T. Smith & Son, 1904]

c. 1825

An Account of the Most Ancient and Noble Family of the De Veres, Earls of Oxford.

1836

Wright, Thomas. *The History and Topography of the County of Essex*. London: G. Virtue.

1842

Robinson, William. *The History and Antiquities of the Parish of Hackney, in the County of Middlesex*. London: J. B. Nichols & Son.

1848

Hart, Joseph C. *The Romance of Yachting*. New York: Harper.

1857

Bacon, Delia. *The Philosophy of the Plays of Shakspere Unfolded*. With a preface by Nathaniel Hawthorne. London: Groombridge and Sons. Repr. in 1970: New York, AMS Press. ["Edward Earl of Oxford" mentioned on page lx]

1872

Poems of Thomas, Lord Vaux; Edward, Earl of Oxford; Robert, Earl of Essex; and Walter, Earl of Essex. Printed for private circulation.

Grosart, Alexander B. *Miscellanies of the Fuller Worthies' Library*. London. [vol. 4 includes a collection of 23 poems by the Earl of Oxford]

1875

Dowden, Edward. *Shakespeare: A Critical Study of His Mind and Art*. Elibron Classics Replica Edition, 2005.

1881

Morgan, Appleton. *The Shakespearean Myth: William Shakespeare and Circumstantial Evidence*. Cincinnati: R. Charles & Co.

1886

O'Connor, William Douglas. *Hamlet's Notebook*. Boston: Houghton, Mifflin.

1888

Markham, Clements R. *The Fighting Veres*. Boston and New York: Mifflin and Co.

1889

O'Connor, William Douglas. *Mr. Donnelly's Reviewers*. Chicago: Belford, Carke.

Whitman, Walt. *Complete Poe7ms and Prose of Walt Whitman, 1855-1888*. Camden, NJ: W. Whitman. [see especially "What Lurks Behind Shakespeare's Historical Plays?" in Part 4, "November Boughs"]

1895

Maude, Francis C. *Bacon or Shakespeare?: Enquiries as to the Authorship of the Plays of Shake-speare*. [pamphlet]

1897

Schucking, Levin L. *The Meaning of Hamlet*. Translated from the German by Graham Rawson. Oxford: The Clarendon Press. Repr. in 1966: New York: Barnes & Noble. Repr. in 1969: London: Allen & Unwin.

1898

Dictionary of National Biography. London: Smith, Elder, & Co. 1885-1901. Revised 1920-22. [see esp. vol. 58, entry for "Edward de Vere," by Sir Sidney Lee]

Lee, Sidney, Sir. *A Life of William Shakespeare*. London: Macmillan & Co. [rev. version 1922]

1899

Herford, Oliver. *An Alphabet of Celebrities*. Boston: Small, Maynard.

1900

Edwards, William H. *Shaksper Not Shakespeare*. Cincinnati: The Robert Clarke Company.

1901

James, Henry. 'Note from Lamb House, June 12, 1901,' in *The Complete Notebooks of Henry James*. Edited by Leon Edel and Lyall H. Powers. New York and Oxford: Oxford University Press, 1987.

1902

Bompas, George, C. *The Problem of the Shakespeare Plays*. London: S. Low, Marston & Co.

1903

Begley, Walter. *Is It Shakespeare?* London: John Murray.

James, Henry. "Letter to Miss Violet Hunt, August 26, 1903." In *The Letters of Henry James*. Selected and edited by Percy Lubbock. New York: Octagon Books. Repr. in 1970.

1904

Collins, J. Churton. *Studies in Shakespeare: The Bacon – Shakespeare Mania*. Westminster: A. Constable. [excerpt reprinted in BTC, vol. 1: 147-152]

Majendie, Severne Andrew Ashhurst. *Some Account of the Family of De Vere, the Earls of Oxford, and of Hedingham Castle in Essex*. London: H. T. Smith & Son. [see also *An Account of Hedingham Castle in the County of Essex*, by Lewis Majendie, 1796]

Stotsenburg, John H. *An Impartial Study of the Shakespeare Title*. Louisville, KY: J. P. Morgan & Co. Repr. in 1970: Port Washington, NY: Kennikat Press.

1908

Greenwood, George G. *The Shakespeare Problem Restated*. London, New York: John Lane Company.

1909

Greenwood, George G. *In re Shakespeare: Beeching v. Greenwood: Rejoinder on Behalf of the Defendant*. London: John Lane.

Harris, Frank. *The Man Shakespeare and His Tragic Life-story*. New York: Mitchell Kennerley. Repr. in 1921: Girard, KS: Haldeman-Julius Co. Repr. in 1969: New York: Horizon Press.

Twain, Mark. *Is Shakespeare Dead?* New York: Harper & Bros.

1910

Courthope, W. J. *History of English Poetry*, vol. II. New York/London: Macmillan and Co.

1911

Greenwood, George G. *The Vindicators of Shakespeare: A Reply to Critics, Together with Some Remarks on Dr. Wallace's "New Shakespeare Discoveries."* London: Sweeting and Co.

1914

Mason, David. *Shakespeare Personally*. London: Smith, Elder & Co. [see p. 17: states that Shakspere left London in 1604]

1915

Baxter, James Phinney. *The Greatest of Literary Problems: The Authorship of the Shakespeare Works: An Exposition of All Points at issue from Their Inception to the Present Moment.* Boston: Houghton Mifflin. Repr. in 1971: New York: AMS Press.

1916

Greenwood, George G. *Is There A Shakespeare Problem?* London, New York: John Lane Company.

Greenwood, George G. *Sir Sidney Lee's New Edition of A Life of William Shakespeare: Some Words of Criticism.* London: John Lane.

Greenwood, George G. *Shakespeare's Law and Latin—How I was "Exposed" by Mr. J. M. Robertson*, M.P. London: Watts & Co.

1918-19

Lefranc, Abel. *Sous le Masque de "William Shakespeare:" William Stanley, Vle Comte de Derby.* [*Behind the Mask Of "William Shakespeare": William Stanley, Earl of Derby*] Paris: Payot & Cie.

[pub. as *Under the Mask of William Shakespeare*, translation by Cecil Cragg: Braunton, Devon: Merlin Books, 1988]

[pub. as *Behind the Mask of William Shakespeare*, translation by Frank Lawler. Cary, NC: Veritas Publications, 2022]

– -- ---- -------- ---------------- -------- ---- -- -

1918

Looney, J. Thomas. *Shakespeare" Identified: A Preliminary Notice.* [printed privately, Dec. 14]

1920

Greenwood, George G. *Shakespeare's Handwriting.* London: John Lane.

Greenwood, George G. *Shakespeare's Law.* London: Cecil Palmer.

[excerpts repr. in *Shakespeare and the Law* (Stritmatter 2022), p. 41-62]

Looney, J. Thomas. *"Shakespeare" Identified in Edward De Vere, the Seventeenth Earl of Oxford.* London: Cecil Palmer.

Looney, J. Thomas. *"Shakespeare" Identified in Edward De Vere, the Seventeenth Earl of Oxford.* New York: Frederick A. Stokes Company.

1921

Greenwood, George G. *Ben Jonson and Shakespeare.* London: Cecil Palmer. [see esp. p. 45-54]

[excerpt repr. in *Shakespeare Authorship Sourcebook* (Stritmatter 2019, 2022), p. 237-44]

Looney, J. Thomas (editor). *The Poems of Edward De Vere, Seventeenth Earl of Oxford.* London: Cecil Palmer.

Still, Colin. *Shakespeare's Mystery Play: A Study of The Tempest.* London: Cecil Palmer.

1922

Hookham, George. *Will o' the Wisp, or The Elusive Shakespeare.* Oxford: B. Blackwell. [mentions J. T. Looney and Edward de Vere, p. 60]

Lee, Sir Sidney. *A Life of William Shakespeare* [rev. version]. London: J. Murray.

Lefranc, Abel. *Le Secret de William Stanley.* Bruxelles: L'Edition du Flambeaux.

Smithson, E. W., and George Greenwood. *Baconian Essays.* London: Cecil Palmer. Repr. in 1970: Port Washington, NY: Kennikat Press. [two chapters and the Introduction and Final Note are by Greenwood]

Squire, John Collings. [published under pseud. Solomon Eagle] *Essays at Large.* New York: H. Doran Company. [see esp. "Shakespeare and the Second Chamber," p. 130-134]

1923

Chambers, E. K. *The Elizabethan Stage*, vol. I-III. Oxford: The Clarendon Press.

Greenwood, George G. *Shakespeare and a Tertium Quid.* London: Cecil Palmer.

Holland, Hubert H. (Admiral). *Shakespeare Through Oxford Glasses.* London: Cecil Palmer.

Times Book Club. *Catalogue of Books Added to the Library from January, 1915, to June, 1923.* [pamphlet] [list includes *"Shakespeare" Identified*]

Ward, Bernard Rowland (Colonel). *The Mystery of "Mr. W. H."* London: Cecil Palmer.

1924

Chambers, E. K. *The Disintegration of Shakespeare: Annual Shakespeare Lecture of the British Academy.* [pamphlet] London: Oxford University Press for the British Academy.

Greenwood, George G. *Shakespeare's Signatures and Sir Thomas More.* London: Cecil Palmer.

Richert, Edith. *Political Propaganda and Satire in A Midsummer Night's Dream*. [pamphlet: repr. from *Modern Philology*, vol. XXI, no. 1 (August) and 2 (November) 1923]

Sydenham, Lord & H. Crouch Batchelor. *The Shakespeare Myth: A Challenge*. [pamphlet] [repr. from *The English Review* (Aug. 1924), p. 221-29]

1925

Chambers, E. K. A Shakespeare Reference Library. [pamphlet; prepared with Sir Sidney Lee]

Greenwood, George G. *The Stratford Bust and the Droeshout Engraving*. London: Cecil Palmer.

Greg. W. W. *English Literary Autographs, Part I, Dramatists, 1550-1650*. Oxford University Press.

Harman, Edward G. *The "Impersonality" of Shakespeare Examined and Discussed*. London: Cecil Palmer.

Lawrence, Basil E. *Notes on the Authorship of Shakespeare's Plays and Poems*. London: Gay and Hancock.

Lee, Sir Sidney & Sir Edmund Chambers. *A Shakespeare Reference Library*. [pamphlet]

Ward, Capt. Bernard M. *The Authorship of The Arte of English Poesie, A Suggestion*. [pamphlet: repr. from *The Review of English Studies*, vol. 1, no. 3 (July 1925)]

1926

Clark, Eva Turner. *Axiophilus, or Oxford Alias Shakespeare*. New York: Knickerbocker Press.

Connes, Georges. *Le Mystere Shakespearien*. Paris: Bovin & Cie.

Rollins, Hyder (editor). *Gorgeous Gallery of Gallant Inventions by Thomas Proctor*. Cambridge: Harvard University Press. [1578] [see 3 poems by Edward de Vere]

Steele, Mary Susan. *Plays and Masques at Court During the Reigns of Elizabeth, James and Charles*. New Haven: Yale University Press.

Ward, Bernard Mordaunt (Captain) (editor). *A Hundreth Sundrie Flowres; From the Original Edition of 1573, by George Gascoigne*. With an intro. by the editor. London: F. Etchells and H. Macdonald.

Ward, Capt. Bernard M. *George Gascoigne and His Circle*. [pamphlet] [repr. from *Review of English Studies*, vol. II, no. 5 (Jan. 1926)]

1927

Connes, Georges A. *The Shakespeare Mystery, Abridged and Translated into English By a Member of the Shakespeare Fellowship*. London: Cecil Palmer.

Dawtrey, John. *The Falstaff Saga*. [pamphlet] [published privately]

Rollins, Hyder E. (editor). *Paradise of Dainty Devices*. Cambridge: Harvard University Press. [1576-1606] [see p. lviii-liv, lx, 244-46]

1928

Allen, Percy. *Shakespeare, Jonson, and Wilkins as Borrowers*. London: Cecil Palmer. Repr. in 1972: New York: Russell & Russell.

Allen, Percy. *Shakespeare as a Topical Dramatist*. [pamphlet published by *The Poetry League*]

Greg, W. W. *Review of A Hundreth Sundry Flowres* edited by Capt. Bernard M. Ward. [pamphlet] [repr. from *Transactions of the Bibliographical Society*, New Series, vol. VII, no. 3 (Dec. 1927)]

Ward, Bernard M. (Captain). *The Seventeenth Earl of Oxford, 1550-1604, From Contemporary Documents*. London: J. Murray.

Ward, Bernard M. (Captain) *The Famous Victories of Henry V*. [pamphlet] [repr. from *Review of English Studies*, vol. IV, no. 15 (July 1928)]

1929

Allen, Percy. *Shakespeare and Chapman as Topical Dramatists*. London: Cecil Palmer.

Allen, Percy. *Manifesto of Conversion*. [pamphlet] [June]

Rendall, Canon Gerald H. *Ben Jonson and the First Folio of Shakespeare's Plays*. [pamphlet]

1930

Allen, Percy. *The Case for Edward de Vere, 17th Earl of Oxford, as "William Sh."* [booklet] London: Cecil Palmer.

Allen, Percy. *The Case for Edward de Vere, 17th Earl of Oxford, as "Shakespeare."* London: Cecil Palmer.

Clark, Eva Turner. *Shakespeare's Plays in the Order of Their Writing*. London: Cecil Palmer. [published in the United States as *Hidden Allusions in Shakespeare's Plays*]

Eagle, Roderick L. *Shakespeare: New Views for Old*. London: Cecil Palmer.

Kittle, William. *G. Gascoigne or Edward De Vere, Seventeenth Earl of Oxford*. Washington, D. C.: W. F. Roberts Company.

Parsons, J. Denham. *Report on the Poet Shakespeare's Identity Submitted to the Trustees of the British Museum*. [pamphlet]

Rendall, Gerald H. (Canon). *Shakespeare's Sonnets and Edward de Vere*. London: J. Murray.

Standen, Gilbert. *Shakespeare Authorship: A Summary of Evidence*. London: Cecil Palmer.

Ward, Col. Bernard R. *The Elizabethan Chronicle Play as War Propaganda*. [pamphlet] [repr. from *The Royal Engineers Journal* (March 1930), p. 14-16]

Ward, Col. Bernard R. *Shakespeare's Sonnets: A Suggested Interpretation*. [pamphlet] [repr. from *Poetry and the Play*, Winter 1929-1930 issue]

Ward. Col. Bernard R., *Shakespeare and Elizabethan War Propaganda*. [pamphlet] [repr. from *Royal Engineers Journal*, vol. XLIII (Dec. 1928), p. 658-668]

1931

Allen, Percy. *The Oxford-Shakespeare Case Corroborated*. London: Cecil Palmer.

Clark, Eva Turner. *Hidden Allusions in Shakespeare's Plays*. New York: W. F. Payson. [published in England as *Shakespeare's Plays In the Order of Their Writing*]

Douglas, Montagu W. (Colonel). *The Earl of Oxford as "Shakespeare:" An Outline of the Case*. London: Cecil Palmer.

Frisbee, George. *Edward De Vere: A Great Elizabethan*. London: Cecil Palmer.

Goldsworthy, W. Lansdown. *Ben Jonson and the First Folio*. London: Cecil Palmer.

Rendall, Gerald H. *Shake-speare: Handwriting and Spelling*. London: Cecil Palmer. Repr. in 1971: New York: Haskell House.

Rendall, Gerald H. *Autograph Letter and Signatures of Edward de Vere* [pamphlet]. [date is approximate]

Rollins, Hyder E. (editor). *The Phoenix Nest*. Cambridge: Harvard Univ. Press. [1593] [see. p. 161-62, 194-95, 200]

Singleton, Esther. *The Shakespeare Garden*. With an introduction by Eva Turner Clark. New York: W. F. Payson.

Slater, Gilbert. *Seven Shakespeares: A Discussion of the Evidence for Various Theories With Regard to Shakespere's Identity*. London: Cecil Palmer. Repr. in 1972: Folcroft, PA: Folcroft Library Editions. Repr. in 1977: Philadelphia: R. West.

Theobald, Bertram G. *Exit Shakspere*. London: Cecil Palmer.

1932

Allen, Percy. *The Life Story of Edward de Vere as "William Shakespeare."* Introduction by Capt. B. M. Ward. London: Cecil Palmer.

Chambers, E. K. *The Oxford Book of Sixteenth Century Verse*. London: Oxford University Press. [see p. vi-vii: "The most hopeful of the courtier poets was Edward de Vere." The collection includes three of his poems, selected by "a standard of absolute poetry, rather than one of merely historic interest" (vii).]

Phillips, Gerald W. *The Tragic Story of "Shakespeare:" Disclosed in the Sonnets*. London: Cecil Palmer.

Wilson, John Dover. *The Essential Shakespeare: A Biographical Adventure*. Cambridge: Cambridgee University Press.

1933

Allen, Percy. *The Plays of Shakespeare & Chapman in Relation to French History*. London: Denis Archer. "Introduction" by Marjorie Bowen.

Allen, Percy and Ernest Allen. *Lord Oxford and Shakespeare: A Reply to John Drinkwater*. London: Denis Archer.

Clark, Eva Turner. *The Satirical Comedy: Love's Labour's Lost*. New York: W. F. Payson.

Drinkwater, John. *Shakespeare*. London: Duckworth.

Fort, J. A. *The Order and Chronology of Shakespeare's Sonnets*. [pamphlet] [repr. from *Review of English Studies*, vol. IX, no. 33 (Jan. 1933)]

Holland, Hubert H. (Admiral). *Shakespeare, Oxford, and Elizabethan Times*. London: Denis Archer. Repr. in 1974: Folcroft, PA: Folcroft Library Editions.

Rollins, Hyder E. (editor), *Brittons Bowre of Delights*. Cambridge: Harvard University Press. [1591] [see p. 95, 105]

1934

Allen, Percy. *Anne Cecil, Elizabeth & Oxford*. London: Denis Archer.

Douglas, Montague W. (Colonel). *Lord Oxford was "Shakespeare:" A Summing Up*. London: Rich & Cowan, Lt

Hart, Alfred. *Shakespeare and the Homilies, and Other Pieces of Research into the Elizabethan Drama*. Melbourne: Melbourne University Press. Repr. in 1970: New York: Octagon Books. Repr. in 1971: New York: AMS Press.

Rendall, Gerald H. (Canon). *Personal Clues in Shakespeare Poems & Sonnets*. London: John Lane.

1935

Eggar, Katharine E. *The Seventeenth Earl of Oxford as Musician, Poet and Controller of the Queen's Revels*. [pamphlet] [repr. from *The Proceedings of the British Musical Association*, vol. LXI (Jan. 17, 1935), p. 39-59]

Freud, Sigmund. *An Autobiographical Study*. New York: W. W. Norton and Co. [compare with the 1998 edition edited by James Strachey]

Kittle, William. *Edward de Vere, Seventeenth Earl of Oxford, 1550-1604*. Washington, D. C.: The Buchanan Company.

Phillips, Gerald W. *Sunlight on Shakespeare's Sonnets*. London: T. Butterworth, Ltd.

Rollins, Hyder E. (editor). *England's Helicon*. Cambridge, MA: Harvard University Press. [1600, 1614] [in vol. 1, see p. 120, 130-32, 166; vol. 2, p. 239 and index, in which Edward de Vere is listed as "alias Shakespeare"]

Spurgeon, Caroline. *Shakespeare's Imagery and What It Tells Us*. Cambridge: Cambridge Univ. Press.

1936

Allen, Percy and Bernard M. Ward. *An Enquiry into the Relations Between Lord Oxford as "Shakespeare," Queen Elizabeth and the Fair Youth*. [pamphlet]. London: Percy Allen.

Cairncross, Andrew S. *The Problem of Hamlet: A Solution*. London: Macmillan. Repr. in 1970, 1975, 1978: Norwood, PA: Norwood Editions.

O'Hagan, Thomas. *What Shakespeare is Not*. Toronto: The Hunter-Rose Co., Ltd. [Chapter II, titled "Shakespeare Identified," is a response to J. Thomas Looney and his book, though neither is mentioned]

Phillips, Gerald W. *Lord Burghley in Shakespeare: Falstaff, Sly and Others*. London: T. Butterworth.

1937

Allen, Ernest. *When Shakespeare Died*. [pamphlet]

Bénézet, Louis P. *Shakspere, Shakespeare, and De Vere*. Manchester, NH: Granite State Press.

Brooks, Alden. *Will Shakespeare: Factotum and Agent*. New York: Round Table Press. Repr. in 1974: AMS Press.

Clark, Eva Turner. *The Man Who Was Shakespeare*. New York: R. R. Smith. Repr. in 1970: New York: AMS Press. [excerpt repr. in TOX; vol. 16: 46-54]

Golding, Louis Thorn. *An Elizabethan Puritan: Arthur Golding the Translator of Ovid's Metamorphoses and also of John Calvin's Sermons*. New York: Richard R. Smith.

Lucas, Edward V. *All of a Piece: New Essays*. Philadelphia, New York: J. B. Lippincott Company.

Ranson, F. Lingard. *Lavenham, Suffolk*. Printed privately. Foreword by Lt. Col. Montagu W. Douglas.

1938

Dawbarn, C. Y. C. *Oxford and the Folio Plays. A Supplement*. [pamphlet] [repr. from *Baconiana* (Oct. 1938)]

1939

Brown, Ivor and George Fearon. *This Shakespeare Industry: Amazing Monument*. New York: Harper & Row. Repr. in 1969: Westport, CT: Greenwood Press. [an examination of the effect that discrediting Shakspere as the author would have on his home town] [see esp. p. 201-205]

Rendall, Gerald H. (Canon). *Ben Jonson and the First Folio Edition of Shakespeare's Plays*. Colchester: Benham & C.

1940

Barrell, Charles Wisner. *Elizabethan Mystery Man: A Digest of Evidence Connecting Edward de Vere with the Literary Activities of "Mr. William Shakespeare."* New York: A. Gauthier. [contains two articles: "Elizabethan Mystery Man" originally published in *The Saturday Review of Literature*, and "Shakespearean Detective Story" never before published]

Porohovshikov, Pierre. S. *Shakespeare Unmasked*. New York: Savoy Book Publishers.

Rendall, Gerald H. *The "Ashbourne" Portrait of Shakespeare*. Colchester: Benham & Co.

1941

Frye, Albert Myrton, and Albert William Levi. *Rational Belief: An Introduction to Logic*. New York: Harcourt, Brace.

Rendall, Canon Gerald H. *Arthur Golding, Translator – Personal and Literary – Shakespeare and Edward de Vere*. [pamphlet] [repr. from *Essex Review* (April 1941)]

1942

Bridgewater, H. *Bacon or Shakspere: Does It Matter?* [pamphlet]

Hart, Alfred. *Stolne and Surreptitious Copies: A Comparative Study of Shakespeare's Bad Quartos*. Melbourne: Melbourne University Press.

Kittle, William. *Edward de Vere, Seventeenth Earl of Oxford, and Shakespeare*. Baltimore: Monumental Printing.

Tillyard, E. M. W. *The Elizabethan World Picture*. New York: Vintage.

1943

Allen, Percy. *Who Were the Dark Lady and Fair Youth of the Sonnets?* [pamphlet printed privately]

Brooks, Alden. *Will Shakspere and the Dyer's Hand*. New York: C. Scribner's Sons.

Eagle, Roderick L. *Shakespeare: New Views for Old*. London, New York: Rider & Co.

1944

Rendall, Gerald H. (Canon). *Shakespeare in Essex and East Anglia*. [pamphlet] [May]

1945

Lefranc, Abel. *A la Découverte de Shakespeare*. Paris: Albin Michel.

1946

Eggar, Katharine E. *The Musical Condition of Man*. [pamphlet] [from the *Proceedings of the Royal Musical Association*, Session LXXIII]

Foster, Thomas H. *Shakespeare—Man of Mystery: An Address Delivered at McCormick Theological Seminary, Chicago, Ill., October 24, 1946*. Cedar Rapids, IA: Torch Press.

1947

Dodd, Alfred. *Who Was Shake-speare?: Was He Francis Bacon, the Earl of Oxford, or William Shaksper?* London: G. Lapworth & Co.

Allen, Percy. *Talks with Elizabethans: Revealing the Mystery of William Shakespeare*. London, New York: Rider and Company. [The Library of Congress lists Hester Dowden as the author]

Johnson, Edward D. *The Shakespeare Illusion, 3rd ed*. London: Mitre Press.

Kent, William. *Edward de Vere, the Seventeenth Earl of Oxford: The Real Shakespeare*. [a 40-page pamphlet; two chapters by William Kent, a third by "Another"] Shakespeare Fellowship.

Kent, William. *The Lost Treasures of London*. London: Phoenix House.

Ogburn, Dorothy & Charlton Ogburn. *The Renaissance Man of England*. New York. Repr. in 1949. Newly Corrected and Augmented edition published in 1955: New York: Coward-McCann, Inc. [published in German translation as *Der Wahre Shakespeare* by Origo-Verlag Zurich]

1948

Lawrence, Sir H. S. and T. M. Aitken. *The Inspiration of Shakespeare*. [pamphlet] Printed privately at the University Press, Oxford.

1949

Freud, Sigmund. *An Outline of Psychoanalysis*. [Abriss der Psycho-Analyse] Authorized translation by James Strachey (1949). New York: W. W. Norton. [see esp. p. 96, 164, 165, 172] [excerpt repr. in *Sh. and His Rivals* (McMichael & Glenn 1962), p. 192]

Galland, Joseph S., and Burton A. Milligan. *Digesta Anti-Shakespeareana*. [contains more than 4,500 entries]. UMI Dissertation Information Service. [completed by Milligan after Galland's untimely death]

Grillo, Ernesto. *Shakespeare and Italy*. Glasgow: R. Maclehose, University Press. Repr. in 1973: New York: Haskell House.

Halliday, Frank E. *Shakespeare and His Critics*. London: Gerald Duckworth.

Looney, J. Thomas. *"Shakespeare" Identified in Edward De Vere, The Seventeenth Earl of Oxford*. Introduction by William McFee; Afterword by Charles Wisner Barrell. New York: Duell, Sloan and Pearce.

1950

Bénézet, Louis P. "Vere, Earls of Oxford," in vol. 1: 301+; and "Shakespeare Authorship Theories," in vol. 9: 326-28, *Grolier Encyclopaedia*. New York: The Grolier Society. [The authorship piece is a 2,400-word article commissioned by Grolier] [repr. in SON, vol. 24/4: 8-10 (Fall 1988); in SON, vol. 29/4: 19 (Fall 1993); and in BTC, vol. 6: 366-69]

Mez, John R. (translator). *Der Wahre Shakespeare, XVII. Earl of Oxford*. Stuttgart: Origo-Verlag Zurich [translation of Charlton and Dorothy's *The Renaissance Man of England*]

Van Moorkorkan, P. H. *Achtar hot Monbakhus* [*Behind the Mask*]. Ansterden: G. A. Van Oorschoot, Uitgovor.

1951

Bowen, Gwynneth M. *Shakespeare's Farewell: The Date and Authorship of The Tempest*. [pamphlet] Inglethorpe, Buxton: printed privately.

Eggar, Katherine E. *Shakespeare In His True Colors*. [pamphlet]. London: R. Ridgill Trout.

1952

Douglas, Montague W. (Colonel). *The Earl of Oxford as "Shakespeare."* Oxford: Alden Press. [revision of *Lord Oxford and the Shakespeare Group: A Summary of Evidence*, 1934]

Le Riche, Kathleen. *Shakespeare in Essex*. [pamphlet] [repr. from *Essex Review*, vol. LXI (Oct. 1952)]

Mez, John R. *Edward de Vere – or "Shakespeare": A Bibliography Compiled by J. R. Mez*. Ruvigliana, Switzerland: printed privately.

Miller, Nathan L. *A Lawyer's Evaluation of the Evidence Related to the Authorship of the Shakespeare Literature*. New York: Nathan Miller.

Ogburn, Dorothy and Charlton. *This Star of England: "William Shake-speare," Man of the Renaissance*. New York: Coward-McCann, Inc. Repr. in 1972: Westport, CT: Greenwood Press.

Titherley, A. W., *Shakespeare's Identity: William Stanley, 6th Earl of Derby*. Winchester, England: Warren & Son.

1954

Beaton, Cecil and Kenneth Tyson. *Persona Grata*. New York: G. P. Putman's Sons. [quotes Orson Welles on Oxford]

Eggar, Katharine E. *The Unlifted Shadow: Some Misunderstood Features in the Life of Edward de Vere*. [pamphlet] [Eggar's toast to Edward de Vere at the Annual Dinner of the Sh. Fellowship, 23rd April, 1954]

Lambin, Georges. *Shakespeare et Tournon*. [pamphlet]

Phillips, Gerald W. *Shakespeare's Sonnets*. [pamphlet]

1955

Amphlett, Hilda. *Who Was Shakespeare? A New Enquiry*. With an introduction by Christmas Humphreys. London: Heinemann. Repr. in 1970: New York: AMS Press.

Ogburn, Dorothy and Charlton Ogburn. *The Renaissance Man of England, Newly Corrected and Augmented*. New York: Coward-McCann, Inc.

Read, Conyers. *Mr. Secretary Cecil and Queen Elizabeth*. London: Cape.

1956

Evans, Alfred J. *Shakespeare's Magic Circle*. London: A. Barker. Repr. in 1970.

Lambin, Georges. *Explorations Sur la Trace d'un Shakespeare inconnu*. [pamphlet]

Lowell, Stanley P. *A Mystery Beyond Words*. [pamphlet]

Sweet, George E. *Shakespeare: The Mystery*. Stanford.

1957

Kent, William & Others. *Edward de Vere . . . The Real Shakespeare*. Second edition. [pamphlet;] [see description under first edition, 1947]

1958

Bénézet, Louis P. *The Six Loves of "Shake-Speare*. New York: Pageant Press.

Churchill, Reginald C. *Shakespeare and His Betters: A History and a Criticism of the Attempts Which Have Been Made to Prove that Shakespeare's Works Were Written By Others*. With collaboration in bibliography and research by Maurice Hussey. Foreword by Ivor Brown. London: M. Reinhardt. Printed in 1959 by Bloomington: Indiana University Press.

Wadsworth, Frank. *The Poacher from Stratford*. Berkeley: University of California Press.

1960

Hoffmann, Calvin. *The Murder of the Man Who Was Shakespeare*. New York: Grosset & Dunlap. [excerpt repr. in *Sh. Authorship Sourcebook* (Stritmatter 2019, 2020): 157-60]

Read, Conyers. *Lord Burghley and Queen Elizabeth*. New York: Knopf.

1961

Bentley, Richard (editor). *Shakespeare Cross-Examination*. American Bar Association.

Blumenthal, Walter H. *Paging Mr. Shakespeare: A Critical Challenge*. New York: University Publishers.

Le Riche, Kathleen. *Shakespeare in Essex*. London: printed privately. [pamphlet] [repr. from *Essex Review 61* (Oct. 1952): 187] [reprinted in 1962]

Pitcher, Seymour. *The Case for Shakespeare's Authorship of "The Famous Victories of Henry V."* New York: State University of New York. [see esp. de Vere material not SAQ-related]

1962

Gibson, H. N. *The Shakespearean Claimants: A Critical Survey of the Four Principal Theories Concerning the Authorship of the Shakespearean Plays*. London: Methuen. New York: Barnes & Noble. [excerpt repr. in *Shakespeare Criticism, vol. 41* (Lee & Barnes 1998), p. 67-76]

Lambin, Georges. *Voyages de Shakespeare en France et en Italie*. Geneve: E. Droz. [English translation by Talmadge Gartley Wilson (completed by Wendy G. and Vance E. Adams, Beorn S. Hall, Anne Lander; W. Ron Hess, general editor) in *The Dark Side of Shakespeare*, vol. 1, Appendix A, p. 355-535, by W. Ron Hess]
[excerpt repr. in *Hidden Allusions*, Eva Turner Clark, 3rd ed., Ruth Loyd Miller, editor, 1974, p. 120-24]

Non-fiction Books and Pamphlets

McManaway, James G. *The Authorship of Shakespeare*. [pamphlet] Washington, D.C.: Folger Shakespeare Library.

McMichael, George L. and Edgar M. Glenn (editors). *Shakespeare and His Rivals: A Casebook on the Authorship Controversy*. New York: Ody6ssey Press.

Ogburn, Dorothy and Charlton Ogburn, Jr. *Shake-speare: The Man Behind the Name* [on dust jacket of hardback version, subtitle is "The Real Man Behind the Name"). New York: Morrow.

1963

Blumenthal, Walter H. *Shakespeare: Veneration vs. Verity: Critical Comments From a Sceptic.* Lexington.

Breitwieser, Ludwig. *Der falsche und der wahre Shakespeare*. Offenbach.

Marder, Louis. *His Exits and His Entrances: The Story of Shakespeare's Reputation*. Philadelphia: Lippincott. [excerpt repr. in *Shakespeare Criticism, vol. 41* (Lee & Barnes 1998), p. 5-18]

1964

Brewster, Eleanor. *Oxford, Courtier to the Queen: A Biography*. New York: Pageant Press.

Chaplin, Charles. *My Auto-Biography*. New York: Simon and Schuster. [see esp. p. 364]

Dewar, Mary. *Sir Thomas Smith: A Tudor Intellectual in Office*. London: Athlone Press.

Holland, Norman N. *Psychoanalysis and Shakespeare*. New York: McGraw-Hill. [see esp. Freud's Mar. 23, 1930 letter to Theodore Reik, quoted on p. 56-57]

Johnson, Edward D. *The Shakespeare Quiz: 100 Questions for Stratfordians to Answer*. [pamphlet] [perhaps a reprint of an edition in 1950]

Kott, Jan. *Shakespeare, Our Contemporary*. Translated by Boleslaw Taborski from *Szkice o Szekspirze*. [first edition in the U.S.] Garden City: Doubleday.

Ogburn (Jr.), Charlton. *Shakespeare and the Man of Stratford*. [pamphlet published by the Shakespeare Oxford Society]

1965

Blumenthal, Walter H. *Who Knew Shakespeare? What Was His Reputation in His Lifetime?* Iowa City, IA: Prairie Press.

Martin, Milward W. *Was Shakespeare Shakespeare? A Lawyer Reviews the Evidence*. New York: Cooper Square Publishers.

Troxell, Edward L. *Scientists Search For Shakespeare*. Winter Park, FL: Rollins Press.

1966

Harbage, Alfred. *Conceptions of Shakespeare*. Cambridge, MA: Harvard University Press.

Tweedale, Ralph L. *Wasn't Shakespeare Someone Else? New Evidence in the Very Words of the Bard Himself about his True Identity*. Southfield, MI: Verity Press. Repr. in 1971.

Wainewright, Ruth M. D. *On the Poems of Edward de Vere*. [pamphlet published by the Shakespearean Authorship Society]

1967

Stone, Lawrence. *Crisis of the Aristocracy, 1558-1641*. London: Oxford University Press.

1968

Akrigg, G. P. V. *Shakespeare and the Earl of Southampton*. London: H. Hamilton. Cambridge: Harvard University Press.

Bevington, David M. *Tudor Drama and Politics: A Critical Approach to Topical Meaning*. Cambridge: Harvard Univ. Press.

Carr, Francis. *The Shakespeare Controversy: A Digest of Comment in recently published books on Stratford and the Shakespeare Controversy*. London: Carr Publications. [compiled from issues of "The Stratford Tragi-Comedy"]

Edwards, Francis (Father). *Marvellous Chance: Thomas Howard, Fourth Duke of Norfolk, and the Ridolphi Plot, 1570-1572*. London: Hart-Davis. [excerpt (Appendix 5) repr. in SAR, issue #26: 9-13 (Summer 1972)]

1970

de Luna, B. N. *The Queen Declined: An Interpretation of Willobie His Avisa, with the Text of the Original Edition*. Oxford: Clarendon Press.

Freud, Ernest L., editor. *The Letters of Sigmund Freud & Arnold Zweig*. Translated by Elaine and William Robson-Scott. New York: Harcourt Brace Jovanovich.

1971

Huston, Craig. *The Shakespeare Authorship Question: Evidence for Edward de Vere, 17th Earl of Oxford*. Philadelphia: Dorrance. [excerpt reprinted in *Oxfordian Vistas*, within pages 107 to 120]

Simmons, Roger D. *The Non-Psychoanalytic Literature in Sigmund Freud's Library*. Chicago: University of Chicago Dissertations.

1972

Feldman, A. Bronson. *Secrets of Shakespeare: Four Chapters from a Subversive History*. Philadelphia: Lovelore Press. [privately published in mimeograph] [see review by Gordon C. Cyr in SON (Winter 1977), p. 7-8] [two chapters ("The Lion and the Lance," and "The Woman Tamer") reprinted in *Early Shakespeare* (Feldman/Hope 2019), p. 123-98] [two chapters ("Kit Sly and the Unknown Lord" and "the Making of William Shakespeare") reprinted in *Shakespeare, Marlowe, . . .* (2022), p. 34-80]

1973

Addison, William W. *Essex Worthies: A Biographical Companion to the County*. London: Phillimore.

Barsi-Greene, Margaret (compiler and arranger). *I, Prince Tudor, Wrote Shakespeare: An Autobiography from His Two Ciphers in Poetry and Prose*. Boston: Branden Press.

Hurstfield, Joel. *The Queen's Wards: Wardship and Marriage Under Elizabeth I*. London: Frank Cass.

1974

Clark, Eva Turner. *Hidden Allusions in Shakespeare's Plays: A Study in the Early Court Revels and Personalities of the Times*. Ruth Loyd Miller, editor. 3rd revised edition, with introduction and additional notes by the editor and others. Port Washington, NY: Kennikat Press.

Holland, Hubert H. (Admiral). *Shakespeare, Oxford, and Elizabethan Times*. Folcroft, PA: Folcroft Library Editions.

1975

Miller, Ruth Loyd (editor). *"Shakespeare" Identified in Edward de Vere, Seventeenth Earl of Oxford* [by J. Thomas Looney], 3rd revised, annotated ed.; and, *The Poems of Edward de Vere* [with biographical notes] by J. Thomas Looney [2nd ed.] Published in one volume, along with a second volume of articles, *Oxfordian Vistas*. Port Washington, NY: Kennikat Press for Minos Pub. Co.

Ward, Bernard M. *A Hundreth Sundrie Flowres: From the Original Edition of 1573, by George Gascoigne, with an Introduction by the Editor*. Second edition, edited by Ruth Loyd Miller, with additional notes by the editor and others. Port Washington, NY: Published by Kennikat Press for Minos Pub. Co.

1977

Feldman, A. Bronson. *Hamlet Himself*. Philadelphia: Lovelore Press. [privately published in mimeograph]

Lavater-Sloman, Mary. *Gefährte der Königin: Elisabeth I., Edward Earl of Oxford und das Geheimnis um Shakespeare*. Zurich und München: Artemis Verlag.

1978

Berg, Scott A. *Max Perkins: Editor of Genius*. New York: E. P. Dutton. Repr. in 2015: New York: New American Library.

1979

Ward, Bernard M. (editor). *The Seventeenth Earl of Oxford, 1550-1604, From Contemporary Documents*. [authorized photocopy made available by Ruth Loyd Miller]

1980

Van Doren, Charles. *Shakespeare: Reading and Talking*. Minos Publishing.
[presents David Hasen's theory that de Vere did not die in 1604 but instead came to the New World and buried his manuscripts in a trunk in a pit on Oak Island off Newfoundland]

Halle, Louis J. *The Search for an Eternal Norm: As Represented by Three Classics*. Washington, D.C.: University Press of America.

1980s

Shakespeare Oxford Society. *An Inquirer's Guide to the Shakespearean Authorship Problem and the Case for Edward de Vere*. Baltimore: Shakespeare Oxford Society. [probably written by Gordon and/or Helen Cyr]

1981

Alvis, John and Thomas G. West (editors). *Shakespeare as Political Thinker*. Durham, NC: Carolina Academic Press. 2nd edition, revised and expanded, 2000: ISI Books.

1982

Gohn, Jack Benoit. *Richard II: Shakespeare's Legal Brief on the Royal Prerogative and the Succession to the Throne*. [pamphlet] [repr. from *Georgetown Law Review*, vol. 70, no. 3 (Feb. 1982)]

1983

Cyr, Helen W. *Lexical Choices and Morphological Variables in the Shakespeare and Oxford Corpora: A Preliminary Study*. [pamphlet] Baltimore: Shakespeare Oxford Society.

Rowse, A. L. *Eminent Elizabethans*. Athens: University of Georgia Press.

Non-fiction Books and Pamphlets

1984

Fiehler, Rudolph. *The Key to the Great Shake-speare Whodunit*. [pamphlet: date is approximate, between 1982 and mid 1986]

Ogburn, (Jr.), Charlton. *The Mysterious William Shakespeare: The Myth and the Reality*. Foreword by David McCullough. New York: Dodd, Mead.

Patterson, Annabel M. *Censorship and Interpretation: The Conditions of Writing and Reading in Early Modern England*. Madison, WI: University of Wisconsin Press.

1985

Appleton, Elizabeth (Elizabeth Appleton van Druenen). *Edward de Vere and the War of Words*. Toronto: Elizabethan Press.

Buckley, Jr., William F. *Firing Line: The Mysterious William Shakespeare* [pamphlet; transcript of the program with Charlton Ogburn and Prof. Maurice Charney taped on 11 Dec. 1984] Columbia, SC: Southern Educational Communication Assoc. [see also article by Gordon Cyr, in SON, vol. 21/1: 7-8 (Winter, 1985)]

Sweet, George E. *Shake-speare: The Mystery*, rev. ed. New York: Vantage Press.

1986

Appleton, Elizabeth (Elizabeth Appleton van Druenen). *William Shakespeare, a Nom de Guerre Shaped by a War of Words*. Toronto: Elizabethan Press.

Fowler, William P. *Shakespeare Revealed in Oxford's Letters*. Portsmouth, NH: Peter E. Randall.

Fowler, William P. *Shake-speare's "Phoenix and Turtle": An Interpretation* (with a supplementary exegesis by Dorothy Ogburn, repr. from *This Star of England*). [pamphlet] Portsmouth, NH: Peter E. Randall.

Shakespeare Oxford Society. *The Shakespeare Identify Crisis: A Reference Guide*. [pamphlet] [perhaps by Gordon and/or Dorothy Cyr]

1987

Edwards, Francis, J.S. *The Strange Case of the Poisoned Pommel: Richard Walpole, S.J., and the Squire Plot, 1597-1598*. [pamphlet] [repr. from Archivum Historicum Societatis Iesu, vol. LVI (1987)]

Fleet, Preston M. *Hue & Cry: Unraveling the Shake-speare Myth*. Templeton, CA: Preston M. Fleet.

Garber, Marjorie. *Shakespeare's Ghost Writers: Literature as Uncanny Causality*. New York and London: Methuen.

Ogburn, Charlton, Jr. *The Man Who Was Shakespeare*. [pamphlet] ["an extremely abbreviated version of the case presented in *The Mysterious William Shakespeare*"]

1988

The Authorship Question: The Case Against William Shakespeare of Stratford and the Case for Edward de Vere, 17th Earl of Oxford. [pamphlet]

International Shakespeare Globe Centre. *The Shakespeare Moot: Who as Between Edward de Vere, 17TH Earl of Oxford, and William Shakespeare of Stratford-upon-Avon, is More Likely to Have Written the Works of William Shakespeare?* [pamphlet]

Lefranc, Abel. *Under the Mask of William Shakespeare*. Translation by Cecil Cragg of *Sous le Masque de "William Shakespeare": William Stanley, Vle Comte de Derby*. Braunton, Devon: Merlin Books, Ltd.

Marcus, Leah S. *Puzzling Shakespeare: Local Reading and Its Discontents*. Berkeley: University of California Press.

Ogburn, (Jr.), Charlton. *The Mystery of William Shakespeare*. Abridged version of TMWS. Foreword by Lord Vere. London: Cardinal Books.

1989

Bacon, Deborah. *Words, Words, Words: Some Usages and Meanings in Shakespeare's Sonnets*. Harrisville, MI: Candlebeam Press.

Caruana, Stephanie and Elisabeth Sears. *Oxford's Revenge: "Shakespeare's" Dramatic Development from Agamemnon to Hamlet*. [pamphlet]

1990

Clare, Janet. *'Art Made Tongue-tied by Authority': Elizabethan and Jacobean Dramatic Censorship*. Manchester, UK: Manchester University Press.

Gay, Peter. *Reading Freud: Explorations & Entertainments*. New Haven and London: Yale University Press. [see esp. "Freud and the Man from Stratford," p. 5-53, which was translated into German by Elisabeth Vorspohl as "Freud, Shakespeare und Looney," *Psyche: Zeitschrift für Psychoanalyse und ihre Anwendungen* 45 (1991), 649-74]

Green, Nina. *The Marprelate Tracts: Martin's Epistle*. Kelowna, BC, Canada: Devere Press.

Honan, Park. *Authors' Lives: On Literary Biography and the Arts of Language*. New York: St. Martin's Press.

Sammartino, Peter. *The Man Who Was William Shakespeare*. New York: Cornwall Books.

1991

Green, Nina. *The Langham Letter: A Modern Spelling Edition*. Kelowna, BC, Canada. De Vere Press.

Hunt, Douglas. *The Riverside Guide to Writing*. Boston: Houghton Mifflin. [see chapter "Arguing When the Facts are Disputed"]

May, Steven W. *The Elizabethan Courtier Poets: The Poems and Their Contexts*. Columbia: University of Missouri Press. Repr. in 1999: Asheville, NC: Pegasus Press. [excerpt repr. in LC, p. 11-15]

Schoenbaum, Samuel. *Shakespeare's Lives*. New York: Clarendon Press. [see esp. "Deviations," p. 385-451] [excerpt repr. in *Shakespeare Criticism, vol. 41* (Lee & Barnes 1998), p. 8-32]

Sears, Elisabeth (Betty). *Shakespeare & the Tudor Rose*. Consolidated Press Printing Company.

1992

Hanson, David J. *"Shake-speare's" Treatise on Verse*. Mill Valley, CA: De Vere Foundation.

Hart, Michael H. *The 100: A Ranking of the Most Influential Persons in History, Revised and Updated for the Nineties*. New York: Citadel Press.

Haynes, Alan. *Invisible Power: The Elizabethan Secret Services, 1570-1603*. New York: St. Martin's Press.

Hope, Warren and Kim Holston. *The Shakespeare Controversy: An Analysis of the Claimants to Authorship, and Their Champions and Detractors*. Jefferson, NC: McFarland. [excerpt repr. in *Sh. Authorship Sourcebook* (Stritmatter 2019, 2022), p. 51-67]

Ogburn, (Jr.), Charlton. *The Mysterious William Shakespeare: The Myth and the Reality*. Foreword by David McCullough. 2nd edition. McLean, VA: EPM Publications. [excerpt repr. in *Shakespeare Criticism, vol. 41* (Lee & Barnes 1998), p. 2-5]

Ogburn, (Jr.), Charlton. *Shakespeare's Self-Portrait: A Summary* [pamphlet]. Northampton, MA: Oxenford Press.

1993

Anderson, Verily. *The De Veres of Castle Hedingham*. Lavenham, Suffolk, UK: Terence Dalton.

Boyle, Charles. *To Catch the Conscience of the King: Leslie Howard and the 17th Earl of Oxford*. [pamphlet] Northampton, MA: Oxenford Press. [revised and repr. in *Another Hamlet*]

DeVere, Rollin. *A Hawk From a Handsaw: A Student's Guide to the Shakespeare Mystery*. Hunting Valley, OH: University School Press.

Hughes, Stephanie H. *Oxford & Byron* [pamphlet]. Portland, OR: Paradigm Press.

Kennedy, Richard J. *Between the Lines* [pamphlet].

Phillips, Graham and Martin Keatman. *The Shakespeare Controversy*. London: Century. [excerpt repr. in *Shakespeare Criticism, vol. 41* (Lee & Barnes 1998): 67-76]

Wright, Daniel L. *The Anglican Shakespeare: Elizabethan Orthodoxy in the Great Histories*. Vancouver, WA: Pacific-Columbia Books.

1994

Bloom, Howard. *The Western Canon: The Books and School of the Ages*. New York: Riverhead Books. [see esp. p. 56-7, 347-49]

Chiljan, Katherine V. (editor). *Dedication Letters to the Earl of Oxford*. Northridge, CA: K. Chiljan.

Haynes, Colin. *The Shakespeare Dilemma*. Bisbee, AZ: Pequeno Press. Illustrated by Pat Baldwin.

Dams, Christopher & Iris Krass. *Discovering the True Shake-speare*. [pamphlet] The De Vere Society. [2nd ed. pub. in 1996]

Matus, Irvin L. *Shakespeare, In Fact*. New York: Continuum. Repr. in 1999 by Continuum. Repr. in 2012: Mineola, NY: Dover Publications.

Plunkett, Paul M. *Shacksper of Stratford: A Monumental Deception*. NY: Vantage Press.

Whalen, Richard F. *Shakespeare—Who Was He? The Oxford Challenge to the Bard of Avon*. Westport, CT: Praeger. [excerpt (p. 62-102) repr. in LC, p. 19-36]

1995

Ogburn, (Jr.), Charlton. *The Man Who Was Shakespeare: A Summary of the Case Unfolded in The Mysterious William Shakespeare: The Myth and the Reality*. McLean, VA: EPM Publications.

Lasocki, David and Roger Prior. *The Bassanos: Venetian Musicians and Instrument Makers in England*. Aldershot, England: Scolar Press. Brookfield, VT: Ashgate Pub. Co. [Chapter 8 repr. in DVN, vol. 2/2: 1-4]

Myers, Alan. *Myers' Literary Guide: The North East* (Lives & Letters). Mid Northumberland Arts Group. Careanet Press.

Non-fiction Books and Pamphlets

1996

Barron, Randall. *The Great Shakespeare Hoax*. Bloomington: 1st Books Library.

Challinor, Arthur M. *Alternative Shakespeare: A Modern Introduction*. Sussex, England: Book Guild.
[excerpt repr. in *Shakespeare Criticism, vol. 41* (Lee & Barnes 1998), p. 42-48]

Dams, Christopher & Iris Krass. *Discovering the True Shake-speare*. [pamphlet] De Vere Society. [2nd ed.]

Richardson, David A. (ed.) *Sixteenth-Century British Nondramatic Writers: Fourth Series*. Detroit: Gale. [see especially p. 181-91: "Edward de Vere, Seventeenth Earl of Oxford" by Dennis Kay]

Michell, John. *Who Wrote Shakespeare?* New York: Thames and Hudson.
[excerpt repr. in *Shakespeare Criticism, vol. 41* (Lee & Barnes 1998), p. 2-5]
[translated into German by Reinhard Kaiser as *Wer schrieb Shakespeare?* Frankfurt am Main: Aweitausendeins, 2001.]
[translated into Japanese by Kenji Takahashi as *Sheikusupia wa Dokoniiru?* Tokyo: Bungei Shunju, 2000.]

Stritmatter, Roger A. *There's Not the Smallest Orb, But in His Motion Like an Angel Sings*. Northampton, MA: Stritmatter.

1997

Baron, Dennis. *De Vere is Shakespeare: Evidence From the Biography and Wordplay*. Introduction by Christopher H. Dams. Cambridge: Oleander Press.

Bond, Jonathan. *The De Vere Code*.

Clegg, Cyndia S. *Press Censorship in Elizabethan England*. New York: Cambridge University Press.

Hughes, Stephanie Hopkins. *The Great Reckoning: Who Killed Christopher Marlowe, and Why*. Portland, OR: Paradigm Press. [repr. in TOX, vol. 18 (2016): 101-132]

Londré, Felicia H. *Love's Labour's Lost: Critical Essays*. New York: Garland Pub.

Sears, Elisabeth (Betty). *The Darling Buds of May*. [pamphlet] Published privately by Elisabeth Sears.

Sobran, Joseph. *Alias Shakespeare: Solving the Greatest Literary Mystery of All Time*. New York: Free Press.
[translated into German as *Genannt Shakespeare: die Lösung des grössten literarischen Rätsels*. Cologne: Dumont, 2002] [translated into *Japanese by Yushi Odashima and Noriko Odashima as Sheikusupia Misuteri*. Toyko: Asahi Shinbun Sha, 2000]

1998

Allen, Ron. *Who Were Shake-speare? The Ultimate Who-dunit*. San Diego: Silverado.

Hughes, Stephanie H. *The Relevance of Robert Greene to the Oxfordian Thesis*. Portland, OR: Paradigm Press.

Lee, Michelle & Dana Ramel Barnes. *Shakespeare Criticism, vol. 41: Authorship Controversy*. Gale.

1999

Brazil, Robert. *The True Story of the Shakespeare Publications, vol. 1: Edward de Vere and the Shakespeare Printers*.

Dunn, Jonni Koonce. *The Literary Patronage of Edward de Vere, The Seventeenth Earl of Oxford* [Master of Arts in English Thesis]. University of Texas, Arlington.

Eldredge, Joe. *Tilt Tournai & No Barriers*. [pamphlet] West Tisbury, MA: Humility Press.

Sexton, Mildred B (Pidge). *As You Like It* (part of the "What Shakespeare's Audiences Knew" pamphlet series). St. Louis: Mildred B. Sexton [written from an Oxfordian perspective]

Sexton, Mildred B. (Pidge). *Hamlet* (part of the "What Shakespeare's Audiences Knew" pamphlet series). St. Louis: Mildred B. Sexton [written from an Oxfordian perspective]

Sexton, Mildred B. *Much Ado About Nothing* (part of the "What Shakespeare's Audiences Knew" pamphlet series). St. Louis: Mildred B. Sexton [written from an Oxfordian perspective]

Sexton, Mildred B. (Pidge). *Twelfth Night* (part of the "What Shakespeare's Audiences Knew" pamphlet series). St. Louis: Mildred B. Sexton [written from an Oxfordian perspective]

Sexton, Mildred B. (Pidge) *The Winter's Tale* (part of the "What Shakespeare's Audiences Knew" pamphlet series). St. Louis: Mildred B. Sexton [written from an Oxfordian perspective]

2000

Alvis, John and Thomas G. West (editors). *Shakespeare as Political Thinker, 2nd Edition, Revised and Expanded*. Wilmington, DE: ISI Books.

Barron, Randall. *Shakespeare and the Queen*. Bloomington, IN: 1st Books.

Barron, Randall. *Shakespeare Through the Looking Glass*. Bloomington, IN: 1st Books.

Pearson, Daphne. *Edward de Vere, Seventeenth Earl of Oxford, 1550-1604: An Evaluation of the Financial Problems and the Changing Political Role of an Elizabethan Aristocrat*. Sheffield: University of Sheffield.

2001

Appleton, Elizabeth (Elizabeth Appleton van Druenen). *An Anatomy of the Marprelate Controversy, 1588-1596, Retracing Shakespeare's Identity and that of Martin Marprelate*. Prefaces by Francis Edwards and Daniel Wright. Lewiston, NY: Edwin Mellen Press.

Dickinson, Warren. *The Wonderful Shakespeare Mystery: Will the Paradigm Shift?* Nashville, TN: OMNI PublishXpress.

Gray, Marilyn Savage. *The Real Shakespeare*. iUniverse.com.

Holmes, Edward. *Discovering Shakespeare: A Handbook for Heretics*. Durham: Mycroft Books.

Price, Diana. *Shakespeare's Unorthodox Biography: New Evidence of an Authorship Problem*. Westport, CT: Greenwood Press.

Streitz, Paul. *Oxford, Son of Queen Elizabeth*. Darien, CT: Oxford Institute Press.

Stritmatter, Roger A. *The Marginalia of Edward de Vere's Geneva Bible: Providential Discovery, Literary Reasoning, and Historical Consequence*: A Dissertation submitted to the University of Massachusetts Amherst. Repr. in June 2003: Northampton, MA: Oxenford Press.

2002

Brame, Michael K. and Galina Popova. *Shakespeare's Fingerprints*. Vashon Island, WA: Adonis Editions.

Croft, Pauline. *Patronage, Culture and Power: The Early Cecils, 1558-1612* (editor). New Haven: Yale Univ. Press.

Er, Odysseus. *Paradigm Shift, Shake-speare: Jonson's Introductory Poems to the 1623 Folio, and Oxford as Shake-speare*. St. Paul: Nonconformist Press.

Hess, W. Ron. *The Dark Side of Shakespeare, vol. 1: An Iron-Fisted Romantic in England's Most Perilous Times*. New York: Writers Club Press.

Kirsch, Hans-Christian. *Oxford oder der Mann, der Shakespeares Stücke schrieb*. Mit Bildern von Christina Nagel. Blieskastel: Gollenstein. [German]

Love, Harold. *Attributing Authorship: An Introduction*. Cambridge: Cambridge University Press.

Sears, Elisabeth. *Shakespeare & the Tudor Rose*. With an introduction by Hank Whittemore and additional appendixes. Marshfield Hills, MA: Meadow Geese Press.

2003

Drumbolis, Nick. *The Pseudonym William Shakespeare*. Toronto: Letters Bookshop.

Er, Odysseus. *Hamlet-Christ*. St. Paul, MN: Nonconformist Press.

Hess, W. Ron. *The Dark Side of Shakespeare, vol. 2: An Elizabethan Courtier, Diplomat, Spymaster & Epic Hero*. Foreword by Gordon C. Cyr. New York: Writers Club Press.

Koz'minius; Melechcii. *Shekspir: Tainaja Istorija [Shakespeare: The Secret History]*. St. Petersburg: Neva.

McIntosh, P. D. *Shakespeare's Sonnets: An Elizabethan Love Story*. Tasmania, Australia: Otakou Press.

Nelson, Alan H. *Monstrous Adversary: The Life of Edward de Vere, 17th Earl of Oxford*. Liverpool: Liverpool University Press. [excerpt repr. in LC, p. 83-106]

North, Marcy L. *The Anonymous Renaissance: Cultures of Discretion in Tudor-Stuart England*. Chicago: University of Chicago Press.

Purdy, Gilbert W. *Edward de Vere Was Shake-speare: At Long Last, the Proof*.

Sinkevich, Ekaterina. *Razvitie Shekspirovskogo voprosa v sovremennom literaturovedenii Anglii I ShA [The Development of the Shakespearean Question in the Contemporary Literary Studies of Great Britain and the USA]*. [Russian] Kherson: Vyd-vo KhDU.

Willis, Charles. *Shakespeare and George Puttenham's Art of English Poesie*. Upso.

2004

Dictionary of National Biography. Oxford: Oxford University Press. [see esp. "Vere, Edward de" by Alan H. Nelson]

Garber, Marjorie. *Shakespeare After All*. New York: Anchor Books.

Greenblatt, Stephen. *Will in the World: How Shakespeare Became Shakespeare*. New York: W. W. Norton. [published in German as *Will in der Welt. Wie Shakespeare zu Shakespeare wurde*. Berlin: Berlin Verlag]

Helsloot, Pieter N. *Edward de Vere: Onvermijdelijk Shakespeare*. Zaltbommel: Aprilis. [Dutch]

Klier, Walter. *Der Fall Shakespeare – Die Autorschaftsdebatte und der 17. Graf von Oxford als der wahre Shakespeare: Bisher bekannt als Das Shakespeare-Komplott [The Case of Shakespeare – The Author's Edition and the 17th Earl of Oxford as the True Shakespeare: So Far Known as The Shakespeare Plot*. Uwe Laugwitz. [German]

Malim, Richard (general editor). *Great Oxford: Essays on the Life and Work of Edward de Vere, 17th Earl of Oxford, 1550-1604*. Tunbridge, Wells, Kent, UK: Parapress.

Vickers, Brian. *Shakespeare, Co-Author: A Historical Study of Five Collaborative Plays*. Oxford: Oxford University Press.

Non-fiction Books and Pamphlets

Yuhas, David. *The Shakespeare-Cervantes Code*. Boulder: Columbine Paperbacks.

2005

Anderson, Mark [Margo] K. *"Shakespeare" By Another Name: The Life of Edward de Vere, Earl of Oxford, the Man Who Was Shakespeare*. Foreword by Derek Jacobi. New York: Gotham Books.

Asquith, Clare. *Shadowplay: The Hidden Beliefs and Coded Politics of William Shakespeare*. New York: PublicAffairs.

Detobel, Robert. *Wie aus William Shaxsper; William Shakespeare wurde*. Verlag Uwe Laugwitz. [published as vol. 10 of *Neues Shakes-speare Journal* (July 2005)]

Fields, Bertram. *Players: The Shakespeare Mystery*. New York: Harper Perennial/Regan Books.

Gordon, Helen Heightsman. *The Secret Love Story in Shakespeare's Sonnets*. Xlibris Corporation.

Iacovou, Andreas. *Shakespeare Unparadised: Defining Shakespeare: An Essay Concerning Human Stupidity* (text selected and edited by Antonios Iacovou). Victoria, BC, Canada: Trafford Publishing.

James, Brenda and William D. Rubinstein. *The Truth Will Out: Unmasking the Real Shakespeare*. Harlow, England; New York: Longman/Pearson Education. Repr. in 2006: Regan.

Kreiler, Kurt (translator). *Edward de Veres Gedichte* [*The Poems of Edward de Vere*] [German and English]. Buchholz: Laugwitz.

McCrea, Scott. *The Case for Shakespeare: The End of the Authorship Question*. Westport, CT: Praeger.

Pearson, Daphne. *Edward de Vere: The Crisis and Consequences of Wardship*. Aldershot, Hants, England; Burlington, VT: Ashgate.

Whittemore, Hank. *The Monument*. Marshfield Hills, MA: Meadow Geese Press.

Whittemore, Hank. *The Monument: An Abridged Introduction to the 918-page First Reference Edition*.

Willis, Charles. *George Puttenham and the Authorship of Shakespeare's Sonnets*. Upso.

2006

Farina, William. *De Vere as Shakespeare: An Oxfordian Reading of the Canon*. Foreword by Felicia Londré. Jefferson, NC: McFarland & Co. [three chapters (*Macbeth, Julius Caesar, Romeo and Juliet*) repr. in *Sh. Authorship Sourcebook* (Stritmatter 2019, 2022), p. 271-300]

Friberg, Gösta & Helena Brodin Friberg. *Täcknamn Shakespeare: Edward de Veres hemliga liv*. Stockholm: Albert Bonniers Förlag. [Finnish]

Kreiler, Kurt (translator). *Edward de Vere: Fortunatus im Unglück. Die Aventiuren des Master F. I.* Frankfurt am Main: Insel-Verlag.

McCarthy, Penny. *Pseudonymous Shakespeare*. Burlington, VT: Ashgate Publishing Company.

Rosenbaum, Ron. *The Shakespeare Wars: Clashing Scholars, Public Fiascoes, Palace Coups*. New York: Random House.

Usher, Peter. *Hamlet's Universe*. Aventine Press.

Williams, Robin P. *Sweet Swan of Avon: Did a Woman Write Shakespeare?* Berkeley, CA: Wilton Circle Press.

Willis, Charles. *Behind Shakespeare's Mask*. Upso.

2007

American Council of Trustees and Alumni (ACTA). *The Vanishing Shakespeare*. Washington, D.C.: ACTA.

Cheney, Patrick (ed.), Hadfield, Andrew (ed.), Sullivan, Garrett A., Jr. (ed.) *Early Modern English Poetry: A Critical Companion*. New York: Oxford University Press. [see esp. p. 60-69: Steven May: "Early CourtierVerse: Oxford, Dyer, and Gascoigne"]

Mullan, John. *Anonymity: A Secret History of English Literature*. London: Faber and Faber. Princeton: Princeton University Press.

Shakespeare Oxford Society. *Report My Cause Aright: Fiftieth Anniversary Anthology, 1957-2007*. Shakespeare Oxford Society.

2008

Bate, Jonathan. *The Genius of Shakespeare*. 10th Anniversary Edition. New York: Oxford University Press. [see esp. "Ch. 3: The Authorship Controversy," p. 65-100]

Broderick, James F. and Darren H. Miller. *Web of Conspiracy: A Guide to Conspiracy Theory Sites on the Internet*. Medford, NJ: Information Today.

Caruso, Carl. *The Mystery of Hamlet*. PublishAmerica.

McClinton, Brian. *The Shakespeare Conspiracies: Untangling a 400-Year Web of Myth and Deceit*. Belfast: Shanway Press.

Nicholson, Adam. *Earls of Paradise: England and the Dream of Perfection*. New York: CarperCollins.

Roper, David L. *Proving Shakespeare: The Looming Identity Crisis*. Cornwall, UK: Orvid Books.

2009

Altrocchi, Paul H. and Hank Whittemore (editors). *Building the Case for Edward de Vere as Shakespeare*. iUniverse.com.

   vol. 1: The Great Shakespeare Hoax.

   vol. 2: Nothing Truer Than Truth.

   vol. 3: Shine Forth.

   vol. 4: My Name Be Buried.

   vol. 5: So Richly Spun.

Bond, Jonathan. *The De Vere Code: Proof of the True Author of Shake-speares Sonnets*. Canterbury: Real Press.

Hackett, Helen. *Elizabeth and Shakespeare: The Meeting of Two Minds*. Princeton: Princeton Uniersity Press.

Hill, Tracey. *Anthony Munday and Civic Culture: Theatre, History and Power in Early Modern London 1580-1633*. Manchester University Press.

Hope, Warren and Kim Holston. *The Shakespeare Controversy: An Analysis of the Authorship Theories, 2nd ed.* Jefferson, NC: McFarland & Co. [excerpt repr. in *Sh. Authorship Sourcebook* (Stritmatter 2019, 2022): 51-67]

Hughes, Stephanie H. *Robert Greene, King of the Paper Stage.*

Kreiler, Kurt. *Der Mann, der Shakespeare erfand: Edward de Vere, Earl of Oxford* [*The Man Who Invented Shakespeare*]. Frankfurt am Main: Insel Verlag.

Maltby, Arthur. *Shakespeare As a Challenge for Literary Biography*. Lewiston: The Edwin Mellen Press. [see esp. p. 180, 190-192]

Moore, Peter R. *The Lame Storyteller, Poor and Despised*. Edited by Gary B. Goldstein. Buchholz, Germany: Verlag Uwe Laugwitz. [Special Editions #1 of *Neues Shake-speare Journal*]

Tassinari, Lamberto. *John Florio: The Man Who Was Shakespeare*. Giano Books.

Wilkinson, Heward. *The Muse as Therapist: A New Poetic Paradigm for Psychotherapy*. Karnak Books. [also Routledge, 2018]

Wright, Daniel L. (editor). *Discovering Shakespeare: A Festschrift in Honor of Isabel Holden*. Portland, OR: Concordia University Bookstore.

2010

Altrocchi, Paul H. *Malice Aforethought: The Killing of a Unique Genius*. Xlibris.

Beauclerk, Charles. *Shakespeare's Lost Kingdom: The True History of Shakespeare and Elizabeth*. New York: Grove Press.

Bevington, David M. *Shakespeare and Biography*. Oxford and New York: Oxford University Press.

Detobel, Robert. *Shakespeare: The Concealed Poet*. English version assisted by K. C. Ligon. Buchholz in der Nordheide, Germany: Laugwitz. [Special editions no. 8 of *Neues Shake-speare Journal*]

Detobel, Robert. *Will – Wunsch und Wirklichkeit: James Shapiro's "Contested Will."* [*Wish and Reality: A Critical Examination of James Shapiro's "Contested Will."* Buchholz, Germany: Verlag Uwe Laugwitz. [Special Editions no. 2 of *Neues Shake-speare Journal*]

Draya, Ren (editor, with Richard F. Whalen). *Othello the Moor of Venice. Fully Annotated from an Oxfordian Perspective*. Horatio Editions.

Feldman, A. Bronson. *Hamlet Himself*. Bloomington: iUniverse.com.

Gilvary, Kevin (editor). *Dating Shakespeare's Plays: A Critical Review of the Evidence*. Turnbridge Wells, Kent, UK: Parapress.

Laugwitz, Uwe, Hanno Wember, and Robert Detobel (editors*). John Thomas Looney und Sigmund Freud* (includes the article by Richard M. Waugaman, "Psychoanalyse und die Verfasserschaftsfrage")

Leahy, William. *Shakespeare and His Authors*. London and New York: Continuum.

Roper, David L. *Shakespeare: To Be or Not To Be?* Carnwall, UK: Orvid Books.

Shapiro, James S. *Contested Will: Who Wrote Shakespeare?* New York: Simon & Schuster.

Twain, Mark. *"1601" and "Is Shakespeare Dead?"* Foreword by Shelley Fisher Fishkin. Introduction by Erica Jong. Afterword by Leslie A. Fiedler. New York: Oxford University Press.

Whalen, Richard F. (editor, with Ren Draya). *Othello the Moor of Venice. Fully Annotated from an Oxfordian Perspective*. Horatio Editions.

Whittemore, Hank. *Shakespeare's Son and His Sonnets*. Groton, MA: Martin and Lawrence Press.

Non-fiction Books and Pamphlets

2011

Boyle, Charles. *Another Hamlet: The Mystery of Leslie Howard*. Revised ed. Somerville, MA: Forever Press.

Chiljan, Katherine. *Shakespeare Suppressed: The Uncensored Truth about Shakespeare and His Works: A Book of Evidence and Explanation*. San Francisco: Faire Editions. [2nd ed., 2016]

Danner, Bruce. *Edmund Spenser's War on Lord Burghley*. New York: Palgrave Macmillan.

Dickson, Peter W. *Bardgate: Shake-speare and the Royalists Who Stole the Bard*. Mount Vernon, OH: Printing Arts Press.

Edmondson, Paul & Stanley Wells. *Shakespeare Bites Back: Not So Anonymous* [e-book].

Feldman, Sabrina. *The Apocryphal William Shakespeare: A 'Third Way' Shakespeare Authorship Scenario*. Indianapolis: Dog Ear Publishing.

Kreiler, Kurt. *Anonymous Shake-Speare – The Man Behind*. München: Dölling.

Kreiler, Kurt (translator). *William Shakespeare – Die Lieder und Gedichte aus den Stücken*. Berlin: Insel-Verlag.

McClarran, Steven [Steven Steinburg]. *I Come To Bury Shaksper: A Deconstruction of the Fable of the Stratfordian Shakespeare and the Supporting Scholarship: An Oxfordian Perspective*.

Measom, Christopher (editor). *Anonymous: William Shakespeare Revealed*. Introduction by Roland Emmerich. Designed by Timothy Shaner. New York: Newmarket Press.

Pointon, A. J. *The Man Who Was Never Shakespeare: The Theft of William Shakspere's Identity*. Turnbridge Wells, Kent, UK: Parapress.

Roe, Richard P. *The Shakespeare Guide to Italy: Retracing the Bard's Unknown Travels*. New York: Harper Perennial. [excerpt repr. in TOX, vol. 16: 73-77]

Roper, David L. *Proving Shakespeare: Verifying Ben Jonson's Vow that Edward de Vere was William Shakespeare* (revised and updated paperback edition). Cornwall, UK: Orvid Books.

Starner, Janet W. and Barbara H. Traister. *Anonymity in Early Modern England: "What's in a Name?"* Burlington, VT: Ashgate.

Trudeau, Lawrence J. (editor). *Literature Criticism 1400 to 1800*, vol. 193. Gale Cengage Publishing. [collection of articles, mostly Oxfordian in nature]

2012

A'Dair, Mike. *Four Essays on the Shakespeare Authorship Question*. Willits, CA: Verisimilitude Press.

Alford, Stephen. *The Watchers: A Secret History of the Reign of Elizabeth I*. Allen Lane.

Detobel, Robert and Hanno Wember (editors). *Stratford's Fragestunde*. Introduction by Michael York. Buchholz, Germany: Verlag Uwe Laugwitz. [Translation of *Exposing an Industry in Denial: Authorship Doubters Respond to "60 Minutes with Shakespeare,"* edited by John M. Shahan and published by The Shakespeare Authorship Coalition] [Special Editions #6 of *Neues Shake-speare Journal*]

Ellis, David. *The Truth About William Shakespeare: Fact, Fiction and Modern Biographies*. Edinburgh: Edin. Univ. Press.

Fox, Robin. *Shakespeare's Education: Schools, Lawsuits, Theater and the Tudor Miracle* (edited by Gary B. Goldstein). Buchholz, Germany: Verlag Uwe Laugwitz. [Special Editions #5 of *Neues Shake-speare Journal*]

Malim, Richard. *The Earl of Oxford and the Making of "Shakespeare": The Literary Life of Edward de Vere in Context*. London: McFarland & Co.

Price, Diana. *Shakespeare's Unorthodox Biography: New Evidence of an Authorship Problem*. Published with corrections, revisions, and additions. Westport, CT: Shakespeare-authorship.com. [excerpt repr. in *Sh. Authorship Sourcebook* (Stritmatter 2019, 2022): 192-95]

Rubinstein, William D. *Who Wrote Shakespeare's Plays?* Stroud: Amberley.

Sharkey, Michael. *Apollo in George Street: The Life of David McKee Wright*. Glebe, NSW, Australia: Puncher & Wattmann.

Warren, James A. *An Index to Oxfordian Publications*. Somerville, MA: Forever Press.

Whittemore, Hank. *Twelve Years in the Life of Shakespeare*. Edited by William E. Boyle. Somerville, MA: Forever Press.

2013

Bergman, Martin S. *The Unconscious in Shakespeare's Plays*. Karnac Books.

Boyle, Charles. *Another Hamlet: The Mystery of Leslie Howard*. Revised ed/ Somerville, MA: Forever Press.

Boyle, William E. *A Poet's Rage: Understanding Shakespeare Through Authorship Studies*. Somerville, MA. Forever Press.

Brazil, Robert S. *Angel Day, The English Secretary, and the Seventeenth Earl of Oxford*. Cortical Output.

Edmondson, Paul and Stanley Wells. *Shakespeare Beyond Doubt: Evidence, Argument, Controversy*. Cambridge; New York: Cambridge University Press.

Gontar, David P. *Hamlet Made Simple: and Other Essays*. Nashville: New English Review Press.

Kreiler, Kurt. *Hundert Gedichte von Edward de Vere, Earl of Oxford*. Berlin: Insel Verlag.

Purdy, Gilbert W. *Edward de Vere Was Shake-speare: At Long Last, the Proof*. CreateSpace.

Shahan, John M. and Alexander Waugh (editors). *Shakespeare Beyond Doubt? Exposing an Industry in Denial*. Tamarac, FL: Llumina Press

Steinburg, Steven. *I Come to Bury Shakespeare II: A Deconstruction of the Fable of the Stratfordian Shake-speare and the Supporting Scholarship. An Oxfordian Perspective*. CreateSpace.

Stritmatter, Roger A. and Lynne Kositsky. *On the Date, Sources and Design of Shakespeare's The Tempest*. Foreword by William S. Niederkorn. Jefferson, NC: McFarland & Co. [exerpt repr. in *Sh. Authorship Sourcebook* (Stritmatter 2022), p. 429-49]

Sturrock, Peter A. *AKA Shakespere: A Scientific Approach to the Authorship Question*. Palo Alto: Exoscience.

Warren, James A. *An Index to Oxfordian Publications. Second Edition*. Somerville, MA: Forever Press.

Whalen, Richard F. (editor). *Macbeth, Annotated from an Oxfordian Perspective*. [2nd edition, revised and expanded] Horatio Editions.

2014

Altrocchi, Paul H. (editor). *Building the Case for Edward de Vere as Shakespeare*. iUniverse.com

    Vol. 6: Wonder of Our Stage

    Vol. 7: Avalanche of Falsity

    Vol. 8: To All the World Must Die

    Vol. 9: Soul of the Age

    Vol. 10: Moniment

Black, Pauline and Michael. *Shakespeare Unraveled—Court Plays: The 1623 Deception*. Published by Pauline and Michael Black.

Brook, Peter. *The Quality of Mercy: Reflections on Shakespeare*. New York: Theatre Communications Group. [see esp. "Alas, Poor Yorick, or What if Shakespeare Fell off the Wall?" p. 3-17]

Cutler, Keir. *The Shakespeare Authorship Question: A Crackpot's View*. Amazon Digital Services, Inc.

Graves, Charles L. *27 Essays on Edward de Vere and William Shakespeare*. CreateSpace.

Hudson, John. *Shakespeare's Dark Lady: Amelia Bassano Lanier: The Woman Behind Shakespeare's Plays*. Amberley Publishing.

Jolly, Margrethe (Eddi). *The First Two Quartos of Hamlet: A New View of the Origins and Relationship of the Texts*. Jefferson, NC: McFarland.

Lavater-Sloman, Mary. *Shakespeare – Ein Leben im Gedicht: Edward de Vere, der 17. Earl of Oxford* (German edition). Romerhof Verlag.

Magri, Noemi. *Such Fruits Out of Italy: The Italian Renaissance in Shakespeare's Plays and Poems*. Edited by Gary B. Goldstein. Buchholz, Germany: Verlag Uwe Laugwitz. [Special Editions #3 of *Neues Shake-speare Journal*]

Mena, Ricardo. *Ver, Begin*. Preface by Hank Whittemore. Amazon Digital Services, Inc.

Montee, David. *Translating Shakespeare: A Guide for Young Actors*. Hanover, NH: Smith and Kraus.

    [excerpt repr. in *Sh. Authorship Sourcebook* (Stritmatter 2019, 2022): 99-115]

Rollett, John M. *William Stanley as Shakespeare: Evidence of Authorship by the Sixth Earl of Derby*. McFarland.

Waugaman, Richard M. *It's Time to Re-Vere the Works of "Shakespeare": A Psychoanalyst Reads the Works of Edward de Vere, Earl of Oxford*. Oxfreudian Press.

Waugaman, Richard M. *Newly Discovered Works by "William Shake-speare": A.K.A. Edward de Vere, Earl of Oxford*. Oxfreudian Press. Republished in 2017.

Waugh, Alexander. *Shakespeare in Court*. Amazon Digital Services, Inc.

2015

American Council of Trustees and Alumni (ACTA). *The Unkindest Cut: Shakespeare in Exile 2015*. Washington, D.C.: ACTA.

Delahoyde, Michael (editor). *Anthony and Cleopatra, edited, introduced, and fully annotated from an Oxfordian Perspective.*

Eyre, Geoffrey. *The Case for Edward de Vere as Shakespeare*. Published by Geoffrey Eyre.

Feldman, Sabrina. *Thomas Sackville and the Shakespearean Glass Slipper: Book Two of A 'Third Way' Shakespeare Authorship Scenario*. CreateSpace.

Gilvary, Kevin. *Shakespearean Biografiction: How Modern Biographers Rely on Context, Conjecture and Inference to Construct a Life of the Bard*. London: Brunel University. [Ph.D. thesis]

Gontar, David P. *Unreading Shakespeare*. Nashville: New England Review Press.

Gray, Marilyn Savage. *The Real Shakespeare, Rev. ed.* iUniverse.

Rush, Peter. *Hidden in Plain Sight: The True History Revealed in Shake-speare's Sonnets*. Foreword by Hank Whittemore. Leesburg, VA: Real Deal Publications.

Steinburg, Steven. *The Shakespeare Puzzles: The Hidden Autobiography of Edward de Vere*. CreateSpace.

Stelting, Michelle. Redating Pericles: *A Re-examination of Shakespeare's Pericles as an Elizabethan Play*. University of Missouri at Kansas City, Department of Theatre, Master's Thesis.

Stritmatter, Roger A. *The Marginalia of Edward de Vere's Geneva Bible* [4th imprint]

Sturrock, Peter A. *Late Night Thoughts About Science*. Exoscience Publishing.

Warren, James A. *An Index to Oxfordian Publications and Oxfordian Articles in Non-Oxfordian Publications. Third Edition*. Somerville, MA: Forever Press. [Jan.]

Wittek, Stephen. *The Media Players: Shakespeare, Middleton, Jonson, and the Idea of News*. University of Michigan Press.

2016

Anderson, Mark K., Alex McNeil and Alexander Waugh (editors). 2016. *Contested Year: An Anthology of Critical Reviews and Corrections to Each Chapter of James Shapiro's "The Year of Lear: Shakespeare in 1606."* Kindle Edition.

Benson, Jon. *The Reader's Companion to The Death of Shakespeare, Part One*. Annapolis, MD: Nedward, LLC. [see also *The Death of Shakespeare As It Was Accomplisht in 1616 & The Causes Thereof, Part One* in the fiction book list]

Browning, Keith. *Shakespeare Re-invented: Challenging 400 Years of Shakespeare Fantasy!!*. Kingsbridge, Devon, UK: Aged Sportsman Publishing.

Chiljan, Katherine. *Shakespeare Suppressed: The Uncensored Truth about Shakespeare and His Works: A Book of Evidence and Explanation, 2nd ed.* San Francisco: Faire Editions. [2011]

Dickson, Peter W. *Bardgate II: Shakespeare, Catholicism and the Politics of the First Folio of 1623*. Mount Vernon, OH: Printing Arts Press.

Dutton, Richard. *Shakespeare, Court Dramatist*. Oxford: Oxford University Press.

Goldstein, Gary B. *Reflections on the True Shakespeare*. Buchholz, Germany: Verlag Uwe Laugwitz. [Special Editions #6 of *Neues Shake-speare Journal*]

Hosking, Tony. *Shakespeare as Philosopher and the Shakespearean Tragedy of Edward de Vere*. Shogi Foundation.

Lake, Peter. *How Shakespeare Put Politics on the Stage: Power and Succession in the History Plays*. New Haven: Yale University Press.

McDonnell, Tom. *Sweete Wittie Soules: Shakespeare's Connections to Oxford, Town, Gown & Shire*. Oxford: Autolycus Bks.

Moser, Franz. *Shakespere ist nicht Shake-speare? Uber den wahren Autor des Shakespeare-Kanons Edward de Vere, Earl of Oxford* [*Shakespeare is Not Shake-speare?: About the True Author of Shakespeare's Canon, Edward de Vere, Earl of Oxford*]. Uwe Laugwitz. [German]

Rush, Peter. *Hidden in Plain Sight: The True History Revealed in Shake-speare's Sonnets Second Edition, Revised*. Leesburg, VA: Real Deal Publications. [foreword by Hank Whittemore]

Story, Ted. *The Shakespeare Fraud: The Politics Behind the Pen*. Somerville, MA: Forever Press.

Stritmatter, Roger A. *The 1623 Shakespeare First Folio: A Minority Report*. [a special issue of *Brief Chronicles*] SOF.

Whittemore, Hank. *100 Reasons Shake-speare was the Earl of Oxford*. Somerville, MA: Forever Press.

2017

A'Dair, Mike. *The Ashbourne Saga: A Cinematic Epic in Fourteen Episodes*. Lulu.

Barber, Ros (editor). *Know-It-All Shakespeare*. London: Quarto Publishing.

Berney, Charles V. *Shakespeare Confidential*. Somerville, MA: Forever Press.

Dowdey, David (editor). *Secret Whispers: Searching for the Truth of Shakespeare*. Traveler Books.

Eyre, Geoffrey. *The Shakespeare Authorship Mystery Explained*. Mardle Publications.

Gray, Joshua. *The Life and Death of King Edward*. Forever Press.

Quealy, Gerit. *Botanical Shakespeare*. Harper Design.

Rosenblum, Joseph (editor). *The Definitive Shakespeare Companion*. Santa Barbara: Greenwood. [see esp. "The Authorship Questions"]

Taylor, Gary & Gabriel Egan (editors). *The New Oxford Shakespeare Authorship Companion*. Oxford: Oxford Univ. Press.

Wallace, David Rains. *Shakespeare's Wilderness*. Independent Publishing Platform.

Warren, James A. (editor). *An Index to Oxfordian Publications and Oxfordian Articles in Non-Oxfordian Publications. Fourth Edition*. Somerville, MA: Forever Press.

2018

Asquith, Clare. *Shakespeare and the Resistance: The Earl of Southampton, the Essex Rebellion, and the Poems that Challenged Tudor Tyranny*. New York: Public Affairs.

Cutting, Bonner Miller. *Necessary Mischief: Exploring the Shakespeare Authorship Question*. Jennings, LA: Minos Publishing Company.

Gilvary, Kevin. *The Fictional Lives of Shakespeare*. London: Routledge.

Jiménez, Ramon. *Shakespeare's Apprenticeship: Identifying the Real Playwright's Earliest Works*. Jefferson, NC: McFarland & Co., Inc.

Leahy, William (editor). *My Shakespeare: The Authorship Controversy*. Edward Everett Root, Publishers.

Looney. J. Thomas. *"Shakespeare" Identified*. Centenary edition edited by James A. Warren. Somerville, MA: Forever Press. Re-released by Veritas Publications in 2019.

McCarthy, Dennis. *A Brief Discourse of Rebellion and Rebels by George North: A Newly Uncovered Manuscript Source for Shakespeare's Plays*. Cambridge: D. S. Brewer.

Roper, David L. *How Science Proved Edward de Vere was William Shakespeare*. Cornwall, UK: Orvid Editions.

Steinburg, Steven. *Renaissance of Lies: Part 2 of the Autobiography of Edward de Vere, 17th Earl of Oxford*.

Vedi, Sten F. & Gerold Wagner. *Hamlet's Elsinore Revisited: The Author's Sources of Knowledge about Elsinore and Denmark*. Buchholz, Germany: Laugwitz Verlag. [Special issue no. 7 of *Neues Shake-speare Journal*]

Wainwright, Michael. *The Rational Shakespeare: Peter Ramus, Edward de Vere, and the Question of Authorship*. Palgrave Macmillan.

Whalen, Richard F. (editor). *Hamlet. Fully annotated from an Oxfordian perspective*. Horation Editions.

2019

Bate, Jonathan. *How the Classics Made Shakespeare*. Princeton: Princeton University Press.

Feldman, A. Bronson. *Early Shakespeare*. Edited by Warren Hope. Laugwitz Verlag. [Special issue no. 8 of *Neues Shake-speare Journal*]

Looney, J. Thomas. *"Shakespeare" Identified*. Centenary edition edited by James A. Warren. Cary, NC: Veritas Publications.

Looney, J. Thomas. *"Shakespeare" Revealed: The Collected Articles and Published Letters of J. Thomas Looney*. Edited by James A. Warren. Cary, NC: Veritas Publications.

Steinburg, Steven. *I Come to Bury Shakspere* (fifth edition).

Stritmatter, Roger (general editor). *The Poems of Edward de Vere, 17th Earl of Oxford . . . and the Shakespeare Authorship Question. Vol. 1: He that Takes the Pain to Pen the Book*. Shakespeare Oxford Fellowship.

Stritmatter, Roger (editor). *The Shakespeare Authorship Sourcebook: A Workbook for Educators and Students*. Shakespeare Oxford Fellowship.

Wildenthal, Bryan. *Early Shakespeare Authorship Doubts*. San Diego: Zindabad Press.

2020

Baker, John Milnes. *The Case for Edward de Vere as the Real William Shakespeare: A Challenge to Conventional Wisdom*. iUniverse.

Beauclerk, Charles & Sarah. *Take Physic, Pomp!*

Destro, Ron (editor). *The Shakespeare Masterclass*. New York and Oxford: Routledge.

Gilbert, Sky. *Shakespeare Beyond Science*. Toronto: Guernica Editions.

Johnson, Ian. *Renaissance Man: The World of Thomas Watson*. New Generation Publishing.

Ostrowski, Donald. *Who Wrote That? Authorship Controversies from Moses to Sholokhov*. Ithica: Northern Illinois University Press.

Roper, David L. *How Science Proved Edward de Vere was William Shakespeare*. [2nd ed. of the 2018 pub.]. First Proofs.

Waugaman, Richard M. *Let's Re-Vere the Works of Shake-speare*. [2nd ed. of the 2014 pub.] Independent.

2021

Blanding, Michael. *North by Shakespeare: A Rogue Scholar's Quest for the Truth Behind the Bard's Works*. New York: Hachette Books.

Delahoyde, Michael. *Twelfth Night. Edited, introduced and fully annotated from an Oxfordian Perspective*.

Gilvary, Kevin (editor). *Dating Shakespeare's Plays, 2nd ed*. Portsea Press.

Steinburg, Steven. *A Lover's Complaint: Part 3 of the Autobiography of Edward de Vere, 17th Earl of Oxford*.

Stepniewski, Michael and Spencer. *Shakespeare's Will . . . In what he hath left us*.

Usher, Peter. *Shakespeare's Knowledge of Astronomy and the Birth of Modern Cosmology*. Peter Lang.

Non-fiction Books and Pamphlets

Warren, James A. (editor). *Shakespeare Investigated: Publications of the Shakespeare Fellowship, 1922-1936*. Cary, NC: Veritas Publications.

Warren, James A. *Shakespeare Revolutionized: The First Hundred Years of J. Thomas Looney's "Shakespeare" Identified*. Cary, NC: Veritas Publications.

Whittemore, Hank. *100 Reasons Shake-speare was the Earl of Oxford*. With a New Introduction by the Author. GMJ Global Media. [excerpts reprinted in *Sh. Authorship Sourcebook* (Stritmatter 2019, 2022), p. 315-24]

2022

Allen, Percy. *Complete Writings on Shakespeare* (7 volumes). Edited by James A. Warren. Cary, NC: Veritas Publications.

> *Vol. 1: Borrowings and Topicality in Elizabethan Drama, 1928-1929.*

> *Vol. 2: The Case for Edward de Vere as "Shakespeare," 1923-0930.*

> *Vol. 3: The Oxford-Shakespeare Case Corroborated, 1930-1932.*

> *Vol. 4: The Life Story of Edward de Vere as "William Shakespeare," 1932-1933.*

> *Vol. 5: The Plays of Shakespeare in Relation to French History, 1933-1936.*

> *Vol. 6: Anne Cecil & the Dynastic Successioin Theory, 1934-1943.*

> *Vol. 7: Later Writings on Shakespeare, 1937-1953.*

Brennan, Michael G. (editor). *English Travellers to Venice 1450-1600*. London: Routledge. [with a nine-page essay on Edward de Vere]

Feldman, A. Bronson. *Shakespeare, Marlowe, and Other Elizabthans*. Edited by Warren Hope. Laugwitz Verlag. [Special issue no. 9 of *Neues Shake-speare Journal*]

Greatorex, Jane. *Manors, Mills & Manuscripts series: John de Vere, 16th Earl of Oxford*.

Hamill, John. *The Secret Shakespeare Sex Scandals: Bisexuality and Bastardy*.

Hughes, Stephanie Hopkins. *Educating Shakespeare: What he knew and how and where he learned it*. Cary, NC: Veritas Publications.

Jiménez, Ramon (editor). *The Famous Victories of Henry V*. [an early play by the real William Shakespeare, Edward de Vere, seventeenth Earl of Oxford] [Introduced, edited and fully annotated from an Oxfordian perspective]

Lawler, Frank (translator). *Behind the Mask of William Shakespeare by Abel Lefranc. A new translation by Frank Lawler*. Cary, NC: Veritas Publications.

Lefranc, Abel. *Behind the Mask of William Shakespeare. A new translation by Frank Lawler*. Cary, NC: Veritas Publications.

Malim, Richard. *Shakespeare's Revolution*. London: Austin Macauley Publishers.

Nelson, Jane E. *Shakespeare and religio mentis: A Study of Christian Hermetism in Four Plays*. Brill.

Prechter, Robert R., Jr. *Oxford's Voices: What Shakespeare Wrote Before He was Shakespeare*. [online]

Steinburg, Steven. *Amoretti: Children of the Virgin Queen: Part 4 of the Autobiography of Edward de Vere, 17th Earl of Oxford*.

Stritmatter, Roger (editor). *The Shakespeare Authorship Sourcebook: A Workbook for Educators and Students*. 2nd edition. Shakespeare Oxford Fellowship.

Stritmatter, Roger (editor). *Shakespeare and the Law: How the Bard's Legal Knowledge Affects the Authorship Question*. Shakespeare Oxford Fellowship.

Whittemore, Hank. *The Living Record: Shakespeare, Succession, and the Sonnets*. GMJ Global Media.

2023

Delahoyde, Michael (editor). *The Comedy of Errors. Edited, introduced and fully annotated from an Oxfordian Perspective*.

Durkee, Lee. *Stalking Shakespeare: A Memoir of Madness, Murder, and My Search for the Poet Beneath the Paint*. New York: Scribner.

Greenhill, Rima. *Elizabeth and Ivan: The Role of English-Russian Relations in Love's Labour's Lost*. Jefferson, NC: McFarland.

Rendall, Gerald H. *Shakespeare Sonnets and Edward de Vere & Personal Clues in Shakespeare Poems and Sonnets*. New editions of both books in one volume, edited by James A. Warren. Cary, NC: Veritas Publications.

Slater, Gilbert. *Seven Shakespeares: A Discussion of the Evidence for Various Theories with Regard to Shakespeare's Identity*. Modern edition edited by James A. Warren. Cary, NC: Veritas Publications.

Stritmatter, Roger (general editor). *The Poems of Edward de Vere, 17th Earl of Oxford . . . and the Shakespeare Question. Vol. 1: He that Takes the Pain to Pen the Book*. Shakespeare Oxford Fellowship.

Stritmatter, Roger (general editor). *The Poems of Edward de Vere, 17th Earl of Oxford . . . and the Shakespeare Question. Vol. 2: As It Fell Upon a Day: Poems from The Passionate Pilgrim*. Shakespeare Oxford Fellowship.

Stritmatter, Roger (editor). *The First Folio: A Shakespearean Enigma. The 1623 First Folio and the Authorship Question*.

Shakespeare Oxford Fellowship.

Ward, Captain Bernard M. *The Seventeenth Earl of Oxford 1550-1604*. Modern edition edited by James A. Warren. Cary, NC: Veritas Publications.

Warren, James A. (editor). *An Index to Oxfordian Publications, including Oxfordian books and selected articles from Non-Oxfordian periodicals. Fifth edition*. Cary: NC: Veritas Publications.

Winkler, Elizabeth. *Shakespeare Was a Woman and Other Heresies: How Doubting the Bard Became the Biggest Taboo in Literature*. New York: Simon and Schuster.

* * * * *

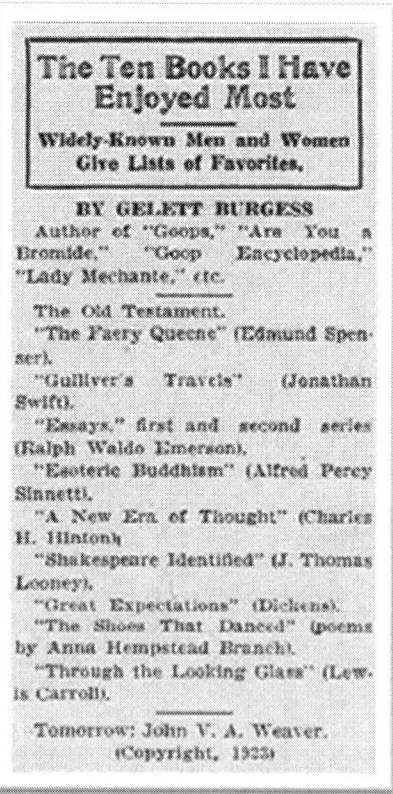

IIIB. Oxford Editions of Shakespearean Era Plays

Anthony and Cleopatra. Edited, introduced and fully annotated from an Oxfordian perspective by Michael Delahoyde. 2015.

The Comedy of Errors. Edited, introduced and fully annotated from an Oxfordian perspective by Michael Delahoyde. 2023.

The Famous Victories of Henry the Fifth, an early play by the real William Shakespeare, Edward de Vere, seventeenth Earl of Oxford. Introduced, edited and fully annotated from an Oxfordian perspective by Ramon Jiménez. 2022.

Hamlet. Fully annotated from an Oxfordian perspective by Richard F. Whalen. Horatio Editions. 2018.

Macbeth, second edition, revised and expanded. Fully annotated from an Oxfordian perspective by Richard F. Whalen. Horatio Editions. 2013. [first edition, 2007]

Othello the Moor of Venice. Fully annotated from an Oxfordian Perspective by Ren Draya and Richard F. Whalen. Horatio Editions. 2010.

Twelfth Night. Edited, introduced and fully annotated from an Oxfordian perspective by Michael Delahoyde. 2021.

Verus Publishing editions of the plays and poems of Edward de Vere (2019-2020)

Anthonie and Cleopatra

A Midsummer Night's Dream

The Merchant of Venice

Much Ado About Nothing

Richard the Third

The Tragedie of Hamlet (2020)

The Tragedie of Julius Caesar

The Tragedie of King Lear

The Tragedie of Macbeth

The Tragedie of Othello

The Tragedie of Romeo and Juliet

The Taming of the Shrew

The Tempest (2020)

Twelfth Night of What You Will

The Poetry of Edward de Vere

IIIc. Imaginative Works Inspired [at least partially] by the Shakespeare Authorship Question

(Chronological order) (See also movies and TV shows in Part IV.)

1645

Anon. *The Great Assizes Holden on Parnassus by Apollo and His Assessors*.

1687

Ravenscroft, Edward. [an adaptation of] *Titus Andronicus*.

1769

Lawrence, Herbert. *The Life and Adventures of Common Sense: An Historical Allegory*. Two volumes. [2nd edition, 1774: New York: Garland Press]

1786

An Officer of the Royal Navy. *The Story of a Learned Pig*. London: R. Jameson.

1827

Ward, Robert Plumer. *De Vere, or, The Man of Independence*. London: H. Colburn.

1837

Disraeli, Benjamin. *Venetia*. London: H. Colburn. Republished several times.

1860

O'Connor, William Douglas. *Harrington: A Story of True Love*. Boston: Thayer & Eldridge.

1903

James, Henry. "The Birthplace," a story in *The Better Sort*, p. 403-465. London: Methuen & Co.

- -- ---- -------- ---------------- -------- ---- -- -

1928

Galsworthy, John. *The White Monkey*. New York: Charles Scribner's Sons.

1929

Singleton, Esther. *Shakespearian Fantasias, Adventures in the Fourth Dimension*. Norwood, MA: Priv. print.

1940

Munsell, Warren P., Jr. *By Any Other Name* [dramatization of the life of Edward Earl of Oxford]

Grotyohann, Walter. *The Man Who Was Shakespeare* [a play]

1949

Boyce, Burke. *Cloak of Folly*. New York: Harper.

1954

O'Neal, Cothburn. *The Dark Lady: A Novel*. New York: Crown Publishers, Inc.

1960?

Amphlett, Hilda. *The Seventeenth Earl of Oxford: A Play*. [unpublished]

1961

Baker, Norman. *William Shakespeare's Conspiracy: A Play*.

1965

Blatty, William P. *I, Billy Shakespeare*. Garden City, NY: Doubleday.

Ford, Gertrude C. *A Rose By Any Name*. Intro. by Francis T. Carmody. New York: A. S. Barnes.

1968

Ford, Gertrude C. *Shakespeare and Elizabeth Unmasked*

Simak, Clifford D. *The Goblin Reservation*. New York: Putnam.

1971

Gale, Gertrude. *Masquerade*. [a play based on Prince Tudor themes]

1972

Brewster, Eleanor. *Oxford and His Elizabethan Ladies*. Philadelphia: Dorrance.

Imaginative Works

1975

Messner, Rhoda Henry. *Absent Thee From Felicity: The Story of Edward de Vere, Seventeenth Earl of Oxford, A Biographical Novel*. Shaker Heights, OH: The Corinthian Press.

1976

Simak, Clifford D. *Shakespeare's Planet*. New York: Berkley.

1977

Blake, Darrol. *Nothing Truer Than Truth: The Life and Times of Edward de Vere, Sometimes Known as William Shakespeare*. [a play, pub. in 2019]

Lavater-Sloman, Mary. *Gefährte der Königin: Elisabeth I, Edward Earl of Oxford und das Geheimnis um Shakespeare*. A novel. Zurich, Munchen: Artemis-Verlag.

1983

Hoyt, Richard. *The Siskiyou Two-Step*. New York: William Morrow and Company, Inc.

1987

Batiuk, Tom. *Funky Winkerbean*. [comic strip mentions Edward de Vere] (Oct. 27, 1987).

1988

Ferlita, Ernest. *The Truth of the Matter: A Play in Two Acts*. New Orleans: Loyola University Drama Department.

Frazer, Winifred L. *Truth is Stranger*. [a play/musical about a grad student who is an Oxfordian trying to get a Ph.D. in English literature, with songs by David Stryker]

Nassivera, John. *All the Queen's Men*. [a two-act play]

Wood, O. M. Ironside. *Proud Passionate Boy*. [a play]

1990

Field, Andrew. *The Lost Chronicle of Edward de Vere*. London, New York: Viking.
[Translated into German by Hans J. Schütz as *Die geheimen Aufzeichnungen des Edward de Vere, Grosskämmerer, Siebzehnter Earl of Oxford, Dichter und Stücheschreiber, genannt Shakespeare*. Stuttgart: Klett-Cotta, 1994]

1992

Desper, Richard. *Star-Crossed Lovers: A Play in Three Acts*. Action, MA: Published by the Author.

Fey, Jerry. *Oxford's Will: A Play*.

Kelly, Walt. *Pogo*. [comic strip about spellings of Shaksper] [repr. in SON, vol. 28/4a: 10]

1993

Bridgers, Sue E. *Keeping Christina*. New York: HarperCollinsPublishers.

1995

D'Artagnan, Robert. *Against This Rage*. London: 1st Books Library.

1996

Peer, Michael. *The Shakespeare Conspiracy: A Play*.

1997

Hovey, Alan J. *Aye, Shakespeare: The Dramatist Unmasked*. [a one-man play] Green Spring, WV.

Imlay, Elizabeth. *Edward de Vere, Part 1* [a play].

1998

Spark, Muriel. *A Far Cry from Kensington*. New York: New Directions Books. [A character in a publishing firm is sure that Shakspere was not the author, and that he, in the next world, must be laughing up his sleeve at what is going on in Stratford today.]

1999

Hagger, Nicholas. *Prince Tudor: A Verse Drama*.

2000

Mankoff, Bob. Cartoon with caption: "I'm confused now. Was Shakespeare somebody else or was somebody else Shakespeare?" *New Yorker*, June 19. [repr. in DVN (July 2000), p. 30]

Altrocchi, Paul H. *Most Greatly Lived: A Biographical Novel of Edward de Vere, Seventeenth Earl of Oxford, Whose Pen Name was William Shakespeare*. Philadelphia: Xlibris Corp.

Howe, Norma. *Blue Avenger Cracks the Code*. New York: Holt.

Kositsky, Lynne. *A Question of Will*. Montreal: Roussan Publishers, Inc. [repub. In 2019]

2001

Coates, George. *The Crazy Wisdom Sho*. [a musical about the life of Edward de Vere]

D'Artagnan, Robert. *Oxford Summer: Shakespeare's Dark Lady Tells All*. London: 1st Books Library.

Dorian, Bill. *A Rose By Any Other Name: A Play*.

Flint, Eric. *1632* [a science-fiction novel]. Riverdale, NY: Baen. Distributed by Simon & Schuster.

Jones, Graham and Jepke Goudsmit. *Shake-speare*. [a play about the life of Edward de Vere']

2002

Baker, Elliott. *Delia*. Philadelphia: Xlibris.

Brown, Patricia Carroll. *Edward de Vere, aka William Shakespeare: A Life in Two Acts*. Toronto: Patricia Brown.

Buckley, Marion. *By Any Other Name* [a humorous dramatization of the life and times of Edward de Vere].

Howe, Norma. *Blue Avenger Cracks the Code*. New York: Harper Tempest.

Matchett, Robin. *The Lion Bats the Bvtterfly, or, The True and Tragicke Historie of Shake-speare*. Toronto: J. Piercemore Books.

Sherwood, James W. *Shakespeare's Ghost: An Historical Mystery Novel*. New York: Opus Books.

Wall, Alan. *School of Night* [a novel]. New York: Thomas Dunne Books/St. Martin's Press.

2003

Smith, Sarah. *Chasing Shakespeares*. New York: Atria Books.

2004

Freed, Amy. *The Beard of Avon*. New York: S. French.

Graves, Gary. *The Mysterious Mr. Looney* [a fictional confrontation between J. Thomas Looney & Sir Sidney Chambers]

Llewellyn, Sally Hazelton. *Edward's Presents: An Oxfordian Play on London's Bankside*.

Llewellyn, Sally Hazelton. *Return to a Forbidden Planet*.

Young, Louise. [a play about Oxford; title not known]

2005

Boyle, James. *The Shakespeare Chronicles: A Novel*. Lulu Press.

Broach, Elise. *Shakespeare's Secret*. New York: Henry Holt and Co.

2007

Carrell, Jennifer Lee. *Interred With Their Bones*. New York: Dutton.

Carrell, Jennifer Lee. *The Shakespeare Secret*. London: Little, Brown Book Group

Smith, Sarah. *Chasing Shakespeares: The Play*.

2008

Fry, Simon. *Paper Trail*.

Garcia, Emanuel E. "Sherlock and the Mystery of *Hamlet*," in *Sherlock Holmes & the Three Poisoned Pawns*. Edited by Anthony J. Richards. Cambridge: Breese Books.

Langford, Michael. *The de Vere Papers*. Turnbridge, Wells, Kent, UK: Parapress.

2009

Dillon, George. *The Man Who Was Hamlet*.

Dorward, Lisa L. *Whose Worth's Unknown: The Life of Edward de Vere, The Man Who Was Shakespeare: A Novel*. [submitted as a thesis to Eberly College of Arts. West Virginia University]

Gladstone, Ryan. *The Shakespeare Show or How an Illiterate Son of a Glover Became the Greatest Playwright in the World. Penned by Edward de Vere*. [a play] [de Vere, dying, charges horse-holder Will Shakespeare with telling his story]

Hampton, Aubrey. *Elizabeth and Edward*. [a play about you-know-who as the real author of Shakespeare's plays.]

Navarre, Alan. *The Crown Signature*. [a three-act play based on the life of Edward de Vere]

2010

Bacino, Ted. *The Shakespeare Controversy: A Novel About the Greatest Literary Deception of All Time*. AuthorHouse.

Carrell, Jennifer Lee. *Haunt Me Still*. New York: Dutton.

Evans, Scott. *First Folio: A Literary Mystery*. AuthorHouse.

Grant, Barry. *Sherlock Holmes and the Shakespeare Letter* [a novel]

Whittemore, Hank & Ted Story. *Shakespeare's Treason: The True Story of King Henry IX, Last of the Tudors* [a one-man show based on *The Monument*]

Imaginative Works

2011

Austin, Al. *The Cottage*. Bloomington: iUniverse.

Emmerich, Roland, Director; John Orloff, Writer. *Anonymous*.

Fry, Simon. *The Shakespeare File: A Novel*. Pub. by Imprimata.

Jouannic, Brünhilde. *Shakespeare, c'est moi: La confession d'Edward de Vere*. Paris: Milo.

Kositsky, Michael. *Detective Superintendent Blattshap Gets His Man*. [a play in one act]

2012

Barber, Ros. *The Marlowe Papers: A Novel in Verse*. London: Sceptre. Repr. in 2013: New York: St. Martin's Press.

Gilbert, Sky. *Come Back*. Toronto: ECW Press.

Hildebrandt, Peter. *The Rest is Silence: A Novel*.

Rylance, Mark. *The Big Secret Live 'I am Shakespeare' Webcam Daytime Chatroom Show!: A Comedy of the Shakespearean Identity Crisis*. London: Hick Hern Books.

Taylor, Lynda. *Or Not To Be*.

2013

Becker, Margaret. *Snatches From History: A Play in Five Acts* [Acts 1-3 printed in *Sh. Matters*, vol. 12/3: 20-27 (Summer 2013); Acts 4-5 printed in vol. 12/4: 29-33 (Fall 2013)]

Creager, Melora. *Fa La La – The Bastardy of Shakespeare's Madrigals*. [a song cycle for four cellos, three voices, percussion and digital looping; songs are drawn from Shakespeare's plays and credited to Edward de Vere]

Hutchison, Bruce. *Love's Labor Lost: The Man Who was Shakespeare*. CreateSpace.

Kline, Syril Levin. *Shakespeare's Changeling: A Fault Against the Dead*. CreateSpace.

2014

Frohlich, Newton. *The Shakespeare Mask*. Tucson, AZ: Blue Bird Press.

Plummer, Christopher. *Nothing Truer Than Truth* (Vero Nihil Verius) [MA Thesis: Oxfordian story in the form of a drama]. Regent University.

Streitz, Paul. *Shakespeare and the Courtesan*. CreateSpace.

2016

Benson, Jon. *The Death of Shakespeare As It Was Accomplisht in 1616 & The Causes Thereof, Part One*. Annapolis, MD: Nedward, LLC. [see also *The Reader's Companion to The Death of Shakespeare, Part One*, on the non-fiction book list]

Hoke, Phil. *Truth; Will Out. A Play*.

Warren, James A. *Summer Storm: A Novel of Ideas*. Veritas Publications.

Sharratt, Mary. *The Dark Lady's Mask*. Marriner Books.

2017

A'Dair, Mike. *The Ashbourne Saga: A Cinematic Epic in Fourteen Episodes*. Published by Lulu.

Todd, Eliza. *Bethy*.

2018

Chaunes. *Le Vrai Shakespeare* [a drama in the form of five acts]. Independent Publisher.

Tatum, Aaron F. *Shakespeare's Secrets*. WaveCloud Corporation.

2019

Blake, Darrol. *Nothing Truer Than Truth: the Life and Times of Edward de Vere, Sometimes Known as William Shakespeare*. [a play writtin in 1977, pub. in 2019]

Kositsky, Lynne. *A Question of Will*. [new edition by the Sh. Ox. Fellowship, from 2001]

Singleton, Esther. *Shakespearian Fantasias: Adventures in the Fourth Dimension*. (modern edition edited by James A. Warren) [1929]

2020

Elton, Ben. *The Upstart Crow*. [a play] [2020?]

2021

Vaughan-Davies, Richard. *In the Shadow of Shakespeare*. Mitford Oak Press. [a novel]

2022

Kenseth, Lars. [cartoon references Edward de Vere] New Yorker, October 31, 2022, p. 28.

2023

Benson, Jon. *The Death of Shakespeare As It Was Accomplisht in 1616 & the Causes Thereof: A Novel, Part Two*. Annapolis: Nedward, LLC.

Clark, Sally. *The King of Nothing*. [a play about Edward de Vere]

Destro, Ron. *The Starre, the Moone, the Sunne: What if Everything You Ever Learned about Willian Shakespeare Was a Lie?* Contempo Publishing.

Light, Leigh. *The Which of Shakespeare's Why: A Novel of the Authorship Mystery Near Solution Today*.

O'Loughlin, Rosemary. *A Rose by Any Other Name* (a play). [2022?]

Post, Douglas. *By My Will*. [a play on the authorship question] [2023 is date of performance]

Undated works

Caruana, Stephanie. *Edward Oxenford: Spear-shaker*. [a play]

Crafts, Daniel Steven. *Bury My Name* [a theatrical presentation of the Oxfordian idea, with songs by Shakespeare and Edward de Vere]

Crafts, Daniel Steven. *The Real Shakespeare*. [song cycle setting poems by Edward de Vere]

Ligon, K. C. *Isle of Dogs* [a play about Edward de Vere]

IIID. CONTENTS OF COLLECTIONS OF ARTICLES
BY OXFORDIAN AUTHORS

Contents of

Building the Case for Edward de Vere as Shakespeare:

A Series of Volumes Devoted to Shakespeare Authorship Research (BTC)
Volumes 1-5 compiled and edited by Paul H. Altrocchi and Hank Whittemore
Volumes 6-10 compiled and edited by Paul H. Altrocchi

Volume 5: So Richly Spun: Four Hundred Years of Deceit Are Enough. Edward de Vere Is Shakespeare.

Building the Case (BTC)

Volume 5 (continued)

124-129	Bowen, Gwynneth M.	Review of Seymour M. Pitcher's Book *The Case for Shakespeare's Authorship of 'The Famous Victories'* (1961) [from SAR, no. 10 (Autumn 1963)]
130-131	Cutner, Herbert	Obituary of William Kent (1886-1963) [from SAR, no. 10 (Aut. 1963)]
132-133	Bowen, Gwynneth M.	Stratfordian Quatercentenary [from SAR, no. 11 (Spring 1964)]
134-140	Vessey, David W. T.	Some Early References to Shakespeare [from SAR, no. 11 (Spring 1964)]
141-143	Wainewright, Ruth M. D.	Summary of Gwynneth Bowen's Lecture: "New Evidence for Dating the Plays" [from SAR, no. 11 (Spring 1964)]
144-145	Amphlett, Hilda	Summary of G. Cimino's Lecture "The Golden Age of Padua" [from SAR, no. 11 (Spring 1964)]
146-149	Bowen, Gwynneth M.	Reverberations [from SAR, no. 12, (Autumn 1964)]
150-152	Vessey, David W. T.	After the Pageant: A Meditation for 1965 [from SAR, no. 13 (Spring 1965)]
153-155	Walker, James	The Pregnant Silence [from SAR, no. 13 (Spring 1965)]
156-159	Ferguson, W. A.	The *Sonnets* of Shakespeare: The 'Oxfordian' Solution [from SAR, no. 13 (Spring 1965)]
160-167	Bowen, Gwynneth M.	Hackney, Harsnett, and the Devils in *King Lear* [from SAR, no. 14 (Autumn, 1965); also in OXV, p. 237-43]
168-169	Patience, Harold W.	Topical Allusions in *King John* [from SAR, no. 14 (Autumn 1965)]
170-172	McGeoch, I. L.	Review of A. F. Falconer's Book *Shakespeare and the Sea* [from SAR, no. 14 (Autumn 1965)]
173	Wainewright, Ruth M. D.	Review of Eleanor Brewster's Book *Oxford Courtier to the Queen* (1964) [from SAR, no. 14 (Autumn 1965)]
174-175	Wainewright, Ruth M. D.	Summary of Gwynneth Bowen's Lecture "The Merchant and the Jew" [from SAR, no. 14 (Autumn 1965
176-178	Bowen, Gwynneth M.	Summary of Ruth Wainewright's Lecture "Conflicting Dates for Various Candidates" [from SAR, no. 14 (Autumn 1965)]
179-182	Rendall, Canon Gerald	Flashback: A 1930 Toast to Edward de Vere [from SAR, no. 15 (Spring 1966)]
183-187	Bowen, Gwynneth M.	Sir Edward Vere and His Mother, Anne Vavasor [from SAR, no. 15 (Spring 1966)]
188-190	Carr, Frances	Summary of Marlowe Society Members' Lecture Death of Kit Marlowe: A Reconstruction [from SAR, no. 15 (Spring, 1966)]
191-192	Carr, Frances	Summary of Gwynneth Bowen's Lecture "Who Was Kyd's and Marlowe's Lord?" [from SAR, no. 15 (Spring 1966)]
193-212	Wainewright, Ruth M. D.	On the Poems of Edward de Vere [from SAR, no. 16 (Autumn 1966)]
213	Editor	Another False Painting: the "Flower Portrait" [from SAR, no. 16 (Autumn 1966)]
214-215	Patience, W. T.	Shakespeare and "Authority" [from SAR, no. 16 (Autumn 1966)]
216-224	Bowen, Gwynneth M.	Oxford's Letter to Bedingfield and Shake-speare's *Sonnets* [from SAR, no. 17 (Spring 1967)]
225-229	Trout, R. Ridgill	Edward de Vere to Robert Cecil: Commentary From His Unpublished book *Twenty Earls and Shakespeare* [from SAR, no. 17 (Spring 1967)]
230-231	Editor	Summary of T. Bokenham's Lecture: "Ben Jonson, Shakespeare and the 1623 *Folio*" [from SAR, no. 17 (Spring 1967)]
232-233	Vessey, David W. T. C.	Summary of his Lecture "Shakespeare's Classical Learning" [from SAR, no. 17 (Spring 1967)]
234-235	Bowen, Gwynneth M.	Summary of her Lecture "Shakespeare Portraits and the Earl of Oxford" [from SAR, no. 17 (Spring 1967)]

Volume 7 (continued)

95-98	Johnson, Morse	A Letter From Morse Johnson [from SON, vol. 28/1: 7-8 (Winter 1992)]
99-105	Duffey, Edith	An Oxfordian Stratfordian [from SON, vol. 28/2: 12-15 (Spring 1992)]
106-108	Ogburn, Charlton	An Interchange of Letters in the *New York Review of Books* Between Charlton Ogburn and Professor E. A. Honigmann [from SON, vol. 28/2, p. 16-17 (Spring 1992)]
109	Lovell, Stanley P.	Lyly and Shakespeare [from SON, vol. 28/2: 16-17 (Spring 1992)]
110-118	Johnson, Morse	Correspondence re the Oxford p. in *The Shakespeare Newsletter* [from SON, vol. 28/3: 13-18 (Summer 1992)]
119-124	Nelson, Paul A.	Walt Whitman on Shakespeare [from SON, vol. 28/4A: 1-4 (Fall 1992)]
125-126	Bénézet, Louis P.	The Stratford Defendant Compromised By His Own Advocates [from SON, vol. 28/4A: 6 (Fall 1992); repr. from SFQ (July 1945)]
127	Frazer, Winifred L.	"Transvestite Shakespeare" [from SON, vol. 28/4A: 7 (Fall 1992)]
128	Johnson, Morse	Signs of a Turning Tide [from SON, vol. 28/4A: 7-8 (Fall 1992)]
129-130	Howerton, Jr., Philip	Shakespeare Newsletter Correspondence: Shakspere as Shakespeare is a Myth [from SON, vol. 28/4A: 7-8 (Fall 1992)]
131-145	Ogburn, Charlton	Shakespeare's Self-Portrait [from SON, vol. 28/4B: 1-10 (Fall 1992)]
146-147	Mixter, Clara	"Flights of Angels sing thee to thy rest" (Excerpts from obituary of William Plumer Fowler by his daughter) [from SON, vol. 29/1A: 4 (Winter 1993)]
148-149	Johnson, Morse	Shake-speare Could Only Have Been a Pseudonym [from SON, vol. 29/1A: 5-6 (Winter 1993)]
150-151	Gill, James	The Play's the Thing, But Is It Mr. Shakespeare's? [from SON, vol. 29/1A: 7-8 (Winter 1993); repr. from *New Orleans Times Picayune*]
152	Livacari, Gary	Letter to Morse Johnson, Editor [from SON, vol. 29/1A: 8 (Wntr. 1993)]
153	Johnson, Morse	Peregrine Bertie's Startling Report [from SON, vol. 29/1A: 18 (Winter 1993)]
154-158	Saliani, Dom	Letter to SOS Newsletter Editor, Morse Johnson [from SON, vol. 29/2A: 7-9 (Spring 1993)]
159-163	Johnson, Morse	Relevant Addenda [from SON, vol. 29/2A: 9-11 (Spring 1993)]
164-171	Hannas, Andrew	Gabriel Harvey and the Genesis of "William Shakespeare" [from SON, vol. 29/1B: 1-8 (Winter 1993)]
172-173	Johnson, Morse	Letter from Morse Johnson to the Shakespeare Birthplace Trust [from SON, vol. 29/2A: 13 (Spring 1993)]
174-175	Johnson, Morse	Lord Burford Reaches 15,000 with the Case for Oxford [from SON, vol. 29/2A: 14 (Spring 1993)]
176-185	Greenwood, George	Excerpts from *The Shakespeare Problem Restated* (1908) [from SON, vol. 29/2B: 1-7 (Spring 1993)]
186-187	Johnson, Morse	"Contradictory Factual Evidence *Is* Unearthed" [from SON, vol. 29/2B: 12-13 (Spring 1993)]
188-200	Frazer, Winifred L.	A Realistic Look at *Groats-Worth of Wit* [from SON, vol. 29/3B: 1-8 (Summer 1993)]
201-205	Barron, Randall	Edward de Vere's Will [from SON, vol. 29/4: 1-3 (Fall 1993)]
206-211	McLatchie, Linda B.	De Vere and the Battle of Bosworth [from SON, vol. 29/4: 4-7 (Fall 1993)]
212-213	Sobran, Joseph	Bible Holds Proof of Shakespeare's Identity [from *The Herald* (July 31, 1993)] [also in SON, vol. 29/4: 8-9 (Fall 1993); and EVR, vol. 1 (Fall 1995)]

Early Shakespeare (ES)

By A. Bronson Feldman. Editor: Warren Hope. Laugwitz Verlag (2019)

Great Oxford: Essays on the Life and Work of Edward de Vere (GO)

General Editor: Richard C. W. Malim; Editorial Team: Kevin Gilvary, Elizabeth Imlay, Eddi Jolly.
Published by Parapress, Ltd., Kent UK (2004)

The Lame Storyteller, Poor and Despised (LS)

By Peter R. Moore, edited by Gary B. Goldstein, published by Verlag Uwe Laugwitz (2009)

Necessary Mischief: Exploring the Shakespeare Authorship Question (NM)

By Bonner Miller Cutting. Published by Minos Publishing Company (2018).

Reflections on the True Shakespeare (REF)

Articles by Gary Goldstein

Published as Special Issue no. 6 of *Neues Shake-speare Journal* by Verlag Uwe Laugwitz (2016)

233   Goldstein, Gary   Oxfordian Scholars Are Now a Major Presence in Libraries Worldwide
                                         [from SON, vol. 52/3: 34-35 (Summer 2016)]

Future Directions
240   Goldstein, Gary   Future Directions

Report My Cause Aright:
The Shakespeare Oxford Society Fiftieth Anniversary Anthology (1957-2007) **(RCA)**

Published by the Shakespeare Oxford Society (2007)

Shakespeare, Marlowe and Other Elizabethans (2022)

A collection of articles by A. Bronson Feldman, edited by Warren Hope
Published as Special Issue no. 8 of *Neues Shake-speare Journal*
by Verlag Uwe Laugwitz, Buchholz, Germany

Shakespeare's Education: Schools, Lawsuits, Theater, and the Tudor Miracle (SE)

Articles by Robin Fox, compiled and edited by Gary B. Goldstein,
and published as Special issue no. 5 of *Neues Shake-speare Journal* by Verlag Uwe Laugwitz (2012)

Such Fruits Out of Italy: The Italian Renaissance in Shakespeare's Plays and Poems (SF)

by Noemi Magri, edited by Gary B. Goldstein, published by Laugwitz Verlag (2014)

Twelve Years in the Life of Shakespeare (2012) (TYLS)

by Hank Whittemore, edited by William E. Boyle, published by Forever Press (Somerset, MA)

IIIE. OTHER OXFORDIAN BOOKS
WITH PIECES BY MULTIPLE AUTHORS

The 1623 Shakespeare First Folio: A Minority Report:
A Special Issue of Brief Chronicle (SFF)

Editor: Roger Stritmatter. Managing Editor: Michael Delahoyde. Spring 2016

Contested Year: Errors, Omissions and Unsupported Statements in James Shapiro's The Year of Lear: Shakespeare in 1606 (CY)

edited by Mark K. Anderson, Alexander Waugh & Alex McNeil
Kindle Edition. February 9, 2016

Dating Shakespeare's Plays: A Critical Review of the Evidence (DSP)

Kevin Gilvary, Editor. Tunbridge Wells, UK: Parapress (2010)

Discovering Shakespeare: A Festschrift in Honor of Isabel Holden (DS)

Daniel Wright, Editor. Published by Concordia University Bookstore (2009)

The First Folio—A Shakespearean Enigma (TFF)
Brief Chronicles, vol. 8

Edited by Roger Stritmatter. Published by the Shakespeare Oxford Fellowship (August 2023)

Hidden Allusions in Shakespeare's Plays by Eva Turner Clark.
3rd Revised Edition, Ruth Loyd Miller, Editor (1974)

* Eva Turner Clark's *The Satirical Comedy, Love's Labour's Lost* (1933) is reprinted in Ruth Loyd Miller's edition of Clark's *Hidden Allusions*, in three disjointed segments:

The "Introduction" is reprinted on pages 125-162, but in a version with so much material added to it that it is five times as long as the original. No notice is given to the reader concerning the additions.

The main body of the book is reprinted as in the first edition, on pages 163-238.

The notes are also reprinted as in the first edition, on pages 242-251, but they are separated from the text to which they refer by a piece on Julio Romano inserted by the editor.

My Shakespeare: The Authorship Controversy:
Experts examine the arguments for Bacon, Neville, Oxford, Marlowe, Mary Sidney, Shakspere, and Shakespeare.

Edited by William Leahy
2018

Oxfordian Vistas (OXV)
Vol. II of *"Shakespeare" Identified & The Poems of Edward de Vere*
by J. Thomas Looney,
Third Edition, Annotated and Illustrated (1975)
Ruth Loyd Miller, Editor

Port Washington, New York-London: Kennikat Press Corp.; Jennings, Louisiana:
Minos Publishing Company

* These pieces are extended excerpts only, and the excerpts have often been extensively edited, with additions and deletions and paraphrasings not indicated by the editor.

The Poems of Edward de Vere, 17th Earl of Oxford . . . and the Shakespeare Question.
Vol. 1: He that Takes the Pain to Pen the Book . . .
Earliest "Canonical" Poems, c. 1566-1580

edited by Roger Stritmatter
2019, 2nd edition, 2023

The Poems of Edward de Vere, 17th Earl of Oxford . . . and the Shakespeare Question.
Vol. 2: As It Fell Upon a Day
Poems from The Passionate Pilgrim

edited by Roger Stritmatter, 2023

A Poet's Rage: Understanding Shakespeare Through Authorship Studies (PR)

Edited by William E. Boyle, Published by Forever Press, Somerville, Massachusetts (2013)

Shakespeare and His Authors: Critical Perspectives on the Authorship Question (SA)

Edited by William Leahy, 2010

Shakespeare and the Law: How the Bard's Legal Knowledge Affects the Authorship Question (SAL)

Edited by Roger Stritmatter, 2022

The Shakespeare Authorship Sourcebook: A Workbook for Educators and Students (SAS)

Edited by Roger Stritmatter
Shakespeare Oxford Fellowship, 2019, 2022.

Shakespeare Beyond Doubt? Exposing an Industry in Denial (SBD?)

Edited by John M. Shahan & Alexander Waugh for The Shakespeare Authorship Coalition (2013)

- - - - - - -

Detailed list of Doubter Responses (pages 152-223):

THE TENNESSEE LAW REVIEW (FALL 2004) (TLR)

Symposium: Who Wrote Shakespeare? An Evidentiary Puzzle
vol. 72, no. 1 (Fall, 2004)

IIIF. OXFORDIAN PIECES (AND OTHERS OF SPECIAL INTEREST) IN NON-OXFORDIAN BOOKS

Literature Criticism 1400 to 1800, vol. 193 (2011)

A Gale Cengage collection of essays mostly Oxfordian in nature edited by Lawrence J. Trudeau

Shakespeare and His Rivals: A Casebook on the Authorship Controversy (1962)

By George McMichael & Edgar M. Glenn. New York: The Odyssey Press, Inc. (SAH)

Shakespeare Criticism, vol. 41: Authorship Controversy (SCV)
Excerpts from the criticism of William Shakespeare's plays and poetry, from the first published appraisals to current evalutation.

Edited by Michelle Lee and Dana Ramel Barnes. (1998)

Shakespeare Cross-Examination:
A Compilation of Articles First Appearing in The American Bar Association Journal (SC)

Published by The American Bar Association (1961)

Other Books with Oxfordian Pieces

Akhtar, Salman (editor). *Betrayal: Developmental, Clinical, and Literary Realms*. London: Karnac Books. 2013.
83-87: "The Theme of Betrayal in the Works of 'William Shakespeare'" by Richard Waugaman.

Akhtar, Salman (editor). *Greed: Developmental, Cultural, and Clinical Realms*. London: Karnac Books. 2015.
69-86: "Greed in the Life of William Shakspere—And Generosity in the Life of Edward de Vere, a.k.a. "Shakespeare" by Richard Waugaman.

Akhtar, Salman (editor). *Truth: Developmental, Cultural, and Clinical Realms*. Phoenix. 2023.
Includes "Nothing is Truer than Truth in Shakespeare" by Richard Waugaman.

Edmondson, Paul & Stanley Wells (editors). *Shakespeare Beyond Doubt: Evidence, Argument, Controversy*. Cambridge University Press. 2013.
29-38: "The Case for Marlowe" by Charles Nicholl.
39-48: "The Life and Theatrical Interests of Edward de Vere, Seventeenth Earl of Oxford" by Alan H. Nelson.

O'Neil, Mary Kay & Salman Akhtar (editors). *Jealousy: Developmental, Cultural, and Clinical Realms*. London: Karnac Books. 2018.
101-12: "Shakespeare and the 'Green-Eyed Monster' of Jealousy" by Richard Waugaman.

Richardson, David A (editor). *Sixteenth-Century British Nondramatic Writers: Fourth Series*. Gale. 1996. [*Dictionary of Literary Biography*, vol. 172]
181-191: "Edward de Vere" by Dennis Kay.

Rosenblum, Joseph (editor). *The Definitive Shakespeare Companion: A Comprehensive Guide for Students*. Santa Barbara: Greenwood. 2017.
Includes "The Authorship Question" by Joseph Rosenblum.

Sengupta, Ednakshi & Patrick Blessinger (editors). *Teaching and Learning Practices for Academic Freedom*. Bingley, UK: Emerald. 2021.
123-144: "With Swinish Phrase Soiling Their Edition: Epistemic Injustice, Academic Freedom, and the Shakespeare Oxford Question" by Michael Dudley.

Stone, James & James Newlin (editors). *New Psychoanalytic Readings of Shakespeare: Cool Reason and Seething Brains*. New York: Routledge. 2023.
215-230: "Psychological Complexity in Shakespeare" by Richard Waugaman.

Pieces in Dictionaries, Encyclopedias, Almanacs, etc.

Almanac of Famous People. Detroit: Gale Research, Inc. (June 2011)
"Edward de Vere, Earl of Oxford"

Britannica Concise Encyclopedia. Chicago: Encyclopedia Britannica. (2017)
"Oxford, Edward de Vere, 17th Earl of"

Cambridge History of Elizabethan Literature. (1928)
[excerpt on the authorship question; repr. in DVN, July 2001, p. 22-23]

Columbia Encyclopedia. (2018)
"Oxford, Edward de Vere, 17th Earl of"

Concise Dictionary of National Biography. edited by Sidney Lee. Oxford Univ. Press: London: Humphrey Milford. 1920.
p. 1337   "Vere, Edward de, seventeenth Earl of Oxford (1550-1604)"

Concise Oxford Companion to English Literature, 3rd ed. Oxford University Press. (2007)
"Oxford, Edward de Vere, 17th earl of"

Continuum Encyclopedia of British Literature. 2006.
"Oxford, Edward de Vere, Seventeenth Earl of"

Dictionary of Literary Biography, vol. 172 [*Sixteenth-Century British Nondramatic Writers: Fourth Series*, David A. Richardson (editor)] Gale. 1996.
p. 181-191:   "Edward de Vere" [Dennis Kay]

Dictionary of National Biography, 11th edition, edited by Sidney Lee. London: Smith, Elder & Co. 1910.
vol. 51: 348-397   "Shakespeare, William (1564-1616)" [Sidney Lee]
vol. 58: 225-229   "Vere, Edward de, Seventeenth Earl of Oxford (1550-1604)" [Sidney Lee]

Dictionary of National Biography, current. [2005?]
"Vere, Edward de" [Alan H. Nelson] [repr. in *De Vere Society Newsletter*, Jan. 2005, p. 8-13]

Encyclopedia Britannica: A Dictionary of Arts, Sciences, Literature and General Information, *11th edition.* Cambridge University Press. 1910-1911.
vol. 24: 772-797   "Shakespeare
vol. 27: 1019-1020   "Vere" [J. H. R.]

Encyclopedia Britannica, 15th edition. (1975)

Encyclopaedia Britannica, current. [still known as the 15th edition, but articles are updated from time to time]
2010   "Oxford, Edward de Vere, 17th Earl of," in *The New Encyclopaedia Britannica, Micropaedia: Ready Reference* (2010), p. 29.
2010   "Shakespeare, William," in *Macropaedia: Knowledge in Depth*, vol. 27: 253-272. [see esp. "Question of authorship," p. 264] by John Russell Brown, John Bew Spencer and David Bevington. [repeats many points rebutted by Oxfordians many times since 1920, with no notice of the rebuttals]

Encyclopedia of English Renaissance Literature, vol. 1. (2012)
"De Vere, Earl of Oxford" [David Kathman]

Encyclopedia of Tudor England. (2011)
"Vere, Edward de, Earl of Oxford"

Grolier Encyclopedia Yearbook. New York: The Grolier Society (1950)
vol. 11: 301+   "Veres, Earls of Oxford" [a 2,400-word piece by Louis P. Bénézet] [repr. in SON, vol. 24/4 (Fall 1988): 8-10; in SON, vol. 29/4 (Fall 1993): 19; and in BTC, vol. 6: 366-69]
vol. 9: 326-28   "Shakespeare Authorship Theories" [Louis P. Bénézet] [excerpt repr. in SON, vol. 24/4 (Summer 1988): 8-10; in SON, vol. 29/4: 19; and in BTC, vol. 6: 366-69]

Hutchinson Unabridged Encyclopedia. (2018)
"Oxford, Edward de Vere, 17th Earl of"

LawPundit (2016)
> "Shakespeare as Marlowe, as Anthony Munday Under Patronage of Edward de Vere, Earl of Oxford"
> [later included in the entry "William Shakespeare" [Andis Kaulins]

National Encyclopaedia: A Dictionary of Universal Knowledge by Writers of Eminence in Literature, Science and Art. London: W. Mackenzie. 1884.
> vol. 11: 607-615   "Shakespeare, William" [states that he returned to Statford in 1604]

Wiley-Blackwell Encyclopedia of Literature: The Encyclopedia of English Renaissance Literature. (2012)
> "de Vere, Edward, Earl of Oxford"

Other Misc. Materials

District Court of the United States for the District of Columbia
> 1948   Charles Wisner Barrell, Plaintiff v. Giles E. Dawson, Defendant: Action for Damages for Libel. [Civil Action No. 2698-48, filed July 1]

Frazer, Winifred
> 1992   Oral History [transcript of an Oral History interview conducted on April 7 by the University of Florida, in which Frazer describes how she became an Oxfordian] [http://ufdc.ufl.edu/UF00006130/00001/]

The Mercury Shakespeare. New York: Harper. [see "Introduction," p. 17+] (1939).

Sobran, Joseph [unpublished pieces available at http://sobran.com/oxfordlibrary.shtml]
> 1998   David Kathamn and the "Historical Record."
>   [reply to Kathman's review of *Alias Shakespeare*]
> 1999   How Old was Oxford's Daughter, and When Did William Lose His Hair?
>   [additional reply to Alan Nelson]

Sobran, Joseph [syndicated columns available at http://sobran.com/oxfordlibrary.shtml]

1997, May 15	The Shakespeare Riddles
1997, Sept.	The Debate Rages On
1999, Nov. 25	Giving Away the Game
2000, Feb. 24	Honoring the True Bard
2000, Feb. 29	Who are the Snobs?
2000, April 13	Happy Birthday, 'Shakespeare'!
2000, May 23	The Rivals
2000, July 27	Making Sense of Shakespeare
2001, March 8	Shakespeare and DNA
2001, April 17	Whose Testiony?
2002, April 9	Shakespeare and the Snobs
2002, June 20	Rejoice!
2002, Nov. 12	Shakespeare and the Directors
2003, April 17	Shakespeare's Social Life
2003, May 1	Olivier and His Successors
2003, May 1	Titus and Lucrece
2004, Jan. 22	Burton's Lost *Hamlet*
2004, June 24	The Death of Shakespeare
2005, Feb. 10	The Baker Street Shakespeareans
2005, May 12	Kyd Stuff
2005, June 16	The Language of Lear

Standen, Gilbert
> 1927?   An album with hundreds of Baconian articles pasted in.
> 1929   The first of the two Oxfordian albums, with Oxfordian ephemera from 1922 to 1929. Includes a wealth of Oxfordian items not known to exist anywhere else, including letters, SF Circulars, published articles, and invitations to SF annual dinners. More than 470 items are pasted into these two Oxfordian albums.
> 1936   The second of the two Oxfordian albums, with ephemera from 1929 to 1936.

Trout, R. Ridgill
> 1958   *Twenty Earls and Shakespeare*. [a large album with hundreds of pages of notes and clippings on the lives of the de Veres, Earls of Oxford, collected from various sources between 1938 and 1958]

PART IV: SOURCES – AUDIO-VISUAL AND OTHER

IVA. Selected Audio and Video Recordings of Interest to Oxfordians
(Chronological Order)

[Film adaptations of Shakespeare's plays (and other films and TV programs about the Elizabethan era) are not included here unless there is an Oxfordian angle to them. Reviews of films, music CDs and broadcasts in Oxfordian periodicals are listed in the Reviews section. Radio discussions for which no recordings are known to exist are not included.]

1941
Mister V/Pimpernel Smith

A film by Leslie Howard in which he twice holds up a copy of J. Thomas Looney's *"Shakespeare" Identified* and declares that Shakespeare's works had been written by Edward de Vere]

1974
Who is Shakespeare?

Panel discussion with David A. More arguing for Christopher Marlowe, Steven Marble for Francis Bacon, and Charles Vere for Edward de Vere broadcast on British TV.

1981, January 21
Perspective

This segment of the BBC program, broadcast before a performance of *All's Well That Ends Well*, mentions the Earl of Oxford and the "bed trick."

1984, December 11
Firing Line: The Mysterious William Shakespeare

This episode of the Public Television (PBS) program hosted by William F. Buckley, included guests author Charlton Ogburn, Jr. and Rutgers University Professor Maurice Charney. A DVD copy is in the Flathead Valley Community College Library, Laispell Campus Library

1984, December 18
Call in Program

WJNO Radio (Palm Beach) phone interview with Charlton Ogburn, Jr.

1985, January 7
Voice of America broadcast

Pro-Ogburn comments by Gordon C. Cyr and anti-Ogburn comments by David Kasten. Broadcast four more times.

1985, January 17
Midday with Sondra Gair

National Public Radio (NPR), Chicago interview with Charlton Ogburn, Jr.

1986
Head of the Class

U.S. TV Sitcom. A character in a Fall 1986 episode who is an Oxfordian raises the authorship issue.

1987, Date, details
Moot Court

Broadcast by C-SPAN. [The Washington College of Law, American University, has a copy of the video.]

1989, April 18
Frontline "The Shakespeare Mystery"

This episode of the Public Television (PBS) program, produced by Al Austin, focuses on the possibility of Edward de Vere as the pen behind the name William Shakespeare. See also Austin's "Who Wrote Shakespeare?" in the Boston PBS station's magazine for its subscribers.

First Tuesday

"In Search of the Bard." The Hon. Enoch Powell presents the case for the doubters in this episode of the BBC TV program.

1989, July 2
Tuesday

[Charles Vere and A. L. Rowse clash on a TV program]

Audio-Visual Broadcasts and Recordings

1990, Nov. 20
    Seinfeld, "The Nose Job" — Season 3, Episode 9. NBC TV program. (Columbia Pictures TV/Castle Rock Entertainment. [One character contends that Sh. was an impostor.]

1992, March 9
    Charles Burford talk, Russell Stage College — VHS tape exists.

1992, September 17
    Frontline: Uncovering Shakespeare: An Update — An interactive videoconference on VisNet hosted by Willian F. Buckley, Jr., with 15 guests, including Charles Boyle, Warren Hope, Felicia Londré, Roger Stritmatter and Charles Vere. Produced by John Mucci and Gary Goldstein.

    Who Was William Shakespeare? — Talk by Charles Burford, University of Washington, Seattle, VHS

1993?
    The Authorship Question: Was Sh. a Fraud? — Charles Burford talk, Cleveland State University Library, VHS

1994
    Trial of William Shakespeare — Coverage of the American Inns of Court Conference Moot Court. Scenario is that Shakspere has filed suit against Edward de Vere because of his claims of authorship.

    Who is Shakespeare? — SAR Roundtable, VHS take with Charles Champlin, Charles Vere, Hannon Library, S. Oregon University Library

1994, October
    National Public Radio (NPR) — Call in program featuring Charles Vere.
    Bard on the Box: Battle of Wills — Hour-long BBC program. Charles Vere defends Oxfordian authorship against laims for Bacon, Marlowe and Shakspere.

1995
    Shakespeare Mystery: Who, in Fact, Was He? — WGBH Educational Foundation, Boston

1995, Spring
    Jeopardy — Contestant Alex McNeil describes the Shakespeare Oxford Society, mentions Edward de Vere, and wins the round.
    Academy Awards — Actor Anthony Hopkins, in presenting the award for best screenplay, notes that scholars have argued about whether or not Shakespeare wrote the plays.

1995, June 1
    Talk of the Nation — Charles Vere debates Stratfordian scholrs in this two-hour National Public Radio (NPR) program.

1996
    The Food of Love – Words and Music for Shakespeare's Theatre — A CD by the Gesualdo Consort

1997
    Conversations with Charlton Ogburn, Jr. — Recorded by Lisa and Laura wilson, 1604 Productions.

1998
    Shakespeare in Love — Film directed by John Madden. Written by Marc Norman and tom Stoppard.

2000
    Sabrina the Teenage Witch [U.S. TV program] — [On one episode, Sabrina, finding Shakespeare's advice too hard to follow, dismisses him with "Yeah, like you wrote your own plays!"]

2001, late June
    710 AM Talk Radio (Kansas City) — Professor Felicia Londré discusses the authorship question in this 45-minute program.

2002, early
    Malcolm in the Middle — American TV sitcom with a regular character who was an Oxfordian.

2002
    Frontline — "Much Ado About Something: Marlowe's Case for Shakespeare." This episode, produced by Mike Rubbio, has much to say about the possibility of Edward de Vere's authorship as well as Marlowe's.

    Much Ado About Something: Marlowe's Case — PBS *Frontline* documentary produced by Mike Rubbio.

for Authorship

2003, April 27
National Public Radio (NPR)   Interview with Diana Price.

2004
The Shakespeare Enigma   In this production by Films for the Humanities and Sciences, Stanley Wells
                                                argues for Shakspere, Francis Carr and Mark Rylance for Francis Bacon,
                                                A. D. Wright for Christopher Marlowe, and Elizabeth Imlay for Edward
                                                de Vere.

2004, March 4, 11, 18
The Breakfast Show   "Looking for the Real Shake-speare" episode, broadcast on WDR TV
                                                (Germany).

2006
The Letters of Edward de Vere   CD, Oxford's letters, read by Derek Jacobi, narrated by Joan Walker, edited
                                                by Stephanie Hopkins Hughes.

2007
My Lord of Oxenford's Maske   *See review, DVN, 2007, Occt., p. 33 for info*

2008, July 3
Morning Edition   "Who Wrote Shakespeare's Plays? The Debate Goes On." In this episode of
                                                the National Public Radio (NPR) program, Renee Montagne, host, talks
                                                with guests Daniel Wright, Diana Price and Steven Greenblatt.

2008, July 4
Morning Edition   "The Real Shakespeare? Evidence Points to Earl." Renee Montagne, host,
                                                talks with James Shapiro, Mark Rylance, Charles Beauclerk, Mark
                                                Anderson, Daniel Wright, Kenneth Branagh.

2008-09
The Shakespeare Enigma   Steve Orme, Films Media Group, North Carolina State University

2011
Anonymous   Feature film directed by Roland Emmerich that portrays Edward de Vere,
                                                Earl of Oxford, as the pen behind the front William Shakespeare.

The Shakespeare Conspiracy   A documentary film directed by Michael Peer.

2011, October 28
Morning Edition   "For *Anonymous* Scribe, a Shakespearean Speculation." Ari Shapiro, host,
                                                with John Orloff, Derek Jacobi, Rhys Ifans, on this PBS program.

2012
Last Will. & Testament   An 84-minute documentary by Lisa Wilson and Laura Wilson Matthias (and
                                                Folio Pictures) about the Authorship Question, featuring interviews with
                                                film director Roland Emmerich, and with Shakespearean actors Derek
                                                Jacobi, Vanessa Redgrave and Mark Rylance. Emmerich served as
                                                Executive Producer.

The Naked Shakespeare   English language version of *Der Nackte Shakespeare*, a German language
                                                documentary film by Claus Bredenbrock.

The Shakespeare Enigma   ADF/Atlantis Films [presented by Derek Jacobi]
Time Team: Series 19, episode 7:   Tony Robinson and the team rip up the pristine lawns of Paul Whight's
                                                stately home at Earls Colne in Essex in search of the secrets of its
                                                illustrious former owners: the de Veres, who built a priory here in the
                                                12ᵗʰ century. And to explore the rumour that the dissolute 17ᵗʰ Earl of
                                                Oxford, Edward de Vere, wrote at least some of William Shakespeare's
                                                plays, and could be buried here, along with his ancestors and
                                                descendants.

2012, March 22
Jeopardy   Question about the Shakespeare authorship question: "The 2011 film
                                                Anonymous claimed it was this man, not Shakespeare, who actually
                                                wrote the works." No contestant even ventured a guess as to the right
                                                answer, "Edward de Vere, Earl of Oxford."

2012, April 12
Jeopardy   Host Alex Trebeck referred to doubts about Shakspere's authorship in off-

the-cuff remarks during a question on Shakespeare.

2013

Fa La La – The Bastardy of Shakespeare's Madrigals

Recording of Melora Creager's song cycle for four cellos, three voices, percussion and digital looping.

Shakespeare Uncovered

A six-part series produced by the BBC examining the performance history of Shakespeare's plays.

2014

Granite Flats

American TV sitcom with an Oxfordian character played by Christopher Lloyd.

The Gambler

[A movie, in which the Oxfordian theory is mentioned briefly]

2015

Nothing is Truer than Truth

An early version of the documentary film by Cheryl Eagan-Donovan. See description in 2018.

2016

Shakespeare's Tomb

A BBC documentary broadcast in early 2016.

The Shakespeare Conspiracy

Documentary presented by Derek Jacobi. Investigating the lives of both Edward de Vere and William Shaksper of Stratford-upon-Avon, the documentary also examines modern attitudes of scholars with a vested interest in the Stratfordian myth and their suppression of relevant facts to this day.

The Shakespeare Enigma (also 2011)

Documentary presented by Derek Jacobi. Investigating the lives of both Edward de Vere and William Shaksper of Stratford-upon-Avon, the documentary also examines modern attitudes of scholars with a vested interest in the Stratfordian myth and their suppression of relevants to this day.

2016, April 25

Morning Edition

"Two Shakespearean Actors Revive Debate Over the Bard's Identity." National Public Radio (NPR) program. Ari Shapiro, host, with Mark Rylance and Derek Jacobi.

2016, April 29

Morning Edition

"Listener Responses" to the April 25, 2016 episode with Mark Rylance and Derek Jacobi. [Transcript is available on the NPR website]

2017

Will Power: Portrait of a Natural Wit

A ten-part TNT series.

2017, Sept. 21

Who Wrote Shakespeare?

Sir Jonathan Bate & Alexander Waugh debate.

2018

All is True

A film directed by Kenneth Branagh.

Nothing is Truer than Truth

A feature-length documentary by Cheryl Eagan-Donovan about Edward de Vere, seventeenth Earl of Oxford. [Released in the UK in 2022 under the title *Shakespeare: The Man Behind the Name*]

2020

SHAKESPEARE: The Truth Behind the Name.

A film written by and staring Robin Phillips Groundbreaker Films

2023

The King of Nothing

Audio recording of Sally Clark's play about Edward de Vere.

IVB. Other: Online

Online Oxfordian pieces

Meyers, Bob
    2016-current   How I Became an Oxfordian [column edited by Meyers on the Shakespeare Fellowship website]
Steinburg, Steven
    2019   The Rainbow Portrait & A Lover's Complaint—More Evidence of the Catastrophic Failure of "Professional" Scholarship.
Wright, Daniel
    2008, Oct.   All My Children: Royal Bastards and Royal Policy [presentation at the SOS conference]

Websites of Major Authorship Organizations:

The Shakespeare Oxford Fellowship – shakespeareoxfordfellowship.org

De Vere Society – deveresociety.co.uk

Shakespearean Authorship Trust – shakespeareanauthorshiptrust.org

Shakespeare Authorship Coalition – doubtaboutwill.org

Shakespeare Authorship Roundtable – shakespeareauthorship.org [Carole Sue Lipman]

Other Oxfordian Websites and Blogs

New England Shakespeare Oxford Library (NESOL) – shakespeareoxfordlibrary.org [Bill Boyle]

Shakespeare Online Authorship Resources (SOAR) – opac.libraryworld.com.opac/home.php [Bill Boyle]

ShakesVere – facebook.com/shakesvere

Shake-speare's Bible – shake-speares-bible.com [Roger Stritmatter]

"Shakespeare" By Another Name – shakespearebyanothername.blogspot.com [Mark/Margo Anderson]

Shakespeare Authorship Research Centre – authorshipstudies.org [Daniel Wright]

Edward Oxenford Review – edwardoxenford.org [Marie Merkel]

Hank Whittemore's Shakespeare Blog – hankwhittemore.com [Hank Whittemore]

The Oxford Authorship Site – oxford-shakespeare.com [Nina Green]

Authorship Sourcebook Website – sourcetext.com/sourcebook [Mark Alexander]

Shakespeare Authorship Question – shakespeareauthorshipquestion.org

OxfraudFraud – Oxfraudfraud.com

Politicworm – politicworm.com [Stephanie Hopkins Hughes]

The Festival Robe: A Post Stratfordian Shake-speare Blog – thefestivalrobe.com [Chris Carolan]

Quake-speare Shorterly – lookingforshakespeare.globspot.com [Rambler]

Podcasts

Don't Quill the Messenger – dragonwagonradio.com/dontquillthemessenger [Steven Sabel]

The Shakespeare Underground – shakespeareunderground.com [Jennifer Newton]

YouTube Channels

Alexander Waugh channel   @alexanderwaugh7036
Shakespeare Oxford Fellowship channel   @shakespeareoxfordfellowship
De Vere Society channel   @thedeveresociety2948

PART V: CODA

PLEASE STAND UP!

Taylor, Thomas
1992, March 8   "WILL THE REAL ..." *Washington Post*, p. 14.

[author not named]
2008, Aug. 12   "WILL THE REAL SHAKESPEARE PLEASE STAND UP?" *Star-News*
                     (Wilmington, NC).

Crane, Lelia
1989, July 17   "WILL REAL SHAKESPEARE PLEASE STAND!" review of a performance
                     of John Nassivera's play *All the Queen's Men*," in *The Hour*
                     (Norwalk, CT).

Dederer, Claire
2003, June 15   "WILL THE REAL BARD PLEASE STAND UP?" *Seattle Times*, p. L10.

DeMott, Benjamin
1970, Nov. 7   "WILL THE REAL SHAKESPEARE PLEASE STAND UP?" *Saturday
                     Review of Literature*, p. 35.

Gabriel, Helen
2002, June 25   "WOULD THE REAL LITERARY GENIUS PLEASE STAND UP?"
                     Birmingham Daily Post, p. 2.

Goldstein, Gary B.
1989, July 21   "Shakespeare Sleuths: WILL THE REAL BARD PLEASE STAND UP?"
                     The Stamford Advocate.

Gore-Langton, Robert,
2014, October 14   "WILL THE REAL MR. SHAKESPEARE PLEASE STAND UP?"
                     The Daily Express, p. 13.

Gross, John
2005, March   "WILL THE REAL SHAKESPEARE PLEASE STAND UP?" *Commentary*,
                     vol. 119/4.

LaBelle, Jenijoy
1991   "The Authorship Question, or WILL THE REAL WILLIAM
                     SHAKESPEARE PLEASE STAND UP?" *Engineering and Science,*
                     vol. 45/1: 22-29.

Satchell, Michael
2000, July 24-31   "Hunting For Good Will: WILL THE REAL SHAKESPEARE PLEASE
                     STAND UP?" *U.S. News & World Report*, p. 71-72.

Smith, Scott S.
1992, Dec.   "WILL THE REAL SHAKESPEARE STAND UP?" *Sky* (Delta Airlines),
                     p. 96, 98+.

Talcott, Christina
2005, Oct. 21   "WILL THE REAL 'BEARD OF AVON' PLEASE STAND UP? Review of
                     The Beard of Avon by Amy Freed," *The Washington Post*, p. T26.

Werner, Hans
2010, May 9   "WILL THE REAL WILL PLEASE STAND UP? Review of *Contested Will*
                     by James Shapiro," *The Toronto Star*, p. 6.

*   *   *   *   *   *   *

WHO-DUN-IT?

Fiehler, Rudolph
 Mid 1980s *The Key to the Great Shake-speare **WHODUNIT*** [pamphlet]

Adler, Tony
 1994, Nov. "The Big **WHODUNNIT**," *Stagebill*, p. 14.

Alter, Alexandra
 2011, April 2 "Just Asking: The Shakespeare **WHODUNIT**: A Scholar Tackles
   Doubters on Who Wrote the Plays; Hollywood Weighs In: Review
   of *Anonymous*," *Wall Street Journal*, p. W4.

Basso, Hamilton
 1950, April 8 "The Big **WHO-DONE-IT**: Review of *"Shakespeare" Identified* by J.
   Thomas Looney," *The New Yorker*, p. 113-14, 117-19.

Bentley, Richard
 1959, Feb. "Elizabethan **WHODUNIT**: Who was "William Shakespeare"?" *American
   Bar Association Journal*, vol. 45/2: 204-08

Hamblin, Dora Jane
 1964, April 24 "History's Biggest Literary **WHODUNIT**," *Life*, vol. 56/17.

Niederkorn, William S.
 2002, Feb. 10 *"A Historic **WHODUNIT**: If Shakespeare Didn't, Who Did?," New York
   Times.*

Patterson, Donald
 1995, Sept. 28 "A Literary **WHODUNIT** – Was Shakespeare Up to the Task?"
   Greensboro News-Record, p. D1.

Quirke, Kieron
 2007, Sept. 3 "So **WHODUNIT**, Will? [review of *The Big Secret Live* by Mark
   Rylance and Matthew Warchus], *The Evening Standard*, p. 1.

* * * * * * *

THE AUTHORSHIP QUESTION USED AS AN EXAMPLE OR ANALOGY IN PUBLICATIONS UNRELATED TO LITERATURE AND HISTORY

Bjerring, Jens-Christian
 2014 "Problems in Epistemic Space," in *Journal of Philosophic Logic*. Feb., p. 153-70.

   The author discusses the usefulness of the concept of "epistemic space" in
   resolving several questions, one of which is whether Edward de Vere was the
   author of "Shakespeare's" works.

Bridges, Linda and William F. Richenbacker
 1991 *The Art of Persuasion: a National Review Rhetoric for Writers*. Introduction by
   William F. Buckley, Jr. New York: Continuum.

   The authors note that they were "persuaded by the Ogburn arguments that the
   works attributed to the bumpkin 'Shakspere' were from the hand of Edward de
   Vere."

Frye, Albert and Albert Levi
 1941 *Rational Belief: An Introduction to Logic* New York: Harcourt, Brace.

   In their discussion of logical thinking, the authors state their belief that "De
   Vere is with a high degree of probability the author."

Furner, Jonathan
 2004 "Conceptual Analysis: A Method for Understanding Information as Evidence, and
   Evidence as Information," *Archival Science*, vol. 4/3-4: 233-35.

In his effort to develop a conceptual framework for "evidentiariness" in archival science, the author cites the appropriateness of a comparison of the stylistic similarities of Edward de Vere's surviving letters with Shakespeare's plays as a means for resolving the question of who wrote Shakespeare's works.

Hunt, Douglas

1991   *The Riverside Guide to Writing*. Boston: Houghton Mifflin.

The author uses Edward de Vere's authorship of the works of Shakespeare as the principal example in Chapter 6, "Arguing When the Facts are Disputed."

Li, Jiexun, et. al.

2006   "From Fingerprint to Writeprint: Identifying the Key Features to Help Identify and Trace Online Authorship," *Communications of the ACH*, vol. 49, no. 4 (April), p. 76-82.

In their discussion of how crime investigators can identify and track those committing crimes online, the authors note the validity of comparing the poems of Shakespeare with those of Edward de Vere, "the leading candidate as the true author of the works credited to Shakespeare."

*   *   *   *   *   *   *

PROGRESS? A FEW SNAPSHOTS ALONG THE WAY

1920, May 21

Looney, J. Thomas. "The Identity of Shakespeae," *Bookman's Journal*, May 21, p. 17.

[Two and a half months after publication of *"Shakespeare" Identified*]
"The ordeal has been passed through; I have watched anxiously every criticism and suggestion that has been made, and what is the result? . . . not a single really formidable or destructive objection to the theory has yet put in an appearance. To the contrary, those critics and reviewers who have mad themselves most intimate with the many-sidedness of the evidence, have confessed themselves most impressed and "almost-persuaded," sometimes apparently against their evident wish."

1930, July 19

Christian Science Monitor, "De Vere as Shakespeare," p. 6.

"It is, probably, no exaggeration to say that belief in the Stratfordian authorship of the Shakespearean poems and plays, though still accepted by the vast majority, is rapidly being discarded by inquiring and thoughtful scholars throughout the English-speaking world."

1935

Rollins, Hyder E. (editor). *England's Helicon, vol. 2*. Cambridge, MA: Harvard University Press.

Its index lists Edward de Vere as "alias Shakespeare."

1939, February 10

Allen, Percy, "who Was Shakespeare?" *John O'London's Weekly*, p. 821.

"The orthodox, traditional "Stratfordian" case is finished. It will no longer bear examination, whether from chronological, topical, or other view-points. It no longer fits either the known facts, or the obvious inferences to be drawn therefrom. It is fast being rejected throughout the English-speaking world. . . . The case for Oxford, as we can now present it, is substantially complete. It has never been answered, and is, in my judgment, unanswerable."

1944, July

Editor. "Oxfordian News: Progress and a Handicap," *Shakespeare Fellowship Quarterly*,
vol. V, no. 3, p. 48.

> "Some thirty of the leading public, university and college libraries of the
> United States have not only recently subscribed to our publication, but have
> placed orders for all copies printed, beginning with vol. 1, no. 1."

1948, Sept.

Cutner, Herbert "Are We Progressing?" *Shakespeare Fellowship Newsletter* (English), p. 6-7.

> "It is obvious that . . . we of the Fellowship have got a great fight against the
> almost universal belief that the plays were written by Shakspere of Stratford. The work of
> Sir George Greenwood seems to be quite forgotten or unread. The credulity of the average
> Shakspere believer is almost incredible, but it is there. Before saying anything about
> Oxford . . . we have to show that it was impossible for the Stratford man to have written a
> line of the plays, that there is no evidence whatever to "wed" him to them."

1969, February 28

Horne, Jr., Richard C.   "Letter to SOS Members." *Shakespeare Oxford Newsletter*, vol. 5/1,
p. 1-6, 8-9.

> "When can we reasonably expect to see light at the end of the tunnel? In 1969? Hardly;
> barring a miracle. The present tactics are not noticeably productive of results. We are
> talking to each other, converting the already converted. It is seriously doubted if there are
> as many active propagandists, lecturers, debaters, and writers for the cause as there were
> in the Thirties, Forties and Fifties."

1970, March 31

Horne, Jr., Richard C.   "Progress Report: Recent Oxfordian News," *Shakespeare Oxford
Newsletter*, vol. 6/1, p. 1-17. [repr. in *Building the Case*, vol. 6, p. 8-34]

> "The rate of our progress in recent years toward gaining recognition of Lord
> Oxford as Shakespeare among the uncommitted and open-minded, can best be
> described as one small step forward, and two giant steps backwards."

1985, Winter

Crinkley, Richmond. "New Perspectives on the Authorship Question, *Shakespeare Quarterly*,
vol. 36/4, p. 515-22.

> Crinkley quotes a statement by E. A. J. Honigmann about Charlton Ogburn and
> comments that this "is the first time in my memory that a Stratfordian has made
> adulatory (or even courteous!) acknowledgement of an anti-Stratfordian work.
> . . . Shakespeare scholarship owes an enormous debt to Charlton Ogburn."

1992

Hart, Michael H. *The 100: A Ranking of the Most Influential Persons in History: Revised and
Updated for the Nineties*. (New York: Citadel Press. CCT105 H32 1992

> Entry no. 31 is "Edward de Vere, better known as William Shakespeare."
> "Another revision [to the 1992 revised edition] . . . is my inclusion of Edward de Vere as
> the real 'William Shakespeare' rather than the man from Stratford-on-Avon, who is
> described as the author by most 'orthodox' textbooks. This change was only made
> reluctantly. It represents an admission that I made a serious error in the first edition when,
> without carefully checking the facts, I simply 'followed the crowd' and accepted the
> Stratford man as the author of the plays. Since then, I have carefully examined the
> arguments on both sides of the question and have concluded that the weight of the
> evidence is heavily against the Stratford man and in favor of de Vere."

Coda

1999, Fall

Paster, Gail Kern. "From the Editor," *Shakespeare Quarterly*, vol. 50/3, p. iii-iv.

> Paster quotes Alan Nelson's lament that "Establishment Shakespeareans . . . are losing the public debate over the 'authorship question." (The Nelson quote is from his review of *Alias Shakespeare* in the same issue of SQ, p. 376-82.)

1999, Winter

Whalen, Richard F. "Authorship and Orthodoxy: Ogburn's legacy can be found in how institutions such as the Folger now treat authorship," *Shakespeare Oxford Newsletter*, vol. 34/4, p. 9. [repr. in *Building the Case*, vol. 8, p. 43-45]

> The title says it all.

2007, Fall

Whalen, Richard F. "Letter: Progress among Stratfordians," *Shakespeare Oxford Newsletter*, vol. 43/4, p. 19-20.

> Whalen cites a dozen examples of greater acceptance of the authorship issue in academia and the media, then concludes that "the extent of these examples just from the past decade is unprecedented. Nothing like it occurred in academia before the mid-1990s."

2008

Broderick, James F. and Darren W. Miller. *Web of Conspiracy: A Guide to Conspiracy Theory Sites on the Internet*. Medford, NJ: Information Today. HV6275 B76 2008

> "What I discovered [in investigating conspiracy theories] is that most do not hold up under scrutiny. The more one digs, the shakier and less credible they become. The Authorship Question was different. The more I dug, the more credible it seemed, until I became fully convinced of its validity. What I had set out expecting to debunk turned out to be the most compelling, fact-based "conspiracy" I had ever researched."

2014, October 27

Gore-Langton, Robert. "Could the Real Mr. Shakespeare Please Stand Up?," *The Daily Express*, p. 13 [repr. in *The De Vere Society Newsletter*, vol. 21/3: 3-5.

> After reading Alexander Waugh's *Shakespeare in Court*, Gore-Langton writes that "The greatest literary ongoing whodunit now has more academics, bloggers and detectives on the case than ever before. . . . I for one will approach the Shakespeare deniers without the dismissive sneer I used to."

* * * * * * *

SHAKESPEARE REVOLUTIONIZED

The First Hundred Years of
J. Thomas Looney's
"Shakespeare" Identified

James A. Warren

ABOUT THE EDITOR

James A. Warren is the author of *Shakespeare Revolutionized: The First Hundred Years of J. Thomas Looney's "Shakespeare" Identified* (2021) and the creator of *An Index to Oxfordian Publications*, now in its fifth edition (2023). He is also the editor of the Centenary edition of Looney's *"Shakespeare" Identified* (2018) and *"Shake-speare" Revealed: The Collected Articles and Published Letters of J. Thomas Looney*, and of the seven-volume collection of Percy Allen's complete writings on Shakespeare. His hardback edition of Bernard M. Ward's the Seventeenth Earl of Oxford 1550-1604 was published in 2023, and his novel on an Oxfordian theme, *Summer Storm: A Novel of Ideas*, was released in 2016.

Warren has given presentations at a dozen Oxfordian conferences and his articles have appeared in *Brief Chronicles*, *The Oxfordian*, *The Shakespeare Oxford Newsletter* and *Shakespeare Matters*. In October 2020 he was named the Shakespeare Oxford Fellowship's Oxfordian of the Year; in 2013 the Shakespeare Authorship Research Centre at Concordia University conferred upon him its Vero Nihil Verius Award for Scholarly Excellence.

As a Foreign Service officer with the U.S. Department of State, Warren served in Public Diplomacy positions at U.S. embassies in eight countries, mostly in Asia. He later served as Executive Director of the Association for Diplomatic Studies and Training (ADST) and as Regional Director for Southeast Asia for the Institute of International Education (IIE). Since 2016 he has been a Fellow at the Center for the Study of the Great Ideas.

VERITAS PUBLICATIONS

Bringing Hidden Truths to Light

The publications listed below are part of Veritas Publications' effort to resurrect important but long forgotten lines of evidence supporting the Oxfordian claim that Edward de Vere was the principal author of the works attributed to "William Shakespeare."

"Shakespeare" Identified
J. Thomas Looney, 1920
Edited by James A. Warren, 2019
ISBN 978-1-7335894-1-3
Paperback, 6x9, 520 pages, $24

Even more than a century after its publication, *"Shakespeare" Identified* is still the most revolutionary book on Shakespeare ever written. Looney's classic account of how he uncovered Edward de Vere's authorship remains essential reading even today. This "Centenary" edition, based on the version published by Cecil Palmer in London in 1920, is the first American edition with the complete text as Looney intended it to be published. It's also the first edition in a modern format, and, with notes identifying more than 230 passages Looney quoted from other works, it's the edition most useful for scholars as well as general readers making their way for the first time through the book that novelist John Galsworthy called the best detective story he had ever read.

Shakespeare Revolutionized: The First Hundred Years of J. Thomas Looney's "Shakespeare" Identified
By James A. Warren, 2021
ISBN 978-1-7335894-3-7
Paperback, 7x10, 784 pages, $40

Shakespeare Revolutionized tells the amazing story of how Looney uncovered de Vere's authorship and how his book inspired generations of brilliant scholars to dig deeper into the circumstances that led him to create the literary masterpieces now known as "Shakespeare's." It also chronicles the influence the Oxfordian idea has had on public opinion and academia over the past century, and shows why so many Shakespeare scholars today resist examining the Oxfordian claim even as it becomes the unacknowledged nucleus around which much of their work revolves.

Shakespeare Investigated: Publications of the Shakespeare Fellowship 1922-1936
Edited by James A. Warren, 2021
ISBN 978-1-7335894-4-4
Paperback, 7x10, 642 pages, $27

Scholars inspired by Looney's pioneering work made one startling discovery after another regarding Shakespeare's plays and the conditions in which they had been written and first performed. These discoveries were reported on in more than 330 articles published by the Shakespeare Fellowship from 1922 to 1936. These pieces, almost lost to history until now, fill an important gap in our understanding of scholarly work on the issue of Shakespearean authorship.

"Shakespeare" Revealed: The Collected Articles and Published Letters of J. Thomas Looney
Edited by James A. Warren, 2019
ISBN 978-0-578-43034-8
Paperback, 6x9, 326 pages, $20

Only a handful of the fifty-three shorter pieces Looney wrote on the issue of Shakespearean authorship after *"Shakespeare" Identified* have ever been reprinted—until now. This collection of forty-two "new" articles and published letters, together with the dozen or so pieces already known of, makes clear for the first time just how intensely Looney continued to defend and enrich his ideas over the final two decades of his life.

The Seventeenth Earl of Oxford 1550-1604
Captain Bernard M. Ward, 1928
Edited by James A. Warren, 2023
ISBN 979-8-9861351-6-8
Hardback, 6x9, 451 pages, $30

Edward de Vere was perhaps the most brilliant of the many extraordinary courtiers who, together with their queen, made the Elizabethan era one of the most fascinating periods in English history. He was also, many believe, the real author of the works attributed to "William Shakespeare." With the release of this new edition of  Ward's book, his fascinating presentation of the life of one of the most provocative figures in English history—and of the time in which he lived — in now readily available for new generations of readers and scholars to enjoy.

Complete Writings on Shakespeare (7 volumes)
Percy Allen, 1923-1953
Edited by James A. Warren, 2022
Paperback, 6x9, $18 each

Percy Allen was the most brilliant of that intrepid band of independent-minded scholars who suddenly appeared in England in the 1920s and 1930s to challenge the entrenched dogma held by professors of English that the uneducated William Shakspere of Stratford-upon-Avon was the great playwright and poet William Shakespeare.

Building on the work of J. Thomas Looney and analyzing newly-uncovered evidence free from the restraints of authority and conventional wisdom, Allen showed that the principal author of Shakespeare's works couldn't have been anyone other than de Vere, who was recognized in his time as the best writer in England of comedies and tragedies and the most active sponsor of other writers and poets during England's remarkable renaissance in language and literature during Queen Elizabeth I's reign.

This seven-volume collection of Allen's works includes nine books, five booklets and 120 shorter works on the authorship question introduced and edited by James Warren, and a Foreword by Don Rubin.

- Vol. 1: Borrowings and Topicality in Elizabethan Drama, 1928-1929
- Vol. 2: The Case for Edward de Vere as "Shakespeare," 1923-1930
- Vol. 3: The Oxford-Shakespeare Case Corroborated, 1930-1932
- Vol. 4: The Life Story of Edward de Vere as "William Shakespeare, 1932-1933
- Vol. 5: The Plays of Shakespeare in Relation to French History, 1933-1936
- Vol. 6: Anne Cecil & the Dynastic Succession Theory, 1934-1943
- Vol. 7: Later Writings on Shakespeare, 1937-1953

Shakespeare Sonnets and Edward de Vere &
Personal Clues in Shakespeare Poems & Sonnets
(in one volume)
Gerald H. Rendall (1930, 1934)
ISBN 979-8-9861351-3-7
Paperback, 6x9, 422 pages, $22

"Shakespeare's sonnets present the soul of Hamlet shaped by the experiences of Edward de Vere. So concluded Gerald H. Rendall, one of the most eminent British scholars and educators of his day. Through an intense study of Shakespeare's poems, sonnets and plays—and Edward de Vere's life and early poems—he found "coincidences so numerous, so circumstantial, so surprising and illuminating, that it became impossible . . . to refuse to recognize in them the handiwork of Edward de Vere." Readers new to this idea will surely appreciate Rendall's description of his own initial difficulty in overcoming his existing belief in William Shakspere's authorship. This volume contains Rendall's two most important books on the subject of de Vere as the pen behind the pen name "William Shakespeare."

Seven Shakespeares: A Discussion of the Evidence
for Various Theories with Regard to Shakespeare's
Identity
Gerald Slater (1931)
ISBN 979-8-9861351-5-1
Paperback, 310 pages, $15

Slater, one of the most prominent British scholars of the 1930s, examines the claims of the seven authorship candidates most worthy of consideration for authorship of the works attributed to William Shakspere of Stratford-on-Avon. Endeavoring "to think and feel as a conscientious judge and not as an advocate," he concludes that Edward de Vere "was the central figure of the collaborators whose works were collectively known as "Shakespeare's."

Shakespearian Fantasias: Adventures in the Fourth
Dimension
Esther Singleton, 1930
Edited by James A. Warren, 2019
ISBN 978-1-7335894-0-6
Paperback, 5.06x7.81, 280 pages, $15

This delightful novel takes readers on flights of fancy as they accompany the narrator, a woman from the twentieth century, who mysteriously finds herself transplanted into the worlds of eleven of Shakespeare's plays. Among them, the feisty Beatrice is our guide through the complications that arise in matters of the heart in *Much Ado About Nothing*, as is the witty Berowne through the complexities arising from the courtship of four filles from France by four English gentlemen in *Love's Labour's Lost*. *Shakespearian Fantasias* was Singleton's only novel. She completed it during the final year of her life, and described it as "the best work that I have ever done, and the most original."

Summer Storm: A Novel of Ideas
James A. Warren, 2016
ISBN 978-1-7335894-2-0
Paperback, 6x9, 396 pages, $17

"An assured and surprisingly gripping tale about the perils of ideological conformity."
Kirkus Reviews

Literature professor Alan Fernwood's life is turned upside down as he discovers that much of what he had thought was true, isn't. His investigations reveal that William Shakespeare didn't write the works attributed to him, and his efforts to promote recognition of the true author, Edward de Vere, show just how mistaken he was about the security of his job. Further complicating matters are Alan's relationship with the bewitching Amelia Mai. They and other characters ask themselves and each other how it is possible to know anything—a subject, a person, or, most important of all, what we should do right now, at this particular moment, in this unique set of circumstances. And along the way Alan and his students find much of relevance in Shakespeare's plays for those living in the world today.

Behind the Mask of William Shakespeare
A new translation by Frank Lawler (1922) of Abel Lefranc's *Sous le Masque de William Shakespeare: William Stanley, Vie comte de Derby* (1918, 1919)
ISBN 979-8-9861351-4-4
Paperback, 6x9, 485 pages, $23.99

Lefranc (1863-1952), a historian of 16th century French literature, brings a unique and erudite perspective to the issue of Shakespearean authorship. While his theory that William Stanley, 6th Earl of Derby (Edward de Vere's son-in-law) authored Shakespeare's works is outdated, his extensive knowledge of 16th century European life, history, and the Court of Navarre, provides long-overlooked insight to the identity, knowledge, and beliefs of the writer of Shakespeare's works. Lawler's fresh translation is supplemented with many annotations drawing on current scholarly findings and research.

Educating Shakespeare: What he knew and how and where he learned it
Stephanie Hopkins Hughes, 2022
ISBN 978-1-7335894-5-1
Paperback, 6x9, 376 pages, $25

Stephanie Hopkins Hughes, founding editor of *The Oxfordian*, digs deep into the sources used by Edward de Vere in creating the plays and poems we know as Shakespeare's. She contends that a deep understanding of his works and the historical context in which they were produced leads inevitably to acceptance of the truth of Oxford's authorship. In seeking answers to what exactly he knew and from whom he learned it, Hughes tells the fascinating story of how the supreme genius of the Elizabethan age created the London stage and the English language we speak today.

In Preparation

The Historical Setting in Which Shakespeare's History Plays Were First Performed on the Public Stage: Selected Articles by Colonel Bernard R. Ward & Captain Bernard M. Ward (1928-1930)
Edited by James A. Warren

Shake-speare: Handwriting and Spelling
By Gerald H. Rendall (1931)
New edition edited by James A. Warren

The Shakspere Signatures and "Sir Thomas More"
By Sir George Greenwood (1924)
New edition edited by James A. Warren

Shakespeare Discussed: The Oxfordian Correspondence of J. Thomas Looney, together with that of other early Oxfordians, 1920-1945
Edited by James A. Warren

A collection of more than 500 letters in which early Oxfordian scholars shared their discoveries and thoughts about progress made in promoting the Oxfordian idea among traditional scholars and the public. More than half are to or from J. Thomas Looney. An introduction and annotations by the editor provide the context in which the letters were sent.

Girolamo Cardano's Cardanus Comforte
Edited by James A. Warren

A new edition of the book often referred to as "Hamlet's Book" because of the similarities between themes and phrasings in it and passages in Shakespeare's *Hamlet.* Based on the English translation by Bedingfield published by Commandment of the Earl of Oxford in 1573, revised in 1576, this will be the first edition in a modern layout. With an introduction and annotations incorporating modern scholarship and findings.

Admiral Hubert H. Holland's Writings on Shakespeare: Three Books and Selected Shorter Pieces in One Volume (1923-1951)
Edited by James A. Warren